MODERN HISTORY

FROM THE EUROPEAN AGE
TO THE NEW GLOBAL ERA

MODERN HISTORY

FROM THE EUROPEAN AGE
TO THE NEW GLOBAL ERA

J.M. ROBERTS

DUNCAN BAIRD PUBLISHERS

LONDON

Modern History

J.M. Roberts

First published in the United Kingdom and Ireland in 2007 by
Duncan Baird Publishers Ltd
Sixth Floor
Castle House
75–76 Wells Street
London W1T 3QH

The fourth revised edition of the text used throughout this edition was first published as *The New Penguin History of the World* by Penguin Press/Allen Lane in 2002. For *Modern History* Professor Arne Westad has further revised the text up to 2007.

DUNCAN BAIRD PUBLISHERS
Managing editor: Christopher Westhorp
Managing designer: Daniel Sturges
Designer: Justin Ford
Picture researchers: Julia Ruxton and Louise Glasson
Map artwork: Russell Bell
Decorative borders: Lorraine Harrison

British Library Cataloguing-in-Publication Data.
A CIP record for this book is available from the British Library.

ISBN-13: 978-1-84483-553-9   ISBN-10: 1-84483-553-7

10 9 8 7 6 5 4 3 2 1

Typeset in Sabon 11/15 pt
Color reproduction by Colourscan, Singapore
Printed in Malaysia by Imago

NOTE
The abbreviations CE and BCE are used throughout this book:
CE Common Era (the equivalent of AD)
BCE Before Common Era (the equivalent of BC)

About the author

J.M. Roberts was born in Bath in 1928 and died in 2003 after a prolonged illness. He was a leading historian and the first since H.G. Wells to write a history of the world, published originally by Hutchinson in 1976 and thereafter by Penguin. From it emerged *The Triumph of the West* in 1985, a book and a television series that showed how Western ideas and institutions have shaped the world. In addition to his career as a prolific and gifted writer, he was a formidable, modernizing university manager, serving as Vice-Chancellor of Southampton University between 1979 and 1984, and Warden of Merton College, Oxford, between 1984 and 1994. From 1953 to 1979 he had been Fellow and Tutor in Modern History at Merton College, Oxford, (later Honorary Fellow, 1980–1984 and 1994–2003) introducing generations of young historians not only to the history of Europe but also that of America, India, China, and Japan.

John Morris Roberts was educated at Taunton School and won a scholarship to Keble College, Oxford, where he gained first class honors in Modern History in 1948. After National Service he was elected a Prize Fellow of Magdalen College, Oxford, in 1951. In 1953–1954 he went as a Commonwealth Fund Fellow to Princeton and Yale in the United States and began to look beyond the eighteenth-century revolutionary era to grander ambitions. In 1972 in his most original work *The Mythology of the Secret Societies* he explored the fear of masonic networks and plots that troubled conservatives in the eighteenth and nineteenth centuries. In 1967 he had written *Europe 1880–1945*, an influential textbook that went into a third edition in 2001, and it was this that led to the idea for *History of the World* (1976, first edition), then *A History of Europe* (1996), and *The Twentieth Century* (1999).

Alongside his own writing he edited (from 1967 to 1977) *English Historical Review* and was general editor of two series for Oxford University Press, the *New Oxford History of England* and the *Short Oxford History of the Modern World*. Outside interests included Trustee of the National Portrait Gallery (1984–1998) and Governor of the BBC (1988–1993), and in 1996 he was honored by becoming a CBE (Commander of the British Empire). He was happily married to Judith Armitage for close to forty years and they had a son and two daughters. After a recurrence of illness he died in his beloved Somerset in May 2003.

Consultant for this revised, updated edition:

Professor Odd Arne Westad, Professor of International History, London School of Economics and Political Science (LSE) read, commented on, and updated where necessary all the material produced up to 2002 by J.M. Roberts. Professor Westad is Co-Director of the LSE's Cold War Studies Centre and his areas of expertise are the Cold War and contemporary East Asia. His books include *The Global Cold War* (2005), which won the Bancroft Prize in 2006, and *Decisive Encounters: The Chinese Civil War, 1946–1950* (2003).

CONTENTS

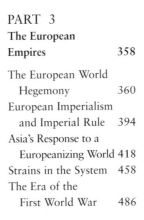

INTRODUCTION

The first edition of this book appeared in 1976, and this is the fourth. There have also been several translations, whose texts have sometimes had to vary slightly from the English originals at the request of their publishers. I think that it is unlikely that I shall now have time to offer the public yet another version. Since, though, this version contains a very substantial revision of the text after a comprehensive reconsideration, it may be helpful to set out once more in a new preface some explanation of what I have tried to do, and why it seemed sensible to do it. At the very least, I feel I should indicate whether the events of more than twenty-five years have led me to change the purposes and perspectives with which I set out to break the ground for this book in the late 1960s.

I have very recently heard it said of world history that "everything changed", or something to that effect, on 11 September 2001. For reasons I have touched on briefly below, and because of certain ideas which have guided me from the outset, I think this is very misleading, untrue in any but a much qualified sense. Yet the first reason why a new edition seemed desirable is that world history for over a decade has been passing through, and continues to pass through, the most recent example of a recurrent phenomenon: a period of turbulent events and kaleidoscopic change. The beginnings of this confused and exciting period were already topics for the last, third, edition of this book, but events in the later 1990s alone made further consideration necessary in case new perspectives had to be taken into account, as well as new facts.

I feared the outcome would be a much enlarged book, but it did not turn out like that. Many changes of detail and style were required, but only the last section of the story underwent major rearrangement and reconstruction. Changes of emphasis were required, of course. There is a little more than in the last edition about recent changes in the position of women, about environmental concerns, about new institutions and assumptions, new questionings of old ones, and about shifts in the formal and informal basis of the international order (these topics are most marked in recent history, and my views on them can be found set out at greater length in my *Penguin History of the Twentieth Century*, published in 1999). But none of this reflects a fundamental change in my standpoint or general outlook, and they can be summed up in much the same terms I have used before and from the outset.

Perhaps my predominant concern, from the start, was to show and recall to a non-specialist readership the weight of the historical past and the importance, even today, of historical inertia in a world we are often encouraged to think we can control and manage. Yet historical forces moulding the thinking and behaviour of modern Americans, Russians, Chinese, Indians and Arabs were laid down centuries before ideas like capitalism or communism were invented. Distant history still clutters our lives, and perhaps even some of what happened in prehistory is still at work in them, too. Yet there has always been tension between such forces and mankind's unique power to produce change. Only recently (it is a matter of

Firefighters in New York City search through the smouldering rubble of the collapsed 110-storey North and South Towers of the World Trade Center on 12 September 2001, just twenty-four hours after a day of dramatic events in the eastern United States during which four airliners were seized in flight by terrorists, including two deliberately crashed into the "Twin Towers" to cause the greatest possible amount of death and destruction.

man's quest for godhood

a few centuries at most) in terms of the six thousand or so years of civilization which make up most of the subject-matter of this book there has also been a growing recognition of mankind's power as a change-maker. What is more, enthusiasm for technical advance now seems universal. Even if very recently indeed some have sought to temper this enthusiasm with qualifications, there is now a widespread notion that most problems can and will be solved by human agency. *the new tower of Babel*

Because in consequence the two phenomena of inertia and innovation continue to operate in all historical developments, it remains my view – as the first edition of this book put it – that we shall always find what happens both more, and less, surprising than we expect. Judgements about the significance of recent or contemporary events, should only be made with this kept firmly in mind. I remain inclined to believe, too, that such judgements will always be influenced very much by temperament, and that our innate optimism or pessimism will tinge any attempt to make predictions. Even if we could handle their abundance, none but the most general statements about likely futures could ever be made from such facts as history provides. Since the last edition of this book, I am aware of a slight shift in my own feelings; I now feel that my children will probably not live in so agreeable a world as I have known, because even greater adjustments in humanity's life everywhere may well be required than I once thought. But I do not claim to know. Historians should never prophesy.

Most of the foregoing I have said before at greater length and need not elaborate further now. It may, though, also still be helpful to new readers of this book if I repeat something of my reasons for choosing the general approach reflected in its layout and contents. I sought from the start to recognize, where they could be discerned, the elements of general influences which had the widest and deepest impact and not just to collect again accounts of traditionally important themes. I wished to avoid detail and to set out instead the major historical processes which affected the largest numbers of human

beings, leaving substantial legacies to the future, and to show their comparative scale and relations with one another. I did not seek to write continuous histories of all major countries or all fields of human activity and believe the place for exhaustive accounts of facts about the past is an encyclopedia.

I have sought to stress the significance of these major influences, and that means chronological and geographical unevenness in allocating space. Although we properly still take time and trouble to gaze at and study the fascinating sites of Yucatán, to ponder the ruins of Zimbabwe or wonder over the mysterious statues of Easter Island, and intrinsically desirable though knowledge of the societies which produced these things may be, they remain peripheral to world history. The early history even of such huge areas as black Africa or pre-Columbian America are only lightly sketched in these pages, because nothing that happened there between very remote times and the coming of Europeans shaped the world as did the cultural traditions in which the legacies of, say, the Buddha, the Hebrew prophets and Christianity, Plato and Confucius were for centuries living and shaping influences for millions of people and often still are.

I also tried not to write most about those subjects where material was most plentiful. There is not, in any case, the slightest chance of mastering all the relevant bibliography of world history. I have sought to stress matters which seemed important, rather than those about which we knew most. Louis XIV, however prominent in the history of France and Europe, can therefore be passed over more briefly than, say, the Chinese Revolution. In our own day, it is more than ever vital to try to distinguish the wood from the trees and not to mention something because it turns up every day in the "news".

New interpretations of the meanings of events are offered to us all the time. For instance, much has been heard recently about a clash of civilizations, presumed to be under way or on its way. This assertion, of course, has been heavily influenced by the new awareness of both the distinctiveness and the new excitability of the Islamic world in the last few decades. I have indicated in what follows my own reason for rejecting this view, at least in its most unqualified presentations, as inadequate and over-pessimistic. But no one could fail to recognize that there are, indeed, multiple tensions building up between what is loosely called the "West" and many Islamic societies. Both with conscious intention and unconsciously, sometimes even accidentally, profoundly disturbing influences from the West have now been at work to disrupt and trouble other traditions, Islam only one among them, for the last few centuries (the notion of "globalization" is emphatically not to be seen in terms of merely the last few years). That process began, of course, with the activities of Europeans and that is why I have given considerable space to the evolution of Europe and its centrality until 1945 in world history.

No doubt such an emphasis reflects the most fundamental impulses arising from my own historical heritage and cultural formation. I cannot but write as an elderly, white, middle-class, British male. If that seems a shortcoming too grave to overcome, other approaches can be found, but the reader must weigh them, too, in similar scales before he or she comes to a judgement. I hope none the less that my efforts to be aware of what I might too easily take for granted may have made it possible to provide what the immensely learned historian Lord Acton termed a history "which is distinct from the combined history of all countries", but which also indicates the variety and richness of the great cultural traditions which determine its structure.

In earlier prefaces, I have identified the many friends and colleagues who in various ways gave me help at earlier stages. I shall always be grateful to them but, because they are on record, I shall not repeat their names here. But I must add to theirs the name of Professor Barry Cunliffe, who was specifically of great help with this edition, and whom I thank most warmly. I continue, too, to owe thanks to the correspondents who have continued to write to me over the years, offering specific advice, suggestion, denunciation and encouragement, too numerous though they are to name here. But none of these friends and critics bears any responsibility for what I chose to do with what they told me, and therefore none should be blamed for anything in what I have written; the responsibility for it is wholly my own.

Finally, though the matter is somewhat personal, I feel I must point out that the final stages of my work of revision were carried out in the months since September last, when plans and schedules were thrown awry by a sudden and unanticipated collapse of health which necessitated frequent and disruptive stays in hospital. It must be obvious that this put considerable strain on others than myself. Very obviously, too, one of the most prominent among them is my editor at Penguin, Simon Winder. At a very difficult time, he continued to show me great patience and to offer encouragement as he has always done. I find it hard to express my appreciation of, and gratitude for, his calmness and helpfulness. I owe him special thanks.

Over those same months, though, more than to anyone else I owe thanks to my family, for the care they offered me, and the love with which they supported me, my children sometimes making long and transoceanic journeys to see me. But in my family, I must single out above all my wife, to whom earlier editions of this book have, in principle, been dedicated. This one is more than ever for her. To the encouragement, advice, judgement and taste she has always made available to me, I must now also recognize that the nearly forty years of devotion she has shown to me and to our children has made possible my own career. Now she has added to her previous tasks those of a full-time nurse. There is no one to whom I owe more and I hope she can find in my offering of this book to her some small evidence of how completely I recognize that.

J.M. Roberts
Timwood, March 2002

THEA
TRVM
ORBIS
TERRA
RVM

THE MAKING OF
THE EUROPEAN AGE

ROUND ABOUT 1500, there were many signs that a new age of world history was beginning. The rise of large continental empires, the discoveries in the Americas and the first shoots of European enterprise in Asia are all among them. At the outset they provide hints about the dual nature of a new age – that it is increasingly an age of truly world history and that it is one whose story is dominated by the astonishing success of one civilization among many, that of Europe. These are two aspects of the same process; there is a more and more continuous and organic interconnection between events in all countries, but it is largely to be explained by the efforts of Europeans and their empires. They eventually became masters of the globe and they used their mastery – sometimes without knowing it – to make the world one. As a result, world history has for the last two or three centuries a growing identity and unity of theme.

In a famous passage, the English historian Macaulay once spoke of red men scalping one another on the shores of the Great Lakes so that a European king could rob his neighbour of a province he coveted. This was one striking side of the story we must now embark upon – the gradual entanglement of struggles with one another the world over in greater and greater wars – but politics, empire-building and military expansion were only a tiny part of what was going on. The economic integration of the globe was another part of the process; more important still was the spreading of common assumptions and ideas. The result was to be, in one of our cant phrases, "One World" – of sorts. The age of independent or at least autonomous civilizations has come to a close.

Given our world's immense variety, this may seem at first sight a wildly misleading exaggeration. National, cultural and racial differences have not ceased to produce and inspire appalling conflicts; the history of the centuries since 1500 can be (and often is) written mainly as a series of wars and violent struggles and those who live in different countries obviously do not feel much more like one another than did their predecessors centuries ago. Yet they are much more alike than their ancestors of, say, the tenth century and show it in hundreds of ways ranging from the superficialities of dress to the forms in which they get their living and organize their societies. The origins, extent and limits of this change make up most of the story which follows. It is the outcome of something still going on in many places, which we sometimes call modernization. For centuries it has been grinding away at differences between cultures and it is the deepest and most fundamental expression of the growing integration of world history. Another way of describing the process is to say that the world is Europeanized, for modernization is above all a matter of ideas and techniques which are European in origin. Whether "modernization" is the same as "Europeanization", though, can be left for discussion elsewhere; perhaps it is only a matter of verbal preferences. What is obvious is that, chronologically, it is with the creation of a new Europe that the unification of world history begins. A great change in Europe was the starting point of modern history.

Europe seated on her throne, on the cover of *Theatrum Orbis Terrarum*, a book produced in Antwerp in 1572, holds both a sceptre, representing world power, and an orb decorated with a crucifix, representing Christianity. Europe clearly dominates the three other feminine figures at her feet: these symbolize Asia, in elaborate dress; Africa, who is half naked; and America, who, entirely naked, brandishes a human head as a sign of her cannibalism, which was encountered in Brazil and elsewhere in the 16th century.

1 A NEW KIND OF SOCIETY: EARLY MODERN EUROPE

THE TERM "modern history" is a familiar one, but it does not always mean the same thing. There was a time when modern history was what had happened since the "ancient" history whose subject-matter was the story of the Jews, Greeks and Romans; this is a sense which, for example, was used in my day to define a course of study at Oxford which includes the Middle Ages. Then it came to be distinguished from "medieval" history, too. Now a further refinement is often made, for historians have begun to make distinctions within it and sometimes speak of an "early modern" period. By this they are really drawing our attention to a process, for they apply it to the era in which a new Atlantic world emerged from the tradition-dominated, agrarian, superstitious and confined western Christendom of the Middle Ages, and this took place at different times in different countries. In England it happened very rapidly; in Spain it was far from complete by 1800, while much of eastern Europe was still hardly affected by it even a century later. But the reality of the process is obvious, for all the irregularity with which it expressed itself. So

is its importance, for it laid the groundwork for a European world hegemony.

A useful starting-point for thinking about what was involved is to begin with the simple and obvious truth that for most of human history most people's lives have been deeply and cruelly shaped by the fact that they have had little or no choice about the way in which they could provide themselves and their families with shelter and enough to eat. The possibility that things might be otherwise has only recently become a conceivable one to even a minority of the world's population, and it became a reality for any substantial number of people only with changes in the economy of early modern Europe, for the most part, west of the Elbe. Another point to be borne in mind is that medieval Europe, like most of the world at that time, still consisted of societies in which, for the most part, surpluses of production over and above the needs of consumption, were obtained from those who produced them – peasants – by social or legal institutions rather than by the operation of the market. When we can recognize the existence of a "modern" Europe, this has changed; the extraction and mobilization of those surpluses has become one of the tasks of a protean entity often labelled "capitalism", which operates largely through cash transactions in increasingly complex markets.

This metal calculating machine was built by the French mathematician, physicist, writer and theologian Blaise Pascal (1623–1662) and was patented in 1647. He invented the machine in order to assist his father with his accountancy work.

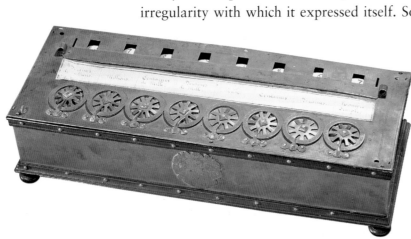

AN AGE OF MEASUREMENT

WE CAN FOLLOW SOME of these economic changes as we can follow no earlier ones because, for the first time, there is reasonably plentiful and continuous quantified data. In one important respect, historical evidence gets much more informative in the last four or five centuries: it becomes much more statistical. Measurement therefore becomes easier. The source of new statistical material was often government. For many reasons, governments wanted to know more and more about the resources or potential resources at their disposal. But private records, especially of business, also give us much more numerical data after 1500. The multiplication of copies as paper and printing became more common meant that the chance of their survival was enormously increased. Commercial techniques appeared which required publication of data in collated forms; the movements of ships, or reports of prices, for example. Moreover, as historians have refined their techniques, they have attacked even poor or fragmentary sources with much greater success than was possible even a few years ago.

THE LIMITATIONS OF STATISTICAL EVIDENCE

All this data has provided much knowledge of the size and shape of change in early modern Europe, though we must be careful not to exaggerate either the degree of precision such material permits or what can be learnt from it. For a long time the collection of good statistics was very difficult. Even quite elementary questions, about, for example, who lived in a certain place, were very difficult to answer accurately until recent times. One of the great aims of reforming monarchs in the eighteenth century was merely to carry out accurate listings of land within their states, cadastral surveys, as they were called, or even to find out how many subjects they had. It was only in 1801 that the first cen-

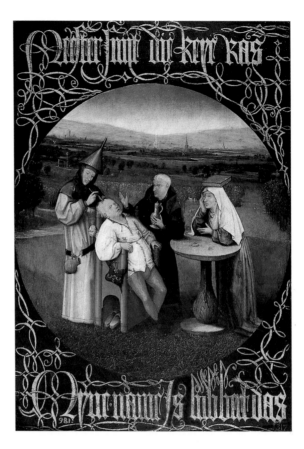

This painting by the Dutch artist Hieronymus Bosch (c.1453–1516), entitled *The Extraction of the Stone of Madness*, caricatures the co-existence of superstition, faith, knowledge and primitive surgery in 15th-century society.

sus was held in Great Britain, nearly eight centuries after the Domesday Book. France did not have her first official census until 1876 nor the Russian Empire her only one until 1897. Such delays are not really surprising. A census or a survey requires a complex and reliable administrative machine. It may arouse strong opposition (when governments seek new information, new taxes often follow). Such difficulties are enormously increased where the population is as illiterate as it was in much of Europe for the greater part of modern history.

New statistical material can also raise as many historical problems as it solves. It can reveal a bewildering variety of contemporary phenomena which often makes generalization harder; it has become much harder to say anything at all about the French peasantry of the eighteenth century since research revealed the diversity hidden by that simple term and that perhaps there was no such thing as *a*

Demographic growth

The lack of any reliable population census during most of this period – the few surveys that were carried out at the beginning of the 18th century were estimations for economic or military use – has meant that records of births and deaths in local parish registers are the principal source of evidence for historians studying the demography of the early modern era. Population growth had been moderate and irregular in the 16th and 17th centuries. However, in spite of short life expectancy, later marriages and a high rate of infant mortality, there can be no doubt that the rate of growth of the European population in the second half of the 18th century began to quicken.

This was due to several factors. By the mid-18th century, improved farming and husbandry meant that nutrition was better and fewer people were dying of hunger. Transport facilities, which played an important role in grain distribution, had also improved.

From the middle of the 16th century, and partly because of the interest of the Renaissance painters, numerous illustrated books on anatomy were published, which helped to improve medical knowledge. By the end of the 17th century, clear descriptions of the symptoms of diseases such as rickets, diabetes, gout and tuberculosis were available, and the circulation of the blood had been discovered. But only very few people were treated by qualified doctors. The peasant masses continued to rely on local "quacks" or travelling practitioners.

The last epidemic of the plague struck in 1713, after which it became a local phenomenon. Growing experience in the use of preventative measures to avoid contagion (vigilance at the ports, and the introduction of quarantine and sanitary cordons) had helped to achieve this. However, typhoid, smallpox, tuberculosis, diphtheria and malaria continued to wreak havoc.

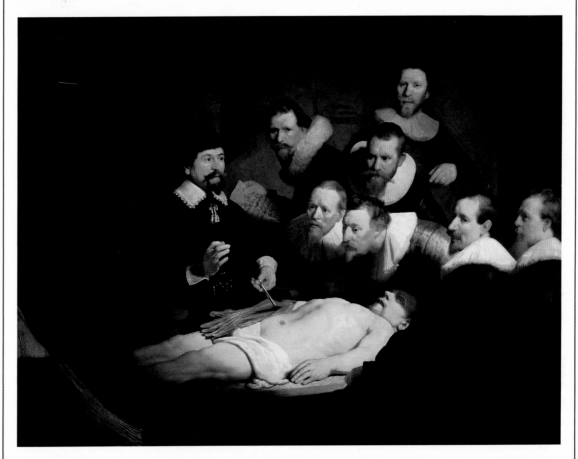

The Anatomy Lesson, *painted in 1632 by the Dutch artist Rembrandt (1606–1669). Anatomical research led to medical advances which, in turn, eventually contributed to an increased life expectancy in Europe.*

The French artist Louis Le Nain (c.1593–1648) and his brothers Antoine (c.1588–1648) and Matthieu (c.1607–1677) painted numerous scenes depicting peasant life. Works such as *Peasant Family at Home* provide an insight into the living conditions of rural workers in 17th-century Europe.

French peasantry, but only several different ones. Finally, too, statistics can illuminate facts while throwing no light at all on causes. Nevertheless after 1500 we are more and more in an age of measurement and the overall effect of this is to make it easier to make defensible statements about what was happening than in earlier times at other places.

POPULATION TRENDS IN EUROPE

DEMOGRAPHIC HISTORY is the most obvious example of a subject that we are able to discuss with more certainty. At the end of the fifteenth century European population was poised on the edge of growth which has gone on ever since. After 1500 we may crudely distinguish two phases. Until about the middle of the eighteenth century the

increase of population was (except for notable local and temporary interruptions) relatively slow and steady; this roughly corre-

The population of Europe 1500–1800

Demographic growth of around 40 per cent occurred in Europe between 1500 and 1700, although during the 17th century there was a negative demographic balance in Spain, several regions of southern Italy and central Germany. This overall growth was less than half of that which was to take place during the 18th century. The estimated population of various European countries during this period is shown in millions in this chart.

	1500	1600	1700	1800
Spain and Portugal	9.3	11.3	10	14.6
Italy	10.5	13.3	13.3	18.1
France (inc. Lorraine and Savoy)	16.4	18.5	21	26.9
Benelux countries	1.9	2.9	3.4	5.2
British Isles	4.4	6.8	9.3	15.9
Scandinavian countries	1.5	2.4	2.8	3.2
Germany	12	15	15	24.5
Switzerland	0.8	1	1.2	1.8
Russia	9	15.5	17.5	
Total for Europe	65.8	86.7	92.5	110.2 (without Russia)

sponds to "early modern" history and was one of the things characterizing it. In the second phase the increase much accelerated and great changes followed. Only the first phase concerns us here, because it regulated the way in which modern Europe took shape. The general facts and trends within it are clear enough. Though they rely heavily on estimates, the figures are much better based than in earlier times, in part because there was almost continuous interest in population problems from the early seventeenth century onwards. This contributed to the foundation of the science of statistics (then called "Political Arithmetic") at the end of the seventeenth century, mainly in England. It produced some remarkable work, though not much more than a tiny island of relatively rigorous method in a sea of guesses and inferences. Nevertheless the broad picture is clear. In 1500 Europe had about eighty million inhabitants, two centuries later she had less than 150 million and in 1800 slightly less than 200 million. Before 1750 Europe had grown fairly steadily at a rate which maintained her share of the world's population at about one-fifth until 1700 or so, but by 1800 she had nearly a quarter of the world's inhabitants.

THE BIRTH-RATE AND LIFE EXPECTANCY

For a long time, obviously, there were no such startling disparities as appeared later between the rate of growth in Europe and that elsewhere. It seems reasonable to conclude that this meant that in other ways, too, European and non-European populations were less different than they were to come to be after 1800. The usual age of death among Europeans, for example, still remained low. Before 1800 they were on the average always much younger than nowadays, because people died earlier. At birth a French peasant of the eighteenth century had a life expectancy of about twenty-two years and only a roughly one-in-four chance of surviving infancy. Then chances were much the same as those of an Indian peasant in 1950 or an Italian under imperial Rome. Comparatively few people would have survived their forties, and, since they were less well fed than we are, they would have looked old to us at that age, and probably rather small in stature and unhealthy-looking. As in the Middle Ages, women tended still to die before men. This meant that many men made a second or even a third marriage, not, as today, because of divorce, but because they were soon widowers. The average European couple had a fairly short married life. West of a line running roughly from the Baltic to the Adriatic, they had shorter marriages than east of it, moreover, because those who lived there tended to make their first marriage later in their twenties, and this was long to be a habit making

Diagram by Mallet and Malthus

Research carried out by the Swiss doctor E. Mallet in Geneva and by the English economist Thomas Malthus (1766–1834) produced slightly different figures for life expectancy during the mid-16th to 18th centuries, as shown in these charts. Short life expectancy is linked to a high mortality rate among women and children, owing to a general lack of hygiene and poor sanitary conditions and nutrition, as well as to natural or human disasters.

Average life span

	Mallet	Malthus
Mid-16th century	21 years, 2 months	18 years, 6 months
17th century	25 years, 8 months	23 years, 4 months
18th century	32 years, 9 months	32 years, 3 months

Life expectancy at birth

	Mallet	Malthus
Mid-16th century	8 years, 7 months	4 years, 10 months
17th century	13 years, 3 months	11 years, 7 months
18th century	27 years, 9 months	27 years, 2 months

for different population patterns east and west. Generally, though, if Europeans were well-off they could afford a fairly large family; the poor had smaller ones. There is strong inferential evidence both that some form of family limitation was already taking place in some places in the seventeenth century and that other methods of achieving it than abortion and infanticide were in use. Further cultural and economic facts are needed to explain this mysterious topic. It remains one of those areas where a largely illiterate society is almost impossible to penetrate historically. We can say very little with confidence about early birth control and still less about its implications – if there were any – for the ways in which early modern Europeans thought about themselves and their control over their own lives.

TOWNS AND CITIES

OVERALL, DEMOGRAPHY ALSO reflected the continuing economic predominance of agriculture. For a long time it produced only slightly more food than was needed and could feed only a slowly growing population. In 1500 Europe was still largely a rural continent of villages in which people lived at a pretty low level of subsistence. It would have seemed very empty to modern eyes. England's population, heavy in relation to area by comparison with the rest of the continent, was in 1800 only about a sixth of today's; in eastern Europe there were huge empty spaces for which population was eagerly sought by rulers who encouraged immigration in all sorts of ways. Yet the towns and cities managed to grow in number and size, one or two of them spectacularly faster than the population as a whole. Amsterdam reached a total of about 200,000 inhabitants in the eighteenth century. Paris

Urbanization in Europe

The growth of European cities resulted partly from the expansion of traditional activities and partly from the development of new functions. Towns thrived around ports, markets, manufacturing or mining centres and the headquarters of secular government or church dignitaries. After 1600, trade and banking centres also attracted ever-increasing populations. Spa towns began to appear and larger fortified towns were founded, as were new naval bases.

However, the size of urban centres was very different from that of modern cities. In around 1600 only about 5 per cent of the total population lived in cities with between 20,000 and 30,000 inhabitants. Of every ten Europeans, seven lived in the rural areas and two in small country towns.

The distribution of urban centres on the European map was very unbalanced, with the highest concentration of towns to be found on the coastal plains of the North Sea.

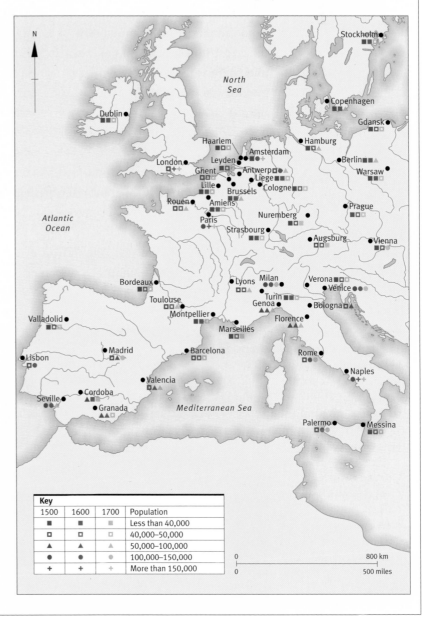

Key			
1500	1600	1700	Population
■	■	■	Less than 40,000
□	□	□	40,000–50,000
▲	▲	▲	50,000–100,000
●	●	●	100,000–150,000
+	+	+	More than 150,000

0   800 km
0   500 miles

probably doubled in size between 1500 and 1700, and rose to slightly less than half a million. London shot ahead of Paris by going up from about 120,000 to nearly 700,000 in the same two centuries; in the much smaller English population this, of course, meant a much bigger shift to urban life. A significant new word came into use in English: suburbs. But it is not easy to generalize about medium-sized and smaller towns. Most were quite small, still under 20,000 in 1700, but the nine European cities of more than 100,000 in 1500 had become at least a dozen two hundred years later. Yet Europe's predominance in urbanization was not so marked in these centuries as it was to become and there were still many great cities in other continents. The city of Mexico, for example, outdid all European cities of the sixteenth century with its population of 300,000.

DIFFERENTIATION IN EUROPEAN GROWTH

Neither urbanization nor population growth was evenly spread. France remained the largest west European nation in these years;

she had about twenty-one million inhabitants in 1700, when England and Wales had only about six million. But it is not easy to make comparisons because estimates are much less reliable for some areas than others and because boundary changes often make it hard to be sure what we are talking about under the same name at different times. Some certainly underwent checks and possibly setbacks in their population growth in a wave of seventeenth-century disasters. Spain, Italy and Germany all had bad outbreaks of epidemic disease in the 1630s and there were other celebrated local attacks such as the Great Plague of London of 1665. Famine was another sporadic and local check; we hear even of cannibalism in the middle seventeenth century in Germany. Poor feeding and the lower resistance it led to quickly produced disaster when coupled to the disruption of the economy which could follow a bad harvest. When accentuated by warfare, of which there was always a great deal in central Europe, the result could be cataclysmic. Famine and the diseases which followed armies about in their baggage-trains could quickly depopulate a small area. Yet this in part reflected the degree to which economic life was still localized; the

The Italian city-states were the most dynamic in the Mediterranean in the 16th century. They were thriving trade and industrial centres and had commercial ties with both the Near East and western Europe. Known as the *Carta della Catena*, this view of the city of Florence dates from 1480.

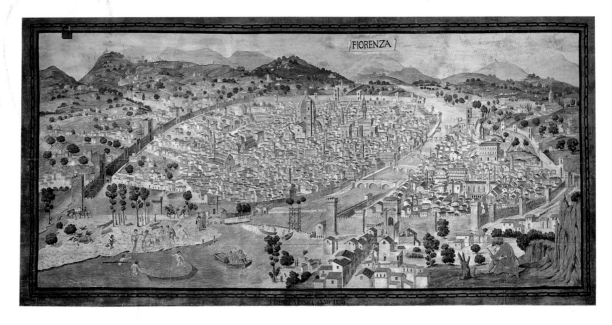

For most 16th-century Europeans, the great religious festivals and the seasonal agrarian tasks, with their cyclical rhythms, served to mark the passing of time. One of the most important activities of the year is depicted in this painting, *Hay Making in July*, by Pieter Brueghel the Elder (c.1520–1569).

converse was that a particular town might get off unscathed even in a campaigning zone if it escaped siege or sack, while only a few miles away another was devastated. The situation was always precarious until population growth began to be overtaken by increases in productivity.

AGRICULTURAL ADVANCES

In PRODUCTIVITY LEVELS, as in so many things, different countries have different histories. A renewed expansion of agriculture seems to have got under way in the middle of the fifteenth century. One sign was the resumption of land which had reverted to waste in the depopulation of the fourteenth century. Yet this had made little headway in any but a few places before 1550 or so. It remained confined to them for a long time,

An August corn harvest is depicted in this engraving from a French Book of Hours (c.1520). At harvest-time, debts were settled, exchanges were made at markets and fairs, taxes were paid and preparations were made for winter. If the harvest failed, however, disaster inevitably followed.

though by then there had already been important improvements in techniques which raised the productivity of land, mainly by the application of labour, that is by intensive cultivation. Where their impact was not felt the medieval past long lingered in the countryside. Even the coming of money was slow in breaking into the near self-sufficiency of some communities. In eastern Europe serfdom actually extended its range when it was dying out elsewhere. Yet by 1800, taking Europe as a whole and a few leading countries in particular, agriculture was one of the two economic sectors where progress was most marked (commerce was the other). Overall, it had proved capable of sustaining a continuing rise of population at first very slowly, but at a quickening rate.

Agricultural life was slowly changed by increasing orientation towards markets, and by technical innovation. They were interconnected. A large population in the neighbourhood meant a market and therefore an incentive. Even in the fifteenth century the inhabitants of the Low Countries were already leaders in the techniques of intensive cultivation. It was in Flanders, too, that better drainage opened the way to better pasture and to a larger animal population. Another area with relatively large town populations was the Po valley; in north Italy new crops were introduced into Europe from Asia. Rice, for example, an important addition to the European larder, appeared in the Arno and Po valleys in the fifteenth century. On the other hand not all crops enjoyed instant success. It took about two centuries for the potato, which came to Europe from America, to become a normal item of consumption in England, Germany and France, in spite of its obvious nutritional value and much promotional folklore stressing its qualities as an aphrodisiac and value in the treatment of warts.

ENGLISH AGRICULTURAL PROWESS

From the Low Countries agricultural improvements spread in the sixteenth century to eastern England where they were slowly elaborated further. In the seventeenth century London became a corn-exporting port and in the next continental Europeans would come to England to learn how to farm. The eighteenth century also brought better husbandry and animal breeding. Such improvements led to yields on crops and a quality of livestock now taken for granted but until then unimaginable. The appearance of the countryside and its occupants was transformed. Agriculture provided the first demonstration of what might be done by even rudimentary science – by experiment, observation, record, and experiment again – to increase human

The Europe of this time was a rural continent; the majority of its population lived in the countryside and most economic activity was related to working the land. Farm labourers are shown working and resting in the fields during the wheat harvest in this 16th-century manuscript illustration.

This portrait by Thomas Gainsborough (1727–1788), entitled *Mr and Mrs Andrews*, was painted in 1748 and reflects the subjects' wealth and social position. Behind the rich landowner and his wife lie rows of neat enclosed fields – the product of the steady transformation of English agricultural methods.

control of the environment more rapidly than could the selection imposed by custom. Improvement favoured the reorganization of land in bigger farms, the reduction of the number of smallholders except on land which specially favoured them, the employment of wage-labour, and high capital investment in buildings, drainage and machinery. The speed of change must not be exaggerated. One index of change in England was the pace of "enclosure", the consolidation for private use of the open fields and common lands of the traditional village. It was only at the end of the eighteenth century and the beginning of the nineteenth that the Acts of Parliament authorizing this became frequent and numerous. The complete integration of agriculture with the market economy and the treatment of land simply as a commodity like any other would have to wait for the nineteenth century, even in England, the leader of world agriculture until the opening of the transoceanic cornlands. Yet by the eighteenth century the way ahead was beginning to appear.

THE RETREAT OF FAMINE

Greater agricultural productivity in the end eliminated the recurrent dearths which so long retained their power to destroy demographic advance. Perhaps the last moment when European population seems to have pressed on resources so as to threaten another great calamity like that of the fourteenth century came at the end of the sixteenth century. In the next bad spell, in the middle decades of the following century, England and the Netherlands escaped the worst. Thereafter, famine and dearth became in Europe local and national events, still capable, it is true, of causing large-scale demographic damage, but gradually succumbing to the increasing availability of imported grain. Bad harvests, it has been said, made France "one great hospital" in 1708–9, but that was in wartime. Later in the century some Mediterranean countries depended for their flour on corn from the Baltic lands. True, it would be a long time before import would be a sure resource; often it could not operate quickly enough,

A plentiful meal, such as the one depicted in *The Wedding Feast* by the Flemish painter Pieter Brueghel the Elder (c.1520–1569), would have been a rare treat in the daily lives of most European peasants.

especially where land transport was required. Some parts of France and Germany were to suffer dearth even in the nineteenth century, and in the eighteenth century the French population grew faster than production so that the standard of living of many French people then actually fell back. For the English rural labourer, though, some of that century was later looked back to as a golden age of plentiful wheaten bread and even meat on the table.

EMIGRATION TO THE NEW WORLD

In the late sixteenth century one response to the obscurely felt pressure of an expanding population upon slowly growing resources had been the promotion of emigration. By 1800, Europeans had done much to people lands overseas. Though far from so great a one as was to come, this has to be taken into account in their demographic history. In 1751 an American reckoned that North America contained a million persons of British origin; modern calculations are that about 250,000 British emigrants went to the New World in the seventeenth century, one and a half million in the next. There were also Germans (about 200,000) there, and a few French in Canada. By 1800 it seems reasonable to suppose that something like two million Europeans had gone to America north of the Rio Grande. South of it there were about 100,000 Spaniards and Portuguese.

THE NEW COMMERCIAL WORLD

F EAR THAT THERE WAS NOT ENOUGH to eat at home helped to initiate these great migrations and reflected the continuing pre-eminence of agriculture in all thinking about economic life. There were important changes in three centuries in the structure and scale of all the main sectors of the European economy, but it was still true in 1800 (as it had been true in 1500) that the agricultural sector predominated even in France and England, the two largest Western countries where commerce and manufacture had much progressed. Moreover, nowhere was anything but a tiny part of the population engaged in industry entirely unconnected with agriculture. Brewers, weavers, and dyers all depended on it, while many who grew crops or cultivated land also spun, wove or dealt in commodities for the market. Apart from agriculture, it is only in the commercial sector that we can observe sweeping change. Here there is from the second half of the fifteenth century a visible quickening of tempo. Europe was then regaining something like the commercial vigour first displayed in the thirteenth century and it showed in scale, technique and direction. Again there is a connection with the growth of towns. They both needed and provided a living for specialists. The great fairs and markets of the Middle Ages still continued. So did medieval laws on usury and the restrictive practices of guilds. Yet a whole new commercial world came into existence before 1800.

It was already discernible in the sixteenth century when there began the long expansion of world commerce which was to last, virtually uninterrupted except briefly by war, until 1930, and then to be resumed again after another world war. It started by carrying further the shift of economic gravity from southern to northwestern Europe, from the Mediterranean to the Atlantic, which has already been remarked. One contribution to this was made by political troubles and wars such as ruined Italy in the early sixteenth century; others are comprised in tiny, short-lived but crucial pressures like the Portuguese harassment of Jews which led to so many of them going, with their commercial skills, to the Low Countries at about the same time.

In 17th-century England and France, the poor spent up to 80 per cent of their incomes on fresh foodstuffs. Although bartering was still predominant in some rural areas, perishable goods were increasingly bought and sold at weekly markets. This scene, depicting an open-air market in the Quai des Grands-Augustins in Paris, dates from c.1660.

The great commercial success story of the sixteenth century was that of Antwerp, though it collapsed after a few decades in political and economic disaster. In the seventeenth century Amsterdam and London surpassed it. In each case an important trade based on a well-populated hinterland provided profits for diversification into manufacturing industry, services and banking. The old banking supremacy of the medieval Italian cities passed first to Flanders and the German bankers of the sixteenth century and then, finally, to Holland and London. The Bank of Amsterdam and even the Bank of England, founded only in 1694, were soon international economic forces. About them clustered other banks and merchant houses undertaking operations of credit and finance. Interest rates came down and the bill of exchange, a medieval invention, underwent an enormous extension of use and became the primary financial instrument of international trade.

Money was used for an ever greater diversity of transactions by the 16th century. The amount of trade on credit increased as drafts, letters of credit and bills of exchange became acceptable. Many specialized dealers, such as those portrayed by Marinus van Reymerswaele in *The Money Changer and his Wife* (c.1540), flourished, and speculation and fraud were rife.

THE APPARATUS OF MODERN CAPITALISM

The growing importance of the bill of exchange marked the beginning of the increasing use of paper, instead of bullion. In the eighteenth century came the first European paper currencies and the invention of the cheque. Joint stock companies generated another form of negotiable security, their own shares. Quotation of these in London coffee-houses in the seventeenth century was overtaken by the foundation of the London Stock Exchange. By 1800 similar institutions existed in many other countries. New schemes for the mobilization of capital and its deployment proliferated in London, Paris and Amsterdam. Lotteries and tontines at one time enjoyed a vogue; so did some spectacularly disastrous investment booms, of which the most notorious was the great English South Sea "Bubble". But all the time the world was growing more commercial, more used to the idea of employing money to make money, and was supplying itself with the apparatus of modern capitalism.

One effect quickly appeared in the much greater attention paid to commercial questions in diplomatic negotiation from the later seventeenth century and in the fact that countries were prepared to fight over them. The English and Dutch went to war over trade in 1652. This opened a long era during which they, the French and the Spanish, fought again and again over quarrels in which questions of trade were important and often paramount.

Governments not only looked after their merchants by going to war to uphold their interests, but also intervened in other ways in the working of the commercial economy. Sometimes they themselves were entrepreneurs and employers; the arsenal at Venice, it has been said, was at one time in the sixteenth century the largest single manufacturing enterprise in the world. They could also offer monopoly privileges to a company under a charter; this made the raising of capital easier by offering better security for a return. In the end people came to think that chartered companies might not be the best way of securing economic advantage and they fell into disfavour (enjoying a last brief revival at the end of the nineteenth century). None the less, such activities closely involved government and so the concerns of businessmen came to shape policy and law.

THE FIRST COMMERCIAL LIFE INSURANCE

Occasionally the interplay of commercial development and society seems to throw light on changes with very deep implications

As the rate of wholesale trade increased and became more complex, representatives and intermediaries became more common, building up reputations based on their specialization, for the region in which they worked, or for the company to which they belonged. *Portrait of Gisze the Merchant* was painted by Hans Holbein the Younger (1497–1543).

indeed. One example came when a seventeenth-century English financier for the first time offered life insurance to the public. There had already begun the practice of selling annuities on individuals' lives. What was new was the application of actuarial science and the newly available statistics of "political arithmetic" to this business. A reasonable calculation instead of a bet was now possible on a matter hitherto of awe-inspiring uncertainty and irrationality: death. With increasing refinement men would go on to offer (at a price) protection against a widening range of disasters. This would, incidentally, also provide another and very important device for the mobilization of wealth in large amounts for further investment. But the timing of the discovery of life insurance, at the start of what has sometimes been called the "Age of Reason", suggests also that the dimensions of economic change are sometimes very far-reaching indeed. It was one tiny source and expression of a coming secularizing of the universe.

INTERNATIONAL TRADE

THE MOST IMPRESSIVE structural development in European commerce was the sudden new importance to it of overseas trade from the second half of the seventeenth century onwards. This was part of the shift of economic activity from Mediterranean to northern Europe already observable before 1500, which first made visible the lineaments of a future world economy. Until about 1580, though, these were still largely the work of the Iberian peoples. They not only dominated the South Atlantic and Caribbean trades, but after 1564 there were regular sailings of "Manila galleons" from Acapulco to the Philippines; so China was brought into commercial touch with Europeans from further east, even as the Portuguese established themselves from the west. Global commerce was beginning to eclipse the old Mediterranean trade. By the late seventeenth century, while the closed trade of Spain and Portugal with their transatlantic colonies was still important, overseas commerce was dominated by the Dutch and their increasingly successful rivals, the English. Dutch success had grown out of the supply of salted herrings to European markets and the possession of a particularly suitable bulk-carrying vessel, the "flute" or "fly-boat". With this the Dutch first dominated the Baltic trade; from it they advanced to become the carriers of Europe. Though often displaced by the English in the

The Atlantic coastal ports enjoyed a level of trade equal to that of the Baltic and the Mediterranean in variety and intensity, but were also the departure points for transoceanic trade – the most spectacular of the age. The port of Lisbon is portrayed in this 16th-century painting.

OLISIPO. SIVE VT PERVE: TVSTÆ LAPIDVM INSCRIP: TIONES HABENT, VLYSIPPO, VVLGO LISBONA FLORENTIS. SIMVM PORTVGALLIÆ EMPORIV.

Together with Lisbon, the port of Seville, depicted in this painting, played a crucial role in the link between the Old and the New worlds. It was also a distribution centre for precious metals, which were dispersed from Seville throughout the rest of Europe and the world.

later seventeenth century, they maintained a far-flung network of colonies and trading stations, especially in the Far East, where they overpowered the Portuguese. The basis of English supremacy, though, was the Atlantic. Fish were important here, too; the English caught the nutritious cod on the Newfoundland banks, dried it and salted it ashore, and then sold it in Mediterranean countries, where fish was in great demand because of the practice of fasting on Fridays. *Bacalao*, as it was called, can still be found on the tables of Portugal and southern Spain, away from the tourist coast. Gradually, both Dutch and English broadened and diversified their carrying trade and became dealers themselves, too. Nor was France out of the race; her overseas trade doubled in the first half of the seventeenth century.

Rising populations and some assurance of adequate transport (water was always cheaper than land carriage) slowly built up an international trade in cereals. Shipbuilding itself promoted the movement of such commodities as pitch, flax or timber, staples first of Baltic trade and later important in the economy of North America. More than European consumption was involved; all this took place in a setting of growing colonial empires. By the eighteenth century we are already in the presence of an oceanic economy and an international trading community which does business – and fights and intrigues for it – around the globe.

BLACK SLAVERY

IN THE NEW GLOBAL ECONOMY an important and growing part was played by slaves. Most of them were black Africans, the first of whom to be brought to Europe were sold at Lisbon in 1444. In Europe itself, slavery had by then all but withered away, mostly because of a self-generated supply of labour (although Europeans were still being enslaved and sold into slavery by Arabs and Turks). Now it was to undergo a vast extension in other continents. Within two or three years over a thousand more blacks had been sold by the Portuguese, who soon set up a permanent slaving station in West Africa. Such figures show the rapid discovery of the profitability of the new traffic but gave little hint of the scale of what was to come. What was already clear was the brutality of the business (the Portuguese quickly noted that the seizure of children usually ensured the docile captivity

This 17th-century painting, entitled *Dance of the Negro Slaves*, depicts black slave workers on a Brazilian plantation.

of the parents) and the complicity of Africans in it; as the search for slaves went further inland, it became simple to rely on local potentates who would round up captives and barter them wholesale.

For a long time, Europe and the Portuguese and Spanish settlements in the Atlantic islands took almost all the slaves West Africa supplied. Then came a change. From the mid-sixteenth century African slaves were shipped across the Atlantic to Brazil, the Caribbean islands and the North American mainland. The trade thus entered upon a long period of dramatic growth whose demographic, economic and political consequences are still with us. African slaves are by no means the only ones important in modern history, nor were Europeans the only slavers. None the less, black slavery based on the selling by Africans of other Africans to Portuguese, Englishmen, Dutchmen and Frenchmen, and their subsequent sale to other Europeans in the Americas, is a phenomenon whose repercussions have been much more profound than the enslavement of Europeans by Ottomans or Africans by Arabs. The approximate numbers of those enslaved, too, have seemed easier to establish, if only approximately. Much of the labour which made American colonies possible and viable was supplied by black slaves, though

for climatic reasons the slave population was not uniformly spread among them. Always the great majority of slaves worked in agriculture or domestic service: black craftsmen or, later, factory workers were unusual.

SLAVE LABOUR

The slave trade was commercially very important, too. Huge profits were occasionally made – a fact which partly explains the crammed and pestilential holds of the slaveships in which were confined the human cargoes. They rarely had a death rate per voyage of less than 10 per cent and sometimes suffered much more appalling mortality. The supposed value of the trade made it a great and contested prize, though the normal return on capital has been much exaggerated. For two centuries it provoked diplomatic wrangling and even war as nation after nation sought to break into it or monopolize it. This testified to the trade's importance in the eyes of statesmen, whether it was economically justified or not.

MECHANICAL ENGINEERING SKILLS IN EUROPE

It was once widely held that the slave trade's profits provided the capital for European industrialization, but this no longer seems plausible. Industrialization was a slow process. Before 1800, though examples of industrial concentration could be found in several European countries, the growth of both manufacturing and extractive industry was still in the main a matter of the multiplication of small-scale artisan production and its technical elaboration, rather than of radically new methods and institutions. Europe had by 1500 an enormous pool of wealth to draw on in her large numbers of skilled craftsmen, already used to investigating new process and exploring new techniques. Two centuries of gunnery had brought mining and metallurgy to a high pitch. Scientific instruments and mechanical clocks testified to a wide diffusion of skill in the making of precision goods. Such advantages as these shaped the early pattern of the industrial age and soon began to reverse a traditional relationship with Asia. For centuries oriental craftsmen had astounded Europeans by their skill and the quality of their work. Asian textiles and ceramics had a superiority which lives in our everyday language: china, muslin, calico, shantung are still familiar words. Then, in the fourteenth and fifteenth centuries, supremacy in some forms of craftsmanship had passed to Europe, notably in mechanical and engineering skills. Asian potentates began to seek Europeans who could teach them how to make effective firearms; they even collected mechanical toys which were the commonplaces of European fairs. Such a reversal of roles was based on Europe's accumulation of skills in traditional occupations and their extension into new fields. This happened usually in towns; craftsmen often travelled from one to another, following demand. So much it is easy to see. It is harder to see what it was in the European mind that pressed the European craftsman forward and also stimulated the interest of his social betters so that a craze for mechanical engineering is as important an aspect of the age of the Renaissance as is the work of its architects and goldsmiths. After all, this did not happen elsewhere.

INDUSTRIAL GROWTH

EARLY INDUSTRIAL AREAS grew by accretion, not only around the centres of established European manufactures (such as textiles or brewing) closely related to agriculture but in the countryside. This long continued to be true. Old trades created concentrations of supporting industry. Antwerp had been the great port of entry to Europe for English cloth; as a result, finishing and dyeing establishments appeared there to work up further the commodities flowing through the port. Meanwhile, in the English countryside, wool merchants shaped the early pattern of industrial growth by "putting out" to peasant spinners and weavers the raw materials they needed. The presence of minerals was another locating factor; mining and metallurgy were the most important industrial activities independent of agriculture and were widely dispersed. But industries could stagnate or even, sometimes, collapse. This seems to have happened to Italy. Its medieval industrial pre-eminence disappeared in the sixteenth century while that of the Flemish Low Countries and western and southern Germany – the old Carolingian heartland – lasted another century or so until it began to be clear that England, the Dutch Netherlands and Sweden

Carved by a Danish woodworker c.1600, this bas-relief shows skilled clockmakers building a mechanical clock.

Dating from 1801, this painting portrays the English Coalbrookdale iron-smelting works by night. The works was founded by the pioneering iron master Abraham Darby (c.1678–1717), who was the first person successfully to use coke to smelt iron. His grandson, also called Abraham Darby (1750–1791), designed and produced the world's first cast-iron bridge, at the Coalbrookdale foundry in 1779.

were the new manufacturing leaders. In the eighteenth century Russia's extractive industries would add her to the list of industrial countries. By then, too, other factors were beginning to enter the equation; organized science was being brought to bear on industrial techniques and state policy was shaping industry both consciously and unconsciously.

INFLATION

The long-term picture of overall expansion and growth obviously requires much qualification. Dramatic fluctuations could easily occur even in the nineteenth century, when a bad harvest could lead to runs on banks and a contraction of demand for manufactured goods big enough to be called a slump. This reflected the growing development and integration of the economy. It could cause new forms of distress. Not long after 1500, for example, it began to be noticed that prices were rising with unprecedented speed.

Locally this trend was sometimes very sharp indeed, doubling costs in a year. Though nothing like this rate was maintained anywhere for long the general effect seems to have been a roughly fourfold rise in European prices in a century. Given twentieth-century inflation, this does not seem very shocking, but it was quite novel and had great and grave repercussions. Some property owners benefited and some suffered. Some landowners reacted by putting up rents and increasing as much as possible the yields from their feudal dues. Some had to sell out. In this sense, inflation made for social mobility, as it often does. Among the poor, the effects were usually harsh, for the price of agricultural produce shot up and money wages did not keep pace. Real wages therefore fell. This was sometimes made worse by local factors, too. In England, for example, high wool prices tempted landlords to enclose common land and thus remove it from common use in order to put sheep on it. The wretched peasant grazier starved and, thus, as one famous contemporary comment put it, "sheep ate men". Everywhere in the central third of the century there were popular revolts and a running disorder which reveal both the incomprehensibility and the severity of what was going on. Everywhere it was the extremes of society which felt the pinch of inflation most sharply; to the poor it brought starvation while kings were pinched because they had to spend more than anyone else.

Much ink has been spent by historians on explaining this century-long price rise. They no longer feel satisfied with the explanation first put forward by contemporary observers, that the essential cause was a new supply of bullion which followed the opening of the New World mines by the Spanish; inflation was well under way before American bullion began to arrive in any significant quantity, even if gold later aggravated things. Probably the fundamental pressure always came from a population whose numbers were increasing when big advances in productivity still lay in the future. The rise in prices continued until the beginning of the seventeenth century. Then it began occasionally even to show signs of falling until a slower increase was resumed around 1700.

A NEW SOCIAL ORDER

IN OUR OWN DAY we need no reminders that social change can quickly follow economic change. We have little belief in the immutability of social forms and institutions. Three hundred years ago, many men and women believed them to be virtually God-given and the result was that although social changes took place in the aftermath of inflation (and, it must be said, for many other reasons) they were muffled and masked by the persistence of old forms. Superficially and nominally much of European society remained

By the Flemish painter David Teniers the Younger (1610–1690), this portrayal of *Peasants in the Tavern* dates from the second half of the 17th century. Not everyone had equal access to the food-stuffs that became increasingly available as international trade grew. The peasant's diet was limited, monotonous and generally lacking in meat. However, the consumption of wine, beer, cider and liquor became a common way of filling empty hours and stomachs.

Painted by Caravaggio (1571–1610), *The Fortune-Teller* dates from c.1594. Despite people's greater knowledge of the world, the cultivation of reason and the advance of science, strong superstitious beliefs remained common in 16th-century Europe.

unchanged between 1500 and 1800 or thereabouts. Yet the economic realities underlying it changed a great deal. Appearances were deceptive.

Rural life had already begun to show this in some countries before 1500. As agriculture became more and more a matter of business (though by no means only because of that), traditional rural society had to change. Forms were usually preserved, and the results were more and more incongruous. Although feudal lordship still existed in France in the 1780s it was by then less a social reality than an economic device. The "seigneur" might never see his tenants, might not be of noble blood, and might draw nothing from his lordship except sums of money which represented his claims on his tenants' labour, time and produce. Further east, the feudal relationship remained more of a reality. This in part reflected an alliance of rulers and nobles to take advantage of the new market for grain and timber in the growing population of western and southern Europe. They tied peasants to the land and exacted heavier and heavier labour services. In Russia serfdom became the very basis of society.

THE ENGLISH NOBILITY

In England even the commercialized "feudalism" which existed in France had gone long before 1800, and noble status conferred no legal privilege beyond the rights of peers to be summoned to a parliament (their other legal distinction was that like most of the other subjects of King George III, they could not vote in the election of a Member of Parliament). The English nobility was a tiny set; until the end of the eighteenth century the House of Lords had fewer than two hundred hereditary members, whose status could only be transmitted to their one direct heir.

Consequently, there did not exist in England the large class of noble men and women, all enjoying extensive legal privileges separating them from the rest of the population, such as there was almost universally elsewhere in Europe. In France there were perhaps a quarter of a million nobles on the eve of the Revolution. All had important legal and formal rights; the corresponding legal order in England could comfortably have been assembled in the hall of an Oxford college and would have had rights correspondingly less impressive.

On the other hand, the wealth and social influence of English landowners was immense. Below the peerage stretched the ill-defined class of English gentlemen, linked at the top to the peers' families and disappearing at the other end into the ranks of prosperous farmers and merchants who were eminently respectable but not "gentlefolk". Its permeability was of enormous value in promoting cohesion and mobility. Gentlemanly status could be approached by enrichment, by professional distinction, or by personal merit. It was essentially a matter of a shared code of behaviour, still reflecting the aristocratic concept of honour, but one civilized by the purging away of its exclusiveness, its gothicisms and its legal supports. In the seventeenth and eighteenth centuries the idea of the gentleman became one of the formative cultural influences of English history.

CHANGES IN EUROPEAN RULING HIERARCHIES

In fact, ruling hierarchies differed from country to country. Contrasts could be drawn right across Europe. There would be nothing tidy about the result. None the less, a broad tendency towards social change which strained old forms is observable in many countries by 1700. In the most advanced countries it brought new ideas about what constituted status and how it should be recognized. Though not complete, there was a shift from personal ties to market relationships as a way of defining people's rights and expectations, and a shift from a corporate vision of society to an individualist one. This was most notable in the United Provinces, the republic which emerged

This 16th-century engraving shows Queen Elizabeth I of England presiding over a meeting of Parliament. The commoners were already beginning to challenge policies laid down by the Crown and its noble councillors.

in the Dutch Netherlands during this era. It was in effect ruled by merchants, particularly those of Amsterdam, the centre of Holland, its richest province. Here the landed nobility had never counted for as much as the mercantile and urban oligarchs.

RESPECT FOR ARISTOCRATS

Nowhere else in Europe had social change gone as far by 1789 as in Great Britain and the United Provinces. Elsewhere questioning of traditional status had barely begun. Figaro, the valet-hero of a notably successful eighteenth-century French comedy, jibed that his aristocratic master had done nothing to deserve his privileges beyond giving himself the trouble to be born. This was recognized at the time as a dangerous and subversive idea, but hardly caused much alarm. Europe was still soaked in the assumptions of aristocracy (and was to be for a long time, even after 1800). Degrees of exclusiveness varied, but the distinction between noble and non-noble remained crucial. Though alarmed aristocrats accused them of doing so, kings would nowhere ally with commoners against them even in the last resort. Kings were aristocrats, too; it was their trade, one of them said. Only the coming of a great revolution in France changed things much and then

hardly at all outside that country before the end of the century. As the nineteenth century began, it looked as if most Europeans still respected noble blood. All that had changed was that not so many people still automatically thought it was a distinction which ought to be reflected in laws.

Just as some people began to feel that to describe society in terms of orders, with legally distinct rights and obligations, no longer expressed its reality, so also a few of them were beginning to feel less sure that religion upheld a particular social hierarchy. It was still for a long time possible to believe that:

The rich man in his castle,
the poor man at his gate,
God made them, high and lowly,
and ordered their estate

as an Ulsterwoman put it in the nineteenth century, but this was not quite the same thing as saying that a fixed unchanging order was the expression of God's will. Even by 1800 a few people were beginning to think God rather liked the rich man to show the wisdom of God's way by having made his own way in the world rather than by inheriting his father's place. "Government is a contrivance of human wisdom for the satisfaction of human wants," said an eighteenth-century Irishman, and he was a

conservative, too. A broad utilitarianism was coming to be the way more and more people assessed institutions in advanced countries, social institutions among them.

STRAINS

The old formal hierarchies were under most pressure where strain was imposed upon them by economic change – increasing mobility, the growth of towns, the rise of a market economy, the appearance of new commercial opportunities – but also the spread of literacy and social awareness. Broadly speaking, three situations can be distinguished. In the East, in Russia, and almost to the same extent in Poland or east Prussia and Hungary, agrarian society was still so little disturbed by

new developments that the traditional social pattern was not only intact but all but unchallenged at the end of the eighteenth century. In these landlocked countries, safe from the threats to the existing order implicit in the commercial development of maritime Europe, the traditional ruling classes not only retained their position but had often showed that they could actually enlarge their privileges. In a second group of countries, there was enough of a clash between the economic and social worlds which were coming into being and the existing order to provoke demands for change. When political circumstances permitted its resolution, these would demand satisfaction, though they could be contained for a time. France was the outstanding example, but in some of the German states, Belgium and parts of Italy there were signs of

The 16th century was a desperate time for France. The government went bankrupt, inflation soared and the country was plagued by the terror and cruelty of a religious civil war. However, the French court maintained its lavish rituals, as shown by this painting, which dates from 1581 and depicts a dance at the court of King Henry III.

London's role as a centre for national and international commerce brought the city considerable wealth. This painting by the English artist William Marlow (1740–1813) shows a busy wharf close to London Bridge.

the same sort of strain. The third group of countries were those relatively more open societies, such as England, the Netherlands and, across the sea, British North America, where the formal distinctions of society already meant less by comparison with wealth (or even talent), where legal rights were widely diffused, economic opportunity was felt to be widespread, and wage-dependency was very marked. Even in the sixteenth century, English society seems much more fluid than that of continental countries and, indeed, when the North Americans came to give themselves a new constitution in the eighteenth century they forbade the conferring of hereditary titles. In these countries individualism had a scope almost untrammelled by law, whatever the real restraints of custom and opportunity.

THE "ADVANCED" EUROPEAN COUNTRIES

It is only too easy in a general account such as this to be overprecise, over-definite. Even the suggested rough tripartite division blurs too much. There were startling contrasts within societies which we might misinterpret if we think of them as homogeneous. In the advanced countries there was still much that we should find strange, even antediluvian. The towns of England, France and Germany were for the most part wrapped in a comfortable provincialism lorded over by narrow merchant oligarchies, successful guildsmen or cathedral chapters. Yet Chartres, contentedly rooted in its medieval countryside and medieval ways, its eighteenth-century population still the same size as five hundred years earlier, was part of the same country as Nantes or Bordeaux, thriving, bustling ports which were only two of several making up the dynamic sector of the French economy. Even the nineteenth century would find its immediate forebears unprogressive; far be it from us, therefore, to predicate the existence of a mature and clearly defined individualist and capitalist society wholly conscious of itself as such in any European country. What marked the countries we might call "advanced" was a tendency to move further and faster in that direction than the great majority of the rest of the world.

Sometimes this won them admiration by would-be reformers. One great questioner of the status quo, Voltaire, was greatly struck by the fact that even in the early eighteenth century a great merchant could be as esteemed and respected in England as was a nobleman. He may have slightly exaggerated and he certainly blurred some important nuances, yet it is remarkable – and a part of the story of the rise of Great Britain to world power – that the political class which governed eighteenth-century England was a landed class and fiercely reflected landed values, yet constantly took care to defend the commercial interests of the country and accepted the leadership and guidance in this of the collective wisdom of the City of London. Though people went on talking of a political division between the "moneyed" and the "landed" interest, and though politics long remained a matter of disputed places and conflicting traditions within the landed class, interests which in other countries would have conflicted with these nevertheless prospered and were not alienated. The explanations must be complex. Some, like the commercialization of British agriculture, go far back into the history of the previous century; some, such as the growth of facilities for private investment in the government and commercial world, were much more recent.

THE DOMINANT NORTHWESTERN STATES

The coincidence of the advanced social evolution of the Netherlands and Great Britain with their economic, and especially their commercial, success is striking. This was once largely attributed to their religion: as a result of a great upheaval within Christendom both had ceased to be dominated by the Catholic Church. Anti-clericals in the eighteenth century and sociologists in the twentieth sought to explore and exploit this coincidence; Protestantism, it was said, provided an ethic for capitalism. This no longer seems plausible. There were too may Catholic capitalists, for one thing, and they were often successful. France and Spain were still important trading countries in the eighteenth century and the first seems to have enjoyed something like the same rates of growth as Great Britain, though she was later to fall behind. They were both countries with Atlantic access, and it was those which had tended to show economic

The busy market and washing place of Antwerp, Flanders, were painted by Joost de Momper in 1443. The success of the annual regional and national festivals that were held in Antwerp had attracted new wealth and inhabitants to the growing city.

growth ever since the sixteenth century. Yet this is not an explanation which goes very far, either. Scotland – northern, Protestant and Atlantic – long remained backward, poor and feudal. There was more to the differences separating Mediterranean and eastern Europe from the north and west than simple geographical position and more than one factor to the explanation of differing rates of modernization. The progress of English and Dutch agriculture, for example, may owe more to the relative scarcity of land in each country than to anything else.

THE EUROPEAN EAST

The European East remained mostly unaffected by these changes. Its social and economic structure remained fundamentally unchanged until the nineteenth century. Deep-rooted explanations have been offered – that, for example, a shorter growing season and less rich soils than were to be found further

west gave it from the start a poorer return on seed, and therefore handicapped it economically in the crucial early stages of agricultural growth. It had man-made handicaps, too. Settlement there had long been open to disturbance by Central Asian nomads, while on its southern flank lay the Balkans and the frontier with Turkey, for many centuries a zone of warfare, raiding and banditry. In some areas (Hungary for example) the effects of Turkish rule had been so bad as to depopulate the country. When it was reacquired for Europe, care was taken to tie the peasantry to the land. In the Russia which emerged from Muscovy in this period, too, the serf population grew larger as a proportion of the whole. Harsher law put state power behind the masters' control of the peasants. In other eastern countries (Prussia was one), the powers of landlords over tenants were strengthened. This was more than just a kingly indulgence of aristocracies which might, if not placated, turn against royal authority. It was also a device for economic development. Not for the first time, nor the last, economic progress went with social injustice; serfdom was a way of making available one of the resources needed if land was to be made productive, just as forced labour was in many other countries at many other times.

One result, which is still in some degree visible, was a Europe divided roughly along the Elbe. To the west lay countries evolving slowly by 1800 towards more open social forms. To the east lay authoritarian governments presiding over agrarian societies where a minority of landholders enjoyed great powers over a largely tied peasantry. In this area towns did not often prosper as they had done for centuries in the west. They tended to be overtaxed islands in a rural sea, unable to attract from the countryside the labour they needed because of the dead hand of serfdom. Over great tracts of Poland and Russia even a

This painting by Jan Vermeer of Delft (1632–1675), entitled *The Visit*, depicts two members of the settled and orderly middle class that was characteristic of the Netherlands by the 17th century. Most Dutch people from this social background appreciated fine fabrics, works of art and elegant pieces of furniture, while retaining their sense of the spiritual value of austerity.

A reading from a tragedy by the celebrated writer Voltaire is given in Madame Geoffrin's drawing-room, or *salon*, in 1775. French noblewomen and ladies of the upper bourgeoisie organized conferences, concerts and scientific experiments, which, in some cases, converted their drawing-rooms into distinguished academies.

money economy barely existed. Much of later European history was implicit in this difference between east and west.

WOMEN IN EUROPE

The east–west divide was discernible in informal institutions, too, in the way, for example, in which women were treated, though here another division could be drawn, that between Mediterranean Europe and the north, which was in due course extended to run between Latin and North America. Formally and legally, little changed anywhere in these centuries; the legal status of women remained what it had been and this was only to be questioned right at the end of this period. Nevertheless, the real independence of women and, in particular, of upper-class women, does seem to have been extended in the more advanced countries. Even in the fifteenth century it had been remarked by foreigners that Englishwomen enjoyed

unusual freedom. This lead does not seem to have diminished, but in the eighteenth century there are signs that in France, at least, a well-born woman could enjoy considerable real independence.

This was in part because the eighteenth century brought the appearance of a new sort of upper-class life, one which had room for other social gatherings than those of a royal court, and one increasingly independent of religious and family ritual. At the end of the seventeenth century we hear of men in London meeting in the coffee-houses from which the first clubs were to spring. Soon there appears the salon, the social gathering of friends and acquaintances in a lady's drawing-room which was especially the creation of the French; some eighteenth-century salons were important intellectual centres and show that it had become proper and even fashionable for a woman to show an interest in things of the mind other than religion. On one of the occasions on which Madame de Pompadour, the mistress of Louis

XV, was painted, she chose to have included in the picture a book – Montesquieu's sociological treatise, *De l'esprit des lois*. But even when women did not aspire to blue stockings, the salon and the appearance of a society independent of the court presented them with a real, if limited, escape from the confinement of the family, which, together with religious and professional gatherings, had until then been virtually the only structures within which even men might seek social variety and diversion.

THE UNQUESTIONED CERTAINTIES OF EUROPEAN SOCIETY

By the end of the eighteenth century we have arrived at the age of the female artist and novelist and of acceptance of the fact that spinsterhood need not mean retirement to a cloister. Where such changes came from is not easy to see. In the early years of the century the English *Spectator* already thought it worthwhile to address itself to women readers as well as men, which suggests that we should look a fair way back. Perhaps it helped that the eighteenth century produced such conspicuous examples of women of great political influence – an English queen and four empresses (one Austrian and three Russian) all ruled in their own right, often with success. But it is not possible to say so with confidence for the prehistory of female emancipation still largely awaits study.

Finally, none of this touched the life of the overwhelming majority in even the most advanced societies of early modern Europe. There had not yet come into being the mass industrial jobs which would provide the first great force to prize apart the unquestioned certainties of traditional life for most men and women alike. Though they may have weighed most heavily in the primitive villages of Poland or in a southern Spain where Moorish influences had intensified the subordination and seclusion of women, those certainties were everywhere still dominant in 1800.

Madame de Pompadour (1721–1764) is depicted in this portrait by the celebrated French painter François Boucher (1703–1770). The influential mistress of Louis XV, Madame de Pompadour befriended Boucher and played an important role in his career, commissioning countless paintings from him. In return, he painted her portrait on numerous occasions.

2 AUTHORITY AND ITS CHALLENGERS

IN 1800 MANY EUROPEANS still held ideas about social and political organization which would have been comprehensible and appropriate four hundred years earlier. The "Middle Ages" no more came to a sudden end in this respect than in many others. Ideas about society and government which may reasonably be described as "medieval" survived as effective forces over a wide area and during the centuries more and more social facts had been fitted into them. Broadly speaking, what has been called a "corporate" organization of society – the grouping of men in bodies with legal privileges which protected their members and defined their status – was still the rule in eighteenth-century continental Europe. Over much of its central and eastern zones, as we have noted, serfdom had grown more rigid and more widespread.

Many continuities in political institutions were obvious. The Holy Roman Empire still existed in 1800 as it had done in 1500; so did the temporal power of the pope. A descendant of the Capetians was still king of France (though he no longer came from the same branch of the family as in 1500 and, indeed, was in exile). Even in England and as late as 1820, a king's champion rode in full armour into Westminster Hall at the coronation banquet of King George IV, to uphold that monarch's title against all comers. In most countries it was still taken for granted that the state was a confessional entity, that religion and society were intertwined and that the authority of the Church was established by law. Although such ideas had been much challenged and in some countries had undergone grievous reverses, in this as in many

In this 15th-century Italian picture of a battle, the prince is still represented as the leader of his men as his troops come face to face with soldiers from another faction. From this period onward, however, it became increasingly common for kings and princes to employ generals to lead their armies.

Machiavelli on the use of power

"From this arises the following question: whether it is better to be loved than feared, or the reverse. The answer is that one would like to be both the one and the other; but because it is difficult to combine them, it is far better to be feared than loved if you cannot be both. ... Men worry less about doing an injury to one who makes himself loved than to one who makes himself feared. The bond of love is one which men, wretched creatures that they are, break when it is to their advantage to do so; but fear is strengthened by a dread of punishment which is always effective.

"The prince must none the less make himself feared in such a way that, if he is not loved, at least he escapes being hated. For fear is quite compatible with an absence of hatred; and the prince can always avoid hatred if he abstains from the property of his subjects and citizens and from their women. If, even so, it proves necessary to execute someone, this is to be done only when there is proper justification and manifest reason for it. But above all a prince must abstain from the property of others; because men sooner forget the death of their father than the loss of their patrimony."

An extract from *The Prince* by Niccolò Machiavelli (1469–1527), translated by George Bull.

matters the weight of history was still enormous in 1800 and only ten years earlier it had been even heavier.

STATE AUTHORITY

When all the continuity in European history is acknowledged, it was nevertheless the general tendency of the three centuries between 1500 and 1800 to dissolve or at least weaken old social and political bonds characteristic of medieval government. Power and authority had instead tended to flow towards the central concentration provided by the state, and away from "feudal" arrangements of personal dependence. (The very invention of the "feudal" idea as a technical term of law was in fact the work of the seventeenth century and it suggests the age's need to pin down something whose reality was ebbing away.) The idea of Christendom, too, though still important in emotional, even subconscious, ways effectively lost any political reality in this period. Papal authority had begun to suffer at the hands of national sentiment in the age of the Schism and that of the Holy Roman emperors had been of small account since the fourteenth century. Nor did any new unifying principle emerge to integrate Europe. The test case was the Ottoman threat. Christian princes exposed to the Muslim onslaught

The Italian statesman and writer Niccolò Machiavelli, one-time adviser to the powerful Medici rulers of Florence, is considered by many as the originator of a pragmatic and ruthless political ethos in which the end justifies the means.

might appeal to their fellow Christians for help, popes might still use the rhetoric of crusade, but the reality, as the Turks well knew, was that Christian states would follow their own interest and ally with the infidel, if necessary. This was the era of *Realpolitik*, of the conscious subordination of principle and honour to intelligent calculation of the interests of the state. It is curious that in an age in which Europeans more and more agreed that greater distinctions of culture separated them (to their credit, they were sure) from other civilizations they paid little attention to institutions (and did nothing to create new ones) which

acknowledged their essential unity. Only the occasional visionary advocated the building of something which transcended the state. Perhaps, though, it is just in a new awareness of cultural superiority that the explanation lies. Europe was entering an age of triumphant expansion and did not need shared institutions to tell her so. Instead, the authority of states, and so the power of their governments, waxed in these centuries. It is important not to be misled by forms. For all the arguments about who should exercise it and a mass of political writing which suggested all sorts of limits on it, the general trend was towards acceptance of the idea of legislative sovereignty – that is, Europeans came to feel that, provided the authority of the state were in the right hands, there should be no restriction upon its power to make laws.

QUESTIONING THE EXISTENCE OF FUNDAMENTAL LAWS

Even given the proviso, this was an enormous break with the thinking of the past. To a medieval European the idea that there might not be rights and rules above human interference, legal immunities and chartered freedoms inaccessible to change by subsequent lawmakers, fundamental laws which would always be respected, or laws of God which could never be contravened by those of human beings, would have been social and juridical, as well as theological, blasphemy. English lawyers of the seventeenth century floundered about in disagreement over what the fundamental laws of the land might be, but all thought some must exist. A century later the leading legal minds of France were doing just the same. Nevertheless, in the end there emerged in both countries (as, to a greater or lesser degree, in most others) the acceptance of the idea that a sovereign, legally

European officials who drew up and authenticated public or private documents required a good legal and cultural education. A room in the College of Public Notaries is depicted in this 16th-century French manuscript.

unrestrained lawmaking power was the characteristic mark of the state. Yet this took a long time. For most of the history of early modern Europe the emergence of the modern sovereign state was obscured by the fact that the most widely prevalent form of government was monarchy. Struggles about the powers of rulers make up much of European history in these centuries and sometimes it is hard to see exactly what is at stake. The claims of princely rulers, after all, could be challenged on two quite distinct grounds: there was resistance based on the principle that it would be wrong for any government to have powers such as some monarchs claimed (and this might be termed the medieval or conservative defence of freedom) and there was resistance based on the principle that such powers could properly exist, but were being gathered into the wrong hands (and this can be called the modern or liberal defence of freedom). In practice, the two claims are often inextricably confused, but the confusion is itself a significant indicator of changing ideas.

THE RISE OF ABSOLUTE MONARCHY

Once away from legal principle, the strengthening of the state showed itself in the growing ability of monarchs to get their way. One indicator was the nearly universal decline in the sixteenth and seventeenth centuries of the representative institutions which had appeared in many countries in the later Middle Ages. By 1789, most of western (if not central and eastern) Europe was ruled by monarchs little hindered by representative bodies; the main exception was in Great Britain. Monarchs began in the sixteenth century to enjoy powers which would have seemed remarkable to medieval barons and burghers. The phenomenon is sometimes

described as the rise of absolute monarchy. If we do not exaggerate a monarch's chances of actually getting his wishes carried out (for many practical checks on his power might exist which were just as restricting as medieval immunities or a representative assembly), the term is acceptable. Almost everywhere, the relative strength of rulers *vis-à-vis* their rivals increased greatly from the sixteenth century onwards. New financial resources gave them standing armies and artillery to use against great nobles who could not afford them. Sometimes the monarchy was able to ally itself with the slow growth of a sense of nationhood in imposing order on the over-mighty. In many countries the late

King Louis XIV of France (1638–1715), shown here visiting the Académie Royale des Sciences in 1667, saw himself as a role model for Europe's absolute monarchs. "L'état c'est moi," he once declared – "I am the state."

fifteenth century had brought a new readiness to accept royal government if it would guarantee order and peace. There were special reasons in almost every case, but nearly everywhere monarchs raised themselves further above the level of the greatest nobles and buttressed their new pretensions to respect and authority with cannon and taxation. The obligatory sharing of power with great subjects, whose status entitled them *de facto* and sometimes *de jure* to office, ceased to weigh so heavily upon monarchs. England's Privy Council under the Tudors was at times a meritocracy almost as much as a gathering of magnates.

THE "RENAISSANCE STATE"

Changes in the structures of monarchy in Europe during the sixteenth and early seventeenth centuries brought about the appearance of what some have called the "Renaissance State". This is a rather grandiose term for swollen bureaucracies, staffed by royal employees and directed by aspirations to centralization, but clear enough if we remember the implied antithesis: the medieval kingdom, whose governmental functions were often in large measure delegated to feudal and personal dependents or to corporations (of which the Church was the greatest).

Of course, neither model of political organization existed historically in a pure form. There had always been royal officials, "new men" of obscure origin, and governments today still delegate tasks to non-governmental bodies. There was no sudden transition to the modern "state": it took centuries and often used old forms. In England, the Tudors seized on the existing institution of royal Justices of the Peace to weld the local gentry into the structure of royal government. This was yet another stage in a long process of undermining seigneurial authority, which elsewhere still had centuries of life before it. Even in England, noblemen had long to be treated with care if they were not to be fatally antagonized.

Rebellion was not an exceptional but a continuing fact of life for the sixteenth-century statesman. Royal troops might prevail in the end, but no monarch wanted to be reduced to reliance on force. As a famous motto had it, artillery was the *last* argument of kings. The history of the French nobility's turbulence right down to the middle of the seventeenth century, of antagonized local interests in England during the same period, or of Habsburg attempts to unify their territories at the expense of local magnates, all show this. The United Kingdom had its last feudal rebellion in 1745; other countries had theirs still later.

In many European countries the birth of the "Renaissance State" was accompanied by a reorganization of the army, the judiciary and the economy. This 16th-century miniature depicts a session of the Chamber of the Exchequer in Paris, an institution created to oversee the French financial system.

TAXATION

Taxation, too, because of the danger of rebellion and the inadequacy of administrative machinery to collect it, could not be pressed very far, yet officials and armies had to be paid for. One way was to allow officials to charge fees or levy perquisites on those who needed their services. For obvious reasons, this was not a complete answer. The raising of greater sums by the ruler was therefore necessary. Something might still be done

A new body of professional diplomats emerged during the Renaissance. These French ambassadors were painted by Hans Holbein the Younger.

The collection of taxes, the revenue from which had almost always been spent in advance, was usually in the hands of money-lenders or bankers. These, in turn, sent their intermediaries to collect the money. This 16th-century painting of a pair of tax collectors is by Marinus van Reymerswaele.

by exploiting royal domains. But all monarchs, sooner or later, were driven back to seek new taxation and it was a problem few could solve. There were technical problems here which could not be dealt with until the nineteenth century or even later, but for three centuries great fertility of imagination was to be shown in inventing new taxes. Broadly speaking, only consumption (through indirect taxes such as customs and excise or taxes on sale, or through requiring licences and authorizations to trade which had to be paid for) or real property could be tapped by the tax-gatherer. Usually, this bore disproportionately upon the poorest, who spent a larger part of their small disposable income on necessities than the wealthy. Nor is it ever easy to stop a landowner from passing his tax burdens along to the man at the bottom of the property pyramid. Taxation, too, was particularly hindered by the surviving medieval idea of legal immunity. In 1500 it was generally accepted that there were areas, persons and spheres of action which were specially protected from invasion by the power of the rule. They might be defended by an irrevocable royal grant in past ages, such as were the privileges of many cities, by contractual agreement such as the English Magna Carta was said to be, by immemorial custom, or by divine law. The supreme example was the Church. Its properties were not normally subject to lay taxation, it had jurisdiction in its courts of matters inaccessible to royal justice, and it controlled important social and economic institutions – marriage, for example. But a province, or a profession, or a family might also enjoy immunities, usually from royal jurisdiction or taxation. Nor was royal standing uniform. Even the French king was only a duke in Brittany and that made a difference to what he was entitled to do there. Such facts were the realities which the "Renaissance State" had to live with. It could do no other than accept their survival, even if the future lay with the royal bureaucrats and their files.

HERESY AND HUMANISM

IN THE EARLY SIXTEENTH CENTURY, a great crisis, which shook Western Christianity and destroyed forever the old medieval unity of the faith, much accelerated the consolidation of royal power. The Protestant Reformation began as just one more dispute over religious authority, the calling in question of the papal claims whose formal and theoretical structure had successfully survived

This painting, from the school of Hans Holbein the Younger, depicts Sir Thomas More (1478–1535), the English Roman Catholic humanist, statesman and author of *Utopia* (1516). More sympathized with Erasmus of Rotterdam's proposals for the reform of the Church.

so many challenges. Thus, in origin at least, it was a thoroughly medieval phenomenon. But important as that was, that was not to be the whole story and far from exhausts the political significance of the Reformation. Given that it also detonated a cultural revolution, there is no reason to question its traditional standing as the start of modern history.

ERASMIAN IDEAS

There was nothing new about demands for reform. The sense that papacy and *curia* did not necessarily serve the interests of all Christians was well grounded by 1500. Some critics had already gone on from this to doctrinal dissent. The deep, uneasy devotional swell of the fifteenth century had expressed a search for new answers to spiritual questions but also a willingness to look for them outside the limits laid down by ecclesiastical authority. Heresy had never been blotted out, it had only been contained. Popular anti-clericalism was an old and widespread phenomenon. There had also appeared in the

fifteenth century another current in religious life, perhaps more profoundly subversive than heresy, because, unlike heresy, it contained forces which might in the end cut at the roots of the traditional religious outlook itself. This was the learned, humanistic, rational, sceptical intellectual movement which, for want of a better word, we may call Erasmian after the man who embodied its ideals most clearly in the eyes of contemporaries, and who was the first Dutchman to play a leading role in European history. He was profoundly loyal to his faith; he knew himself to be a Christian and that meant, unquestionably, that he remained within the Church. But of that Church he had an ideal which embodied a vision of a possible reformation. He sought a simpler devotion and a purer pastorate.

Erasmus of Rotterdam (1467–1536) is shown at his desk, in a portrait by Hans Holbein the Younger (c.1497–1543).

This portrait of Martin Luther (1483–1546), the German theologian who was the leading figure of the German Reformation, dates from the first half of the 16th century.

Martin Luther's theses

5. The Pope cannot and does not intend to pardon any sentence either dictated by him or imposed by canonical laws.
21. Consequently, those who preach of pardons are wrong when they say that through papal pardons man is free of all sentence and is saved.
32. Those who believe their salvation to be guaranteed through indulgences will be condemned forever with their masters.
82. For example: Why does the Pope not empty purgatory as an act of holy charity and taking into account the utmost necessity of these souls – the most justified of motives – if with the ill-fated money destined for the construction of the basilica – the most banal motive – he redeems infinite souls?

Extracts from Martin Luther's 95 theses against indulgences ("Disputatio pro declarationes virtutis indulgentiarum"), 1517.

Though he did not challenge the authority of the Church or papacy, in a subtler way he challenged authority in principle, for his scholarly work had implications which were deeply subversive. So was the tone of the correspondence which he conducted with colleagues the length and breadth of Europe. They learnt from him to disentangle their logic and therefore the teaching of the faith from the scholastic mummifications of Aristotelian philosophy. In his Greek New Testament he made available a firm basis for argument on doctrine at a time when a knowledge of Greek was again becoming widespread. Erasmus, too, was the exposer of the spuriousness of texts on which bizarre dogmatic structures had been raised.

Yet neither he nor those who shared his viewpoint attacked religious authority outright, nor did they turn ecclesiastical into universal issues. They were good Catholics. Humanism, like heresy, discontent with clerical behaviour and the cupidity of princes, was something in the air at the beginning of the sixteenth century, waiting – as many things had long waited – for the man and the occasion which would make them into a religious revolution. No other term is adequate to describe what followed the unwitting act of a German monk. His name was Martin Luther and in 1517 he launched a movement which was to end by fragmenting a Christian unity intact in the West since the disappearance of the Arians.

MARTIN LUTHER

Unlike Erasmus, the international man, Luther lived all his life except for brief absences in a small German town, Wittenberg, almost at the back of beyond on the Elbe. He was an Augustinian monk, deeply read in theology, somewhat tormented in spirit, who had already come to the conclusion that he must preach the Scriptures in a new light, to present God as a forgiving God, not a punitive one. This need not have made him a revolutionary; the orthodoxy of his views was never in question until he quarrelled with the papacy. He had been to Rome, and he had not liked what he saw there, for the papal city seemed a worldly place and its ecclesiastical rulers no better than they should be. This did not dispose him to feel warmly towards an itinerant Dominican who came to Saxony only as a pedlar of indulgences – papal certificates whose possessor, in consideration of payment (which went towards the building of the new and magnificent St Peter's then rising in Rome), was assured that some of the penalties incurred by him for sin would be remitted in the next world. Accounts of the preaching of this man were brought to Luther by peasants who had heard him and bought their indulgences. Research has made it clear that what had been said to them was not only misleading but outrageous; the crudity of the transaction promoted by the preacher displays one of the most unattractive faces of medieval Catholicism. It infuriated Luther, almost obsessed as he was by the overwhelming seriousness of the transformation necessary in a person's life before he or she could be sure of redemption. He formulated his protests against this and certain other papal practices in a set of ninety-five theses setting out his positive views. In the tradition of the scholarly disputation he posted them in Latin on the door of the castle church in Wittenberg on 21 October 1517. He had also sent the theses to the Archbishop of Mainz, primate of Germany, who passed them to Rome with a request that Luther be forbidden by his order to preach on this theme. By this time the theses had been put into German and the new information technology had transformed the situation; they were printed and circulated everywhere in Germany. So Luther got the debate he sought. Only the protection of Frederick of Saxony, the ruler of Luther's state, who refused to surrender him, kept him out of danger of his life. The delay in scotching the chicken of heresy in the egg was fatal. Luther's monastic order abandoned him, but his university did not. Soon the papacy found itself confronted by a German national movement of grievance against Rome sustained and inflamed by Luther's own sudden discovery that he was a literary genius of astonishing fluency and productivity, the first to exploit the huge possibilities of the printed pamphlet.

THE REFORMATION

WITHIN TWO YEARS, Luther was being called a Hussite. The Reformation had by then become entangled in German politics. Even in the Middle Ages would-be reformers had looked to secular rulers for help. This did not necessarily mean going outside the fold of the faith; the great Spanish churchman Ximenes had sought to bring to bear the authority of the Catholic monarchs on the problems facing the Spanish Church. Rulers were not meant to protect heretics; their duty was to uphold the true faith. Nevertheless, an appeal to lay authority could open the way to changes which went further perhaps than their authors had intended, and this, it seems, was the case with Luther. His arguments had rapidly carried him beyond the desirability and grounds of reform in practice to the questioning of, first,

The evolution of printing

Printing played a prominent role in the expansion of literacy. By the 17th century, books had become commonplace in the homes of wealthy people who had received some education, and the ownership of a private library became a status symbol for the rich and cultured. Most early books were on religious themes: the Reformation and the Counter-Reformation and the controversies that preoccupied Roman Catholics and Protestants at that time acted as a strong stimulus to the production of books. Bibles, prayer books and doctrinal works were, for a long time, the main printed works.

Secular works made ground only gradually. The works of the humanists, with the exception of Erasmus, and the publication of works by classical authors never had more than a limited public. However, published treatises and law compendiums became increasingly common, as the study of law came to be considered an essential part of a gentleman's education. Political works became popular, as did scientific treatises accompanied by illustrations on

metallurgy, mining, machines, mechanical applications, chemistry, agriculture, architecture, urban planning and the building of dykes and canals. Books on the subjects of commercial arithmetic, bookkeeping and other business skills also sold well, although the practical value of such publications was extremely variable.

In the first century of its history, printing was carried out by individuals who combined the roles of typographer, printer, editor and bookseller. They would travel from city to city in search of wealthy patrons and a readership. From the middle of the 16th century, there was a tendency towards a concentration of larger firms and the specialization of functions. Thus, educated scholars composed the page, typesetting became the work of firms with expertise in that process; the owner of a workshop limited himself to administration and proofreading; and the printing was left to skilled, strong men, who, by the beginning of the 18th century, were capable of producing 3,000 pages a day.

This 17th-century woodcut depicts the interior of a printing works in Nuremberg, Germany.

papal authority and, then, of doctrine. The core of his early protests had not been theological. Nevertheless, he came to reject transubstantiation (replacing it with a view of the eucharist even more difficult to grasp) and to preach that mortals were justified – that is, set aside for salvation – not by observance of the sacraments only ("works", as this was called), but by faith. This was, clearly, an intensely individualist position. It struck at the root of traditional teaching, which saw no salvation possible outside the Church. (Yet, it may be noted, Erasmus, when asked for his view, would not condemn Luther; it was known, moreover, that he thought Luther to have said many valuable things.) In 1520 Luther was excommunicated. Before a wondering audience he burnt the bull of excommunication in the same fire as the books of canon law. He continued to

preach and write. Summoned to explain himself before the imperial Diet, he refused to retract his views. Germany seemed on the verge of civil war. After leaving the Diet under a safe-conduct, he disappeared, kidnapped for his own safety by a sympathetic prince. In 1521 Charles V, the emperor, placed him under the Imperial Ban; Luther was now an outlaw.

Luther's doctrines, which he extended to condemnations of confession and absolution and clerical celibacy, by now appealed to many Germans. His followers spread them by preaching and by distributing his German translation of the New Testament. Lutheranism was also a political fact; the German princes, who entangled it in their own complicated relations with the emperor and his vague authority over them, ensured this. Wars ensued and the word "Protestant"

This engraving, dating from 1555, depicts the Diet of Augsburg, held on 30 June 1548, during which the German princes met in the presence of the emperor Charles V. The factional fighting between Catholics and Protestants that followed continued until the Peace of Augsburg of 1555.

This portrait depicts Huldreich Zwingli (1484–1531), the priest who introduced the Reformation to Switzerland. The optimism and equality of Zwingli's Christian humanism contrasted with Calvin's beliefs, which were founded in the concept of human beings as sinners facing the omnipotent power of God.

came into use. By 1555, Germany was irreparably divided into Catholic and Protestant states. This was recognized in agreement at the Diet of Augsburg that the prevailing religion of each state should be that of its ruler, the first European institutionalizing of religious pluralism. It was a curious concession for an emperor who saw himself as the defender of universal Catholicism. Yet it was necessary if he was to keep the loyalty of Germany's princes. In Catholic and Protestant Germany alike, religion now looked as never before to political authority to uphold it in a world of competing creeds.

CALVINISM

By 1555, other varieties of Protestantism had emerged from the evangelical ferment. Some drew on social unrest. Luther soon had to dis-

John Calvin the Younger (1509–1564), like other religious leaders, was convinced of the veracity of his own beliefs and the falsity of those of his opponents.

tinguish his own teaching from the views of peasants who invoked his name to justify rebellion. One radical group were the Anabaptists, persecuted by Catholic and Protestant rulers alike. At Münster in 1534 their leaders' introduction of communism of property and polygamy confirmed their opponents' fears and brought a ferocious suppression upon them. Of other forms of Protestantism, only one demands notice in so general an account as this. Calvinism was to be Switzerland's most important contribution to the Reformation, but it was the creation of a Frenchman, John Calvin. He was a theologian who formulated his essential doctrines while still a young man: the absolute depravity of man after the Fall of Adam and the impossibility of salvation except for those few, the Elect, predestined by God to salvation. If Luther, the Augustinian monk, spoke with the voice of Paul, Calvin evoked the tones of Augustine. It is not easy to understand the attractiveness of this gloomy creed. But to its efficacy, the history not only of

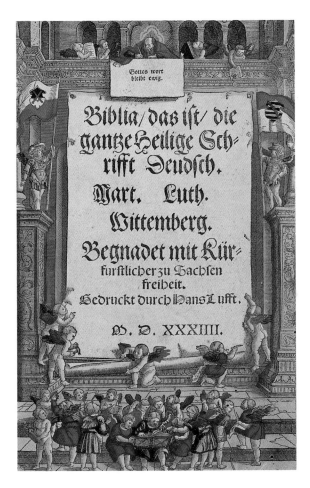

This illustrated title page is from the 1533 edition of Luther's German translation of the Bible, produced by the printer Hans Lufft and, as the inscription states, with the permission of the elector of Saxony. Luther's Bibles became vital to the expansion of Protestantism.

drowned, men beheaded (an apparent reversal of the normal penal practice of a male-dominated European society where women, considered weaker vessels morally and intellectually, were usually indulged with milder punishments than men). Severe punishments, too, were reserved for those guilty of heresy.

From Geneva, where its pastors were trained, the new sect took root in France, where it won converts among the nobility and had more than 2,000 congregations by 1561. In the Netherlands, England and Scotland and, in the end, Germany, it challenged Lutheranism. It spread also to Poland, Bohemia and Hungary. Thus in its first century it showed a remarkable vigour, surpassing that of Lutheranism which, except in Scandinavia, was never strongly entrenched beyond the German lands which first adopted it.

Geneva, but of France, England, Scotland, the Dutch Netherlands, and British North America all witnessed. The crucial step was conviction of membership of the Elect. As the signs of this were outward adherence to the commandments of God and participation in the sacraments, it was less difficult to achieve such conviction than might be imagined.

Under Calvin, Geneva was not a place for the easy-going. He had drawn up the constitution of a theocratic state which provided the framework for a remarkable exercise in self-government. Blasphemy and witchcraft were punished by death, but this would not have struck contemporaries as surprising. Adultery, too, was a crime in most European countries and one punished by ecclesiastical courts. But Calvin's Geneva took this offence much more seriously and imposed the death penalty for it; adulterous women were

THE CONSEQUENCES OF THE REFORMATION

The variety of the Protestant Reformation still defies summary and simplification. Complex and deep-rooted in its origins, it also owed much to circumstance and was very rich and far-reaching in its effects. If the name "Protestantism" can be taken seriously as an indicator of fundamental identity beneath the disorder of its many expressions, that identity is to be found in its influence and effect. It was disruptive. In Europe and the Americas it created new ecclesiastical cultures founded on the study of the Bible and preaching, to which it gave an importance sometimes surpassing that of the sacraments.

Henry VIII of England (1491–1547), here depicted in a portrait by Hans Holbein the Younger, renounced his subordination to the Catholic Church of Rome in order to establish his leadership of the Church of England, over which he was to have complete control. Although the Protestant reformers paved the way for other European sovereigns to make similar breaks with Rome, it seems likely that the medieval unity of the Church was already doomed, even before the Reformation.

ANNO · ÆTATIS ·   · SVÆ · XLIX ·

It was to shape the lives of millions by accustoming them to a new and an intense scrutiny of private conduct and conscience (thus, ironically, achieving something long sought by Roman Catholics) and it re-created the non-celibate clergy. Negatively, it slighted or at least called in question all existing ecclesiastical institutions and created new political forces in the form of churches which princes could now manipulate for their own ends – often against popes whom they saw simply as princes like themselves. Rightly, Protestantism was to come to be seen, by friend and foe alike, as one of the forces determining the shape of modern Europe and therefore of the world.

This anonymous portrait of Catherine of Aragon (1485–1536) dates from 1530 – three years after Henry VIII began to seek an annulment of their marriage. Although Henry remarried in 1533, Catherine never accepted her situation and fought the Act of Succession, which declared her daughter by Henry illegitimate.

royal pen (his descendant still bears that title). But the assertion of the royal supremacy opened the way to an English Church separate from Rome. A vested interest in it was soon provided by a dissolution of monasteries and some other ecclesiastical foundations and the sale of property to buyers among the aristocracy and gentry.

POLITICS AND THE CHURCH IN ENGLAND AND EUROPE

Churchmen sympathetic to new doctrines sought to move the Church in England significantly towards continental Protestant ideas

THE CHURCH OF ENGLAND

CURIOUSLY, NEITHER LUTHERANISM nor Calvinism provoked the first rejection of papal authority by a nation-state. In England a unique religious change arose almost by accident. A new dynasty originating in Wales, the Tudors, had established itself at the end of the fifteenth century and the second king of this line, Henry VIII, became entangled with the papacy over his wish to dissolve the first of his six marriages in order to remarry and get an heir, an understandable preoccupation. This led to a quarrel and one of the most remarkable assertions of lay authority in the whole sixteenth century; it was also one fraught with significance for England's future. With the support of his parliament, which obediently passed the required legislation, Henry VIII proclaimed himself Head of the Church in England. Doctrinally, he conceived no break with the past; he was, after all, entitled Defender of the Faith by the pope because of a refutation of Luther from the

Mary I (Mary Tudor), Queen of England from 1553 to 1558, was the daughter of Catherine of Aragon and Henry VIII and the wife of Philip II of Spain. She attempted to re-convert her English subjects to Roman Catholicism, unleashing, perhaps unwittingly, a terrible campaign of persecution against Protestants. Mary's early death may have saved her country from civil war.

in the next reign. Popular reactions were mixed. Some saw this as the satisfaction of old national traditions of dissent from Rome; some resented innovations. From a confused debate and murky politics emerged a literary masterpiece, the Book of Common Prayer, and some martyrs both Catholic and Protestant. There was a reversion to papal authority (and the burning of Protestant heretics) under the fourth Tudor, the unfairly named and unhappy Bloody Mary, perhaps England's most tragic queen. By this time, moreover, the question of religion was thoroughly entangled with national interest and foreign policy, for the states of Europe drew apart more and more on religious grounds.

This 16th-century painting represents the St Bartholomew's Day Massacre, which took place in Paris during the night of 23–24 August, 1572. The horror that ensued, as Catholics murdered Protestant Huguenots, made many people question the value of beliefs that could lead to such a blood-bath.

THE REFORMATION AND THE ENGLISH PARLIAMENT

The English Reformation, which, like the German, was a landmark in the evolution of a national consciousness, was also notable for other reasons. It had been carried out by Act of Parliament and a constitutional question was implicit in the religious settlement: were there any limits to legislative authority? With the accession of Mary's half-sister, Elizabeth I,

the pendulum swung back, though for a long time it was unclear how far. Yet Elizabeth insisted, and her parliament legislated, that she retain the essentials of her father's position; the English Church, or Church of England, as it may henceforth be called, claimed to be Catholic in doctrine but rested on the royal supremacy. More important still, because that supremacy was recognized by Act of Parliament, England would before long be at war with a Catholic king of Spain, who was well known for his determination to root out heresy in the lands he subjugated. So another national cause was identified with that of Protestantism.

Reformation helped the English parliament to survive when other medieval representative bodies were going under before monarchical power, though this was far from the whole story. A kingdom united since Anglo-Saxon times and without provincial assemblies which might rival it made it much easier for Parliament to focus national politics than any similar body elsewhere. Royal carelessness helped, too; Henry VIII had squandered a great opportunity to achieve a sound basis for absolute monarchy when he rapidly liquidated the mass of property – about a fifth of the land of the whole kingdom – which he held briefly as a result of the dissolutions. Nevertheless, all such imponderables duly weighed, the fact that Henry chose to seek endorsement of his will from the national representative body in creating a national church still seems one of the most crucial decisions in Parliament's history.

THE FRENCH WARS OF RELIGION

Catholic martyrs died under Elizabeth because they were judged traitors, not because they were heretics – but England was far less divided by religion than Germany and France. Sixteenth-century France was tormented and torn between Catholic and Calvinist interests. Each was in essence a group of noble clans, who fought for power in the Wars of Religion, of which nine have been distinguished between 1562 and 1598. At times their struggles brought the French monarchy very low; the nobility of France came near to winning the battle against the centralizing state. Yet, in the end, their divisions benefited a Crown which could use one faction against another. The wretched population of France had to bear the brunt of disorder and devastation until there came to the throne in 1589 (after the murder of his predecessor) a member of a junior branch of the royal family, Henry, king of the little state of Navarre, who became Henry IV of France and inaugurated the Bourbon line whose descendants still claim the French throne. He had been a Protestant, but accepted Catholicism as the condition of his succession, recognizing that Catholicism was the religion most French people would cling to – a continuing strain in the identity of nationhood. The Protestants were assured special guarantees which left them a state within a state, the possessors of fortified towns where the king's writ did not run; this very old-fashioned sort of solution assured protection for their religion by creating new immunities. Henry and his successors could then turn to the business of re-establishing the authority of a throne badly shaken by assassination and intrigue. But the French nobility were still far from tamed.

Reformation and Counter-Reformation Europe

In the second half of the 16th century, the time of religious reconciliation came to an end. Old conflicts re-emerged and new conflicts began to appear, in the form of confessional confrontations between Reformed and Catholic forces. Political divisions within individual countries began to polarize depending on the different factions' religious leanings: these divisions crossed class barriers and affected every level of society. Thus, political struggles tended to become civil wars and civil wars invited foreign intervention. The year 1562, which marked the outbreak of the Wars of Religion in France, saw the beginning of what some contemporaries called "the century of iron". The map shows the predominantly Protestant and Roman Catholic regions of Europe in about 1600.

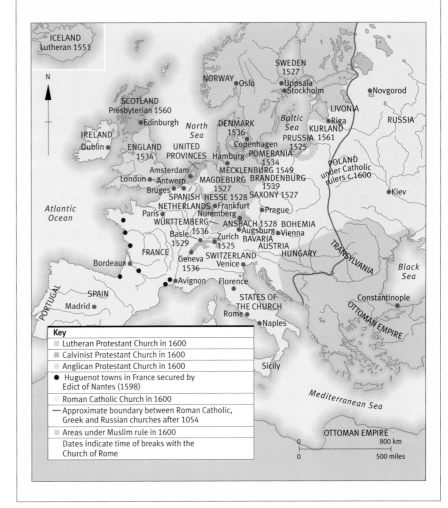

Key
- Lutheran Protestant Church in 1600
- Calvinist Protestant Church in 1600
- Anglican Protestant Church in 1600
- ● Huguenot towns in France secured by Edict of Nantes (1598)
- Roman Catholic Church in 1600
- — Approximate boundary between Roman Catholic, Greek and Russian churches after 1054
- Areas under Muslim rule in 1600
- Dates indicate time of breaks with the Church of Rome

THE COUNTER-REFORMATION

LONG BEFORE THE REIGN of Henry IV of France, religious struggles had been further inflamed by the wave of internal reassessment and innovation within the Roman Church, which is called the Counter-Reformation. Its formal expression was a general council, the Council of Trent, summoned in 1545 and meeting in three sessions over the next eighteen years. Bishops from

From the Venetian school of painting, this 16th-century work depicts one of the sessions of the Council of Trent. Hopes that in this general council of the Roman Catholic Church a compromise acceptable to all Christians would be reached were quickly thwarted.

Italy and Spain dominated it. This mattered, for the Reformers challenged Catholicism little in Italy and not at all in Spain. The result was somewhat to accentuate the intransigence of the Council's decisions. They not only became the touchstone of orthodoxy in doctrine and discipline until the nineteenth century, providing a standard to which Catholic rulers could rally, but also initiated institutional change. Bishops were given more authority and parishes took on new importance. More remarkably still (though almost unnoticed), it answered by implication an old question about the headship of Catholic Europe; from this time, it indisputably lay with the pope. Like the Reformation, the Counter-Reformation went beyond forms and legal principles. It expressed and gave direction to a new devotional intensity and rejuvenated the fervour of laity and clergy alike. It made attendance at mass each week obligatory and regulated baptism and marriage more strictly; it also ended the selling of indulgences by "pardoners" – the very practice which had detonated the Lutheran explosion.

THE JESUITS

Papal authority was not the only source of Catholic reform nor was the Counter-Reformation just a response to the Protestant challenge. The spirituality and spontaneous fervour already apparent among the faithful in the fifteenth century lay behind it, too. One of the most potent expressions of its spirituality, as well as an institution which was to prove enduring was the invention of a Spaniard, the soldier Ignatius Loyola. By a curious irony he had been a student at the same Paris college as Calvin in the early 1530s, but it is not recorded that they ever met. In 1534 he and a few companions took vows; their aim was missionary work and as they trained for it Loyola devised a rule for a new religious order. In 1540 it was recognized by the pope and named the Society of Jesus. The Jesuits, as they soon came to be called, were to have an importance in the history of the Church akin to that of the early Benedictines or the Franciscans of the thirteenth century. Their warrior-founder liked to think of them as the militia of the Church, utterly disciplined and completely subordinate to papal authority through their general, who lived in Rome. They transformed Catholic education. They were in the forefront of a renewed missionary effort which carried their members to every part of the world. In Europe their intellectual eminence and political skill raised them to high places in the courts of kings.

ROMAN CATHOLIC SPAIN

THOUGH IT BROUGHT new instruments to the support of papal authority, the Counter-Reformation (like the Reformation) could also strengthen the authority of lay rulers over their subjects. The new dependence of religion upon political authority –

This fresco in Toledo Cathedral in Spain depicts Cardinal Francisco Ximenez de Cisneros (1436–1517). With the support of the Catholic Monarchs, Ximenez prematurely undertook the reformation of the Spanish clergy's customs and training, with limited success.

that is to say, upon organized force – further extended the grip of the political apparatus. This was most obvious in the Spanish kingdoms. Here two forces ran together to create an unimpeachably Catholic monarchy long before the Council of Trent. The Reconquest so recently completed had been a crusade; the title of the Catholic Monarchs itself proclaimed the identification of a political process with an ideological struggle. Secondly, the Spanish monarchy had the problem of suddenly absorbing great numbers of non-Christian subjects, both Muslims and Jews. They were feared as a potential threat to security in a multiracial society. The instrument deployed against them was a new one: an Inquisition not, like its medieval forerunner, under clerical control, but under

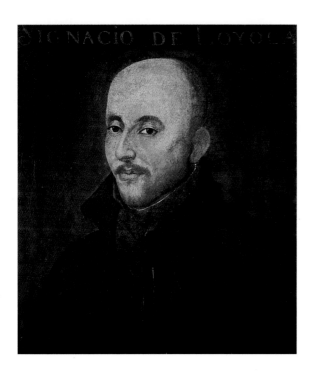

The Spanish soldier Ignatius de Loyola founded the Society of Jesus, which was the Catholic Church's most effective intellectual weapon against the Protestants. The Jesuits became university professors, advisers to popes, and confessors of princes and missionaries.

Philip II (1527–1598), King of Spain from 1556, favoured orthodox Catholicism and employed the Spanish Inquisition as a tool against reformers and Protestants. His violent campaigns to end religious heresy left the Spanish dominions bitterly divided at his death.

that of the Crown. Established by papal bull in 1478, the Spanish Inquisition began to operate in Castile in 1480. The pope soon had misgivings; in Catalonia lay and ecclesiastical authority alike resisted, but to no avail. By 1516, when Charles I, the first ruler to hold both the thrones of Aragon and Castile, became king, the Inquisition was the only institution in the Spanish domains which, from a royal council, exercised

authority in all of them – in the Americas, Sicily and Sardinia, as much as in Castile and Aragon. The most striking effects had already been what was later called "ethnic cleansing", the expulsion from them of the Jews and a severe regulation of the Moriscoes (converted Moors).

This gave Spain a religious unity unbreakable by a handful of Lutherans with whom the Inquisition found it easy to deal.

The cost to Spain was in the end to be heavy. Yet already under Charles, a fervent Catholic, Spain was, in religion as in her secular life, aspiring to a new kind of centralized, absolutist monarchy, the Renaissance state *par excellence* in fact, and, incidentally, the first administrative organism ever having to take decisions about events all over the globe. The residues of formal constitutionalism within the peninsula hardly affected this. Spain was a model for Counter-Reformation states elsewhere and one to be imposed upon much of Europe by force or example in the century after 1558, when Charles died after a retirement spent largely at his devotions in a remote monastery in Estremadura.

PHILIP II OF SPAIN

Of all the European monarchs who identified themselves with the cause of the Counter-Reformation as extirpators of heresy, none was more determined and bigoted than Charles I's son and successor, Philip II of Spain, widower of Mary Tudor. To him had come half his father's empire: Spain, the Indies, Sicily and the Spanish Netherlands. (In 1581 he acquired Portugal, too, and it remained Spanish until 1640.) The results of his policies of religious purification in Spain have been variously interpreted. What is not open to dispute is the effect in the Spanish Netherlands, where they provoked the emergence of the first state in the world to break away from the old domination of monarchy and landed nobility.

THE REVOLT OF THE NETHERLANDS

WHAT SOME CALL the "Revolt of the Netherlands" and the Dutch call the "Eighty Years' War" has been, like many other events at the roots of nations, a great source of myth-making, some of it conscious. Even this, though, may have been less misleading than the assumption that because in the end a very modern sort of society emerged, it was a very "modern" sort of revolt, dominated by a passionate struggle for religious toleration and national independence. That could hardly be less true. The troubles of the Netherlands arose in a very medieval setting, the Old Burgundian inheritance of the lands of the richest state in northern Europe, the duchy which had passed to the Habsburgs by marriage. The Spanish Netherlands, seventeen provinces of very different sorts, formed part of it. The southern provinces, where many of the inhabitants spoke French, included the most urbanized part of Europe and the great Flemish commercial centre of Antwerp. They had long been troublesome and the Flemish towns had at one moment in the late fifteenth century seemed to be trying to turn themselves into independent city-states. The northern provinces were more agricultural and maritime. Their inhabitants showed a peculiarly tenacious feeling for their land, perhaps because they had actually been recovering it from the sea and making polders since the twelfth century.

North and South were to be the later Netherlands and Belgium, but this was inconceivable in 1554. Nor could a religious division between the two then be envisaged. Though the Catholic majority of the south grew somewhat as many Protestants emigrated northwards, the two persuasions were mixed upon both sides of a future boundary. Early sixteenth-century Europe was much more tolerant of religious divisions than it would be after the Counter-Reformation got to work.

Philip's determination to enforce the decrees of the Council of Trent explains

This allegory of the tyranny of the Spanish Duke of Alva (c.1600) was painted to justify the Dutch rebellion against Spanish rule. Alva, who has enchained figures representing the Dutch provinces, is shown being crowned by the devil, while outside the executions of the counts Egmont and Horn, condemned to death by the duke, are carried out.

something of what followed, but the origins of trouble went back a long way. As the Spaniards strove to modernize the relations of central government and local communities (which meant tapping a growing prosperity through more effective taxation), they did so with more up-to-date methods and perhaps less tact than the Burgundians had shown. Spanish royal envoys came into conflict first with the nobility of the southern provinces. As prickly and touchy as other nobilities of the age in defence of their symbolic "liberties" – that is, privileges and immunities – they felt threatened by a monarch more remote than the great Charles who, they felt, had understood them (he spoke their language), even if he was Charles's son. The Spanish commander, the Duke of Alva, they argued, was further violating local privilege by interfering with local jurisdictions in the pursuit of heretics. Catholic though they were, they had a stake in the prosperity of the Flemish cities where Protestantism had taken root and feared the introductions to them of the Spanish Inquisition. In addition, they were as uneasy as other noblemen of the times about the pressures of inflation.

WILLIAM THE SILENT

Resistance to Spanish government began in thoroughly medieval forms, in the Estates of Brabant, and for a few years the brutality of the Spanish army and the leadership of one of their number, William, Prince of Orange, united the nobles against their lawful ruler. Like his contemporary, Elizabeth Tudor, William (nicknamed the "Silent" because of his reputed refusal to allow unguarded anger to escape him when he learnt of his ruler's determination to bring his heretic subjects to heel) was good at suggesting sympathy for popular causes. But there was always a potential rift between noblemen and Calvinist townsmen who had more at stake. Better political tactics by Spanish governors and the victories of the Spanish armies were in the end enough to force it open. The nobles fell back into line and thus, without knowing it, the Spanish armies defined modern Belgium. The struggle continued only in the northern provinces (though still under the political direction of William the Silent until he was assassinated in Delft in 1584, by a Catholic Frenchman and supporter of Philip II.

THE NEW DUTCH NATION

The Dutch (as we may now call them) had much at stake and were not encumbered as their southern co-religionists had been with the ambiguous dissatisfactions of the nobility. But they were divided among themselves; the provinces could rarely come easily to agreement. On the other hand, they could use the cry of religious freedom and a broad toleration to disguise their divisions. They benefited, too, from a great migration northwards of Flemish capital and talent. Their enemies had difficulties; the Spanish army was formidable but could not easily deal with an enemy which retired behind its town walls and surrounded them with water by opening the dykes and flooding the countryside. The Dutch, almost by accident, transferred their main effort to the sea where they could do a great deal of damage to the Spanish on more equal terms. Spanish communications with the Netherlands were more difficult once the northern sea route was harried by the rebels. It was expensive to maintain a big army in Belgium by the long road up from Italy and even more expensive when other enemies had to be beaten off. That was soon the case. The Counter-Reformation had infected international politics with a new ideological element. Together with their interest in maintaining a balance of power on the continent and preventing the complete success of the Spanish, this led the English first to a diplomatic and then to a military and naval struggle against Spain, which brought the Dutch allies.

The war created, almost fortuitously and incidentally, a remarkable new society, a loose federation of seven little republics with a weak central government, called the United Provinces. Soon, its citizens discovered a forgotten national past (much as decolonized Africans did in the twentieth century) and celebrated the virtues of Germanic tribesmen

dimly discernible in Roman accounts of rebellion; relics of their enthusiasm remain in the paintings commissioned by Amsterdam magnates depicting attacks upon Roman camps (this was in the era we remember for the work of Rembrandt). The distinctiveness of a new nation thus consciously created is now more interesting than such historical propaganda. Once survival was assured, the United Provinces enjoyed religious tolerance, great civic freedom and provincial independence; the Dutch did not allow Calvinism the upper hand in government.

ELIZABETHAN ENGLAND

Later generations came to think they saw a similar linkage of religious and civic freedom in Elizabethan England; this was anachronistic, although comprehensible given the way

Elizabeth I (1533–1603) reigned as Queen of England at a time when her country was emerging as a world power. She skilfully maintained the unity of her realm in the face of attack by the Spanish Armada and threats to her own life by Catholic supporters of her cousin Mary Stuart. Her image as the "Virgin Queen" was carefully preserved by her portrait painters; throughout her long reign, she was consistently depicted in flattering terms.

English institutions were to evolve over the next century or so. Paradoxically, one part of this was a great strengthening of the legislative authority of the state, one which carried the limitation of privilege so far that at the end of the seventeenth century it was regarded with amazement by other Europeans. For a long time this cannot have seemed a likely outcome. Elizabeth had been an incomparable producer of the royal spectacle. As the myths of beauty and youth faded she had acquired the majesty of those who outlive their early counsellors. In 1603 she had been queen for forty-five years, the centre of a national cult fed by her own Tudor instinct for welding the dynasty's interest to patriotism, by poets of genius, by mundane devices such as the frequent travel (which kept down expenses, since she stayed with her nobility) which made her visible to her people, and by her astonishing skill with her parliaments. Nor did she persecute for religion's sake; she did not, as she put it, want to make "windows into men's souls". It is hardly surprising that the accession day of Good Queen Bess became a festival of patriotic opposition to government under her successors. Unhappily, she had no child to whom to bequeath the glamour she brought to monarchy, and she left an encumbered estate. Like all other rulers of her day, she never had a big enough income. The inheritance of her debts did not help the first king of the Scottish house of Stuart, who succeeded her, James I. The shortcomings of the males of that dynasty are still difficult to write about with moderation; the Stuarts gave England four bad kings in a row. Still, James was neither as foolish as his son nor as unprincipled as his grandsons. It was probably his lack of tact and alien ways rather than more serious defects that did most to embitter politics in his reign.

In defence of the Stuarts, it can be agreed that this was not the only troubled monarchy. In the seventeenth century there was a roughly contemporaneous crisis of authority in several countries, and one curiously parallel to an economic crisis which was Europe-wide. The two may have been connected, but it is not easy to be sure what the nature of the connection was. It is also interesting that these civil struggles coincided with the last phase of a period of religious wars which had been opened by the Counter-Reformation. We may at least assume that a contemporaneous breakdown of normal political life in a number of countries, notably England, France and Spain, owed something to the needs of governments forced to take part in them.

The reign of James VI (1566–1625), King of Scotland from 1567 and of Great Britain and Ireland (as James I) from 1603, was dogged by financial crises, struggles between Protestant, Puritan and Catholic factions in both of his kingdoms, and clashes with Parliament.

Charles I (1600–1649), King of Great Britain and Ireland, is depicted in a portrait after Sir Anthony van Dyck, the Flemish painter who was knighted by the king. Charles I was tried for treason after his supporters were defeated in the second phase of the English Civil War in 1648. He refused to plead at his trial, claiming that the court was illegitimate, and was condemned to death by beheading. He is remembered for the great courage and dignity with which he died.

CIVIL WAR IN ENGLAND

In England the crisis came to a head in civil war, regicide and the establishment of the only republic in English history. Historians still argue about where lay the heart of the quarrel and the point of no return in what became armed conflict between Charles I and his parliament. One crucial moment came when he found himself at war with one set of his subjects (for he was King of Scotland, as well as of England), and had to call Parliament to help him in 1640. Without new taxation, England could not be defended. But by then some of its members were convinced that there was a royal scheme to overturn from within the Church by law established and to reintroduce the power of Rome. Parliament harried the king's servants (sending the two most conspicuous to the scaffold).

Charles decided in 1642 that force was the only way out and so the Civil War began. In it he was defeated. Parliament was uneasy, as were many Englishmen, for if you stepped outside the ancient constitution of King, Lords and Commons, where would things end? But Charles threw away his advantage by seeking a foreign invasion in his support (the Scots were to fight for him this time). Those who dominated Parliament had had enough and Charles was tried and executed – in the eyes of contemporaries, an outstanding outcome. His son went into exile.

THE ENGLISH REPUBLIC

AFTER THE EXECUTION of Charles I, there followed in England an interregnum during which the dominant figure, until his death in 1658, was one of the most remarkable of all Englishmen, Oliver Cromwell. He was a country gentleman who had risen in the parliamentary side's councils by his genius as a soldier. This gave him great power, for provided his army stood by him he could dispense with the politicians, but also imposed limitations on him, for he could not risk losing the army's support. The result was an English republic astonishingly fertile in new constitutional schemes, as Cromwell cast about to find a way of governing through Parliament without delivering England to an intolerant Protestantism. This was the Commonwealth.

PURITANISM

The intolerance of some parliamentarians was one expression of a many-sided strain in English (and American) Protestantism which has been named Puritanism. It was an ill-defined but growing force in English life since Elizabeth's reign. Its spokesmen had originally sought only a particularly close and austere interpretation of religious doctrine and ceremony. Most early Puritans were Anglicans but some of them were impatient over the Church's retention of much from the Catholic past; as time went by it was to this second tendency that the name was more and more applied. By the seventeenth century the epithet "puritan" also betokened, besides rigid doctrine and disapproval of ritual, the reform of manners in a strongly Calvinistic sense. By the time of the republic, many who had been on the parliament's side in the Civil War appeared to wish to use its victory to impose Puritanism, both doctrinal and moral, by law not only on conservative and royalist Anglicans, but on dissenting religious minorities – Congregationalists, Baptists, Unitarians – which had found their voice under the Commonwealth. There was nothing politically or religiously democratic about Puritanism. Those who were of the Elect might freely choose their own elders and act as a self-governing community, but from outside the self-designated circle of the saved they looked (and were) an oligarchy claiming to know God's will for others, and therefore all the more unacceptable. It was a few, untypical minorities, not the dominant Protestant establishment, which threw up the democratic and levelling ideas which contributed so much to the great debate of the republican years.

THE RESTORATION OF THE ENGLISH MONARCHY

The publication of more than twenty thousand books and pamphlets (a word which entered English usage in the 1650s) on political and religious issues would by itself have made the Civil War and Commonwealth years a great epoch in English political education. Unfortunately, once Cromwell had died, the institutional bankruptcy of the republic

This 17th-century painting portrays Oliver Cromwell (1599–1658) who, after the abolition of the monarchy, the House of Lords, the bishops and finally the House of Commons (1653), ruled as Lord Protector of England and the Commonwealth.

Charles II, son of the executed Charles I, was crowned king in Scotland in 1651, but spent nine years in exile in the aftermath of the Civil War. He returned to England in triumph in 1660, when the monarchy was restored.

was clear. The English could not agree in sufficient numbers to uphold any new constitution. But most of them, it turned out, would accept the old device of monarchy. So the story of the Commonwealth ended with the restoration of the Stuarts in 1660. England in fact had her king back on unspoken conditions: in the last resort, Charles II came back because Parliament said so, and believed he would defend the Church of England. Counter-Reformation Catholicism frightened the English as much as did revolutionary Puritanism. Although the struggle of monarch and Parliament was not over, there would be no absolute monarchy in England; henceforth the Crown was on the defensive.

Historians have tried to see much more than this in so great an episode of English history and have argued lengthily about what the so-called "English Revolution" expressed. Clearly, religion played a big part in it. Extreme Protestantism was given a chance to have an influence on the national life it was never again to have; this earned it the deep dislike of Anglicans and made political England anti-clerical for centuries. It was not without cause that the best English historian of the struggle has spoken of the "Puritan Revolution". But religion no more exhausts the meaning of these years than does the constitutional quarrel. Others have sought a class struggle in the Civil War. Of the interested motives of many of those engaged there can be no doubt, but it does not fit any clear general pattern. Still others have seen a struggle between a swollen "Court", a governmental nexus of bureaucrats, courtiers and politicians, all linked to the system by financial dependence upon it, and "Country", the local notables who paid for this. But localities often divided: it was one of the tragedies of the Civil War that even families could be split by it. It remains easier to be clear about the results of the English Revolution than about its origins or meaning.

CARDINAL RICHELIEU

Most continental countries were appalled by the trial and execution of Charles I, but they had their own bloody troubles. A period of conscious assertion of royal power in France by Cardinal Richelieu not only reduced the privileges of the Huguenots (as French Calvinists had come to be called) but had installed royal officials in the provinces as the direct representatives of royal power; these were the *intendants*. Administrative reform was an aggravation of the almost continuous suffering of the French people in the 1630s and 1640s. In the still overwhelmingly agricultural economy of France, Richelieu's measures were bound to hurt the poor most. Taxes on the peasant doubled and sometimes trebled in a few years. An eruption of popular rebellion, mercilessly repressed, was the result. Some parts of France, moreover, were devastated by the campaigns of the last phase of the great struggle for Germany and central Europe called the Thirty Years' War, the phase in which it became a Bourbon-Habsburg conflict. Lorraine, Burgundy and much of eastern France were reduced to ruins, the population of some areas declining by a quarter or a third. The claim that the French monarchy sought to impose new and (some said) unconstitutional taxation finally detonated political crisis under Richelieu's successors. The role of defender of the traditional constitution was taken up by special interests, notably the *parlement* of Paris, the corporation of lawyers who sat in and could plead before the first law court of the kingdom. In 1648 they led an insurrection in Paris (soon named the Fronde). A compromise settlement was followed after an uneasy interval by a second, much more dangerous Fronde, led this time by great noblemen. Though the *parlement* of Paris did not long maintain a united front with them, these men could draw on the anti-centralist feelings of the provincial nobility, as regional rebellions showed. Yet the Crown survived (and so did the *intendants*). In 1660 the absolute monarchy of France was still essentially intact.

CIVIC UNREST IN THE RENAISSANCE STATES

In Spain, too, taxation provoked troubles. An attempt by a minister to overcome the provincialism inherent in the formally federal structure of the Spanish state led to revolt in Portugal (which had been absorbed into Spain with promises of respect for her liberties from Philip II), among the Basques and in Catalonia. The last was to take twelve years to suppress. There was also a revolt in 1647 in the Spanish kingdom of Naples.

In all these instances of civic turbulence, demands for money provoked resistance. In the financial sense, then, the Renaissance state was far from successful. The appearance of standing armies in most states in the seventeenth century did not mark only a military revolution. War was a great devourer of taxes. Yet the burdens of taxation laid on the French seem far greater than those laid on the English: why, then, did the French monarchy appear to suffer less from the "crisis"? England, on the other hand, had civil war and the overthrow (for a time) of her monarchy without the devastation which went with foreign invasion. Nor were her occasional riots over high prices to be compared with the

Cardinal Richelieu (1585–1642), principal minister to King Louis XIII of France, was a great promoter of the absolute authority of the state and the founder of a French national foreign policy.

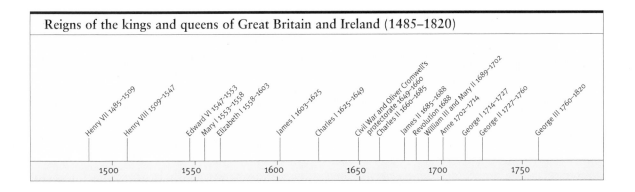

Reigns of the kings and queens of Great Britain and Ireland (1485–1820)

Henry VII 1485–1509
Henry VIII 1509–1547
Edward VI 1547–1553
Mary I 1553–1558
Elizabeth I 1558–1603
James I 1603–1625
Charles I 1625–1649
Civil War and Oliver Cromwell's protectorate 1649–1660
Charles II 1660–1685
James II 1685–1688
Revolution 1688
William III and Mary II 1689–1702
Anne 1702–1714
George I 1714–1727
George II 1727–1760
George III 1760–1820

1500   1550   1600   1650   1700   1750

in 1685, in no sense menaced the state. This makes it all the more striking, in retrospect, that people remained so unwilling to admit the reality of sovereignty. The English solemnly legislated a series of defences of individual liberty in the Bill of Rights, yet even in 1689 it was hard to argue that what one king in Parliament had done, another could not undo. In France everyone agreed the king's power was absolute, yet lawyers went on saying that there were things he could not legally do.

HOBBES

One thinker at least, the greatest of English political philosophers, Thomas Hobbes, showed in his books, notably in the *Leviathan* of 1651, that he recognized the way society was moving. Hobbes argued that the disadvantages and uncertainties of not agreeing that someone should have the last word in deciding what was law clearly outweighed the danger that such power might be tyrannically employed. The troubles of his times deeply impressed him with the need to know certainly where authority was to be found. Even when they were not continuous, disorders were always liable to break out: as Hobbes put it (roughly), you do not have to live all the time under a torrential downpour to say that the weather is rainy. The recognition that legislative power – sovereignty – rested, limitless, in the state and not elsewhere, and that it could not be restricted by appeals to immunities, customs, divine law or anything else without the danger of falling into anarchy, was Hobbes's contribution to political theory, though he got small thanks for it and had to wait until the nineteenth century for due recognition. Though, in practice, people often acted as though they accepted his views, he was almost universally condemned.

Free food is distributed to victims of the Frondes at the gates of a Parisian abbey, depicted in an 18th-century watercolour from the French school.

appalling bloodshed of the peasant risings of seventeenth-century France. In England, too, there was a specific challenge to authority from religious dissent. In Spain this was non-existent and in France it had been contained long before. The Huguenots, indeed, were a vested interest; but they saw their protector in the monarchy and therefore rallied to it in the Frondes. Regionalism was important in Spain, to a smaller extent in France where it provided a foothold for conservative interests threatened by governmental innovation, but seems to have played very little part in England. The year 1660, when the young Louis XIV assumed full powers in France and Charles II returned to England, was, in fact, something of a turning-point. France was not to prove ungovernable again until 1789 and was to show, in the next half-century, astonishing military and diplomatic power. In England there was never again to be, in spite of further constitutional troubles and the deposition of another king, a civil war. After 1660 there was an English standing army, and the last English rebellion, by an inadequate pretender and a few thousand deluded yokels

Hobbes' *Leviathan*

"The finall Cause, End, or Designe of men (who naturally love Liberty, and Dominion over others), in the introduction of that restraint upon themselves (in which wee see them live in Commonwealths) is the foresight of their own preservation ... that is to say, of getting themselves out from that miserable condition of Warre, which is necessarily consequent ... to the naturall Passions of men, when there is no visible Power to keep them in awe, and tye them by feare of punishment to the performance of their Covenants, and observation of those Lawes of Nature ... .

For the Lawes of Nature (as *Justice, Equity, Modesty, Mercy,* and (in summe) *doing to others, as wee would be done to,*) of themselves, without the terrour of some Power, to cause them to be observed, are contrary to our naturall Passions, that carry us to Partiality, Pride, Revenge, and the like."

An extract from Chap. 17, Part II ("Of Commonwealth") of the *Leviathan* by Thomas Hobbes, 1651, edited by C. B. Macpherson.

This was the title page for the first edition of the *Leviathan* by the English philosopher Thomas Hobbes (1588–1679).

CONSTITUTIONAL ENGLAND

Constitutional England was in fact one of the first states to operate on Hobbes's principles. By the early eighteenth century, the English (the Scots were less sure, even when they came under the parliament at Westminster after the Act of Union of 1707) accepted in principle and sometimes showed in practice that there could be no limits except practical ones to the potential scope of law. This conclusion was to be explicitly challenged even as late as Victorian times, but was implicit when in 1688 England at last rejected the direct descent of the Stuart male line, pushed James II off the throne and put his daughter and her consort on it on conditions. Already, one of the indexes of the strengthening of Parliament had been the growth for a century or more of the need for the Crown to manage Parliament; with the creation of a contractual monarchy England at last broke with her *ancien régime* and began to function as a constitutional state. Effectively, centralized power was shared; its major component lay with a House of Commons which represented the dominant social interest, the landowning classes. The king still kept important powers of his own but his advisers, it soon became clear, must possess the confidence of the House of Commons. The legislative sovereign, the Crown in Parliament, could do anything by statute. No such immunity as still protected privilege in continental countries existed nor any body which could hope to become a rival to Parliament. The English answer to the danger posed by such a concentration of authority was to secure, by revolution if necessary, that the authority should only act in accordance with the wishes of the most important elements in society.

THE "GLORIOUS REVOLUTION" OF 1688

This 17th-century engraving depicts the coronation of William III and Mary II, which took place in 1689.

The year 1688 gave England a Dutch king, Queen Mary's husband, William III, to whom the major importance of the "Glorious Revolution" of that year was that England could be mobilized against France, now threatening the independence of the United Provinces. There were too many complicated interests at work in them for the Anglo-French wars which followed to be interpreted in merely constitutional or ideological terms. Moreover, the presence of the Holy Roman Empire, Spain and various German princes in the shifting anti-French coalitions of the next quarter-century would certainly make nonsense of any neat contrast of political principle between the two sides. Nevertheless, it rightly struck some contemporaries that there was an ideological element buried somewhere in the struggle. England and Holland were more open societies than the France of Louis XIV. They allowed and protected the exercise of different religions. They did not censor the press but left it to be regulated by the laws which protected persons and the state against defamation. They were governed by oligarchies representing the effective possessors of social and economic power. France was at the opposite pole.

LOUIS XIV

UNDER LOUIS XIV, absolute government reached its climax in France. It is not easy to pin his ambitions down in familiar categories; for him personal, dynastic and national greatness were hardly distinguishable. Perhaps that is why he became a model for all European princes. Politics was reduced effectively to administration; the royal councils, together with the royal agents in the provinces, the *intendants* and military commanders, took due account of such social facts as the existence of the nobility and local immunities, but the reign played havoc with the real independence of the political forces so powerful hitherto in France. This was the era of the establishment of royal power throughout the country and some later saw it as a revolutionary one; in the second half of the century the frame which Richelieu had knocked together was at last filled up by administrative reality. Louis XIV tamed aristocrats by offering them the most glamorous court in Europe; his own sense of social hierarchy made him happy to caress them with honours and pensions, but he never forgot the Frondes and controlled the nobility as had Richelieu. Louis's relatives were excluded from his council, which contained non-noble ministers on whom he could safely rely. The *parlements* were restricted to their judicial role; the French Church's independence of Roman authority was asserted, but only to bring it the more securely under the wing of the Most Christian King (as one of Louis's titles had it). As for the Huguenots, Louis was determined, whatever the cost, not to be a ruler of heretics; those who were not exiled were submitted to a harsh persecution to bring them to conversion.

THE PERFECT ABSOLUTE MONARCHY

The coincidence with a great age of French cultural achievement still seems to make it hard for the French to recognize the harsh face of the reign of Louis XIV. He ruled a hierarchical, corporate, theocratic society which, even if up-to-date in methods, looked to the past for its goals. Louis even hoped to become Holy Roman Emperor. He refused to allow the philosopher Descartes, the defender of religion, to be given religious burial in France because of the dangers of his ideas. Yet for a long time his kind of government seems to have been what most French people wanted. The process of effective government could be brutal, as Huguenots who were coerced into conversion by having soldiers billeted on them, or peasants reluctant to pay taxes who were visited by a troop of cavalry for a month or so, both knew. Yet life may have been better than life a few decades previously, in spite of some exceptionally hard years. The reign was the end of an era of disorder, not the start of one. France was largely free from invasion and there was a drop in the return expected from investment in land which lasted well into the eighteenth century. These were solid realities to underpin the glittering façade of an age later called the *Grand Siècle*.

Louis's European position was won in large measure by success in war (though by the end of the reign, he had undergone serious setbacks), but it was not only his armies and diplomacy which mattered. He carried French prestige to a peak at which it was long to remain because of the model of monarchy he presented; he was the perfect absolute monarch. The physical setting of the Ludovican achievement was the huge new palace of Versailles. Few buildings or the lives lived in them can have been so aped and

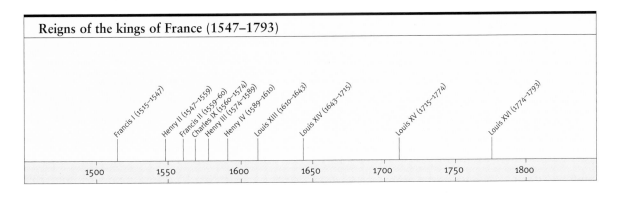

Reigns of the kings of France (1547–1793)

Francis I (1515–1547)
Henry II (1547–1559)
Francis II (1559–60)
Charles IX (1560–1574)
Henry III (1574–1589)
Henry IV (1589–1610)
Louis XIII (1610–1643)
Louis XIV (1643–1715)
Louis XV (1715–1774)
Louis XVI (1774–1793)

1500   1550   1600   1650   1700   1750   1800

imitated. In the eighteenth century Europe was to be studded with miniature reproductions of the French court, painfully created at the expense of their subjects by would-be "grands monarques" in the decades of stability and continuity which almost everywhere followed the upheavals of the great wars of Louis's reign.

ENLIGHTENED DESPOTISM

THERE WERE BETWEEN 1715 and 1740 no important international tensions to provoke internal change in states, nor were there great ideological divisions such as those of the seventeenth century, nor rapid economic and social development with their consequential strain. Not surprisingly, therefore, governments changed little and everywhere society seemed to settle down after a turbulent century or so. Apart from Great Britain, the

United Provinces, the cantons of Switzerland and the fossil republics of Italy, absolute monarchy was the dominant state form. It remained so for most of the eighteenth century, sometimes in a style which came to be called "enlightened despotism" – a slippery term, which neither has nor ever had a clear meaning any more than terms like "Right" or "Left" have today. What it indicates is that from about 1750 the wish to carry out practical reforms led some rulers to innovations which seemed to be influenced by the advanced thought of the day. Such innovations, when effective, were imposed none the less by the machinery of absolute monarchical power. If sometimes humanitarian, the policies of "enlightened despots" were not necessarily politically liberal. They were, on the other hand, usually modern in that they undermined traditional social and religious authority, cut across accepted notions of social hierarchy or legal rights, and helped to concentrate law-making power in the state and assert its unchallenged authority over its subjects, who were treated increasingly as an aggregate of individuals rather than as members of a hierarchy of corporations.

Not surprisingly, it is almost impossible to find an example which in practice perfectly fulfils this general description, just as it is impossible to find a definition of a "democratic" state today, or a "fascist" state in the 1930s, which fits all examples. Among Mediterranean and southern countries, for example, Naples, Spain, Portugal and some other Italian states (and even at times the Papal States) had ministers who sought economic reform. Some of these were stimulated by novelty; others – Portugal and Spain – turned to enlightened despotism as a way to recover lost status as great powers. Some encroached on the powers of the Church. Almost all of them served rulers who were part of the Bourbon family connection. The involvement of one of the smallest of them, Parma, in a quarrel with the papacy led to a general attack in all of these countries on the right arm of the Counter-Reformation papacy, the Society of Jesus. In 1773 the pope was driven by them to dissolve the Society, a great symbolic defeat, as important for its demonstration of the strength of advanced anti-clerical principles even in Catholic Europe as for its practical effects.

EASTERN EUROPEAN ABSOLUTISM

Among these states only Spain had any pretension to great power status and she was in decline. Of the eastern enlightened despotisms, on the other hand, three out of four certainly had. The odd man out was Poland, the sprawling ramshackle kingdom where reform on "enlightened" lines came to grief on constitutional rocks; the enlightenment

was there all right, but not the despotism to make it effective. More successfully, Prussia, the Habsburg empire and Russia all managed to sustain a façade of enlightenment while strengthening the state. Once more, the clue to change can be found in war, which cost far more than building even the most lavish replica of Versailles. In Russia, modernization of the state went back to the earliest years of the century, when Peter the Great sought to guarantee her future as a great power through technical and institutional change. In the second half of the century, the empress Catherine II reaped many of the benefits of this. She also gave the régime a thin veneer of up-to-the-minute ideas by advertising widely her patronage of letters and humanitarianism. This was all very superficial; the traditional ordering of society was unchanged. Russia was a conservative despotism whose politics were largely a matter of the struggles of noble factions and families. Nor did enlightenment much change things in Prussia, where there was a well-established tradition of efficient, centralized, economical administration embodying much

King Philip V of Spain (1683–1746), who is portrayed with his family in this 18th-century painting, considered himself to be an enlightened despot.

This portrait by the French painter Jean-Marc Nattier (1685–1766) depicts Peter I (1672–1725). Known as Peter the Great, the emperor made the Westernization of Russia his principal aim.

of what reformers sought elsewhere. Prussia already enjoyed religious toleration and the Hohenzollern monarchy ruled a strongly traditional society virtually unchanged in the eighteenth century. The Prussian king was obliged to recognize – and willingly did so – that his power rested on the acquiescence of his nobles and he carefully preserved their legal and social privilege. Frederick II remained convinced that only noblemen should be given commissioned rank in his army and at the end of his reign there were more serfs in Prussian territory than there had been at the beginning.

THE HABSBURG EMPIRE

COMPETITION WITH PRUSSIA was a decisive stimulus to reform in the Habsburg dominions. There were great obstacles in the way. The dynasty's territories were very diverse, in nationality, language, institutions; the emperor was King of Hungary, Duke of Milan, Archduke of Austria, to name only a few of his many titles. Centralization and greater administrative uniformity were essential if this variegated empire was to exercise its due weight in European affairs. Another problem was that, like the Bourbon states, but unlike Russia or Prussia, the Habsburg empire was overwhelmingly Roman Catholic. Everywhere the power of the Church was deeply entrenched; the Habsburg lands included most of those outside Spain where the Counter-Reformation had been most successful. The Church also owned huge properties; it was everywhere protected by tradition, canon law and papal policy, and it had a monopoly of education. Finally, the Habsburgs provided almost without interruption during these centuries the successive occupants of the throne of the Holy Roman Empire. In consequence they had special responsibilities in Germany.

HABSBURG REFORM

This background was always likely to give modernization in the Habsburg dominions an "enlightened" colour. Everywhere practical reform seemed to conflict with entrenched social power or the Church. The empress Maria Theresia was herself by no means sympathetic to reform which had such implications, but her advisers were able to present a persuasive case for it when, after the 1740s, it became clear that the Habsburg monarchy would have to struggle for supremacy with Prussia. Once the road to fiscal and consequently administrative reform had been entered upon, it was in the end bound to lead to conflict between Church and State. This came to a climax in the reign of Maria Theresia's son and successor, Joseph II, a man who did not share the pieties of his mother and who was alleged to have advanced views. His reforms became especially associated with measures of secularization. Monasteries lost their property, religious appointments were interfered with, the right of sanctuary was removed and education was taken out of the hands of the clergy. So far as it went, this awoke angry opposition, but mattered less than the fact that by 1790 Joseph had antagonized to the point of open defiance the nobles of Brabant, Hungary and Bohemia. The powerful local institutions – estates and diets – through which those lands could oppose his policies paralysed government in many of Joseph's realms at the end of his reign.

RESISTANCE TO FRENCH REFORM

Differences in the circumstances in which they were applied, in the preconceptions which governed them, in the success they achieved and in the degree to which they did or did not embody "enlightened" ideas, all show how misleading is any idea that there was, anywhere, a "typical" enlightened despotism to serve as a model. The government of France, clearly touched by reforming policies and aspirations, only confirms this. Obstacles to change had, paradoxically, grown stronger after the death of Louis XIV. Under his successor (whose reign began as a minority under a regency), the real influence of the privileged had grown and increasingly there grew up in the *parlements* a tendency to criticize laws which infringed special interest and historic privilege. There was a new and growing resistance to the idea that there rested in the Crown any right of unrestricted legislative sovereignty. As the century wore on, France's international role imposed heavier and heavier burdens on her finances and the issue of reform tended to crystallize in the issue of finding new tax revenue – an exercise that was bound to encourage resist-

Frederick II of Prussia (1712–1786), known as Frederick the Great, called himself "the first servant of the state", a phrase which was quickly adopted in other royal circles.

ance. Onto this rock ran most of the proposals for reform within the French monarchy.

Paradoxically, France was in 1789 the country most associated with the articulation and diffusion of critical and advanced ideas, yet also one of those where it seemed most difficult to put them into practice. But this was an issue which was Europe-wide in the traditional monarchies of the end of the eighteenth century. Wherever reform and modernization had been tried, the hazards of vested historical interest and traditional social structure threw obstacles in the way. In the last resort, it was unlikely that mon-archical absolutism could have solved this problem anywhere. It could not question historical authority too closely for this was what it rested upon itself. Unrestricted legislative sovereignty seemed still in the eighteenth century to call too much in question. If historic rights were infringed, could not property be? This was a fair point, though Europe's most successful ruling class, the English, seemed to accept that nothing was outside the sphere of legislative competence, nothing beyond the scope of reform, without fears that such a revolutionary idea was likely to be used against them.

THE GROWTH OF STATE POWER

With this important qualification, though, enlightened despotism, too, embodies the theme already set out – that at the heart of the complex story of political evolution in many countries over a period of three centuries, continuity lies in the growth of the power of the state. The occasional successes of those who tried to put the clock back almost always proved temporary. True, even the most determined reformers and the ablest statesmen had to work with a machinery of state which to any modern bureaucrat would seem woefully inadequate. Though the eighteenth-century state might mobilize resources much greater than had done its predecessors

it had to do so with no revolutionary innovations of technique. Communications as the eighteenth century ended depended just as they had done three hundred years earlier on wind and muscle; the "telegraph" which came into use in the 1790s was only a semaphore system, worked by pulling ropes. Armies could move only slightly faster than three centuries earlier, and if their weapons were improved, they were not improved out of recognition. No police force such as exists today existed in any country; income tax lay still in the future. The changes in the power of the state which are already observable came about because of changes in ideas and because of the development to greater efficiency of well-known institutions, rather than because of technology. In no major state before 1789 could it even be assumed that all its subjects would understand the language of government, while none, except perhaps Great Britain and the United Provinces, succeeded in so identifying itself with its subjects as to leave its government more concerned to protect them against foreigners than itself against them. Nowhere else on the eastern side of the Atlantic did any sovereign power look much like a modern nation-state.

Empress Maria Theresia (1717–1780), the daughter of the emperor Charles VI, was Archduchess of Austria and Queen of Hungary and Bohemia from 1740. Her husband, Francis I, became Holy Roman Emperor in 1745, and her eldest son, Joseph II, succeeded him in 1765. One of her daughters, Marie Antoinette, was married to the future French king Louis XVI in 1770.

3 THE NEW WORLD OF GREAT POWERS

AMONG THE INSTITUTIONS which took their basic shape in the fifteenth and sixteenth centuries, and are still with us today, are those of resident diplomacy. Rulers had sent messages to one another and negotiated, but there were always many ways of doing this and of understanding what was going on. The Chinese, for example, used the idea that their emperor was ruler of the world and that all embassies to him were therefore of the nature of petitions or tributes by subjects.

Medieval European kings had sent one another heralds, about whom a special ceremonial had grown up and whom special rules protected, or occasional missions of ambassadors. After 1500, it slowly became the practice to use in peacetime the standard device we still employ, of a permanently resident ambassador through whom all ordinary business is at least initially transacted and who has the task of keeping his own rulers informed about the country to which he is accredited.

MAXIMILIANVS I IMP
ARCHIDVX AVSTRIÆ.
DVX BVRGVNDIÆ

PHILIPPVS HISP. REX.I.
ARCHIDVX AVSTRIÆ.

MARIA DVCISSA
BVRGVNDIÆ MAX: VXOR.

FERDINANDVS. I. IMP.
ARCHIDVX AVSTRIÆ.

CAROLVS. V. IMP.
ARCHIDVX AVSTRIÆ.

LVDOVIVS REX
IVNG MAS

THE NEW DIPLOMATIC SYSTEM

The first notable examples of permanent ambassadors were Venetian. It is not surprising that a republic so dependent on trade and the maintenance of regular relationships should have provided the first examples of the professional diplomat. More changes followed. Gradually, the hazards of the life of earlier emissaries were forgotten as diplomats were given a special status protected by privileges and immunities. The nature of treaties and other diplomatic forms also became more precise and regularized. Procedure became more standardized. All these changes came about slowly, when they were believed to be useful. For the most part, it is true, the professional diplomat in the modern sense had not yet appeared by 1800, ambassadors were

This 15th-century painting depicts the emperor Maximilian (1459–1519) and his family. The Habsburgs' diplomatic and matrimonial policies turned the House of Austria into a major European force and eventually resulted in the division of the dynasty into two branches – Spanish and Austrian.

then still usually noblemen who could afford to sustain a representative role, not paid civil servants. None the less, the professionalization of diplomacy was beginning. It is another sign that after 1500 a new world of relationships between sovereign powers was replacing that of feudal ties between persons and the vague supremacies of pope and emperor.

The most striking characteristic of this new system is the expression it gave to the assumption that the world is divided into sovereign states. This idea took time to emerge; sixteenth-century Europe was certainly not seen by contemporaries as a set of independent areas, each governed by a ruler of its own, belonging to it alone. Still less were its components thought to have in any but a few cases any sort of unity which might be called "national". That this was so was not only because of the survival of such museums of past practice as the Holy Roman Empire. It was also because the dominating principle of early modern Europe's diplomacy was dynasticism.

DYNASTICISM

In the sixteenth and seventeenth centuries, the political units of Europe were less states than landed estates. They were accumulations of property put together over long or short periods by aggressiveness, marriage and inheritance – by the same processes and

forces, that is to say, by which any private family's estate might be built up. The results were to be seen on maps whose boundaries continually changed as this or that portion of an inheritance passed from one ruler to another. The inhabitants had no more say in the matter than might the peasants living on a farm which changed hands. Dynasticism accounts for the monotonous preoccupation of negotiations and treaty-making with the possible consequences of marriages and the careful establishment and scrutiny of lines of succession.

Besides their dynastic interests, rulers also argued and fought about religion and, increasingly, trade or wealth. Some of them acquired overseas possessions; this, too, became a complicating factor. Occasionally, the old principles of feudal superiority might still be invoked. There were also always map-making forces at work which fell outside the operation of these principles, such as settlement of new land or awakening national sentiment. Nevertheless, broadly speaking, most rulers in the sixteenth and seventeenth centuries saw themselves as the custodians of inherited rights and interests which they had to pass on. In this they behaved as was expected; they mirrored the attitudes of other men and other families in their societies. It was not only the Middle Ages which were fascinated by lineage, and the sixteenth and seventeenth centuries were the great age of genealogy.

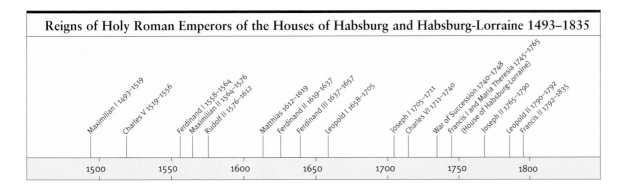

Reigns of Holy Roman Emperors of the Houses of Habsburg and Habsburg-Lorraine 1493–1835

The Catholic
Monarchs in
Spain, like most royal
European dynasties,
used marriage as a
means of extending
their rule. Isabella of
Castile and Ferdinand II
of Aragon arranged a
double marriage with
the House of Austria:
that of John with
Marguerite and that of
their daughter the
Infanta Joanna with
Philip I, known as the
Handsome. The latter
couple, depicted on
these 16th-century
panels, had two sons
(later the emperors
Charles V and
Ferdinand I), who
inherited a vast empire.

In 1500 the dynastic map of Europe was about to undergo a major transformation. For the next two centuries, two great families were to dispute much of Europe as they were already at that date disputing Italy. These were the house of Habsburg and the ruling house of France, first Valois, then after the accession of Henry IV in 1589, Bourbon. The one would come to be predominantly Austrian and the other's centre would always be France. But both would export rulers and consorts of rulers to many other countries. The heart of their quarrel when the sixteenth century began was the Burgundian inheritance. Each of them was then far from playing a wider European role. Indeed, there was not a great deal to distinguish them at that date in power – though much in antiquity – from other dynasties, the Welsh Tudors, for example, whose first ruler, Henry VII, had ascended the throne of England in 1485.

TOWARDS THE NATIONAL STATE

Only in England, France and perhaps Spain and Portugal could there be discerned any real national cohesion and sentiment to sustain political unity. England, a relatively unimportant power, was a well-developed example. Insular, secluded from invasion and rid, after 1492, of continental appendages other than the seaports of Calais (finally lost only in 1558), her government was unusually centralized. The Tudors, anxious to assert the unity of the kingdom after the long period of disorder labelled the "Wars of the Roses", consciously associated national interest with that of the dynasty. Shakespeare quite naturally uses the language of patriotism (and, it may be remarked, says little about religious differences). France, too, had already come some way along the road to national cohesion. The house of Valois-Bourbon had greater problems than the Tudors, though, in the continued survival of immunities and privileged enclaves within its territories over which its monarchs did not exercise full sovereignty as kings of France. Some of their subjects did not even speak French. Nevertheless, France was well on the way to becoming a national state.

This miniature portrays Ferdinand I of Habsburg (1503–1564) and is taken from his Book of Hours. Already First Regent of the patrimonial states of the House of Habsburg (the Austrian Archduchies), Ferdinand was named King of the Romans in 1531. He became Holy Roman Emperor in 1558.

HABSBURG PRE-EMINENCE

SPAIN WAS ALSO becoming a national state, though its two crowns were not united until the grandson of the Catholic monarchs, Charles of Habsburg, became co-ruler with his insane mother in 1516 as Charles I. He had still carefully to distinguish the rights of Castile from those of Aragon, but Spanish nationality was made more self-conscious during his reign because, although at first popular, Charles obscured the national identity of Spain in a larger Habsburg empire and, indeed, sacrificed Spanish interest to dynastic aims and triumphs. The great diplomatic event of the first half of the century was his election in 1519 as Charles V, Holy Roman Emperor. He succeeded his grandfather Maximilian, who had sought his election, and careful marriages in the past had by then already made him the ruler of the furthest-flung territorial empire the world had ever seen, to which the imperial title supplied a fitting crown. From his mother he inherited the Spanish kingdoms, and therefore both the Aragonese interest in Sicily, and the Castilian in the newly discovered Americas. From his father, Maximilian's son, came the Netherlands which had been part of the duchy of Burgundy, and from his grandfather the Habsburg lands of Austria and the Tyrol, with Franche-Comté, Alsace and a bundle of claims in Italy. This was the greatest dynastic accumulation of the age, and the crowns of Bohemia and Hungary were held by Charles's brother, Ferdinand, who was to succeed him as emperor. Habsburg pre-eminence was the central fact of European politics for most of the sixteenth century. Its real and unreal pretensions are well shown in the list of Charles's titles when he ascended the imperial throne: "King of the Romans; Emperor-elect; semper Augustus; King of Spain, Sicily, Jerusalem, the Balearic Islands, the Canary Islands, the Indies and the mainland on the far side of the Atlantic; Archduke of Austria; Duke of Burgundy, Brabant, Styria, Carinthia, Carniola, Luxemburg, Limburg, Athens and Patras; Count of Habsburg, Flanders and Tyrol; Count Palatine of Burgundy, Hainault, Pfirt, Roussillon; Landgrave of Alsace; Count of Swabia; Lord of Asia and Africa."

Charles I of Spain and V of Germany (1500–1558) is shown here in a portrait by Titian.

THE IMPERIAL AMBITIONS OF CHARLES I

Whatever the conglomeration ruled by Charles I represented, it was not nationality. It fell, for practical purposes, into two main blocks: the Spanish inheritance, rich through the possession of the Netherlands and irrigated by a growing flow of bullion from the Americas, and the old Habsburg lands, demanding an active role in Germany to maintain the family's pre-eminence there. Charles, though, saw from his imperial throne much more than this. Revealingly, he liked to call himself "God's standard-bearer" and campaigned like a Christian paladin of old against the Turk in Africa and up and down the Mediterranean. In his own eyes he was still the medieval emperor, much more than one ruler among many; he was leader of Christendom and responsible only to God for his charge. He may have felt he had a better claim to be called "Defender of the Faith" than his Tudor rival Henry VIII, another aspirant to the imperial throne. Germany, Spain and Habsburg dynastic interest were all to be sacrificed in some degree to Charles's vision of his role. Yet what he sought was impossible. The dream of ruling such an empire was beyond the powers of any man given the strains imposed by the Reformation and the inadequate apparatus of sixteenth-century communication and administration. Charles, moreover, strove to rule personally, travelling ceaselessly in pursuit of this futile aim and thereby, perhaps, he ensured also that no part of his empire (unless it was the Netherlands) felt identified with his house. His aspiration reveals the way in which the medieval world still lived on, but also his anachronism.

The Holy Roman Empire was, of course, distinct from the Habsburg family possessions. It, too, embodied the medieval past, but at its most worm-eaten and unreal. Germany, where most of it lay, was a chaos supposedly united under the emperor and his tenants-in-chief, the imperial Diet. Since the Golden Bull the seven electors were virtually sovereign in their territories. There were also a hundred princes and more than fifty imperial cities, all independent. Another three hundred or so minor statelets and imperial vassals completed the patchwork, which was what was left of the early medieval empire. As the sixteenth century began, an attempt to reform this confusion and give Germany some measure of national unity failed; this suited the lesser princes and the cities. All that emerged were some new administrative institutions. Charles's election as emperor in 1519 was by no means a foregone conclusion; rightly, people feared that German interests in the huge Habsburg dominions might be overridden or neglected. Heavy bribery of the

electors was needed before he prevailed over the king of France (the only other serious candidate, for nobody believed that Henry VIII would be able to pay enough). Habsburg dynastic interest was thereafter the only unifying principle at work in the Holy Roman Empire until its abolition in 1806.

THE "ITALIAN" WARS

Italy, one of the most striking geographical unities in Europe, was also still fragmented into independent states, most of them ruled

Francis I of France (1494–1547), shown here in a portrait attributed to the French painter Jean Clouet (c.1485–c.1541), was Charles V's opponent in disputes over the control of territories including Burgundy, Milan, Genoa and Naples. Both were warring monarchs who fought personally in battle.

Emperor Charles V is shown entering the conquered city of Tunis in this 16th-century engraving. With its expansion from the western Mediterranean to the African Barbary Coast, however, the Turkish Empire also threatened Italy. Charles' conquest of Tunis in 1535 brought a brief halt to attacks by Barbary pirates supported by the Turks.

their own ancestral lands. The divisions of the peninsula made it an attractive prey and a tangle of family relationships gave French and Spanish rulers excuses to dabble in affairs there. For the first half of the sixteenth century the main theme of European diplomatic history is provided by the rivalry of Habsburg and Bourbon, and its main theatre and its prizes lay in Italy.

The Habsburg–Valois wars in Italy, which began in 1494 with a French invasion reminiscent of medieval adventuring and raiding (decked out as a crusade), lasted until 1559. There were altogether six "Italian" wars and they were more important than they might at first appear. They constitute a distinct period in the evolution of the European states system. Charles V's accession and the defeat of Francis in the imperial election brought out the lines of dynastic competition more clearly. To Charles the ruler of the empire they were a fatal distraction from the Lutheran problem in Germany, and to Charles the king of Spain they were the start of a fatal draining of their country's power. To the French, they brought impoverishment and invasion, and to their kings, in the end, frustration, for Spain was left dominant in Italy. To the inhabitants of that country, the wars brought a variety of disasters. For the first time since the age of the barbarian invasions, Rome was sacked (in 1527, by a mutinous imperial army) and Spanish hegemony finally ended the great days of the city republics. At one time, the coasts of Italy were raided by French and Turkish ships in concert; the hollowness of the unity of Christendom was revealed by a formal alliance of a French king with the Sultan.

Perhaps these were good years only for the Ottomans. Venice, usually left to face the Turks alone, watched her empire in the eastern Mediterranean begin to crumble away. Spain, enthralled by the mirage of dominating Italy and the illusions bred by a seemingly

by princely despots, and some of them dependencies of external powers. The pope was a temporal monarch in the states of the Church. A king of Naples of the house of Aragon ruled that country. Sicily belonged to his Spanish relatives. Venice, Genoa and Lucca were republics. Milan was a large duchy of the Po valley ruled by the Sforza family. Florence was theoretically a republic but from 1509 really a monarchy in the hands of the Medici, a former banking house. In north Italy the dukes of Savoy ruled Piedmont, on the other side of the Alps from

endless flow of treasure from the Americas, had abandoned her earlier Moroccan conquests. Both Charles V and his son were defeated in African enterprises and while defeat of the Turks at Lepanto in 1571 was only a momentary success, three years later they took back Tunis from the Spanish. The struggle with the Ottomans and the support of the Habsburg cause in Italy had by then overburdened even Spain's wealth. In his last years, Charles V was crippled by debt.

THE ABDICATION OF CHARLES

Charles V abdicated in 1556, just after the first settlement at Augsburg of the religious disputes of Germany, to be succeeded as emperor by his brother, who took the Austrian inheritance, and as ruler of Spain by his son, Philip II, a Spaniard born and bred. Charles had been born in the Netherlands and the ceremony which ended the great emperor's reign took place there, in the Hall of the Golden Fleece; he was moved to tears as he left the assembly, leaning on the shoulder of a young nobleman, William of Orange. This division of the Habsburg inheritance marks the watershed of European affairs in the 1550s.

What followed was the blackest period of Europe's history for centuries. With a brief lull as it opened, European rulers and their people indulged in the seventeenth century in an orgy of hatred, bigotry, massacre, torture and brutality which has no parallel until the twentieth. The dominating facts of this period were the military pre-eminence of Spain, the ideological conflict opened by the Counter-Reformation, the paralysis of Germany and, for a long time, France, by internal religious quarrels, the emergence of new centres of power in England, the Dutch Netherlands and Sweden, and the first adumbrations

of the overseas conflicts of the next two centuries. Only with the end of this period did it appear that the power of Spain had dwindled and that France had inherited her continental ascendancy.

THE DUTCH REVOLT

The best starting-point in an assessment of seventeenth-century Europe is the Dutch Revolt. Like the Spanish Civil War of 1936–9 (but for much longer) it mixed up outsiders in a confusion of ideological, political, strategic and economic quarrels. France could not be

Philip II of Spain (1527–1598), the son of Charles I, was known as "Defender of the Faith". However, Philip, like his father, did not hesitate to enter into conflict with the papacy, for which he was excommunicated.

easy while Spanish armies might invade her from Spain, Italy and Flanders. England's involvement arose in other ways. Though Protestant, she was only just Protestant, and Philip tried to avoid an outright break with Elizabeth I. He was for a long time unwilling to sacrifice the chance of reasserting the English interests he had won by marriage to Mary Tudor, and at first thought to retain them by marrying a second English queen. Moreover he was long distracted by campaigns against the Ottomans. But national and religious feeling were inflamed in England by Spanish responses to English piracy at the expense of the Spanish empire; Anglo-Spanish relations decayed rapidly in the 1570s and 1580s. Elizabeth overtly and covertly helped the Dutch, whom she did not want to see go under, but did so without enthusiasm; being a monarch, she did not like rebels. In the end, armed with papal approval

for the deposition of Elizabeth, the heretic queen, a great Spanish invasion effort was mounted in 1588. "God blew and they were scattered" said the inscription on an English commemorative medal; bad weather completed the work of Spanish planning and English seamanship and gunnery (though not a ship on either side was actually sunk by gunfire) to bring the Armada to disaster. War with Spain went on long after its shattered remnants had limped back to Spanish harbours but a great danger was over. Also, almost incidentally, an English naval tradition of enormous importance was born.

THE THIRTY YEARS' WAR

James I strove sensibly to avoid a renewal of the conflict once peace had been made and succeeded, for all the anti-Spanish prejudices

The Congress of Münster of 15 May 1648, a scene from which is depicted in this 17th-century painting, was one of two parallel conferences that marked the start of the European peace process to end the Thirty Years' War. The conference in Münster was attended by representatives of the Catholic powers, while the envoys from the Protestant states met in Osnabrück.

France and Spain continued fighting after the signing of the Peace of Westphalia (1648). Hostilities between them did not end until 1659, by which time French predominance in western Europe was firmly established. In this engraving, Louis XIV of France and Navarre and Philip IV of Spain meet in 1659 to ratify the Peace of the Pyrenees, which put an end to the fighting.

of his subjects. England was not sucked into the continental conflict when the revolt of the Netherlands, re-ignited after a Twelve Years' Truce, was merged into a much greater struggle, the Thirty Years' War. At its heart was a Habsburg attempt to rebuild the imperial authority in Germany by linking it with the triumph of the Counter-Reformation. This called in question the Peace of Augsburg and the survival of a religiously pluralistic Germany. It was seen, too, as an attempt to buttress an over-ambitious House of Habsburg. Once again, cross-currents confused the pattern of ideological conflict. As Habsburg and Valois had disputed Italy in the sixteenth century, Habsburg and Bourbon disputed Germany in the next. Dynastic interest brought Catholic France into the field against the Catholic Habsburgs. Under the leadership of a cardinal, the "eldest daughter of the Church", as France was claimed to be, allied with Dutch Calvinists and Danish and Swedish Lutherans to assure the rights of German princes. Meanwhile the unhappy inhabitants of much of central Europe had often to endure the whims and rapacities of quasi-independent warlords. Cardinal Richelieu has a better claim than any other man to be the creator of a foreign policy of stirring up trouble beyond the Rhine which was to serve France well for over a century. If anyone still doubted it, with him the age of *Realpolitik* and *raison d'état*, of simple, unprincipled assertion of the interest of the sovereign state, had clearly arrived.

The Peace of Westphalia which ended the Thirty Years' War in 1648 was in several ways a registration of change. Yet it showed traces still of the fading past. This makes it a good vantage-point. It was the end of the era of religious wars in Europe; for the last time European statesmen had as one of their main concerns in a general settlement the religious future of their peoples. It also marked the end of Spanish military supremacy and of the dream of reconstituting the empire of Charles V. It closed, too, an era of Habsburg history. In Germany a new force had appeared

Europe at the time of the Treaty of Westphalia, 1648

The peace of Westphalia undoubtedly meant the end of Habsburg domination in Europe and particularly of its Spanish branch. However, although a "European balance" was now spoken of for the first time, new great powers emerged after the treaties: France and Sweden. At first, a policy of religious tolerance was introduced; the empire was divided into a confederation of independent states where the individual princes' power was much greater than that of the emperor. But these treaties did not bring about general peace in Europe, since the Baltic problems remained unresolved and the war between France and Spain continued.

in the Electorate of Brandenburg, with which later Habsburgs would contend, but the frustration of Habsburg aims in Germany had been the work of outsiders, Sweden and France. Here was the real sign of the future: a period of French ascendancy was beginning in Europe west of the Elbe. In a still longer perspective it opened a period during which the underlying issues of European diplomacy were to be the balance of power in Europe, both east and west, the fate of the Ottoman empire, and the distribution of global power.

THE RISE OF COLONIAL INTEREST

A century and a half after Columbus, when Spain, Portugal, England, France and Holland all already had important overseas empires, these were apparently of no interest to the authors of the peace of 1648. England was not even represented at either of the centres of negotiation; she had hardly been concerned in events once the first phase of the war was over. Preoccupied by internal quarrels and troubled by her Scottish neighbours,

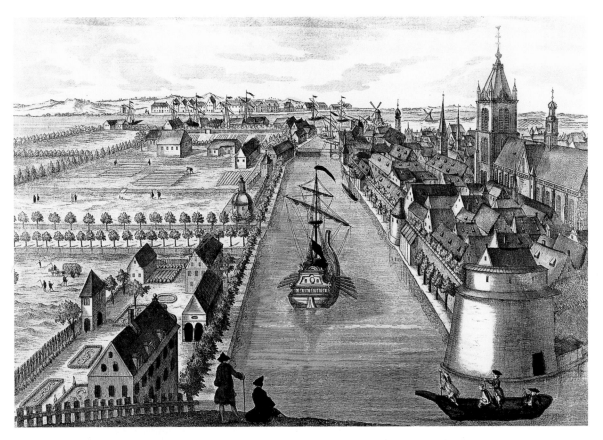

The port of Rotterdam near Delft, in Holland, is shown in this engraving. Rotterdam was one of Holland's thriving commercial ports during the 16th and 17th centuries.

her foreign policy was directed towards ends more extra-European than European – though it was these ends which soon led her to fight the Dutch (1652–4). Although Cromwell quickly restored peace, telling the Dutch there was room in the world for both of them to trade, English and Dutch diplomacy was already showing more clearly than that of other nations the influence of commercial and colonial interest. For both of them, the ocean was seen as their means of expansion, rather than the traditional routes through continental Europe.

THE FRANCE OF LOUIS XIV

FRENCH ASCENDANCY on the continent was founded on solid natural advantages. France was the most populous state of western Europe and on this simple fact rested French military power until the nineteenth century; it would always require the assembling of great international forces to contain it. France, however miserably poor its inhabitants may seem to modern eyes, had great economic resources, and was able to sustain a huge efflorescence of power and prestige under Louis XIV. His reign began formally in 1643, but actually in 1661 when, at the age of twenty-two, he announced his intention of managing his own affairs. This assumption of supreme power was a great fact in international as well as French history; Louis was the most consummate exponent of the trade of kingship who has ever lived. Only for convenience may his foreign policy be distinguished from other aspects of his reign. The building of Versailles, for example, was not only the gratification of a personal taste, but an exercise in building a prestige essential to his diplomacy. Similarly, though they may be separated, his foreign and domestic policy were closely entwined with one another and with

The Palace of Versailles is depicted in this 18th-century engraving. Louis XIV (the "Sun King") intended the palace to glorify the French monarchy, which meant that art of every kind was collected on an unrestrained scale. The court of the Sun King and the salons of Paris were copied throughout Europe. In Germany, Poland and Russia such imitation went so far as the adoption of French as the second, or even the first, language of educated society.

ideology. Louis might wish to improve the strategical shape of France's northwestern frontier, but also (though he might buy millions of tulip bulbs a year from them for Versailles) he despised the Dutch as merchants, disapproved of them as republicans, and detested them as Protestants. In him lived the spirit of the militant Counter-Reformation. Nor was that all. Louis was a legalistic man – kings had to be – and he felt easier when there existed legal claims good enough to give respectability to what he was doing. This was the complicated background to a foreign policy of expansion. Though in the end it cost his country dearly, it carried France to a pre-eminence from which she was to freewheel through half the eighteenth century, and created a legend to which the French still look back with nostalgia.

FRENCH AGGRESSION

Louis's first aim was an improved frontier. This meant conflict with Spain, still in possession of the Spanish Netherlands and the Franche-Comté. The defeat of Spain opened the way to war with the Dutch. The Dutch held their own, but the war ended in 1678 with a peace usually reckoned the peak of Louis's achievement in foreign affairs. He now turned to Germany. Besides territorial conquest, he sought the imperial crown and to obtain it was willing to ally with the Turk. A turning-point came in 1688, when William of Orange, the stadtholder of Holland, took his wife Mary Stuart to England to replace her father on the English throne. From this time Louis had a new and persistent enemy across the Channel, instead of the complaisant Stuart kings. Dutch William could deploy the resources of the leading Protestant country and for the first time since the days of Cromwell, England fielded an army on the continent in support of a league of European states (even the pope joined it secretly) against Louis. King William's war (also called the war of the League of Augsburg) brought together Spain and Austria, as well as the Protestant states of Europe, to contain the overweening ambition of the French king. The peace which ended it was the first in which he had to make concessions.

THE WAR OF THE SPANISH SUCCESSION

In 1700 Charles II of Spain died childless. It was an event Europe had long awaited, for he had been a sickly, feeble-minded fellow. Enormous diplomatic preparations had been made for his demise because of the great danger and opportunity which it must present. A huge dynastic inheritance was at stake. A tangle of claims arising from marriage alliances in the past meant that the Habsburg emperor and Louis XIV (who had passed his rights in the matter on to his grandson) would have to dispute the matter. But everyone was interested. The English wanted to know what would happen to the trade of Spanish America, the Dutch the fate of the Spanish Netherlands. The prospect of an undivided inheritance going either to Bourbon or Habsburg alarmed everybody. The ghost of Charles V's empire walked again. Partition treaties had therefore been made. But Charles II's will left the whole Spanish inheritance to Louis's grandson. Louis accepted it, setting aside the agreements into which he had entered. He also offended the English by recognizing the exiled Stuart Pretender as James III of England. A Grand Alliance of emperor, United Provinces and

England was soon formed, and there began the War of the Spanish Succession, twelve years' fighting which eventually drove Louis to terms. By treaties signed in 1713 and 1714 (the Peace of Utrecht), the crowns of Spain and France were declared for ever incapable of being united. The first Bourbon king of Spain took his place on the Spanish throne, though, taking with Spain the Indies but not the Netherlands, which went to the emperor as compensation and to provide a tripwire defence for the Dutch against further French aggression. Austria also profited in Italy.

The king of Spain is depicted attending mass in this painting entitled *Adoration of the Sacred Host by Charles II.*

The Battle of Almansa in southeast Spain, depicted here, was a turning point mid-way through the War of the Spanish Succession. A Bourbon victory on April 24, 1707, consolidated Philip V's reign as King of Spain. But French reverses elsewhere soon ensured that Philip would not retain all Spain's possessions nor ever combine the thrones of Spain and France.

France made concessions overseas to Great Britain (as it was after the union of England with Scotland in 1707). The Stuart Pretender was expelled from France and Louis recognized the Protestant succession in England.

THE STABILIZATION OF WESTERN POLITICAL BOUNDARIES

The terms of the Peace of Utrecht assured the virtual stabilization of western continental Europe until the French Revolution seventy-five years later. Not everyone liked it (the emperor refused to admit the end of his claim to the throne of Spain) but to a remarkable degree the major definitions of western Europe north of the Alps have remained what they were in 1714. Belgium, of course, did not exist, but the Austrian Netherlands occupied much of what is now that country, and the United Provinces corresponds to the modern Netherlands. France would keep Franche-Comté and, except between 1871

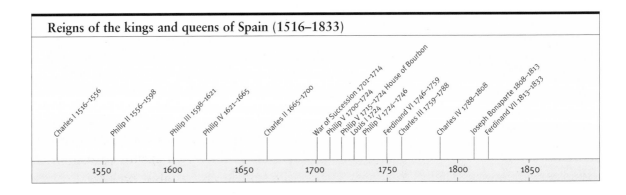

Reigns of the kings and queens of Spain (1516–1833)

Charles I 1516–1556
Philip II 1556–1598
Philip III 1598–1621
Philip IV 1621–1665
Charles II 1665–1700
War of Succession 1701–1714
Philip V 1700–1724
Philip V 1715–1724 House of Bourbon
Louis I 1724
Philip V 1724–1746
Ferdinand VI 1746–1759
Charles III 1759–1788
Charles IV 1788–1808
Joseph Bonaparte 1808–1813
Ferdinand VII 1813–1833

1550　　1600　　1650　　1700　　1750　　1800　　1850

and 1918, the Alsace and Lorraine which Louis XIV had won for her. Spain and Portugal would after 1714 remain separate within their present boundaries; they still had large colonial empires but were never again to be able to deploy their potential strength so as to rise out of the second rank of powers. Great Britain was the new great power in the West; since 1707, England no longer had to bother about the old Scottish threat, although once more attached by a personal connection to the continent because after 1714 her rulers were also electors of Hanover. South of the Alps, the dust took longer to settle. A still disunited Italy underwent another thirty-odd years of uncertainty, minor representatives of European royal houses shuffling around it from one state to another in attempts to tie up the loose ends and seize the leftovers of the age of dynastic rivalry. After 1748 there was only one important native dynasty left in the peninsula, that of Savoy, which ruled Piedmont on the south side of the Alps and the island of Sardinia. The Papal States, it is

true, could since the fifteenth century be regarded as an Italian monarchy, though only occasionally a dynastic one, and the decaying republics of Venice, Genoa and Lucca also upheld the tattered standard of Italian independence. Foreign rulers were installed in the other states.

THE AGE OF NATIONAL POLITICS

Western political geography was thus set for a long time. Immediately, this owed much to the need felt by all statesmen to avoid for as long as possible another conflict such as that which had just closed. For the first time a treaty of 1713 declared the aim of the signatories to be the security of peace through a balance of power. So practical an aim was an important innovation in political thinking. There were good grounds for such realism; wars were more expensive than ever and even Great Britain and France, the only countries in the eighteenth century capable of sustaining war

Under the long sultanate of Suleiman the Magnificent (1520–1566) the Turkish Empire managed to threaten Europe from the east by advancing towards the Balkans, occupying Hungary after the Battle of Mohács (1527) in which King Louis II died, and in 1529 closing in on Vienna for the first time. In 1532, it took all the efforts of the Holy Roman Emperor, Charles V, to end the siege of that city, as shown in this engraving.

against other great powers without foreign subsidy, had been strained. But the end of the War of the Spanish Succession also brought effective settlements of real problems. A new age was opening. Outside Italy, much of the political map of the twentieth century was already visible in western Europe. Dynasticism was beginning to be relegated to the second rank as a principle of foreign policy. The age of national politics had begun, at least for some princes who felt they could no longer separate the interests of their house from those of their nation.

East of the Rhine (and still more east of the Elbe) none of this was true. Great changes had already occurred there and many more were to come before 1800. But their origins have to be traced back a long way, as far as the beginning of the sixteenth century. At that time Europe's eastern frontiers were guarded by Habsburg Austria and a vast Polish-Lithuanian kingdom ruled by the Jagiellons, which had been formed by marriage in the fourteenth century. They shared with the mar-

itime empire of Venice the burden of resistance to Ottoman power, the supreme fact of eastern European politics at that moment.

THE OTTOMAN EXPANSION

THE PHRASE "Eastern Question" had not then been invented; if it had been, it would have meant then the problem of defending Europe against Islam. The Turks would be winning victories and making conquests as late as the eighteenth century, though by then their last great effort was spent. For more than two centuries after the capture of Constantinople, nevertheless, they set the terms of eastern European diplomacy and strategy. That capture was followed by more than a century of naval warfare and Turkish expansion, from which the main sufferer was Venice. While it long remained rich by comparison with other Italian states, Venice suffered a relative decline, first in military and then in commercial power. The first, which led to the second, was the result of a long losing battle against the Turks, who in 1479 took the Ionian islands and imposed an annual charge for trade in the Black Sea. Though Venice acquired Cyprus two years later, and turned it into a major base, it was in its turn lost in 1571. By 1600, though still (thanks to her manufacturers) a rich state, Venice was no longer a mercantile power at the level of the United Provinces or even England. First Antwerp and then Amsterdam had eclipsed her. Turkish success was interrupted in the early seventeenth century but then resumed; in 1669 the Venetians had to recognize that they had lost Crete. Meanwhile, Hungary became in 1664 the last Turkish conquest of a European kingdom, though the Ukrainians soon acknowledged Turkish suzerainty and the Poles had to give up Podolia. In 1683 the Turks opened their

Sultan Mehmet II ("the Conqueror") (1429–1481), is portrayed in this painting of 1480 by Gentile Bellini (c.1429–1507). Mehmet II established the capital of the Ottoman Empire in Istanbul, began the expansion towards the Balkans and attacked Venetian possessions.

second siege of Vienna (the first had been a century and a half before) and Europe seemed in its greatest danger for over two centuries. In fact it was not. This was to be the last time Vienna was besieged, for the great days of Ottoman power were over.

OTTOMAN DECLINE

In effect, the effort which began with the conquest of Hungary had been the last heave of a long-troubled power. The Ottoman army was no longer abreast of the latest military technology: it lacked the field artillery which had become the decisive weapon of the seventeenth-century battlefield. At sea, the Turks clung to the old galley tactics of ramming and boarding and were less and less successful against the Atlantic nations' technique of using the ship as a floating artillery battery (unfortunately for themselves, the Venetians were conservative too). Turkish power was in any case badly overstretched. It had saved Protestantism in Germany, Hungary and Transylvania, but it was pinned down in Asia (where the conquest of Iraq from Persia in 1639 brought almost the whole Arab-Islamic world under Ottoman rule) as well as in Europe and Africa, and the strain was too much for a structure allowed to relax by inadequate or incompetent rulers. A great vizier had pulled things together in the middle of the century to make the last offensives possible. But there were weaknesses which he could not correct, for they were inherent in the nature of the empire itself.

More a military occupation for purposes of plunder than a political unity, the Ottoman empire was geared to continual expansion and the gathering of new resources in taxes and manpower. Moreover, it was dangerously dependent on subjects whose loyalty it could not win. The Ottomans usually respected the customs and institutions of non-Muslim communities, which were ruled under the *millet* system, through their own authorities. The Greek Orthodox, Armenians and Jews were the most important and each had their own arrangements, the Greek Christians having to pay a special poll-tax, for example, and being ruled, ultimately, by their own patriarch in Constantinople. At lower levels, such arrangements as seemed best were made with leaders of local communities for the support of the plunder machine. In the end this bred over-mighty subjects as pashas feathered their

The Ottoman sultan Selim I (1467–1520), shown in this manuscript illustration on a sailing outing, conquered Syria, Arabia and Egypt and ordered the Turkish siege of Vienna.

Sultan Mustafa II, son of Mehmet IV, ruled the Ottoman Empire from 1695 to 1703. His reign was plagued by confrontations with the members of the Holy League (Austria, Venice, Poland and Russia), with whom he signed the Peace of Karlowitz in 1699. From that time, the power of the Ottoman Empire began to diminish.

own nests amid incoherence and inefficiency. It gave the subjects of the sultan no sense of identification with his rule but, rather, alienated them from it while the Ottoman lands in Europe grew poorer.

THE OTTOMAN RETREAT IN EUROPE

The year 1683, although a good symbolic date as the last time that Europe stood upon the defensive against Islam before going over to the attack, was a less dangerous moment than it looked. Afterwards the tide of Turkish power was to ebb almost without interruption until in 1918 it was once more confined to the immediate hinterland of Constantinople and the old Ottoman heartland, Anatolia. The relief of Vienna by the king of Poland, John Sobieski, was followed

In 1683 the Turkish siege of Vienna was broken by a multinational army led by John Sobieski, the king of Poland. From the time of their humiliating defeat, a scene from which is depicted in this 17th-century painting, the Turks were on the defensive, although their decline was a slow one.

by the liberation of Hungary. The dethronement of an unsuccessful sultan in 1687 and his incarceration in a cage proved no cure for Turkish weakness. In 1699 Hungary became part of the Habsburg dominions again, after the first peace the Ottomans signed as a defeated power. In the following century Transylvania, the Bukovina, and most of the Black Sea coasts would follow it out of Ottoman control. By 1800, the Russians had asserted a special protection over the Christian subjects of the Ottomans and had already tried promoting rebellion among them. In the eighteenth century, too, Ottoman rule ebbed in Africa and Asia; by the end of it, though forms might be preserved, the Ottoman caliphate was somewhat like that of the Abbasids in their declining days.

The beginning of the Ottoman retreat in Europe

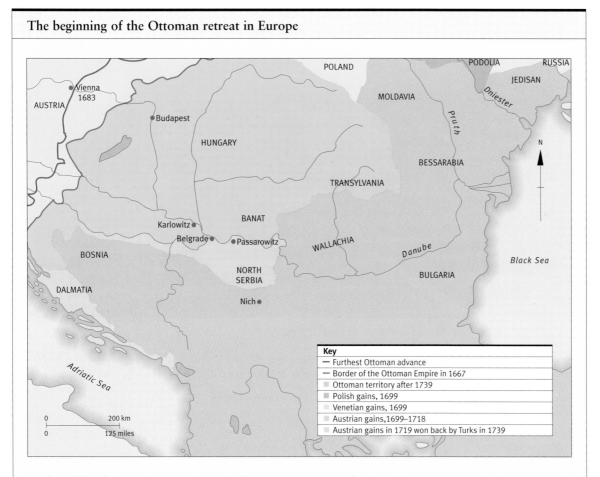

Key
— Furthest Ottoman advance
— Border of the Ottoman Empire in 1667
▪ Ottoman territory after 1739
▪ Polish gains, 1699
▪ Venetian gains, 1699
▪ Austrian gains,1699–1718
▪ Austrian gains in 1719 won back by Turks in 1739

By the middle of the 16th century, the Turkish Empire practically equalled Justinian's Byzantine Empire in size, and was governed from a resplendent Istanbul. The great pillars of the Ottoman Empire were a well-disciplined, highly skilled army, access to plentiful human and natural resources and a stable leadership provided by the dynastic and governmental institutions. However, when expansion ground to a halt and then went into reverse in the 18th century, these pillars disintegrated – a process accompanied by misery and oppression. The Ottoman Empire became a target for the European monarchies. The Treaty of Karlowitz, signed in 1699, ended the "Vienna War" and forced the Ottomans to concede land to Poland, Austria and Venice. At Passarowitz in 1718 a treaty was signed giving the Habsburg emperor more Ottoman territories, although Austria was forced to return some land to the Ottoman Empire by the Treaty of Belgrade in 1739. Only the rivalries between the various European powers allowed the Ottoman Empire, which was almost incapable of defending itself by 1800, to survive until the 19th century.

Morocco, Algeria, Tunis, Egypt, Syria, Mesopotamia and Arabia were all in varying degrees independent or semi-independent.

POLAND

It was not the traditional guardians of eastern Europe, the once-great Polish-Lithuanian commonwealth and the Habsburgs, who were the legatees of the Ottoman heritage, nor they who inflicted the most punishing blows as the Ottoman Empire crumbled. The Poles were in fact nearing the end of their own history as an independent nation. The personal union of Lithuania and Poland had been turned into a real union of the two countries too late. In 1572, when the last king of the Jagiellon line died without an heir, the throne had become not only theoretically but actually elective. A huge area was up for grabs. His successor was French and for the next century Polish magnates and foreign kings disputed each election, while their country was under grave and continuing pressure from Turks, Russians and Swedes. Poland prospered against these enemies only when they were embarrassed elsewhere. The Swedes descended on her northern territories during the Thirty Years' War and the last of the Polish coast was given up to them in 1660. Internal divisions had worsened, too; the Counter-Reformation brought religious persecution to the Polish Protestants and there were risings of Cossacks in the Ukraine and continuing serf revolts.

THE POLISH SOCIAL STRUCTURE

The election as king of the heroic John Sobieski was the last which was not the outcome of machinations by foreign rulers. He had won important victories and managed to preside over Poland's curious and highly decentralized constitution. The elected kings had very little legal power to balance that of the landowners. They had no standing army and could rely only on their own personal troops when factions among the gentry or magnates fell back on the practice of armed rebellion ("Confederation") to obtain their wishes. In the Diet, the central parliamentary body of the kingdom, a rule of unanimity stood in the way of any reform. Yet reform was badly needed, if a geographically ill-defined, religiously divided Poland, ruled by a narrowly selfish rural gentry, was to survive. Poland was a medieval community in a modernizing world.

John Sobieski could do nothing to change this. Poland's social structure was strongly resistant to reform. The nobility or gentry were effectively the clients of a few great families of extraordinary wealth. One clan, the Radziwills, owned estates half the size of Ireland and held a court which outshone that of Warsaw; the Potocki estates covered 6,500 square miles (roughly half the area of the Dutch Republic). The smaller landowners could not stand up to such grandees. Their estates made up less than a tenth of Poland in 1700. The million or so gentry who were legally the Polish "nation" were for the most part poor, and therefore dominated by great magnates reluctant to surrender their power to arrange a confederation or manipulate a Diet. At the bottom of the pile were the peasants, some of the most miserable in Europe, in 1700 unendingly battling the feudal dues demanded of them, over whom landlords still had rights of life and death. The towns were powerless. Their total population was only half the size of the gentry and they had been devastated by the seventeenth-century wars. Yet Prussia and Russia also rested on backward agrarian and feudal infrastructures and survived. Poland was the only one of the three eastern states to go under completely. The principle of election blocked the emergence of Polish Tudors or Bourbons who could identify their own dynastic instincts of self-aggrandizement with those of the nation. Poland entered the eighteenth century under a foreign king, the Elector of Saxony, who was chosen to succeed

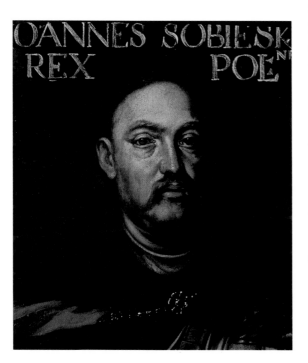

John III of Poland (1624–1696), known as John Sobieski, is portrayed in this 17th-century painting. A highly distinguished soldier, he was elected king of Poland in 1674. When Poland, Saxony, Bavaria and many other small German principalities sent troops to defend Vienna against the Turks in 1683, John Sobieski led the army to victory, thereby becoming a hero of Christian Europe.

John Sobieski in 1697, soon deposed by the Swedes, and then put back again on his throne by the Russians.

RUSSIAN POWER AND IVAN THE TERRIBLE

RUSSIA WAS THE COMING new great power in the East. Her national identity had been barely discernible in 1500. Two hundred years later her potential was still only beginning to dawn on most Western statesmen, though the Poles and Swedes were already alive to it. It now requires an effort to realize how rapid and astonishing was the appearance as a major force of what was to become one of the two most powerful states in the world. At the beginning of the European age,

when only the ground-plan of the Russian future had been laid out by Ivan the Great, such an outcome was inconceivable, and so it long remained. The first man formally to bear the title of "Tsar" was his grandson Ivan IV, crowned in 1547; and the conferment of the title at his coronation was meant to say that the Grand Prince of Muscovy had become an emperor ruling many peoples. In spite of a ferocious vigour which earned him his nickname "the Terrible", he played no significant role in European affairs.

So little was Russia known even in the next century that a French king could write to a tsar, not knowing that the prince whom he addressed had been dead for ten years. The shape of a future Russia was determined slowly, and almost unnoticed in the West. Even after Ivan the Great, Russia had remained territorially ill-defined and exposed. The Turks had pushed into southeast Europe. Between them and Muscovy lay the Ukraine, the lands of the Cossacks, peoples who fiercely protected their independence. So long as they had no powerful neighbours, they found it easy to do so. To the east of Russia, the Urals provided a theoretical though hardly a realistic frontier. Russia's rulers have always found it easy to feel isolated in the middle of hostile space. Almost instinctively, they have sought natural frontiers at its edges or a protective glacis of clients.

The first steps had to be the consolidation of the gains of Ivan the Great which constituted the Russian heartland. Then came penetration of the wilderness of the north. When Ivan the Terrible came to the throne, Russia had a small Baltic coast and a vast territory stretching up to the White Sea, thinly inhabited by scattered and primitive peoples, but providing a route to the west; in 1584 the port of Archangel was founded. Ivan could do little on the Baltic front but

The Cathedral of St Basil the Blessed was built between 1554 and 1560 outside the Kremlin in Moscow, following Ivan IV's victory over the Tatars (Mongols) of Kazan and Astrakhan.

successfully turned on the Tatars after they burned Moscow yet again in 1571, allegedly slaughtering 150,000 in the process. He drove them from Kazan and Astrakhan and won control of the whole length of the Volga, carrying Muscovite power as far as the Caspian Sea.

ASIAN EXPANSION UNDER IVAN

The other great thrust which began in his reign was across the Urals, into Siberia, and was to be less one of conquest than of settlement. Even today, most of the Russian republic is in Asia, and for nearly two centuries a world as

During the reign of Ivan III, known as Ivan the Great, Moscow (seen here in a 16th-century illustration) was a commercial centre that exported cereals, linen and fodder. The creation of the English Muscovy Company later brought the city increasingly under Western influence. In the 17th century, numerous European merchants lived in a special district called the Sloboda.

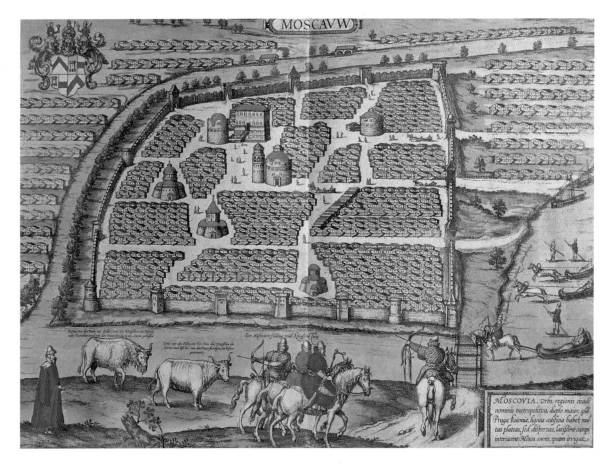

well as a European power was ruled by the tsars and their successors. The first steps towards this outcome were an ironic anticipation of what was to be a theme of the major Siberian frontier in later times: the first Russian settlers across the Urals seem to have been political refugees from Novgorod. Among those who followed were others fleeing from serfdom (there were no serfs in Siberia) and aggrieved Cossacks. By 1600 there were Russian settlements as much as 600 miles beyond the Urals, closely supervised by a competent bureaucracy out to assure the state tribute in furs. The rivers were the keys to the region, more important even than those of the American frontier. Within fifty years a man and his goods could travel by river with only three portages from Tobolsk, 300 miles east of the Urals, to the port of Okhotsk, 3,000 miles away. There he would be only 400 miles by sea from

Sakhalin, the northernmost of the major islands of the chain which makes up Japan – a sea-passage about as long as that from Land's End to Antwerp. By 1700 there were 200,000 settlers east of the Urals: it had by then been possible to agree the treaty of Nerchinsk with the Chinese, and some Russians, we are told, talked of the conquest of China.

RUSSIA AND THE WEST

The movement eastward was not much affected by the upheavals and dangers of the "Time of Troubles" which followed Ivan's death, though in the west there were moments when the outlet to the Baltic was lost and when even Moscow and Novgorod were occupied by Lithuanians or Poles. Russia was still not a serious European power in the early seventeenth century. The then rising strength of Sweden was thrown against her and it was not until the great war of 1654–67 that the tsars finally regained Smolensk and Little Russia, not to be lost again (and then only briefly) until 1812. Maps and treaties now began to define Russia in the west in a way which had some reality. By 1700, though she still had no Black Sea coast, her southwestern frontier ran on the western side of the Dnieper for most of its length, embracing the great historic city of Kiev and the Cossacks who lived on the east bank. They had appealed to the tsar for protection from the Poles and were granted special, semi-autonomous governmental arrangements which survived until Soviet times. Most Russian gains had been at the expense of Poland, long preoccupied with fighting off Turk and Swede. But Russian armies joined the Poles in alliance against the Ottomans in 1687; this was a historic moment, too, for it was the beginning of the classical Eastern Question which was to trouble European statesmen until 1918, when they found that the problem of deciding what limit, if any, should be placed upon Russian encroachment on the Ottoman Empire had at last disappeared with the protagonists themselves.

The making of Russia was overwhelmingly a political act. The monarchy was its centre and motor; the country had no racial unity to preordain its existence and precious little geographical definition to impose a shape. If it was united by Orthodoxy, other Slavs were Orthodox, too. The growth of the personal domain and power of the tsars was the key to the building of the nation. Ivan the Terrible was an administrative reformer. Under him appeared the beginnings of a nobility owing military service in return for their estates, a development of a system employed by the princes of Muscovy to obtain levies to fight the Tatars. It made possible the raising of an army which led the king of Poland to warn the English queen, Elizabeth I, that if they got hold of Western technical skills the Russians would be unbeatable; the danger was remote, but this was prescient.

THE ROMANOVS AND THE TAMING OF THE CHURCH

From time to time Russia suffered setbacks, though the survival of the state does not seem in retrospect to have been at stake. The last tsar of the house of Rurik died in 1598. Usurpation and the disputing of the throne between noble families and Polish interventionists went on until 1613, when the first tsar of a new house, Michael Romanov, emerged. Though a weak ruler who lived in the shadow of his dominating father, he founded a dynasty which was to rule Russia for three hundred years, until the tsarist state itself collapsed. His immediate successors

The boyars, wealthy landowners, constituted Russia's upper nobility. The picture shows a group of boyars who were sent to the court of the Holy Roman Emperor Maximilian II in 1576. They are bearing gifts from Russia for the emperor, including furs.

fought off rival nobles and humbled the great ones among them, the boyars, who had attempted to revive a power curbed by Ivan the Terrible. Beyond their ranks the only potential internal rival was the Church. In the seventeenth century it was weakened by schism and in 1667 a great step in Russian history was taken when the patriarch was deprived after a quarrel with the tsar. There was to be no Investiture Contest in Russia. After this time the Russian Church was structurally and legally subordinated to a lay official. Among believers there would emerge plenty of spontaneous doctrinal and moral opposition to current Orthodoxy, and there began the long-lived and culturally very important movement of underground religious dissent called the *raskol,* which would eventually feed political opposition. But Russia was never to know the conflict of Church and State which was so creative a force in western Europe, any more than she was to know the stimulus of the Reformation.

TSARIST AUTOCRACY

The outcome of the subordination of the Russian Church to royal authority was the final evolution of the enduring Russian governmental form, tsarist autocracy. It was characterized by the personification in the ruler of a semi-sacrosanct authority unlimited by clear legal checks, by an emphasis on the service owed to him by all subjects, by the linking of landholding to this idea, by the idea that all institutions within the state except the Church derived from it and had no independent standing of their own, by the lack of a distinction of powers and the development of a huge bureaucracy, and by the paramountcy of military needs. These qualities, as the scholar who listed them pointed out, were not all present at the start, nor were all of them

equally operative and obvious at all times. But they clearly mark tsardom off from monarchy in Western Christendom where, far back in the Middle Ages, towns, estates of the realm, guilds and many other bodies had established the privileges and liberties on which later constitutionalism was to be built. In old Muscovy, the highest official had a title which meant "slave" or "servant" at a time when, in neighbouring Poland-Lithuania, his opposite number was designated "citizen". Even Louis XIV, though he might believe in Divine Right and aspire to unrivalled power, always conceived it to be a power explicitly restricted by rights, by religion, by divinely ordained law. Though his subjects knew he was an absolute monarch, they were sure he was not a despot. In England an even more startlingly different monarchy was developing, one under the control of Parliament. Divergent from one another though English and French monarchical practice might be, they both accepted practical and theoretical limitations inconceivable to tsardom; they bore the stamp of a Western tradition Russia had never known. For the whole of its existence the Russian autocracy was to be in the West a byword for despotism.

Yet it suited Russia. Moreover, the attitudes which underlay it seem in some measure to suit Russia still. Eighteenth-century sociologists used to suggest that big, flat countries favoured despotism. This was over-simple, but there were always latent centrifugal tendencies in a country so big as Russia, embracing so many natural regions and so many different peoples. The tsars' title, significantly, was "Tsar of all the Russias", and to this day events have reflected this diversity. Russia had always to be held together by a strong pull towards the centre if the divergences within it were not to be exploited by the enemies on the borders.

THE RUSSIAN NOBILITY

The humbling of the boyars left the ruling family isolated in its eminence. The Russian nobility was gradually brought to depend on the state on the grounds that nobility derived from service, which was indeed often rewarded in the seventeenth century with land and later with the grant of serfs. All land came to be held on the condition of service to the autocracy as defined in a Table of Ranks in 1722. This effectively amalgamated all categories of nobility into a single class. The obligations laid on noblemen by it were very large, often extending to a man's lifetime, though in the eighteenth century they came to be progressively diminished and were finally removed altogether. Nevertheless, service still continued to be the route to an automatic ennoblement, and Russian nobles never acquired quite such independence of their monarch as those of other countries. New privileges were conferred upon them but no closed caste emerged. Instead, nobility grew hugely by new accessions and by natural increase. Some of its members were very poor, because there was neither primogeniture nor entail in Russia and property could be much subdivided in three or four generations. Towards the end of the eighteenth century most nobles owned fewer than a hundred serfs.

PETER THE GREAT

Of all imperial Russia's rulers the one who made the most memorable use of the autocracy and most deeply shaped its character was Peter the Great. He came to the throne as a ten-year-old child and when he died something had been done to Russia which could never be quite eradicated. In one way he resembled twentieth-century strong men who have striven ruthlessly to drag traditional societies into modernity, but he was very much a monarch of his own day, his attention focused on victory in war – Russia was only at peace for one year in his entire reign – and he accepted that the road to that goal ran through westernizing and modernizing. His ambition to win a Russian Baltic coast supplied the driving force behind the reforms which would open the way to it. That he should be sympathetic to such a course may owe something to his childhood, growing up as he did in the "German" quarter of Moscow where foreign merchants and their retinues lived. A celebrated pilgrimage he made to Western Europe in 1697–8 showed that his interest in technology was real. Probably in his own mind he did not distinguish the urge to modernize Russians from the urge to free them forever from the fear of their neighbours. Whatever the exact balance of his motives, his reforms have ever since served as something of an ideological touchstone; generation after generation of Russians were to look back with awe and ponder what he had done and its meaning for

This statue, known as "The Bronze Horseman", dates from 1782 and represents Peter the Great (1672–1725). The tsar looks out over St Petersburg, the city he built as his capital and the symbol of his drive to Westernize Russia.

Count Golovkin, depicted here in a portrait dating from 1720, accompanied the tsar Peter I on his trip to western Europe. The count took charge of foreign affairs in 1706; three years later he was appointed State Chancellor of Russia.

Russia. As one of them wrote in the nineteenth century, "Peter the Great found only a blank page . . . he wrote on it the words Europe and Occident."

EXPANSION UNDER PETER

Peter the Great's territorial achievement is the easiest to assess. Though he sent expeditions off to Kamchatka and the oases of Bokhara and ceased to pay to the Tatars a tribute levied on his predecessors, his driving ambition was to reach the sea to the west. For a while he had a Black Sea fleet and annexed Azov, but had to abandon it later because of distractions elsewhere, from the Poles and, above all, the Swedes. The wars with Sweden for the Baltic outlet were a struggle to the death. The Great Northern War, as contemporaries termed the last of them, began in 1700 and lasted until 1721. The world recognized that something decisive had happened when in 1709 the Swedish king's army, the best in the world, was destroyed far away from home at Poltava, in the middle of the Ukraine where its leader had sought to find allies among the Cossacks. The rest of Peter's reign drove home the point and at the peace Russia was established firmly on the Baltic coast, in Livonia, Estonia and the Karelian isthmus. Sweden's days as a great power were over; she had been the first victim of a new one.

A few years before this, the French *Almanach Royale* for the first time listed the Romanovs as one of the reigning families of Europe. Victory had opened the way to further contact with the West, and Peter had

This engraving shows the Swedish city of Stockholm during the reign of King Charles XII (1697–1718). Although Charles was a great warrior king, his persistent efforts to establish Swedish control of the Baltic were thwarted by Peter the Great of Russia.

Russian Expansion 1500–1800

Territorial expansion towards the east in the 16th century allowed Russia to control the Volga valley as far as the Caspian Sea and the trade routes towards Central Asia, at the expense of the Mongols. Then the conquest of Siberia began: by the end of the 17th century the Russians had reached the Pacific Ocean.

Russian expansion towards the south was more difficult, however, as it was opposed by the armies of the Ottoman Empire and the highly skilled Cossack warriors. Westward expansion was even more complicated – the Baltic states' naval power and military organization was still superior to that of the Russian forces. However, Russian territory was to expand towards both the south and the west from the reign of Peter the Great to the end of the 18th century. This confirmed the words that one of the 16th-century kings of Poland had once written to Elizabeth I of England:

"... in so much as you bring them [the Russians] not only merchandise, but also arms, which up until now they have not known, as well as arts and crafts; by which means they will make themselves stronger in order to vanquish all others ... . For this, we who know them better, and who have them on our borders, warn other Christian princes in time, not to hand over their dignity, liberty and life, nor those of their subjects, to such a barbaric and cruel enemy."

(As quoted by H. G. Koenigsberger in *The Modern World 1500–1789*).

These maps show Russia's expansion between 1500 and 1689 (above) and between 1689 and 1812 (below).

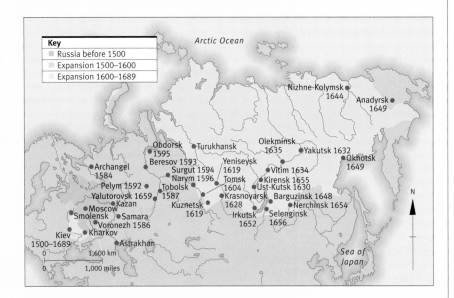

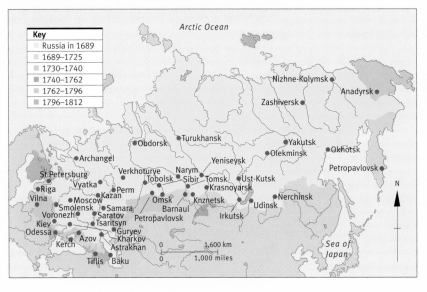

already anticipated the peace by beginning in 1703 to build, on territory captured from the Swedes, St Petersburg, the beautiful new city which was to be for two centuries the capital of Russia. The political and cultural centre of gravity thus passed from the isolation of Muscovy to the edge of Russia nearest the developed societies of the West. Now the Westernizing of Russia could go ahead more easily. It was a deliberate break with the past.

WESTERNIZING RUSSIA

Even Muscovy, of course, had never been completely isolated from Europe. A pope had helped to arrange Ivan the Great's marriage, hoping he would turn to the Western Church. There was always intercourse with the neighbours, the Roman Catholic Poles, and English merchants had made their way to Moscow under Elizabeth I, where to this day they are commemorated in the Kremlin by the

presence of a magnificent collection of the work of English silversmiths. Trade continued, and there also came to Russia the occasional foreign expert from the West. In the seventeenth century the first permanent

embassies from European monarchs were established. But there was always a tentative and suspicious response among Russians; as in later times, efforts were made to segregate foreign residents.

Peter threw this tradition aside. He wanted experts – shipwrights, gun founders, teachers, clerks, soldiers – and he gave them privileges accordingly. In administration he broke with the old assumption of inherited family office and tried to institute a bureaucracy selected on grounds of merit. He set up schools to teach technical skills and founded an Academy of Sciences, thus introducing the idea of science to Russia, where all learning had hitherto been clerical. Like many other great reformers he also put much energy into what might be thought superficialities. Courtiers were ordered to wear European clothes; the old long beards were cut back and women were told to appear in public in German fashions. Such psychological shocks were indispensable in so backward a country. Peter was virtually without allies in what he

was trying to do and in the end such things as he achieved had to be driven through. They rested on his autocratic power and little else. The old Duma of the boyars was abolished and a new senate of appointed men took its place. Peter began to dissolve the tie between land ownership and state power, between sovereignty and property, and launched Russia on a march towards a new identity as a multi-ethnic empire. Those who resisted were ruthlessly broken, but it was less easy for Peter to dispose of a conservative cast of mind; he had at his disposal only an administrative machine and communications that would seem inconceivably inadequate to any modern government.

The most striking sign of successful modernization was Russia's new military power. Another was the virtual reduction of the Church to a department of state. More complicated tests are harder to come by. The vast majority of Russians were untouched by Peter's educational reforms, which only obviously affected technicians and a few among the upper class. The result was a fairly Westernized higher nobility, focused at St Petersburg; by 1800 its members were largely French-speaking and sometimes in touch with the currents of thought which arose in western Europe. But they were often resented by the provincial gentry and formed a cultural island in a backward nation. The mass of the nobility for a long time did not benefit from the new schools and academies. Further down the social scale, the Russian masses remained illiterate; those who learnt to read did so for the most part at the rudimentary level offered by the teaching of the village priest, often only one generation removed from illiteracy himself. A literate Russia had to wait for the twentieth century.

SERFDOM IN RUSSIA

Russia's social structure, too, tended more and more to mark her off. She was to be the last country in Europe to abolish serfdom; among Christian countries only Ethiopia and the United States kept bonded labour for longer. While the eighteenth century saw the institution weakening almost everywhere, in

Dating from 1815, this engraving of a military parade taking place in front of the imperial palace in St Petersburg illustrates the Westernized dress of both the troops and the upper-class civilians watching the proceedings.

The Russian artist Mikhail Shibanov came from a Serb family. He specialized in depicting peasant life. *The Betrothal* shows a scene from the celebration of a marriage contract and dates from 1789.

Russia it spread. This was largely because labour was always scarcer than land; significantly, the value of a Russian estate was usually assessed in the number of "souls" – that is, serfs – tied to it, not its extent. The number of serfs had begun to go up in the seventeenth century, when the tsars found it prudent to gratify nobles by giving them land, some of which already had free peasants settled on it. Debt tied them to their landlords and many of them entered into bondage to the estate to work it off. Meanwhile, the law imposed more and more restrictions on the serf and rooted the structure of the state more and more in the economy. Legal powers to recapture and restrain serfs were steadily increased and landlords had been given a special interest in using such powers when Peter

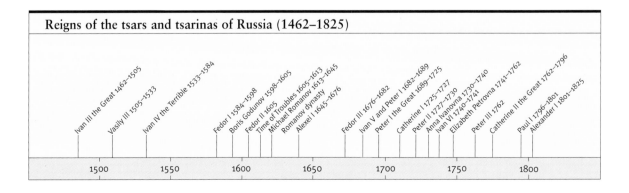

Reigns of the tsars and tsarinas of Russia (1462–1825)

Ivan III the Great 1462–1505
Vasily III 1505–1533
Ivan IV the Terrible 1533–1584
Fedor I 1584–1598
Boris Godunov 1598–1605
Fedor II 1605
Time of Troubles 1605–1613
Michael Romanov 1613–1645
Romanov dynasty
Alexei 1645–1676
Fedor III 1676–1682
Ivan V and Peter I 1682–1689
Peter I the Great 1689–1725
Catherine I 1725–1727
Peter II 1727–1730
Anna Ivanovna 1730–1740
Ivan VI 1740–1741
Elizabeth Petrovna 1741–1762
Peter III 1762
Catherine II the Great 1762–1796
Paul I 1796–1801
Alexander I 1801–1825

1500   1550   1600   1650   1700   1750   1800

had made them responsible for the collection of the poll-tax and for military conscription. Thus, economy and administration were bound together in Russia more completely than in any Western country. Russia's aristocrats tended to become hereditary civil servants, carrying out tasks for the tsar.

Formally, by the end of the eighteenth century, there was little that a lord could not do to his serfs short of inflicting death on them. If they were not obliged to carry out heavy labour services, money dues were levied upon them almost arbitrarily. There was a high rate of desertion, serfs making for Siberia or even volunteering for the galleys. About a half of the Russian people were in bondage to their lords in 1800, a large number of the rest owing almost the same services to the Crown and always in danger of being granted away to nobles by it.

As new lands were annexed, their populations, too, passed into serfdom even if they had not known it before. The result was a huge inertia and a great rigidifying of society. By the end of the century, Russia's greatest problem for the next hundred years was already there: what to do with so huge a population when both economic and political demands made serfdom increasingly intolerable, but when its scale presented colossal problems of reform. It was like the man riding an elephant; it is all right so long as he keeps going but there are problems when he wants to get off.

POPULATION AND ECONOMY

Servile labour had become the backbone of the economy. Except in the famous Black Earth zone, only beginning to be opened up in the eighteenth century, Russian soil is by no means rich, and even on the best land farming methods were poor. It seems unlikely that pro-

duction ever kept pace with population until the twentieth century though periodic famine and epidemics were the natural restoratives of balance. Population nearly doubled in the eighteenth century, about seven million of the thirty-six million or so at which it stood at the end having been acquired with new territories, the rest having accumulated by natural increase. This was a faster rate of growth than in any other European country. Of this population, only about one in twenty-five at most lived in towns.

Yet the Russian economy made striking progress during the century and was unique in utilizing serfdom to industrialize. Here, it

A Russian peasant woman in festive dress is depicted in this portrait dating from 1784.

may be thought, was one of Peter's unequivocal successes; though there had been beginnings under the first two Romanovs, it was he who launched Russian industrialization as a guided movement. True, the effect was not quickly apparent. Russia's starting level was very low, and no eighteenth-century European economy was capable of rapid growth. Though grain production went up and the export of Russian cereals (later a staple of Russian foreign trade) began in the eighteenth century, it was done by the old method of bringing more land under cultivation and perhaps by the more successful appropriation of the surplus by the landlord and tax-collector. The peasant's consumption declined. This was to be the story throughout most of the imperial era and sometimes the load was crushing: it has been estimated that taxes took 60 per cent of the peasant's crop under Peter the Great. The techniques were not there to increase productivity and the growing rigidity of the system held it down more and more firmly. Even in the second half of the nineteenth century the typical Russian peasant wasted what little time was left to him after work for his lord by trudging around the collection of scattered strips which made up his holding. Often he had no plough, and crops had to be raised from the shallow scratching of the soil which was all that was possible.

None the less, this agricultural base somehow supported both the military effort which made Russia a great power, and the first phase of her industrialization. By 1800 Russia produced more pig-iron and exported more iron ore than any other country in the world. Peter, more than any other man, was responsible for this. He grasped the importance of Russia's mineral resources and built the administrative apparatus to grapple with them. He initiated surveys and imported the miners to exploit them. By way of incentive, the death penalty was prescribed for landlords who concealed mineral deposits on their estates or tried to prevent their use. Communications were developed to allow access to these resources and slowly the centre of Russian industry shifted towards the Urals. The rivers were crucial. Only a few years after Peter's death the Baltic was linked by water to the Caspian.

INDUSTRIALIZATION

Manufacturing grew up around the core of extractive mineral and lumber industry which

This portrait of a member of the Russian Demidov family was painted in 1773. The Demidovs' wealth came from the mining companies and metal works they owned in the Urals and in Siberia.

A s Empress of Russia, the daughter of Peter the Great and Catherine I, Elizabeth Petrovna (1709–1762), continued her parents' policies of economic reform and waged war against Sweden and Prussia. This portrait of the empress on horseback was painted in 1743.

encouraged mine-owners, the need of such encouragement shows that the stimuli for maintained growth, which were effective elsewhere, were lacking in Russia.

PETER'S SUCCESSORS

After Peter, in any case, there was a notable flagging of state innovation. The impetus could not be maintained; there were not enough educated men to allow the bureaucracy to keep up the pressure once his driving power had gone. Peter had not named a successor (he had his own son tortured to death). Those who followed him faced a renewed threat of hostility from the great noble families without his force of character and the terror he had inspired. The direct line

ensured Russia a favourable balance of trade for the whole century. Less than a hundred factories in Peter's reign became more than 3,000 by 1800. After 1754, when internal customs barriers were abolished, Russia was the largest free-trade area in the world. In this, as in the granting of serf labour or of monopolies, the state continued to shape the Russian economy; Russian industry did not emerge from free enterprise, but from regulation, and this had to be, for industrialization ran against the grain of Russian social fact. There might be no internal customs barriers, but nor was there much long-distance internal trade. Most Russians lived in 1800 as they had done in 1700, within self-sufficient local communities, depending on their artisans for a small supply of manufactures and hardly emerging into a money economy. Such "factories" as there were seem sometimes to have been little more than agglomerations of artisans. Over huge areas labour service, not rent, was the basis of tenure. Foreign trade was still mainly in the hands of foreign merchants. Moreover, though state grants to exploit their resources and allocations of serfs

D uring the reign of Elizabeth Petrovna, the Italian architect Bartolomeo Rastrelli was commissioned to build the Winter Palace in St Petersburg. The work was carried out between 1754 and 1762, and the result is shown in this engraving from 1891.

This 18th-century portrait of Catherine the Great (1729–1796) shows the empress in traditional Russian dress.

twenty years later) in favour of Elizabeth, daughter of Peter the Great, who relied on the support of the Guards regiments and Russians irritated by foreigners. She was succeeded in 1762 by a nephew who reigned barely six months before he was forced to abdicate. The mistress of the overmighty subject who subsequently murdered the deposed tsar was the new tsarina and widow of the deposed victim, a German princess who became Catherine II and known, like Peter, as "the Great".

CATHERINE THE GREAT

THE GLITTER WITH WHICH Catherine the Great surrounded herself masked a great deal and took in many of her contemporaries. Among the things it almost hid was the bloody and dubious route by which she came to the throne. It may be true, though, that she rather than her husband might have been the victim if she had not struck first. In any case, the circumstances of her accession and of those of her predecessors showed the weakening the autocracy had undergone since Peter. The first part of her reign was a ticklish business; powerful interests existed to exploit her mistakes and for all her identification with her new country (she had renounced her Lutheran religion to become Orthodox) she was a foreigner. "I shall perish or reign," she once said, and reign she did, to great effect.

Though Catherine's reign was more spectacular than that of Peter the Great, its innovatory force was less. She, too, founded schools and patronized the arts and sciences. The difference was that Peter was concerned with practical effect; Catherine rather to associate the prestige of enlightened thinkers with her court and legislation. The forms were often forward-looking while the reality was reactionary. Close observers were not taken

was broken in 1730 when Peter's grandson died. Yet factional quarrels could be exploited by monarchs, and his replacement by his niece, Anna, was something of a recovery for the Crown. Though put on the throne by the nobles who had dominated her predecessor, she quickly curbed them. Symbolically, the court returned to St Petersburg from Moscow, to which (to the delight of the conservatives) it had gone after Peter's death. Anna turned to foreign-born ministers for help and this worked well enough until her death in 1740. Her successor and infant grand-nephew was within a year set aside (to be kept in prison until murdered more than

in by legislative rhetoric; the reality was shown by the exile of the young Radischev, who had dared to criticize the régime and has been seen as Russian's first dissentient intellectual. Such reforming impulses as Catherine showed perceptibly weakened as the reign went on and foreign considerations distracted her.

The Cossack Yemelian Pugachev led an uprising in southern Russia while claiming to be Peter III, Catherine the Great's assassinated husband. Pugachev was eventually captured and was executed in 1775.

Her essential caution was well shown by her refusal to tamper with the powers and privileges of the nobility. She was the tsarina of the landlords, giving them greater power over the local administration of justice and taking away from their serfs the right to petition against their masters. Only twenty times in Catherine's thirty-four-year reign did the government act to restrain landlords abusing their powers over their serfs. Most significant of all, the obligation to service was abolished in 1762 and a charter of rights was later given to the nobility which sealed a half-century of retreat from Peter's policies towards them. The gentry were exempted from personal taxation, corporal punishment and billeting, could be tried (and be deprived of their rank) only by their peers, and were given the exclusive right to set up factories and mines. The landowner was in a sense taken into partnership by the autocracy.

SOCIAL OSSIFICATION

In the long run the close relationship between the nobility and the autocracy was pernicious. Under Catherine, Russia began to truss herself more and more tightly in the corset of her social structure at a time when other countries were beginning to loosen theirs. This would increasingly make Russia unfit to meet the challenges and changes of the next half-century. One sign of trouble was the scale of serf revolt. This had begun in the seventeenth century, but the most frightening and dangerous crisis came in 1773, the rebellion of Pugachev, the worst of the great regional uprisings which studded Russian agrarian history before the nineteenth century. Later, better policing would mean that revolt was usually local and containable, but it continued through almost the whole of the imperial era. Its recurrence is hardly surprising. The load of labour services piled on the peasant rose sharply in the Black Earth zone during Catherine's reign. Soon critics would appear among the literate class and the condition of the peasant would be one of their favourite themes, thus providing an early demonstration of a paradox evident in many developing countries in the next two centuries. It was becoming clear that modernization was more than a matter of technology; if you borrowed Western ideas, they could not be confined in their effect. The first critics of Orthodoxy and autocracy were beginning to appear. Eventually the need to preserve an ossifying social system would virtually bring to a halt the changes which Russia needed to retain the place that courageous and unscrupulous leadership and seemingly inexhaustible military manpower had given her.

CATHERINE'S LEGACY

By 1796, when Catherine died, Russia's position was indeed impressive. The most solid ground of her prestige was her armies and diplomacy. She had given Russia seven million new subjects. She said she had been well treated by Russia, to which she had come "a poor girl with three or four dresses", but that she had paid her debts to it with Azov, the Crimea and the Ukraine. This was in the line of her predecessors. Even when the monarchy was weak, the momentum of Peter's reign carried the foreign policy of Russia forward along two traditional lines of thrust, into Poland and towards Turkey. It helped that Russia's likely opponents laboured under growing difficulties for most of the eighteenth century. Once Sweden was out of the running, only Prussia or the Habsburg empire could provide a counter-weight, and since these two were often at loggerheads Russia could usually have her own way both over an ailing Poland and a crumbling Ottoman Empire.

PRUSSIA

I N 1701 THE ELECTOR OF BRANDENBURG, with the consent of the emperor, became a king; his kingdom, Prussia, was to last until 1918.

Frederick William of Prussia (1620–1688), depicted in this 18th-century portrait, was victorious in the Thirty Years' War, acquiring Magdeburg and Pomerania. He went on to create a centralized adminis-tration, with close links to the army and the landowning nobility (known as "the Junkers").

The Hohenzollern dynasty had provided a continuous line of electors since 1415, steadily adding to their ancestral domains, and Prussia, then a duchy, had been united to Brandenburg in the sixteenth century, after a Polish king had ousted the Teutonic Knights who ruled it. Religious toleration had been Hohenzollern policy after an elector was converted to Calvinism in 1613, while his subjects remained Lutheran. One problem facing the Hohenzollerns was the spread and variety of their lands, which stretched from East Prussia to the west bank of the Rhine. The Swedes provided infilling for this scatter of territories in the second half of the seventeenth century, though there were setbacks even for the "Great Elector", Frederick William, the creator of the Prussian standing army and winner of the victories against the Swedes, which were the basis of the most enduring military tradition in modern European history. Arms and diplomacy continued to carry forward his successor to the kingly crown he coveted and to participation in the Grand Alliance against Louis XIV. Prussia was by that fact alone clearly a power. This imposed a heavy cost but careful housekeeping had again built up the best army and one of the best-filled treasuries in Europe by 1740, when Frederick II came to the throne.

FREDERICK II

Frederick II was to be known as "the Great" because of the use he made of Prussia's wealth and fine army, largely at the expense of the Habsburgs and the kingdom of Poland, though also at the expense of his own people whom he subjected to heavy taxation and exposed to foreign invasion. It is difficult to decide whether he was more or less attractive than his brutal father (whom he hated). He

This 18th-century painting shows Frederick the Great of Prussia (1712–1786), accompanied by the Marquis of Argens, visiting the construction site of the Sans-Souci Palace in Potsdam.

was certainly malicious, vindictive and completely without scruple. But he was also highly intelligent and cultivated, playing and composing for the flute, and enjoying the conversation of clever men. He was like his father in his utter devotion to the interests of his dynasty, which he saw as the extension of its territories and the magnification of its prestige.

Frederick gave up some possessions too remote to be truly incorporated in the state, but added to Prussia more valuable territories. The opportunity for the conquest of Silesia came when the emperor died in 1740, leaving a daughter whose succession he had sought to assure but whose prospects were uncertain. This was Maria Theresia. She remained Frederick's most unforgiving opponent until her death in 1780 and her intense personal dislike for him was fully reciprocated. A general European war "of the Austrian Succession" left Prussia holding Silesia. It was not to be lost in later wars and in the last year

This 18th-century engraving shows the centre of Vienna, capital of Austria.

of his reign Frederick formed a League of German Princes to thwart the attempts of Maria Theresia's son and successor, Joseph II, to negotiate the acquisition of Bavaria as a recompense for the Habsburg inheritance.

This episode matters more to European history as a whole than might be expected of a contest for a province, however rich, and for the leadership of the princes of Germany. At first sight a reminder of how alive still in the eighteenth century were the dynastic preoccupations of the past, it is also, and more importantly, the opening of a theme with a century of life to it, and consequences great for Europe. Frederick launched a struggle between Habsburg and Hohenzollern for the mastery of Germany, which was only to be settled in 1866. That is further ahead than may be usefully considered at present; but this context gives perspective to the Hohenzollern appeal to German patriotic sentiment against the emperor, many of whose essential interests were non-German. There would be periods of good relations, but in the long struggle which began in 1740 Austria's great handicap would always be that she was both more and less than a purely German state.

THE CRIMEA

The disadvantages of the spread of Maria Theresia's interests were made very obvious during her reign. The Austrian Netherlands were an administrative nuisance rather than a strategic advantage, but it was in the east that the worst distractions from German problems arose, and they became increasingly pressing as the second half of the century brought more and more clearly into view the likelihood of a long and continuing confrontation with Russia over the fate of the Ottoman Empire. For thirty years or so Russo-Turkish relations had been allowed to slumber with only occasional minor eruptions over the building of a fort or the raids of the Crimean Tatars, one of the peoples originating in a fragment of the Golden Horde and under Turkish suzerainty. Then, between 1768 and 1774, Catherine fought her most successful war. A peace treaty with the Ottomans, signed in an obscure Bulgarian village called Kutchuk Kainarji, was one of the most important of the whole century. The Turks gave up their suzerainty over the Crimean Tatars (an important loss both materially, because of their military manpower, and morally, because this was the first Islamic people over which the Ottoman Empire ceded control), and Russia took the territory between the Bug and Dnieper, together with an indemnity, and the right of free navigation on the Black Sea and through the straits. In some ways the most pregnant with future opportunity of the terms was a right to take up with the Turks the interests of "the church to be built in Constantinople and those who serve it". This meant that the Russian government was recognized as the guarantor and protector of new rights granted to the Greek – that is, Christian – subjects of the Sultan. It was to prove a blank cheque for Russian interference in Turkish affairs.

Almost at once it became clear that this was a beginning, not an end. In 1783 Catherine annexed the Crimea, and after another war with the Turks her armies carried her frontier up to the line of the Dniester river. The next obvious boundary ahead was the Pruth, which meets the Danube a hundred miles or so from the Black Sea. The possibility of Russia's installation at the mouth of the Danube was to remain an Austrian nightmare, but the danger which appeared in the east before this was that Russia would swallow Poland. With the eclipse of Sweden, Russia had effectively had her own way at Warsaw, happy to leave her interests to be secured through a compliant Polish king. The factions of the magnates and their quarrels blocked the road to reform and without reform Polish independence would be a fiction because effective resistance to Russia was impossible. When there seemed to be for a moment a slight chance of reforms these were checkmated by skilful Russian exploitation of religious divisions to produce confederations which speedily reduced Poland to civil war.

THE PARTITIONING OF POLAND

The last phase of Poland's independent history had opened when the Turks declared war on Russia in 1768, with the excuse that they wished to defend Polish liberties. Four years later, in 1772, came the first "Partition" of Poland, in which Russia, Prussia and Austria shared between them about one-third of Poland's territory and one-half of her inhabitants. The old international system, which had somewhat artificially preserved Poland, had now disappeared. After two more partitions Russia had done best on the map, absorbing something like 180,000 square miles of territory (though in the next century it would be clear that the population of dissident Poles which went with it was by no means an unambiguous gain) but Prussia also did well, emerging from the division of booty with more Slav than German subjects. Nevertheless, so huge a prize set the seal on Russian success; the transformation of eastern Europe since 1500 was complete and the stage was set for the nineteenth century, when there would be no booty left to divert Austria and Russia from the Ottoman succession problem. Meanwhile, independent Poland disappeared for a century and a quarter.

DAWN OF A NEW AGE

Catherine rightly claimed to have done much for Russia, but she had only deployed a strength already apparent. Even in the 1730s, one Russian army had been as far west as the Neckar; in 1760 another marched into Berlin. In the 1770s there was a Russian fleet in the Mediterranean. A few years later a Russian army was campaigning in Switzerland and, after twenty years, another was to enter Paris. The paradox at the heart of such evidences of strength was that this military power was based on a backward social and economic structure. Perhaps this was inherent in what Peter had done. The Russian state rested on a society with which it was fundamentally incompatible, and later Russian critics would make much of this theme. Of course, this did not mean that the clock could be put back. The Ottoman Empire was for ever gone as a serious competitor for power while Prussia's emergence announced a new age as much as did Russia's. The future international weight of the United Provinces and Sweden had been unimaginable in 1500, but their importance, too, had come and gone by 1800; they were then still important nations, but of the second rank. France was still to be a front-rank power in an age of national states as she had been in the days of sixteenth-century dynastic rivalry; indeed, her power was relatively greater and the peak of her dominance in western Europe was still to come. But she faced a new challenger, too, and one which had already defeated her. From the little English kingdom of 1500, cooped up in an island off the coast of Europe under an upstart dynasty, had emerged the world power of Great Britain.

This was a transformation almost as surprising and sudden as Russia's. It transcended the old categories of European diplomacy quite as dramatically. From what some historians have called "the Atlantic Archipelago" of islands and kingdoms, ruled intermittently in varying measure and extent by Tudor and Stuart monarchs, had emerged a new oceanic power. Besides its new unity, it enjoyed unique institutional and economic advantages in deploying its influence worldwide. In three hundred years, the major zones of European conflict and dispute had migrated from the old battlegrounds of Italy, the Rhine and the Netherlands, moving from them to central and eastern Germany, the Danube valley, Poland and Carpathia, and the Baltic, but also – greatest change of all – across the oceans. A new age had indeed begun, signalled not only by the remaking of eastern Europe, but in the wars of Louis XIV, the first world wars of the modern era, imperial and oceanic in their scope.

A contemporary print represents the first partition of Poland by the eastern European monarchs, who are shown dividing the spoils.

4 EUROPE'S ASSAULT ON THE WORLD

THE CHANGE WHICH CAME ABOUT in world history after 1500 was quite without precedent. Never before had one culture spread over the whole globe. Even in prehistory, the cultural tide had seemed set towards differentiation. Now it began to turn. Even by the end of the eighteenth century, the essentials of what was going on were evident. European nations, including Russia, had already laid claim to more than half the world's land surface. They actually controlled (or said they controlled) about a third of it. Never before had those sharing one particular civilization managed to acquire for their own use so great a territory. The consequences, moreover, had already begun to be shown in irreversible changes. Europeans had already transplanted crops and animal species to begin what was to be the greatest reshaping of ecology ever to take place. To the western hemisphere they sent populations which, already in 1800, constituted new centres of civilization, equipped with European institutions of government, religion and learning. A new nation had emerged from former British possessions in North America, while to the south the Spanish had destroyed two mature civilizations to implant their own. To the east, the story was different, but equally impressive. Once past the Cape of Good Hope (where something like 20,000 Dutch lived), an Englishman travelling on an East Indiaman in 1800 would not land at European colonial communities like those of the Americas unless he wandered as far off course as Australia, just beginning to receive its settlers. But in East Africa, Persia, India, Indonesia he would find Europeans coming to do business and then, in the long or short run, planning to return home to enjoy the profits. They could even be found in Canton, or, in very small numbers, in the closed island kingdom of Japan. Only the interior of Africa, still protected by disease and climate, seemed impenetrable.

Geographers, such as this one portrayed by Diego Velázquez between 1624 and 1626, were highly respected figures during the 16th and 17th centuries.

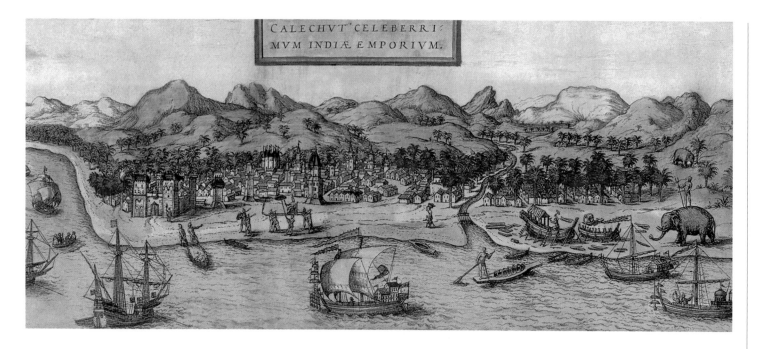

CALECHVT CELEBERRI:
MVM INDIÆ EMPORIVM.

EUROPE LOOKS OUTWARD

The remarkable transformation thus begun (and to go much further) was mostly a one-way process. Europeans went out to the world, only to a limited extent did it come to them. In the sixteenth, seventeenth and eighteenth centuries, few non-Europeans other than Turks entered Europe except as exotic imports or slaves. Yet the Arabs and Chinese were by no means unskilful sailors. They had made oceanic voyages and knew about the compass, while the island peoples of the Pacific made long sea crossings on their mysterious errands. None the less, the ships which came around the Horn or the tip of Africa to Atlantic ports were European and homeward bound, not Asiatic ones.

This was a great transformation of world relationships and it was the work of Europeans. Underpinning it lay layer upon layer of exploration, enterprise, technical advantage and governmental patronage. The trend seemed irreversible by the end of the eighteenth century and, in a sense, so it was to prove, even if direct European rule was to dissolve more quickly than it was built up.

No civilization had been more rapidly and dramatically successful, so untroubled in its expansion by any but temporary and occasional setbacks.

MIXED MOTIVES FOR EUROPEAN EXPANSION

One advantage possessed by Europeans had been the powerful motives they had to succeed. The major thrust behind the Age of Reconnaissance had been their wish to get into easier and more direct contact with the Far East, the source of things badly wanted in Europe, at a time when the Far East wanted virtually nothing Europe could offer in exchange. When Vasco da Gama showed what he had brought to give to a king, the inhabitants of Calicut laughed at him; he had nothing to offer which could compare with what Arab traders had already brought to India from other parts of Asia. It was indeed just the legendary superiority of so much of the civilization of the Orient that spurred Europeans on to try to reach it on some more regular and assured basis than the occasional

Calicut, in southern India, was the first Indian port to be reached by the Portuguese – Vasco da Gama landed there in 1498. This engraving shows Calicut as it was c.1572.

This painting, dating from c.1520, shows a fleet of Portuguese carracks – galleons that served as merchantmen in the Mediterranean during the 15th and 16th centuries.

trip of a Marco Polo. Coincidentally, China, India and Japan were at something like a cultural peak in the sixteenth and seventeenth centuries. The land blockade of eastern Europe by the Turk made them even more attractive to Europeans than they had been before. There were huge profits to be made and great efforts could be justified.

If the expectation of reward is a good recipe for high morale, so is the expectation of success. By 1500 enough had been done for the business of exploration and new enterprise to be attacked confidently; there was a cumulative factor at work, as each successful voyage added both to knowledge and to the certainty that more could be done. As time went by, there would also be profits for the financing of future expansion. Then there was the psychological asset of Christianity. Soon after the establishment of settlement this found a vent in missionary enterprises, but it was always present as a cultural fact, assuring Europeans of their superiority to the peoples with whom they began to come into contact for the first time. In the next four centuries, it was often to have disastrous effects.

Confident in the possession of the true religion, Europeans were impatient and contemptuous of the values and achievements of the peoples and civilizations they disturbed. The result was always uncomfortable and often brutal. It is also true that religious zeal could blur easily into less avowable motives. As the greatest Spanish historian of the American conquests put it when describing why he and his colleagues had gone to the Indies, they thought "to serve God and his Majesty, to give light to those who sat in darkness and to grow rich as all men desire to do".

Greed quickly led to the abuse of power, to domination and exploitation by force. In the end this led to great crimes – though they were often committed unconsciously. It sometimes brought about the destruction of whole societies, but this was only the worst aspect of a readiness to dominate which was present from the outset in European enterprise. The adventurers who first reached the coasts of India were soon boarding Asian merchantmen, torturing and slaughtering their crews and passengers, looting their cargoes and burning the ravaged hulks. Europeans could usually exact what they wanted in the end because of a technical superiority which exaggerated the power of their tiny numbers and for a few centuries turned the balance against the great historic agglomerations of population.

SHIPS AND GUNS

The next Portuguese captain after da Gama to go to India provided a fitting symbol of this by bombarding Calicut. A little later, when in 1517 the Portuguese reached Canton, they fired a salute as a gesture of friendship and respect, but the noise of their guns horrified the Chinese (who at first called them *folangki* – a remote corruption of "Franks"). These weapons were much more powerful than anything China had. There had long been guns in Asia, and the Chinese had known about gunpowder centuries before Europe, but the technology of artillery

had stood still there. European craftsmanship and metallurgy had in the fifteenth century made great strides, producing weapons better than any available elsewhere in the world. There were still more dramatic improvements to come, so that the comparative advantage of Europeans was to increase, right down to the twentieth century. This progress had been and was to be, again, paralleled in other fields, notably by the developments in shipbuilding and handling which have already been touched upon. When combined, such advances produced the remarkable weapon with which Europe opened up the world, the sailing-ship which was a gun-carrier. Again, evolution was far from complete in 1517, but already the Portuguese had been able to fight off the fleets organized by the Turks to keep them out of the Indian Ocean. (The Turks had more success in the Red Sea, in whose narrower waters the oar-propelled galley, which closed with its enemies to grapple and board, retained more of its usefulness. Even there,

From the *Gallery of Maps*, this illustration, which was commissioned by Pope Gregory XIII between 1580 and 1583, shows a 16th-century galleon. These sailing ships, with their fine lines, high forecastles and sternposts, were the first to mount bow-chasers – guns firing forward – as well as guns mounted traditionally, broadside.

though, the Portuguese were able to penetrate as far north as the Suez isthmus.) The Chinese war-junk would do no better than the rowed galley. The abandonment of the oar for propulsion and the mounting, broadside, of large numbers of guns, enormously multiplied the value of Europe's scanty manpower.

This European advantage was clear to contemporaries. As early as 1481 the pope forbade the sale of arms to Africans. The Dutch in the seventeenth century were very anxious to keep to themselves the secrets of gun-founding and not to allow them to pass into the hands of Asiatics. Yet pass they did. There had been Turkish gunners in India in the fifteenth century and before they reached China the Portuguese were supplying the Persians with cannon and teaching them how to cast more in order to embarrass the Turks. In the seventeenth century their knowledge of gun-founding and gunnery was one of the attractions which kept the Jesuit Fathers in favour with the Chinese authorities.

EUROPEAN CONFIDENCE

Yet even when, as the Dutch feared, the knowledge of up-to-date gun founding penetrated oriental societies it did not offset the European advantage. Chinese artillery remained inferior in spite of the Jesuits' training. There was more to the technological disparity of Europe and the world than mere

European trading stations and possessions in Africa and Asia c.1750

During the 17th century the Persian and Ottoman empires entered a long period of decline. The Dutch, English and French gradually replaced the Portuguese in the Indian Ocean and in Asia, where the colonial forces increased commercial exploitation. Meanwhile, the Spanish and Portuguese continued their colonization and exploitation of Central and South America, and the French, English and Dutch began to establish themselves in the West Indies and on the coasts of North America.

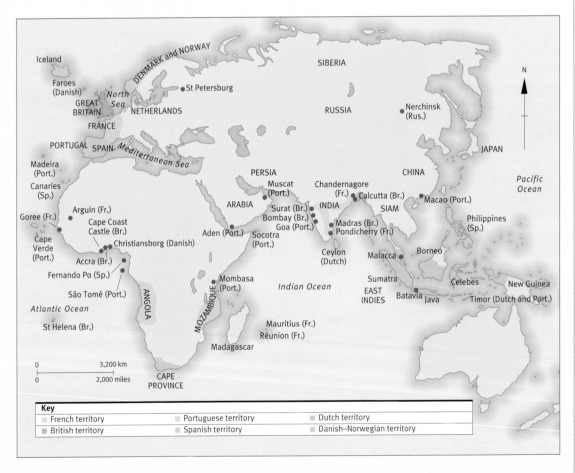

know-how. One of the assets Europe enjoyed at the beginning of her era was not only new knowledge, but an attitude to knowledge different from that of other cultures. There was a readiness to bring it to bear upon practical problems, a technological instinct for the useful. In it lay the roots of another psychological characteristic of Europeans, their growing confidence in the power to change things. Here, perhaps, was the most fundamental difference of all between them and the rest of the world. Europe was open to the future and its possibilities in a way that other cultures were not. On this confidence would rest a psychological advantage of the greatest importance. Even in 1500 some Europeans had seen the future – and it worked.

PORTUGUESE IMPERIALISM

AFRICA AND ASIA were the first targets against which Europeans' advantages were deployed. In these continents, the Portuguese led for a century and more. They figured so largely and were so successful in the opening of routes to the East that their king took the title (confirmed by the pope) "Lord of the conquest, navigation and commerce of India, Ethiopia, Arabia and Persia", which sufficiently indicates both the scope and the eastern bias of Portuguese enterprise, though slightly misleading in its reference to Ethiopia, with which Portuguese contacts were small. Penetration of Africa was impossible on any more than a tiny and hazardous basis. The Portuguese suggested that God had especially set a barrier around the African interior with its mysterious and noxious diseases (which were to hold Europeans at bay until the end of the nineteenth century). Even the coastal stations of West Africa were unhealthy and could only be tolerated because of their importance in

This 19th-century engraving is a copy of a 16th-century image of the *St Catherine of Mount Sinai*, the flagship of Vasco da Gama's squadron.

the slave trade and the substructure of long-range commerce. The East African stations were less unhealthy, but they, too, were of interest not as jumping-off points for the interior, but because they were part of a commercial network created by Arabs, whom the Portuguese deliberately harried so as to send up the cost of the spices passed by way of the Red Sea and the Middle East to the Venetian merchants of the eastern Mediterranean. The successors of the Portuguese were to leave the interior of Africa alone as they had done, and the history of that continent for another two centuries was still to move largely to its own rhythms in the obscure fastnesses of its forests and savannahs, its inhabitants only coming into corrosive and stimulating con-

Africa in the early modern era

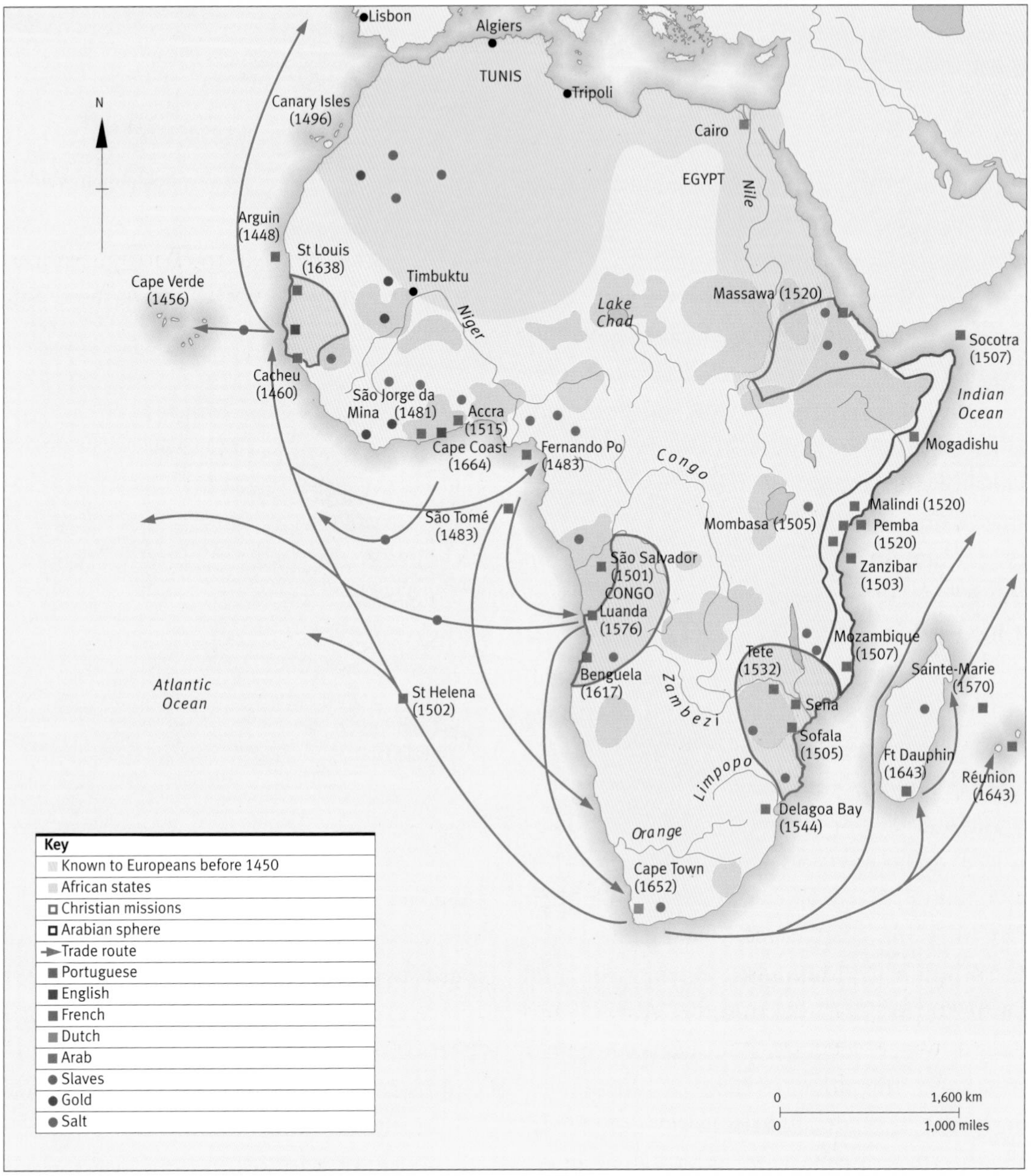

Lisbon
Algiers
TUNIS
Tripoli
Cairo
N
Canary Isles
(1496)
EGYPT
Nile
Arguin
(1448)
St Louis
(1638)
Cape Verde
(1456)
Timbuktu
Massawa (1520)
Lake
Chad
Niger
Socotra
(1507)
Cacheu
(1460)
Indian
Ocean
São Jorge da
Mina   (1481)   Accra
(1515)
Cape Coast   Fernando Po
(1664)   (1483)
Congo
Mogadishu
Malindi (1520)
São Tomé
(1483)
Mombasa (1505)   Pemba
(1520)
São Salvador
(1501)
CONGO
Luanda
(1576)
Zanzibar
(1503)
Atlantic
Ocean
St Helena
(1502)
Benguela
(1617)
Zambezi
Tete
(1532)
Mozambique
(1507)
Sainte-Marie
(1570)
Sena
Sofala
(1505)
Ft Dauphin
(1643)
Réunion
(1643)
Limpopo
Delagoa Bay
(1544)
Orange
Cape Town
(1652)

Key

	Known to Europeans before 1450
	African states
	Christian missions
	Arabian sphere
	Trade route
	Portuguese
	English
	French
	Dutch
	Arab
	Slaves
	Gold
	Salt

0   1,600 km
0   1,000 miles

At the beginning of the 15th century, having Christianized various newly discovered lands and acquired profitable trade routes, the Portuguese began the exploration and colonization of the Azores and Madeira. With the encouragement of Prince Henry the Navigator, the Portuguese naval forces risked visiting the uncharted western African coast, in search of a new route towards the East, the source of the spices and wonders of which Marco Polo had written.

Spanish sailors followed the Portuguese example; the Spanish also occupied the Canary Islands. Both nations established small settlements along the African coast – secure harbours where their ships could break their journeys. By the end of the 15th century, many of these had grown into important European trading posts and power bases, and the French, English and Dutch – the great European empire-builders of the Modern Age – also had commercial interests in the region.

tact with Europeans at its fringes. It is also true, though, that the opening of the European age in Asia showed that none of the powers concerned was in the first place interested in the subjugation or settlement of large areas. The period down to the middle of the eighteenth century was marked by the multiplication of trading posts, concessions in port facilities, protective forts and bases on the coast, for these by themselves would assure the only thing early imperialism sought in Asia, secure and profitable trade.

THE PORTUGUESE TRADE MONOPOLY

The Portuguese dominated trade with Asia in the sixteenth century; their fire-power swept all before them and they rapidly built up a chain of bases and trading posts. Twelve years after Vasco da Gama arrived at Calicut the Portuguese established their main Indian Ocean trading station some 300 miles further up the western Indian coast, at Goa. It was to become a missionary as well as a commercial centre; once established, the Portuguese Empire strongly supported the propagation of the faith, and the Franciscans played a large part in this. In 1513 the first Portuguese ships reached the Moluccas, the legendary spice islands, and the incorporation of Indonesia, Southeast Asia, and islands as far south as Timor within the European horizon began.

Four years later the first Portuguese ships reached China and opened direct European trade by sea with that empire. Ten years later they were allowed to use Macao; in 1557 they obtained a permanent settlement there. When Charles V gave up to them the rights which Spain had claimed as a result of exploration in the Moluccas, keeping only the Philippines in the Far East, and renouncing any interest in the Indian Ocean area, the Portuguese were in possession of a monopoly of eastern empire for the next half-century.

It was a trading monopoly, but not only one of trade with Europe; there was much business to be done as carriers between Asian countries. Persian carpets went to India, cloves from the Moluccas to China, copper and silver from Japan to China, Indian cloth to Siam. Both the Portuguese and their successors found this a profitable source of income to offset some of the costs of Europe's unfavourable balance of trade with Asia, whose inhabitants long wanted little from Europe except silver. The only serious competitors at sea were the Arabs and they were controlled effectively by Portuguese squadrons operating from the East African bases, from Socotra, at the mouth of the Red Sea, where they had established themselves in 1507, from Ormuz, on the northern coast of the entrance to the Persian Gulf, and from Goa. From these places the Portuguese expanded their commerce further and were eventually to trade into the Red Sea as far as

A town in Goa is depicted in this 16th-century Dutch engraving. Goa was occupied by Affonso d'Albuquerque in 1510 and formed part of Portuguese India until 1961, when it was annexed by the Union of India.

The Portuguese traders often commissioned African artisans to produce luxury objects. This 16th-century Benin-style salt cellar is made of ivory. Figures of Portuguese warriors decorate the base, and the lid is crowned by a model of a Portuguese caravel.

Massawa and up to the head of the Persian Gulf, where they established a factory at Basra. They had also secured privileges in Burma and Siam and in the 1540s were the first Europeans to land in Japan. This network was supported by a diplomacy of agreements with local rulers and the superiority of Portuguese fire-power at sea. Even if

they had wished to do so, they could not have developed this power on land because they lacked men, so that a commercial empire was not only economic sense but was all that could be created with the means available.

PORTUGUESE WEAKNESS

Portugal's supremacy in the Indian Ocean disguised fundamental weaknesses, a lack of manpower and a shaky financial base. It lasted only until the end of the century and was then replaced by that of the Dutch, who carried the technique and institutions of commercial empire to their furthest point. The Dutch were the trading imperialists *par excellence*, though in the end they also carried out some settlement in Indonesia. Their opportunity arose when Portugal was united with Spain in 1580. This change provided a stimulus to Dutch seamen now excluded from the profitable re-export trade of oriental goods from Lisbon to northern Europe which had been mainly in their hands. The background of the Eighty Years' War with Spain was an additional incentive for the Dutch to enter areas where they might make profits at the expense of the Iberians. Like the Portuguese they were few, barely two million people, and their survival depended on a narrow base; commercial wealth was therefore vitally important to them. Their advantages lay in the pool of naval manpower, ships, wealth and experience built up by their ascendancy in fishing and carrying in northern waters, while commercial expertise at home made it easy to mobilize resources for new enterprises. The Dutch were assisted, too, by the simultaneous recovery of the Arabs, who took back the East African stations north of Zanzibar as Portuguese power wavered in the aftermath of the Spanish union.

The first decades of the seventeenth

century therefore brought the collapse of much of the Portuguese Empire in the East and its replacement by the Dutch. For a time, too, the Dutch established themselves in Pernambuco, the sugar-producing region of Portuguese Brazil, though they were not able to retain it. The main objective of the Dutch was the Moluccas. A brief period of individual voyages (sixty-five in seven years, some around the Straits of Magellan, some around Africa) ended when in 1602, at the initiative of the States General, the government of the United Provinces, there was set up the Dutch United East India Company, the organization which was to prove the decisive instrument of Dutch commercial supremacy in the East. Like the Portuguese before them,

the company's servants worked through diplomacy with native rulers to exclude competitors, and through a system of trading stations. How unpleasant the Dutch could be to rivals was shown in 1623, when ten Englishmen were murdered at Amboyna; this ended any English attempt to intervene directly in the spice trade. Amboyna had been one of the first Portuguese bases to be seized in a rapid sweeping-up of Portuguese interests, but it was not until 1609, when a resident governor-general was sent to the East, that the reduction of the major Portuguese forts could begin. The centre of these operations was the establishment of the Dutch headquarters at Jakarta (renamed Batavia) in Java, where it was to remain until

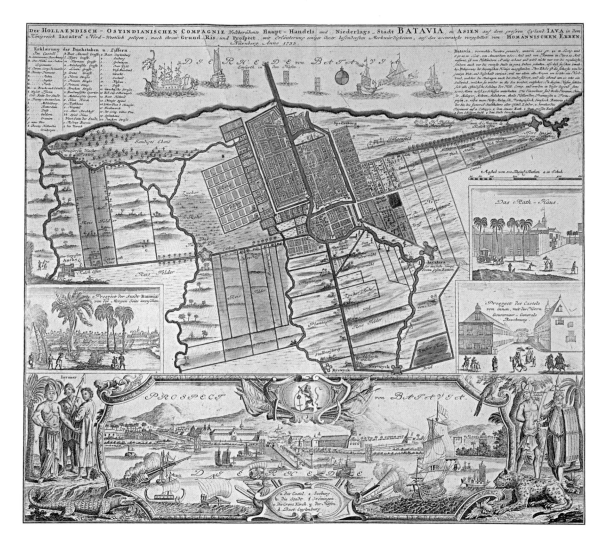

This 18th-century engraving shows Batavia (Jakarta), the capital of the Dutch colony on the Indonesian island of Java and site of the headquarters of the Dutch East India Company.

the end of Dutch colonial rule. It became the centre of an area of settlement, where Dutch planters could rely upon the company to back them up in a ruthless control of their labour force. The early history of the Dutch colonies is a grim one of insurrection, deportation, enslavement and extermination. The trade of local shippers – and of the Chinese junks – was deliberately destroyed in order to concentrate all sources of profit in the hands of the Dutch.

DUTCH TRADE

The spice trade to Europe was the centre of Dutch attention and was a huge prize. It accounted during most of the century for over two-thirds of the values of the cargoes sent back to Amsterdam. But the Dutch also set about replacing the Portuguese in the valuable East Asian trade. They could not expel the Portuguese from Macao, although they sent expeditions against it, but succeeded in setting themselves up in Formosa, from which they built up an indirect trade with the mainland of China. In 1638 the Portuguese were expelled from Japan and the Dutch succeeded them there. In the next two decades, the Portuguese were replaced by the Dutch in Ceylon, too. Their successful negotiation of a monopoly of trade to Siam, on the other hand, was overtaken by another power, France. This country's connection with the area was opened by accident in 1660 when circumstance took three French missionaries to the Siamese capital. Thanks to their establishment of a mission centre and the presence of a Greek adviser at the Siamese court there followed a French diplomatic and military mission in 1685. But these promising beginnings ended in civil war and failure and Siam again moved out of the sphere of European influence for another two centuries.

In the early eighteenth century there thus existed a Dutch supremacy in the Indian Ocean and Indonesia, and an important Dutch interest in the China seas. To a remarkable degree this reproduced the earlier Portuguese pattern, although there survived Portuguese stations such as Goa and Macao. The heart of Dutch power was the Malacca Strait, from which it radiated through Malaysia and Indonesia, to Formosa and the trading links with China and Japan, and down to the southeast to the crucial Moluccas. This area was by now enjoying an internal trade so considerable that it was beginning to be self-financing, with bullion from Japan and China providing its flow of currency rather than bullion from Europe as in the early days. Further

A contemporary oil painting shows the fleet of the Dutch East India Company returning to the port of Amsterdam in the early 17th century, carrying spices and other valuable commodities from the East.

west, the Dutch were also established at Calicut, in Ceylon and at the Cape of Good Hope, and had set up factories in Persia. Although Batavia was a big town and the Dutch were running plantations to grow the goods they needed, this was still a littoral or insular commercial empire, not one of internal dominion over the mainland. In the last resort it rested on naval power and it was to succumb, though not to disappear, as Dutch naval power was surpassed.

THE ENGLISH IN INDIA

DUTCH NAVAL SUPERIORITY was clearly beginning to be threatened in the last decades of the seventeenth century. The unlikely challenger for Indian Ocean supremacy was England. At an early date the English had sought to enter the spice trade. There had been an East Indian Company under James I, but its factors had got bloody noses for their pains, both when they tried to cooperate with the Dutch and when they fought them. The upshot of this was that by 1700 the English had in effect drawn a line under their accounts east of the Malacca Strait. Like the Dutch in 1580, they were faced with a need to change course and did so. The upshot was the most momentous event in British history between the Protestant Reformation and the onset of industrialization – the acquisition of supremacy in India.

In India the main rivals of the English were not the Dutch or Portuguese, but the French. What was at stake did not emerge for a long time. The rise of British power in India was very gradual. After the establishment of Fort St George at Madras and the acquisition of Bombay from the Portuguese as a part of the dowry of Charles II's queen, there was no further English penetration of India until the end of the century. From their early footholds (Bombay was the only territory they held in full sovereignty) Englishmen conducted a trade in coffee and textiles less glamorous than the Dutch spice trade, but one which

This contemporary illustration depicts Akbar, the Moghul emperor of India, crossing the Ganges river. When Akbar died in 1605, his huge empire was already under threat, not only from internal religious struggles, but also from growing interference by Europeans trading in India.

grew in value and importance. It also changed their national habits, and therefore society, as the establishment of coffee-houses in London showed. Soon, ships began to be sent from India to China for tea; by 1700 the English had acquired a new national beverage and a poet would soon commemorate what he termed "cups that cheer but not inebriate".

THE COLLAPSE OF THE MOGHUL EMPIRE

As a defeat of the East India Company's forces in 1689 showed, military domination in India was unlikely to prove easy. Moreover, it was not necessary to prosperity. The company therefore did not wish to fight if it could avoid it. Though at the end of the century a momentous acquisition was made when the company was allowed to occupy Fort William, which it had built at Calcutta, the directors in 1700 rejected the idea of acquiring fresh territory or planting colonies in India as quite unrealistic. Yet all preconceptions were to be changed by the collapse of the Moghul Empire after the death of Aurungzebe in 1707. The consequences emerged slowly, but their total effect was that India dissolved into a collection of autonomous states with no paramount power.

The Moghul Empire had already before 1707 been troubled by the Marathas. The centrifugal tendencies of the empire had always favoured the *nawabs*, or provincial governors, too, and power was divided between them and the Marathas with increasing obviousness. The Sikhs provided a third focus of power. Originally appearing as a Hindu sect in the sixteenth century, they had turned against the Moghuls but had also drawn away from orthodox Hinduism to become virtually a third religion with it and Islam. The Sikhs formed a military brotherhood, had no castes,

and were well able to look after their own interests in a period of disunion. Eventually a Sikh empire appeared in northwest India which was to endure until 1849. Meanwhile, there were signs in the eighteenth century of an increasing polarity between Hindu and Muslim. The Hindus withdrew more into their own communities, hardening the ritual practices which publicly distinguished them. The Muslims reciprocated. On this growing dislocation, presided over by a Moghul military and civil administration which was conservative and unprogressive, there fell also a Persian invasion in the 1730s and consequent losses of territory.

RIVALRY BETWEEN BRITAIN AND FRANCE

There were great temptations to foreign intervention in the disintegration of the Moghul Empire. In retrospect it seems remarkable that both British and French took so long to take advantage; even in the 1740s the British East India Company was still less wealthy and powerful than the Dutch. This delay is a testimony to the importance still attached to trade as their main purpose. When they did begin to intervene, largely moved by hostility to the French and fear of what they might do, the British had several important advantages. The possession of a station at Calcutta placed them at the door to that part of India which was potentially the richest prize – Bengal and the lower Ganges valley. They had assured sea communications with Europe, thanks to British naval power, and ministers listened to the East India merchants in London as they did not listen to French merchants at Versailles. The French were the most dangerous potential competitors but their government was always likely to be distracted by its European continental

The meeting between Robert Clive and the nawab (prince) of Bengal's General Mir Jafar after the Battle of Plassey in 1757 is depicted in this painting. The British victory, which was secretly aided by Jafar, led to their acquisition of Bengal. Jafar was rewarded when the British placed him on the defeated nawab's throne.

commitments. Finally, the British lacked missionary zeal; this was true in the narrow sense that Protestant interest in missions in Asia quickened later than Catholic, and also, more generally, in that they had no wish to interfere with native custom or institution but only – somewhat like the Moghuls – to provide a neutral structure of power within which Indians could carry on their lives as they wished, while the commerce from which the company profited prospered in peace.

CONFLICT IN THE CARNATIC

The way into an imperial future led through Indian politics. Support for rival Indian princes was the first, indirect, form of conflict between French and British. In 1744

this led for the first time to armed struggle between British and French forces in the Carnatic, the southeastern coastal region. India had been irresistibly sucked into the worldwide conflict between British and French power. The Seven Years' War (1756–63) was decisive. Before its outbreak, there had in fact been no remission of fighting in India, even while France and Great Britain were officially at peace after 1748. The French cause had prospered under a brilliant French governor in the Carnatic, Dupleix, who caused great alarm to the British by his extension of French power among native princes by force and diplomacy. But he was recalled to France and the French Indian company was not to enjoy the wholehearted support of the metropolitan government which it needed to emerge as the new paramount power. When war broke out again, in 1756, the *nawab* of Bengal attacked and captured Calcutta. His treatment of his English prisoners, many of whom were suffocated in the soon legendary "Black Hole", gave additional offence. The East India Company's army, commanded by its employee, Robert Clive, retook the city from him, seized the French station at Chandernagore and then on 22 June 1757 won a battle over the *nawab*'s much larger armies at Plassey, about a hundred miles up the Hooghly from Calcutta.

It was not very bloody (the *nawab*'s army was suborned) but it was one of the decisive battles of world history. It opened to the British the road to the control of Bengal and its revenues. On these was based the destruction of French power in the Carnatic; that opened the way to further acquisitions which led, inexorably, to a future British monopoly of India. Nobody planned this. The British government, it is true, had begun to grasp what was immediately at stake in terms of a threat to trade and sent out a battalion of regular troops to help the company; the gesture is doubly revealing, both because it recognized that a national interest was involved, but also because of the tiny scale of this military effort. A very small number of European troops with European field artillery could be decisive. The fate of India turned on the company's handful of European and European-trained soldiers, and on the diplomatic skills and acumen of its agents on the spot. Upon this narrow base and the need for government in a disintegrating India was to be built the British Raj.

EARLY BRITISH RULE IN INDIA

In 1764 the East India Company became the formal ruler of Bengal. This had by no means been the intention of the company's directors who sought not to govern but to trade. However, if Bengal could pay for its own government, then the burden could be undertaken. There were now only a few scattered French bases; the peace of 1763 left five trading posts on condition that they were not fortified. In 1769 the French Compagnie des Indes was dissolved. Soon after, the British took Ceylon from the Dutch and the stage was cleared for a unique example of imperialism.

The road would be a long one and was for a long time followed reluctantly, but the East India Company was gradually drawn on by its revenue problems and by the disorder of native administrations in contiguous territories to extend its own governmental aegis. The obscuring of the company's primary commercial role was not good for business. It also gave its employees even greater opportunities to feather their own nests. This drew the interest of British politicians, who first cut into the powers of the directors of the company and then brought it firmly under the control of the Crown, setting up in 1784 a system of "dual control" in India which was to last until 1858. In the same Act were provisions against further interference in native affairs; the British government hoped as fervently as the company to avoid being dragged any further into the role of imperial power in India. But this was what happened in the next half-century, as many more acquisitions followed. The road was open which was to lead eventually to the enlightened despotism of the nineteenth-century Raj. India was quite unlike any other dependency so far acquired by a European state in that hundreds of millions of subjects were to be added to the empire without any conversion or assimilation of them being envisaged except by a few visionaries and at a very late date. The character of the British imperial structure would be profoundly

The growth of British power in India

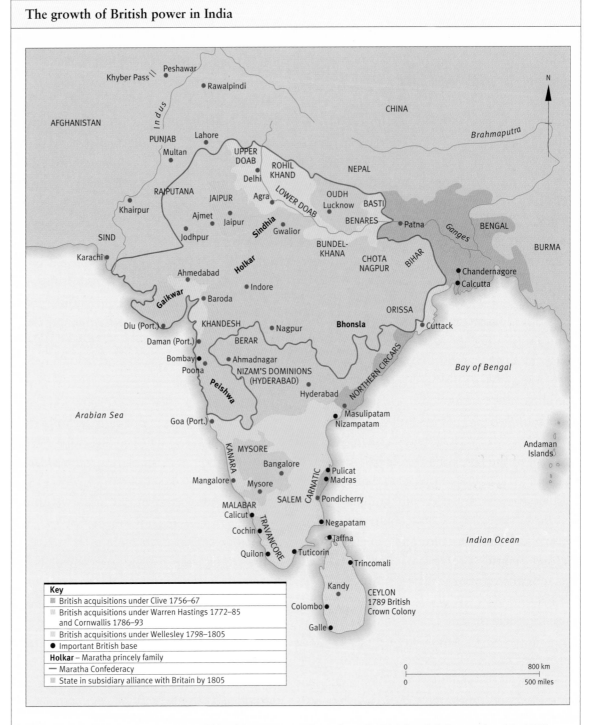

Key
- ■ British acquisitions under Clive 1756–67
- ■ British acquisitions under Warren Hastings 1772–85 and Cornwallis 1786–93
- ■ British acquisitions under Wellesley 1798–1805
- ● Important British base
- **Holkar** – Maratha princely family
- — Maratha Confederacy
- ■ State in subsidiary alliance with Britain by 1805

The decline of the Moghul Empire and bloody battles between Muslims and Hindus facilitated the establishment of new European trading bases. The French East India Company (founded in 1664) competed with the British East India Trading Company until 1746. Anglo-French commercial disputes tended to be settled through diplomatic channels until 1744, but fighting escalated in 1754 when war broke out between the two powers in North America, the West Indies and western Africa as well as in India. In 1757 the English victory over the nawab of Bengal at the Battle of Plassey assured British ascendancy and put an end to the French expansion on Indian territory.

transformed by this, and so, eventually, would be British strategy, diplomacy, external trade patterns and even outlook.

SPANISH CONQUISTADORES IN THE AMERICAS

EXCEPT IN INDIA AND DUTCH INDONESIA, no territorial acquisitions in the East in these centuries could be compared to the vast seizures of lands by Europeans in the Americas. Columbus's landing had been followed by a fairly rapid and complete exploration of the major "West Indian" islands. It was soon clear that the conquest of American lands was attractively easy by comparison with the struggles to win north Africa from the Moors which had immediately followed the fall of Granada and the completion of the Reconquest on the Spanish mainland. Settlement rapidly made headway, particularly in Hispaniola and Cuba. The cornerstone of the first cathedral in the Americas was laid in 1523; the Spaniards, as their city-building was intended to show, had come to stay. Their first university (in the same city, Santo Domingo) was founded in 1538 and the first printing-press was set up in Mexico in the following year.

The Spanish settlers looked for land, as agriculturalists, and gold, as speculators. They had no competitors and, indeed, with the exception of Brazil, the story of the opening up of Central and South America remains Spanish until the end of the sixteenth century. The first Spaniards in the islands were often Castilian gentry, poor, tough and ambitious. When they went to the mainland they were out for booty, though they spoke as well of the message of the Cross and the greater glory of the Crown of Castile. The first penetration of the mainland had come in Venezuela in 1499. Then, in 1513, Balboa

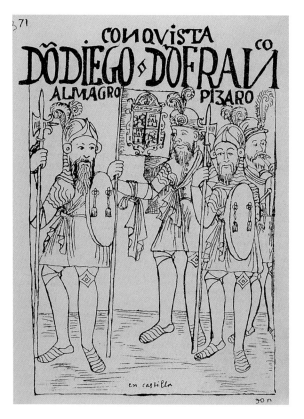

crossed the isthmus of Panama and Europeans for the first time saw the Pacific. His expedition built houses and sowed crops; the age of the *conquistadores* had begun. One among them whose adventures captured and held the imagination of posterity was Hernán Cortés.

CORTES AND PIZARRO

Late in 1518 Cortés left Cuba with a few hundred followers. He was deliberately flouting the authority of its governor and subsequently justified his acts by the spoils he brought to the Crown. After landing on the coast of Vera Cruz in February 1519, he burnt his ships to ensure that his men could not go back and then began the march to the high central plateau of Mexico, which was to provide one of the most dramatic stories of the whole history of imperialism. When they reached the city of Mexico itself, they were

The Spanish conquistadores Diego de Almagro (1475–1538) and Francisco Pizarro (c.1475–1541) conquered the Inca Empire between 1531 and 1535 and began the Spanish colonial-ization of Peru. Almagro and his men went on to conquer Chile between 1535 and 1536. They then returned to Peru to dispute Pizarro's occupation of Cuzco, thus instigating a civil war between the rival Spanish forces.

Royal councils, such as the one depicted in this 17th-century illustration, were gradually set up in the Spanish Americas to administer justice and to advise the Crown. With the viceroys, they formed the basic pillars of Spanish colonial administration and government.

This painting dates from 1716 and is entitled *Entry into the City of Lima of the Viceroy of Peru, Nicholas Caracciolo*. Until Charles III's reforms of 1776, the viceroy of a Spanish American colony was an extremely powerful figure. He acted as the president of the city's royal council, the captain general of the troops, the official head of the treasury and the ecclesiastical vice-patron.

astounded by the civilization they found there. Besides its wealth of gold and precious stones, it was situated in a land suitable for the kind of estate cultivation familiar to Castilians at home.

Though Cortés's followers were few and their conquest of the Aztec Empire which dominated the central plateau heroic, they had great advantages and a lot of luck. The people upon whom they advanced were technologically primitive, easily impressed by the gunpowder, steel and horses the *conquistadores* brought with them. Aztec resistance was hampered by an uneasy feeling that Cortés might be an incarnation of their god, whose return to them they one day expected. The Aztecs were very susceptible to imported diseases, too. Furthermore, they were themselves an exploiting race and a cruel one; their Indian subjects were happy to welcome the new conquerors as liberators or

at least as a change of masters. Circumstances thus favoured the Spaniards. Nevertheless, in the end their own toughness, courage and ruthlessness were the decisive factors.

In 1531 Pizarro set out upon a similar conquest of Peru. This was an even more remarkable achievement than the conquest of Mexico and, if possible, displayed even more dreadfully the rapacity and ruthlessness of the *conquistadores*. Settlement of the new empire began in the 1540s and almost at once there was made one of the most important mineral discoveries of historical times, that of a mountain of silver at Potosí, which was to be Europe's main source of bullion for the next three centuries.

THE SPANISH EMPIRE

BY 1700, THE SPANISH EMPIRE in the Americas nominally covered a huge area from the modern New Mexico to the River Plate. By way of Panama and Acapulco it was linked by sea to the Spanish in the Philippines. Yet this huge extent on the map was misleading. The Californian, Texan and New Mexican lands north of the Rio Grande were very thinly inhabited; for the most part occupancy meant a few forts and trading posts and a larger number of missions. Nor, to the south, was what is now Chile well settled. The most important and most densely populated regions were three: New Spain (as Mexico was called), which quickly became the most developed part of Spanish America, Peru, which was important for its mines and intensively occupied, and some of the larger and long-settled Caribbean islands. Areas unsuitable for settlement by Spaniards were long neglected by the administration.

The Indies were governed by viceroys at Mexico and Lima as sister kingdoms of Castile and Aragon, dependent upon the Crown of Castile. They had a royal council of their own through which the king exercised direct authority. This imposed a high degree of centralization in theory; in practice, geography and topography made nonsense of such a pretence. It was impossible to control

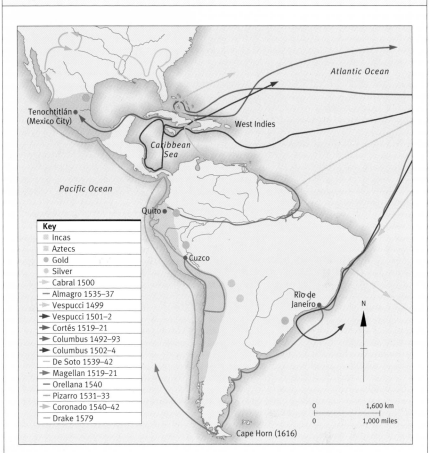

Exploration of the Americas

Key
- Incas
- Aztecs
- Gold
- Silver
- Cabral 1500
- Almagro 1535–37
- Vespucci 1499
- Vespucci 1501–2
- Cortés 1519–21
- Columbus 1492–93
- Columbus 1502–4
- De Soto 1539–42
- Magellan 1519–21
- Orellana 1540
- Pizarro 1531–33
- Coronado 1540–42
- Drake 1579

With the idea that the earth was spherical, the search for a sea route to the Orient began. It was this quest that led to the discovery of the American mainland by Christopher Columbus in 1498. European influence in the Americas increased significantly during the 17th century, when the acquisition of large empires in that region transformed Spain and Portugal into great powers. As a result of European colonialization in the Americas, worldwide trade increased, farming was transformed, precious metals started to flood into Europe and great population movements and mixtures began. For several centuries, America would be not only a great investment, but also a land of opportunity and hope for many Europeans.

New Spain or Peru closely from Spain with the communications available. The viceroys and captains-general under them enjoyed an effective independence in their day-to-day business. But the colonies could be run by Madrid for fiscal advantage and, indeed, the Spaniards and Portuguese were the only powers colonizing in the western hemisphere for

During the conquest of Mexico, Hernán Cortés (1485–1547) and his followers often treated the native peoples with great brutality. The Cholula people, who had refused to supply provisions to the members of a Spanish expedition, were accused of treason. Their attempts, shown in this contemporary illustration, to resist the Spanish forces were in vain: the Cholula were ruthlessly massacred.

over a century who managed to make their American possessions not only pay for themselves but return a net profit for the metropolis. This was largely because of the flow of precious metals. After 1540 silver flooded across the Atlantic, to be dissipated, unfortunately for Spain, in the wars of Charles V and Philip II. By 1650, 16,000 tons of silver had come to Europe, to say nothing of 180 tons of gold objects.

THE ECONOMY OF EMPIRE

Whether Spain got economic benefits other than gold and silver bullion from her colonies is harder to say. She shared with other colonizing powers of the age the belief that there was only a limited amount of trade to go around; it followed that trade with her colonies should be reserved to her by regulation and force of arms. Furthermore, she endorsed another commonplace of early colonial economic theory, the view that colonies should not be allowed to develop industries which might reduce the opportunities available to the home country in their markets. Unfortunately, Spain was less successful than other countries in drawing advantage from this. Though they successfully prevented the development of any but

extractive or handicraft industry in America, the Spanish authorities were increasingly unable to keep out foreign traders (interlopers as they came to be called) from their territories. Spanish planters soon wanted what metropolitan Spain could not supply: slaves, especially. Apart from mining, the economy of the islands and New Spain rested on agriculture. The islands soon came to depend on slavery; in the mainland colonies, a Spanish government unwilling to countenance the enslavement of the conquered populations evolved other devices to assure the supply of labour. The first, started in the islands and extended to Mexico, was a kind of feudal lordship: a Spaniard would be given an *encomienda*, a group of villages over which he extended protection in return for a share of their labour. The general effect was not always easily distinguishable from serfdom, or even from slavery, which soon came to mean black African slavery.

THE TREATMENT OF NATIVE POPULATIONS

The presence from the start of large pre-colonial native populations to provide labour did as much as the nature of the occupying power to differentiate the colonialism of Central and South America from that of the north. Centuries of Moorish occupation had accustomed the Spanish and Portuguese to the idea of living in a multiracial society. There soon emerged in Latin America a population of mixed blood. In Brazil, which the Portuguese finally secured from the Dutch after thirty years' fighting, there was much interbreeding, both with the indigenous peoples and with the growing black population of slaves. They had first been imported to work on the sugar plantations in the sixteenth century. In Africa, too, the Portuguese showed no concern at racial interbreeding, and its lack of a colour bar has been alleged to have been a palliative feature of Portuguese imperialism.

None the less, though the establishment of racially mixed societies over huge areas was one of the enduring legacies of the Spanish and Portuguese empires, these societies were stratified along racial lines. The dominant classes were always the Iberian-born and the Creoles, persons of European blood born in the colonies. As time passed, the latter came to feel that the former, called *peninsulares*, excluded them from key posts and were antagonistic towards them. From the Creoles there led downwards a blurred incline of increasing gradations of blood to the poorest and most oppressed, the pure Indians and black slaves. Though Indian languages survived, often thanks to the efforts of the Spanish missionaries, the dominant languages of the continent became, of course, those of the conquerors. This was the greatest single formative influence making for the cultural unification of the continent, though another of comparable importance was Roman Catholicism.

NEW WORLD CATHOLICISM

THE CHURCH PLAYED AN enormous part in the opening of Spanish (and Portuguese) America. The lead was taken from the earliest years by the missionaries of the mendicant orders – Franciscans, in particular – but for three centuries their successors worked away at the civilization of native Americans. They took Indians from their tribes and villages, taught them Christianity and Latin (the early friars often kept them from learning Spanish, to protect them from corruption by the settlers), put them in trousers and sent them back to spread the light among their compatriots. The mission stations of the frontier determined the shapes of countries which

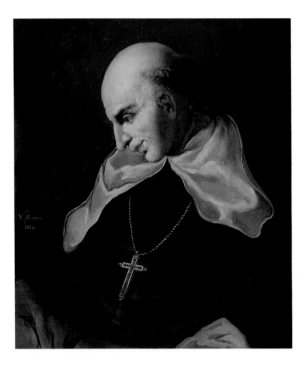

Bartolomé de las Casas, the Spanish priest who fought to protect the rights of the native population in the Spanish Americas, is thought to be the figure portrayed in this 19th-century painting.

would only come into existence centuries later. They met little resistance. Mexicans, for example, enthusiastically adopted the cult of the Blessed Virgin, assimilating her with the native goddess, Tonantzui.

For good and ill the Church saw itself from the start as the protector of the Indian subjects of the Crown of Castile. The eventual effect of this would only be felt after centuries had brought important changes in the demographic centre of gravity within the Roman communion, but it had many implications visible much earlier than this. It was in 1511 that the first sermon against the way the Spanish treated their new subjects was preached (by a Dominican) at Santo Domingo. From the start, the monarchy proclaimed its moral and Christian mission in the New World. Laws were passed to protect the Indians and the advice of churchmen was sought about their rights and what could be done to secure them. In 1550 an extraordinary event took place when the royal government held a theological and philosophical enquiry by debate into the principles on which the New World peoples were to be

was probably the main cause of the demographic disaster of the first century of Spanish empire in America.

The Church, meanwhile, was almost continuously at work to convert the natives (two Franciscans baptised 15,000 Indians in a single day at Xocomilcho) and then to throw around them the protection of the mission and the parish. Others did not cease to make representations to the Crown. The name of one, Bartolomé de las Casas, a Dominican, cannot be ignored. He had come out as a settler, only to become the first priest ordained in the Americas and thereafter, as theologian and bishop, he spent his life trying to influence Charles V's government, and not without success. He brought to bear the discipline of refusing absolution even in the last rites to those whose confessions left him unsatisfied over their treatment of Indians, and argued against opponents on a thoroughly medieval basis. He assumed, with Aristotle, that some human beings indeed were "by nature" slaves (he had black slaves of his own) but denied that the Indians were among them. He was to pass into historical memory, anachronistically, as one of the first critics of colonialism, largely because of the use made of his writings two hundred years later by a publicist of the Enlightenment.

THE CATHOLIC MONOPOLY

For centuries, the preaching and rituals of the Church were virtually the only access to European culture for the Amerindian peasant, who found some of Catholicism's features sympathetic and comprehensible. To European education, only a few had access; Mexico had no native bishop until the seventeenth century, and education, except for the priesthood, did not take a peasant much further than the catechism. The Church tended,

The English navigator Sir Francis Drake (c.1540–1596) led English pirates in attacks on Spanish and Portuguese trade monopolies in the West Indies.

governed. But America was far away, and enforcement of laws difficult. It was all the harder to protect the native population when a catastrophic drop in its numbers created a labour shortage. The early settlers had brought smallpox to the Caribbean (its original source seems to have been Africa) and one of Cortés's men took it to the mainland; this

in fact, for all the devoted work of many of its clergy, to remain an imported, colonial church. Ironically, even the attempts of churchmen to protect the native Christians had the effect of isolating them (by, for instance, not teaching them Spanish) from the routes to integration with the possessors of power in their societies.

Perhaps this was inevitable. The Catholic monopoly in Spanish and Portuguese America was bound to mean a large measure of identification of the Church with the political structure: it was an important reinforcement for a thinly spread administrative apparatus and it was not only crusading zeal which made the Spanish enthusiastic proselytizers. The Inquisition was soon set up in New Spain and it was the Church of the Counter-Reformation which shaped American Catholicism south of the Rio Grande. This had important consequences much later; although some priests were to play important parts in the revolutionary and independence movements of South America, and though in the eighteenth century the Jesuits were to incur the wrath of the Portuguese settlers and government of Brazil for their efforts to protect the natives, the Church as an organization never found it easy to adopt a progressive stance. In the very long run, this meant that in the politics of independent Latin America, liberalism would take on the associations of anti-clericalism it was to have in Catholic Europe. This was all in marked contrast to the religiously pluralistic society which was taking root contemporaneously in British North America.

AGRICULTURE IN THE CARIBBEAN

For all the spectacular inflow of bullion from the mainland colonies, the New World was probably of the greatest economic importance to Europe throughout most of the early modern period because of the Caribbean islands. This importance rested on their agricultural produce, above all on sugar, introduced first by the Arabs to Europe, in Sicily and Spain, and then carried by Europeans first to Madeira and the Canaries, and then to the New World. Both the Caribbean and Brazil were transformed economically by this crop. Medieval man had sweetened his food with honey; by 1700 sugar, though still expensive, was a European necessity and was, with tobacco, hardwood and coffee, the main product of the islands and the tap-root of the African slave trade. Together, these exports gave the planters great importance in the affairs of their metropolitan countries.

The story of large-scale Caribbean agriculture began with the Spanish settlers, who quickly started growing fruit (which they had brought from Europe) and raising cattle.

In this 18th-century engraving black slave workers are shown processing tobacco in Santo Domingo, the capital of the present-day Dominican Republic, then the Spanish colony of Hispaniola.

1. Negre qui ejambe le tabac.
2. Negre qui torque le tabac.
3. Negre qui le met en rolle.
4. Tabac a la pente.

When they introduced rice and sugar, production was for a long time held back by a shortage of labour, as the native populations of the islands succumbed to European ill-treatment and disease. The next economic phase was the establishment by later arrivals of parasitic industries: piracy and smuggling. The Spanish occupation of the larger Caribbean islands – the Greater Antilles – still left hundreds of smaller islands unoccupied, most of them on the Atlantic fringe. These attracted the attention of English, French and Dutch captains who found them useful as bases from which to prey on Spanish ships going home from New Spain, and for contraband trade with the Spanish colonists who wanted their goods. European settlements appeared, too, on the Venezuelan coast where there was salt for preserving meat. Where individuals led, governmental enterprises – English royal concessions and the Dutch West India Company – followed in the seventeenth century.

ENGLISH SETTLEMENTS

By the early seventeenth century, the English had for decades been looking for suitable places for what contemporaries called "plantations" – that is, settler colonies – in the New World. They tried the North American mainland first. Then, in the 1620s they established their first two successful West Indian colonies, on St Christopher in the Leeward Isles, and Barbados. Both prospered; by 1630 St Christopher had about 3,000 inhabitants and Barbados about 2,000. This success was based on tobacco, the drug which, with syphilis (believed to have been in Europe at Cadiz in 1493) and the cheap automobile, some have thought to be the New World's revenge for its violation by the old. These tobacco colonies rapidly became of great importance to England not only because of the customs revenue they supplied, but also because the new growth of population in the

Cane sugar was one of the most profitable products traded between the New World and the Old. In the 17th century it became an affordable commodity and there was great competition among sugar producers and importers. This 17th-century engraving shows a sugar mill in the West Indies.

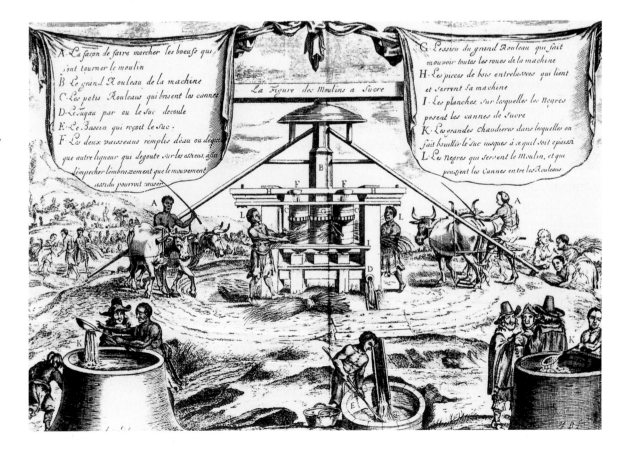

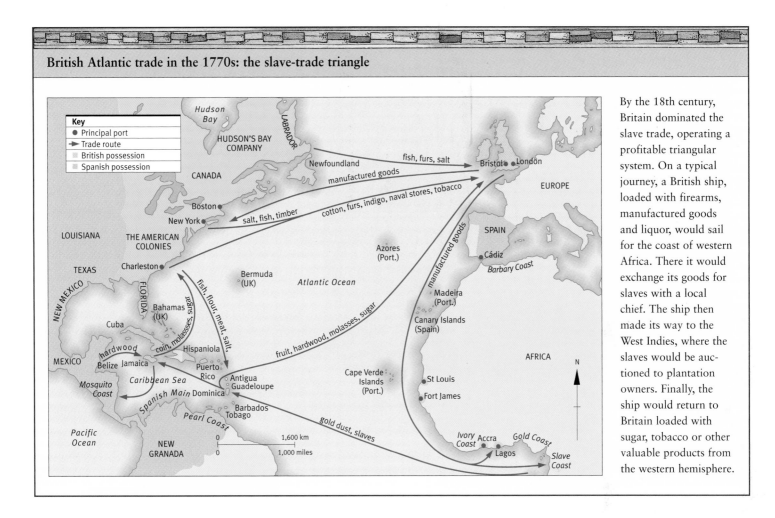

British Atlantic trade in the 1770s: the slave-trade triangle

By the 18th century, Britain dominated the slave trade, operating a profitable triangular system. On a typical journey, a British ship, loaded with firearms, manufactured goods and liquor, would sail for the coast of western Africa. There it would exchange its goods for slaves with a local chief. The ship then made its way to the West Indies, where the slaves would be auctioned to plantation owners. Finally, the ship would return to Britain loaded with sugar, tobacco or other valuable products from the western hemisphere.

Caribbean stimulated demand for exports and provided fresh opportunities for interloping in the trade of the Spanish Empire. Soon the English were joined by the French in this lucrative business, the French occupying the Windward Isles, the English the rest of the Leewards. In the 1640s there were about 7,000 French in the West Indies, and over 50,000 English.

SUGAR AND SLAVES

After the mid-seventeenth century the tide of English emigration to the New World was diverted to North America and the West Indies were not again to reach such high figures of white settlement. This was partly because sugar joined tobacco as a staple crop.

Tobacco can be produced economically in small quantities; it had therefore suited the multiplication of small holdings and the building up of a large immigrant population of whites. Sugar was economic only if cultivated in large units; it suited the big plantation, worked by large numbers, and these were likely to be black slaves, given the decline of local population in the sixteenth century. The Dutch supplied the slaves and aspired to the sort of general commercial monopoly in the western hemisphere which they were winning in the Far East, working out of a base at the mouth of the Hudson river, New Amsterdam. This was the beginning of a great demographic change in the Caribbean. In 1643 Barbados had 37,000 white inhabitants and only 6,000 black African slaves; by 1660 there were over 50,000 of the latter.

This 16th-century engraving shows trade ships preparing to depart from Lisbon, Portugal, bound for the West Indies, North America and Brazil.

With the appearance of sugar, the French colonies of Guadeloupe and Martinique took on a new importance and they, too, wanted slaves. A complex process of growth was under way. The huge and growing Caribbean market for slaves and imported European goods was added to that already offered by a Spanish Empire increasingly unable to defend its economic monopoly. This fixed the role of the West Indies in the relationships of the powers for the next century. They were long a prey to disorder, the Caribbean an area where colonial frontiers met and policing was poor and there were great prizes to be won (in one year a Dutch captain took the great *flota* bearing home the year's treasure from the Indies to Spain). Not surprisingly, they became the classical and, indeed, legendary hunting-ground of pirates, whose heyday was the last quarter of the seventeenth century. Gradually, the great powers fought out their disputes until they arrived at acceptable agreements, but this was to take a long time. Meanwhile, through the eighteenth century the West Indies and Brazil provided the great market for slaves and sustained most of that trade. As time passed, it too became involved in another economy besides those of Europe, Africa and New Spain: that of a new North America.

NORTH AMERICA IS SETTLED

FOR A LONG TIME, by all the standards of classical colonial theory, settlement in North America was a poor second in attractiveness to Latin America or the Caribbean. Precious metals were not discovered there and though there were furs in the north, there seemed to be little else that Europe wanted from that region. Yet there was nowhere else to go, given the Spanish monopoly to the south, and a great many nations tried it. The Spanish expansion north of the Rio Grande need not concern us, for it was hardly an occupation, more of a missionary exercise, while Spanish Florida's importance was strategical, for it gave some protection to Spanish communications with Europe by the northern outlet from the Caribbean. It was the settlement of the Atlantic coast which drew other Europeans. There was even briefly a New Sweden, taking its place beside New Netherlands, New England and New France.

The motives for settling North America were often those which operated elsewhere, though the crusading, missionary zeal of the Reconquest mentality was almost entirely missing further north. For most of the sixteenth century the Englishmen, who were the most frequent explorers of North American possibilities, thought there might be mines there to rival those of the Spanish Indies. Others believed that population pressure made emigration desirable and increasing knowledge revealed ample land in temperate climates with, unlike Mexico, very few native inhabitants. There was also a constant pull in the lure of finding a northwest passage to Asia.

EUROPEAN SETTLERS

By 1600, there had been much exploration, but only one (unsuccessful) settlement north of Florida, at Roanoke, Virginia. The English were too weak, the French too distracted, to achieve more. With the seventeenth century there came more strenuous, better-organized and better-financed efforts, the discovery of the possibility of growing some important staples on the mainland, a set of political changes in England which favoured emigration, and the emergence of England as a great naval power. Between them, these facts brought about a revolutionary transformation of the Atlantic littoral. The wilderness of 1600, inhabited by a few Indians, was a hundred years later an important site of civilization. In many places settlers had pushed as far inland as the mountain barrier of the Alleghenies. Meanwhile the French had established a line of posts along the valley of the St Lawrence and the Great Lakes. In this huge right-angle of settlement lived about a half-million white people, mainly of British and French stock.

Spain claimed all North America, but this had long been contested by the English on the ground that "prescription without possession availeth nothing". The Elizabethan adventurers had explored much of the coast and gave the name "Virginia", in honour of their queen, to all the territory north of thirty degrees of latitude. In 1606 James I granted a charter to a Virginia company to establish colonies. This was only formally the beginning; the company's affairs soon required revision of its structure and there were unprofitable initiatives in plenty, but in 1607 there was already established the first English settlement in America which was to survive, at Jamestown, in modern Virginia. It only just came through its early trials but by 1620 its "starving time" was far behind it and it prospered. In 1608, the year after Jamestown's foundation, the French explorer Samuel de Champlain built a small fort at Quebec. For the immediate future the French colony was so insecure that its food had to be brought from France, but it was the beginning of settlement in Canada. Finally, in 1609, the Dutch sent an English explorer, Henry Hudson, to find a northeast passage to Asia. When he was unsuccessful he turned completely around and sailed across the Atlantic to look for a northwestern one. Instead, he discovered the river that bears his name and established a preliminary Dutch

At the beginning of the 18th century, the British establishments in North America were located on a narrow coastal strip where there were still areas that had not been colonized. This 18th-century engraving shows a view of the British colony of New York.

claim by doing so. Within a few years there were Dutch settlements along the river, on Manhattan and on Long Island.

ENGLISH SUCCESSES

The English were in the lead in North America and remained so. They prospered because of two new facts. One was the technique, of which they were the first and most successful exponents, of transporting whole communities, men, women and children. These set up agricultural colonies which worked the land with their own labour and soon became independent of the mother country for their livelihood. The second was the discovery of tobacco, which became a staple first for Virginia and then for Maryland, a colony whose settlement began in 1634. Further north, the availability of land which could be cultivated on European lines assured the survival of the colonies; although interest in the area had originally been awoken by the prospects of fur-trading and fishery there was soon a small surplus of grain for export. This was an attractive prospect for land-hungry Englishmen in a country widely believed in the early seventeenth century to be over-populated. Something like 20,000 went to "New England" in the 1630s.

Another distinctive feature of the New England colonies was their association with religious dissent and Calvinistic Protestantism. They would not have been what they were without the Reformation. Although the usual economic motives were at work in the settlements, the leadership among immigrants to Massachusetts in the 1630s of men associated with the Puritan wing of English Protestantism bore fruit in a group of

The Seven Years' War for control of the French settlement of Quebec in Canada ended with the British victory at the Battle of Quebec in 1759. Under General James Wolfe, British troops sailed up the St Lawrence River and scaled steep cliffs to launch an attack on the French battalions, as shown in this contemporary engraving.

colonies whose constitutions varied from theocratic oligarchy to democracy. Though sometimes led by members of the English gentry, they shed more rapidly than the southern colonies their inhibitions about radical departures from English social and political practice, and their religious nonconformity did as much as the conditions in which they had to survive to bring this about. At some moments during the English constitutional troubles of the mid-century it even seemed that the colonies of New England might escape from the control of the Crown altogether, but this did not happen.

CANADIAN ORIGINS

After the Dutch settlements of what was subsequently New York State had been swallowed up by the English, the North American littoral in 1700 from Florida north to the Kennebec river was organized as twelve colonies (a thirteenth, Georgia, appeared in 1732) in which lived some 400,000 whites and perhaps a tenth as many black slaves. Further north lay still disputed territory and then lands that were indisputably French. In these, colonists were much thinner on the ground than in the English settlements. There were perhaps 15,000 French in North America in all and they had benefited from no such large migrations of communities as had the English colonies. Many of them were hunters and trappers, missionaries and explorers, strung out over the length of the St Lawrence and dotted about in the Great Lakes region and even beyond. New France was a huge area on the map, but outside the St Lawrence valley and Quebec it was only a scatter of strategically and commercially important forts and trading posts. Nor was density of settlement the only difference between the French and English colonial

An episode from one of the first English expeditions to the Arctic is depicted in this illustration dating from 1587. The native Inuit are shown attempting to defend themselves from the European guns by firing arrows at their attackers.

zones. New France was closely supervised from home; after 1663 a company structure had been abandoned in favour of direct royal rule and Canada was governed by a French governor with the advice of the *intendant* much as a French province was governed at home. There was no religious liberty; the Church in Canada was monopolistic and missionary. Its history is full of glorious examples of bravery and martyrdom, and also of bitter intransigence. The farms of the settled area were grouped in *seigneuries*, a device which had some value in decentralizing administrative responsibility. Social forms therefore reproduced those of the Old World much more than those in the English settlements, even to the extent of throwing up a nobility with Canadian titles.

LIFE IN THE EARLY COLONIES

The English colonies were very diverse. Strung out as they were over almost the whole Atlantic seaboard, they contained a great variety of climate, economy and terrain.

Their origins reflected a wide range of motives and methods of foundation. They soon became somewhat ethnically mixed, for after 1688 Scottish, Irish, German, Huguenot and Swiss emigrants had begun to arrive in appreciable numbers, though for a very long time the predominance of the English language and the relatively small numbers of non-English-speaking immigrants would maintain a culture overwhelmingly Anglo-Saxon. There was religious diversity and even by 1700 a large measure of effective religious toleration, though some of the colonies had close association with specific religious denominations. All this increased the colonies' difficulty in seeing themselves as one society. They had no American centre; the Crown and the home country were the foci of the colonies' collective life, as English culture was still their background. None the less, it was already obvious that the English North American colonies offered individuals opportunities for advancement unavailable either in the more strictly and closely regulated society of Canada or at home in Europe.

By 1700, some colonies had already shown a tendency to grasp whatever freedom fromn royal control was available to them. It is tempting to look back a long way for evidence of the spirit of independence which was later to play so big a part in popular tradition. In fact, it would be a misconception to read the prehistory of the United States in these terms. The "Pilgrim Fathers" who landed at Cape Cod in 1620 were not rediscovered or inserted in their prominent place in the national mythology until the end of the eighteenth century. Yet they had, indeed, wanted to make a *New* England. What can be seen much earlier than the idea of independence is the emergence of facts which would in the future make it easier to think in terms of independence and unity. One was the slow strengthening of a representative tradition in the first century of settlement. For all their initial diversity, in the early eighteenth century each colony settled down to work through some sort of representative assembly which spoke for its inhabitants to a royal governor appointed in London. Some of the settlements had needed to cooperate with one another against the Indians at an early date, and in the French wars this had become even more important. When the French loosed their Huron allies against the British colonists, it helped to create a sense of common interest among the individual colonies (as well as spurring on the British to enlist on their side the Iroquois, the hereditary foes of the Huron).

ECONOMICS AND GOVERNMENT

From economic diversity, too, a measure of economic inter-relatedness was emerging. The middle and southern colonies produced plantation crops of rice, tobacco, indigo and timber; New England built ships, refined and distilled molasses and grain spirits, grew corn and fished. There was a growing and apparent logic in thinking that the Americans might perhaps be able to run their affairs in their own interest – including that of the West Indian colonies – better than in that of the mother country. Economic growth was changing attitudes, too. The northern mainland colonies of New England were on the whole underprized and even disliked in the mother country. They competed in shipbuilding and, illegally, in the Caribbean trade; unlike plantation colonies, they produced nothing that the mother country wanted. Besides, they were full of religious dissenters.

In the eighteenth century British America made great progress in wealth and civilization. The total colonial population had continued to grow and was well over a million by halfway through the century. It was being pointed out in the 1760s that the mainland colonies were going to be worth much more to Great Britain than the West Indies had been. By 1763, Philadelphia could rival many European cities in stylishness and cultivation. A great uncertainty had been removed in 1763, too, for Canada had been conquered and was by the peace treaty of that year to remain British. This changed the outlook of many Americans both towards the value of the protection afforded by the imperial government and towards the question of further expansion to the west.

As farming settlers tended to fill up the coastal plain they came to press through the mountain barrier and down the river valleys beyond, eventually to the upper Ohio and the northwest. The danger of conflict with the French as a result was now removed, but this was not the only consideration which faced the British government in handling this movement after 1763. There were the rights and the likely reactions of the Native American Indians to take into account. To antagonize them would be to court danger, but if Indian wars were to be avoided by holding the colonists back, then the frontier would have to be policed by British troops for that purpose, too. The result was a decision of government in London to impose a western land policy which would limit expansion, to raise taxes in the colonies to pay for the costs of defending forces, and to tighten up the commercial system and cease to wink at infringements in its working. It was unfortunate that all this was coming to a head in the last years in which the old assumptions about the economics of colonial dependencies and their relationship to the mother country were accepted without demur by the makers of colonial policy in London.

THE CONSEQUENCES OF COLONIALISM IN THE AMERICAS

By the end of the eighteenth century about two and a half centuries had gone by since European settlement in the New World began. The overall effect of expansion in the Americas upon European history had already been immense, but is far from easy to define. Eventually, it is clear, all the colonial powers had, by this time, been able to extract some economic profit from their colonies, though they did so in different ways. The flow of silver to Spain was the most obvious, and this had, of course, implications for the European economy as a whole and even for Asia. Growing colonial populations also helped to stimulate European exports and manufactures. In this respect the English colonies were of the greatest importance, pointing the way to a growing flow of people from Europe, which was to culminate in the last of that continent's major folk-migrations in the nineteenth and early twentieth centuries. To colonial expansion, too, must be linked the enormous growth of European shipping and shipbuilding. Whether engaged in slaving,

Tea, coffee and chocolate from the colonies became fashionable drinks in many parts of Europe, as reflected in this 18th-century painting. The first chocolate shop in London was opened by a Frenchman in 1657.

contraband trading, legal import and export between metropolis and colony or fishing to supply new consumer markets, shipbuilders, shipowners and captains benefited. There was an incremental and incalculable effect at work. It is thus very hard to sum up the total effect of the possession of American colonies on the imperialist powers in the first age of imperialism.

Of the overriding cultural and political importance of that fact in the long run we can speak with more confidence: the western hemisphere was to be culturally European. Spanish, Portuguese and English might be very different, but they offered edited versions of the same text. They all brought selections from European civilization with them. Politically, that was to mean that from Tierra del Fuego to Hudson Bay two continents would eventually be organized on European legal and administrative principles even when they ceased to remain dependent on colonial power. The hemisphere was also going to be Christian; when Hinduism or Islam eventually made their appearance there, it would be as the possession of small minorities, not as rivals to a basically Christian culture.

THE ENGLISH INHERITANCE

More specifically within these generalities, great political importance was to lie in the further differentiation of the Americas, north and south. It was always true that in cultural terms North American native life could offer no such impressive human achievements as the civilizations of Central and South America. But colonialism was a differentiating fact, too. It is not fanciful to recall ancient parallels. The colonies of the ancient Greek cities were set up by their parent states as communities largely independent, in a way similar to the English settlements of the North American littoral. Once established, they tended to evolve towards a self-conscious identity of their own. The Spanish empire displayed the deployment of a regular pattern of institutions essentially metropolitan and imperial, rather as had done the provinces of imperial Rome. It took time for it to be clear that the basic forms already given to the evolution of British North America were to shape the kernel of a future world power. That evolution was therefore to prove a shaper of world as well as American history. Two great transforming factors had still to operate before the North American future was fixed in its main lines: the differing environments revealed as the northern continent filled up by movement to the west, and a much greater flow of non-Anglo-Saxon immigration. But these forces would flow into and around moulds set by the English inheritance, which would leave its mark on the future United States as Byzantium left its own on Russia. Nations do not shake off their origins, they only learn to view them in different ways. Sometimes outsiders can see this best. It was a German statesman who remarked towards the end of the nineteenth century that its most important international fact was that Great Britain and the United States spoke the same language.

The British American colonies' economic resources in the 18th century

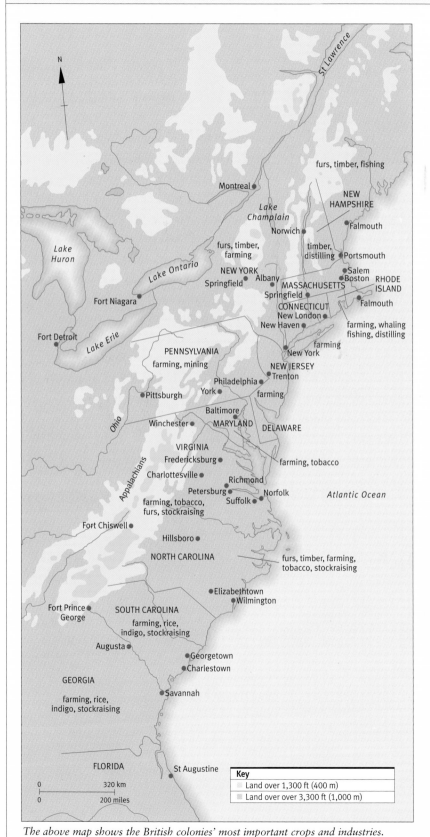

The above map shows the British colonies' most important crops and industries.

Population growth and high birth rates in North America throughout the 18th century (in 1763 there were around two million inhabitants) allowed large areas of land to be colonized, stimulating economic growth. At the beginning of the century, the North American economy was based on subsistence farming. However, by 1750, much settled land was given over to the cultivation of cash crops for export to a world market.

Although wheat was a staple in all of them, the 13 colonies in British America developed very diverse economies. The New England colonies' forests and streams supported fur and timber industries; the latter, combined with the region's natural harbours, produced a major shipbuilding industry. Fishing and whaling were similarly important. Pennsylvania was one of the richest colonies by the end of the 18th century, mainly due to the high levels of immigration to the fertile Delaware valley. The middle colonies produced grain and flour for export, while in the southern colonies large plantations, usually run on slave labour, became commonplace. The exception to this was North Carolina, cut off from international trade by its harsh coastline, where small farms were prevalent. This colony also became an important supplier of naval stores. South Carolina's more navigable coastline meant that it enjoyed trade with England and the West Indies, producing rice and, from 1742, indigo for export around the world. (Entrepreneurs in both Georgia and the Carolinas tried and failed to produce silk.) The economies of Virginia and Maryland were almost entirely reliant on tobacco which had been introduced there in the early 17th century. Both colonies were hit hard by the British Navigation Act of 1760, which stated that tobacco could be exported only to Britain.

By 1770, the total value to Great Britain of export from the North American colonies exceeded £1,000,000 sterling per annum – almost four times the total value of export in 1710.

5 WORLD HISTORY'S NEW SHAPE

IN 1776 THERE BEGAN IN AMERICA the first of a series of colonial revolts which were to take several decades to work themselves out. Besides marking an epoch in the history of the American continents these upheavals also provide a convenient vantage-ground from which to consider the first phase of European hegemony as a whole. In other parts of the world, too, something of a change of rhythm was marked by such facts as the elimination of serious French competition to the British in India, and the opening of Australasia, the last discovered and habitable continent, to settlement. At the end of the eighteenth century there is a sense of completing one era and opening another; it is a good point for assessment of the difference made by the previous three centuries to the history of the globe.

ATLANTIC EUROPE'S IMPERIALISM

Between the sixteenth and eighteenth centuries, outright conquest and occupation were the main form of European hegemony. They provided wealth Europe could use to increase still further its relative superiority over other civilizations and they set up political structures which diffused other forms of European influence. They were the work of a handful of European states which were the first world powers in the geographical range of their interests, even if not in their strength: the Atlantic nations to which the age of discoveries had given opportunities and historical destinies distinct from those of other European states.

The first to seize these opportunities had been Spain and Portugal, the only great

In 1503 the House of Contracts in Seville, Spain, was founded to deal with trade and navigation with Africa and the East. Officials here controlled virtually every aspect of this trade, including commercial traffic, the organization of the fleets, the payment and supervision of port entry taxes and nautical training. They also acted as mediators in trade disputes.

colonial powers of the sixteenth century. They had long passed their zenith by 1763, when the Peace of Paris, which ended the Seven Years' War, was signed. This treaty is a convenient marker of a new world order which had already replaced that dominated by Spain and Portugal. It registered the ascendancy of Great Britain in the rivalry with France overseas, which had preoccupied her for nearly three-quarters of a century. The duel was not over, and the French could still be hopeful that they would recover lost ground. Great Britain, none the less, was the great imperial power of the future. These two nations had eclipsed the Dutch, whose empire had been built, like theirs, in the seventeenth century, in the era of declining Portuguese and Spanish power. But Spain, Portugal and the United Provinces all still held important colonial territories and had left enduring marks on the world map.

OVERSEAS ISSUES IN DIPLOMACY

The five major European colonial nations had by the eighteenth century been differentiated by their oceanic history, both from the land-locked states of central Europe and from those of the Mediterranean so important in earlier centuries. Their special colonial and overseas trade interests had given their diplomats new causes and places over which to compete. Most other states had been slower to recognize how important issues outside Europe might be, and so, indeed, had even some of these five at times. Spain had fought grimly enough first for the Habsburgs in Italy, then against the Ottomans, and finally for European supremacy in the Thirty Years' War, to waste the treasure of the Indies in the process. In their long duel with the British, the French were always more liable than their rivals to distraction and the diversion of their

This engraving, entitled *The Discoveries of Captain Cook and de la Pérouse*, dates from c.1798. After Cook's death, a French research expedition was led by de la Pérouse in 1785. Britain's Vancouver Expedition was commissioned in the 1790s to complete Cook's hydrographical work in New Zealand, Australia and Oceania and on the Pacific coast of North America.

resources to continental ends. At the outset, the discernment that extra-European issues might be intrinsically tangled with European interests in diplomacy had, after all, barely existed. Once the Spanish and Portuguese had demarcated their interests to their own satisfaction there was little to concern other European nations. The fate of a French Huguenot settlement in Florida or the flouting of the vague Spanish claims, which was implicit in the Roanoke voyages, hardly troubled the minds of European diplomats, let alone shaped their negotiations. This situation began to change when English pirates and adventurers countenanced by Elizabeth I began to inflict real damage on the Spanish fleets and colonies. They were soon joined by the Dutch and from this time one of the great themes of the diplomacy of the next century was apparent; as a French minister wrote under Louis XIV, "Trade is the cause of a perpetual combat in war and in peace between the nations of Europe". So much had things changed in two hundred years.

Rulers had, of course, always been concerned with wealth and the opportunity of increasing it. Venice had long defended her commerce by diplomatic means and the English had often safeguarded their cloth exports to Flanders by treaty. It was widely accepted that there was only so much profit to go around and that one country could therefore only gain at the expense of others. But it was a long time before diplomacy had to take account of the pursuit of wealth outside Europe. There was even an attempt to segregate such matters; in 1559 the French and Spanish agreed that what their captains

This 16th-century gold medallion, bearing a bust of Queen Elizabeth I of England, commemorates the British victory over the Spanish Armada in 1588.

did to one another "beyond the line" (which meant at that time west of the Azores, and south of the Tropic of Cancer) should not be taken as a reason for hostility between the two states in Europe.

TRADE WARS

THE CHANGE TO A NEW SET of diplomatic assumptions, if that is the way to put it, began in conflicts over trade with the Spanish Empire. Contemporary thinking took it for granted that in the colonial relationship the interests of the metropolitan power were always paramount. In so far as those interests were economic, settlement colonies were intended to produce, either by exploiting their mineral and natural resources, or by their balance of trade with the mother country, a net advantage to the latter and, if possible, self-sufficiency, while her trading bases gave her the domination of certain areas of international traffic. By 1600 it was clear that claims would be settled by sea-power, and since the defeat of the Armada Spanish sea-power no longer commanded the respect it had done. Essentially, Philip was caught in a dilemma: the dispersal of his effort and interest between Europe – where the struggle with the Valois and Elizabeth, the Dutch Revolt, and the Counter-Reformation all claimed his resources – and the Indies, where safety could have lain only in sea-power and the organization of effective Spanish supply of the colonists' needs. The choice was to try to keep the empire, but to use it to pay for European policies. This was to underrate the difficulties of controlling so huge an empire through sixteenth-century bureaucracy and communications. Nevertheless a huge and complicated system of regular sailings in convoy, the concentration of colonial trade in a few authorized ports and policing by coastguard squadrons were ways in which the Spanish tried to keep the wealth of the Indies to themselves.

It was the Dutch who first made it clear that they were prepared to fight for a share of such prizes and therefore first forced diplomats to turn their attention and skills to regulating matters outside Europe. For the Dutch, predominance in trade overrode other considerations. What they would do for it was made clear from the start of the seventeenth century, in the East Indies, the Caribbean, and Brazil, where they engaged great fleets against the Spanish–Portuguese defence of the world's chief producer of sugar. The last provided their only serious failure, for in 1654 the Portuguese were able to evict the Dutch garrisons and resume control without subsequent challenge.

ANGLO-DUTCH TRADE WARS

The quest for commercial wealth cut across the wishes of the most Protestant of English seventeenth-century governments; England had been an ally of the Dutch rebels in the previous century and Cromwell would have liked nothing better than the leadership of a Protestant alliance against Catholic Spain. Instead he found himself fighting the first of three Anglo-Dutch wars. The first (1652–4) was essentially a trade war. What was at issue was the English decision to restrict imports to England to goods travelling in English ships or those of the country producing the goods. This was a deliberate attempt to encourage English shipping and put it in a position to catch up with the Dutch. It struck at the heart of Dutch prosperity, its European carrying trade and, in

particular, that in Baltic goods. The Commonwealth had a good navy and won. The second round came in 1665, after the Dutch had been further provoked by the English seizure of New Amsterdam. In this war the Dutch had the French and Danes as allies and also had the best of it at sea. At the peace they were therefore able to win an easing of the English restrictions on imports, although they left New Amsterdam to the English in exchange for an offshoot of Barbados at Surinam. This was decided by the Treaty of Breda (1667), the first multilateral European peace settlement to say as much about the regulation of extra-European affairs as European. By it France surrendered West Indian islands to England and received in return recognition of her possession of the uninhabited and uninviting but strategically important territory of Acadia. The English had done well; the new

By the late 17th century Amsterdam was the main distribution centre in Europe and most Dutch cities were governed by the wealthiest merchants or by the descendants of great merchant families. This portrait, painted in 1669 by Bartholomeus van der Helst (1613–1670), depicts the Dutch merchant Daniel Bernhard.

t' Fort nieuw Amsterdam op de Manhatans.

In 1626 the governor of the Dutch West India Company, Peter Minuit, bought the island of Manhattan from the Indians and created a colony, New Amsterdam, which is depicted in this detail from a contemporary engraving. New Amsterdam passed into English hands in 1664.

Caribbean acquisitions followed in a tradition established under the Commonwealth, when Jamaica had been taken from Spain. It was England's first transoceanic acquisition of territory by conquest.

Cromwell's policies have been seen as a decisive turn towards conscious imperial policy. This may be attributing too much to his vision. The returned Stuarts indeed kept intact most of the "Navigation" system for the protection of shipping and colonial trade, as well as hanging on to Jamaica and continuing to recognize the new importance of the West Indies. Charles II gave a charter to a new company, named after Hudson Bay, to contest with the French the fur trade of the north and west. He and his in other ways inadequate successor, James II, at least maintained (even if with some setbacks) English naval strength so that it was available to William of Orange in his wars with Louis XIV.

THE ANGLO-FRENCH STRUGGLE

It would be tedious to trace the detailed changes of the century and a half after 1660 when the new imperial emphasis, first of English and then of British diplomacy, came to maturity. A brief third Anglo-Dutch war (it had virtually no important consequences) does not really belong to this epoch, which is dominated by the long rivalry of England and France. The War of the League of Augsburg (or King William's War, as it was called in America) brought much colonial fighting, but no great changes. The War of the Spanish Succession was very different. It was a world war, the first of the modern era, about the fate of the Spanish Empire as well as about French power. At its close, the British not only won Acadia (henceforth Nova Scotia) and other acquisitions in the western hemisphere from the French, but also the right to supply slaves to the Spanish colonies and to send one ship a year with merchandise to trade with them.

GLOBAL WARFARE

Overseas matters loomed larger and larger in British foreign policy after the War of the Spanish Succession. European considerations mattered less, in spite of the change of dynasty in 1714, when the elector of Hanover became the first king of Great Britain. Though there were some embarrassing moments, British policy remained remarkably consistent, always swinging back to the goals of promoting, sustaining and extending British commerce. Often this was best done by seeking to maintain a general peace, sometimes by diplomatic pressure (as when the Habsburgs were persuaded to withdraw a scheme for an Ostend company to trade with Asia), sometimes by fighting to maintain privileges or strategical advantage.

The importance of war became clearer and clearer. The first time that two European powers ever went to war on a purely non-European issue came in 1739 when the British government began hostilities with

Spain over, in essence, the Spanish right of search in the Caribbean – or, as the Spanish might have put it, over the steps they properly took to secure their empire against abuse of the trading privileges granted in 1713. This was to be remembered as the "War of Jenkins' Ear" – the organ produced in pickle by its owner in the House of Commons, whose sensitive patriotism was inflamed and outraged to hear of the alleged mutilation by a Spanish coastguard. The conflict soon became caught up with the War of the Austrian Succession, and therefore became an Anglo-French struggle. The peace of 1748 did not much change the respective territorial position of the two rivals, nor did it end fighting in North America, where the French appeared to be about to cut off the British settlements for ever from the American west by a chain of forts. The British government sent regular contingents to America for the first time in order to meet this danger, but were unsuccessful; only in the Seven Years' War did a British minister grasp that the chance of a final decision in the long duel existed because of France's commitment to her ally Austria in Europe. Once British resources were allocated accordingly, sweeping victories in North America and India were followed by others in the Caribbean, some at the expense of Spain. A British force even seized the Philippines. It was global war.

THE FIRST BRITISH EMPIRE

THE PEACE OF 1763 DID NOT in fact go so far in crippling France and Spain as many Britons had wanted. But it virtually eliminated French competition in North America and India. When it was a question of retaining Canada or Guadeloupe, a sugar-producing island, one consideration in favour of keeping Canada was that competition from increased sugar production within the empire was feared by Caribbean planters already under the British flag. The result was a huge new British empire. By 1763, the whole of eastern North America and the Gulf Coast as far west as the mouth of the Mississippi was British. The elimination of French Canada had blown away the threat – or, from the French point of view, the hope – of a French empire of the Mississippi valley, stretching from the St Lawrence to New Orleans, which had been created by the great French explorers of the seventeenth century. Off the continental coast the Bahamas were the northern link of an island chain that ran down through the lesser Antilles to Tobago,

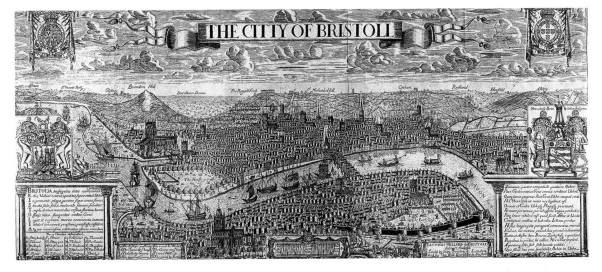

The English city of Bristol, an important port since the 13th century, is shown in this 17th-century engraving.

England's numerous well-protected ports played a key role in its economic growth. This 18th-century painting depicts the bustling docks and quay at the port of Bristol.

and all but enclosed the Caribbean. Within it, Jamaica, Honduras and the Belize coast were British. In the Peace of 1713, the British had exacted a limited legal right to trade in slaves with the Spanish Empire, which they quickly pressed far beyond its intended limits. In Africa there were only a few British posts on the Gold Coast but these were the bases of the huge African slave trade. In Asia the direct government of Bengal was about to provide a start to the territorial phase of British expansion in India.

THE MERCHANT MARINE

British imperial supremacy was based on sea-power. Its ultimate origins could be sought in the ships built by Henry VIII, among the greatest warships of the age (the *Harry Grâce à Dieu* carried 186 guns), but this early start was neglected under his successors until the reign of Elizabeth I. Her captains, with little financing available either from Crown or commercial investors, built both a fighting tradition and better ships from the profits of operations against the Spanish. Again, there was an ebbing of interest and effort under the early Stuart kings. The royal administration could not afford ships (and paying for new ones was, indeed, one of the causes of the royal taxes Parliament had raged over). It was only under the Commonwealth, ironically, that the serious and continuing interest in naval power which sustained the Royal Navy of the future began. By that time, the connexion between Dutch superiority in merchant shipping and their naval strength had been taken to heart and the upshot was the Navigation Act which provoked the first Anglo-Dutch war. A strong merchant marine provided a nursery of seamen for fighting vessels and the flow of trade whose taxation by customs dues would finance the upkeep of specialized warships. A strong merchant marine could only be built upon carrying the goods of other nations: hence the importance of competing, if necessary by gunfire, and of breaking into such reserved areas as the Spanish American trade.

MARITIME TECHNOLOGY

The machines which were evolved to do the fighting in the competition for trade underwent steady improvement and specialization, but no revolutionary change, between the fifteenth and nineteenth centuries. Once square-rigging and broadside firing had been adopted, the essential shape of vessels was determined, though individual design could still do much to give sailing superiority and the French usually built better ships than Great Britain during the eighteenth-century duel between the two countries. In the sixteenth century, under English influence, ships grew longer in proportion to their beam. The relative height of the forecastle and poop above the deck gradually came down, too, over the whole period. Bronze guns reached a high level of development even in the early seventeenth century; thereafter gunnery changed by improvement in design, accuracy and weight of shot. There were two significant eighteenth-century innovations, the short-range but large-calibre and heavy-shotted iron carronade, which greatly increased the power of even small

vessels, and a firing mechanism incorporating a flintlock, which made possible more precise control of the guns.

Specialization of function and design between warships and merchant vessels was accepted by the middle of the seventeenth century, though the line was still somewhat blurred by the existence of older vessels and the practice of privateering. This was a way of obtaining naval power on the cheap. In time of war, governments authorized individual private captains or their employers to prey upon enemy shipping, taking profits from the prizes they made. It was a form of regularized piracy and English, Dutch and French privateers all operated at various times with great success against one another's traders. The first great privateering war was that fought unsuccessfully against the English and Dutch under King William by the French.

Other seventeenth-century innovations were tactical and administrative. Signalling became formalized and the first Fighting Instructions were issued to the Royal Navy. Recruitment became more important; the press-gang appeared in England (the French used naval conscription in the maritime provinces). In this way large fleets were manned and it became clear that, given equality of

A commercial port began to develop around the estuary of Plymouth Sound in the 16th century. At the end of the 17th century a military base, Devonport, was founded nearby and by the 18th century the large naval shipyard depicted in this contemporary painting had been established.

skill and the limited damage which could be done even by heavy guns, numbers were always likely to be decisive in the end.

BRITISH SEA-POWER

From the seminal period of development in the seventeenth century there emerged a naval supremacy which was to last over two centuries and underpin a worldwide *pax Britannica*. Dutch competition dropped away as the Republic bent under the strain of defending its independence on land against the French. The important maritime rival of the English was France and here it is possible to see that a decisive point had been passed by the end of King William's reign. By then, the dilemma of being great on land or sea had been decided by the French in favour of the land. From that time, the promise of a French naval supremacy was never to be revived, though French shipbuilders and captains would still win victories by their skill and courage. The English were not so distracted from oceanic power; they had only to keep their continental allies in the field, not to keep up great armies themselves. But there was a little more to it than a simple concentration of resources. British maritime strategy also evolved in a way very different from that of other sea-powers. Here, the French loss of interest in the navy of Louis XIV is relevant, for it came after the English had inflicted a resounding defeat in a fleet action in 1692, which discredited the French admirals. It was the first of many such victories which demonstrated an appreciation of the strategic reality that sea-power was in the end a matter of commanding the surface of the sea so that friendly ships could move on it in safety while those of the enemy could not. The key to this desirable end was the neutralization of the enemy's fleet. So long as it was there, a danger existed. The early defeat of the enemy's fleet in battle therefore became the supreme aim of British naval commanders for a century during which it gave the Royal Navy almost uninterrupted command of the seas and a formidable offensive tradition.

Naval strategy fed imperial enterprise indirectly as well as directly because it made more and more necessary the acquisition of bases from which squadrons could operate. This was particularly important in building the British Empire. In the late eighteenth century, too, that empire was about to undergo the loss of much of its settled territory and this would bring further into relief the way in which European hegemony was, outside the New World, still in 1800 a matter of trading stations, island plantations and bases, and the control of carrying trade, rather than of occupation of large areas.

Stock exchanges were founded in Amsterdam, London, Paris, Hamburg and Frankfurt during the 17th century. The Amsterdam Exchange is seen in this painting by Emmanuel de Witte (1617–1692).

A WORLD ECONOMY IN THE MAKING

Less than three centuries of even a limited form of imperialism revolutionized the world economy. Before 1500, there had been hundreds of more or less self-supporting and self-contained economies, some of them linked by trade. The Americas and Africa were almost, Australasia was entirely, unknown to Europe, communication within them was tiny in proportion to their huge extent, and there was a thin flow of luxury trade from Asia to Europe. By 1800, a world-wide network of exchange had appeared. Even Japan was a part of it and central Africa, though still mysterious and unknown, was linked to it through slavery and the Arabs. Its first two striking adumbrations had been the diversion of Asian trade with Europe to the sea routes dominated by the Portuguese and the flow of bullion from America to Europe. Without that stream, above all of silver, there could hardly have been a trade with

Precious metals extracted from Peruvian mines, such as the one shown in this 18th-century illustration, were highly sought after and quickly made an impact on the European economy. Other products, including foodstuffs, livestock, plants and minerals, were slowly introduced to early modern Europe, with varying degrees of success.

Asia for there was almost nothing produced in Europe that Asia wanted. This may have been the main importance of the bullion from the Americas, whose flow reached its peak at the end of the sixteenth century and in the early decades of the next.

Although a new abundance of precious metals was the first and most dramatically obvious economic effect of Europe's new interplay with Asia and America, it was less important than the general growth of trade, of which slaves from Africa for the Caribbean and Brazil formed a part. The slave-ships usually made their voyage back to Europe from the Americas loaded with the colonial

This illustration shows the boiling of bamboo shoots in 16th-century China to produce paper paste for export to Europe. The aim of trade with Asia was not to find new markets for European goods, but to supply Europe with luxury products. Except for arms and munitions, the only European commodity wanted in the East was silver.

At the beginning of the 16th century, tobacco was grown in medicinal gardens in Europe. By the 1850s the amount of tobacco imported from North America had exceeded that produced in Europe. This engraving of a tobacco plant dates from the late 18th century.

Tabaco — EST. CXLVI

Tea was first brought to Europe from China by the Dutch East India Company in 1609. In 1646 the English East India Company began to import it and the first shop to specialize in retailing tea was probably Twinings, which opened in London in 1713. This painting, dating from 1764, portrays a group of French aristocrats enjoying English-style tea in the Palais du Temple in Paris.

produce which more and more became a necessity to Europe. In Europe, first Amsterdam and then London surpassed Antwerp as international ports, in large measure because of the huge growth of the re-export trade in colonial goods which were carried by Dutch and English ships. Around these central flows of trade there proliferated branches and sub-branches, which led to further specializations and ramifications. Shipbuilding, textiles and, later, financial services such as insurance all prospered together, sharing in the consequences of a huge expansion in sheer volume. Eastern trade in the second half of the eighteenth century made up a quarter of the whole of Dutch external commerce and during that century the number of ships sent out by the East India Company from London went up threefold. These ships, moreover, thanks to improvements in design, carried more and were worked by fewer men than those of earlier times.

CHANGES IN EUROPEAN LIFESTYLE

The material consequences of Europe's new involvement with the world are much easier to measure than some of the others. European diet remains one of the most varied in the world and this came about in the early modern age. The coming of tobacco, coffee, tea and sugar alone brought about a revolution in taste, habit and housekeeping. The potato was to change the lives of many countries by sustaining much larger populations than its predecessors. Scores of drugs were added to the European pharmacopoeia, mainly from Asia.

INTELLECTUAL IMPACT

Beyond the material effects of Europe's colonialization it is harder to proceed. The interplay of new knowledge of the world with European mentality is especially hard to pin down. Minds were changing, as the great increase in the numbers of books about discoveries and voyages in both East and West had showed as early as the sixteenth century. Oriental studies may be said to have been founded as a science in the seventeenth century, although Europeans only begin to show the impact of knowledge of the anthropologies of other people towards its close. Such developments were intensified in the unrolling of their effects by the fact that they took place in an age of printing, too, and this makes the novelty of interest in the world outside Europe hard to evaluate. By the early eighteenth century, though, there were signs of an important intellectual impact at a deep level. Idyllic descriptions of savages who lived moral lives without the help of Christianity provoked reflection; an English philosopher, John Locke, used the evidence of other continents to show that humans did not share any God-given innate ideas. In particular, an idealized and sentimentalized picture of China furnished examples for speculation on the relativity of social institutions, while the penetration of Chinese literature (much aided by the studies of the Jesuits) revealed a chronology whose length made nonsense of traditional calculations of the date of the Flood described in the Bible as the second beginning of humanity.

As its products became more easily available, China also provoked in Europe an eighteenth-century craze for oriental styles in furniture, porcelain and dress. As an artistic and intellectual influence this has remained more obvious than the deeper perspective given to the observation of European life by an awareness of different civilizations with different standards elsewhere. But while such comparisons may have had some disquieting aspects, revealing that Europe had, perhaps,

Painted in 1793, this watercolour shows the Chinese emperor Ts'ien-lung and his entourage at a reception ceremony for the first British ambassador to China, Lord Macartney.

less to be proud of in its attitude to other religions than China, there were still others suggested by exploits such as those of the *conquistadores* which fed Europeans' notions of their superiority.

THE IMPACT OF EUROPE ON THE WORLD

THE IMPACT OF EUROPE on the world is no easier to encapsulate in a few simple formulae than that of the world upon Europe, but it is, in some of its manifestations at least, at times more dramatically obvious. It is an appalling fact that almost nowhere in the world can most of those in non-European countries be shown to have benefited materially from the first phase of Europe's expansion; far from it, many of them suffered terribly. Yet this was not always something for which blame attaches to the Europeans – unless they should be blamed for being there at all. In an age with no knowledge of infectious disease beyond the most elementary, the devastating impact of smallpox or other diseases brought from Europe to the Americas could not have been anticipated. But it was disastrous. It has been calculated that the population of Mexico fell by three-quarters in the sixteenth century; that of some Caribbean islands was wiped out altogether.

Such facts as the ruthless exploitation of those who survived, on the other hand, whose labour was so much more valuable after this demographic collapse, are a different matter. Here is expressed that *leitmotiv* of subjection and domination which runs through well-nigh every instance of Europe's early impact on the rest of the world. Different colonial environments and different European traditions present little but gradations of oppression and exploitation. Not all colonial societies were based on the same extremes of brutality and horror. But all were tainted. The wealth of the United Provinces and its magnificent seventeenth-century civilization were fed by roots which, at least in the spice islands and Indonesia, lay in bloody ground. Long before expansion in North America went west of the Alleghenies, the brief good relations of the first English settlers of Virginia with the Native North Americans had soured and extermination and eviction had begun. Though the populations of Spanish America had been in some measure protected by the state from the worst abuses of the *encomienda* system, they had for the most part been reduced to peonage, while determined efforts were made (for the highest motives) to destroy their culture. In South Africa the fate of the Hottentot, and in Australia that of the Aborigine, would repeat the lesson that European culture could devastate those whom it touched, unless they had the protection of old and advanced civilizations such as those of India or China. Even in those great countries, much damage would be done, nor would they be able to resist the Europeans once they decided to bring sufficient force to bear. But it was the settled colonies that showed most clearly the pattern of domination.

THE COSTS OF SLAVERY

THE PROSPERITY OF MANY European colonies long depended on the African slave trade, whose economic importance has already been touched upon. Since the eighteenth century it has obsessed critics who have seen in it the most brutal example of the inhumanity of man to man, whether that of white to black, of European to non-European, or of capitalist to labourer. It has properly dominated much of the historiography of Europe's expansion and American civilization, for it was a major fact in both. Less use-fully, it has, because of its importance in shaping so much of the New World, diverted attention from other forms of slav-ery at other times – or even alternative fates to slav-ery, such as the extermination, intentional or unintentional, which overtook other peoples.

Outlets in the New World settler colonies dominated the direction of the slave trade until its abolition in the nineteenth century. First in the Caribbean islands and then on the American mainland north and south, the slavers found their most reliable customers. The Portuguese who had first dominated the trade were soon elbowed out of the Caribbean by the Dutch and then by Elizabeth I's "sea-dogs", but Portuguese cap-tains turned to importing slaves to Brazil instead as the sixteenth century went on. Early in the seventeenth century the Dutch founded their West Indies company to ensure a regular supply of slaves to the West Indies, but by 1700 their lead had been overtaken by French and English slavers who had estab-lished posts on the "slave coast" of Africa. Altogether, their efforts sent between nine and ten millions of black slaves to the western hemisphere, 80 per cent of them after 1700. The eighteenth century saw the greatest pros-perity of the trade; some six million slaves were shipped then. European ports like Bristol and Nantes built a new age of commercial wealth on slavery. New lands were opened as black slave labour made it possible to work them. Larger-scale production of new crops brought, in turn, great changes in European demand, manufacturing and trading patterns. Racially, too, we still live with the results.

CRUELTY AND DESTRUCTION

What has disappeared and can now never be measured is the human misery involved, not

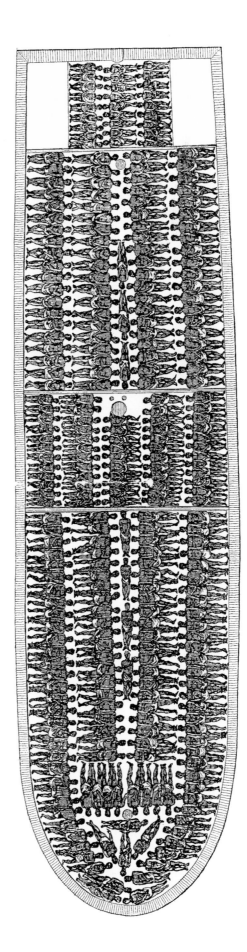

This plan of an 18th-century slave ship shows how tightly African slaves were packed into the vessel's hull in order to max-imize the numbers the ship could carry. Conditions during the long journeys under-taken by such ships were horrendous and death rates of more than 40 per cent among the slaves were not uncommon.

Slave merchants are shown negotiating the sale of two black slaves in Gorée, in Senegal, Africa, in an illustration dated 1796.

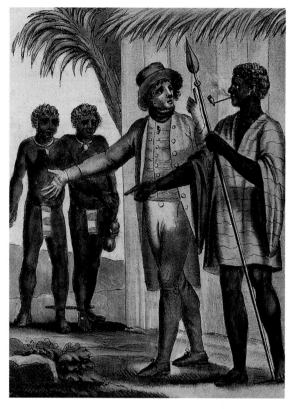

merely in physical hardship (a black man might live only a few years on a West Indian plantation even if he survived the horrible conditions of the voyage) but in the psychological and emotional tragedies of this huge migration. Historians still debate whether slavery "civilized" blacks in the Americas by bringing them into contact, willy-nilly, with higher civilizations, or whether it retarded them in quasi-infantile dependence. The question seems as insoluble as the degree of cruelty involved is incalculable; on the one hand is the evidence of the fetters and the whipping-block, on the other the reflection that these were commonplaces of European life too, and that, a priori, self-interest should have prompted the planters to care for their investment. That it did not always do so, slave rebellions showed. Revolt, though, was infrequent other than in Brazil, a fact which also bears consideration. It is unlikely that the debate will end.

Estimates of the almost unrecorded damage done in Africa are even harder to arrive at, for the evidence is even more subject to conjecture. The obvious demographic loss may (as some historians have hazarded) be balanced against the introduction to Africa of new foodstuffs from America. Conceivably, such by-products of a European contact determined by the hunt for slaves actually led to population growth, but the hypothesis can hardly be weighed against the equally immeasurable effects of imported disease.

EUROPEAN ACCEPTANCE OF THE SLAVE TRADE

It is notable that the African slave trade for a long time awoke no misgivings such as those which had been shown by Spanish churchmen in defence of the American Indians, and the arguments with which some Christians actually resisted any restriction of this traffic still retain a certain gruesome fascination. Feelings of responsibility and guilt began to be shared widely only in the eighteenth century and mainly in France and England. One expression of it was the British acquisition of another dependency in 1787, Sierra Leone, soon adopted by philanthropists as a refuge for African slaves freed in England. Given a favourable political and economic conjuncture, the current of public feeling educated by humanitarian thought would in the next century destroy the slave trade and, in the European world, slavery. But that is part of a different story. In the unfolding of European world power, slavery was a huge social and economic fact. It was to become a great mythical one, too, symbolizing at its harshest the triumph of force and cupidity over humanity. Sadly, it was also only the outstanding expression of a general dominance by force of advanced societies over weaker ones.

French law on the treatment of slaves

Art. 16: We forbid slaves belonging to different masters to gather together, by day or by night, under pain of corporal punishment which will be no less than flogging or a fleur-de-lis (branding on the back); and in the case of frequent repetition of the offence and other aggravating circumstances, the slave can be condemned to death, which we leave to the discretion of the judges. We entrust all our subjects with the persecution of those who violate the law, of detaining them and taking them to prison, although they are not officials and although there is no decree of arrest.

Art. 33: Any slave who hits his master, or his master's wife, his mistress or the husband of his mistress, or their children causing bruising or bloodshed, will be punished with death.

Art. 38: A fugitive slave who has been on the run for a month from the day of being reported to the court by his master, will have his ears cut off and will be marked by a fleur-de-lis on his shoulder; and if he repeats the offence from the day of being reported he will have the back of his knees cut and will be marked with a fleur-de-lis on the other shoulder; on the third time he will be punished with death.

Art. 44: We decree that slaves are furniture, and as such they become property, that consequently they cannot be leased, that they are divided into equal parts amongst the co-inheritors, without testimonial preferences nor right of primogeniture, that they are not subject to the usual widow's pension, to a feudal and dependent's pension, to feudal rights, to the formalities of decrees nor to the reductions of the four fifths, in the case of settlements of any last will and testament.

Extracts from the code of law on the policy of the Islands of the Archipelago, Versailles, March 1685. From *Recueil général des anciennes lois françaises* by Isambert.

CATHOLIC MISSIONARIES

Some Europeans recognized the inhuman nature of the slave trade but none the less believed that any evil was outweighed by what they offered to the rest of the world, above all, by the bringing of Christianity. It was a bull of Paul III, the pope who summoned the Council of Trent, which proclaimed that "the Indians are truly men and … are not only capable of understanding the Catholic faith but according to our information, they desire exceedingly to receive it". Such optimism was not merely an expression of the Counter-Reformation spirit, for the missionary impulse had been there from the start in the Spanish and Portuguese possessions. Jesuit missionary work began in Goa in 1542 and radiated from there all over the Indian Ocean and Southeast Asia and even reached Japan. Like the other Catholic powers, the French, too, emphasized missionary work, even in areas where France was not herself economically or politically involved. A new vigour was none the less given to missionary enterprise in the sixteenth and seventeenth centuries and may be acknowledged as one invigorating effect of the Counter-Reformation. Formally at least, Roman Christianity took in more converts and greater tracts of territory in the sixteenth century than in any earlier. What this really meant is harder to assess, but what little protection the Native American had was often only provided by the Roman Catholic Church, whose theologians kept alive the only notion of trusteeship towards subject peoples which existed in early imperial theory.

PROTESTANT MISSIONARIES

Protestantism lagged far behind Catholicism in concern about the natives of settlement

Christian missionary activity in the European colonies

By the beginning of the 19th century, Roman Catholic missions were firmly established in most of the French, Spanish and Portuguese colonies in Asia and Africa. Protestant missionary activity had been less common until this period, when British colonial expansion (and the influence of Evangelical Revivalism) resulted in the presence of Protestant missionaries in every part of the British Empire.

The success rates of European missionaries in the colonies were very mixed. Islam, Hinduism, Buddhism and Confucianism proved too highly resistant to the Christian creeds, unlike many native African religions.

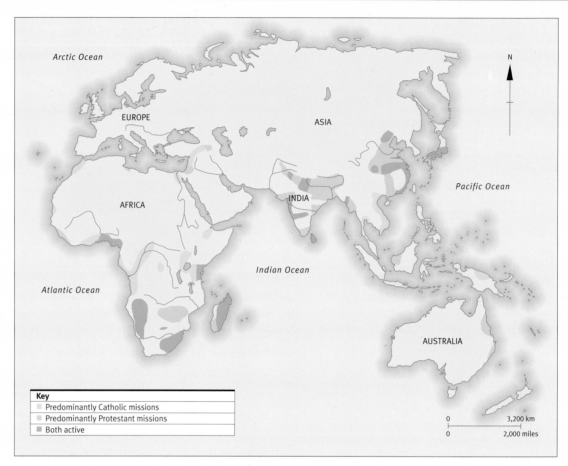

Key
Predominantly Catholic missions
Predominantly Protestant missions
Both active

0   3,200 km
0   2,000 miles

This map shows areas of colonial missionary activity in 19th-century Africa and Asia.

colonies, as it did in missionary work. The Dutch hardly did anything and the English American colonists not only failed to convert, but actually enslaved some of their Native North American neighbours (the Quakers of Pennsylvania were laudable exceptions). The origins of the great Anglo-Saxon overseas missionary movements are not to be detected until the end of the seventeenth century. Furthermore, even in the gift of the Gospel to the world when it came there lay a tragic ambiguity. It, too, was a European export of enormously corrosive potential, challenging and undermining traditional structures and ideas, threatening social authority, legal and moral institutions, family and marriage patterns. The missionaries, often in spite of themselves, became instruments of the process of domination and subjugation which runs through the story of Europe's intercourse with the rest of the globe.

EUROPEAN TRANSPLANTS

Perhaps there was nothing Europeans brought with them which would not in the end turn out to be a threat, or at least double-edged. The food plants which the Portuguese carried from America to Africa in the sixteenth century – these included cassava, sweet potatoes and maize – may have improved African diet, but (it has been argued) may also have provoked population growth which led to social disruption and upheaval. Plants taken to the Americas, on the other hand, founded new industries which then created a demand for slaves; coffee and sugar were commodities of this sort. Further north, wheat-growing by British settlers did not require slaves, but intensified the demand for land and added to the pressures driving the colonists into the ancestral hunting-grounds of the Indians, whom they ruthlessly pushed out of the way.

The lives of generations unborn – when such transplants were first made – were to be shaped by them, and a longer perspective than one confined by 1800 is helpful here. Wheat was, after all, ultimately to make the western hemisphere the granary of European cities; in the twentieth century even Russia and Asian countries drew on it. A still-flourishing wine industry was implanted by the Spanish in the Madeiras and America as early as the sixteenth century. When bananas were established in Jamaica, coffee in Java and tea in Ceylon, the groundwork was laid of much future politics. All such changes, moreover, were in the nineteenth century complicated by variations in demand, as industrialization increased the demand for old staples such as cotton (in 1760 England imported two and a half million pounds of raw cotton – in 1837 the figure was 360 million) and sometimes created new ones; it was a consequence of this that rubber was to be successfully transplanted from South America to Malaya and Indo-China, a change fraught with great strategic significance for the future.

In the Cape of Good Hope in southern Africa, the Dutch East India Company discouraged export, considering the region to be a strategic base and a centre for the supply of food to its traders rather than a colony. This painting shows a Boer family's house located in the north of the Cape.

ECOLOGICAL CHANGE

The scope of such implications for the future in the early centuries of European hegemony will appear sufficiently in what follows. Here it is only important to note one more, often-repeated, characteristic of this pattern, its unplanned, casual nature. It was the amalgam of many individual decisions by comparatively few men. Even their most innocent innovations could have explosive consequences. It is worth recalling that it was the importation of a couple of dozen rabbits in 1859 which led to the devastation of much of rural Australia by millions of them within a few decades. Similarly, but on a smaller scale, Bermuda was to be plagued with English toads.

Conscious animal importations, though, were even more important (the first response to the Australian rabbit scourge was to send for English stoats and weasels; a better answer had to wait for myxomatosis). Almost the entire menagerie of European domesticated animals was settled in the Americas by 1800. The most important were cattle and horses. Between them they would revolutionize the

The European-style buildings in this view of 18th-century Canton in southern China are testimony to the presence of French, North American, English and Dutch commercial companies.

life of the Plains Indians; later, after the coming of refrigerated ships, they were to make South America a great meat exporter just as Australasia was to be made one by the introduction of sheep the English had themselves imported originally from Spain. And, of course, the Europeans brought human bloodstock, too. Like the British in America, the Dutch for a long time did not encourage the mixing of races. Yet in Latin America, Goa and Portuguese Africa the effects were profound. So, in an entirely different and negative way, were they in British North America, where racial intermarriage was not significant and the near-exact coincidence of colour and legally servile status bequeathed an enormous legacy of political, economic, social and cultural problems to the future.

PROBLEMS OF IMPERIAL GOVERNMENT

The creation of large colonial populations shaped the future map, but also presented problems of government. The British colonies

nearly always had some form of representative institution which reflected parliamentary tradition and practice while France, Portugal and Spain all followed a straightforward authoritarian and monarchical institutional system. None of them envisaged any sort of independence for their colonies, nor any need to safeguard their interests against those of the mother country, whether these were conceived as paramount or complementary. This would in the end cause trouble and by 1763 there were signs at least in the British North American colonies that it might be on lines reminiscent of seventeenth-century England's struggles between Crown and Parliament. And in their struggles with other nations, even when their governments were not formally at war with them, the colonists always showed a lively sense of their own interests. Even when Dutch and English were formally allied against France their sailors and traders would fight one another "beyond the line".

Problems of imperial government in the eighteenth century were, though, largely a matter of the western hemisphere. That was

The English explorer Captain James Cook is portrayed in this 18th-century painting. On his first voyage, Cook left Tahiti to travel round New Zealand and chart eastern Australia. His second journey began in 1772 and crossed the Atlantic and Pacific oceans, with four scouting expeditions below 60° latitude south. The third trip completed charts from the Bering Strait to California; on this final trip Cook aimed to discover the elusive Northwest Passage (a long-sought sea passage along the northern coast of North America), but he was killed in Hawaii in 1779.

where the settlers had gone. Elsewhere in the world in 1800, even in India, trade still mattered more than possession and many important areas had still to feel the full impact of Europe. As late as 1789 the East India Company was sending only twenty-one ships in the year to Canton; the Dutch were allowed two a year to Japan. Central Asia was at that date still only approachable by the long land routes used in the days of Chinghis Khan and the Russians were still far from exercising effective influence over the hinterland. Africa was protected by climate and disease. Discovery and exploration still had to complete that continent's map before European hegemony could become a reality.

EUROPEANS REACH AUSTRALIA

In the Pacific and "South Seas", things were moving faster. The voyage of Dampier, a Somerset man, in 1699, had begun the integration of Australasia, an unknown continent, within established geography, though it took another century to complete.

The last discoveries

During the 17th and 18th centuries, the discovery of new lands continued to be a major preoccupation for the European powers; scouting expeditions multiplied and a large number of exciting new finds were made. Although the search for wealth and power, as well as evangelizing zeal, continued to play an important role, other more concrete reasons for exploration emerged during this period, such as trade and scientific research. Leading explorers also had better technical, nautical and financial backing.

The Pacific was one of the main objectives of this continual discovery effort. In 1605 the Portuguese navigator Pedro Fernández de Quirós began a voyage to the Pacific which would take him to the New Hebrides. The Spaniard Diego de Prados and his colleague Luis Vaez de Torres continued the search and touched the Australian mainland at Cape York. In 1642, a Dutch expedition, led by Abel Tasman, sailed around the Australian coast and discovered Tasmania and New Zealand. Another Dutchman, Jacob Roggeveen, discovered Easter Island in 1721 on a round-the-world voyage from Brazil. In the late 18th century, England sent two teams to Australia to improve nautical charts: John Byron (from 1764 to 1766) and Samuel Wallis and Philip Carteret (from 1766 to 1768) charted the positions of several islands.

This illustration shows Queen Oberea of Tahiti in conversation with the newly arrived Captain Samuel Wallis (1728–1795), who discovered Tahiti and the Wallis Islands during his circumnavigation of the globe from 1766 to 1768.

In the north, the existence of the Bering Straits had been demonstrated by 1730. The voyages of Bougainville and Cook, in the 1760s and 1770s, added Tahiti, Samoa, eastern Australia, Hawaii and New Zealand to the last New World to be opened. Cook even penetrated the Antarctic Circle. In 1788 the first cargo of convicts, 717 of them, was landed in New South Wales. British judges were calling into existence a new penal world to redress the balance of the old, since the American colonies were now unavailable for dumping English undesirables, and were incidentally founding another new nation. More important still, a few years later the first sheep arrived and so was founded the industry to ensure that nation's future. Along with animals, adventurers and ne'er-do-wells there came to the South Pacific, also, the Gospel. In 1797 the first missionaries arrived in Tahiti. With them, the blessings of European civilization may be reckoned at last to have appeared, at least in embryonic form, in every part of the habitable world.

This notice board, promising equal justice to blacks and whites alike, was addressed to the Aboriginal population of Van Diemen's Land (Tasmania), Australia, c.1828. In spite of such assurances, the British governor of the island, Sir George Arthur (1785–1854), actually tried (but failed) to restrict the Aborigines to the southeastern peninsula behind a "Black Line". By the second half of the 19th century, Tasmania's Aboriginal population had been practically wiped out.

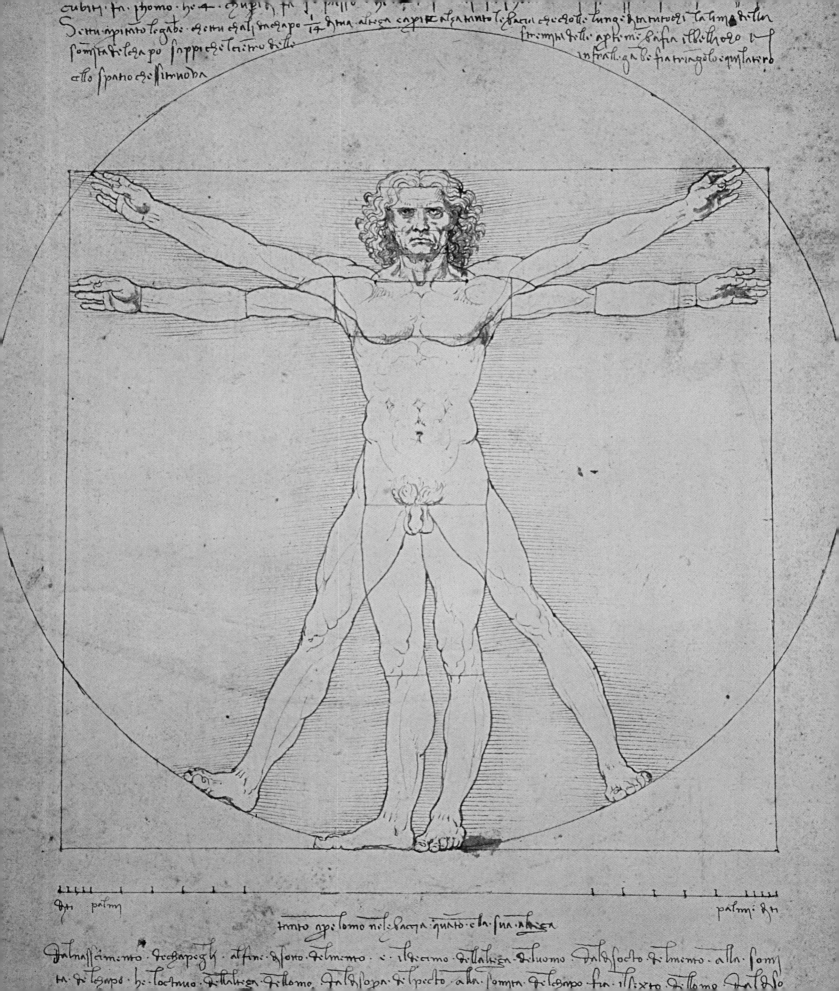

THE AGE OF REVOLUTION

BETWEEN 1500 AND 1800, significant changes took place in the way educated Europeans saw their society. Important scientific discoveries were made and the Enlightenment brought a new sense of responsibility and reason. In spite of such changes, however, in the middle of the eighteenth century most people in the world (and probably most Europeans) could still believe that history would go on much as it had always done. The weight of the past was everywhere enormous and often it was immovable: some of the European efforts to shake it off have been touched upon, but nowhere outside Europe was even the possibility of doing so grasped. Though in many parts of the world a few people's lives had begun to be revolutionized by contact with Europeans, most of it was unaffected and much of it was untouched by such contamination of traditional ways.

Yet even in the eighteenth century, the idea of historical change was already to be found spreading among thinking Europeans. By 1900 it was obvious that in Europe and the European world of settlement change had irreversibly cut off much of the traditional past. A fundamentally progressive view of history became more widely shared. If never questioned, the myth of progress more and more gave meaning to events.

Just as important, impulses from northern Europe and the Atlantic countries also radiated outwards to transform both Europe's relations with the rest of the world and the very foundations of their lives for many of its peoples, however much some of them regretted and resisted it. By the end of the nineteenth century a world once regulated by tradition was on a new course. Its destiny was now to be continuing and accelerating transformation and the second adjective was as important as the first. A man born in 1800 who lived out the psalmist's span of three-score years and ten, could have seen the world more changed in his lifetime than it had been in the previous thousand years. History was speeding up.

The consolidation of the European world hegemony was central to these changes and one of the great motors propelling them. They might not always agree on what was most important about it but few Europeans could deny that it had produced wealth on an unprecedented scale and that it dominated the rest of the globe by power and influence as no previous civilization had ever done. Europeans (or their descendants) ran the world. Much of their domination was political, a matter of direct rule. Large areas of the world had been peopled by European stocks. As for the non-European countries still formally and politically independent of Europe, most of them had in practice to defer to European wishes and accept European interference in their affairs. Few indigenous peoples could resist, and if they did Europe often won its subtlest victory of all, for successful resistance required the adoption of European practices and, therefore, Europeanization in another form.

Leonardo da Vinci (1452–1519), whose *Diagram of the proportions of the body* is seen here, was an accomplished architect, sculptor, painter, writer, engineer, scientist and inventor – the definitive all-round "Renaissance man". The ideas of the Renaissance and its spirit of enquiry were profoundly influential on Europe's development.

1 IDEAS OLD AND NEW

THE ESSENCE OF THE CIVILIZATION Europe was exporting to the rest of the globe between 1500 and 1800 lay in ideas. The limits they imposed and the possibilities they offered shaped the way in which that civilization operated and the way it saw itself. What is more, although the twentieth century has done great damage to them, the leading ideas adumbrated by Europeans during that period still provide most of the sign-posts by which we make our way. European culture was then given a secular foundation; it was then, too, that there took hold a progressive notion of historical development as movement towards an apex at which Europeans felt themselves to stand. Finally it was then that there grew up a confidence that scientific knowledge used in accordance with utilitarian criteria would make possible limitless progress. In short, the civilization of the Middle Ages at last came to an end in the minds of thinking men and women.

THE WEIGHT OF THE PAST

Things rarely happen cleanly and neatly in history, and few Europeans would have been aware of any change in popular consciousness by 1800. In a couple of centuries there had been little change in the way most of them saw things and behaved. The traditional institutions of monarchy, hereditary status, society and religion still held sway over most of the continent in that year. Only a hundred years before there had been no civil marriage anywhere in Europe and there was still none over most of it. Barely twenty years before 1800 the last heretic had been burned in Poland and even in England an eighteenth-century monarch had, like medieval kings, been touched for the king's evil (scrofula). The seventeenth century, indeed, had in one or two respects even shown regression. In both Europe and North America there was an epidemic of witch-hunting far more widespread than anything in the Middle Ages (Charlemagne had condemned witch-burners to death and canon law had forbidden belief in the night flights and other supposed pranks of witches as pagan). Nor was this the end of superstition. The last English wizard was harried to his death by his neighbours well after 1700 and a Protestant Swiss was legally executed by his countrymen for witchcraft in 1782. The Neapolitan cult of St Januarius

Known as the "Tempietto", this colonnade in the courtyard of St Peter's Church in Monteno, Rome, was commissioned by Ferdinand and Isabella of Spain and built c.1502 by Donato Bramante (c.1444–1514). During the Renaissance and Enlightenment periods, the Roman Catholic Church – the only Christian Church to have its own territorial state – consciously presented itself as a solid, monumental institution and this was reflected in its architecture.

This view of St Peter's in Rome was painted by the Dutch artist Gaspar van Wittel (1653–1736).

was still of political importance in the era of the French Revolution because the successful or unsuccessful liquefaction of the saint's blood was believed to indicate divine pleasure or displeasure at what the government was doing. Penology was still barbarous; some crimes were thought so atrocious as to merit punishment of exceptional ferocity and it was as parricides that the assassin of Henry IV of France and the attempted assassin of Louis XV suffered their abominable torments. The second died under them in 1757, only a few years before the publication of the most influential advocacy of penal reform that has ever been written. The glitter of modernity in the eighteenth century can easily deceive us; in societies which produced art of exquisite refinement and outstanding examples of chivalry and honour, popular amusements focused on the pleasures of bear-baiting, cock-fighting or pulling the heads off geese.

ORGANIZED RELIGION

If popular culture often shows most obviously the weight of the past, until almost the end of these three centuries much of the formal and

Many Europeans long remained fascinated with superstition, fortune-telling and witchcraft. This Spanish painting, *The Witches' Coven, was* painted by Francisco de Goya in 1821–1822.

institutional apparatus which upheld the past also remained intact over most of Europe. The most striking example to modern eyes would be the primacy still enjoyed almost everywhere in the eighteenth century by organized religion. In every country, Catholic, Protestant and Orthodox alike, even ecclesiastical reformers took it for granted that religion should be upheld and protected by the law and the coercive apparatus of the state. Only a very few advanced thinkers questioned this. In much of Europe there was still no toleration for views other than those of the established Church. The coronation oath taken by a French king imposed on him the obligation to stamp out heresy, and only in 1787 did non-Catholics in France gain any recognized civic status and therefore the right to legitimize their children by contracting legal marriage. In Catholic countries the censorship, though often far from effective, was still supposed and sometimes strove to prevent the dissemination of writings inimical to Christian belief and the authority of the Church. Although the Counter-Reformation spirit had ebbed and the Jesuits were dissolved, the Index of prohibited books and the Inquisition which had first compiled it were maintained. The universities everywhere were in clerical hands; even in England, Oxford and Cambridge were closed to nonconformist dissenters and Roman Catholics. Religion also largely determined the content of their teaching and the definition of the studies they pursued.

THE GROWTH OF NEW INSTITUTIONS

The institutional fabric of society also showed the onset of innovation. One of the reasons why universities lost importance in these centuries was that they no longer monopolized the intellectual life of Europe. From the middle of the seventeenth century there appeared in many countries, and often under the highest patronage, academies and learned societies such as the English Royal Society, which was given a charter in 1662, or the French Académie des Sciences, founded four years later. In the eighteenth century such associations greatly multiplied; they were diffused through smaller towns and

Freemasons gather to discuss the exposure of a fraud in their midst. This meeting was held at a London Masonic lodge in 1786, at a time when Masonic membership was rising fast.

founded with more limited and special aims, such as the promotion of agriculture. A great movement of voluntary socialization was apparent; though most obvious in England and France, it left few countries in western Europe untouched. Clubs and societies of all sorts were a characteristic of an age no longer satisfied to exhaust its potential in the social institutions of the past, and they sometimes attracted the attention of government. Some of them made no pretension to have as their sole end literary, scientific or agricultural activity, but provided gatherings and meeting-places at which general ideas were debated, discussed or merely chatted about. In this way they assisted the circulation of new ideas. Among such associations the most remarkable was the international brotherhood of Freemasons. It was introduced from England to continental Europe in the 1720s

and within a half-century spread widely; there may have been more than a quarter-million Masons by 1789. They were later to be the object of much calumny; the myth was propagated that they had long had revolutionary and subversive aims. This was not true of the craft as a body, however true it may have been of a few individual Masons, but it is easy to believe that so far as Masonic lodges, like other gatherings, helped in the publicity and discussion of new ideas, they contributed to the breaking up of the ice of tradition and convention.

LITERACY

THE INCREASED CIRCULATION of ideas and information did not, of course, rest primarily on meetings held by clubs and societies, but on the diffusion of the written word through print. One of the crucial transformations of Europe after 1500 was that it became more literate; some have summed it up as the change from a culture focused on the image to one focused on the word. Reading and writing (and especially the former), though not universally diffused, had, nevertheless, become widespread and in some places common. They were no longer the privileged and arcane knowledge of a small élite, nor were they any longer mysterious in being intimately and specially connected with religious rites.

In assessing this change we can emerge a little way from the realm of imponderables and enter that of measurable data which shows that somehow, for all the large pools of illiteracy which still existed in 1800, Europe was by then a literate society as it was not in 1500. That is, of course, not a very helpful statement as it stands. There are many degrees of attainment in both reading and writing. Nevertheless, however we define our terms, Europe and its dependencies in 1800 had a higher proportion of literates than any other cultures. This was a critical historical change. By then, Europe was well into the age of the predominance of print, which eventually superseded, for most educated people, the spoken word and images as the primary means of instruction and direction, and lasted until the twentieth century restored oral and visual supremacy by means of radio, cinema and television.

DIFFERING LEVELS OF LITERACY

The sources for assessing literacy are not good until the middle of the nineteenth century – when, it appears, somewhere about half of all Europeans still could neither read nor write – but they all suggest that the improvement from about 1500 was cumulative but uneven. There were important differences between countries, between the same countries at different periods, between town and country, between the sexes, and between occupations. All this is still true, though in diminished degree, and it greatly simplifies the problem of making general statements: none but the vaguest are possible until recent times. But specific facts are suggestive about trends.

The first signs of the educational effort underlying the increase of literacy can be seen before the invention of printing. They appear to be another part of that revival and invigoration of urban life between the twelfth and thirteenth centuries whose importance has

This painting of a graduation ceremony at the University of Leyden in the Netherlands dates from 1649. By that time, the social promotion that knowledge could bring meant that a good education was a valuable asset.

already been noted. Some of the earliest evidence of the commissioning of schoolmasters and provision of school places comes from the Italian cities which were then the vanguard of European civilization. In them there soon appeared a new appreciation, that literacy is an essential qualification for certain kinds of office. We find, for example, provisions that judges should be able to read, a fact with interesting implications for the history of earlier times.

The early lead of the Italian cities had given way by the seventeenth century to that of England and the Netherlands (both countries with, for the age, a high level of urbanization). These have been thought to be the European countries with the highest levels of literacy in about 1700; the transfer of leadership to them illustrates the way in which the history of rising literacy is geographically an uneven business. Yet French was to be the international language of eighteenth-century publication and the bedrock of the public

which sustained this must surely have been found in France. It would not be surprising if levels of literacy were higher in England and the United Provinces, but the numbers of the literate may well have been larger in France, where the total population was so much bigger.

PRINTING AND THE REFORMATION

An outstanding place in the overall trend to literacy must surely be given to the spread of printing. By the seventeenth century there was in existence a corpus of truly popular publishing, represented in fairy stories, tales of true and unrequited love, almanacs and books of astrology, and hagiographies. The existence of such material is evidence of demand. Printing had given a new point to being literate, too, for the consultation of manuscripts had necessarily been difficult and

Popular entertainment, such as theatre, was aided by the rise in literacy and the dissemination of printed matter. A performance of Molière's *Le Malade imaginaire* is depicted in this engraving dated 1673.

The first known edition of *El ingenioso hidalgo don Quijote de la Mancha*, the cover of which is shown here, was printed by Juan de la Cueva in Madrid in 1605. The work of a little-known writer called Miguel de Cervantes (1547–1616), *Don Quijote* was to bring its author long-lasting fame, but not wealth.

was a great force for enlightenment; it was both a stimulus to reading and a focus for intellectual activity. In England and Germany its importance in the making of a common culture can hardly be exaggerated, and in each country it produced a translation of the Bible which was a masterpiece.

EDUCATION AND PUBLICATIONS

As the instance of the reformers shows, authority was often in favour of greater literacy, but this was not confined to the Protestant countries. In particular, the legislators of innovating monarchies in the eighteenth century often strove to promote education – which meant in large measure primary education. Austria and Prussia were notable in this respect. Across the Atlantic the puritan tradition had from the start imposed in the New England communities the obligation to provide schooling. In other countries education was left to the informal and unregulated operation of private enterprise and charity (as in England), or to the Church. From the sixteenth century begins the great age of particular religious orders devoted to teaching (as in France).

An important consequence, promoter and concomitant of increased literacy was the rise of the periodical press. From broadsheets and occasional printed newsletters there evolved by the eighteenth century journals of regular publication. They met various needs. Newspapers began in seventeenth-century Germany, a daily coming out in London in 1702, and by the middle of the century there was an important provincial press and millions of newspapers were being printed each year. Magazines and weekly journals began to appear in England in the first half of the eighteenth century and the most important of them, the *Spectator*, set a model for journal-

time-consuming, because of their relative inaccessibility. Technical knowledge could now be made available in print very quickly and this meant that it was in the interest of the specialist to read in order to maintain his skill in his craft.

Another force making for literacy was the Protestant Reformation. Almost universally, the reformers themselves stressed the importance of teaching believers how to read; it is no coincidence that Germany and Scandinavia both reached higher levels of literacy than many Catholic countries by the nineteenth century. The Reformation made it important to read the Bible and it had rapidly become available in print in the vernaculars which were thus strengthened and disciplined by the diffusion and standardization which print brought with it. Bibliolatry, for all its more obviously unfortunate manifestations,

ism by its conscious effort to shape taste and behaviour. Here was something new. Only in the United Provinces did journalism have such success as in England; probably this was because all other European countries enjoyed censorships of varying degrees of efficacy as well as different levels of literacy. Learned and literary journals appeared in increasing numbers, but political reporting and comment were rarely available. Even in eighteenth-century France it was normal for the authors of works embodying advanced ideas to circulate them only in manuscript; in this stronghold of critical thought there was still a censorship, although one arbitrary and unpredictable and, as the century wore on, less effective in its operation.

THE "DANGERS" OF LITERACY

It may have been a growing awareness of the subversive potential of easily accessible journalism which led to a change of wind in official attitudes to education. Until the eighteenth century there was no very widespread feeling that education and literacy might be dangerous and should not be widely extended. Though formal censorship had always been a recognition of the potential dangers brought by literacy, there was a tendency to see this in predominantly religious terms; one duty of the Inquisition was to maintain the effectiveness of the Index. In retrospect it may well seem that the greater opportunity which literacy and printing gave for the criticism and questioning of authority in general was a more important effect than their subversion of religion. Yet this was not their only importance. The diffusion of technical knowledge also accelerated other kinds of social change. Industrialization would hardly have been possible without greater literacy and a part of what has been called a

"scientific revolution" in the seventeenth century must be attributed to the simple cumulative effect of more rapidly and widely circulated information.

THE SCIENTIFIC REVOLUTION

THE FUNDAMENTAL SOURCES of the "scientific revolution" lie deeper than the increased availability of information, in changed intellectual attitudes. Their core was a changed view of man's relation to nature. From a natural world observed with bemused awe as evidence of God's mysterious ways, human beings somehow made the great step

This painting by Dutch artist Adriaen van Ostade (1610–1685) depicts a village schoolmaster and his pupils.

*T*he Alchemist at *Work* is portrayed by David Teniers the Elder (1582–1649). Alchemy first emerged in ancient China, India and Greece, and became widespread in medieval Europe. The science of alchemy – more than merely the search for a means to turn base metal into gold (although in that debased form it became notorious) – was the forerunner of chemistry, and alchemists made some important findings, including the discovery of mineral acids and alcohol.

to a conscious search for the means to achieve its manipulation. Although the work of medieval scientists had been by no means as primitive and uncreative as it was once the fashion to believe, it suffered from two critical limitations. One was that it provided very little knowledge that was of practical use and this inhibited attention to it. The second was its theoretical weakness; it had to be surpassed at a conceptual as well as a technical level. In spite of its beneficial irrigation by ideas from the Arab world and a healthy emphasis on definition and diagnosis in some of its branches, medieval science rested on assumptions which were untested, in part because the means of testing them could not be grasped, in part because the wish to test them did not exist. The dogmatic assertion of the theory that the four elements, fire, air,

earth and water, were the constituents of all things, for example, went unrefuted by experiment. Although experimental work of a sort went on within the alchemical and hermetic traditions, and with Paracelsus came to be directed towards other ends than a search for gold, it was still directed by mythical, intuitive conceptions.

DESCRIPTIVE STUDIES

The tendency to rely on medieval scientific assumptions continued until the seventeenth century. The Renaissance had its scientific manifestations but they found expression usually in descriptive studies (an outstanding example was that of Vesalius's human anatomy of 1543) and in the solution of practical problems in the arts (such as those of perspective) and mechanical crafts. One branch of this descriptive and classificatory work was particularly impressive, that addressed to making sense of the new geographical knowledge revealed by the discoverers and cosmographers. In geography, said a French physician of the early sixteenth century, "and in what pertains to astronomy, Plato, Aristotle, and the old philosophers made progress, and Ptolemy added a great deal more. Yet, were one of them to return today, he would find geography changed past recognition." Here was one

of the stimuli for a new intellectual approach to the world of nature.

It was not a stimulus quick to operate. A tiny minority of educated men, it is true, would already in 1600 not have found it easy to accept the conventional world picture based on the great medieval synthesis of Aristotle and the Bible. Some of them felt an uneasy loss of coherence, a sudden lack of bearings, an alarming uncertainty. But for most of those who considered the matter at all, the old picture still held true, the whole universe still centred on the earth, and the life of the earth upon human beings, its only

Only a century or so after Raphael (1483–1520) painted *The School of Athens (Philosophy)* in the Vatican, the classical world-view would prove inadequate as knowledge became ever more sophisticated and based on rational, observed truths.

rational inhabitants. The greatest intellectual achievement of the next century was to make it impossible for an educated person to think like this. It was so important that it has been seen as the essential change to the modern from the medieval world.

FRANCIS BACON

The English statesman and philosopher Francis Bacon (1561–1626) is depicted in this anonymous 17th-century portrait.

Early in the seventeenth century something new is already apparent in science. The changes which then manifested themselves meant that an intellectual barrier was crossed and the nature of civilization was altered for ever. There appeared in Europe a new attitude, deeply utilitarian, encouraging the curious to invest time, energy and resources to master nature by systematic experiment. When a later age came to look back for its precursors in this attitude they found the outstanding one to have been Francis Bacon, sometime Lord Chancellor of England, fondly supposed by some later admirers to be the author of the plays of Shakespeare, a man of outstanding intellectual energy and many unlikeable personal traits. His works seem to have had little or no contemporary effect but they attracted posterity's attention for what seemed a prophetic rejection of the authority of the past. Bacon advocated a study of nature based upon observation and induction and directed towards harnessing it for human purposes. "The true and lawful end of the sciences," he wrote, "is that human life be enriched by new discoveries and powers." Through them could be achieved a "restitution and reinvigorating [in great part] of man to the sovereignty and power ... which he had in his first state of creation". This was ambitious indeed – nothing less than the redemption of mankind from the consequences of Adam's Fall – but Bacon was sure it was possible if scientific research was effectively organized; in this, too, he was a prophetic figure, precursor of later scientific societies and institutions.

The modernity of Bacon was later exaggerated and other men – notably his contemporaries Kepler and Galileo – had much more to say which was of importance in the advance of science. Nor did his successors adhere so closely as he would have wished to a programme of practical discovery of "new arts, endowments, and commodities for the bettering of man's life" (that is, to a science dominated by technology). Nevertheless, he rightly acquired something of the status of a mythological figure because he went to the heart of the matter in his advocacy of observation and experiment instead of deduction from *a priori* principles. Appropriately, he is said even to have achieved scientific martyrdom, having caught cold while stuffing a fowl with snow one freezing March day, in order to observe the effects of refrigeration upon the flesh. Forty years later, his central ideas were the commonplace of scientific discourse. "The management of this great machine of the world," said an English scientist in the 1660s, "can be explained only by the experimental and mechanical philosophers." Here were ideas which Bacon would have understood and approved and which are central to the world which we still inhabit. Ever since the seventeenth century it has been

a characteristic of the scientist that he answers questions by means of experiment and for a long time it was to lead to new attempts to understand what was revealed by these experiments by constructing systems.

EXPERIMENTAL METHOD

The use of experimentation led at first to concentration on the physical phenomena which could best be observed and measured by the techniques available. Technological innovation had arisen from the slow accretion of skills by European workmen over centuries; these skills could now be directed to the solution of problems which would in turn permit the solution of other, intellectual problems. The invention of logarithms and calculus was a part of an instrumentation which had among other components the building of better clocks and optical instruments. When the clockmaker's art took a great stride forward with the seventeenth-century introduction of the pendulum as a controlling device it in turn made the measurement of time by precision instruments, and therefore astronomy, much easier. With the telescope came new opportunities to scrutinize the heavens; Harvey discovered the circulation of the blood as the result of a theoretical investigation by experiment, but *how* circulation took place was only made comprehensible when the microscope made it possible to see the tiny vessels through which blood flowed. Telescopic and microscopic observation were not only central to the

The mirror telescope was first constructed by Isaac Newton in 1671. This instrument, later perfected by William Herschel (1738–1822), produced large images and reflected a great deal of light, allowing the user to study distant heavenly bodies.

Microscopes, such as this late 18th-century model, made possible the study of major new scientific fields. For example, with the discovery of the existence of "animalcules" – infinitesimally minute living creatures, later called bacteria – microbiology was born.

Chemistry

Chemistry was a practical subject which perfected the use of metals and their alloys, dyes, pottery, gunpowder, salts and many other substances. It was in the field of alchemy, in which outstanding Arab achievements were followed in the 16th century by the Western alchemists, that investigation of such topics began. Modern chemistry began in the 17th century, along with new methods, knowledge and definitions, expounded by scientists such as Robert Boyle, Johann Glauber, Jean-Baptiste van Helmont, Friedrich Hoffmann, Wilhelm Homberg, Johan Kunckel, Nicolas Lémery and Jean Rey. In the 18th century, thanks to the work of Antoine Lavoisier, chemical theory was born and fundamental laws began to be grasped.

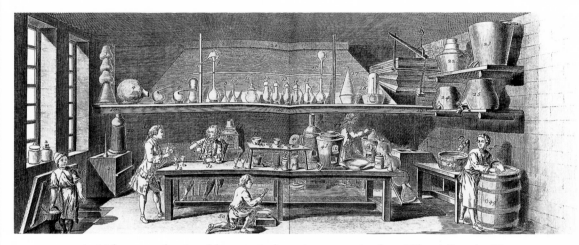

An 18th-century chemistry laboratory is shown in an engraving from Diderot's Encyclopédie.

discoveries of the scientific revolution, moreover, but made visible to laymen something of what was implied in a new world outlook.

THE NEW SCIENTIFIC COMMUNITY

What was not achieved for a long time was the line of demarcation between the scientist and philosopher which we now recognize. Yet a new world of scientists had come into being, a true scientific community and an international one, too. Here we come back to printing. The rapid diffusion of new knowledge was very important. The publication of scientific books was not its only form; the *Philosophical Transactions* of the Royal Society were published and so were, increasingly, the memoirs and proceedings of other learned bodies. Scientists moreover kept up voluminous private correspondences with one another, and much of the material they recorded in them has provided some of the most valuable evidence for the way in which scientific revolution actually occurred. Some of these correspondences were published; they were more widely intelligible and read than would be the exchanges of leading scientists today.

One feature of the scientific revolution remarkable to the modern eye is that it was something in which amateurs and part-time enthusiasts played a big part. It has been suggested that one of the most important facts explaining why science progressed in Europe while stagnation overtook even outstanding technical achievement in China, was the association with it in Europe of the social prestige of the amateur and the gentleman.

The membership of the learned societies which began to appear more widely at about the mid-seventeenth century was full of gentlemanly dabblers who could not by any stretch of imagination have been called professional scientists but who lent to these bodies the indefinable but important weight of their standing and respectability whether or not they got their hands dirty in experimental work.

LIMITATIONS

By 1700 specialization between the major different branches of science already existed though it was by no means as important as it was to become. Nor was science in those days relentlessly demanding on time; scientists could still make major contributions to their study while writing books on theology or holding administrative office. This suggests some of the limitations of the seventeenth-century revolution; nor could it transcend the limits of the techniques available which, while they permitted great advances in some fields, tended to inhibit attention to others. Chemistry, for example, made relatively small progress (though few still accepted the Aristotelian scheme of four elements which had still dominated thinking about the constituents of matter in 1600), while physics and cosmology went ahead rapidly and indeed arrived at something of a plateau of consolidation which resulted in less spectacular but steady advance well into the nineteenth century, when new theoretical approaches reinvigorated them.

SCIENCE AND GOD

Altogether, the seventeenth-century scientific achievement was a huge one. First and

foremost, it replaced a theory of the universe which saw phenomena as the direct and often unpredictable operation of divine power by a conception of it as a mechanism, in which change proceeded regularly from the uniform and universal working of laws of motion. This was still quite compatible with belief in God. His majesty was not perhaps shown in daily direct intervention but in his creation of a great machine; in the most celebrated analogy God was the great watch-maker. Neither the typical student of science nor the scientific world view of the seventeenth century was anti-religious or anti-theocentric. Though it was indubitably important that new views on astronomy, by displacing human beings from the centre of the universe, implicitly challenged their uniqueness (it was in 1686 that a book appeared arguing that there might be more than one inhabited world), this was not what preoccupied the men who made the cosmological revolution. For them it was only an accident that the authority of the Church became entangled with the proposition that the sun went round the earth. The new views they put forward

The English artist Joseph Wright (1734–1797) specialized in scientific subjects. In this painting, entitled *An Experiment on a Bird in the Air Pump*, he depicts a physicist creating a vacuum. Wright's work illustrates the growing fashion in élite circles for public scientific demonstrations.

merely emphasized the greatness and mysteriousness of God's ways. They took for granted the possibility of christening the new knowledge as Aristotle had been christened by the Middle Ages.

THE COPERNICAN UNIVERSE

Long before the German philosopher Kant coined the phrase "Copernican revolution" at the end of the eighteenth century, the roll of the makers of a new cosmology was recognized to begin with the name of Copernicus, a Polish cleric whose book, *On the Revolutions of the Celestial Orbs*, was published in 1543. This was the same year as Vesalius's great work on anatomy (and, curiously, of the first edition of the works of Archimedes); Copernicus was a Renaissance humanist rather than a scientist – not surprisingly, considering when he lived. In part for philosophic and aesthetic reasons he hit upon the idea of a universe of planets moving around the sun, explaining their motion as a system of cycles and epicycles. It was (so to

Tycho Brahe (1546–1601), the Danish astronomer for whom King Frederick II built an observatory, is depicted in this engraving dated 1586.

speak) a brilliant guess, for he had no means of testing the hypothesis and most common-sense evidence told against it.

The first true scientific data in support of heliocentricity was in fact provided by a man who did not accept it, the Dane Tycho Brahe. Besides possessing the somewhat striking distinction of an artificial nose, Brahe began recording the movements of planets, first with rudimentary instruments and then, thanks to a munificent king, from the best-equipped observatory of his age. The result was the first systematic collection of astronomical data to be made within the orbit of the Western tradition since the Alexandrian era. Johannes Kepler, the first great Protestant scientist, who was invited by Brahe to assist him, went on to make even more careful observations of his own and provide a second major theoretical step forward. He showed that the movements of planets could be explained as regular if their courses followed ellipses at irregular speeds. This broke at last with the Ptolemaic frame-

Nicholas Copernicus (1473–1543), the Polish theologian, astronomer and mathematician, caused a great scandal when he asserted that the earth rotated round the sun once a year, and on its own axis once a day.

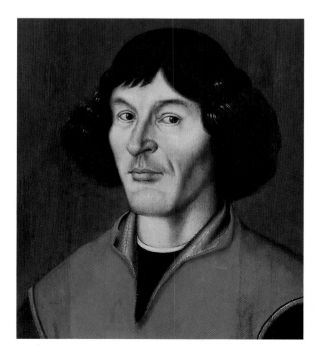

work within which cosmology had been more and more cramped and provided the basis of planetary explanation until the twentieth century. Then came Galileo Galilei, who eagerly seized upon the telescope, an instrument seemingly discovered about 1600, possibly by chance. Galileo was an academic, professor at Padua of two subjects characteristically linked in early science: physics and military engineering. His use of the telescope finally shattered the Aristotelian scheme; Copernican astronomy was made visible and the next two centuries were to apply to the stars what was known of the nature of the planets.

GALILEO

Galileo's major work was not in observation but in theory and in linking it to technical practice. He first described the physics which made a Copernican universe possible by providing a mathematical treatment of the movement of bodies. With his work, mechanics left the world of the craftsman's know-how, and entered that of science. What is more, Galileo came to his conclusions as a result of systematic experiment. On this rested what Galileo called "two new sciences", statics and dynamics. The published result was the book in which has been seen the first statement of the revolution in scientific thought, Galileo's *Dialogue on the Two Great Systems of the World* (that of Ptolemy and that of Copernicus) of 1632. Less remarkable than its contents, but still interesting, are the facts that it was written not in Latin but in the vernacular Italian, and dedicated to the pope; Galileo was undoubtedly a good Catholic. Yet the book provoked an uproar, rightly, for it meant the end of the Christian–Aristotelian world view which was the great cultural triumph of the medieval Church. Galileo's trial followed. He was con-

demned and recanted, but this did not diminish the effect of his work. Copernican and heliocentric views henceforth dominated scientific thinking.

ISAAC NEWTON

In the year that Galileo died, Isaac Newton was born. It was his achievement to provide the physical explanation of the Copernican universe; he showed that the same mechanical laws explained both what Kepler and what Galileo had said, and finally brought together terrestrial and celestial knowledge. He employed a new mathematics, the "method of fluxions" or, in later terminology, the infinitesimal calculus. Newton did not invent this;

The Italian astronomer and physicist Galileo Galilei (1564–1642), who was forced publicly to recant his heretical views under threat of torture from the Inquisition, is portrayed in this contemporary painting.

Newton thus in due time became, with Francis Bacon, the second of the canonized saints of a new learning. There was little exaggeration in this in Newton's case. He was a man of almost universal scientific interests and, as the phrase has it, touched little that he did not adorn. Yet the full significance of much of Newton's work must always elude the non-scientist. Manifestly, he completed the revolution begun with Copernicus. A dynamic conception of the universe had replaced a static one. His achievement was great enough to provide the physics of the next two centuries and to underpin all the other sciences with a new cosmology.

THE CONFLICT OF SCIENCE AND RELIGION

WHAT WAS NOT ANTICIPATED by Newton and his predecessors was that their work might presage an insoluble conflict of science and religion. Newton, indeed, seems even to have been pleased to observe that the law of gravity did not adequately sustain the view that the universe was a self-regulated system, self-contained once created; if it was not just a watch, its creator could do more than invent it, build it, wind it up and then stand back. He welcomed the logical gap which he could fill by postulating divine intervention, for he was a passionate Protestant apologist. Churchmen, especially Catholic, nevertheless did not find it easy to come to terms with the new science. In the Middle Ages clerics had made important contributions to science, but from the seventeenth to the mid-nineteenth century, very little first-rank scientific work was done by churchmen. This was truer, certainly, of the countries where the Counter-Reformation had triumphed than those where it had not. In the seventeenth century there opened that split

he applied it to physical phenomena. It provided a way of calculating the positions of bodies in motion. His conclusions were set out in a discussion of the movements of the planets contained in a book which was to prove the most important and influential scientific work since that of Euclid. The *Principia*, as it is called for short (or, anglicized, *The Mathematical Principles of Natural Philosophy*), demonstrated how gravity sustained the physical universe. The general cultural consequences of this discovery were comparable with those within science. We have no proper standard of measurement, but perhaps they were even greater. That a single law, discovered by observation and calculation, could explain so much was an astonishing revelation of what the new scientific thinking could achieve. Pope has been quoted to excess, but his epigram still best summarizes the impact of Newton's work on the European mind:

Nature and Nature's laws lay hid in night:
God said, "Let Newton be!" and all was light.

between organized religion and science which has haunted European intellectual history ever since, whatever efforts have from time to time been made to patch it up. One symbolic crisis was that of the Neapolitan Bruno. He was not a scientist but a speculator, formerly a Dominican monk who broke with his order and wandered about Europe publishing controversial works, dabbling in a magical "secret science" supposedly derived from ancient Egypt. In the end the Inquisition took him and after eight years in its hands he was burned at Rome for heresy. His execution became one of the foundations of the later historical mythology of the development of "free thought", of the struggle between progress and religion as it was to come to be seen.

DEFENDERS OF RELIGIOUS BELIEF AND THE CHURCH

In the seventeenth century an antithesis between progress and religion was not much felt by scientists and philosophers. Newton, who wrote copiously on biblical and theological topics and believed his work on the prophetical books to be as flawless as the *Principia*, seems to have held that Moses knew about the heliocentric theory and recommended his readers to "beware of Philosophy and vain deceit and oppositions of science falsely so called" and to have recourse to the Old Testament. Napier, the inventor of logarithms, was delighted to have in them a new tool to deploy in deciphering the mysterious references in the Book of Revelation to the Number of the Beast. The French philosopher Descartes formulated what he found to be satisfactory philosophical defences of religious belief and Christian truth coherent with his technically sceptical approach to his subject. This did not prevent him (or the philosophical movement which took its name

from him, Cartesianism) from attracting the hostility of the Church. The traditional defenders of religious belief correctly recognized that what was at stake was not only the conclusions people arrived at, but the way that they arrived at them. A rationally argued acceptance of religious belief, which started from principles of doubt and demonstrated they could satisfactorily be overcome, was a poor ally for a Church which taught that truth was declared by authority. The Church was quite logical in setting aside as irrelevant Descartes' own devotion and Christianity and correctly (from its own point of view) put all his works on the Index.

The argument from authority was taken up by a French Protestant clergyman of the

The occasional co-existence of scientific experimentation, religion and superstition is demonstrated in this 18th-century painting by Joseph Wright entitled *The Alchymist, in Search of the Philosopher's Stone, Discovers Phosphorus, and Prays for the Successful Conclusion of his Operation, as was the custom of the Ancient Chymical.*

The German philosopher Immanuel Kant is portrayed in this 18th-century lithograph.

later seventeenth century, Pierre Bayle, who pointed out that it had an unsatisfactory open-endedness. What authority prescribed the authority? In the end it seemed to be a matter of opinion. Every dogma of traditional Christianity, he suggested, might be refuted if not in accordance with natural reason. With such ideas a new phase in the history of European thought announced itself; it has been called the Enlightenment.

THE ENLIGHTENMENT

THE WORD ENLIGHTENMENT and similar ones were used in the eighteenth century in most European languages to characterize the thinking which Europeans felt distinguished their own age and cut it off from what had gone before. The key image is of the letting in of light upon what was dark, but when the German philosopher Kant asked the question "What is enlightenment?" in a famous essay he gave a different answer: liberation from self-imposed tutelage. At its heart lay a questioning of authority. The great heritage to be left behind by the Enlightenment was the generalizing of the critical attitude. From this time, everything was exposed to scrutiny. Some felt – and it came in the very long run to be true – that nothing was sacred, but this is somewhat misleading. Enlightenment had its own authority and dogmas; the critical stance itself long went unexamined. Furthermore, Enlightenment was as much a bundle of attitudes as a collection of ideas and here lies another difficulty in coming to terms with it. Many streams flowed into this result but by no means did they all follow the same course. The roots of Enlightenment are as confused as its development, which always resembled a continuing debate – sometimes a civil war – much more than the advance of a united army of the enlightened.

Descartes had argued that systematic doubt was the beginning of firm knowledge. Fifty years later, the English philosopher John Locke provided an account of the psychology of knowledge which reduced its primary constituents to the impressions conveyed by the senses to the mind; there were not, he argued against Descartes, ideas innate in human nature. The mind contained only sense-data and the connections it made between them. This was, of course, to imply that humanity had no fixed ideas of right and wrong; moral values, Locke taught, arose as the mind experienced pain and pleasure. There was to be an enormous future for the development

Kant's *What is Enlightenment?*

"For enlightenment of this kind, all that is needed is *freedom* ... freedom to make *public use* of one's reason in all matters. But I hear on all sides the cry: *Don't argue*! The officer says: Don't argue, get on parade! The tax-official: Don't argue, pay! The clergyman: Don't argue, believe! ... All this means restrictions on freedom everywhere. ... But by the public use of one's own reason I mean that use which anyone may make of it *as a man of learning* addressing the entire *reading public*. ... Thus it would be very harmful if an officer receiving an order from his superiors were to quibble openly, while on duty ... . He must simply obey. But he cannot reasonably be banned from making observations as a man of learning on the errors in the military service, and from submitting these to his public for judgement. The citizen cannot refuse to pay the taxes imposed upon him; presumptuous criticisms of such taxes ... may be punished as an outrage which could lead to general insubordination. Nonetheless, the same citizen does not contravene his civil obligations if, as a learned individual, he publicly voices his thoughts on the impropriety or even injustice of such fiscal measures."

An extract from *An Answer to the Question: "What is Enlightenment?"* by Immanuel Kant (1724–1804), translated by H.B. Nisbet.

Descartes' *Discourse on Method*

" ... I believed I would have sufficient in the four following rules, so long as I took a firm and constant resolve never once to fail to observe them.

"The first was never to accept anything as true that I did not know to be evidently so: that is to say, carefully to avoid precipitancy and prejudice, and to include in my judgements nothing more than what presented itself so clearly and distinctly to my mind that I might have no occasion to place it in doubt.

"The second, to divide each of the difficulties that I was examining into as many parts as might be possible and necessary in order best to solve it.

"The third, to conduct my thoughts in an orderly way, beginning with the simplest objects and the easiest to know, in order to climb gradually, as by degrees, as far as the knowledge of the most complex, and even supposing some order among those objects which do not precede each other naturally.

"And the last, everywhere to make such complete enumerations and such general reviews that I would be sure to have omitted nothing."

An extract from *Discourse on Method* (1637) by René Descartes (1596–1650), translated by F.E. Sutcliffe.

of such ideas; from them would flow theories about education, about society's duty to regulate material conditions and about many other derivations from environmentalism. There was also a huge past behind them: the dualism which Descartes and Locke both expressed in their distinctions of body and mind, physical and moral, have their roots in Plato and Christian metaphysics. Yet what is perhaps most striking at this point is that his ideas could still be associated by Locke with the traditional framework of Christian belief.

AN OPTIMISTIC CREED

Incoherences were always to run through the Enlightenment, but its general trend is clear. The new prestige of science, too, seemed to promise that the observations of the senses were, indeed, the way forward to knowledge, and to a knowledge whose value was proved by its utilitarian efficacy. It could make possible the improvement of the world in which human beings lived. Its techniques could unlock the mysteries of nature and reveal their logical, rational foundations in the laws of physics and chemistry.

All this was long an optimistic creed (the word *optimistie* entered the French language in the seventeenth century). The world was getting better and would continue to do so. In 1600 things had been very different. Then, the Renaissance worship of the classical past had combined with the upheavals of war and the always latent feeling of religious men that

The German mathematician, rationalist philosopher and logician Gottfried Leibniz (1646–1716) saw evil as the consequence of a series of "misunderstandings". Voltaire invented the term *optimistie* to describe Leibniz, who believed that once such "misunderstandings" were resolved, universal peace would reign.

the end of the world could not long be delayed, to produce a pessimistic mood and a sense of decline from a great past. In a great literary debate over whether the achievements of the ancients excelled those of modern times the writers of the late seventeenth century crystallized the idea of progress which emerged from the Enlightenment. It was also a non-specialists' creed. In the eighteenth century it was still possible for an educated man to tie together in a manner satisfactory at least for himself the logic and implications of many different studies. Voltaire was famous as a poet and playwright, but wrote at length on history (he was for a time the French historiographer royal) and expounded Newtonian physics to his contemporaries. Adam Smith was renowned as a moral philosopher before he dazzled the world with his *Wealth of Nations*, a book which may reasonably be said to have founded the modern science of economics.

RELIGION AND THE ENLIGHTENMENT

In such eclecticism religion, too, found a place, yet (as Gibbon put it) "in modern times, a latent, and even involuntary, scepticism adheres to the most pious disposition". In "enlightened" thought there seemed to be

---

D'Alembert and philosophy of the Enlightenment era

"Our time likes to call itself 'the era of philosophy'. Indeed, if we examine the current situation of our knowledge, without prejudice, we cannot deny that philosophy has made great progress among us. The science of nature daily acquires new riches, geometry widens its frontiers and carries its torch into the domains of physics, closest to it; at last, the true system of the world is revealed, developed and perfected. The science of nature widens its vision from Earth to Saturn, from the history of the skies to that of insects. And with it, all the other sciences take on new life. But the discovery and use of a new method of philosophy has awakened, however, through the enthusiasm which accompanies all great discoveries, a general increase of ideas. All these causes have contributed to producing a vital effervescence of all spirits. This effervescence, which spreads everywhere, violently attacks anything which stands up to it ... . Everything has been discussed, analysed, stirred up, from the principles of science to the fundaments of religion, from the problems of metaphysics to those of taste, from music to morals, from theological questions to those of economy and trade, from politics to civil rights. As the fruit of this general effervescence of spirits, a new light is being shed on many objects and a new darkness covers them, as in the ebb and flow of the tide beaching unexpected things on the shore and pulling others away with it."

The French philosopher and physicist d'Alembert (1717–1783) is depicted in this 18th-century engraving.

An extract from *Essay on the Elements of Philosophy* by Jean le Rond d'Alembert, 1758.

L'EGIDE DE MINERVE

This allegory of the the Enlightenment in France, painted by an anonymous artist c.1780, shows representatives of the main religions deep in discussion. Around them is evidence of the dissemination of books and journals.

small room for the divine and the theological. It was not just that educated Europeans no longer felt hell gaping about them. The world was becoming less mysterious; it also promised to be less tragic. More and more troubles seemed not inseparable from being, but man-made. Awkward problems, it was true, might still be presented by appalling natural disasters such as earthquakes, but if the relief of most ills was possible and if, as one thinker put it, "Man's proper business is to seek happiness and avoid misery", what was the relevance of the dogmas of Salvation and Damnation? God could still be included in a perfunctory way in the philosopher's account of the universe, as the First Cause that had started the whole thing going and the Great Mechanic who prescribed the rules on which it ran, but was there any place for his subsequent intervention in its working, either directly by incarnation or indirectly through his Church and the sacraments it conveyed? Inevitably, the Enlightenment brought revolt against the Church, the supreme claimant to intellectual and moral authority.

Denis Diderot (1713–1784), portrayed here in 1784, was commissioned to direct the *Encyclopédie* (1751–1776), a demonstration of the triumph of the rationalist spirit.

REJECTION OF THE AUTHORITY OF THE PAST

Here was a fundamental conflict. The rejection of authority by the thoughtful in the seventeenth and eighteenth centuries was only rarely complete, in the sense that new authority was sought and discovered in what were believed to be the teachings of science and reason. Yet increasingly and more and more emphatically the authority of the past was rejected. As the literary argument over ancient and modern culture advanced the destruction of the authority of classical teaching, so had the Protestant Reformation exploded the authority of the Catholic Church, the other pillar of traditional European culture. When the Protestant reformers had replaced old priest by new presbyter (or by the Old Testament) they could not undo the work of undermining religious authority which they had begun and which the men of the Enlightenment were to carry much further.

CONFIDENCE IN THE ENLIGHTENMENT

The implications of the Enlightenment took some time to emerge, whatever the quickly formulated and justified misgivings of churchmen. The characteristics of advanced thought in the eighteenth century tended to express themselves in fairly practical and everyday recommendations which in a measure masked their tendency. They are probably best summarized in terms of the fundamental beliefs which underlay them and of which they were consequences. At the basis of all others was a new confidence in the power of mind; this was one reason why the Enlightened so much admired Bacon, who shared this with them, yet even the creative giants of the Renaissance did not do so much to give Europeans a conviction of intellectual power as did the eighteenth century. On this rested the assurance that almost indefinite improvement was possible. Most thinkers of the age were optimists who saw it as the apex of history. Confidently they looked forward to the improvement of the lot of mankind by the manipulation of nature and the unfolding to human beings of the truths which reason had written in their hearts. Innate ideas bundled out of the front door crept in again by the back stairs. Optimism was qualified only by the realization that there were big practical obstacles to be overcome. The first of these was simply ignorance. Perhaps a knowledge of final causes was impossible (and certainly science seemed to suggest this as it revealed more and more complexity in nature) but this was not the sort of ignorance which worried the enlightened. They had a more everyday level of experience in mind and the combination of reason and knowledge gave confidence that ignorance could be dispersed. The greatest literary embodiment of Enlightenment had precisely this aim.

The great *Encyclopédie* of Diderot and D'Alembert was a huge compilation of information and propaganda in twenty-one volumes published between 1751 and 1765. As some of its articles made clear, another great obstacle to enlightenment was intolerance – especially when it interfered with freedom of publication and debate. The *Encyclopédie*, said one of its authors, was a "war machine", intended to change minds as well as inform them. Parochialism was yet another barrier to happiness. The values of the Enlightenment, it was assumed, were those of all civilized society. They were universal. Never, except perhaps in the Middle Ages, has the European intellectual élite been more cosmopolitan or shared more of a common language. Its cosmopolitanism was increased by knowledge of other societies, for which the Enlightenment showed an extra-

These first editions of the encyclopedia compiled by Denis Diderot and Jean le Rond d'Alembert once formed part of Louis XVI's private collection.

Jovellanos on the value of education

"Is it not education which develops intellectual faculties and which increases man's physical strength? Without it, his intellect is like an unlit torch; with it, he illuminates all the kingdoms of nature, discovering the deepest, hidden caverns, and subjects them to his will. Calculations by an inexpert man with dark strength will have little results, but with the help of nature, what methods can he not use? What obstacles can he not remove? What prodigies can he not produce? This is how education improves human beings, the only beings which can be perfected by it, the only ones gifted with the capacity for perfection. This is the greatest gift that he has received from his ineffable Creator. Education prepares him, gives him the means for his welfare and comfort, and is, finally, the basic origin of individual happiness. It is also the origin of public prosperity which can only be understood as the sum of result of the happiness of individuals who make up the social body."

An extract from *A Thesis on Public Education* (1802) by Gaspar de Jovellanos (1744–1811).

ordinary appetite. In part this was because of genuine curiosity; accounts of travel and discovery brought to public notice unfamiliar ideas and institutions and thus awoke interest in social and ethical relativities. They provided new grounds for criticism. What was thought to be a humane and enlightened China particularly captured the imagination of eighteenth-century Europeans, a fact which perhaps suggests how superficial was their acquaintance with its realities.

THE INSTITUTIONALIZATION OF CRITICISM

Once ignorance, intolerance and parochialism were removed, it was assumed that the unimpeded operation of the laws of nature, uncovered by reason, would promote the reform of society in everyone's interest except that of those wedded to the past by their blindness or their enjoyment of indefensible privilege. The *Lettres persanes* of the French author Montesquieu began the tradition of suggesting that the institutions of existing societies – in his case the laws of France – could be improved by comparison with the laws of nature. In articulating such a programme, the men of the Enlightenment were appointing themselves as the priesthood of a new social order. In their vision of their role as critics and reformers there emerged for the first time a social ideal which has been with us ever since, that of the intellectual. Moralists, philosophers, scholars, scientists already existed; their defining characteristic was specialized competence. What the Enlightenment invented was the ideal of the generalized critical intellect. Autonomous, rational, continuous and universal criticism was institutionalized as never before and the modern "intellectual" is the outcome.

THE PHILOSOPHERS

The eighteenth century did not use this term. It had the type, but called its exemplars simply "philosophers". This was an interesting adaptation and broadening of a word already familiar; it came to connote not the specialized mental pursuit of philosophical studies but the acceptance of a common outlook and critical stance. It was a term with moral and evaluative tones, used familiarly by enemies as well as friends to indicate also a zeal to propagate the truths revealed by critical insight to a large and lay public. The archetypes were a group of French writers soon lumped together in spite of their differences and referred to as *philosophes*. Their numbers and celebrity correctly suggest the preponderance of France in the central period of Enlightenment thought. Other countries neither produced so many and such conspicuous figures within this tradition, nor did they usually confer such prestige and eminence on those they had. Yet the presiding deities of the early Enlightenment were the English Newton and Locke; it could be reasonably claimed too that the philosopher who expressed the most extreme development of Enlightenment ideals and methods was Bentham, and that its greatest historiographical monument is Gibbon's work. Further north, Scotland had a great eighteenth-century cultural efflorescence and produced in Hume one of the most engaging as well as the most acute of the Enlightenment's technical philosophers, who combined extreme intellectual scepticism with good nature and social conservatism, and in Adam Smith the author of one of the great creative books of modern times. Among Latin countries, Italy was, outside France, most prolific in its contribution to the Enlightenment in

spite of the predominance there of the Roman Church. The Italian Enlightenment would be assured of a remembrance even if it had thrown up only Beccaria, the author of a book which founded penal reform and the criticism of penology and gave currency to one of the great slogans of history, "the greatest happiness of the greatest number". The German Enlightenment was slower to unroll and less productive of figures who won universal acclaim (possibly for linguistic reasons) but produced in Kant a thinker who, if he consciously sought to go beyond the Enlightenment, nevertheless embodied in his moral recommendations much of what it stood for. Only Spain seemed to lag conspicuously. It was not an unfair impression even

This 18th-century painting portrays the French author and *philosophe* Voltaire at his desk.

Montesquieu's *The Spirit of the Laws*

"When legislative power is united with executive power in a single person or in a single body of the magistracy, there is no liberty, because one can fear that the same monarch or senate that makes tyrannical laws will execute them tyrannically.

"Nor is there liberty if the power of judging is not separate from legislative power and from executive power. If it were joined to legislative power, the power over the life and liberty of the citizens would be arbitrary, for the judge would be the legislator. If it were joined to executive power, the judge could have the force of an oppressor."

An extract from *The Spirit of the Laws* by Montesquieu, 1748, translated by Anne M. Cohler, Basia C. Miller and Harold S. Stone.

Empress Maria Theresia of Austria (1717–1780) is shown with her French-speaking family in 1772. French was the common language of intellectual Europe during the Enlightenment period.

allowing for the work of one or two enlightened statesmen; Spanish universities in the eighteenth century were still rejecting Newton.

FRENCH CULTURAL PRIMACY

Important though the work of other nations was for the history of civilization, that of the French struck contemporaries the most forcefully. There were many reasons: one lay simply in the glamour of power; France under Louis XIV had won an enduring prestige. Another reason is the magnificent instrument for the diffusion of French culture which lay to hand in the French language. It was in the eighteenth century the *lingua franca* of Europe's intellectuals and its people of fashion alike; Maria Theresia and her children used it for their family correspondence and Frederick II wrote (rather bad) verses in it. A European audience was assured for any book written in French and it seems likely that the

success of that language actually held back cultural advance in the German tongue.

A shared language made propaganda, discussion and critical comment possible, but what would actually be achieved by way of practical reform in the short term was bound to depend on political circumstance. Some statesmen attempted to put "enlightened" ideas into practice, because there were coincidences between the interests of states and the aims of philosophers. This was especially apparent when "enlightened despotisms" found themselves running into opposition from vested interest and conservatism. Such conflicts were obvious in the enforcement of educational reform at the expense of the Church inside the Habsburg dominions, or in Voltaire's attacks, written to the brief of a royal minister, on the *parlement* of Paris when it stood in the way of fiscal innovation. Some rulers, like Catherine the Great of Russia, ostentatiously paraded the influence of Enlightenment ideas on their

Dated 1850, this painting is an evocation of Frederick II of Prussia (1712–1786), centre, at lunch at his Sans Souci palace. His guests are depicted as including famous artists and philosophers; the figure on the far right is Voltaire.

legislation. Perhaps the most important and influential impact of such ideas, apart from those of utilitarian reform which were deployed against the Church, was always in educational and economic matters. In France, at least, the economic recommendations of enlightened thinkers made their mark on administration.

ATTACKS ON THE CHURCH

Religious questions drew the attention of the *philosophes* with unique power. The Church and the effects of its teaching were, of course, still inseparable from every side of Europe's life. It was not just that the Church claimed authority in so much, but also that it was

Jean Calas, the French Protestant merchant who was executed in Toulouse in 1762 for heresy, is depicted saying his farewells to his family in an illustration dated 1767.

physically omnipresent as a great corporate interest, both social and economic; it was involved in some measure in every aspect of society to which the attention of reformers might be drawn. Whether it was because the abuse of sanctuary or clerical privilege stood in the way of judicial reform, or mortmain impeded economic improvement, or a clerical monopoly of education encumbered the training of administrators, or dogma prevented the equal treatment of loyal and valued subjects, the Church seemed to find itself always opposing improvement. But this was not all that drew the fire of the *philosophes*. Religion could also lead, they thought, to crime. One of the last great scandals of the era of religious persecution was the execution of a Protestant at Toulouse in 1762 on the charge of converting Catholics to heresy. For this he was tortured, tried, convicted and executed. Voltaire made this a *cause célèbre*. His efforts did not change the law, but it is impossible not to believe that, for all the violence of feeling which continued to divide Catholic and Protestant in southern France, they made it impossible for such a judicial murder ever to be repeated. Yet France did not give even a limited legal toleration to Protestants until 1787 and then did not extend it to Jews. By that time Joseph II had already introduced religious toleration into his Catholic territories.

THE ENLIGHTENMENT'S LEGACY

The continuing power of the Church suggests an important limit to the practical success of enlightenment. For all its revolutionary power, it had to operate within the still very restrictive institutional and moral framework of the *ancien régime*. Its relationship with despotism was ambiguous: it might struggle against the imposition of censorship or the practice of religious intolerance in a theocratic monarchy, but could also depend on despotic power to carry out reform. Nor, it must be remembered, were enlightened ideas the only stimulus to improvement. The English institutions Voltaire admired did not stem from enlightenment and many changes in eighteenth-century England owed more to religion than to "philosophy".

The greatest political importance of the Enlightenment lay in its legacies to the future. It clarified and formulated many of the key demands of what was to be called "liberalism", though here, too, its legacy is ambiguous, for the men of the Enlightenment sought not freedom for its own sake but freedom for the consequences it would bring. The possibility of contriving that human beings should be happy on earth was the great insight of the eighteenth century; the age may be said, indeed, not merely to have invented earthly happiness as a feasible goal but also the thought that it could be measured (Bentham wrote of a "felicific calculus") and that it could be promoted through the exercise of reason. Above all, the Enlightenment diffused the idea that knowledge, in its social tendency, was fundamentally benign and progressive, and therefore that it should be trusted. Those ideas all had profound political implications.

ANTI-CLERICALISM

Apart from the invention of the concept of earthly happiness, the age made its best-known contribution to the future European liberal tradition in a more specific and negative form; the Enlightenment created classical anti-clericalism. Criticism of what the Church had done led to support for attacks by the state upon ecclesiastical organizations and authority. The struggles of Church and State had many roots other than philosophical, but

could always be presented as a part of a continuing war of enlightenment and rationality against superstition and bigotry. In particular, the papacy attracted criticism – or contempt; Voltaire seems to have once believed that it would in fact disappear before the end of the century. The greatest success of the *philosophes* in the eyes of their enemies and of many of their supporters was the papal dissolution of the Society of Jesus.

A few *philosophes* carried their attacks on the Church beyond institutions to an attack on religion itself. Out-and-out atheism (together with deterministic materialism) had its first serious expression in the eighteenth century, but it remained unusual. Most of those during the Enlightenment era who thought about these things were probably

Joseph II of Austria (1741–1790), whose coronation banquet in Frankfurt in 1765 is shown here, reduced the power of the Church, advocated religious toleration and abolished serfdom.

sceptical about the dogmas of the Church, but kept up a vague theism. Certainly, too, they believed in the importance of religion as a social force. As Voltaire said, "one must have religion for the sake of the people". He, in any case, continued throughout his life to assert, with Newton, the existence of God and died formally at peace with the Church.

ROUSSEAU

Something always in danger of being lost to sight in the Enlightenment is the importance of the non-intellectual and non-rational side of human nature. The most prophetic figure of the century in this respect and one who quarrelled bitterly with many of the leading figures among the "enlightened" and the *philosophes* was the Genevan Rousseau. His importance in the history of thought lies in his impassioned pleas that due weight be given to the feelings and the moral sense, both in danger of eclipse by rationality.

In his *Social Contract* of 1762, the Swiss-born philosopher Jean-Jacques Rousseau (1712–1778) expounded many of the ideas on democracy and government that would later form the basis of the French Revolution. In this engraving dating from the year of his death he is portrayed gathering herbs in Ermenonville.

Because of this, he thought, the men of his day were stunted creatures, partial and corrupt beings, deformed by the influence of a society which encouraged this eclipse.

European culture was to be deeply marked by Rousseau's vision, sometimes perniciously. He planted (it has been well said) a new torment in every soul. There can be found in his writings a new attitude to religion (which was to revivify it), a new psychological obsession with the individual which was to flood into art and literature, the invention of the sentimental approach to nature and natural beauty, the origins of the modern doctrine of nationalism, a new child-centredness in educational theory, a secularized puritanism (rooted in a mythical view of ancient Sparta), and much else besides. All these things had both good and bad consequences; Rousseau was, in short, the key figure in the making of what has been called Romanticism. In much he was an innovator, and often one of genius. Much, too, he shared with others. His distaste for the Enlightenment erosion of community, his sense that men were brothers and members of a social and moral whole was, for example, expressed just as eloquently by the Irish author Edmund Burke, who nevertheless drew from it very different conclusions. Rousseau was in some measure voicing views beginning to be held by others as the age of Enlightenment passed its zenith. Yet of Rousseau's central and special importance to Romanticism there can be no doubt.

ROMANTICISM

Romanticism is a much used and much misused term. It can be properly applied to things which seem diametrically opposed. Soon after 1800, for example, some would deny any value to the past and would seek to overthrow its legacies just as violently as men of the Enlightenment had done, while at the same time others tenaciously defended historic institutions. Both can be (and have been) called Romantics, because in each of them moral passion counted for more than intellectual analysis. The clearest link between such antitheses lay in the new emphasis of romantic Europe on feeling, intuition, and, above all, the natural. Romanticism, whose

The Wanderer Over the Sea of Clouds was painted in 1818 by one of the early European Romantic artists, Caspar David Friedrich (1774–1840).

expressions were to be so manifold, started almost always from some objection to enlightened thought, whether from disbelief that science could provide an answer to all questions, or from a revulsion against rational self-interest. But its positive roots lay deeper than this, in the Reformation's displacement of so many traditional values by the one supreme value of sincerity; it was not entirely wrong to see Romanticism as some Catholic critics saw it, as a secularized Protestantism, for above all it sought authenticity, self-realization, honesty, moral exaltation. Unhappily it did so all too often without regard to cost. The great effects were to reverberate through the nineteenth century, usually with painful results, and in the twentieth century would affect many other parts of the world as one of the last manifestations of the vigour of European culture.

The Decline of the Carthaginian Empire, by the English painter Joseph Turner (1775–1851), was first exhibited in 1817 and is one of the great masterpieces of the Romantic era.

2 LONG-TERM CHANGE

IN 1798 THOMAS MALTHUS, an English clergyman, published an *Essay on Population* which was to prove the most influential book ever written on the subject. He described what appeared to be the laws of population growth but his book's importance transcended this apparently limited scientific task. Its impact on, for example, economic theory and biological science was to be just as important as the contribution it made to demographic studies. Here, though, such important consequences matter less than the book's status as an indicator of a change in thinking about population. Roughly speaking, for two centuries or so European statesmen and economists had agreed that a rising population was a sign of prosperity. Kings and queens should seek to increase the number of their subjects, it was thought, not merely because this would provide more tax-payers and soldiers but because a bigger population both quickened economic life and was an indication that it had done so. Obviously, larger numbers showed that the economy was providing a living for more people. This view was in its essentials endorsed by no less an authority than the great Adam Smith himself, whose *Wealth of Nations*, a book of huge influence, had agreed as recently as 1776 that an increase in population was a good rough test of economic prosperity.

This illustration, which depicts a busy marketplace at Louth in Lincolnshire, England, dates from the time when Thomas Malthus (1766–1834) was writing about population growth.

THOMAS MALTHUS

Malthus doused the view that population growth signified prosperity with very cold water. Whatever the consequences for society as a whole might be judged to be, he concluded that a rising population sooner or later spelt disaster and suffering for most of its members, the poor. In a famous demonstration he argued that the produce of the earth had finite limits, set by the amount of land available to grow food. This in turn set a limit to population. Yet population always tended to grow in the short run. As it grew, it would press increasingly upon a narrowing margin of subsistence. When this margin was exhausted, famine must follow. The population would then fall until it could be maintained with the food available. This mechanism could only be kept from operating if men and women abstained from having children (and prudence, as they regarded the consequences, might help them by encouraging late marriage) or by such horrors as the natural checks imposed by disease or war.

Much more could be said about the complexity and refinement of this gloomy thesis. It aroused huge argument and counter-argument, and whether true or false, a theory attracting such attention must tell us much about the age. Somehow, the growth of population had begun to worry people so that even prose so unattractive as that of Malthus had great success. People had become aware of population growth as they had not been aware of it before and had done so just as it was to become faster than ever. In the nineteenth century, in spite of what Malthus

The Scottish economist Adam Smith (1723–1790), whose portrait adorns this 1787 medallion, firmly believed that economic freedom was beneficial for society.

had said, the numbers of some divisions of the human race went up with a rapidity and to levels hitherto inconceivable.

POPULATION GROWTH

A LONG VIEW IS BEST for measuring such a change; there is nothing to be gained and much to be lost by worrying about precise dates and the overall trends run on well into the twentieth century. If we include Russia (whose population has until very recent times to be estimated from very poor statistics) then a European population of about 190 million in 1800 rose to about 420 million a century later. As the rest of the world seems to have grown rather more slowly, this represented a rise in Europe's share of the total population of the world from about one-fifth to one-quarter; for a little while, her disadvantage in numbers by comparison with the great Asiatic centres of population was reduced (while she continued to enjoy her technical and psychological superiority). Moreover, at the same time, Europe was sustaining a huge emigration of her stocks. In the 1830s European emigration overseas first passed the figure of 100,000 a year; in 1913 it was over a million and a half. Taking an even longer view, perhaps fifty million people left Europe to go overseas between 1840 and 1930, most of them to the western hemisphere. All these people *and their descendants* ought to be added to the totals in order to grasp how much European population growth accelerated in these years.

This growth was not shared evenly within Europe and this made important differences to the standing of great powers. Their strength was usually reckoned in terms of military manpower and it was a crucial change that in 1871 Germany replaced France as the largest mass of population under one government west of Russia. Another way of looking at such changes would be to compare the respective shares of Europe's population enjoyed by the major military powers at different dates. Between 1800 and 1900, for example, that of Russia grew from 21 to 24 per cent of the total, Germany's from 13 to 14, while France's fell from 15 to 10 per cent, and that of Austria slightly less, from 15 to 12. Few increases, though, were as dramatic as that of the United Kingdom, which rose from about eight million when Malthus wrote, to twenty-two million by 1850 (it was to reach thirty-six million by 1914).

FALLING MORTALITY RATES

Population grew everywhere, though at different rates at different times. The poorest agrarian regions of Eastern Europe, for example, experienced their highest growth rates only in the 1920s and 1930s. This is because the basic mechanism of population increase in this period, underlying change everywhere, was a fall in mortality. Never in history has there been so spectacular a fall in death rates as in the last hundred years, and it showed first in the advanced countries of Europe in the nineteenth century. Roughly speaking, before 1850 most European countries had birth rates which slightly exceeded death rates and both were about the same in all countries. They showed, that is to say, how little impact had been made by that date upon the fundamental determinants of human life in a still overwhelmingly rural society. After 1880 this changed rapidly. The death rate in advanced European countries fell pretty steadily, from about thirty-five per thousand inhabitants per year to about twenty-eight by 1900; fifty years later it would be about eighteen. Less advanced countries still maintained rates of thirty-eight per thousand between 1850 and 1900, and thirty-two down to 1950. This produced a striking inequality between two Europes, in the richer of which expectation of life was much higher. Since, in large measure, advanced European countries lay in the west, this was (leaving out Spain, a poor country with high mortality) a fresh intensification of older divisions between East and West, a new accentuation of the imaginary frontier from the Baltic to the Adriatic.

INCREASED LIFE EXPECTANCY

Other factors besides lower mortality helped. Earlier marriage and a rising birth rate had showed themselves in the first phase of expansion, as economic opportunity increased, but now they mattered much more, since from the nineteenth century onwards, the children of earlier marriages were much more likely to survive, thanks to greater humanitarian concern, cheaper food, medical and engineering progress, and better public

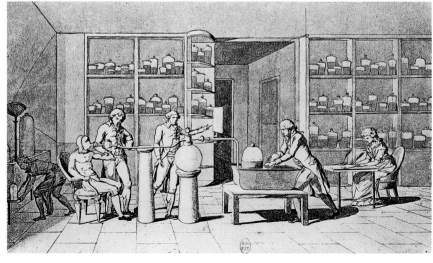

The work of scientists such as Antoine Lavoisier (1743–1794) made possible the medical advances that increased life expectancy. Here, in a drawing by his wife, Lavoisier is shown in his laboratory carrying out research on the human respiratory system.

health provision. Of these, medical science and the provision of medical services were the last to influence population trends. Doctors only came to grips with the great killing diseases from about 1870 onwards; these were the child-killers: diphtheria, scarlet fever, whooping-cough, typhoid. Infant mortality was thus dramatically reduced and expectation of life at birth greatly increased. But earlier than this, social reformers and engineers had already done much to reduce the incidence of these and other diseases (though not their fatality) by building better drains and devising better cleaning arrangements for the growing cities. Cholera was eliminated in industrial countries by 1900, though it had devastated London and Paris in the 1830s and 1840s. No western European country had a major plague outbreak after 1899. As such changes affected more and more countries, their general tendency was everywhere to raise the average age of death with, in the long run, dramatic results. By the second quarter of the twentieth century, men and women in North America, the United Kingdom, Scandinavia and industrial Europe could expect to live two or three times as long as their medieval ancestors. Immense consequences flowed from this.

FAMILY LIMITATION

Just as accelerated population increase first announced itself in those countries which were economically the most advanced, so did the slowing down of growth which was the next discernible demographic trend. This was produced by a declining number of births, though it was for a long time masked because the fall in the death rate was even faster. In every society this showed itself first among the better-off; to this day, it remains a good rough working rule that fecundity varies

inversely with income (celebrated exceptions among wealthy American political dynasties notwithstanding). In some societies (and in western rather than eastern Europe) this was because marriage tended to be put off longer so that women were married for less of their fertile lives; in some it was because couples chose to have fewer children – and could now do so with confidence, thanks to effective contraceptive techniques. Possibly there had been some knowledge of such techniques in some European countries; it is at least certain that the nineteenth century brought improvements in them (some made possible by scientific and technical advance in manufacturing the necessary devices) and propaganda which spread knowledge of them. Once more, a social change touches upon a huge ramification of influences, because it is difficult not to connect such spreading knowledge with, for example, greater literacy, and with rising expectations. Although people were beginning to be wealthier than their ancestors, they were all the time adjusting their notion of what was a tolerable life – and therefore a tolerable size of family. Whether they followed the calculation by putting off the date of

Entitled *The Origin of the Vaccine*, this contemporary cartoon caricatures Edward Jenner (1749–1823), the pioneer of vaccination. Jenner noticed that people who had suffered from cowpox did not develop the more serious disease smallpox, an observation that led him deliberately to infect subjects with cowpox in order to protect them against smallpox.

marriage (as French and Irish peasants did) or by adopting contraceptive techniques (as the English and French middle classes seem to have done) was shaped by other cultural factors.

THE EFFECTS OF POPULATION GROWTH

Changes in the ways men and women died and lived in their families transformed the structures of society. On the one hand, the Western countries in the nineteenth and twentieth centuries had absolutely more young people about and, for a time, also had them about in a greater proportion than ever before. It is difficult not to attribute much of the expansiveness, buoyancy and vigour of nineteenth-century Europe to this. On the other hand, advanced societies gradually found a higher proportion of their members surviving into old age than ever before. This increasingly strained the social mechanisms which had in earlier centuries maintained the old and those incapable of work; the problem grew worse as competition for industrial employment became more intense. By 1914, in almost every European or North American country much thought had been given to ways of confronting the problems of poverty and dependence, however great the differences in scale and success of efforts to cope with them.

Such trends would not begin to show in eastern Europe until after 1918, when their general pattern was already well established in the advanced Western countries. Death rates long continued to fall more sharply than did the birth rate, even in advanced countries, so that down to the present the population of Europe and the European world has continued to rise. It is one of the most important themes in the history of the era, linked to almost every other. Its material consequences can be seen in unprecedented urbanization and the rise of huge consumer markets for manufacturing industry. The social consequences range from strife and unrest to changing institutions to grapple with them. There were international repercussions as statesmen took into account population figures in deciding what risks they could (and which they had to) take, or as people became more and more alarmed about the consequences of overcrowding. Worries in the nineteenth-century United Kingdom over the prospect of too many poor and unemployed led to the encouragement of emigration which, in its turn, shaped people's thinking and feelings about empire. Later, the Germans discouraged emigration because they feared the loss of military potential, while the French and Belgians pioneered the award of children's allowances for the same reason.

MALTHUS SEEMS TO BE DISPROVED

The introduction of measures designed to influence population levels suggests, correctly, that the gloomy prophecies of Malthus tended to be forgotten as the years went by and the disasters he feared did not take place. The nineteenth century still brought demographic calamities to Europe; Ireland and Russia had spectacular famines and near-famine conditions occurred in many other places. But such disaster grew rarer. As famine and dearth were eliminated from advanced countries, this in turn helped to make disease demographically less damaging. Meanwhile Europe north of the Balkans enjoyed two long periods of virtually undisturbed peace from 1815 to 1848 and from 1871 to 1914; war, another of Malthus's checks, also seemed to be less of a scourge. Finally, his diagnosis actually seemed to be disproved when a rise in population was accompanied by higher standards of living – as rises in the average age of death seemed to show. Pessimists could only reply (reasonably) that Malthus had not been answered; all that had happened was that there had turned out to be much more food available than had been feared. It did not follow that supplies were limitless.

A REVOLUTION IN FOOD PRODUCTION

IN FACT, there was occurring another of those few great historical changes which have truly transformed the basic conditions of human life. It can reasonably be called a food-producing revolution. Its beginnings have already been traced. In the eighteenth century European agriculture was already capable of obtaining about two and a half times the yield on its seed normal in the Middle Ages. Now even greater agricultural improvement was at hand. Yields would go up to still more spectacular levels. From about 1800, it has been calculated, Europe's agricultural productivity grew at a rate of about 1 per cent a year, dwarfing all previous advance. More important still, as time passed European industry and commerce would make it possible to tap huge larders in other parts of the world. Both of these changes were aspects of a single process, the accelerating investment in productive capacity which made Europe and North America by 1870 clearly the greatest concentration of wealth on the face of the globe. Agriculture was fundamental to it. People have spoken of an "agricultural revolution" and provided this is not thought of as implying rapid change, it is an acceptable term; nothing much less strong

will describe the huge surge in world output achieved between 1750 and 1870 (and, later, even surpassed). But it was a process of great complexity, drawing on many different sources and linked to the other sectors of the economy in indispensable ways. It was only one aspect of a worldwide economic change which involved in the end not merely continental Europe, but the Americas and Australasia as well.

This illustration from Diderot's *Encyclopédie* (1751–1776) depicts traditional agricultural processes and implements.

Until the latter half of the 19th century, grain was the single most important crop in most of Europe and this is reflected in countless paintings. The English artist John Constable (1776–1837), painted *The Wheatfield* in 1826.

ENGLISH AGRICULTURE

Once important qualifications have been stated, it is possible to particularize. By 1750 England had the best agriculture in the world. The most advanced techniques were prac-tised and the integration of agriculture with a commercial market economy had gone fur-

thest in England, whose lead was to be main-tained for another century or so. European farmers went there to observe methods, buy stock and machinery, and seek advice. Meanwhile, the English farmer, benefiting from peace at home (that there were no large-scale and continuous military operations on British soil after 1650 was of literally incalculable benefit to the economy) and a rising population to buy his produce, generated profits which provided capital for further improvement. His willingness to invest them in this way was, in the short run, an optimistic response to the likely commercial prospects but also says something deeper about the nature of English society. The benefits of better farming went in England to individuals who owned their own land or held it securely as leaseholding tenants on terms shaped by market realities. English agriculture was part of a capitalist market economy in which land was even by the eighteenth century treated almost as a commodity like any other. Restraints on its use familiar in European countries had disappeared faster and faster ever since Henry VIII's sequestration of ecclesiastical property. After 1750, the last great stage of this came with the spate of Enclosure Acts at the turn of the century (significantly coincident with high prices for grain) which mobilized for private profit the English peasant's traditional rights to pasture, fuel or other economic benefits. One of the most striking contrasts between English and European agriculture in the early nineteenth century was that the traditional peasant all but disappeared in England. England had wage labourers and smallholders, but the huge European rural populations of individuals with some, if minuscule, legal rights linking them to the soil through communal usages and a mass of tiny holdings, did not exist.

THE TRANSFORMATION OF ENGLISH FARMING METHODS

Inside the framework provided by prosperity and English social institutions, technical progress was continuous. For a long time, much of this was hit-and-miss. Early breeders of better animals succeeded not because of a knowledge of chemistry, which was in its infancy, or of genetics, which did not exist, but because they backed hunches within long-established practice. Even so, the results were remarkable. The appearance of the livestock inhabiting the landscape changed; the scraggy medieval sheep whose backs resembled, in section, the Gothic arches of the monasteries which bred them, gave way to the fat, square, contented-looking animals familiar today. "Symmetry, well-covered" was an eighteenth-century farmer's toast. The appearance of farms changed as draining and hedging progressed and big, open medieval fields with their narrow strips, each cultivated by a different peasant, gave way to enclosed fields worked in rotation and made a huge patchwork of the English countryside. In some of these fields machinery was at work even by 1750. Much thought was given to its use and improvement in the eighteenth century, but it does not seem that it really made much of a contribution to output until after 1800, when more and more large fields became available, and it became more productive in relation to cost. It was not long before steam engines were driving threshers; with their appearance in English fields, the way was open which

This 19th-century engraving shows a steam-powered threshing machine. Most agricultural tasks, however, were carried out by hand until the late 19th century.

The hard working conditions of the rural peasant are depicted in this painting entitled *Working in the Fields* by the Italian artist Arnaldo Ferraguti (1850–1924). The use of centuries-old farming methods, including three-yearly crop rotation and the fallow field system, continues today in some of the more traditional parts of Europe.

would lead eventually to an almost complete replacement of muscular by machine power on the twentieth-century farm.

species, and much else. Change on so comprehensive a basis often had to work against the social and political grain, too.

RURAL CHANGE IN CONTINENTAL EUROPE

AGRICULTURAL IMPROVEMENTS and changes spread, *mutatis mutandis* and with a lag in time, to continental Europe. Except by comparison with earlier centuries of quasi-immobility, progress was not always rapid. In Calabria or Andalusia, it might be imperceptible over a century. Nevertheless, rural Europe changed, and the changes came by many routes. The struggle against the inelasticities of food supply was in the end successful, but it was the outcome of hundreds of particular victories over fixed crop rotations, outdated fiscal arrangements, poor standards of tillage and husbandry, and sheer ignorance. The gains were better stock, more effective control of plant blight and animal disease, the introduction of altogether new

FRANCE

The French formally abolished serfdom in 1789; this probably did not mean much, for

This painting by Francisco de Goya (1748–1828) is entitled *The Grape Harvest.* Intensive farming existed in parts of northern Europe by 1800, but traditional crops and farming methods persisted in most Mediterranean regions, as did the peasant's precarious way of life.

The Corn Sifters was painted by Gustave Courbet in 1854. The harsh living and working conditions of many European peasants, labourers, smallholders, sharecroppers, and tenant-farmers prompted many to emigrate to the cities or to other continents during the 19th century.

there were few serfs in France at that date. The abolition of the "feudal system" in the same year was a much more important matter. What was meant by this vague term was the destruction of a mass of traditional and legal usages and rights which stood in the way of the exploitation of land by individuals as an investment like any other. Almost at once, many of the peasants who had thought they wanted this discovered that they did not altogether like it in practice; they discriminated. They were happy to abolish the customary dues paid to the lord of the manor, but did not welcome the loss of customary rights to common land. The whole change was made still more confusing and difficult to measure by the fact that there took place at the same time a big redistribution of property. Much land previously belonging to the Church was sold within a few years to private individuals. The consequent increase in the number of people owning land outright and growth in the average size of properties should, on the English analogy, have led to a period of great agricultural advance for France, but it did not. There was very slow progress and little consolidation of properties on the English pattern.

THE GERMANIC LANDS

Generalizations about the pace and uniformity of what was happening should be cautious and qualified. For all the enthusiasm Germans were showing for travelling exhibitions of agricultural machinery in the 1840s, theirs was a huge country and one of those

(France was the other) of which a great economic historian commented that "broadly speaking, no general and thorough-going improvement can be registered in peasant life before the railway age". Yet the dismantling of medieval institutions standing in the way of agricultural improvement did go on steadily before that and prepared the way for it. It was accelerated in some places by the arrival during the Napoleonic period of French armies of occupation, which introduced French law, and after this by other forces, so that by 1850 peasants tied to the soil and obligatory labour had disappeared from most of Europe. This did not mean, of course, that attitudes from the *ancien régime* did not linger after its institutions had disappeared. Prussian, Magyar and Polish landlords seem, for good and ill, to have maintained much of their more or less patriarchal authority in the manor even after its legal supports had vanished, and did so as late as 1914. This was important in assuring a continuity of conservative aristocratic values in a much more intense and concentrated way in these areas than in western Europe. The Junker often accepted the implications of the market in planning his own estate management, but not in his relations with his tenants.

SERFS AND SLAVES

The longest resistance to change in traditional legal forms in agriculture came in Russia. There, serfdom itself persisted until abolished in 1861. This act did not at once bring Russian agriculture entirely under the operation of individualist and market economy principles, but with it an era of European history had closed. From the Urals to Corunna there no longer survived in law any substantial working of land on the basis of serfdom, nor were peasants any longer bound to landlords whom they could not leave. It was the end of a system which had been passed from antiquity to Western Christendom in the era of the barbarian invasions and had been the basis of European civilization for centuries. After 1861, Europe's rural proletariat everywhere worked for wages or keep; the pattern which had begun to spread in England and France with the fourteenth-century agricultural crisis had become universal.

Formally, the medieval usage of bond labour lasted longest in some of the American countries forming part of the European world. Obligatory labour in its most unqualified form, slavery, was legal in some of the United States until the end of a great civil war in 1865, when its abolition (though promulgated by the victorious government two years before) became effective throughout the whole republic. The war which had made this possible had been in some measure a distraction from the already rapid development of the country, now to be resumed and to become of vital significance to Europe. Even before the war, cotton-growing, the very agricultural operation which had been at the centre of debates over slavery, had already shown how the New World might supplement European agriculture on such a scale as to become almost indispensable. After the war the way was open for the supply to Europe not merely of products such as cotton, which she could not easily grow, but also of food.

ADVANCES IN FOOD DISTRIBUTION

The United States – and Canada, Australia and New Zealand, the Argentine and Uruguay – were soon to show they could offer food at much cheaper prices than Europe herself. Two things made this pos-

This painting by Claude-Joseph Vernet (1714–1789) shows a road being built through mountainous country-side in France. Improved communications would prove to be a vital factor in the transformation of European agriculture.

sible. One was the immense extent of these new lands, now added to Europe's own resources. The American plains, the huge stretches of pasture in the South American pampas and the temperate regions of Australasia provided vast areas for the growing of grain and the raising of livestock. The second was a revolution in transport which made them exploitable for the first time. Steam-driven railways and ships came into service in increasing numbers from the 1860s. These quickly brought down transport costs and did so all the faster as lower prices bred growing demand. Thus further profits were generated to be put into more capital investment on the ranges and prairies of the New World. On a smaller scale the same

phenomenon was at work inside Europe, too. From the 1870s the eastern European and German farmers began to see that they had a competitor in Russian grain, able to reach the growing cities much more cheaply once railways were built in Poland and western Russia and steamships could bring it from Black Sea ports. By 1900 the context in which European farmers worked, whether they knew it or not, was the whole world; the price of Chilean guano or New Zealand lamb could already settle what went on in their local markets.

Even in such a sketch the story of agricultural expansion bursts its banks; after first creating civilization and then setting a limit to its advance for thousands of years,

The Manchester to Liverpool train is shown transporting cattle, sheep and pigs across northern England in 1831.

The spinning-jenny, a machine that spun and wound yarn on to spindles, was invented by James Hargreaves in 1764. It was to revolutionize the British cotton and wool industries.

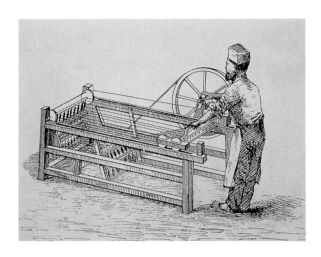

agriculture suddenly became its propellant; within a century or so it suddenly demonstrated that it could feed many more people than ever before. The demand of the growing cities, the coming of railways, the availability of capital, all point to its inseparable interconnection with other sides of a growing transoceanic economy between 1750 and 1870. For all its chronological primacy and its huge importance as a generator of investment capital, the story of agriculture in this period should only for convenience be separated from that of overall growth registered in the most obvious and spectacular way by the appearance of a whole new society, one based on large-scale industrialization.

INDUSTRIALIZATION

INDUSTRIALIZATION is another colossal subject. It is not even easy to see just how big it is. It produced the most striking change in European history since the barbarian inva-

Curious onlookers gather round George Stephenson's locomotive, the *Rocket*, in 1825. Wagons and rails had been used since ancient times in mining, but the combination of rails, wagons and the locomotive produced something entirely new: the railway.

sions, but it has been seen as even more important, as the biggest change in human history since the coming of agriculture, iron or the wheel. Within a fairly short time – a century and a half or so – societies of peasants and craftsmen turned into societies of machine-tenders and book-keepers. Ironically, it ended the ancient primacy of agriculture from which it had sprung. It was one of the major facts turning human experience back from the differentiation produced by millennia of cultural evolution to common experiences, which would tend once more towards cultural convergence.

Even to define it is by no means easy, although the processes which lie at its heart are obvious around us. One is the replacement of human or animal labour by machines driven by power from other, increasingly mineral, sources. Another is the organization of production in much larger units. Another is the increasing specialization of manufacturing. But all these things have implications and ramifications which quickly take us far beyond them. Although it embodied countless conscious decisions by countless entrepreneurs and customers, industrialization also looks like a blind force sweeping across social life with transforming power, one of the "senseless agencies" a philosopher once detected as half the story of revolutionary change. Industrialization implied new sorts of towns, needed new schools and new forms of higher learning, and, very quickly, new patterns of daily existence and living together.

SOURCES OF INDUSTRIALIZATION

The roots which made such a change possible go back far beyond the early modern age. Capital for investment had been accumulated slowly over many centuries of agricultural and commercial innovation. Knowledge had been built up, too. Canals were to provide the first network of communication for bulk transport once industrialization got under way, and from the eighteenth century they began to be built as never before in Europe (in China, of course, the story was different). Yet even Charlemagne's men had known how to build them. Even the most startling technical innovations had roots deep in the past. The men of the "Industrial Revolution" (as a Frenchman of the early nineteenth century named the great upheaval of his era) stood on the shoulders of innumerable craftsmen and artificers of pre-industrial times who had slowly built up skills and experience for the future. Fourteenth-century Rhinelanders, for example, learnt to make cast iron; by 1600 the gradual spread of blast furnaces had begun to remove the limits hitherto set to the use of iron by its high cost and in the eighteenth century came the inventions making it possible to use coal instead of wood as fuel for some processes. Cheap iron, even in what were by later standards small quantities, led to experiment with new ways of using it; further changes would then follow. New demand meant that areas where ore was easily to be found became important. When new techniques of smelting permitted the use of mineral rather than vegetable fuel, the location of supplies of coal and iron began to fashion the later industrial geography of Europe and North America. In the northern hemisphere lies much of the discovered coal supply of the world, in a great belt running from the basin of the Don, through Silesia, the Ruhr, Lorraine, the north of England and Wales, to Pennsylvania and West Virginia.

This painting by William Powell Frith (1819–1909) portrays the crowded throng of London's Paddington Station in 1862, a time when the railways were enjoying rapid expansion.

This early steam engine was built in 1767. In 1774, James Watt and Matthew Boulton improved the steam engine and reduced its size, so that it could be applied to other apparatus. The first steam-powered machines were so large they had to be built at the site where they were going to be used.

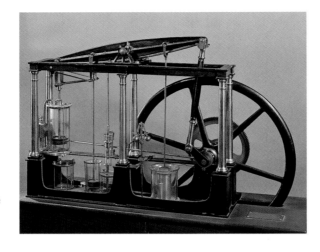

STEAM AND METALLURGY

BETTER METAL AND RICHER FUEL made their decisive contribution to early industrialization with the invention of a new source of energy, the steam engine. Again, the roots are very deep. That the power of steam could be used to produce movement was known in Hellenistic Alexandria. Even if (as some believe) there existed the technology to develop this knowledge, contemporary economic life did not make it worthwhile to strain to do so. The eighteenth century brought a series of refinements to the

This scene from a large French textile factory in Orléans dates from 1874.

technology so important that they can be considered as fundamental changes, and did so when there was money to invest in them. The result was a source of power rapidly recognized as of revolutionary importance. The new steam engines were not only the product of coal and iron, they also consumed them, directly both as fuel and as materials used in their own construction. Indirectly they stimulated production by making possible other processes which led to increased demand for them. The most obvious and spectacular was railway-building. It required huge quantities of first iron and then steel for rails and rolling-stock. But it also made possible the movement of goods at much lower cost. What the new trains moved might well again be coal, or ore, thus allowing these materials to be used cheaply far from where they were easily found and dug. New industrial areas grew up near to the lines, and the railway could carry away goods from them to distant markets.

THE ADVENT OF STEAM AND OCEAN TRANSPORT

The railway was not the only change steam made to transport and communications. The first steamship went to sea in 1809. By 1870, though there were still many sailing-ships and navies were still building battleships with a full spread of sail, regular ocean sailings by "steamers" were commonplace. The economic effect was dramatic. Oceanic transport's real cost in 1900 was a seventh of what it had been a hundred years earlier. The shrinking of costs, of time spent in transit, and of space, which steamships and railways produced, overturned conventional ideas of the possible. Since the domestication of the horse and the invention of the wheel, people and goods had been conveyed at speeds which certainly varied according to the local roads available, but probably only within limits of no more than one and five miles per hour over any considerable distance. Faster travel was possible on water and this had perhaps increased somewhat over the millennia in which ships underwent quite considerable modification. But all such slow improvement was dwarfed when in a man's lifetime he could witness the difference between travel on horseback and in a train capable of forty or even fifty miles an hour for long periods.

THE GRADUAL APPEARANCE OF FACTORIES

We have now lost one of the most pleasant of industrial sights, the long, streaming plume of steam from the funnel of a locomotive at speed, hanging for a few seconds behind it against a green landscape before disappearing. It greatly struck those who first saw it and so, less agreeably, did other visual aspects of the industrial transformation. One of the most terrifying was the black industrial town, dominated by a factory with smoking chimneys, as the pre-industrial town had been by the spire of church or cathedral. So dramatic and novel was the factory, indeed, that it has often gone unremarked that it was an unusual expression of the early stages of industrialization, not a typical one. Even in the middle of the nineteenth century most English industrial workers worked in manufacturing enterprises employing fewer than fifty. For a long time great agglomerations of labour were to be found only in textiles; the huge Lancashire cotton mills, which first gave that area a visual and urban character distinct from earlier manufacturing towns, were startling because they were unique. Yet by 1850 it was apparent that in more and more manufacturing processes the trend was towards the centralization under one roof, made attractive by economies of transport, specialization of function, the use of more powerful machinery and the imposition of effective work discipline.

A contemporary illustration shows the use of steam-powered machinery at an early 19th-century English mine.

This 19th-century painting is entitled *Conference of Engineers at Britannia Bridge, c.1850* and depicts a time when British industrialists and engineers were filled with optimism and pride in their country's technological revolution and led the world with their skill and expertise.

INDUSTRIAL BRITAIN IN THE NINETEENTH CENTURY

In the middle of the nineteenth century the changes of which these were the most striking had only created a mature industrial society in one country: Great Britain. Long and unconscious preparation lay behind this. Domestic peace and less rapacious government than on the continent had bred confidence for investment. Agriculture had provided its new surpluses first in England. Mineral supplies were easily available to exploit the new technological apparatus resulting from two or three generations of remarkable invention. An expanding overseas commerce generated further profits for investment and the basic machinery of finance and banking was already in being before industrialization needed to call on it.

Society seemed to have readied itself psychologically for change; observers detected an exceptional sensitivity to pecuniary and commercial opportunity in eighteenth-century England. Finally, an increasing population was beginning to offer both labour and a rising demand for manufactured goods. All these forces flowed together and the result was unprecedented and continuing industrial growth, first apparent as something totally new and irreversible in the second quarter of the nineteenth century. By 1870 Germany, France, Switzerland, Belgium and the United States had joined Great Britain in showing the capacity for self-sustained economic growth but she was still first among them both in the scale of her industrial plant and in her historic primacy. The inhabitants of "the workshop of the world", as the British liked to think of themselves, were fond of running over the figures which showed how wealth and power had followed upon industrialization. In 1850 the United Kingdom owned half the world's ocean-going ships and contained half the world's railway track. On those railways trains ran with a precision and regularity and even a speed not much improved upon for a hundred years after. They were regulated by "timetables" which were the first examples of their kind (and occasioned the first use of the word) and their operation relied on the electric telegraph. They were ridden in by men and women who had a few years before only ridden in stagecoaches or carters' wagons. In 1851, a year when a great international exhibition at London advertised her new supremacy, Great Britain smelted two and a half million tons of iron. It does not sound much, but it was five times as much as the United States of America and ten times as much as Germany. At that moment, British steam engines could produce more than 1.2 million horsepower, more than half that of all Europe together.

RATES OF INDUSTRIALIZATION

By 1870 a change had already started to appear in relative positions. Great Britain was still in most ways in the lead, but less decisively, and was not long to remain there. She still had more steam horsepower than any other European country, but the United States (which had already had more in 1850) was ahead of her and Germany was coming up fast. In the 1850s both Germany and France had made the important transition already made in Great Britain from smelting most of their iron by charcoal to smelting with mineral fuels. British superiority in manufacturing iron was still there and her pig-iron output had gone on rising, but now it was only three and a half times that of the United States and four times that of Germany. These were still huge superiorities, none the less, and the age of British industrial dominance had not yet closed.

The industrial countries of which Great Britain was the first were puny creatures in

The mining and building industries, foundries and shipyards grew bigger than ever before and employed large numbers of labourers. This view of a French open-cast mine was painted in 1854.

Sheffield in Yorkshire was Britain's major steel producer. This view of the city dates from c.1885.

comparison with what they were to become. Among them only Great Britain and Belgium had a large majority of their population living in urban districts in the middle of the nineteenth century. The census of 1851 showed that agriculture was still the biggest single employer of labour among British industries (rivalled only by domestic service). But in these countries the growing numbers engaged in manufacturing industries, the rise of new concentrations of economic wealth and a new scale of urbanization all made very visible the process of change which was going forward.

URBANIZATION

The life of whole regions was changed as workers poured into them; mills were built and chimneys shot up, transforming even the physical appearance of such places as the West Riding of Yorkshire, the Ruhr and Silesia, as new towns multiplied. They grew

at a spectacular rate in the nineteenth century, particularly in its second half, when the appearance of big centres that would be the nuclei of what a later age would call "conurbations" was especially marked. For the first time, some European cities ceased to depend on rural immigration for their growth. There are difficulties in reckoning indices of urbanization, largely because in different countries urban areas were defined in different ways, but this does not obscure the main lines of what was happening. In 1800 London, Paris and Berlin had, respectively, about 900,000, 600,000 and 170,000 inhabitants. In 1900 the corresponding figures were about 4.7 million, 3.6 million and 2.7 million. In that year, too, Glasgow, Moscow, St Petersburg and Vienna also had more than a million inhabitants each. These were the giants; just behind them were sixteen more European cities with over 500,000, a figure passed only by London and Paris in 1800. These great cities and the smaller ones, which were still immeasurably

In late 19th-century Russia, life in the rapidly expanding industrial cities was particularly harsh. For this working-class family, photographed in St Petersburg in the 1890s, home was the rented corner of a room.

bigger than the old ones they overshadowed, were still attracting immigrants in large numbers from the countryside, notably in Great Britain and Germany. This reflected the tendency for urbanization to be marked in the relatively few countries where industrialization first made headway, because it was the wealth and employment generated by industry which to begin with drew workers to them. Of the twenty-three cities of more than a half-million inhabitants in 1900, thirteen were in four countries: the United Kingdom (six), Germany (three), France (three) and Belgium (one).

LIFE IN THE NEW CITIES

Opinion about cities has undergone many changes. As the eighteenth century ended, something like a sentimental discovery of rural life was in full swing. This coincided with the first phase of industrialization, and

the nineteenth century opened with the tide of aesthetic and moral comment on the turn against a city life which was indeed about to reveal a new and often unpleasant face. That urbanization was seen as an unwelcome, even unhealthy, change by many people was a tribute to the revolutionary force of what was going on. Conservatives distrusted and feared cities. Long after European governments had demonstrated the ease with which they could control urban unrest, the cities were regarded suspiciously as likely nests of revolution. This is hardly surprising; conditions in many of the new metropolitan centres were often harsh and terrible for the poor. The East End of London could present appalling evidence of poverty, filth, disease and deprivation to anyone who chose to penetrate its slums. A young German businessman, Friedrich Engels, wrote in 1844 one of the most influential books of the century, *The Condition of the Working Class in England*, to expose the appalling conditions in which lived the poor of Manchester, and many English-born writers were drawn to similar themes. In France the phenomenon of the "dangerous classes" (as the Parisian poor were called) preoccupied governments for the first half of the century, and misery fired a succession of revolutionary outbreaks between 1789 and 1871. Clearly, it was not unreasonable to fear that the growing cities could breed resentment and hatred of society's rulers and beneficiaries, and that this was a potentially revolutionary force.

THE PLACE OF RELIGION IN THE NEW CITIES

It was also reasonable to predicate that the city made for ideological subversion. It was the great destroyer of traditional patterns of behaviour in nineteenth-century Europe and a crucible of new social forms and ideas, a huge and anonymous thicket in which men and women easily escaped the scrutiny of priest,

squire and neighbours, which had been the regulator of rural communities. In it (and this was especially true as literacy slowly spread downwards) new ideas were brought to bear upon long-unchallenged assumptions. Upper-class nineteenth-century Europeans were particularly struck by the seeming tendency of city life to atheism and infidelity, and one of the usual responses was to build more churches. More was at stake, it was felt, than religious truth and sound doctrine (about which the upper classes themselves had long comfortably tolerated disagreement). Religion was the great sustainer of morals and the support of the established social order. A revolutionary writer, Karl Marx, sneered that religion was "the opium of the people"; the possessing classes would hardly have put it in the same terms, but they acknowledged the importance of religion as social cement. One result was a long-continued series of attempts, both in Catholic and Protestant countries, to find a way of recapturing the towns for Christianity. The effort was misconceived in so far as it presumed that the Churches had ever had any footing in the urban areas, which had long since swamped the traditional parish structures and religious institutions of the old towns and villages at their hearts. But it had a variety of expressions, from the building of new churches in industrial suburbs to the creation of missions combining evangelism and social service which taught churchmen the facts of modern city life. By the end of the century the religious-minded were at least well aware of the challenge they faced, even if their predecessors had not been. One great English evangelist used in the title of one of his books words precisely calculated to emphasize the parallel with missionary work in pagan lands overseas: *Darkest England*. His answer was to found a quite new instrument of religious propaganda, designed to appeal specifically

An illustration dated 1881 shows a service held at the Salvation Army headquarters in Whitechapel Road, London. The Salvation Army was founded as an institution for evangelistic and social work by William Booth (1829–1912) in 1878 and quickly spread around the world.

to a new kind of population and to combat specifically the ills of urban society, the Salvation Army.

THE URBAN POPULATION

The revolution brought by industrialization had an impact far beyond material life. It is an immensely complicated problem to distinguish how modern civilization, the first, so far as we know, which does not have some formal structure of religious belief at its heart, came into being. Perhaps we cannot separate the role of the city in breaking down traditional religious observance from, say, that of science and philosophy in corrupting the belief of the educated. Yet a new future was visible already in the European industrial population of 1870, much of it literate, alienated from traditional authority, secular-minded and beginning to be conscious of itself as an entity. This was a different basis for civilization from anything yet seen.

THE NEW PACE OF LIFE

To talk of a new basis for civilization is to anticipate, but legitimately, for it suggests once again how rapid and deep was the impact of industrialization on every side of life. Even the rhythm of life changed. For the whole of earlier history, the economic behaviour of most of humanity had been regulated fundamentally by the rhythms of nature. In an agricultural or pastoral economy they imposed a pattern on the year which dictated both the kind of work which had to be undertaken and the kind which could be. Operating

From 1840, the number of labourers employed in mines, quarries, steel and iron industries, and machinery and naval industries grew unchecked. Although wages tended to be higher in these industries, fluctuations in demand for products such as those made at this Berlin laminating workshop in 1875 meant that unemployment was a constant threat.

within the framework set by the seasons were the subordinate divisions of light and darkness, fair weather and foul. Tenants lived in great intimacy with their tools, their animals and the fields in which they won their bread. Even the relatively few town dwellers lived, in large measure, lives shaped by the forces of nature; in Great Britain and France a bad harvest could still blight the whole economy well after 1850. Yet by then many people were already living lives whose rhythms were dictated by quite different pace-makers. Above all they were set by the means of production and their demands – by the need to keep machines economically employed, by the cheapness or dearness of investment capital, by the availability of labour. The symbol of this was the factory whose machinery set a pattern of work in which accurate time-keeping was essential. Men and women began to think in a quite new way about time as a consequence of their industrial work.

As well as imposing new rhythms, industrialism also related labourers to their work in new ways. It is difficult, but important, to avoid sentimentalizing the past in assessing this. At first sight the disenchantment of the factory workers with their monotonous routine, with its exclusion of personal involvement and its background of the sense of working for another's profit, justifies the rhetoric it has inspired, whether in the form of regret for a craftsman's world that has vanished or analysis of what has been identified as the alienation of the worker from the product. But the life of the medieval peasant was monotonous, too, and much of it was spent working for another's profit. Nor is an iron routine necessarily less painful because it is set by sunset and sunrise instead of an employer, or more agreeably varied by drought and tempest than by commercial slump and boom. Yet the new disciplines involved a revolutionary transformation of the ways many men and women won their livelihood, however we may evaluate the results by comparison with what had gone before.

CHILD LABOUR

A CLEAR EXAMPLE of the changes that transformed the workplace can be found in what soon became notorious as one of the persistent evils of early industrialism, its abuse of child labour. An English generation, morally braced by the abolition of slavery and by the exaltation that accompanied it, was also one intensely aware of the importance of religious training – and therefore of anything which might stand between it and the young – and one disposed to be sentimental about children in a way earlier generations had not been. All this helped to create an awareness of this problem (first, in the United Kingdom), which perhaps distracted attention from the fact that the brutal exploitation of children in factories was only one part of a total transformation of patterns of employment. About the use of children's labour in itself there was nothing new. Children had for centuries provided

This illustration depicts child workers and their abusive foreman in a London factory in 1848.

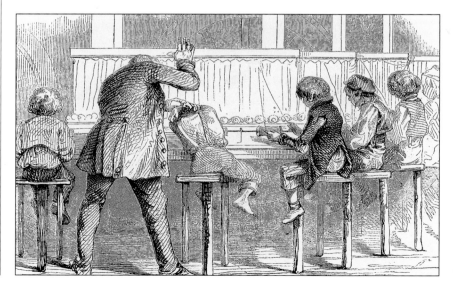

swineherds, birdscarers, gleaners, maids-of-all-work, crossing-sweepers, prostitutes and casual drudges in Europe (and still do in most non-European societies). The terrible picture of the lot of unprotected children in Hugo's great novel *Les Misérables* (1862) is a picture of their life in a *pre*-industrial society. The difference made by industrialism was that their exploitation was regularized and given a quite new harshness by the institutional forms of the factory. Whereas the work of children in an agricultural society had per-force been clearly differentiated from that of adults by their inferior strength, there existed in the tending of machines a whole range of activity in which children's labour competed directly with that of adults. In a labour market normally over-supplied, this meant that there were irresistible pressures upon the parent to send the child into the factory to earn a contribution to the family income as soon as possible, sometimes at the age of five or six. The consequences were not only often terrible for the victims, but also revolutionary in that the relation of child to society and the structure of the family were blighted. This was one of the "senseless agencies" of history at its most dreadful.

EARLY LEGISLATION

The problems created by industrialization were too pressing to remain without attention and a start was soon made in taming its most obvious evils. By 1850, the law of England had already begun to intervene to protect, for example, women and children in mines and factories; in all the millennia of the history of agriculturally based economies, it had still been impossible by that date to eradicate slavery even in the Atlantic world. Given the unprecedented scale and speed of social trans-formation, early industrial Europe should not

The floor in the City of London's New Stock Exchange in 1809 is shown in this engraving taken from a drawing by Thomas Rowlandson.

be blamed without qualification for not act-ing more quickly to remedy ills whose outlines could only dimly be grasped. Even in the early stage of English industrialism, when, perhaps, the social cost was most heavy, it was difficult to cast off the belief that the liberation of the economy from legal interference was essential to the enor-mous generation of new wealth which was going on.

ECONOMIC IDEAS

IT IS ALMOST IMPOSSIBLE to find economic theorists and publicists of the early industrial period who advocated absolute non-interference with the economy. Yet there was a broad, sustaining current which favoured the view that much good would result if the market economy was left to operate without the help or hindrance of politicians and civil servants. One force

working this way was the teaching often
summed up in a phrase made famous by a
group of Frenchmen: *laissez-faire*. Broadly
speaking, economists after Adam Smith had
said with growing consensus that the
production of wealth would be accelerated,
and therefore the general well-being would
increase if the use of economic resources
followed the "natural" demands of the
market. Another reinforcing trend was individualism, embodied in both the assumption

that individuals knew their own business best
and the increasing organization of society
around the rights and interests of individuals.

FREE TRADE IN BRITAIN

Individualism and laissez-faire were the
sources of the long-enduring association
between industrialism and liberalism; they
were deplored by conservatives who regretted

a hierarchical, agricultural order of mutual obligations and duties, settled ideas and religious values. Yet liberals who welcomed the new age were by no means taking their stand on a simply negative and selfish base. The creed of "Manchester", as it was called because of the symbolic importance of that city in English industrial and commercial development, was for its leaders much more than a matter of mere self-enrichment. A great political battle which for years preoccupied Englishmen in the early nineteenth century made this clear. Its focus was a campaign for the repeal of what were called the "Corn Laws", a tariff system originally imposed to provide protection for the British farmer from imports of cheaper foreign grain. The "repealers", whose ideological and political leader was a none-too-successful businessman, Richard Cobden, argued that much was at stake. To begin with, retention of the duties on grain demonstrated the grip upon the legislative machinery of the agricultural interest, the traditional ruling class, who ought not to be allowed a monopoly of power. Opposed to it were the dynamic forces of the future which sought to liberate the national economy from such distortions in the interest of particular groups. Back came the reply of the anti-repealers: the manufacturers were themselves a particular interest who only wanted cheap food imports in order to be able to pay lower wages; if they wanted to help the poor, what about improving the conditions under which they employed women and children in factories? There, the inhumanity of the production process showed a callous disregard for the obligations of privilege which would never have been tolerated in rural England. To this, the repealers responded that cheap food would mean cheaper goods for export. And in this, for someone like Cobden, much more than profit was involved. A worldwide

Women working in a British textile mill are shown in an illustration dating from 1851.

expansion of free trade, untrammelled by the interference of mercantilist governments, would lead to international progress both material and spiritual, he thought; trade brought peoples together, exchanged and multiplied the blessings of civilization and increased the power in each country of its progressive forces. On one occasion Cobden even committed himself to the view that free trade was the expression of the divine will (though even this was not to go as far as the British consul at Canton, who had proclaimed that "Jesus Christ is Free Trade, and Free Trade is Jesus Christ").

THE REPEAL OF THE CORN LAWS

There was much more to the free trade issue in Great Britain (of which the Corn Law debate was the focus) than a brief summary can do justice to. The more it is expounded, the more it becomes clear that industrialism involved creative, positive ideologies, which implied intellectual, social and political challenge to the past. This is why it should not be the subject of simple moral judgments, though both conservatives and liberals thought it could be at the time. The same man might resist legislation to protect the workman against long hours while proving himself a model employer, actively supporting educational and political reform and fighting the corruption of public interest by privileged birth. His opponent might struggle to protect children working in factories and act as a model squire, a benevolent patriarch to his tenants, while bitterly resisting the extension of the franchise to those not members of the established Church or any reduction of the political influence of landlords. It was all very muddled. In the specific issue of the Corn Laws the outcome was paradoxical, too, for a Conservative prime minister was in the end convinced by the arguments of the repealers. When he had the opportunity to do so without too obvious an inconsistency he persuaded Parliament to make the change in 1846. His party contained men who never forgave him and this

This view of Saltaire near Bradford in Yorkshire dates from c.1860. The complex of woollen mills was built on the banks of the Leeds and Liverpool Canal by the English industrialist and Liberal politician Sir Titus Salt (1803–1876). In 1853 he built one of the earliest examples of a model village in the valley for his employees.

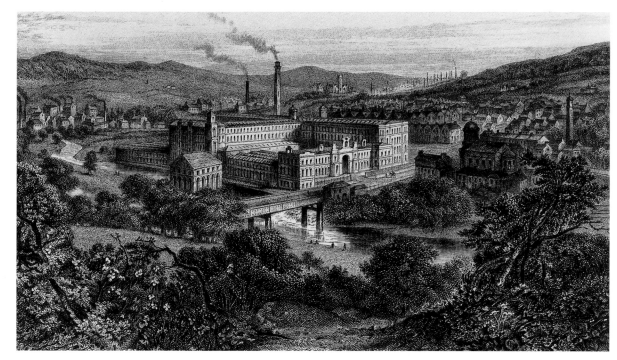

The inside of this 1844 "Corn Law Repeal Hat" is decorated with graphic representations of what campaigners saw as the many blessings that free trade would bring to Britain.

great climax of Sir Robert Peel's political career, for which he was to be revered by his Liberal opponents once he was safely out of the way, came shortly before he was dismissed from power by his own followers.

THE BRITISH EXAMPLE AND EUROPEAN OPTIMISM

Only in England was the free trade issue fought out so explicitly and to so clear-cut a conclusion. In other countries, paradoxically, the protectionists soon turned out to have the best of it. Only in the middle of the century, a period of expansion and prosperity, especially for the British economy, did free trade ideas get much support outside the United Kingdom, whose prosperity was regarded by believers as evidence of the correctness of their views and even mollified their opponents; free trade became a British political dogma, untouchable until well into the twentieth century. The prestige of British economic leadership helped to give it a brief popularity elsewhere, too. The prosperity of the era in fact owed as much to other influences as to this ideological triumph, but the belief added to the optimism of economic liberals. Their creed was the culmination of the progressive view of human potential, whose roots lay in Enlightenment ideas.

The solid grounds for this optimism can nowadays be too easily overlooked. In assessing the impact of industrialism we labour under the handicap of not having before us the squalor of the past it left behind. For all the poverty and the slums (and the very worst was over by then), the people who lived in the great cities of 1900 consumed more and lived longer than their ancestors. This did not, of course, mean they were either tolerably off, by later standards, or contented. But they were often, and probably for the most part, materially better off than their predecessors or most of their contemporaries in the non-European world. Amazing as it may seem, they were part of the privileged minority of mankind. Their lengthening lives were the best evidence of it.

A poster dated 1886 shows what the completed Eiffel Tower will look like and proclaims that it will be the "main attraction at the Exposition Universelle in Paris in 1889". For many people, the tower symbolized the great optimism and belief in progress that prevailed during this era.

3 POLITICAL CHANGE IN THE AGE OF REVOLUTION

IN THE EIGHTEENTH CENTURY the word "revolution" came to have a new meaning. Traditionally it meant only a change in the composition of government and not necessarily a violent one (though one reason why the English "Glorious Revolution" of 1688 was thought glorious was that it had been non-violent, the English learnt to believe). Observers could speak of a "revolution" occurring at a particular court when one minister replaced another. After 1789 this changed. People came to see that year as the beginning of a new sort of revolution, a real rupture with the past, perhaps characterized by violence, but also by limitless possibilities for radical change, social, political and economic, and began to think, too, that this new phenomenon might transcend national boundaries and have something universal and general about it. Even those who disagreed very much about the desirability of such a revolution could none the less agree that this new sort of revolution was a phenomenon of the politics of their age.

British rule in North America

In the 18th century, the subjects of the English colonies in North America enjoyed much more independence and involvement in decision-making than the citizens of most European countries. The colonists could decide on town improvements, hold

King George III of Britain (1738–1820) supported his ministers in their hard-line attitude to the inhabitants of the North American colonies. He considered those who declared independence to be nothing short of rebels.

public discussions, practise any religion, start up any business and petition their regional assemblies. They were conscious of their dignity, as they saw it, and were accustomed to taking decisions collectively.

The British government, however, made its presence felt. For example, it did not allow the colonies to join together to defend themselves. The British parliament reserved for itself the control of general legal issues, and its intervention from time to time with commerce occasionally caused friction (although this usually stopped short of open conflict).

In the second half of the 18th century, the population, size and wealth of the American colonies were growing rapidly. Problems arose when the British government insisted on keeping a tight rein on territorial, trading, legal and political issues in the face of American demands for greater self-determination. From 1763, a series of restrictive laws was passed, culminating in the 1765 Stamp Act, which was to result in North America's declaration of independence.

POLITICS AND REVOLUTION

It would be misleading to seek to group all the political changes of this period under the rubric of "revolution" conceived in such terms as these. But we can usefully speak of an "age of revolution" for two other reasons. One is that there were indeed within a century or so many more political upheavals than hitherto, which could be called revolutions in this extreme sense, even though many of them failed and others brought results far different from those they had led people to expect. In the second place, if we give the term a little more elasticity, and allow it to cover examples of greatly accelerated and fundamental political change which certainly go beyond the replacement of one set of governors by another, then there are many less dramatic political changes in these years which are distinctly revolutionary in their effect. The first and most obvious was the dissolution of the first British empire, whose central episode later became known as the American Revolution.

BRITISH COLONIES IN NORTH AMERICA

IN 1763 BRITISH IMPERIAL POWER in North America was at its height. Canada had been taken from the French; the old fear of a Mississippi valley cordon of French forts enclosing the thirteen colonies had been blown away. This might seem to dispose of

This 18th-century woodcut depicts slaves supposedly greeting a wealthy plantation owner and his family in the state of Virginia.

any grounds for future misgiving, yet some prophets had already suggested, even before the French defeat, that their removal might not strengthen but weaken the British grasp on North America. In the British colonies, after all, there were already more colonists then there were subjects in many sovereign states of Europe. Many were neither of English descent nor native English-speakers. They had economic interests not necessarily congruent with those of the imperial power. Yet the grip of the British government on them was bound to be slack, simply because of the huge distances which separated London from the colonies. Once the threat from the French (and from the Native North Americans whom the French had egged on) was gone, the ties of empire might have to be allowed to grow slacker still.

Time chart (1765–1814)

		1767 Townshend Acts	1774 First Continental Congress in Philadelphia	1783 End of the War of Independence	1803 The Louisiana Purchase
1750					**1800**
	1765 Stamp Act	1773 Boston Tea Party	1775 Outbreak of the War of Independence	1787 Constitution of the United States of America	1812–14 War against Great Britain and Canada

THE POTENTIAL FOR AMERICAN INDEPENDENCE

Difficulties soon appeared. How was the West to be organized? What relation was it to have to the existing colonies? How were the new Canadian subjects of the Crown to be treated? These problems were given urgency by a Native North American revolt in the Ohio valley in 1763 in response to pressure by the colonists who saw the West as their proper domain for settlement and trade. The imperial government immediately proclaimed the area west of the Alleghenies closed to settlement. This, as a start, offended many colonials who had looked forward to the exploitation of these regions, and it was followed by further irritation as British administrators negotiated treaties with Native North Americans and worked out arrangements for a garrisoned frontier to protect the colonists and Native North Americans from one another.

Ten years followed during which the dormant potential for American independence matured and came to a head. Grumbles about grievances turned first into resistance, then rebellion. Time after time, colonial politicians used provocative British legislation to radicalize American politics by making the colonists believe that the practical liberty they already enjoyed was in danger. The pace throughout was set by British initiatives. Paradoxically, Great Britain was ruled at this time by a succession of ministers anxious to carry out reforms in colonial affairs; their excellent intentions helped to destroy a status quo which had previously proved workable. They thus provide one of the first examples of what was to be a frequent phenomenon of the next few decades, the goading of vested interests into rebellion by well-meant but politically ill-judged reform.

TAXATION OF THE COLONIES

One principle firmly grasped in London was that the Americans ought to pay a proper share of the taxes which contributed to their defence and the common good of the empire. There were two distinct attempts to assure this. The first, in 1764–5, took the form of imposing duties on sugar imported to the colonies and a Stamp Act which was to raise money from revenue stamps to be put on various classes of legal documents. The important thing about these was not the amounts they proposed to raise nor even the novelty of taxing the internal transactions of the colonies (which was much discussed) but rather that these were, as both British politicians and American taxpayers saw, unilateral acts of legislation by the imperial parliament. The usual way in which colonial affairs were handled and revenue raised had been by haggling with their own assemblies. What was now brought into question was something so far hardly even formulated as a question:

Benjamin Franklin (1706–1790), philosopher, physicist and North American statesman, was commissioned to take the American protest against the Stamp Act to London. When the British government rejected his demands, Franklin, who had previously believed that it was possible for America to develop freely within the British Empire, returned to North America in 1775 to take an active part in the debate that would lead to the Declaration of Independence the following year.

whether the undoubted legislative sovereignty of the parliament of the United Kingdom also extended to its colonies. Riots, angry protest and non-importation agreements followed. The unhappy officials who held the stamps were given a bad time. Ominously, representatives of nine colonies attended a Stamp Act Congress to protest. The Stamp Act was withdrawn.

The London government then took a different tack. Its second fiscal initiative imposed external duties on paint, paper, glass and tea. As these were not internal taxes and the imperial government had always regulated trade, they seemed more promising. But it proved to be an illusion. Americans were by now being told by their radical politicians that no taxation whatsoever should be levied on them by a legislature in which they were not represented. As George III saw, it was not the Crown but Parliament whose power was under attack. There were more riots and boycotts and one of the first of those influential scuffles which make up so much of the history of decolonization, when the death of possibly five rioters in 1770 was mythologized into a "Boston Massacre".

RADICAL COLONIAL POLITICIANS

Once more, the British government retreated. Three of the duties were withdrawn: that on tea remained. Unfortunately, the issue was by now out of hand; it transcended taxation, as the British government saw, and had become one of whether or not the imperial parliament could make laws enforceable in the colonies. As George III put it a little later: "We must either master them, or totally leave them to themselves." The issue was focused in one place, though it manifested itself throughout the colonies. By 1773, after the destruction of

a cargo of tea by radicals (the "Boston Tea Party"), the crucial question for the British government was: could Massachusetts be governed?

There were to be no more retreats: George III, his ministers and the majority of the House of Commons were agreed on this. A number of coercive acts were passed to bring Boston to heel. The New England radicals were heard all the more sympathetically in the other colonies at this juncture because a humane and sensible measure providing for the future of Canada, the Quebec Act of 1774, stirred up wide feeling. Some disliked the privileged position it gave to Roman Catholicism (it was intended to leave French Canadians as undisturbed as possible in their ways by their change of rulers), while others saw its extension of Canadian boundaries south to the Ohio as another block to expansion in the West. In September the same year a Continental Congress of delegates from the colonies at Philadelphia severed commercial

A contemporary engraving depicts the Boston Massacre of 5 March 1770 – the first recorded violent incident of the American Revolution – in which five people were killed. Of the nine British soldiers later tried for murder, seven were acquitted and two found guilty of manslaughter.

The boycott against
the British tariffs
increased and the
general unrest in the
North American
colonies began to be
channelled through
committees. The
women of Edenton,
North Carolina, who
are represented in this
18th-century engraving,
swore not to drink any
more tea until their
country gained its
freedom.

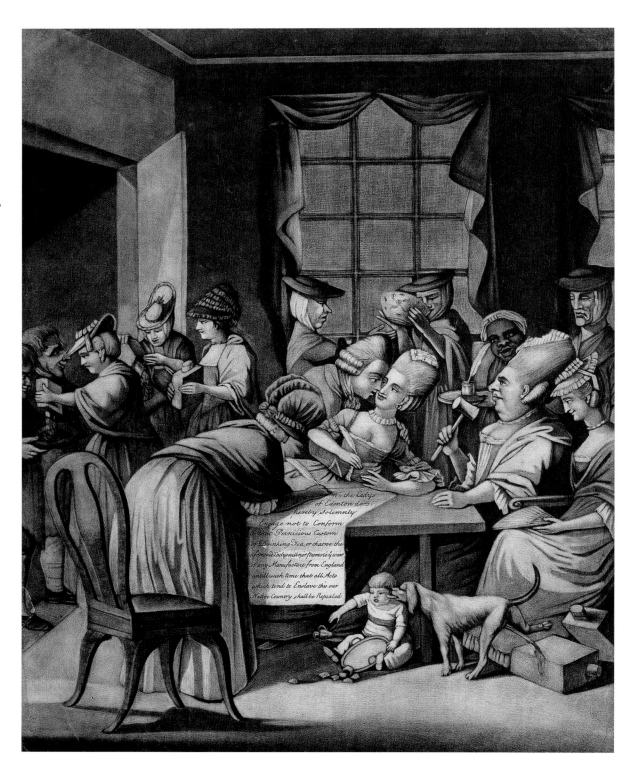

relations with the United Kingdom and
demanded the repeal of much existing legislation, including the Quebec Act. By
this time the recourse to force was probably
inevitable. The radical colonial politicians

had brought out into the open the practical
sense of independence already felt by many
Americans. But it was inconceivable that any
eighteenth-century imperial government could
have grasped this. The British government

was in fact remarkably reluctant to act on its convictions by relying simply on force until disorder and intimidation of the law-abiding and moderate colonials had already gone very far. At the same time, it made it clear that it would not willingly bend on the principles of sovereignty.

THE DECLARATION OF INDEPENDENCE

Arms were gathered in Massachusetts. In April 1775 a detachment of British soldiers sent to Lexington to seize some of them fought the first action of the American Revolution. It was not quite the end of the beginning. It took a year more for the feelings of the colonists' leaders to harden into the conviction that only complete independence from Great Britain would rally an effective resistance. The result was the Declaration of Independence of July 1776, and the debate was transferred to the battlefield.

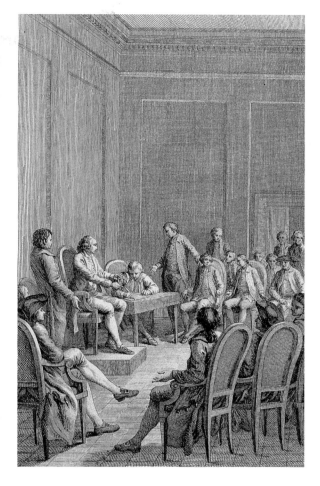

This engraving, dated 1774, depicts the first pan-colonial congress, at Philadelphia, which was attended by delegates from the 13 colonies. They agreed to suspend trade with Britain until the rights that the colonies had enjoyed prior to 1763 were re-established and all legislation since that date rescinded. Resolutions were also passed to pay no taxes to Britain, and to prepare to defend the colonies if British troops attacked them.

The American Declaration of Independence, 4 July 1776

"We hold these truths to be self-evident: that all men are created equal, that they are endowed by their Creator with certain unalienable Rights, that among these are Life, Liberty, and the pursuit of Happiness. That to secure these rights, Governments are instituted among Men, deriving their just powers from the consent of the governed.

"That whenever any Form of Government becomes destructive of these ends, it is the Right of the People to alter or to abolish it, and to institute new Government, laying its foundation on such principles and organizing its powers in such form, as to them shall seem most likely to effect their Safety and Happiness.

"The history of the present King of Great Britain is a history of repeated injuries and usurpations, all having in direct object the establishment of an absolute Tyranny over these States. ...

"We, therefore, the Representatives of the United States of America ... do ... solemnly publish and declare, That these United Colonies are, and of Right ought to be Free and Independent States; that they are Absolved from all Allegiance to the British Crown, and that all political connection between them and the State of Great Britain, is ... totally dissolved; and that as Free and Independent States, they have full Power to levy War, conclude Peace, contract Alliances, establish Commerce, and to do all other Acts ... which Independent States may of right do. And for the support of this Declaration ..., we mutually pledge to each other our Lives, our Fortunes and our ... Honor."

An extract from the Declaration of Independence.

The first armed conflict of the American War of Independence took place on 18 April 1775. This engraving depicts the surrender of Britain's General Burgoyne to the American leader General Gates at Saratoga Springs on 17 October 1777.

The British lost the war which followed because of the difficulties imposed by geography, because American generalship succeeded in avoiding superior forces long enough to preserve an army which could impose its will on them at Saratoga in 1777, because the French entered the war soon afterwards to win a return match for the defeat of 1763, and because the Spanish followed them and thus tipped the balance of naval power. The British had a further handicap; they dared not fight the kind of war which might win military victory by terrorizing the American population and thus encouraging those who wished to remain under the British flag to cut off the supplies and freedom of movement which General Washington's army enjoyed. They could not do this because their overriding aim had to be to keep open the way to a conciliatory peace with colonists willing again to accept British rule. In these circumstances, the Bourbon coalition was fatal. The military decision came in 1781, when a British army found itself trapped at Yorktown between the Americans on land and a French squadron at sea. Only 7,000 or so men were involved, but their surrender was the worst humiliation yet undergone by British arms and the end of an era of imperial rule. Peace negotiations soon began and two years later, at Paris, a treaty was signed in which Great Britain recognized the independence of the United States of America, whose territory the British negotiators had already conceded should run to the Mississippi. This was a crucial decision in the shaping of a new nation; the French, who had envisaged making a recovery in the Mississippi valley, were disappointed. The northern continent was to be shared by the rebels only with Spain and Great Britain, it appeared.

A NEW NATION

FOR ALL THE LOOSE ENDS which had to be tied up, and some boundary disputes which dragged on for decades to come, the appearance of a new state of great potential resources in the western hemisphere was by any standard certainly a revolutionary change. If it was at first often seen as something less than this by foreign observers, that was because the weaknesses of the new nation were at the time more apparent than its potential. Indeed, it was far from clear that it was a nation at all; the colonies were divided and many expected them to fall to quarrelling and disunion. Their great and inestimable advantage was their remoteness. They could work out their problems virtually untroubled by foreign intervention, a blessing crucial to much that was to follow.

Victory in war was followed by a half-dozen critical years during which a handful of American politicians took decisions which were to shape much of the future history of the world. As in all civil wars and wars of independence, new divisions had been created which accentuated political weakness. Among these, those which divided loyalists from rebels were, for all their bitterness,

General George Washington (1732–1799), who was designated commander-in-chief of the American forces, had to face the British troops, the Americans who remained loyal to the British and the warriors of the Native American tribes who had allied themselves with the colonists' enemy. Washington later became the first president of the United States.

John Paul Jones (a naval officer), Benjamin Franklin and George Washington enter Independence Hall, Philadelphia, during the Constitutional Convention of 1787.

perhaps the least important. That problem had been solved, brutally, by emigration of the defeated; something like 80,000 loyalists left the rebel colonies, for a variety of motives ranging from dislike of intimidation and terror to simple loyalty to the Crown. Other divisions were likely to cause more trouble in the future. Class and economic interests separated farmers, merchants and plantation-owners. There were important differences between the new states which had replaced the former colonies and between the regions or sections of a rapidly developing country; one of these, that imposed by the economic importance of black slavery to the southern states, was to take decades to work out. On the other hand, the Americans also had great advantages as they set about nation-building. They faced the future without the incubus of a huge illiterate and backward peasant population such as stood in the way of evolving a democratic system in many other countries. They had ample territory and great economic resources even in their existing areas of occupation. Finally, they had European civilization to draw upon, subject only to the modifications its legacies might undergo in transplantation to a virgin – or near-virgin – continent.

THE AMERICAN CONSTITUTION

The war against the British had imposed a certain discipline. Articles of Confederation had been agreed between the former colonies and came into force in 1781. In them appeared the name of the new nation, the United States of America. The peace brought a growing sense that these arrangements were unsatisfactory. There were two areas of particular concern. One was disturbance arising fundamentally from disagreement about what the Revolution ought to have meant in domestic affairs. The central government came to many Americans to appear to be far too weak to deal with disaffection and disorder. The other arose from a post-war economic depression, particularly affecting external trade and linked to currency problems arising from the independence of individual states. To deal with these as well, the central government seemed ill-equipped. It was accused of neglecting American

economic interests in its conduct of relations with other countries. Whether true or not, this was widely believed. The outcome was a meeting of delegates from the states in a constitutional convention at Philadelphia in 1787. After four months' work they signed a draft constitution which was then submitted to the individual states for ratification. When nine states had ratified it the constitution came into effect in the summer of 1788. In April 1789 George Washington, the former commander of the American forces in the war against the British, took the oath of office as the first president of the new republic, thus inaugurating a series of presidencies which has continued unbroken to this day.

Much was said about the need for simple institutions and principles clear in their intention, yet the new constitution was still to be revealing its potential for development two hundred years later. For all the determination of its drafters to provide a document which would unambiguously resist reinterpretation, they were (fortunately) unsuccessful. The United States constitution was to prove capable of spanning a historical epoch, which turned a scatter of largely agricultural societies into a giant and industrial world

This portrayal of the signing of the constitution of the United States in 1787 was painted in 1940 by Howard Chandler Christy for the Hall of Representatives in Washington, DC.

power. In part this was because of the provision for conscious amendment, but in larger measure it was due to the evolving interpretation of the doctrines it embodied. But also much remained unchanged; though often formal, these features of the constitution are very important. Besides them, too, there were fundamental principles which were to endure, even if there was much argument about what they might mean.

REPUBLICANISM

To begin with the most obvious fact: the constitution was republican. This was by no means normal in the eighteenth century and should not be taken for granted. Some Americans felt that republicanism was so important and so insecure that they even disapproved of the constitution because they thought it (and particularly its installation of a president as the head of the executive) "squinted towards monarchy", as one of

them put it. The ancient republics were as familiar to classically educated Europeans for their tendency to decay and faction as for their legendarily admirable morals. The history of the Italian republics was unpromising, too, and much more unedifying than that of Athens and Rome. Republics in eighteenth-century Europe were few and apparently unflourishing. They seemed to persist only in small states, though it was conceded that the remoteness of the United States might protect republican forms which would elsewhere ensure the collapse of a large state. Still, observers were not sanguine about the new nation. The later success of the United States was therefore to be of incalculable importance in reversing opinion about republicanism. Very soon, its capacity to survive, its cheapness and a liberalism thought to be inseparable from it focused the attention of critics of traditional governments all over the civilized world. European advocates of political change soon began to look to America for inspiration; soon, too, the influence of repub-

The inauguration of President George Washington, depicted here, took place in New York's Old City Hall on 30 April 1789. Washington went on to be re-elected as president in 1793 and remained in office until 1797.

The centre of American political life was to be the Capitol, pictured here towards the final stages of its construction. George Washington, who laid its first stone in 1792, also participated in the planning of the federal capital city that bears his name. Congress moved into the Capitol building in Washington, DC in 1800.

lican example was to spread from the northern to the southern American continent.

THE BRITISH INFLUENCE

The second characteristic of the new constitution, which was of fundamental importance, was that its roots lay largely in British political experience. Besides the law of England, whose Common Law principles passed into the jurisprudence of the new state, this was true also of the actual arrangement of government. The founding fathers had all grown up in the British colonial system in which elected assemblies had debated the public interest with monarchical governors. They instituted a bicameral legislature (although they excluded any hereditary element in its composition) on the English model, to offset a president. They thus followed English constitutional theory in putting a monarch, albeit an elected one, at the head of the executive machinery of government. Though, in a different sense, the British had an elected monarchy, this was not how the British constitution of the eighteenth century actually worked, but it was a good approximation to its appearance. The founding fathers took, in fact, the best constitution they knew, purged it of its corruptions (as they saw them) and added modifications appropriate to American political and social circumstance. What they did not do was to emulate the alternative principle of government available in contemporary Europe – monarchical absolutism – even in its enlightened form. The Americans wrote a constitution for free citizens because they believed that the British already lived under one. They thought it had failed only in so far as it had been corrupted, and that it had been improperly employed to deprive Americans of the rights they too ought to have exercised under it. Because of this, the same principles of government (albeit in much evolved forms)

The bustling streets of New York City are depicted on the morning of Inauguration Day, 1789.

debate about what were the proper relations of the central government and the individual states. It was a debate which would in the end come within an inch of destroying the Union. Federalism would also promote a major readjustment within the constitution, the rise of the Supreme Court as an instrument of judicial review. Outside the Union, the nineteenth century would reveal the appeal of federalism to many other countries, impressed by what appeared to have been achieved by the Americans. Federalism was to be seen by European liberals as a crucial device for reconciling unity with freedom and British governments found it a great standby in their handling of colonial problems.

would one day be propagated and patronized in areas which shared none of the cultural assumptions of the Anglo-Saxon world on which they rested.

FEDERALISM

One way in which the United States differed radically from most other existing states and diverged consciously from the British constitutional model was in adherence to the principle of federalism. This was indeed fundamental to it, since only large concessions to the independence of individual states made it possible for the new union to come into existence at all. The former colonies had no wish to set up a new central government which would bully them as they believed the government of King George had done. The federal structure provided an answer to the problem of diversity – *e pluribus unum*. It also dictated much of the form and content of American politics for the next eighty years. Question after question whose substance was economic or social or ideological would find itself pressed into the channels of a continuing

DEMOCRACY

Finally, in any summary, however brief, of the historic significance of the constitution of the United States, attention must be given to its opening words: "We the People" (even though they seem to have been included almost casually). The actual political arrangements in several of the states of 1789 were by no means democratic, but the principle of popular sovereignty was enunciated clearly from the start. In whatever form the mythology of a particular historical epoch might cloak it, the popular will was to remain the ultimate court of appeal in politics for Americans. Here was a fundamental departure from British constitutional practice, and it owed something to the way in which seventeenth-century colonists had sometimes given themselves constitutions. Yet British constitutionalism was prescriptive; the sovereignty of king in parliament was not there because the people had once decided it should be, but because it was there and was unquestioned. As the great English constitutional historian Maitland once put it, Englishmen had taken the authority of the Crown as a substitute for the theory of the state. The new constitution broke with this and with every other prescriptive theory (although not with British political thinking, for Locke had said in the 1680s that governments held their powers on trust and that the people could upset governments which abused that trust, and on this ground, among others, some Englishmen had justified the Glorious Revolution).

The American adoption of a democratic theory that all governments derive their just powers from the consent of the governed (as it had been put in the Declaration of Independence) was epoch-marking. But it by no means solved the problems of political authority at a stroke. Many Americans feared what a democracy might do and sought to restrict the popular element in the political system right from the start. Another problem was suggested by the fundamental rights set out in the first ten amendments to the constitution at the end of 1789. These were presumably as much open to reamendment at the hands of popular sovereignty as any other part of the constitution. Here was an important source of disagreement for the future: Americans have always found it easy to be somewhat confused (especially in the affairs of other countries but even in their own at times) about whether democratic principles consist in following the wishes of the majority or in upholding certain fundamental rights. Nevertheless, the *de facto* adoption of the democratic principle in 1787 was immensely important and justifies the consideration of the constitution as a landmark in world history. For generations to come the new United States would become the focus of the aspirations of those longing to be free the world over – "the world's last, best hope", as one American once memorably said. Even today, when America so often appears conservative and inward-looking, the democratic ideal of

which for so long it was the custodian and exemplar retains its power in many countries, and the institutions it fertilized are still working.

FRANCE IN THE REVOLUTIONARY ERA

PARIS WAS THE CENTRE of social and political discussion in Europe. To it returned some of the French soldiers who had helped to bring to birth the young American Republic. It is hardly surprising, then, that although most European nations responded in some measure to the transatlantic revolution, the French were especially aware of it. American example and the hopes it raised were a contribution, though a subsidiary one, to the huge release of forces which is still, after two hundred years and many subsequent risings, called *the* French Revolution. Unfortunately, this all-too-familiar and simple term puts obstacles in the way of

This anti-royalist caricature from the era of the French Revolution is entitled *La Chasse aux Aristocrates*. The imagery of this turbulent period abounds with depictions of nobles and clerics being hounded and ridiculed by revolutionaries.

The ill-fated King Louis XVI (1754–1793) reigned to see the French monarchy replaced by a republic.

understanding. Politicians and scholars have offered many different interpretations of what the essence of the Revolution was, have disagreed about how long it went on and what were its results, and even about when it began. They agree about little except that what began in 1789 was very important. Within a very short time, indeed, it changed

The Swiss-born banker Jacques Necker (1732–1804) was director-general of French finance from 1777. His reform programmes incurred the queen's wrath and resulted in his dismissal in 1781. Necker was recalled to office in 1788, and recommended the summoning of the Estates General.

the whole concept of revolution, though there was much in it that looked to the past rather than the future. It was a great boiling-over of the pot of French society and the pot's contents were a jumbled mixture of conservative and innovating elements much like those of the 1640s in England, and equally confused in their mixture of consciousness and unconsciousness of direction and purposes, too.

FINANCIAL PROBLEMS

Confusion was the symptom of big dislocations and maladjustments in the material life and government of France. She was the greatest of European powers and her rulers neither could nor wished to relinquish her international role. The first way in which the American Revolution had affected her was by providing an opportunity for revenge; Yorktown was the retaliation for defeat at the hands of the British in the Seven Years' War, and to deprive them of the Thirteen Colonies was some compensation for the French loss of India and Canada. Yet the successful effort was costly. The second great consequence was that for no considerable gain beyond the humiliation of a rival, France added yet another layer to the huge and accumulating debt piled up by her efforts since the 1630s to build and maintain a European supremacy.

Attempts to liquidate this debt and cut the monarchy free from the cramping burden it imposed (and it was becoming clear after 1783 that France's real independence in foreign affairs was narrowing sharply because of it) were made by a succession of ministers under Louis XVI, the young, somewhat obtuse, but high-principled and well-meaning king who came to the throne in 1774. None of them succeeded in even arresting the growth of the debt, let alone in reducing it. What was worse, their effects only advertised the facts of failure. The deficit could be measured and the figures published as would never have been possible under Louis XIV. If there was a spectre haunting France in the 1780s, it was not that of revolution but of state bankruptcy. The whole social and political structure of France stood in the way of tapping the wealth of the better-off, the only sure way of emerging from the financial impasse. Ever since the days of Louis XIV himself, it had proved impossible to levy a due weight of taxation on the wealthy without resorting to force, for French legal and social assumptions and the mass of privileges, special immunities

Time chart (1789–1815)				
	1791 Constitution Legislative Assembly	1804 Napoleon becomes Emperor	1814 Paris Peace Treaty Louis XVIII King of France	
1750				1850
	1789 National Assembly	1792 The National Convention declares the Republic	1799 The Consulate	1815 Battle of Waterloo Napoleon banished to St Helena

and the prescriptive rights they upheld, blocked the way ahead. The paradox of eighteenth-century European government was at its most evident in France; a theoretically absolute monarchy could not infringe the mass of liberties and rights which made up the essentially medieval constitution of the country without threatening its own foundations. Monarchy itself rested on prescription.

POLARIZATION

To more and more Frenchmen it appeared that France needed to reform her governmental and constitutional structure if she was to emerge from her difficulties. But some went further. They saw in the inability of government to share fiscal burdens equitably between classes the extreme example of a whole range of abuses which needed reform. The issue was more and more exaggerated in terms of polarities: of reason and superstition, of freedom and slavery, of humanitarianism and greed. Above all, it tended to concentrate on the symbolic question of legal privilege. The class which focused the anger this aroused was the nobility, an immensely diverse and very large body (there seem to have been between 200,000 and 250,000 noble males in France in 1789) about which cultural, economic or social generalization is impossible, but whose members all shared a legal status which in some degree conferred privilege at law.

THE ESTATES GENERAL MEETS

While the logic of financial extremity pushed the governments of France more and more towards conflict with the privileged, there was a natural unwillingness on the part of many of the royal advisers, themselves usually noblemen, and of the king himself, to proceed except by agreement. When in 1788 a series of failures nerved the government to accept that conflict was inevitable, it still sought to

An engraving after an original contemporary drawing by a court painter shows the opening of the Estates General meeting in Versailles on 5 May 1789.

confine it to legal channels, and, like Englishmen in 1640, turned to historic institutions for means to do so. Not having Parliament to hand, they trundled out from the attic of French constitutionalism the nearest thing to a national representative body that France had ever possessed, the Estates General. This body of representatives of nobles, clergy and commoners had not met since 1614. It was hoped that it would provide sufficient moral authority to squeeze agreement from the fiscally privileged for the payment of higher taxes. It was an unimpeachably constitutional step, but as a solution had the disadvantage that great expectations were aroused while what the Estates General could legally do was obscure. More than one answer was given. Some were already saying that the Estates General could legislate for the nation, even if historic and undoubted legal privileges were at issue.

SOCIAL STRAINS

This very complicated political crisis was coming to a head at the end of a period in which France was also under other strains. One was population growth. Since the second quarter of the century this had risen at what a later age would think a slow rate, but was still fast enough to outstrip growth in the production of food. This sustained a long-run inflation of food prices, which bore most painfully upon the poor, the vast majority who were peasants with little or no land. Given the coincidence of the fiscal demands of governments – which for a long time staved off the financial crisis by borrowing or by putting up the direct and indirect taxes which fell most heavily on the poor – and the efforts of landlords to protect themselves in inflationary times by holding down wages and putting up rents and dues, the life of the

poor was growing harsher and more miserable for most of the century. To this general impoverishment should be added the special troubles, which from time to time afflicted particular regions or classes, but which, coincidentally, underwent something of an intensification in the second half of the 1780s. Bad harvests, cattle disease, and recession, which badly affected the areas where peasants' families produced textiles as a supplement to their income, all sapped the precarious health of the economy in the 1780s. The sum effect was that the elections to the Estates General in 1789 took place in a very excited and embittered atmosphere. Millions of French people were desperately

Entitled *The Village Man, Born into Hard Labour*, this 18th-century French engraving aims to show the harsh conditions in which peasants worked and bemoans the fact that most of their meagre incomes went to rent and tax collectors.

seeking some way out of their troubles, were eager to seek and blame scapegoats, and had quite unrealistic and inflated notions of what good the king, whom they trusted, could do for them.

Thus a complex interplay of governmental impotence, social injustice, economic hardship and reforming aspiration brought about the French Revolution. But before this complexity is lost to sight in the subsequent political battles and the simplifying slogans they generated, it is important to emphasize that almost no one either anticipated this outcome or desired it. There was much social injustice in France, but no more than many other eighteenth-century states found it possible to live with. There was a welter of expectant and hopeful advocates of particular reforms, ranging from the abolition of the censorship to the prohibition of immoral and irreligious literature, but no one doubted that such changes could easily be carried out by the king, once he was informed of his people's wishes and needs. What did not exist was a party of revolution clearly confronting a party of reaction.

THE REVOLUTIONARY DECADE

Parties only came into existence when the Estates General had met. This is one reason why the day on which they did so, 5 May 1789 (a week after George Washington's inauguration), is a date in world history, because it opened an era in which to be for or against the Revolution became the central political question in most continental countries, and even tainted the very different politics of Great Britain and the United States. What happened in France was bound to matter elsewhere. At the simplest level this was because she was the greatest European power; the Estates General would either

On 20 June 1789 the new National Assembly met in the tennis court at Versailles (having been barred from their usual meeting place), and swore "never to part again ... until the constitution of the kingdom is established on firm foundations". The Tennis Court Oath, as this event became known, is depicted in this illustration by Jacques-Louis David (1748–1825), dated 1791.

By the middle of the summer of 1789, popular hostility towards the Crown was rife and rumours that the king's troops had been ordered to storm the capital were circulating. Unrest broke out on the streets of Paris during the night of 12–13 July, as portrayed in this illustration, and culminated in the storming of the Bastille on 14 July.

paralyse her (as many foreign diplomats hoped) or liberate her from her difficulties to play again a forceful role. Beyond this, France was also the cultural leader of Europe. What her writers and politicians said and did was immediately accessible to people elsewhere because of the universality of the French language, and it was bound to be given respectful attention because people were used to looking to Paris for intellectual guidance.

THE NEW NATIONAL ASSEMBLY

In the summer of 1789 the Estates General turned itself into a national assembly claiming sovereignty. Breaking with the assumption that it represented the great medieval divisions of society, the majority of its members claimed to represent all Frenchmen without distinction. It was able to take this revolutionary step because the turbulence of France frightened the government and those deputies to the assembly who opposed such a change. Rural revolt and Parisian riot alarmed ministers no longer sure that they could rely upon the army. This led first to the monarchy's abandonment of the privileged classes, and then to its concession, unwillingly and uneasily, of many other things asked for by the politicians who led the new National Assembly. At the same time these concessions created a fairly clear-cut division between those who were for the Revolution and those who were against it; in language to go round the world they were soon called Left and Right (because of the places in which they sat in the National Assembly).

The main task which that body set itself was the writing of a constitution, but in the process it transformed the whole institutional structure of France. By 1791, when it dispersed, it had nationalized the lands of the Church, abolished what it termed "the feudal system", ended censorship, created a system

On the night of 4 August 1789 the National Assembly abolished feudal rights in the meeting depicted. On 26 August the Declaration of the Rights of Man and of the Citizen received the Assembly's approval.

On 14 July 1789 the people of Paris stormed the state prison, the Bastille, as this engraving shows. Lafayette took charge of the newly created National Guard. In the provinces the peasants revolted and revolutionary town councils were created.

of centralized representative government, obliterated the old provincial and local divisions and replaced them with the "departments" under which the French still live, instituted equality before the law, and separated the executive from the legislative power. These were only the most remarkable things done by one of the most remarkable parliamentary bodies the world has ever seen. Its failures tend to mask this huge achievement; they should not be allowed to do so. Broadly speaking, they removed the legal and institutional checks on the modernization of France. Popular sovereignty, administrative centralization, and individual legal equality were from this time poles towards which her institutional life always returned.

Many in France did not like all this; some liked none of it. By 1791 the king had given clear evidence of his own misgivings, the

goodwill which had supported him in the early Revolution was gone and he was suspected as an anti-revolutionary. Some noblemen had already disliked enough of

In 1791, strikes were organized in Parisian cafés such as this one on the Boulevard du Temple.

Maximilien de Robespierre (1758–1794), deputy in the Estates General for the commoners, represented the extreme left in his democratic convictions and became a leader of the radical Jacobins. Elected to the ruling Committee for Public Safety in 1793, he lost its support the following year when fellow committee members sent him to the guillotine for his role in the Terror.

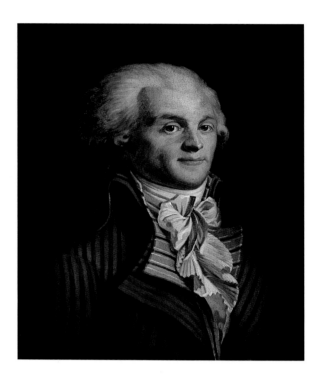

The Rights of Man and of the Citizen

1. Men are born and remain free and equal in rights; social distinctions may be based only upon general usefulness.
2. The aim of every political association is the preservation of the natural and inalienable rights of man; these rights are liberty, property, security, and resistance to oppression.
3. The source of all sovereignty resides essentially in the nation; no group, no individual may exercise authority not emanating expressly therefrom. ...
9. Since every man is presumed innocent until declared guilty ... all unnecessary severity for securing the person of the accused must be severely repressed by law.
10. No one is to be disquieted because of his opinions, even religious, provided their manifestation does not disturb the public order established by law.
11. Free communication of ideas and opinions is one of the most precious of the rights of man. Consequently, every citizen may speak, write, and print freely, subject to responsibility for the abuse of such liberty in the cases determined by law. ...
16. Every society in which the guarantee of rights is not assured or the separation of powers not determined has no constitution at all.

Extracts from the Declaration of the Rights of Man and of the Citizen, as published by the National Assembly on 27 August, 1789.

what was going on to emigrate; they were led by two of the king's brothers, which did not improve the outlook for royalty. But most important of all, many of the French turned against the Revolution when, because of papal policy, the National Assembly's settlement of Church affairs was called in question. Much in it had appealed deeply to many in France, churchmen among them, but the pope rejected it and this raised the ultimate question of authority. French Catholics had to decide whether the authority of the pope or that of the French constitution was supreme for them. This created the most important division which came to embitter revolutionary politics.

THE END OF THE FRENCH MONARCHY

As 1792 began, the British prime minister expressed his confidence that fifteen years of peace could reasonably be expected to lie ahead. In April, France went to war with Austria and was at war with Prussia soon after. The issue was complicated but many French people believed that foreign powers wished to intervene to bring the Revolution to an end and put the clock back to 1788. By the summer, as things went badly and shortages and suspicion mounted at home, the king was discredited. A Parisian insurrection overthrew the monarchy and led to the summoning of a new assembly to draw up a new and, this time, republican constitution. This

Popular demonstrations on 10 August 1792 in Paris convinced Robespierre that the only legality was that of the people. These revolutionary-era drawings represent Parisian *sans-culottes*, so called because the men wore long trousers rather than the knee breeches of the nobility under the old régime.

body, remembered as the Convention, was the centre of French government until 1796. Through civil and foreign war and economic and ideological crisis it achieved the survival of the Revolution. Most of its members were politically not much more advanced in their views than their predecessors. They believed in the individual and the sanctity of property (they prescribed the death penalty for anyone proposing a law to introduce agrarian communism) and that the poor are always with us, although they allowed some of them a small say in affairs by supporting direct universal adult male suffrage. What distinguished them from their predecessors was that they were willing to go rather further to meet emergencies than earlier French assemblies (especially when frightened by the possibility of defeat); they also sat in a capital city, which was for a long time manipulated by more extreme politicians to push them into measures more radical than they really wanted, and into using very democratic language. Consequently, they frightened Europe much more than their predecessors had done.

THE TERROR

The Convention's symbolic break with the past came when it voted for the execution of the king in January 1793. The judicial murder of kings had hitherto been believed to be an English aberration; now the English were as shocked as the rest of Europe. They, too, now went to war with France, because they feared the strategical and commercial result of French success against the Austrians in the Netherlands. But the war looked more and more like an ideological struggle and to win it the French government appeared increasingly bloodthirsty at home. A new instrument for

The reign of Louis XVI ended in September 1792 when a republic was proclaimed, ruled by a National Convention. Its Jacobin wing accused the king of conspiring to overthrow the republic and he was narrowly found guilty of treason. His execution took place on 21 January 1793.

humane execution, the guillotine (a characteristic product of pre-revolutionary enlightenment, combining as it did technical efficiency and benevolence in the swift, sure death it afforded its victims), became the symbol of the Terror, the name soon given to a period during which the Convention strove by intimidation of its enemies at home to assure survival to the Revolution. There was much that was misleading in this symbolism. Some of the Terror was only rhetoric, the hot air of politicians trying to keep up their own spirits and frighten their opponents. In practice it often reflected a jumble of patriotism, practical necessity, muddled idealism, self-interest and petty vengefulness, as old scores were settled in the name of the republic. Many people died, of course – something over 35,000, perhaps – and many emigrated to avoid danger, yet the guillotine killed only a minority of the victims, most of whom died in the

provinces, often in conditions of civil war and sometimes with arms in their hands. In eighteen months or so the Frenchmen whom contemporaries regarded as monsters killed about as many of their countrymen as died in ten days of street-fighting and firing-squads in Paris in 1871. To take a different but equally revealing measure, the numbers of those who died in this year and a half are roughly twice those of the British soldiers who died on the first day of the battle of the Somme in 1916. Such bloodshed drove divisions even deeper between French groups, but their extent should not be exaggerated. All noblemen, perhaps, had lost something in the Revolution, but only a minority of them found it necessary to emigrate. Probably the clergy suffered more, man for man, than the nobility, and many priests fled abroad. Yet fewer fled from France during the Revolution than from the American colonies after 1783.

A much larger proportion of Americans felt too intimidated or disgusted with their Revolution to live in the United States after independence than the proportion of French people who could not live in France after the Terror.

CHANGES IN REVOLUTIONARY POLITICS

The Convention won victories and put down insurrection at home. By 1797, only Great Britain had not made peace with France, the Terror had been left behind, and the republic was ruled by something much more like a parliamentary régime, under the constitution whose adoption closed the Convention era in 1796. The Revolution was safer than ever. But it did not seem so. Abroad, the royalists strove to get allies with whom to return and also intrigued with malcontents inside France. The return of the old order was a prospect which few in France would welcome, though. On the other hand, there were those who argued that the logic of democracy should be pressed further, that there were still great divisions between rich and poor, which were as offensive as had been the old distinctions of legally privileged and unprivileged, and that the Parisian radicals should have a greater say in affairs. This was almost as alarming as fears of a restoration to those who had benefited from the Revolution or simply wanted to avoid further bloodshed. Thus pressed from Right and Left, the

Following the *coup d'état* of 9 November 1799 the inauguration of a State Council, with Napoleon Bonaparte as First Consul, took place on 25 December. This event, which was to have such great significance for the whole of Europe, is portrayed here in one of the many later and non-contemporary pictures which glorified different episodes in what became the Napoleonic legend.

Directory (as the new régime was called) was in a way in a good position, though it made enemies who found the (somewhat zigzag) *via media* it followed unacceptable. In the end it was destroyed from within when a group of politicians intrigued with soldiers to bring about a *coup d'état* which instituted a new régime in 1799.

POST-REVOLUTIONARY FRANCE

IN 1799, TEN YEARS after the meeting of the Estates General, it was at least clear to most observers that France had for ever broken with the medieval past. In law this happened very rapidly. Nearly all the great

The prominent *sans-culotte* Pierre Chaumette (1763–1794) unveils the Altar to Reason in the cathedral of Notre Dame in November 1793.

reforms underlying it were legislated at least in principle in 1789. The formal abolition of feudalism, legal privilege and theocratic absolutism and the organization of society on individualist and secular foundations, were the heart of the "principles of '89" then distilled in the Declaration of the Rights of Man and of the Citizen which prefaced the constitution of 1791. Legal equality and the legal protection of individual rights, the separation of Church and State and religious toleration were their expressions. The derivation of authority from popular sovereignty acting through a unified National Assembly, before whose legislation no privilege of locality or group could stand, was the basis of the jurisprudence which underlay them. It showed both that it could ride out financial storms far worse than those the old monarch had failed to master (national bankruptcy and the collapse of the currency among them), and that it could carry out administrative change of which enlightened despotism had only dreamed. Other Europeans watched aghast or at least amazed as this powerful legislative engine was employed to overturn and rebuild institutions at every level of French life. Legislative sovereignty was a great instrument of reform, as the enlightened despots had known. Judicial torture came to an end, and so did titular nobility, juridical inequality and the old corporate guilds of French workmen. Incipient trades unionism was nipped in the bud by legislation forbidding association by workers or employers for collective economic ends. In retrospect, the signposts to market society seem pretty plain. Even the old currency based on units in the Carolingian ratios of 1:20:12 (*livres, sous* and *deniers*) gave way to a decimal system of *francs* and *centimes*, just as the chaos of old-fashioned weights and measures was (in theory) replaced by the metric system later to become almost universal.

A church is desecrated during the French Revolution. In Paris, many important Christian icons were removed from churches or converted into revolutionary images by sculptors or painters. This included the changing of stone Bibles, held by statues of saints, into copies of the Declaration of the Rights of Man.

REVOLUTION AND THE CHURCH

Such great changes were bound to be divisive, the more so because minds can change more slowly than laws. Peasants who eagerly welcomed the abolition of feudal dues were much less happy about the disappearance of the communal usages from which they benefited and which were also part of the "feudal" order. Such conservatism was especially hard to interpret in religious affairs, yet was very important. The holy vessel kept at Rheims, from which the kings of France had been anointed since the Middle Ages, was publicly destroyed by the authorities during the Terror, an altar to Reason replaced the Christian one in the cathedral of Notre Dame and many priests underwent fierce personal persecution. Clearly, the France which did this was no longer Christian in the traditional sense, and the theocratic monarchy went unmourned by most people. Yet the treatment of the Church aroused popular opposition to the Revolution as nothing else had done, the cults of quasi-divinities such as Reason and the Supreme Being which some revolutionaries promoted were a flop, and many Frenchmen (and perhaps most Frenchwomen) would happily welcome the official restoration of the Catholic Church to French life when it eventually came. By then, it had long been restored *de facto* in the parishes by the spontaneous actions of church-goers.

A NEW DEBATE

The divisions aroused by revolutionary change in France could no more be confined within its borders than could the principles of '89. These had at first commanded much admiration and not much explicit condemnation or distrust in other countries, though this soon changed, in particular when French governments began to export their principles by propaganda and war. Change in France rapidly generated debate about what should happen in other countries. Such debate was bound to reflect the terminology and circumstances in which it arose. In this way France gave her politics to Europe and this is the second great fact about the revolutionary decade. That is when Modern European politics began, and the terms Right and Left have been with us ever since. Liberals and conservatives (though it was to be a decade or so before those terms were used) came into political existence when the French Revolution provided what appeared to be a touchstone or litmus paper for political standpoints. On one side were republicanism, a wide suffrage, individual rights, free speech and free publication; on the other were order, discipline and emphasis on duties rather than rights, the recognition of the social function of hierarchy and a wish to temper market forces by morality.

The Tree of Liberty with the Devil Tempting John Bull was etched by British cartoonist James Gillray (1757–1815) to illustrate the failure of supposed attempts by English politicians to spread the revolution to Britain.

THE REVOLUTION'S EFFECTS BEYOND FRANCE

Some in France had always believed that the French Revolution had universal significance. In the language of enlightened thought they advocated the acceptance by other nations of the recipes they employed for the settlement of French problems. This was not entirely arrogant. Societies in pre-industrial and traditional Europe still had many features in common; all could learn something from France. In this way the forces making for French influence were reinforced by conscious propaganda and missionary effort. This was another route by which events in France entered universal history.

That the Revolution was of universal, unprecedented significance was not an idea confined to its admirers and supporters. It also lay at the roots of European conservatism as a self-conscious force. Well before 1789, it is true, many of the constituent elements of modern conservative thought were lying about in such phenomena as irritation over the reforming measures of enlightened despotism, clerical resentment of the prestige and effect of "advanced" ideas, and the emotional reaction from the fashionable and consciously rational which lay at the heart of romanticism. Such forces were especially prevalent in Germany, but it was in England that there appeared the first and in many ways the greatest statement of the conservative, anti-revolutionary argument. This was the *Reflections on the Revolution in France*, published in 1790 by Edmund Burke. As might easily be inferred from his former role as defender of the rights of the American colonists, this book was far from a mindless defence of privilege. In it a conservative stance shook itself clear of the legalistic defence of institutions and expressed itself in a theory of society as the creation of more

This contemporary illustration, entitled *Planting the Tree of Liberty*, shows one typical symbolic interpretation of the French Revolution much enacted by enthusiasts.

than will and reason and the embodiment of morality. The Revolution, by contrast, was condemned as the expression of the arrogance of the intellect, of arid rationalism, and of pride – deadliest of all the sins.

The new polarization, which the Revolution brought to Europe's politics, promoted also the new idea of revolution itself, and that was to have great consequences. The old idea that a political revolution was merely a circumstantial break in an essential continuity was replaced by one which took it as radical, comprehensive upheaval, leaving untouched no institution and limitless in principle, tending, perhaps, even to the subversion of such basic institutions as the family and property. According to whether people felt heartened or dismayed by this prospect, they sympathized with or deplored revolution wherever it occurred as a manifestation of a universal phenomenon. In the nineteenth century they came even to speak of *the* Revolution as a universally, eternally present

force. This idea was the extreme expression of an ideological form of politics which is by no means yet dead. There are still those who, broadly speaking, feel that all insurrectionary and subversive movements should, in principle, be approved or condemned without regard to the particular circumstances of cases. This mythology has produced much misery, but first Europe and then the world which Europe transformed have had to live with those who respond emotionally to it, just as earlier generations had to live with the follies of religious divisions. Its survival, unhappily, is testimony still of the impact of the French Revolution.

NAPOLEON BONAPARTE

MANY DATES CAN BE CHOSEN as the "beginning" of the French Revolution; a specific date to "end" it would be meaningless. The year 1799 none the less was an

This anonymous oil-painting shows the young Napoleon Bonaparte at Arcole (near Verona), where he defeated the Austrian army in November 1796.

important punctuation mark in its course. The *coup d'état*, which then swept the Directory away, brought to power a man who quickly inaugurated a dictatorship which was

to last until 1814 and turn international relations upside-down. This was Napoleon Bonaparte, formerly general of the republic, now First Consul of the new régime and soon to be the first Emperor of France. Like most of the leading figures of his age, he was still a young man when he came to power. He had already shown exceptional brilliance and ruthlessness as a soldier. His victories combined with a shrewd political sense and a readiness to act in an insubordinate manner to win him a glamorous reputation; in many ways he now seems the greatest example of the eighteenth-century type of "the adventurer". In 1799 he had a great personal prestige and popularity. No one except the defeated politicians much regretted it when he shouldered them aside and assumed power. Immediately he justified himself by defeating the Austrians (who had joined again in a war against France) and making a victorious peace for France (as he had done once already). This removed the threat to the Revolution; no one doubted Bonaparte's

Napoleon and his wife Joséphine are shown visiting the Sévane Brothers' factory in Rouen in November 1802.

The coronation of Napoleon Bonaparte (1769–1821) in Notre Dame is depicted by Jacques-Louis David.

own commitment to its principles. His consolidation of them was his most positive achievement.

NAPOLEONIC RULE

Although Napoleon (as he was called officially after 1804, when he proclaimed his empire) reinstituted monarchy in France, it was in no sense a restoration. Indeed, he took care so to affront the exiled Bourbon family that any reconciliation with it was inconceivable. He sought popular approval for the empire in a plebiscite and got it. This was a monarchy Frenchmen had voted for; it rested on popular sovereignty, that is, on the Revolution. It assumed the consolidation of the Revolution which the Consulate had already begun. All the great institutional reforms of the 1790s were confirmed or at least left intact; there was no disturbance of the land sales which had followed the confiscation of Church property, no resurrection of the old corporations, no questioning of the principle of equality before the law. Some measures were even taken further, notably when each department was given an administrative head, the prefect, who was in his powers something like one of the emergency emissaries of the Terror (many former revolutionaries became prefects). Such further centralization of the administrative structure would, of course, have been approved also by the enlightened despots. In the actual working of government, it is true, the principles of the Revolution were often infringed in practice. Like all his predecessors in power since 1793, Napoleon controlled the press by a punitive censorship, locked up people without trial and in general gave short shrift to the Rights of Man so far as civil liberties were concerned. Representative bodies existed under consulate and empire, but not much attention was paid to them. Yet it seems that this was what the French wanted, as they had wanted Napoleon's shrewd recognition of reality in, for instance, a concordat with the pope which

Painted by Jacques-Louis David in 1801, this heroic portrait shows Napoleon crossing the Alps in April 1797, following in the path of Hannibal nearly 2,000 years before. Napoleon, always very aware of the importance of his public image, had instructed the great artist to portray him as a calm, strong figure astride a wild horse.

reconciled Catholics to the régime by giving legal recognition to what had already happened to the Church in France.

All in all, this amounted to a great consolidation of the Revolution and one guaranteed at home by firm government and by military and diplomatic strength abroad. Both were eventually to be eroded by Napoleon's huge military efforts. These for a time gave France the dominance of Europe; her armies fought their way to Moscow in the east and Portugal in the west and garrisoned the Atlantic and northern coast from Corunna to Stettin. Nevertheless, the cost of this was too great; even ruthless exploitation of occupied countries was not enough for France to sustain this hegemony indefinitely against the coalition of all the other European countries which Napoleon's arrogant assertion of his power aroused. When he invaded Russia in 1812, and the greatest army he ever led crumbled into ruins amid the snows of the winter, he was doomed unless his enemies should fall out with one another. This time they did not. Napoleon himself blamed the British, who had been at war with him (and, before him, with the Revolution) with only one short break since 1792. There is something in this; the Anglo-French war was the last and most important round in a century of rivalry, as well as a war of constitutional monarchy against military dictatorship. It was the Royal Navy at Aboukir in 1798 and at Trafalgar in 1805 which confined Napoleon to Europe, British money which financed the allies when

they were ready to come forward, and a British army in the Iberian peninsula which kept alive there from 1809 onwards a front which drained French resources and gave hope to other Europeans.

NAPOLEON'S LEGACY

BY THE BEGINNING of 1814, Napoleon could defend only France. Although he did so at his most brilliant, the resources were not available to fight off Russian, Prussian and Austrian armies in the east, and a British invasion in the southwest. At last his generals and ministers were able to set him aside and make peace without a popular outcry, even though this meant the return of the Bourbons. But it could not by then mean the return of anything else of significance from the years before 1789. The Concordat remained, the departmental system remained, equality before the law remained, a representative sys-

The Prussian victory over the Napoleonic army at Katzbach, on 26 August 1813, is depicted in this painting.

tem remained; the Revolution, in fact, had become part of the established order in France. Napoleon had provided the time, the social peace and the institutions for that to happen. Nothing survived of the Revolution except what he had confirmed.

This makes him very different from a monarch of the traditional stamp, even the most modernizing – and, in fact, he was often very conservative in his policies, distrusting innovation. In the end he was a democratic despot, whose authority came from the people, both in the formal sense of the plebiscites, and in the more general one that he had needed (and won) their goodwill to keep his armies in the field. He is thus nearer in style to twentieth-century rulers than to Louis XIV. Yet he shares with that monarch the credit for carrying French international power to an unprecedented height and because of this both of them have retained the admiration of their countrymen. But again there is an important, and twofold, difference: Napoleon not only dominated Europe as Louis XIV never did, but because the

Revolution had taken place his hegemony represented more than mere national supremacy, though this fact should not be sentimentalized. The Napoleon who was supposed to be a liberator and a great European was the creation of later legend. The most obvious impact he had on Europe between 1800 and 1814 was the bloodshed and upheaval he brought to every corner of it, often as a consequence of megalomania and personal vanity. But there were also important side-effects, some intentional, some not. They all added up to the further spread and effectiveness of the principles of the French Revolution.

THE REORGANIZATION OF GERMANY

The most obvious expression of the side-effects of Napoleon's rule was on the map. The patchwork quilt of the European state system of 1789 had undergone some revolutionary revision already before Napoleon took power, when French armies in Italy, Switzerland and the United Provinces had created new satellite republics. But these had proved incapable of survival once French support was withdrawn and it was not until French hegemony was re-established under the Consulate that there appeared a new organization which would have enduring consequences in some parts of Europe.

The most important of these were in west Germany, whose political structure was revolutionized and medieval foundations swept away. German territories on the left bank of the Rhine were annexed to France for the whole of the period from 1801 to 1814, and this began a period of destroying historic German polities. Beyond the river, France provided the plan of a reorganization which secularized the ecclesiastical states, abolished

Symbols of Napoleonic power are represented in this 19th-century illustration, which is now housed in the Biblioteca Nazionale in Turin, Italy.

Napoleonic Europe and the collapse of the French Empire

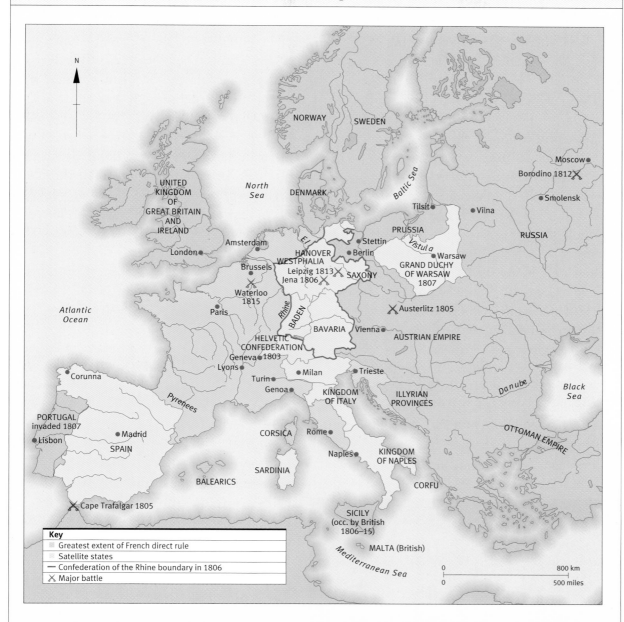

Key
- ▪ Greatest extent of French direct rule
- ▫ Satellite states
- — Confederation of the Rhine boundary in 1806
- ✕ Major battle

In 1812, the Napoleonic Empire had reached its greatest extent, but national feeling, both in the name of the *ancien régime* and in that of liberty and equality, was steadily building up against it. At home, the empire could win over neither the old French aristocracy nor the republicans, who could remember a time of greater freedom.

The Napoleonic bureaucracy was unable to control the smuggling and corruption that had emerged as a result of the continental blockade by Britain. Nor could it prevent prices from rising and the growing, dangerous opposition it faced from bankers. These divisive forces were underlined by the start of the Russian campaign which encouraged the formation of a new coalition (the sixth) between Russia, Britain and Prussia in 1813. At the beginning of the following year, the combined armies of Britain, Russia, Prussia, Austria and Sweden invaded France and by March they had occupied Paris. Napoleon abdicated and was exiled by the victors to the island of Elba.

nearly all the free cities, gave extra territory to Prussia, Hanover, Bavaria and Baden to compensate them for losses elsewhere, and abolished the old independent imperial nobility. The practical effect was to diminish the Catholic and Habsburg influence in Germany while strengthening the influence of its larger princely states (especially Prussia). The constitution of the Holy Roman Empire was revised, too, to take account of these changes. In its new form it lasted only until 1806, when another defeat of the Austrians led to more changes in Germany and its abolition. So came to an end the institutional structure which, however inadequately, had given Germany such political coherence as it had possessed since Ottonian times. A Confederation of the Rhine was now set up which provided a third force balancing that of Prussia and Austria. Thus were triumphantly asserted the national interests of France in a great work of destruction. Richelieu and Louis XIV would have enjoyed the contemplation of a French frontier on the Rhine with, beyond it, a Germany divided into interests likely to hold one another in

check. But there was another side to it; the old structure, after all, had been a hindrance to German consolidation. No future rearrangement would ever contemplate its resurrection. When, finally, the allies came to settle post-Napoleonic Europe, they too provided for a German Confederation. It was different from Napoleon's. Prussia and Austria were members of it in so far as their territories were German, but there was no going back on the fact of consolidation. More than three hundred political units with different principles of organization in 1789 were reduced to thirty-eight states in 1815.

THE REORGANIZATION OF ITALY AND OTHER STATES

Reorganization was less dramatic in Italy and its effect less revolutionary. The Napoleonic system provided in the north and south of the peninsula two large units which were nominally independent, while a large part of it (including the Papal States) was formally incorporated in France and organized in departments. None of this survived 1815, but neither was there a complete restoration of the old régime. Notably, the ancient republics of Genoa and Venice were left in the tombs to which the armies of the Directory had first consigned them. They were absorbed by bigger states, Genoa by Sardinia, Venice by Austria. Elsewhere in Europe, at the height of Napoleonic power, France had annexed and governed directly a huge block of territory whose coasts ran from the Pyrenees to Denmark in the north and from Catalonia almost without interruption to the boundary between Rome and Naples in the south. Lying detached from it was a large piece of modern Yugoslavia. Satellite states and vassals of varying degrees of real independence, some of them ruled over by members of Napoleon's

In this 19th-century painting an Austrian soldier bids his family farewell as he leaves to fight the Napoleonic army during the Austrian rebellion against French rule of 1813–1815.

own family, divided between them the rest of Italy, Switzerland and Germany west of the Elbe. Isolated in the east was another satellite, the "grand duchy" of Warsaw, which had been created from former Russian territory.

THE FRENCH EMPIRE

In most of these countries similar administrative practices and institutions provided a large measure of shared experience. That experience, of course, was of institutions and ideas which embodied the principles of the Revolution. They hardly reached beyond the Elbe except in the brief Polish experiment, and thus the French Revolution came to be another of those great shaping influences which again and again have helped to differentiate eastern and western Europe.

Within the French Empire, Germans, Italians, Illyrians, Belgians and Dutch were all governed by the Napoleonic legal codes; the bringing of these to fruition was the result of Napoleon's own initiative and insistence, but the work was essentially that of revolutionary legislators who had never been able in the troubled 1790s to draw up the new codes so many in France had hoped for in 1789. With the codes went concepts of family, property, the individual, public power and others, which were thus generally spread through Europe. They sometimes replaced and sometimes supplemented a chaos of local, customary, Roman and ecclesiastical law. Similarly, the departmental system of the empire imposed a common administrative practice, service in the French armies imposed a common discipline and military regulation, and French weights and measures, based on

A contemporary illustration depicts Napoleon landing on the French coast in February 1815, after his flight from exile in Elba.

the decimal system, replaced many local scales. Such innovations exercised an influence beyond the actual limits of French rule, providing models and inspiration to modernizers in other countries. The models were all the more easily assimilated because French officials and technicians worked in many of the satellites while many nationalities other than French were represented in the Napoleonic service.

THE DISPERSION OF REVOLUTIONARY IDEALS

Changes took time to produce their full effect in the French Empire, but it was a deep one and was revolutionary. It was by no means necessarily liberal; even if the Rights of Man formally followed the tricolour of the French armies, so did Napoleon's secret police, quartermasters and customs officers. A more subtle revolution, deriving from the

Napoleonic impact, lay in the reaction and resistance it provoked. In spreading revolutionary principles the French were often putting a rod in pickle for their own backs. Popular sovereignty lay at the heart of the Revolution and it is an ideal closely linked to that of nationalism. French principles said that peoples ought to govern themselves and that the proper unit in which they should do so was the nation: the revolutionaries had proclaimed their own republic "one and indivisible" for this reason. Some of their foreign admirers applied this principle to their own countries; manifestly, Italians and Germans did not live in national states, and perhaps they should. But this was only one side of the coin. French Europe was run for the benefit of France, and it thus denied the national rights of other Europeans. They saw their agriculture and commerce sacrificed to French economic policy, found they had to serve in the French armies, or to receive at the hands of Napoleon French (or Quisling) rulers and viceroys. When even those who had welcomed the principles of the Revolution felt such things as grievances, it is hardly surprising that those who had never welcomed them at all should begin to think in terms of national resistance, too. Nationalism in Europe was given an immense fillip by the Napoleonic era, even if governments distrusted it and felt uneasy about employing it. Germans began to think of themselves as more than Westphalians and Bavarians, and Italians began to believe they were more than Romans or Milanese, because they discerned a common interest against France. In Spain and Russia the identification of patriotic resistance with resistance to the Revolution was virtually complete.

THE BATTLE OF WATERLOO

In the end, then, though the dynasty Napoleon hoped to found and the empire he set up both proved ephemeral, his work was of great importance. He unlocked reserves of energy in other countries just as the Revolution had unlocked them in France, and afterwards they could never be quite shut up again. He ensured the legacy of the Revolution its maximum effect and this was his greatest achievement, whether he desired it or not.

His unconditional abdication in 1814 was not quite the end of the story. Just under a year later the emperor returned to France from Elba where he had lived in a pensioned exile, and the restored Bourbon régime crumbled at a touch. The allies none the less determined to overthrow him, for he had frightened them too much in the past. Napoleon's attempt to anticipate the gathering of overwhelming forces against him came to an end at Waterloo, on 18 June 1815, when the threat of a revived French Empire was destroyed by the Anglo-Belgian and Prussian armies. This time the victors sent him to St Helena, thousands of miles away in the South Atlantic, where he died in 1821. The fright that he had given them strength-

The Battle of Waterloo finally broke the power of Napoleon's army. The French suffered 25,000 casualties, and the allies nearly as many – a scene from the battle is depicted in this contemporary illustration.

ened their determination to make a peace that would avoid any danger of a repetition of the quarter-century of almost continuous war which Europe had undergone in the wake of the Revolution. Thus Napoleon still shaped the map of Europe, not only by the changes he had made in it, but also by the fear France had inspired under his leadership.

This detail from a 19th-century French painting depicts an imaginary scene of Napoleon being greeted by his soldiers on his return from Elba in February 1815.

4 POLITICAL CHANGE: A NEW EUROPE

WHATEVER CONSERVATIVE statesmen hoped in 1815, an uncomfortable and turbulent era had only just begun. This can be seen most easily in the way the map of Europe changed in the next sixty years. By 1871, when a newly united Germany took its place among the great powers, most of Europe west of a line drawn from the Adriatic to the Baltic was organized in states claiming to be based on the principle of nationality, even if some minorities denied it. Even to the east of that line there were states which were already identified with nations. By 1914 the triumph of nationalism was to go further still, and most of the Balkans would be organized as nation-states, too.

NATIONALISM

Nationalism, one aspect of a new kind of politics, had origins which went back a long way, to the examples set in Great Britain and some of Europe's smaller states in earlier times. Yet its great triumphs were to come after 1815, as part of the appearance of a new politics. At their heart lay an acceptance of a new framework of thought, which recognized the existence of a public interest greater than that of individual rulers or privileged hierarchies. It also assumed that competition to define and protect that interest was legitimate. Such competition was thought increasingly to require special arenas and institutions; old

A contemporary illustration depicts the 1815 Congress of Vienna, which followed the defeat of the Napoleonic Empire. Every important decision at the congress was taken by the victors, although France was allowed to attend. Prussia was allotted new provinces in the Rhineland, the mineral resources of which later helped Prussia to become the strongest German power.

juridical or courtly forms no longer seemed sufficient to settle political questions.

An institutional framework for this transformation of public life took longer to emerge in some countries than others. Even in the most advanced it cannot be identified with any single set of practices. It always tended, though, to be strongly linked with the recognition and promotion of certain principles. Nationalism was one of them which went most against older principles – that of dynasticism, for instance. It was more and more a commonplace of European political discourse, as the nineteenth century went on, that the interests of those recognized to be "historic" nations should be protected and promoted by governments. This was, of course, wholly compatible with bitter and prolonged disagreement about which nations were historic, how their interests should be defined, and to what extent they could and should be given weight in statesmen's decisions.

THE GROWING POWER OF THE STATE

There were also other principles in play besides nationalism. Terms like democracy and liberalism do not help very much in defining them, though they must be used in default of better ones and because contemporaries used them. In most countries there was a general trend towards accepting representative institutions as a way of associating (even if only formally) more and more people with the government. Liberals and democrats almost always asked for more people to be given votes and for better electoral representation. More and more, too, the individual became the basis of political and social organization in economically advanced countries. The individual's membership of communal,

Political liberty in post-Napoleonic Europe was championed by the English poet Lord Byron, shown here in a portrait that captures his romantic aura. He died of malaria at the age of 36, attempting to aid the Greek struggle to throw off Turkish rule.

Time chart (1789–1870)

1789 The French Revolution	1848 Revolutions across Europe	1853–1856 The Crimean War	1861 Abolition of serfdom in Russia War of Secession in America	1870 Franco-Prussian War Third Republic in France

1800   **1900**

1815 Waterloo Vienna Congress: Restoration	1830 July Revolution in Paris	1852 Second Empire in France	1859 Beginning of the unification of Italy	1863 Polish uprising	1866 Austro-Prussian War

religious, occupational and family units came to matter much less than his or her individual rights. Though this led in some ways to greater freedom, it sometimes led to less. The state became much more juridically powerful in relation to its subjects in the nineteenth century than ever before, and slowly, as its apparatus became technically more efficient, came to be able to coerce them more effectively.

THE IMPACT OF THE FRENCH REVOLUTION

The French Revolution had been of enormous importance in actually launching such changes but its continuing influence as example and a source of mythology mattered just as much. For all the hopes and fears that the Revolution was over by 1815, its full Europe-wide impact was then still to come. In many other countries, institutions already swept away in France invited criticism and demolition. They were the more vulnerable because other forces of economic and social change were also at work. This gave revolutionary ideas and traditions new opportunities. There was a widespread sense that all Europe faced, for good or ill, potential revolution. This encouraged both the upholders and would-be destroyers of the existing order to sharpen political issues and fit them into the frameworks of the

Europe in 1815

In Vienna, Europe was shared out, and France lost a large portion of the territory she had occupied between 1792 and 1814. Prussia, Austria and Russia increased their territories; Belgium and the Netherlands became the United Netherlands, and Norway and Sweden were united. The Grand Duchy of Warsaw disappeared. A new Germanic Confederation of 38 sovereign states and three kingdoms appeared, and Britain retained Malta and the Ionian Islands.

Key
— German Confederation boundary

principles of 1789: nationalism and liberalism. By and large, these ideas dominated the history of Europe down to about 1870 and provided the dynamic of its politics. They did not achieve all their advocates hoped. Their realization in practice had many qualifications, they frequently and thwartingly got in one another's way, and they had many opponents. Yet they remain useful guiding threads in the rich and turbulent history of nineteenth-century Europe, already a political laboratory whose experiments, explosions and discoveries were changing the history of the rest of the world.

THE TREATY OF VIENNA

The influences of nationalism and liberalism could already be seen at work in the negotiations shaping the foundation deed of the nineteenth-century international order, the Treaty of Vienna of 1815, which closed the era of the French wars. Its central aim was to prevent their repetition. The peacemakers sought the containment of France and the avoidance of revolution, using as their materials the principle of legitimacy which was the ideological core of conservative Europe and certain practical territorial arrangements against future French aggression. Thus Prussia was given large acquisitions on the Rhine, a new northern state appeared under a Dutch king ruling both Belgium and the Netherlands, the kingdom of Sardinia was given Genoa, and Austria not only recovered her former Italian possessions, but kept Venice and was allowed a virtually free hand in keeping the other Italian states in order. In most of these cases legitimacy bowed to expediency; those despoiled by the revolutionaries or Napoleon did not obtain restoration. But the powers talked legitimacy all the same, and (once the arrangements were complete) did so

with some success. For nearly forty years the Vienna settlement provided a framework within which disputes were settled without war. Most of the régimes installed in 1815 were still there, even if some of them were somewhat shaken, forty years later.

This owed much to the salutary fear of revolution. In all the major continental states the restoration era (as the years after 1815 have been termed) was a great period for policemen and plotters alike. Secret societies proliferated, undiscouraged by failure after failure. This record showed, though, that there was no subversive threat that could not be handled easily enough. Austrian troops dealt with attempted coups in Piedmont and Naples, French soldiers restored the power of a reactionary Spanish king hampered by a liberal constitution, the Russian empire survived a military conspiracy and a Polish revolt. The Austrian predominance in Germany was not threatened at all and it is difficult in retrospect to discern any very real danger to any part of the Habsburg monarchy before 1848. Russian and Austrian power, the first in reserve, the second the main force in central Europe and Italy from 1815 to 1848, were the two rocks on which the Vienna system rested.

A satirical French cartoon depicts the key protagonists of the Congress of Vienna. The British foreign secretary Robert Castlereagh (second left) fought for the creation of the Quadruple Alliance of Britain, Austria, Prussia and Russia. Representatives of these four countries were to meet regularly in order to guarantee "the maintenance of the peace of Europe".

Mistakenly, liberalism and nationalism were usually supposed to be inseparable; this was to prove terribly untrue in later times, but in so far as a few people did seek to change Europe by revolution before 1848, it is broadly true that they wanted to do so by advancing both the political principles of the French Revolution – representative government, popular sovereignty, freedom of the individual and the press – and those of nationality. Many confused the two; the most famous and admired of those who did so was Mazzini, a young Italian. By advocating an Italian unity most of his countrymen did not want and conspiring unsuccessfully to bring it about, he became an inspiration and model for other nationalists and democrats in every continent for over a century and one of the first idols of radical chic. The age of the ideas he represented had not yet come, though.

RESTORATION IN FRANCE

To the west of the Rhine, where the writ of the Holy Alliance (the term given to the group of three conservative powers: Russia, Austria and Prussia) did not run, the story was different; there, legitimism was not to last long. The very restoration of the Bourbon dynasty in 1814 had itself been a compromise with the principle of legitimacy. Louis XVIII was supposed to have reigned like any other king of France since the death of his predecessor, Louis XVII, in a Paris prison in 1795. In fact, as everyone knew but legitimists tried to conceal, he came back in the baggage train of the Allied armies which had defeated Napoleon and he only did so on terms acceptable to the French political and military élites of the Napoleonic period and, presumably, tolerable by the majority of the French. The

This heroic portrayal of the July Revolution of 1830 in France, *Liberty Leading the People*, was painted by Eugène Delacroix (1798–1863).

An English painting depicts Louis XVIII's return to France in 1814 after 23 years in exile. His 10-year reign was characterized by moderation and respect for the revolutionary institutions and the Napoleonic Code.

restored régime was regulated by a charter which created a constitutional monarchy, albeit with a limited suffrage. The rights of individuals were guaranteed and the land settlement resulting from revolutionary confiscations and sales was unquestioned; there was to be no return to 1789.

Nevertheless, there was some uncertainty about the future; battle between Right and Left began with arguments about the charter itself – was it a contract between king and people, or a simple emanation of the royal benevolence which might therefore be withdrawn as easily as it had been granted? – and went on over a whole range of issues, which raised questions of principle (or were thought to do so) about ground won for liberty and the possessing classes in the Revolution.

CHARLES X IS DEPOSED

What was implicitly at stake was what the Revolution had actually achieved. One way of describing that would be to say that those who had struggled to be recognized as having a voice in ruling France under the *ancien régime* had won; the political weight of the "notables", as they were sometimes called, was assured and they, whether drawn from the old nobility of France, those who had done well out of the Revolution, Napoleon's lackeys, or simply substantial landowners and businessmen, were now the real rulers of France. Another change had been the nation-making brought about in French institutions; no person or corporation could now claim to stand outside the operative sphere of the national government of France. Finally and crucially, the Revolution had changed political thinking. Among other things, the terms in which French public affairs would be discussed and debated had been transformed. Wherever the line was to be drawn between Right and Left, conservatives or liberals, it was on that line that political battle now had to be centred, not over the privilege of counselling a monarch by divine right. This was just what the last king of the direct Bourbon line, Charles X, failed to see. He foolishly attempted to break out of the constitutional limitations which bound him, by what was virtually a *coup d'état*. Paris rose against him in the "July Revolution" of 1830, liberal politicians hastily put themselves at its head, and to the chagrin of republicans, ensured that a new king replaced Charles.

LOUIS PHILIPPE

Louis Philippe was head of the junior branch of the French royal house, the Orléans family, but to many conservative eyes he was the Revolution incarnate. His father had voted for the execution of Louis XVI (and went to the scaffold himself soon after) while the new king had fought as an officer in the republican armies. He had even been a member of the notorious Jacobin club, which was widely believed to have been a deep-rooted conspiracy, and certainly had been a forcing-house for some of the Revolution's most prominent leaders. To liberals Louis Philippe was attractive for much the same reasons; he reconciled the Revolution with the stability provided by

This scene is from the "glorious days" of the French "July Revolution" of 1830. There was substantial popular feeling against Charles X in Paris at a time when widespread recession and unemployment meant that more than 25 per cent of the city's inhabitants were claiming public assistance.

Restoration

"Once Napoleon was dead, divine and human powers recovered, but there was no faith in them. ...

"Until then, there had been people who hated nobles, cried out against the clergy, who conspired against kings; there had been shouts against abuse and prejudice, but it was a great novelty to see the people smile. If a noble, a clergyman or a king went by, the peasants who had fought in the war began to shake their heads and say, 'Oh we've seen him at another place and time, but he had a different face!', and when the throne and the altar were mentioned, they answered, 'Those are only a few lengths of wood, we have nailed them together and unnailed them', and when they were told, 'People, you have mended your ways, you have called back your kings and your clergy', they answered, 'We didn't, not those charlatans', and when it was suggested, 'People, forget the past, work and obey', they shifted in their seats and there was a dull sound of resentment. It was no more than a rusty, nicked sword shaking in the corner of the hut, but then, one hurried to add, 'At least stay where you are; if no-one troubles you, don't look for trouble.' Unfortunately, they were content with that.

"All the sicknesses of the current century come from two sources: the people who have gone through '93 and 1814 have two wounds in their hearts. All that was, is no longer; and that will be, is not yet. Do not look any further for the secret of our troubles."

An extract from *Confessions of a Child of the Century* (1835) by Alfred de Musset (1810–1857).

monarchy, though the left wing were disappointed. The régime over which he was to preside for eighteen years proved unimpeachably constitutional and preserved essential political freedoms, but protected the interests of the well-to-do. It vigorously suppressed urban disorder (of which poverty produced

Louis Philippe
d'Orléans
(1773–1850) and his
five sons are depicted
leaving Versailles after a
military parade in this
picture by the French
painter Horace Vernet
(1789–1863).

plenty in the 1830s) and this made it unpopular with the Left. One prominent politician told his fellow countrymen to enrich themselves – a recommendation much ridiculed and misunderstood, although all he was trying to do was to tell them that the way to obtain the vote was through the qualification which a high income conferred (in 1830 only about a third as many Frenchmen as Englishmen had a vote for their national representatives, while the population of France was about twice that of England). Nevertheless, in theory, the July Monarchy rested on popular sovereignty, the revolutionary principle of 1789.

EUROPE IN THE 1830s

The July Monarchy's revolutionary base gave it a certain special international standing in a Europe divided by ideology. In the 1830s there were sharply evident differences between a Europe of constitutional states – Britain, France, Spain and Portugal – and that of the legitimist, dynastic states of the East, with their Italian and German satellites. Conservative governments had not liked the July revolution. They were alarmed when the Belgians rebelled against their Dutch king in 1830, but could not support him because the British and French favoured the Belgians and

The fall of Missolonghi to the Turks in 1826 is represented by this personification of Greece on the ruins of the city, by Eugène Delacroix. In 1827 Britain, France and Russia sent a navy against the Turkish fleet in an effort to help the Greeks gain their independence.

Russia had a Polish rebellion on her hands. It took until 1839 to secure the establishment of an independent Belgium, and this was until 1848 the only important change in the state system created by the Vienna settlement, although the internal troubles of Spain and Portugal caused ripples which troubled European diplomacy.

THE EASTERN QUESTION

Elsewhere, in southeast Europe, the pace of change was quickening. A new revolutionary era was opening there just as that of western Europe moved to its climax. In 1804 a well-to-do Serbian pork dealer had led a revolt by his countrymen against the undisciplined Turkish garrison of Belgrade. The Ottoman régime was willing to countenance his actions in order to bridle its own mutinous soldiers and put down the Christian peasants who set about the massacre of urban Muslims. But the

One of the first Turkish reactions to the Greek declaration of independence was the Massacre of Chios in 1822. Eugène Delacroix produced moving paintings of the massacre – such as this one – which epitomized the Romantic school of painting.

eventual cost to the empire was the establishment of an autonomous Serbian princedom in 1817. By then the Turks had also ceded Bessarabia to Russia, and had been forced to recognize that their hold on much of Greece and Albania was little more than formal, real power being in the hands of the local pashas.

This was, though hardly yet visibly so, the opening of the Eastern Question of the nineteenth century: who or what was to inherit the fragments of the crumbling Ottoman Empire? It was to take more than a century and a world war to solve the question in Europe; in the Balkans and what were the Asiatic provinces of the empire, wars of the Ottoman succession are still going on today. Racial, religious, ideological, and diplomatic issues were entangled from the start. The Ottoman territories were populated by peoples and communities scattered over wide areas in logic-defying patterns and the Vienna settlement did not include them among those it covered by guarantees of the great powers. When there began what was represented as a "revolution" of "Greeks" (that is, Orthodox Christian subjects of the sultan, many of whom were bandits and pirates) against Ottoman rule in 1821, Russia abandoned her conservative principles and favoured the rebels. Religion and the old pull of Russian strategic aims towards southeastern Europe made it impossible for the Holy Alliance to support an Islamic ruler as it did other rulers, and in the end the Russians even went to war with the sultan. The new kingdom of Greece which emerged in 1832, its boundaries settled by outsiders, was bound to give ideas to other Balkan peoples and it was evident that the nineteenth-century Eastern Question was going to be complicated by the specious claims of nationalism as it had not been in the eighteenth century. The outlook was not good, for at its outset the Greek revolt had prompted massacres of Greeks by Turks in Constantinople and Smyrna, to be followed, rapidly, by Greek massacres of Turks in the Peloponnese. The problems of the next two centuries in the Balkans were poisoned at their roots by such examples of what would later be called "ethnic cleansing".

THE REVOLUTIONS OF 1848

In 1848 came a new revolutionary explosion. Briefly, it seemed that the whole 1815 settlement was in jeopardy. The 1840s had been years of economic hardship, food shortages and distress in many places, particularly in Ireland where, in 1846, there was a great famine, and then in central Europe and France in 1847, where a commercial slump

Czechs, Croats, Slovaks, Poles, Hungarians, Italians and Austrians rebelled in 1848, demanding independence from the Austrian government and recognition of their national identities. This 1848 painting shows the national guard trying to restore order to the streets of Vienna.

A united Italy is proclaimed in 1849. Led by Giuseppe Mazzini, the Roman Republic, as it was known, forced Pope Pius IX to flee, but the uprising was defeated by French troops in 1850. Mazzini's influence declined, although he became an inspiration to later Italian patriots.

starved the cities. Unemployment was widespread. This bred violence which gave new edge to radical movements everywhere. One disturbance inspired another; example was contagious and weakened the capacity of the international security system to deal with further outbreaks. The symbolic start came in February, in Paris, where Louis Philippe abdicated after discovering the middle classes would no longer support his continued opposition to the extension of the suffrage. By the middle of the year, government had been swept aside or was at best on the defensive in every major European capital except London and St Petersburg. When a republic appeared in France after the February Revolution every revolutionary and political exile in Europe had taken heart. The dreams of thirty years' conspiracies seemed realizable. The *Grande Nation* would be on the move again and the armies of the Great Revolution might march once more to spread its principles. What happened, though, was very different. France made a diplomatic genuflection in the direction of martyred Poland, the classical focus of liberal sympathies, but the only military operations it undertook were in defence of the pope, an unimpeachably conservative cause.

This was symptomatic. The revolutionaries of 1848 were provoked by very different situations, and many different aims, and followed divergent and confusing paths. In most of Italy and central Europe they rebelled against governments which they thought oppressive because they were illiberal; there, the great symbolic demand was for constitutions to guarantee essential freedoms. When such a revolution occurred in Vienna itself, the chancellor Metternich, architect of the conservative order of 1815, fled into exile. Successful revolution at Vienna meant the paralysis and therefore the dislocation of the whole of central Europe. Germans were now free to have their revolutions without fear of Austrian intervention in support of the *ancien régime* in the smaller states. So were other peoples within the Austrian dominions; Italians (led by an ambitious but apprehensive conservative king of Sardinia) turned on the Austrian armies in Lombardy and Venetia, Hungarians revolted at Budapest, and Czechs at Prague. This much complicated things. Many of these revolutionaries wanted national independence rather than constitutionalism, though constitutionalism seemed for a time the way to independence because it attacked dynastic autocracy.

THE FAILURES OF 1848

If the liberals were able to get constitutional governments installed in central Europe and Italy, then it followed there would actually come into existence nations hitherto without their own state structures, or at least without them for a very long time. If Slavs achieved their own national liberation then states previously thought of as German would be shorn of huge tracts of their territory, notably in

Poland and Bohemia. It took some time for this to sink in. The German liberals suddenly fell over this problem in 1848 and quickly drew their conclusions; they chose nationalism. (The Italians were still grappling with their own version of the dilemma in the South Tyrol a hundred years later.) The German revolutions of 1848 failed, essentially, because the German liberals decided that German nationalism required the preservation of German lands in the east. Hence, they needed a strong Prussia and must accept its terms for the future of Germany. There were other signs, too, that the tide had turned before the end of 1848. The Austrian army had mastered the Italians. In Paris a rising aiming to give the Revolution a further shove in the direction of democracy was crushed with great bloodshed in June. The republic was, after all, to be a conservative one. In 1849 came the end. The Austrians overthrew the Sardinian army which was the only shield of the Italian revolutions, and monarchs all over the peninsula then began to withdraw the constitutional concessions they had made while Austrian power was in abeyance. German rulers did the same, led by Prussia. The pressure was kept up on the Habsburgs by the Croats and Hungarians, but then the Russian army came to its ally's help.

SPRINGTIME OF THE NATIONS

Liberals saw 1848 as a "springtime of the nations". If it was one, the shoots had not lived long before they withered. By the end of 1849 the formal structure of Europe was once again much as it had been in 1847, in spite of important changes within some countries. Nationalism had certainly been a popular cause in 1848, but it had been neither strong

The Italian nationalist leader Giuseppe Mazzini (1805–1872), pictured here, continued to campaign for an Italian republic after the country was unified as a monarchy.

Six hundred delegates attended the meeting of the German National Assembly in Frankfurt in 1848. The assembly had a significantly nationalistic character – some of its members proposed the formation of a Greater Germany, which would include the Tyrol, Bohemia, Alsace, Switzerland and the Netherlands.

High levels of unemployment and rapid inflation caused starvation in Poland during 1845–1847, which led to rioting in the cities. This contemporary painting shows angry crowds storming the public bakery in Breslau Market.

enough to sustain revolutionary governments nor obviously an enlightened force. Its failure shows the charge that the statesmen of 1815 "neglected" to give it due attention is false; no new nation emerged from 1848 for none was ready to do so. The basic reason for this was that although nationalities might exist, over most of Europe nationalism was still an abstraction for the masses; only relatively few and well-educated, or at least half-educated, people much cared about it. Where national differences also embodied social issues there was sometimes effective action by people who felt they had an identity given them by language, tradition or religion, but it did not lead to the setting up of new nations. The Ruthene peasants of Galicia in 1847 had happily murdered their Polish landlords when the Habsburg administration allowed them to do so. Having thus satisfied themselves they remained loyal to the Habsburgs in 1848.

POPULAR UPRISINGS

There were some genuinely popular risings in 1848. In Italy they were usually revolts of townsmen rather than peasants; the Lombard peasants, indeed, cheered the Austrian army when it returned, because they saw no good for them in a revolution led by the aristocrats who were their landlords. In parts of Germany, over much of which the traditional structures of landed rural society remained intact, the peasants behaved as their predecessors had done in France in 1789, burning their landlords' houses, not merely through personal animus but in order to destroy the hated and feared records of rents, dues and labour services.

Such outbreaks frightened urban liberals as much as the Parisian outbreak of despair and unemployment in the June Days frightened the middle classes in France. There, because the peasant was since 1789 (speaking broadly) a conservative, the government was assured of the support of the provinces in crushing the Parisian poor who had given radicalism its brief success.

But conservatism could be found within revolutionary movements, too. German working-class turbulence alarmed the better-off, but this was because the leaders of German workers talked of "socialism" while actually seeking a return to the past. They had the safe world of guilds and apprenticeships in mind, and feared machinery in factories, steamboats on the Rhine, which put boatmen out of work, the opening of unrestricted entry to trades – in short, the all-too-evident signs of the onset of market society. Almost always, liberalism's lack of appeal to the masses was shown up in 1848 by popular revolution.

THE REPERCUSSIONS OF 1848

Altogether, the social importance of 1848 is as complex and escapes easy generalization as much as its political content. It was probably in the countryside of eastern and central Europe that the revolutions changed society most. There, liberal principles and the fear of popular revolt went hand in hand to impose change on the landlords. Wherever outside Russia obligatory peasant labour and bondage to the soil survived, it was abolished as a result of 1848. That year carried the rural social revolution launched sixty years earlier in France, to its conclusion in central and most of eastern Europe. The way was now open for the reconstruction of agricultural life in Germany and the Danube valley on individualist and market lines. Though many of its practices and habits of mind were still to

The Venetian Republic is proclaimed in St Mark's Square on 23 March 1848, freeing Venice from Austrian rule.

linger, feudal society was in effect now coming to an end all over Europe. The political components of French revolutionary principles, though, would have to wait longer for their expression.

THE CRIMEAN WAR

In the case of nationalism this was not very long. A dispute over Russian influence in the Near East in 1854 ended the long peace between great powers which had lasted since 1815. The Crimean War, in which the French and British fought as allies of the Ottoman sultan against the Russians, was in many ways a notable struggle. Fighting took place in the Baltic, in southern Russia, and in the Crimea, the last theatre attracting most attention. There, the allies had set themselves to capture Sebastopol, the naval base which was the key to Russian power in the Black Sea. Some of the results were surprising. The British army fought gallantly, as did its opponents and allies, but was especially distinguished by the inadequacy of its administrative arrangements; the scandal these caused launched an important wave of radical reform at home. Incidentally the war also helped to found the prestige of a new profession for women, that of nursing, for the collapse of British medical services had been

A montage illustrates the defence of Sebastopol, the Crimean port that was captured from the Russians in September 1855 after a long struggle. The Crimean War was notable for its enormous number of casualties – more than resulted from any other European war between 1815 and 1914. Of the 675,000 fatalities of the Crimean War, more than 80 per cent were caused by disease or infected wounds.

The consequences of the Crimean War

The Crimean War broke out in 1853. The conflict escalated in the following year and lasted until 1856. Russian interest in the Turkish Straits, which would allow them an outlet to the Mediterranean, brought them into direct conflict with the British, who claimed that the Straits must be kept open to international traffic (a position that was vital for a country like Britain, which drew its strength from maritime control and from its powerful navy).

By 1855, the Russian troops were clearly fighting a losing battle against the Turkish, British and French allied forces. When Tsar Nicholas I died that year, his successor, Alexander II, recognized that he had no choice but to sue for peace.

The signatories of the peace treaty of Paris in 1856 agreed to maintain "the integrity of the Turkish Empire". Russia ceded the left bank of the mouth of the Danube to Moldavia. Moldavia and Wallachia (which was united with Romania in 1858) and Serbia were recognized as self-governing principalities under the protection of the European powers. Russia ceased to have the right to maintain warships in the Black Sea and the Danube was to be open to commercial navigation from every nation.

A British position to the east of Sebastopol is depicted in this Crimean War engraving.

particularly striking. Florence Nightingale's work launched the first major extension of the occupational opportunities available to respectable women since the creation of female religious communities in the Dark Ages. The conduct of the war is also noteworthy in another way as an index of modernity: it was the first between major powers in which steamships and a railway were employed, and it brought the electric telegraph cable to Istanbul.

Some of these things were portentous. Yet they mattered less in the short run than what the war did to international relations. Russia was defeated and her long enjoyment of a power to intimidate Turkey was bridled for a time. A step was taken towards the establishment of another new Christian nation,

Romania, which was finally brought about in 1862. Once more, nationality triumphed in former Ottoman lands. But the crucial effect of the war was that the Holy Alliance had disappeared. The old rivalry of the eighteenth century between Austria and Russia over what would happen to the Ottoman inheritance in the Balkans had broken out again when Austria warned Russia not to occupy the Danube principalities (as the future Romania was termed) during the war and

then occupied them herself. This was five years after Russia had intervened to restore Habsburg power by crushing the Hungarian revolution. It was the end of friendship between the two powers. The next time Austria faced a threat she would have to do so without the Russian policeman of conservative Europe at her side.

NAPOLEON III

In 1856, when peace was made, few people can have anticipated how quickly the next threat to Austria would come. Within ten years Austria lost in two short, sharp wars her hegemony both in Italy and in Germany, and those countries were united in new national states. Nationalism had indeed triumphed, and at the cost of the Habsburgs, as had been prophesied by enthusiasts in 1848, but in a totally unexpected way. Not revolution, but the ambitions of two traditionally expansive monarchical states, Sardinia and Prussia, had led each to set about improving its position at the expense of Austria, whose isolation was at that moment complete. Not only had she sacrificed the Russian alliance, but after 1852 France was ruled by an emperor who again bore the name Napoleon (he was the nephew of the first to do so). He had been elected president of the Second Republic, whose constitution he then set aside by *coup d'état*. The name Napoleon was itself terrifying. It suggested a programme of international reconstruction – or revolution. Napoleon III (the second was a legal fiction, a son of Napoleon I who had never ruled) stood for the destruction of the anti-French settlement of 1815 and therefore of the Austrian predominance which propped it up in Italy and Germany. He talked the language of nationalism with less inhibition than most rulers and seems to have believed

Napoleon III (1808–1873), formerly Louis-Napoleon Bonaparte, was president of the French Republic and in 1852 proclaimed himself ruler of the Second Empire.

in it. With arms and diplomacy he forwarded the work of two great diplomatic technicians, Cavour and Bismarck, the prime ministers respectively of Sardinia and of Prussia.

UNITY IN ITALY AND GERMANY

In 1859 Sardinia and France fought Austria; after a brief war the Austrians were left with only Venetia in Italy. Cavour now set to work to incorporate other Italian states into Sardinia, a part of the price being that Sardinian Savoy had to be given to France. Cavour died in 1861, and debate still continues over what was the real extent of his aims, but by 1871 his successors had produced a united Italy under the former king of Sardinia, who was thus recompensed for the loss of Savoy, the ancestral duchy of his house. In that year Germany was united, too. Bismarck had begun by rallying German liberal sentiment to the Prussian cause once

again in a nasty little war against Denmark in 1864. Two years later Prussia defeated Austria in a lightning campaign in Bohemia, thus at last ending the Hohenzollern–Habsburg duel for supremacy in Germany begun in 1740 by Frederick II. The war which did this was rather a registration of an accomplished fact than its achievement, for since 1848 Austria had been much weakened in German affairs. In that year, German liberals had offered a German crown, not to the emperor, but to the king of Prussia. Nevertheless, some states had still looked to Vienna for leadership and patronage, and they were now left alone to meet Prussian bullying. The Habsburg empire now became wholly Danubian and its foreign policy was preoccupied with southeast Europe and the Balkans. It had retired from the Netherlands in 1815, Venetia had been exacted by the Prussians for the Italians in 1866, and now it left Germany to its own devices, too. Immediately after the peace the Hungarians

A contemporary painting depicts the triumphal entry of Victor Emmanuel II of Sardinia, Piedmont and Savoy and Napoleon III into Milan on 8 June 1859. Count Cavour's influence on plebiscites held in 1860 resulted in the incorporation of Parma, Modena, Romagna and Tuscany into the Italian union, under the crown of Victor Emmanuel II.

seized the opportunity to inflict a further defeat on the humiliated monarchy by obtaining a virtual autonomy for the half of the Habsburg monarchy made up of the lands of the Hungarian Crown. The empire thus became, in 1867, the Dual or Austro Hungarian monarchy, divided rather untidily into two halves linked by little more than the dynasty itself and the conduct of a common foreign policy.

THE PRUSSIAN SECOND REICH

German unification required one further step. It had gradually dawned on France that the assertion of Prussian power beyond the Rhine was not in the French interest; instead of a disputed Germany, she now faced one dominated by an important military power. The Richelieu era had crumbled away unnoticed. Bismarck used this new awareness, together with Napoleon III's weaknesses at home and

international isolation, to provoke France into a foolish declaration of war in 1870. Victory in this war set the coping-stone on the new edifice of German nationality, for Prussia had taken the lead in "defending" Germany against France – and there were still Germans alive who could remember what French armies had done in Germany under an earlier Napoleon. The Prussian army destroyed the Second Empire in France (it was to be the last monarchical régime in that country) and created the German Empire, the Second Reich, as it was called, to distinguish it from the medieval empire. In practice, it was a Prussian domination cloaked in federal forms, but as a German national state it satisfied many German liberals. It was dramatically and appropriately founded in 1871 when the king of Prussia accepted the crown of united Germany (which his predecessor had refused to take from German liberals in 1848) from his fellow princes in the palace of Louis XIV at Versailles.

REVOLUTIONARY TENDENCIES BEGIN TO WANE

There had been in fifty years a revolution in international affairs and it would have great consequences for world, as well as European, history. Germany had replaced France as the dominant land-power in Europe as France had replaced Spain in the seventeenth century. This fact was to overshadow Europe's international relations until they ceased to be determined by forces originating within her. It owed just a little to revolutionary politics in the narrow and strict sense. The conscious revolutionaries of the nineteenth century had achieved nothing comparable with the work of Cavour, Bismarck and, half in spite of himself, Napoleon III. This is very odd, given the

hopes entertained of revolution in this period, and the fears felt for it. Revolution had achieved little except at the fringes of Europe and had even begun to show signs of flagging. Down to 1848 there had been plenty of revolutions, to say nothing of plots, conspiracies and *pronunciamientos* which did not justify the name. After 1848 there were very few. Another Polish revolution took place in 1863, but this was the only outbreak of note in the lands of the great powers until 1871.

An ebbing of revolutionary effort by then is understandable. Revolutions seemed to have achieved little outside France and had there brought disillusion and dictatorship. Some of their goals were being achieved in other ways. Cavour and his followers had created a united Italy, after all, greatly to the chagrin of Mazzini, since it was not one of which that revolutionary could approve, and Bismarck had done what many of the German liberals of 1848 had hoped for by providing a Germany which was indisputably

a great power. Other ends were being achieved by economic progress; for all the horrors of the poverty which it contained, nineteenth-century Europe was getting richer and was giving more and more of its peoples a larger share of its wealth. Even quite short-term factors helped here. The year 1848 was soon followed by the great gold discoveries of California, which provided a flow of bullion to stimulate the world economy in the 1850s and 1860s; confidence grew and unemployment fell in these decades and this was good for social peace.

THE GROWING POWER OF CENTRAL GOVERNMENT

A more fundamental reason why revolutions were less frequent was, perhaps, that they became more difficult to carry out. Governments were finding it steadily easier to grapple with them, largely for technical

The Place de la Concorde in Paris was renamed that in 1830 to distance the site from its bloody past when, as the Place de la Révolution, it had been the site of the infamous guillotine. After that, the statue of Louis XV was replaced by the two fountains and the obelisk of Luxor – all three of which can be seen here in Boulanger's 1871 painting *Battle in the Place de la Concorde*, when the area was the scene of another outbreak of bloodshed after the communards of Paris attacked government forces.

reasons. The nineteenth century created modern police forces. Better communications by rail and telegraph gave new power to central government in dealing with distant revolt. Above all, armies had a growing technical superiority to rebellion. As early as 1795 a French government showed that once it had control of the regular armed forces, and was prepared to use them, it could master Paris. During the long peace from 1815 to 1848 many European armies in fact became much more instruments of security, directed potentially against their own populations, than means of international competition, directed against foreign enemies. It was only the defection of important sections of the armed forces which permitted successful revolution in Paris in 1830 and 1848; once such forces were available to the government, battles like that of the June Days of 1848 (which one observer called the greatest slave-war in history) could only end with the defeat of the

rebels. From that year, indeed, no popular revolution was ever to succeed in a major European country against a government whose control of its armed forces was unshaken by defeat in war or by subversion, and which was determined to use its power.

THE PARIS COMMUNE

The power of an effective army was vividly and bloodily demonstrated in 1871, when a rebellious Paris was once again crushed by a French government in little more than a week, with a toll of dead as great as that exacted by the Terror of 1793–4. A popular régime, which drew to itself a wide range of radicals and reformers, set itself up in the capital as the "Commune" of Paris, a name evocative of traditions of municipal independence going back to the Middle Ages and, more important, to 1793, when the

This French drawing entitled *Le Mur des Fédérés* shows the execution of communards on 28 May, 1871, the day after the fall of the Paris Commune.

Commune (or city council) of Paris had been the centre of revolutionary fervour.

The Commune of 1871 was able to take power because in the aftermath of defeat by the Germans the French government could not disarm the capital of the weapons with which it had successfully withstood a siege, and because the same defeat had inflamed many Parisians against the government they believed to have let them down. During its brief life (there were a few weeks of quiet while the government prepared its riposte) the Commune did very little, but it produced a lot of left-wing rhetoric and was soon seen as the embodiment of social revolution. This gave additional bitterness to the efforts to suppress it. Those moves came when the government had reassembled its forces from returning prisoners of war to reconquer Paris, which became the scene of brief but bloody street-fighting. Once again, regularly consti-tuted armed forces overcame workmen and shopkeepers manning hastily improvised bar-ricades. If anything could do so, the ghastly failure of the Paris Commune should have killed the revolutionary myth, both in its power to terrify and its power to inspire. Yet it did not. If anything, it strengthened it.

SOCIALISM

CONSERVATIVES FOUND IT a great standby to have the Commune example to hand in evoking the dangers lurking always ready to burst out from under the surface of society. Revolutionaries had a new episode of heroism and martyrdom to add to an apostolic succession of revolutionaries run-ning already from 1789 to 1848. But the Commune also revivified the revolutionary mythology because of a new factor whose importance had already struck both Left and Right. This was socialism.

This portrayal of early rail travel by the French artist Honoré Daumier (1808–1878) is entitled *The Third Class Carriage.*

This word (like its relative, "socialist") has come to encompass a great many things, and did so almost from the start. Both words were first commonly used in France around about 1830 to describe theories and men opposed to a society run on market principles and to an economy operated on *laissez-faire* lines, of which the main beneficiaries (they thought) were the wealthy. Economic and social egalitarianism is fundamental to the socialist idea, as are broad political participation and arrangement for general welfare. Most socialists have been able to agree on that. They have usually believed that in a good society there would be no class oppressing another through the advantages given by the ownership of wealth. All socialists, too, could agree that there was nothing sacred about property, whose rights buttressed injustice; some sought its complete abolition and were called communists. "Property is theft" was one very successful slogan.

SOCIALIST THOUGHT

Such ideas might be frightening, but were not very novel. Egalitarian ideas have fascinated human beings throughout history and the Christian rulers of Europe had managed without difficulty to reconcile social arrangements resting on sharp contrasts of wealth with the practice of a religion, one of whose greatest hymns praised God for filling the hungry with good things and sending the rich away empty. What happened in the early nineteenth century was that such ideas seemed to become at once more dangerous, linked to the idea of revolution in the new style, and more widespread. There was also a need for new thinking because of other developments. One was that the success of liberal political reform appeared to show that legal equality was not enough, if it was deprived of content by dependence on the economically powerful, or denatured by poverty and atten-

dant ignorance. Another was that already in the eighteenth century a few thinkers had seen big discrepancies of wealth as irrationalities in a world which could and should (they thought) be regulated to produce the greatest good of the greatest number. In the French Revolution some thinkers and agitators already pressed forward demands in which later generations would see socialist ideas. Egalitarian ideas none the less only became socialism in a modern sense when they began to grapple with the problems of the new epoch of economic and social change, above all with those presented by industrialization.

This often required a great perspicacity, for these changes were very slow in making their impact outside Great Britain and Belgium, the first continental country to be industrialized in the same degree. Yet perhaps because the contrast they presented with traditional society was so stark, even the small beginnings of concentration in capitalist finance and manufacturing were remarked. One of the first men to grasp their potentially very great implications for social organization was a French nobleman, Claude Saint-Simon. His seminal contribution to socialist thought was to consider the impact on society of technological and scientific advance. Saint-Simon thought that they not only made planned organization of the economy imperative, but implied (indeed, demanded) the replacement of the traditional ruling classes, aristocratic and rural in their outlook, by élites representing new economic and intellectual forces. Such ideas influenced many thinkers (most of them French), who in the 1830s advocated greater egalitarianism; they seemed to show that on rational as well as ethical grounds such change was desirable. Their doctrines made enough impact and considerations were enough talked about to terrify the French possessing classes in 1848, who thought they saw in the June Days a "socialist" revolution. Socialists willingly identified themselves for the most part with the tradition of the French Revolution, picturing the realization of their ideals as its next phase, so the misinterpretation is understandable.

THE COMMUNIST MANIFESTO

In 1848, at this juncture, there appeared a pamphlet which is the most important document in the history of socialism. It is always known as *The Communist Manifesto* (though this was not the title under which it was published). It was largely the work of Karl Marx, a young German of Jewish birth (though himself baptized), and with it the point is reached at which the prehistory of socialism can be separated from its history. Marx proclaimed a complete break with what he called the "utopian socialism" of his predecessors. Utopian socialists attacked industrial capital-

Count Claude de Saint-Simon (1760– 1825) is often cited as the founder of French socialism.

Karl Marx (1818–1883) is shown at work in his study in this 19th-century drawing.

ism because they thought it was unjust; Marx thought this beside the point. Nothing, according to Marx, could be hoped for from arguments to persuade people that change was morally desirable. Everything depended on the way history was going, towards the actual and inevitable creation of a new working class by industrial society, the rootless wage-earners of the new industrial cities, whom he termed the industrial proletariat. This class was bound, according to Marx, to act in a revolutionary way. History was working upon them so as to generate revolutionary capacity and mentality. It would present them with conditions to which revolution was the only logical outcome and that revolution would be, by those conditions, guaranteed success. What mattered was not that capitalism was morally wrong, but that it was already out of date and therefore historically doomed. Marx asserted that every society had a particular system of property rights and class relationships, and these accordingly shaped its particular political arrangements. Politics were bound to express economic forces. They would change as the particular organization of society changed under the influence of economic developments, and therefore, sooner or later (and Marx seems to have thought sooner), the revolution would sweep away capitalist society and its forms in as capitalist society had already swept away feudal.

A SECULAR RELIGION

There was much more to Marx than the theory of historical inevitability, but this was a striking and encouraging message, which gave him domination of the international socialist movement that emerged in the next twenty years. The assurance that history was on their side was a great tonic to revolutionaries. They learnt with gratitude that the cause to which they were impelled anyway by motives ranging from a sense of injustice to the promptings of envy was predestined to triumph. This was essentially a religious faith. For all its intellectual possibilities as an analytical instrument, Marxism came to be above all a popular mythology, resting on a view of history which said that human beings were bound by necessity because their institutions were determined by the evolving methods of production, and on a faith that the working class were the chosen people whose pilgrimage through a wicked world would end in the triumphal establishment of a just society in which necessity's iron law would cease to operate. Social revolutionaries could thus feel confident of scientifically irrefutable arguments for irresistible progress towards the socialist millennium, while clinging to a revolutionary activism it seemed to make unnecessary. Marx himself seems to have followed his teaching more cautiously, applying it only to the broad, sweeping changes in history which individuals are powerless to resist and not to its detailed unfolding. Perhaps it is not surprising that, like many masters, he did not recognize all his pupils: he later protested that he was not a Marxist.

MARXIST MOVEMENTS

This new religion was an inspiration to working-class organization. Trades unions and cooperatives already existed in some countries; the First International organization of working men appeared in 1863. Though it included many who did not subscribe to Marx's views (anarchists, among others), his influence was paramount within it (he was its secretary). Its name frightened conservatives, some of whom blamed the Paris Commune on it. Whatever their justification, their instincts were right. What happened in the years after 1848 was that socialism captured the revolutionary tradition from the liberals, and a belief in the historical role of an industrial working class, still barely visible outside England (let alone predominant in most countries), was tacked on to the tradition which held that, broadly speaking, revolution could not be wrong. Forms of thinking about politics evolved in the French Revolution were thus transferred to societies to which they would prove increasingly inappropriate. How easy such a transition could be was shown by

Bakunin *versus* Marx

"Marx is an authoritarian, centralist communist. He wants what we want: the triumph of economic and social equality, but through the State and by the power of the State; by the dictatorship of a powerful and, one could say, despotic provisional government, that is to say, denying liberty. His economic ideal is that of a State converted into the sole owner of all land and all capital, cultivating the former through agricultural associations, well-remunerated and managed by its civil engineers, and collectivizing the latter through industrial and commercial associations.

"We want that same triumph of economic and social equality to come through the abolition of the State and everything known as Legal Rights, which, in our view, is the permanent negation of human rights. We want to rebuild society and to build human unity, not from top to bottom with the aid of any authorities, but from bottom to top, through the free federation of all types of workmen's associations, freed from the yoke of the State."

An extract from a private letter written in 1872 by Russian anarchist Mikhail Bakunin (1814–1876).

the way Marx snapped up the drama and mythical exaltation of the Paris Commune for socialism. In a powerful tract he annexed it to his own theories, though it was, in fact, the product of many complicated and differing forces and expressed very little in the way of egalitarianism, let alone "scientific" socialism. It emerged, moreover, in a city which, though huge, was not one of the great manufacturing centres in which he predicted proletarian revolution would mature. These remained, instead, stubbornly quiescent. The Commune was, in fact, the last and greatest example of traditional Parisian radicalism. It was a great failure (and socialism suffered from it, too, because of the repression it provoked), yet Marx made it central to socialist mythology.

NICHOLAS I OF RUSSIA

RUSSIA SEEMED, except in her Polish lands, immune to the disturbances troubling other continental great powers. The French

The domestic policy of Nicholas I (1796–1855), portrayed here, reflected that of his ancestors: despotism propped up by the power of the military. His pan-Slavism – he aimed to Russify all the peoples of his empire – led to Roman Catholics and Protestants being encouraged to become part of the Russian Orthodox Church.

Byron on the tsar of Russia

Referring to the tsar of Russia's interference in Greece's struggle for independence from the Ottoman Empire, Byron wrote:

"The aid evaded, and the cold delay,
Prolong'd but in the hope to make a prey;–
These, these shall tell the tale, and Greece can show
The false friend is worse than the infuriate foe.
But this is well: Greeks only should free Greece,
Not the barbarian, with his mask of peace.
How should the autocrat of bondage be
The king of serfs, and set the nations free?
Better still serve the haughty Mussulman,
Than swell the Cossaque's prowling caravan ...
Better still toil for masters, than await,
The slave of slaves, before a Russian gate,–
Number'd by hordes, a human capital,
A live estate, existing but for thrall,
Lotted by thousands, as a meet reward
For the first courtier in the Czar's regard;
While their immediate owner never tastes
His sleep, *sans* dreaming of Siberia's wastes:
Better succumb even to their own despair,
And drive the camel than purvey the bear."

An extract from v. 6 of *The Age of Bronze* by Lord Byron, 1823.

Revolution had been another of those experiences which, like feudalism, Renaissance or Reformation, decisively shaped western Europe and passed Russia by. Although Alexander I, the tsar under whom Russia met the 1812 invasion, had indulged himself with liberal ideas and had even thought of a constitution, nothing seemed to come of this. A formal liberalization of Russian institutions did not begin until the 1860s, and even then its source was not revolutionary contagion. It is true that liberalism and revolutionary ideologies did not quite leave Russia untouched before this. Alexander's reign had seen something of an opening of a Pandora's box of

ideas and it had thrown up a small group of critics of the régime who found their models in western Europe. Some of the Russian officers who went there with the armies which pursued Napoleon to Paris were led by what they saw and heard to make unfavourable comparisons with their homeland; this was the beginning of political opposition. In an autocracy opposition was bound to mean conspiracy. Some of them took part in the organization of secret societies which attempted a coup amid the uncertainty caused by the death of Alexander in 1825; this was called the "Decembrist" movement. It soon collapsed but only after giving a fright to Nicholas I, a tsar who decisively and negatively affected Russia's historical destiny at a crucial moment by ruthlessly turning on polit-

ical liberalism and seeking to crush it. In part because of the immobility which he imposed, Nicholas's reign influenced Russia's destiny more than any since that of Peter the Great. A dedicated believer in autocracy, he confirmed the Russian tradition of authoritarian bureaucracy, the management of cultural life, and the rule of the secret police just when the other great conservative powers were, however unwillingly, beginning to move in the opposite direction. There was, of course, much to build on already in the historical legacies which differentiated Russian autocracy from western European monarchy. But there were also great challenges to be met and Nicholas's reign was a response to these as well as a simple deployment of the old methods of despotism by a man determined to use them.

Moscow is depicted by Fiodor Alexeyev in 1811, during the reign of Tsar Alexander I (1777–1825).

The Russian nobility became ever more Europeanized during the 19th century. The intelligentsia began to identify with German idealism, utopian French socialism and Romanticism. Here, intellectuals are shown taking tea in a St Petersburg salon in 1830.

OFFICIAL IDEOLOGY

The ethnic, linguistic and geographical diversity of the empire had begun to pose problems far outrunning the capacity of Muscovite tradition to deal with them. The population of the empire itself more than doubled in the forty years after 1770. This ever-diversifying society none the less remained overwhelmingly backward; its few cities were hardly a part of the vast rural expanses in which they stood and often seemed insubstantial and impermanent, more like huge temporary encampments than settled centres of civilization. The greatest

expansion had been to the south and southeast; here new élites had to be incorporated in the imperial structure and to stress the religious ties between the Orthodox was one of the easiest ways to do this. As the conflict with Napoleon had compromised the old prestige of things French and the sceptical ideas of the Enlightenment associated with that country, a new emphasis was now given to religion in the evolution of a new ideological basis for the Russian Empire under Nicholas. "Official Nationality", as it was called, was Slavophile and religious in doctrine, bureaucratic in form and strove to give Russia an ideological unity it had lost since outgrowing its historic centre in Muscovy.

The importance of official ideology was from this time one of the great differences between Russia and western Europe. Until the last decade of the twentieth century Russian governments were never to give up their belief in ideology as a unifying force. Yet this did not mean that daily life in the middle of the century, either for the civilized classes or the mass of a backward population, was much different from that of other parts of eastern and central Europe. Yet Russian intellectuals argued about whether Russia was or was not a European country, and this is not surprising; Russia's roots were different from those of countries further west. What is more, a decisive turn was taken under Nicholas, from the beginning of whose reign possibilities of change, which were at least being felt in other dynastic states in the first half of the nineteenth century were simply not allowed to appear in Russia. It was the land *par excellence* of censorship and police. In the long run this was bound to exclude certain possibilities of modernization (though other obstacles rooted in Russian society seem equally important), but in the short run it was highly successful. Russia passed through the whole nineteenth century without revolution; revolts in Russian Poland in 1830–31 and 1863–4 were ruthlessly suppressed, the more easily because Poles and Russians cherished traditions of mutual dislike.

RUSSIAN EXPANSION

The other side of the coin was the almost continuous violence and disorder of a savage and primitive rural society, and a mounting and more and more violent tradition of conspiracy, which perhaps incapacitated Russia even further for normal politics and the

Pushkin describes St Petersburg

"I love you, Peter's own creation;
I love your stern, your stately air,
Nevá's majestical pulsation,
the granite that her quaysides wear,
your railings with their iron shimmer,
your pensive nights in the half-gloom,
translucent twilight, moonless glimmer,
when, sitting lampless in my room,
I write and read; when, faintly shining,
the streets in their immense outlining
are empty, given up to dreams;
when Admiralty's needle gleams;
when not admitting shades infernal
into the golden sky, one glow
succeeds another, and nocturnal
tenure has one half-hour to go;
I love your brutal winter, freezing
the air to so much windless space;
by broad Nevá the sledges breezing;
brighter than roses each girl's face; ...
... I love it when some warlike duty
livens the Field of Mars, and horse
and foot impose on that concourse
their monolithic brand of beauty;
above the smooth-swaying vanguard
victorious, tattered flags are streaming,
on brazen helmets light is gleaming,
helmets that war has pierced and scarred.
I love the martial detonation,
the citadel in smoke and roar,
when the North's Empress to the nation
has given a son for empire, or
when there's some new triumph in war
victorious Russia's celebrating;
or when Nevá breaks the blue ice,
sweeps it to seaward, slice on slice,
and smells that days of spring are waiting.
    "Metropolis of Peter, stand,
steadfast as Russia, stand in splendour!
Even the elements by your hand
have been subdued and made surrender;
let Finland's waves forget the band
of hate and bondage down the ages,
nor trouble with their fruitless rages
Peter the Great's eternal sleep!"

Extract from *The Bronze Horseman* by Alexander Pushkin, 1833, translated by Charles Johnston.

shared assumptions they required. Unfriendly critics variously described Nicholas's reign as an ice age, a plague zone and a prison, but not for the last time in Russian history the preservation of a harsh and unyielding despotism at home was not incompatible with a strong international role. This rested upon Russia's huge military superiority. When armies contended with muzzle-loaders and no important weaponry distinguished one from another her vast numbers were decisive. On Russian military strength rested the anti-revolutionary international security system, as 1849 showed. But Russian foreign policy had other successes, too. Pressure was consistently kept up on the central Asian khanates and on China. The left bank of the Amur became Russian and in 1860 Vladivostok was founded. Great concessions were exacted from Persia and during the nineteenth century Russia absorbed Georgia and a part of Armenia. For a time there was even a deter-

mined effort to pursue Russian expansion in North America, where there were forts in Alaska and settlements in northern California until the 1840s.

The major effort of Russian foreign policy, nevertheless, was directed to the southwest, towards Ottoman Europe. Wars in 1806–12 and 1828 carried the Russian frontier across Bessarabia to the Pruth and the mouth of the Danube. It was by then clear that the partition of the Ottoman Empire in Europe would be as central to nineteenth-century diplomacy as the partition of Poland had been to that of the eighteenth, but there was an important difference: the interests of more powers were involved this time and the complicating factor of national sentiment among the subject peoples of the Ottoman Empire would make an agreed outcome much more difficult. As it happened, the Ottoman Empire survived far longer than might have been expected, and an eastern question is still bothering statesmen.

The railway at Balaklava is depicted in this English illustration of the port after its capture from the Russians during the Crimean War.

A PERIOD OF CHANGE IN IMPERIAL RUSSIA

Some of the complicating factors of the Eastern Question led to the Crimean War, which began with a Russian occupation of Ottoman provinces on the lower Danube. In Russia's internal affairs the war was more important than in those of any other country. It revealed that the military colossus of the 1815 restoration now no longer enjoyed an unquestioned superiority. She was defeated on her own territory and obliged to accept a peace which involved the renunciation for the foreseeable future of her traditional goals in the Black Sea area. Fortunately, in the middle of the war Nicholas I had died. This simplified the problems of his successor; defeat meant that change had to come. Some modernization of Russian institutions was unavoidable

if Russia was again to generate a power commensurate with her vast potential, which had become unrealizable within her traditional framework. When the Crimean War broke out there was still no Russian railway south of Moscow. Russia's once important contribution to European industrial production had hardly grown since 1800 and was now far outstripped by others. Her agriculture remained one of the least productive in the world and yet her population steadily rose, pressing harder upon its resources. It was in these circumstances that Russia at last underwent radical change. Though less dramatic than many upheavals in the rest of Europe it was in fact more of a revolution than much that went by that name elsewhere, for what was at last uprooted was the institution which lay at the very roots of Russian life, serfdom.

The Orthodox Church played a central role in the lives of the vast majority of Russia's rural population in the 19th century. Here, a painting of 1878 depicts the arrival of an icon in a Russian village.

Russian peasants are shown tilling the soil in spring in this scene dating from 1820–1830.

THE EMANCIPATION OF THE SERFS

Its extension had been the leading characteristic of Russian social history since the seventeenth century. Even Nicholas had agreed that serfdom was the central evil of Russian society. His reign had been marked by increasingly frequent serf insurrections, attacks on landlords, crop-burning and cattle-maiming. The refusal of dues was almost the least alarming form of popular resistance to it. Yet it was appallingly difficult for the rider to get off the elephant. The vast majority of Russians were serfs. They could not be transformed overnight by mere legislative *fiat* into wage labourers or smallholders, nor could the state accept the administrative burden, which would suddenly be thrown upon it if the services discharged by the manorial system should be withdrawn and nothing put in their place. Nicholas had not dared to proceed. Alexander II did. After years of study of the evidence and possible advantages and disadvantages of different forms of abolition, the tsar issued in 1861 the edict which marked an epoch in Russian history and won him the title of the "Tsar Liberator". The one card Russian government could play was the unquestioned authority of the autocrat and it was now put to good use.

The edict gave the serfs personal freedom and ended bond labour. It also gave them allotments of land. But these were to be paid for by redemption charges whose purpose was to make the change acceptable to the landowners. To secure the repayments and offset the dangers of suddenly introducing a

Russian canal workers tow barges along the Volga river in the 1870s in a scene by the great Russian naturalist painter Ilya Repin (1844–1930).

free labour market, peasants remained to a considerable degree subject to the authority of their village communities, which were given the charge of distributing the land allotments on a family basis.

It would not be long before a great deal would be heard about the shortcomings of this settlement. Yet there is much to be said for it and in retrospect it seems a massive achievement. Within a few years the United States would emancipate its black slaves. There were far fewer of them than there were Russian serfs and they lived in a country of much greater economic opportunity, yet the effect of throwing them on the labour market, exposed to the pure theory of *laissez-faire* economic liberalism, was to exacerbate a problem with whose ultimate consequences the United States was still grappling a century later. In Russia the largest measure of social

engineering in recorded history down to this time was carried out without comparable dislocation and it opened the way to modernization for what was potentially one of the strongest powers on earth. It was the indispensable first step towards making the peasant look beyond the estate for available industrial employment.

REFORM

More immediately, liberation opened an era of reform; there followed other measures which by 1870 gave Russia a representative system of local government and a reformed judiciary. When, in 1871, the Russians took advantage of the Franco-Prussian War to denounce some of the restrictions placed on their freedom in the Black Sea in 1856, there

A religious procession takes place in Kursk province c.1880, portrayed by Ilya Repin.

was almost a symbolic warning to Europe in what they did. After tackling her greatest problem and beginning to modernize her institutions Russia was again announcing that she would after all be master in her own house. The resumption of the most consistently and long-pursued policies of expansion in modern history was only a matter of time.

A Russian nobleman with some of his serfs is somewhat sentimentally depicted in a French publication of 1861.

5 POLITICAL CHANGE: THE ANGLO-SAXON WORLD

BY THE END OF THE nineteenth century the United Kingdom had created an identifiable sub-unit within the ambit of European civilization, with an historical destiny diverging from that of the continent. The components of this Anglo-Saxon world included growing British communities in Canada, Australia, New Zealand and South Africa (the first and last containing other important national elements, too) and at the heart of it were two great Atlantic nations, one the greatest world power of the nineteenth century, one that of the next.

Painted by Ford Madox Brown in 1855, *The Last Farewell to England* conveys something of both the sadness and the hope of emigrants leaving Europe for the New World.

BRITAIN AND THE UNITED STATES: SIMILARITIES

SO MANY PEOPLE FOUND IT profitable to keep on pointing it out how different they were that it is easy to overlook how much the United Kingdom and the young United States of America had in common for much of the nineteenth century. Though one was a monarchy and the other a republic, both countries escaped first the absolutist and then the revolutionary currents of continental Europe. Anglo-Saxon politics, of course, changed quite as radically as those of any other countries in the nineteenth century. But they were not transformed by the same political forces as those of continental states nor in the same way.

Their similarity arose in part because for all their differences the two countries shared more than they usually admitted. One aspect of their curious relations was that Americans could still without a sense of paradox call England the mother country. The heritage of English culture and language was for a long time paramount in the United States; immigration from other European countries only became overwhelming in the second half of the nineteenth century. Though by the middle of the century many Americans – perhaps most – already had the blood of other nations in their veins, the tone of society was long set by those of British stock. It was not until 1837 that there was a president who did not have an English, Scotch, or Irish surname (the next would not be until 1901, and there have been only four down to the present day).

COMMERCE AND MUTUAL FASCINATION

Post-colonial problems made, as they did in far later times, for emotional, sometimes violent, and always complex relations between the United States and the United Kingdom. But they were also much more than this. They were, for example, shot through with economic connections. Far from dwindling (as had been feared) after independence, commerce between the two countries had gone on from strength to strength. English capitalists found the United States an attractive place for investment even after repeated and unhappy experiences with the bonds of defaulting states. British money was heavily invested in American railroads, banking, and insurance. Meanwhile the ruling élites of the two countries were at once fascinated and repelled by each other. Some English people commented acidly on the vulgarity and rawness of American life but others warmed as if by instinct to its energy, optimism

and opportunity; Americans found it hard to come to terms with monarchy and hereditary titles but sought to penetrate the fascinating mysteries of English culture and society no less eagerly for that.

PHYSICAL ISOLATION

More striking than the huge differences between them was what the United Kingdom and the United States had in common when considered from the standpoint of continental Europe. Above all, both were able to combine liberal and democratic politics with spectacular advances in wealth and power. They did this in very different circumstances, but at least one was common to both, the fact of isolation: Great Britain had the Channel between herself and Europe, the United States had the Atlantic Ocean. This physical remoteness long masked from Europeans the potential strength of the young republic and the huge opportuni-

Transatlantic trade was crucial to the growth of the United States' economy. The transatlantic steamship *Great Western* is seen departing from Bristol in Rhode Island in 1850.

ties facing it in the West, whose exploitation was to be the greatest achievement of American nationalism. At the peace of 1783 the British had defended the Americans' frontier interests in such a way that there inevitably lay ahead a period of expansion for the United States; what was not clear was how far it might carry nor what other powers it might involve. This was in part a matter of geographical ignorance. No one knew for certain what the western half of the continent might contain. For decades the huge spaces just across the eastern mountain ranges would provide a big enough field of expansion. In 1800 the United States was still psychologically and actually very much a matter of the Atlantic seaboard and the Ohio valley.

AMERICAN DIPLOMATIC ISOLATION

If at first the United States' political frontiers were ill-defined, they imposed relations with

France, Spain and the United Kingdom. None the less, if frontier disputes could be arranged, then a practical isolation might be attained, for the only other interests which might involve Americans in the affairs of other countries were, on the one hand, trade and the protection of her nationals abroad, and, on the other, foreign intervention in the affairs of the United States. The French Revolution appeared briefly to pose the chance of the latter, and caused a quarrel, but for the most part it was frontiers and trade which preoccupied American diplomacy under the young republic. Both also aroused powerful and often divisive or potentially divisive forces in domestic politics.

The American aspiration to non-involvement with the outside world was already clear in 1793, when the troubles of the French revolutionary war led to a Neutrality Proclamation rendering American citizens liable to prosecution in American courts if they took any part in the Anglo-French war. The bias of American policy already expressed in this received its classical formulation in 1796. In the course of Washington's Farewell Address to his "Friends and Fellow Citizens" as his second term as president drew to a close, he chose to comment on the objectives and methods which a successful republican foreign policy should embody, in language to be deeply influential both on later American statesmen and on the national psychology. In retrospect, what is now especially striking about Washington's thoughts is their predominantly negative and passive tone. "The great rule of conduct for us," he began, "in regard to foreign nations is, in extending our commercial relations, to have with them as little political connection as possible." "Europe has a set of primary interests," he continued, "which to us have none, or a very remote relation ... Our detached and distant situation invites and enables us to pursue a different course ... It is our true policy to steer clear of permanent alliances with any portion of the foreign world." Moreover, Washington also warned Americans against assumptions of permanent or special hostility or friendship with any other nation. In all this there was no hint of America's future destiny as a world power (Washington did not even consider other than European relations; America's future Pacific and Asian role was inconceivable in 1796).

WAR WITH BRITAIN

By and large, a pragmatic approach, case by case, to the foreign relations of the young republic was indeed the policy pursued by Washington's successors in the presidency. There was only one war with another great power, that between the United States and Great Britain in 1812. Besides contributing to the growth of nationalist feeling in the young republic, the struggle led both to the appearance of Uncle Sam as the caricature embodiment of the nation and to the composition of the "Star-spangled Banner", which became the national anthem. More importantly, it marked an important stage in the evolving relations of the two countries. Officially, British interference with trade during the struggle with the Napoleonic blockade had caused the American declaration of war, but more important had been the hopes of some Americans that the conquest of Canada would follow. It did not, and the failure of military expansion did much to determine that the future negotiation of the boundary problems with the British should be by peaceful negotiation. Though Anglophobia had been aroused again in the United States by the war, the fighting (which had its humiliations for both sides) cleared the air. In future boundary disputes it was tacitly understood that neither American nor British governments were willing to consider war except under extreme provocation. In this setting the northern boundary of the United States was soon agreed as far west as the "Stony Mountains" (as the Rockies were then called); in 1845 it was carried further west to the sea and by then the disputed Maine boundary, too, had been agreed.

Because news of the peace treaty of Ghent, signed on 28 December 1814, was slow to reach the battlefield, General Jackson took on the British army at New Orleans on 8 January 1815. Jackson's use of earthworks and cotton bales as barricades was so effective that the battle lasted only half an hour. The defeated British army suffered more than 2,000 casualties and Jackson became a national hero.

THE LOUISIANA PURCHASE

The greatest change in American territorial definition was brought about by the Louisiana Purchase. Roughly speaking, "Louisiana" was the area between the Mississippi and the Rockies. In 1803 it belonged, if somewhat theoretically, to the French, the Spanish having ceded it to them in 1800. This change had provoked American interest; if Napoleonic France envisaged a revival of French American empire, New Orleans, which controlled the mouth of the river down which so much American commerce already passed, was of vital importance. It was to buy freedom of navigation on the Mississippi that the United States entered a negotiation, which ended with the purchase of an area larger than the then total area of the republic. On the modern map it includes Louisiana, Arkansas, Iowa, Nebraska, both the Dakotas, Minnesota west of the Mississippi, most of Kansas, Oklahoma, Montana, Wyoming and a big piece of Colorado. The price was $11,250,000.

This was the largest sale of land of all time and its consequences were appropriately huge. It transformed American domestic history. The opening of the way to the trans-Mississippi West was to lead to a shift in demographic and political balance of revolutionary import for the politics of the young republic. This shift was already showing itself in the second decade of the century when the population living west of the Alleghenies more than doubled. When the Purchase was rounded off by the acquisition of the Floridas from Spain, the United States had by 1819 legal sovereignty over territory bounded by the Atlantic and Gulf coasts from Maine to the Sabine river, the Red and Arkansas rivers, the Continental Divide and the line of the 49th Parallel agreed with the British.

THE MONROE DOCTRINE

The United States was already the most important state in the Americas. Though

A contemporary engraving depicts the port of New Orleans in the mid-19th century. The South's huge exports of raw cotton, tobacco and rice played a crucial role in the national economy of the United States.

The use of steam boats along the Mississippi and its tributaries from 1811 ensured safe, regular traffic linking the farming areas of the West and the Southern plantations to the markets in New Orleans. Water transport largely gave way to railways after the Civil War.

there were still some European colonial possessions there, a major effort would be required to contest this fact, as the British had discovered in war. None the less, alarm about a possible European intervention in Latin America, together with Russian activity in the Pacific northwest, led to a clear American statement of the republic's determination to rule the roost in the western hemisphere. This was the "Monroe doctrine" of 1823, which said that no future European colonization in the hemisphere could be considered and that intervention by European powers in its affairs would be seen as unfriendly to the United States. As this suited British interests, the Monroe doctrine was easily maintained. It had the tacit underwriting of the Royal Navy and no European power could conceivably mount an American operation if British seapower was used against it.

The Monroe doctrine remains the bedrock of American hemisphere diplomacy to this day. One of its consequences was that

other American nations would not be able to draw upon European support in defending their own independence against the United States. The main sufferer before 1860 was

James Monroe (1758–1831) served as the fifth president of the USA between 1817 and 1825. His declaration, known as the Monroe doctrine, that further European colonization of the Americas would be seen as a direct threat to the United States, echoed a theme from Washington's farewell speech of 1796.

The emergence and consolidation of the USA

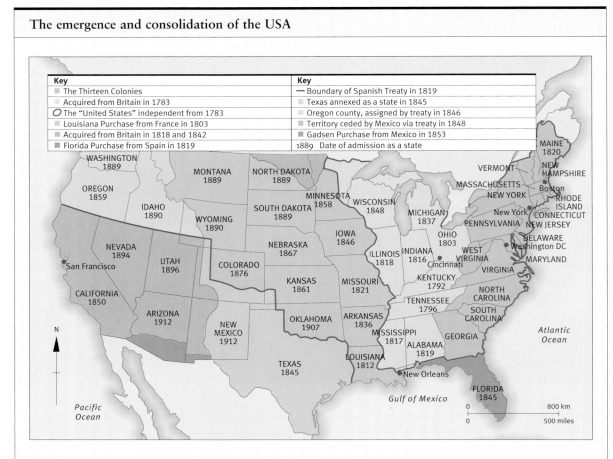

Key
- The Thirteen Colonies
- Acquired from Britain in 1783
- ◯ The "United States" independent from 1783
- Louisiana Purchase from France in 1803
- Acquired from Britain in 1818 and 1842
- Florida Purchase from Spain in 1819

Key
- — Boundary of Spanish Treaty in 1819
- Texas annexed as a state in 1845
- Oregon county, assigned by treaty in 1846
- Territory ceded by Mexico via treaty in 1848
- Gadsden Purchase from Mexico in 1853
- 1889   Date of admission as a state

Between 1820 and 1860, the number of states rose from 23 to 33, and the population of the United States increased by 9.6 million to total 31.3 million inhabitants. There was continuous westward expansion during this period. The French territories in the Mississippi valley were purchased in 1803. Spanish territories were forcibly incorporated into the United States during the Florida campaign, in which annexation was disguised as purchase in 1819. The Oregon Treaty of 1846 fixed the 49th Parallel as the lower limit for the border with Canada. Texas, which had declared itself independent of Mexico, was annexed in 1845. After a successful war (1846–1848), the United States took New Mexico and California from Mexico. Large territories were taken from the Native North Americans through various treaties.

When a sufficient number of settlers requested it, a new acquisition became a territory; when it had more than 60,000 settlers, it could be formally recognized as a State and request admission to the Union.

Mexico. American settlers within its borders rebelled and set up an independent Texan republic which was subsequently annexed by the United States. In the war that followed Mexico did very badly. The peace of 1848 stripped her, in consequence, of what would one day become Utah, Nevada, California and most of Arizona, an acquisition of territory which left only a small purchase of other Mexican land to be made to round off the mainland territory of the modern United States by 1853.

WESTWARD SETTLEMENT

In the seventy years after the Peace of Paris the republic expanded to fill half a continent. Less than four million people in 1790 had become nearly twenty-four million by 1850.

Most of these still lived east of the Mississippi, it was true, and the only cities with more than 100,000 inhabitants were the three great Atlantic ports of Boston, New York and Philadelphia: none the less, the centre of gravity of the nation was moving westward. For a long time the political, commercial and cultural élites of the eastern seaboard would continue to dominate American society. But from the moment that the Ohio valley had been settled a western interest had been in existence; Washington's farewell address had already recognized its importance. The West was an increasingly decisive contributor to the politics of the next seventy years, until there came to a head the greatest crisis in the history of the United States and one which settled her destiny as a world power.

SLAVERY IN THE UNITED STATES

EXPANSION, both territorial and economic, shaped the history of the United States as profoundly as the democratic bias of her political institutions. Its influence on those institutions, too, was very great and sometimes glaring; sometimes they were transformed. Slavery is the outstanding example. When Washington began his presidency there were a little under 700,000 black slaves within the territories of the Union. This was a large number, but the framers of the constitution paid no special attention to them, except in so far as questions of political balance between the different states were involved. In the end it had been decided that a slave should count as three-fifths of a free

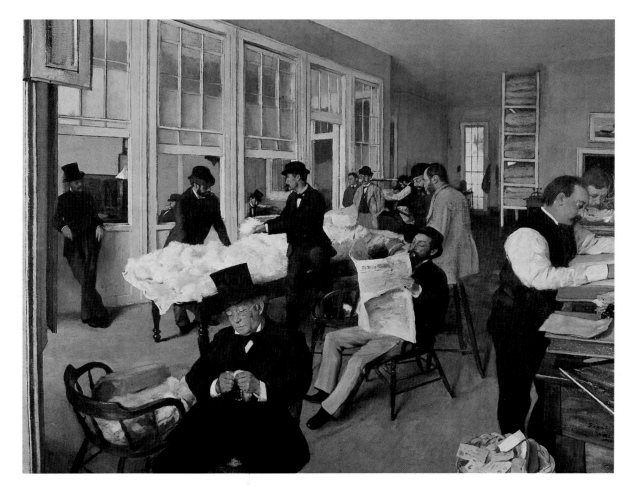

Edgar Degas' famous painting depicts cotton trading in New Orleans in 1873. Around this time, falling cotton prices began to result in increased poverty in the South.

man in deciding how many representatives each state should have.

Within the next half-century three things revolutionized this state of affairs. The first was an enormous extension of slavery. It was driven by a rapid increase in the world's consumption of cotton (above all in its consumption by the mills of England). This led to a doubling of the American crop in the 1820s and then its doubling again in the 1830s: by 1860, cotton provided two-thirds of the value of the total exports of the United States. This huge increase was obtained largely by cropping new land, and new plantations meant more labour. By 1820 there were already a million and a half slaves, by 1860 about four million. In the Southern states slavery had become the foundation of the economic system. Because of this, Southern society became even more distinctive; it had always been aware of the ways it differed from the more mercantile and urban northern states, but now its "peculiar institution", as slavery was

called, came to be regarded by Southerners as the essential core of a particular civilization. By 1860 many of them thought of themselves as a nation, with a way of life they idealized and believed to be threatened by tyrannous interference from the outside. The expression and symbol of this interference was, in their view, the growing hostility of Congress to slavery.

THE EVOLUTION OF AMERICAN POLITICS

That slavery became a political issue was the second development changing its role in American life. It was part of a general evolution in American politics evident also in other ways. The early politics of the republic had reflected what were to be later called "sectional" interests and the farewell address itself had drawn attention to them. Roughly speaking, they produced political parties reflecting, on the one hand, mercantile and business interests, which tended to look for strong federal government and protectionist legislation, and on the other, agrarian and consumer interests which tended to assert the right of individual states and cheap money policies. At that stage slavery was hardly a political question although politicians sometimes spoke of it as an evil which must succumb (though no one quite knew how) with the passage of time. Such quiescence had gradually to change, partly as a result of the inherent tendencies of American institutions, partly because of social change. Judicial interpretation gave a strongly national and federal emphasis to the constitution. At the same time as congressional legislation was thus given new potential force, the law-makers were becoming more representative of American democracy; the presidency of Andrew Jackson has traditionally been seen

The French political analyst Alexis de Tocqueville (1809–1859) produced a major study of the young United States, entitled *Democracy in America*, in 1835.

Democracy in America

"I don't think there is any country in the world where, proportionately, there are fewer ignorant people nor fewer wise people than in America. Primary education is available for everyone; higher education, for practically nobody … . Americans cannot spend more than the first few years of their lives on the general education of their intelligence. At fifteen, they start to work. Thus, their education tends to finish just at the moment when ours begins. If this education is taken further, it is directed to special, lucrative matters; science is studied much the same way as one might choose a trade, learning no more about it than those applications which currently have well-known practical uses.

"In America, most of the rich people start off being poor; almost all those who do not work, were extremely busy in their youth. Therefore, when one could feel passion for study, there is no time to spend on it, and when one has time, there is no inclination to do so … . There are, then, a large number of people who have more or less the same notions on subjects such as religion, history, sciences, economic policies, law, government."

An extract from Volume I of *Democracy in America* by Alexis de Tocqueville, 1835.

as especially important in this. The growing democratization of politics reflected other changes; the United States was not to be troubled by an urban proletariat of those driven off the land, because in the West the possibility long existed of realizing the dream of independence; the social ideal of the independent smallholder could remain central to the American tradition. The opening up of the western hinterland by the Louisiana Purchase was as important in revolutionizing the distribution of wealth and population which shaped American politics as was the commercial and industrial growth of the North.

THE WIDENING OF THE SLAVERY DEBATE

Above all, the opening of the West transformed the question of slavery. There was great scope for dispute about the terms on which new territories should be joined to the Union. As the organization first of the Louisiana Purchase and then territory taken from Mexico had to be settled, the inflammatory question was bound to be raised: was slavery to be permitted in the new territories? A fierce anti-slavery movement had arisen in the North, which dragged the slavery issue to the forefront of American politics and kept it there until it overshadowed every other question. Its campaign for the ending of the slave trade and for the eventual emancipation of the slaves stemmed from much the same forces which had produced similar demands in other countries towards the end of the eighteenth century. But the American movement was importantly different, too. In the first place it was confronted with a *growth* of slavery at a time when it was disappearing elsewhere in the Europeanized world, so that the universal trend seemed to be at least checked, if not reversed, in the United States. Secondly, it involved a tangle of constitutional questions because of argument about the extent to which private property could be interfered with in individual states where local laws upheld it, or even in territories that were not yet states. Moreover, the anti-slavery politicians brought forward a question which lay at the heart of the constitution, and, indeed, of the political life of every European country, too: who was to have the last word? The people were sovereign, that was clear enough: but was the "people" the majority of its representatives in Congress, or the populations of individual states acting through their state legislatures and asserting the indefeasibility of their rights even against Congress?

Thus slavery came by mid-century to be entangled with almost every question raised by American politics.

THE MISSOURI COMPROMISE

The great issues raised by slavery were just contained so long as the balance of power between the Southern and Northern states remained roughly the same. Although the North had a slight preponderance of numbers, the crucial equality in the Senate (where each state had two senators, regardless of its population or size) was maintained. Down to 1819, new states were admitted to the Union on an alternating system, one slave, one free; there were then eleven of each. Then came the first crisis, over the admission of the state of Missouri. In the days before the Louisiana Purchase French and Spanish law permitted slavery there and its settlers expected this to continue. They were indignant, and so were representatives of the Southern states when a

Northern congressman proposed restrictions upon slavery in the new state's constitution. There was great public stir and debate about sectional advantage; there was even talk of secession from the Union, so strongly did some Southerners feel. Yet the moral issue was muted. It was still possible to reach a political answer to a political question by the "Missouri Compromise", which admitted Missouri as a slave state, but balanced her by admitting Maine at the same time, and prohibiting any further extension of slavery in United States territory north of a line of latitude 36° 30'. This confirmed the doctrine that Congress had the right to keep slavery out of new territories if it chose to exercise it, but there was no reason to believe that the question would again arise for a long time. Indeed, so it proved until a generation had passed. But already some had foreseen the future: Thomas Jefferson, a former president and the man who drafted the Declaration of Independence, wrote that he "considered it at once as the knell of the Union", and another

Black slaves, such as those depicted here unloading provisions from a Mississippi steamship, constituted around one-third of the South's population and made up the labour force on the plantations. In the mid-19th century, 80 per cent of the white population in the South had no slaves and only around 3,000 planters owned more than 100 slaves. In spite of this, the South almost unanimously asserted its right to retain slavery.

The United States and the slavery issue

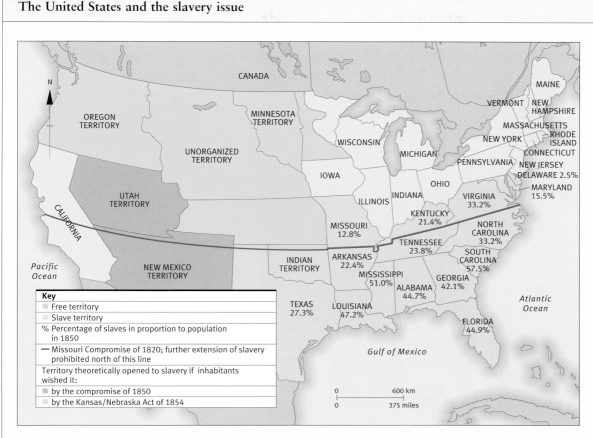

Key
- Free territory
- Slave territory
- % Percentage of slaves in proportion to population in 1850
- — Missouri Compromise of 1820; further extension of slavery prohibited north of this line
- Territory theoretically opened to slavery if inhabitants wished it:
- by the compromise of 1850
- by the Kansas/Nebraska Act of 1854

In 1815, those living south of the line that separated Maryland from Pennsylvania comprised half of the total population of the United States, and the South was expanding rapidly. Kentucky had become a state in 1792, Tennessee in 1796, Mississippi, Alabama and Missouri in 1821, Arkansas in 1836 and Florida and Texas in 1845. In the west and the north, nine new states had come from the Louisiana Purchase. Moreover, increasing numbers of immigrants were settling in the free states in the North. This meant that the Missouri Compromise of 1820, which banned slavery north of parallel 36° 30', and guaranteed a North–South balance, had become obsolete. In 1850, the political balance broke down. When the discovery of gold in California unleashed the gold rush, California applied for admission as a free state without having first been recognized as a territory, and was admitted into the Union. Although the interests of the North weighed heavily in Congress, the Senate was more evenly balanced between North and South, until 1859, when the incorporation of Kansas tipped the scales in favour of the North and the abolitionists.

(future) president wrote in his diary that the Missouri question was "a mere preamble – a title-page to a great, tragic volume".

THE ABOLITIONIST CAMPAIGN

The tragedy did not come to a head for another forty years. In part this was because Americans had much else to think about – territorial expansion above all – and in part because no question arose of incorporating territories suitable for cotton-growing, and therefore requiring slave labour, until the 1840s. But there were soon forces at work to agitate public opinion and they would be effective when the public was ready to listen. It was in 1831 that a newspaper was established in Boston to advocate the unconditional emancipation of black slaves. This was the beginning of the "abolitionist" campaign of increasingly embittered propaganda, electoral pressure upon politicians in the North, assistance to runaway slaves and opposition to their return to their owners after recapture, even when the law courts said they must be sent back. Against the background abolitionists provided, a struggle raged in the 1840s over the terms on which

territory won from Mexico should be admitted. It ended in 1850 in a new Compromise, but one not to last long. From this time, politics were strained by increasing feelings of persecution and victimization among the Southern leaders and a growing arrogance on their part in the defence of their states' way of life. National party allegiances were already affected by the slavery issue; the Democrats took their stand on the finality of the 1850 settlement.

DESCENT TO DISASTER

The 1850s brought the descent to disaster. The need to organize Kansas blew up the truce which rested on the 1850 Compromise and brought about the first bloodshed as abolitionists strove to bully pro-slavery Kansas into accepting their views. There emerged a Republican party in protest against the proposal that the people living in the territory should decide whether Kansas should be slave or free: Kansas was north of the 36° 30' line. The anger of abolitionists now mounted, too, whenever the law supported the slave-owner, as it did in a notable Supreme Court decision in 1857 (in the "Dred Scott" case), which returned a slave to his master. In the South, on the other hand, such outcries were seen as incitements to disaffection among the blacks and a determination to use the electoral system against Southern liberties – a view which was, of course, justified, because the abolitionists, at least, were not men who would compromise, though they could not get the Republican party to support them. The Republican presidential candidate in the election of 1860 campaigned on a programme which, in so far as it concerned slavery, envisaged the exclusion of slavery only from territories to be brought into the Union in the future.

THE AMERICAN CIVIL WAR

THE 1860 CAMPAIGN PLATFORM was already too much for some Southerners. Although the Democrats were divided, the country voted on strictly sectional grounds in 1860; the Republican candidate Abraham Lincoln, who was to prove the greatest of American presidents, was elected by Northern states, together with the two Pacific coast ones. This was the end of the line for many Southerners. South Carolina formally seceded from the Union as a protest against the election. In February 1861 it was joined by six other states, and the Confederate States of America, which they set up, had its provisional government and president installed a month before President Lincoln was inaugurated in Washington.

Each side accused the other of revolutionary designs and behaviour. It is very difficult not to agree with both of them. The heart of the Northern position, as Lincoln saw, was that democracy should prevail, a claim assuredly of potentially limitless revolutionary implication. In the end, what the North achieved was indeed a social revolution in the South. On the other side, what the South was asserting in 1861 (and three more states joined the Confederacy after the first shots were fired) was that it had the same right to organize its life as had, say, revolutionary Poles or Italians in Europe. It is unfortunate, but generally true, that the coincidence of nationalist claims with liberal institutions is rarely exact, or even close, and never complete, but the defence of slavery was also a defence of self-determination. At the same time, though such great issues of principle were certainly at stake, they presented themselves in concrete, personal and local terms which make it very difficult to state clearly the actual lines along which the republic divided for the great crisis of its history and identity. They ran through families, towns and villages, religions, and sometimes around groups of different colours. It is the tragedy of civil wars to be like that.

Two runaway slaves about to be returned to slavery are marched through the streets of Boston to a steamer bound for South Carolina, whence they had fled. Some of the watching abolitionists weep as the manacled slaves are led past.

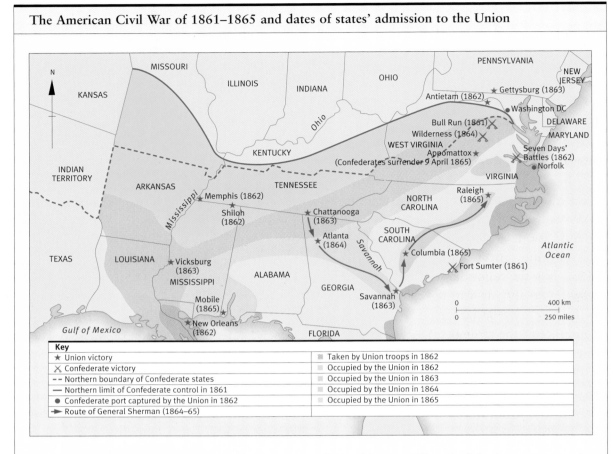

The American Civil War of 1861–1865 and dates of states' admission to the Union

Key

★ Union victory	Taken by Union troops in 1862
X Confederate victory	Occupied by the Union in 1862
-- Northern boundary of Confederate states	Occupied by the Union in 1863
— Northern limit of Confederate control in 1861	Occupied by the Union in 1864
● Confederate port captured by the Union in 1862	Occupied by the Union in 1865
→ Route of General Sherman (1864–65)	

In 1860 Abraham Lincoln, candidate for the Republican Party which had been established a few years earlier, was elected president. His electoral platform had included promises to increase tariffs and to prevent slavery from being introduced into the new western states. In February 1861, seven of the slave states agreed on secession and set up the Confederate States of America. When the federal government took steps to reinforce its garrisons in the South, the Southerners' attack on Fort Sumter started the Civil War. At first, the Confederates appeared to have the upper hand in the war, but as the fighting dragged on, the North's industrial and demographic superiority came to the fore.

LINCOLN'S CHANGING OBJECTIVES

Once under way, war has a revolutionary potential of its own. Much of the particular impact of what one side called "the Rebellion" and the other side "the War between the States" grew out of the necessities of the struggle. It took four years for the Union forces to beat the Confederacy and in that time an important change had occurred in Lincoln's aims. At the beginning of the war he had spoken only of restoring the proper order of affairs: there were things happening in the Southern states, he told the people, "too powerful to be suppressed by the ordinary course of judicial proceedings" and they would require military operations. This view broadened into a consistent reiteration that the war was fundamentally about preserving the Union; Lincoln's aim in fighting was to reunite the states which composed it. For a long time this meant that he failed to satisfy those who sought from the war the abolition of slavery. But in the end he came round to it. In 1862 he could still say in a public letter that:

"If I could save the Union without freeing any slave, I would do it; and if I could save it by freeing all the slaves I would do it; and if I could save it by freeing some and leaving others alone, I would also do that,"

but he did so at a moment when he had already decided that he must proclaim the emancipation of slaves in the rebel states. That became effective on New Year's Day 1863; thus the nightmare of Southern politicians was reality at last, though only because of the war they had courted. It transformed the nature of the struggle, though not at once very obviously. In 1865 the final step was taken in an amendment to the constitution which prohibited slavery anywhere in the

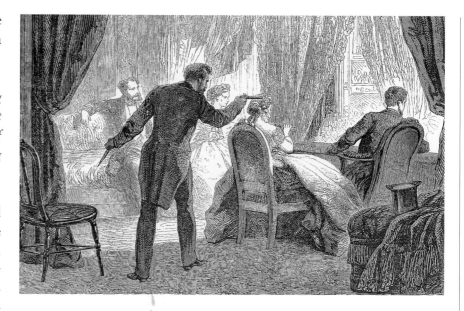

United States. By that time the Confederacy was defeated, Lincoln had been murdered and the cause which he had imperishably summed up as "government of the people, by the people, for the people" was safe.

President Lincoln is assassinated by a Southern fanatic, John Wilkes Booth, at Ford's Theatre in Washington.

Unionist soldiers pose with one of their guns during the Petersburg campaign against Confederates in Virginia, which lasted from June 1864 until April 1865.

The cabinet responsible for the proclamation of emancipation is depicted in an illustration of 1864. Lincoln, seated, is third from the left.

THE IMPLICATIONS OF THE NORTHERN VICTORY

In the aftermath of its military victory Lincoln's cause could hardly appear as an unequivocally noble or righteous one to all Americans, but its triumph was pregnant with importance not only for America but for all humanity. It was the only political event of the century whose implications were as far-reaching as, say, the Industrial Revolution. The war settled the future of the continent; one great power would continue to dominate the Americas and exploit the resources of the richest untapped domain yet known to be open to settlement. That fact in due course settled the outcome of two world wars and therefore the history of the world. The Union armies also decided that the system which would prevail in American politics would be

the democratic one; this was not, perhaps, always true in the sense of Lincoln's words but the political institutions which in principle provided for the rule of the majority were henceforth secure from direct challenge. This was to have the incidental effect of linking democracy and material well-being closely in the minds of Americans; industrial capitalism in the United States would have a great pool of ideological commitment to draw upon when it faced its later critics.

THE SOCIAL CONSEQUENCES OF EMANCIPATION

There were other domestic consequences of emancipation, too. The most obvious was the creation of a new colour problem. In a sense there had been no colour problem while slavery existed. Servile status was the barrier separating the overwhelming majority of blacks (there had always been a few free among them) from whites, and it was upheld by legal sanctions. Emancipation swept away the framework of legal inferiority and replaced this with the framework, or myth, of democratic equality when very few Americans were ready to give this social reality. Millions of blacks in the South were suddenly free. They were also for the most part uneducated, largely untrained except for field labour, and virtually without leadership of their own race. For a little while in the Southern states they leant for support on the occupying armies of the Union; when this prop was removed blacks disappeared from the legislatures and public offices of the Southern states to which they had briefly aspired. In some places they disappeared from the polling-booths, too. Legal disabilities were replaced by a social and physical coercion which was sometimes harsher than had been the old régime of slavery. Slaves at least had the value to their master of being an investment of capital; they were protected like other property and were usually ensured a minimum security and maintenance. Competition in a free labour market at a moment when the economy of large areas of the South was in ruins, with impoverished whites struggling for subsistence, was disastrous for the blacks. By the end of the century they had been driven by a poor white population bitterly resentful of defeat and emancipation into social subordination and economic deprivation. From this was to stem emigration to the North and new racial problems in the twentieth century.

THE TWO-PARTY SYSTEM

As another consequence of the war the United States retained a two-party system. Between

Emancipation did not guarantee freed slaves access to American justice. In this engraving, dated 1911, a white Southern mob murders an ex-slave accused of killing a white woman.

them, Republicans and Democrats have continued to divide the presidency to this day, not often threatened by third parties. There was nothing to make this probable before 1861. Many parties had come and gone, reflecting different movements in American society. But the war was to rivet upon the Democratic party a commitment to the Southern cause which at first was a grave handicap because it carried the stigma of disloyalty (no Democrat was president until 1885). Correspondingly, it won for the Republicans the loyalty of Northern states and the hopes of radicals who saw in them the saviours of the Union and democracy, and the liberators of the slave. Before the inadequacy of these stereotypes was clear, the parties were so deeply rooted in certain states that their predominance in them, let alone survival, was unchallengeable. Twentieth-century American politics would proceed by internal transformation of the two great parties which long reflected their primitive origins.

For the moment the Republicans of 1865 had it all their own way. Perhaps they would have found a way to reconcile the South if Lincoln had lived. As it was, the impact of their policies upon a defeated and devastated South made the "Reconstruction" years bitter

ones. Many Republicans strove honestly to use the power they had to ensure democratic rights for the blacks; thus they ensured the future hegemony of the Democrats in the South. But they did not do too badly. Soon the economic tide was with them as the great expansion interrupted briefly by the war was resumed.

A GROWING ECONOMY

American expansion had been going on for seventy years and was already prodigious. Its most striking manifestation had been territorial; it was about to become economic. The phase of America's advance to the point at which her citizens would have the highest per capita income in the world was just opening in the 1870s. In the euphoria of this huge blossoming of confidence and expectation, all political problems seemed for a while to have been solved. Under Republican administrations Americans turned, not for the last time, to the assurance that the business of America was not political debate but business. The South remained largely untouched by the new prosperity and slipped even further behind the North; it had no political leverage until an issue capable of bringing support to the Democrats in other sections turned up.

THE MAGNETISM OF THE UNITED STATES

Meanwhile, the North and West could look back with confidence that the astonishing changes of the previous seventy years promised even better times ahead. Foreigners could feel this, too; that is why they were coming to the United States in growing numbers – two and a half million in the 1850s alone. They fed a population which had grown from just

The winning of the Far West

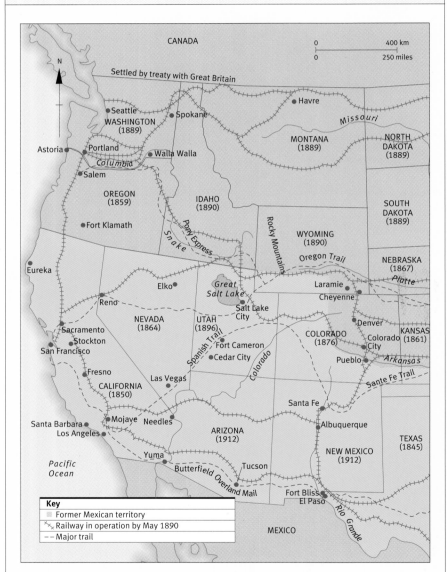

The development of the North American economy in the last 30 years of the 19th century was spectacular. For vast numbers of Europeans who lived in poverty the United States became, more than ever, the promised land. Transcontinental railways reinforced the national unity that had been won on the battlefields. In 1869 the first coast-to-coast rail link was completed and by 1900 there were three more, making the settlement of the West much easier. It also signalled the end of the North American Indians' way of life – they fought their final, desperate battles in these years.

over five and a quarter million in 1800 to nearly forty million in 1870. About half of them by then lived west of the Alleghenies and the vast majority of them in rural areas. The building of railroads was opening the Great Plains to settlement and exploitation which had not yet really begun. In 1869 the golden spike was driven, which marked the completion of the first transcontinental railroad link. In the new West the United States would find its greatest agricultural expansion; already, thanks to the shortage of labour experienced in the war years, machines were being used in numbers which pointed to a quite new scale of farming, the way to a new phase of the world's agricultural revolution which would make North America a granary for Europe (and, one day, for Asia, too). There were a quarter of a million mechanical reapers alone at work by the end of the war. Industrially, too, great years lay ahead; the United States was not yet an industrial power to compare with Great Britain (in 1870 there were still fewer than two million Americans employed in manufacturing), but the groundwork was done. With a large, increasingly well-off domestic market the prospects for American industry were bright.

Poised on the brink of their most confident and successful era, Americans were not being hypocritical in forgetting the losers. They understandably found it easy to do so in the general sense that the American system worked well. The blacks and the poor whites of the South now joined the Native North Americans, who had been losers steadily for two centuries and a half, as the forgotten failures. The new poor of the growing Northern cities should probably not be regarded, comparatively, as losers; they were at least as well off, and probably better, than the poor of Andalusia or Naples. Their willingness to come to the United States showed that it was already a magnet of great power. Nor was

that power only material. Besides the "wretched refuse", there were the "huddled masses yearning to breathe free". The United States was in 1870 still a political inspiration to political radicals elsewhere, though perhaps her political practice and forms had more impact in Great Britain – where people

A Union Pacific Railroad poster from 1869 advertises the opening of the USA's first transcontinental railroad. "Now is the time to seek your Fortune…" proclaims the poster, which also promotes the "luxurious cars and eating houses" the railroad has to offer.

The "Peterloo Massacre", pictured in this 19th-century painting, took place in Manchester, England, in 1819 when local magistrates sent the yeomanry (cavalry force) to St Peter's Fields to control a peaceful public meeting of supporters of political reform. Eleven people were killed and hundreds were injured in the ensuing panic. In the aftermath of the event, the Whigs called for parliamentary reform.

linked (both approvingly and disapprovingly) democracy with the "Americanization" of British politics – than in continental Europe.

DEMOCRATIZING BRITISH POLITICS

VARIOUS TRANSATLANTIC influences and connections were aspects of the curious, fitful, but tenacious relations between the two Anglo-Saxon countries. They both underwent revolutionary change though in wholly different ways. Yet here, perhaps, the achievement of Great Britain in the early nineteenth century is even more remarkable than the transformation of the United States. At a time of unprecedented and potentially dislocating social upheaval, which turned her within a single lifetime into the first industrialized and urbanized society of modern times, Great Britain managed to maintain an astonishing constitutional and political continuity. At the same time, she was acting as a world and European power as the United States never had to, and ruled a great empire. In this setting she began the democratization of her

institutions while retaining most of her buttresses of individual liberty.

Socially the United Kingdom was far less democratic than the United States in 1870 (if the blacks are set aside as a special case). Social hierarchy (conferred by birth and land if possible, but if not, money would often do) stratified the United Kingdom; every observer was struck by the assured confidence of the English ruling classes that they were meant to rule. There was no American West to offset the deep swell of deference with the breeze of frontier democracy; Canada and Australia attracted restless emigrants, but in so doing removed the possibility of their changing the tone of English society. Political democracy developed faster than social, on the other hand, even if the universal male suffrage already long-established in the United States would not be introduced until 1918; the democratization of English politics was already past the point of reversibility by 1870.

THE ENLARGEMENT OF THE ELECTORATE

The democratization of English politics had come about within a few decades. Though it had deeply libertarian institutions – equality at law, effective personal liberty, a representative system – the English constitution of 1800 had not rested on democratic principles. Its basis was the representation of certain individual and historic rights and the sovereignty of the Crown in Parliament. The accidents of the past produced from these elements an electorate large by contemporary European standards, but as late as 1832, the word "democratic" was a pejorative one and few thought it indicated a desirable goal. To most English people, democracy meant the French Revolution and military despotism. Yet the most important step towards democracy in the English political history of the century was taken in 1832. This was the passing of a Reform Act which was not itself democratic and was, indeed, intended by many of those who supported it to act as a barrier to democracy. It carried out a great revision of the representative system, removing anomalies (such as the tiny constituencies which had been effectively controlled by patrons), to provide parliamentary constituencies which better (though still far from perfectly) reflected the needs of a country of growing industrial cities, and above all to make more orderly the franchise. It had been based on a jumble of different principles in different places; now, the main categories of persons given the vote were freeholders in the rural areas, and householders who owned or paid rent for their house at a middle-class level in the towns. The model elector was the man with a stake in the country, although dispute about the precise terms of the franchise still

left some oddities. The immediate result was an electorate of about 650,000 and a House of Commons which largely resembled its predecessor. None the less, dominated by the aristocracy as it still was, it marked the beginning of nearly a century during which British politics were to be completely democratized, because once the constitution had been changed in this way, then it could be changed again and the House of Commons more and more claimed the right to say what should be done. In 1867, another Act produced an electorate of about two million and in 1872 the decision that voting should take place by secret ballot followed: a great step.

PEEL AND CONSERVATISM

The process of democratizing English politics would not be completed before the twentieth century, but it soon brought other changes in

This contemporary satire is entitled *The Reformers' Attack on the Old Rotten Tree.* The Reform Act of 1832, which, as well as extending the franchise, eliminated many of the "Rotten Boroughs", is widely thought to have prevented the threat of a British revolution from being realized.

the nature of British politics. Slowly, and somewhat grudgingly, the traditional political class began to take account of the need to organize parties which were something more than family connections or personal cliques of Members of Parliament. This was much more obvious after the emergence of a really big electorate in 1867. But the implication – that there was a public opinion to be courted which was more than that of the old landed class – was grasped sooner than this. All the greatest of English parliamentary leaders in the nineteenth century were men whose success rested on their ability to catch not only the ear of the House of Commons, but that of important sections of society outside it. The first and possibly most significant example was Sir Robert Peel, who created English Conservatism. By accepting the verdicts of public opinion he gave Conservatism a pliability which always saved it from the

intransigence into which the right was tempted in so many European countries.

The great political quarrel of Corn Law repeal demonstrated this. It was not only about economic policy; it was also about who should govern the country, and was in some ways a complementary struggle to that for parliamentary reform before 1832. By the middle of the 1830s the Conservatives had been brought by Peel to accept the consequences of 1832, and in 1846 he was just able to make them do the same over the protective Corn Laws, whose disappearance showed that landed society no longer had the last word. Vengefully, his party, the stronghold of the country gentlemen who considered the agricultural interests the embodiment of England and themselves the champions of the agricultural interest, turned on Peel soon afterwards and rejected him. They were right in sensing that the whole tendency of his

A Summer's Day in Hyde Park was painted by John Ritchie in 1858. A new degree of middle-class wealth was one sign of mid-Victorian social changes.

policy had been directed to the triumph of the free trade principles which they associated with the middle-class manufacturers. Their decision divided their party and condemned it to paralysis for twenty years, but Peel had in fact rid them of an incubus. He left it free when reunited to compete for the electorate's goodwill untrammelled by commitment to the defence of only one among several economic interests.

VICTORIAN ACHIEVEMENTS

The redirection of British tariff and fiscal policies towards free trade was one side, though in some ways the most spectacular, of a general alignment of British politics towards reform and liberalization in the central third of the century. During this time a beginning was made with local government reform (significantly, in the towns, not in the countryside where the landed interest was still the master), a new Poor Law was introduced, factory and mining legislation was passed and began to be effectively policed by inspection, the judicial system was reconstructed, disabilities on Protestant nonconformists, Roman Catholics and Jews were removed, the ecclesiastical monopoly of matrimonial law, which went back to Anglo-Saxon times, was ended, a postal system was set up, which became the model on which other nations would shape theirs, and a beginning was even made with tackling the scandalous neglect of public education. All this was accompanied by unprecedented growth in wealth, whose confident symbol was the holding in 1851 of a Great Exhibition of the world's wares in London under the patronage of the queen herself and the direction of her consort. If the British were inclined to bumptiousness, as they seem to have been in the central decades of Victoria's reign, then it may be said that

they had grounds. Their institutions and economy had never looked healthier.

Not that everyone was pleased. Some moaned about a loss of economic privilege: in fact, the United Kingdom continued to display extremes of wealth and poverty as great as any other country's. There was somewhat more substance to the fear of creeping centralization. Parliamentary legislative sovereignty led to bureaucracy invading more and more areas which had previously been immune to government intervention in practice. England in the nineteenth century was very far from concentrating power in her state apparatus to the degree which has now

Dated 1858, this view of the interior of the House of Commons, inside London's new Houses of Parliament, was painted by Joseph Nash (1802–1878).

Governments and the middle classes loved progress and showed it. The Crystal Palace in London, pictured in this contemporary illustration, was the venue for the Great Exhibition, the first of its kind in the world, which opened on 1 May, 1851.

become usual in all countries. Yet some people felt worried that she might be going the way of France, a country whose highly centralized administration was taken to be sufficient explanation of the failure to achieve liberty which had accompanied the French success in establishing equality. In offsetting such a tendency, the Victorian reforms of local government, some of which came only in the last two decades of the century but drove it further towards democracy, were crucial.

AVOIDING REVOLUTION

Some foreigners admired the British political system. Most wondered how, in spite of the appalling conditions of its factory towns, the United Kingdom had somehow navigated the rapids of popular unrest, which had proved fatal to orderly government in other states. Britain had deliberately undertaken huge reconstructions of its institutions at a time when the dangers of revolution were clearly apparent elsewhere, and had emerged unscathed, its power and wealth enhanced and the principles of liberalism even more apparent in its politics. British statesmen and historians gloried in reiterating that the essence of the nation's life was freedom, in a famous phrase, "broadening down from precedent to precedent". The English seemed fervently to believe this, yet it did not lead to license. The country did not have the advantages of geographical remoteness and almost limitless land which were enjoyed by the United States – and even the United States had fought one of the bloodiest wars in human history to contain a revolution. How, then, had Great Britain done it?

This was a leading question, though one historians still sometimes ask without thinking about its implications: that there exist certain conditions which make revolution

likely and that British society seems to have fulfilled them. It may be, rather, that no such propositions need to be conceded. Perhaps there never was a potentially revolutionary threat in this rapidly changing society. Many of the basic changes which the French Revolution brought to Europe had already existed in Great Britain for centuries, after all. The fundamental institutions, however rusty or encrusted with inconvenient historic accretion they might be, offered large possibilities. Even in unreformed days, the House of Commons and House of Lords were not the closed corporate institutions which were all that was available in many European states. Already before 1832, they had shown their capacity to meet new needs, even if slowly and belatedly; the first Factory Act (not, admittedly, a very effective one) had been passed as early as 1801. Once 1832 was past, then there were good grounds for thinking that if Parliament were only pressed hard enough from the outside, it would carry out any reforms that were required. There was no legal restraint on its power to do so. Even the oppressed and angry seem to have seen this. There were many outbreaks of desperate violence and many revolutionaries about in the 1830s and 1840s (which were especially hard times for the poor) but it is striking that the most important popular movement of the day, the great spectrum of protest gathered together in what was called "Chartism", asked in the People's Charter which was its programme for measures which would make Parliament more responsive to popular needs, not for its abolition.

TRADITIONAL PATTERNS OF BEHAVIOUR

It is not likely that Parliament would have been called upon to provide reform unless

Queen Victoria, whose coronation is pictured here, reigned from 1837 to her death in 1901. Her long rule became the symbol of an era of British progress, certainty, conquest and wealth.

other factors had operated. Here it is perhaps significant that the great reforms of Victorian England were all ones which interested the middle classes as much as the masses, with the possible exception of factory legislation. The English middle class came to an early share in political power as its continental counterparts had not and could therefore use it to obtain change; it was not tempted to ally with revolution, the recourse of desperate individuals to whom other avenues were closed. But in any case it does not seem that the English masses were themselves very revolutionary. At any rate, their failure to act in a revolutionary way has caused much distress to later left-wing historians. Whether this is because their sufferings were too great, not great enough or whether simply there were too many differences between different sections of the working class has been much disputed. But it is at least worth noticing, as did contemporary visitors, that in England traditional patterns of behaviour died hard; it was long to remain a country with habits of deference to social superiors which forcibly struck foreigners – especially Americans. Moreover, there were working-class organizations which provided alternatives to

revolution. They were often "Victorian" in their admirable emphasis on self-help, caution, prudence, sobriety. Of the elements making up the great English Labour movement, only the political party which bears that name was not in existence already before 1840; the others were mature by the 1860s. The "friendly societies" for insurance against misfortune, the cooperative associations and, above all, the trades unions all provided effective channels for personal participation in the improvement of working-class life, even if at first only to a few and slowly. This early maturity was to underlie the paradox of English socialism, its later dependence on a very conservative and unrevolutionary trade-union movement, for a long while the largest in the world.

Once the 1840s were over, economic trends may have helped to allay discontent. At any rate working-class leaders often said so, almost regretfully; they, at least, thought that betterment told against a revolutionary danger in England. As the international economy picked up in the 1850s good times came to the industrial cities of a country which was the workshop of the world and its merchant, banker, and insurer, too. As employment and wages rose, the support which the Chartists had mustered crumbled away and they were soon only a reminiscence.

A DOMESTICATED MONARCHY

The symbols of the unchanging form, which contained so much change, were the central institutions of the kingdom: Parliament and the Crown. When the Palace of Westminster was burned down and a new one was built, a mock-medieval design was chosen to emphasize the antiquity of what would come to be called "the Mother of Parliaments".

The violent changes of the most revolutionary era of British history thus continued to be masked by the robes of custom and tradition. Above all, the monarchy continued. Already in 1837, when Victoria ascended the throne, it was second only to the papacy in antiquity among the political institutions of Europe; yet it was much changed in reality, for all that. It had been brought very low in public esteem by George III's successor, the worst of English kings, and not much enhanced by his heir. Victoria and her husband were to make it unquestionable, except by a very few republicans. In part this was against the grain for the queen herself; she did not pretend to like the political neutrality appropriate to a constitutional monarch when the Crown had withdrawn above the political battle. None the less, it was in her reign that this withdrawal was seen to be made. She also domesticated the monarchy; for the first time since the days of the young George III the phrase "the Royal Family" was a reality and could be seen to be such. It was one of many ways in which her German husband, Prince Albert, helped her, though he got little thanks for it from an ungrateful English public.

THE IRISH FAILURE

Only in Ireland did their capacity for imaginative change seem always to fail the British people. They had faced a real revolutionary danger and had had to put down a rebellion there in 1798. In the 1850s and 1860s things were quiet. But the reason was in large measure an appalling disaster which overtook Ireland in the middle of the 1840s, when the failure of the potato crop was followed by famine, disease and thus, brutally, a Malthusian solution to Ireland's over-population. For the moment, the demand for the repeal of the Act of Union,

which had joined her to Great Britain in 1801, was muted, the dislike of her predominantly Catholic population for an alien and established Protestant Church was in abeyance and there was no serious disturbance among a peasant population feeling no loyalty to absentee English landlords (or, for that matter, to the resident but equally grasping and more numerous Irish landlords) who exploited tenant and labourer alike. Problems none the less remained and the Liberal government which took office in 1868 addressed itself above all else to them. All that emerged was a new Irish nationalism movement, based on the Roman Catholic peasantry and demanding "Home Rule". Dispute over what this might – let alone ought to – mean was to

Anti-British demonstrations took place in Dublin's Phoenix Park during the unrest that followed the suspension of habeas corpus in 1882. In the face of the arrest of anti-British activists in Ireland, two British ministers were assassinated in Dublin.

haunt British politics, overturn their combinations and wreck attempts to settle the Irish Question for a century and more. In the short run, it promoted two rival Irish revolutionary movements north and south and contributed to the wrecking of British liberalism. Thus Ireland, after a thousand years, began again to make a visible mark on world history, though, of course, she had already made one less obviously earlier in the century through the emigration of so many of her people to the United States of America.

Evicted tenants in County Kerry, Ireland, watch while their homes are burned. During the Irish Land War of 1879–1881, tenant farmers struggled against rising rents and evictions following an agricultural depression and eventually persuaded the British prime minister, William Gladstone, to meet their demands, in the Irish Land Act of 1881.

THE EUROPEAN EMPIRES

HISTORICAL SUCCESS sometimes encourages short-term perspectives and judgments. The bald fact that in so many ways Europe ran the world at the beginning of the twentieth century encouraged Europeans to overlook the recent nature of their hegemony, and the very brief time for which it had been in existence. Not many of them could guess, either, how precarious that success might prove. For the moment, none the less, the domination of the interests of a minority of the world's population over the vast majority seemed assured. Only a few of them saw that the spread of European ideas, institutions and technology must in the end weaken European hegemony, even if only in its political expressions. One reason why its ephemeral, brief nature (in the long run of history, though more widespread than the hegemony of Rome, it did not last as long) went unrecognized was the richness and multiplicity of the ways in which it was expressed and worked. European hegemony was always much more than political or military domination, important and visible though these were. In diversity, in fact, lay its strength and the explanation why it lasted as long as it did. Similarly, the explanation of its waning and passing has to be sought in facts much more diverse than simple changes in power. A cultural tradition often itself appearing self-questioning and divided, Europe's own huge intestinal wars, the drifting away of economic power to new centres, all played their part – and all were in some measure visible to astute observers even before the twentieth century began.

By the end of the 19th century, the British Empire was the largest European empire in the world, and India was the "jewel in the crown" of that empire. Lord Curzon (1859–1925), shown here with his wife taking the lead role in a royal durbar (formal assembly) to show the strength of the British Raj in 1903, was viceroy of India from 1898 until 1905. Like many European colonialists of his generation, Curzon was convinced that he knew what was best for India and held the Indian Congress Party and the mood of growing nationalism in utter contempt. By 1918, however, when the British government conceded the principle of self-rule to India, European empires around the globe were threatened by increasingly insistent demands for independence.

1 THE EUROPEAN WORLD HEGEMONY

French officials pose with local Algerian leaders in front of a police station in Boghari in French-ruled Algeria. When this picture was taken (c.1900), European influence over the rest of the world was at its height and vast expanses of Asia, Africa and Oceania were under direct European control.

BY 1900 THE PEOPLES of Europe and European stocks overseas dominated the globe. They did so in many different ways, some explicit and some implicit, but the qualifications matter less than the general fact. For the most part, the world responded to European initiatives and marched increasingly to European tunes. It is easy to overlook the fact that this was a unique development in world history. For the first time, one civilization established itself as a leader right around the globe. One minor consequence is that the remainder of this book will be increasingly concerned with a single, global, history.

It is important not to think only of the direct formal rule of the majority of the world's land surface by European states (some people would prefer the term "Western" but this is unnecessarily finicky – the Americas and Antipodes are dominated by culture of European origin, not of Asian or African – and is also liable to suggest too much, because of the use of that word recently in a narrow political sense). There is economic and cultural hegemony to be considered, and European ascendancy was often expressed in influence as well as in overt control. The important distinction is between European forces which are aggressive, shaping, manipulative, and indigenous cultures and peoples, which are the objects of those forces, and not often able to resist them effectively. It was by no means always to the disadvantage of non-Europeans that this was so, but they tended almost always to be the underdogs, those who had to adapt to the Europeans' world. At times they did so willingly, when they succumbed to the attractive

Time chart (1818–1888)

		1839 The French complete their conquest of Algeria	1842 China is opened to the West		1868 The "Meiji Restoration" begins in Japan	1884–1885 A conference on Africa is held in Berlin
1800				**1850**		**1900**
	1818 India becomes a British dominion	1834 Slavery is abolished in the British colonies		1869 The Suez Canal is opened		1888 Slavery is abolished in Brazil

The British Empire (and Protected Territories) 1815–1914

Key

Growth of British Empire:

- Empire by 1815
- Gains 1815–1914

Canada, Union of South Africa, Australia and New Zealand received dominion status and self-government before 1914

During the 19th century, the British expanded the territorial gains they had already made, mainly in Canada and India, to create the most important of the European colonial empires. At the height of the imperialist era, it was often remarked (as it had been earlier of the empire of Charles V) that the sun never set on the British Empire, so extensive was its reach.

force of Europe's progressive ideals or, most subtly of all, to new sets of expectations aroused by European teaching and example.

SPHERES OF EUROPEAN INFLUENCE

ONE WAY OF ENVISAGING the Europeans' world of 1900 is as a succession of concentric circles. The innermost was old Europe itself, which had grown in wealth and population for three centuries thanks to an increasing mastery first of its own and then of the world's resources. Europeans distinguished themselves more and more from other human beings by taking and consuming a growing share of the world's goods and by the energy and skill they showed in manipulating their environment. Their civilization was already rich in the nineteenth century and was all the time getting richer. Industrialization had confirmed its self-feeding capacity to open up and create new resources; furthermore, the power generated by new wealth made possible the appropriation of the wealth of other parts of the world. The profits of Congo rubber, Burmese teak or Persian oil would not for a long time be reinvested in those countries. The poor European and American benefited from low prices for raw materials, and improving mortality rates tell the story of an industrial civilization finding it possible to give its peoples a richer life. Even the European peasant could buy cheap manufactured clothes and tools while his contemporaries in Africa and India still lived in the Stone Age.

This wealth was shared by the second circle of European hegemony, that of the European cultures transplanted overseas. The United States is the greatest example; Canada,

Australia, New Zealand, South Africa and the countries of South America make up the list. They did not all stand on the same footing towards the Old World, but together with Europe proper they were what is sometimes called the "Western world", an unhelpful expression, since they are scattered all around the globe. Yet it seeks to express an important fact: the similarity of the ideas and institutions from which they were sprung. Of course, these were not all that had shaped them. They all had their distinctive frontiers, they all had faced special environmental challenges and unique historical circumstances. But what they had in common were ways of dealing with these challenges, institutions which different frontiers would reshape in different ways. They were all formally Christian – no one ever settled new lands in the name of atheism until the twentieth century – all regulated their affairs by European systems of law, and all had access to the great cultures of Europe with which they shared their languages.

THE IMPOSITION OF EUROPEAN VALUES

In 1900 the Europeanized world was sometimes called the "civilized world". It was called that just because it was a world of shared standards; the confident people who used the phrase could not easily see that there was much else deserving of the name of civilization in the world. When they looked for it, they tended to see only heathen, backward, benighted peoples or a few striving to join the civilized. This was one reason why Europeans were so successful; what were taken to be demonstrations of the inherent superiority of European ideas and values nerved individuals to fresh assaults on the world and inspired fresh incomprehension of it. The progressive values of the eighteenth century provided new arguments for superiority to reinforce those originally stemming from religion. By 1800, Europeans had lost most of the respect they had once showed for other civilizations. Their own social practice seemed obviously

The kingdom of Tonga in the Pacific Ocean was a British protectorate from 1900 until 1970. This photograph, which dates from c.1900, shows a British missionary in Tonga standing outside the Catholic Mission, accompanied by a group of local girls in European-style dress.

Las Esclavas de Buē. Ayꝰ Demuestran ser Libres y Gratas à su Noble Libertador.

By 1830, most Latin American states had banned the slave trade, although slavery itself continued for several more decades. The abolition of slavery in Argentina by Juan Manuel de Rosas, dictator from 1835 to 1852, is commemorated in this 19th-century painting.

superior to the unintelligible barbarities found elsewhere. The advocacy of individual rights, a free press, universal suffrage, the protection of women, children (and even animals) from exploitation, have been ideals pursued right down to our own day in other lands by Europeans and Americans, often wholly unconscious that they might be inappropriate.

Philanthropists and progressives long continued to be confident that the values of European civilization should be universalized, as were its medicine and sanitation, even when deploring other assertions of European superiority. Science, too, has often appeared to point in the same direction, to the destruction of superstition and the bringing of the blessings of a rational exploitation of resources, the provision of formal education and the suppression of backward social customs. During the colonial era there was a well-nigh universal assumption that the values of European civilization were better than indigenous ones (obviously, too, they often were) and a large obliviousness to any disruptive effects they might have.

SUBJECT PEOPLES

Fortunately, it was thought, for the peoples of some of the lands over which "thick darkness brooded yet" (as the Victorian hymn put it), they were by 1900 often ruled directly by Europeans or European stocks: subject peoples formed the third concentric circle through which European civilization radiated outwards. In many colonies enlightened administrators toiled to bring the blessings of railways, Western education, hospitals, law and order to peoples whose own institutions had clearly failed (it was taken as evidence of their inadequacy that they had failed to stand up to the challenge and competition of a superior civilization). Even when native institutions were protected and preserved, it was from a position which assumed the superiority of the culture of the colonial power.

COLONIALISTS ABOLISH SLAVERY

A consciousness of superiority is no longer admired or admissible, even if secretly cherished. In one respect, it achieved an end, nevertheless, which the most scrupulous critics of colonialism still accept as good, even when suspecting the motives behind it. This was the abolition of slavery in the European world and the deployment of force and diplomacy to combat it even in countries Europeans did not control. The crucial steps were taken in 1807 and 1834, when the British parliament abolished first the trade in slaves and then slavery itself within the British Empire. This action by the major naval, imperial and commercial power was decisive; similar measures were soon enforced by other European nations, and slavery finished in the United States in 1865. The end of the process may be reckoned to be the emancipation of slaves in Brazil in 1888, at which date colonial governments and the Royal Navy were pressing hard on the operations of Arab slave-traders in the African continent and the Indian Ocean. Many forces, intellectual, religious, economic and political, went into this great achievement, and debate about their precise individual significance continues. It is perhaps worth pointing out here that though it was

only after three hundred years and more of large-scale slave-trading that abolition came, Europe's is also the only civilization which has ever eradicated slavery for itself. Though in the present century slavery briefly returned to Europe, it could not be sustained except by force, nor was it openly avowable as slavery. It cannot have been much consolation to their unhappy occupants, but the forced-labour camps of our own century were run by men who had to pay the tribute of hypocrisy to virtue either by denying their existence or by disguising their slaves as the subjects of re-education or judicial punishment.

BEYOND THE EUROPEAN SPHERE

BEYOND THIS OUTERMOST CIRCLE of directly ruled territories lay the rest of the world. Its peoples were shaped by Europe, too. Sometimes their values and institutions were corroded by contact with it – as was the case in the Chinese and Ottoman empires – and this might lead to indirect European political

The Meiji emperor Mitsuhito and his wife are depicted at the opening of the 1904 industrial fair in Tokyo. During Mitsuhito's reign (1868–1912), Japan's economy was transformed by the adoption of new ideas and technology from the West.

interference as well as the weakening of traditional authority. Sometimes they were stimulated by such contacts and exploited them: Japan is the only example of an important nation doing this with success. What was virtually impossible was to remain untouched by Europe. The busy, bustling energy of the European trader would alone have seen to that. In fact, it is the areas which were not directly ruled by Europeans which make the point of European supremacy most forcibly of all. European values were transferred on the powerful wings of aspiration and envy. Geographical remoteness was almost the only security (but even Tibet was invaded by the British in 1904). Ethiopia is virtually the solitary example of successful independence; it survived British and Italian invasion in the nineteenth century, but, of course, had the important moral advantage of claiming to have been a Christian country, albeit not a Western one and only intermittently, for some fourteen centuries.

MISSIONARY ACTIVITY

Whoever opened the door, a whole civilization was likely to try to follow them through it, but one of the most important agencies bringing European civilization to the rest of the world had always been Christianity, because of its virtually limitless interest in all sides of human behaviour. The territorial spread of the organized churches and the growth in their numbers of official adherents in the nineteenth century made this the greatest age of Christian expansion since apostolic times. Much of this was the result of a renewed wave of missionary activity; new orders were set up by Catholics, new societies for the support of overseas missions appeared in Protestant countries. Yet the paradoxical effect was the intensifying of the European

flavour of what was supposedly a creed "for all sorts and conditions of men," as the *English Book of Common Prayer* puts it. This is why Christianity was long seen as just one more aspect of European civilization, rather than as a spiritual message. Another interesting if trivial example was the concern missionaries often showed over dress. Whereas the Jesuits in seventeenth-century China had discreetly adopted the costume of their hosts, their nineteenth-century successors set to work with zeal to put Bantus and Solomon Islanders into European garments which were often of almost freakish unsuitability. This was one way in which Christian missionaries diffused more than a religious message. Often, too, they brought important material and technical benefits: food in time of famine, agricultural techniques, hospitals and schools, some of which could be disruptive of the societies which received them. Through them filtered the assumptions of a progressive civilization.

MILITARY SUPERIORITY

The ideological confidence of Europeans, missionaries and non-missionaries alike,

This engraving, which dates from 1882, depicts the African port of Lagos. Although the port was frequented by large numbers of European ships, the surrounding area appears to have been untouched by Westernization, even in the late 19th century. Lagos is now the capital of Nigeria and one of the largest cities in Africa.

The colonial armies were mainly made up of native soldiers led by European commanding officers, as shown in this engraving of a French African frontier post in 1891.

could rest in the last resort on the knowledge that they could not be kept away, even from countries which were not colonized. There appeared to be no part of the world where Europeans could not, if they wished, impose themselves by armed strength. The development of weapons in the nineteenth century gave Europeans an even greater relative advantage than they had enjoyed when the first Portuguese broadside was fired at Calicut. Even when advanced devices were available to other peoples, they could rarely deploy them effectively. At the battle of Omdurman in the Sudan in 1898 a British regiment opened fire on its opponents at 2,000 yards' range with the ordinary magazine rifle of the British army of the day. Soon afterwards, shrapnel shell and machine-guns were shredding to pieces the masses of the Mahdist army, who never reached the British line. By the end of the battle 10,000 of them had been killed for a loss of forty-eight British and Egyptian soldiers. It was not, though, as an Englishman put it soon afterwards, simply the case that

Whatever happens, we have got
The Maxim gun, and they have not

for the Khalifa had machine-guns in his armoury at Omdurman, too. He also had telegraph apparatus to communicate with his forces and electric mines to blow up the British gunboats on the Nile. But none of these things was properly employed; not only a technical, but a mental transformation was required before non-European cultures could turn the instrumentation of the Europeans against them.

There was also one other sense, more benevolent and less disagreeable, in which European civilization rested upon force. This was because of the *Pax Britannica* which throughout the whole nineteenth century stood in the way of European nations fighting each other for mastery of the non-European world. There was to be no re-run of the colonial wars of the seventeenth and eighteenth centuries in the nineteenth, although the greatest extension of direct colonial rule in modern times was then going on. Traders of all nations could move without let or hindrance on the surface of the seas. British naval supremacy was a precondition of the informal expansion of European civilization.

A WORLD ECONOMY

BRITISH NAVAL STRENGTH guaranteed, above all, the international framework of trade whose centre, by 1900, was Europe. The old peripheral exchanges by a few merchants and enterprising captains had, from the

Military superiority was crucial to the European empires' rapid expansion. This engraving depicts Anglo-Egyptian troops entering the Sudanese city of Omdurman in 1898. Led by Commander-in-Chief Kitchener, they had easily defeated the Mahdist army.

seventeenth century onwards, been replaced gradually by integrated relationships of inter-dependence based on a broad distinction of role between industrial and non-industrial countries; the second tended to be primary producers meeting the needs of the increas-ingly urbanized populations of the first. But this crude distinction needs much qualifica-tion. Individual countries often do not fit it; the United States, for example, was both a great primary producer and the world's lead-ing manufacturing power in 1914, with an output as great as those of Great Britain, France and Germany together. Nor was this distinction one which ran exactly between nations of European and non-European cul-ture. Japan and Russia were both indus-trializing faster than China or India in 1914, but Russia, though European, Christian and imperialist, could certainly not be regarded as a developed nation, and most Japanese (like most Russians) were still peasants. Nor could a developed economy be found in Balkan Europe. All that can be asserted is that in 1914 a nucleus of advanced countries existed with social and economic structures quite

different from those of traditional society, and that these were the core of an Atlantic group of nations which was increasingly the world's main producer and consumer.

THE PIVOTAL ROLE OF GREAT BRITAIN

The world economy came to a sharp focus in London, where the financial services which sustained the flow of world trade were centred. A huge amount of the world's business was transacted by means of the sterling bill of exchange; it rested in turn upon the international gold standard which sustained confidence by ensuring that the main currencies remained in fairly steady relationships with one another. All major countries had gold currencies and travel any where in the world was possible with a bag of gold sovereigns, five-dollar pieces, gold francs or any other major medium of exchange, without any doubts about their acceptability.

London was also in another sense the centre of the world economy because although the United Kingdom's gross output

Attempting to fight the Europeans meant acquiring their weapons. This engraving, dated 1884, shows Sudanese Mahdist soldiers carrying European guns. Without the Western armies' tactics and discipline, however, such weapons brought only brief success.

The Royal Exchange building, seen in this late 19th-century image, was at the heart of the London Stock Exchange.

always the unique instance of the United States, little involved in export, but gradually commanding a greater and greater share of its own domestic market for manufactured goods, and still a capital importer.

FREE TRADE

Most British economists believed in 1914 that the prosperity which this system enjoyed and the increasing wealth which it made possible showed the truth of free trade doctrine. Their own country's prosperity had grown most rapidly in the heyday of such ideas. Adam Smith had predicted that prosperity would continue if a closed imperial system reserving trade to the mother country were abandoned and so, in the case of America, it had soon proved, for a big expansion had come to the Anglo-American trade within a few years of the peace of 1783. By 1800 a majority of British exports were already going outside Europe and there then still lay ahead the greatest period of expansion of trade in India and East Asia. British imperial policy was directed less to the potentially embarrassing acquisition of new colonies than to the opening of areas closed to trade, for that was where prosperity was deemed to lie. One flagrant example was the Opium War of 1839–42. The outcome was the opening of five Chinese ports to European trade and the *de facto* cession to Great Britain of Hong Kong as a base for the exercise of a jurisdiction inseparable from the management of commerce.

In the middle of the nineteenth century there had been for a couple of decades a high tide of free trade ideas when more governments seemed willing to act upon them than ever before or after. In this phase, tariff barriers were demolished and the comparative advantage of the British – first among

was by 1914 overtaken in important respects by that of the United States and Germany, she was the greatest of trading nations. The bulk of the world's shipping and carrying trade was in British hands. She was the main importing and exporting nation and the only one which sent more of its manufactures to non-European nations than to European. Great Britain was also the biggest exporter of capital and drew a huge income from her overseas investments, notably those in the United States and South America. Her special role imposed a roughly triangular system of international exchange. The British bought goods, manufactured and otherwise, from Europe and paid for them with their own manufactures, cash and overseas produce. To the rest of the world they exported manufactures, capital and services, taking in return food and raw materials and cash. This complex system illustrates how little the European relationship with the rest of the world was a simple one of exchanging manufactures for raw materials. And there was, of course,

This photograph was taken c.1900 in an opium den in China. Although the opium trade had been banned in 1800, it has been estimated that there may have been as many as 10 million Chinese addicts by 1830. The mainly British merchants who imported the drug to China from India, where it was produced, could earn enormous profits.

trading and manufacturing nations – had continued. But this era passed in the 1870s and 1880s. The onset of a worldwide recession of economic activity and falling prices meant that by 1900 Great Britain was again the only major nation without tariffs for protection and even in that country questioning of the old free trade dogmas was beginning to be heard as competition from Germany grew fiercer and more alarming.

ECONOMIC INTEGRATION

The economic world of 1914 still seems to be one of astonishing economic freedom and in

retrospect confidence. A long European peace provided the soil in which trading connections could mature. Stable currencies assured great flexibility to a world price system; exchange control existed nowhere in the world and Russia and China were by then as

This painting, entitled *Oil Creek Valley in 1871*, depicts rigs for extracting crude oil in Pennsylvania in the United States. The first oil well had been sunk in Pennsylvania in 1857 and it was the first region in the world to boast a large-scale operation to extract oil.

completely integrated into this market as other countries. Freight and insurance rates had grown cheaper and cheaper, food prices had shown a long-term decline and wages had shown a long-term rise. Interest rates and taxation were low. It seemed as if a capitalist paradise might be achievable.

As this system had grown to incorporate Asia and Africa, it, too, came to be instrumental in a diffusion of ideas and techniques originally European, but soon acclimatized in other lands. Joint stock companies, banks, commodity and stock exchanges spread around the world by intrusion and imitation; they began to displace traditional structures of commerce. The building of docks and railways, the infrastructures of world trade, together with the beginnings of industrial employment, began in some places to turn peasants into an industrial proletariat.

Sometimes the effects on local economies could be bad; the cultivation of indigo in India, for example, more or less collapsed when synthetic dyes became available in Germany and Great Britain. The economic history of Southeast Asia and its strategic importance were transformed by the British introduction of the rubber-tree there (a step which also, incidentally, ruined the Brazilian rubber industry). Isolation first disturbed by explorers, missionaries and soldiers was destroyed by the arrival of the telegraph and the railway; in the twentieth century the motor car would take this further. Deeper relationships were being transformed, too; the canal opened at Suez in 1869 not only shaped British commerce and strategy, but gave the Mediterranean new importance, not this time as a centre of a special civilization, but as a route.

The British built an extensive railway network in India from the mid-19th century. This early 20th-century photograph shows the entrance to the Barogh Tunnel on the Kalka–Simla Railway, north of Delhi. The narrow-gauge railway, which was completed in 1903, connected the town of Kalka with the hill station of Simla, where the British government of India convened every summer from 1865 until 1939.

The Suez Canal

In the 7th century BCE the Egyptian king Necho II was the first ruler to try, in vain, to link the Red Sea to the Mediterranean. In 522 BCE, the Persian king Darius I restored and completed the canal, thus creating a crucial direct maritime link between Egypt and Persia. Although the canal was improved during Roman times, little by little it silted up until it became unnavigable and it was abandoned.

In 1854, the French diplomat Ferdinand de Lesseps was granted permission by Muhammad Said Pasha, the viceroy of the Ottoman Empire, to start work on a canal that would link Suez directly to the Mediterranean. With financial support from French shareholders, work began in 1859, despite attempts by the British government to prevent the project from going ahead. Although prisoners were initially used to carry out the construction work, they were eventually replaced by mechanical excavators; some 3 million cubic metres (3.9 million cubic yards) of sand were dug out in total. A fresh-water canal had to be built to supply the 25,000 workers with drinking water and a new city, named Port Said, was established at the Mediterranean end of the canal.

In November 1869 the Suez Canal was finally completed. The opening ceremony was attended by 6,000 guests, including the French empress Eugénie and other figureheads of European royalty. The finished canal was 105 miles (169km) long, 190ft (58m) wide at the surface and 72ft (22m) wide at the bottom, and had an average depth of 26ft (8m). It allowed maritime traffic to travel between the Red Sea and the Mediterranean, thus cutting the distance between European and Asian ports by more than 4,350 miles (7,000km).

In 1875, Great Britain acquired the majority of the shares of the company, which it kept until Nasser, the Egyptian president, nationalized the canal in 1956. More recently, during the Six Day War between Egypt and Israel in 1967, the canal was blocked by sunken ships, and it remained closed until 1975.

The first ships sail through the Suez Canal on its opening day, 17 November 1869. Because it drastically reduced the sailing time between Europe and Asia, the canal became an essential route for Europe's commercial expansion and a vital axis of the British Empire.

Members of the Japanese army are pictured c.1875, with their German military advisers. The Japanese soldiers are dressed in European-style uniforms that are modelled on those of the Germans. Many Japanese saw the adoption of European dress as a sign of progress.

THE CULTURAL IMBALANCE

Economic integration and institutional change were inseparable from cultural contamination. The formal instruments of missionary religion, educational institutions and government policy are only a tiny part of this story. European languages, which were used officially, for example, took with them European concepts and opened to educated élites in non-European countries the heritage not only of Christian civilization, but of secular and "enlightened" European culture, too. Missionaries spread more than dogma or medical and educational services; they also provoked the criticism of the colonial régime itself, because of the gap between its performance and the pretensions of the culture it imposed.

In the perspectives of the twentieth century, much of what is most durable and important in the impact of Europe on the world can be traced to such unintended, ambiguous effects as these. Above all, there was the simple urge to imitate, whether expressed ludicrously in the adoption of European dress or, much more importantly, in the conclusion drawn by many who sought to resist European hegemony that to do so it was necessary to adopt European ways. Almost everywhere, radicals and reformers advocated Europeanization. The ideas of 1776, 1789 and 1848 are still at work in Asia and Africa and the world still debates its future in European terms.

This extraordinary outcome is too often overlooked. In its unravelling, 1900 is only a vantage point, not the end of the story. The Japanese are a gifted people who have inherited exquisite artistic traditions, yet they have adopted not only Western industrialism (which is understandable enough) but Western art forms and Western dress in preference to their own. The Japanese now find whisky and claret fashionable and the Chinese still officially revere Marx, a German philosopher who articulated a system of thought rooted in nineteenth-century German idealism and English social and economic facts, rarely spoke of Asia except with contempt, and never went east of Prussia in his life. This suggests another curious fact: the balance sheet of cultural influence is overwhelmingly one-sided. The world gave back to Europe occasional fashions, but no idea or institution of comparable effect to those Europe gave to the world. The teaching of Marx was long a force throughout twentieth-century Asia; the last non-European whose words had any comparable authority in Europe was Jesus Christ.

THE GREAT RESETTLEMENT

ONE PHYSICAL TRANSMISSION of culture was achieved by the movement of Europeans to other continents. Outside the United States, the two largest groups of European communities overseas were (as they still are) in South America and the former British colonies of white settlement which, though formally subject to London's direct rule for much of the nineteenth century, were in fact long oddly hybrid, not quite independent nations, but not really colonies either. Both groups were fed during the nineteenth century, like the United States, by the great diaspora of Europeans whose numbers justify one name which has been given to this era of European demography: the Great Resettlement. Before 1800, there was little European emigration except from the British Isles. After that date, something like sixty million Europeans went overseas, and this tide began to flow strongly in the 1830s. In the nineteenth century most of it went to North America, and then to Latin America (especially Argentina and Brazil), to

At the end of the 19th century, emigration to America seemed, to many Europeans, to offer opportunities that did not exist in the Old World. This engraving from 1878 shows emigrants in Hamburg, Germany, boarding a transatlantic liner bound for the United States.

Australia and South Africa. At the same time a concealed European emigration was also occurring across land within the Russian empire, which occupied one-sixth of the world's land surface and which had vast spaces to draw migrants in Siberia. The peak of European emigration overseas actually came on the eve of the First World War, in 1913, when over a million and a half left Europe; over a third of these were Italians, nearly 400,000 were British and 200,000 Spanish. Fifty years earlier, Italians figured only to a minor degree, Germans and Scandinavians loomed much larger. All the time, the British Isles contributed a steady flow; between 1880 and 1910 eight and a half million Britons went overseas (the Italian figure for this period was just over six million).

The greatest number of British emigrants went to the United States (about 65 per cent of them between 1815 and 1900), but large numbers went also to the self-governing colonies; this ratio changed after 1900 and by 1914 a majority of British emigrants was going to the latter. Italians and Spaniards also went to South America in large numbers, and Italians to the United States. That country remained the greatest of the receivers for all other nationalities; between 1820 and 1950 the United States benefited by the arrival of over thirty-three million Europeans.

REASONS FOR EUROPEAN AND ASIAN MIGRATION

Explanations of the striking demographic evolution caused by migration are not far to seek. Politics sometimes contributed to the flow, as it did after 1848. Rising populations in Europe always pressed upon economic possibilities as the discovery of the phenomenon of "unemployment" shows. In the last decades of the nineteenth century, too, when emigration was rising fastest, European farmers were pressed by overseas competition. Above all, it mattered that for the first time in human history there were obvious opportunities in other lands, where labour was needed, at a moment when there were suddenly easier and cheaper means of getting there. The steamship and railroad greatly changed demographic history and they both began to produce their greatest effect after 1880. They permitted much greater local mobility, so that temporary migrations of labour and movements within continents became much easier. Great Britain exported Irish peasants, Welsh miners and steelworkers and English farmers; she took in at the end of the nineteenth century an influx of Jewish communities from Eastern Europe which was long to remain a distinguishable element in British society. To the seasonal migration of labour, which had always characterized such border districts as southern France, were now added longer-term movements as Poles came to France to

The large numbers of immigrants arriving in the United States during the second half of the 19th century produced xenophobic reactions. In this cartoon, dated 1888, a mixed group of immigrants gawps at the "last genuine Yankee" in a street where foreign shops advertise themselves as American. In spite of prejudice, the integration of people of diverse origins into the American culture was broadly successful.

work in coal-mines and Italian waiters and ice-cream men became part of British folk-lore. When political changes made the North African shore accessible, it, too, was changed by short-range migration from Europe; Italians, Spanish and French were drawn there to settle or trade in the coastal cities and created a new society with interests distinct both from those of the societies from which the migrants had come and from those of the native societies beside which they had settled.

Easier travel did not only ease European migration. Chinese and Japanese settlement on the Pacific coasts of North America was already important by 1900. Chinese migrants also moved down into Southeast Asia, Japanese to Latin America; the spectacle frightened Australians, who sought to preserve a "White Australia" by limiting immigration by racial criteria. The British Empire provided a huge framework within which Indian communities spread around the world. But these movements, though important, were subordinate to the major phenomenon of the nineteenth century, the last great *Völkerwanderung* of the European peoples, and one as decisive for the future as the barbarian invasions had been.

SPANISH AMERICA

I N "LATIN AMERICA" (the term was invented in the middle of the nineteenth century), which attracted in the main Italians and Spaniards, southern Europeans could find much that was familiar. There was the framework to cultural and social life provided by Catholicism; there were Latin languages and social customs. The political and legal framework also reflected the imperial past, some of whose institutions had persisted through an era of political upheaval at the beginning of the nineteenth

century which virtually ended Spanish and Portuguese colonial rule on the mainland. This happened because events in Europe had led to a crisis in which weaknesses in the old empires proved fatal.

This was not for want of effort, at least on the part of the Spanish. In contrast to the British in the north, the metropolitan government had attempted sweeping reforms in the eighteenth century. When the Bourbons replaced the last Habsburg on the Spanish throne in 1701 a new era of Spanish imperial development had begun, though it took some decades to become apparent. When changes came they led first to reorganization and then to "enlightened" reform. The two viceroyalties of 1700 became four, two more appearing in New Granada (Panama and the area covered by Ecuador, Colombia and Venezuela), and La Plata, which ran from the mouth of the river across the continent to the border of Peru. This structural rationalization was followed by relaxations of the closed commercial system, at first unwillingly conceded and then consciously promoted as a means to prosperity. These stimulated the

For poor 19th-century emigrants, such as these Irish families, the long journey to America was often undertaken in dire conditions.

economy both of the colonies and of those parts of Spain (notably the Mediterranean littoral) which benefited from the ending of the monopoly of colonial trade hitherto confined to the port of Seville.

None the less, these healthy tendencies were offset by grave weaknesses which they did not touch. A series of insurrections revealed deep-seated weaknesses in the Spanish empire. In Paraguay (1721–35), Colombia (1781) and, above all, Peru (1780) there were real threats to colonial government which could only be contained by great military efforts. Among others, these required levies of colonial militia, a double-edged expedient, for it provided the *creoles* with military training which they might turn against Spain. The deepest division in Spanish colonial society was between the Indians and the colonists of Spanish descent, but that between the *creoles* and *peninsulares* was to have more immediate political importance. It had widened with the passage of time. Resentful of their exclusion from high office, the *creoles* noted the success of the British colonists of North America in shaking off imperial rule. The French Revolution, also, at first suggested possibilities rather than dangers.

This watercolour celebrates the proclamation of Agustín de Iturbide as emperor of the newly independent Mexico (1822). Two years later, Iturbide was dethroned by a republican uprising. For a long time, life in the new Latin American states was characterized by political instability and civil conflict.

THE WARS OF INDEPENDENCE

As insurrections threatened the colonies, the Spanish government was embarrassed in other ways. In 1790 a quarrel with Great Britain led at last to surrender of the remnants of the old Spanish claim to sovereignty throughout the Americas, when it conceded that the right to prohibit trade or settlement in North America only extended within an area of thirty miles around a Spanish settlement. Then came wars, first with France, then with Great Britain (twice), and finally with France again, during the Napoleonic invasion. These wars not only cost Spain Santo Domingo, Trinidad and Louisiana, but also its dynasty, which was forced by Napoleon to abdicate in 1808. The end of Spanish sea-power had already come at Trafalgar. In this state of disorder and weakness, when, finally, Spain itself was engulfed by French invasion, the *creoles* decided to break loose and in 1810 the Wars of Independence began with risings in New Granada, La Plata and New Spain. The *creoles* were not at first successful and in Mexico they found that they had a racial war on their hands when the Indians took the opportunity to turn on all whites. But the Spanish government was not able to win them over nor to muster sufficient strength to crush further waves of rebellion. British sea-power guaranteed that no conservative European power could step in to help the Spanish and thus practically sustained the Monroe doctrine. So, there emerged from the fragments of the former Spanish Empire a collection of republics, most of them ruled by soldiers.

In Portuguese Brazil the story had gone differently, for though a French invasion of Portugal had in 1807 provoked a new departure, it was different from that of the Spanish empire. The prince regent of Portugal had himself removed from Lisbon to Rio de

Slave labour played an important role in the economy of colonial Brazil. In this 18th-century engraving, slaves working in a diamond mine are watched by white foremen brandishing whips.

Janeiro, which thus became the effective capital of the Portuguese Empire. Though he went back to Portugal as king in 1820 he then left behind his son, who took the lead in resisting an attempt by the Portuguese government to reassert its control of Brazil and, with relatively little trouble, became the emperor of an independent Brazil in 1822.

Post-colonial South America

Key

▨ Main block of territory disputed and changing hands during the wars of the 19th century

▨ European possessions

All dates refer to year of independence

| 0 | | 1,600 km |
| 0 | | 1,000 miles |

In 1819, following his victories against the Spanish, the independence movement leader Simón Bolívar (1783–1830) was declared president of the Republic of Colombia (present-day Venezuela, Colombia and Ecuador). Upper Peru was named Bolivia in his honour.

SOUTH AMERICA AFTER INDEPENDENCE

Between 1810 and 1822, the whole of South America, except for the Guyanas, proclaimed its independence. The new borders, which were often drawn through regions that were almost totally uninhabited, took time to become established and gave rise to several conflicts. In the 19th century, the most important of these were the Triple Alliance War (1864–1870) in which Argentina, Brazil and Uruguay defeated Paraguay, and the Pacific War (1878–1883), in which Chile defeated Peru and Bolivia.

A glance at the map of contemporary South America reveals the most obvious of many great differences between the revolution in North and South America: no United States of South America emerged from the Wars of Independence. Although the great hero and leader of independence, Simon Bolívar, hoped for much from a Congress of the new states at Panama in 1826, nothing came of it. It is not difficult to understand why. For all the variety of the thirteen British colonies and difficulties facing them, they had after their victory relatively easy intercommunication by sea and few insurmountable obstacles of terrain. They also had some experience of co-operation and a measure of direction of their own affairs even while under imperial rule. With these advantages, their divisions still remained important enough to impose a constitution which gave very limited powers to the national government. It is hardly surprising that the southern republics could not achieve continental unity for all the advantages of the common background of Spanish rule which most of them shared.

The absence of unifying factors may not have been disadvantageous, for the Latin Americans of the early nineteenth century faced no danger or opportunity which made unity desirable. Against the outside world, other than the United States, they were protected by Great Britain. At home the problems of post-colonial evolution were far greater than had been anticipated and were unlikely to be tackled more successfully by the creation of an artificial unity. Indeed, as in Africa a century and a half later, one legacy of colonial rule was that geography and community did not always suit political units which corresponded to the old administrative divisions. The huge, thinly populated states which emerged from the Wars of Independence were constantly in danger of disintegrating into small units as the urban minorities who had guided the independence movement found it impossible to control their followers. Some did break up. There were racial problems, too; the social inequalities they gave rise to were not removed by independence. Not every country experienced them in the same way. In Argentina, for example, the relatively small Indian population underwent near-extermination at the hands of the army. That

country was celebrated by the end of the nineteenth century for the extent to which it resembled Europe in the domination of European strains in its population. At the other extreme, Brazil had a population the majority of which was black and, at the time of independence, much of it still in slavery. Intermarriage was not frowned upon, and the result is a population which may well be the most successfully integrated ethnic mix in the world today. Finally, an important part of South America's colonial inheritance was a set of economic relationships with the outside world which would be slow to change. They would lead later to denunciation of the continent's economic "dependency". But the legacy had another side to it; much of the continent's

Benito Juárez, a Mexican of indigenous Indian blood, was one of the instigators of Mexico's progressive constitution of 1857 and was elected president in 1861. Juárez fought against the French invasion, which temporarily made Maximilian of Austria emperor of Mexico. After defeating Maximilian in 1870, Juárez once again took the office of president, which he held until his death in 1872.

Military force has often decided Latin American political struggles. This scene from the brief civil war that took place in Chile in 1891 shows the navy attacking the port of Valparaiso in support of a conservative congress against the reformist president José Manuel Balmaceda.

wealth would never have been there but for colonialism. Every plantation crop grown in Brazil had been brought there by Europeans from overseas – sugar, coffee, chocolate, cattle, wheat.

POLITICAL DIFFICULTIES

The new Latin American states could not draw upon any tradition of self-government in facing their many problems, for the colonial administrations had been absolutist and

had not thrown up representative institutions. For the political principles they sought to apply, the leaders of the republics looked in the main to the French Revolution, but these were advanced ideas for states whose tiny élites did not even share among themselves agreement about accepted practice; they could hardly produce a framework of mutual tolerance. Worse still, revolutionary principles quickly brought the Church into politics, a development which was perhaps in the long run inevitable, given its huge power as a landowner and popular influence, but unfortunate in adding anti-clericalism to the woes of the continent. In these circumstances, it was hardly surprising that during most of the century each republic found that its affairs tended to drift into the hands of *caudillos*, military adventurers and their cliques who controlled armed forces sufficient to give them sway until more powerful rivals came along.

The cross-currents of civil war and wars between the new states – some very bloody – led by 1900 to a map which is still much the same today. Mexico, the most northern of the former Spanish colonies, had lost vast areas in the north to the United States. Four mainland Central American republics had appeared and two island states, the Dominican Republic and Haiti. Cuba was on the point of achieving independence. To the south were the ten states of South America. All of these countries were republican; Brazil had given up its monarchy in 1889. Though all had been through grave civic disorders, they represented very different degrees of stability and constitutional propriety. In Mexico, an Indian had indeed become president, to great effect, in the 1860s, but everywhere there remained the social divisions between Indians, *mestizos* (those of mixed blood), and those of European blood (much reinforced in numbers when immigration became more rapid after 1870). The

Latin American countries had contained about nineteen million people in 1800; a century later they had sixty-three million.

LATIN AMERICAN WEALTH

Large-scale immigration argues a certain increase in wealth. Most of the Latin American countries had important natural resources in one form or another. Sometimes they fought over them for such advantages became even more valuable as Europe and the United States became more industrialized. Argentina had space and some of the finest pasture in the world: the invention of refrigerator ships in the 1880s made it England's butcher and later grain grower as well. At the end of the nineteenth century, it was the richest of the Latin American countries. Chile had nitrates (taken from Bolivia and Peru in the "War of the Pacific" of 1879–83) and Venezuela had oil; both grew more important in the twentieth century. Mexico had oil, too. Brazil had practically everything (except oil), above all coffee and sugar. The list could be continued but would confirm that the grow-

ing wealth of Latin America came above all from primary produce. The capital to exploit this came from Europe and the United States and this produced new ties between these European nations overseas and Europe itself.

This increase in wealth nevertheless was connected with two related drawbacks. One was that it did nothing to reduce the disparities of wealth to be found in these countries; indeed, they may have increased. In conse-

A street in Rio de Janeiro in 1827 is portrayed in this contemporary scene. The slaves' elegant livery was an external sign of the great wealth of the city's élite Europeanized families.

This engraving, which is dated 1854, depicts the Plaza de la Independencia in Santiago de Chile. The square is lined with imposing European-style buildings.

quence, social, like racial, tensions remained largely unresolved. An apparently Europeanized urban élite lived lives wholly unlike those of the Indian and *mestizo* masses. This was accentuated by the dependence of Latin America on foreign capital. Not unreasonably, foreign investors sought security. They by no means always got it, but it tended to lead them to support of the existing social and political authorities, who thus enhanced still further their own wealth. It would take only a few years of the twentieth century for conditions resulting from this sort of thing to produce social revolution in Mexico.

RELATIONS WITH THE UNITED STATES

The irritation and disappointment of foreign investors who could not collect the debts due to them led sometimes to diplomatic conflicts and even armed intervention. The collection of debt was, after all, not seen as a revival of colonialism and European governments sent stiff messages and backed them up with force on several occasions during the century. When in 1902 Great Britain, Germany and Italy together instituted a naval blockade of Venezuela in order to collect debts due to their subjects who had suffered in revolutionary troubles, this provoked the United States to go further than the Monroe doctrine.

From the days of the Texan republic onwards, the relations of the United States with its neighbours had never been easy: nor are they today. Too many complicating factors were at work. The Monroe doctrine expressed the basic interest of the United States in keeping the hemisphere uninvolved with Europe, and the first Pan-American Congress was another step in this direction when the United States organized it in 1889. But this could no more prevent the growth of economic links with Europe than could the Revolution sever those of the United States with Great Britain (and North Americans were among the investors in South American countries and soon had their own special pleas to make to their government). Moreover, as the century came to an end, it was clear that the strategic situation which was the background to the Monroe doctrine had changed. Steamships and the rise of American interest in the Far East and the Pacific made the United States much more sensitive, in particular, to developments in Central America and the Caribbean, where an isthmian canal was more and more likely to be built.

This 19th-century view of Mexico City, with a peasant family's encampment in the foreground, illustrates the contrast between the country's expanding urban centres and the traditional rural way of life.

UNITED STATES INTERVENTION IN LATIN AMERICA

The outcome of the changing strategic situation was greater heavy-handedness and even arrogance in United States policy towards its neighbours in the early twentieth century. When, after a brief war with Spain, the United States won Cuba its independence (and took Puerto Rico from Spain for itself), special restraints were incorporated in the new Cuban constitution to ensure it would remain a satellite. The territory of the Panama Canal was obtained by intervention in the affairs of Colombia. The Venezuelan debt affair was followed by an even more remarkable assertion of American strength – a "corollary" to the Monroe doctrine. This was the announcement (almost at once given practical expression in Cuba and the Dominican Republic) that the United States would exercise a right of intervention in the affairs of any state in the western hemisphere whose internal affairs were in such disorder that they might tempt European intervention. Later, one American president sent marines to Nicaragua in 1912 on this ground and another occupied the Mexican port of Vera Cruz in 1914 as a way of coercing a Mexican government. In 1915 a protectorate was established by treaty over Haiti which was to last forty years.

This was not the end of an unhappy story of relations between the United States and its neighbours, though far enough to take it for the moment. Their importance here, in any case, is only symptomatic of the ambiguous standing of the Latin American states in relation to Europe. Rooted in its culture, tied to it by economics, they none the less were constrained politically to avoid entanglement with it. This did not, of course, mean that they did not stand, so far as Europeans were concerned, on the white man's side of the great distinction more and more drawn between those within the pale of European civilization and those outside it. When Europeans thought of "Latin Americans" they thought of those of European descent, the urban, literate, privileged minority, not the Indian and black masses.

KITH AND KIN.

Canada (to Britannia). "If I can be of any assistance, command me." (And so say Victoria and New South Wales.)

This cartoon, which appeared in the British magazine *Punch* on 21 February 1885, shows a personification of the Dominion of Canada loyally offering to fight for Britannia.

BRITISH COLONIALISM

THE CRUMBLING of the Spanish Empire so soon after the defection of the thirteen colonies led many people to expect that the other settler colonies of the British Empire would soon throw off the rule of London, too. In a way, this happened, but hardly as had been anticipated. At the end of the nineteenth century, the British magazine *Punch* printed a patriotic cartoon in which the British Lion looked approvingly at rows of little lion-cubs, armed and uniformed, who represented the colonies overseas. They were appropriately dressed as soldiers, for the volunteer contingents sent from other parts of the empire to fight for the British in the war they were then engaged upon in South Africa were of major importance. A century earlier, no one could have foreseen that a single colonial soldier would be available to the mother country. The year 1783 had burnt deep into the consciousness of British statesmen. Colonies, they thought they had learnt, were tricky things, costing money, conferring few

In Montreal, in the British Dominion of Canada, a train crosses the frozen St Lawrence River in 1880. Thick beams have been laid across the ice to support the sleepers – a remarkable technical feat for any age.

benefits, engaging the metropolitan country in fruitless strife with other powers and native peoples and in the end usually turning around to bite the hand that fed them. The distrust of colonial entanglements which such views engendered helped to swing British imperial interest towards the East at the end of the eighteenth century, towards the possibilities of Asian trade. It seemed that in the Far East there would be no complications caused by European settlers and in eastern seas no need for expensive forces which could not easily be met by the Royal Navy.

SELF-GOVERNING DEPENDENCIES

Broadly speaking, wariness about potentially problematic colonies was to be the prevailing attitude in British official circles during the whole nineteenth century. It led them to tackle the complicated affairs of each colony in ways which sought, above all else, economy and the avoidance of trouble. In the huge spaces of Canada and Australia this led, stormily, to the eventual uniting of the individual colonies in federal structures with responsibility for their own government. In

1867 the Dominion of Canada came into existence, and in 1901 there followed the Commonwealth of Australia. In each case, union had been preceded by the granting of responsible government to the original colonies and in each case there had been special difficulties. In Canada the outstanding one was the existence of a French Canadian community in the province of Quebec, in Australia the clashes of interest between settlers and convicts – of whom the last consignment was delivered in 1867. Each, too, was a huge, thinly populated country which could only gradually be pulled together to generate a sense of nationality. In each case the process was slow: it was not until 1885 that the last spike was driven on the transcontinental line of the Canadian Pacific Railway, and transcontinental railways in Australia were delayed for a long time by the adoption of different gauges in different states. In the end, nationalism was assisted by the growth of awareness of potential external threats – United States economic strength and Asian immigration – and, of course, by bickering with the British.

New Zealand also achieved responsible government, but one less decentralized, as befitted a much smaller country. Europeans had arrived there from the 1790s onwards and they found a native people, the Maori, with an advanced and complex culture, whom the visitors set about corrupting. Missionaries followed, and did their best to keep out settlers and traders. But they arrived just the same. When it seemed that a French entrepreneur was likely to establish a French interest, the British government at last reluctantly gave way to the pressure brought upon it by missionaries and some of the settlers and proclaimed British sovereignty in 1840. In 1856 the colony was given responsible government and only wars with the Maoris delayed the withdrawal of British soldiers until 1870. Soon afterwards, the old provinces lost their remaining legislative powers. In the later years of the century, New Zealand governments showed remarkable independence and vigour in the pursuit of advanced social welfare policies and achieved full self-government in 1907.

That was the year after a Colonial Conference in London had decided that the name "Dominion" should in future be the term used for all the self-governing dependencies, which meant, in effect, the colonies of white settlement. One more remained to be given this status before 1914, the Union of South Africa, which came into existence in 1910. This was the end of a long and unhappy chapter – the unhappiest in the history of the British Empire and one which closed only to open another in the history of Africa which within a few decades looked even more bleak.

SOUTH AFRICA

NO BRITISH COLONISTS had settled in South Africa until after 1814, when Great Britain for strategic reasons retained the former Dutch colony at the Cape of Good Hope. This was called "Cape Colony" and soon there arrived some thousands of British settlers who, though outnumbered by the Dutch, had the backing of the British government in introducing British assumptions and law. This opened a period of whittling away of the privileges of the Boers, as the Dutch farmers were called. In particular, they were excited and irked by any limitation of their freedom to deal with the native African as they wished. Their especial indignation was aroused when, as a result of the general abolition of slavery in British territory, some 35,000 of their black slaves were freed with, it was said, inadequate compensation. Convinced that the British

After defeating the Zulus in South Africa, the British authorities came to an agreement with them. The Zulu king, Cetewayo, was restored to the throne in 1883 in the ceremony shown in this engraving. King Cetewayo can be distinguished from his subjects by his European-style clothes.

Paul Kruger, President of the Boer Republic of Transvaal from 1883 to 1900, is portrayed in this 19th-century engraving. Kruger led the Boers into war with Britain (1899–1902).

THE EXTENSION OF BRITISH TERRITORY

A Boer republic in Natal was soon made a British colony, in order to protect the Africans from exploitation, and prevent the establishment of a Dutch port which might some day be used by a hostile power to threaten British communications with the Far East. Another exodus of Boers followed, this time north of the Vaal river. This was the first extension of British territory in South Africa but set a pattern which was to be repeated. Besides humanitarianism, the British government and the British colonists on the spot were stirred by the need to establish good relations with African peoples which would otherwise (as the Zulus had already shown against the Boers) present a continuing security problem (not unlike that posed by Indians in the American colonies in the previous century). By mid-century, there existed two Boer republics in the north (the Orange Free State and the Transvaal), while Cape Colony and Natal were under the British flag, with elected assemblies for which the few black men who met the required economic tests could vote. There were also native states under British protection. In one of these, Basutoland, this actually placed Boers under black jurisdiction, which was felt by many of them to be an especially galling subjection.

Happy relations were unlikely in these circumstances and, in any case, British governments were often in disagreement with the colonists at the Cape, who, after 1872, had responsible government of their own. New facts arose, too. The discovery of diamonds led to the British annexation of another piece of territory which, since it lay north of the Orange, angered the Boers. British support for the Basutos, whom the Boers had defeated, was a further irritant. Finally, the governor of Cape Colony

would not abandon a policy favourable to the native African – and, given the pressures upon British governments, this was a reasonable view – a great exodus of Boers took place in 1835. This "Great Trek" north across the Orange river was of radical importance in forming the Afrikaner consciousness. It was the beginning of a long period during which Anglo-Saxon and Boer struggled to live sometimes apart, sometimes together, but always uncomfortably, their decisions as they did so dragging in their train others about the fate of the black African.

committed an act of folly by annexing the Transvaal republic. After a successful Boer rising and a nasty defeat of a British force, the British government had the sense not to persist and restored independence to the republic in 1881, but from this moment Boer distrust of British policy in South Africa was probably insurmountable.

THE BOER WAR

Within twenty years of the restoration of independence, tension between the Boers and the British led to war, largely because of two further unanticipated changes. One was a small-scale industrial revolution in the Transvaal republic, where gold was found in 1886. The result was a huge influx of miners and speculators, the involvement of outside financial interests in the affairs of South Africa, and the possibility that the Afrikaner State might have the financial resources to escape from the British suzerainty it unwillingly accepted. The index of what had happened was Johannesburg, which grew in a few years to become the only city of 100,000 in Africa south of the Zambezi. The second change was that other parts of Africa were being swallowed in the 1880s and 1890s by other European powers and the British government was reacting by stiffening in its determination that nothing must shake the British presence at the Cape, deemed essential to the control of sea routes to the East and increasingly dependent on traffic to and from the Transvaal for its revenues. The general effect was to make British governments view with concern any possibility of the Transvaal obtaining independent access to the Indian

British soldiers are depicted fighting in the Transvaal in the first year of the Boer War.

This contemporary engraving shows Boer troops attacking a British armour-plated train in 1899.

Ocean. This concern made them vulnerable to the pressure of an oddly assorted crew of idealistic imperialists, Cape politicians, English demagogues and shady financiers, who provoked a confrontation with the Boers in 1899 which ended in an ultimatum from the Transvaal's president, Paul Kruger, and the outbreak of the Boer War. Kruger had a deep dislike of the British; as a boy he had gone north on the Great Trek.

BRITISH VICTORY AND CONCESSIONS TO THE BOERS

The well-known traditions of the British army of Victorian times were amply sustained in the last war of the reign, both in the level of ineptness and incompetence shown by some higher commanders and administrative services and in the gallantry shown by regimental officers and their men in the face of a brave and well-armed enemy whom their training did not prepare them to defeat. But of the outcome there could be no doubt; as the queen herself remarked, with better strategic judgment than some of her subjects, the possibilities of defeat did not exist. South Africa was a theatre isolated by British sea-power; no other European nation could help the Boers and it was only a matter of time before greatly superior numbers and resources were brought to bear upon them. This cost a great deal – over a quarter of a million soldiers were sent to South Africa – and aroused much bitterness in British domestic politics; further, it did not present a very favourable picture to the outside world. The Boers were regarded as an oppressed nationality; so they were, but the nineteenth-century liberal obsession with nationality in this case as in others blinded observers to some of the shadows it cast. Fortunately, British statesmanship recovered itself sufficiently to make a generous treaty to end the war in 1902 when the Boers had been beaten in the field.

This was the end of the Boer republics. But concession rapidly followed; by 1906 the Transvaal had a responsible government of its own, which in spite of the large non-Boer population brought there by mining, the Boers controlled after an electoral victory the following year. Almost at once they began to legislate against Asian immigrants, mainly Indian. (One young Indian lawyer, Mohandas Gandhi, now entered politics as the champion of his community.) When, in 1909, a draft constitution for a South African Union was agreed, it was on terms of equality for the Dutch and English languages and, all-important, it provided for government by an elected assembly to be formed according to the electoral regulations decided in each province. In the Boer provinces the franchise was confined to white men.

At the time, there was much to be said for the settlement. When people then spoke of a "racial problem" in South Africa they meant the problem of relations between the British and Boers, whose conciliation seemed the most urgent need. The defects of the settlement would take some time to appear. When they did it would be not only because the historical sense of the Afrikaner proved to be tougher than people had hoped, but also because the transformation of South African society which had begun with the industrialization of the Rand could not be halted and would give irresistible momentum to the issue of the black Africans.

RESOURCES IN THE BRITISH DOMINIONS

In its economic development, South Africa's future had been just as decisively influenced as had those of all the other British white dominions by being caught up in the trends of the whole world economy. Canada, like the

United States, had become, with the building of the railroads on her plains, one of the great granaries of Europe. Australia and New Zealand first exploited their huge pastures to produce the wool for which European factories were increasingly in the market; then, with the invention of refrigeration, they used them for meat and, in the case of New Zealand, dairy produce. In this way these new nations found staples able to sustain economies much greater than those permitted by the tobacco and indigo of the seventeenth-century plantations. The case of South Africa was to be different in that she was to reveal herself only gradually (as much later would Australia) as a producer of minerals. The beginning of this was the diamond industry, but the great step forward was the Rand gold discovery of the 1880s. The exploitation of this sucked in capital and expertise to make possible the eventual exploitation of other minerals. The return which South Africa provided was not merely in the profits of European companies and shareholders, but also an augmentation of the world's gold supply which stimulated European commerce much as had done the California discoveries of 1849.

Prospectors are depicted filtering the soil on a river bank in this 19th-century illustration of a diamond field in Britain's South African Cape Colony.

A Maori chief and his wife are portrayed in this engraving dating from the mid-19th century. The Maoris of New Zealand, who were of Polynesian origin, were more adaptable, had more advanced technology and were more warlike than the Australian Aborigines.

THE TREATMENT OF NATIVE POPULATIONS

THE GROWTH OF HUMANITARIAN and missionary sentiment in England and the well-founded Colonial Office tradition of distrust of settler demands made it harder to forget the native populations of the white dominions than it had been for Americans to sweep aside the Plains Indians. Yet in several of the British colonies, modernity made its impact not upon ancient civilizations like those of India or South America but on primitive societies, some of which were at a very

low stage of achievement indeed, Neolithic if not Palaeolithic, and correspondingly vulnerable. The Canadian Indians and Eskimos were relatively few and presented no such important obstacle to the exploitation of the west and northwest as had done the Plains Indians' struggle to keep their hunting-grounds. The story in Australia was far bloodier. The hunting and gathering society of the Aborigines was disrupted by settlement, tribes were antagonized and provoked into violence by the uncomprehending brutality of the white Australians, and new diseases cut fast into their numbers. The early decades of each Australian colony are stained by the blood of massacred Aborigines; their later years are notorious for the neglect, bullying and exploitation of the survivors. There is perhaps no other population inside former British territory which underwent a fate so like that of the North American Indian. In New Zealand, the arrival of the first white men brought guns to the Maori, who employed them first on one another, with disruptive effects upon their societies. Later came wars with the government, whose essential origin lay in the settlers' displacement of the Maori from their lands. At their conclusion, the government took steps to outlaw the most fraudulent tactics of land acquisition, but the introduction of English notions of individual ownership led to the disintegration of the tribal holdings and the virtual loss of their lands by the end of the century. The Maoris, too, declined in numbers, but not so violently or irreversibly as did the Australian Aborigines. There are now many more Maoris than in 1900 and their numbers grow faster than those of New Zealanders of European stock.

As for South Africa, the story is a mixed one. British protection enabled some of its native peoples to survive into the twentieth century on their ancestral lands living in ways

In this scene from the mid-19th century, Australian Aborigines perform a ceremonial dance. When the British arrived in Australia, it was inhabited by several hundred thousand Aborigines who survived by hunting and gathering. By the beginning of the 20th century the Aborigines' numbers had been reduced to 50,000.

which changed only slowly. Others were driven off or exterminated. In all cases, though, the crux of the situation was that in South Africa, as elsewhere, the fate of the native inhabitants was never in their own hands. They depended for their survival upon the local balance of governmental interest and benevolence, settler needs and traditions, economic opportunities and exigencies. Although in the short run they could sometimes present formidable military problems (as did the Zulus of Cetewayo, or the guerrilla warfare of the Maoris) they could not in the end generate from their own resources the means of effective resistance any more than had the Aztecs been able successfully to resist Cortés. For non-European peoples to do that, they would have to Europeanize. The price of establishing the new European nations beyond the seas always turned out to be paid by the native inhabitants, often to the limit of their ability.

EUROPEAN SELF-JUSTIFICATION

The damage done to the aboriginal peoples under their rule by Europeans should not be quite the last word about colonialism. There remains the puzzle of self-justification: Europeans witnessed the disruption and, often, destruction of native societies and did not stop it. It is too simple to explain this by saying they were all bad, greedy individuals (and, in any case, the work of the humanitarians among them makes the blackest judgment untenable). The answer must lie somewhere in mentality. Something was due to lack of insight or simple ignorance. Many Europeans who could recognize that the native populations were damaged, even when the white contact with them was benevolent in intention, could not be expected to understand the corrosive effect of this culture on established structures. This requires an anthropological knowledge and insight

Europe had still to achieve. It was all the more difficult when, clearly, a lot of native culture was simple savagery and the Europeans' missionary confidence was strong. They *knew* they were on the side of "progress" and "improvement", and many still saw themselves as on the side of the Cross, too. This was a confidence which ran through every side of European expansion, whether in the white settler colonies and directly ruled possessions or in the arrangements made with dependent and "protected" societies. The confidence in belonging to a higher civilization was not only a licence for predatory habits as Christianity had earlier been, but the nerve of an attitude akin, in many cases, to that of crusaders. It was their sureness that they brought something better that blinded Europeans all too often to the actual and material results of substituting individual freehold for tribal rights, of turning the hunters and gatherers, whose possessions were what they could carry, into wage-earners.

This engraving from the English *Illustrated London News* shows Queen Victoria (1819–1901) visiting the South Australia Exhibit at the Colonial and Indian Exhibition in May 1886.

2 EUROPEAN IMPERIALISM AND IMPERIAL RULE

THE RULING OF ALIEN PEOPLES and other lands by Europeans was the most impressive evidence that they ran the world. In spite of continuing argument about what imperialism was and is, it seems helpful to start with the simple notion of direct and formal overlordship, blurred though its boundaries with other forms of power over the non-European world may be. This neither raises nor answers questions about causes or motives, on which much time, ink and thought have been spent. From the outset different and changing causes were at work, and not all the motives involved were unavowable or self-deceiving.

Imperialism was not the manifestation of only one age, for it has gone on all through history; nor was it peculiar to Europe's relations with non-Europeans overseas, for imperial rule had advanced overland as well as across the seas and some Europeans have ruled others and some non-Europeans have ruled Europeans. None the less, in the nineteenth and twentieth centuries the word came to be particularly associated with European expansion and the direct domination of Europeans over the rest of the world had by then become much more obvious than ever before. Although the American revolutions suggested that the European empires built up over the preceding three centuries were in decline, in the next hundred years European imperialism was carried much further and became more effective than ever before. This happened in two distinguishable phases, and one running down to about 1870 can conveniently be considered first. Some of the old imperial powers then continued to enlarge their empires impressively; such were Russia, France and Great Britain. Others stood still or found theirs reduced; these were the Dutch, Spanish and Portuguese.

RUSSIAN EXPANSION

The Russian expansion has at first sight something in common both with the American experience of filling up the North American continent and dominating its weaker neighbours, and something with that of the British in India, but was in fact a very special case. To the west Russia confronted matured, established European states where there was little hope of successful territorial gain. The same was only slightly less true of expansion into the Turkish territories of the Danubian regions, for here the interests of

A French expedition crosses the Tonkin mountains, in Indo-China in 1884. The armed escort is made up entirely of natives.

Imperialism

Imperialism – the rule, often originating in armed conquest, of one people over others – has existed since the beginning of the first civilizations, in various parts of the world. The term imperialism, however, only came into use in the second half of the 19th century, as a label for the great European colonial expansion that was then taking place.

In the on-going debate about the causes of imperialism, some historians have proposed political explanations, such as the need to divert public attention from domestic problems and gain international prestige. Others favour economic causes – many 19th-century imperialists believed, often erroneously, that empires provided lucrative markets. Some claim that imperialists are motivated by psychological and social issues. Social Darwinism, the once popular theory that Europeans are naturally superior to other races and have a duty to rule over them, was often cited by empire-builders. But many empires have grown from simple international rivalry.

A review of the native cavalry in French Indo-China, in August 1903 is shown. For the most part, order in the colonies was maintained by native troops, organized in European military units and under the command of European officers.

other powers were always likely to come into play against Russia and check her in the end. She was much freer to act to the south and eastwards; in both directions the first three-quarters of the nineteenth century brought great acquisitions. A successful war against Persia (1826–8) led to the establishment of Russian naval power on the Caspian as well as gains of territory in Armenia. In Central Asia an almost continuous advance into Turkestan and towards the central oases of Bokhara and Khiva culminated in the annexation of the whole of Transcaspia in 1881. In Siberia, aggressive expansion was followed by the exaction of the left bank of the Amur down to the sea from China and the founding in 1860 of Vladivostok, the Far Eastern capital. Soon after, Russia liquidated its commitments in America by selling Alaska to the United States; this seemed to show it sought to be an Asian and Pacific, but not an American, power.

THE ERA OF BRITISH NAVAL SUPREMACY

The other two dynamic imperial states of this era besides Russia, France and Great Britain, expanded overseas. Yet many of the British gains were made at the expense of France; the Revolutionary and Napoleonic Wars proving in this respect the final round of the great colonial Anglo-French contest of the eighteenth century. As in 1714 and 1763, many of Great Britain's acquisitions at a victorious peace in 1815 were intended to reinforce maritime strength. Malta, St Lucia, the Ionian Islands, the Cape of Good Hope, Mauritius and Trincomalee were all kept for this reason. Soon afterwards, steamships began to appear in the Royal Navy and the situation of bases had to take coaling into account; this now led to further acquisitions. In 1839, an internal upheaval in the Ottoman Empire gave the British the opportunity to seize Aden, a base

Victoria, Queen of England, is depicted with her daughter Princess Beatrice in 1880. The British Empire reached its height during Victoria's long reign (1837–1901). In 1876 she was crowned Empress of India.

the world's greatest commercial power undertake a policing of the seas from which all could benefit.

Naval supremacy guarded the trade which gave the British colonies participation in the fastest-growing commercial system of the age. Already before the American Revolution British policy had been more encouraging to commercial enterprise than the Spanish or French. Thus the old colonies themselves had grown in wealth and prosperity and the later dominions were to benefit. On the other hand, settlement colonies went out of fashion in London after the American Revolution; they were seen mainly as sources of trouble and expense. Yet Great Britain was the only European country sending out new settlers to existing colonies in the early nineteenth century, and those colonies sometimes drew the mother country into yet further extensions of territorial rule over alien lands.

BRITISH IMPERIAL RULE IN INDIA

IN SOME BRITISH ACQUISITIONS (notably in South Africa) there can be seen at work a new concern about strategy and communication with Asia. This is a complicated business. No doubt American independence and the Monroe doctrine diminished the attractiveness of the western hemisphere as a region of imperial expansion, but the origins of a shift of British interest to the East can be seen before 1783, in the opening up of the South Pacific and in a growing Asian trade. War with the Netherlands, when it was a French satellite, subsequently led to new British enterprise in Malaya and Indonesia. Above all, there was the steadily deepening British involvement in India. By 1800 the importance of the Indian trade was already a central axiom of British commercial and colonial

of strategic importance on the route to India, and others were to follow. No power could successfully challenge such action after Trafalgar. It was not that resources did not exist elsewhere which, had they been assembled, could have wrested naval supremacy form Great Britain. But to do so would have demanded a huge effort. No other nation operated either the number of ships or possessed the bases which could make it worth while to challenge this thalassocracy. There were advantages to other nations in having

thinking. By 1850, it has been urged, much of the rest of the empire had only been acquired because of the strategical pull exercised by India. By then, too, the extension of British control inside the subcontinent itself was virtually complete. It was and remained the centrepiece of British imperialism.

This had hardly been expected or even foreseeable. In 1784 the institution of "Dual Control" had been accompanied by decisions to resist further acquisition of Indian territory; the experience of American rebellion had reinforced the view that new commitments were to be avoided. Yet there was a continuing problem, for through its revenue management the East India Company's affairs inevitably became entangled in native administration and politics. This made it more important than ever to prevent excesses by its individual officers, such as had been tolerable in the early days of private trading; slowly, agreement emerged that the government of India was not only of interest to Parliament

because it might be a great source of patronage, but also because the government in London had a responsibility for the good government of Indians. There began to be articulated a notion of trusteeship. It should not be surprising that, during a century in which the idea that government should be for the benefit of the governed was gaining ground in Europe, the same principle should be applied, sooner or later, to rule over colonial peoples. Since the days of Las Casas, exploitation of indigenous peoples had its vociferous critics. In the mid-eighteenth century, a bestselling book by the *abbé* Raynal (it went through thirty editions and many translations in twenty years) had put the criticisms of the churchmen into the secular terms of enlightenment humanitarianism. Against this deep background Edmund Burke in 1783 put it to the House of Commons in a debate on India that "all political power which is set over men ... ought to be some way or other exercised ultimately for their benefit".

The influence of British colonization is already evident in this street in Mandalay, Upper Burma, in 1887.

Soldiers from a Bengal infantry regiment are shown taking the town of Minhla in Burma in this engraving, dated 1886. In the same year, the British annexed Upper Burma to complete their conquest of the country.

Warren Hastings, governor-general of India from 1773 to 1784, was tried by the House of Lords for corruption after his resignation from the post. Corruption was then endemic among British officials in India, although Hastings himself was eventually absolved of the charge.

NEW ATTITUDES TO INDIAN AFFAIRS

The background against which Indian affairs were considered was changing. Across two centuries, the awe and amazement inspired by the Moghul court in the first merchants to reach it had given way rapidly to contempt for what was seen on closer acquaintance as backwardness, superstition and inferiority. But now there were signs of another change. While Clive, the victor of Plassey, never learnt to speak with readiness in any Indian tongue, Warren Hastings, the first governor-general of India, strove to get a chair of Persian set up at Oxford, and encouraged the introduction of the first printing-press to India and the making of the first fount of a vernacular (Bengali) type. There was greater appreciation of the complexity and variety of Indian culture. In 1789 there began to be published in Calcutta the first journal of oriental studies, *Asiatick Researches*. Meanwhile, at the more practical level of government, East India Company judges were already enjoined to follow Islamic law in family cases involving Muslims, while the revenue authority of Madras both regulated and funded Hindu temples and festivals. From 1806 Indian languages were taught at the East India Company's college, Haileybury.

The periodic renewals of the Company's charter took place, therefore, in the light of changing influences and assumptions about Anglo-Indian relationships. Meanwhile, government's responsibilities grew. In 1813 renewal strengthened London's control further, and abolished the Company's monopoly of trade with India. By then, the wars with France had already led to the extension of British power over south India through annexation and the negotiation of treaties with native rulers which secured control of their foreign policy. By 1833, when the charter was again renewed, the only important block of territory not ruled directly or indirectly by the Company was in the northwest. The annexation of the Punjab and Sind followed in the 1840s and with their paramountcy established in Kashmir, the British held sway over virtually the whole subcontinent.

THE EAST INDIA COMPANY GOVERNS

The East India Company had by then ceased to be a commercial organization and had become a government. The 1833 charter took away its trading functions (not only those with India but the monopoly of trade with China and it was confined to an administrative role); in sympathy with current thinking, Asian trade was henceforth to be free trade. The way was open to the consummation of many real and symbolic breaks with India's past and the final incorporation of the subcontinent in a modernizing world. The name of the Moghul emperor was removed from the coinage, but it was more than a symbol that Persian ceased to be the legal language of record and justice. This step not only marked the advance of English as the official language (and therefore of English education), but also disturbed the balance of forces between Indian communities. Anglicized Hindus would prove to do better than less enterprising Muslims. In a subcontinent so divided in so many ways, the adoption of English as the language of administration was complemented by the important decision in principle to provide primary education through instruction given in English, few though the Indians would be who received it.

At the same time an enlightened despotism exercised by successive governors-general began to impose material and institutional improvement. Roads and canals were built and the first railway followed in 1853. Legal codes were introduced. English officials for the Company's service began to be trained specially in the college established for this purpose. The first three universities in India were founded in 1857. There were other educational structures, too; as far back as 1791 a Scotsman had founded a Sanskrit college at Benares, the Lourdes of Hinduism. Much of the transformation which India was gradually undergoing arose not from the direct work of government but from the increasing freedom with which these and other agencies were allowed to operate. From 1813 the arrival of missionaries (the Company had hitherto kept them out) gradually built up another constituency at home with a stake in what happened in India – often to the embarrassment of official India. Two philosophies, in effect, were competing to make government act positively. Utilitarians looked for the promotion of happiness, evangelical Christians to the salvation

of souls. Both were arrogantly sure they knew what was best for India. Both subtly changed British attitudes as time passed.

THE EXPATRIATE COMMUNITY

The coming of the steamship was influential, in that it brought India nearer. More English and Scots people began to live and make their careers there. This gradually transformed the nature of the British presence. The comparatively few officers of the eighteenth-century Company had been content to live the lives of exiles, seeking rewards in their commercial opportunities and relaxation in a social life sometimes closely integrated with that of the Indians. They often lived much in the style of Indian gentlemen, some of them taking to Indian dress and food, some to Indian wives and concubines. Reform-minded officials, intent on the eradication of the backward and barbaric in native practice – and in such

Hider Ali-Khan, Muslim prince of Mysore, is shown receiving the French admiral Pierre de Suffren in 1782. Their collaboration in the struggle against Hastings' British forces failed to save them from defeat.

This 18th-century Indian miniature depicts the maharaja Ranjit Singh (1780–1839), also known as "the Lion of the Punjab", who succeeded his father as a minor Sikh leader in 1792. With the help of an army trained by Western soldiers (the maharaja was a firm ally of the British), Ranjit Singh captured Lahore in 1799 and created a very powerful independent Sikh state in the Punjab region.

English officials and their wives mingle at a tennis party in 19th-century India. Most of the Indians in the picture are servants rather than guests. The English participants' clothes, the furniture and the event itself all signify a determination on the part of the colonialists to cling to the British way of life.

practices as female infanticide and suttee they had good cause for concern – missionaries with a creed to preach, which was corrosive of the whole structure of Hindu or Muslim society and, above all, the Englishwomen who arrived to make homes in India while their husbands worked there, often did not approve of the ways of John Company's men. They all changed the temper of the British community, which drew more and more apart from the natives, more and more convinced of a moral superiority, which sanctioned the ruling of Indians who were culturally and morally inferior. The rulers grew consciously more alien from those they ruled. One of them spoke approvingly of his countrymen as representatives of a "belligerent civilization" and defined their task as "the introduction of the essential parts of European civilization into a country densely peopled, grossly ignorant, steeped in idolatrous superstition, unenergetic, fatalistic, indifferent to most of what we regard as the evils of life and preferring the response of submitting to them to the trouble of encountering and trying to remove them". This robust creed was far from that of the

Englishmen of the previous century who had innocently sought to do no more in India than make money. Now, while new laws antagonized powerful native interests, the British had less and less social contact with Indians; more and more they confined the educated Indian to the lower ranks of the administration and withdrew into an enclosed, but conspicuously privileged, life of their own. Earlier conquerors had been absorbed by Indian society in greater or lesser measure; the Victorian British, thanks to a modern technology which continuously renewed their contacts with the homeland and their confidence in their intellectual and religious superiority, remained immune, increasingly aloof, as no earlier conqueror had been. They could not be untouched by India, as many legacies to the English language and the English breakfast and dinner table still testify, but they created a civilization that confronted India as a challenge, though not wholly English; "Anglo-Indian" in the nineteenth century was a word applied not to persons of mixed blood, but to Englishmen who made careers in India, and it indicated a cultural and social distinctiveness.

The mythology of the Mutiny is depicted in this 19th-century engraving of a battle between British and Indian troops.

THE INDIAN MUTINY

THE SEPARATENESS of Anglo-Indian society from India was made virtually absolute by the appalling damage done to British confidence by the rebellions of 1857 called the Indian Mutiny. Essentially, this was a chain reaction of outbreaks, initiated by a mutiny of Hindu soldiers who feared the polluting effect of using a new type of cartridge, greased with animal fat. This detail is significant. Much of the rebellion was the spontaneous and reactionary response of traditional society to innovation and modernization. By way of reinforcement there were the irritations of native rulers, both Muslim and Hindu, who regretted the loss of their privileges and thought that the chance might have come to recover their independence; the British were after all very few. The response of those few was prompt and ruthless. With the help of loyal Indian soldiers the rebellions were crushed, though not before there had been some massacres of British captives and a British force had been under siege at Lucknow, in rebel territory, for some months.

THE MUTINY'S MYTHICAL IMPORTANCE

The Mutiny and its suppression were disasters for British India, though not quite unmitigated. It did not much matter that the Moghul Empire was at last formally brought to an end by the British (the Delhi mutineers had proclaimed the last emperor their leader). Nor was there, as later Indian nationalists were to suggest, a crushing of a national liberation movement whose end was a tragedy for India. Like many episodes important in the making of nations, the Mutiny was to be important as a myth and an inspiration; what it was later believed to have been was more important than what it actually was, a jumble of essentially reactionary protests. Its really disastrous and important effect was the wound it gave to British goodwill and confidence. Whatever the expressed intentions of British policy, the consciousness of the British in India was from this time suffused by the memory that Indians had once proved almost fatally untrustworthy. Among Anglo-Indians as well as Indians the mythical importance of the Mutiny grew with time. The atrocities actually committed were bad enough, but others, which had never occurred, were also alleged as grounds for a policy of repression and social exclusiveness. Immediately and institutionally, the Mutiny also marked an epoch because it ended the government of the Company. The governor-general now became the queen's viceroy, responsible to a British cabinet minister. This structure provided the framework of the British Raj for its life of ninety years.

TRADE

The Mutiny changed Indian history, but by thrusting it more firmly in a direction to which it already tended. Another fact, which was equally revolutionary for India, was much more gradual in its effects. This was the nineteenth-century flowering of the economic connection with Great Britain. Commerce was the root of the British presence in the subcontinent and it continued to shape its destiny. The first major development came when India became the essential base for the China trade. Its greatest expansion came in the 1830s and 1840s when, for a number of reasons, access to China became much easier. It was at about the same time that there took place the first rapid rise in British exports to India, notably of textiles, so that, by the time of the Mutiny, a big Indian commercial interest existed, which involved many more

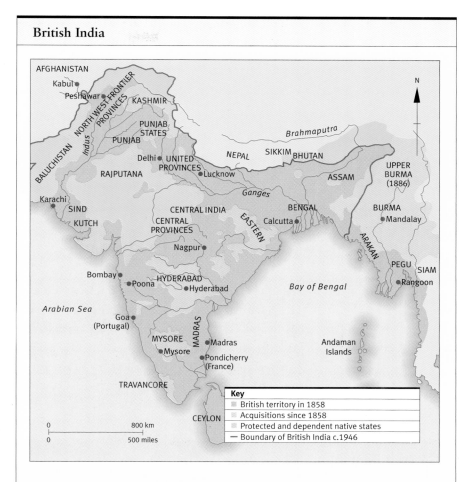

British India

Once the rebellions of the Indian Mutiny had been quashed in 1858, the old British East India Company was dissolved and India became a direct dominion of the British Crown.

However, the Indian principalities, ruled independently by their princes, survived until the end of the colonial period, although they were subject to British protectorate.

Englishmen and English commercial houses than the old Company had ever done.

The story of Anglo-Indian trade was now locked into that of the general expansion of British manufacturing supremacy and world commerce. The Suez Canal brought down the costs of shipping goods to Asia by a huge factor. By the end of the century the volume of British trade with India had more than quadrupled. The effects were felt in both countries, but were decisive in India, where a check was imposed on an industrialization which might have gone ahead more rapidly without British competition. Paradoxically, the growth of trade thus delayed India's modernization and alienation from its own past. But there were other forces at work, too. By the end of the century the framework provided by the Raj and the stimulus of the cultural influences it permitted had already made impossible the survival of wholly unmodernized India.

FRENCH IMPERIALISM

NO OTHER NATION in the early nineteenth century so extended its imperial possessions as Great Britain, but the French had also made substantial additions to the empire with which they had been left in 1815. In the next half-century France's interests elsewhere (in West Africa and the South Pacific, for example) were not lost to sight but the first clear sign of a reviving French imperialism came in Algeria. The whole of North Africa was open to imperial expansion by European predators because of the decay there of the formal overlordship of the Ottoman sultan. Right around the southern and eastern Mediterranean coasts the issue was posed of a possible Turkish partition. French interest in the area was natural; it went back to a great extension of the country's Levant trade in the eighteenth century. But a more precise marker had been an expedition to Egypt under Bonaparte in 1798, which opened the question of the Ottoman succession in the extra-European sphere.

Algeria's conquest began uncertainly in 1830. A series of wars not only with its native inhabitants but with the sultan of Morocco followed until, by 1870, most of the country had been subdued. This was, in fact, to open

This picture was painted in 1834 by the French artist Emile Vernet. Entitled *Arab Chiefs Meeting in Council*, it shows a scene from the French conquest of Algeria.

a new phase of expansion, for the French then turned their attention to Tunis, which accepted a French protectorate in 1881. To both these sometime Ottoman dependencies there now began a steady flow of European immigrants, not only from France, but from Italy and, later, Spain. This built up substantial settler populations in a few cities which were to complicate the story of French rule. The day was past when the African Algerians might have been exterminated or all but exterminated, like the Aztecs, American Indians or Australian Aborigines. Their society, in any case, was more resistant, formed in the crucible of an Islamic civilization which had once contested so successfully with Christendom. None the less, they suffered, notably from the introduction of land law which broke up their traditional usages and impoverished the peasants by exposing them to the full blast of market economics.

EGYPT

At the eastern end of the African littoral a national awakening in Egypt led to the emergence there of the first great modernizing nationalist leader outside the European world, Mehemet Ali, pasha of Egypt. Admiring Europe, he sought to borrow its ideas and techniques while asserting his independence of the sultan. When he was later called upon for help by the sultan against the Greek revolution, Mehemet Ali went on to attempt to seize Syria as his reward. This threat to the Ottoman Empire provoked an international crisis in the 1830s in which the French took his side. They were not successful, but thereafter French policy continued to interest itself in the Levant and Syria too, an interest which was eventually to bear fruit in the brief establishment in the twentieth century of a French presence in the area.

THE LAST IMPERIAL WAVE

The feeling that Great Britain and France had made good use of their opportunities in the early part of the nineteenth century was no doubt one reason why other powers tried to follow them from 1870 onwards. But envious emulation does not go far as an explanation of the extraordinary suddenness and vigour of what has sometimes been called the "imperialist wave" of the late nineteenth century. Outside Antarctica and the Arctic less than a fifth of the world's land surface was not under a European flag or that of a country of European settlement by 1914; and of this small fraction only Japan, Ethiopia and Siam enjoyed real autonomy.

Why this happened has been much debated. Clearly one part of the story is that of the sheer momentum of accumulated forces. The European hegemony became more and more irresistible as it built upon its own strength. The theory and ideology of imperialism were up to a point mere rationalizations of the huge power the European world suddenly found itself to possess. Practically, for example, as medicine began to master tropical infection and steam provided

The French infantry shoot at a band of retreating Algerian horsemen in November 1836. In spite of their apparent military superiority, however, the 1836 campaign was a disaster for the French.

quicker transport, it became easier to establish permanent bases in Africa and to penetrate its interior; the Dark Continent had long been of interest but its exploitation began to be feasible for the first time in the 1870s. Such technical developments made possible and attractive a spreading of European rule which could promote and protect trade and investment. The hopes such possibilities aroused were often ill-founded and usually disappointed. Whatever the appeal of "undeveloped estates" in Africa (as one British statesman imaginatively but misleadingly put it), or the supposedly vast market for consumer goods constituted by the penniless millions of China, industrial countries still found other industrial countries their best customers and trading partners. Former or existing colonies attracted more overseas capital investment than new acquisitions. By far the greatest part of British money invested abroad went to the United States and South America; French investors preferred Russia to Africa, and German money went to Turkey.

IMPERIAL RIVALRY

Economic expectation excited many individuals. Because of them, imperial expansion always had a random factor in it which makes it hard to generalize about. Explorers, traders and adventurers on many occasions took steps which led governments, willingly or not, to seize more territory. They were often popular heroes, for this most active phase of European imperialism coincided with a great growth of popular participation in public affairs. By buying newspapers, voting, or cheering in the streets, the masses were more and more involved in politics, which, among other things, emphasized imperial competition as a form of national rivalry. The

---

The "burden" of colonialism

The English author Rudyard Kipling (1865–1936) wrote a well-known exaltation of colonialism, which he portrayed as a burden taken on by the colonizers for the benefit of the colonized, in a poem in which he exhorted the United States to take on this role in the Philippines. It begins:

"Take up the White Man's Burden–
Send forth the best ye breed–
Go bind your sons to exile
To serve your captives' need;
To wait in heavy harness
On fluttered folk and wild–
Your new-caught, sullen peoples,
Half devil and half child.

"Take up the White Man's Burden–
In patience to abide,
To veil the threat of terror
And check the show of pride;
By open speech and simple,
A hundred times made plain,
To seek another's profit,
And work another's gain.

"Take up the White Man's Burden–
The savage wars of peace–
Fill full the mouth of Famine
And bid the sickness cease;
And when your goal is nearest
The end for others sought,
Watch Sloth and heathen Folly
Bring all your hope to nought."

The first three verses of "The White Man's Burden" by Rudyard Kipling, 1899.

---

new cheap press often pandered to this by dramatising exploration and colonial warfare. Some also thought that social dissatisfactions might be soothed by the contemplation of the extension of the rule of the national flag over new areas even when the experts knew that nothing was likely to be forthcoming except expense.

But cynicism is no more the whole story than is the profit motive. The idealism which inspired some imperialists certainly salved the conscience of many more. Those who believed that they possessed true civilization were bound to see the ruling of others for their good as a duty. Kipling's famous poem urged Americans to take up the White Man's Burden, not his Booty.

Many diverse elements were thus tangled together after 1870 in a context of changing inter-national relationships which imposed its own logic on colonial affairs. The story need not be explained in detail, but two continuing themes stand out. One is that, as the only truly worldwide imperial power, Great Britain quarrelled with other states over colonies more than anyone else – its possessions were everywhere. The centre of concerns was more than ever India; the acquisition of African territory to safeguard the Cape route and the new one via Suez, and frequent alarms over dangers to the lands which were India's northwestern and western glacis both showed this. Between 1870 and 1914 the only crises over non-European issues, which made war between Great Britain and another great power seem possible, arose over Russian dabblings in Afghanistan and a French attempt to establish themselves on the Upper Nile. British officials were also much concerned about French penetration of West Africa and Indo-China, and Russian influence in Persia.

IMPERIALISM AND EUROPEAN RELATIONS

International disagreements about colonial issues indicate the second continuing theme. Though European nations quarrelled about what happened overseas for forty years or so, and though the United States went to war with one of them (Spain), the partition by the great powers of the non-European world was amazingly peaceful. When a Great War at last broke out in 1914, Great Britain, Russia and France, the three nations which had quarrelled with one another most over imperial difficulties, would be on the same side; it was not overseas colonial rivalry which caused the conflict. Only once after 1900, in Morocco, did a real danger of war occasioned by a quarrel over non-European lands arise between two European great powers and here the issue was not really one of colonial rivalry, but of whether Germany could bully France without fear of her being supported by others. Quarrels over non-European affairs

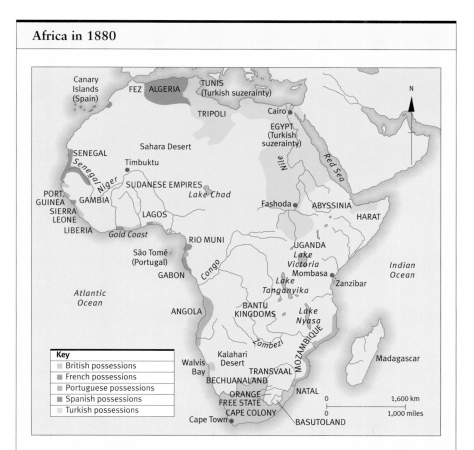

Africa in 1880

In 1880, European presence was limited to narrow coastal strips, with the exception of Algeria and Senegal and the British and the Boers in South Africa. The Turkish dominion over many areas was more theoretical than real. In little more than a decade, the panorama would change drastically, with most of the continent coming under European rule.

Africa in 1914

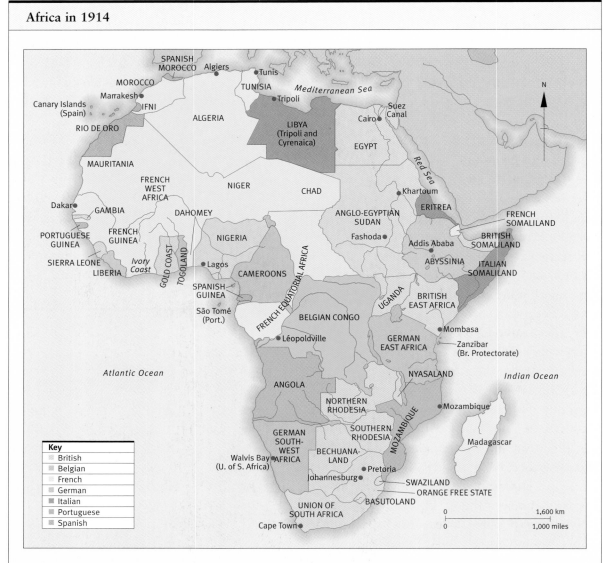

By 1914 all of Africa was under European domination, except for Liberia, which an American society had founded in 1816 as a state in which emancipated slaves could settle, and Abyssinia (Ethiopia), a Christian kingdom which defeated one Italian invasion attempt in 1896, only to succumb to a second in 1936.

before 1914 seem in fact to have been a positive distraction from the more dangerous rivalries of Europe itself; they may even have helped to preserve European peace.

THE SCRAMBLE FOR AFRICA

IMPERIAL RIVALRY had its own momentum. When one power got a new concession or a colony, it almost always spurred on others to go one better. The imperialist wave was in this way self-feeding. By 1914 the most striking results were to be seen in Africa. The activities of explorers, missionaries, and the campaigners against slavery early in the nineteenth century had encouraged the belief that extension of European rule in the "Dark Continent" was a matter of spreading enlightenment and humanitarianism – the blessings of civilization, in fact. On the African coasts, centuries of trade had shown that desirable products were available in the interior. The whites at the Cape were already pushing further inland (often because of Boer resentment of British rule). Such facts made up an explosive mixture, which was set off in 1881 when a British force was sent to Egypt to secure that country's government against a nationalist revolution whose success (it was feared) might threaten the safety of the Suez Canal. The corrosive power of European culture – for this was the source of the ideas of the Egyptian nationalists – thus both touched off another stage in the decline of the Ottoman Empire of which Egypt was still formally a part and launched what was called the "Scramble for Africa".

THE PARTITION OF AFRICA

The British had hoped to withdraw their soldiers from Egypt quickly; in 1914 they were still there. British officials were by then virtually running the administration of the country while, to the south, Anglo-Egyptian rule had been pushed deep into the Sudan. Meanwhile, Turkey's western provinces in Libya and Tripoli had been taken by the Italians (who felt unjustly kept out of Tunisia by the French protectorate there), Algeria was French, and the French enjoyed a fairly free hand in Morocco, except where the Spanish were installed. Southwards from Morocco to the Cape of Good Hope, the coastline was entirely divided between the British, French, Germans, Spanish, Portuguese and Belgians, with the exception of the isolated black republic of Liberia. The empty wastes of the Sahara were French; so was the basin of the Senegal and much of the northern side of that of the Congo. The Belgians were installed in the rest of it on what was soon to prove some

of the richest mineral-bearing land in Africa. Further east, British territories ran from the Cape up to Rhodesia and the Congo border. On the east coast they were cut off from the sea by Tanganyika (which was German) and Portuguese East Africa. From Mombasa, Kenya's port, a belt of British territory stretched through Uganda to the borders of the Sudan and the headwaters of the Nile. Somalia and Eritrea (in British, Italian and French hands) isolated Ethiopia, the only African country other than Liberia still independent of European rule. The ruler of this ancient but Christian polity was the only non-European ruler of the nineteenth century to avert the threat of colonization by a military success, the annihilation of an Italian army at Adowa in 1896. Other Africans did not have the power to resist successfully, as the French suppression of Algerian revolt in 1871, the Portuguese mastery (with some difficulty) of insurrection in Angola in 1902 and again in 1907, the British destruction of the Zulu and Matabele, and, worst of all, the German massacre of the Herrero of South West Africa in 1907, all showed.

An Egyptian garrison prepares to defend a fortress in Sudan from the approach of Mahdist troops in an engraving dated 1884. Two years earlier, Egypt had become a British protectorate. At that time, Egyptian rule of Sudan, an inheritance from the Ottoman era, was threatened by an uprising led by a religious leader, the Mahdi. He died in 1885 and in 1898, his successor, the Khalifa, was defeated by the British.

This photograph of Adjiki-Toffia, King of Dahomey, was taken in 1908. The king, with his subjects prostrated before him, is wearing a European uniform – his kingdom had been conquered by the French in 1892.

THE EFFECTS OF COLONIALISM

The colossal extension of European power, for the most part achieved after 1881, transformed African history. It was the most important change since the arrival in the continent of Islam. The bargains of European negotiators, the accidents of discovery and the convenience of colonial administrations in the end settled the ways in which modernization came to Africa. The suppression of intertribal warfare and the introduction of even elementary medical services released population growth in some areas. As in America centuries earlier, the introduction of new crops made it possible to feed more people. Different colonial régimes had different cultural and economic impact, however. Long after the colonialists had gone, there would be big distinctions between countries where, say,

French administration or British judicial practice had taken root. All over the continent Africans found new patterns of employment, learnt something of European ways through European schools or service in colonial regiments, saw different things to admire or hate in the white man's ways which now came to regulate their lives. Even when, as in some British possessions, great emphasis was placed on rule through native institutions, they had henceforth to work in a new context. Tribal and local unities would go on asserting themselves but more and more did so against the grain of new structures created by colonialism and left as a legacy of independent Africa. Christian monogamy, entrepreneurial attitudes, new knowledge (to which the way had been opened by European languages, the most important of all the cultural implants), all contributed finally to a new self-consciousness and greater individualism. From such influences would emerge the new African élites of the twentieth century. Without imperialism, for good or ill, those influences could never have been so effective so fast.

AFRICA'S IMPACT ON EUROPE

Europe, by contrast, was hardly changed by the African adventure. Clearly, it was important that Europeans could lay their hands on yet more easily exploitable wealth, yet probably only Belgium drew from Africa resources making a real difference to its national future. Sometimes, too, the exploiting of Africa aroused political opposition in European countries; there was more than a touch of the *conquistadores* about some late nineteenth-century adventurers. The administration of the Congo by the Belgian king Leopold and forced labour in Portuguese Africa were notorious examples, but there were other places where Africa's natural resources – human and material – were ruthlessly exploited or despoiled in the interests of profit by Europeans with the connivance of imperial authorities, and this soon created an anti-colonial movement. Some nations recruited African soldiers, though not for service in Europe, where only the French hoped to employ them to offset the weight of German numbers. Some countries hoped for outlets for emigration which would ease social problems, but the opportunities presented by Africa for European residence were very mixed. There were two large blocks of white settlement in the south, and the British would later open up Kenya and Rhodesia, where there were lands suitable for white farmers. Apart from this, there were the Europeans in the cities of French North Africa, and a growing community of Portuguese planters in Angola. The hopes

entertained of Africa as an outlet for Italians, on the other hand, were disappointed, while German immigration was tiny and almost entirely temporary. Some European countries – Russia, Austria, Hungary and the nations of Scandinavia – sent virtually no settlers to Africa at all.

IMPERIALISM IN ASIA AND THE PACIFIC

Of course, there was much more than Africa to the story of nineteenth century imperial-

Under colonial rule, some aspects of the traditional African way of life remained practically unchanged. These Nubian children, depicted protecting their crops from birds, were painted by the French artist Maurice Berchère.

ism. The Pacific was partitioned less dramatically but in the end no independent political unit survived among its island peoples. There was also a big expansion of British, French and Russian territory in Asia. The French established themselves in Indo-China, the British in Malaya and Burma, which they took to safeguard the approaches to India. Siam retained her independence because it suited both powers to have a buffer between them. The British also asserted their superiority by an expedition to Tibet, with similar considerations of Indian security in mind. Most of these areas, like much of the zone of Russian overland expansion, were formally under Chinese suzerainty. Their story is part of that of the crumbling Chinese Empire, a story which paralleled the corrosion of other empires, such as the Ottoman, Moroccan and Persian, by European influence, though it had

greater importance still for world history. At one moment it looked as if a Scramble for China might follow the partition of Africa. That story is better considered elsewhere. Here it is convenient to notice that the imperialist wave in the Chinese sphere as in the Pacific was also importantly different from that in Africa because the United States of America took part.

AMERICAN IMPERIALISM

AMERICANS HAD ALWAYS been uneasy and distrustful over imperial ventures outside the continent they long regarded as God-given to them. Even at its most arrogant, imperialism had to be masked, muffled and muted in the republic in a way unnecessary in Europe. The very creation of the United States had

In the 19th century, the Pacific islands became a refuge for many Europeans in search of a new life far away from "civilization". The French post-Impressionist painter Paul Gauguin (1848–1903), whose *Tahitian Women at the Beach* is shown here, settled in Tahiti in 1891 and remained there for most of the rest of his life.

The port of Pago Pago, the capital of American Samoa, is depicted in 1886.

been by successful rebellion against an imperial power. The constitution contained no provision for the ruling of colonial possessions and it was always very difficult to see what could be the position under it of territories which could not be envisaged as eventually moving towards full statehood, let alone that of non-Americans who stayed under American rule. On the other hand, there was much that was barely distinguishable from imperialism in the nineteenth-century territorial expansion of the United States, although Americans might not recognize it when it was packaged as a "Manifest Destiny". The most blatant examples were the war of 1812 against the British and the treatment of Mexico in the middle of the century. But there was also the dispossession of the Indians to consider and the dominating implications of the Monroe doctrine.

In the 1890s the overland expansion of the United States was complete. It was announced that the continuous frontier of domestic settlement no longer existed. At this moment, economic growth had given great importance to the influence of business interests in American government, sometimes expressed in terms of economic nationalism and high tariff protection. Some of these interests directed the attention of American

public opinion abroad, notably to Asia. The United States was thought by some to be in danger of exclusion from trade there by the European powers. There was an old connection at stake (the first American Far Eastern squadron had been sent out in the 1820s) as a new era of Pacific awareness dawned with California's rapid growth in population. A half-century's talk of a canal across Central America also came to a head at the end of the century; it stimulated interest in the doctrines of strategists who suggested that the United States might need an oceanic glacis in the Pacific to maintain the Monroe doctrine.

RAPID EXPANSION

All these currents flowed into a burst of expansion which has remained to this day a unique example of American overseas imperialism because, for a time, it set aside traditional restraint on the acquisition of new territory overseas. The beginnings lie in the increased opening of China and Japan to American commerce in the 1850s and 1860s and to participation with the British and the Germans in the administration of Samoa (where a naval base obtained in 1878 has remained a United States possession). This was followed by two decades of growing intervention in the affairs of the kingdom of Hawaii, to which the protection of the United States had been extended since the 1840s. American traders and missionaries had established themselves there in large numbers. Benevolent patronage of the Hawaiians then gave way to attempts to engineer annexation to the United States in the 1890s. Washington already had the use of Pearl Harbor as a naval base but was led to land marines in Hawaii when a revolution occurred there. In the end, the government had to give way to the forces set in motion by the settlers and a short-lived Hawaiian Republic was annexed as a United States Territory in 1898.

SPANISH COLONIES FALL TO AMERICA

In 1898, a mysterious explosion destroyed an American cruiser, the USS *Maine*, in Havana harbour. This led to a war with Spain. In the background was both the long Spanish failure to master revolt in Cuba, where American business interests were prominent and American sentiment was aroused, and the growing awareness of the importance of the Caribbean approaches to a future canal across the isthmus. In Asia, American help was given to another rebel movement against the Spaniards in the Philippines. When American rule replaced Spanish in Manila, the rebels turned against their former allies and a guerrilla war began. This was the first phase of a long and difficult process of disentangling the United States from her first Asian colony. At that moment, given the likelihood of the collapse of the Chinese Empire, it seemed best in Washington not to withdraw. In the Caribbean, the long history of Spanish empire in the Americas at last came to an end. Puerto Rico passed to the United States and Cuba obtained its independence on terms which guaranteed its domination by the

A merican soldiers and native Muslims on the Philippine island of Mindanao are seen in a photograph dating from 1900. Having usurped Spain as the ruling colonial power, the Americans had to face the same guerrillas who had fought against Spain.

United States. American forces went back to occupy the island under these terms from 1906 to 1909, and again in 1917.

THE PANAMA CANAL

The end of Spanish rule in the Caribbean was the prelude to the last major development in this wave of American imperialism. The building of an isthmian canal had been canvassed since the middle of the nineteenth century and the completion of Suez gave it new plausibility. American diplomacy negotiated a way around the obstacle of possible British participation; all seemed plain sailing but a snag arose in 1903 when a treaty providing for the acquisition of a canal zone from Colombia was rejected by the Colombians. A revolution was engineered in Panama, where the canal was to run. The United States prevented its suppression by the Colombian government and a new Panamanian republic emerged, which gratefully bestowed upon the United States the necessary territory together with the right to intervene in its affairs to maintain order. The work could now begin and the canal was opened in 1914.

The Panama Canal

The Portuguese seafarer Antonio Galvao was the first person to suggest the idea of opening a canal in the Isthmus of Darién in Panama, in a book he wrote in 1550. As for the Suez Canal, it was a group of French financiers who obtained the concession to build a canal which would join Colón on the Atlantic coast to Panama on the Pacific. Ferdinand de Lesseps, the French diplomat who had spearheaded the Suez project, formed the Compagnie Universelle du Canal Interocéanique in 1879. Work began the following year on the canal, but the enterprise, having cost 287 million dollars and more than 20,000 lives, had to be abandoned in 1889 when the company went bankrupt.

In 1903, the United States government supported Panama's independence and obtained in exchange permission to open up the canal. The chief engineer of the US Isthmian Canal Commission, John F. Stevens, drew up the final plans in 1906. He favoured a high-level rather than a sea-level canal – a system of interconnecting lakes and six pairs of enormous locks were built to enable vessels to navigate the 85ft (26m) difference between sea level and the level of the highest lake, Lake Gatún.

Although the workers were mainly spared the bouts of malaria and yellow fever that had cursed the French project, technical problems dogged the construction process. The worst of these occurred at the Gaillard Cut, where an 8 mile (12km) artificial canyon had to be dug through the mountain. Internal pressure forced the excavated earth upwards and caused landslides in the canyon walls. What was initially planned as a narrow gorge became a huge valley with gently sloping sides.

Since the canal's official opening in 1914, it has been controlled by the United States. Under the terms of the 1977 Treaty of Panama, sovereignty of the canal passed to the Republic of Panama in the year 2000. It is feared, however, that a recent fall in the volume of water in its tributaries may endanger the canal's system in the coming years.

The SS Ancon *approaches the Cucaracha Slide on 15 August, 1914. The* Ancon *was the first ship to pass through the Panama Canal.*

The possibility of transferring ships rapidly from one ocean to another made a great difference to American naval strategy. It was also the background to the "corollary" to the Monroe doctrine proposed by President Theodore Roosevelt; when the Canal Zone became the key to the naval defence of the hemisphere, it was more important than ever to assure its protection by stable government and United States predominance in the Caribbean states. A new vigour in American intervention in them was soon evident.

THE COLONIAL WORLD

Though its motives and techniques were different – for one thing, there was virtually no permanent American settlement in the new possessions – the actions of the United States can be seen as part of the last great seizure of territories carried out by the European peoples. Almost all of them had taken part except the South Americans; even the Queenslanders had tried to annexe New Guinea. By 1914 a third of the world's surface was under two flags, those of the United Kingdom and Russia (though how much Russian territory should be regarded as colonial is, of course, debatable). To take a measure which excludes Russia, in 1914 the United Kingdom ruled 400 million subjects outside its own borders, France over fifty million and Germany and Italy about fourteen million each; this was an unprecedented aggregation of formal authority.

At that date, though, there were already signs that imperialism overseas had run out of steam. China had proved a disappointment and there was little left to divide, though Germany and Great Britain discussed the possibility of partitioning the Portuguese Empire, which seemed to be about to follow the Spanish. The most likely area left for further European imperialism was the decaying Ottoman Empire, and its dissolution seemed at last to be imminent when the Italians seized Tripoli in 1912 and a Balkan coalition formed against Turkey took away almost all that was left of her European territories in the following year. Such a prospect did not seem likely to be so free from conflict between great powers as had been the partition of Africa; much more crucial issues would be at stake in it for them.

King George V and Queen Mary of Britain appear on the wall of the Red Fort in Delhi in 1911 during the Coronation Durbar. This was the first visit to India by a reigning British monarch and it was hoped that the dazzling spectacle would revive Indian subjects' loyalty to the Crown. The event failed, however, to curtail the Indian independence movement, which was already well under way.

3 ASIA'S RESPONSE TO A EUROPEANIZING WORLD

A PERCEPTIVE CHINESE OBSERVER might have found something revealing in the disgrace which in the end overtook the Jesuits, at first so acceptable, at K'ang-hsi's court. For more than a century these able men had judiciously and discreetly sought to ingratiate themselves with their hosts. To begin with they had not even spoken of religion, but had contented themselves with studying the language of China. They had even worn Chinese dress, which, we are told, created a very good impression. Great successes had followed. Yet the effectiveness of their mission was suddenly paralysed; their acceptance of Chinese rites and beliefs and their Sinicizing of Christian teaching led to the sending of two papal emissaries to China to check improper flexibility. Here, for historians, if not for contemporaries, was a sign that Europeans, unlike other intruders, might not in the end succumb to its cultural pull.

There was a message for all Asia in this revelation of the intransigence of European culture. It was going to be more important to what was about to happen in Asia – and was already under way there – than even the technology of the newcomers. It was certainly more decisive than any temporary or special weaknesses of the Eastern empires, as China's own history was to show. Under K'ang-hsi's immediate successors, the Manchu empire was already past its peak; its slow and eventually fatal decline would not have in itself been surprising given the cyclical pattern of dynastic rise and fall in the past. What made the fate of the Ch'ing (Qing) dynasty different from that of its predecessors was that it survived long enough to preside over the country while it faced a quite new threat, one from a culture stronger than that of traditional China. For the first time in nearly two thousand years, Chinese society would have to change, not the imported culture of a new wave of barbarian conquerors. The Chinese Revolution was about to begin.

A Ch'ing emperor is depicted in the gardens of his harem. The Ch'ing (Qing) dynasty, of Manchu origins, ruled China from 1644 to 1912.

CHINESE CONFIDENCE

In the eighteenth century, no Chinese official could have been expected to predict the eventual decline of the Manchu empire. When Lord Macartney arrived in 1793 to ask for equality of diplomatic representation and free trade, the confidence of centuries was unshaken. The first Western advances and encroachments had been successfully rebuffed or contained. The representative of George III could only take back polite but unyielding messages of refusal to what the Chinese emperor was pleased to call "the lonely remoteness of your island, cut off from the world by intervening wastes of sea". It can hardly have made the message more palatable that George was also patted on the back for his "submissive loyalty in sending this tribute mission" and encouraged to "show even greater devotion and loyalty in future".

The assumption of their own cultural and moral superiority came naturally to the educated Chinese as it was to do to the European and American missionaries and philanthropists of the next century who unconsciously patronized the people they came to serve. It embodied the Chinese world view, in which all nations paid tribute to the emperor, possessed of the Mandate of Heaven, and took it for granted that China already had all the materials and skills needed for the highest civilization and would only waste her time and energy in indulging relations with Europe going beyond the limited trade tolerated at Canton (where by 1800 there were perhaps a thousand Europeans). Nor was this obviously nonsense. Nearly three centuries of trade with China had failed to reveal any manufactured goods from Europe which the Chinese

This 19th-century engraving depicts the preparations for a wedding in a luxurious Chinese mansion. Although Western influences were present in many parts of China at the time, they had hardly touched the traditional Chinese way of life.

wanted except the mechanical toys and clocks they found amusing. European trade with China rested on the export to her of silver or other Asian products. As a British merchant concisely put it in the middle of the eighteenth century, the "East India trade ... exports our bullion, spends little of our product or manufactures and brings in commodities perfectly manufactured which hinder the consumption of our own".

POPULATION PRESSURE AND INFLATION

Yet for all official China's confidence in her internal régime and cultural superiority, signs

Time chart (1839–1912)

	1850–1864 The Taiping insurrection in China	1885 The Indian National Congress is founded	1899–1900 Boxer Rebellion in China	1911–1912 Chinese Republican revolution
1800	**1850**			**1900**
1839–1842 The first Opium War	1868 "Meiji Restoration" in Japan	1894–1895 Sino-Japanese War	1904–1905 War between Russia and Japan	

of future difficulties can be discerned in retrospect. The secret societies and cults, which kept alive a smouldering national resentment against a foreign dynasty and the central power, still survived and even prospered. They found fresh support as the surge of population became uncontainable; in the century before 1850 numbers seem to have more than doubled to reach about 430 million by 1850. Pressure on cultivated land became much more acute because the area worked could be increased only by a tiny margin; times grew steadily harder and the lot of the peasantry more and more miserable. There had been warning signs in the 1770s and 1780s, when a century's internal peace was disturbed by revolts of a regional and religious nature. Early in the next century anti-government activity became more frequent and destructive. To make matters worse, these political disturbances were accompanied by another economic deterioration, inflation in the price of the silver in which taxes had to be paid. Most daily transactions (including the payment of wages) were carried out in copper, so this added to the crushing burdens already suffered by the poor. Yet none of this seemed likely to be fatal, except, possibly, to the

dynasty. It could all be fitted into the traditional pattern of the historic cycle. All that was required was that the service gentry should remain loyal, and even if they did not, then, though a collapse of government might follow, there was no reason to believe that in due course another dynasty would not emerge to re-enlist their loyalty and preserve the imperial framework of an unchanging China. This time, though, it was not to happen like that, because of the drive and power of the nineteenth-century barbarian challenge.

THE OPIUM WAR

The inflation itself was a result of China's changing relations with the outside world which within a few decades made nonsense of the reception given to Macartney. Before 1800 the West could offer China little that she wanted except silver, but within the next three decades of the nineteenth century this ceased to be so, largely because British traders at last found a commodity the Chinese wanted and India could supply: opium. Naval expeditions forced the Chinese to open their country to sale (albeit at first under certain restrictions) of this drug, but the "Opium War", which began in 1839, ended in 1842 with a treaty which registered a fundamental change in China's relations with the West. The Canton monopoly and the tributary status of the foreigner came to an end together. Once the British had kicked ajar the door to Western trade, others were to follow them through it.

GROWING SUBVERSION

Unwittingly, the government of Queen Victoria had launched the Chinese Revolution. The 1840s opened a period of

A British ship, the HMS *Leopard*, is pictured in dock at Shanghai in the mid-19th century. The whole Yangtze valley area came under British influence when China was forced to open up to international trade.

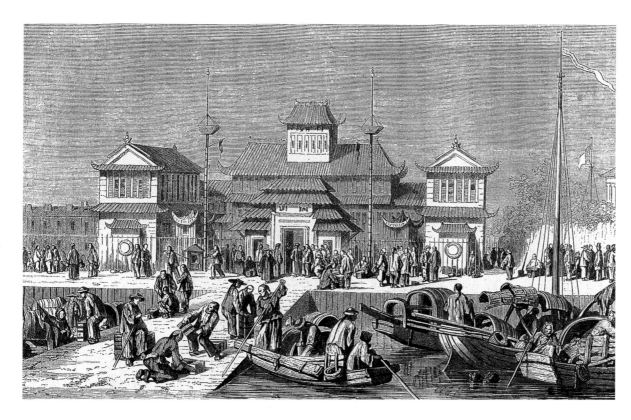

This contemporary engraving shows how busy Shanghai's customs wharf was by the 1850s.

upheaval which took over a century to come to completion. The revolution would slowly reveal itself as a double repudiation, both of the foreigner and of much of the Chinese past. The first would increasingly express itself in the nationalist modes and idioms of the progressive European world. Because such ideological forces could not be contained within the traditional framework, they would in the end prove fatal to it, when the Chinese sought to remove the obstacles to modernization and national power. More than a century after the Opium War the Chinese Revolution finally shattered for good a social system which had been the foundation of Chinese life for thousands of years. By that time, though, much of old China would already have vanished. By that time, too, it would appear that China's troubles had also been a part of an ever wider upheaval, a Hundred Years' War of Asia and the West whose turning-point came in the early twentieth century.

HOSTILITY TO WESTERNERS

The implications of the growing European influence in China matured only slowly. In the beginning, Western encroachments in China usually produced only a simple, xenophobic hostility and even this was not universal. After all, for a long time very few Chinese were directly or obviously much concerned with the coming of the foreigners. A few (notably Canton merchants involved in the foreign trade) even sought accommodation with them. Hostility was a matter of anti-British mobs in the towns and of the rural gentry. At first many officials saw the problem as a limited one: that of the addiction of the subjects of the empire to a dangerous drug. They were humiliated, in particular, by the weaknesses which this revealed in their own people and administration; there was much connivance and corruption involved in the opium trade. They do not at first seem to have seen the deeper

Manchu China 1644–1912

In 1644, the invasion of China by the Manchus put an end to the Ming dynasty. The invaders founded the new Ch'ing dynasty, which was to rule over this vast country for two and a half centuries. It was not long before the Ch'ing emperors were facing Russian pressure on China's northern frontiers. However, the pressure exerted by the rest of the Western world, which increased significantly by the mid-19th century, represented a much greater threat to political stability in Manchu China.

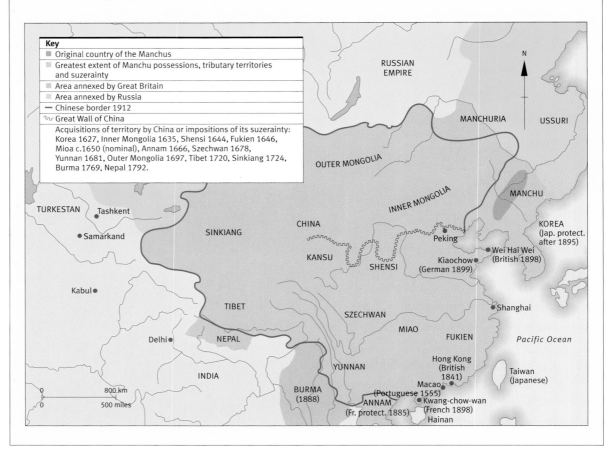

Key
- Original country of the Manchus
- Greatest extent of Manchu possessions, tributary territories and suzerainty
- Area annexed by Great Britain
- Area annexed by Russia
- Chinese border 1912
- Great Wall of China

Acquisitions of territory by China or impositions of its suzerainty: Korea 1627, Inner Mongolia 1635, Shensi 1644, Fukien 1646, Mioa c.1650 (nominal), Annam 1666, Szechwan 1678, Yunnan 1681, Outer Mongolia 1697, Tibet 1720, Sinkiang 1724, Burma 1769, Nepal 1792.

issue of the future, that of the questioning of an entire order, or have sensed a cultural threat; China had suffered defeats in the past and its culture had survived unscathed.

The first portent of a deeper danger came when, in the 1840s, the imperial government had to concede that missionary activity was legal. Though still limited, this was obviously corrosive of tradition. Officials in the Confucian mould who felt its danger stirred up popular feeling against missionaries – whose efforts made them easy targets – and there were scores of riots in the 1850s and 1860s. Such demonstrations often made things worse. Sometimes foreign consuls would be drawn in; exceptionally a gunboat would be sent. The Chinese government's prestige would suffer in the ensuing exchange of apologies and punishment of culprits. Meanwhile, the activity of the missionaries was steadily undermining the traditional society in more direct and didactic ways by preaching an individualism and egalitarianism alien to it and by acting as a magnet to converts to whom it offered economic and social advantages. The inability of the imperial government to stamp out Christianity was a telling indicator of the limits if its power.

PEASANT REVOLTS

The process of undermining China also went forward directly by military and naval means; there were further impositions of concessions by force. But there was a growing ambiguity in the Chinese response. The authorities did not always resist the arrival of the foreigners. First the gentry of the areas immediately concerned and then the Peking (Beijing) government came round to feeling that foreign soldiers might not be without their value for the régime. Social disorder was growing. It could not be canalized solely against the foreigners and was threatening the establishment; China was beginning to undergo a cycle of peasant revolts which were to be the greatest in the whole of human history. In the middle decades of the century the familiar indicators multiplied: banditry, secret societies. In the 1850s the "Red Turbans" were suppressed only at great cost. Such troubles frightened the establishment, and threw it on to the defensive, leaving it with little spare capacity to resist the steady gnawing of the West. These great rebellions were fundamentally caused by hunger for land and the most important and distinctive of them was the Taiping rebellion or, as it may more appropriately be called, revolution, which lasted from 1850 to 1864.

THE TAIPING REBELLION

THE HEART of this great convulsion, which cost the lives of more people than died the world over in the First World War, was a traditional peasant revolt. Hard times and a succession of natural disasters had helped to provoke it. It drew on a compound of land hunger, hatred of tax-gatherers, social envy and national resentment against the Manchus (though it is hard to see exactly what this meant in practice, for most of the officials who actually administered the empire were, of course, themselves Chinese). It was also a regional outbreak, originating in the south and even there promoted by an isolated minority of settlers from the north. The new feature behind the revolt, and one which made it ambiguous in the eyes of both Chinese and Europeans, was that its leader, Hung Hsiu-ch'uan, had a superficial but impressive acquaintance with the Christian religion in the form of American Protestantism. This led him not only to rewrite the Decalogue with a new emphasis on filial piety, but, among other things, to denounce the worship of other gods and destroy idols and to talk of establishing the kingdom of God on earth. He felt rejected by his own culture, for he had been unsuccessful in the examinations which conferred status on low-born Chinese. Within the familiar framework of one of the periodic peasant upheavals of old China, that is to say, a new ideology was at work and showing itself subversive of the traditional culture and state. Some of its opponents at once grasped this and saw the movement as an ideological as well as a social challenge. Thus the Taiping rebellion can be seen as an epoch in the Western disruption of China.

TAIPING IDEOLOGY

The Taiping army at first had a series of spectacular successes. By 1853 they had captured Nanking and established there the court of Hung Hsiu-ch'uan, now proclaimed the "Heavenly King". In spite of alarm

The Heavenly Kingdom of the Taiping

The Taiping rebellion, inspired by its curious mixture of Chinese traditions and Protestant Christian influences, resulted in the bloodiest internal struggle in Chinese history.

The Taiping leader Hung Hsiu-ch'uan had convinced himself, through reading Christian texts and from visions he claimed to have had during an illness, that he was the younger brother of Christ and that his Father had charged him with the mission of liberating the Chinese people from the diabolical Manchu domination and showing them how to live in accordance with God's divine plan: the Great Peace. Hung Hsiu-ch'uan recruited a large army of discontented peasants, miners and charcoal workers from

the district of central Kwangsi. This army eventually took the important city of Nanking in 1853.

Although his followers executed homosexuals and prostitutes in the name of their leader's strict sexual morals, the "Heavenly King", once installed at Nanking, retired with his dozens of wives to a court made up exclusively of women. His officers soon began to fight among themselves. The movement's popularity waned: local people were alienated by its anti-Confucian stance; the poor Taiping followers felt let down by failure of the land redistribution scheme. In 1864, the imperial troops, armed with Western weapons and partly under the command of foreign generals, seized Nanking and quashed the rebellion.

This contemporary painting depicts the imperial Chinese troops launching their attack on the Taiping rebels at Tai. The rebels, outnumbered and ill-equipped, are shown beating a hasty retreat.

further north, though, this was as far as they went. After 1856 the revolution was on the defensive. Nevertheless, it announced important social changes (which were to be praised later by Chinese reformers) and although it is by no means clear how widely these were effective or even appealing, they had real

disruptive ideological effects. The basis of Taiping social doctrine was not private property but communal provision for general needs. The land was in theory distributed for working in plots graded by quality to provide just shares. Even more revolutionary was the proclaimed extension of social and educational equality to women. The traditional binding of their feet was forbidden and a measure of sexual austerity marked the movement's aspirations (though not the conduct of the "Heavenly King" himself). All this reflected the mixture of religious and social elements which lay at the root of the Taiping cult and threatened the traditional order.

CHINESE CONCESSIONS TO EUROPEANS

The Taiping movement benefited at first from the demoralization brought about in the Manchu forces by their defeats at the hands of the Europeans and from the usual weaknesses shown by central government in China in a region relatively remote and distinct. As time passed and the Manchu forces were given abler (sometimes European) commanders, the bows and spears of the Taipings proved insufficient. The foreigners, too, came to see the movement as a threat but kept up their pressure on the imperial government while it grappled with the Taipings. Treaties with France and the United States, which followed that with Great Britain, guaranteed the toleration of Christian missionaries and began the process of reserving jurisdiction over foreigners to consular and mixed courts. The danger from the Taiping brought yet more concessions: the opening of more Chinese ports to foreign trade, the introduction to the Chinese customs administration of foreign superiors, the legalization of the sale of opium and the cession to the Russians of the province in which Vladivostok was to be built. It is hardly surprising that in 1861 the Chinese decided for the first time to set up a new department to deal with foreign affairs. The old myth that all the world recognized the Mandate of Heaven and owed tribute to the imperial court was dead.

In the end, the foreigners joined in against the Taipings. Whether their help was needed to end it is hard to say; certainly the movement was already failing. In 1864 Hung died and shortly afterwards Nanking fell to the Manchu. This was a victory for traditional China: the rule of the bureaucratic gentry had survived one more threat from below. None the less, an important turning-point had been reached. A rebellion had offered a revolutionary programme announcing a new danger, that the old challenge of peasant rebellion might be reinforced by an ideology from

This 1882 engraving depicts a Catholic missionary school in Peking. The image of Christ is surrounded by inscriptions in Chinese characters.

POTTIN.DEL.

Dated 1879, this engraving shows a Chinese market. Even in the latter part of the 19th century, there was still practically no Western presence in most of China.

outside deeply corrosive to Confucian China. Nor did the end of the Taiping rebellion mean internal peace; from the middle of the 1850s until well into the 1870s there were great Muslim risings in the northwest and southwest as well as other rebellions.

A KIND OF COLONIALISM

IMMEDIATELY AFTER THE SUPPRESSION of the Taiping rebellion, China showed even greater weakness in the face of the Western barbarians. Large areas had been devastated in the fighting; in many of them the soldiers were powerful and threatened the control of the bureaucracy. If the enormous loss of life did something to reduce pressure on land, this was probably balanced by a decline in the prestige and authority of the dynasty. Concessions had already had to be made to the Western powers under and because of these disadvantaged conditions; between 1856 and 1860 British and French forces were engaged every year against the Chinese.

A treaty in 1861 brought to nineteen the number of "treaty ports" open to Western merchants and provided for a permanent British ambassador at Peking. Meanwhile, the Russians exploited the Anglo-French successes to secure the opening of their entire border with China to trade. Further concessions would follow. It was evident that methods which had drawn the sting of nomadic invaders were not likely to work with confident Europeans, whose ideological assurance and increasing technical superiority protected them from the seduction of Chinese civilization. When Roman Catholic missionaries were given the right to buy land and put up buildings Christianity was linked to economic penetration; soon the wish to protect converts meant involvement in the internal affairs of public order and police. It was impossible to contain the slow but continuous erosion of Chinese sovereignty. Never formally a colony, China was beginning none the less to undergo a measure of colonization.

Then there were territorial losses as the century wore on. In the 1870s the Russians seized the Ili valley (though they later handed much of it back) and in the next decade the French established a protectorate in Annam. Loosely asserted but ancient Chinese suzerainty was being swept away; the French began to absorb Indo-China and the British annexed Burma in 1886. The worst blow came from another Asiatic state; in the war of 1894–5 the Japanese took Formosa and the Pescadores, while China had to recognize the independence of Korea, from which they had received tribute since the seventeenth century. Following the Japanese success came further encroachments by other powers, provoked by the Russians, who established themselves in Port Arthur. Britain, France and Germany all extracted long leases of ports at the end of the century. Before this, the Portuguese, who had been in China longer than any other

Europeans, converted their tenure of Macao into outright ownership. Even the Italians were in the market, though they did not actually get anything. And long before this, concessions, loans and agreements had been exacted by Western powers to protect and foster their own economic and financial interests. It is hardly surprising that when a British prime minister spoke at the end of the century of two classes of nation, the "living and the dying", China was regarded as an outstanding example of the second. Statesmen began to envisage her partition.

ATTEMPTS AT REFORM

Before the end of the nineteenth century it became clear to many Chinese intellectuals and civil servants that the traditional order would not generate the energy necessary to resist the new barbarians. Attempts along the old lines had failed. New tendencies began to appear. A "society for the study of self-strengthening" was founded to consider Western ideas and inventions which might be helpful. Its leaders cited the achievements of Peter the Great and, more significantly, those of contemporary reformers in Japan, an example all the more telling because of the superiority shown by the Japanese over China in war in 1895. Yet the would-be reformers still hoped that they would be able to root change in the Confucian tradition, albeit one purified and invigorated. They were members of the gentry and they succeeded in obtaining the ear of the emperor; they were thus working within the traditional framework and machinery of power to obtain administrative and technological reform without compromising the fundamentals of Chinese culture and ideology.

Unfortunately this meant that the Hundred Days of Reform of 1898 (as the

brief ascendancy of the reformers came to be known) was almost at once tangled up in the court politics of the rivalry between the emperor and the dowager empress, to say nothing of Chinese–Manchu antagonism. Though a stream of reform edicts was published, they were swiftly overtaken by a *coup d'état* by the empress, who locked up the emperor. The basic cause of the reformers' failure was the provocation offered by their inept political behaviour. Yet although they had failed, it was important that their initiative had taken place at all. It was to be a great stimulus to wider and deeper thinking about China's future.

A scene near the city wall in Peking is portrayed in this French engraving dated 1879.

THE BOXER MOVEMENT

For the moment, though, China seemed to have turned back to older methods of confronting the threat from outside, as a dramatic episode, the "Boxer movement",

German sailors fight the Boxers, as depicted by an illustration in a contemporary French magazine.

showed. Exploited by the empress, this was essentially a backward-looking and xenophobic popular upheaval, which was given official encouragement. Missionaries and converts were murdered, a German minister killed and the foreign legations at Peking besieged; the Boxers once more revealed the hatred of foreigners which was waiting to be tapped. Yet their efforts showed how little could be hoped for from the old structure, for its most conservative forces had dominated the movement, not the few reformers who became involved in it. The Boxers were in due course suppressed by a military intervention which provides the only example in history of the armed forces of all the great powers

operating under the same commander (a German, as it happened) and the sequel was yet another diplomatic humiliation for China; an enormous indemnity was settled on customs henceforth under foreign direction.

SUN YAT-SEN

THE ENDING of the Boxer movement left China still more unstable. Reform had failed in 1898; so now had reaction. Perhaps only revolution lay ahead. Officers in the parts of the army which had undergone reorganization and training on Western lines began to think about it. Students in exile had already begun to meet and discuss their country's future, above all in Tokyo. The Japanese were happy to encourage subversive movements which might weaken their neighbour; in 1898 they had set up an "East Asian

In defence of Westernization

One of the defenders of the new reformist movement in China, which advocated the embracing of Western innovations, was the scholar Yen Fu (1854–1921), who translated the works of Adam Smith and John Stuart Mill. He wrote:

"There is not time to ask oneself if knowledge is Chinese or Western, or if it is new or old. If one path leads us to ignorance, and, therefore, to poverty and weakness, although it comes down from our ancestors or is based on the authority of our governors and masters ... we should leave it aside. If another path effectively conquers ignorance, and therefore frees us from our poverty and weakness, we should follow it although it comes from the barbarians ... ."

An extract from the writings of Yen Fu, 1900.

Cultural Union" from which emerged the slogan "Asia for the Asians". The Japanese had great prestige in the eyes of the young Chinese radicals as Asians who were escaping from the trap of traditional backwardness which had been fatal to India and seemed to be about to engulf China. Japan could confront the West on terms of equality. Other students looked elsewhere for support, some to the long-enduring secret societies. One of them was a young man called Sun Yat-sen. His achievement has often been exaggerated, but nevertheless he attempted revolution ten times altogether. In the 1890s, he and others were asking only for a constitutional monarchy, but that was a very radical demand at the time.

Discontented exiles drew on support from Chinese businessmen abroad, of whom there were many, for the Chinese had always been great traders. They helped Sun Yat-sen to form in 1905 in Japan a revolutionary alliance aiming at the expulsion of the Manchus and the initiation of Chinese rule, a republican constitution, land reform. It sought to conciliate the foreigners, at this stage a wise tactical move. Its programme

A popular Chinese print from 1891 encourages the people to fight against foreign influences.

showed the influence of Western thinkers (notably that of the English radical John Stuart Mill and the American economic reformer Henry George). Once again the West was providing the stimulus and some of the ideological baggage of a Chinese reform movement and it was the launching of the party eventually to emerge as dominant in the Chinese Republic.

Its formation, though, may well be thought less significant than another event of the same year, the abolition of the traditional examination system. More than any other institution, the examination system had held Chinese civilization together by providing the bureaucracy it recruited with its internal homogeneity and cohesion. This would not quickly wane, but the distinction between the mass of Chinese subjects and the privileged ruling class was now gone. Meanwhile, returning students from abroad, dissatisfied with what they found and no longer under the necessity of accommodating themselves to it by going through the examination procedure if they wished to enter government

In 1894 Sun Yat-sen (1866–1925), pictured here, founded the Association for the Regeneration of China, which was a revolutionary movement principally calling for national independence, agrarian reform and the formation of a republic.

The end of imperial China

Widespread discontent in early 20th-century China eventually allowed republican ideals (expressed by the growing group of young Chinese people who had been educated in the West) to triumph over the Manchu dynasty. Revolution broke out almost by chance in 1911, when a group of officers took up arms after being implicated in the preparations for a revolution. A large number of cities rapidly joined the uprising and the defection of high-ranking army officers led to the collapse of the dynasty.

It was extremely difficult for republican democracy to take root in China – the country lacked not only the tradition of a representative government but also a public judiciary that was more than just a penal system. On Yuan Shih-kai's death in 1916 China would sink into unrest once more.

Yuan Shih-kai (1859–1916) was the second president of China, after Sun Yat-sen.

service, exercised a profoundly disturbing influence. They much increased the rate at which Chinese society began to be irradiated by Western ideas. Together with the soldiers in a modernized army, more and more of them looked to revolution for a way ahead.

THE CHINESE REPUBLIC

There were a number of rebellions (some directed by Sun Yat-sen from Indo-China with French connivance) before the empress and her puppet emperor died on successive days in 1908. The event raised new hopes but the Manchu government continued to drag its feet over reform. On the one hand it made important concessions of principle and promoted the flow of students abroad; on the other it showed that it could not achieve a decisive break with the past or surrender any of the imperial privileges of the Manchus. Perhaps more could not have been asked for. By 1911, the situation had deteriorated badly. The gentry class showed signs of losing its cohesion: it was no longer to back the dynasty in the face of subversion as it had done in the past. Governmentally, there existed a near-stalemate of internal power, the dynasty effectively controlling only a part of China. In October a revolutionary headquarters was discovered at Hankow. There had already been revolts which had been more or less contained earlier in the year. This precipitated one which at last turned into a successful revolution. Sun Yat-sen, whose name was used by the early rebels, was in the United States at the time and was taken by surprise.

The course of the revolution was decided by the defection from the régime of its military commanders. The most important of these was Yuan Shih-kai; when he turned on the Manchus, the dynasty was lost. The Mandate of Heaven had been withdrawn until on 12 February 1912 the six-year-old – and last – Manchu emperor abdicated. A republic had already been proclaimed, with Sun Yat-sen its president, and a new national-ist party soon appeared behind him. In March he resigned the presidency to Yuan Shih-kai; thus acknowledging where power really lay in the new republic and inaugurating a new phase of Chinese government, in which an ineffective constitutional régime at Peking disputed the practical government of China by warlords. China had still a long way to travel before she would be a modern nation-state. None the less, she had begun the half-century's march, which would recover for her an independence lost in the nineteenth century to foreigners.

JAPAN

At the beginning of the nineteenth century, there was little to show a super-ficial observer that Japan might adapt more successfully than China to challenges from the West. She was to all appearances deeply conservative. Yet much had already changed since the establishment of the shogunate and there were signs that the changes would cut deeper and faster as the years went by. It was a paradox that this was in part attributable to the success of the Tokugawa era itself. It had brought peace. An obvious result was that

Japan's military system became old-fashioned and inefficient. The samurai themselves were evidently a parasitic class; warriors, there was nothing for them to do except to cluster in the castle-towns of their lords, consumers with-out employment, a social and economic problem. The prolonged peace also led to the surge of growth, which was the most pro-found consequence of the Tokugawa era. Japan was already a semi-developed, diversi-fying society, with a money economy, the beginnings of a quasi-capitalist structure in agriculture, which eroded the old feudal

A Japanese lady and her maid are portrayed in an 18th-century print. Thanks to the popularity at that time of such scenes from daily life, there is a wealth of graphic documentation on the Tokugawa era.

relationships, and a growing urban population. Osaka, the greatest mercantile centre, had between 300,000 and 400,000 inhabitants in the last years of the shogunate. Edo may have had a million. These great centres of consumption were sustained by financial and mercantile arrangements, which had grown enormously in scale and complication since the seventeenth century. They made a mockery of the old notion of the inferiority of the merchant order. Even their techniques of salesmanship were modern; the eighteenth-century house of Mitsui (two centuries later still a pillar of Japanese capitalism) gave free umbrellas decorated with their trademark to customers caught in their shops by the rain.

POLITICAL AND ECONOMIC INSTABILITY

Many of the changes that had taken place in Japan registered the creation of new wealth from which the shogunate had not itself benefited, largely because it was unable to tap it at a rate which kept pace with its own growing needs. The main revenue was the rice tax which flowed through the lords, and the rate at which the tax was levied remained fixed at the level of a seventeenth-century assessment. Taxation therefore did not take away the new wealth arising from better cultivation and land reclamation and, because this remained in the hands of the better-off peasants and village leaders, this led to sharpening contrasts in the countryside. The poorer peasantry was often driven to the labour markets of the towns. This was another sign of disintegration in the feudal society. In the towns, which suffered from an inflation made worse by the shogunate's debasement of the coinage, only the merchants seemed to prosper. A last effort of economic reform failed in the 1840s. The lords grew poorer and their retainers lost confidence; before the end of the Tokugawa, some samurai were beginning to dabble in trade. Their share of their lord's tax yield was still only that of their seventeenth-century predecessors; everywhere could be found impoverished, politically discontented swordsmen – and some aggrieved families of great lords who recalled the days when their race had stood on equal terms with the Tokugawa.

OPENNESS TO WESTERN INFLUENCES

The obvious danger of Japan's potential instability was all the greater because insulation against Western ideas had long since ceased to be complete. A few learned men had interested themselves in books which entered Japan through the narrow aperture of the Dutch trade. Japan was very different from China in its technical receptivity. "The Japanese are sharp-witted and quickly learn anything they see," said a sixteenth-century Dutchman. They had soon grasped and exploited, as the Chinese never did, the advantages of European firearms, and began to make them in quantity. They copied the European clocks, which the Chinese treated as toys. They were eager to learn from Europeans, as unhampered by their traditions as the Chinese seemed bogged down in theirs. On the great fiefs there were notable schools or research centres of "Dutch studies". The shogunate itself had authorized the translation of foreign books, an important step in so literate a society, for education in Tokugawa Japan had been almost too successful: even young samurai were beginning to enquire about Western ideas. The islands were relatively small and communications good, so that new ideas got about easily. Thus, Japan's posture when she suddenly had to face a new and unprecedented challenge from the West was less disadvantageous than that of China.

The first period of Western contact with Japan had ended in the seventeenth century, with the exclusion of all but a few Dutchmen allowed to conduct trade from an island at Nagasaki. Europeans had not then been able to challenge this outcome. That this was not likely to continue to be the case was shown in the 1840s by the fate of China, which some of Japan's rulers observed with increasing alarm. The Europeans and North Americans seemed to have both a new interest in breaking into Asian trade and new and irresistible strength to do it. The Dutch king warned the shogun that exclusion was no longer a realistic policy. But there was no agreement among Japan's rulers about whether resistance or concession was the better. Finally, in 1851 the president of the United States sent a naval officer, Commodore Perry, to open relations with Japan. Under him, the first foreign squadron to sail into Japanese waters entered Edo Bay in 1853. In the following year it returned and the first of a series of treaties with foreign powers was made by the shogunate.

THE END OF THE SHOGUNATE

Perry's arrival could be seen in Confucian terms as an omen that the end of the shogunate was near. No doubt some Japanese saw it in that way. Yet this did not at once follow and there were a few years of somewhat muddled response to the barbarian threat. Japan's rulers did not straightway come around to a wholehearted policy of concession (there was

The signing of a trade treaty between France and Japan is depicted in this engraving dated 1860.

one further attempt to expel foreigners by force) and Japan's future course was not set until well into the 1860s. Within a few years the success of the West was none the less embodied in and symbolized by a series of so-called "unequal treaties". Commercial privileges, extra-territoriality for Western residents, the presence of diplomatic representatives and restrictions on the Japanese export of opium were the main concessions won by the United States, Great Britain, France, Russia and the Netherlands. Soon afterwards the shogunate came to an end; its inability to resist the foreigner was one contributing factor and another was the threat from two great aggregations of feudal power, which had already begun to adopt Western military techniques in order to replace the Tokugawa by a more effective and centralized system under their control. There was fighting between the Tokugawa and their opponents, but it was followed not by a relapse into disorder and anarchy but by a resumption of power by the imperial court and administration in 1868 in the so-called "Meiji Restoration".

This English engraving illustrates the opening of the Japanese parliament by the emperor on 29 November 1890. It had been made clear to the members of the new legislature and to the Japanese public that the constitution of 1889 emanated from and could only be amended by the emperor's will.

THE MEIJI RESTORATION

The re-emergence of the emperor from centuries of ceremonial seclusion, and the widespread acceptance of the revolutionary renewal which followed, was attributable above all to the passionate desire of most literate Japanese to escape from a "shameful inferiority" to the West which might have led them to share the fate of the Chinese and Indians. In the 1860s both the *bakufu* and some individual clans had already sent several missions to Europe. Anti-foreign agitation was dropped in order to learn from the West the secrets of its strength. There was a paradox in this. As in some European countries, a nationalism rooted in a conservative view of society was to dissolve much of the tradition it was developed to defend.

The transference of the court to Edo was the symbolic opening of the Meiji "Restoration" and the regeneration of Japan; its indispensable first stage was the abolition of feudalism. What might have been a difficult and bloody business was made simple by the voluntary surrender to the emperor of their lands by the four greatest clans, who set out their motives in a memorial they addressed to the emperor. They were returning to the emperor what had originally been his, they said, "so that a uniform rule may prevail throughout the empire. Thus the country will be able to rank equally with the other nations of the world." This was a concise expression of the patriotic ethic which was to inspire Japan's leaders for the next half-century and was widely spread in a country with a large degree of literacy where local leaders could make possible the acceptance of national goals to a degree impossible elsewhere. True, such expressions were not uncommon in other countries. What was peculiar to Japan was the urgency which observation of the fate of China lent to the programme, the emotional support given to the idea by Japanese social and moral tradition, and the fact that in the imperial throne there was available within the established structure a source of moral authority not committed merely to maintaining the past. These conditions made possible a Japanese 1688: a conservative revolution opening the way to radical change.

JAPANESE "WESTERNIZATION"

Following the "Meiji Restoration", Japan rapidly adopted many of the institutions of Western government and Western society. A prefectorial system of administration, posts, a daily newspaper, a ministry of education, military conscription, the first railway, religious toleration and the Gregorian calendar all arrived within the first five years. A representative system of local government was inaugurated in 1879 and ten years later a new constitution set up a bicameral parliament (a peerage had already been created in preparation for the organization of the upper house). In fact, this was less revolutionary than it might appear, given the strong authoritarian strain in the document. At about the same time, too, the innovatory passion was beginning to show signs of flagging; the period when things Western were a craze was over; no such enthusiasm was to be seen again until the second half of the twentieth century. In 1890 an imperial Rescript on Education, subsequently to be read on great days to generations of Japanese schoolchildren, enjoined the observation of the traditional Confucian duties of filial piety and obedience and the sacrifice of self to the state if need be.

Much – perhaps the most important part – of old Japan was to survive the Meiji revolution and was to do so very obviously; this is in part the secret of modern Japan. But

Japanese versus Western civilization

The conservative point of view on the contrast between the dynamics of Western culture and the immobility of Eastern culture is explained in this paragraph from a famous Japanese novel:

"Monarchy is not convenient, so parliamentary procedures are tried, which also disappoint and on to another thing. A river irritates, so a bridge is built; a mountain annoys, a tunnel is drilled. If communications are difficult, a railway line is built. But they never achieve total satisfaction. How far can man push forward his will in a positive way? Western civilization can be positive, progressive, but in the end it is a civilization created by people who are never satisfied. Japanese civilization does not look for satisfaction through changing things, but in man himself. Where this differs deeply from the West is in that it has been developed on the great assertion that it is not necessary to make fundamental changes in our surroundings. If relationships between parents and children are not the best, our civilization does not try to find harmony by changing those relationships, as the Europeans do. The relationships are thought to be unalterable and a means to restore serenity within them is sought."

An extract from *I Am A Cat* by Natsume Soseki (1906).

much, too, had gone. Feudalism could never be restored, generously compensated with government stock though the lords might be. Another striking expression of the new direction was the abolition of the old ordered class system. Care was shown in removing the privileges of the samurai; some of them could find compensation in the opportunities offered to them by the new bureaucracy, in business – no longer to be a demeaning activity – and in the modernized army and navy. For these foreign instruction was sought, because the Japanese sought proven excellence. Gradually they dropped their French military advisers and took to employing Germans after the Franco-Prussian War; the British provided instructors for the navy. Young Japanese were sent abroad to learn at first hand other secrets of the wonderful and threatening puissance of the West. It is still hard not to be moved by the ardour of many of these young men and of their elders and impossible not to be impressed by their achievement, which went far beyond Japan and their own time. The *shishi* (as some of the most passionate and dedicated activists of reform were called) later inspired national leaders right across Asia, from India to China. Their spirit was still at work in the young officers of the 1930s, who were to launch the last and most destructive wave of Japanese imperialism.

ECONOMIC CHANGE

The crudest indexes of the success of the reformers are the economic, but they are very striking. They built on the economic benefits of the Tokugawa peace. It was not only the borrowing of Western technology and expertise which ensured the release in Japan of a current of growth achieved by no other non-Western state. The country was lucky in being already well-supplied with entrepreneurs who took for granted the profit motive and it was undoubtedly richer than, say, China. Some of the explanation of the great leap forward by Japan lay also in the overcoming of inflation and the liquidation of feudal restraints, which had made it hard to tap Japan's full potential. The first sign of change was a further increase in agricultural production, little though the peasants, who made up four-fifths of the population in 1868, benefited from it. Japan managed to feed a growing population in the nineteenth century by bringing more land under cultivation for rice and by cultivating existing fields more intensively. Though the dependence on the land tax lessened as a bigger portion of the revenue could be found from other sources, it was still upon the peasant that the cost of the new Japan fell most heavily. As late as 1941, Japanese farmers

This view of the Japanese city of Osaka was published in an English newspaper in 1891.

saw few of the gains from modernization. Relatively they had fallen behind; their ancestors only a century earlier had a life expectancy and income approximating to that of their British equivalents, but even by 1900 this was far from true of their successors. There were few non-agricultural resources. It was the increasingly productive tax on land which paid for investment. Consumption remained low, though there was not the suffering of, say, the later industrialization process of Stalin's Russia. A high rate of saving (12 per cent in 1900) spared Japan dependence on foreign loans but, again, restricted consumption. This was the other side of the balance sheet of expansion, whose credit entries were clear enough: the infrastructure of a modern state, an indigenous arms industry, a usually high credit rating in the eyes of foreign investors and a big expansion of cotton-spinning and other textiles by 1914.

SOCIAL UPHEAVAL

In the end a heavy spiritual cost had to be paid for these successes. Even while seeking to learn from the West, Japan turned inward. The "foreign" religious influences of Confucianism and even, at first, Buddhism, were attacked by the upholders of the state Shintoist cult, which, even under the shogunate, had begun to stress and enhance the role of the emperor as the embodiment of the divine. The demands of loyalty to the emperor as the focus of the nation came to override the principles embodied in the new constitution which might have been developed in liberal directions in a different cultural setting. The character of the régime expressed itself less in its liberal institutions than in the repressive actions of the imperial police. Yet it is difficult to see how an author-

Prince Ito Hirobumi (1841–1909) headed the commission that prepared the Japanese constitution, travelling to Europe to study Western democratic models. He was a key figure in the Westernization of Japan and held office as prime minister from 1886 intermittently until 1901.

itarian emphasis could, in fact, have been avoided, given the two great tasks facing the statesmen of the Meiji Restoration. The modernization of the economy meant not planning in the modern sense but a strong governmental initiative and harsh fiscal policies. The other problem was order. The imperial power had once before gone into eclipse because of its failure to meet the threat on this front and now there were new dangers, because not all conservatives could be reconciled to the new model Japan. Discontented *ronin* – rootless samurai without masters – were one source of trouble. Another was peasant misery; there were scores of agrarian revolts in the first decade of the Meiji era. In the Satsuma rebellion of 1877 the government's new conscript forces showed that they could handle conservative resistance. It was the last of several rebellions against the Restoration and the last great challenge from conservatism.

The energies of the discontented samurai

Japanese expansion 1895–1942

For half a century, Japan carried out an aggressive policy of military expansion. The wars with China (1894–1895) and Russia (1904–1905) allowed Japan to occupy Formosa and Korea. In 1931, the Japanese seized Manchuria from China; six years later they attacked China itself. In 1941, when Germany appeared to be winning the Second World War, Japan entered the war against the United States and Great Britain, in an attempt to impose Japanese rule over the whole of eastern Asia.

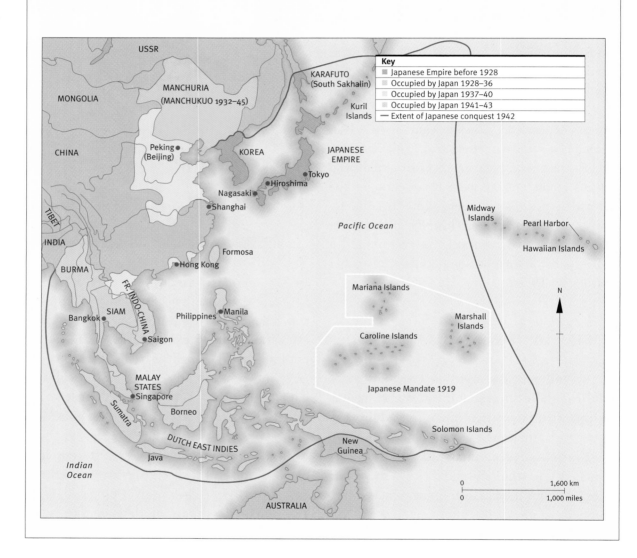

Key
- ■ Japanese Empire before 1928
- Occupied by Japan 1928–36
- Occupied by Japan 1937–40
- Occupied by Japan 1941–43
- — Extent of Japanese conquest 1942

were gradually to be siphoned off into the service of the new state, but this did not mean that the implications for Japan were all beneficial. They intensified in certain key sectors of the national life an assertive nationalism which was to lead eventually to aggression abroad. Immediately, this was likely to find expression not only in resentment of the West but also in imperial ambitions directed towards the nearby Asian mainland. Modernization at home and adventure abroad were often in tension in Japan after the Meiji Restoration, but in the long run they pulled in the same direction. The popular and democratic movements especially felt the tug of imperialism.

RELATIONS WITH CHINA AND KOREA

China was the predestined victim of imperialist urges and was to be served much more harshly by her fellow Asians than by any of the Western states. At first she was threatened only indirectly by Japan. Just as China's supremacy over the dependencies on her borders was challenged in Tibet, Burma and Indo-China by Europeans, so the Japanese menaced it in the ancient empire of Korea, long a tributary of Peking. Japanese interests there went back a long way. In part they were strategic; the Tsushima straits were the place where the mainland was nearest. But the Japanese were also concerned over the possible Far Eastern ambitions of Russia, particularly in Manchuria, and over China's inability to resist them. In 1876 an overt move was made; under the threat of military and naval action (like those deployed by Europeans against China, and by Perry against Japan), the Koreans agreed to open three of their ports to the Japanese and to exchange diplomatic representatives. This was an affront to China. Japan was treating Korea as an independent country and negotiating with it over the head of the imperial court in Peking, which claimed sovereignty over Korea. Some Japanese wanted even more. They remembered earlier Japanese invasions of Korea and successful piracy on its coasts, and coveted the mineral and natural wealth of the country. The statesmen of the Restoration did not at once give way to such pressure, but in a sense they were only making haste slowly. In the 1890s another step forward was taken which led Japan into her first major war since the Restoration, and it was against China. It was sweepingly successful, but was followed by national humiliation when in 1895 a group of Western powers forced Japan to accept a peace treaty

much less advantageous than the one she had imposed on the Chinese (which had included a declaration of Korea's independence).

WESTERN ACCEPTANCE OF JAPAN

At this point resentment of the West fused with enthusiasm for expansion in Asia. Popular dislike of the "unequal treaties" had been running high and the 1895 disappointment brought it to a head. The Japanese government had its own interests in backing Chinese revolutionary movements and now it had a slogan to offer them: "Asia for the Asians." It was becoming clear, too, to the Western powers that dealing with Japan was a very different matter from bullying China. Japan was increasingly recognized to be a "civilized" state, not to be treated like other non-European nations. One symbol of the change was the ending in 1899 of one humiliating sign of European predominance, extra-territoriality. Then, in 1902, came the clearest acknowledgement of

This Japanese illustration of an episode in the war against China (1894–1895) emphasizes the overwhelming energy of the Japanese troops, whose modern uniforms contrast with the more traditional garb of the Chinese.

Japanese customs reach the West

From 1853, Western travellers were allowed to visit Japan for the first time in more than two centuries. The first Westerners to take advantage of this new openness were amazed to discover a highly refined Japanese culture. The mementos that visitors brought back with them made Japanese culture very fashionable in Europe in the latter part of the 19th century. European ladies took to wearing kimonos in private, and there was great interest in Japanese woodcuts, which inspired artists such as Van Gogh.

Some Japanese traditions were to become that country's identifying traits in the eyes of the rest of the world. These included the tea ceremony, with its detailed rituals and the beautiful, simplistic design of the objects used; Kabuki theatre; the elegance of the geishas; and the martial arts.

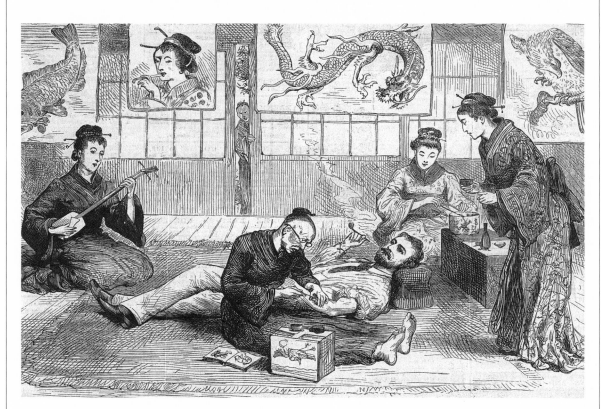

A European receives a tattoo in Nagasaki in 1882, attended by several geishas. Many Western visitors to 19th-century Japan were fascinated by the country's customs.

Japan's acceptance as an equal by the West, an Anglo-Japanese alliance. Japan, it was said, had joined Europe.

WAR WITH RUSSIA

At the beginning of the twentieth century Russia was the leading European power in the Far East. In 1895 her role had been decisive; her subsequent advance made it clear to the Japanese that the longed-for prize of Korea might elude them if they delayed. Railway-building in Manchuria, the development of Vladivostok, and Russian commercial activity in Korea – where politics was little more than a struggle of pro-Russian and pro-Japanese factions – were alarming. Most serious of all, the Russians had leased the naval base of Port Arthur from the enfeebled Chinese. In 1904 the Japanese struck. The result, after a year of war in Manchuria, was a humiliating defeat for the Russians. It was the end of tsarist pretensions in Korea and South Manchuria, where Japanese influence was henceforth dominant, and other territories passed into Japanese possession to remain there until 1945. But there was more to the Japanese victory than that. For the first time since the Middle Ages, non-Europeans had defeated a European power in a major war. The reverberations and repercussions were colossal.

A TURNING-POINT IN ASIA

The formal annexation of Korea by Japan in 1910, together with the Chinese Revolution of the following year and the end of Manchu rule, can now be seen as a milestone, the end of the first phase of Asia's response to the West, and as a turning-point. Asians had shown very differing reactions to Western challenges. One of the two states which were to be the great Asian powers of the second half of the century was Japan, and she had inoculated herself against the threat from the West by accepting the virus of modernization. The other, China, had long striven not to do so.

In each case, the West provided both direct and indirect stimulus to upheaval, though in one case it was successfully contained and in the other it was not. In each case, too, the fate of the Asian power was shaped not only by its own response, but by the relations of the Western powers among themselves. Their rivalries had generated the scramble in China which had so alarmed and tempted the Japanese. The Anglo-Japanese alliance assured them that they could strike at their great enemy, Russia, and find her unsupported. A few years more and Japan and China would both be participants as formal equals with other powers in the First World War. Meanwhile, Japan's example and, above

The Japanese fleet is depicted in action against the Russians, off Port Arthur in Manchuria in 1904.

all, its victory over Russia, were an inspiration to other Asians, the greatest single reason for them to ponder whether European rule was bound to be their lot. In 1905 an American scholar could already speak of the Japanese as the "peers of Western peoples"; what they had done, by turning Europe's skills and ideas against her, might not other Asians do in their turn?

Everywhere in Asia European agencies launched or helped to launch changes which speeded up the crumbling of Europe's political hegemony. They had brought with them ideas about nationalism and humanitarianism, the Christian missionary's dislocation of local society and belief, and a new exploitation not sanctioned by tradition; all of which helped to ignite political, economic and social change. Primitive, almost blind, responses like the Indian Mutiny or the Boxer Rebellion were the first and obvious outcome, but there were others which had a much more important future ahead. In particular, this was true in India, the biggest and most important of all colonial territories.

This engraving dates from 1889 and depicts a visit to Bombay by the viceroy, Lord Lansdowne, who held office from 1888 to 1893.

COLONIAL INDIA

IN 1877 PARLIAMENT had bestowed the title of "Empress of India" upon Queen Victoria; some of her subjects laughed and a few disapproved, but it does not seem that there were many who thought it mattered much. Most took the British supremacy there to be permanent or near-permanent and were not much concerned about names. They would have agreed with their compatriot who said "we are not in India to be pleasant" and held that only a severe and firm government could be sure to prevent another Mutiny. Others would also have agreed with the British viceroy, who declared as the twentieth century began, that: "As long as we rule India, we are the greatest power in the world. If we lose it, we shall drop straightaway to a third-rate power." Two important truths underlay this assertion. One was that the Indian taxpayer paid for the defence of much of the British Empire; Indian troops had been used to sustain it from Malta to China and in the subcontinent there was always a strategical reserve. The second was that Indian tariff policy was subordinated to British commercial and industrial realities.

IDEAS OF RACIAL SUPERIORITY

The economic and strategic importance of British India were the harsh facts whose weight was harder and harder to ignore. Yet they were not the whole story of the Raj. There was more to the government of a fifth of humankind than just fear, greed, cynicism or the love of power. Human beings do not find it easy to pursue collective purposes without some sort of myth to justify them; nor did the British in India. Some of them saw themselves as the heirs of the Romans whom a classical education taught them to admire, stoically bearing the burden of a lonely life in an alien land to bring peace to the warring and law to peoples without it. Others saw in Christianity a precious gift with which they must destroy idols and cleanse evil custom. Some never formulated such clear views but were simply convinced that what they brought was better than what they found and therefore what they were doing was good. At the base of all these views there was a conviction of superiority and there was nothing surprising about this; it had always animated some imperialists. But in the later nineteenth century it was especially reinforced by fashionable racialist ideas and a muddled reflection of what was thought to be taught by current biological science about the survival of the fittest. Such ideas provided another rationale for the much greater social separation of the British in India from native Indians after the shock of the Mutiny. Although there was a modest intake of nominated Indian landlords and native rulers into the legislative branch of government, it was not until the very end of the century that these were joined by elected Indians. Moreover, though Indians could compete to enter the civil service, there were important practical obstacles in the way of their entry to the ranks of the decision-makers. In the army,

Imperial expansion in Southeast Asia (1850–1914)

Southeast Asia was divided between the main Western powers during the 19th century. The Dutch, who had settled in Java in the early 18th century, completed their domination of present-day Indonesia. The British established their rule over Burma, Malaya and the northern part of Borneo, while the French took over Indo-China. In 1899, the United States replaced Spain as a colonial power in the Philippines. Uniquely, the kingdom of Siam (now Thailand) maintained its independence.

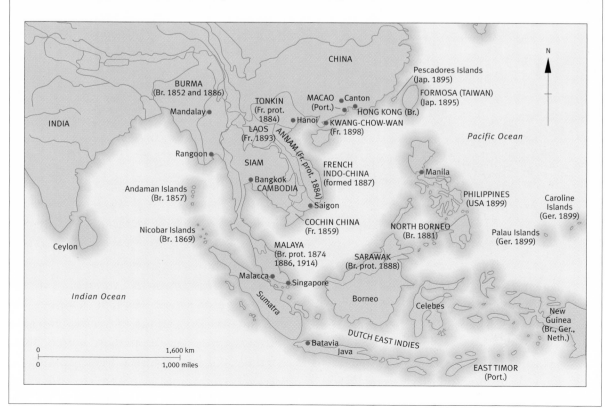

Painted in the Moghul tradition, this 19th-century portrait represents the Indian maharaja Gulab Singh. Having signed a treaty with the British at the end of the Sikh War in 1846, Singh became ruler of the combined states of Jammu and Kashmir in northwestern India. Kashmir, a region rich in wildlife, became popular with British hunters.

too, Indians were kept out of the senior commissioned ranks.

The largest single part of the British army was always stationed in India, where its reliability and monopoly of artillery combined with the officering of the Indian regiments by Europeans to ensure that there would be no repetition of the Mutiny. The coming of railways, telegraphs and more advanced weapons in any case told in favour of government in India as much as in any European country. But armed force was not the explanation of the self-assuredness of British rule, any more than was a conviction of racial superiority. The Census Report of 1901 recorded that there were just under 300 million Indians. These were governed by about 900 white civil servants. Usually there was about one British soldier for every 4,000 Indians. As an Englishman once put it, picturesquely, had all the Indians chosen to spit at the same moment, his countrymen would have been drowned.

THE ADMINISTRATION OF THE RAJ

THE RAJ RESTED on carefully administered policies. One assumption underlying them after the Mutiny was that Indian society should be interfered with as little as possible. Female infanticide, since it was murder, was forbidden, but there was to be no attempt to prohibit polygamy or child marriage (though after 1891 it was not legal for a marriage to be consummated until the wife was twelve years old). The line of the law was to run outside what was sanctioned by Hindu religion. This conservatism was reflected in a new attitude towards the native Indian rulers. The Mutiny had shown that they were usually loyal; those who turned against the government had been provoked by resentment against British annexation of their lands. Their rights were therefore scrupulously respected after the Mutiny; the princes ruled their own states independently and virtually irresponsibly, checked only by their awe of the British political officers resident at their courts. The native states included over a fifth of the population. Elsewhere, the British cultivated the native aristocracy and the landlords. This was part of a search for support

from key groups of Indians, but often led the British to lean on those whose own leadership powers were already being undermined by social change. Enlightened despotism at their expense, but in the interests of the peasantry (such as had been shown earlier in the century) none the less now disappeared. These were all some of the unhappy consequences of the Mutiny.

A RISING TIDE OF DISCONTENT

No more than any other imperial government was the Raj able permanently to ensure itself against change. Its very success told against it. The suppression of warfare favoured the growth of population – and one consequence was more frequent famine. But the provision of ways of earning a living other than by agriculture (which was a possible outlet from the problem of an overpopulated countryside) was made very difficult by the obstacles in the way of Indian industrialization. These arose in large measure from a tariff policy in the interest of British manufactures. A slowly emerging class of Indian industrialists did

The British army in India is shown during training exercises in 1891. This army was the ultimate defence of the security of India from the time of the failed Mutiny until Indian independence.

not, therefore, feel warmly towards government, but were increasingly antagonized by it. The alienated also came to include many of the growing number of Indians who had received an education along English lines and had subsequently been irritated to compare its precepts with the practice of the British community in India. Others, who had gone to England to study at Oxford, Cambridge or the Inns of Court, found the contrast especially galling: in late nineteenth-century England there were even Indian Members of Parliament, while an Indian graduate in India might be slighted by a British private soldier, and there had been uproar among British

residents when, in the 1880s, a viceroy wished to remove the "invidious distinction" which prevented a European from being brought before an Indian magistrate. Some, too, had pondered what they read at their mentors' behest; John Stuart Mill and Mazzini were thus to have a huge influence in India and, through its leaders, in the rest of Asia.

THE HINDU NATIONALIST MOVEMENT

Resentment was especially felt among the Hindus of Bengal, the historic centre of British power: Calcutta was the capital of India. In 1905 this province was divided in two. This partition for the first time brought the Raj into serious conflict with something which had not existed in 1857, an Indian nationalist movement.

The growth of a sense of nationality was slow, fitful and patchy. It was part of a complex set of processes, which formed modern Indian politics, and was far from the most important in many localities and at many levels. Moreover, at every stage, national feeling was itself strongly influenced by non-Indian forces. British orientalists, at the beginning of the nineteenth century, had begun the rediscovery of classical Indian culture which was essential both to the self-respect of Hindu nationalism and the overcoming of the subcontinent's huge divisions. Indian scholars then began to bring to light, under European guidance, the culture and religion embedded in the neglected Sanskrit scriptures; through these they could formulate a conception of a Hinduism far removed from the rich and fantastic, but also superstitious, accretions of its popular form. By the end of the nineteenth century this recovery of the Aryan and Vedic past – Islamic India was virtually disregarded – had gone far enough for Hindus to meet

Food is handed out in India during a drought, in a drawing published by an Italian newspaper in 1902. The huge population growth that occurred in India under British rule played its part in making famine more frequent and serious.

with confidence the reproaches of Christian missionaries and offer a cultural counter-attack; a Hindu emissary to a "Parliament of Religions" in Chicago in 1893 not only awoke great personal esteem and obtained serious attention for his assertion that Hinduism was a great religion capable of revivifying the spiritual life of other cultures, but actually made converts.

National consciousness, like the political activity it was to reinforce, was for a long time confined to a few. The proposal that Hindi should be India's language seemed wildly unrealistic when hundreds of languages and dialects fragmented Indian society and Hindi could only appeal to a small élite seeking to strengthen its links across a sub-continent. The definition of its membership was education rather than wealth: its backbone was provided by those Hindus, often Bengali, who felt especially disappointed at the failure of their educational attainments to win them an appropriate share in the running of India; by 1887 only a dozen Indians had entered the Indian Civil Service through the competitive examination. The Raj seemed determined to maintain the racial predominance of Europeans and to rely upon such conservative interests as the princes and landlords, to the exclusion and, possibly even more important, the humiliation of the *babu*, the educated, middle-class, urban Hindu.

THE INDIAN NATIONAL CONGRESS

A new cultural self-respect and a growing sense of grievance over rewards and slights were the background to the formation of the Indian National Congress. The immediate prelude was a flurry of excitement over the failure of the government proposals – because of the outcry of European residents – to equalize the treatment of Indians and

The strength of the Hindu faith

A French traveller who visited India in 1864 to 1868 was amazed by the great religious tolerance the Hindus showed:

"In what country can one contemplate the spectacle offered before our eyes that day in the square in Benares [Varanasi]. Ten paces from all that the Indian holds most sacred in his religion, between the fountain of Wisdom and the idol of Shiva, under a tree, a Protestant missionary stood on a chair, and preached in native languages about the Christian religion and the errors of paganism. I heard his screeching voice when he said to the crowd, who stood round him respectfully, 'You are idolatrizers! That stone you worship was chiselled out of a quarry and is as inert, as impotent as the post on the corner of my street.' These words did not cause even a murmur; they listened impassively to the missionary, but they were following his speech because now and again one of them asked a question, which the evangelist tried to answer as best he could. Perhaps the missionary's courage would be more admirable if the Indians' tolerance were not so well known. One of them said to me one day, 'Our work is useless, because one can never convert a man who is so confident of his own faith that he can listen to our attacks against it without becoming upset.'"

An extract from *Rajas' Travels in India* by Louis Rousselet.

Europeans in the courts. Disappointment caused an Englishman, a former civil servant, to take the steps which led to the first conference of the Indian National Congress in Bombay in December 1885. Vice-regal initiatives, too, had played a part in this, and Europeans were long to be prominent in the administration of Congress. And they would patronize it for even longer with protection and advice in London. It was an appropriate symbol of the complexity of the European impact on India that some Indian delegates

The Indian National Congress

The organization that was to lead India to independence in 1947, and which would govern as the leading party for the first decades of independence, was established in Bombay in December 1885. The 70 delegates who founded the Indian National Congress did not contest British rule. However, in the years that followed, Indian nationalist feelings grew and Congress (although it was always careful to stay within the law) became a voice of opposition to British politics in India.

At the beginning of the 20th century, the increasing tension between Hindus and Muslims considerably complicated the Indian political situation. Although extreme nationalists opted for the use of terrorism, Congress long remained loyal to Great Britain.

Founder members of the Indian National Congress are portrayed in this 19th-century photograph.

attended in European dress, improbably attired in morning-suits and top-hats of comical unsuitability to the climate of their country, but the formal attire of its rulers.

Congress was soon committed by its declaration of principles to national unity and regeneration: as in Japan already and China and many other countries later, this was the classical product of the impact of European ideas. But it did not at first aspire to self-government. Congress sought, rather, to provide a means of communicating Indian views to the viceroy and proclaimed its "unswerving loyalty" to the British Crown.

Only after twenty years, in which much more extreme nationalist views had won adherents among Hindus, did it begin to discuss the possibility of independence. During this time its attitude had been soured and stiffened by the vilification it received from British residents who declared it unrepresentative, and the unresponsiveness of an administration which endorsed this view and preferred to work through more traditional and conservative social forces. Extremists became more insistent. In 1904 came the inspiring victories of Japan over Russia. The issue for a clash was provided in 1905 by the partition of Bengal.

THE PARTITION OF BENGAL

The purpose of the partition was twofold: it was administratively convenient and it would undermine nationalism in Bengal by producing a West Bengal where there was a Hindu majority, and an East Bengal with a Muslim majority. This detonated a mass of explosive situations that had long been accumulating. Immediately, there was a struggle for power in Congress. At first a split was avoided by agreement on the aim of *swaraj*, which in practice might mean independent self-government such as that enjoyed by the white dominions: their example was suggestive. The extremists were heartened by anti-partition riots. A new weapon was deployed against the British, a boycott of goods, which, it was hoped, might be extended to other forms of passive resistance such as non-payment of taxes and the refusal of soldiers to obey orders. By 1908 the extremists were excluded from Congress. By this time, a second consequence was apparent: extremism was producing terrorism. Again, foreign models were important. Russian revolutionary terrorism now joined the works of Mazzini and the biography of Garibaldi, the guerrilla leader hero of Italian independence, as formative influences on an emerging India. The extremists argued that political murder was not ordinary murder. Assassination and bombing were met with special repressive measures.

MUSLIMS AND HINDUS

The third consequence of partition was perhaps the most momentous. It brought out into the open the division of Muslim and Hindu. For reasons which went back to the percolation of Muslim India before the Mutiny by an Islamic reform movement, the Arabian Wahhabi sect, Indian Muslims had for a century felt themselves more and more distinct from Hindus. Distrusted by the British because of attempts to revivify the Moghul Empire in 1857, they had little success in winning posts in government or on the judicial bench. Hindus had responded more eagerly than Muslims to the educational opportunities offered by the Raj; they were of more commercial weight and had more influence on government. But Muslims too had found their British helpers, who had established a new, Islamic college, providing the English education they needed to compete with Hindus, and had helped to set up Muslim political organizations. Some English civil servants began to grasp the potential for balancing Hindu pressure which this could give the Raj. Intensification of Hindu ritual practice, such as a cow protection movement, was not likely to do anything but increase the separation of the two communities.

Nevertheless, it was only in 1905 that the split became, as it remained, one of the fundamentals of the subcontinent's politics. The anti-partitionists campaigned with a strident display of Hindu symbols and slogans. The British governor of eastern Bengal favoured Muslims against Hindus and strove to give them a vested interest in the new province. He was dismissed, but his inoculation had taken: Bengal Muslims deplored his removal. An Anglo-Muslim *entente* seemed in the making. This further inflamed Hindu terrorists. To make things worse, all this was taking place during five years (from 1906 to 1910) in which prices rose faster than at any time since the Mutiny.

COMMUNAL POLITICS

An important set of political reforms conceded in 1909 did not do more than

A temple to the Hindu goddess Kali in Calcutta is depicted in this illustration dated 1887. Worshippers of the goddess could descend the temple steps to bathe in the purifying waters of the Hooghly river , one of the tributaries of the Ganges delta.

change somewhat the forms with which to operate the political forces which were henceforth to dominate the history of India until the Raj came to an end nearly forty years later. Indians were for the first time appointed to the council which advised the British minister responsible for India and, more important, further elected places were provided for Indians in the legislative councils. But the elections were to be made by electorates which had a communal basis; the division of Hindu and Muslim India, that is to say, was institutionalized.

In 1911, for the first and only time, a reigning British monarch visited India. A great imperial durbar was held at Delhi, the old centre of Moghul rule, to which the capital of British India was now transferred from Calcutta. The princes of India came to do homage; Congress did not question its duty to the throne. The accession to the throne of George V that year had been marked by the conferring of real and symbolic benefits, of which the most notable and politically significant was the reuniting of Bengal. If there was a moment at which the Raj was at its apogee, this was it.

MUSLIM DISCONTENT

Yet India was far from settled. Terrorism and seditious crime continued. The policy of favouring the Muslims had made Hindus more resentful while Muslims now felt that the government had gone back on its understandings with them in withdrawing the partition of Bengal. They feared the resumption of a Hindu ascendancy in the province. Hindus, on the other hand, took the concession as evidence that resistance had paid and began to press for the abolition of the communal electoral arrangements which the Muslims prized. The British had therefore done much to alienate Muslim support when a further strain appeared. The Indian Muslim élites, which had favoured cooperation with the British, were increasingly under pressure from more middle-class Muslims susceptible to the violent appeal of a pan-Islamic movement. The pan-Islamists could point to the fact that the British had let the Muslims down in Bengal, but also noted that in Tripoli (which the Italians attacked in 1911) and the Balkans in 1912 and 1913, Christian powers were attacking Turkey, the seat of the Caliphate, the institutional embodiment of the spiritual leadership of Islam, and Great Britain was, indisputably, a Christian power. The intense susceptibilities of lower-class Indian Muslims were excited to the point at which even the involvement of a mosque in the replanning of a street could be presented as a part of a deliberate plot to harry Islam. When in 1914 Turkey decided to go to war with Great Britain, though the Muslim League remained loyal, some Indian Muslims accepted the logical consequence of the Caliphate's supremacy, and began to prepare revolution against the Raj. They were few. What was more important for the future was that by that year not two but three forces were making the running in Indian politics: the British, Hindus and Muslims. Here was the origin of the future partition of the only complete political unity the subcontinent had ever known and, like that unity, it was as much the result of the play of non-Indian as of Indian forces.

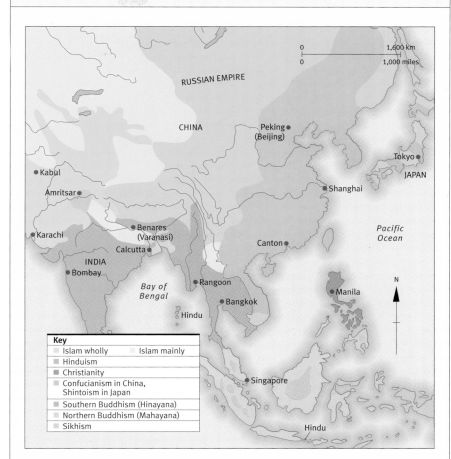

The major religions of Asia in the early 20th century

Key
- Islam wholly
- Islam mainly
- Hinduism
- Christianity
- Confucianism in China, Shintoism in Japan
- Southern Buddhism (Hinayana)
- Northern Buddhism (Mahayana)
- Sikhism

The religious composition of Asia in the early 20th century was the result of thousands of years of history. Hinduism, which predominates in India, has inherited a tradition which is more than 3,000 years old. Islam entered India in the 11th century and Indonesia in the 13th century. The Buddha's preaching in India 2,500 years ago gave rise to two branches of Buddhism, one of which spread through Tibet, China, Korea and Japan, and the other through Ceylon and Indo-China. In China and Japan the ancient traditions of Confucianism and Shintoism, respectively, survived the influx of new creeds. In the 15th century, Sikhism was founded by Guru Nanak and began to take root in the Indian region of the Punjab. Finally Christianity reached the Philippines in the 16th century.

SOUTHEAST ASIA

INDIA WAS THE LARGEST single mass of non-European population and territory under European rule in Asia, but to the southeast and in Indonesia, both part of the Indian cultural sphere, lay further imperial posses-sions. Few generalizations are possible about so huge an area and so many peoples and religions. One negative fact was observable: in no other European possession in Asia was there such transformation before 1914 as in India, though in all of them modernization had begun the corrosion of local tradition. The forces which produced this were those which have already been noted at work else-where: European aggression, the example of Japan, and the diffusion of European culture. But the first and last of these forces operated in the region for a shorter time before 1914 than in China and India. In 1880 most of mainland Southeast Asia was still ruled by native princes who were independent rulers, even if they had to make concessions in "unequal treaties" to European power. In the following decade this was rapidly changed by the British annexation of Burma and continu-ing French expansion in Indo-China. The sultans of Malaya acquired British residents at their courts, who directed policy through the native administration, while the "Straits settlements" were ruled directly as a colony. By 1900 only Siam was left as an independent kingdom in the region, those of Indo-China having succumbed to French imperialism.

FRENCH INDO-CHINA

Cambodia and Laos had been shaped by reli-gious and artistic influences flowing from India, but one of the countries of Indo-China

was much more closely linked to China by its culture. This was Vietnam. It had three parts: Tonkin in the north, Annam, its central area, and Cochin in the south. Vietnam had a long tradition of national identity and a history of national revolt against Chinese imperial rule. It is not surprising, therefore, that it was here that resistance to Europeanization was most marked. Europe's connections with Indo-China had begun with seventeenth-century Christian missionaries from France (one of them devised the first romanization of the Vietnamese language) and it was the persecu-tion of Christians which provided the excuse for a French expedition (briefly assisted by Spanish forces) to be sent there in the 1850s. There followed diplomatic conflict with China, which claimed sovereignty over the country. In 1863 the emperor of Annam ceded part of Cochin under duress to the French. Cambodia, too, accepted a French protectorate. This was followed by further French advance and the arousing of Indo-Chinese resistance. In the 1870s the French occupied the Red River delta; soon, other quarrels led to a war with China, the para-mount power, which confirmed the French grip on Indo-China. In 1887 they set up an Indo-Chinese Union which disguised a centralized régime behind a system of protec-torates. Though this meant the preservation of native rulers (the emperor of Annam and the kings of Cambodia and Laos), the aim of French colonial policy was always assimila-tion. French culture was to be brought to new French subjects whose élites were to be gallicized as the best way to promote modern-ization and civilization.

OPPOSITION TO FRENCH RULE

The centralizing tendencies of French administration soon made it clear that the

Indian troops cross a river after having fought rebel tribes in Manipur, near the Burmese frontier. Upper Burma was integrated into the British Empire in 1886.

Of European origin, this 19th-century engraving shows Christians being beheaded in Cochin China.

formal structure of native government was a sham. Unwittingly, the French thus sapped local institutions without replacing them with others enjoying the loyalty of the people. This was a dangerous course. There were also other important by-products of the French presence. It brought with it, for example, French tariff policy, which was to slow down industrialization. This eventually led Indo-Chinese businessmen, like their Indian equivalents, to wonder in whose interests their country was run. Moreover, the conception of an Indo-China, which was integrally a part of France, whose inhabitants should be turned into French citizens, also brought problems. The French administration had to grapple with the paradox that access to French education could lead to reflection on the inspiring motto to be found on official buildings and documents of the Third Republic: "liberty, equality and fraternity."

Finally, French law and notions of property broke down the structure of village land-holding and threw power into the hands of money-lenders and landlords. With a growing population in the rice-growing areas, this was to build up a revolutionary potential for the future.

Japan and China provided catalysts for Indo-Chinese grievances embodied in these facts and the legacy of traditional Vietnamese nationalism soon made itself felt. The Japanese victory over Russia led several young Vietnamese to go to Tokyo, where they met Sun Yat-sen and the Japanese sponsors of "Asia for the Asians". After the Chinese Revolution of 1911, one of them organized a society for a Vietnamese Republic. None of this much troubled the French who were well able to contain such opposition before 1914, but it curiously paralleled conservative opposition to them among the Vietnamese

In the kingdom of Tonkin, which was part of French Indo-China, the regional colonial commander receives local petitioners in front of his residence in the early 1900s.

Confucian scholar class. Though they opened a university in 1907, the French had to close it almost at once and it remained closed until 1918 because of fears of unrest among the intellectuals. This important section of Vietnamese opinion was already deeply alienated by French rule within a couple of decades of its establishment.

INDONESIA

To the south of Indo-China, too, French history had already had an indirect impact in Indonesia. By the end of the nineteenth century there were some sixty million Indonesians; population pressure had not yet produced there the strains that were to come, but it was the largest group of non-Europeans ruled by a European state outside India. Their ancestors had nearly two centuries of sometimes bitter experience of Dutch rule before the French Revolution led to the invasion of the United Provinces, the setting up of a new revolutionary republic there in 1795 and the dissolving of the Dutch East India Company and, soon afterwards, a British occupation of Java. The British troubled the waters by important changes in the revenue system, but there were also other influences now at work to stir up Indonesia. Though originally an outcropping of the Hindu civilization of India, it was also part of the Islamic world, with large numbers of at least nominal Muslims among its peoples, and commercial ties with Arabia. In the early years of the nineteenth century this had new importance. Indonesian pilgrims, some of them of birth and rank, went to Mecca and then sometimes went on to Egypt and Turkey. There they found themselves directly in touch with reforming ideas from further west.

ANTI-DUTCH FEELING

The instability of the situation in Indonesia was revealed when the Dutch returned and had, in 1825, to fight a "Java War" against a dissident prince which lasted five years. It damaged the island's finances so that the Dutch were constrained to introduce further changes. The result was an agricultural system which enforced the cultivation of crops for the government. The workings of this system led to grave exploitation of the peasant which began in the later nineteenth century to awaken among the Dutch an uneasiness about the conduct of their colonial government. This culminated in a great change of attitude; in 1901 a new "Ethical Policy" was announced which was expressed in decentralization and a campaign to achieve improvement through village administration. But this programme often proved so paternalistic and interventionist in action that it, too, sometimes stimulated hostility. This was utilized by the first Indonesian nationalists, some of them inspired by Indians. In 1908 they formed an organization to promote national education. Three years later an Islamic association appeared, whose early activities were directed as much against Chinese traders as against the Dutch. By 1916 it had gone so far as to ask for self-government while remaining in union with the Netherlands. Before this, however, a true independence party had been founded in 1912. It opposed Dutch authority in the name of native-born Indonesians, of any race; a Dutchman was among its three founders and others followed him. In 1916 the Dutch took the first step towards meeting the demands of these groups by authorizing a parliament with limited powers for Indonesia.

THE LEGACY OF IMPERIALISM IN ASIA

Though European ideas of nationalism were by the early years of the twentieth century at work in almost all Asian countries, they took their different expressions from different possibilities. Not all colonial régimes behaved in the same way. The British encouraged nationalists in Burma, while the Americans doggedly pursued a benevolent paternalism in

The European influence is unmistakable in this illustration of a street in Java in 1886.

the Philippines after suppressing insurrection originally directed against their Spanish predecessors. Those same Spanish, like the Portuguese elsewhere in Asia, had vigorously promoted Christian conversion, while the British Raj was very cautious about interference with native religion. History also shaped the futures of colonial Asia, because of the different legacies the various European régimes played there. Above all, the forces of historical possibilities and historical inertia showed themselves in Japan and China, where European influence was just as dramatic in its effects as in directly-ruled India or Vietnam. In every instance, the context in which that influence operated was decisive in shaping the future; at the end of a couple of centuries of European activity in Asia much (perhaps most) of that context remained intact. A huge residue of customary thought and practice remained undisturbed. Too much history was present for European expansion alone to explain twentieth-century Asia. The catalytic and liberating power of that expansion, none the less, was what brought Asia into the modern era.

Albert Sarraut, the governor of French Indo-China, poses with Emperor Khai Dai of Annam. Khai Dai's son Bao Dai (who was born in 1913) ruled as the last emperor of Annam from 1932 until 1945, when he was deposed and the Republic of Vietnam was declared.

4 STRAINS IN THE SYSTEM

Early incubators are used to care for babies in a Parisian maternity hospital in 1884. Premature babies were laid in wooden structures which were then placed over metal containers full of hot water to keep the infants at the correct temperature. The use of incubators contributed to the drop in the infant mortality rate in Europe in the late 19th and early 20th centuries.

ONE HISTORICAL TREND very obvious as the twentieth century opened was the continuing increase of population in the European world. In 1900 Europe itself had about 400 million inhabitants – a quarter of them Russians – the United States about seventy-six million and the British overseas dominions about fifteen million between them. This kept the dominant civilization's share of world population high. On the other hand, growth was already beginning to slow down in some countries in the first decade of this century. This was most obvious in the advanced nations, which were the heart of western Europe, where growth

depended more and more on falling death-rates. In them there was evidence that keeping your family small was a practice now spreading downwards through society. Traditional contraceptive knowledge of a sort had long been available, but the nineteenth century had brought to the better-off more effective techniques. When these were taken up more widely (and there were soon signs that they were), their impact on population structure would be very great.

FEARS OF WORLD OVERPOPULATION

In eastern and Mediterranean Europe, on the other hand, major changes in the population structure were far away. There, rapid growth was only just beginning to produce grave strains. The growing availability of outlets though emigration in the nineteenth century had made it possible to overcome them; there might be trouble to come if those outlets ceased to be so easily available. Further afield, even more pessimistic reflections might be prompted by considering what would happen when the agencies at work to reduce the death-rate in Europe came to spread to Asia and Africa. In the world civilization the

Time chart 1853–1903					
1853–1856 The Crimean War	1861 Unification of Italy	1870–1871 Franco-Prussian War	1876 Telephone invented	1886 First automobiles	1903 The Wright brothers' aeroplane
1850		1870			1900
	1859 *The Origin of Species* by Charles Darwin	1867 *Das Kapital* by Karl Marx	1877–1888 War between Russia and Turkey	1889 Second Socialist International	

nineteenth century had created, this could not be prevented. In that case, Europe's success in imposing itself would have guaranteed the eventual loss of the demographic advantage recently added to her technical superiority. Worse still, the Malthusian crisis once feared (but lost to sight as the nineteenth-century economic miracle removed the fear of over-population) might at last become a reality.

RAPID ECONOMIC GROWTH

It had been possible to set aside Malthus's warnings because the nineteenth century brought about the greatest surge in wealth creation the world had ever known. Its sources lay in the industrialization of Europe, and the techniques for assuring the continuance of this growth were far from exhausted or compromised in 1900. There had not only been a vast and accelerating flow of commodities available only in (relatively) tiny quantities a century before, but whole new ranges of goods had come into existence. Oil and electricity had joined coal, wood, wind and water as sources of energy. A chemical industry existed which could not have been envisaged in 1800. Growing power and wealth had been used to tap seemingly inexhaustible natural resources, both agricultural and mineral – and not only in Europe; its demand for raw materials changed the economies of other continents. The needs of the new electrical industry gave Brazil a brief rubber boom, but changed for ever the history of Malaysia and Indo-China.

The daily life of millions changed, too. Railways, electric trams, steamships, motor cars and bicycles gave individuals a new control over their environment; they quickened travel from place to place and speeded up land transport for the first time since animals had been harnessed to carts thousands of years

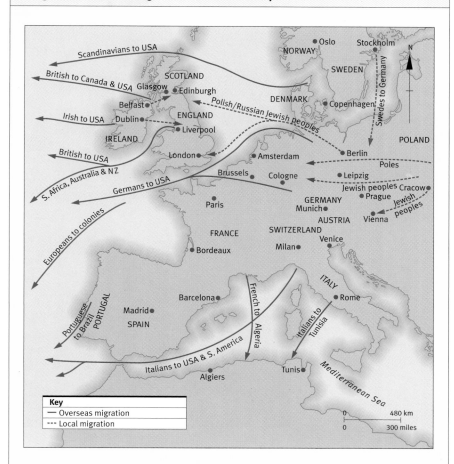

Migration from Europe in the 19th century

During the 19th century, the main population movement was that of the Europeans emigrating to America. The sparsely populated territories of the United States, and to a lesser extent South American countries such as Argentina and Brazil, offered wonderful opportunities to immigrants. Many Japanese and Chinese people also emigrated to America. The colonies seemed less attractive to European settlers, although there were some exceptions, including Australia.

Within Europe itself, the main population movement was that of the Jews, who left the hostile tsarist Russian Empire in large numbers to settle in the western European states.

before. The overall result of such changes had been that in many countries a growing population had been easily carried on an even faster growing production of wealth; between 1870 and 1900, for example, Germany's output of pig-iron increased sixfold, but her population rose only by about a third. In terms of consumption, or of the services to which they had access, or in the enjoyment of

This painting, entitled *The Forge*, dates from 1893. At that time, the iron and steel industries were enormously important in Europe: economic and military power could not be achieved without them.

better health, even the mass of the population in developed countries was much better off in 1900 than their predecessors a hundred years before. This still left out people like the Russian or Andalusian peasants (though an assessment of their condition is by no means easy to make nor the result a foregone conclusion). But, none the less, the way ahead looked promising even for them, inasmuch as a key to prosperity had been found which could be made available to all countries.

POVERTY IN INDUSTRIAL EUROPE

In spite of the cheerful picture presented by growing prosperity, doubts could break in. Even if what might happen in the future were

ignored, contemplation of the cost of the new wealth and doubts about the social justice of its distribution were troubling. Most people were still terribly poor, whether or not they lived in rich countries where the incongruity of this was more striking than in earlier times. Poverty was all the more afflicting when society showed such obvious power to create new wealth. Here was the beginning of a change of revolutionary import in expectations. Another change in the way Europeans thought about their condition arose over their power to get a livelihood at all. It was not new that wage-earners should be without work. What was new was that situations should suddenly arise in which the operation of blind forces of boom and slump produced millions of men without work concentrated in great towns. This was "unemployment", a new phenomenon for which a new word had been needed. Some economists thought that it might be an inevitable concomitant of capitalism. Nor were the cities themselves yet rid of all the evils which had so struck the first observers of industrial society. By 1900 the majority of Western Europeans were town-dwellers. By 1914 there were more than 140 cities of over 100,000 inhabitants. In some of them, millions of people were cramped, ill-housed, underprovided with schools and fresh air, let alone amusement other than that of the streets, and this often in sight of the wealth their society helped to produce. "Slums" was another word invented by the nineteenth century. Two converging conclusions were often drawn from contemplating them. One was that of fear; many sober statesmen at the end of the nineteenth century still distrusted the cities as centres of revolutionary danger, crime and wickedness.

The other was hopeful: the condition of the cities gave grounds for assurance that revolution against the injustice of the social and economic order was inevitable. What both these responses neglected, of course, was the accumulating evidence of experience that revolution in western Europe was in fact less and less likely.

DISORDER AND THE FEAR OF REVOLUTION

The fear of revolution was fed also by disorder, even if its nature was misinterpreted and exaggerated. In Russia, a country which was clearly a part of Europe if it is contrasted with the rest of the world, but one which had not moved forward rapidly along the lines of economic and social progress, reform had not gone far enough and there was a continuing

The novel in the 19th century

As a genre, the novel achieved during the 19th century the predominant status it holds today. The great novels of that era constitute an outstanding record of 19th-century society's virtues and vices. Realist writing, in which the circumstances of human life in different social classes were explored, began to become prominent in the 1830s: Honoré de Balzac in France and Charles Dickens in England launched the trend, which later spread throughout the Western world from Leo Tolstoy's Russia to the United States of Henry James. Some of the most significant novels published during the 19th century include:

1813	Jane Austen: *Pride and Prejudice*
1814	Walter Scott: *Waverley*
1825–1827	Alessandro Manzoni: *I Promessi Sposi*
1830	Stendhal: *Le Rouge et le Noir*
1833	Honoré de Balzac: *Eugénie Grandet*
1835	Honoré de Balzac: *Le Père Goriot*
1837	Charles Dickens: *The Pickwick Papers*
1837–1839	Charles Dickens: *Oliver Twist*
1842	Nikolai Gogol: *Dead Souls*
1847	Honoré de Balzac: *La Cousine Bette*
1847	Emily Brontë: *Wuthering Heights*
1851	Herman Melville: *Moby Dick*
1852–1853	Charles Dickens: *Bleak House*
1857	Gustave Flaubert: *Madame Bovary*
1862	Ivan Turgenev: *Fathers and Sons*
1865–1869	Leo Tolstoy: *War and Peace*
1866	Fyodor Dostoyevsky: *Crime and Punishment*
1870	Gustave Flaubert: *L'Education sentimentale*
1871–1872	George Eliot: *Middlemarch*
1875–1877	Leo Tolstoy: *Anna Karenina*
1875	Joao Maria Eça de Queiróz: *Father Amaro's Crime*
1879–1880	Fyodor Dostoyevsky: *The Brothers Karamazov*
1880	Emile Zola: *Nana*
1881	Giovanni Verga: *I Malavoglia*
1884–1885	Leopoldo Alas: *La Regenta*
1885	Emile Zola: *Germinal*
1886	Henry James: *The Bostonians*
1886–1887	Benito Pérez Galdós: *Fortunata y Jacinta*
1895	Thomas Hardy: *Jude the Obscure*
1895	Stephen Crane: *The Red Badge of Courage*
1895	Theodor Fontane: *Effi Briest*
c.1899	Thomas Mann: *Buddenbrooks*

SUNDAY MORNING
WORKMANS HOME
LEATHER LANE

Published in 1875, this image of a London worker's home illustrated a magazine article denouncing the miserable conditions in which many labourers and their families lived.

revolutionary movement. It broke out in terrorism – one of whose victims was a tsar – and was assisted by continuing and spontaneous agrarian unrest. Peasant attacks on landlords and their bailiffs reached a peak in the early years of this century. When there ensued defeat in war at the hands of the

Japanese and the momentary shaking of the régime's confidence, the result was a revolution in 1905. Russia might be, and no doubt was, a special case, but Italy, too, had something that some observers thought of as barely contained revolution in 1898 and again in 1914, while one of the great cities of Spain, Barcelona, exploded into bloody street-fighting in 1909. Strikes and demonstrations could become violent in industrialized countries without revolutionary traditions, as the United States amply showed in the 1890s; even in Great Britain deaths sometimes resulted from them. This was the sort of data which, when combined with the sporadic activities of anarchists, kept policemen and respectable citizens on their toes. The anarchists especially succeeded in pressing themselves on the public imagination. Their acts of terrorism and assassinations during the 1890s received wide publicity; the importance of such acts

At the end of the 19th century a wave of anarchist attacks took place across Europe – seen here is the aftermath of an explosion at the Véry restaurant in Paris on 25 April 1892. This attack led to the detention of François Ravachol, who was later executed for several terrorist crimes.

transcended success or failure because the growth of the press had meant that great publicity value could be extracted from a bomb or a dagger-stroke. In using such methods, not all anarchists shared the same aims, but they were children of their epoch: they protested not only against the state in its governmental aspects, but also against a whole society which they judged unjust. They helped to keep the old fear of revolution alive, though probably less than the rhetoric of their old rivals, the Marxists.

THE SOCIALIST MOVEMENT

B Y 1900 SOCIALISM almost everywhere meant Marxism. An important alternative tradition and mythology existed only in England, where the early growth of a numerous trade-union movement and the possibilities of working through established political parties favoured a non-revolutionary radicalism. The supremacy of Marxism among continental socialists, by contrast, was formally expressed in 1896, when the "Second International", an international working-class movement set up seven years before to coordinate socialist action in all countries, expelled the anarchists who had until then belonged to it. Four years later, the International opened a permanent office in Brussels. Within this movement, numbers, wealth and theoretical contributions made the German Social Democratic Party preponderant. This party had prospered in spite of police persecution thanks to Germany's rapid industrialization, and by 1900 was an established fact of German politics, their first truly mass organization. Numbers and wealth alone would have made it likely that Marxism, the official creed of the German party, would be that of the international socialist movement, but Marxism also had its own intellectual and

emotional appeal. This lay above all in its assurance that the world was already going the way socialists hoped, and the emotional satisfaction it provided of participating in a struggle of classes, which, Marxists insisted, must end in violent revolution.

REVISIONIST MARXISTS

Though Marxist mythology confirmed the fears of the established order, some intelligent Marxists had noticed that after 1880 or so the facts by no means obviously supported it. Manifestly, great numbers of people had been able to obtain a higher standard of living within the capitalist system. The unfolding of

In their union building in Milan in 1905, railway workers vote on whether to take strike action. Trade unions had formed in several countries by this time. Many were legally recognized and had their own premises and press.

Jean Jaurès (1859–1914), the founder of the French Socialist Party, is depicted speaking in the Chamber of the National Assembly in Paris. In 1904, Jaurès helped to create the socialist newspaper *L'Humanité*, which he edited until his assassination in 1914.

towards the transformation of society by socialism. If people liked to call that transformation, when it came, a revolution, then only an argument about usage was involved. Inside this theoretical position and the conflict it provoked was a practical issue which came to a head at the end of the century: whether socialists should or should not sit as ministers in capitalist governments.

SPLITS WITHIN SOCIALISM

The debate which divisions in the socialist movement aroused took years to settle. What emerged in the end was explicit condemnation of revisionism by the Second International while national parties, notably the Germans, continued to act on it in practice, doing deals with the existing system as it suited them. Their rhetoric continued to be about revolution. Many socialists even hoped that this might be made a reality by refusing to fight as conscripts if their governments tried to make them go to war. One socialist group, the majority in the Russian party, continued vigorously to denounce revisionism and advocate violence; this reflected the peculiarity of the Russian situation, where there was little to hope for from parliamentary politics and a deep tradition of revolution and terrorism. This group was called Bolshevik, from the Russian word meaning a majority, and more was to be heard of it.

INDUSTRIAL CONSERVATISM AND STATE INTERFERENCE

Socialists claimed to speak for the masses. Whether they did so or did not, by 1900 many conservatives worried that the advances gained by liberalism and democracy in the nineteenth century might well prove

that system in all its complexity was not simplifying and sharpening class conflict in the way Marx had predicted. Moreover, capitalist political institutions had been able to serve the working class. This was very important; in Germany, above all, but also in England, important advantages had been won by socialists using the opportunities provided by parliaments. The vote was available as a weapon and they were not disposed to ignore it while waiting for the revolution. This led some socialists to attempt to restate official Marxism so as to take account of such trends; they were called "revisionists" and, broadly speaking, they advocated a peaceful advance irresistible except by force. A few of them still lived in a mental world which was pre-nineteenth rather than pre-twentieth century. In much of eastern Europe quasi-patriarchal relationships and the traditional authority of the landowner over his estates were still intact. Such societies could still produce aristocratic conservatives who were opposed in spirit not merely to encroachments upon their material privilege, but to all the values and assumptions of what was to be called "market society". But this line was more and more blurred and, for the most part, conservative thinking tended to fall back upon the defence of capital, a position which, of course, would in many places half a century earlier have been regarded as radically liberal, because individualist. Capitalist, industrial and conservative Europe opposed itself more and more vigorously to the state's interference with its wealth, an interference which had grown steadily with the state's acceptance of a

larger and larger role in the regulation of society. There was a crisis in England on the issue, which led to a revolutionary transformation of what was left of the 1688 constitution, in 1911 by the crippling of the power of the House of Lords to restrain an elected House of Commons. In the background were many issues, among them higher taxation of the rich to pay for social services. Even France had by 1914 accepted the principle of an income tax.

WOMEN IN A CHANGING SOCIETY

CONSTITUTIONAL CHANGES registered the logic of the democratizing of politics in advanced societies. By 1914, universal adult male suffrage existed in France, Germany and several smaller European countries; Great Britain and Italy had electorates big enough

Telephone switchboard operators are shown at work in France at the beginning of the 20th century. As more and more jobs became available to women and their traditional role in society began to change, their demand to be enfranchised won support in many European countries.

to come near to meeting this criterion. This brought forward another disruptive question: if men had, should not women have the vote in national politics? The issue was already causing uproar in English politics. But in Europe only Finland and Norway had women in their parliamentary electorates by 1914, though, further afield, New Zealand, two Australian states and some in the United States had given women the franchise by then. The issue was to remain open in many countries for another thirty years.

THE EARLY FEMINIST MOVEMENT

Political rights were one aspect of a larger question of women's rights in a society whose overall bias, like that of every other great civilization which had preceded it, was towards the interests and values of men. Yet discussion of women's role in society in Europe had begun in the eighteenth century and it was not long before cracks appeared in the structure of assumptions which had so long

Feminism

Women have been subjected to masculine supremacy in virtually every civilization, including those of the Western world. Women's natural role was long perceived to be that of the home-maker; their participation in public affairs was, at best, limited and their freedom of action was restricted by being under the tutelage of their fathers or husbands. Criticism of this inequality began in the atmosphere of intellectual and social change that accompanied the French Revolution. Among the first publications to advocate a new social role for women were *On the Admission of Women to the Right to Sovereignty* (1790) by the Marquis de Condorcet, *Declaration of the Rights of Women and Citizens* (1791) by Olympia de Gouges and *A Vindication of the Rights of Women* (1792) by Mary Wollstonecraft. However, even the Assemblies of revolutionary France did not support greater freedom for women and the Civil Code drawn up under Napoleon perpetuated discrimination.

The situation began to change from the mid-19th century, and particularly during the 20th century. At least in the Western world, women have gradually achieved civil and political equality, access to higher education and to better-paid jobs, and a greater personal freedom, although many believe that this process is not yet complete. The right to vote, which was an essential vindication of the early feminists, was first obtained in some of the world's youngest states: the North American territory of Wyoming (1869), the British dominions of New Zealand (1893) and Australia (1902) and the newly independent Norway (1913).

A feminist protest in France in 1908 is depicted on the cover of a magazine. French women did not obtain the right to vote until after the Second World War.

enclosed it. Women's rights to education, to employment, to control of their own property, to moral independence, even to wear more comfortable clothes, had increasingly been debated in the nineteenth century. Ibsen's play *A Doll's House* was interpreted as a trumpet-call for the liberation of women instead of, as the author intended, a plea for the individual. The bringing forward of such issues implied a real revolution. The claims of women in Europe and North America threatened assumptions and attitudes which had not merely centuries, but even millennia, of institutionalization behind them. They awoke complex emotions, for they were linked to deep-seated notions about the family and sexuality. In these ways, they troubled some people – men and women alike – more deeply than the threat of social revolution or political democracy. People were right to see the question in this dimension. In the early European feminist movement was the seed of something whose explosive content would be even greater when transferred (as it soon was) to other cultures and civilizations as a part of the assault by Western values.

NEW OPPORTUNITIES FOR WOMEN

The politicization of women, and political attacks on the legal and institutional structures which were felt by them to be oppressive, probably did less for women than did some other changes. Three of these were of slowly growing but, eventually, gigantic importance in undermining tradition. The first was the growth of the advanced capitalist economy. By 1914 this already meant great numbers of new jobs – as typists, secretaries, telephone operators, factory hands, department store assistants and teachers – for women in some countries. Almost none of

these had existed a century earlier. They brought a huge practical shift of economic power to women: if they could earn their own living, they were at the beginning of a road which would eventually transform family structures. Soon, too, the demands of warfare in the industrial societies would accelerate this advance as the need for labour opened an even wider range of occupations to them. Meanwhile, for growing numbers of girls even by 1900, a job in industry or commerce at once meant a chance of liberation from parental regulation and the trap of married drudgery. Most women did not by 1914 so benefit, but an accelerating process was at work, because such developments would stimulate other demands, for example, for education and professional training.

The second great transforming force was even further from showing its full potential to change women's lives by 1914. This was contraception. It had already decisively

This pottery figure of a woman on horseback is entitled *Liberty* and dates from 1905. The figure's dynamism reflects a new vision of women.

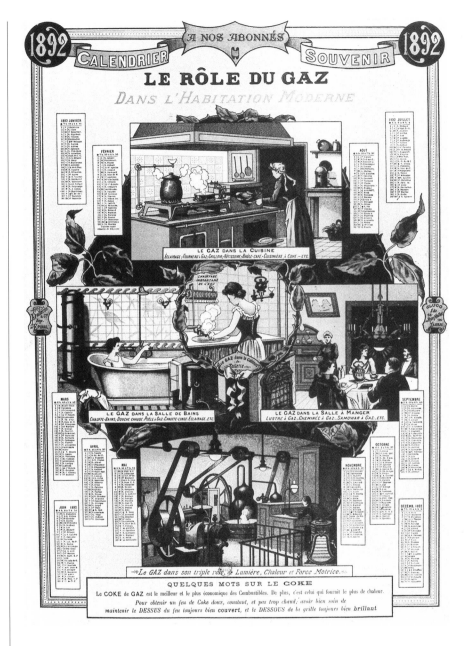

An advertising poster from 1892 shows the various ways in which gas could be used in the modern home. The consumption of gas was on the increase: it was used to power machines, to provide light and heat in houses and to cook food.

TECHNOLOGY AND WOMEN'S LIBERATION

To the third great force moving women imperceptibly but irresistibly towards liberation from ancient ways and assumptions it is much harder to give an identifying single name, but if it has a governing principle, it is technology. It was a process made up of a vast number of innovations, some of them already slowly accumulating for decades before 1900 and all tending to cut into the iron time-tables of domestic routine and drudgery, however marginally at first. The coming of piped water, or of gas for heating and lighting, are among the first examples; electricity's cleanliness and flexibility was later to have even more obvious effects. Better shops were the front line of big changes in retail distribution, which not only gave a notion of luxury to people other than the rich, but also made it easier to meet household needs. Imported food, with its better processing and preserving, slowly changed habits of family catering once based – as they are still often based in India or Africa – on daily or twice daily visits to the market. The world of detergents and easily cleaned artificial fibres still lay in the future in 1900, but already soap and washing soda were far more easily and cheaply available than a century before, while the first domestic machines – gas cookers, vacuum cleaners, washing machines – began to make their appearance at least in the homes of the rich early in this century.

affected demography. What lay ahead was a revolution in power and status as more women absorbed the idea that they might control the demands of childbearing and rearing, which hitherto had throughout history dominated most women's lives; beyond that lay an even deeper change, only beginning to be discerned in 1914, as women came to see that they could pursue sexual satisfaction without necessarily entering the obligation of lifelong marriage.

FEMALE SUFFRAGE

Historians who would recognize at once the importance of the introduction of the stirrup or the lathe in earlier times have none the less strangely neglected the cumulative force of such humble commodities and instruments as

A suffragette is arrested by police after chaining herself to the railings of London's Buckingham Palace in 1914. The campaign for women's suffrage provoked unexpectedly powerful reactions in Britain on both sides of the debate. Women over the age of 30 in the United Kingdom were finally granted the vote in 1918.

these. Yet they implied a revolution for half the world. It is more understandable that their long-term implications interested fewer people at the beginning of this century than the antics of the "suffragettes", as women who sought the vote were called in England.

The immediate stimulus to their activity was the evident liberalization and democratization of political institutions in the case of men. This was the background which their campaign presupposed. Logically, there were grounds for pursuing democracy across the

This contemporary magazine illustration shows campaigners putting up election propaganda posters in Milan in 1911. Political propaganda techniques developed alongside wider access to the vote and greater literacy.

boundaries of sex even if this meant doubling the size of electorates.

NEW MASS POLITICS

The formal and legal structure of politics was not the whole story of their tendency to show more and more of a "mass" quality. The masses had to be organized. By 1900 there had appeared to meet this need the modern political party, with its simplifications of issues in order to present them as clear choices, its apparatus for the spread of political awareness, and its cultivation of special interests. From Europe and the United States it spread around the world. Old-fashioned politicians deplored the new model of party

and by no means always did so insincerely, because it was another sign of the coming of mass society, the corruption of public debate and the need for traditional élites to adapt their politics to the ways of the man in the street.

The importance of public opinion had begun to be noticed in England early in the nineteenth century. It had been thought decisive in the struggles over the Corn Laws. By 1870, the French emperor felt he could not resist the popular clamour for a war which he feared and was to lose. Bismarck, the quintessential conservative statesman, felt soon afterwards that he must give way to public opinion and promote Germany's colonial interests. The manipulation of public opinion, too, seemed to have become possible (or so, at least, many newspaper owners and statesmen believed). Growing literacy had two sides to it. It had been believed on the one hand that investment in mass education was necessary in order to civilize the masses for the proper use of the vote. What seemed to be the consequence of rising literacy, however, was that a market was created for a new cheap press, which often pandered to emotionalism and sensationalism, and for the sellers and devisers of advertising campaigns, another invention of the nineteenth century.

NATIONALISM

THE POLITICAL PRINCIPLE which undoubtedly still had the most mass appeal was nationalism. Moreover, it kept its revolutionary potential. This was clear in a number of places. In Turkish Europe, from the Crimean War onwards, the successes of nationalists in fighting Ottoman rule and creating new nations had never flagged. Serbia, Greece and Romania were solidly established by 1870. By the end of the century they had been joined by Bulgaria and Montenegro. In 1913, in the last wars of the Balkan states against Turkey before a European conflict swallowed the Turkish question, there appeared Albania, and by then an autonomous Crete already had a Greek governor. These nationalist movements had at several times dragged greater states into their affairs and always presented a potential danger to peace. This was not so true of those within the Russian Empire, where Poles, Jews, Ukrainians and Lithuanians felt themselves oppressed by the Russians. War, though, seemed a more likely outcome of strains in the Austro-Hungarian Empire, where nationalism presented a real revolutionary danger in the lands within the Hungarian half of the monarchy. Slav majorities there looked across the border to Serbia for help against Magyar oppressors. Elsewhere in the empire – in Bohemia and Slovakia, for example – feeling was less high, but nationalism was no less the dominant question. Great Britain faced no such dangers as these, but even she had a nationalist problem, in Ireland. Indeed, she had two.

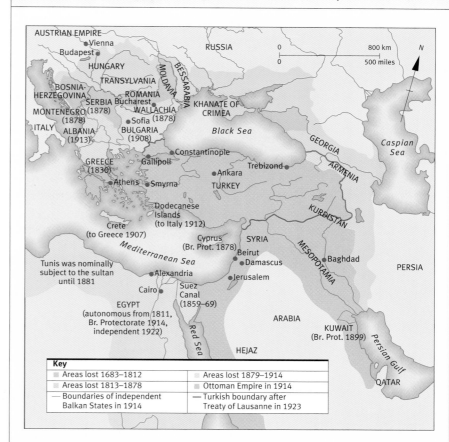

Ottoman decline and the emergence of modern Turkey 1683–1923

From the late 17th century, the extent of the Ottoman Empire had been reduced, first at the hands of Austria in the Danube valley, and then around the Black Sea by Russia. The Serbian uprising of 1815–1817 led to the Ottoman retreat from the Balkans, which ended in defeat in the wars of 1912–1913. The North African Ottoman territories were seized by the European countries and, at the end of the First World War, the empire lost the remainder of its Arabian lands.

On the above map some of the areas shown as lost include tributary peoples over whom the Ottomans claimed suzerainty, as well as areas of direct Ottoman rule.

That of the Catholic Irish was for most of the nineteenth century the more obvious. Important reforms and concessions had been granted, though they fell short of the autonomous state of "Home Rule" to which

A massacre of Armenians in Turkey is depicted in an Italian illustration dated 1909. The Young Turks' revolt of 1908 was a major step in the modernization of Turkey, but the nationalist fervour which accompanied it had tragic consequences for the Armenian population.

the British Liberal Party was committed. By 1900, however, agricultural reform and better economic conditions had drawn much of the venom from this Irish question, although it was reinstated by the appearance of another Irish nationalism, that of the Protestant majority of the province of Ulster, which was excited to threaten revolution if the government in London gave Home Rule to the Roman Catholic Irish nationalists. This was much more than merely embarrassing. When the machinery of English democracy did finally deliver Home Rule legislation in 1914, some foreign observers were misled into thinking that British policy would be fatally inhibited from intervention in European affairs by revolution at home.

THE GERMAN CHALLENGE

All those who supported expressions of nationalism believed themselves with greater or less justification to do so on behalf of the oppressed. But the nationalism of the great powers was also a disruptive force. France and Germany were psychologically deeply sundered by the transfer of two provinces, Alsace and Lorraine, to Germany in 1871. French politicians whom it suited to do so, long and assiduously cultivated the theme of *revanche*. Nationalism in France gave especial bitterness to political quarrels because they seemed to raise questions of loyalty to great national institutions. Even the supposedly sober British from time to time grew excited about national symbols. There was a brief but deep enthusiasm for imperialism and always great sensitivity over the preservation of British naval supremacy. More and more this appeared to be threatened by Germany, a power whose obvious economic dynamism caused alarm by the danger it presented to British supremacy in world commerce. It did not matter that the two countries were one another's best customers; what was more important was that they appeared to have interests opposed in many specific ways. Additional colour was given to this by the stridency of German nationalism under the reign of the third emperor, Wilhelm II. Conscious of Germany's potential, he sought to give it not only real but symbolic expression. One effect was his enthusiasm for building a great navy; this especially annoyed the British who could not see that it could be intended for use against anyone but them. But there was a generally growing impression in Europe, far from unjustified, that the Germans were prone to throw their weight about unreasonably in international affairs. National stereotypes cannot be summarized in a phrase, but because they helped to impose terrible simplifications upon public reactions they are part of the story of the disruptive power of nationalist feeling at the beginning of the twentieth century.

Kaiser Wilhelm II in 1900. Emperor of Germany from 1888 until 1918, Wilhelm favoured an aggressive foreign policy which contributed to the outbreak of the First World War.

Before the First World War it was believed that any conflict would be limited by its cost. Tragically, this belief turned out to be unfounded, as European industry supplied the armies with an unprecedented number of weapons; this image of a British armaments factory during the First World War gives some idea of the immense output. At the same time, the mass conscription of men led to the incorporation of women into manufacturing sectors where they had not previously been employed.

"CIVILIZED WARFARE"

Those who felt confident could point to the diminution of international violence in the nineteenth century; there had been no war between European great powers since 1876 (when Russia and Turkey had come to blows) and, unhappily, European soldiers and statesmen failed to understand the portents of the American Civil War, the first in which one commander could control over a million men, thanks to railway and telegraph, and the first to show the power of modern mass-produced weapons to inflict huge casualties. While such facts were overlooked, the summoning of congresses in 1899 and 1907 to halt competition in armaments could be viewed optimistically, though they failed in their aim. Certainly acceptance of the practice of

international arbitration had grown and some restrictions on the earlier brutality of warfare were visible. A significant phrase was used by the German emperor when he sent off his contingent to the international force fielded against the Chinese Boxers. Stirred to anger by reports of atrocities against Europeans by Chinese, Wilhelm urged his soldiers to behave "like Huns". The phrase stuck in people's memories. Though thought to be excessive even at the time, its real interest lies in the fact that he should have believed such an instruction was needed. Nobody would have had to tell a seventeenth-century army to behave like Huns, because it was in large measure then taken for granted that they would. By 1900, European troops were not expected to behave in this way and had therefore to be told to do so. So far had the humanizing of war come.

"Civilized warfare" was a nineteenth-century concept and far from a contradiction in terms. In 1899 it had been agreed to forbid, albeit for a limited period, the use of poison gas, dum-dum bullets and even the dropping of bombs from the air.

THE CHURCH IN DECLINE

THE RESTRAINT EXERCISED on European rulers by the consciousness of any tie other than that of a common resistance to revolution had, of course, long since collapsed together with the idea of Christendom. Nineteenth-century religion was in international relations at most a palliative or mitigation of conflict, a minor and indirect force, reinforcing a humanitarianism and pacifism fed from other sources. Christianity had proved as feeble a check to violence as would the hopes of socialists that the workers of the world would refuse to fight one another in the interests of their masters. Whether this was a result of a general loss of power by organized churches is not clear. Certainly much misgiving was felt by 1900 about their declining force in regulating behaviour. This was not because a new religion of traditional form challenged the old Christian churches. There had been, rather, a continuing development of trends observable in the eighteenth century and much more marked since the French Revolution. Almost all the Christian communions seemed more and more touched by the blight of one or other of the characteristic intellectual and social advances of the age. Nor did they seem able to exploit new devices – the late nineteenth-century appearance of mass-circulation newspapers, for instance – which might have helped them. Indeed, some of them, above all the Roman Catholic Church, positively distrusted such developments.

Pius IX was pope from 1846 to 1878, at a time when the Church of Rome seemed to repudiate the new liberal civilization. He condemned liberalism in the Syllabus of 1864 and refused to accept the incorporation of the Papal States into the newly united Italy.

THE PAPACY LOSES PRESTIGE

Though all the Christian communions felt a hostile current, the Roman Catholic Church was the most obvious victim, the papacy having especially suffered both in its prestige and power. It had openly proclaimed its hostility to progress, rationality and liberalism in statements which became part of the dogmas of the Church. Politically, Rome had begun to suffer from the whittling away of the Temporal Power in the 1790s, when the French revolutionary armies brought revolutionary principles and territorial change to Italy and invasion of the papal territories. Often, later infringements of the papacy's rights were to be justified in terms of the master ideas of the age: democracy, liberalism, nationalism. Finally, in 1870, the last territory of the old Papal States, still outside the Vatican itself, was taken by the new kingdom of Italy and the papacy became almost entirely a purely spiritual and ecclesiastical authority. This was the end of an era of temporal authority stretching back to Merovingian times and some felt it to be an inglorious one for an institution long the centre of European civilization and history.

In fact, it was to prove a blessing. Nevertheless, at the time the spoliation confirmed both the hostility to the forces of the century which the papacy had already expressed and the derision in which it was held by many progressive thinkers. Feeling on both sides reached new heights when in 1870 it became a part of the dogma of the Church that the pope, when he spoke *ex cathedra* on faith and morals, did so with infallible authority. There followed two decades in which anticlericalism and priest-baiting were more important in the politics of Germany, France, Italy and Spain than ever before. National sentiment could be mobilized against the Church in most Roman Catholic countries other than Poland. Governments took advantage of anti-papal prejudice to advance their own legal powers over the Church, but they were also increasingly pushing into areas where the Church had previously been paramount – above all, elementary and secondary education.

Persecution bred intransigence. In conflict, it emerged that whatever view might be taken on the abstract status of the teachings of the Roman Church, it could still draw on vast loyalty among the faithful. Moreover, these were still being recruited by conversion in the mission field overseas and would soon be added to in still greater numbers by demographic trends. Though organized religion might not make much progress anywhere among the new city-dwellers of Europe,

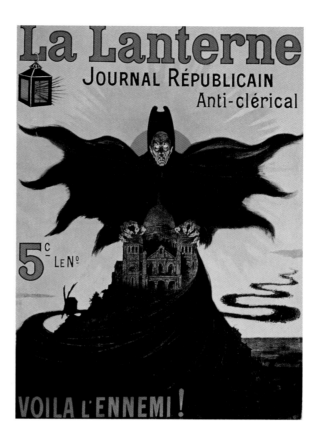

This anticlerical French cartoon illustrates the confrontation between the Church and its opponents that played a key role in political and intellectual life in the 19th and early 20th centuries.

untouched by inadequate ecclesiastical machinery and paganized by the slow stain of the secular culture in which they were immersed, it was far from dying, let alone dead, as a political and social force. Indeed, the liberation of the papacy from its temporal role made it easier for Roman Catholics to feel uncompromised loyalty towards it.

THE QUESTIONING OF TRADITIONAL BELIEFS

The Roman Catholic Church is one of the most demanding of the Christian denominations in its claims on believers and was in the forefront of the battle of religion with the age, but the claims of revelation and the authority of priest and clergyman were everywhere questioned. This was one of the most striking features of the nineteenth century, all the more so because so many Europeans and

Americans still retained simple and literal beliefs in the dogmas of their churches and the story contained in the Bible. They felt great anxiety when such beliefs were threatened, yet this was happening increasingly and in all countries. Traditional belief was at first obviously threatened only among an intellectual élite which often consciously held ideas drawn from Enlightenment sources: "Voltairean" was a favourite nineteenth-century adjective to indicate anti-religious and sceptical views. As the nineteenth century

What is a nation?

The liberal concept of a nation – seen as a community based not on race or language but on the popular will of people prepared to work together towards a common goal – was expounded in a speech by Ernest Renan:

"A nation is a great solidarity, created by the sense of sacrifices which have been made and those which people are prepared to make in the future. It presupposes a past; but it is summarized in the present in a concrete fact: the consent, the desire freely expressed, to continue to live together. A nation's existence is a daily plebiscite, the same as the existence of an individual is a perpetual affirmation of life … . It will be objected that secession and eventually the decline of nations would be the consequences of a system which leaves old organizations at the mercy of the will of people who are often unenlightened. Clearly, in matters such as this, no principle can be taken to extremes … nations are not eternal. They had a beginning and they will probably have an end. They will probably be replaced by a European confederation. But this is not the law of the century in which we live. At present, the existence of nations is good and even necessary."

An extract from *What is a Nation?* by Ernest Renan, 1882.

proceeded, such ideas were reinforced by two other intellectual currents, both also at first a concern of élites, but increasingly with a wider effect in an age of growing mass literacy and cheap printing.

One new intellectual challenge came from biblical scholars, the most important of them German, who from the 1840s onwards not only demolished many assumptions about the value of the Bible as historical evidence, but also, and perhaps more fundamentally, brought about something of a psychological change in the whole attitude to the scriptural text. In essence this change made it possible henceforth simply to regard the Bible as an historic text like any other, to be approached critically. An immensely successful (and scandal-provoking) *Life of Jesus*, published in 1863 by a French scholar, Ernest Renan, brought such an attitude before a wider public than ever before. The book that had been the central text of European civilization since its emergence in the Dark Ages was never to recover its position.

THE ROLE OF SCIENCE

A SECOND SOURCE of ideas damaging to traditional Christian faith – and therefore to the morality, politics, and economics for so long anchored in Christian assumptions – was natural science. Enlightenment attacks on internal and logical inconsistency in the teaching of the Church became much more alarming when science began to produce empirical evidence that things said in the Bible (and therefore based on the same authority as everything else in it) plainly did not fit observable fact. The starting-point was geology; ideas which had been about since the end of the eighteenth century were given a much wider public in the 1830s by the publication of *Principles of Geology* by Scottish

Darwin's theory of evolution

"It is interesting to contemplate a tangled bank, clothed with many plants of many kinds, with birds singing on the bushes, with various insects flitting about, and with worms crawling through the damp earth, and to reflect that these elaborately constructed forms, so different from each other, and dependent upon each other in so complex a manner, have all been produced from laws acting around us. These laws, taken in the largest sense, being Growth and Reproduction; Inheritance which is almost implied by reproduction; Variability from the indirect and direct action of the conditions of life, and from use and disuse: a ratio of increase so high as to lead to a struggle for life, and as a consequence to Natural Selection, entailing divergence of character and the extinction of less improved forms. Thus, from the war of nature, from famine and death, the most exalted object which we are capable of conceiving, namely, the production of the higher animals, directly follows. There is grandeur in this view of life, with its several powers, having been originally breathed by the Creator into a few forms or into one; and that, whilst this planet has gone cycling on according to the fixed law of gravity, from so simple a beginning endless forms most beautiful and most wonderful have been, and are being evolved."

An extract from the concluding chapter of *The Origin of Species* by Charles Darwin, 1876 edition.

That biblical chronology was simply untrue in relation to humanity was increasingly suggested by discoveries of stone tools in British caves along with the fossilized bones of extinct animals. The argument that the human race was much older than the biblical account allowed may perhaps be regarded as officially conceded when, in 1859, British learned societies heard and published papers establishing "that in a period of antiquity remote beyond any of which we have hitherto found traces", human beings had lived in Palaeolithic societies in the Somme valley.

CHARLES DARWIN

It is an over-simplification, but not grossly distorting, to say that the year 1859 brought

Charles Darwin (1809–1882) applied his theory of evolution, which had first been published in 1859, specifically to the human species in 1871. His work revolutionized concepts about living beings.

scientist Charles Lyell. This book explained landscape and geological structure in terms of forces still at work, that is, not as the result of a single act of creation, but of wind, rain and so on. Moreover, Lyell pointed out that if this were correct, then the presence of fossils of different forms of life in different geological strata implied that the creation of new animals had been repeated in each geological age. If this were so, the biblical account of creation was clearly in difficulties.

many of these questions to a head by an approach along a different line – "the biological" – when an English scientist, Charles Darwin, published one of the seminal books of modern civilization, the book called, for short, *The Origin of Species*. Much in it he owed, without acknowledgment, to others. Its publication came at a moment and in a country where it was especially likely to cause a stir; the issue of the rightfulness of the traditional dominance of religion (for example, in education) was in the air. The word "evolution" with which Darwin's name came especially to be connected was by then already familiar, though he tried to avoid using it and did not let it appear in *The Origin of Species* until its fifth edition, ten years after the first. Nevertheless, his book was the greatest single statement of the evolutionary hypothesis – namely, that living things were what they were because their forms had undergone long evolution from simpler ones. This, of course, included human beings, as he made explicit in another book, *The Descent of Man*, in 1871. Different views were held about how this evolution had occurred. Darwin, impressed by Malthus's vision of the murderous competition of humanity for food, took the view that the qualities which made

The British physicist Michael Faraday (1791–1867), depicted here in his laboratory, advanced the study of electricity and its possible practical applications considerably when he discovered the law of electromagnetic induction in 1831.

success likely in hostile environments ensured the "natural selection" of those creatures embodying them: this was a view to be vulgarized (and terribly misrepresented) by the use as a slogan of the phrase "survival of the fittest". But, important though many aspects of his work were to be in inspiring fresh thought, here it is important rather to see that Darwin dealt a blow against the biblical account of creation (as well as against the assumption of the unique status of the human race) which had wider publicity than any earlier one. In combination with biblical criticism and geology, his book made it impossible for any conscientious and thoughtful reader to accept – as was still possible in 1800 – the Bible as literally true.

THE NEW STATUS OF SCIENCE

The undermining of the authority of scripture remains the most obvious single way in which science affected formulated beliefs. Yet just as important, if not more so, was a new, vague but growing prestige which science was coming to have among a public more broadly based than ever before. This was because of its new status as the supreme instrument for the manipulation of nature, which was seen as increasingly powerless to resist. Here was the beginning of what was to grow into a mythology of science. Its essence lay in the fact that while the great achievements of seventeenth-century science had not often resulted in changes in the lives of ordinary men and women, those of the nineteenth century increasingly did. People who understood not a word of what might be written by Joseph Lister, who established the need for (and technique of using) antiseptics in surgery, or by Michael Faraday, who more than anyone else made possible the generation of electricity, knew none the less that the

medicine of 1900 was different from that of their grandparents and often saw electricity about them in their work and homes. By 1914, radio messages could be sent across the Atlantic, flying-machines which did not rely upon support by bags of gas of lower density than air were common, aspirins were easily available and an American manufacturer was selling the first cheap mass-produced automobile. The growing power and scope of science were by no means adequately represented by such facts, but material advance of this sort impressed the average person and led him or her to worship at a new shrine.

Popular awareness of science came through technology because for a long time this was almost the only way in which science had a positive impact on the lives of most people. Respect for it therefore usually grew in proportion to spectacular results in engineering or manufacture and even now, though science makes its impact in other ways, it still makes it very obviously through industrial processes. But though deeply entwined in this way with the dominant world civilization and so interwoven with society, the growth of science meant much more than just a growth of sheer power. In the years down to 1914 the foundations were laid for what would be evident in the second half of the twentieth century, a science which was as much as anything the mainspring of the dominant world culture. So rapid has been the advance to this state of affairs that science has already affected every part of human life while people are still trying to grapple with some of its most elementary philosophical implications.

SCIENTIFIC INSTITUTIONS

The easiest observations of the changing role of science which can be made (and the easiest

Some major scientific and technological advances 1815–1905	
1815	Theory of light waves, Augustin-Jean Fresnell
1818	Atomic weights, Jöns Berzelius
1827	Law of electrical conductivity, Georg Ohm
1831	Law of electromagnetic induction, Michael Faraday
1835	Telegraph, Samuel Morse
1839	Photography, Louis-Jacques Daguerre
1846	Anaesthetics, William Morton
1847	Rotary printing press, Richard Hoe
1856	First synthetic dye, Sir William Perkin
1859	Theory of evolution, Charles Darwin
1860–1865	Electromagnetics, James Clerk Maxwell
1865	Principles of heredity, Gregor Mendel
1865	Antisepsis, Joseph Lister
1866	Dynamo, Werner von Siemens
1869	Periodic table of the elements, Dimitri Mendeleyev
1870s	Statistical mechanics and thermodynamics, Ludwig Boltzmann
1876	Telephone, Alexander Graham Bell
1878	Incandescent electric lamp, Thomas Edison
1882	Tuberculosis bacillus, Robert Koch
1885	Anti-rabies vaccine, Louis Pasteur
1885	Automobile, Gottlieb Daimler and Carl Benz
1885–1889	Electrical waves, Heinrich Hertz
1895	Cinematograph, Auguste and Louis Lumière
1896	Radio-telegraphy, Guglielmo Marconi
1897	Electron, Sir Joseph Thompson
1898	Isolation of radium, Marie and Pierre Curie
1900	Quantum theory, Max Planck
1901	Mutation theory, Hugo de Vries
1902	Radioactivity, Ernest Rutherford
1903	Aeroplane, Wilbur and Orville Wright
1905	Special theory of relativity, Albert Einstein

to take as a starting-point) are those which display its status as a social and material phenomenon in its own right. From the moment when the first great advances in physics were made, in the seventeenth century, science was already a social fact. Institutions were then created in which men came together to study nature in a way which a later age could recognize as scientific, and scientists even then were sometimes employed by rulers to bring to bear their expertise on specific problems. It was noticeable, too, that in the useful arts –

and they were more usually called arts than sciences – such as navigation or agriculture, experiment by those who were not themselves practising technicians could make valuable contributions. But a terminological point helps to set this age in perspective and establish its remoteness from the nineteenth century and after: at this time scientists were still called "natural philosophers". The word "scientist" was not invented until about a third of the way through the nineteenth century, when it was felt that there was need to distinguish a rigorous experimental and observational investigation of nature from speculation on it by unchecked reason. Even then, though, there was little distinction for most people between the man who carried out such an investigation and the applied scientist or technologist who was the much more conspicuous representative of science in an age of engineering, mining and manufacturing on an unprecedented scale.

The nineteenth century was none the less the first in which science was taken for granted by the educated as a specialized field of study, whose investigators had professional standing. Its new status was marked by the much larger place given to science in educa-

tion, both by the creation of new departments at existing universities, and by the setting up in some countries, notably France and Germany, of special scientific and technical institutions. Professional studies, too, incorporated larger scientific components. Such developments accelerated as the effects of science on social and economic life became increasingly obvious. The sum effect was to carry much further an already long established trend. Since about 1700 there has been a steady and exponential increase in the world population of scientists: their numbers have doubled roughly every fifteen years (which explains the striking fact that ever since then there have always been, at any moment, more scientists alive than dead). For the nineteenth century, other measurements of the growth of science can be used (the establishment of astronomical observatories, for example) and these, too, provide exponential curves.

SCIENCE IN PRACTICE

The ever increasing number of scientists underlay the growing control of his environment and the improvement of his life, which

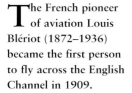

The French pioneer of aviation Louis Blériot (1872–1936) became the first person to fly across the English Channel in 1909.

were so easily grasped by the layman. This was what made the nineteenth century the first in which science truly became an object of religion – perhaps of idolatry. By 1914, educated Europeans and Americans could take for granted anaesthetics, the motor car, the steam turbine, harder and specialized steels, the aeroplane, the telephone, the wireless and many more marvels which had not existed a century previously; their effects were already very great. Perhaps the most widely apparent were those stemming from the availability of cheap electrical power; it was already shaping cities by making electric trams and trains available to suburban householders, work in factories through electric motors, and domestic life through the electric light. Even animal populations were affected: the 36,000 horses pulling trams in Great Britain in 1900 had only 900 successors in 1914. Of course, the practical application of science was by no means new. There has never been a time since the seventeenth century when there has not been some obvious technological fall-out from scientific activity though, to begin with, it was largely confined to ballistics, navigation and map-making, agriculture and a few elementary industrial processes. But only in the nineteenth century did science begin to play a truly important role in sustaining and changing society other than through a few obviously striking and spectacular accomplishments. The chemistry of dyeing, for example, was a vast field in which nineteenth-century research led to sweeping innovations, which flooded through the manufacture of drugs, explosives, antiseptics – to mention only a few. These had human and social, as well as economic, repercussions. The new fast dyes themselves affected millions of people; the unhappy Indian grower of indigo found that his market dried up on him, and the industrial working classes of the West found they could buy marginally less drab clothes and thus began to move slowly forward along the road at the end of which mass-production methods and man-made fibres all but obliterated visible difference between the clothes of different classes.

MEDICAL ADVANCES

This already takes us across the boundary between sustaining life and changing it. Fundamental science was to go on changing society, though some of what was done before 1914 – in physics, for example – is better left for discussion at a later point. One area in which effects are easier to measure was medicine. By 1914, advances had been made which were huge. In a century, a skill had become a science. Great bridgeheads had been driven into the theory and control of infection; antiseptics, having been introduced by Lister only in the 1860s, were taken for

Louis Pasteur (1822–1895) is portrayed carrying out an immunological experiment on a dog. Pasteur discovered anaerobic bacteria and made important contributions to the fight against various infectious diseases, including rabies, for which he produced a vaccine in 1885.

granted a couple of decades later, and he and his friend Louis Pasteur, the most famous and greatest of French chemists, laid the foundations of bacteriology. Queen Victoria herself had been a pioneer in the publicizing of new medical methods; the use of anaesthetics during the birth of a prince or princess was important in winning quick social acceptance for techniques only in their infancy in the 1840s. Fewer people, perhaps, would have been aware of the importance of such achievements as the discovery in 1909 of Salvarsan, a landmark in the development of selective treatment of infection, or the identification of the carrier of malaria, or the discovery of "X-rays". Yet all these advances, though of great importance, were to be far surpassed in the next fifty years – with, incidentally, huge rises in the cost of medicine, too.

THE MYTHOLOGY OF SCIENCE

Enough impact was made by science even before 1914 to justify the conclusion that it generated its own mythology. In this context, "mythology" implies no connotations of fiction or falsity. It is simply a convenient way of calling attention to the fact that science, the vast bulk of its conclusions no doubt validated by experiment and therefore "true", has also come to act as an influence shaping the way we look at the world, just as great religions have done in the past. It has, that is to say, come to be important as more than a method for exploring and manipulating nature. It has been thought also to provide guidance about metaphysical questions, the aims human beings ought to pursue, the standards they should employ to regulate

These motor cars and omnibuses were photographed in London's Oxford Street in 1911. By that time, although horse-drawn carriages were still the main means of transport in almost every city in the world, the mass production of cheap cars had already begun in the United States.

Science and the idea of progress

The 19th century saw a dramatic improvement in the ability of science to explain the physical and biological world, and to apply the knowledge acquired to the development of technology. This led, in the whole of the Western world and later also in Japan, India and China, to a widespread confidence that many human problems could be solved through scientific reasoning and experimentation.

Thinkers such as Jeremy Bentham (1748–1832), Auguste Comte (1798–1857), Karl Marx (1818–1883) and Herbert Spencer (1820–1903) defended the need to make a scientific study of human behaviour and of society itself. Bentham tried to define the principles of social organization based on measuring human behaviour with respect to pleasure and pain. Marx built a system around deterministic materialism. Comte set down the foundations of positivism and defined sociology as a science. Spencer tried to justify capitalism scientifically by asserting that competition played the same role in human progress as natural selection did in the evolution of the species.

Some dissidents spoke out against such ideas. A leading Darwinist, Thomas Huxley (1825–1895) none the less took the view that human society should be based on totally different rules from those of a brutal natural selection.

behaviour. Above all it has been a pervasive influence in shaping popular attitudes. All this, of course, has no intrinsic or necessary connection with science as the pursuit of scientists. But the upshot in the longest term was a civilization whose élites had, except vestigially, no dominant religious belief or transcendent ideals. It was a civilization whose core, whether or not this was often articulated, lay in the belief in the promise of what can be done by manipulating nature. In principle, it believed that there is no problem which need be regarded as insoluble, given sufficient resources of intellect and money; it had room for the obscure, but not for the essentially mysterious. Many scientists have drawn back from this conclusion. All of its implications are still far from being grasped. But it is the assumption on which a dominant world view now rests and it was already formed in essentials before 1914.

THE STUDY OF SOCIETY

Confidence in science in its crudest form has been called "scientism", but probably very few people held it with complete explicitness and lack of qualification, even in the late nineteenth century, its heyday. Equally good evidence of the prestige of the scientific method, though, is provided by the wish shown by intellectuals to extend it beyond the area of the natural sciences. One of the earliest examples can be detected in the wish to found "social sciences", which can be seen in the utilitarian followers of the English reformer and intellectual, Jeremy Bentham, who hoped to base the management of society upon calculated use of the principles that people responded to pleasure and pain, and that pleasure should be maximized and pain minimized, it being understood that what was to be taken into account were the sensations of the greatest number and their intensity. Later in the nineteenth century, Marx (who was greatly impressed by the work of Darwin) also exemplified the wish to found a science of society. A name for one was provided by the French philosopher Auguste Comte – sociology. These (and many other) attempts to emulate the natural sciences proceeded on a basis of a search for general quasi-mechanical laws; that the natural sciences were at that moment abandoning the search for such laws does not signify here, the search itself still testifying to the scientific model's prestige.

OLD VALUES RECONSIDERED

Paradoxically, science, too, was contributing by 1914 to an ill-defined sense of strain in European civilization. This showed most obviously in the problems posed to traditional religion, without doubt, but it also operated in a more subtle way; in determinisms such as those many drew from thinking about Darwin, or through a relativism suggested by anthropology or the study of the human mind, science itself sapped the confidence in the values of objectivity and rationality which had been so important to it since the eighteenth century. By 1914 there were signs that liberal, rational, enlightened Europe was under strain just as much as traditional, religious and conservative Europe.

EUROPEAN INTERRELATIONSHIPS

Doubt must not loom too large. The most obvious fact about early twentieth-century Europe is that although Europeans might be sceptical or fearful about its future, it was almost never suggested that it would not continue to be the centre of the world's affairs, the greatest concentration of political power in the globe and the real maker of the world's destinies. Diplomatically and politically, European statesmen could usually ignore the rest of the world, except in the western hemisphere, where another nation of European origins, the United States, was paramount, and the Far East, where Japan was increasingly important and the Americans had interests which they might require others to respect. It was their relationships with one another that fascinated most European statesmen in 1900; for most of them there was nothing else so important to worry about at this time.

This political cartoon mocking the German domination of European diplomacy appeared in a 1908 edition of the British publication *Punch*. Entitled *A Rival Attraction*, the cartoon depicts a neglected artiste (a performer on the European concertina) complaining that she will never have her chance to appear on stage, "what with all these Berlin knock-about extra turns!".

5 *THE ERA OF THE FIRST WORLD WAR*

Emperor Franz Josef attends a ball in Vienna at the beginning of the 20th century. During Franz Josef's reign (1848–1916), Austria's empire (which became the Austro-Hungarian Empire in 1867) suffered from fierce nationalist pressures.

AGAINST THE ONE CLEAR favourable fact that great wars had been successfully averted by European states ever since 1870, could be set some political evidence that the international situation was none the less growing dangerously unstable by 1900. Some major states had grave internal problems, for example, which might imply external repercussions. For all the huge difference between them, united Germany and united Italy were new states; they had not existed forty years earlier and this made their

rulers especially sensitive to internal divisive forces and consequently willing to court chauvinistic feeling. Some of Italy's leaders went in for disastrous colonial ventures, keeping alive suspicion and unfriendliness towards Austria-Hungary (formally Italy's ally, but the ruler of territories still regarded by Italians as "unredeemed") and finally plunged their country into war with Turkey in 1911. Germany had the advantages of huge industrial and economic success to help it, yet after the cautious Bismarck had been sent into retirement its foreign policy was conducted more and more with an eye to winning the impalpable and slippery prizes of respect and prestige – a "place in the sun", as some Germans summed it up. Germany had also to face the consequences of industrialization. The new economic and social forces it spawned were increasingly difficult to reconcile with the conservative character of its constitution, which gave so much weight in imperial government to a semi-feudal, agrarian aristocracy.

PROBLEMS IN RUSSIA

Internal tensions were not confined to new states. The two great dynastic empires of

Time chart (1867–1922)				
	1867 Austro-Hungarian Empire founded	1894 Franco-Russian alliance	1917 Russian Revolution	1918 End of the First World War
1850		1900		1950
	1879 Alliance of Germany and Austria-Hungary		1914 Start of the First World War	1922 Triumph of Fascism in Italy

Russia and Austria-Hungary each faced grave internal problems; more than any other states they still fitted the assumption of the Holy Alliance era, that governments were the natural opponents of their subjects. Yet both had undergone great change in spite of apparent continuity. The Habsburg monarchy in its new, hyphenated form was itself the creation of a successful nationalism, that of the Magyars. In the early years of the twentieth century there were signs that it was going to be more and more difficult to keep the two halves of the monarchy together without provoking other nations inside it beyond endurance. Moreover, here, too, industrialization (in Bohemia and Austria) was beginning to add new tensions to old. Russia, as has been indicated, actually exploded in political revolution in 1905, and was also changing

more deeply. Autocracy and terrorism between them destroyed the liberal promise of the reforms of Alexander II, but they did not prevent the start of faster industrial growth by the end of the century. This was the beginning of an economic revolution to which the great emancipation had been the essential preliminary. Policies designed to exact grain from the peasant provided a commodity for export to pay for the service of foreign loans. With the twentieth century, Russia began to show at last a formidable rate of economic advance. The quantities were still small – in 1910 Russia produced less than a third as much pig-iron as the United Kingdom and only about a quarter as much steel as Germany. But these quantities had been achieved at a very high rate of growth. Probably more important, there were

The picture shows the Russian squadron in the French Mediterranean port of Toulon in 1893. The following year, both countries' distrust of Germany led to a Franco-Russian alliance.

A peasant gathering takes place in rural Russia in 1910. The seated man at the left of the picture appears to be literate, which was extremely rare among the rural population at that time.

strong. Russia was still dependent on foreign suppliers for the capital it needed, as well.

FRANCE

Most of Russia's capital came from its ally, France. With the United Kingdom and Italy, the Third Republic represented liberal and constitutional principles among Europe's great powers. Socially conservative, France was, in spite of its intellectual vitality, uneasy and conscious of weakness. In part, a superficial instability was a matter of bitter exchanges between politicians; in part it was because of the efforts of some who strove to keep alive the revolutionary tradition and rhetoric. Yet the working-class movement was weak. France moved only slowly towards industrialization and, in fact, the Republic was probably as stable as any other régime in Europe, but slow industrial development indicated another handicap of which the French were very aware, their military inferiority. The year 1870 had shown that the French could not on their own beat the German army. Since then, the disparity of the two countries' positions had grown ever greater. In manpower, France had fallen further still behind and in economic development, too, it had been dwarfed by its neighbour. Just before 1914, France was raising about one-sixth as much coal as Germany, made less than a third as much pig-iron and a quarter as much steel. If there was ever to be a return match for 1870, the French knew they would need allies.

signs that by 1914 Russian agriculture might at last have turned the corner and be capable of producing a grain harvest which would grow faster than population. A determined effort was made by one minister to provide Russia with a class of prosperous independent farmers whose self-interest was linked to raising productivity, by removing the last of the restraints on individualism imposed by the terms of serfdom's abolition. Yet there was still much backwardness to overcome. Even in 1914 fewer than 10 per cent of Russians lived in towns and only about three million out of a total population of more than 150 million worked in industry. The debit side still loomed large in foreign estimates of Russia's progress. Russia might be a potential giant, but still one entangled with grievous handicaps. The autocracy governed badly, reformed unwillingly and opposed all change (though forced to make constitutional concessions in 1905). The general level of culture was low and unpromising; industrialization would demand better education and that would cause new strains. Liberal traditions were weak; terrorist and autocratic traditions were

BRITAIN IN 1900

An ally for France was not, in 1900, to be looked for across the Channel. This was mainly because of colonial issues; France (like

Russia) came into irritating conflict with the United Kingdom in a great many places around the globe where British interests lay. For a long time, the United Kingdom found it could remain clear of European entanglements; this was an advantage, but it, too, had troubles at home. The first industrial nation was also one of the most troubled by working-class agitation and, increasingly, by uncertainty about its relative strength. By 1900 some British businessmen were clear that Germany was a major rival; there were plenty of signs that in technology and method German industry was greatly superior to British. The old certainties began to give way; free trade itself was called in question. There were even signs, in the violence of Ulstermen and suffragettes, and the embittered struggles over social legislation with a House of Lords determined to safeguard the interests of wealth, that parliamentarianism itself might be threatened. There was no longer a sense of the sustaining consensus of mid-Victorian politics. Yet there was a reassuring solidity about British institutions and political habits. Parliamentary monarchy had proved able to carry through vast changes since 1832 and there was little reason for fundamental doubt that it could continue to do so.

THE GROWING POWER OF THE UNITED STATES

Only a perspective which the British of the day found hard to recognize reveals the fundamental change that had come about in the international position of the United Kingdom within the preceding half-century

The end of an era for Britain came when Queen Victoria, who had reigned for almost 64 years, died in 1901. This photograph shows her funeral cortège passing through the streets of Cowes on the Isle of Wight.

Immigrants continued to flood into the United States after the turn of the century. Those pictured here are arriving at the main immigrant gateway of New York's Ellis Island.

or so. This is provided by a view from Japan or the United States, the two great extra-European powers. The Japanese portent was the more easily discerned of the two, perhaps, because of the military victory over Russia, yet there were signs for those who could interpret them that the United States would shortly emerge as a power capable of dwarfing Europe, and as the most powerful nation in the world. The nineteenth-century expansion of the United States had come to a climax with the establishment of its supremacy on an unquestionable footing of power in its own hemisphere. The war with Spain and the building of the Panama Canal rounded off the process. American domestic, social and econ-omic circumstances were such that the political system proved easily able to handle the problems it faced once the great mid-century crisis was surmounted. Amongst these, some of the gravest resulted

from industrialization. The confidence that all would go well if the economically strongest were simply allowed to drive all others to the wall first began to be questioned towards the end of the nineteenth century. But this was after an industrial machine of immense scale had already matured. It would be the bedrock of future American power. By 1914 American production of pig-iron and steel was more than double that of Great Britain and Germany together; the United States mined almost enough coal to outpace them, too, and made more motor cars than the rest of the world put together. At the same time the standard of living of its citizens con-tinued to act as a magnet to immigration; in its natural resources and a stream of cheap, highly motivated labour lay two of the sources of America's economic might. The other was foreign capital. It was the greatest of debtor nations.

Though its political constitution was older in 1914 than that of any major European state except Great Britain or Russia, the arrival of new Americans helped to give the United States the characteristics and psychology of a new nation. A need to integrate new citizens often led to the expression of strong nationalist feeling. But because of geography, a tradition of rejecting Europe, and the continuing domination of American government and business by élites formed in the Anglo-Saxon tradition, this did not take violent forms outside the western hemisphere. The United States in 1914 was still a young giant waiting in the wings of history, whose full importance would only become manifest when Europe needed to involve America in its quarrels.

THE TWO WORLD WARS

IN 1914 A WAR BEGAN as a result of Europe's internal quarrels. Though it was not the bloodiest nor the most prolonged war in history, nor strictly, as it was later termed, the "first" world war, it was the most intensely fought struggle and the greatest in geographical extent to have occurred down to that time. Nations from every continent took part. It was also costlier than any earlier war and made unprecedented demands upon resources. Whole societies were mobilized to fight it, in part because it was also the first war in which machines played an overwhelmingly important part; war was for the first time transformed by science. The best name to give it remains the simple one used by those who fought in it: the *Great* War. This is sufficiently justified by its unprecedented psychological effect alone.

It was also the first of two wars whose central issue was the control of German power. The damage they did ended Europe's

political, economic and military supremacy. Each of these conflicts originated in essentially European issues and the war always had a predominantly European flavour; like the next great struggle detonated by Germany, though, it sucked into it other conflicts and jumbled together a whole anthology of issues. But Europe was the heart of the matter and self-inflicted damage in the end finished off its world hegemony. This did not happen by 1918, when the Great War ended (though irreparable damage had already been done, even by then), but it was obvious in 1945, at the end of a "second world war". That left behind a continent whose pre-1914 structure had vanished. It has led some historians to speak of the whole era from 1914 to 1945 as an entity, as a European "civil war" – not a bad metaphor, provided it is borne in mind that it is a metaphor. Europe had never been free from wars for long and the containment of internal disorder is the fundamental presupposition of a state: Europe had never been united and could not therefore have a true civil war. But it was the source and

This painting shows a Mk V tank going into action in the First World War. Tanks, which could not be stopped by barbed wire or machine-gun fire, were developed by the British and were used for the first time on the Western Front in 1916.

seat of a civilization which was a unity; Europeans saw themselves as having more in common with other Europeans than with black, brown or yellow peoples. Furthermore, it was a system of power which in 1914 was an economic unity and had just experienced its longest period of internal peace. These facts, all of which were to vanish by 1945, make the metaphor of civil war vivid and acceptable; it signifies the self-destructive madness of a civilization.

A DELICATE PEACE

A European balance had kept the peace between great states for over forty years. By 1914 this was dangerously disturbed. Too many people had come to feel that the chances of war might offer them more than a continued peace. This was especially so in the ruling circles of Germany, Austria-Hungary and Russia. By the time that they had come to feel this, there existed a complicated set of ties, obligations and interests between states which so involved them with one another that it was unlikely that a conflict could be limited to two, or even to a few of them. Another force making for instability was the existence of small countries enjoying special relations with larger ones; some of them were in a position to take the effective power to make decisions from the hands of those who would have to fight a major war.

EUROPE COURTS DANGER

The delicate European situation in 1914 was made all the more dangerous by the psychological atmosphere in which statesmen by then had to work. It was an age when mass emotions were easily aroused, in particular by nationalist and patriotic stimuli. There was widespread ignorance of the dangers of war, because nobody, except a tiny minority, foresaw a war which would be different from that of 1870; they remembered the France of that year, and forgot how, in Virginia and Tennessee only a few years earlier, modern war had first shown its face in prolonged slaughter and huge costs (more Americans died in the Civil War than have died in all the other wars in which the United States has taken part, even to the present day). Everyone knew that wars could be destructive and violent, certainly, but also believed that in the twentieth century they would be swiftly over. The very cost of armaments made it inconceivable that civilized states could sustain a prolonged struggle such as that with Napoleonic France; the complex world economy and the taxpayer, it was said, could not survive one. This perhaps diminished

This poster urged British women to encourage their husbands and sons to fight in the First World War. The extensive British propaganda campaign appears to have been almost unnecessary until 1916, such was the level of popular support for the cause. It was not uncommon, for example, for young men to lie about their age in order to be accepted as volunteers. Of those who went to war, however, an unprecedented number never returned – the scale of the slaughter on both sides was enormous.

misgivings about courting danger. There are even signs, too, that many articulate Europeans were bored by their lives in 1914 and saw in war an emotional release purging away a sense of decadence and sterility. Revolutionaries, of course, welcomed international conflict because of the opportunities they thought it might bring. Finally, it is worth remembering that the success of diplomats in negotiating grave crises without war was itself a danger. Their machinery had worked so many times that when it was presented with facts more than ordinarily recalcitrant in July 1914, their significance for a time seemed to escape many of those who had to deal with them. On the very eve of conflict, statesmen were still finding it difficult to see why another conference of ambassadors or even a European congress should not extricate them from their problems.

REVOLUTIONARY NATIONALISM

One of the conflicts which came to a head in 1914 went back a very long way. This was the old rivalry of Austria-Hungary and Russia in southeastern Europe. Its roots lay deep in the eighteenth century, but its last phase was dominated by the accelerated collapse of the Ottoman Empire in Europe from the Crimean War onwards. For this reason the First World War is from one point of view to be seen as another war of the Ottoman succession. After the Congress of Berlin in 1878 had pulled Europe through one dangerous moment, Habsburg and Romanov policy had settled down to a sort of understanding by the 1890s. This lasted until Russian interest in the Danube valley revived after the checking of Russian imperial ambition in the Far East by the Japanese. At that moment, events outside the Habsburg and Turkish empires were giving a new aggressiveness to Austro-Hungarian policy, too.

At the root of this was revolutionary nationalism. A reform movement looked for a while as if it might put the Ottoman Empire together again and this provoked the Balkan nations to try to undo the status quo established by the great powers and the Austrians to look to their own interests in a situation

This contemporary engraving shows the main participants in the 1878 Congress of Berlin. The foreground is dominated by the tall figure of the German chancellor, Prince von Bismarck, who is depicted shaking hands with the Russian representative Count Shuvalov. On the left, shown leaning on his cane, is Benjamin Disraeli, the British prime minister, with Emperor Franz Josef of Austria-Hungary.

once again fluid. They offended and humiliated the Russians by a mismanaged annexation of the Ottoman province of Bosnia in 1909; the Russians had not been given a corresponding and compensating gain. Another consequence of Bosnia's annexation was that the Dual Monarchy acquired more Slav subjects. There was already discontent among the monarchy's subject peoples, in particular the Slavs who lived under Magyar rule. More and more under the pressure of Magyar interests, the government in Vienna had shown itself hostile to Serbia, a nation to which these Slav subjects might look for support. Some of them saw Serbia as the nucleus of a future state embracing all South Slavs, and its rulers seemed unable (and perhaps

This French illustration depicts the assassination in 1903 of the king of Serbia, Alexander I, and his wife. The inset portrays Alexander's successor, Peter I. Internal and external strife made the Balkans the most unstable area in Europe.

unwilling) to restrain South Slav revolutionaries who used Belgrade as a base for terrorism and subversion in Bosnia. Lessons from history are often unfortunate; the Vienna government was only too ready to conclude that Serbia might play in the Danube valley the role that Sardinia had played in uniting Italy. Unless the serpent were scotched in the egg, many servants of the empire felt another loss of Habsburg territory would follow. Having been excluded from Germany by Prussia and from Italy by Sardinia, a potential new South Slav state, whether a greater Serbia or something else, now seemed to some Habsburg counsellors to threaten the empire with exclusion from the lower Danube valley. This would mean its end as a great power and an end, too, of Magyar supremacy in Hungary, for fairer treatment of Slavs who remained in Hungarian territory would be insisted upon by South Slavdom. The continuing subsidence of the Ottoman Empire could then only benefit Russia, the power which stood behind Serbia, determined there should not be another 1909.

EUROPEAN POWERS ARE DRAWN INTO THE CONFLICT

Into this complicated situation the other powers were pulled by interest, choice, sentiment and formal alliances. Of these, the last were perhaps less important than was once thought. Bismarck's efforts in the 1870s and 1880s to ensure the isolation of France and the supremacy of Germany had spawned a system of alliances unique in peacetime. Their common characteristic was that they defined conditions on which countries would go to war to support one another, and this seemed to cramp diplomacy. But in the end they did not operate as planned. This does not mean that they did not contribute to the coming of war, but that formal arrangements can only be effective if people want them to be, and other factors decided that in 1914.

At the root of the alliances was the German seizure of Alsace and Lorraine from France in 1871, and the consequent French restlessness for revenge. Bismarck guarded against this first by drawing together Germany, Russia and Austria-Hungary on the common ground of dynastic resistance to revolutionary and subversive dangers, which France, the only republic among the major states, was still supposed to represent; there were after all still alive in 1871 people born before 1789 and many others who could remember the comments of those who had lived through the years of the great Revolution, while the upheaval of the Paris Commune revived all the old fears of international subversion. The conservative alliance none the less lapsed in the 1880s, essentially because Bismarck felt he must in the last resort back Austria-Hungary if a conflict between her and Russia proved unavoidable. To Germany and the Dual Monarchy was then added Italy; thus was formed in 1882 the Triple Alliance. But Bismarck still kept a separate "Reinsurance" treaty with Russia, though he seems to have felt uneasy about the prospect of keeping Russia and Austria-Hungary at peace in this way.

TWO CAMPS IN EUROPE

A conflict between Russia and Austria-Hungary did not again look likely until after 1909. By then, Bismarck's successors had allowed his Reinsurance treaty to lapse and Russia had become in 1892 an ally of France. From that date the road led away from Bismarck's Europe, where everyone else had been kept in equilibrium by Germany's

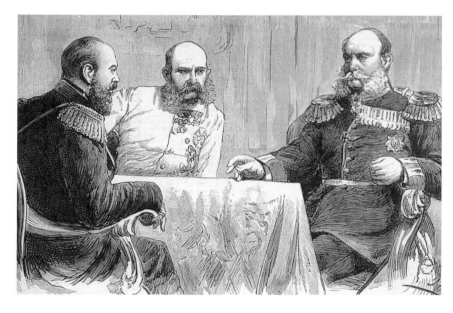

central role, to a Europe divided into two camps. This was made worse by German policy. In a series of crises, it showed that it wanted to frighten other nations with its displeasure and make itself esteemed. In particular, in 1905 and 1911 irritation was directed against France, and commercial and colonial issues were used as excuses to show by displays of force that France had not won the right to disregard German wishes by making an ally of Russia. German military planning had already by 1900 accepted the need to fight a two-front war if necessary, and made preparations to do so by a quick overthrow of France while the resources of Russia were slowly mobilized.

As the twentieth century opened, it had therefore become highly probable that if an Austro-Russian war broke out, Germany and France would join in. Moreover, Germans had within a few years made this more likely by patronizing the Turks. This was much more alarming to the Russians than it would have been earlier, because a growing export trade in grain from Russia's Black Sea ports had to pass through the Straits. The Russians began to improve their fighting-power. One essential step in this was the completion of

Tsar Alexander III of Russia, Emperor Franz Josef of Austria-Hungary and Emperor Wilhelm I of Germany meet at the Warsaw Conference in 1884. Prince von Bismarck, then German chancellor, made great efforts during the conference to maintain the alliance with Russia, which Wilhelm II would later renounce.

a railway network which would make possible the mobilization and delivery to the battlefields of eastern Europe of Russia's vast armies.

BRITISH INVOLVEMENT IN THE CONFLICT

There was no obvious need for Great Britain to be concerned in a potential Austro-Russian struggle, had not German policy perversely antagonized it. At the end of the nineteenth century Great Britain's quarrels were almost all with France and Russia. They arose where imperial ambitions clashed, in Africa and Central and Southeast Asia. Anglo-German relations were more easily managed, if occasionally prickly. As Great Britain entered the new century it was still preoccupied with empire, not with Europe. The first peacetime alliance it had made since the eighteenth century was with Japan, to safeguard its interests in the Far East. Then came a

settlement of long outstanding disputes with France in 1904; this was in essence an agreement about Africa, where France was to be given a free hand in Morocco in return for Great Britain having one in Egypt – a way of settling another bit of the Ottoman succession – but it rounded up other colonial quarrels the world over, some going back as far as the Peace of Utrecht. A few years later, Great Britain made a similar (though less successful) agreement with Russia about spheres of interest in Persia. But the Anglo-French settlement grew into much more than a clearing away of grounds for dispute. It became what was called an *entente*, or special relationship.

This was Germany's doing. Irritated by the Anglo-French agreement, the German government decided to show France that it would have to have its say in Morocco's affairs at an international conference. They got it, but bullying France solidified the *entente*; the British began to realize that they would have to concern themselves for the first time in decades with the continental balance of power. If they did not, Germany would dominate it. At the end of this road would be their acceptance of a role as a great military power on land, a change of the assumptions which British strategy had followed since the days of Louis XIV and Marlborough, the last age in which the country had put its major weight into prolonged effort on the continent. Secret military talks with the French explored what might be done to help their army against a German invasion through Belgium. This was not going far, but Germany then threw away the chance to reassure British public opinion, by pressing forward with plans to build a great navy. It was inconceivable that such a step could be directed against any power except Great Britain. The result was a naval race which most British were determined to win (if they

This cartoon, which appeared in the British publication *Punch* in March 1906 with the caption "Sitting Tight", makes fun of the German attempt to limit French control in Morocco.

could not end it) and therefore the further inflammation of popular feeling. In 1911, when the gap between the two countries' fleets was narrowest and most felt in Great Britain, German diplomacy provoked another crisis over Morocco. This time, a British minister said publicly something that sounded very much like an assertion that Great Britain would go to war to protect France.

THE OUTBREAK OF THE GREAT WAR

When war came, it was in the South Slav lands. Serbia did well in the "Balkan Wars" of 1912–13, in which the young Balkan nations first despoiled the Ottoman Empire of most that was left of its European territory and then fell out over the spoils. But Serbia might have got more had the Austrians not objected. Behind Serbia stood Russia, launched on the programme of rebuilding

and expanding its forces. But that would take three or four years to bring to fruition. If South Slavs were to be shown that the Dual Monarchy could humiliate Serbia so that they could not hope for its support, then the sooner the better. Given that Germany was the Dual Monarchy's ally it, in turn, was unlikely to seek to avoid fighting Russia while there was still time to feel sure of winning.

The crisis came when an Austrian archduke was assassinated by a Bosnian terrorist at Sarajevo in June 1914. The Austrians believed that the Serbians were behind it. They decided that the moment had come to teach Serbia a lesson and kill for ever the pan-Slav agitation. The Germans supported them. The Austrians declared war on Serbia on 28 July. A week later all the great powers were at war (though, ironically, the Austro-Hungarians and Russians were then still at peace with one another; it was only on 6 August that the Dual Monarchy at last declared war on its old rival). German

The Great War of 1914–1918

At the start of the First World War, Austria-Hungary and Germany were at war with Serbia, Russia, France, Belgium and Great Britain – other countries joined the conflict as the war progressed. The Western Front was soon established, after an initial German advance, while on the Eastern Front the Austro-Hungarians and Germans managed to occupy Serbia, Romania and some provinces of imperial Russia. Following the Russian Revolution in 1917, after which the Bolsheviks sued for peace in early 1918, the Germans moved most of their troops to the Western Front, where the outcome of the war was eventually decided.

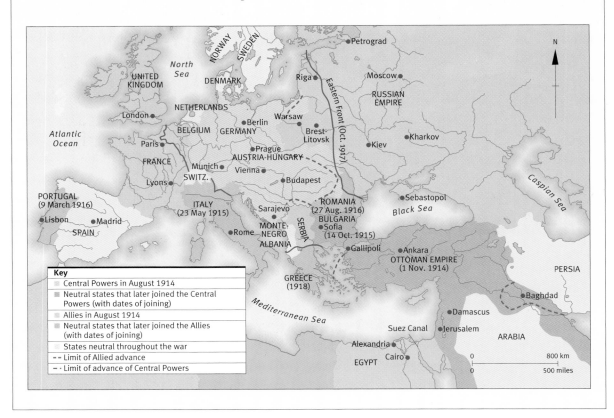

military planning had dictated the timetable of events. The key decision to dispose of France before Russia had been made years before; German planning required an attack on France to be made through Belgium, whose neutrality the British among others had guaranteed. Thereafter the sequence of events fell almost automatically into place. When Russia mobilized to bring pressure on Austria-Hungary for Serbia's protection, the Germans declared war on Russia. Having done that, they had to attack the French and, finding a pretext, formally declared war on them. Thus, the Franco–Russian alliance never

actually operated. By Germany's violation of Belgian neutrality, the British government, uneasy about a German attack on France, but not seeing clearly on what grounds they could justify intervention to prevent it, was given an issue to unite the country and take it into war against Germany on 4 August.

THE THEATRE OF WAR

Just as the duration and intensity of the war were to outrun all expectations, so did its geographical spread. Japan and the Ottoman

Empire joined in soon after the outbreak; the former on the side of the Allies (as France, Great Britain and Russia were called) and Turkey on that of the Central Powers (Germany and Austria-Hungary). Italy joined the Allies in 1915, in return for promises of Austrian territory. Other efforts were made to pick up new supporters by offering cheques to be cashed after a victorious peace; Bulgaria joined the Central Powers in September 1915 and Romania the Allies in the following year. Greece became an Ally in 1917. Portugal's government had tried to enter the war in 1914 but, though unable to do so because of internal troubles, was finally faced with a German declaration of war in 1916. Thus, by the end of that year, the original issues of Franco–German and Austro–Russian rivalry had been thoroughly confused by other struggles. The Balkan states were fighting a third Balkan war (the war of the Ottoman succession in its European theatre), the British a war against German naval and commercial power, the Italians the last war of the Risorgimento, while outside Europe the British, Russians and Arabs had begun a war of Ottoman partition in Asia, and the Japanese were pursuing another cheap and highly profitable episode in the assertion of their hegemony in the Far East.

A NEW KIND OF WARFARE

One reason why there was a search for allies in 1915 and 1916 was that the war then showed every sign of getting bogged down in a stalemate no one had expected. The nature of the fighting had surprised almost everyone. It had opened with a German sweep into northern France. This did not achieve the lightning victory which was its aim but gave the Germans possession of all but a tiny scrap of Belgium and much French territory, too. In the east, Russian offensives had been stopped

by the Germans and Austrians. Thereafter, though more noticeably in the west than the east, the battlefields settled down to siege warfare on an unprecedented scale. This was because of two things. One was the huge killing-power of modern weapons. Magazine rifles, machine-guns and barbed wire could stop any infantry attack not preceded by pulverizing bombardment. Demonstrations of this truth were provided by the huge casualty lists. By the end of 1915 the French army alone had lost 300,000 dead; that was bad enough, but in 1916 one seven-month battle before Verdun added another 315,000

At his First World War headquarters, Kaiser Wilhelm II discusses tactics with Germany's greatest strategists: Hindenburg (left) and Ludendorff.

The French president Georges Clemenceau (1841–1929) visits the trenches. Clemenceau's personal energy helped to sustain French morale in the face of the horrors of war.

to this total. In the same battle 280,000 Germans died. While it was going on, another struggle further north, on the Somme, cost the British 420,000 casualties and the Germans about the same. The first day of that battle, 1 July, remains the blackest in the history of the British Army, when it suffered 60,000 casualties, of whom more than a third died.

Such figures made nonsense of the confident predictions that the cost of modern war would be bound to make the struggle a short one. This was a reflection of the second surprise, the revelation of the enormous war-making power of industrial societies. Plenty of people were weary by the end of 1916, but by then the warring states had already amply demonstrated a capacity greater than had been imagined to organize their peoples as never before in history to produce unprecedented quantities of material and furnish the recruits for new armies. Whole societies were engaged against one another; the international solidarity of the working class might never have been thought of for all the resistance it opposed to this, nor the international interests of ruling classes against subversion.

GLOBAL CONFLICT

The inability to batter one another into submission on the battlefields accelerated the strategic and technical expansion of the struggle. This was why diplomats had sought new allies and generals new fronts. The Allies in 1915 mounted an attack on Turkey at the Dardanelles in the hope, not to be realized, of knocking her out of the war and opening up

A British tank drags a cannon, seized from the enemy, to the British lines during the Battle of Cambrai in November 1917.

communication with Russia through the Black Sea. The same search for a way round the French deadlock later produced a new Balkan front at Salonika; it replaced the one which had collapsed when Serbia was over-run. Colonial possessions, too, had ensured from the first that there would be fighting all around the globe, even if on a small scale. The German colonies could be picked up fairly easily, thanks to the British command of the seas, though the African ones provoked some lengthy campaigning. The most important and considerable extra-European operations, though, were in the eastern and southern parts of the Turkish empire. A British and Indian army entered Mesopotamia. Another force advanced from the Suez Canal towards Palestine. In the Arabian desert, an Arab revolt against the Turks provided some of the few romantic episodes to relieve the brutal squalor of industrial war.

WAR ON A HUGE SCALE

The technical expansion of the war was most noticeable in its industrial effects and in the degeneration of standards of behaviour. The American Civil War a half-century before had prefigured the first of these, too, in revealing the economic demands of mass war in a dem-ocratic age. The mills, factories, mines and furnaces of Europe now worked as never before. So did those of the United States and Japan, both accessible to the Allies but not to the Central Powers because of the British naval supremacy. The maintenance of mil-lions of men in the field required not only arms and ammunition, but food, clothing, medical equipment, and machines in huge quantities. Though a war in which millions of animals were needed, it was also the first war of the internal-combustion engine; trucks and tractors swallowed petrol as avidly as horses

and mules ate their fodder. Many statistics illustrate the new scale of war but one must suffice; in 1914 the whole British Empire had 18,000 hospital beds and four years later it had 630,000.

The repercussions of this vast increase in demand rolled outwards through society, leading in all countries in varying measure to the governments' control of the economy, conscription of labour, the revolutionizing of women's employment, the introduction of new health and welfare services. They also

The British soldier and agent Thomas Edward Lawrence (1888–1935), who become famous as Lawrence of Arabia, played a crucial role in the Arab rebellion against the Ottoman Empire during the First World War. This portrait of Lawrence in Arabian dress was painted in Damascus in 1918.

rolled overseas. The United States ceased to be a debtor nation; the Allies liquidated their investments there to pay for what they needed and became debtors in their turn. Indian industry received the fillip it had long required. Boom days came to the ranchers and farmers of the Argentine and the British white Dominions. The latter also shared the military burden, sending soldiers to Europe and fighting the Germans in their colonies.

WHOLE SOCIETIES AS TARGETS

Technical expansion also made the war more frightful. This was not only because machine-guns and high explosive made possible such terrible slaughter. It was not even because of new weapons such as poison gas, flame-throwers or tanks, all of which made their appearance as soldiers strove to find a way out of the deadlock of the battlefield. It was also because the fact that whole societies were engaged in warfare brought with it the realization that whole societies could be targets for warlike operations. Attacks on the

A t Ypres in 1915 the Germans made the first attempt to use poison gas attacks to break the stalemate. Here, German soldiers are pictured testing gas masks in preparation for an attack.

morale, health and efficiency of civilian workers and voters became desirable. When such attacks were denounced, the denunciations were themselves blows in another sort of campaign, that of propaganda. The possibilities of mass literacy and the recently created cinema industry supplemented and overtook such old standbys as pulpit and school in this kind of warfare. To British charges that the Germans, who carried out primitive bombing raids on London by airship, were "baby-killers", Germans retorted that the same could be said of the sailors who sustained the British blockade. The rising figures of German infant mortality bore them out.

BLOCKADES AND THE INVENTION OF SUBMARINES

In part because of the slow but apparently irresistible success of the British blockade, and because of its unwillingness to risk the fleet whose building had done so much to poison pre-war feeling between the two countries, the German High Command devised a new use for a weapon whose power had been underrated in 1914, the submarine. It was launched at Allied shipping and the ships of neutrals who were supplying the Allies, attacks often being made without warning and on unarmed vessels. This was first done early in 1915, though few submarines were then available and they did not do much damage. There was an outcry when a great British liner was torpedoed that year, with the loss of 1,200 lives, many of them Americans, and the unrestricted sinking of shipping was called off by the Germans. It was resumed at the beginning of 1917. By then it was clear that if Germany did not starve Great Britain first, it would itself be choked by British blockade. During that winter there was famine in Balkan countries and people were starving in

the suburbs of Vienna. The French had by then suffered 3,350,000 casualties and the British over a million, the Germans had lost nearly two and a half million and were still fighting a war on two fronts. Food riots and strikes were becoming more frequent; infant mortality was rising towards a level 50 per cent higher than that of 1915. There was no reason to suppose that the German army, divided between east and west, would be any more likely to achieve a knockout than had been the British and French and it was in any case more favourably placed to fight on the defensive. In these circumstances the German general staff chose to resume unrestricted submarine warfare, the decision which brought about the first great transformation of the war in 1917, the entry into it of the

United States. The Germans knew this would happen, but gambled on bringing Great Britain to its knees – and thus France – before American weight could be decisive.

THE USA ENTERS THE WAR

American opinion, by no means favourable to one side or the other in 1914, had come a long way since then. Allied propaganda and purchases had helped; so had the first German submarine campaign. When the Allied governments began to talk about war aims, which included the reconstruction of Europe on the basis of safeguarding the interests of nationalities, it had an appeal to "hyphenated" Americans. The resumption of

These British soldiers in France, blinded by gas in the German offensive of April 1918, are queuing for medical treatment.

Some of the 1,200,000 American soldiers who fought in the First World War are pictured on their way to Europe in autumn 1917. The intervention of the United States played a crucial role in the Allies' victory.

unrestricted submarine warfare was decisive; it was a direct threat to American interests and the safety of her citizens. When it was also revealed to the American government that Germany hoped to negotiate an alliance with Mexico and Japan against the United States, the hostility aroused by the submarines was confirmed. Soon, an American ship was sunk without warning and the United States declared war shortly afterwards.

THE HORRORS OF 1917

The impossibility of breaking the European deadlock by means short of total war had thus sucked the New World into the quarrels of the Old, almost against its will. The Allies

were delighted; victory was now assured. Immediately, though, they faced a gloomy year. The year 1917 was even blacker for Great Britain and France than 1916. Not only did the submarine take months to master but a terrible series of battles in France (usually lumped under one name, Passchendaele) inflicted an ineffaceable scar upon the British national consciousness and cost another 400,000 men to gain five miles of mud. Worn out by heroic efforts in 1916, the French army underwent a series of mutinies. Worst of all for the Allies, the Russian empire collapsed and Russia ceased, by the end of the year, to be a great power for the foreseeable future.

THE BOLSHEVIK REVOLUTION

THE RUSSIAN STATE was destroyed by the war. This was the beginning of the revolutionary transformation of central and eastern Europe, too. The makers of what was called a "revolution" in Russia in February 1917 were the German armies, who had in the end broken the hearts of even the long-enduring Russian soldiers, who had behind them cities starving because of the breakdown of the transport system and a government of incompetent and corrupt men who feared constitutionalism and liberalism as much as defeat. At the beginning of 1917 the security forces themselves could no longer be depended upon. Food riots were followed by mutiny and the autocracy was suddenly seen to be powerless. A provisional government of liberals and socialists was formed and the tsar abdicated. The new government itself then failed, in the main because it attempted the impossible, the continuation of the war; the Russians wanted peace and bread, as Lenin, the leader of the Bolsheviks, saw. His determination to take power from the moderate provisional government was the second reason for their failure. Presiding over a disintegrating country, administration and army, still facing the unsolved problems of privation in the cities, the provisional government was itself swept away in a second change, the coup called the October Revolution which, together with the American entry into the war, marks 1917 as a break between two eras of European history. Previously, Europe had settled its own affairs; now the United States would be bound to have a large say in its future. There had come into being a state which was committed by the beliefs of its founders to the destruction of the whole pre-war European order, a truly and consciously revolutionary centre for world politics.

RUSSIA LEAVES THE WAR

The immediate and obvious consequence of the establishment of the Union of Soviet Socialist Republics (USSR), as Russia was now called, after the workers' and soldiers' councils which were its basic political institution after the revolution, was a new strategic situation. The Bolsheviks consolidated their *coup d'état* by dissolving (since they did not control it) the only freely elected representative body based on universal suffrage Russia ever had and by trying to secure the peasant's loyalties by promises of land and peace. This was essential if they were to survive; the backbone of the party, which now strove to assert its authority over Russia,

This contemporary painting shows Vladimir Ilyich Lenin (1870–1924) addressing the crowds in Petrograd in 1920. The Bolshevik leader's determination and energy were central to his party's ability to cling to power in the chaos that followed the October Revolution. Large areas of Russia had been devastated by the war.

German and Russian representatives are depicted at the preliminary peace negotiations held in Brest-Litovsk in December 1917. Trotsky deliberately prolonged the talks, hoping that the proletarian revolution would spread throughout Europe. The failure of this revolution to materialize and the revival of the German advance through its territory in February eventually forced the Soviet Union to accept Germany's harsh conditions.

Leon Trotsky (1879–1940) was the Soviet commissar of war from the beginning of 1918 and founded the Red Army. Here he is shown haranguing his troops during the Civil War of 1918–1921.

was the very small industrial working class of a few cities. Only peace could provide a safer and broader foundation. At first the terms demanded by the Germans were thought so objectionable that the Russians stopped negotiation; they then had to accept a much more punitive outcome, the Treaty of Brest-Litovsk, in March 1918. It imposed severe losses of territory, but gave the new order the peace and time it desperately needed to tackle its internal troubles.

ALLIED HOSTILITY TO RUSSIA

The Allies were furious with the Bolsheviks, whose action they saw as a treacherous defection. Nor was their attitude towards the new régime softened by the intransigent revolutionary propaganda it directed against their citizens. The Russian leaders expected a revolution of the working class in all the advanced capitalist countries. This gave an extra dimension to a series of military interventions in the affairs of Russia by the Allies. Their original purpose was strategic, in that they hoped to stop the Germans exploiting the advantage of being able to close down their eastern front, but they were quickly interpreted by many people in the capitalist countries and by all Bolsheviks as anti-communist crusades. Worse still, they became entangled in a civil war which seemed likely to destroy the new régime. Even without the doctrinal filter of Marxist theory through which Lenin and his colleagues saw the world, these episodes would have been likely to have soured relations between Russia and the capitalist countries for a long time; once translated into Marxist terms they seemed a confirmation of an essential and ineradicable hostility. Memories of this influenced Russian leaders for the next fifty years. They also helped to justify the Russian revolution's turn downwards into authoritarian government. Fear of the invader as a restorer of the old order and patron of landlords combined with Russian traditions of autocracy and police terrorism to stifle any liberalization of the régime.

THE EXPLOITATION OF NATIONALISM

The Russian communists' conviction that revolution was about to occur in central and western Europe was in one sense correct, yet crucially wrong. In its last year, war's revolutionary potential indeed became plain, but in national, not class, forms. The Allies were provoked (in part by the Bolsheviks) to a revolution strategy of their own. The military situation looked bleak for them at the end of 1917. It was obvious that they would face a German attack in France in the spring

General Kornilov, the Cossack commander-in-chief of the Russian army, is seen here reviewing his troops. He led a muddled *coup d'état* in the summer of 1917 and was later one of the main organizers of the first White Army which confronted the Bolsheviks. He died in combat at the beginning of the Russian Civil War.

without the advantage of a Russian army to draw off their enemies, and that it would be a long time before American troops arrived in large numbers to help them in France. But they could adopt a revolutionary weapon. They could appeal to the nationalities of the Austro-Hungarian empire and no longer had to stand by their treaty of agreement with tsarist Russia. This had the additional advantage of emphasizing in American eyes the ideological purity of the Allied cause now that it was no longer tied to tsardom. Accordingly, in 1918, subversive propaganda was directed at the Austro-Hungarian armies and encouragement was given to Czechs and South Slavs in exile. Before Germany gave in, the Dual Monarchy was already dissolving under the combined effects of reawakened national sentiment and a Balkan campaign which at last began to provide victories. This was the second great blow to old Europe. The political structure of the whole area bounded by the Urals, the Baltic and the Danube valley was now in question as it had not been for centuries. There was even a Polish army again in existence. It was patronized by the Germans as a weapon against Russia, while the American president announced that an independent Poland was an essential of Allied peacemaking. All the certainties of the past century seemed to be in the melting-pot.

THE PRICE OF WAR

The crucial battles were fought against an increasingly revolutionary background. By the summer, the Allies had managed to halt the last great German offensive. It had made huge gains, but not enough. When the Allied armies began to move forward victoriously in their turn, the German leaders sought an end: they, too, thought they saw signs of revolutionary collapse at home. When the kaiser abdicated, the third of the dynastic empires had fallen; the Habsburgs had already gone, so that the Hohenzollerns just outlasted their old rivals. A new German government requested an armistice and the fighting came to an end.

The cost of this huge conflict has never been adequately computed. One figure which is approximate indicates its scale: about ten million men had died as a result of direct military action. Yet typhus probably killed another million in the Balkans alone. Nor do even these horrible figures indicate the physical cost in maiming, blinding, or the loss to families of fathers and husbands, the spiritual havoc in the destruction of ideals, confidence and goodwill. Europeans looked at their huge cemeteries and were appalled at what they had done. The economic damage was immense, too. Over much of Europe people starved. A year after the war manufacturing output was still nearly a quarter below that of 1914; Russia's was only 20 per cent of what it had then been. Transport was in some countries almost impossible to procure. Moreover,

all the complicated, fragile machinery of international exchange was smashed and some of it could never be replaced. At the centre of this chaos lay, exhausted, a Germany which had been the economic dynamo of central Europe. "We are at the dead season of our fortunes," wrote J.M. Keynes, a young British economist at the peace conference. "Our power of feeling or caring beyond the immediate questions of our own material well-being is temporarily eclipsed ... We have been moved beyond endurance, and need rest. Never in the lifetime of men now living has the universal element in the soul of man burnt so dimly."

THE PEACE

DELEGATES TO A PEACE CONFERENCE began to assemble at the end of 1918. It was once the fashion to emphasize their failures, but perspective and the recognition of the magnitude of their tasks imposes a certain respect for what they did. It was the greatest settlement since 1815 and its authors had to reconcile great expectations with stubborn facts. The power to make the crucial decisions was remarkably concentrated: the British and French prime ministers and the American president, Woodrow Wilson, dominated the negotiations. These took place between the victors; the defeated Germans were subsequently presented with their terms. In the diverging interests of France, aware above all of the appalling danger of any third repetition of German aggression, and of the Anglo-Saxon nations, conscious of standing in no such peril, lay the central problem of European security, but many others surrounded and obscured it. The peace settlement had to be a world settlement. It not only dealt with territories outside Europe – as earlier great settlements had done – but many

Crowds watch the Victory Parade in Paris in 1919. The satisfaction of victory did not last long in France, where the fear of possible retribution by Germany surfaced a few years later.

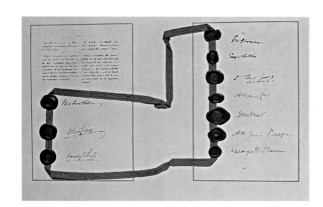

Technically, the peace settlement consisted of a group of distinct treaties made not only with Germany, but with Bulgaria, Turkey and the "succession states" which claimed the divided Dual Monarchy. Of these a resurrected Poland, an enlarged Serbia called the "kingdom of the Serbs, Croats and Slovenes" (and, later, Yugoslavia) and an entirely new Czechoslovakia were present at the conference as allies, while a much reduced Hungary and the Germanic heart of old Austria were treated as defeated enemies with whom peace had to be made. All of this posed difficult problems. But the main concern of the Peace Conference was the settlement with Germany embodied in the Treaty of Versailles signed in June 1919.

THE TREATY OF VERSAILLES

The Treaty of Versailles was a punitive settlement and explicitly stated that the Germans were responsible for the outbreak of war. But most of the harshest terms arose not from this moral guilt but from the French wish, if possible, so to tie Germany down that any third German war was inconceivable. This was the purpose of economic reparations, which were the most unsatisfactory part of the settlement. They angered Germans and made acceptance of defeat even harder. Moreover they were economic nonsense. Nor was the penalizing of Germany supported by arrangements to ensure that Germany might not one day try to reverse the decision by force of arms, and this angered the French. Germany's territorial losses, it went without saying, included Alsace and Lorraine, but were otherwise greatest in the east, to Poland. In the west the French did not get much more reassurance than an undertaking that the German bank of the Rhine should be "demilitarized".

Guards watch over German prisoners-of-war in a French camp at the end of the First World War.

non-European voices were heard in its making. Of twenty-seven states whose representatives signed the main treaty, a majority, seventeen, lay in other continents. The United States was the greatest of these; with Japan, Great Britain, France and Italy she formed the group described as the "principal" victorious powers. For a world settlement, nevertheless, it was ominous that no representative attended from Russia, the only great power with both European and Asian frontiers.

The last page of the Treaty of Versailles contains the signatures and seals of the delegates of the United States, headed by President Wilson.

The signing of the peace in the Hall of Mirrors in Versailles (28 June 1919) is depicted in this famous painting by Sir William Orpen (1878–1931).

PROBLEMS OF NATIONALITY

The second leading characteristic of the peace was its attempt where possible to follow the principles of self-determination and nationality. In many places this merely meant recognizing existing facts; Poland and Czechoslovakia were already in existence as states before the peace conference met, and Yugoslavia was built around the core of the former Serbia. By the end of 1918, therefore, these principles had already triumphed over much of the area occupied by the old Dual Monarchy (and were soon to do so also in the

The Romanian royal family sits for a photograph at home in 1922. Romania, which had fought on the Allies' side during the war and had seen great tracts of its land occupied by the enemy, was treated favourably in the Paris peace treaty. It was allowed to annex the vast and ethnically diverse region of Transylvania, which had previously belonged to Hungary.

former Baltic provinces of Russia). After outlasting even the Holy Roman Empire, the Habsburgs were gone at last and in their place appeared states which, though not uninterruptedly, were to survive most of the rest of the century. The principle of self-determination was also followed in providing that certain frontier zones should have their destiny settled by plebiscite.

Unfortunately, the principle of nationality could not always be applied. Geographical, historical, cultural and economic realities cut across it. When it prevailed over them – as in the destruction of the Danube's economic unity – the results could be bad; when it did not they could be just as bad because of the aggrieved feelings left behind. Eastern and central Europe were studded with national minorities embedded resentfully in nations to which they felt no allegiance. A third of Poland's population did not speak Polish; more than a third of Czechoslovakia's consisted of minorities of Poles, Russians, Germans, Magyars and Ruthenes; an enlarged Romania now contained over a million Magyars. In some places, the infringement of the principle was felt with especial acuteness as an injustice. Germans resented the existence of a "corridor" connecting Poland with the sea across German lands, Italy was disappointed of Adriatic spoils held out to her by her allies when they had needed her help, and the Irish had still not got Home Rule after all.

THE LEAGUE OF NATIONS

The most obvious non-European question concerned the disposition of the German colonies. Here there was an important innovation. Undisguised colonial greed was not acceptable to the United States; instead, tutelage for non-European peoples, formerly under German or Turkish rule, was provided by the device of trusteeship. "Mandates" were given to the victorious powers (though the United States declined any) by a new

"League of Nations" to administer these territories while they were prepared for self-government; it was the most imaginative idea to emerge from the settlement, even though it was used to drape with respectability the last major conquests of European imperialism.

The League of Nations owed much to the enthusiasm of the American president, Woodrow Wilson, who ensured its Covenant – its constitution – pride of place as the first part of the Peace Treaty. It was the one instance in which the settlement transcended the idea of nationalism (even the British Empire had been represented as individual units, one of which, significantly, was India).

It also transcended that of Europe; it is another sign of the new era that twenty-six of the original forty-two members of the League were countries outside Europe. Unfortunately, because of domestic politics Wilson had not taken into account, the United States was not among them. This was the most fatal of several grave weaknesses, which made it impossible for the League to satisfy the expectations it had aroused. Perhaps these were all unrealizable in principle, given the actual state of world political forces. None the less, the League was to have its successes in handling matters which might, without its intervention, have

The League of Nations

On 28 April 1919 the delegates of the Paris peace conference signed the pact of the League of Nations, which took effect in January 1920. The League's objective was to "promote international cooperation and to achieve international peace and security".

From the start, the League of Nations was disadvantaged by the absence of the United States. Also, neither the countries defeated in the First World War nor Soviet Russia were members. The Soviet Union joined in 1934. Germany joined in 1926, but in 1933 Hitler withdrew its membership and his gesture

was copied by Mussolini for Italy in 1937. Japan had also withdrawn in 1933. This meant that there were always important absentees.

The League of Nations had its seat in Geneva. It was made up of the General Assembly, comprised of all the member nations; the Council, made up of four permanent members (Great Britain, France, Italy and Japan) and others elected for three-year periods; and the Secretariat, which prepared agendas and reports. The League's powers were limited: unable to decree military interventions, it could only oppose aggression with economic sanctions. Its subsidiary bodies included the International Labour Organization, which campaigned for governments to pass legislation on minimum wages and maximum working hours.

In spite of its restrictions, the League sometimes succeeded in averting international conflict: in 1921, for example, when Yugoslavia invaded Albania, and in 1925, when Bulgaria invaded Greece. Its failure to have any effect, however, when Japan invaded Manchuria in 1931, and when Italy invaded Ethiopia in 1935, led Great Britain and France to reject suggestions that it could be used against Nazi Germany. During the Second World War, the idea of replacing the League with a more effective organization dominated discussion and eventually gave rise to the United Nations.

The driving force behind the League of Nations was the United States president Woodrow Wilson (1856–1924).

proved dangerous. If exaggerated hopes had been entertained that it might do more, it does not mean it was not a practical as well as a great and imaginative idea.

RUSSIA'S ABSENCE FROM THE PEACE CONFERENCE

Russia was absent from the League just as it was from the peace conference. Probably the latter was the more important. The political arrangements to shape the next stage of European history were entered into without consulting Russia, though in eastern Europe this meant the drawing of boundaries in which any Russian government was bound to be vitally interested. It was true that the Bolshevik leaders did all they could to provide excuses for excluding them. They envenomed relations with the major powers by revolutionary propaganda, for they were convinced that the capitalist countries were

determined to overthrow them. The British prime minister, Lloyd George, and Wilson were in fact more flexible – even sympathetic – than many of their colleagues and electors in dealing with Russia. Their French colleague, Clemenceau, on the other hand, was passionately anti-Bolshevik and had the support of many French ex-soldiers and investors in being so; Versailles was the first great European peace to be made by powers all the time aware of the dangers of disappointing democratic electorates. But however the responsibility is allocated, the outcome was that Russia, the European power which had, potentially, the greatest weight of all in the affairs of the continent, was not consulted in the making of a new Europe. Though for the time being virtually out of action, it was bound eventually to join the ranks of those who wished to revise the settlement or overthrow it. It only made it worse that its rulers detested the social system it was meant to protect.

The new Irish Free State was plagued by a civil war (1922–1923) between the provisional government and the Irregulars, who opposed the terms of the Anglo-Irish Treaty. Members of the Irish Republican Army (the armed wing of those who opposed the treaty) can be seen here marching through the streets during the Dublin Battle of July 1922.

THE WEAKNESSES OF THE PEACE

Huge hopes had been entertained of the peace settlement. They were often unrealistic, yet in spite of its manifest failures, the peace has been over-condemned, for it had many good points. When it failed, it was for reasons which were for the most part beyond the control of the men who made it. In the first place, the days of a European world hegemony in the narrow political sense were over. The peace treaties of 1919 could do little to secure the future beyond Europe. The old imperial policemen were now too weakened to do their job inside Europe, let alone outside; some had disappeared altogether. In the end the United States had been needed to ensure Germany's defeat but now she plunged into a period of artificial isolation. Nor did Russia wish to be involved in the continent's stabilizing.

The isolationism of the one power and the sterilization of the other by ideology left Europe to its own inadequate devices. When no revolution broke out in Europe, the Russians turned in on themselves; when Americans were given the chance by Wilson to be involved in Europe's peace-keeping, they refused it. Both decisions are comprehensible, but their combined effect was to preserve an illusion of European autonomy which was no longer a reality and could no longer be an adequate framework for handling its problems. Finally, the settlement's gravest immediate weakness lay in the economic fragility of the new structures it presupposed. Here its terms were more in question: self-determination often made nonsense of economics. But it is difficult to see on what grounds self-determination could have been set aside. Ireland's problems are still with us to some extent more than eighty years after an independent Irish Free State appeared in 1922.

ILLUSIONS OF SUCCESS

The situation was all the more likely to prove unstable because many illusions persisted in Europe and many new ones arose. Allied victory and the rhetoric of peace-making made many think that there had been a great triumph of liberalism and democracy. Four autocratic anti-national illiberal empires had collapsed, after all, and to this day the peace settlement retains the distinction of being the only one in history made by great powers all of which were democracies. Liberal optimism also drew strength from the ostentatious stance taken by Wilson during the war; he had done all he could to make it clear that he saw the participation of the United States as essentially different in kind from that of the other Allies, being governed (he reiterated) by high-minded ideals and a belief that the world could be made safe for democracy if other nations would give up their bad old ways. Some thought that he had been shown to be right;

This British cartoon, dating from 1927, mocks communist propaganda. The speaker, who does not look as proletarian as the sparse public he is addressing, is surrounded by posters bearing slogans such as "Against King and Country!" and "Up the Reds!".

the new states, above all the new Germany, adopted liberal, parliamentary constitutions and often republican ones, too. Finally, there was the illusion of the League; the dream of a new international authority, which was not an empire seemed at last a reality.

EUROPE'S FEAR OF COMMUNIST REVOLUTION

IDEAS OF THE PEACE SETTLEMENT as a triumph of liberalism and democracy were rooted in fallacy and false premise. Since the peacemakers had been obliged to do much more

than enthrone liberal principles – they had also to pay debts, protect vested interests, and take account of intractable facts – those principles had been much muddied in practice. Above all, they had left much unsatisfied nationalism about and had created new and fierce nationalist resentments in Germany. Perhaps this could not be helped, but it was a soil in which things other than liberalism could grow. Further, the democratic institutions of the new states – and the old ones, too, for that matter – were being launched on a world whose economic structure was terribly damaged. Everywhere, poverty, hardship and unemployment exacerbated political

Communism

Proposals for the organization of social life based on collective property have been made from ancient times. Although he was far from being a communist philosopher, Plato, in the 4th century BCE, maintained that in an ideal state the ruling class should have neither property nor family. In the 16th century, the Englishman Thomas More described for the first time, in his book *Utopia*, an imaginary society where not just a minority but all its members shared collective property. During the French Revolution Gracchus Babeuf proposed the establishment of a communist society through a revolutionary conspiracy.

Modern communism emerged with the *Communist Manifesto* (1848) of Karl Marx and Friedrich Engels. According to Marx, history was leading inevitably towards the establishment of a communist society, in which the disappearance of private property and state structures would make people completely free. Lenin's dream of creating a society in which he could put Marx's theories into practice was realized when the Bolsheviks seized power in Russia in 1917. The following year, the Bolshevik Party became the Communist Party, and in 1919 the Communist International, or Comintern, was founded. However, by the time the Communist Party lost power in Russia in 1991, the countries ruled by communist governments were more characterized by an immense state bureaucracy than by the "withering away" of the state envisaged by Marx.

Vladimir Ilyich Lenin (left), founder of the Soviet Union and of the international communist movement, is photographed with his successor, Joseph Stalin.

struggle and in many places they were made worse by the special dislocations produced by respect for national sovereignty. The crumbling of old economic patterns of exchange in the war made it much more difficult to deal with problems like peasant poverty and unemployment, too; Russia, once the granary of much of western Europe, was now inaccessible economically. This was a background which revolutionaries could exploit. The communists were happy and ready to do this, for they believed that history had cast them for this role, and soon their efforts were reinforced in some countries by another radical phenomenon, fascism.

INTERNATIONAL COMMUNISM

Communism threatened the new Europe in two ways. Internally, each country soon had a revolutionary communist party. They effected little that was positive, but caused great alarm. They also did much to prevent the emergence of strong progressive parties. This was because of the circumstances of their birth. A "Comintern", or Third International, was devised by the Russians in March 1919 to provide leadership for the international socialist movement, which might otherwise, they feared, rally again to the old leaders, whose lack of revolutionary zeal they blamed for a failure to exploit the opportunities of the war. The test of socialist movements for Lenin was adherence to the Comintern, whose principles were deliberately rigid, disciplined and uncompromising, in accordance with his view of the needs of an effective revolutionary party. In almost every country this divided socialists into two camps. Some adhered to the Comintern and took the name communist; others, though sometimes claiming still to be Marxists, remained in the rump

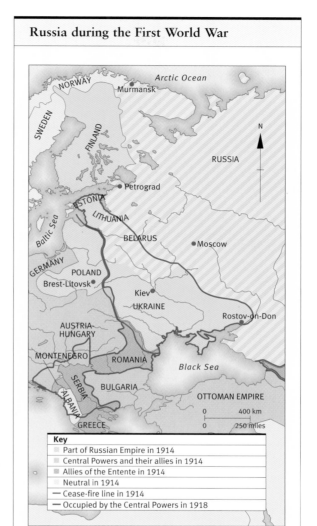

Russia during the First World War

When the Russian communist government signed the Brest-Litovsk Peace Treaty with the Central Powers in March 1918, the latter had occupied a vast territory on the western fronts of the old tsarist empire. As a result of the defeat of Germany, the communists regained the Ukraine and Belarus which, in 1922, were integrated into the Union of Soviet Socialist Republics together with Russia and Transcaucasia. Finland, the three Baltic states and Poland, on the other hand, consolidated their independence.

national parties and movements. They competed for working-class support and fought one another bitterly.

The new revolutionary threat on the Left was all the more alarming to many Europeans

In the aftermath of the First World War, the October Revolution and the Civil War, famine inflicted further misery on millions of Russians, such as this family of starving peasants.

because there were plenty of revolutionary possibilities for communists to exploit. The most conspicuous led to the installation of a Bolshevik government in Hungary, but more startling, perhaps, were attempted communist coups in Germany, some briefly successful. The German situation was especially ironical, for the government of the new republic, which emerged there in the aftermath of defeat, was dominated by socialists who were forced back to reliance upon conservative forces – notably the professional soldiers of the old army – in order to prevent revolution. This happened even before the founding of the Comintern and it gave a special bitterness to the divisions of the Left in Germany. But everywhere, communist policy made united resistance to conservatism more difficult, frightening moderates with revolutionary rhetoric and conspiracy.

FEAR OF RUSSIA IN EASTERN EUROPE

In eastern Europe, the social threat was often seen also as a Russian threat. The Comintern was manipulated as an instrument of Soviet foreign policy by the Bolshevik leaders; this was justifiable, given their assumption that the future of world revolution depended upon the preservation of the first socialist state as a citadel of the international working class. In the early years of civil war and slow consolidation of Bolshevik power in Russia that belief led to the deliberate incitement of disaffection abroad in order to preoccupy capitalist governments. But in eastern and central Europe there was more to it than this, because the actual territorial settlement of that area was in doubt long after the Versailles treaty. The First World War did not end there until in March 1921 a peace treaty between Russia and the new Polish Republic provided frontiers lasting until 1939. Poland was the most anti-Russian by tradition, the most anti-Bolshevik by religion, as well as the largest and most ambitious of the new nations. But all of them felt threatened by a recovery of Russian power, especially now that it was tied up with the threat of social revolution. This connection helped to turn many of these states before 1939 to dictatorial or military governments which would at least guarantee a strong anti-communist line.

POST-REVOLUTIONARY RUSSIA

FEAR OF COMMUNIST REVOLUTION in eastern and central Europe was most evident in the immediate post-war years, when economic collapse and uncertainty about the outcome of the Polish–Russian war (which, at one time, appeared to threaten Warsaw itself) provided the background. In 1921, with peace at last and, symbolically, the establishment of orderly official relations between the USSR and Great Britain, there was a noticeable relaxation. This was connected with the Russian government's own sense of emerging from a period of acute danger in the civil war. It did not produce much in the way of better diplomatic manners, and revolutionary propaganda and denunciation of capitalist countries did not cease, but the Bolsheviks could now turn to the rebuilding of their own shattered land. In 1921 Russian pig-iron production was about one-fifth of its 1913 level, that of coal a tiny 3 per cent or so, while the railways had less than half as many locomotives in service as at the start of the war. Livestock had declined by over a quarter and cereal deliveries were less than two-fifths of those of 1916. On to this impoverished economy there fell in

Proletarian dictatorship

Lenin defined the new Russian régime as a proletarian dictatorship, but it soon became clear that it was a dictatorship not by the working masses, but by a centralized and disciplined party.

"The dictatorship of the proletariat means a most determined and most ruthless war waged by the new class against a more powerful enemy, the bourgeoisie, whose resistance is increased tenfold by their overthrow (even if only in a single country), and whose power lies, not only in the strength of international capital, the strength and durability of their international connections, but also in the force of habit, in the strength of small-scale production. Unfortunately, small-scale production is still widespread in the world, and small-scale production engenders capitalism and the bourgeoisie continuously, daily, hourly, spontaneously, and on a mass scale. All these reasons make the dictatorship of the proletariat necessary, and victory over the bourgeoisie is impossible without a long, stubborn and desperate life-and-death struggle which calls for tenacity, discipline and a single and inflexible will."

An extract from Ch. 2 of *"Left-Wing"* *Communism: an Infantile Disorder* by Vladimir Ilyich Lenin (1920).

1921 a drought in south Russia. More than two million died in the subsequent famine and even cannibalism was reported.

INTERNAL POLITICAL STRIFE

Liberalization of the economy brought about a turnround. By 1927 both industrial and agricultural production were nearly back to pre-war levels. The régime in these years was undergoing great uncertainty in its leadership. This had already been apparent before Lenin died in 1924, but the removal of a man whose acknowledged ascendancy had kept forces within it in balance opened a period of evolution and debate in the leadership of the Communist Party. This was not about the centralized, autocratic nature of the régime which had emerged from the 1917 revolution, for none of the protagonists considered that political liberation was conceivable or that the use of secret police and the party's dictatorship could be dispensed with in a world of hostile capitalist states. But they could disagree about economic policy and tactics and personal rivalry sometimes gave extra edge to this.

Broadly speaking, two viewpoints emerged. One emphasized that the revolution depended on the goodwill of the mass of Russians, the peasants; they had first been allowed to take the land, then antagonized by attempts to feed the cities at their expense, then conciliated again by the liberalization of the economy and what was known as "NEP", the New Economic Policy which Lenin had approved as an expedient. Under it, the peasants had been able to make profits for themselves and had begun to grow more food and to sell it to the cities. The other viewpoint showed the same facts in a longer perspective. To conciliate the peasants would slow down industrialization, which Russia needed to survive in a hostile world. The Party's proper course, argued those who took this view, was to rely upon the revolutionary militants of the cities and to exploit the still non-Bolshevized peasants in their interest while pressing on with industrialization and the promotion of revolution abroad. The communist leader Trotsky took this view.

This painting by Yuri Pimenov is entitled *New Moscow* and gives an unusually light-hearted impression of life in the Soviet Union under Stalin. In fact the 1930s brought the imprisonment or execution of millions of Soviet citizens, many of them veteran communists, in Stalin's so-called purges.

Joseph Stalin, sitting fifth from the left in the front row, is pictured among the delegates of the 8th Congress of the Soviets in 1936. On the left of the front row is Nikita Khruschev, who would denounce Stalin's crimes 20 years later. At the other end of the row is Marshal Mikhail Tukhachevsky, who became a victim of the purges in 1937.

STALIN AND INDUSTRIALIZATION

What happened was roughly that Trotsky was shouldered aside, but his view prevailed. From the intricate politics of the Communist Party there emerged eventually the ascendancy of a member of its bureaucracy, Joseph Stalin, a man far less attractive intellectually than either Lenin or Trotsky, equally ruthless, and of greater historical importance. Gradually arming himself with a power, which he used against former colleagues and old Bolsheviks as willingly as against his enemies, he carried out the real Russian revolution to which the Bolshevik seizure of power had opened the way and created a new élite on which a new Russia was to be based. For him industrialization was paramount. The road to it lay through finding a way of forcing the peasant to pay for it by supplying the grain he would rather have eaten if not offered a good profit. Two "Five Year Plans"

carried out an industrialization programme from 1928 onwards, and their roots lay in the collectivization of agriculture. The Communist Party now for the first time conquered the countryside. In a new civil war millions of peasants were killed or transported, and grain levies brought back famine. But the towns were fed, though the police apparatus kept consumption down to the minimum. There was a fall in real wages. But by 1937, 80 per cent of Russian industrial output came from plant built since 1928. Russia was again a great power and the effects of this alone would assure Stalin a place in history.

The price in suffering was enormous. The enforcement of collectivization was only made possible by brutality on a scale far greater than anything seen under the tsars and it made Russia a totalitarian state far more effective than the old autocracy had been. Stalin, though himself a Georgian, looks a very Russian figure, a despot whose ruthless use of power is anticipated by an Ivan the Terrible or a Peter the Great. He was also a somewhat paradoxical claimant to Marxist orthodoxy, which taught that the economic structure of society determined its politics. Stalin precisely inverted this; he demonstrated that if the will to use political power was there, the economic substructure could be revolutionized by force.

ITALIAN FASCISM

CRITICS OF LIBERAL CAPITALIST society in other countries often held up Soviet Russia, of which they had a very rosy picture,

as an example of the way in which a society might achieve progress and a revitalization of its cultural and ethical life. But this was not the only model offered to those who found the civilization of the West disappointing. In the 1920s in Italy a movement appeared calling itself Fascism. It was to lend its name to a number of other and only loosely related radical movements in other countries which had in common a rejection of liberalism and strong anti-Marxism.

The Great War had badly strained constitutional Italy. Though poorer than other countries regarded in 1914 as great powers, Italy's share of fighting had been disproportionately heavy and often unsuccessful and

Fascism in Italy and Germany

Fascism was a political movement founded in Italy by Benito Mussolini in 1919. It greatly changed Europe during the period between the wars, when several other political parties, influenced by the Italian example, were established, including the German National Socialist Party. The Italian fascists and similar parties in other countries claimed to be against all the other political movements then in existence. They were anti-liberal and anti-socialist, fiercely anti-communist and to a certain degree, anti-conservative, although in many cases they allied themselves with the conservative right-wing parties.

The objective of the Italian and German fascists was to establish nationalist, authoritarian states, which would intervene in economic, social and cultural affairs. They aspired to territorial expansion through conflict. They were aggressive and secular; they glorified youth, masculinity and war, and paid homage to charismatic leaders with carefully manipulated cults of personality.

Germany and Italy's defeat in the Second World War – and the memory of the atrocities committed by their fascist régimes – completely undermined any prestige the doctrine had acquired in the pre-war era. However, neo-fascist movements have recently emerged in several European countries, often as a result of rising levels of youth unemployment.

Benito Mussolini (1883–1945) (left) is pictured with the writer Gabriele d'Annunzio, who actively promoted ultra-nationalistic attitudes at the end of the First World War.

much of it had taken place on Italian territory. Inequalities had accentuated social divisions as the war went on. With peace came even faster inflation, too. The owners of property, whether agricultural or industrial, and those who could ask higher wages because of a labour shortage, were more insulated against it than the middle classes and those who lived on investment or fixed incomes. Yet these were on the whole the most convinced supporters of the unification completed in 1870. They had sustained a constitutional and liberal state while conservative Roman Catholics and revolutionary socialists had long opposed it. They had seen the war Italy entered in 1915 as an extension of the Risorgimento, the nineteenth-century struggle to unite Italy as a nation, a crusade to remove Austria from the last soil she ruled which was inhabited by those of Italian blood or speech. Like all nationalism, this was a muddled, unscientific notion, but it was powerful.

Peace brought to Italians disappointment and disillusion; many nationalist dreams were left unrealized. Moreover, as the immediate post-war economic crisis deepened, the socialists grew stronger in parliament and seemed more alarming now that a socialist revolutionary state existed in Russia. Disappointed and frightened, tired of socialist anti-nationalism, many Italians began to cast loose from liberal parliamentarianism and to look for a way out of Italy's disappointments. Many were sympathetic to intransigent nationalism abroad (for example, to an adventurer, Gabriele d'Annunzio, who seized the Adriatic port of Fiume which the Peace Conference had failed to give to Italy) and violent anti-Marxism at home. The second was bound to be attractive in a Roman Catholic country, but it was not only from the traditionally conservative Church that the new leadership against Marxism came.

Mussolini is depicted at the head of the Fascist militia in an idealized portrayal of the "March on Rome" of 1922. In reality, Mussolini did not march on Rome at all, but travelled by train in comfort, arriving before his followers.

BENITO MUSSOLINI

In 1919 a journalist and ex-serviceman, who had before the war been an extreme socialist, Benito Mussolini, formed a movement called the *fascio di combattimento*, which can be roughly translated as "union for struggle". It sought power by any means, among them violence by groups of young thugs, directed at first against socialists and working-class organizations, then against elected authorities. The movement prospered. Italy's constitutional politicians could neither control it nor tame it by cooperation. Soon the Fascists (as they came to be called) often enjoyed official or quasi-official patronage and protection from local officials and police. Gangsterism was semi-institutionalized. By 1922 they had not only achieved important electoral success but had virtually made orderly government impossible in some places by terrorizing their political enemies, especially if they were communist or socialist. In that year, other politicians having failed to master the Fascist challenge, the king called Mussolini to form a government; he did so, on a coalition basis, and the violence came to an end. This was what was called in later Fascist mythology the "March on Rome", but was not quite the end of constitutional Italy. Mussolini only slowly turned his position into a dictatorship. In 1926 government by decree began; elections were suspended. There was little opposition.

FASCIST GOVERNMENT

The new régime had terrorism in plenty at its roots, and it explicitly denounced liberal ideals, yet Mussolini's rule was far short of totalitarian and was much less brutal than the Russian (of which he sometimes spoke admiringly). He undoubtedly had aspirations to revolutionary change, and many of his followers much stronger ones, but revolution turned out in practice to be largely a propaganda claim; Mussolini's own temperamental impatience with an established society from which he felt excluded lay behind it, as much as real radical pressure in his movement. Italian Fascism in practice and theory rarely achieved coherence; instead, it reflected more and more the power of established Italy. Its

Cardinal Gasbarri signs the Lateran treaties in 1929, while Mussolini (seated on right) looks on.

Mussolini's Fascist doctrines

"Above all, Fascism ... does not believe in the possibility nor the usefulness of perpetual peace .... Only war takes all human energy to its maximum pressure and stamps the seal of nobility on those peoples who have the courage to confront it ... .

"This conception of life makes Fascism totally opposed to the doctrine, based on so-called scientific and Marxist socialism, which is the materialist concept of history. ... Fascism, now and always, believes in sanctity and heroism; that is to say, in actions which are not influenced by direct or indirect economic motives. ... Fascism denies the validity of the equation welfare equals happiness, which would reduce men to the level of animals ... .

"As well as socialism, Fascism fights the whole complex system of democratic ideology ... . Fascism refuses to accept that the majority, by the simple fact of being a majority, can lead human society ... and affirms the immutable, beneficial and advantageous inequality of humankind ... .

"The basis of Fascism is its concept of state. Fascism sees the state as an absolute, compared to which all individuals or groups are relative ... .

An extract from *Fascist Doctrines* by Benito Mussolini, 1932.

greatest domestic step was a diplomatic agreement with the papacy, which in return for substantial concessions to the authority of the Church in Italian life (which persist to this day) recognized the Italian state officially for the first time. For all Fascism's revolutionary rhetoric, the Lateran treaties of 1929, which embodied this agreement, were a concession to the greatest conservative force in Italy. "We have given back God to Italy and Italy to God," said the pope. Just as unrevolutionary were the results of Fascist criticism of free enterprise. The subordination of individual interest to the state boiled down to depriving trades unions of their power to protect their members' interests. Few checks were placed on the freedom of employers and Fascist economic planning was a mockery. Only agricultural production notably improved.

AUTHORITARIANISM ELSEWHERE IN EUROPE

The same divergence between style and aspiration on the one hand and achievement on the other was also to be marked in movements elsewhere, which have been called fascist. Though indeed reflecting something new and post-liberal – they were inconceivable except as expressions of mass society – such movements almost always in practice made compromising concessions to conservative influences. This makes it difficult to speak of the phenomenon "fascism" at all precisely; in many countries régimes appeared which were authoritarian – even totalitarian in aspiration – intensely nationalist, and anti-Marxist. But fascism was not the only possible source of such ideas. Such governments as those which emerged in Portugal and Spain, for example, drew upon traditional and conservative forces rather than upon those which arose from the new phenomenon of mass politics. In them, true radicals who were fascists often felt discontented at concessions made to the existing social order. Only in Germany, in the end, did a movement some termed "fascist" succeed in a revolution which mastered historical conservatism. For such reasons, the label of fascism sometimes confuses as much as it clarifies.

DEMOCRACY THWARTED

Perhaps it is best merely to distinguish two separable phenomena of the twenty years

after 1918. One is the appearance (even in stable democracies such as Great Britain and France) of ideologists and activists who spoke the language of a new, radical politics, emphasized idealism, will-power and sacrifice, and looked forward to rebuilding society and the state on new lines without respect to vested interests or concessions to materialism. This was a phenomenon which, though widespread, triumphed in only two major states, Italy and Germany. In each of these, economic collapse, outraged nationalism and anti-Marxism were the sources of success,

Mussolini is accompanied by top military aides. The Fascist leader's decision to take part in the Second World War was fatal both for him and for his régime.

Admiral Miklos Horthy (1868–1957) was head of state in Hungary from 1920 until 1944, having commanded the troops which overthrew Béla Kun's communist régime in 1919. Horthy's was one of many conservative dictatorships that were established in Europe in the period between the wars.

though that in Germany did not come until 1933. If one word is wanted for this, let it be fascism. In other countries, usually under-developed economically, it might be better to speak of authoritarian, rather than fascist, régimes, especially in eastern Europe. There, large agricultural populations presented problems aggravated by the peace settlement. Sometimes alien national minorities appeared to threaten the state. Liberal institutions were only superficially implanted in many of the new countries and traditional conservative social and religious forces were strong. As in Latin America, where similar economic conditions could be found, their apparent constitutionalism tended to give way sooner or later to the rule of strong men and soldiers. This proved the case before 1939 in the new

General Miguel Primo de Rivera (1870–1930) led a military *coup d'état* in Spain in 1923, supported by the king and the army. He acted as dictator until 1930, when the loss of the army's support forced him to resign.

Baltic states, Poland and all the successor states of the Dual Monarchy except Czechoslovakia, the one effective democracy in central Europe or the Balkans. The need of these states to fall back on such régimes demonstrated both the unreality of the hopes entertained of their political maturity in 1918 and the new fear of Marxist communism, especially acute on Russia's borders. Such pressure operated also – though less acutely – in Spain and Portugal, where the influence of traditional conservatism was even stronger and Catholic social thinking counted for more than fascism.

ECONOMIC RECOVERY

The failures of democracy between the wars did not proceed at an even pace; in the 1920s a bad economic start was followed by a gradual recovery of prosperity in which most of Europe outside Russia shared, and the years

General Carmona, president of the Portuguese republic from 1928 to 1951, is greeted by enthusiastic crowds in 1941. Next to him is Antonio de Oliveira Salazar, prime minister and the real dictator of Portugal from 1932 to 1968.

from 1925 to 1929 were on the whole good ones. This permitted optimism about the political future of the new democratic nations. Currencies emerged from appalling inflation in the first half of the decade and were once more stable; the resumption by many countries of the gold standard was a sign of confidence that the old pre-1914 days were returned. In 1925 the production of food and raw materials in Europe for the first time passed the 1913 figure and a recovery of manufacturing was also under way. With the help of a worldwide recovery of trade and huge investment from the United States, now an exporter of capital, Europe reached in 1929 a level of trade not to be touched again until 1954.

GERMAN ECONOMIC WEAKNESS

Yet collapse followed the boom of the 1920s. Economic recovery had been built on insecure foundations. When faced with a sudden crisis, the new prosperity crumbled rapidly. There followed not merely a European but a world economic crisis, which was the single most important event between two world wars.

The complex but remarkably efficient economic system of 1914 had in fact been irreparably damaged. International exchange was hampered by a huge increase of restrictions immediately after the war as new nations strove to protect their infant economies with tariffs and exchange control, and bigger and older nations tried to repair their enfeebled ones. The Versailles treaty made things worse by saddling Germany, the most important of all the European industrial states, with an indefinite burden of reparation in kind and in cash. This not only distorted her economy and delayed its recovery for years, but also took away much of the incentive to make it work. To the east, Germany's greatest potential market, Russia, was almost

A French soldier accompanies a cargo of German coke to France as part of the reparations Germany was ordered to make to her former enemy at the end of the First World War.

entirely cut off behind an economic frontier which little trade could penetrate; the Danube valley and the Balkans, another great area of German enterprise, was divided and impoverished. Temporarily, these difficulties were gradually overcome by the availability of American money, which Americans were willing to supply (though they would not take European goods and retired behind their tariff walls). But this brought about a dangerous dependence on the continued prosperity of the United States.

AMERICAN BOOM AND SLUMP

In the 1920s the United States produced nearly 40 per cent of the world's coal and over half the world's manufactures. This wealth, enhanced by the demands of war, had transformed the life of many Americans, the first people in the world to be able to take for granted the possession of family automobiles. Unfortunately, American domestic prosperity carried the world. On it depended the confidence which provided American capital for export. Because of this, a swing in the business cycle turned into a world economic disaster. In 1928 short-term money began to be harder to get in the United States. There were also signs that the end of the long boom might be approaching as commodity prices began to fall. These two factors led to the calling in of American loans from Europe. Soon some European borrowers were in difficulties. Meanwhile, demand was slackening in the United States as people began to think a severe slump might be on the way. The Federal Reserve Bank now began to make its own contribution to disaster by raising interest rates and continuing to do so. Almost accidentally, there was a particularly sudden and spectacular stock market collapse in October 1929. It did not matter that there

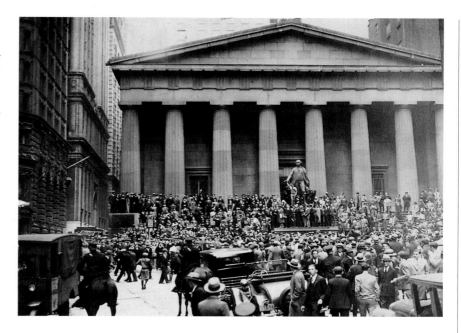

was thereafter a temporary rally and that great bankers bought to restore confidence. It was the end of American business confidence and of overseas investment. After a last brief rally in 1930 American money for investment abroad dried up. The world slump began.

THE WORLD ECONOMY COLLAPSES

Economic growth came to an end because of the collapse of investment, but another factor was soon operating to accelerate disaster. As the debtor nations tried to put their accounts in order, they cut imports. This caused a drop in world prices, so that countries producing primary goods could not afford to buy abroad. Meanwhile, at the centre of things, both the United States and Europe went into a financial crisis; as countries struggled, unsuccessfully, to keep the value of their currencies steady in relation to gold (an internationally acceptable means of exchange – hence the expression "gold standard") they adopted deflationary policies to balance their books which again cut demand. So

Horrified crowds gather in front of the Treasury Building on New York's Wall Street in 1929 as news of the stock market crash breaks.

An American soup kitchen distributes free food to the poor during the Depression.

government intervention ensured that recession would become disaster. By 1933 all the major currencies, except the French, were off gold. This was the symbolic expression of the tragedy, the dethronement of one old idol of liberal economics. Its reality was a level of unemployment which may have reached thirty million in the industrial world. In 1932 (the worst year for industrial countries) the index of industrial production for the United States and Germany was in each case only just above half of what it had been in 1929.

The effects of economic depression rolled outwards with a ghastly and irresistible logic. The social gains of the 1920s, when many people's standard of living had improved, were almost everywhere wiped out. No country had a solution to unemployment and though it was at its worst in the United States and Germany it existed in a concealed form all around the world in the villages and farmlands of the primary producers. The national income of the United States fell by 38 per cent between 1929 and 1932; this was exactly the figure by which the prices of manufactured goods fell, but at the same time raw material

prices fell by 56 per cent and foodstuffs by 48 per cent respectively. Everywhere, therefore, the poorer nations and the poorer sectors of the mature economies suffered disproportionately. They may not always have seemed to do so, because they had less far to fall; an eastern European or an Argentinian peasant may not have been absolutely much worse off for he had always been badly off, while an unemployed German clerk or factory hand certainly was worse off and knew it.

THE DECAY OF EUROPEAN HEGEMONY

There was to be no world recovery before another great war. Nations cut themselves off more and more behind tariffs (the 1930 United States tariff raised average duties on imports to 59 cents) and strove in some cases to achieve economic self-sufficiency by an increasing state control of their economic life. Some did better than others, some very badly. The disaster was a promising setting for the communists and fascists who expected or advocated the collapse of liberal civilization and now began to flap expectantly about the enfeebled carcass. The end of the gold standard and the belief in non-interference with the economy mark the collapse of a world order in its economic dimension as strikingly as the rise of totalitarian régimes and the rise of nationalism to its destructive climax mark it in its political. Liberal civilization, frighteningly, had lost its power to control events. Many Europeans still found it hard to see this, though, and they continued to dream of the restoration of an age when that civilization enjoyed unquestioned supremacy. They forgot that its values had rested on a political and economic hegemony which, remarkably though it had worked for a time, was already visibly in decay all around the world.

New York's Broadway is pictured in 1928 – the year before the bubble burst. The carefree 1920s, when America and Europe enjoyed a period of relative prosperity, were almost over. Such untroubled times would soon become a distant memory, as the world prepared to enter another devastating global war.

EMERGING
POWERS

I N 1900 EUROPEANS COULD LOOK BACK on two, perhaps three, centuries of astonishing growth. Most of them would have said that it was growth for the better – that is, progress. Their history since the Middle Ages looked very much like a continuing advance to evidently worthwhile goals questioned by few. Whether the criteria were intellectual and scientific, or material and economic (even if they were moral and aesthetic, some said, so persuasive was the gospel of progress), a look at their own past assured them that they were set on a progressive course – which meant that the world was set on a progressive course, for their civilization was now spread worldwide. What was more, limitless advance seemed to lie ahead. Europeans showed in 1900 much the same confidence in the continuing success of their culture as the Chinese élite had shown in theirs a century earlier. The past, they were sure, proved them right.

Even so, a few did not feel so confident. They felt that the evidence could equally well imply a pessimistic conclusion. Though there were far fewer pessimists than optimists, they numbered in their ranks men of acknowledged standing and powerful minds. Some of them argued that the civilization in which they lived had yet to reveal its full self-destructive potential and sensed that the time when it would do so might not be far away. Some of them saw a civilization more and more obviously drifting away from its moorings in religion and moral absolutes, carried along by the tides of materialism and barbarity – probably to complete disaster.

As it turned out, neither optimists nor pessimists were wholly right, perhaps because their eyes were glued too firmly to what they thought were the characteristics of European civilization. They looked to its own inherent powers, tendencies or weaknesses for guidance about the future; not many of them paid much attention to the way Europe was changing the world in which her own ascendancy had been built and was thus to alter once again the balance between the major centres of civilization. Few looked further than Europe and Europe beyond the seas except the unbalanced cranks who fussed about the "Yellow Peril", though Napoleon had a century earlier warned that China was a sleeping giant best left undisturbed.

It is tempting to say in retrospect that the pessimists have had the best of the argument; it may even be true. But hindsight is sometimes a disadvantage to the historian; in this instance it makes it difficult to see how the optimists could once have felt so sure of themselves. Yet we should try to do so. For one thing, there were men of vision and insight among them; for another, optimism was for so long an obstacle to the solution of certain problems in the twentieth century that it deserves to be understood as a historical force in its own right. And much of what the pessimists said was wrong too. Appalling though the disasters of the twentieth century were, they fell on societies more resilient than those shattered by lesser troubles in earlier times, and they were not always those feared nearly a century ago. In 1900, optimists and pessimists alike had to work with data which could be read in more than one way. It is not reprehensible, merely tragic, that they found it so hard to judge exactly what lay ahead. With better information available to us, we have not been so successful in shorter-term prediction that we are in a position to condemn them.

The sense of optimism about the future that many Europeans had felt in the late 19th century was swept
away by the outbreak of the First World War in 1914. This image of Verdun, France, four years later
shows a scene of the devastation suffered by so many French cities and towns. Material disaster and
unprecedented slaughter in 1914–1918 bequeathed poisonous legacies to the inter-war years.

1 A NEW ASIA IN THE MAKING

Industrial expansion meant that Japanese cities grew increasingly crowded during the 1920s, as this traffic jam in Tokyo's slum district of Honjo shows.

EUROPE'S TROUBLES COULD NOT be confined to one continent. They were bound soon to cramp her ability to dominate affairs elsewhere and the earliest signs of this came in Asia. European colonial power in Asia was, in the perspective of world history, only very briefly unchallengeable and unchallenged. By 1914 one European power, Great Britain, had made an ally of Japan in order to safeguard her interests in the Far East, rather than rely on her own resources. Another, Russia, had been beaten by Japan in war and had turned back towards Europe after twenty years of pressure towards the Yellow Sea. A century's bullying of China which had seemed likely to prove fatal at the time of the Boxer rebellion was coming to an end; she lost no more territory to European imperialists after that. Unlike India or Africa, China had somehow hung on to her independence into an era where European power in Asia was ebbing. As tensions in Europe mounted and the difficulty of frustrating Japanese ambitions indefinitely became clear, European statesmen realized that the time for acquiring new ports or dreaming of partitions of the "sick man" of the Far East was over. It would suit everyone better to turn to what was always, in effect, British policy, that of an "open door" through which all countries might seek their own commercial advantage. That advantage, too, showed signs of being much less spectacular than had been thought in the sanguine days of the 1890s and that was another reason to tread more softly in the Far East.

THE TWILIGHT OF COLONIALISM

Not only was the high tide of the European onslaught on Asia past by 1914 but the revolutionizing of Asia by colonialism, cultural interplay, and economic power had already produced defensive reflexes which had to be taken seriously. As early as 1881, a Hawaiian king had proposed to the Meiji emperor the creation of a "Union and Federation of Asiatic Nations and Sovereigns"; this was only a straw in the wind, but already such reflexes were now apparent in Japan. Their indirect operation as catalysts of modernization, channelled through this local and Asian force, set the pace of the next phase of the Hundred Years' War of East and West. Japanese dynamism dominates Asian history in the first forty years of the twentieth century; China's revolution had no similar impact until after 1945 when, together with new change-making forces from outside, that country would once more surpass Japan in importance as a shaper of Asian affairs and would close the Western age in Asia.

JAPAN

JAPAN'S DYNAMISM manifested itself both in economic growth and territorial aggressiveness. For a long time the first was more obvious. It was part and parcel of an overall process of what was seen as "Westernizing", which could in the 1920s still sustain a mood of liberal hopefulness about Japan and helped to mask Japanese imperialism. In 1925 universal suffrage was introduced and in spite of much evidence from European states that this had no necessary connection with liberalism or moderation, it seemed to confirm once again a pattern of steady constitutional progress that had begun in the nineteenth century.

POST-WAR INDUSTRIAL EXPANSION

Confidence in Japan's constitutional progress, shared both by foreigners and by Japanese, was for a time helped by its industrial growth, notably in the mood of expansive optimism awoken by the Great War, which gave it great opportunities: markets (especially in Asia) in which it had been faced by heavy Western competition were abandoned when their former exploiters found they could not meet the demands of the war in their own countries; the Allied governments ordered great quantities of munitions from Japanese factories; a world shipping shortage gave its new shipyards the work they needed. The Japanese gross national product went up by 40 per cent during the war years. Though interrupted in

During an election campaign in Japan in 1914 a speaker, who is wearing Western-style clothes, addresses an audience, most of whom are dressed in traditional Japanese attire.

Time chart (1911–1937)				
		1919 Paris Peace Treaty	1937 Japanese invasion of China	
1900				1940
	1911–1912 Chinese Revolution	1926–1927 KMT expedition to the north	1934–1935 The Long March	

1920 expansion was resumed later in the decade and in 1929 the Japanese had an industrial base which (though it still engaged less than one in five of the population) had in twenty years seen its steel production rise almost tenfold, its textile production triple, and its coal output double. Its manufacturing sector was beginning to influence other Asian countries, too; it imported iron ore from China and Malaya, coal from Manchuria. Still small though its manufacturing industry was by comparison with that of the Western powers, and though it coexisted with an enduring small-scale and artisan sector, Japan's new industrial strength was beginning to shape both domestic politics and foreign relations in the 1920s. In particular, it affected its relations with mainland Asia.

The 1911 Chinese Revolution ended the Ch'ing dynasty. Pu-Yi (1906–1967), who ruled as the last emperor of China from 1908 to 1912, is pictured right with his father, Prince Chun Tsai-Feng and his younger brother. Pu-Yi was forced to abdicate in February 1912 but later ruled, under the name of K'ang Te, as Japan's puppet emperor of Manchukuo from 1934 to 1945.

CHINA AFTER THE 1911 REVOLUTION

A CONTRAST TO THE PRE-EMINENT and dynamic role of Japan was provided there by the continuing eclipse of China, potentially the greatest of Asian and world powers. The 1911 revolution had been of enormous importance, but did not by itself end this eclipse. In principle, it marked an epoch far more fundamentally than the French or Russian revolutions: it was the end of more than two thousand years of history during which the Confucian state had held China together and Confucian ideals had dominated Chinese culture and society. Inseparably intertwined, Confucianism and the legal order fell together. The 1911 revolution proclaimed the shattering of the standards by which traditional China lived. On the other hand, the revolution was limited, in two ways especially. In the first place, it was destructive rather than constructive. The monarchy had held together a vast country, virtually a continent, of widely different regions. Its collapse meant that the centrifugal regionalism, which so often expressed itself in Chinese history, could again have full rein. Many of the revolutionaries were animated by a bitter envy and distrust of Peking (Beijing). Secret societies, the gentry and military commanders were only too ready to step forward and take a grip of affairs in their own regions. These tendencies were somewhat masked while Yuan Shih-k'ai remained at the head of affairs (until 1916), but then burst out. The revolutionaries were split between a group around Sun Yat-sen called the Chinese National People's Party, or Kuomintang (KMT), and those who upheld the central government based on the parliamentary structure at Peking. Sun's support was drawn mainly from Canton businessmen and certain soldiers in the south. Against this background warlords

The republic presided over by Yuan Shih-k'ai (1859–1916) – shown here in full military regalia – was in fact a dictatorship. Political power was in the hands of the military leaders and this was to continue. Between 1916 and 1919 a series of armed struggles between regional governors and warlords plagued the country and made life even harsher for the poverty-stricken Chinese people.

thrived. They were soldiers who happened to have control of substantial forces and arms at a time when the central government was continuously weak. Between 1912 and 1928 there were some 1,300 of them, often controlling important areas. Some of them carried out reforms. Some were simply bandits. Some had considerable status as plausible pretenders to government power. It was a little like the end of the Roman Empire, though less drawn out. When no one took the place of the old scholar-bureaucrats, the soldiers hastened to fill the void. Yuan Shih-k'ai himself can be regarded as the outstanding example of the type.

"NEW YOUTH" REFORMERS

The second limitation of the revolution of 1911 was that it provided no basis of agreement for further progress. Sun Yat-sen had said that the solution of the national question

The Kuomintang (KMT)

The Kuomintang, the Chinese National People's Party, was the centre of the Chinese nationalist revolution of 1911. Comprising members of the upper- and middle-class bourgeoisie, workers and peasants, the Kuomintang was strongest in the industrial coastal areas, which left the rural areas as fertile ground for communist agitation.

Between 1927 and 1937 China was governed by the Kuomintang, which unified the country, consolidating a nationalist government and becoming an authoritarian, military power, linked to Western neo-colonial interests. The government was able to balance the budget and it abolished special privileges for foreigners. However, when Japan attacked China in 1937 the Kuomintang proved incapable of resolving the situation. In 1949 the Chinese Communist Party triumphed over the Kuomintang, which they saw as a liberal-bourgeois body.

Members of the Kuomintang are pictured in 1927, shortly after the conference that unified "left" and "right" factions.

would have to precede that of the social. But even about the shape of a nationalist future there was much disagreement, and the removal of the dynasty took away a common enemy that had delayed its emergence. Although eventually creative, the intellectual confusion marked among the revolutionaries in the first decade of the Chinese Revolution was deeply divisive and symptomatic of the huge task awaiting China's would-be renovators.

From 1916 a group of cultural reformers began to gather particularly at the university of Peking. The year before, one of them, Ch'en Tu-hsiu, had founded a journal called *New Youth* which was the focus of the debate they ignited. Ch'en preached to Chinese youth, in whose hands he believed the revolution's destiny to lie, a total rejection of the old Chinese cultural tradition. Like other intellectuals who talked of Huxley and Dewey and introduced their bemused compatriots to the works of Ibsen, Ch'en still thought the key lay in the West; in its Darwinian sense of struggle, its individualism and utilitarianism, it still seemed to offer a way ahead. But important though such leadership was and enthusiastic though its disciples might be, an emphasis on a Western re-education for China was a handicap. Not only were many educated and patriotic Chinese sincerely attached to the traditional culture, but Western ideas were only sure of a ready welcome among the most untypical elements of Chinese society, the seaboard city-dwelling merchants and their student offspring, often educated abroad. The mass of Chinese could hardly be touched by such ideas and appeals, and the demand of other reformers for a vernacular literature was one evidence of this fact.

POVERTY AMONG THE PEASANTS

In so far as they were touched by nationalist feeling the Chinese were likely to turn against the West and against the Western-inspired capitalism which, for many of them, meant one more kind of exploitation and was the most obvious constituent of the civilization some modernizers urged them to adopt. But for the most part China's peasant masses seemed after 1911 relapsed in passivity, apparently unmoved by events and unaware of the agitation of angry and Westernized young men. It is not easy to generalize about their economic state: China was too big and too varied. But it seems clear that while the population steadily increased, nothing was done to meet the peasants' hunger for land; instead, the number of the indebted and

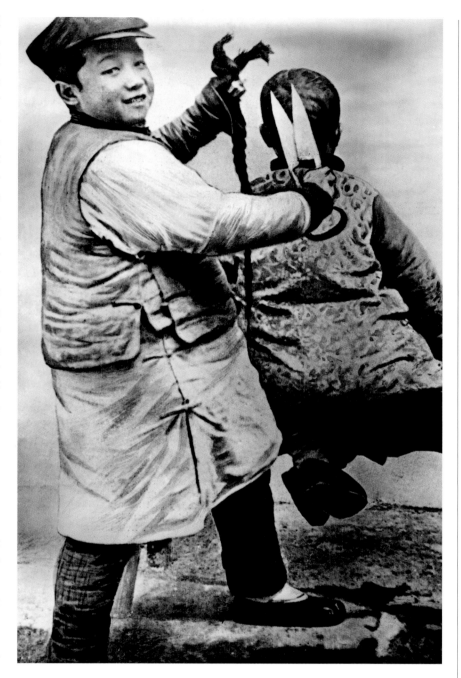

landless grew, their wretched lives frequently made even more intolerable by war, whether directly, or through its concomitants, famine and disease. The Chinese Revolution would only be assured success when it could activate these people, and the cultural emphasis of the reformers sometimes masked an unwillingness to envisage the practical political steps necessary for this.

The revolution of 1911 created a class of intellectuals and reformers, whose campaign against the traditional symbols of the old imperial régime included cutting off Manchu-style pigtails.

JAPAN'S DEMANDS ON CHINA

China's weakness remained Japan's opportunity. A world war was the occasion to push forward again her nineteenth-century ambitions. The advantages offered by the Europeans' quarrels with one another could be exploited. Japan's allies could hardly object to her seizure of the German ports in China; even if they did, they could do nothing about it while they needed Japanese ships and manufactures. There was always the hope, too, that the Japanese might send their own army to Europe to fight, though nothing like this happened. Instead, the Japanese finessed by arousing fears that they might make a separate peace with the Germans and pressed ahead in China.

Early in 1915 the Japanese government presented to the Chinese government a list of twenty-one demands and an ultimatum. In effect, this amounted to a proposal for a Japanese protectorate over China. The United Kingdom and United States did what diplomacy could do to have the demands reduced but, in the end, the Japanese got much of what they asked for as well as further confirmation of their special commercial and leasehold rights in Manchuria. Chinese patriots were enraged, but there was nothing they could do at a moment when their internal politics were in disorder. They were so confused that Sun Yat-sen was himself at this moment seeking Japanese support. The next Japanese intervention in China came in 1916, when Japanese pressure was brought to bear on the British to dissuade them from approving Yuan Shih-k'ai's attempt to restore stability by making himself emperor. In the following year came another treaty, this time extending the recognition of Japan's special interests as far as Inner Mongolia.

In August 1917 the Chinese government went to war with Germany, partly in the hope of winning goodwill and support which would ensure her an independent voice at the peace, but only a few months later the United States formally recognized the special interests of Japan in China in return for endorsement of the principle of the "open door" and a promise to maintain Chinese integrity and independence. All that the Chinese had got from the Allies was the ending of German and Austrian extra-territoriality and the concession that payment of Boxer indemnities to the Allies should be delayed. The Japanese, moreover, secured more concessions from China in secret agreements in 1917 and 1918.

THE PEACE SETTLEMENT

Yet, when the peace came, it deeply disappointed Chinese and Japanese alike. Japan was now indisputably a world power; it had in 1918 the third largest navy in the world. It was true, too, that it won solid gains at the peace: it retained the former German rights in Shantung (promised by the British and French in 1917), and was granted a mandate over many of the former German Pacific islands and a permanent seat on the Council of the League of Nations. But the gain in "face" implied in such recognition was offset in Asian eyes by a failure to have a declaration in favour of racial equality written in to the Covenant of the League. On this line (the only one on which Japanese and Chinese stood shoulder to shoulder at Paris), Woodrow Wilson rejected a majority vote, ruling that approval should be unanimous. With the United Kingdom, Australia and New Zealand against it, it fell by the wayside. The Chinese had much more to feel aggrieved about, too, for in spite of widespread sympathy over the Twenty-One Demands (notably in the United States) they were unable to obtain a reversal of the Shantung decision. Disappointed of American diplomatic support and crippled by the divisions within their own delegation between the representatives of the Peking government and those of the Kuomintang at Canton, the Chinese refused to sign the treaty.

THE MAY 4TH MOVEMENT

AN ALMOST IMMEDIATE consequence was an upheaval in China to which some commentators have given an importance as great as that of the 1911 revolution itself. This was the "May 4th Movement" of 1919. It stemmed from a student demonstration in Peking against the peace, which had been planned for 7 May, the anniversary of China's acceptance of the 1915 demands, but was brought forward to anticipate action by the authorities. It escalated, although at first only into a small riot and the resignation of the head of the university. This then led to a nationwide student movement (one of the first political reflections of the widely spread establishment in China of new colleges and universities after 1911). This in turn spread to embrace others than students and to manifest itself in strikes and a boycott of Japanese goods. A movement, which had begun with intellectuals and their pupils, spread to include other city-dwellers, notably industrial workers and the new Chinese capitalists who had benefited from the war. It was the most important evidence yet seen of the mounting rejection of Europe by Asia.

CHINESE INDUSTRIALIZATION

For the first time, an industrial China entered the scene. China, like Japan, had enjoyed an economic boom during the war. Though a decline in European imports to China had been partly offset by increased Japanese and American sales, Chinese entrepreneurs in the ports had found it profitable to invest in production for the home market. The first important industrial areas outside Manchuria began to appear. They belonged to progressive capitalists who sympathized with revolutionary ideas all the more when the return of peace brought renewed Western competition and evidence that China had not earned her liberation from tutelage to the foreigner. The workers, too, felt this resentment: their jobs were threatened. Many of them were first-generation town-dwellers, drawn into the new industrial areas from the countryside by the promise of employment. An uprooting from the tenacious soil of peasant

Sun Yat-sen, pictured here in 1925, was the founder of the Kuomintang. He was a particularly westernized Chinese leader. Unlike this rare image, most photographs of Sun Yat-sen show him in European-style dress.

tradition was even more important in China than in Europe a century before. Family and village ties were especially strong in China. The migrant to the town left behind patriarchal authority and the reciprocal obligations of the independent producing unit, the household: this was a further great weakening of the age-old structure which had survived the revolution and still tied China to the past. New material was thus made available for new ideological deployments.

THE SEEDS OF FURTHER REVOLUTION

The May 4th Movement first showed what could be made of new ideological forces by creating the first broadly based Chinese revolutionary coalition. Progressive Western liberalism had not been enough; implicit in the movement's success was the disappoint-ment of the hopes of many of the cultural reformers. Capitalist Western democracy had been shown up by the Chinese government's helplessness in the face of Japan. Now, that government faced another humiliation from its own subjects: the boycott and demonstration forced it to release the arrested students and dismiss its pro-Japanese ministers. But this was not the only important consequence of the May 4th Movement. For all their limited political influence, reformers had for the first time, thanks to the students, broken through into the world of social action. This aroused enormous optimism and greater popular political awareness than ever before. This is the case for saying that contemporary Chinese history begins positively in 1919 rather than 1911.

Yet ultimately the explosion had come because of an Asian force, Japanese ambition. That force, not in itself a new one in China's affairs, was by 1919 operating on a China

In this scene from Shanghai in April 1919 coolies carry luggage to the wharf where foreigners are waiting to depart, anxious about the growing political unrest.

whose cultural tradition was dissolving fast. The ending of the examination system, the return of the westernized exiles and the great literary and cultural debate of the war years had all pushed things too far for any return to the old stable state. The warlords could provide no new authority to identify and sustain orthodoxy. And now even the great rival of the Confucian past, Western liberalism, was under attack because of its association with the exploiting foreigner. Western liberalism had never had mass appeal; now its charm for intellectuals was threatened just as another rival ideological force from the West had appeared on the scene. The Bolshevik revolution gave Marxism a homeland to which its adherents abroad could look for inspiration, guidance, leadership and, sometimes, material support, a great new factor now introduced into an already dissolving historical epoch, and bound to accelerate its end.

MARXISM IN CHINA

BOTH THE FEBRUARY 1917 REVOLUTION and the Bolshevik victory had been warmly welcomed by one of the contributors to *New Youth*, Li Ta-chao, who was from 1918 a librarian at Peking University. Soon he came to see in Marxism the motive force of world revolution and the means to vitalize the Chinese peasantry. At that moment of disillusion with the West, Russia was very popular among Chinese students. It seemed that the successors of the tsar had driven out the old imperialist Adam, for one of the first acts of the Soviet government had been a formal renunciation of all extra-territorial rights and jurisdictions enjoyed by the tsarist state. In the eyes of the nationalists, Russia, therefore, had clean hands. Moreover, her revolution – a revolution in a great peasant society –

claimed to be built upon a doctrine whose applicability to China seemed especially plausible in the wake of the industrialization provoked by the war. In 1918 there had begun to meet at Peking University a Marxist study society of whose members some had been prominent in the May 4th Movement. One of them was an assistant in the university library, Mao Tse-tung. By 1920 Marxist texts were beginning to appear in student magazines and in that year the first complete Chinese translation of the *Communist Manifesto* appeared. Now, too, the first attempts were made to deploy Marxist and Leninist principles by organizing strikes in support of the May 4th Movement.

Yet Marxism opened divisions between the reformers. Ch'en Tu-hsiu himself turned to it as a solution for China's problems in 1920. He threw his energies into helping to organize the emerging Chinese Left around Marxism. The liberals were beginning to be left behind. The Comintern observed its opportunities and had sent its first man to

The Chinese Communist Party was founded in June 1921. Among its founding members was Mao Tse-tung (1893–1976), seen here in a photograph taken in 1967. The CCP's beginnings were extremely modest: it had very few card-carrying members, no national organization, no funds and no experience, and many of the details of the founding of the party remain obscure.

China in 1919 to help Ch'en and Li Ta-chao. The effects were not entirely happy; there were quarrels. Nevertheless, in circumstances still obscure – we know precisely neither names nor dates – the Chinese Communist Party was formed in Shanghai in 1921 by delegates from different parts of China (Mao Tse-tung among them).

CHINESE COMMUNISM

With the foundation of the Chinese Communist Party began the last stage of the Chinese Revolution and the latest twist of that curious dialectic which has run through the relations of Europe with Asia. Once more an alien Western idea, Marxism, born and shaped in a society totally unlike the traditional societies of the East, embodying a background of assumptions whose origins were rooted in Judaeo-Christian culture, was taken up by an Asian people and put to their use. It was to be deployed not merely against the traditional sources of inertia in China, in the name of the Western goals of modernization, efficiency and universal human dignity and equality, but against the source from which it, too, came – the European world.

Communism benefited enormously in China from the fact that capitalism could easily be represented as the unifying, connecting principle behind foreign exploitation and aggression. In the 1920s, China's divisions were thought to make it of little account in international affairs, though nine powers with Asiatic interests were got to guarantee its territorial integrity and Japan agreed to hand back former German territories in China which it had taken in the Great War. This was part of a complicated set of agreements made at Washington whose core was the international limitation on naval strength (there was great uneasiness about the cost of armaments); these in the end left Japan relatively stronger. The four major powers guaranteed one another's possessions, too, and thus provided a decent burial for the

In this view of late 19th-century Shanghai the European-style buildings housing foreign commercial companies and embassies can be seen.

Anglo-Japanese alliance, whose ending had long been sought by the Americans. But the guarantee to China, everyone knew, was worth no more than the preparedness of the Americans to fight to support it; the British had been obliged by the treaties *not* to build a naval base at Hong Kong. Meanwhile, foreigners continued to administer the customs and tax revenues on which the Peking government of an "independent" China depended and foreign agents and businessmen dealt directly with the warlords when it suited them. Though American policy had further weakened the European position in Asia, this was not apparent in China.

THE KMT MOVES TOWARDS MARXISM

The apparently continuing grip of the foreign devils on China's life was one reason why Marxism's appeal to intellectuals went far beyond the boundaries of the formal structure of the Chinese Communist Party. Sun Yat-sen stressed his doctrinal disagreement with it but adopted views which helped to carry the KMT away from conventional liberalism and in the direction of Marxism. In his view of the world, Russia, Germany and Asia had a common interest as exploited powers against their oppressors and enemies, the four imperialist powers (Germany was well regarded after it had undertaken in 1921 to place its relations with China on a completely equal footing). He coined a new expression, "hypo-colony", for the state of affairs in which China was exploited without formal subordination as a dependency. His conclusion was collectivist: "On no account must we give more liberty to the individual," he wrote; "let us secure liberty instead for the nation." This was to give new endorsement to the absence of individual liberty which had always been present in the

classical Chinese outlook and tradition. The claims of family, clan and state had always been paramount and Sun Yat-sen envisaged a period of one-party rule in order to make possible mass indoctrination to reconfirm an attitude which had been in danger of corruption by Western ideas.

When this photograph was taken of Chiang K'ai-shek (1887–1975), Chiang was still merely a high-ranking soldier of the new régime.

COOPERATION BETWEEN THE CCP AND THE KMT

There was apparently, then, no grave obstacle to the cooperation of the Chinese Communist Party (CCP) and the KMT. The behaviour of the Western powers and of the warlords provided common enemies and the Russian government helped to bring them together.

Cooperation with the anti-imperialist power with which China had its longest land frontier seemed at least prudent and potentially very advantageous. The policy of the Comintern, for its part, favoured cooperation with the KMT to safeguard Russian interests in Mongolia and as a step towards holding off Japan. The USSR had been left out of the Washington conferences, though no power had greater territorial interests in Asia. For her, cooperation with the likely winners in China was an obvious course even if Marxist doctrine had not also fitted such a policy. From 1924 onwards the CCP was working with the KMT under Soviet patronage, in spite of some doubts among Chinese communists. As individuals, though not as a party, they could belong to the KMT. Sun Yat-sen's able young soldier, Chiang K'ai-shek, was sent to Moscow for training, and a military academy was founded in China to provide ideological as well as military instruction.

KMT SUCCESSES

In 1925 Sun Yat-sen died; he had made communist cooperation with his followers easier, and the united front still endured. Sun Yat-sen's will (which Chinese schoolchildren learnt by heart) had said that the revolution was not yet complete and while the communists made important advances in winning peasant support for the revolution in certain provinces, the new revolutionary army led by idealistic young officers made headway against the warlords. By 1927 something of a semblance of unity had been restored to the country under the leadership of the KMT. Anti-imperialist feeling supported a successful boycott of British goods, which led the British government, alarmed by the evidence of growing Russian influence in China, to surrender its concessions at Hankow and

Kiukiang. It had already promised to return Wei-hai-wei to China (1922), and the United States had renounced its share of the Boxer indemnity. Such successes added to signs that China was on the move at last.

RURAL REVOLUTION

One important aspect of the Chinese Revolution long went unremarked. Theoretical Marxism stressed the indispensable revolutionary role of the industrial proletariat. The Chinese communists were proud of the progress they had made in politicizing the new urban workers, but the mass of Chinese were peasants. Still trapped in the Malthusian vice of rising numbers and land shortage, their centuries of suffering were, if anything, intensified by the breakdown of central authority in the warlord years. Some Chinese communists saw in the peasants a revolutionary potential which, if not easy to reconcile with contemporary Marxist orthodoxy (as retailed by the Moscow theorists), none the less embodied Chinese reality. One of them was Mao Tse-tung. He and those who agreed with him turned their attention away from the cities to the countryside in the early 1920s and began an unprecedented effort to win over the rural masses to communism. Paradoxically, Mao seems to have continued to cooperate with the Kuomintang longer than other Chinese communists just because it was more sympathetic to the organization of the peasants than was his own party.

A great success followed. It was especially marked in Hunan, but altogether some ten million or so peasants and their families were by 1927 organized by the communists. "In a few months," wrote Mao, "the peasants have accomplished what Dr Sun Yat-sen wanted, but failed to accomplish in the forty years he devoted to the national revolution." Organization made possible the removal of many of the ills that beset the peasants. Landlords were not dispossessed, but their rents were often reduced. Usurious rates of interest were brought down to reasonable levels. Rural revolution had eluded all previous progressive movements in China and this was identified by Mao as the key shortcoming of the 1911 revolution; the communist success in reaching this goal was based on the discovery that it could be brought about by using the revolutionary potential of the peasants themselves. This had enormous significance for the future, for it implied new possibilities of historical development throughout Asia. Mao grasped this. "If we allot ten points to the democratic revolution," he wrote, "then the achievements of the urban dwellers and the military units rate only three points, while the remaining seven points should go to the peasants in their rural revolution." In an image twice-repeated in a report on the Hunan movement he compared the peasants to an elemental force; "the attack is just like a tempest or hurricane; those who submit to it survive, those who resist perish." Even the image is significant; here was something rooted deeply in Chinese tradition and the long struggle against landlords and bandits. If the communists tried hard to set aside tradition by eradicating superstition and breaking family authority, they nevertheless drew upon it, too.

THE KMT "RIGHT" TURNS ON THE COMMUNISTS

Communism's rural lodgement was the key to its survival in the crisis which overtook its relations with the KMT after Sun Yat-sen's

---

Chiang K'ai-shek

As a young man, Chiang K'ai-shek studied at military academies in Peking and Tokyo. After failing in business in Shanghai, he joined Sun Yat-sen, whom he had met during his two-year stay in Japan, and became one of the most outstanding officers in the Kuomintang. On Sun's death in 1925, he took over the presidency of the party and initiated the reunification of China by launching an expedition against the warlords who had controlled the north. Chiang, representing capitalist interests, broke off the alliance with the Chinese Communist Party and the Kuomintang's own left wing and began brutally to persecute the communists. He was defeated in the civil war (1945–1949) and took refuge with his followers in Formosa (present-day Taiwan), where he installed a Nationalist government. As the elected president of the republic – a post he held from 1950 until his death – Chiang led the efforts to create a modern industrialized state in Taiwan.

Chiang K'ai-shek (1887–1975) is pictured here in 1949.

A British naval unit marches up Nanking Road in Shanghai's international settlement in 1927. Sailors sometimes formed some of the forces stationed in Shanghai to protect the European and US business interests in the city during the period of unrest; this parade was intended as a display of force.

death. Sun's removal permitted a rift to open in the KMT between a "left" and a "right" wing. The young Chiang, who had been seen as a progressive, now emerged as the military representative of the "right", which reflected mainly the interests of capitalists and, indirectly, landlords. Differences within the KMT over strategy were resolved when Chiang, confident of his control of his troops, committed them to destroying the left factions and the Communist Party's organization in the cities. This was accomplished with much bloodshed in Shanghai and Nanking in 1927, under the eyes of contingents of European and American soldiers, who had been sent to China to protect the concessions. The CCP was proscribed, but this was not quite the end of its cooperation with the KMT, which continued in a few areas for some months, largely because of Russian unwillingness to break with Chiang. This had already made easier the destruction of the city communists; the Comintern in China, as elsewhere,

myopically pursued what were believed to be Russian interests refracted through the mirror of dogmatic Marxism. These interests were for Stalin in the first place domestic; in external affairs, he wanted someone in China who could stand up to the British, the greatest imperialist power, and the KMT seemed the best bet for that. Theory fitted these choices; the bourgeois revolution had to precede the proletarian one, according to Marxist orthodoxy. Only after the triumph of the KMT was clear did the Russians withdraw their advisers from the CCP, which gave up open politics to become a subversive, underground organization.

Chinese nationalism had in fact done well out of Russian help even if the CCP had not. Nevertheless, the KMT was left with grave problems and a civil war on its hands at a time when the revolution needed to satisfy mass demands if it was to survive. The split within the revolution was a setback, making it impossible to dispose finally of the warlord problem and, more serious, weakening the anti-foreign front. Pressure from Japan had continued in the 1920s after the temporary relaxation and handing back of Kiao-chou. Its domestic background was changing in an important way.

JAPANESE ECONOMIC DEPRESSION

When the wartime economic boom finally ended in 1920, hard times and growing social strains followed, even before the onset of the world economic depression. By 1931, half of Japan's factories were idle; the collapse of European colonial markets and the entrenchment of what remained of them behind new tariff barriers had a shattering effect as Japanese exports of manufactures went down by two-thirds. Japan's export outlets on the Asian mainland were now crucial. Anything that seemed to threaten them provoked intense irritation. The position of the Japanese peasant deteriorated, too, millions being ruined or selling their daughters into prostitution in order to survive. Grave political consequences were soon manifest, though less in the intensification of class conflict than in the provocation of nationalist extremism. The forces which were to pour into this had for a long time been absorbed in the struggle against the "unequal treaties". With those out of the way, a new outlet was needed, and the harsh operation of industrial capitalism in times of depression provided anti-Western feeling with fresh fuel.

JAPAN'S CUE TO ACT

The circumstances seemed propitious for further Japanese aggression in Asia. The Western colonial powers were clearly on the defensive, if not in full retreat. The Dutch faced rebellions in Java and Sumatra in the 1920s, the French a Vietnamese revolt in 1930; in both places there was the sinister novelty of communist help to nationalist rebels. The British were not in quite such difficulties in India. Yet although some in Britain were not yet reconciled to the idea that India must move towards self-government, it was by now the proclaimed aim of British policy. In China the British had already shown in the 1920s that they wanted only a quiet accommodation with a nationalist movement they found hard to assess, and not too grave a loss of face. Their Far Eastern policies looked even feebler after economic collapse, which also knocked the stuffing out of American opposition to Japan. Finally, Russian power, too, seemed in the eclipse after its attempt to influence events in China. Chinese nationalism, on the contrary, had won notable successes, showed no sign of retreat and was considered to be beginning to threaten the long-established Japanese presence in Manchuria. All these factors were present in the calculations made by Japanese statesmen as the depression deepened.

Chaos reigned in post-revolutionary China, not only on a political and social level, but also when natural disasters, such as the flooding of the Yangtze river in 1931, took place. In Hankow, pictured here, the entire population of the region was forced to carry its household goods to safety on improvised rafts.

Japanese imperialism

Japanese imperialist tendencies were already emerging in the period between the two world wars. Since her victory in the war with Russia in 1905, Japan had become a great industrial nation, dependent on a large amount of foreign trade. Ideological values influenced by traditional religious feelings, militarism and extreme right-wing nationalism combined with the failure of multi-party government in domestic politics to create a favourable environment in which the new Japanese imperial spirit could flourish.

In eastern Asia, Japan took on a dominant role, although it had abandoned, for a time, its designs on China. This was mainly thanks to the moderation of the minister for foreign affairs, Kijuro Shidehara, who, during his terms in office (from 1924 to 1927 and again from 1929 to 1931), urged economic rather than military expansion. But by the late 1920s, the Japanese were concerned with keeping their rights over Port Arthur, Darien and the south of Manchuria, and therefore, in 1927, Tokyo sent troops to Tsingtao, the Shantung port that it had renounced in 1922, and the Japanese invasion of northern China started in 1931.

By that time, the international peace system was deteriorating all over the world. The Japanese armed forces had always been a powerful group with political interests. Disillusionment with multi-party politics had been growing, particularly among the young officers who focused their activities on secret societies and the Kwantung expeditionary force in Manchuria. At the beginning of the 1930s, an authoritarian régime was established and an aggressive foreign policy adopted. Particularly in the region of Manchuria, the liberal-bourgeois parties gave way to the rising nationalist force of the military High Command and of the patriotic secret societies.

Japan took control of Manchuria in 1931, renaming it Manchukuo and running it as a puppet state. This photograph captures a moment in the Japanese occupation.

THE MANCHURIAN CRISIS

Manchuria was the crucial theatre. A Japanese presence there went back to 1905. Heavy investment had followed. At first the Chinese acquiesced, but in the 1920s began to question it, with support from the Russians who foresaw danger from the Japanese pushing their influence towards Inner Mongolia. In 1929 the Chinese in fact came into conflict with the Russians over control of the railway, which ran across Manchuria and was the most direct route to Vladivostok, but this can only have impressed the Japanese with the new vigour of Chinese power; the nationalist KMT was reasserting itself in the territories of the old empire. There had been armed conflict in 1928 when the Japanese had tried to prevent KMT soldiers from operating against warlords in north China whom they found it convenient to patronize. Finally, the Japanese government was by no means unambiguously in control on the spot. Effective power in Manchuria rested with the commanders of the Japanese forces there, and when in 1931 they organized an incident near Mukden, which they used as an excuse for taking over the whole province, those in Tokyo who wished to restrain them could not do so.

There followed the setting up of a new puppet state, Manchukuo (to be ruled by the last Manchu emperor), an outcry against Japanese aggression at the League of Nations, assassinations in Tokyo, which led to the establishment there of a government much more under military influence, and the expansion of the quarrel with China. In 1932 the Japanese replied to a Chinese boycott of their goods by landing forces at Shanghai; in the following year they came south across the Great Wall to impose a peace, which left Japan dominating a part of historic China itself and trying unsuccessfully to organize a secessionist north China. There matters stood until 1937.

From Manchukuo, whose puppet emperor Pu-Yi (known as K'ang Te) appears in the photograph, the Japanese continued to attack Chinese territory. They advanced along the coast to the outskirts of Peking. Their troops also overran the five northern provinces, which until 1937 supplied Japanese industry with iron and coal.

THE COMMUNISTS ORGANIZE THE PEASANTS

The KMT government proved unable, after all, to resist imperialist aggression. Yet from its new capital, Nanking, it appeared to control successfully all save a few border areas. It continued to whittle away at the treaties of inferiority and was helped by the fact that as the Western powers saw in it a means of opposing communism in Asia, they began to show themselves somewhat more accommodating. These achievements, considerable though they were, none the less masked important weaknesses which compromised the KMT's domestic success. The crux was that though the political revolution might have continued, the social revolution had come to a stop. Intellectuals withdrew their moral support from a régime which had not provided reforms, of which a need to do something about land was the

China 1918–1949

The area controlled by the Kuomintang up to 1937 was mainly along the country's east coast. The CCP was strong in specific areas all over China. An important step came when, in search of a safe sanctuary, Mao Tse-tung moved the Kiangsi Soviet from the central southern region to the far north. Participants in this "Long March" covered more than 6,000 miles (9,650km) on foot in order to penetrate the mountainous region of Shansi, which was better suited to guerrilla activities.

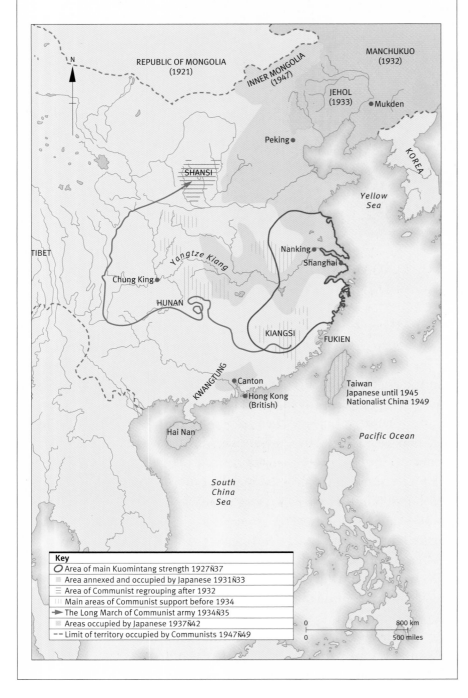

REPUBLIC OF MONGOLIA (1921)

INNER MONGOLIA (1947)

MANCHUKUO (1932)

JEHOL (1933)

●Mukden

Peking●

SHANSI

Yellow Sea

KOREA

TIBET

Yangtze Kiang

Nanking●
Shanghai●

Chung King●

HUNAN

KIANGSI

FUKIEN

KWANGTUNG

●Canton
●Hong Kong (British)

Taiwan
Japanese until 1945
Nationalist China 1949

Hai Nan

Pacific Ocean

South China Sea

Key

⬭	Area of main Kuomintang strength 1927–37
▪	Area annexed and occupied by Japanese 1931–33
≡	Area of Communist regrouping after 1932
⦀	Main areas of Communist support before 1934
➤	The Long March of Communist army 1934–35
▪	Areas occupied by Japanese 1937–42
--	Limit of territory occupied by Communists 1947–49

0 ____ 800 km
0 ____ 500 miles

most pressing. The peasants had never given the KMT their allegiance as some of them had given it to the communists. Unfortunately for the régime, Chiang fell back more and more at this juncture upon direct government through his officers and showed himself increasingly conservative at a time when the traditional culture had decayed beyond repair. The régime was tainted with corruption in the public finances, often at the highest level. The foundations of the new China were therefore insecure. And there was once more a rival waiting in the wings.

THE LONG MARCH

The central leadership of the Chinese Communist Party (CCP) for some time continued to hope for urban insurrection; in the provinces, none the less, individual Communist leaders continued to work along the lines indicated by Mao in Hunan. They dispossessed absentee landlords and organized local soviets, a shrewd appreciation of the value of the traditional peasant hostility to central government. By 1930 they had done better than this, by organizing an army in Kiangsi, where a Chinese Soviet Republic ruled fifty million people, or claimed to. In 1932 the CCP leadership abandoned Shanghai to join Mao in this sanctuary. KMT efforts were now directed towards destroying the communist army, but always without success. This meant fighting on a second front at a time when Japanese pressure was strongest. The last great KMT effort, it is true, drove the communists out of their sanctuary, thus forcing them on the "Long March" to Shansi, which began in 1934, the epic of the Chinese Revolution and an inspiration ever since. Once there, the 7,000 survivors found local communist support but were still hardly safe; only the demands of resistance to the

Japanese troops enter Peking's Forbidden City in 1937. By the end of the following year, Japan ruled over the most important areas of economic activity and controlled territory inhabited by 42 per cent of the Chinese population.

Japanese prevented the KMT from doing more to harass them.

JAPAN ATTACKS CHINA

Consciousness of the external danger explains why there were tentative essays in cooperation between CCP and KMT again in the later 1930s. They owed something, too, to another change in the policies of the Comintern; it was an era of "Popular Fronts" elsewhere which allied communists with other parties. The KMT was also obliged to mute its anti-Western line and this won it a certain amount of easy sympathy in England and, above all, the United States. But neither the cooperation of communists nor the sympathies of Western liberals could prevent the Nationalist régime from being forced on the defensive when the Japanese launched their attack in 1937.

The "China incident", as the Japanese continued to call it, was to take eight years' fighting and inflict grave social and physical damage on China. It has been seen as the opening of the Second World War. At the end of 1937 the Chinese government removed itself for safety's sake to Chungking in the far west while the Japanese occupied all the important northern and coastal areas. League condemnation of Japan and Russian deliveries of aircraft seemed equally unable to stem the onslaught. The only bonus in the first black years was an unprecedented degree of patriotic unity in China; communists and nationalists alike saw that the national revolution was at stake. This was the view of the Japanese, too; significantly, in the area they occupied, they encouraged the re-establishment of Confucianism. Meanwhile, the Western powers felt deplorably unable to intervene. Their protests, even on behalf of their own citizens when they were menaced and manhandled, were brushed aside by the Japanese who by 1939 made it clear that they were prepared to blockade the foreign settlements if recognition of the Japanese new order in Asia was not forthcoming. For British and French weakness there was an obvious explanation: they had troubles enough elsewhere. American ineffectiveness had deeper roots; it went back to a long-established fact that however the United States might talk about mainland Asia, Americans would not fight for it, perhaps wisely. When the Japanese bombed and sank an American gunboat near Nanking the State Department huffed and puffed but eventually swallowed Japanese "explanations". It was all very different from what had happened to the USS *Maine* in Havana harbour forty years before, though the Americans did send supplies to Chiang K'ai-shek.

CHINA HUMILIATED

By 1941, China was all but cut off from the outside world, though on the eve of rescue. At the end of that year its struggle would at last be merged with a world war. By then, though, China had been badly damaged. In the long duel between the potential Asian rivals, Japan was by then clearly the winner. On the debit side of Japan's account had to be placed the economic cost of the struggle and the increasing difficulty experienced by its occupying forces in China. On the other hand, its international position had never seemed stronger; this was demonstrated by humiliating Western residents in China and by forcing the British in 1940 to close the Burma Road by which supplies reached China, and the French to admit an occupying army to Indo-China. Here was a temptation to further adventure, and it was not likely to be resisted while the

A child cries alone in the aftermath of a Japanese bombardment of Shanghai. The Japanese bombed the city extensively during the Sino-Japanese War of 1937–1945, with the intention of destroying the foreign concessions that were based there.

A Japanese officer, standing on Nanking's historic wall in 1938 and holding the Rising Sun flag, symbolizes the Japanese conquest of China. The war, however, had severe repercussions in Japan; what was called the "China incident" required general military mobilization and centralized economic planning.

prestige of the military and their power in government remained as high as it had been since the mid-1930s.

DECOLONIALIZATION BEGINS

There was also a negative side to Japanese military success. Aggression made it more and more imperative for Japan to seize the economic resources of Southeast Asia and Indonesia. Yet it also slowly prepared the Americans psychologically for armed defence of their interest. It was clear by 1941 that the United States would have to decide before long whether it was to be an Asian power at all and what that might mean. In the background, though, lay something even more important. For all its aggression against China, it was with the window-dressing slogan of "Asia for the Asians" that Japan advanced on the crumbling Western position in Asia. Just as its defeat of Russia in 1905 marked an epoch in the psychological relations of Europe and Asia, so did the independence and power which Japan showed in 1938–41. When followed by the overthrow of the European empires, as it was to be, it would signal the beginning of the era of decolonialization; thus fittingly inaugurated by the one Asian power at that time successful in its "Westernization".

2 THE OTTOMAN HERITAGE AND THE WESTERN ISLAMIC LANDS

DURING THE NINETEENTH CENTURY the Ottoman Empire all but disappeared in Europe and Africa. In each continent, the basic causes were the same: the disintegrating effect of nationalism and the predatory activities of European powers. The Serbian revolt of 1804 and Mehemet Ali's establishment of himself as the governor of Egypt in 1805 together opened the final, though long drawn out, era of Turkish decline. In Europe the next milestone was the Greek revolt; from that time the story of the Ottoman Empire in Europe can be told in the dates of the establishment of new nations, until in 1914 Turkey in Europe meant only eastern Thrace. In Islamic Africa the decline of Ottoman power had by then gone even further and faster; much of North Africa had already been virtually independent of the sultan's rule early in the nineteenth century.

EGYPT UNDER MEHEMET ALI

One result of the decline of Ottoman power in the region was that when nationalism began to appear in Islamic Africa it tended to be directed more against Europeans than the

Fighting in the name of a disappearing empire: young Turkish recruits are photographed in 1914 in Istanbul. Following its defeat in the First World War, the Ottoman Empire lost all its non-Turkish territories.

Ottomans. It was also linked with cultural innovation. The story again begins with Mehemet Ali. Though he himself never went further west than his birthplace, Kavalla, in Rumelia, he admired European civilization and thought Egypt could learn from it. He imported technical instructors, employed foreign consuls to direct health and sanitation measures, printed translations of European books and papers on technical subjects, and sent boys to study in France and England. Yet he was working against the grain. His practical achievements disappointed him, though he opened Egypt to European influence as never before. Much of it flowed through educational and technical institutions and reflected an old French interest in the trade and affairs of the Ottoman Empire. French was soon the second language of educated Egyptians and a large French community grew up in Alexandria, one of the great cosmopolitan cities of the Mediterranean.

PAN-ARABISM

Few modernizing statesmen in the non-European world have been able to confine their borrowings from the West to technical knowledge. Soon, young Egyptians began to pick up political ideas, too; there were plenty of those available in French. A compost was forming which would in the end help to transform Europe's relations with Egypt. Egyptians would draw the same lesson as Indians, Japanese and Chinese: the European

disease had to be caught in order to generate the necessary antibodies against it. So, modernization and nationalism became inextricably intertwined. Here lay the origin of an enduring weakness in Middle Eastern nationalism. It was long to be the creed of advanced élites cut off from a society whose masses lived in an Islamic culture still largely uncorroded by Western ideas. Paradoxically, the nationalists were usually the most Europeanized members of Egyptian, Syrian and Lebanese societies, and this was true until well into the twentieth century. Yet their ideas were to come to have wider resonance. It was among Christian Arabs of Syria that there seems first to have appeared the idea of pan-Arabian or Arab nationalism (as opposed to Egyptian, Syrian or some other kind), an assertion that all Arabs, wherever they were, constituted a nation. Pan-Arabism was an idea distinct from that of the brotherhood of Islam, which not only embraced millions of non-Arabs, but also excluded many non-Muslim Arabs. The potential complications of this for any attempt actually to realize an Arab nation in practice were, like other weaknesses of pan-Arabist ideas, not to appear until well into the twentieth century.

ISMAIL LEADS EGYPT INTO DEBT

Another landmark in the history of the former Ottoman lands was the opening of the Suez Canal in 1869. This did more in the long run (though indirectly) than any other single

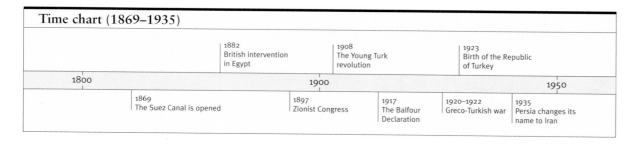

Time chart (1869–1935)					
	1882 British intervention in Egypt	1908 The Young Turk revolution	1923 Birth of the Republic of Turkey		
1800		1900			1950
	1869 The Suez Canal is opened	1897 Zionist Congress	1917 The Balfour Declaration	1920–1922 Greco-Turkish war	1935 Persia changes its name to Iran

fact to doom Egypt to intervention by foreigners. Yet the canal was not the immediate cause of the start of nineteenth-century interference by Europeans in Egypt's government. That came about because of the actions of Ismail (the first ruler of Egypt to obtain from the sultan the title of khedive, in recognition of his substantial *de facto* independence). Educated in France, Ismail liked Frenchmen and up-to-date ideas, and travelled much in Europe. He was very extravagant. When he became ruler in 1863, the price of cotton, Egypt's main export, was high because of the American Civil War and Ismail's financial prospects therefore looked good. Unhappily, his financial management was less than orthodox. The results were to be seen in the rise in the Egyptian national debt; £7 million at Ismail's accession, it stood at nearly £100 million only thirteen years later. The interest charges amounted to £5 million a year, in an age when such sums mattered. In 1876 the Egyptian government was bankrupt and ceased to pay its debts, so foreign managers were sent in. Two controllers, one British, one French, were appointed to make sure that Egypt was governed by Ismail's son with the

priority of keeping up revenue and paying off the debt. They were soon blamed by nationalists for the huge burdens of taxation laid upon the Egyptian poor in order to provide the revenue to pay debt interest as well as for economies, such as the reduction of government salaries. The European officials who worked in the name of the khedive were, in the nationalists' eyes, simply the agents of foreign imperialism. There was growing resentment of the privileged legal position of foreigners in Egypt and their special courts.

BRITISH INTERVENTION IN EGYPT

Grievances against European officials led to nationalist conspiracy and eventually to revolution. As well as the Westernizing xenophobes there were others now urging the reform of Islam, the unity of the Muslim world and a pan-Islamic movement adapted to modern life. Some were simply antagonized by the preponderance of Turks in the khedive's entourage. But such divisions mattered less after a British intervention frustrating a revolution in 1882. This was not intervention for financial reasons. It took place because British policy, even under a Liberal prime minister who favoured nationalism in other parts of the Ottoman Empire, could not accept the danger that the security of the canal route to India might be jeopardized by an unfriendly government at Cairo. It was unthinkable at the time, but British soldiers were only at last to leave Egypt in 1956, tied down until then as they were by strategical dogma.

After 1882, therefore, the British became the prime targets of nationalist hatred in Egypt. They said they wanted to withdraw as soon as a dependable government was available, but could not do so because none was acceptable to them. Instead, British adminis-

Dated 1882 – the year of the British army's intervention to put down an Egyptian revolution – this illustration depicts English soldiers in Alexandria searching Arabs for hidden weapons.

trators took on more and more of the government of Egypt. This was not wholly deplorable; they reduced the debt and mounted irrigation schemes, which made it possible to feed a growing population (it doubled to about twelve million between 1880 and 1914). They antagonized Egyptians, though, by keeping them out of government service in the interests of economy, by imposing high taxes and by being foreign. After 1900 there was growing unrest and violence. The British and the puppet Egyptian government proceeded firmly against agitation, and also sought ways out through reform. At first administrative, this led in 1913 to a new constitution providing for more representative elections to a more powerful legislative assembly. Unfortunately, the assembly met only for a few months before it was suspended at the outbreak of war. The Egyptian government was pushed into war with Turkey, a khedive suspected of anti-British plotting was replaced, and at the end of the year the British proclaimed a protectorate. The khedive now took the title of sultan.

In 1875 the British prime minister Benjamin Disraeli (1804–1881) bought shares in the Suez Canal from the khedive of Egypt. Having acquired control of this major strategic waterway, Great Britain had more reason than ever to intervene in Egyptian political affairs.

The first part of this meant that they wished to end the despotic rule of Abdul Hamid and restore a liberal constitution granted in 1876 and subsequently withdrawn. But they wanted this less for its own sake than because they thought it would revive and reform the empire, making possible modernization and an end to the process of decay. Both this programme and the Young Turks' methods of conspiracy owed much to Europe; they used, for example, masonic lodges as cover and organized secret societies such as those which had flourished among European liberals in the days of the Holy Alliance. But they much resented the increasing interference in Ottoman internal affairs by Europeans, notably in the management of finance, for, as in Egypt, the securing of interest on money lent for internal development had been

THE YOUNG TURK MOVEMENT

BY THE TIME WAR BROKE OUT, the Ottoman government had also lost Tripolitania to the Italians, who had invaded it in 1911 partly because of another manifestation of reforming nationalism, this time in Turkey itself. In 1907 a successful rebellion had been started there by the "Young Turk" movement, which had a complicated history, but a simple purpose. As one Young Turk put it: "we follow the path traced by Europe … even in our refusal to accept foreign intervention."

This engraving, which dates from 1879, shows the traditional irrigation system at work on the banks of the Nile in Upper Egypt.

followed by loss of independence. European bullying had also resulted (they felt) in the Ottoman government's humiliating retreat from the Danube valley and the Balkans.

THE COUP AND THE REFORMS

After a series of mutinies and revolts, the sultan gave way over the constitution in 1908. Liberals abroad smiled on constitutional Turkey; it seemed that misrule was at last to end. But an attempted counter-revolution led to a Young Turk coup which deposed Abdul Hamid and installed a virtual dictatorship. From 1909 to 1914 the revolutionaries ruled with increasingly dictatorial means from behind the façade of constitutional monarchy. Ominously, one of them announced that "there are no longer Bulgars, Greeks, Romanians, Jews, Muslims … we glory in being Ottoman". This was something quite new: the announcement of the end of the old multinational régime.

The Young Turks

The Young Turks were the first group to succeed in modernizing the Ottoman political system. Led by a minister and a high-ranking army officer, and taking advantage of the turbulent times both nationally and internationally, the Young Turks managed to convince the sultan, Abdul Hamid II, to rework a constitution first granted and then suspended in 1876. This instituted a parliament and ministers who would answer to it (although the first elected parliament only lasted for a year).

Turkey's younger generation had been increasingly exposed to European ideas. Young people gradually became sceptical about the legitimacy of the traditional Ottoman institutions, which led them to consider the possibility of deposing the greatest exponent of that power, the sultan himself. In 1908 a group of Young Turks (army officers garrisoned in Macedonia) began an uprising which spread rapidly and was joined by the troops sent to quash it.

Although the 1876 constitution was restored and the sultan deposed, the Young Turks' government was unable to prevent army interference in politics, especially when the Balkan Wars broke out in 1912. Factional infighting led to the forcible ejection of a more conservative wing of the movement in January 1913 and the emergence of a Young Turk dictatorship.

The Young Turks hesitated between neutrality and alliance with Germany as the First World War approached. Here, their minister of war, Enver Pasha (formerly Enver Bey), is seen in conversation with the British ambassador's military attaché.

With hindsight, the Young Turks seem more comprehensible than they did at the time. They faced problems like those of many modernizers in non-European countries and their violent methods have been emulated by many since from necessity or imagined necessity. They threw themselves into reform of every branch of government (importing many European advisers). To seek (for instance) to improve the education of girls was a significant gesture in an Islamic country. But they took power in an empire displaying blatant signs of backwardness and during a shattering succession of diplomatic humiliations which weakened their appeal and led them to rely on force.

After the Habsburg annexation of Bosnia, the ruler of Bulgaria won an acknowledgement of Bulgarian independence, and the Cretans announced their union with Greece. A brief pause then was followed by the Italian attack on Tripoli, and then the Balkan Wars and further military defeat.

REFORMISTS RESORT TO TYRANNY

Under such strain, it was soon apparent that the post-reform harmony among the peoples to which liberals had looked forward was a chimera. Religion, language, social custom and nationality still fragmented even what was left of the empire. The Young Turks were driven back more and more upon the assertion of one nationalism among many, that of the Ottomans. This, of course, led to resentment among other peoples. The result was once more massacre, tyranny and assassination, the time-honoured instruments of rule at Constantinople; from 1913 they were deployed by a triumvirate of Young Turks who ruled as a collective dictatorship until the outbreak of the First World War.

In January 1913 a group of Young Turk officers, led by Colonel Enver Bey, crossed the Sublime Gateway in Constantinople, as depicted in this contemporary illustration, and announced the overthrow of the cabinet installed by another army faction just the year before.

Though they had disappointed many of their admirers, these men had the future on their side. They represented the ideas which would one day remake the Ottoman heritage: nationalism and modernization. They had even – willy-nilly – done something towards this by losing most of the little that was left of the Ottoman Empire in Europe, thus releasing themselves from a burden. But their heritage was still too encumbering in 1914. Before them lay no better alternative as a vehicle for reform than nationalism. How little pan-Islamic ideas would mean was to be shown by what happened after 1914 in the largest remaining block of Ottoman territory, the largely Muslim provinces of Asia.

ASIA'S MUSLIM PROVINCES

IN 1914 THE MUSLIM PROVINCES of Asia covered a large and strategically very important area. From the Caucasus the frontiers with Persia ran down to the Gulf near

Theodor Herzl (1816–1904) established political Zionism and the movement to found a Jewish homeland. In 1896, in his pamphlet *The Jewish State*, he proposed that a world council of nations should be created to settle the Jewish political question.

Basra, at the mouth of the Tigris. On the southern shore of the Gulf Ottoman rule ran around Kuwait (with an independent sheik and under British protection) and then back to the coast as far south as Qatar. From here the coasts of Arabia right around to the entrance of the Red Sea were in one way or another under British influence, but the whole interior and Red Sea coast were Ottoman. Under British pressure the Sinai desert had been surrendered to Egypt a few years before, but the ancient lands of Palestine, Syria and Mesopotamia were still all Turkish. This was the heartland of historical Islam, and the sultan was still caliph, its spiritual leader.

This heritage was to crumble as the strategy and politics of world war played upon it. Even within the historic Islamic heartland, there had been signs before 1914 that new political forces were at work. In part, they stemmed from old-established European cultural influences, which operated in Syria and the Lebanon much more strongly than in Egypt. French influence had been joined in those countries by American missionary efforts and the foundation of schools and colleges to which there came Arab boys, both Muslim and Christian, from all over the Arab world. The Levant was culturally advanced and literate. On the eve of the world war over a hundred Arabic newspapers were published in the Ottoman Empire outside Egypt.

GROWING DISSENT

An important crystallization had followed the triumph of the Young Turks and their Ottomanizing tendencies. Secret societies and open groups of dissidents were formed among Arab exiles, notably in Paris and Cairo. In the background was another

uncertain factor: the rulers of the Arabian peninsula, whose allegiance to the sultan was shaky. The most important of them was Hussein, sherif of Mecca, in whom by 1914 the Turkish government had no confidence. A year earlier there had also been the ominous sign of a meeting of Arabs in Persia to consider the independence of Iraq. Against this, the Turks could only hope that the divisiveness of the different interests represented among the Arabs would preserve the status quo.

ZIONISM

Finally, although it did not present an immediate danger, the latest converts to the culture of territorial nationalism were the Jews. Their history had taken a new turn when, in 1897, there appeared a Zionist Congress whose aim was the securing of a national home. Thus, in the long history of Jewry, assimilation, still barely achieved in many European countries after the liberating age of the French Revolution, was now replaced as an ideal by nationalism. The desirable location had not at once been clear; Argentina, Uganda were suggested at different times, but by the end of the country Zionist opinion had come to rest finally on Palestine. Jewish immigration there had begun, though still on a small scale. The unrolling of the war was to change its significance.

THE FIRST WORLD WAR

CURIOUS PARALLELS EXISTED between the Ottoman and Habsburg empires in 1914. Both sought war, seeing it, in part, as a solution to their problems. Yet both were bound to suffer from it, because too many people inside and outside their borders saw in

The Young Turk government's leanings towards Germany were obvious as it began the rearmament and training of the Turkish army. Although the Ottoman Empire had been exhausted by the Balkan Wars, Enver Pasha insisted that Turkey enter the First World War as Germany's ally. This announcement led to anti-war demonstrations in the streets of Constantinople, such as this one in October 1914.

war an opportunity to score at their expense. In the end, both empires were to be destroyed by it. Even at the outset, Russia, the historic enemy, seemed likely to benefit since Turkey's entry to the war evaporated the last of the tradition of resistance of the British and French to the establishment of tsarist power at Constantinople. For their part, the French had their own fish to fry in the Middle Eastern pan. Though their irritation over a British presence in Egypt had subsided somewhat with the making of the entente and a free hand for France in Morocco, there was a tradition of a special French role in the Levant. The evocations of St Louis and the crusaders, with which some enthusiasts made play, did not have to be taken seriously, but, undeniably, French governments had for a hundred years claimed to exercise a special protection of Catholicism in the Ottoman Empire, especially in Syria, to which Napoleon III had sent a French army in the 1860s. There was also the cultural predominance evinced by the wide use of the French language among the educated in the Levant, and much French capital was invested there. These were not forces which could be overlooked.

Nevertheless, in 1914 Turkey's main military antagonists outside Europe were likely to be Russia in the Caucasus, and Great Britain at Suez. The defence of the canal was the foundation of British strategic thinking in the area, but it soon became clear that no great danger threatened it. Then events occurred revealing new factors, which would in the end turn the Middle and Near East upside-down. At the end of 1914 an Indian-British army landed at Basra to safeguard oil supplies from Persia. This was the beginning of the interplay of oil and politics in the historical destiny of this area, though it was not to show itself fully until well after the Ottoman Empire had ceased to exist. On the other hand, an approach which the British governor of Egypt made to Hussein in October 1914 bore fruit very quickly. This was the first attempt to use the weapon of Arab nationalism.

AN ARABIAN ALLIANCE

The attraction of striking a blow against Germany's ally became all the greater as fighting went on bloodily but indecisively in Europe. An attempt in 1915 to force the Dardanelles by combined naval and land operations, in the hope of taking Constantinople, became bogged down. By then Europe's civil war had already set in train forces one day to be turned against her. But there was a limit to what could be offered to Arab allies. Terms were not agreed with Hussein until the beginning of 1916. He had demanded independence for all the Arab lands south of a line running along the 37th degree of latitude – this was about eighty miles north of a line from Aleppo to Mosul and included, in effect, the whole of the Ottoman Empire outside Turkey and Kurdistan. It was much more than the British could take at the gallop. The French had to be consulted, too, because of their special interest in Syria. When an agreement was made between the British and French on spheres of influence in a partitioned Ottoman Empire it left many questions still unsettled

British troops are pictured at a makeshift position during the disastrous Dardanelles campaign of 1915, in which the Allies invaded the Gallipoli peninsula. But they failed to achieve their aim of occupying the northern side of the Dardanelles channel and then Istanbul (Constantinople). British Commonwealth casualties alone totalled more than 214,000, and the defeat led Winston Churchill to resign as first lord of the Admiralty.

for the future, including the status of Iraq, but an Arab nationalist political programme looked like becoming a reality.

THE ARAB REVOLT

The future of such undertakings was soon in doubt. The Arab revolt began in June 1916 with an attack on the Turkish garrison of Medina. The rising was never to be more than a distraction from the main theatres of war, but it prospered and became a legend. Soon the British felt they must take the Arabs more seriously; Hussein was recognized as king of the Hejaz. Their own troops pressed forwards in 1917 into Palestine, taking Jerusalem. In 1918 they were to enter Damascus together with the Arabs. Before this, though, two

Edmund Allenby (1861–1936), the British commander-in-chief of the Egypt expeditionary force against the Turks, launched an offensive to take Jerusalem in 1917. On entering the city, he was warmly welcomed by the Jewish community.

The Balfour Declaration

"I have much pleasure in conveying to you, on behalf of His Majesty's Government, the following declaration of sympathy with Jewish Zionist aspirations which has been submitted to, and approved by, the Cabinet.

"His Majesty's Government view with favour the establishment in Palestine of a national home for the Jewish people, and will use their best endeavours to facilitate the achievement of this object, it being clearly understood that nothing shall be done which may prejudice the civil and religious rights of existing non-Jewish communities in Palestine, or the rights and political status enjoyed by Jews in any other country.

"I should be grateful if you would bring this declaration to the knowledge of the Zionist Federation."

A letter from Arthur James Balfour, the British foreign secretary, to Lord Rothschild, dated 2 November, 1917.

other events had further complicated the situation. One was the American entry into the war; in a statement of war aims President Wilson said he favoured "an absolute unmolested opportunity of development" for the non-Turks of the Ottoman Empire. The other was the Bolshevik publication of their predecessors' secret diplomacy; this revealed Anglo-French proposals for spheres of influence in the Middle East. One part of this agreement had been that Palestine should be administered internationally. Another irritant was added when it was announced that British policy favoured the establishment of a national home in Palestine for the Jewish people. The "Balfour Declaration" can be accounted the greatest success of Zionism down to this time. It was not strictly incompatible with what had been said to the Arabs, and President Wilson had joined in the good work by introducing to it qualifications to protect Palestinians who were not Jews, but it

Lawrence of Arabia

In 1916, when the British tried to advance into Sinai to protect their access to the Suez Canal, Hussein, the sherif of Hejaz, began an uprising against the Turks. Keen to support him, the British sent two Arab specialists into Hejaz: Ronald Storrs and Thomas Edward Lawrence. The latter, a captain attached to the British army, was to become a fierce defender of the cause of Faisal, Hussein's son.

Lawrence persuaded Faisal to abandon the siege of Medina and centre his activities on severing Turkish communications along the railway line to Damascus. Together, they conquered Aqaba and entered Palestine; his heroic adventures won the British captain the nickname "Lawrence of Arabia". At the end of the war Lawrence acted as adviser to the Arab delegation at the Paris Peace Conference, but failed to achieve Faisal's great hope of creating a pan-Arab state that would cover the whole of the Middle East. Lawrence was killed in a motorcycle accident in 1935.

T.E. Lawrence (1888–1935) is pictured in Arabia.

is almost inconceivable that it could ever have operated unchallenged, especially when further British and French expressions of goodwill towards Arab aspirations followed in 1918. On the morrow of Turkish defeat, the outlook was thoroughly confused.

MIDDLE EASTERN MANDATES

Following the Turkish defeat Hussein was recognized as king of the Arab peoples by Great Britain, but this did little for him. It was not Arab nationalists but the British and French, with the help of the League of Nations, who were to lay out the map of the modern Arab world. During a confused decade the British and French then became embroiled with the Arabs whom they had themselves conjured on to the stage of world politics, while the Arab leaders quarrelled among themselves. The mirage of Islamic

unity once more faded away, but, mercifully, so did the Russian threat (even if only briefly), and only two great powers were left engaged in the Middle East. They distrusted one another, but could agree, roughly, on the basis that if the British had their way in Iraq, the French could have theirs in Syria. This was legitimized by the League of Nations awarding mandates for Arab lands to them. Palestine, Transjordan and Iraq went to the British and Syria to the French, who governed high-handedly from the start, having to install themselves by force after a national congress had asked for independence or a British or American mandate. They evicted the king the Arabs had chosen, Hussein's son, and subsequently had to face a full-scale insurrection. The French were still holding their own by force in the 1930s, though there were by then signs that they would concede some power to the nationalists. Unfortunately, the Syrian situation soon also showed the disintegrating power of national-ism when the Kurdish people of north Syria revolted against the prospect of submergence in an Arab state, so introducing to Western diplomats another Middle Eastern problem with a long life before it.

INDEPENDENCE FOR THE PENINSULA STATES

The Arabian peninsula was meanwhile racked by a struggle between Hussein and yet another king with whom the British had negotiated a treaty (his followers, to make things more difficult still, were members of a particularly puritanical Islamic sect who added religious to dynastic and tribal con-flict). Hussein was displaced, and in 1932 the new kingdom of Saudi Arabia emerged in the place of the Hejaz. From this flowed other problems, for sons of Hussein were by this time kings of Iraq and Transjordan. After heavy fighting had shown the difficulties ahead, the British had moved as fast as they dared towards the ending of the mandate over Iraq, seeking only to secure British strategic interests by preserving a military and air force presence. In 1932, accordingly, Iraq entered the League as an independent and fully sovereign state. Earlier, Transjordan had been recognized as independent by the British in 1928, again with some retention of military and financial powers.

THE PALESTINIAN PROBLEM

Palestine was much more difficult. From 1921, when there were anti-Jewish riots by Arabs alarmed over Jewish immigration and Jewish acquisition of Arab land, that unhappy country was never to be long at peace. More was at stake than merely religious or national feeling. Jewish immigra-tion meant the irruption of a new Western-izing and modernizing force, its operation changing economic relationships and impos-ing new demands on a traditional society. The British mandatory power was caught between the outcry of the Arabs if it did not restrict Jewish immigration, and the outcry of the Jews if it did. Arab governments now had to be taken into account, too, and they occupied lands which were economically and strategi-cally important to British security. World opinion was becoming involved. The question became more inflamed than ever when in 1933 a régime came to power in Germany which persecuted Jews and began to take away the legal and social gains they had been making since the French Revolution. By 1937 there were pitched battles between Jews and Arabs in Palestine. Soon a British army was trying to hold down an Arab insurrection.

BRITISH ECONOMIC INTERESTS

The collapse of the paramount power in the Arab lands had often in the past been followed by a period of disorder. What was unclear this time was whether disorder would be followed – as earlier periods of anarchy had eventually been – by the establishment of a new imperial hegemony. The British did not want that role; after a brief spell of imperial intoxication in the aftermath of victory, they desired only to secure their own fundamental interests in the area, the protection of the Suez Canal and the swelling flow of oil from Iraq and Iran. Between 1918 and 1934 a great pipeline had been built from northern Iraq across Transjordan and Palestine to Haifa, thus giving yet another new twist to the future of these territories. The consump-tion of oil in Europe was not yet so large that there was any general dependence on it, nor had the great discoveries been made which would again change the political position in the 1950s. But a new factor was making itself felt; the Royal Navy had turned over to oil for its ships.

INDEPENDENT EGYPT

The British believed Suez to be best secured by keeping forces in Egypt, but this caused increasing trouble. The war had intensified Egyptian feeling. Armies of occupation are never popular; when the war sent up prices the foreigner was blamed. Egyptian nationalist leaders attempted in 1919 to put their case to the Paris Peace Conference but were pre-

vented from doing so; there followed a rising against the British which was quickly put down. But the British were in retreat. The protectorate was ended in 1922 in the hope of getting ahead of nationalist feeling. Yet the new kingdom of Egypt had an electoral system which returned nationalist majority after nationalist majority, thus making it impossible for an Egyptian government to come to terms on safeguards for British interests which any British government would find acceptable. The result was a prolonged constitutional crisis and intermittent disorder until in 1936 the British finally agreed to be content with a right to garrison the Canal Zone for a limited number of years. An end was also announced to the jurisdictional privileges of foreigners.

PAN-ARAB FEELING GROWS

These concessions were among other signs of the beginning of a British retreat from empire which can be detected elsewhere after 1918; it was in part a reflection of an overstretching of power and resources, as British foreign policy began to be preoccupied by other challenges. Changes in world relationships far from the Middle East thus helped to shape post-Ottoman developments in Islamic lands. Another novel factor was Marxist communism. During the whole of the years between the wars, Russian radio broadcasting to the Arab countries supported the first Arab communists. But for all the worry they caused, communism showed no sign of being able to displace the strongest revolutionary influence of the area, still that of Arab nationalism, whose focus had come by 1938 to be Palestine. In that year a congress was held in Syria to support the Palestinian Arab cause. Arab resentment of the brutality of the French in Syria was beginning to be evident,

The Druzes, a group of whom are shown here, revolted against the French in 1926. The rebellion reached Damascus, and continued throughout the summer, but – after several bombings of Damascus – most of the trouble had died out by the following summer.

Jubilant Turkish nationalists celebrate Turkey's success in reclaiming the town of Smyrna (now Izmir) from Greece during the war between Greece and Turkey of 1921–1922.

too, as well as an Arab response to the outcry of the Egyptian nationalists against the British. In pan-Arab feeling lay a force which some thought might in the end override the divisions of the Hashemite kingdoms.

influence. This was the most blatant imperialism and a far harsher settlement than that imposed on Germany at Versailles. To drive home the point, European financial control was re-established.

EUROPEANS IN TURKEY AFTER THE WAR

Allied agreements during the war also complicated the history of the Ottoman homeland, Turkey (as it was soon to be renamed) itself. The British, French, Greeks and Italians had all agreed on their shares of the booty; the only simplification brought by the war had been the elimination of the Russian claim to Constantinople and the Straits. Faced with French, Greek and Italian invasion, the sultan signed a humiliating peace. Greece was given large concessions, Armenia was to be an independent state, while what was left of Turkey was divided into British, French and Italian spheres of

THE END OF THE OTTOMAN EMPIRE

THIS DIVISION of historic Turkey was followed by the first successful revision of any part of the peace settlement. It was largely the work of one man, a former Young Turk and the Ottomans' only victorious general, Mustafa Kemal, who drove out French and Greeks in turn after frightening away the Italians. With Bolshevik help he crushed the Armenians. The British decided to negotiate and so a second treaty was made with Turkey in 1923. It was a triumph of nationalism over the decisions at Paris, and it was the only part of the peace settlement which was negotiated between equals and not imposed on the defeated. It was also the only one in which Russian negotiators took part and it lasted better than any of the other peace treaties. The capitulations and financial controls disappeared. Turkey gave up her claims to the Arab lands and the islands of the Aegean, Cyprus, Rhodes and the Dodecanese. A big exchange of Greek and Turkish population followed (380,000 Muslims left Greece for Turkey and 1.3 million Orthodox Christians left Turkey for Greece) and thus the hatred of these peoples for one another was reinforced. Yet in the light of subsequent events this outcome could be reckoned one of the more fruitful exercises in ethnic cleansing in the region, leaving a less dangerous situation behind it than it found. So the Ottoman Empire outside Turkey was wound up after six centuries. A new republic then came into existence in 1923 as a national state. Appropriately, the caliphate followed the empire into history in 1924. This was the end of the Ottoman era; of Turkish history, it was a new beginning. The Anatolian Turks were now for the first time in five or six centuries the majority people of their state. Symbolically, the capital was moved from Istanbul to Ankara.

The Turkish sultan Muhammad VI (centre) is shown offering prayers to Allah at the tomb of Muhammad the Conqueror in Istanbul in 1922. When the sultan was forced into exile and the caliphate was abolished, there were uprisings all over Turkey and negative reactions from the Islamic communities.

ATATÜRK'S MODERNIZATION OF TURKEY

Kemal, as he tended to call himself (the name meant "Perfection"), was something of a Peter the Great (though he was not interested in territorial expansion after the successful revision of the dictated peace) and something of a more enlightened despot. He was also one of the century's most effective modernizers. The law was secularized (on the model of the Napoleonic code), the Muslim calendar abandoned, and in 1928 the constitution was amended to remove the statement that Turkey was an Islamic state. Polygamy was forbidden. In 1935 the weekly day of rest, formerly Friday, the Islamic holy day, became Sunday and a new word entered the language: *vikend* (the period from 1p.m. Saturday to midnight Sunday). Schools ceased to give religious instruction. The fez was forbidden; although it had come from Europe it was considered Muslim. Kemal was conscious of the radical nature of the modernization he wished to achieve and such symbols mattered to him. They were signs, but signs of something very important, the replacement of traditional Islamic society by a European one. One Islamic ideologist urged his fellow Turks to "belong to the Turkish nation, the Muslim religion and European civilization" and did not appear to see difficulties in achieving that. The alphabet was latinized and this had great importance for education, henceforth obligatory at the primary level. A national past was rewritten in the schoolbooks; it was said that Adam had been a Turk.

Kemal – on whom the National Assembly conferred the name of Atatürk, or "Father of the Turks" – was an immensely significant figure. He was what Mehemet Ali perhaps wanted to be, the first transformer of an Islamic state by modernization. He remains strikingly interesting; until his death in 1938

Mustafa Kemal

Mustafa Kemal twice made history. He won the crucial battle of the Dardanelles campaign and, after the war ended, he brought his Turkish-speaking Muslim compatriots to see themselves as citizens of a republic and members of a new Turkish nation.

Kemal's landing in Samsun in 1919, after the Greek invasion, is generally thought to represent the start of the Turkish revolution. By 1920, he was head of the civil government in Ankara. He was also commander-in-chief of the army, which carried out a successful counter-attack against the Greeks in the Battle of Sakarya in 1921.

As president of the People's Republican Party, Kemal officially proclaimed the Republic of Turkey on 29 October 1923, and became its first president. He upheld a firm belief in progress and science, but was also aware of the importance of historical, ethnic and cultural forces in society. Although he wielded a vast amount of personal power, Kemal also managed to win wide support in the republic's assembly.

Mustafa Kemal (1880–1938) is pictured as commander-in-chief of the Turkish army in 1922.

---

he seemed determined not to let his revolution congeal. The result was the creation of a state in its day and in some ways among the most advanced in the world. In Turkey, a much greater break with the past was involved in giving a new role to women than in Europe, but in 1934 Turkish women received the vote and they were encouraged to enter the professions.

PERSIA

THE MOST IMPORTANT Islamic country, neither under direct imperial rule by Europeans nor Ottomans before 1914, was Persia. The British and Russians had both interfered in her affairs after agreeing over spheres of influence in 1907, but Russian power had lapsed with the Bolshevik revolu-

tion. British forces continued to operate on Persian territory until the end of the war. Resentment against the British was excited when a Persian delegation was not allowed to state its case to the Peace Conference. There was a confused period during which the British struggled to find means of maintaining resistance to the Bolsheviks after withdrawal of their forces. There could be no question of retaining Persia by force, given the over-taxing of British strength. Almost by accident, a British general had already discovered the man who was to do this, though hardly in the way anticipated.

REZA KHAN'S REFORMS

Reza Khan was an officer who carried out a *coup d'état* in 1921 and at once used the

Bolshevik fear of the British to get a treaty conceding all Russian rights and property in Persia and the withdrawal of Russian forces. Reza Khan then went on to defeat separatists who had British support. In 1925 he was given dictatorial powers by the national assembly and a few months later was proclaimed "shah of shahs". He was to rule until 1941 (when the Russians and the British together turned him off the throne), somewhat in the style of an Iranian Kemal. The abolition of the veil and religious schools showed secularist aims, though they were not pressed so far as in Turkey. In 1928 the capitulations were abolished, an important symbolic step; meanwhile industrialization and the improvement of communications were pressed forward. A close association with Turkey was cultivated. Finally, the Persian strong man won in 1933 the first notable success in a new art, the diplomacy of oil, when the concession held by the Anglo-Persian Oil Company was cancelled. When the British government took the question to the League of Nations, another and more favourable concession was Reza Shah's greatest victory and the best evidence of the independence of Persia. A new era had opened in the Gulf, fittingly marked in 1935 by an official change of the name of the state: Persia became Iran. Two years later, the Shah's wife for the first time appeared unveiled.

The shah of Iran, Reza Khan (1878–1944), portrayed here, admired Mustafa Kemal and imitated many of the methods that Kemal had used to modernize Turkey.

3 THE SECOND WORLD WAR

THE DEMONSTRATION that the European age was at last over was made in another world war. It began (in 1939) like its predecessor, as a European struggle, and like it became a combination of wars. To a far greater degree than any of its predecessors it made unprecedented demands; this time they were on a scale which left nothing untouched, unmobilized, undisturbed. It was realistically termed "total" war.

ECONOMIC DISINTEGRATION

By 1939, there were already many signs for those with eyes to see that a historical era was ending. Though 1919 had brought a few last extensions of territorial control by colonial powers, the behaviour of the greatest of them, Great Britain, showed that imperialism was on the defensive, if not already in retreat. The vigour of Japan meant that Europe was no longer the only focus of the international power system; a prescient South African statesman said as early as 1921 that "the scene has shifted away from Europe to the Far East and to the Pacific". His prediction now seems more than ever justified and it was made when the likelihood that China might soon again exercise her due weight was far from obvious. Ten years after he spoke, the economic foundations of Western

French refugees flee during the bombing of Dunkirk in northern France in 1940. When Dunkirk was liberated in 1945 only a quarter of its buildings were still standing.

preponderance had been shaken even more plainly than the political; the United States, greatest of industrial powers, had still ten million unemployed. Though none of the European industrial countries was by then in quite such straits, the confidence, which took for granted the health of the basic foundations of the economic system, had evaporated for ever. Industry might be picking up in some countries – largely because rearmament was stimulating it – but attempts to find recovery by international cooperation came to an end when a World Economic Conference broke down in 1933. After that, each nation had gone its own way; even the United Kingdom at last abandoned free trade. *Laissez-faire* was dead, even if people still talked about it. Governments were by 1939 deliberately interfering with the economy as they had not done since the heyday of mercantilism.

CHANGING INTELLECTUAL AND MORAL TRENDS

IF THE POLITICAL AND ECONOMIC assumptions of the nineteenth century had gone, so had many others. It is more difficult to speak of intellectual and spiritual trends than of political and economic, but though many people still clung to old shibboleths, for the élite which led thought and opinion the old foundations were no longer firm. Many people still attended religious services – though only a minority, even in Roman Catholic countries – but the masses of the

industrial cities lived in a post-Christian world in which the physical removal of the institutions and symbols of religion would have made little difference to their daily lives. So did intellectuals; they perhaps faced an even greater problem than that of loss of religious belief, because many of the liberal ideas, which had helped to displace Christianity from the eighteenth century, were by now being displaced in their turn. In the 1920s and 1930s, the liberal certainties of the autonomy of the individual, objective moral criteria, rationality, the authority of parents, and an explicable mechanical universe all seemed to be going under along with the belief in free trade.

The "Roaring Twenties" were a time of economic recovery during which many people felt able to enjoy a new lease of life after the horrors and deprivation of the First World War. Nightclubs such as the Charleston Contest Parody Club, shown here in 1926, became very popular.

Time chart (1919–1945)

			1939
	1931	1933	The German-Soviet pact is signed
	Japanese invasion of	Hitler comes to power	Poland is divided
	Manchuria	Roosevelt's New Deal	The Second World War begins

1900					1950

	1919–1920	1929	1936–1939	1941	1945
	Peace Treaties of the Paris	The Wall	The Spanish Civil War	The Japanese attack	Atomic bombs are dropped on Hiroshima and Nagasaki
	Conference	Street Crash	Germany takes Czechoslovakia	Pearl Harbor	End of the Second World War
	The Weimar Republic is established		Creation of the Anschluss		The UN is created

Art and changing values

In the early 20th century, recent major scientific discoveries and theories began to undermine the solid scientific and cultural paradigms of the previous century. The new ideas derived from Darwin's theory of evolution had a widespread impact, as did Freud's uncovering of a new field of knowledge, the unconscious mind. The formulation of relativist theories also transformed prevailing attitudes: humanity began to seem ever less significant in relation to other species (we are just one more of them), in relation to ourselves (we are not governed only by rational forces) and in relation to the universe (time and space do not have an absolute value).

The late 19th-century philosophers, in particular Arthur Schopenhauer and Friedrich Nietzsche, had considerable impact both on literature and on music. Artists, influenced by the spirit of the time, moved away from naturalism and immersed themselves in a private world. In literature, Virginia Woolf, James Joyce and Franz Kafka explored the human ego and laid the foundations of 20th-century narrative. In music, dodecaformism, or the twelve-tone technique, which was first used by Arnold Schoenberg in 1923, emerged as an alternative to classical tonal systems. In painting, after Impressionism came Cubism, Dadaism and Surrealism.

Animal Composition *was painted by the Spanish artist Joan Miró (1893–1983), who became a leading figure in the field of abstract art and Surrealist fantasy.*

THE ARTS

Change was most obvious in the arts. For three or four centuries, since the age of humanism, Europeans had believed that the arts expressed aspirations, insights and pleasures accessible in principle to ordinary men, even though they might be raised to an exceptional degree of fineness in execution, or be especially concentrated in form so that not everyone would always enjoy them. At any rate, it was possible for the whole of that time to retain the notion of the cultivated individual who, given time and study, could discriminate with taste among the arts of his or her time because they were expressions of a shared culture with shared standards. This idea was somewhat weakened when the nineteenth century, in the wake of the Romantic movement, came to idealize the artist as genius – Beethoven was one of the first examples – and formulated the notion of the *avant-garde*. By the first decade of the twentieth century, though, it was already very difficult for even trained eyes and ears to recognize art in much of what was done by contemporary artists. The most vivid symbol of this was the dislocation of the image in painting. Here, the flight from the representational still kept a tenuous link with tradition as late as Cubism, but by then it had long ceased to be apparent to the average "cultivated man" – if he still existed. Artists retired into a less and less accessible chaos of private visions, whose centre was reached in the world of Dada and Surrealism. The years after 1918 are of the greatest interest as something of a culmination of disintegration in the arts; in Surrealism even the notion of the objective disappeared, let alone its representation. As one Surrealist put it, the movement meant "thought dictated in the absence of all control exerted by reason, and outside all aesthetic or moral preoccupations". Through chance, symbolism, shock, suggestion and violence the Surrealists sought to go beyond consciousness itself. In so doing, they were only exploring what many writers and musicians were trying to do at the same time.

Such phenomena provide evidence in different forms of the decay of liberal culture, which was the final outcome of the high civilization of the European age. It is significant that such disintegratory movements were often prompted by a sense that the traditional culture had been too limited in its exclusion of the resources of emotion and experience which lay in the unconscious. Probably few of the artists who would have agreed with this would actually have read the work of the man who, more than any other, gave the twentieth century a language and stock of metaphors with which to explore this area and the confidence that it was there that life's secrets lay.

THE ROLE OF SIGMUND FREUD

Sigmund Freud was the founder of psychoanalysis. He thought he had a place in the history of culture beside Copernicus or Darwin, for he changed the way educated men and women thought of themselves. Freud himself made conscious comparisons, describing the idea of the unconscious as the third great "insult" to the narcissism of humanity, after those delivered by heliocentricity and evolutionary theory. He introduced several new ideas into ordinary discourse: the special meanings we now give to the words "complex" and "obsession", and the appearance of the familiar terms "Freudian slip" and "libido" are monuments to the power of his teaching. His influence quickly spread into literature, personal relations, education, politics. Like the words of

The work carried out by Sigmund Freud (1856–1939) in Vienna transformed thinking about the human consciousness around the world. Because Freud was Jewish, his books were among the first to be burned by the Nazis following Hitler's annexation of Austria.

many prophets, his message was often distorted. What he was believed to have said was much more important than the specific clinical studies which were his contribution to science. Like that of Newton and Darwin, Freud's importance lay beyond science – where his influence was less than theirs – in providing a new mythology. It was to prove highly corrosive.

The message people took from Freud suggested that the unconscious was the real source of most significant behaviour, that moral values and attitudes were projections of the influences which had moulded this unconscious, that, therefore, the idea of responsibility was at best a myth and probably a dangerous one, and that perhaps rationality itself was an illusion. It did not matter much that Freud's own assertions would have been nonsense had this been true. This was what many people believed he had proved – and many still believe. Such a bundle of ideas called in question the very foundation of liberal civilization itself, the idea of the rational, responsible, consciously motivated individual, and this was its general importance.

Freud's teaching was not the only intellectual force contributing to the loss of certainty and the sense that human beings had little firm ground beneath their feet. But it was the most apparent in the intellectual life of the interwar period. From grappling with the insights he brought, or with the chaos of the arts, or with the incomprehensibility of a world of science, which seemed suddenly to have abandoned Laplace and Newton, men and women - plunged worriedly into the search for new mythologies and standards to give them bearings. Politically, this led to fascism, Marxism, and the more irrational of the old certainties, extreme nationalism, for example. People did not feel inspired or excited by tolerance, democracy, and the old individual freedoms.

THE GERMAN PROBLEM

THE SWING AWAY FROM the old liberal assumptions made it all the more difficult to deal with the deepening uncertainty and foreboding clouding international relations in the 1930s. The heart of this lay in Europe, in the German problem which threatened a greater upheaval than could Japan. Germany had not been destroyed in 1918; it was a logical consequence, therefore, that it would one day again exercise its due weight. Geography, population and industrial power all meant that in one way or another a united Germany must dominate central Europe and overshadow France. What was at issue fundamentally was whether this could be faced without war; only a few cranks thought it might be disposed of by dividing again the Germany united in 1871.

Germans soon began to demand the revision of the settlement of Versailles. This demand eventually became unmanageable, although in the 1920s it was tackled in a hopeful spirit. The real burden of reparations was gradually whittled away and the Treaty of Locarno was seen as a great landmark

The German delegation, lead by Dr Gustav Streseman, leaves Berlin to join the representatives of other European governments for the signing of the Treaty of Locarno in 1925. The treaty represented a high point in the successful use of diplomacy to solve international conflicts peacefully.

Friedrich Ebert (1871–1925), the first president of Germany's Weimar Republic, is pictured delivering an address to the National Constituent Assembly in March 1919.

because by it Germany gave her consent to the Versailles territorial settlement in the west. But it left open the question of revision in the east and behind this loomed the larger question: how could a country potentially so powerful as Germany be related to its neighbours in a balanced, peaceful way, given the particular historical and cultural experience of the Germans?

THE FRAGILE WEIMAR REPUBLIC

Most people hoped the German issue had been settled by the creation of a democratic German republic, whose institutions would gently and benevolently reconstruct German society and civilization. It was true that the constitution of the Weimar Republic (as it was called from the place where its constituent assembly met) was very liberal, but too many Germans were out of sympathy

with it from the start. That Weimar had solved the German problem was revealed as an illusion when economic depression shattered the narrow base on which the German republic rested and set loose the destructive nationalist and social forces it had masked.

When this happened, the containment of Germany again became an international problem. But for a number of reasons, the 1930s were a very unpromising decade for containment to be easy. To begin with, some of the worst effects of the world economic crisis were felt in the relatively weak and agricultural economies of the new states of eastern and central Europe. France had always looked for allies against a German revival there, but such allies were now gravely weakened. Furthermore, their very existence made it doubly difficult to involve Russia, again an indisputable (if mysterious) great power, in the containment of Germany. Her ideological distinction presented barriers

The 1929 Wall Street Crash

By the 1920s, the United States had become an industrialized nation. In the post-war years of economic boom, an atmosphere of optimism and complete confidence in the country's financial security reigned in America. Many investors believed that the time had come in which they could make their fortunes by investing in Wall Street. Even for those who were not familiar with the stock exchange, it was more profitable to speculate on the stock market than to wait for a particular company to pay dividends.

In spring 1928, the New York Stock Exchange rose by 25 points owing to highly optimistic forecasts made by influential figures in industry and agriculture. Speculation on the stock exchange pushed the index up another 30 points in January 1929. During that summer, millions of investors bought shares, often on credit, in the hope of selling them on at a higher price. However, in October, crisis struck. People began to

sell their shares and prices started to sink at an alarming speed. The worst came on 29 October, when the general index dropped 43 points. Panic-selling led to 16 million shares being sold on that day, for a fraction of their original value. On 13 November, the industrial index was worth half its value of two months earlier.

The stock exchange crash triggered a series of repercussions. Many banks were not able to cover the loans their ruined clients had taken out and closed one by one as their funds ran out: in 1929, 642 banks closed; in 1930 there were 1,945 closures; and in 1931, 2,298. This brought about similar disasters in Europe, where many banks were closely linked to the North American system through war loans and money lent for reconstruction in the post-war period. When American capital was urgently recalled, the crisis spread across Europe.

After the Wall Street Crash, those who had bought shares on credit during the stock market boom had to pay for their lost shares in cash. Many speculators, such as this man in New York in October 1929, were forced to sell their possessions. The newspapers were full of tales of the resounding ruin of seemingly indestructible fortunes and there was more than a touch of truth in comedian Will

Rogers' quip about having to queue for a hotel window from which to jump (11 financiers committed suicide on 29 October, known as "Black Thursday"). Haunting images of the ensuing Great Depression – the long lines of the unemployed queueing at soup kitchens in the American cities and starving people in rural areas – were soon seen around the world.

enough to co-operation with the United Kingdom and France, but there was also her strategic remoteness. No Soviet force could reach Central Europe without crossing one or more of the east European states, whose short lives were haunted by fear of Russia and communism: Romania, Poland and the Baltic states, after all, were built from, among other things, former Russian lands.

PRE-WAR AMERICA

THE AMERICANS, LIKE the USSR, could not be relied upon to help contain Germany. The whole trend of American policy since Wilson failed to get his countrymen to join the League had been back towards a self-absorbed isolation which was, of course, suited to traditional ideas. Americans who had gone to Europe as soldiers did not want to repeat the experience. Justified apparently by boom in the 1920s, isolation was paradoxically confirmed by slump in the 1930s. When Americans did not confusedly blame Europe for their troubles – the question of debts from the war years had great psychological impact because it was believed to be tied up with international financial problems (as indeed it was, though not quite as Americans thought) – they felt distrustful of further entanglement. Anyway, the depression left them with enough on their plate. With the election of a Democratic president in 1932 they were, in fact, at the beginning of an era of important change which would in the end sweep away this mood, but this could not be foreseen.

FRANKLIN ROOSEVELT

The next phase of American history was to be presided over by Democrats for five successive presidential terms, the first four of

them after elections won by the same man, Franklin Roosevelt. To stand four successive times as presidential candidate was almost unprecedented (only the unsuccessful socialist, Eugene Debs, also did so); to win, astonishing. To do so with (on each occasion) an absolute majority of the popular vote was something like a revolution. No earlier Democratic candidate since the Civil War had ever had one at all (and no other was to have one until 1964). Moreover, Roosevelt was a rich, patrician figure. It is all the more surprising, therefore, that he should have emerged as one of the greatest leaders of the early twentieth century. He did so in an electoral contest which was basically one of hope versus despair. He offered confidence and the

President Franklin D. Roosevelt (1882–1945) (right) is seen on board the electoral train in 1932. It would take his Republican Party opponents another 20 years to recover from the loss of credibility the Great Depression had brought them.

promise of action to shake off the blight of economic depression. A political transformation followed his victory, the building of a Democratic hegemony on a coalition of neglected constituencies – the South, the poor, the farmer, the black American, the progressive liberal intellectual – which then attracted further support as it seemed to deliver results.

THE NEW DEAL

There was some degree of illusion in Roosevelt's success. The "New Deal" on which the Roosevelt administration embarked was still not grappling satisfactorily with the economy by 1939. None the less it changed the emphasis of the working of American capitalism and its relations with government. A huge programme of unemployment relief with insurance was started, millions were poured into public works, new regulation of finance was introduced, and a great experiment in public ownership was launched in a

The Tennessee Valley Authority emblem is displayed in 1934 shortly after its approval by President Roosevelt. The ambitious government project to develop the enormous Tennessee river basin resulted in the creation of thousands of jobs and significantly increased the national level of electricity production.

hydroelectric scheme in the Tennessee valley. Capitalism was given a new lease of life, and a new governmental setting. The New Deal brought the most important extension of the power of the Federal authorities over American society and the states that had ever occurred in peacetime and it has proved irreversible. Thus American politics reflected the same pressures towards collectivism which affected other countries in the twentieth century. In this sense, too, the Roosevelt era was historically decisive. It changed the course of American constitutional and political history as nothing had done since the Civil War and incidentally offered to the world a democratic alternative to fascism and communism by providing a liberal version of large-scale governmental intervention in the economy. This achievement is all the more impressive in that it rested almost entirely on the interested choices of politicians committed to the democratic process and not on the arguments of economists, some of whom were already advocating greater central management of the economy in capitalist nations. It was a remarkable demonstration of the ability of the American political system to deliver what people felt they wanted.

DIPLOMATIC PROBLEMS IN EUROPE

The American political machinery, of course, could also only deliver as a foreign policy what most Americans would tolerate. Roosevelt was much more aware than the majority of his fellow citizens of the dangers of persistent American isolation from Europe's problems. But he could reveal his own views only slowly. With Russia and the United States unavailable, only the western European great powers remained to confront Germany if she revived. Great Britain and

Italian troops invaded the ancient African kingdom of Ethiopia (then called Abyssinia) in October 1935. In this photograph taken by an Italian soldier, natives of a captured province salute a portrait of Mussolini, whom they knew as the "Great White Father". By May 1936, the Italian annexation of Ethiopia was complete. The kingdom was part of Italian East Africa until 1941.

France were badly placed to act as the policemen of Europe. They had memories of their difficulties in dealing with Germany even when Russia had been on their side. Furthermore, they had been much at odds with one another since 1918. They were also militarily weak. France, conscious of her inferiority in manpower should Germany ever rearm, had invested in a programme of strategic defence by fortification, which looked impressive but effectively deprived her of the power to act offensively. The Royal Navy was no longer without a rival, nor, as in 1914, safe in concentrating its resources in European waters. British governments long pursued the reduction of expenditure on armaments at a time when worldwide commitments were a growing strain on her forces. Economic depression reinforced this tendency; it was

feared that the costs of rearmament would cripple recovery by causing inflation. Many British voters, too, believed that Germany's grievances were just. They were disposed to make concessions in the name of German nationalism and self-determination, even by handing back German colonies. Both Great Britain and France were also troubled by a joker in the European pack, Italy. Under Mussolini, hopes that she might be enlisted against Germany had disappeared by 1938.

ITALY INVADES ETHIOPIA

The realization that Mussolini would not ally his country with Britain and France arose from a belated attempt by Italy to participate in the scramble for Africa when, in 1935, her forces invaded Ethiopia. Such action posed the question of what should be done by the League of Nations; it was clearly a breach of its covenant that one of its members should attack another. France and Great Britain were in an awkward position. As great powers, Mediterranean powers and African colonial powers, they were bound to take the lead against Italy at the League. But they did so feebly and half-heartedly, for they did not want to alienate an Italy they would like to have with them against Germany. The result was the worst possible one. The League failed to check aggression and Italy was alienated. Ethiopia lost its independence, though, it later proved, only for six years.

IDEOLOGY AND INTERNATIONAL RELATIONS

The League's failure to prevent Italy's invasion of Ethiopia was one of several moments at which it later looked as if a fatal

When Stalin took power in 1924, Leon Trotsky's persistent criticism of the Communist Party's increasingly undemocratic organization won him many enemies. He was eventually exiled from the Soviet Union in 1929. During the following decade, Stalin's régime would similarly exile, imprison or execute thousands of Soviet citizens for alleged political dissent. Trotsky was murdered by a Stalinist assassin in Mexico in 1940.

error was committed. But it is impossible to say in retrospect at what stage the situation which developed from these facts became unmanageable. Certainly the emergence of a much more radical and ferociously opportunist régime in Germany was the major turning-point. But the depression had preceded this and made it possible. Economic collapse also had another important effect. It made plausible an ideological interpretation of events in the 1930s and thus further embittered them. Because of the intensification of class conflict which economic collapse brought with it, interested politicians sometimes interpreted the development of international relations in terms of Fascism versus Communism, and even of Right versus Left or Democracy versus Dictatorship. This was easier after Mussolini, angered by British and French reactions to his invasion of Ethiopia, came to ally Italy to Germany and talked of an anti-communist crusade. But this was misleading, too. All ideological interpretations of international affairs in the 1930s tended to obscure the central nature of the German problem – and, therefore, to make it harder to tackle.

RUSSIA BETWEEN THE WARS

Russian propaganda was important, too. During the 1930s her internal situation was precarious. The industrialization programme was imposing grave strains and sacrifices. These were mastered – though perhaps also exaggerated – by a savage intensification of dictatorship which expressed itself not only in the collectivization struggle against the peasants, but in the turning of terror against the cadres of the régime itself from 1934 onwards. In five years millions of Russians were executed, imprisoned or exiled, often to forced labour. The world looked on amazed

Voters gather in Saint-Denis in Paris at the end of the French election day in 1936. The election was won by the leftist-liberal Popular Front coalition government led by Léon Blum, which governed until 1938. Although the French Communist Party supported Blum's government, they did not join it – they knew that further unrest among the French workers would wreak chaos and leave the country exposed to a fascist invasion.

as batches of defendants grovelled with grotesque "confessions" before Soviet courts. Nine out of ten generals in the army went and, it has been estimated, half the officer corps. A new communist élite replaced the old one in these years; by 1939 over half the delegates who had attended the Party Congress of 1934 had been arrested. It was very difficult for outsiders to be sure what was happening, but it was clear to them that Russia was by no means either a civilized, liberal state nor necessarily a very strong potential ally.

More directly, this affected the international situation because of the propaganda which accompanied it. Much of this, no doubt, arose from the deliberate provocation inside Russia of a siege mentality; far from being relaxed, the habit of thinking of the world in terms of Us versus Them which had been born in Marxist dogma and the interventions of 1918–22 was encouraged in the 1930s. As this notion took hold, so, outside, did the preaching of the doctrine of inter-national class struggle by the Comintern. The reciprocal effect was predictable. The fears of conservatives everywhere were intensified. It became easy to think of any concession to left-wing or even mildly progressive forces as a victory for the Bolsheviks. As attitudes thus hardened on the Right, so communists were given new evidence for the thesis of inevitable class conflict and revolution.

THE REJECTION OF COMMUNISM IN EUROPE

In spite of the communists' hopes, though, there was not one successful left-wing revolution. The revolutionary danger had subsided rapidly after the immediate post-war years. Labour governments peacefully and undramatically ruled Great Britain for part of the 1920s. The second ended in financial collapse in 1931, to be replaced by conservative coalitions which had overwhelming electoral support and proceeded to govern with remarkable fidelity to the tradition of progressive and piecemeal social and administrative reform which had marked Great Britain's advance into the "welfare state". This direction had been followed even further in the Scandinavian countries, often held up for admiration for their combination of political democracy and practical socialism, and as a contrast to communism. Even in France, where there was a large and active Communist Party, there was no sign that its aims were acceptable to the majority of the electorate even after the Depression. In Germany the Communist Party before 1933 had been able to get more votes, but it was never able to displace the Social Democrats in control of the working-class movement. In less advanced countries than these, communism's revolutionary success was even smaller. In Spain it had to compete with socialists and anarchists; Spanish conservatives certainly feared it and may have had grounds to fear also what they felt to be a slide towards social revolution under the republic which was established in

Hitler's *Mein Kampf*

"To win the masses for a national resurrection, no social sacrifice is too great. Whatever economic concessions are made to our working class today, they stand in no proportion to the gain for the entire nation if they help to give the broad masses back to their nation. Only pig-headed short-sightedness, such as is often unfortunately found in our employer circles, can fail to recognize that in the long run there can be no economic upswing for them and hence no economic profit, unless the inner national solidarity of our people is restored.

"If during the War the German unions had ruthlessly guarded the interests of the working class, if even during the War they had struck a thousand times over and forced approval of the demands of the workers they represented on the dividend-hungry employers of those days; but if in matters of national defence they had avowed their Germanism with the same fanaticism; and if with equal ruthlessness they had given to the fatherland that which is the fatherland's, the War would not have been lost."

An extract from *Mein Kampf* by Adolf Hitler, 1929, translated by Ralph Manheim.

The German dictator Adolf Hitler (1889–1945) delivers a speech at the opening ceremony of a new Volkswagen car factory in Fallersleben, Germany, in 1936.

1931, but it was hardly Spanish communism that threatened them.

ADOLF HITLER

THE IDEOLOGICAL interpretations had great appeal, even to many who were not communists. They were much strengthened by the accession to power of a new ruler in Germany, Adolf Hitler, whose success makes it very difficult to deny him political genius despite his pursuit of goals which make it difficult to believe him wholly sane. In the early 1920s he was only a disappointed agitator, who had failed in an attempt to overthrow a government (the Bavarian) and who poured out his

Crowds at the 1936 Olympic Games in Berlin greet the Führer. The Nazi régime was determined that the games would be a showcase for Hitler's Germany. The competing German athletes were put under enormous pressure to win the maximum number of medals in order to demonstrate to the world the superiority of the Aryan race. This aim was thwarted, much to Hitler's disgust, by the black American athlete Jesse Owens (1913–1980), who won four gold medals and was declared "Athlete of the Games".

obsessive nationalism and anti-Semitism not only in hypnotically effective speeches but in a long, shapeless, semi-autobiographical book which few people read. In 1933, the National Socialist German Workers Party which he led ("Nazi" for short) was electorally strong enough for him to be appointed chancellor of the German republic. Politically, this may have been the most momentous single decision of the century, for it meant the revolutionizing of Germany, its redirection upon a course of aggression, which ended by destroying the old Europe and Germany too, and that meant a new world.

Though Hitler's messages were simple, his appeal was complex. He preached that Germany's troubles had identifiable sources. The Treaty of Versailles was one. The international capitalists were another. The supposedly anti-national activities of German Marxists and Jews were others. He also said

that the righting of Germany's political wrongs must be combined with the renovation of German society and culture, and that this was a matter of purifying the biological stock of the German people, by excising its non-Aryan components.

THE NAZIS IN POWER

In 1922 Hitler's message took Hitler a very little way; in 1930 it won him 107 seats in the German parliament – more than the communists, who had seventy-seven. The Nazis were already the beneficiaries of economic collapse, and it was to get worse. There are several reasons why the Nazis reaped its political harvest, but one of the most important was that the communists spent as much energy fighting the socialists as their other opponents. This had fatally handicapped the

Berlin's Reichstag (parliament) building went up in flames on 27 February 1933. Marinus van der Lubbe, a mentally disturbed Dutchman and an ex-communist, was later accused of starting the fire. The Nazis claimed that the fire was intended to signal the start of a communist revolution. On 28 February Chancellor Hitler persuaded President Hindenburg to declare a temporary state of emergency (which was to last until 1945). Historians disagree about the true cause of the Reichstag fire. Some believe that Hitler's bodyguards, the SS, had started it and then deliberately implicated van der Lubbe in the crime; others think that van der Lubbe, who was later found guilty and executed, acted alone and that the Nazis merely seized the opportunity to take power.

Left in Germany all through the 1920s. Another reason was that under the democratic republic anti-Semitic feeling had grown. It, too, was exacerbated by economic col-

lapse. Anti-Semitism, like nationalism, had an appeal which cut across classes as an explanation of Germany's troubles, unlike the equally simple Marxist explanation in terms of class war which, naturally, antagonized some as well as (it was hoped) attracting others.

By 1930 the Nazis showed they were a power in the land. They attracted more support, and won backers from those who saw in their street-fighting gangs an anti-communist insurance, from nationalists who sought rearmament and revision of the Versailles peace settlement and from conservative politicians who thought that Hitler was a party leader like any other, who might now be valuable in their own game. The manoeuvres were complicated, but in 1932 the Nazis became the biggest party in the German parliament, though without a majority of seats. In January 1933 Hitler was called to office in due constitutional form by the president of the republic. There followed new elections, in which the régime's monopoly of the radio and use of intimidation still did not secure the Nazis a majority of seats; none the less, they had one when supported by some right-wing members of parliament, who joined them to vote special enabling powers to the government. The most important was that of governing by emergency decree. This was the end of parliament and parliamentary sovereignty. Armed with these powers, the Nazis proceeded to carry out a revolutionary destruction of democratic institutions. By 1939, there was virtually no sector of German society not controlled or intimidated by them. The conservatives, too, had lost. They soon found that Nazi interference with the independence of traditional authorities was likely to go very far.

HITLER'S AMBITIONS UNLEASHED

Like Stalin's Russia, the Nazi régime rested in large measure on terror used mercilessly against its enemies. It was soon unleashed against the Jews and an astonished Europe

found itself witnessing revivals in one of its most advanced societies of the pogroms of medieval Europe or tsarist Russia. This was indeed so amazing that many people outside Germany found it difficult to believe that it was happening. Confusion over the nature of the régime made it even more difficult to deal with. Some saw Hitler simply as a nationalist leader bent, like an Atatürk, upon the regeneration of his country and the assertion of its rightful claims. Others saw him as a crusader against Bolshevism. Even when people only thought he might be a useful barrier against it, that increased the likelihood that politicians of the Left would see him as a tool of capitalism. But no simple formula will contain Hitler or his aims – and there is still great disagreement about what these were – and probably a reasonable approximation to the truth is simply to recognize that he expressed the resentments and exasperations of German society in their most negative and destructive forms and embodied them to a monstrous degree. When his personality was given scope by economic disaster, political cynicism and a favourable arrangement of international forces, he could release these negative

Nazi soldiers in 1935 hold banners warning "Don't buy from Jews". The Nuremberg Laws of 1935 deprived the German Jews (defined as anyone who had at least one Jewish grandparent) of citizenship, barred them from practising a profession, isolated them socially and banned mixed marriages. This was Hitler's first step on the road to his "Final Solution" – the Nazi attempt to exterminate all the Jews in Europe.

qualities at the expense of all Europeans in the long run, his own countrymen included.

THE SPANISH CIVIL WAR

The path by which Germany came to be at war again in 1939 is complicated. Argument is still possible about when, if ever, there was a chance of avoiding the final outcome. One important moment, clearly, was when Mussolini, formerly wary of German ambitions in central Europe, became Hitler's ally. After he had been alienated by British and French policy over his Ethiopian adventure, a civil war broke out in Spain when a group of generals mutinied against the left-wing republic. Hitler and Mussolini both sent contingents to support the man who emerged there as the rebel leader, General Franco.

German war planes, at General Franco's behest, carried out a devastating aerial attack on the small Basque town of Guernica in April 1937. Picasso's depiction of the event expresses his emotional reaction to the bombing and his horror at the terrible human cost of military action, small though the slaughter was by comparison with what was soon to follow.

This, more than any other single fact, gave an ideological colour to Europe's divisions. Hitler, Mussolini and Franco were all now identified as "fascist" and Russian foreign policy began to coordinate support for Spain within Western countries by letting local communists abandon their attacks on other left-wing parties and encouraging "Popular Fronts". Thus Spain came to be seen as a conflict between Right and Left in its purest form; this was a distortion, but it encouraged people to think of Europe as divided into two camps.

RENEWED GERMAN AGGRESSION

BRITISH AND FRENCH GOVERNMENTS were by this time well aware of the difficulties of dealing with Germany. Hitler had already in

Hitler and Mussolini meet in 1940. Their decision to join forces had major implications for international relations.

1935 announced that its rearmament (forbidden at Versailles) had begun. Until their own rearmament was completed, they remained very weak. The first consequence of this was shown to the world when German troops re-entered the "demilitarized" zone of the Rhineland from which they had been excluded by the Treaty of Versailles. No attempt was made to resist this move. After the civil war in Spain had thrown opinion in Great Britain and France into further

disarray, Hitler then seized Austria. The terms of Versailles, which forbade the fusion of Germany and Austria seemed hard to uphold; to the French and British electorates this could be presented as a matter of legitimately aggrieved nationalism. The Austrian republic had also long had internal troubles. The *Anschluss* (as union with Germany was called) took place in March 1938. In the autumn came the next German aggression, the seizure of part of Czechoslovakia. Again, this was justified by the specious claims of self-determination; the areas involved were so important that their loss crippled the prospect of future Czechoslovak self-defence, but they were areas with many German inhabitants. Memel would follow, on the same grounds, the next year. Hitler was gradually fulfilling the old dream which had been lost when Prussia beat Austria – the dream of a united Great Germany, defined as all lands of those of German blood.

In the Sudetenland, a largely German-speaking area of Czechoslovakia, pro-Nazi feelings were running high by 1938, particularly after the Anschluss with Austria. Here, Sudetenland women salute the German troops as they arrive to take power in the region on 12 October 1938.

The dismemberment of Czechoslovakia had been something of a turning-point. It was achieved by a series of agreements at Munich in September 1938 in which Great Britain and Germany took the main parts. This was the last great initiative of British foreign policy to try to satisfy Hitler. The British prime minister was still too unsure of rearmament to resist, but hoped also that the transference of the last substantial group of Germans from alien rule to that of their homeland might deprive Hitler of the motive for further revision of Versailles – a settlement which was now somewhat tattered in any case.

WAR OVER POLAND

But the dismemberment of Czechoslovakia did not satisfy Hitler, who went on to inaugurate a programme of expansion into Slav lands. The first step was the absorption of what was left of Czechoslovakia, in March 1939. This brought forward the question of the Polish settlement of 1919. Hitler resented the "Polish Corridor" which separated East Prussia from Germany and contained Danzig, an old German city given an international status in 1919. At this point the British government, though hesitatingly, changed tack and offered a guarantee to Poland and other East European countries against aggression. It also began a wary negotiation with Russia.

Russian policy remains hard to interpret. It seems that Stalin kept the Spanish Civil War going with support to the republic as long as it seemed likely to tie up German attention, but then looked for other ways of buying time against the attack from the west, which he always feared. To him, it seemed likely that a German attack on Russia might be encouraged by Great Britain and France, who would

---

The German–Soviet Pact of Non-Aggression

By spring 1939, Stalin had probably come to the conclusion that he could not trust France and Great Britain actually to confront Germany and that, when they sought cooperation from the Soviet Union, they were merely hoping to implicate Russia in a war against Germany in which they themselves would not take part. Soviet diplomats therefore began to negotiate separately with both sides, hoping to force them to continue supporting their initial positions: the

Western powers should continue to believe that they could rely on Soviet aid, while Germany was to believe it could count on Russia to remain neutral.

In August 1939, while the French and British delegations were in Moscow, Hitler showed great interest in reaching an immediate agreement with the USSR. This sudden eagerness on the part of the Germans convinced Stalin that attack was imminent. He knew that his own country was not in immediate danger – it had no shared frontier with Germany and it was too late in the year to attack Russia herself. In fact, Germany was planning to attack Poland. Stalin met with Hitler's foreign minister Joachim von Ribbentrop on 23 August and signed the German–Soviet pact. A secret protocol established that Finland, Estonia, Lithuania, a large part of Poland and Bessarabia would become areas of Russian influence. This was the price Germany paid to keep Russia neutral, leaving Hitler free to attack Poland.

Molotov, the Soviet commissar for foreign affairs, signs the German–Soviet Pact of Non-Aggression. Ribbentrop is standing in the centre with Stalin by his side.

German troops in Paris parade along the Champs Elysées towards the Arc de Triomphe in August 1940, two months after Hitler's conquest of France.

see with relief the danger they had so long faced turning against the workers' state. No doubt they would have done. There was little possibility of working with the British or French to oppose Hitler, however, even if they were willing to do so, because no Russian army could reach Germany except through Poland – and this the Poles would never permit. Accordingly, as a Russian diplomat remarked to a French colleague on hearing of the Munich decisions, there was now nothing for it but a fourth partition of Poland. This was arranged in the summer of 1939. After their bitter respective diatribes against Bolshevik–Slav barbarism and fascist–capitalist exploitation, Germany and Russia made an agreement in August which provided for the division of Poland between them; authoritarian states enjoy great flexibility in the conduct of diplomacy. Armed with this, Hitler went on to attack Poland. He thus began the Second World War on 1 September 1939. Two days later the British and French honoured their guarantee to Poland and declared war on Germany.

BRITISH AND FRENCH RELUCTANCE

The British and French governments were not very keen on declaring war, for it was obvious that they could not help Poland. That unhappy nation disappeared once more, divided by Russian and German forces about a month after the outbreak of war. But not to have intervened would have meant acquiescing to the German domination of Europe, for no other nation would have thought British or French support worth having. So, uneasily and without the excitement of 1914, the only two constitutional great powers of Europe found themselves facing a totalitarian régime. Neither their peoples nor their governments had much enthusiasm for this role, and the decline of liberal and democratic forces since 1918 put them in a position much inferior to that of the Allies of 1914, but exasperation with Hitler's long series of aggressions and broken promises made it hard to see what sort of peace could be made which would reassure them. The basic cause

Europe during the Second World War 1939–1945

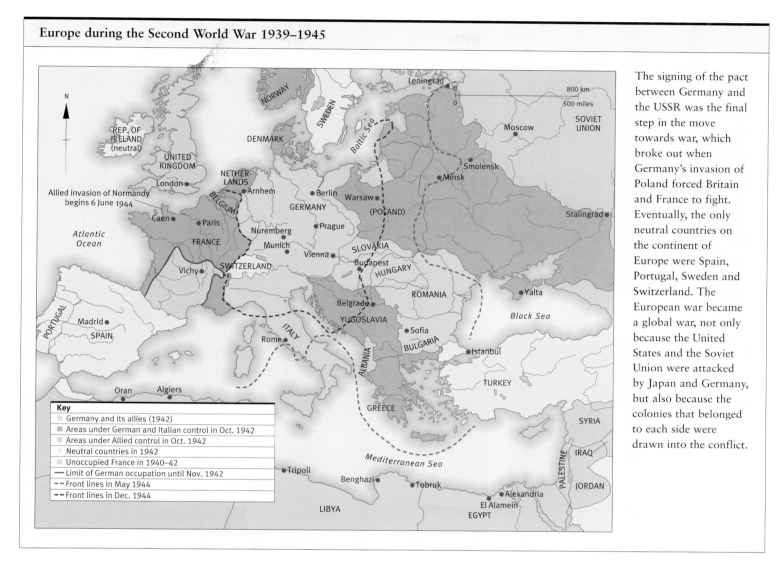

Key
- Germany and its allies (1942)
- Areas under German and Italian control in Oct. 1942
- Areas under Allied control in Oct. 1942
- Neutral countries in 1942
- Unoccupied France in 1940–42
- — Limit of German occupation until Nov. 1942
- -- Front lines in May 1944
- -- Front lines in Dec. 1944

The signing of the pact between Germany and the USSR was the final step in the move towards war, which broke out when Germany's invasion of Poland forced Britain and France to fight. Eventually, the only neutral countries on the continent of Europe were Spain, Portugal, Sweden and Switzerland. The European war became a global war, not only because the United States and the Soviet Union were attacked by Japan and Germany, but also because the colonies that belonged to each side were drawn into the conflict.

of the war was, as in 1914, German nationalism. But whereas then Germany had gone to war because *it* felt threatened, now Great Britain and France were responding to the danger presented by Germany's expansion. *They* felt threatened this time.

BRITAIN IS ISOLATED

To the surprise of many observers, and the relief of some, the first six months of the war were almost uneventful once the short Polish campaign was over. It was quickly plain that mechanized forces and air power were to play a much more important part than between 1914 and 1918. The memory of the slaughter of the Somme and Verdun was too vivid for the British and French to plan anything but an economic offensive; the weapon of blockade, they hoped, would be effective. Hitler was unwilling to disturb them, because he was anxious to make peace. This deadlock was only broken when the British sought to intensify the blockade in Scandinavian waters. This coincided, remarkably, with a German offensive to secure ore supplies, which conquered Norway and Denmark. Its launching on 9 April 1940 opened an astonishing period of fighting. Only a month later

The German army arrives in the Danish town of Horsens in May 1940.

there began a brilliant German invasion, first of the Low Countries and then of France. A powerful armoured attack through the Ardennes opened the way to the division of the Allied armies and the capture of Paris. On 22 June France signed an armistice with the Germans. By the end of the month, the whole European coast from the Pyrenees to the North Cape was in German hands. Italy had joined in on the German side ten days before the French surrender. A new French government at Vichy broke off relations with Great Britain after the British had seized or destroyed French warships they feared might fall into German hands. The Third Republic effectively came to an end with the installation of a French marshal, a hero of the First World War, as head of state. With no ally left on the continent, Great Britain faced a worse strategic situation by far than that in which she had struggled against Napoleon.

ANTI-GERMAN FORCES UNITE

The French armistice was followed by a capitulation which marked a huge change in the nature of the war. Great Britain was not quite alone. There were the dominions, all of which had entered the war on its side, and a number of governments in exile from the overrun continent. Some of these commanded forces of their own and Norwegians, Danes, Dutchmen, Belgians, Czechs and Poles were to fight gallantly, often with decisive effect, in the years ahead. The most important exiled contingents were those of the French, but at this stage they represented a faction within France, not its legal government. A general who had left France before the armistice and was condemned to death *in absentia* was their leader: Charles de Gaulle. He was recognized by the British only as "leader of the Free French" but saw himself as constitutional legatee of the Third Republic and the custodian of France's interests and honour. He soon began to show an independence, which was in the end to make him the greatest servant of his country since Clemenceau.

De Gaulle's position was immediately important to the British because of uncertainties about what might happen to parts of the French Empire where he hoped to find sympathizers who wished to join him to continue the fight. This was one way in which the war was now extended geographically. This was also a consequence of Italy's entry into the war, since her African possessions and the Mediterranean sea-lanes now became operational areas. Finally, the availability of Atlantic and Scandinavian ports to the Germans meant that what was later called the "Battle of the Atlantic", the struggle by submarine, surface, and air attack to sever or wear down British sea communications was now bound to become much fiercer.

WINSTON CHURCHILL

Mounting German aggression in the Atlantic meant that the British Isles immediately faced

The Free French Forces, founded by General Charles de Gaulle (1890–1970), originally consisted of 7,000 exiled French volunteers funded by Great Britain. By 1942, under the new name of the Fighting French, and boosted by soldiers from French colonies, the organization had 400,000 troops. Here General de Gaulle is shown on his triumphant return to France after the liberation in June 1944.

direct attack. The hour had already found the man to brace the nation against such a challenge. Winston Churchill, after a long and chequered political career, had become prime minister when the Norwegian campaign collapsed, because no other man commanded support in all parties in the House of Commons. To the coalition government which he immediately formed he gave vigorous leadership, something hitherto felt to be lacking. More important than this, he called forth in his people, whom he addressed frequently by radio, qualities they had forgotten they possessed. It was soon clear that only defeat after direct assault was going to get the British out of the war.

This was even more certain after a great air battle over southern England in August and September had been won by British science, in the form of radar, and the Royal Air Force. For a moment, the British knew the pride and relief of the Greeks after Marathon. It was true, as Churchill said in a much-quoted speech, that "never in the field of human conflict was so much owed by so many to so few". This victory made a German seaborne invasion impossible (though a successful one was always unlikely). It also established that Great Britain could not be defeated by air bombardment alone. The islands had a bleak outlook ahead, but this victory changed the direction

The British prime minister Winston Churchill (1874–1965) demonstrates his "V for Victory" sign during a visit to the United States in 1946. Throughout the Second World War, Churchill personified the British determination to fight Hitler to the end.

of the war, for it was the beginning of a period in which a variety of influences turned German attention in another direction. In December 1940 planning began for a German invasion of Russia.

THE GERMAN INVASION OF RUSSIA

BY THE END OF 1940, Russia had made further gains in the west, apparently with an eye to securing a glacis against a future German attack. A war against Finland gave her important strategic areas. The Baltic republics of Latvia, Lithuania and Estonia were swallowed in 1940. Bessarabia, which Romania had taken from Russia in 1918, was now taken back, together with the northern Bukovina. In the last case, Stalin was going beyond tsarist boundaries. The German deci-

sion to attack Russia arose in part because of disagreements about the future direction of Russian expansion: Germany sought to keep Russia away from the Balkans and the Straits. It was also aimed at demonstrating, by a quick overthrow of Russia, that further British war-making was pointless. But there was also a deep personal element in the decision. Hitler had always sincerely and fanatically detested Bolshevism and maintained that the Slavs, a racially inferior group, should provide Germans with living space and raw materials in the east. His was a last, perverted vision of the old struggle of the Teuton to impose Western civilization on the Slav East. Many Germans responded to such a theme. It was to justify more appalling atrocities than any earlier crusading myth.

BARBAROSSA

In a brief spring campaign, which provided an overture to the holocaust ahead, the Germans overran Yugoslavia and Greece, with which Italian forces had been unhappily engaged since October 1940. Once again British arms were driven from the mainland of Europe. Crete, too, was taken by a spectacular German airborne assault. Now all was ready for "Barbarossa", as the great onslaught on Russia was named, after the medieval emperor who had led the Third Crusade (and had been drowned during it).

The attack was launched on 22 June 1941 and had huge early successes. Vast numbers of prisoners were taken and the Russian armies fell back hundreds of miles. The German advance guard came within a few miles of entering Moscow. But that margin was not quite eliminated and by Christmas the first successful Russian counter-attacks had announced that in fact Germany was pinned down. German strategy had lost the

Winston Churchill and Franklin D. Roosevelt on board the British battleship *Prince of Wales* on 14 August 1941, where the conference that produced the Atlantic Charter was held. The two leaders met nine times during the war and the mutual admiration and close friendship that developed between them were to have a major impact on the course of events, in spite of their profound differences over some important questions.

initiative. If the British and Russians could hold on and if they could keep in alliance with one another then, failing a radical technical modification of the war by the discovery of new weapons of great power, their access to American production would inexorably increase their strength. This did not, of course, mean that they would inevitably defeat Germany, only that they might bring her to negotiate terms.

JAPAN AND THE UNITED STATES ENTER THE WAR

THE AMERICAN PRESIDENT had believed since 1940 that in the interests of the United States Great Britain had to be supported up to the limits permitted by his own public and the law of neutrality. In fact, he went well beyond both at times. By the summer of 1941, Hitler knew that to all intents and purposes the United States was an undeclared enemy. A crucial step had been the American Lend-Lease Act of March that year which, after British assets in the United States had been liquidated, provided production and services to the Allies without immediate payment. Soon afterwards, the American government extended naval patrols and the protection of its shipping further eastward into the Atlantic. After the invasion of Russia came a meeting between Churchill and Roosevelt which resulted in a statement of shared principles – the Atlantic Charter – in which the leaders of one nation at war and another formally at peace spoke together of the needs of a post-war world "after the final

The American battleships *West Virginia* and *Tennessee* are pictured in flames in Pearl Harbor. President Roosevelt later referred to the surprise Japanese attack on the US naval base in Hawaii as "a day which will live in infamy". During the same month, the Japanese took Hong Kong, Guam, Luzon and Borneo, threatening the other American garrisons in the Philippines, the British in the Moluccas, and even Australia.

destruction of the Nazi tyranny". This was a long way from isolationism and was the background to Hitler's second fateful but foolish decision of 1941, a declaration of war on the United States on 11 December, after a Japanese attack on British and American territories four days earlier. Hitler had earlier promised the Japanese to do this. The war thus became global. The British and American declarations of war on Japan might have left two separate wars to rage, with only Great Britain engaged in both; Hitler's action threw away the chance that American power might have been kept out of Europe and deployed only in the Pacific. Few single acts have so marked the end of an epoch, for this announced the eclipse of European affairs. Europe's future would now be settled not by its own efforts but by the two great powers on its flanks, the United States and Soviet Russia.

The Japanese decision was also a rash one, though the logic of Japanese policy had long pointed towards conflict with the United States. Japan's ties with Germany and Italy, though they had some propaganda value for both sides, did not amount to much in practice. What mattered in the timing of Japanese policy was the resolution of debates in Tokyo about the danger, or lack of it, of a challenge to the United States which must involve war. The crux of the matter was that Japan's needs for a successful conclusion of the war in China included oil which she could only obtain with the tacit consent of the United States that Japan was to destroy China. This no American government could have given.

Instead, in October 1941 the American government imposed an embargo on all trade by United States citizens with Japan.

PEARL HARBOR

After the imposition of the trade embargo, there followed the last stages of a process which had its origins in the ascendancy established in Japan by reactionary and militant forces in the 1930s. The question had by this time become for the Japanese military planners purely strategic and technical; since they would have to take the resources in Southeast Asia which they needed by force, all that had to be settled was the nature of the war against the United States and its timing. Such a decision was fundamentally irrational, for the chances of ultimate success were very small; once arguments of national honour had won, though, the final calculations about the best point and moment of attack were carefully made. The choice was made to strike as hard a blow as possible against American seapower at the outset in order to gain the maximum freedom of movement in the Pacific and South China Sea. The result was the onslaught of 7 December, whose centrepiece was an air attack on the American fleet at Pearl Harbor, which was one of the most brilliantly conceived and executed operations in the history of warfare. Yet it fell just short of complete success, for it did not destroy American naval air power, though it gave the Japanese for months the strategical freedom they sought. After their victory at Pearl Harbor the Japanese faced a prolonged war they were bound to lose in the end. They had united Americans. Isolationism could be virtually ignored after 8 December; Roosevelt had a nation behind him as Wilson never had.

GLOBAL CONFLICT

When even a few Japanese bombs had fallen on the American mainland, it was obvious that this was much more truly a world war than the first had been. The German operations in the Balkans had by the time of Pearl Harbor left Europe with only four neutral

American marines, killed during the Battle of Midway in 1943, are buried at sea. They died when a Japanese kamikaze, or suicide plane, crashed onto the US aircraft-carrier *Lexington*.

Japanese tanks are paraded through the streets of Tokyo in April 1940 as a demonstration to the world of the nation's military might.

countries: Spain, Portugal, Sweden and Switzerland. The war in North Africa raged back and forth between Libya and Egypt. It was extended to Syria by the arrival there of a German mission and to Iraq when a nationalist government supported by German aircraft was removed by a British force. Iran had been occupied by British and Soviet forces in 1941. In Africa, Ethiopia was liberated and the Italian colonial empire destroyed.

With the opening of the Far Eastern war the Japanese wrought destruction on the colonial empires there, too. Within a few months they took Indonesia, Indo-China, Malaya, the Philippines. They pressed through Burma towards the Indian border and were soon bombing the north Australian port of Darwin from New Guinea. Meanwhile, the naval war was fought by German submarine forces, aircraft and surface raiders all over the Atlantic, Arctic, Mediterranean and Indian oceans. Only a tiny minority of countries were left outside this struggle. Its demands were colossal and carried much fur-

ther the mobilization of whole societies than had the First World War. The role of the United States was decisive. Her huge manufacturing power made the material preponderance of the "United Nations" (as the coalition of states fighting the Germans, the Italians and the Japanese was called from the beginning of 1942) incontestable.

A TURNING-POINT FOR THE UNITED NATIONS

In spite of the United Nations' advantages, the way ahead was still a hard one. The first half of 1942 was a very bleak time for the United Nations. Then came the turning-point, in four great and very different battles. In June, a Japanese fleet attacking Midway Island was broken in a battle fought largely by aircraft. Japanese losses in carriers and aircrews were such that Japan never regained the strategical initiative and the long American counter-attack in the Pacific now

The Allied invasion of Normandy

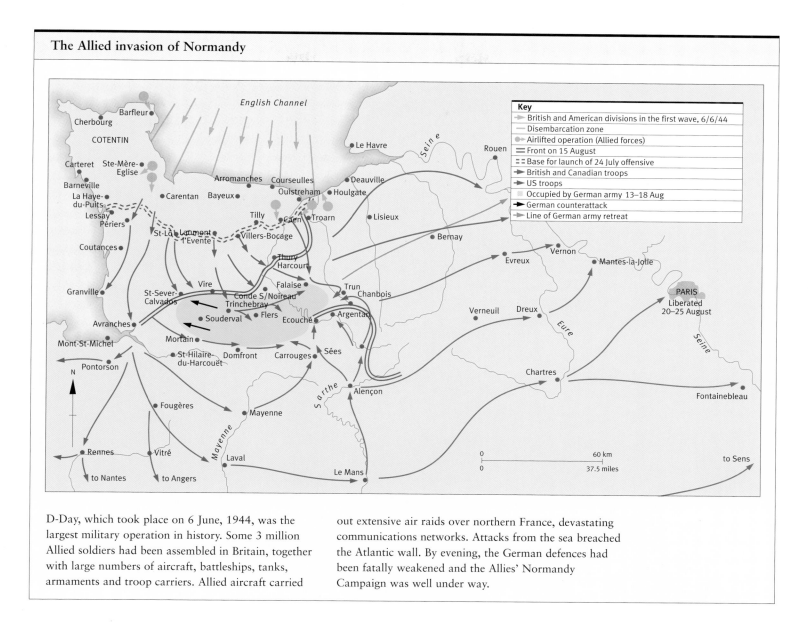

Key
- British and American divisions in the first wave, 6/6/44
- Disembarcation zone
- Airlifted operation (Allied forces)
- Front on 15 August
- Base for launch of 24 July offensive
- British and Canadian troops
- US troops
- Occupied by German army 13–18 Aug
- German counterattack
- Line of German army retreat

D-Day, which took place on 6 June, 1944, was the largest military operation in history. Some 3 million Allied soldiers had been assembled in Britain, together with large numbers of aircraft, battleships, tanks, armaments and troop carriers. Allied aircraft carried out extensive air raids over northern France, devastating communications networks. Attacks from the sea breached the Atlantic wall. By evening, the German defences had been fatally weakened and the Allies' Normandy Campaign was well under way.

began to unroll. Then, at the beginning of November, the British army in Egypt decisively defeated the Germans and Italians and began a march west which was to end with the eviction of the enemy from all North Africa. The Battle of El Alamein had coincided with landings by Anglo-American forces in French North Africa. They subsequently moved eastwards and by May 1943 German and Italian resistance on the continent had ceased. Six months earlier, at the end of 1942, the Russians had bottled up at Stalingrad on the Volga a German army

rashly exposed by Hitler. The remnants surrendered in February in the most demoralizing defeat yet suffered by the Germans in Russia, and yet one which was only part of three splendid months of winter advance which marked the turning-point of the war on the Eastern Front.

THE END OF THE WAR IN EUROPE

The other great Allied victory has no specific date, but was as important as any of these.

The use of the atomic bomb

Although German scientists had discovered the potential to build atom bombs in 1938 it was then widely believed that such weapons would take a long time to develop and would be too heavy to be carried by aircraft. After the outbreak of the Second World War, however, two physicists exiled from Germany in Great Britain prepared a report in which they stated that it may be possible to manufacture portable atom bombs in a relatively short time. Research began in Britain. After its entry into the war in December 1941 the United States concentrated all its scientific might on the construction of atomic bombs under the "Manhattan Project". The first nuclear test was carried out on 16 July 1945 in New Mexico, when a plutonium bomb was exploded.

On 6 August, a B-29 bomber dropped a uranium atom bomb on the Japanese city of Hiroshima. The explosion completely flattened the city, killing around 80,000 people instantly and injuring 70,000. Thousands who survived the initial blast died in the following days of burns, injuries and radiation sickness. Thousands more died in later years from cancer and other radiation-related illnesses.

Three days later, another bomb, made of plutonium, was dropped on Nagasaki, where 40,000 people were killed and 25,000 injured. In the face of this devastating atomic power, Japan surrendered.

Pictured are the ground crew and pilot (centre) of the American bomber that dropped the atom bomb on Hiroshima.

This was the Battle of the Atlantic. Allied merchant shipping losses reached their peak in 1942. At the end of the year nearly eight million tons of shipping had been lost for eighty-seven U-boats sunk. In 1943 the fig-

ures were three and a quarter million tons and 237 U-boats, and during the spring months the battle had been won. In May alone, forty-seven U-boats had been sunk. This was the most crucial battle of all for the United Nations, for on it depended their ability to draw on American production.

Command of the sea also made possible re-entry to Europe. Roosevelt had agreed to give priority to the defeat of Germany, but the mounting of an invasion of France to take the strain off the Russian armies could not in the end be managed before 1944, and this angered Stalin. When it came, the Anglo-American invasion of northern France in June 1944 was the greatest seaborne expedition in history. Mussolini had by then been overthrown by Italians and Italy had already been invaded from the south; now Germany was fighting on three fronts. Soon after the landings in Normandy, the Russians entered Poland. Going faster than their allies, it still took them until next April to reach Berlin. In the west, Allied forces had by then broken out of Italy into central Europe and from the Low Countries into northern Germany. Almost incidentally, terrible destruction had been inflicted on German cities by a great air offensive which, until the last few months of the war, exercised no decisive strategic effect. When, on 30 April, the man who had ignited this conflagration killed himself in a bunker in the ruins of Berlin, historic Europe was literally as well as figuratively in ruins.

JAPAN SURRENDERS

The war in the Far East took a little longer. At the beginning of August 1945 the Japanese government knew it must be defeated. Many of Japan's former conquests had been retrieved, her cities were devastated by American bombing, and her sea power, on which communications and safety from invasion rested, was in ruins. At this moment two nuclear weapons of a destructive power hitherto unapproached were dropped with terrible effect on two Japanese cities by the Americans. Between the explosions, the Russians declared war on Japan. On 2 September the Japanese government abandoned its plan of a suicidal last-ditch stand and signed an instrument of surrender. The Second World War had come to an end.

THE HORRORS OF NAZISM REVEALED

In the immediate aftermath of the war it was difficult to measure the colossal extent of what happened. Only one clear and unambiguous good was at once visible, the overthrow of the Nazi régime. As the Allied armies advanced into Europe, the deepest evils of a system of terror and torture were revealed by the opening of the huge prison camps and the revelations of what went on in them. It was suddenly apparent that Churchill had spoken no more than the bare truth when he told his countrymen that "if we fail, then the whole world, including the United States, including all that we have known and cared for, will sink into the abyss of a new Dark Age made more sinister, and perhaps more protracted, by the lights of perverted science". The reality of this threat could first be seen in Belsen and Buchenwald. Distinctions could hardly be meaningful between degrees of atrocity inflicted on political prisoners, slave labourers from other countries, or some prisoners of war. But the world's imagination was most struck by the belated recognition of the systematic attempt which had been made to wipe out European Jewry, the so-called "Final Solution" sought by Germans, an attempt which was carried far enough to

change the demographic map: the Polish Jews were almost obliterated, and Dutch Jews, too, suffered terribly in proportion to their numbers. Overall, though complete figures may never be available, it is probable that between five and six million Jews were killed, whether in the gas chambers and crematoria of the extermination camps, by shootings and extermination on the spot in east and southeast Europe, or by overwork and hunger.

THE MEANING OF VICTORY

FEW PEOPLE AND NO NATIONS had engaged in the war because they saw it as a struggle against such wickedness. It cannot be doubted, though, that many of them were heartened as it proceeded by the sense that the conflict had a moral dimension. Propaganda contributed to this. Even while Great Britain was the only nation in Europe still on her feet and fighting for her survival, a democratic society had sought to see in the struggle positive ends which went beyond survival and beyond the destruction of

The American soldiers who liberated the Nazis' Buchenwald concentration camp in 1945 were horrified to discover piles of unburied corpses and crude huts packed with starving prisoners. Millions of Jews and other "undesirables" had been forced into slave labour, used as the subjects of macabre medical experiments or simply sent to the gas chambers in death camps such as this.

On 13–15 February 1943, 800 Allied planes dropped more than 3,500 tons of bombs on the German city of Dresden, seen here after the attacks. In those raids, and in others that followed over the next two months, thousands of civilians were killed and the city's unique Baroque architecture was destroyed. Militarily, the Allied attack achieved little.

Nazism. Aspirations to a new world of cooperation between great powers and social and economic reconstruction were embodied in the Atlantic Charter and United Nations. They were encouraged by sentimental goodwill towards allies and a tragic blurring of differences of interest and social ideals which were only too quickly to re-emerge. Much wartime rhetoric boomeranged badly with the coming of peace; disillusionment followed inspection of the world after the guns were silent. Yet for all this, the war of 1939–45 in Europe remains a moral struggle in a way, perhaps, in which no other war between great powers has ever been. It is important to remember this. Too much has been heard of the regrettable consequences of Allied victory, and it is too easily forgotten that it crushed the worst challenge to liberal civilization that has ever arisen.

A SHATTERED EUROPE

Some far-sighted observers could see a deep irony in the anti-liberal nature of the Nazi régime. In many ways, Germany had been one of the most progressive countries in Europe; the embodiment of much that was best in its civilization. That Germany should fall prey to collective derangement on this scale suggested that something had been wrong at the root of that civilization itself. The crimes of Nazism had been carried out not in a fit of barbaric intoxication with conquest, but in a systematic, scientific, controlled, bureaucratic (though often inefficient) way about which there was little that was irrational except the appalling end which it sought. In this respect the Asian war was importantly different. Japanese imperialism replaced the old Western imperialisms for a time, but many among the subject peoples did not much regret the change. Propaganda during the war attempted to give currency to the notion of a "fascist" Japan, but this was a distortion of so traditional a society's character. No such appalling consequences as faced European nations under German rule would have followed from a Japanese victory.

The second obvious result of the war was its unparalleled destructiveness. It was most visible in the devastated cities of Germany and Japan, where mass aerial bombing, one of the major innovations of the Second World War, proved much more costly to life and buildings than had been the bombing of Spanish cities in the Spanish Civil War. Yet even those early essays had been enough to convince many observers that bombing alone could bring a country to its knees. In fact, although often invaluable in combination with other forms of fighting, the huge strategic bombing offensive against Germany, built up by the British Royal Air Force from tiny beginnings in 1940, and steadily supplemented by the United States Air Force from 1942 onwards, up to the point at which their combined forces could provide a target with continuous day and night bombing, achieved very little until the last few months of the war. Nor was the fiery destruction of the Japanese cities strategically so important as the elimination of its sea power.

EAST AND WEST

Not only cities had been shattered. The economic life and communications of Central Europe had also been grievously stricken. In 1945, millions of refugees were wandering about in it, trying to get home. There was a grave danger of famine and epidemic because of the difficulty of supplying food. The tremendous problems of 1918 were upon Europe again, and this time confronted nations demoralized by defeat and occupation; only the neutrals and Great Britain had escaped those scourges. There were abundant arms in private hands, and some feared revo-

lution. These conditions could also be found in Asia, but there the physical destruction was less severe and prospects of recovery better.

In Europe, too, the revolutionary political impact of the war was obvious. The power structure, which had been a reality until 1914 and had an illusory prolongation of life between the two world wars, was doomed in 1941. Two great peripheral powers dominated Europe politically and were established militarily in its heart. This was evident at a meeting of the Allied leaders at Yalta in February 1945 at which Roosevelt secretly agreed with Stalin on the terms on which the USSR would enter the war against Japan. Yalta also provided a basis for agreement between all three great powers which was to be the nearest thing to a formal peace settlement for Europe achieved for decades. Its

The "Big Three", Churchill (left), an ailing Roosevelt (centre) and Stalin (right), pose for the camera during the Yalta Conference on 9 February 1945.

The Yalta Conference

"The United Kingdom, the United States of America and the Union of Soviet Socialist Republics shall possess supreme authority with respect to Germany. In the exercise of such authority they will take such steps, including the complete disarmament, demilitarization and the dismemberment of Germany as they deem requisite for future peace and security."

An extract from "The Dismemberment of Germany", amended Article 12 (a) of the *Surrender Terms for Germany*, Yalta Conference, 11–14 February, 1945.

outcome was that old central Europe would disappear. Europe would be divided into eastern and western halves. Once again a Trieste–Baltic line became a reality, but now new differences were to be layered on top of old. At the end of 1945 there lay to the east a Europe of states which, with the exception of Greece, all had communist governments or governments in which communists shared power with others. The Russian army which had overrun them had proved itself a far better instrument for the extension of international communism than revolution had ever been. The pre-war Baltic republics did not emerge from the Soviet state, of course, and the Soviet Union now also absorbed parts of pre-war Poland and Romania.

THE NEW BALANCE OF THE WORLD ECONOMY

Germany, the centre of the old European power structure, had effectively ceased to exist. A phase of European history which she had dominated was at an end, and Bismarck's creation was partitioned into zones occupied by the Russians, Americans, British and French. The other major political units of western Europe had reconstituted themselves after occupation and defeat, but were feeble; Italy, which had changed sides after Mussolini had been overthrown, had, like France, a much strengthened and enlarged Communist Party which, it could not be forgotten, was still committed to the revolutionary overthrow of capitalism. Only Great Britain retained its stature of 1939 in the world's eyes; it was even briefly enhanced by its stand in 1940 and 1941, and remained for a while the recognized equal of Russia and the United States. (Formally, this was true of France and China, too, but less attention was paid to them.) Yet Great Britain's moment was past. By a huge effort of mobilizing its resources and social life to a degree unequalled outside Stalin's Russia, the country had been able to retain its standing. But it had been let out of a strategic impasse only by the German attack on Russia, and kept afloat only by American Lend-Lease. And this aid had not been without its costs: the Americans had insisted on the sale of British overseas assets to meet the bills before it was forthcoming. Moreover, the sterling area was dislocated. American capital was now to move into the old dominions on a large scale. Those countries had learnt new lessons both from their new wartime strength and, paradoxically, from their weakness in so far as they had relied upon the mother country for their defence. From 1945, they more and more acted with full as well as formal independence.

THE END OF AN ERA

It only took a few years for this huge change in the position of the greatest of the old

The British army's "Desert Rats", who had fought in North Africa during the war, parade through Berlin in July 1945 after the Allied victory.

imperial powers to become clear. Symbolically, when Great Britain made its last great military effort in Europe, in 1944, the expedition was commanded by an American general. Though British forces in Europe for a few months afterwards matched the Americans, they were by the end of the war outnumbered. In the Far East, too, although the British reconquered Burma, the defeat of Japan was the work of American naval and air power. For all Churchill's efforts, Roosevelt was by the end of the war negotiating over his head with Stalin, proposing *inter alia* the dismantling of the British Empire. Great Britain, in spite of its victorious stand alone in 1940 and the moral prestige this gave it, had not escaped the shattering impact of the war on Europe's political structure. Indeed, it was in some ways the power which, with Germany, illustrated it best.

Thus was registered in Europe the passing of the European supremacy also evident at its periphery. In the last and only briefly successful attempt by a British government to thwart American policy, British forces secured Dutch and French territories in Asia just in time to hand them back to their former overlords and prevent the seizure of power by anti-colonial régimes. But fighting with rebels began almost immediately and it was clear that the imperial powers faced a difficult future. The war had brought revolution to the empires, too. Subtly and suddenly, the kaleidoscope of authority had shifted, and it was still shifting as the war came to an end. The year 1945 is not, therefore, a good place at which to pause; reality was then still masked somewhat by appearance. Many Europeans still had to discover, painfully, that the European age of empire was over.

4 *THE SHAPING OF A NEW WORLD*

This aerial view of the United Nations headquarters in New York City was taken in 1950, when the organization symbolized post-war hopes for lasting peace.

such a thing. This was one healthy contrast between the circumstances of the two great attempts of this century to reorder international life. Neither, of course, could start with a clean sheet on which to plan. Events had closed off many roads, and crucial decisions had already been taken, some by agreement, some not, about what should follow victory. One of the most important of the Second World War had been that, once more, an international organization should be set up to maintain international peace. The fact that the great powers saw such an organization in different ways, the Americans as a beginning to the regulation of international life by law and the Russians as a means of maintaining the Grand Alliance, did not prevent them pressing forward. So the United Nations Organization (UNO) came into being at San Francisco in 1945.

THE UNITED NATIONS

Much thought, naturally, had been given to the failure of the League of Nations to come up to expectations. One of its defects was remedied in 1945: the United States and Russia belonged to the new organization from the start. Apart from this, the

After the first world war, it had still been possible to embrace the illusion that an old order might be restored. In 1945, no one in authority could believe

Time chart (1945–1948)		
	1945 The Yalta and Potsdam conferences Surrender of Germany and Japan Proclamation of independence in Vietnam	1948 Gandhi is assassinated Birth of the state of Israel First Arab-Israeli war
1900		1950
	1946 Definitive phase of the civil war in China begins	1947 Independence of India and Pakistan The Marshall Plan is drawn up

The United Nations

At the meetings of the world powers held at Dumbarton Oaks mansion in Washington, DC, in 1944 and in Yalta in 1945, it was agreed that an international organization should be set up in order to help maintain world balance and peace. The 51 states that signed the San Francisco Charter in 1945 made up the first General Assembly of the United Nations Organization. Its inaugural session was held in two parts: in London in February 1946 and in New York in November and December of the same year.

The UN is made up of the General Assembly, the Security Council, the Economic and Social Council, the Secretariat General, the International Tribunal of Justice and other subsidiary organizations, comprising a busy network of commissions, conferences, committees and other specialized groups. The General Assembly is made up of representatives of all the member countries and is the UN's highest deliberative organ. It is a kind of world parliament – a forum for debate and recommendation – which also encourages research into methods of improving international cooperation on a political level. The Security Council has five permanent members with the right to veto out of a total of fifteen. Its jurisdiction is limited to peace-keeping and matters of international security. The Economic and Social Council is a consultative body that depends on the General Assembly, whose mission is to prepare reports and research on economic, social, cultural, educational and other matters. The General Assembly also has the capacity to convoke international conferences on matters under its jurisdiction.

A representative of the Netherlands addresses one of the committees at the San Francisco Conference of 1945.

The International Tribunal is based in The Hague; the magistrates who sit on it are elected independently of their nationality. Its main tasks are to provide voluntary arbitration between countries in conflict and to consult on issues of international law.

basic structure of the United Nations resembled that of the League in outline. Its two essential organs were a small Council and a large Assembly. Permanent representatives of all member states were to sit in the General Assembly. The Security Council had at first eleven members, of whom five were permanent; these were the representatives of the United States, the USSR, Great Britain, France (at the insistence of Winston Churchill) and China. The Security Council was given greater power than the old League Council and this was largely the doing of the Russians. They believed that there was a strong likelihood that they would always be outvoted in the General Assembly – where, at first, fifty-one nations were represented – because the United States could rely not only on the votes of its allies, but also on those of its Latin American satellites. Naturally, not all the smaller powers liked this. They were uneasy about a body on which at any one moment any of them was likely not to have a seat, which would have the last word and in which the great powers would carry the main weight. Nevertheless, the structure the great powers wanted was adopted, as, indeed, it had to be if any organization was to work at all.

A NEW ERA IN INTERNATIONAL POLITICS

The other main issue which caused grave constitutional dispute when the UN was founded was the veto power given to the permanent members of the Security Council. This was a necessary feature if the great powers were to accept the organization, though in the end the veto was restricted somewhat, in that a permanent member could not prevent investigation and discussion of matters which especially affected it, unless they were likely to lead to action inimical to its interests.

In theory the Security Council possessed very great powers, but, of course, their operation was bound to reflect political reality. In its first decades, the importance of the United Nations proved to lie not in its power to act, but rather in the forum it provided for discussion. For the first time, a world public linked as never before by radio and film – and later, by television – would have to be presented with a case made at the General Assembly for

A 1990 session of the United Nations Security Council is pictured.

what sovereign states did. This was something quite new. The United Nations at once gave a new dimension to international politics; it took much longer to provide effective new instrumentation for dealing with its problems. Sometimes, the new publicity of international argument led to feelings of sterility, as increasingly bitter and unyielding views were set out in debates which changed no one's mind. But an educational force was at work. It was important, too, that it was soon decided that the permanent seat of the General Assembly should be in New York; this drew American attention to it and helped to offset the historic pull of isolationism.

In 1946, in London, the United Nations General Assembly met for the first time. At once, bitter debates began; complaints were made about the continued presence of Russian soldiers in Iranian Azerbaijan, occupied during the war, and the Russians promptly replied by attacking Great Britain for keeping forces in Greece. Within a few days the first veto was cast, by the Soviet delegation. There were to be many more. The instrument which the Americans and British had regarded and continued to use as an extraordinary measure for the protection of special interests became a familiar piece of Soviet diplomatic technique. Already in 1946 the United Nations was an arena in which the USSR contended with a still inchoate Western bloc, which its policies were to do much to solidify.

RUSSIAN AND AMERICAN POWER

THOUGH THE ORIGINS OF CONFLICT between the United States and Russia are often traced back a very long way, in the later years of the war the British government had tended to feel that the Americans made too many concessions and were over-friendly to the

Soviet Union. Of course, there was always a fundamental ideological division; if the Russians had not always had a deep preconception about the roots of behaviour of capitalist societies, they would certainly have behaved differently after 1945 towards their wartime ally. It is also true that some Americans never ceased to distrust Russia and saw her as a revolutionary threat. But this did not mean that they had much impact on the making of American policy. In 1945, when the war ended, American distrust of Russian intentions was much less than it later became. Of the two states the more suspicious and wary was the Soviet Union.

At that moment, there were no other true great powers left. The war had catalysed the realization of Tocqueville's intuition a century before, that between them America and Russia would one day dominate the world. For all the legal fictions expressed in the composition of the Security Council, Great Britain was gravely overstrained, France barely risen from the living death of occupation and stricken by internal divisions (a large Communist Party threatened its stability), while Italy had discovered new quarrels to add to old ones. Germany was in ruins and under occupation. Japan was occupied and militarily powerless, while China had never yet been a great power in modern times. The Americans and Russians therefore enjoyed an immense superiority over all possible rivals. They were the only real victors. They alone had made positive gains from the war. All the other victorious states had, at the most, won survival or resurrection. To the United States and the USSR, the war brought new empires.

THE SOVIET UNION IN 1945

Though the empire of the Soviet Union had been won at huge cost, it now had greater

After two months of meetings, held in San Francisco in 1945, the United Nations Charter was passed unanimously and signed by all the representatives. Here the Earl of Halifax, the United Kingdom's ambassador to the United States, is pictured signing the charter during a ceremony held at the Veterans' War Memorial Building on 26 June 1945.

The USA and the post-war global economy

When the Second World War ended, American objectives were focused on creating a globally integrated world economy around the nucleus that its own national economy was to become. This was a logical position for the US government to adopt – the United States then possessed 59 per cent of the world's oil reserves and produced 46 per cent of world industrial production at a time when most of the world depended on American aid in order to survive the shortages of food, coal, machinery and manufactured goods.

strength than it had ever known under the tsars. Her armies dominated a vast European glacis, much of which was sovereign Soviet territory; the rest was organized in states, which were by 1948 in every sense satellites, and one of them was East Germany, a major industrial entity. Beyond the glacis lay Yugoslavia and Albania, the only communist states to emerge since the war without the help of Russian occupation; in 1945 both seemed assured allies of Moscow. This advantageous Soviet position had been won by the fighting of the Red Army, but it also owed much to decisions taken by Western governments and to their commander in Europe during the closing stages of the war, when General Eisenhower had resisted pressure to get to Prague and Berlin before the Russians. The resulting Soviet strategical preponderance in central Europe was all the more menacing because the old traditional barriers to Russian power had gone: in 1914 the Habsburg empire, and now a united Germany. An exhausted Great Britain and

slowly reviving France could not be expected to stand up to the Red Army, and no other conceivable counterweight on land existed if the Americans went home.

Soviet armies also stood in 1945 on the borders of Turkey and Greece – where a communist rising was under way – and occupied northern Iran. In the Far East they had held much of Sinkiang, Mongolia, northern Korea and the naval base of Port Arthur as well as occupying the rest of Manchuria, though the only territory they actually took from Japan was the southern half of the island of Sakhalin and the Kuriles. The rest of their gains had been effectively at China's expense. Yet in China there was already visible at the end of the war the outline of a new communist state which could be expected to be friendly to Moscow. Stalin might have backed the wrong horse there in the past, but the Chinese communists could not hope for moral and material help from anyone else. So it seemed that in Asia, too, a Soviet satellite might be in the making. There was no reason to think that the Soviet leadership had forgotten old Russia's ambition to be a Pacific power.

THE UNITED STATES IN 1945

The new world power of the United States rested much less on occupation of territory than that of the USSR. It, too, had at the end of the war a garrison in the heart of Europe, but American electors in 1945 wanted it brought home as soon as possible. American naval and air bases around much of the Eurasian land mass were another matter. Although Russia was a far greater Asian power than ever, the elimination of Japanese naval power, the acquisition of island airfields and technological changes, which made huge fleet trains possible had together turned the Pacific Ocean into an American lake. Above all, Hiroshima and Nagasaki had demonstrated the power of the new weapon which the United States alone possessed, the atomic bomb. But the deepest roots of American empire lay in its economic strength. Apart from the Red Army, the overwhelming industrial power of the United States had been the decisive material factor behind the Allied victory. America had equipped not only its own huge forces but many of those of its allies. Moreover, by comparison with them, victory had cost it little. American casualties were fewer than theirs; even those of the United Kingdom were heavier and those of Russia colossally so. The home base of the United States had been immune to enemy attack in any but a trivial sense and was undamaged; its fixed capital was intact, its resources greater than ever. Its citizens had seen their standard of living actually rise during the war; the armament programme ended a depression which had not been mastered by Roosevelt's New Deal. America was a great creditor country, with capital to invest abroad in a world where no one else could supply it. Finally, its old commercial and political rivals were staggering under the troubles of recovery. Their economies drifted into the ambit of America because of their own lack of resources. The result was a worldwide surge of indirect American power, its beginnings visible even before the war ended.

SOVIET–AMERICAN RELATIONS

Something of the future implicit in the great power polarization could dimly be seen before the fighting stopped in Europe. It was made clear, for example, that the Russians would not be allowed to participate in the occupation of Italy or the dismantling of its colonial empire, and that the British and Americans could not hope for a Polish settlement other than one wanted by Stalin. Yet (in spite of their record in their own hemisphere)

The photograph shows the remains of Hiroshima after the atom bomb explosion of 6 August 1945. Hundreds of thousands of people died in the Japanese city on that day and in the weeks, months and years that followed, from the effects of the blast. Horrified as the Americans were by the terrible destruction that had been wrought by the bomb, they also believed that its deployment had been necessary to bring a swift end to the war.

the Americans were not happy about explicit spheres of influence; the Russians were readier to take them as a working basis. There is no need to read back into such divergences assumptions which became current a few years after the war, when conflict between the two powers was presumed to have been sought from the start by one or other of them. Appearances can be deceptive. For all the power of the United States in 1945, there was little political will to use it; the first concern of the American military after victory was to achieve as rapid a demobilization as possible. Lend-Lease arrangements with allies had already been cut off even before the Japanese surrender. This further reduced America's indirect international leverage; it simply weakened friends it would soon be needing who now faced grave recovery problems. They could not provide a new security system to replace American strength. Nor could the use of the atomic bomb be envisaged except in the last resort; it was too powerful.

THE USSR ACQUIRES NUCLEAR WEAPONS

It is difficult to be sure of what was going on in Stalin's Russia after the war. Its peoples had clearly suffered appallingly from the conflict, more, certainly, than even the Germans. No one has been able to do more than provide estimates, but it seems likely that over twenty million Soviet citizens may have died. Stalin may well have been less aware of Soviet strength than of Soviet weakness when the war ended. True, his governmental methods relieved him of any need, such as faced Western countries, to demobilize the huge land forces which gave him supremacy on the spot in Europe. But the USSR had no atomic bomb nor a significant strategic bomber force, and Stalin's decision to develop nuclear weapons put a further grave strain on the Soviet economy at a time when general economic reconstruction was desperately needed. The years immediately after the war were to prove

Russian refugees return to their home town in 1944 to find that their house has been obliterated by German bombers.

as grim as had been those of the industrialization race of the 1930s. Yet in September 1949 an atomic explosion was achieved. In the following March it was officially announced that the USSR had an atomic weapon. By then much had changed.

THE DEVASTATED EUROPEAN ARENA

Piecemeal, relations between the two major world powers had deteriorated very badly by 1949. This was largely the result of what happened in Europe, the area most in need of imaginative and coordinated reconstruction in 1945. The cost of the war's destruction there has never been accurately measured. Leaving out the Russians, about fourteen and a quarter million Europeans were dead. In the most-stricken countries those who survived lived amid ruins. One estimate is that about seven and a half million dwellings were destroyed in Germany and Russia. Factories and communications were shattered. There was nothing with which to pay for the imports Europe needed and currencies had collapsed; Allied occupation forces found that cigarettes and bully-beef were better than money. Civilized society had given way not only under the horrors of Nazi warfare, but also because occupation had transformed lying, swindling, cheating and stealing into acts of virtue; they were not only necessary to survival, but they could be glorified as acts of "resistance". The struggles against German occupying forces had bred new divisions; as countries were liberated by the advancing Allied armies, the firing squads got to work in their wake and old scores were wiped out. It was said that in France more perished in the "purification" of liberation than in the great Terror of 1793.

Above all, more finally than in 1918, the economic structure of Europe had disintegrated. The flywheel of much of European economic life had once been industrial Germany. But even if the communications and the productive capacity to restore the machine had been there, the Allies were at first bent on holding down German industrial production to prevent its recovery. Furthermore, Germany was divided. From the start the Russians had been carrying off capital equipment as "reparations" to repair their own ravaged lands – as well they might; the Germans had destroyed 39,000 miles of railway track alone in their retreat in Russia. The Soviet Union may have lost a quarter of its gross capital equipment.

THE EAST–WEST DIVIDE

A POLITICAL DIVISION between eastern and western Europe was coming to be evident before the end of the war. The British, in particular, had been alarmed by what happened to Poland. It seemed to show that the Soviet Union would only tolerate governments in eastern Europe which were subservient. This was hardly what the Americans had envisaged as freedom for eastern Europeans to choose their own rulers, but until the war was over neither government nor public in the United States was much concerned or much doubted they could come to reasonable agreement with the Russians. Broadly speaking, Roosevelt had been sure that America could get on with the Soviet Union; they had common ground in resisting a revival of German power and undermining the old colonial empires. Neither he nor the American public showed any awareness of the historic tendencies of

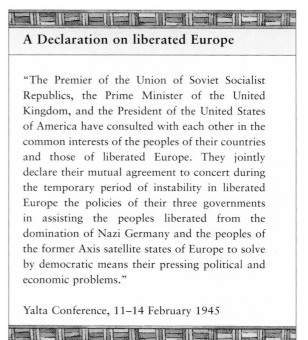

A Declaration on liberated Europe

"The Premier of the Union of Soviet Socialist Republics, the Prime Minister of the United Kingdom, and the President of the United States of America have consulted with each other in the common interests of the peoples of their countries and those of liberated Europe. They jointly declare their mutual agreement to concert during the temporary period of instability in liberated Europe the policies of their three governments in assisting the peoples liberated from the domination of Nazi Germany and the peoples of the former Axis satellite states of Europe to solve by democratic means their pressing political and economic problems."

Yalta Conference, 11–14 February 1945

Russian policy. They disapproved strongly of British forces in Greece fighting the communists who sought to overthrow the monarchy after the German withdrawal. (Stalin did not object: he agreed with Churchill that Great Britain should have a virtually free hand in Greece in return for having one himself in Romania.)

A DIVIDED GERMANY

President Truman (who succeeded Roosevelt on his death in April 1945) and his advisers came to change American policies largely as a result of their experience in Germany. The Russians were punctilious in carrying out their agreement to admit British and American (and later French) armed forces to Berlin and share the administration of the city they had conquered. There is every indication that they wished Germany to be governed as a unit (as envisaged by the victors at Potsdam in July 1945), for this would give them a hand in controlling the Ruhr, potentially a treasure-

From November 1944, Germany was divided into four sectors, ruled by France, Britain, the United States and the Soviet Union. This scene from occupied Berlin gives an impression of the ruined condition of the city at the end of the war.

house of reparations. Yet the German economy soon bred friction between West and East. Russian efforts to ensure security against German recovery led to the increasing practical separation of its zone of occupation from those of the three other occupying powers. Probably this was at first intended to provide a solid and reliable (that is, communist) core for a united Germany, but it led in the end to a solution by partition to the German problem which no one had envisaged. First, the western zones of occupation were for economic reasons integrated, without the eastern zone. Meanwhile Soviet occupation policy aroused increasing distrust. The entrenchment of communism in the Soviet zone of Germany seemed to repeat a pattern seen elsewhere. In 1945 there had been communist majorities only in Bulgaria and Yugoslavia, and in other East European countries the communists only shared power in coalition governments. None the less, it increasingly looked as if those governments could, in fact, do little more than behave as Russian puppets. Something like a bloc was already appearing in eastern Europe in 1946.

POST-WAR SOVIET FOREIGN POLICY

Stalin obviously feared any use of Germany's military and industrial potential against the Soviet Union. One of his main preoccupations after the war was to prevent the United States from eventually controlling all of Germany and, if possible, even to decrease American domination of the western part of the country. While Russia had too many memories of attacks from the west to trust a united Germany, it was the threat from a combination of the Western powers and the most developed part of Germany that Stalin really feared. Elsewhere, though, Soviet policy showed more flexibility. While anxiously organizing eastern Germany on the Russian side of a line slowly appearing across Europe, in China it was still officially supporting the KMT. In Iran, on the other hand, there was an obvious reluctance to withdraw Soviet forces as had been agreed. Even when they finally departed they left behind a satellite communist republic in Azerbaijan – to be later obliterated by the Iranians, to whom, by 1947, the Americans were giving military aid.

In the Security Council the Soviet veto was more and more employed to frustrate its former allies and it was clear that the communist parties of western Europe were manipulated in Russian interests. Yet Stalin's calculations remain in doubt; perhaps he was waiting, expecting or even relying upon economic collapse in the capitalist world.

AN IRON CURTAIN

There had been and still was much goodwill for the USSR among its former allies. When Winston Churchill drew attention in 1946 to the increasing division of Europe by an "iron curtain" he by no means spoke either for all his countrymen or for his American audience; some condemned him. Yet although the British Labour Government elected in 1945 was at first hopeful that "Left could speak to Left", it quickly became more sceptical.

British and American policy began to converge during 1946, as it became clear that the British intervention in Greece had in fact made possible free elections and as American officials had more experience of the tendency of Soviet policy. Nor did President Truman have any prejudices in favour of Russia to shed. The British, moreover, were by now clearly embarked upon a deliberate policy of leaving India; that counted with American official opinion.

THE TRUMAN DOCTRINE

In February 1947 a communication from the British government reached Truman which, perhaps more than any other, conceded the long-resisted admission that Great Britain was no longer a world power. The British economy had been gravely damaged by the huge efforts made during the war; there was

The Marshall Plan

On 5 June 1947 the US secretary of state, General George Marshall, declared that it was imperative for the European countries to draw up a plan for economic recovery, which the United States would whole-heartedly support.

Although the Soviet Union and its satellites refused to participate in the plan, Austria, Belgium, Denmark, France, Great Britain, Greece, Iceland, Ireland, Italy, Luxembourg, the Netherlands, Norway, Portugal, Sweden, Switzerland and Turkey reacted favourably to the scheme. The Organization for European Economic Cooperation was set up to put the Marshall Plan into practice. It took from 15 September 1947 to 1 April 1948 to set up the European Reconstruction Programme, as the Marshall Plan was officially called.

George Marshall (1880–1959) was awarded the Nobel peace prize in 1953.

urgent need for investment at home. The first stages of decolonialization, too, were expensive. One outcome was that by 1947 the British balance of payments could only be maintained if forces were withdrawn from Greece. President Truman decided at once that the United States must fill the gap. It was a momentous decision. Financial aid was to be given to Greece and Turkey, to enable them to survive the pressure they were under from Russia. He deliberately drew attention to the implication; much more than propping up two countries was involved. Although only Turkey and Greece were to receive aid, he deliberately offered the "free peoples" of the world American leadership to resist, with American support, "attempted subjugation by armed minorities or by outside pressures". This was a reversal of the apparent return to isolation from Europe which the United States had seemed to pursue in 1945, and an enormous break with the historic traditions of American foreign policy. The decision to "contain", as it was called, Soviet power was possibly the most important in American diplomacy since the Louisiana Purchase. It was provoked by Russian behaviour and the growing fears Stalin's policy had aroused over the previous eighteen months as well as by British weakness. Ultimately, it was to lead to unrealistic assessments of the effective limits of American power, and, critics were to say, to a new American imperialism, as the policy was extended outside Europe, but this could not be seen at the time.

THE MARSHALL PLAN

A few months after the president's offer of support to the "free peoples" of the world, the "Truman Doctrine" was completed by another and more pondered step, an offer of American economic aid to European nations,

which would come together to plan jointly their economic recovery. This was the Marshall Plan, named after the American secretary of state who announced it. Its aim was a non-military, unaggressive form of checking communism. It surprised everyone. The British foreign secretary, Ernest Bevin, was the first European statesman to grasp its implications. With the French, he pressed for the acceptance of the offer by western Europe. It was made, of course, to all European nations. But the Russians would not participate, nor did they allow their satellites to do so. Instead, they bitterly attacked the plan. When, with obvious regret, the Czechoslovakian coalition government also declined to adhere, that country, the only one in eastern Europe still without a fully communist government and not regarded as a Russian satellite, was visibly regretful in having to toe the Soviet line. Any residual belief in Czechoslovakia's independence was removed by a communist coup, which replaced the government, in February 1948. Another sign of Russian intransigence was an old pre-war propaganda device, the

Armed workers' units march across Prague's Charles Bridge in 1948 in a show of force which ended in a mass demonstration in support of communism. The communist coup had been carefully prepared, with Czechoslovakia's administration, police and army neutralized in advance. The president, desperate to avoid a civil war, accepted the formation of a communist government.

Comintern, revived as the Cominform in September 1947. It at once began the denunciation of what it termed a "frankly predatory and expansionist course ... to establish the world supremacy of American imperialism". Finally, when western Europe set up an Organization for European Economic Cooperation to handle the Marshall Plan, the Russians replied by organizing their own half of Europe in Comecon, a Council for Mutual Economic Assistance, which was window-dressing for the Soviet integration of the command economies of the East.

THE ADVENT OF THE COLD WAR

B Y 1947, THE COLD WAR (as it came to be called) had begun. The first phase of Europe's post-war history was over. The next, a phase in global history, too, was to continue well into the 1960s. In it, two groups of states, one led by the United States and one by Soviet Russia, strove throughout a succession of crises to achieve their own security by all means short of war between the principal contenders. Much of what was said was put into ideological terms. In some countries of what came to be a Western bloc, the Cold War therefore also appeared as civil war or near-war, and as moral debate about values such as freedom, social justice and individualism. Some of it was fought in marginal theatres by propaganda and subversion or by guerrilla movements sponsored by the two great states. Fortunately, they always stopped short of the point at which they would have to fight with nuclear weapons whose increasing power made the notion of a successful outcome more and more unrealistic. The Cold War was also an economic competition by example and by offers of aid to satellites and uncommitted nations. Inevitably, in the

O n 23 October 1956 an uprising against the communist régime took place in Budapest. A dissident who had been expelled from Hungary's Communist Party claimed to head the new government, demanding the withdrawal of the Russian troops from the city and the dismantling of the Warsaw Pact. The Soviet Union reacted swiftly: Russian tanks, seen in this photograph, were sent in to Budapest and the rebellion was quashed within 24 hours.

process much opportunism got mixed up with doctrinaire rigidity. Probably it was unavoidable, but it was a blight which left little of the world untouched, and a seeping source of crime, corruption and suffering for more than thirty years.

THE EFFECTS OF THE COLD WAR

In retrospect, for all the simple brutalities of the language it generated, the Cold War now looks somewhat like the complex struggles of religion in sixteenth- and seventeenth-century Europe, when ideology could provoke violence, passion, and even, at times, mobilize conviction, but could never wholly accommodate the complexities and cross currents of the day. Above all, it could not contain those introduced by national interest. Like the religious struggles of the past, too, though, there was soon every sign that although specific quarrels might die down and disaster be avoided, its rhetoric and mythology could go rolling on long after they ceased to reflect reality.

The first important complication to cut across the Cold War was the emergence of a growing number of new states which showed no firm commitment to one side or the other. Many new nations came into existence within a decade of 1945 as a result of decolonization.

In some parts of the world this caused as much upheaval as the Cold War itself. The United Nations General Assembly mattered more as a platform for anti-colonial than for Cold War propaganda (though they were often confused). Short-lived though European empire had been as a phenomenon of world history, its passing was an immensely complicated phenomenon. Every colony and every colonial power was a special case, for all the generalized rhetoric. In some places – particularly in parts of sub-Saharan Africa – the processes of modernization had barely been

launched and colonialism left behind little on which to build. In others – French North Africa was an outstanding instance – long-established white settler populations could not be ignored by colonial government (and, indeed, Algeria was not technically a colony at all, being governed as a department of metropolitan France). In India, contrastingly, the British demographic presence was of little significance in managing the processes of granting independence. The timing of those processes, too, varied greatly within the rough distinction that European rule had in any significant measure disappeared in Asia by 1954, while Africa emerged from colonialism only in the next decade, the Portuguese hanging on to their colonies even into the 1970s. But Angola and Mozambique were exceptional in southern Africa in other ways, too; like Algeria and Indo-China, for example, they were areas of bitter warfare between the colonial state and the indigenous peasantry, whereas in other African colonies there was a relatively peaceful transfer of power to the successor élites (which were of varying numerical strength and adequacy for the task of government). In some countries – India and Indo-China were outstanding though

This Soviet Cold War propaganda cartoon, which dates from 1953, mock's "Washington's Dove" of peace. Similar anti-Soviet cartoons were common in the American press.

Japanese brutality towards prisoners of war aroused great indignation in Great Britain and the United States, where propaganda such as this was used to spur on the war effort. In the Asian colonies, administrative and economic posts left vacant by the colonists (who had been withdrawn or taken prisoner) were taken over by native local élites.

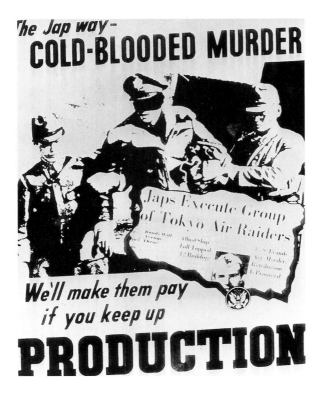

The Jap way – COLD-BLOODED MURDER

Japs Execute Group of Tokyo Air Raiders

We'll make them pay if you keep up PRODUCTION

very different examples – real nationalist sentiment and organization existed before the departure of the imperial rulers (and the British, unlike the French, had made important concessions to it), while in much of Africa nationalism was the creature and consequence of independence, rather than a cause.

POST-WAR ASIA

FOR ALL THE DIFFERENCES of circumstances, though, there was a sense in which the Asian colonial subjects of imperialism had been assured eventual success well before 1945. This was not merely a matter of concession before 1939, but was overwhelmingly a result of defeat in war; Japan had flattened the card castle of European imperialism in 1940 and 1941. It was not only a matter of the displacement of imperial power in specific colonies. The surrender of more than 60,000 British, Indian and Dominion soldiers at Singapore in 1942 was a signal that European

empire in Asia was over. It was far worse than Yorktown and, like that surrender, was irretrievable. Against that background it hardly mattered that the Japanese sometimes squandered advantages by behaving badly in their new conquests. Even their worst brutalities did not alienate all of their new subjects, and they found numerous collaborators, among them nationalist politicians. The Allies' parachute drops of arms to those they thought might resist the Japanese only made it likely that they would be used to resist the Allies' return. Furthermore, by comparison with the upheavals in Europe, which were brought about by bombing, conscription for labour, starvation, fighting and disease, in many Asian villages and in much of the countryside life went on under Japanese rule almost undisturbed. By 1945 the potential for change in Asia was immense.

Imperialism was doomed, too, because the two dominant world powers were against it, at least in the form of other people's empires. For very different reasons, the USA and USSR were committed to undermining colonialism. Long before 1939, Moscow had offered refuge and support to its opponents. The Americans had understood in a very specific sense the Atlantic Charter's declaration of the rights of nations to choose their own governments and it was only a few months after its signature that an American undersecretary of state announced that the "age of imperialism is over". Soviet and United States representatives found no difficulty in together subscribing to the UN Charter's affirmation of the ultimate goal of independence for colonial territories. Yet great power relationships do not remain unchanged. Although they were clearly enough demarcated between the Soviet Union and the United States in 1948 to remain almost unchanged for forty years, the diplomatic shape of the Far East nonetheless was to be in doubt for much longer, partly because of the emergence of new great powers, and partly because of uncertainties introduced by the disappearance of imperial rule.

INDIA

Some had always thought India would become a dominant Asian power once she was self-governing. When, before 1939, the timetable and replacement of British rule was being discussed in general terms, there were many among those Englishmen who favoured Indian independence who hoped to keep a new India linked to the British Commonwealth of Nations; this was the name officially given to the empire after the Imperial Conference of 1926. That conference had also produced the first official definition of "Dominion Status" as independent association with the Commonwealth in allegiance to the Crown, with complete independent control of internal and external affairs. This was a conceivable goal for India, many thought, though not one a British government conceded as an immediate aim until 1940. Yet though unevenly, some progress was made before this and it in part explains the absence in India of so complete a revulsion of anti-Western feeling as had occurred in China.

INDIA BETWEEN THE WARS

Indian politicians had been deeply disappointed after the First World War. They had for the most part rallied loyally to the Crown; India had made big contributions of men and money to the imperial war effort, and Gandhi, later to be seen as the father of the Indian nation, had been one of those who had worked for it in the belief that this would bring a due reward. In 1917, the British government had announced that it favoured a policy of steady progress towards responsible government for India within the empire – Home Rule, as it were – though this was short of what some Indians were beginning to ask for. Reforms introduced in 1918 were none the less very disappointing, though they satisfied some moderates, and even such limited success as they had was soon dissipated. Economics came into play as international trading conditions worsened. In the 1920s the Indian government was already supporting Indian demands to put an end to commercial and financial arrangements favouring the United Kingdom, and soon insisted on the imperial government paying a proper share of India's contribution to imperial defence. Once into the world slump, it became clear that London could no longer be allowed to settle Indian tariff policy so as to suit British industry. Whereas in 1914, Indian textile manufacture had met only a quarter of the country's needs, in 1930 that figure had become half.

In 1930, Gandhi attacked the British government's high tax and production monopoly on salt – an issue that appealed to India's poor. Gandhi is pictured here during his 240-mile march from Satarmati to the shore at Dandi, where he illegally extracted salt by boiling sea water. He was later arrested for this breach of the law.

GANDHI AND INDIAN NATIONALISM

A scene from the aftermath of Hindu–Muslim riots at Cawnpore (Kanpur), India, in 1931. On the right are the ruins of the private residence of a rich Hindu banker, demolished and looted by Muslims.

One factor then still hindering progress was the continuing isolation of the British community in India. Convinced that Indian nationalism was a matter of a few ambitious intellectuals, it pressed for strong measures against conspiracy. This also appealed to some administrators confronted with the consequences of the Bolshevik revolution (though the Indian Communist Party was not founded until 1923). The result, against the wishes of all the Indian members of the legislative council, was the suspension of normal legal safeguards for suspects. This provoked Gandhi's first campaign of strikes and pacifist civil disobedience. In spite of his efforts to avoid violence there were riots. At Amritsar in 1919, after some Englishmen had been killed and others attacked, a general foolishly decided, as an example of his countrymen's determination, to disperse a crowd by force. When the firing stopped, nearly 400 Indians had been killed and over a thousand wounded. An irreparable blow to British prestige was made worse when British residents in India and some Members of Parliament loudly applauded what had been done.

DIVISIONS BETWEEN THE NATIONALISTS

A period of boycott and civil disturbance followed the Amritsar massacre, in which Gandhi's programme was adopted by Congress. Although Gandhi himself emphasized that his campaign was non-violent there was nevertheless much disorder and he was arrested and imprisoned for the first time in 1922 (and was soon released because of the danger that he might die in prison). This was the end of significant agitation in India for the next few years.

In 1927 British policy began to move slowly forward again. A commission was sent to India to look into the working of the last series of constitutional changes (though this caused more trouble because no Indians had been included in it). Much of the enthusiasm which had sustained unity among the nationalists had by now evaporated and there was a danger of a rift bridged only by Gandhi's efforts and prestige between those who stuck to the demand for complete independence and those who wanted to work for dominion status. Congress was, in any case, not so solid a structure as its rhetoric suggested. It was less a political party with deep roots in the masses than a coalition of local bigwigs and interests. Finally, a more grievous division still was deepening between Hindu and Muslim. In the 1920s there had been communal rioting and bloodshed. By 1930 the president of the Muslim political league was proposing that the future constitutional development of India should include the establishment of a separate Muslim state in the northwest.

THE ROLE OF THE CONGRESS PARTY

It was a violent year in 1930. The British viceroy had announced that a conference was to take place with the aim of achieving dominion status, but this undertaking was made meaningless by opposition in Great Britain. Gandhi would not take part, therefore. Civil disobedience was resumed and intensified as distress deepened with the world economic depression. The rural masses were now more ready for mobilization by nationalist appeals; as the Congress movement changed to take account of mass interests, it made Gandhi the first politician to be able to claim an India-wide following.

The wheels of the India Office were by now beginning to turn as they absorbed the lessons of the discussions and the 1927 commission. A real devolution of power and patronage came in 1935, when a Government of India Act was passed which took still further the establishment of representative and responsible government, leaving in the viceroy's sole control only such matters as defence and foreign affairs. Though the

transfer of national power proposed in the Act was never wholly implemented, this was the culmination of legislation by the British. They had by now created the framework for a national politics. It was increasingly clear that at all levels the decisive struggles between Indians would be fought out within the Congress party. The 1935 Act once more affirmed the principle of separate communal representation and almost immediately its working provoked further hostility between Hindu and Muslim. Congress was by now to all intents and purposes a Hindu organization (though it refused to concede that the Muslim League should therefore be the sole representative of Muslims). But Congress had its internal problems, too. Some members still wished to press forward to independence while others – some of them beginning to be alarmed by Japanese aggressiveness – were willing to work the new institutions in cooperation with the imperial government. The evidence that the British were in fact devolving power was bound to be divisive; different interests began to seek to insure themselves against an uncertain future.

The key figures in the fight for Indian independence, Mahatma Gandhi (1869–1948) and Jawarhal Nehru (1889–1964), are seen in discussion during a meeting of the Indian Congress in Bombay in 1946.

THE BRITISH RESPONSE

The tide was thus running fast by 1941. Nearly two decades of representative institutions in local government and the progressive Indianization of the higher civil service had produced a country which could not be governed except with the substantial consent of its élites and one which had undergone a considerable preparatory education in self-government, if not democracy. Though the approach of war made the British increasingly aware of their need of the Indian army, they had already given up trying to make India pay for it and were by 1941 bearing the cost of its modernization. Then the Japanese attack forced the hand of the British government. It offered the nationalists autonomy after the war and a right of secession from the Commonwealth, but this was too late; they now demanded immediate independence. Their leaders were arrested and the British Raj continued. A rebellion in 1942 was crushed much more rapidly than had been the Mutiny nearly a century earlier, but the sands were running out if the British wanted to go peacefully. One new factor was pressure from the United States. President Roosevelt discussed confidentially with Stalin the need to prepare for Indian independence (as well as that of other parts of Asia, including French Indo-China); the involvement of the United States implied revolutionary change in other people's affairs just as in 1917.

PARTITION

In 1945 the Labour Party, which had long had the independence of India and Burma as part of its programme, came to power at Westminster. On 14 March 1946, while India was torn with Hindu–Muslim rioting and its politicians were squabbling over the future, the British government offered full independence. Nearly a year later, it put a pistol to the head of the Indians by announcing that it would hand over power not later than June 1948. The tangle of communal rivalries was cut, and the partition of the subcontinent followed, the greatest degree of governmental unity it had ever enjoyed coming to an end. On 15 August 1947 two new dominions appeared within it, Pakistan and India. The first was Muslim and was itself divided into two slabs of land at the extremities of northern India; the second was officially secular but was overwhelmingly Hindu in composition and inspiration.

Perhaps partition was inevitable. India had never been ruled directly as one entity, even by the British, and Hindu and Muslim had been increasingly divided since the Mutiny. Nevertheless, its cost was tragic. The psychic wound to many nationalists was symbolized when Gandhi was murdered by a Hindu fanatic for his part in it. Huge massacres occurred in areas where there were minorities. Something like two million people fled to where their co-religionists were in control. Almost the only clear political gain on the morrow of independence was the solution, a bloody one, of the communal problem for the immediate future. Apart from this, the assets of the new states were the goodwill (arising from very mixed motives) shown to them by great powers, the inheritance of a civil service already largely native before independence, and an important infrastructure of institutions and services. These inheritances were not, however, equally shared, with India tending to enjoy more of them than Pakistan.

POPULATION GROWTH

In spite of their advantages, the new states could not do much to deal with the subcontinent's economic and social backwardness. The worst problem was demographic. A steady rise in population had begun under British rule. Sometimes it was briefly mitigated by Malthusian disasters like the great influenza epidemic at the end of the First World War, which struck down five million Indians, or a famine in Bengal during the Second World War which carried off millions more. But in 1951 there was famine again in India, and in 1953 in Pakistan. The spectre of it lingered into the 1970s.

The subcontinent's industrialization, although it had made important strides in the twentieth century (notably in the Second World War), did not offset this danger. It could not provide new jobs and earnings fast enough for a growing population. Though the new India had most of what industry there was, her problems were graver in this respect than those of Pakistan. Outside her huge cities, most Indians were landless peasants, living in villages where, for all the

Gandhi is among the participants at the India Conference, which was held in London in 1947 and resulted in the declaration of the terms of Indian independence.

egalitarian aspirations of some of the leaders of the new republic, inequality remained as great as ever. The landlords who provided the funds for the ruling Congress Party and dominated its councils stood in the way of any land reform which could have dealt with this. In many ways, the past lay heavy on a new state proclaiming the Western ideals of democracy, nationalism, secularism and material progress, and it was to encumber the road of reform and development.

CHINA

CHINA HAD FOR A LONG TIME been engaged in fighting off a different imperialism. Success against the Japanese and completion of her long revolution was made possible by the Second World War. The political phase of this transformation began in 1941, when the Sino–Japanese War merged in a world conflict. This gave China powerful allies and a new international standing. Significantly, the last vestiges of the "unequal treaties" with

Great Britain, France and the United States were then swept away. This was more important than the military help the Allies could give; for a long time they were too busy extricating themselves from the disasters of early 1942 to do much for China. A Chinese army, indeed, came instead to help to defend Burma and the land route to China from the Japanese. Still hemmed in to the west, though supported by American aircraft, the Chinese had for a long time to hold out as best they could, in touch with their allies only by air or the Burma Road. None the less a decisive change had begun.

China had at first responded to Japanese attacks with a sense of national unity long desired but never hitherto forthcoming except, perhaps, in the May 4th Movement. In spite of friction between the communists and the nationalists, sometimes breaking out into open conflict, this unity survived, broadly speaking, until 1941. Then, the new fact that the United States was now Japan's major enemy, and would eventually destroy her, subtly began to transform the attitude of

In May 1949 in Shanghai, a Chinese policeman executes communists in the street while Nationalist régime troops look on in the background. The city was soon to fall to the communists.

the Nationalist government. It came to feel that as ultimate victory was certain, there was no point in using up men and resources in fighting the Japanese when they might be husbanded for the struggle against the Communists after the peace. Some of its members went further. Soon the KMT was fighting the communists again.

NATIONALIST AND COMMUNIST CHINA

Two Chinas were emerging. Nationalist China increasingly displayed the lethargy, self-seeking and corruption which had from the early 1930s tainted the KMT because of the nature of the support on which it drew. The régime was repressive and stifled criticism. It alienated the intellectuals. Its soldiers, sometimes badly officered and undisciplined, terrorized the peasant as much as did the Japanese. Communist China was different. In large areas they controlled (often behind the Japanese lines) a deliberate attempt was being made to ensure the support of as wide a spectrum of interests as possible by moderate but unambiguous reform and disciplined behaviour. Outright attacks on landlords were usually avoided, but peasant goodwill was cultivated by enforcing lower rents and abolishing usury. Meanwhile, Mao published a series of theoretical writings designed to prepare the new communist cadres for the task ahead. There was a need for political education as the Communist Party and the army grew steadily in numbers; when the Japanese collapsed in 1945 there were about a million Chinese communist soldiers. In many areas they had been harbouring their strength for a post-war showdown with the KMT.

The suddenness of victory was the second factor that shaped the last stage of the revolution. Huge areas of China had suddenly to be

Chiang K'ai-shek, president of the Republic of China until 1947, is pictured in front of a huge portrait of Sun Yat-sen. Chiang claimed to be Sun's natural successor.

reoccupied and reincorporated into the state. Many of them were already under communist control before 1945 and others could not possibly be reached by nationalist forces before the communists dug in there. The Americans did what they could by sending soldiers to hold some of the ports until the nationalists could take them over. In places the Japanese were told to hold on until the Chinese government could re-establish its authority. But when the final and military phase of the revolution opened, the communists held more territory than they had ever done before and held it in the main with the support of a population who had found that communist rule was by no means as bad as they had heard.

THE DEMISE OF THE KMT

Albeit unwittingly, the Japanese, by launching their attack on the KMT régime, had in the end brought about the very triumph of the Chinese Revolution they had long striven to avoid. It is at least possible that if the nationalists had been undistracted by foreign invasion and had not suffered the crippling damage it inflicted, they might have been able to master Chinese communism in the short run. In 1937 the KMT could still draw heavily on patriotic goodwill; many Chinese believed that it was the authentic carrier of the revolution. The war destroyed the chance of exploiting this, if it were true, but also enabled China to resume at last its long march towards world power from which it had been deflected first by Europeans and then by fellow Asians. The long frustration of Chinese Nationalism was about to end, and the beneficiaries would be the communists.

The defeat of the KMT in the civil war took three years. Although the Japanese usually sought to surrender to the KMT or Americans, the communists had acquired authority in new areas and with it large stocks of arms. The Russians, who had invaded Manchuria in the last days before the Japanese surrender, gave them access to the arms there. Mao made deliberately moderate policy pronouncements and continued to push forward with land reform. This conferred a further advantage on the communists in the civil war which continued until 1949; victory in that was essentially a victory of the countryside over a city-based régime.

Chinese communist troops advance to liberate the people of the province of Guanxi from the Japanese at the end of the Second World War.

THE PEOPLE'S REPUBLIC OF CHINA

American policy was increasingly disillusioned by the revealed inadequacy and corruption of the Chiang K'ai-shek government. In 1947 American forces were withdrawn from China and the United States abandoned the efforts it had hitherto made to mediate between the two Chinas. In the following year, with most of the north in communist hands, the Americans began to cut down the amount of financial and military aid given to the KMT. From this time on, the nationalist government ran militarily and politically downhill; as this became obvious, more and more employees of government and local authorities sought to make terms with the communists while they might still do so. The conviction spread that a new era was dawning. By the beginning of December, no important nationalist military force remained intact on the mainland and Chiang withdrew to Formosa (Taiwan). The Americans cut off their aid while this withdrawal was under way and publicly blamed the inadequacies of the Nationalist régime for the débâcle. Meanwhile, on 1 October 1949, the People's Republic of China was officially inaugurated at Peking and the most populous communist state in the world had come into existence. Once again, the Mandate of Heaven had passed.

SOUTHEAST ASIA AND INDONESIA

IN SOUTHEAST ASIA AND INDONESIA the Second World War was as decisive as elsewhere in ending colonial rule, although the pace was bloodier and faster in Dutch and French colonies than British. The grant of representative institutions by the Dutch in Indonesia before 1939 had not checked the growth of a

nationalist party, and a flourishing communist movement had appeared by then, too. Some nationalist leaders, among them one Achmed Sukarno, collaborated with the Japanese when they occupied the islands in 1942. They were in a favourable position to seize power when the Japanese surrendered, and proclaimed an independent Indonesian republic before the Dutch could return. Fighting and negotiation followed for nearly two years until agreement was reached for an Indonesian republic still under the Dutch Crown; this did not work. Fighting went on again, the Dutch pressing forward vainly with their "police operations" in one of the first campaigns by a former colonial power to attract the full blast of communist and anti-colonial stricture at the United Nations. Both India and Australia (which had concluded that the Dutch would be wise to conciliate the independent Indonesia which must eventually emerge) took the matter to the Security Council. Finally the Dutch gave in. The story begun by the East India Company of Amsterdam three and a half centuries before thus came to an end in 1949 with the creation of the United States of Indonesia, a mixture of more than a hundred million people scattered over hundreds of islands, of scores of races and religions. A vague union with the Netherlands under the Dutch Crown survived, but was dissolved five years later. Three hundred thousand Dutch citizens, white and brown, arrived in the Netherlands from Indonesia in the early 1950s.

HO CHI MINH AND THE VIETNAM REPUBLIC

For a time the French in Indo-China seemed to be holding on better than the Dutch. That area's wartime history had been somewhat

Ho Chi Minh (1892–1969) is pictured during his first year as president of North Vietnam in 1954. Ho Chi Minh was re-elected in 1960 and played a leading role in the war with South Vietnam and the United States during the following decade.

different from that of Malaysia or Indonesia because although the Japanese had exercised complete military control there since 1941 French sovereignty was not formally displaced until March 1945. The Japanese then amalgamated Annam, Cochin China and Tongking to form a new state of Vietnam under the emperor of Annam. As soon as the Japanese surrendered, though, the chief of the local Communist Party, the Viet Minh, installed himself in government at Hanoi and proclaimed the Vietnam republic. This was Ho Chi Minh, a man with long experience in the Communist Party and also in Europe. He had already received American aid and support and believed he had the backing of the Chinese, too. The revolutionary movement quickly spread while Chinese forces entered north Vietnam and British were sent to the south. It was soon evident that if the French wished to re-establish themselves it would not be easy. The British co-operated with them, but the Chinese did not, and dragged their feet over reimposing French authority. A large expeditionary force was sent to Indo-China and a concession was made in that the French recognized the republic of Vietnam as an autonomous state within the French Union. But now there arose the question of giving Cochin, a major rice-producing area, separate status and on this all attempts to agree broke down. Meanwhile, French soldiers were sniped at and their convoys were attacked. At the end of 1946 there was an attack on residents in Hanoi and many deaths. Hanoi was bombarded (6,000 were killed) and reoccupied by French troops and Ho Chi Minh fled.

WAR

With the flight of Ho Chi Minh began a war which was to last thirty years, in which the communists were to struggle essentially for the nationalist aim of a united country, while the French tried to retain a diminished Vietnam which, with the other Indo-Chinese states, would remain inside the French Union. By 1949 they had come round to including Cochin China in Vietnam and recognizing Cambodia and Laos as "associate states". But new outsiders were now becoming interested

and the Cold War had come to Indo-China. The government of Ho Chi Minh was recognized in Moscow and Peking, that of the Annamese emperor, whom the French had set up, by the British and Americans.

Thus in Asia decolonialization quickly burst out of the simplicities Roosevelt had envisaged. As the British began to liquidate their recovered heritage, this further complicated things. Burma and Ceylon became independent in 1947. In the following year, communist-supported guerrilla war began in Malaya; though it was to be unsuccessful and not to impede steady progress towards independence in 1957, it was one of the first of the many post-colonial problems which were to torment American policy. Growing antagonism with the communist world soon cut across visceral anti-colonialism.

THE MIDDLE EAST

ONLY IN THE MIDDLE EAST did things go on seeming clear-cut. In May 1948, a new state, Israel, came into existence in Palestine. This marked the end of forty years during which only two great powers had needed to agree in order to manage the area. France and Great Britain had not found this too difficult. In 1939 the French still held League of Nations mandates in Syria and the Lebanon (their original mandate had been divided into two), and the British retained theirs in Palestine. Elsewhere in the Arab lands the British exercised varying degrees of influence or power over the new Arab rulers of individual states. The most important were Iraq, where a small British force, mainly of air force units, was maintained, and Egypt, where a substantial garrison still protected the Suez Canal. The latter had become more and more important in the 1930s as Italy showed increasing hostility to Great Britain.

A scene from the 1949 "Song Thao" campaign in Vietnam shows a French colonialist military post that has been overrun by troops from the Vietnam People's Army.

ANTI-COLONIAL FEELING

The war of 1939 was to release change in the Middle East as elsewhere, though this was not at first clear. After Italy's entry to the war, the Canal Zone became one of the most vital areas of British strategy and Egypt suddenly found herself with a battlefront for a western border. She remained neutral almost to the end, but was in effect a British base and little else. The war also made it essential to assure the supply of oil from the Gulf and especially from Iraq. This led to intervention when Iraq threatened to move in a pro-German direction after another nationalist coup in 1941. A British and Free French invasion of Syria to keep it out of German hands led in 1941 to an independent Syria. Soon afterwards the Lebanon proclaimed its own independence. The French tried to re-establish their authority at the end of the war, but unsuccessfully, and during 1946 these two countries saw the last foreign garrisons leave. The French also had difficulties further west, where fighting broke out in Algeria in 1945. Nationalists there were at that moment asking only for autonomy in federation with France and the French went some way in this direction in 1947, but this was far from the end of the story.

Where British influence was paramount, anti-British sentiment was still a good rallying-cry. In both Egypt and Iraq there was much hostility to British occupation forces in the post-war years. In 1946 the British announced that they were prepared to withdraw from Egypt, but negotiations on the basis of a new treaty broke down so badly that Egypt referred the matter (unsuccessfully) to the United Nations. By this time the whole question of the future of the Arab lands had been diverted by the Jewish decision to establish a national state in Palestine by force.

THE GROWING CRISIS OVER PALESTINE

The Palestine question has been with us ever since. Its catalyst had been the Nazi revolution in Germany. At the time of the Balfour Declaration 600,000 Arabs had lived in Palestine beside 80,000 Jews – a number already felt by Arabs to be threateningly large. In some years after this, though, Jewish emigration actually exceeded immigration and there was ground for hope that the problem of reconciling the promise of a "national home" for Jews with respect for "the civil and religious rights of the existing non-Jewish communities in Palestine" (as the Balfour Declaration had put it) might be resolved. Hitler changed this.

From the beginning of the Nazi persecution the numbers of those who wished to come to Palestine rose. As the extermination policies began to unroll in the war years, they made nonsense of British attempts to restrict

Crowds of Jewish refugees throng the deck of a ship in the port of Haifa, northwestern Israel, in 1948. During the war with Palestine that followed the foundation of the state of Israel, Haifa was one focus of fighting between the Arabs and the Jewish defence force, the Hagana.

immigration, which was the side of British policy unacceptable to the Jews; the other side – the partitioning of Palestine – was rejected by the Arabs. The issue was dramatized as soon as the war was over by a World Zionist Congress demand that a million Jews should be admitted to Palestine at once. Other new factors now began to operate. The British, in 1945, had looked benevolently on the formation of an "Arab League" of Egypt, Syria, Lebanon, Iraq, Saudi Arabia, the Yemen and Transjordan. There had always been in British policy a strand of illusion – that pan-Arabism might prove the way in which the Middle East could be persuaded to settle down after post-Ottoman confusion, and that the coordination of the policies of Arab states would open the way to the solution of its problems. In fact the Arab League was soon preoccupied with Palestine to the virtual exclusion of anything else.

SUPPORT FOR THE ZIONISTS

The other novelty was the Cold War. In the immediate post-war era, Stalin seems to have taken still the old communist view that Great Britain was the main imperialist prop of the international capitalist system. Attacks on its position and influence therefore followed, and in the Middle East this, of course, coincided with traditional Russian interests, though the Soviet government had shown little interest in the area between 1919 and 1939. Pressure was brought to bear on Turkey at the Straits, and ostentatious Soviet support was given to Zionism, the most dis-

---

The Palestinian refugee crisis of 1949

With the foundation of Israel in 1948, the Arabs born in Palestine found themselves in a terrible position. The Jews not only colonized but expanded the areas they had seized, as a direct result of the war launched against them by the Arab states that had bitterly opposed the partition of Palestine.

The conflict, together with the fresh wave of Jewish immigration that began in 1948, created well over half a million Arab refugees. At the end of the war, in 1949, barely 160,000 Arabs remained in the Israeli-occupied areas of the country in which they had previously been the predominant population. The land that the UN had granted to the Palestinians in the partition of their territory had vanished: some areas, especially in the Negev desert, had been absorbed by Israel, while others were taken over by the Arab states who had fought on the side of the Palestinians. Egypt kept Gaza, and the West Bank (Samaria and Judaea) was annexed by Jordan.

The first problem the displaced Palestinians faced was that of where to go. Those who had families in Judaea, Samaria or Gaza moved there. The rest sheltered in improvised refugee camps, where conditions were so appalling that the UN created an organization to guarantee survival in the Palestinian camps (the Aid and Re-adaptation Organization for Arab Refugees). Some Palestinians managed to improve their lot by finding work in Jordan, Egypt, Syria, Iraq and the United Arab Emirates.

To prevent their disappearance as a people, Palestinians do not take the nationality of any other Arab country: Palestinian nationality is passed on from one generation of refugees to the next. Many of the ever-growing numbers of Palestinian refugees, such as those pictured here in 1993, live in atrocious conditions in camps in Gaza.

ruptive element in the situation. It did not need extraordinary political insight to recognize the implications of a resumption of Russian interest in the area of the Ottoman legacy. Yet at the same moment American policy turned anti-British or, rather, pro-Zionist. This could hardly have been avoided. In 1946 mid-term congressional elections were held and Jewish votes were important. Since the Roosevelt revolution in domestic politics, a Democratic president could hardly envisage an anti-Zionist position.

THE FOUNDATION OF ISRAEL

The British sought to disentangle themselves from the Holy Land. From 1945 they faced both Jewish and Arab terrorism and guerrilla warfare in Palestine. Unhappy Arab, Jewish and British policemen struggled to hold the ring while the British government still strove to find a way acceptable to both sides of bringing the mandate to an end. American help was sought, but to no avail; Truman wanted a pro-Zionist solution. In the end the British took the matter to the United Nations. It recommended partition, but this was still a non-starter for the Arabs. Fighting between the two communities grew fiercer and the British decided to withdraw without more ado. On the day that they did so, 14 May 1948, the state of Israel was proclaimed. It was immediately recognized by the United States (sixteen minutes after the foundation act) and the USSR; they were to agree about little else in the Middle East for the next quarter-century.

Israel was attacked almost at once by Egypt, whose armies invaded a part of Palestine which the United Nations proposal had awarded to Jews. Jordanian and Iraqi forces supported Palestinian Arabs in the territory proposed for them. But Israel fought

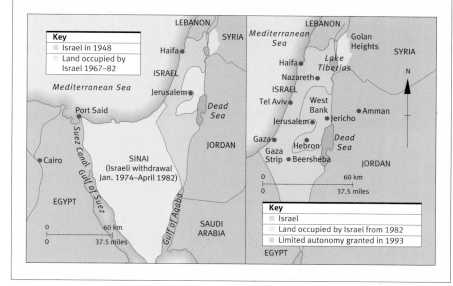

Israel 1948–1967 (left) and 1982–1993 (right)

From 1948 to 1967, despite hundreds of Palestinian assaults on Israelis, Israel consolidated its presence in the region and won important foreign support. In the Six Day War of 1967, Israel won major victories against Egypt, Jordan and Syria, gaining new territories. During the Yom Kippur War of 1973, Israel took yet more land from Egypt and Syria. In 1982 Israel invaded Lebanon and defeated PLO troops there. After six years of Palestinian rebellion (the *intifada*) in Gaza and the West Bank, an Israeli–PLO treaty gave limited self-rule to the Palestinians in the occupied territories.

off her enemies, and a truce, supervised by the United Nations, followed (during which a Zionist terrorist murdered the United Nations mediator). In 1949 the Israeli government moved to Jerusalem, a Jewish national capital again for the first time since the days of imperial Rome. Half of the city was still occupied by Jordanian forces, but this was almost the least of the problems left to the future. With American and Russian diplomatic support and American private money, Jewish energy and initiative had successfully established a new national state where no basis for one had existed twenty-five years before. Yet the cost was long to go on being paid. The disappointment and humiliation of the Arab states assured their continuing hostility to it and therefore opportunities for great power intervention in the future. Moreover, the action of

Israel's first prime minister, David Ben-Gurion, watches British troops preparing to leave the newly established state from the port of Haifa in 1948.

Zionist extremists and Israeli forces in 1948–9 led to an exodus of Arab refugees. Soon there were 750,000 of them in camps in Egypt and Jordan, a social and economic problem, a burden on the world's conscience, and a potential military and diplomatic weapon for Arab nationalists. It would hardly be surprising were it true (as some students believe) that the first president of Israel

quickly encouraged his country's scientists to work on a nuclear energy programme.

AGE-OLD PROBLEMS

Many currents flowed together in a curious and ironical way to swirl in confusion in an area which had always been a focus of world history. Victims for centuries, the Jews were in their turn now seen by Arabs as persecutors. The problems with which the peoples of the area had to grapple were poisoned by forces flowing from the dissolution of centuries of Ottoman power, from the rivalries of successor imperialisms (and in particular from the rise of two new world powers, which dwarfed these in their turn), from the interplay of nineteenth-century European nationalism and ancient religion, and from the first effects of the new dependence of developed nations on oil. There are few moments in the twentieth century so soaked in history as the establishment of Israel. It is a good point at which to pause before turning to the story of the rest of the twentieth century.

A Jew casts his vote in the first general election to be held in the new state of Israel, in January 1949. One month later, the elected constituent assembly decreed that Israel's legislature was to be a one-chamber parliament, which would be known as the Knesset.

5 POPULATION, ECONOMY AND THE MANAGEMENT OF NATURE

The Long-Duration Exposure Facility (LDEF) satellite, which was deployed from the space shuttle *Challenger* on 7 April 1984, was designed to test the long-term effects of exposure to space conditions on electronic systems. The development of communication satellites has revolutionized global communications.

Even as the twenty-first century of the Christian era began to close, it was already easy enough to agree that great and startling changes had come about since, say, 1945. Today, that is even more apparent. But the problems which arise as we try to pin them down as part of the world's history do not go away. They may even become more difficult to solve. The mere narrative of events seems to thicken up suddenly, unaccountably, and of its own accord. It is harder than ever, under the strong impression of recent events, to get our perspective right in treating the last fifty or so years of history in relation to the preceding six thousand or so.

Part of the trouble lies in our reasonable expectations. When we read about times through which we have lived, we expect to come across events we recall, or recall hearing about at an impressionable age, and there is

then a sense of disappointment if they do not turn up in the story. But all history is a selection; it is, in the strictest sense, what any one age finds remarkable in an earlier period, and expectation, legitimate or illegitimate, is only a part of it.

THE PACE AND EXTENT OF CHANGE

Expectation is not the only source of challenge in the history of recent times. The pace of change poses another difficulty. It was only a few centuries ago that the notion of human cultural evolution began to get some grip on writers of history. It is really only very recently, moreover, that historians have begun to take it for granted that generations will differ culturally, that the societies they live in are always changing in very deep and determining ways, and that basic attitudes change with them. Yet any adult alive today has almost certainly lived through examples of radical adaptations which are now taken for granted, absorbed into our consciousness and often go unremarked, though they may be far more profound and far more strikingly rapid than any experienced by our predecessors. The growth of population is the exemplary case; no earlier generation has lived through anything like such a rapid increase in human numbers. Yet few human beings have been conscious of it.

It is not just as a succession of events that history has speeded up. The rapidity of the changes it has brought has often had wider and deeper implications, and more influence than in the past, just because of the speed with which the changes came about. For all the dissatisfactions still felt by many over the extent of advance, the opportunities and freedoms available to women in Western society, to take one example, have grown at a quite different rate and by an order of magnitude dramatically greater than in the previous century or so. As yet, they have not begun to exhaust (or in some places even to exercise) their full effect. The same could be said of many more narrowly technological and material changes, some of which are far from exercising their full potential effects.

NEW PERSPECTIVES

If the history of the last few decades is – because of the rapid and radical changes they have brought – quite different from any earlier history, that makes it harder to write about as part of the same story. In entering it, we seem not merely (in some sense) to have to change gear, but to need to take up a different viewpoint. Much more explanation is required in order to show the special influence of this or that fact or event, especially when it involves technical innovation. More detail is needed to unravel the crumbling and rebuilding of a world political system in the context of the first truly global economic order, or for the weighing of questions about how much irreversible change can now be identified as the outcome of human intervention with nature. Such matters, of course,

In defiance of the homogenizing effect of the global mass media, many countries are now experiencing a reaffirmation of cultural traditions. The *geishas* in Japan are a good example of this.

force themselves on us for consideration in earlier history, too. But in former times the deep and far-reaching implications of the events which embodied them tended only to reveal themselves slowly and at times almost imperceptibly. Now they do so with sometimes surprising, even explosive rapidity, and this, too, makes a steady perspective much harder to achieve.

TURNING-POINTS

Then there is chronology, the bedrock of history. Reflection that history marches into a

Time chart (1900–1969)						
	1903 First flight of the Wright brothers' aeroplane	1905 Special theory of relativity, Einstein	1916 General theory of relativity, Einstein	1953 Discovery of the structure of deoxyribonucleic acid (DNA)	1957 The USSR launches *Sputnik I*	
1900				1950		
	1900 Quantum theory, Planck	1904 Pavlov's theory of conditioned reflexes		1938 Discovery of nuclear fission	1969 The USA lands men on the moon	

A rickshaw rider in Beijing cycles past a billboard in 2005 advertising Adidas and seven of the globally known stars or "galacticos" of Spain's footballing giants Real Madrid – (from the left) Michael Owen, Zinedine Zidane, Raul, David Beckham, Luis Figo, Ronaldo and Roberto Carlos.

new and distinctive phase somewhere in the middle of the twentieth century leaves many of us looking about for what we might treat as turning-points, punctuations, indispensable milestones of chronology, such as we take for granted in earlier history. In thinking of these matters, though, whether 1917 is a more meaningful turning-point than 1919, or whether what happened in Manchuria in 1931 marked a more striking new departure than what happened in Poland in 1939 may not within a few decades seem to matter so

much as once we thought. Possibly neither of those dates should be regarded as more noteworthy than, for example, that of the patent filed in 1951 for a compound effective in controlling fertility in women and capable of being administered safely by mouth. That was a landmark in the development of what soon became known, ten years later, as "the Pill", whose effects have already been immense.

In what follows, I have tried consciously to face such problems and to make them somewhat less intimidating by setting out first – even at some length – the most important general developments which embody or represent long-term themes and influences operating over the last fifty years or so. Only then have I tried to outline a narrative of the events which usually made more of the headlines, divided roughly into short chronological periods. From this, I hope, will emerge the main chronological markers of "contemporary history" – the moments when things might have gone otherwise had history not been history and been therefore "bound" to go the way it did.

ONE CONVERGING WORLD

Of course, there are some general points which we can be fairly sure will emerge, even before we start. It is not difficult, for example, to see that the days of domination of world affairs by Europeans are over; and that we can call the age since 1945 post-European. But there are even more general and sweeping changes to register. The world is now one as never before. This process is one of the ways in which the world has, in a few years, changed faster and perhaps more fundamentally than ever in earlier history. A common civilization is now spread and in many ways shared more widely than any civilization hitherto, but even as we discern that fact, it is changing before our eyes into something else. Indeed, it is a civilization uniquely committed to change, and therefore often of revolutionary impact. We can have far less firm ground for confidence in making guesses about what life will be like in even a few decades than our predecessors had. Greater economic and technological independence and, above all, a hugely increased supply of information and better means of tapping it are among the most obvious reasons for this. Almost anything that happens anywhere in the world can now in principle rapidly produce effects elsewhere; more and more, even if not yet all, political leaders seem to recognize this, whether they are prompted to do so by ideology, calculation or simple fear. Even if sometimes too slowly, most of them come around to recognizing the path history has taken. For convenience, the processes involved are often talked about as "modernization" and the symptoms of it have now spread to every part of the globe, even where they are as yet apparent only as aspirations.

Long ago in prehistory, humanity began its liberation from nature through primitive technologies. During thousands of years it then followed different and diverging paths, which provided it with different ways of life and created highly individual and particular cultures and civilizations. A few centuries ago, those paths began to converge, as there began to spread from one part of the world the processes of modernization. Now we can sense that they are in some senses coming together the world over, even if we cannot say very much that is precise about something happening at so general a level. What we must (and, fortunately, can easily) recognize, though, is that even the most recent history has still to be seen in the light of older history. To do so makes the chance of securing a just perspective on even the greatest changes just a little better.

THE GROWTH OF THE WORLD POPULATION

IN 1974 THE FIRST WORLD conference on population ever to be held took place in Romania. The uneasiness of an informed few about the demographic outlook had for the first time provided a forum for the human race to consider its numbers. A quarter-century later, the unwilled, apparently still uncontrollable and accelerating rise in world population, which had been going on for a couple of centuries or so, was seen by many more to pose global problems, even if their exact nature remained uncertain because of incomplete information.

Accuracy in computing populations still eludes us. We can only estimate to within a couple of hundred millions how many people are now alive. Nonetheless, the likely degree of error probably does not seriously distort our impression of what has happened. In round numbers, a world population of about

This group of schoolgirls is from North Africa, where there has recently been a shift from large to smaller families in recent decades.

A government propaganda poster in Chengdu, China, advocates family planning and endorses the state's one-child-per-family policy, which was launched to control the growth of the country's huge population.

实行计划生育　是我国的一项基本国策
FAMILY PLANNING – A BASIS NATIONAL POLICY OF CHINA

750 million two and a half centuries ago more than doubled in a hundred and fifty years and numbered about 1,600 million in 1900. It then took just a further fifty years to add the next 850 million or so; by 1950 the world had about 2,500 million inhabitants. The next 850 million were added in only twenty years, and now the world's population is more than 6500 million. This huge growth in the numbers of human beings can be set in a still longer timescale. It had taken at least 50,000 years for *Homo sapiens* to number 1,000 million (a number reached in 1840 or thereabouts) while the last 1,000 million of the species has been added in only fifteen years. Until only a few decades ago the total was growing faster and faster, perhaps reaching its peak at a rate over 2 per cent per year in the later 1960s.

ATTEMPTS TO LIMIT POPULATION GROWTH

The rapid rate of population growth made the spectre of Malthusian disaster walk again for some, although as Malthus himself observed, "no estimate of future population or depopulation, formed from any existing rate of increase or decrease, can be depended upon". We cannot be sure what might further change the pattern. Some societies, for instance, have set out to control their size and shape, an effort which, strictly speaking, was not entirely new. In some places, murder and abortion had long been customary ways of holding down demands on scarce resources. Babies were exposed to die in medieval Japan; female infanticide was widespread in nineteenth-century India and returned (or, perhaps, was acknowledged openly again) in China in the 1980s. What was new was that governments began to put resources and authority behind more humane methods of population control. Their aim was positive social and economic improvement instead of the mere avoidance of personal and family distress.

DIFFERENCES IN GROWTH RATES

Only a few governments made such efforts and economic and social facts did not everywhere produce the same response, even to unquestionable advance in technology and knowledge. A new contraceptive technique spread rapidly, with radical impact on behaviour and thinking, in many Western countries in the 1960s, while it has yet to be adopted with anything like the same alacrity by women in the non-Western world. It was one of many reasons why population growth, though worldwide, did not everywhere take the same form or provoke the same responses. Though many non-European countries followed nineteenth-century European patterns (in first showing a fall in death rates without a corresponding fall in birth rates), it would be rash to predict that they will simply go on to repeat the next phase of the population history of developed countries. We cannot assume patterns of declining natality in one place or one society will be repeated elsewhere – but nor can we be sure that they will not be. The dynamics of population growth are exceedingly complex, reflecting limits set to them by ignorance and by personal and social attitudes hard to measure, let alone manipulate, and while we wait for these dynamics to become clearer some poor countries cannot for a long time hope to achieve demographic equilibrium. In Europe,

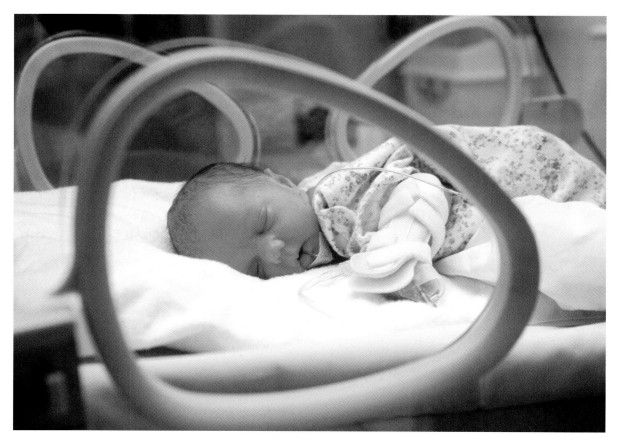

Technological advances in postnatal care have contributed to the fall in the infant mortality rate in the developed world. This one-day-old baby is six weeks' premature and is being kept alive in an incubator in a modern intensive care unit. Between 5 and 10 per cent of all babies born in developed countries are now born before 37 weeks' gestation. Of babies born at 28 weeks' gestation and given specialist care, around 80 per cent survive.

Europe's population is increasingly becoming old as the combined effects are felt of improved life expectancy and decreased fertility. This flower-seller in Dubrovnik, Croatia, is in the fifty-plus age group, which accounts for nearly 40 per cent of Croatia's female population as a whole. The government projects that the population will shrink by more than 10 per cent by 2050.

natality only began to drop in the last couple of centuries when prosperity in a few countries made it attractive to have smaller families; few of today's countries showing fast population growth are anywhere near that point. Better medical, nutritional and, above all, public health provision may well make things worse. Advances have been colossal

since 1900, yet there are many places where they have yet to cut into mortality as dramatically as they had already done in Europe in the century before that. When and where they do, humanity's numbers may rise faster still.

LIFE EXPECTANCY PATTERNS

Infant mortality is a helpful rough indicator of potential for future growth. In the century before 1970 this fell from an average of about 225 per thousand live births to under twenty in developed countries; in 1988 the comparative figures for Bangladesh and Japan were 118 and five. Such discrepancies between rich and poor countries are greater than in the past. There are comparable differences of life expectancy at all ages, too. At birth in developed countries it rose from slightly over forty in 1870 to slightly over seventy a hundred years later. It now shows a remarkable evenness; in 2006, for example, seventy-eight, seventy-nine and eighty-one years respectively in the United States, the United Kingdom and Sweden. Differences between them were insignificant by comparison with those then separating them from Ethiopia (forty-nine) or even India (sixty-four). Yet the Indian baby faces prospects of survival enormously improved over those of his or her predecessor in 1900 – let alone those of French babies in 1789.

In the immediate future, such disparities will present new problems. For most of history, all societies resembled pyramids, with large numbers of young people at their base, and a few old. Now, developed societies are looking like tapering columns; the proportion of much older people is larger than in the past. In poorer countries, the reverse is true. Almost half of Kenya's people are under fifteen. To talk simply of overall population growth therefore obscures important facts.

Population distribution

At the beginning of 1990, world population was distributed roughly as follows:

Population in millions:

Region	Population
Europe (excl. USSR)	549
USSR	285
Asia (excl. USSR)	2943
Africa	610
South America & the Caribbean	430
North America	272
Australasia & Oceania	26

Percentage of total:

11,9
8,4
5,3
0,5
10,7
5,5
57,7

World population goes on growing mightily, but in ways that have very different origins and will have very different historical implications and effects.

POPULATION DISTRIBUTION

Among the various historical effects of population growth are big changes in the way population is shared. The fall from Europe's mid-nineteenth century share of world population (a quarter) is striking. So is the ending of four centuries in which emigrants of European stocks had left the continent to spread around the world; until the 1920s, Europe was still exporting people overseas, notably to the Americas. That outflow was much cut down by restrictions on entry to the United States in that decade, dwindled further during the Great Depression, and has never since recovered its former importance. On the other hand, immigration to the United States from the Caribbean, Central and South America and Asia surged upwards in the last decades of the twentieth century. Moreover, although some European countries still sent out emigrants (in the early 1970s more Britons still left the country each year than there were immigrants to it from abroad), they began also from the 1950s to attract North Africans, Turks, Asians and West Indians, seeking work they could not find at home. Europe is now, overall, an importer of people.

AREAS WITH FAST GROWTH

Present world patterns may not remain unchanged for long. Asia now contains over half of mankind, China a fifth of it, and India a sixth, but some of the huge growth rates that have produced these numbers are at last beginning to fall. In Brazil, where population increase ran at more than twice the world rate in the early 1960s, it does so no longer, though Brazilians continue to grow in number. As in other Latin American countries where standards of living and life expectancy for much of the population are not much better than in Europe at the end of the nineteenth

---

Population density

The world's most heavily population region is Asia, with the highest population density occurring on the islands of Macao, Singapore and Hong Kong. Life expectancy is highest in wealthy, industrialized countries, where infant mortality rates are also the lowest. Life expectancy is shortest in developing countries, which have the highest infant mortality rates.

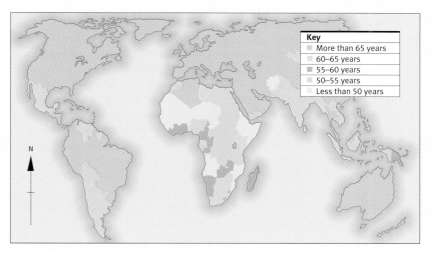

Key
More than 65 years
60–65 years
55–60 years
50–55 years
Less than 50 years

Worldwide life expectancy (the average lifespan, given in years) in the early 1990s.

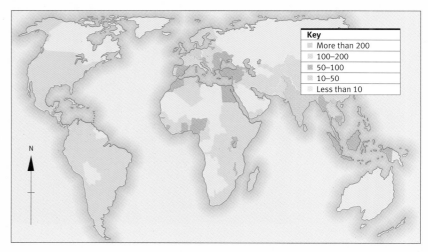

Key
More than 200
100–200
50–100
10–50
Less than 10

Worldwide population density (number of people per square km) in the early 1990s.

century, the Roman Catholic Church has been blamed, because of its long record of opposition to birth control and abortion, but that can hardly be the whole explanation. The attitudes of Latin American males and the social disciplines that impose large families on many poor Latin American women – who were, until recently, almost unquestioningly complaisant – may matter just as much. Meanwhile, the most alarming growth rates are to be found in the Islamic world; Jordan, at the 1990s rate, would double its popula-

tion in sixteen years, and Iraq grew only a little less vigorously at 3.5 per cent per year, while Saudi Arabia's much smaller population grew at a startling annual rate of 5.6 per cent.

POPULATION CONTROL

There is, nonetheless, evidence from some developing countries of reduction in family size in the last thirty years. Undoubtedly, this is partly due to official efforts and partly to increases in wealth. Though communist régimes had never traditionally welcomed ideas of population stabilization or reduction, in the 1960s China began to encourage people to delay marriage and have smaller families. It also pressed forwards with measures of legal regulation, tax incentives and social pressure, though at the cost of the reappearance of condemned practices of female infanticide. The Indian government spent large sums on publicity and propaganda for contraception, and some for sterilization, but with limited success. Revolutionized neither economically as Japan had been, nor by any political attack on its traditional institutions as China had been, India remained a predominantly agrarian society, profoundly conservative in ideas and institutions. Outside a tiny minority within her élites, India maintained, for example, a vast and traditional inequality in the status and employment prospects of men and women. Were attitudes towards women now taken for granted in Europe or North America (and often denounced there as inadequate) even slightly more prevalent in India, they would be likely to raise dramatically the age of women at marriage, thus reducing the number of children in the average family. But such a change would presuppose a break with India's traditional ways, opportunities and structures of authority which would be much more radical

Contraception

For centuries, because infant mortality rates were generally high, governments never saw a need to lower the birth-rate through artificial means.

After the Second World War, when more Western women were working, the average number of children per family began to fall. Medical advances have since widened the range of anti-conceptive methods available, mainly for women. The contraceptive pill, intrauterine devices (IUD), sterilization, diaphragms, spermicide creams,

etc., have allowed couples to choose when to start a family and how many children they want to have. The use of these methods has caused a marked fall in the birth-rate in several countries in the developed world. However, in some developing countries, such as India or China, the birth-rate remains extremely high, in spite of government campaigns to limit the number of children born and attempts to make family planning advice and contraception available to everyone.

This maternity hospital in Shanghai, China, provides women with information about family planning methods.

than the winning of political independence in 1947. Deeply entrenched traditions and culture cannot be got rid of painlessly and no country should be expected to find it easy to shake off so much.

Perhaps we need not be too gloomy. Fertility has tended to fall in developing countries when economic well-being increases. Even when countries like India have not been able to generate obvious improvement in the lot of their masses, Latin America provides evidence that such improvement eases the way to a decline in natality. The still-expanding influence of civilization in the European tradition, however it is packaged on arrival, remains the most powerful solvent of traditional ways that history can show. Change in population structure seems in one way or another to accompany it as unavoidably as the weakening of religious culture, the building of factories or the liberation of women – and such a list could be much extended.

POPULATION AND POWER

Differences of population and changes in them affect the comparative strength of nations, although they are not simply to be equated with differences of power. Resources and culture come into the matter, and power for one purpose is not always power for another. Nonetheless, power and population are related in many ways. China, for example, has a population so large as to make her virtually unconquerable. But there is not always so direct and obvious an equation. A list of the ten largest states in population reveals, on any reckoning, that it contains the three most powerful countries in the world; they were not, of course, the three most powerful a hundred years earlier. Some of the ten are also very poor. While China's social transformation has forged ahead, others on the list

are still sunk in a poverty that for some of them looks insurmountable, whether it is absolute, because natural resources are few (Bangladesh) or relative, in that they are swallowed up by population growth which is too fast (India and Indonesia) and has overtaken the cashing of the cheque of development. Newly generated wealth has in such cases been at best largely consumed in longer life expectancy. But it is not easy, though tempting, to generalize; India's agricultural output doubled between 1948 and 1973 and she was thought to be about to enter a period of self-sufficiency in food, yet this barely held the

In many parts of the Indian subcontinent, the status of women has remained practically unchanged for centuries – they are still expected to live according to ancient traditions. This young Indian dancer is from Jaipur.

India is the second most populous state in the world; in fact, only India and China have more than 1,000 million inhabitants. Pictured here are some of the millions of Hindu pilgrims who travel to the Ganges and Yamuna rivers each year to purify their souls by bathing in the waters.

line for a population growing at the rate of a million a month.

URBANIZATION

World population was changing in another way, too; as the twentieth century ended nearly half of it lived in cities. The city is becoming the typical habitat of *Homo sapiens*. This was a remarkable change from most of human history. It registered the fact that cities have been losing their old killing-power. In the past, the high death rates of city life required constant demographic nourishment by country-born immigrants in order to keep up numbers. In the nineteenth century, city-dwellers in some countries had begun to reproduce themselves in sufficient surviving numbers for cities to grow organically. The results are startling; there are now many cities whose numbers of inhabitants are literally uncountable. Calcutta already had a million in 1900, but now has more than fifteen times as many; Mexico City had only 350,000 inhabitants as the twentieth century began, but ended with over twenty million. Other impressions can be derived from the longer term. The world had only five cities of more than a half-million inhabitants in 1700; in 1900 there were forty-three; and now Brazil alone has seven of more than a million. Sanitary regimes and public health measures have moved more

The world's ten most populous states

At the beginning of the 21st-century the ten most populous states are roughly as shown:

Population in millions:

China	1300
India	1100
USA	300
Indonesia	230
Brazil	180
Pakistan	155
Bangladesh	140
Russia	130
Nigeria	130
Japan	125

slowly in some countries than others to make such changes possible, and the tide of urbanization is far from ebbing.

WORLD RESOURCES

Population and urbanization dynamics both imply a huge growth in world resources. To simplify the question ruthlessly, though many have starved, many more have lived. Millions may have died in famines, but there has so far been no worldwide Malthusian disaster. If the world had not been able to feed them, human numbers would be smaller. Whether this can continue for long is another question. Experts have concluded that we can for a good while to come provide food for growing numbers. There is still hope, too, that population policy may help to stabilize demand. But in such matters we enter the realms of speculation, though the very existence of such hopes interests the historian, for they say something about a present and actual state of the world where what is believed to be possible is important in settling what will happen. In considering that, we have to recognize the major economic fact of modern history, and especially of the last half-century: that it brought about anunprecedented production of wealth.

ECONOMIC GROWTH

Readers of this book are probably used to seeing harrowing pictures of famine and deprivation on their television screens. Yet over much of the world since 1945, continuing economic growth has, for the first time, come to be taken for granted. It has become the "norm", in spite of hiccups and interruptions along the way. Any slowing down in its rate now provokes alarm. What is more, as population figures show, in gross

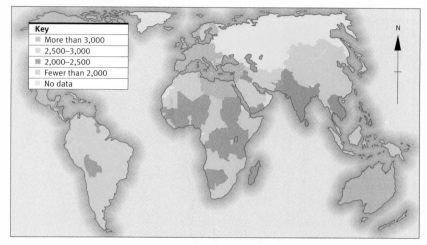

Worldwide daily calorie intake

Africa and South America, which contain the world's largest areas of arable land, also have, proportionally, the smallest areas of land under cultivation. If present economic and socio-political obstacles could be removed in those regions – and if suitable scientific farming methods were applied – the land available would be capable of providing 4,000–5,000 calories per person per day to ten times the world's present population.

Key
- More than 3,000
- 2,500–3,000
- 2,000–2,500
- Fewer than 2,000
- No data

This map shows the average daily calorie intake per person.

terms real economic growth has been the story in most of the underdeveloped world. Against the background of the way the world still thought, even in 1939, this can be accounted a revolution. Yet that story does not just begin with the decades since the end of the Second World War, the golden age of unprecedented growth. The appropriate historical background for the surge in wealth creation, that has successfully carried the burden of soaring world population, is much deeper. One way of measuring it is to reflect that the average human being today commands about nine times the wealth of an average human being in 1500. The world's Gross Domestic Product (GDP) has risen from a base of 100 five centuries ago to a figure of more than 13,000 today – but has, of course, to be shared between many more people.

Wealth and human numbers, indeed, tended to rise more or less in parallel until the nineteenth century. Then some economies began to display much faster growth than others. Even at the beginning of the twentieth century, a new intensification of wealth creation was already under way which, though badly set back by two world wars and the upheavals of the 1930s, was to be resumed after 1945 and has barely ceased since, in spite of serious challenges and striking contrasts between different economies. GDP rose almost everywhere after 1960 and, generally, per capita, too.

DIFFERENTIATION OF WEALTH

For all the huge disparities and setbacks in some countries, economic growth has taken place more widely than ever before. Selected figures must be interpreted cautiously, and they can change very quickly, but they give a truthful impression of the way in which the world has become richer in a century. Yet some of humanity still remains woefully poor.

If the overriding fact is one of wealth creation, it must have helped that the major powers were at peace with one another for so long. The years since 1945 have, of course, been studded with many bloody smaller-scale or incipient conflicts, while men and women have died every day of them, hundreds of thousands in warlike operations or their aftermath. The great powers have had much fighting done for them by surrogates. Yet no such destruction of human and economic capital as that of the two world wars took place. The international rivalry that underlay often notable tension tended, rather, to sustain or provoke economic activity in many countries. It provided much technological spin-off and led to major capital investments and transfers for political motives, some of which did much to increase real wealth.

THE WORLD ECONOMIC ORDER

The first transfers of capital took place in the

The modern National Congress buildings in Brasilia, designed by Oscar Niemeyer. Located in the barren centre of Brazil, the purpose-built 20th-century capital city is a modernistic-looking example of state-directed urban planning and an arguably fitting collection of symbols for a young country with a dynamic and developed economy.

later 1940s, when American aid made possible the recovery of Europe. For this to be successful, the American dynamo had to be available to promote recovery, as it had not been after 1918. The enormous wartime expansion of the American economy that had at last brought it out of the pre-war Depression, together with the immunity of the American home base from physical damage by war, had ensured that it would be.

Explanation for the deployment of American economic strength as aid has to be sought in circumstances (of which the Cold War was an important part). International tension made it seem in America's interest to behave as it did; an imaginative grasp of opportunities was shown by many of its statesmen and businessmen; there was for a long time no alternative source of capital on such a scale; finally, it helped that men of different nations, even before the end of the war, had already set in place institutions for regulating the international economy in order to avoid any return to the near-fatal economic anarchy of the 1930s.

The story of the reshaping of the economic life of the world thus begins before 1945, in the wartime efforts that produced the International Monetary Fund (IMF), the World Bank and the General Agreement on Tariffs and Trade (GATT). The economic

Worldwide Gross Domestic Product

Defined as the total market value of the final goods and services produced per year, GDP is a useful estimate of a country's prosperity. While most world trade remains that in manufactured goods (57% in 1992), since 1960 the fastest growing section of GDP is the service sector (21%), now almost equivalent to the volume of trade in food and raw materials (22%).

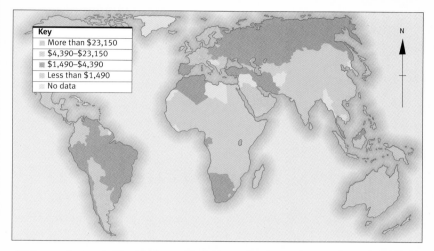

This map shows world-wide Gross Domestic Product per capita in US dollars in 1993.

stability they provided in the non-communist world after 1945 underpinned two decades of growth in world trade at nearly 7 per cent per annum in real terms. Between 1945 and the 1980s the average level of tariffs on manufactured goods fell from 40 per cent to 5 per cent, and world trade multiplied more than fivefold.

Changes in GDP in the 20th century

The following examples reveal the change in GDP *per capita* (in terms of 1988 US dollars) during the 20th century:

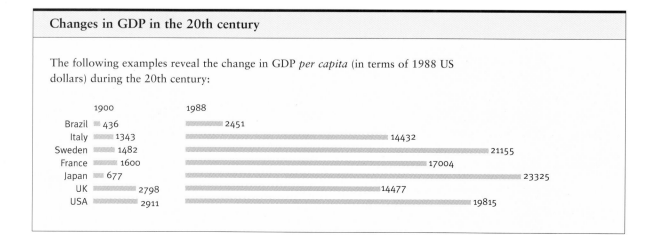

The logos of the World Bank (top) and the International Monetary Fund.

SCIENTIFIC PROGRESS

ANOTHER DECISIVE CONTRIBUTION of human agency to economic growth was less formal, often less visible, and has been made over a much longer term. It was provided by scientists and engineers. The continued application of scientific knowledge through technology, and the improvement and rationalization of processes and systems in the search for greater efficiency, were all very important before 1939. They came dramatically to the fore and began to exercise a quite new order of influence after 1945.

ADVANCES IN AGRICULTURE

Agriculture, where improvement had begun long before industrialization itself was a recognizable phenomenon, is one of the clearest examples of the successful application of scientific knowledge. For thousands of years farmers edged their returns upwards almost entirely by ancient methods, above all by clearing and breaking in new land. There is still a lot left that, with proper investment, could be made to raise crops (and much has been done in recent decades to use such land, even in a crowded country like India). Yet this does not explain why world agricultural output has risen so dramatically. The root explanation is a continuation and acceleration of the agricultural revolution that began in early modern Europe and has been visible at least from the seventeenth century. Two hundred and fifty years later, it was vastly speeded up, thanks, largely, to applied science.

Well before 1939, wheat was being successfully introduced to lands in which, for climatic reasons, it had not been grown hitherto. Plant geneticists had evolved new strains of cereals, one of the first twentieth-century scientific contributions to agriculture

on a scale going far beyond the trial-and-error "improvement" of earlier times; only much later did genetic modification of crop species begin to attract adverse criticism. Greater contributions to world food supplies had by then been made in areas already growing grain by using better chemical fertilizers (of which the first had become available in the nineteenth century). An unprecedented rate of replacement of nitrogen in the soil underlay the larger yields that have become commonplace in countries with advanced agriculture. Their costs include huge energy inputs, though, and fears of ecological consequences began to be expressed in the 1960s. By then better fertilizers had been joined by effective herbicides and insecticides, too, while the use of machinery in agriculture had grown enormously in developed countries. England had in 1939 the most mechanized farming in the world in terms of horsepower per acre cultivated; English farmers nonetheless then still did much of their work with horses, while combine harvesters (already familiar in the United States) were rare. But not only were the fields mechanized. The coming of electricity brought automatic milking, grain-drying, threshing, the heating of animal sheds in winter. Now, the computer and automation have begun to reduce dependence on human labour even more; in the developed world the agricultural workforce has continued to fall while production per acre has risen and genetically modified crops promise even greater yields.

DISPARITIES IN AGRICULTURAL PRODUCTION LEVELS

For all that, paradoxically, there may well be more subsistence farmers in the world today than in 1900, just because there are more people. Their share of cultivated land and of the value of the crops produced, though, has fallen. The 2 per cent of the farmers who live in developed countries now supply about half the world's food. In Europe the peasant is fast disappearing, as he disappeared in Great Britain 200 years ago. But this change has been unevenly spread and easily disrupted. Russia was traditionally one of the great agricultural economies, but as recently as 1947 suffered famine so severe as to provoke outbreaks of cannibalism once more. Local dearth is still a danger in countries with large and rapidly growing populations where subsistence agriculture is the norm and productivity remains low. Just before the First World War, the British yield of wheat per acre was already more than two and a half times that of India; by 1968 it was roughly five times. Over the same period the Americans raised their rice yield from 4.25 to nearly 12 tons an acre, while that of Burma, once the "rice bowl of Asia", rose only from 3.8 to

4.2. In 1968, one agricultural worker in Egypt was providing food for slightly more than one family, while in New Zealand each farm employee was producing enough for forty.

Countries economically advanced in other ways show the greatest agricultural productivity. Countries in greatest need have found it impossible to produce crops more cheaply than can leading industrial economies. Ironic paradoxes result: the Russians, Indians and Chinese, big grain and rice producers, have found themselves buying American and Canadian wheat. Disparities between developed and undeveloped countries have widened in the decades of plenty.

THE USE OF RESOURCES

The most striking measure of the difference between developed and undeveloped coun-

An aerial view of a farm in the Lancaster region of Pennsylvania, which boasts the most productive farming land in the United States. Most North American commercial farms are highly mechanized. Reliance on improved irrigation techniques, fertilizers, seed selection and crop rotation have all contributed to a considerable increase in productivity, while enabling farmers to prevent soil erosion.

Water shortage is one of the basic causes of suffering in many developing countries, usually due to drought but also as a result of poor infrastructure. These Haitian women are carrying bottled water from a UN distribution center in Gonaives, in September 2004, when more than 1,000 people died in floods.

tries is relative consumption of the world's resources. Half of humanity now consumes about six-sevenths of the world's production; the other half shares the rest. Even among wealthy nations there are wide disparities. The United States has been the most extravagant consumer. In 1970 the half-dozen or so Americans in every 100 human beings used about forty of every 100 barrels of oil produced in the world each year. They each consumed roughly a quarter-ton of paper products; the corresponding figure for China was about twenty pounds. The electrical energy used by China for all purposes in a year at that time would (it was said) just have sustained the supply of power to the United States' air conditioners. Electricity production, indeed, is one of the best ways of making comparisons, since relatively little electrical power is traded internationally and most of it is consumed in the country where it is generated. In the late 1980s, the USA produced nearly forty times as much electricity per capita as India, twenty-three times as much as China, but only 1.3 times as much as Switzerland.

RICH AND POOR

In all parts of the world the disparity between rich and poor nations has grown more and more marked since 1945, not usually because the poor have grown poorer, but because the rich have grown much richer. Almost the only exceptions to this were to be found in the comparatively rich (by poor world standards) economies of the USSR and eastern Europe, where mismanagement and the exigencies of a command economy held back growth. With these exceptions, even spectacular accelerations of production (some Asian countries, for example, pushed up their agricultural output between 1952 and 1970 proportionately more than Europe and much more than North America) have rarely succeeded in improving the position of poor countries in relation to that of the rich, because of their rising populations – and rich countries, in any case, began at a higher level.

The Asian-African Conference, 1955

"The Asian-African Conference recommended: the early establishment of the Special United Nations Fund for Economic Development; the allocation by the International Bank for Reconstruction and Development of a greater part of its resources to Asian-African countries; the early establishment of the International Finance Corporation which should include in its activities the undertaking of equity investment, and encouragement to the promotion of joint ventures among Asian-African countries in so far as this will promote their common interest."

Para A3 of the Final Communiqué of the Asian-African Conference, which was held in Bandung, Indonesia, 18–24 April, 1955.

Although their rankings in relation to one another may have changed, most high living-standard countries of 1950 have retained their status, except parts of the former Soviet Union. They have been joined by Japan and some regions in the rest of East Asia. These are the major industrial countries. Their economies are today the richest per capita, and their example spurs poorer countries to seek their own salvation in economic growth, which is too often read as industrialization.

INDUSTRIAL CHANGE

COMPARISONS HAVE become more difficult. Major industrial economies today do not much resemble their nineteenth-century predecessors. The old heavy and manufacturing industries, which long provided the backbone of economic strength, are no longer a simple and satisfactory measures of it. Once-staple industries in leading countries have declined. Of the three major steel-making countries of 1900, the first two (the USA and Germany) were still among the first five world producers eighty years later, but in third and fifth places respectively; the United Kingdom (third in 1900) came tenth in the same world table – with Spain, Romania and Brazil close on her heels. Nowadays, Poland makes more steel than did the USA a century ago. What is more, newer industries often found a better environment for rapid growth in some developing countries than in the mature economies. Thus the people of Taiwan came by 1988 to enjoy per capita GDP nearly eighteen times that of India, while that of South Korea, too, was fifteen times as big.

Twentieth-century economic growth has often been in sectors – electronics and plastics are examples – which barely existed even in 1945 and in new sources of power. Coal replaced running water and wood in the nine-teenth century as the major source of industrial energy, but long before 1939 it was joined by hydro-electricity, oil and natural gas; very recently, power generated by nuclear fission was added to these.

THE MOTOR CAR ECONOMY

Industrial growth has raised standards of living as power costs have come down and with them those of transport. One particular

One of the new sources of power in action – a solar power station produces electricity in California in the United States. Wind and wave power can also now be used to generate electricity.

World energy resources

Of the world production of raw minerals, most is concentrated in just 20 countries. The main importers are Japan, the USA and western Europe, which imports more than two-thirds of what it consumes. The main exporters are in Latin America, Africa, the Middle East, Southeast Asia and Russia. Exported products include crude oil, iron, copper, tin, phosphates and coal.

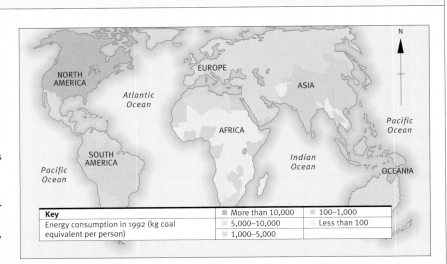

Key	More than 10,000	100–1,000
Energy consumption in 1992 (kg coal equivalent per person)	5,000–10,000	Less than 100
	1,000–5,000	

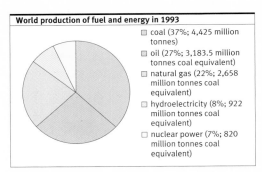

World production of fuel and energy in 1993

- coal (37%; 4,425 million tonnes)
- oil (27%; 3,183.5 million tonnes coal equivalent)
- natural gas (22%; 2,658 million tonnes coal equivalent)
- hydroelectricity (8%; 922 million tonnes coal equivalent)
- nuclear power (7%; 820 million tonnes coal equivalent)

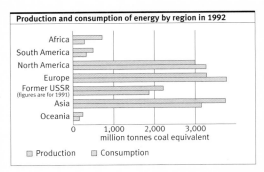

Production and consumption of energy by region in 1992

Africa, South America, North America, Europe, Former USSR (figures are for 1991), Asia, Oceania

million tonnes coal equivalent

☐ Production   ☐ Consumption

The above map shows the use of the world's energy resources; the pie chart (left) shows world production of fuel and energy; the bar chart (right) shows the production and consumption of energy by region (million tonnes coal equivalent).

innovation was of huge importance. In 1885 the first vehicle propelled by internal combustion was made – one, that is to say, in which the energy produced by heat was used directly to drive a piston inside the cylinder of an engine, instead of being transmitted to it via steam made in a boiler with an external flame. Nine years later came a four-wheeled contraption made by the French Panhard Company, which is a recognizable ancestor of the modern car. France, with Germany, dominated the production of cars for the next decade or so and they remained rich men's toys. This is automobile pre-history. Automobile history began in 1907, when American Henry Ford set up a production line for what became his "Model T". Planned deliberately for a mass market, its price was low. By 1915 a million Ford cars were being made each year and by 1926 the Model T cost less than $300 (about £60 in British money at rates then current). An enormous commercial success was underway. So was a social and economic revolution. Ford changed the world. By giving the masses something previously considered a luxury, and a mobility unavailable even to the millionaire fifty years earlier, his impact was as great as the coming of railways. This increase in amenity was to spread around the world, too, with enormous consequences.

WORLDWIDE CAR MANUFACTURING

One result was a worldwide car manufacturing industry, often dominating domestic manufacturing sectors and bringing, eventually, large-scale international integration; in the 1980s eight large producers made three out of four of the world's cars. The industry stimulated huge investment in related sectors; only a few years ago, half the robots employed in the world's industry were welders in car factories, and another quarter painted their products. Over a similarly long term, car production enormously stimulated demand for oil. Huge numbers of people came to be employed in supplying fuel and other services to car owners. Investment in road-building became a major concern of governments, as it had not been since the days of the Roman Empire.

THE BIRTH OF THE ASSEMBLY LINE

Ford, like many other great revolutionaries, had brought other men's ideas to bear on his

Once filled with human workers, high-tech car assembly plants now contain many industrial robots (the Czech word *robota* meant "forced labour"). Japanese manufacturers did much to promote automation in the 1970s when it was feared that the booming Japanese economy would make it increasingly difficult to attract human workers.

History of the automobile

In the 20th century, the car has taken the place of the train as the vital means of transport in the developed world. Once the internal combustion engine had been patented, Carl Friedrich Benz applied it, in 1885, to a tricycle with a top speed of 10mph (15km/ph) – the design of the automobile soon followed.

Automobiles first became popular in the United States and from the start Detroit was the headquarters of the most important automobile manufacturers. Since the appearance of early models, such as the Ford Model-T in the United States, car design has undergone huge changes:

ever higher speeds and increased braking power have been achieved, and the vast range of models now on the market would have been unimaginable at the beginning of the twentieth century.

One of the most remarkable recent changes in the car industry is the growing concern for driver and passenger safety. Companies now compete to offer features such as air bags and automatic braking systems. Even cars designed to give drivers better visibility in the dark (using special night-vision cameras combined with the latest computer technology) will soon be available.

The world's first assembly line in the Ford car factory in 1913.

own. In the process he also transformed the workplace. Stimulated by his example, assembly lines became the characteristic way of making consumer goods. On those set up by Ford, the motor car moved steadily from worker to worker, each one of them carrying out in the minimum necessary time the pre-

cisely delimited and, if possible, simple task in which he (or, later, she) was skilled. The psychological effect on the worker was soon deplored, but Ford saw that such work was very boring and paid high wages (thus also making it easier for his workers to buy his cars). This was a contribution to another fundamental social change, with cultural consequences of incalculable significance – the fuelling of economic prosperity by increasing purchasing power and, therefore, demand.

THE COMPUTER AGE

Some assembly lines nowadays are "manned" entirely by robots. The single greatest technological change to affect the major industrial societies since 1945 has come in the huge field of what is comprehensively called information technology, the complex science of devising, building, handling and managing electronically powered machines that process information. Few innovatory waves in the history of technology have rolled in so fast. Applications of work done only during the Second World War were widely diffused in services and industrial processes over a couple of decades. This was most obvious in the spread of "computers", electronic data processors of which the first only appeared in 1945. Rapid increases in power and speed, reductions in size and improvements in visual display capacity brought a huge increase in the amount of information that could be ordered and processed in a given time. Quantitative change, though, brought qualitative transformation. Technical operations hitherto unfeasible because of the mass of data involved now became possible. Intellectual activity had never been so suddenly accelerated. Moreover, at the same time as there was revolutionary growth in the power of computers, so there was in their availability, cheapness and portability. Within thirty years a "microchip" the size of a credit card was doing the job that had at first required a machine the size of the average British living room. It was observed in 1965 that the processing power of a "chip" doubled every eighteen months; the 2,000 or so transistors carried by a chip thirty years ago have now multiplied to millions. The transforming effects have been felt exponentially, and in every human activity – from money- and war-making, to scholarship and pornography.

IMPROVED COMMUNICATIONS

Computers are, of course, only part of another long story of development and innovation in communication of all kinds, beginning with advances in the physical and mechanical movement of solid objects – goods and people. The major nineteenth-century achievements were the application of steam to land and sea communication, and later electricity and the internal combustion engine. In the air, there had been balloons, and the first "dirigible" airships flew before 1900, but it was only in 1903 that the first flight was made by a man-carrying "heavier than air" machine (that is, one whose buoyancy was not derived from bags of a gas lighter than air). This announced a new age of physical transport; a century later, the value of goods moving through London's biggest airport was greater than that through any British seaport. Millions now regularly travel by air on business and professional concerns, as well as for leisure, and flight has given a command of space to the individual only faintly imaginable as the century began.

The development of mobile telephones and digital photography and video – and the modern fusion between them – means that ordinary people can become media producers as well as consumers. It is estimated that nearly all cellular phones used in Japan now have a digital camera – this was the scene at a launch event in Tokyo in 2004. The rise in ownership of handheld technology among the general public has meant an increasing supply of more immediate imagery to the traditional news media.

The communication of information had already advanced far into another revolution. The essence of this was the separation of the information flow from any physical connection between source and signal. In the middle of the nineteenth century, poles carrying the wires for the electric telegraph were already a familiar sight beside railway lines, and the process of linking the world together with undersea cables had begun. Physical links were still fundamental. Then, Hertz identified the radio-magnetic wave. By 1900, scientists were exploiting electromagnetic theory to make possible the sending of the first, literally, "wireless" messages. The transmitter and the receiver no longer needed any physical connection. Appropriately, it was in 1901, the first year of a new century to be profoundly marked by this invention, that Marconi sent the first radio message across the Atlantic. Thirty years later, most of the millions who by then owned wireless receivers had ceased to believe that they needed to open windows for the mysterious "waves" to reach them and large-scale broadcasting systems existed in all major countries.

A few years before this the first demonstration had been made of the devices on which television was based. In 1936, the BBC opened the first regularly scheduled television broadcasting service; twenty years later the medium was commonplace in leading industrial societies and now that is true worldwide. Like the coming of print, the new medium had huge implications, but for their full measurement they must be placed in the context of the whole modern era of communications development. Like the coming of print, the implications were incalculable, though they were politically and socially neutral or, rather, double-edged. Telegraphy and radio made information more quickly available, and this could be advantageous both to governments and to their opponents. The ambiguities of television became visible even more rapidly. Its images could expose things governments wanted to hide to the gaze of hundreds of millions, but it was also believed to shape opinion in the interests of those who controlled it. By the end of the twentieth century, too, it was clear that the Internet, the latest major advance in information technology, also had ambiguous possibilities. From its origins in the Arpanet – developed by the Advanced Research Projects Agency of the US Department of Defense in 1969 – the Internet by 2000 had 360 million regular users, mostly in the developed countries. By then, the ease of communication that it offered had helped revolutionize world markets and strongly influence world politics, especially in those regions that were moving towards more open political systems. E-commerce – the buying and selling of consumer goods and services through the Internet – became a major part of commerce in the United States in the early 2000s, with companies such as Amazon and E-Bay among the wealthiest and most influential in the market. By 2005, electronic mail had replaced postal services as the preferred way of communication in North

Television sets became common in Western homes from around 1950. Today, television plays an important role in both reflecting and creating social trends in the developed world.

America, Europe, and parts of East Asia. But at the same time much of the ever increasing speed capacity of Internet transfers was used for watching pornographic films or to play interactive games. And with much of its capacity wasted, the social difference between those who spend much of their day on-line and those who have no access to the Internet is increasing rapidly.

SCIENCE AND NATURE

By 1950 MODERN INDUSTRY was already dependent on science and scientists, directly or indirectly, obviously or not, acknowledged or not. Moreover, the transformation of fundamental science into end products was by then often very rapid, and has continued to accelerate in most areas of technology. A substantial generalization of the use of the motor car, after the grasping of the principle of the internal combustion engine, took about half a century; in recent times, the microchip made hand-held computers possible in about ten years. Technological progress is still the only way in which large numbers of people become aware of the importance of science. Yet there have been important changes in the way in which it has come to shape their lives.

THE REPERCUSSIONS OF SCIENCE

In the nineteenth century, most practical results of science were still often by-products of scientific curiosity. Sometimes they were even accidental. By 1900 a change was underway. Some scientists had seen that consciously directed and focused research was sensible. Twenty years later, large industrial companies were beginning to see research as a proper call on their investment,

albeit a small one. Some industrial research departments were in the end to grow into enormous establishments in their own right as petrochemicals, plastics, electronics and biochemical medicine made their appearance later in the century. Nowadays, the ordinary citizen of a developed country cannot lead a life that does not rely on applied science. This all-pervasiveness, coupled with its impressiveness in its most spectacular achievements, was one of the reasons for the ever-growing recognition given to science. Money is one yardstick. The Cavendish Laboratory at Cambridge, for example, in which some of the fundamental experiments of nuclear physics were carried out before 1914, had then a grant from the university of about £300 a year – roughly $1,500 at rates then current. When, during the war of 1939–45, the British and Americans decided that a major effort had to be mounted to produce nuclear weapons, the resulting "Manhattan Project" (as it was called) is estimated to have cost as much as all the scientific research previously conducted by human beings from the beginnings of recorded time.

Plastic products became highly fashionable in the 1950s. Advertisements such as this one emphasized plastic's versatility, colourfulness and practicality.

GOVERNMENT INVESTMENT

Huge sums of money, such as that spent on the "Manhattan Project" – and there were to be even larger bills to meet in the post-war world – mark another momentous change, the new importance of science to government. After being for centuries the object of only occasional patronage by the state, it now became a major political concern. Only governments could provide resources on the scale needed for some of the things done since 1945. One benefit they usually sought was better weapons, which explained much of the huge scientific investment of the United States and the Soviet Union. The increasing interest and participation of governments has not, on the other hand, meant that science has grown more national; indeed, the reverse is true. The tradition of international communication among scientists is one of their most splendid inheritances from the first great age of science in the seventeenth century, but even without it science would, for theoretical and technical reasons, jump national frontiers.

A NEW PHYSICS

ALREADY BEFORE 1914 it was increasingly clear that boundaries between the individual sciences, some of them intelligible and usefully distinct fields of study since the seventeenth century, were tending first to blur and then to disappear. The full implications of this have only begun to appear very lately, however. For all the achievements of the great chemists and biologists of the eighteenth and nineteenth centuries, it was the physicists who did most to change the scientific map of the twentieth century. James Clerk Maxwell, the first professor of experimental physics at Cambridge, published in the 1870s the work in electro-magnetism which first broke effec-

tively into fields and problems left untouched by Newtonian physics. Maxwell's theoretical work and its experimental investigation profoundly affected the accepted view that the universe obeyed natural, regular and discoverable laws of a somewhat mechanical kind and that it consisted essentially of indestructible matter in various combinations and arrangements. Into this picture had now to be fitted the newly discovered electromagnetic fields, whose technological possibilities quickly fascinated laymen and scientists alike.

SPLITTING THE ATOM

The crucial work that followed the investigation of electro-magnetism and that founded modern physical theory was done between 1895 and 1914, by Röntgen who discovered X-rays, Becquerel who discovered radioactivity, Thomson who identified the electron, the Curies who isolated radium, and Rutherford who investigated the structure of the atom. They made it possible to see the physical world in a new way. Instead of lumps of matter, the universe began to look more like an aggregate of atoms, which were tiny solar systems of particles held together by electrical forces in particular arrangements. These particles seemed to behave in a way that blurred the distinction between matter and electro-magnetic fields. Moreover, such arrangements of particles were not fixed, for in nature one arrangement might give way to another and thus elements could change into other elements. Rutherford's work, in particular, was decisive, for he established that atoms could be "split" because of their structure as a system of particles. This meant that matter, even at this fundamental level, could be manipulated. Two such particles were soon identified: the proton and the electron; others were not isolated until after 1932, when Chadwick discovered the neutron. The scientific world now had an experimentally validated picture of the atom's structure as a system of particles. But as late as 1935 Rutherford said that nuclear physics would have no practical implications – and no one rushed to contradict him.

QUANTUM MECHANICS

What this radically important experimental work did not at once do was supply a new theoretical framework to replace the Newtonian system. This only came with a long revolution in theory, beginning in the last years of the nineteenth century and culminating in the 1920s. It was focused on two different sets of problems, which gave rise to the work designated by the terms relativity and quantum theory. The pioneers were Max Planck and Albert Einstein. By 1905 they had provided experimental and mathematical demonstration that the Newtonian laws of motion were an inadequate framework for explanation of a fact no longer to be contested: that energy transactions in the material world took place not in an even flow but in discrete jumps – quanta, as they came to be termed. Planck showed that radiant heat (from, for example, the sun) was not, as Newtonian physics required, emitted continuously; he argued that this was true of all energy transactions. Einstein argued that light was propagated not continuously but in particles. Though much important work was to be done in the next twenty or so years, Planck's contribution had the most profound effect and it was again unsettling. Newton's views had been found wanting, but there was nothing to put in their place.

Meanwhile, after his work on quanta, Einstein had published in 1905 the work for which he was to be most widely, if

One of the most expensive areas of government-funded scientific research is the collection of data about space. These radio telescopes form part of the Very Large Array (VLA) in New Mexico in the United States. This array effectively forms one gigantic radio dish: the data gathered by the 27 telescopes, each of which has a diameter of 82ft (25m), is combined to produce a single image at the National Radio Astronomy Observatory.

While studying the distribution of energy in a black body, in 1900, Max Planck (1858–1947) formulated what he called the quantum theory of energy. This was to have enormous impact on physics, particularly when its application by Albert Einstein and Niels Bohr led to further major discoveries. Planck was awarded the Nobel prize for physics in 1918.

uncomprehendingly, celebrated – his statement of the theory of relativity. This was essentially a demonstration that the traditional distinctions of space and time, and mass and energy, could not be consistently maintained. Instead of Newton's three-dimensional physics, he directed men's attention to a "space-time continuum" in which the interplay of space, time and motion could be understood. This was soon to be corroborated by astronomical observation of facts for which Newtonian cosmology could not properly account, but which could find a place in Einstein's theory. One strange and unanticipated consequence of the work on which relativity theory was based was his demonstration of the relations of mass and energy which he formulated as $E = mc^2$, where E is energy, m is mass and c is the constant speed of light. The importance and accuracy of this theoretical formulation was not to become clear until much more nuclear physics had been done. It would then be apparent that the relationships observed when mass energy was converted into heat energy in the breaking up of nuclei also corresponded to his formula.

A BREAKTHROUGH IN NUCLEAR PHYSICS

While these advances were absorbed, attempts continued to rewrite physics, but they did not get far until a major theoretical breakthrough in 1926 finally provided a mathematical framework for Planck's observations and, indeed, for nuclear physics. So sweeping was the achievement of Schrödinger and Heisenberg, the two mathematicians mainly responsible, that it seemed for a time as if quantum mechanics might be of virtually limitless explanatory power in the sciences. The behaviour of particles in the atom observed by Rutherford and Bohr could now be accounted for. Further development of their work led to predictions of the existence of new nuclear particles, notably the positron, which was duly identified in the 1930s. Quantum mechanics seemed to have inaugurated a new age of physics and the discovery of new particles continued.

A NEW VIEW OF THE UNIVERSE

By mid-century much more had disappeared in science than just a once-accepted set of general laws (and in any case it remained true that, for most everyday purposes, Newtonian physics was still all that was needed). In physics, from which it had spread to other sciences, the whole notion of a general law was being replaced by the concept of statistical probability as the best that could be hoped for. The idea, as well as the content, of science was changing. Furthermore, the boundaries between sciences collapsed under the onrush of new knowledge made accessible by new theories and instrumentation. Any one of the great traditional divisions of science was soon beyond the grasp of any single mind. The conflations involved in importing physical theory into neurology or mathematics into biology put further barriers in the way of attaining that synthesis of knowledge that had been the dream of the nineteenth century, just as the rate of acquisition of new knowledge (some in such quantities that it could only be handled by the newly available computers) became faster than ever.

THE BIOLOGICAL SCIENCES

THE INCREASINGLY COMPLEX nature of scientific research did nothing to diminish either the prestige of the scientists or the faith that they were humanity's best hope for the better management of its future. Doubts, when they came, arose from other sources than their inability to generate an overarching theory as intelligible to lay understanding as Newton's had been. Meanwhile, the flow of specific advances in the sciences continued.

In a measure, the baton passed after 1945 from the physical to the biological or "life" sciences. Their current success and promise has, once again, deep roots. The seventeenth-century invention of the microscope had first revealed the organization of tissue into discrete units called cells. In the nineteenth century investigators already understood that cells could divide and that they developed individually. Cell theory, widely accepted by 1900, suggested that individual cells, being alive themselves, provided a good approach to the study of life, and the application of chemistry to this became one of the main avenues of biological research. The other mainline advance in nineteenth-century biological science was provided by a new discipline, genetics; the study of the inheritance

by offspring of characteristics from parents. Darwin had invoked inheritance as the means of propagation of traits favoured by natural selection. The first steps towards understanding the mechanism that made this possible were those of an Austrian monk, Gregor Mendel. From a meticulous series of breeding experiments on pea plants, Mendel concluded that there existed hereditary units controlling the expression of traits passed from parents to offspring. In 1909 a Dane gave them the name "gene".

THE DISCOVERY OF DNA

Gradually the chemistry of cells became better understood and the physical reality of genes was accepted. In 1873 the presence in the cell nucleus of a substance that might embody the most fundamental determinant of all living matter was already established. Experiments then revealed a visible location for genes in chromosones, and in the 1940s it was shown that genes controlled the chemical structure of protein, the most important constituent of cells. In 1944 the first step was taken towards identifying the specific effective agent in bringing about changes in certain bacteria, and therefore in controlling protein structure. In the 1950s it was at last identified as "DNA", whose physical structure (the double helix) was established in 1953. The crucial importance of this substance (its full name is deoxyribonucleic acid) is that it is the carrier of the genetic information that determines the synthesis of protein molecules at the basis of life. The chemical mechanisms underlying the diversity of biological phenomena were at last accessible. Physiologically, and perhaps psychologically, this implied a transformation of human self-perception unprecedented since the diffusion of Darwinian ideas in the previous century.

THE APPLICATION OF GENETICS

The identification and analysis of the structure of DNA was the most conspicuous

A computer screen at a research centre in Cambridge, England, displays as a series of coloured bands a sequence of human deoxyribonucleic acid – or DNA. The DNA consists of two long strands linked by the interactions of bases along their lengths. Each colour represents a specific base. The sequence of bases makes up the genetic code in the form of genes, or segments of DNA which have specific functions within an organism. By studying these genes, a greater understanding of genetic diseases and heredity can be achieved.

single step towards a new manipulation of nature, the shaping of life forms. Already in 1947, the word "biotechnology" had been coined. Once again, not only more scientific knowledge but also new definitions of fields of study and new applications followed. "Molecular biology" and "genetic engineering", like "biotechnology", quickly became familiar terms. The genes of some organisms could, it was soon shown, be altered so as to give those organisms new and desirable characteristics. By manipulating their growth processes, yeast and other micro-organisms could be made to produce novel substances, too – enzymes, hormones or other chemicals. This was one of the first applications of the new science; the empirical technology and data accumulated informally for thousands of years in making bread, beer, wine and cheese was at last to be overtaken. Genetic modification of bacteria could now grow new compounds. By the end of the twentieth century, three-quarters of the soya grown in the United States was the product of genetically modified seed, while agricultural producers like Canada, Argentina and Brazil were also raising huge genetically modified crops.

More dramatically, by the end of the 1980s there was underway a worldwide collaborative investigation, the Human Genome Project. Its almost unimaginably ambitious aim was the mapping of the human genetic apparatus. The position, structure and function of every human gene – of which there were said to be from 30,000 to 50,000 in every cell, each gene having up to 30,000 pairs of the four basic chemical units that form the genetic code – was to be identified. As the century closed, it was announced that the project had been completed. (Shortly afterwards, the sobering discovery was made that human beings possessed only about twice the number of genes as the fruit fly – substantially fewer than had been expected.)

Life sciences: milestones in biotechnology and genetic engineering

1865 Mendel publishes first accounts of experiments with peas showing the presence of independent factors ("genes").

1909 First use of the term "gene" in a book by Johannsen.

1928 Fleming discovers penicillin – publication of the first paper.

1941 First mass production of antibiotics (penicillin) in the USA (UK production insufficient for demand).

1947 First use of the word "Biotechnology" (USA).

1953 Crick and Watson publish paper showing the structure of DNA. Structure of insulin published (first protein structure to be determined).

1973 Cohen and Boyer discover recombinant rDNA – the basis for genetic engineering.

1975 Milstein publishes the results of cell fusion experiments which lead to the development of monocolonal antibodies.

1982 Commercial production of first genetically engineered drug (insulin).

1983 First publication of gene mapping (Huntington's disease).

1986 Jefferys publishes method of "DNA" fingerprinting", first used forensically 1987.

1989 First isolation (structure determination) of a defective gene (cystic fibrosis).

1990 Goodfellow discovers structure of testis determining gene.

1991 First sex-reversed transgenic animal (mouse) produced.

1997 "Dolly" the sheep is the first mammal cloned from a cell taken from an adult animal.

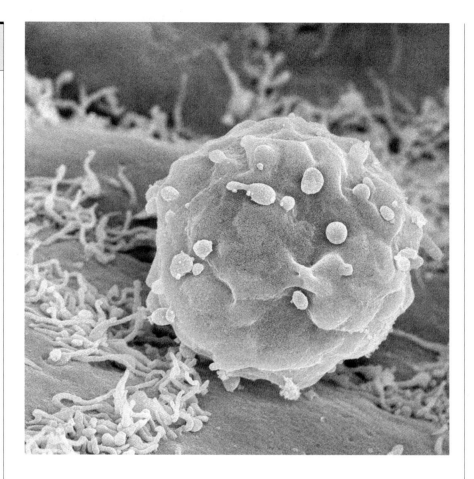

The door had been opened to a great future for manipulation of nature at a new level – and what that might mean was already visible in a Scottish laboratory in the form of the first successfully "cloned" sheep. Already, too, the screening for the presence of defective genes is a reality and the replacement of some of them is possible. The social and medical implications of this are tremendous. At a day-to-day level, what is called DNA "fingerprinting" is now a matter of routine in police work in identifying individuals from blood, saliva or semen samples.

By 2005 it was becoming clear that genetic engineering would shape a substantial part of our future, in spite of the controversy created by many research programmes in this field. The "new" micro-organisms created by geneticists are now patentable and therefore commercially available in many parts of the

Embryonic stem cells (ESCs), in purple, viewed through a high-powered scanning electron micrograph (SEM). ESCs are pluripotent, which means that they can differentiate into any cell type, depending upon the biochemical signals received by the immature cells. This ability makes ESCs a potential source of cells to repair damaged tissue in diseases such as Parkinson's and insulin-dependent diabetes. However, controversy attends the research because it requires the destruction of an embryo.

world. Likewise, genetically modified crops are used to increase yields through the creation of more resistant and more productive strains, thereby giving some regions their first ever opportunity to become self-sufficient in staple foods. But while providing obvious benefits, biotechnology has also come under scrutiny for delivering food products that may not be safe and for the increasing dominance of large multinational corporations in both research and production worldwide. Such concerns have, for obvious reasons, become particularly strong when genetic research on human material has been involved, such as in work on stem cells from embryos. Many scientists fail to realize how the matters they are dealing with raise immense concerns among the public, mostly because of warnings from the history of the twentieth century.

Carl Sagan on our knowledge of space

"We now have, for the first time, the tools to make contact with civilizations on planets of other stars. It is an astonishing fact that the great one-thousand-foot-diameter radio telescope of the National Astronomy and Ionosphere Center, run by Cornell University in Arecibo, Puerto Rico, would be able to communicate with an identical copy of itself anywhere in the Milky Way Galaxy. We have at our command the means to communicate not merely over distances of hundreds or thousands of light-years; we can communicate over tens of thousands of light-years, into a volume containing hundreds of billions of stars. The hypothesis that advanced technical civilizations exist on planets of other stars is amenable to experimental testing. It has been removed from the arena of pure speculation. It is now in the arena of experiment."

An extract from ch. 27 of *The Cosmic Connection* by Carl Sagan, 1973.

THE SPEED OF PROGRESS

Progress in these matters has owed much of its startling rapidity to the availability of new computer power. It is another instance, too, of the tendency for scientific advance to accelerate, and so both to provide faster applications of new knowledge and to challenge more quickly the world of settled assumptions and landmarks with new ideas that must be taken into account by laymen. Yet it remains as hard as ever to see what such challenges imply or may mean. For all the huge recent advances in the life sciences, it is doubtful that even their approximate importance is sensed by more than tiny minorities.

THE SPACE AGE

FOR A BRIEF PERIOD IN THE middle of the twentieth century the power of science was above all visible in the exploration of space. Such an extension of the human environment may well turn out one day to dwarf in significance other historical processes (discussed at greater length in this book) but as yet shows no sign of doing so. Yet it suggests that the capacity of human culture to meet unprecedented challenges is as great as ever and it has provided what is so far the most obvious example of human domination of nature. For most people, the space age began in October 1957 when an unmanned Soviet satellite called *Sputnik I* was launched by rocket and could soon be discerned in orbit around the earth, emitting radio signals. Its political impact was vast: it shattered the belief that Russian technology lagged significantly behind American. The full significance of the event, though, was still obscured, because superpower rivalries swamped other considerations for most observers. In fact, it ended the era when the possibility of human travel in space could still be doubted. Thus, almost incidentally, it marked a break in historical continuity as important as the European discovery of the Americas, or the Industrial Revolution.

EARLY ACHIEVEMENTS

Visions of space exploration could be found in the last years of the nineteenth century and the early years of the twentieth, when they were brought to the notice of the Western public in fiction, notably, in the stories of Jules Verne and H.G. Wells. Its technology went back almost as far. A Russian scientist, K.E. Tsolikovsky, had designed multi-staged rockets and devised many of the basic principles of space travel (and he, too, had written fiction to popularize his obsession) well before 1914. The first Soviet liquid-fuelled rocket went up (three miles) in 1933, and a two-stage rocket six years later. The Second World War prompted a major German rocket programme, which the United States had drawn on to begin its own programme in 1955. It started with more modest hardware than the Russians (who already had a commanding lead) and the first American satellite weighed only three pounds (*Sputnik I* weighed 184 pounds). A much-publicized launch attempt was made at the end of December 1957, but the rocket caught fire instead of taking off. The Americans would soon do much better than this, but within a month of *Sputnik I* the Russians had already put up *Sputnik II*, an astonishingly successful machine, weighing half a ton and carrying the first passenger in space, a black-and-white mongrel dog called Laika. For nearly six months *Sputnik II* orbited the earth, visible to the whole inhabited world and enraging thousands of dog-lovers, for Laika was not to return.

THE SPACE RACE

By early 1958, the Russian and American space programmes had somewhat diverged. The Russians, building on their pre-war experience, had put much emphasis on the power and size of their rockets, which could lift big loads, and here their strength continued to lie. The military implications were more obvious than those (equally profound but less spectacular) which flowed from American concentration on data-gathering and on instrumentation. A competition for prestige was soon underway, but although people spoke of a "space race" the contestants were really running towards different goals. With one great exception (the wish to be first to put a man in space) their technical decisions were probably not much influenced by one another's performance. The contrast was clear enough when *Vanguard*, the American satellite that failed in December 1957, was successfully launched the following March. Tiny though it was, it went much deeper into space than any predecessor and provided more valuable scientific information in proportion to its size than any other satellite. It is likely to be going around for another couple of centuries or so.

New achievements then quickly followed. At the end of 1958 the first satellite for communications purposes was successfully launched (it was American). In 1960 the Americans scored another "first" – the recovery of a capsule after re-entry. The Russians followed this by orbiting and retrieving *Sputnik V*, a four-and-a-half-ton satellite, carrying two dogs, which thus became the first living creatures to have entered space and returned to earth safely. In the spring of the following year, on 12 April, a Russian rocket took off carrying a man, Yuri Gagarin. He landed 108 minutes later after one orbit around the earth. Humanity's life in space had begun, four years after *Sputnik I*.

PRESIDENT KENNEDY'S MOON PROJECT

Possibly spurred by a wish to offset a recent publicity disaster in American relations with Cuba, President Kennedy proposed in May 1961 that the United States should try to land a man on the moon (the first man-made object had already crash-landed there in 1959) and return him safely to earth before the end of the decade. His publicly stated reasons for recommending this compare interestingly with those that led the rulers of fifteenth-century Portugal and Spain to back their Magellans and da Gamas. One was that such a project provided a good national goal; the next that it would be prestigious ("impressive to mankind" were the president's words); the third was that it was of great importance for the exploration of space; and the fourth was (somewhat oddly) that it was of unparalleled difficulty and expense. Kennedy said nothing

of the advancement of science, of commercial or military advantage – or, indeed, of what seems to have been his real motivation: to do it before the Russians did. Surprisingly, the project met virtually no opposition and the first money was soon allocated.

During the early 1960s the Russians continued to make spectacular progress. The world was perhaps most excited when they sent a woman into space in 1963, but their technical competence continued to be best shown by the size of their vehicles – a three-man machine was launched in 1964 – and in the achievement the following year of the first "space walk", when one of the crew emerged from his vehicle and moved about outside while in orbit (though reassuringly attached to it by a lifeline). The Russians were to go on to further important advances in achieving rendezvous for vehicles in space and in engineering their docking, but after 1967 (the year of the first death through space travel, when a Russian was killed on re-entry) the glamour transferred to the Americans. In 1968, they achieved a sensational success by sending a three-man vehicle into orbit around the moon and transmitting television pictures of its surface. It was by now clear that *Apollo*, the moon-landing project, was going to succeed.

THE FIRST MOON LANDING

In May 1969 a vehicle put into orbit with the tenth rocket of the project approached to within six miles of the moon to assess the techniques of the final stage of landing. A few weeks later, on 16 July, a three-man crew was launched. Their lunar module landed on the moon's surface four days later. On the following morning, 21 July, the first human being to set foot on the moon was Neil Armstrong, the commander of the mission. President Kennedy's goal had been achieved with time

Man's first steps on the moon, on 21 July 1969. Millions of spectators worldwide were almost immediately able to see on television this extraordinary event, which, as well as demonstrating the advance of space technology, showed how quickly audiovisual technology was developing. As American astronaut Neil Armstrong (1930–) stepped from his spacecraft onto the surface of the moon, he uttered the phrase for which he will always be remembered: "... a small step for man but a giant leap for mankind."

An American space shuttle is launched in June 1991. Although they are launched by rockets, on their return to the earth, space shuttles are able to land on runways, like aeroplanes.

An American space shuttle is launched in June 1991. Although they are launched by rockets, on their return to the earth, space shuttles are able to land on runways, like aeroplanes.

in hand. Other landings were to follow. In a decade that had opened politically with humiliation for the United States in the Caribbean and was ending in the morass of an unsuccessful war in Asia, it was a triumphant reassertion of what America (and, by implication, capitalism) could do. It was also the outstanding signal of the latest and greatest extension by *Homo sapiens* of his environment, the beginning of a new phase of his history, that to be enacted on other celestial bodies.

THE EXPLORATION AND USE OF SPACE

Even at the time, this wonderful achievement was decried, and now it is difficult to shake off a sense of anti-climax. Its critics felt that the mobilization of resources the programme needed was unjustified, because irrelevant to the real problems of the earth. To some, the technology of space travel has seemed to be our civilization's version of the pyramids, a huge investment in the wrong things in a world crying out for money for education, nutrition, medical research – to name but a few pressing needs. It is not difficult to sympathize with such a view. Yet, the far-reaching scientific and economic effect of the space effort is hardly quantifiable; the use of knowledge of miniaturization needed to make control systems, for example, rapidly spills over into applications of obvious social and economic value. It cannot be said that this knowledge would necessarily have been available had not the investment in space come first. Nor, indeed, can we be confident that the resources lavished on space exploration would have been made available for any other great scientific or social goals, had they not been used in this way. Our social machinery does not operate like that.

The mythical importance of what has happened has also to be considered. However regrettable it may be, modern societies have shown few signs of being able to generate much interest and enthusiasm among their members for collective purposes, except for brief periods (or in war, whose "moral equivalent" – as one American philosopher put it well before 1914 – is still to seek). The imagination of large numbers of people was not really fired by the prospect of adding marginally to the GDP or introducing one more refinement to a system of social services, however intrinsically desirable these things might have been. Kennedy's identification of a national goal was shrewd; in the troubled 1960s Americans had much to agitate and divide them, but they did not turn up to frustrate launchings of the space missions.

THE SPACE SHUTTLE

It was important, too, that space exploration became more international as it went on. Before the 1970s there was little co-operation between the two greatest nations concerned, the United States and Soviet Russia, and much duplication of effort and inefficiencies. Ten years before the Americans planted the American flag on it, a Soviet mission had dropped a Lenin pennant on the moon. This

---

The exploration and use of space: major steps down to 1969

1903 Konstantin Tsolikovsky (1857–1935) publishes paper on rocket space travel using liquid propellants.

1933 1 May: Tsolikovsky predicts that many Soviet citizens will live to see the first space flights.

1944 German V2 rockets used to bombard London.

1954 President Eisenhower announces a small scientific satellite, *Vanguard*, will be launched 1957–8.

1957 1 October: Launch of *Sputnik I* (USSR), weight 184lbs (83.46kg).
3 November: Launch of *Sputnik II*, weight 1,120lbs (508kg), with the dog Laika as passenger.

1958 31 January: Launch of *Explorer* (USA) and discovery of Van Allen radiation belts.
17 March: Launch of *Vanguard 1* (USA), weight 3.25lbs (1.47kg). The first satellite with solar batteries.

1959 13 September: *Luna II* (USSR) crashes on moon, the first man-made object to arrive there.
10 October: *Luna III* photographs far side of moon.

1960 11 August: *Discoverer 13* (USA) recovered after first successful re-entry to atmosphere.
19 August: *Sputnik V* (USSR) orbits earth with two dogs which return unharmed.

1961 12 April: Yuri Gagarin (USSR) orbits the earth.
25 May: President Kennedy commits USA to landing man on moon by 1970.
6 August: *Vostok II* (USSR) makes 17 orbits of earth.

1962 20 February: First manned orbited space flight.
10 July: Launch of *Telstar* (USA) and first television pictures across the Atlantic.

1965 18 March: On *Voskhod II* mission (USSR) Alexey Leonov makes ten-minute "walk in space".
2 May: *Early Bird* (*Intelsat 1*) commercial communication satellite (USA) first used by television.
15 December: Launch of *Gemini 6* (USA) which makes rendezvous with *Gemini 7*, the two craft coming within a foot of one another.

1966 July–November: *Gemini* missions 10, 11, 12 (USA) all achieve "docking" with "Agena" vehicle.

1967 First deaths in US programme.

1968 21–27 December: *Apollo 8* (USA) makes first manned voyage round the moon.

1969 14–17 January: *Soyuz IV* and V (USSR) dock in space and exchange passengers.
21 July: *Apollo 11* (USA) lands two men on the moon.

seemed ominous; there was a basic national rivalry in the technological race itself and nationalism might provoke a "scramble for space". But the dangers of competition were avoided; it was soon agreed that celestial objects were not subject to appropriation by any one state. In July 1975, some 150 miles above the earth, co-operation became a startling reality in a remarkable experiment in which Soviet and American machines connected themselves so that their crews could move from one to the other. In spite of doubts, exploration continued in a relatively benign international setting. The visual exploration of further space was carried beyond Jupiter by unmanned satellite, and 1976 brought the first landing of an unmanned exploration vehicle on the surface of the planet Mars. In 1977 the Space Shuttle, the first reusable space vehicle, made its maiden voyage.

SPACE THE NEW FRONTIER

These achievements were tremendous, yet now they are hardly noticed, so jaded are our imaginations. So rapidly did there grow up a new familiarity with the idea of space travel that by 2000 it seemed only mildly risible that an American should make the first fare-paying flight as a passenger. Yet to land safely on the moon and return was a dazzling affirmation of the belief that we live in a universe we can manage. The instruments for doing so were once magic and prayer; they are now science and technology. But continuity lies in the growing human confidence throughout history that the natural world could be manipulated. Landing on the moon was a landmark in that continuity, an event perhaps of the same order as the mastery of fire, the invention of agriculture or the discovery of nuclear power.

It can be compared also to the great age of terrestrial discovery. The timescales are interestingly different. Something like about eighty years of exploration were needed to take the Portuguese around Africa and India; there were only eight between the launching of the first man into space and the arrival of men on the moon. The target set in 1961 was achieved with about eighteen months to spare. Exploration in space proved safer, too. In spite of a few spectacular accidents, in terms of deaths per passenger-mile travelled it is still the safest form of transport known to man, while fifteenth-century seafaring was a perilous business. Actuarially, the risk of travelling in the *Santa Maria* – or even the *Mayflower* – must have been much greater than that faced by the *Apollo* crews. But there are continuities, too. The age of oceanic discovery was for a long time mainly dominated by one people, the Portuguese, building on a slow accumulation of knowledge. As data was added, piece by piece, to what was known, the base of exploration widened. Da Gama had to pick up an Arab navigator once around the Cape of Good Hope. Unknown seas lay ahead. Five hundred years later, *Apollo* was launched from a far broader but still cumulative base, nothing less than the whole scientific knowledge of mankind. In 1969, the distance to the moon was already known, so were the conditions that would greet men arriving there, most of the hazards they might encounter, the quantities of power, supplies and the nature of the other support systems they would need to return, the stresses their bodies would undergo. Though things might have gone wrong, there was a widespread feeling that they would not. In its predictable, as in its cumulative quality, space exploration epitomizes our science-based civilization. Perhaps this is why space does not seem to have changed minds and imaginations as did former great discoveries.

Behind the increasing mastery of nature achieved in seven or eight thousand years lay the hundreds of millennia during which prehistoric technology had inched forwards from the discovery that a cutting edge could be put on a stone chopper and that fire could be mastered, while the weight of genetic programming and environmental pressure still loomed much larger then than did conscious control. The dawning of consciousness that more than this was possible was the major step in man's evolution after his physical structure had settled into more or less what it is today. With it, the control and use of experience became possible.

ENVIRONMENTAL CONCERNS

ALREADY IN THE 1980s, space exploration was overshadowed in many minds by a new uneasiness about humanity's interference with nature. Within only a few years of *Sputnik I*, doubts were being voiced about the ideological roots of so masterful a view of our relationship to the natural world. This uneasiness, too, could now be expressed with a precision based on observed facts not hitherto available or not considered in that light; it was science itself, which provided the instrumentation and data that led to dismay about what was going on. A recognition of the possible future damage interference with the environment might bring was beginning to arise. It was, of course, the recognition that was new, not the phenomena which provoked it. *Homo sapiens* (and perhaps his predecessors) had always scratched away at the natural world in which he lived, modifying it in many particulars, destroying other species. Millennia later than that, migration southward and the adoption of dryland crops from the Americas had devastated the great forests of southwest China, bringing soil erosion and the consequential silting of the Yangtze drainage system in its train, and so culminating in repeated flooding over wide areas. In the early Middle Ages, Islamic conquest had

The International Space Station (ISS) in 2000 showing its first deployment of a new array of solar array panels. Since then the station has been continuously inhabited by a resident crew. The ISS is a joint project between five space agencies: NASA (USA), Roskosmos (the Russian Federation), JAXA (Japan), CSA (Canada) and ESA (the European Union).

brought goat-herding and tree-felling to the North African littoral on a scale that destroyed a fertility once able to fill the granaries of Rome. But such sweeping changes, though hardly unnoticed, were not understood. The unprecedented rapidity of ecological interference, initiated from the seventeenth century onwards by Europeans, however, was to bring things to a head. The unconsidered power of technology forced the dangers on the attention of human beings in the second half of the twentieth century. People began to reckon up damage as well as achievement, and by the middle of the 1970s

Racked earth in the Khon Kean area of northern Thailand, an agricultural region which experiences an erratic distribution of rainfall, resulting at times in flooding and at others in drought.

it seemed to some of them that even if the story of growing human mastery of the environment was an epic, that epic might well turn out to be a tragic one.

SCEPTICISM

Suspicion of science had never wholly disappeared in Western societies, although tending to be confined to a few surviving primitive or reactionary enclaves as the majesty and implication of the scientific revolution of the seventeenth century gradually unrolled. History can provide much evidence of uneasiness about interference with nature and attempts to control it, but until recently such uneasiness seemed to rest on non-rational grounds, such as the fear of provoking divine anger or nemesis. As time passed, it was steadily eroded by the palpable advantages and improvements that successful interference with nature brought about, most obviously through the creation of new wealth expressed in all sorts of goods, from better medicine to better clothing and food.

In the 1970s, however, it became clear that a new scepticism about science itself was abroad, even though only among a minority and only in rich countries. There, a cynic might have said, the dividends on science had already been drawn. Nonetheless, scepticism manifested itself there first and in the 1980s as "green" political parties sought to promote policies protective of the environment. They were not able to achieve much, but they proliferated; the established political parties and perceptive politicians therefore toyed with "green" themes, too. Environmentalists, as the concerned came to be called, benefited from the new advances in communications, which rapidly broadcast disturbing news even from previously uncommunicative sources. In 1986, an accident occurred at a Ukrainian nuclear power station. Suddenly and horribly, human interdependence was made visible. Grass eaten by lambs in Wales, milk drunk by Poles and Yugoslavs, and air breathed by Swedes, were all contaminated. An incalculable number of Russians, it appeared, were going to die over the years from the slow effects of radiation.

This alarming event was brought home to millions worldwide by television not long after other millions had watched on their screens an American rocket blow up with the loss of all on board. Chernobyl and *Challenger* showed to huge numbers of people for the first time both the limitations and the possible dangers of an advanced technological civilization.

QUESTIONING THE BENEFITS OF SCIENTIFIC PROGRESS

The terrible Chernobyl and *Challenger* accidents reinforced and diffused the new concern with the environment. It soon became tangled with much else. Some of the doubts that have recently arisen accept that our civilization has been good at creating material wealth, but note that by itself that does not necessarily make people happy. This is hardly a new idea but its application to society as a whole instead of to individuals is a new emphasis.

This development led to a wider recognition that improvement of social conditions may not remove all human dissatisfactions and may actually irritate some of them more acutely. Pollution, the oppressive anonymity of crowded cities and the nervous stress and strain of modern work conditions easily erase satisfactions provided by material gain and they are not new problems: 4,000 people died of atmospheric pollution in a week in London in 1952, but the word "smog" had been

invented nearly half a century before that. Scale, too, has now become a problem in its own right. Some modern cities may even have grown to the point at which they present problems that are, for the moment, insoluble.

FINITE RESOURCES

Some fear that resources are now so wastefully employed that we confront a new version of the Malthusian peril. Energy has never been used so lavishly as it is today; one calculation suggests that more has been used by humanity during the last century than during the whole of previous history – say, in the last 10,000 years. Yet the best estimates do not suggest that there is an imminent danger of running out of the fossil fuels that have supplied most of this enormous increase. Nor have we by any means reached the end of our capacity to produce food, though there is more land under cultivation than ever before (and its area doubled in the last century), but there would at once be an impossible situation if the whole world sought to consume other goods than food at the level of developed countries today. There is a limit to what

The town of Pripyat, which overlooks the fourth reactor of the Chernobyl nuclear power plant, was abandoned in 1986 after being heavily contaminated in the wake of the world's worst nuclear disaster to date, when the reactor at the plant exploded and spewed out radioactivity across northern Europe.

The vanishing tropical rainforests

The systematic destruction of the tropical rainforests is symbolic of the havoc that human beings are currently wreaking on the environment. Tropical rainforests are among the most advanced ecological systems on earth, as well as being the most complex, the most diverse and also the most fragile. They take up just 6 per cent of the earth's surface, but they contain 60 per cent of its biological species. It is estimated that around 170 of these species are made extinct in these forests every day. According to a report by UNESCO, 60 per cent of the world's tropical rainforests have already been felled and the destruction is accelerating all the time, at the rate of an area the size of a football pitch every second.

Scenes of devastation, such as this one, are increasingly common in the Amazon rainforests in Brazil.

a human being can eat, but virtually none to what he or she can consume in terms of a better environment, social services, medicine and the like.

We may, too, already have passed the point at which energy consumption is putting unmanageable strains on the environment (for instance, in pollution or damage to the ozone layer), and to further increase those strains would be intolerable. The social and political consequences that might follow from changes that have already occurred have not yet begun to be grasped and we have nothing like the knowledge, technique or consensus over goals such as was available to land men on the moon.

GLOBAL CLIMATIC CHANGE

This became much clearer as a new spectre came to haunt the last decades of the century – the possibility of man-made, irreversible climatic change. The year 1990 had hardly ended before it was being pointed out that it had been the hottest year since climatic records began to be kept. Was this, some asked, a sign of "global warming", of the "greenhouse effect" produced by the release into the atmosphere of the immense quantities of carbon dioxide produced by a huge population burning fossil fuels as never before? One estimate is that there is now some 25 per cent more carbon dioxide in the atmosphere than in pre-industrial times. It may be so (and as the world's output of the stuff is now said to be 6,000 million tons a year, it is not for laymen to dispute the magnitudes). Not that this was the only contributor to the phenomenon of accumulating gases in the atmosphere, whose presence prevents the planet from dissipating heat; methane, nitrous oxide and chlorofluorocarbons all add to the problem. And if global warming is not enough to worry about, then acid rain, ozone depletion leading to "holes" in the ozone layer, and deforestation at unprecedented rates, all provided major grounds for new environmental concern.

The consequences, if no effective countermeasures are forthcoming, could be enormous, expressing themselves in climatic change (average surface temperature on the earth *might* rise by between one and four degrees Celsius over the next century), agricultural transformation, rising sea-levels (six centimetres a year has been suggested as possible and plausible), and major migrations. Beginnings have been made in controlling chlorofluorocarbons, and officials from newly created environment ministries have begun to discuss measures to tackle and avert global climatic change.

The Kyoto Protocol to the UN Framework Convention on Climate Change, which came into force in 2005, is an attempt to deal with these problems through limiting the amount of greenhouse gases that are released into the atmosphere. Thirty-eight industrial nations have pledged to reduce their emissions to below 1990 levels by 2012. But the world's largest polluter, the United States, has refused to sign, while the world's second largest polluter, China, is exempt from most of the regulations because of its status as a developing country. Even if the signatories live up to their commitments, most experts believe that much more is needed to avoid the long-term effects of global warming. By the turn of the century it was abundantly clear that if the major states could eventually come to co-operate rather than compete, there would be plenty of common concerns for humankind to co-operate about – if they could agree on what had to be done.

We are now aware that the price of industrialization can be heavy environmental damage. Here, chimney stacks at a steel mill in Bihar, India, pollute the air in a scene to be found on every continent and known to be partly responsible for global warming.

6 IDEAS, ATTITUDES AND AUTHORITY

Pictured is the Sunday market in a Peruvian village near Cuzco, once an Inca city. In spite of technological progress and the spread of consumer society, millions of people around the world still carry out economic transactions today in the way they have done for centuries in such markets.

HISTORIANS SHOULD NOT pontificate about what goes on in the minds of the majority, for they know no more than anyone else; it is the untypical, who have left disproportionately prominent evidence, whom they know most about. They should be careful, too, about speculating on the effect of what they think are widely held ideas. Obviously, as recent political responses to environmental concerns show, changes in ideas can soon affect our collective life. But this is true even when only a minority know what the ozone layer is. Ideas held more widely, and of a vaguer, less-defined sort, also have historical impact; a Victorian Englishman invented the expression "cake of custom"' to speak of the attitudes, formed by deep-seated and usually unquestioned assumptions, which exercise decisive conser-vative weight in most societies. To be dogmatic about how such ideas operate is even more hazardous than to say how ideas tie up with specific matters (such as environmental change), yet the effort has to be made.

We can now see, for example, that more than any other single influence a growing abundance of commodities has recently shattered what was for millions – still not long ago – a world of stable expectations. This is still happening, most strikingly in some of the poorest countries. Cheap consumer goods and the images of them increasingly available in advertisements, especially on television, bring major social changes in their train. Such goods confer status; they generate envy and ambition, provide incentives to work for wages with which to buy them, and often encourage movement towards towns and centres where those wages are to be had. This severs ties with traditional ways and with the disciplines of ordered, stable life. This is one of many currents feeding the hastening onrush of modernity.

A NEW SENSE OF OPTIMISM

Part of the complicated background to and the process of such changes is an obvious paradox: the last century was one of unprecedentedly dreadful tragedy and disaster on any measurable scale, and yet it appeared to end with more people than ever believing that human life and the condition of the world could be improved, perhaps indefinitely, and therefore that they should be. The origins of such optimistic attitudes lie centuries back in

Europe; until recently, they were confined to cultures rooted in that continent. Elsewhere they have still to make much progress. Few could formulate such an idea clearly or consciously, even when asked; yet it is one shared more widely than ever before and one that is changing behaviour everywhere.

Almost certainly such a change owes less to exhortatory preaching (though there has been plenty of that) than to the material changes whose psychological impact has everywhere helped to break up the cake of custom. In many places they were the first comprehensible sign that change was in fact possible, that things need not always be as they have been. Once, most societies consisted mainly of peasants living in similar bondage to routine, custom, the seasons, poverty. Now, cultural gulfs within humankind – say, those between the European factory-worker and his equivalent in India or China – are often vast. That between the factory-worker and peasant is wider still. Yet even the peasant begins to sense the possibility of change. To have spread the idea that change is not only possible but also desirable is the most important and disruptive of all the triumphs of the culture – European in origin – which we now call "Western".

THE MOMENTUM OF PROGRESS

Technical progress has often promoted such change by undermining inherited ways over very broad areas of behaviour. As already mentioned, an outstanding example has been the appearance over the last two centuries of better forms of contraception, whose apogee was reached in the 1960s with the rapid and wide diffusion of what became (in many languages) known simply as "the pill". Though women in Western societies had long had access to effective techniques and knowledge in these matters, the pill – essentially a chemi-

cal means of suppressing ovulation – implied a greater transference of power to women in sexual behaviour than any earlier device. Although still not taken up by women in the non-Western world so widely as by their Western sisters, and although not legally available on the same basis in all developed countries, it has, through the mere spread of awareness of its existence, marked an epoch in relations between the sexes. But many other instances of the transforming power of science and technology on society could be cited. It is difficult not to feel, for example, that two centuries' changes in communication, and particularly those of the last six or seven decades, imply even more for the history of culture than, say, did the coming of print. Technical progress also operates in a general way through the testimony it provides of the seemingly magical power of science, since there is greater awareness of its importance than ever before. There are more scientists about; more attention is given to science in education; scientific information is

In recent years, the appearance of enormous commercial centres has radically changed shopping habits in the Western world. These sanitized "temples of consumption", as they have been called, attract people not only to shop, but also to be entertained, with the result that small local shops are gradually put out of business.

more widely diffused through the media and more readily comprehensible.

Yet success, paradoxically, as in space, has provided diminishing returns in awe. When more and more things prove possible, there is less that is very surprising about the latest marvel. There is even (unjustifiable) disappointment and irritation when some problems prove recalcitrant. Yet the grip of the master idea of our age, the notion that purposive change can be imposed upon nature if sufficient resources are made available, has grown stronger in spite of its critics. It is a European idea, and the science now carried on around the globe (all based on the European experimental tradition) continues to throw up ideas and implications disruptive of traditional, theocentric views of life. This has accompanied the high phase of a long process of dethroning the idea of the supernatural.

The illiteracy rate is often as high as 50 per cent in developing countries. In an effort to improve this situation, UNESCO has set up literacy and training programmes in many countries.

THE IMPACT OF FAITH IN SCIENCE

Sience and technology have thus both tended to undermine traditional authority, customary ways and accepted ideology. Even when they appear to offer material and technical support to the established order, their resources become available to critics of that order, too. Clear ideas about what scientists do may hardly filter through to the public at large, but even if most of humanity rests undisturbed in traditional pieties and superstition, science, technology and the improvements they bring make it harder to stay in the familiar ruts. This is true not only for the intellectuals who are, of course, disproportionately prominent in histories of thought and culture, but of the inherited assumptions and prejudices with which most of us live. The second effect is more important in recent history than at earlier times because improving communication has pushed new ideas more quickly into mass culture than ever before, though the impact of scientific ideas on élites is easier to trace. In the eighteenth century, Newtonian cosmology had been able to settle down into co-existence with Christian religion and other theocentric modes of thought without troubling the wide range of social and moral beliefs tied to them. As time passed, however, science has seemed harder and harder to reconcile with any fixed belief at all. It has appeared to stress relativism and the pressure of circumstance to the exclusion of any unchallengeable assumption or viewpoint.

PSYCHOLOGY

A VERY OBVIOUS INSTANCE of the tension between science and religion can be seen in one new branch of science – psychology – which evolved in the nineteenth century. After

A Buddhist monk in Punakna in the Himalayan country of Bhutan listens to music through the head-phones of a personal stereo for the first time. Ownership of Western consumer goods such as computers and telephones is limited to an élite in Bhutan, where most of the mainly Buddhist population is dependent on agriculture. The Bhutan government is engaged in a controlled attempt to modernize the country while avoiding the erosion of its cultural traditions.

1900 more began to be heard of it by the lay public, and especially of two of its expressions. One, which eventually took the name "psychoanalysis", can be considered, as an influence on society at large, to begin with the work of Sigmund Freud, which had begun in the clinical observation of mental disorder, a well-established method. His own development of this became, with comparative rapidity, notorious because of its wide influence outside medicine. As well as stimulating a mass of clinical work that claimed to be scientific (though its status was and is contested by many scientists), it undermined many accepted assumptions, above all, attitudes to sexuality, education, responsibility and punishment. Freud's work was based on a belief that therapy could be pursued and relevant clinical data assembled by uncovering patients' unconscious wishes, feelings and thoughts. This was to prove an inspirational gift to artists, teachers, moralists and advertising specialists.

BEHAVIOURISM

Meanwhile, another another psychological approach was that pursued by practitioners of "behaviourism" (like "Freudian" and "psycho-analytical", a word often used somewhat loosely). Its roots went back to eighteenth-century ideas, and it appeared to generate a body of experimental data

The study of human behaviour

In around 1900, the Russian scientist Pavlov started a long study on association in animals. He developed a technique to associate one stimulant with another and to measure the reaction when each of the stimulants was present. One experiment involved associating the aural stimulant of a bell with the stimulant of food proffered. His experiments demonstrated the conditioned reflex, and he applied his findings to an interpretation of human and animal behaviour, which he saw as an interrelated set of such reflexes.

The Russian physiologist Ivan Pavlov (1849–1936), pictured with his team in 1904, demonstrates the conditioned reflex.

certainly as impressive as (if not more impressive than) the clinical successes claimed by psychoanalysis. The pioneer name associated with behaviourism is still that of the Russian, I.P. Pavlov, the discoverer of the "conditioned reflex". This rested on the manipulation of one of a pair of variables in an experiment, in order to produce a predictable result in behaviour through a "conditioned stimulus" (the classical experiment provided for a bell to be sounded before food was given to a dog; after a time, sounding the bell caused the dog to salivate without the actual appearance of food). Refinements and developments of such procedures followed which provided much information and, it was believed, insight into the sources of human behaviour.

Whatever the benefits these psychological studies may have brought with them, what is striking to the historian is the contribution that Freud and Pavlov made to a larger and not easily definable cultural change. The doc-trines of both were bound – like more empirical approaches to the medical treatment of mental disorder by chemical, electrical and other physical interference – to suggest flaws in the traditional respect for moral autonomy and personal responsibility that lay at the heart of European moral culture. In a sharper focus, too, their weight was now added to that of the geologists, biologists and anthropologists in the nineteenth century who contributed to the undermining of religious belief.

RELIGION

THE POWER OF THE OLD IDEA that things mysterious and inexplicable were best managed by magical or religious means now seems to have waned, in Western societies at any rate. It may be conceded that where this has happened it has gone along with a new acceptance, even if halting and elementary, that science was now the way to manage most of life. But to speak of such things demands very careful qualification. When people talk about the waning power of religion, they often mean only the formal authority and influence of the Christian churches; behaviour and belief are quite different matters. No English monarch since Elizabeth I, four and a half centuries ago, has consulted an astrologer about an auspicious day for a coronation. Yet in the 1980s the world was amused (and perhaps a little alarmed) to hear that the wife of the president of the United States liked to seek astrological advice. It seems more revealing, perhaps, that in 1947 the timing of the ceremony marking the establishment of Indian independence was only settled after appropriate consultation with the astrologers, even though India has a constitution that is non-confessional and, theoretically, secular. Around the world, too, confessional states or established religions are now unusual outside Muslim countries. This need not mean, however, that the real power of religious belief or of religions over their adherents has declined. The founders of Pakistan were secular-minded, Westernized men, but in a struggle with the conservative *ulema* after independence, they lost. Pakistan became an orthodox Islamic state, and not a secular democracy on Western lines, which simply respects Islam as the religion of the majority of its people.

THE INTERPLAY OF RELIGION AND SOCIETY

It may well be true that today more people give serious attention to what is said by religious authorities than have ever done so before: there are more people alive, after all. Many people in England were startled in the 1980s when Iranian clergymen denounced a fashionable author as a traitor to Islam and pronounced a sentence of death upon him; it was a surprise to *bien pensant* and progressive circles to discover that, as it were, the Middle Ages were still in full swing in some parts of the world, without their having noticed it. They were even more startled when numbers of their Muslim fellow citizens appeared to agree with the *fatwa*. "Fundamentalism", though, is a word borrowed from American religious sociology. Within Christian churches, too, it expresses a protest against modernization by those who feel threatened and dispossessed by it. Nevertheless, some believe that here as elsewhere Western society has indicated a path that other societies will follow, and that conventional Western liberalism will prevail. It may be so. Equally, it may not be. The interplay of religion and society is very complex and it is best to be cautious. That the numbers of pilgrims travelling to Mecca have risen dramatically may register a new fervour or merely better air travel facilities.

Alarm has been felt recently over the vociferous reassertion of their faith by Muslims. Yet Islam does not seem able to avoid cultural corruption by the technology and materialism of the European tradition, though successfully resisting that tradition's ideological expression in atheistic communism. Radicals in Islamic societies are frequently in conflict with Westernized and laxly observant Islamic élites. Islam is, of course, still an expanding and missionary faith and the notion of Islamic unity is far from dead in Islamic lands. It can still nerve men to political action, too. United with strong social forces, religion produced terrifying massacres in the Indian subcontinent during the months of partition of 1947 and in the struggles of 1971, which led to the breaking away of East Bengal from Pakistan to

Western society, as an instigator of social unrest, is often viewed as an enemy in Islamic societies. However, such perceptions do not mean that there is never conflict among Islamic countries. Here, jubilant Iraqi soldiers are pictured in front of a bullet-riddled portrait of the Iranian leader Ayatollah Khomeini in 1988, during the Iran–Iraq war.

reappear as Bangladesh. In Ulster and the Republic of Ireland, sectarian Irishmen still mouth their hatreds and bitterly dispute the future of their country in the vocabulary of Europe's seventeenth-century religious wars, though marginally less violently than at times in the past. Although the hierarchies and leaders of different religions find it appropriate to exchange public courtesies, it cannot be said that religion has ceased to be a divisive force even if doctrine has become more amorphous. Whether the supernatural content of religion is losing its hold in all parts of the world, and is important today merely as a badge of group membership, is debatable.

What is less doubtful is that within the world whose origins are Christian, which did so much to shape today's world, the decline of sectarian strife has gone along with the general decline of Christian belief and, often, of a loss of nerve. Ecumenism, the movement within Christianity, whose most conspicuous expression was the setting up of a World Council of Churches (which Rome did not join) in 1948, owes much to Christians' growing sense in developed countries that they are living in hostile environments. It also owes something to widespread ignorance and uncertainty about what Christianity is, and what it ought to claim.

ROMAN CATHOLICISM

The only unequivocally hopeful sign of vigour in Christianity has been the growth (largely by natural increase) in numbers of Roman Catholics. Most of them are now non-Europeans, a change dramatized in the 1960s by the first papal visits to South America and Asia and the presence at the Vatican Council of 1962 of seventy-two archbishops and bishops of African descent. By 1980 40 per cent of the world's Roman Catholics lived in Latin America, and a majority of the College of Cardinals came from outside Europe.

Religion is still used to justify social hatred and violence. In a Northern Ireland torn by sectarian conflict, Roman Catholics demonstrate in front of British soldiers in Belfast in 1972.

As for the papacy's historic position within the Roman Church, that seemed to be weakening in the 1960s, some symptoms being provided by the Second Vatican Council itself. Among other things registering its work of *aggiornamento* or updating, for which John XXIII had asked, it went so far as to speak respectfully of the "truths" handed down in the teachings of Islam. But 1978 (a year of three popes) brought to the throne of St Peter John Paul II, the first non-Italian in four and a half centuries, the first Polish pope, and the first whose coronation was attended by an Anglican archbishop of Canterbury. His pontificate soon showed his personal determination to exercise the historic authority and possibilities of his office in a conservative sense; yet he was also the first pope to travel to Greece in search of reconciliation with the Orthodox churches of eastern Europe. The changes in eastern Europe in 1989 – and especially those in his native Poland – owed a great deal to the activism and the moral authority of Pope John Paul II. When he died in 2005, after a pontificate that was the third longest in history, he left a mixed legacy: A staunch conservative on matters of doctrine, the Polish pope had grown increasingly concerned with the materialism that he saw as pervading the contemporary world, not least in the countries he had helped break away from their communist past.

It would be hazardous to project further trends in the history of an institution whose fortunes have fluctuated so much across the centuries as those of the papacy (up with Hildebrandine reform; down with Schism and conciliarism; up with Trent; down with Enlightenment; up with the First Vatican Council). It is safest simply to recognize that one issue at least, posed by twentieth-century advances in the knowledge, acceptability and techniques of contraception, may for the first time be inflicting mortal wounds on the authority of Rome in the eyes of millions of Roman Catholics.

On 6 January 1971, in Vatican City, Pope Paul VI awarded the first Pope John XXIII Peace Prize to Mother Teresa for her work among the sick and impoverished of Calcutta and her founding of an order, the Missionaries of Charity, dedicated to working with the poor.

HALF THE WORLD

Some of the most influential changes of recent times have still to reveal their full weight and implications; after all, the issue of contraception affects, potentially, the whole human race, although we usually think about it as part of the history of women. But the relations of men and women should be considered as a whole, even if it is traditional and convenient to approach the subject from one side only. Much that settles the fate of many women can nonetheless be roughly measured and measurement, even at its crudest, quickly makes it clear that great as the level of change has been, it still has a long way to go. Radical change has occurred only in a few places, and is measurable (if at all) only in the last couple of centuries even there.

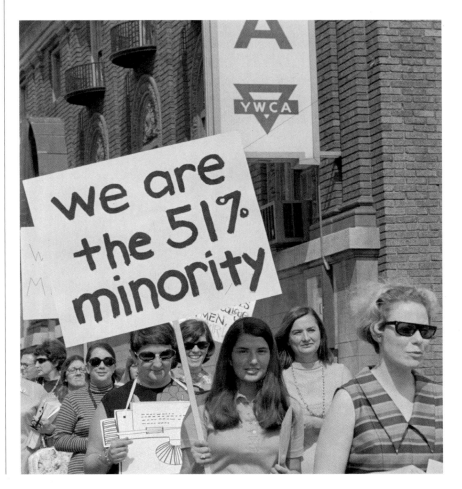

Our recognition of the changes has to be very carefully qualified; most Western women now live lives dramatically unlike those of their great-grandmothers while the lives of women in some parts of the world have been little changed for millennia.

Advances in women's political and legal equality with men are easy to trace. A majority of members of the United Nations now accepts some measure of female suffrage and in most Western (and some other) countries, formal and legal inequalities between the sexes have now been under attack for a long time. Prolonged moral questioning of them has led at least to much compliance with the wishes of egalitarians. The range of legislation attempting to assure equity in the treatment of women has been steadily extended (for instance, into the recognition of disadvantages in employment which had long been ignored). Examples thus set have been noted and influential in non-Western countries, even in the teeth of conservative oppositions. This has been a new operative force in changing perceptions and, of course, it has been all the more influential in a world where women's labour has confronted growing opportunities thanks to technological and economic change. To the huge early opportunities of jobs they could take, which were provided by textile mill and typewriter, were later added literally hundreds of new roles which women could fill as they mastered other technical skills – and, indeed, as opportunities of education were increased to meet their needs.

Such matters continued to unroll in developing societies in the interconnected, interlocking ways in which they had done so since the industrialization wave began. Even the home was transformed as a place of work – piped water and gas were soon followed by electricity and the possibility of easier management of domestic processes, by detergents,

A teacher in a Kabul classroom gives a special accelerated learning class in early 2003 designed in particular to meet the needs of girls who had missed out on a number of years of school due to Taliban restrictions. Approximately 15,000 students attended the three-month long winter classes led by the Afghan Ministry of Education with support from UNICEF.

synthetic fibres and prepared foods, while information became available to women as never before through radio, cinema, television and cheap print. It is tempting to speculate, though, that no such changes arising in more sophisticated societies had anything like the fundamental impact of the appearance in the 1960s of "the pill". Thanks to its convenience and the way in which it was used, it did more than any earlier advance in contraceptive knowledge or technique to transfer power over their own lives in these matters to women. It opened a new era in the history of sexual culture, even if that was obvious only in a few societies three or four decades later.

One concomitant, in the United States in particular, was a new feminism that broke away from the liberal tradition in which its predecessors had been rooted. Arguments for traditional feminism had always had a liberal flavour, saying that for women to live unencumbered by laws and customs, which did not apply to men but only to them, was merely a logical extension of the truth that

freedom and equality were good things unless specific cause otherwise were to be shown. The new feminism took a new tack. It embraced a wider spectrum of causes specific to women – the protection of lesbians, for example – laid particular stress on women's sexual liberation, and above all strove to identify and uncover unrecognized instances of psychological, implicit and institutionalized forms of masculine oppression. Its impact has been varied, even within societies and cultures whose élites are susceptible to modernization and its ideas.

In some traditional societies any feminist advance at all has been fiercely contested. In only one respect has there been a widespread and striking change and it owes as much in specific places to colonialism, Communism and Christianity as to feminism. This is the worldwide retreat of polygamy. Few governments now officially support it. Other institutional expressions of special cultural attitudes towards female emancipation nonetheless remain very striking. This is often

The violent nationalism in the former Yugoslavia shocked the world in the late 20th century. After the death of the communist ruler Tito in 1980, the tensions between ethnic Serbs, Croats, Bosnians, Slovenes, Macedonians and Montenegrins came to the fore and civil war broke out. This building in Sarajevo was destroyed by shelling in 1992.

incompatible with successful support by Islamic scholars for defending certain rights for women. Whether such facts turn out to establish sensible compromise or uneasy equilibrium will differ from one Muslim society to another. It should not be forgotten that violent contrasts in what is thought appropriate behaviour for women have until recently existed in European societies, too. It is not easy to relate such paradoxes as they have sometimes presented to what are supposed to be uniformities of faith.

THE STATE

WHETHER OGANIZED RELIGION and the notion of fixed, unchanging moral law have or have not lost some of their power as social regulators, the state, the third great historic agent of social order, at first sight seems to have kept its end up much better. It has never been so widely taken for granted. There are more states – recognized, geographically defined political units claiming legislative sovereignty and a monopoly of the use of force within their own borders – than ever before. More people than ever before look to government as their best chance of securing well-being rather than as their inevitable enemy. Politics as a contest to capture state power has at times apparently replaced religion (sometimes even appearing to eclipse market economics) as the focus of faith that can move mountains.

THE AGGRANDIZEMENT OF THE STATE

remarked in Western comments on Muslim ways. Yet this, too, is a topic formidably difficult to evaluate. It tempts the observer to subjective and emotional judgement on subjects best not abandoned to quick and generalized reaction. Specification, though, is almost as dangerous as generalization. Only too obviously, the Islamic world maintains restrictions and practices that protect an ultimate male dominance. Many attempts to change this have been thwarted or aborted. Yet not all Muslim societies impose the veil on their women and the wearing of the *chador* in the Iranian Islamic republic is not

One of the most visible institutional marks left by Europe on world history has been the reorganization of international life as basically a matter of sovereign (and now, in name at least, often republican and usually national) states. Beginning in the seventeenth century, this was already in the nineteenth century beginning to look a possible global outcome, and the process was virtually completed in the twentieth century. With it went the diffusion of similar forms of state machinery, sometimes through adoption, sometimes through imposition first by imperial rulers. This was assumed to be a concomitant of modernization. The sovereign state is now taken for granted, as in many places it still was not even a century ago. This has been largely a mechanical consequence of a slow demolition of empires. That new states should come into being to replace them was scarcely questioned at any stage. With the collapse of the USSR almost a half-century after the dissolution of other empires, the global generalization of the constitutional language of the sovereignty of the people, representative institutions and the separation of powers reached its greatest extent.

LIBERAL ASSUMPTIONS LOSE GROUND

The aggrandizement of the state – if we may so put it – thus long met with little effective resistance. Even in countries where governments have traditionally been distrusted or where institutions exist to check them, people tend to feel that they are much less resistible than even a few years ago. The strongest checks on the abuse of power remain those of habit and assumption; so long as electorates in liberal states can assume that governments will not quickly fall back on the use of force, they do not feel very alarmed. But the cause of liberal democracy worldwide does not always look very hopeful; there are now more dictators and more authoritarian political regimes in the world than in 1939 (though, since changes in Greece, Portugal and Spain in the 1970s, and later in eastern European countries, few in Europe). Like the undermining of other liberal assumptions, this is a measure of

The undeniable influence of the mass media means that any attempt to seize power in a Western country is unlikely to be effective if the media cannot also be controlled. Here, anti-Yeltsin demonstrators attack the national television station during the failed coup of October 1993.

In 1991, the tiny region of Chechnya in southwestern Russia declared itself independent from the Russian Federation. Russian troops were sent to capture the Chechen city of Grozny in December 1994, at a huge cost in life to both sides. Here Chechen soldiers wave their flag in front of Grozny's presidential palace after defeating the Russian army in a battle in June 1995.

the narrowing base of what was once thought to be the cause of the future, but seemed to turn out to be only that of a few advanced societies of the nineteenth century. Furthermore, the forms of liberal politics have, indeed, in one sense prospered, for democracy and constitutionalism are more talked about and nationalism is stronger than ever. Yet the substantial freedoms once associated with these ideas are often non-existent or conspicuously in danger and even if most states now claim to be democratic, the lack of any but historical connections between nationalism and liberalism is more obvious than ever.

One reason for this is that those ideas have been exported to contexts inimical to them. It is unhistorical to deplore the outcome; as Burke pointed out long ago, political principles always take their colour from circumstances. Often in the last half-century

it has been shown that representative institutions and democratic forms cannot work properly in societies lacking solid foundations in habits coherent with them, or where powerful divisive influences are at work. In such circumstances, the imposition of an authoritarian style of government has often been the best way of resisting social fragmentation once the discipline imposed by a colonial power is withdrawn. Only too obviously, this has not meant great freedom in most post-colonial countries. Whether greater happiness has followed may be more debatable, but cannot be assumed.

The role played by the urge to modernize in strengthening the state – something prefigured long ago outside Europe in a Mehemet Ali or a Kemal – was an indication of new sources from which the state increasingly drew its moral authority. Instead of relying on

personal loyalty to a dynasty or a supernatural sanction, it has come to rely increasingly on the democratic and utilitarian argument that it is able to satisfy collective desires. Usually these were for material improvement, but sometimes not; now, they appear often to be for greater equality.

THE CONTINUING POWER OF NATIONALISM

If one value more than any other legitimizes state authority today it is in fact nationalism, still the motive and fragmenting force of much of world politics and paradoxically often the enemy of many particular states in the past. Nationalism has been successful in mobilizing allegiance as no other force has been able to do; the forces working the other way, to integrate the world as one political system, have been circumstantial and material, rather than comparably powerful moral

ideas or mythologies. Nationalism was also the greatest single force in the politics of history's most revolutionary century, engaging for most of it with multinational empires as its main opponents. Now, though, it is more often engaged with rival nationalisms and with them continues to express itself in violent and destructive struggles.

When in conflict with nationalism, admittedly, the state often came off badly even when, to all appearances, enormous power had been concentrated in its apparatus. Buttressed by the traditions of communist centralization though they were, both the USSR and Yugoslavia have now disintegrated into national units. Québécois still talk of separating from Canada. There are many other instances of disturbingly violent potential. Yet nationalism has also greatly reinforced the power of government and extended its real scope, and politicians in many countries are hard at work fostering new nationalisms where they do not exist in order to bolster shaky structures that have emerged from decolonization.

Nationalism, too, has often underwritten the moral authority of states, usually by claiming to deliver collective good, if only in the minimal form of order. Even when there is disagreement or debate about exactly what benefits the state should provide in specific instances, modern justifications of government rest at least implicitly on its claim to be able to provide them, and so to protect national interests. Whether states actually did deliver any such good at all, has, of course, often been disputed. Marxist orthodoxy used to argue, and in a few places still does, that the state was a machine for ensuring the domination of a class and, as such, would disappear when overtaken by the march of History. Even Marxist regimes, though, have not always behaved as if that were true. As for the idea that a state might be a private possession of a dynasty or an individual serving private interests, it is now everywhere formally disavowed, whatever the reality in many places.

The European Parliament in Strasbourg is pictured in session. Because of widespread hostility to the idea of a central European "government", the European Union places much emphasis on its democratic institutions and the forum for international debate that it provides.

RESTRAINTS ON STATE POWER

Some states now participate to a degree far surpassing any of their predecessors in elaborate systems, connections and organizations for purposes going well beyond those of simple alliance and requiring concessions of sovereignty. Some are groupings to undertake specific activities in common, some give new opportunities to those who belong to them, while others consciously restrict state power. They differ greatly in their structures and their impact on international behaviour.

The United Nations is made up of sovereign states, but it has organized or authorized collective action against an individual member as the League of Nations or earlier associations never did. On a smaller, but important scale, regional groupings have emerged, requiring the observance of common disciplines. Some, like those of eastern Europe, have proved evanescent, but the European Union, even if many of the visions that attended its birth remain unrealized, inches forward – on 1 January 2002 a new common currency was introduced among twelve of its member states and 300 million people. Nor are formal organizations the whole story. There are some unorganized or only vestigially organized supranational realities that from time to time appear to eclipse the freedom of individual states. Islam has at times been feared or welcomed as such a force, and perhaps the racialist consciousness of pan-Africanism, or of what is called *négritude*, inhibits some nations' actions. The spread of this luxuriant undergrowth to international affairs must make obsolete the old notion that the world consists of independent and autonomous players operating without restraint except that of individual interest. Paradoxically, the first substantial interstate structures emerged from a century in which

The growth of the welfare state

A product of the 20th-century concept of government whereby the state plays a key role in the protection of its citizens' social and financial security, the welfare state is a feature of the most advanced industrialized countries. The fundamental feature of this social care package is social insurance (such as National Insurance in Britain), usually financed by compulsory contributions. This revenue is used to provide unemployment and sickness benefit, old-age pensions, healthcare, housing and, in some countries, anti-poverty schemes and taxation plans.

Most modern versions of the welfare state are based on the measures adopted in Britain in 1948 after the Second World War. These were suggested by Sir William Beveridge in his 1942 report *Social Insurance and Allied Services*, in which he advocated state protection for the individual "from the cradle to the grave". In spite of the inherent difficulties of creating such a national "safety net" – financing the services and accurately gauging adequate individual provision while maintaining an incentive to work – welfare states across Europe thrived until the 1980s. From that period governments began to reconsider or dismantle them: for example, in Britain pension provision, the bedrock of the system, was under review in the late 1990s.

A mother and her children arrive at a new council estate in Liverpool, England, in 1954. At that time the demand for houses in Liverpool was high – thousands of families were on the council waiting lists. On just two estates in the city's Kirkby district, 30 or 40 houses were built every week in the mid-1950s.

more blood was shed by states in quarrels with one another than ever before.

International law, too, now aspires to greater practical control of states' behaviour than previously despite all the notorious examples that remain of failure to comply with it. In part this is a matter of slow and still sporadic change in the climate of opinion. Uncivilized and barbarous regimes go on behaving in uncivilized and barbarous ways, but decency has won its victories, too. The shock of uncovering in 1945 the realities of the Nazi regime in wartime Europe meant that great evils cannot now be launched and

Water cannons from a supply boat bombard the *Brent Spar* oil platform after a helicopter delivered supplies to Greenpeace activists on board the installation in the North Sea in 1995.

carried through without concealment, denial or attempts at plausible justification. In July 1998, representatives of 120 nations – although those of the United States were not among them – agreed to set up a permanent international court to try war crimes and crimes against humanity. In the following year, the highest of the British courts of justice ruled, unprecedentedly, that a former head of state was liable to extradition to another country to answer there charges of crimes alleged against him. In 2001, the former president of Serbia was surrendered to an international court and appeared there in the dock.

It is important not to exaggerate. Many wicked men continue to practise around the world brutalities and cruelties for which there is little practical hope at present of holding them to account. International criminality is a concept that infringes state sovereignty and the United States is not likely under any conceivable presidency to admit the jurisdiction of an international court over its own citizens. But the United States itself also explicitly adopted revolutionary foreign policy goals for quasi-moral ends in the 1990s in seeking to overthrow the governments of Saddam Hussein and Slobodan Milosevic and it is now concerned with the organization of efforts against terrorism, which must imply some further interference with others' sovereignty.

STATE POWER

Nevertheless, at home, governments have for two or three hundred years enjoyed more and more power to do what was asked of them. Lately, economic distress in the 1930s and great wars required huge mobilization of resources and new extensions of governmental power. To such forces have also been added demands that governments indirectly promote the welfare of their subjects and undertake the provisions of services either unknown hitherto or left in the past to individuals or such "natural" units as families and villages. The welfare state was a reality in Germany and Great Britain before 1914. In the last fifty years, the share of GDP taken by the state has shot up almost everywhere. There has also been the urge to modernize. Few countries outside Europe achieved this without direction from above and even in Europe some countries have owed most of their modernization to government. The twentieth century's outstanding examples were Russia and China, two great agrarian societies that sought and achieved modernization through state power. Finally, technology, through better communications, more powerful weapons and more comprehensive information systems, has advantaged those who could spend most on it: governments.

Once, and not long ago, even the greatest of European monarchies could not carry out a census or create a unified internal market. Now, the state has a virtual monopoly of the main instruments of physical control. Even a hundred years ago, the police and armed forces of governments unshaken by war or uncorrupted by sedition gave them a security; technology has only increased their near-certainty. New repressive techniques and weapons, though, are now only a small part of the story. State intervention in the economy, through its power as consumer, investor or planner, and the improvement of mass communications in a form that leaves access to them highly centralized all matter immensely. Hitler and Roosevelt made great use of radio (though for very different ends); and attempts to regulate economic life are as old as government itself.

However, governments in most countries have had to grapple more obviously in recent times with a new integration of the world economy. This goes beyond the operation of supranational institutions like the World Bank or International Monetary Fund (IMF); it is a function of the tendency often now called "globalization" in its latest manifestations. Sometimes institutionalized by international agreement or by the simple economic growth of large companies, but driven by rising expectations everywhere, it is a phenomenon that often dashes the hopes of politicians seeking to direct the societies over which they are expected to preside. Economic and political independence can be hugely infringed by unregulated global financial flows, and even by the operations of great companies, some of which can call on resources far larger than those of many small states. Paradoxically, complaints about the curbing of state independence to which globalization can give rise are sometimes voiced most loudly by those who would urge even more vigorous interference with sovereignty in cases of, for example, abuse of human rights.

The play of such forces is discernible in the pages that follow. Perhaps they are bringing about some reduction in state power, while leaving forms largely intact as power accumulates elsewhere. This is at least more probable than that radical forces will succeed in destroying the state. Such forces exist, and

at times they draw strength from and appear to prosper in new causes – ecology, feminism and a generalized anti-nuclear and "peace" movement have all patronized them. But in forty years of activity they have only been successful when they have been able to influence and shape state policy, change laws and set up new institutions. The idea that major amelioration can be achieved by altogether bypassing so dominant an institution still seems as unrealistic as it was in the days of the anarchistic and utopian movements of the nineteenth century.

Peace protesters have placed a bunch of carnations in the gun carried by this Soviet soldier in Vilnius, Lithuania, in 1991. The Baltic states' emergence from the Soviet Union, following their declaration of their independence, was achieved relatively peacefully.

THE NEW GLOBAL ERA

THE CONTINUING ACCELERATION of historical change which has characterized the last five hundred years or so has been more striking than ever since 1945. For some peoples and societies, the pace of change has literally been intolerable. We live in a world still unsettled by the global revolution in economic and political organization which began during the Second World War and has been going on ever since. Two and a half decades during which the central characteristics of the world political order seemed to be more and more frozen (though revolutionary developments were continuing elsewhere) were to be followed by a renewed quickening of the pace of change in the 1980s. By the end of that decade, landmarks taken for granted for thirty years and more had disappeared (sometimes almost overnight) and others, even more dominating, were already called into question. The whole process was so rapid and continuous as to make divisions in the story unusually artificial, but the historian has to try to analyse and uncover their structure. Some of the forces behind the turmoil were very profound and very mixed. Some, for instance, were rooted in the growing energy needs of industrialized societies already touched upon. Others can be traced ultimately much further back – to, for example, ideas first announced in the French Revolution. But though it is worth striving for as deep a historical perspective as possible, the long-term trends and forces cannot alone explain what happened. Like other great changes throughout history, many of those of the second half of the twentieth century arose almost from accident, circumstance, even personality. They are none the easier to explain for that.

Since 1985, Europe has undergone extraordinary changes much more quickly than most people ever imagined possible. The "Iron Curtain" that once divided western and eastern Europe disappeared in the space of a few short years, giving rise to numerous political, economic, psychological and military disturbances. With the era of *perestroika* (restructuring) and *glasnost* (openness) in the Soviet Union and the fall of the Berlin Wall, political and economic objectives, as well as international relations, were redefined in eastern Europe. Here, East Berliners watch a section of the wall being torn down in late 1989. Many people kept pieces of it as a souvenir of the "wall of shame".

1 *THE POLITICS OF THE NEW WORLD*

By 1950, A PERIOD HAD BEGUN during which the central characteristics of the world political order seemed increasingly to be frozen and irremovable, whatever might be going on elsewhere. Then, after a quarter-century or so, came a quickening of the pace of change, reaching its climax in the 1980s. By 1990, landmarks taken for granted for thirty years and more had disappeared (sometimes almost overnight) while others were already called into question. But this happened after a long time, during most of which a prolonged and bitter Soviet–American antagonism overshadowed almost every other part of international life, casting a blight over most of the world, and constituting a source of crime, corruption and suffering for thirty years. Cold War was far from the only force shaping history, and perhaps not the most fundamental in those years, but it was central to them.

Its first serious struggles took place in Europe, where the initial phase of post-war history was brief and may be thought to have ended with the communist takeover of government in Czechoslovakia. At that moment, the continent's economic recovery had hardly begun. But there were some grounds for hope about other, older problems. The familiar German threat had gone away; there was now no menace from her once-great power. Instead, her former opponents now had to grapple with the vacuum of power in the centre of Europe. Further east, boundary changes, ethnic cleansing and wartime atrocity had left Poland and Czechoslovakia without the problems of racial heterogeneity they had been obliged to live with before 1939. Yet in a new way Europe was divided as never before and that fact was embedded in the worldwide Soviet–American antagonism, whose exact origins have been and can still be much debated. In one sense, after all, it was only a late and spectacular manifestation of the rupture of ideological and diplomatic history in 1917. Communist Russia had from the start approached international affairs in a new and uniquely troublesome way. For it, diplomacy was not just a convenient way of doing business but a weapon for the advance of a revolution. Even that, though, would

have mattered much less if history had not produced by 1945 a new world power, the long-awaited modernized Russia, far better placed than any tsarist empire to have its own way in eastern Europe, and to advance its ambitions in other parts of the world. Soviet diplomacy after Stalin's accession to power often reflected historic ambitions, and Russian national interest, shaped by geography and history, was to prove inseparable from the ideological struggle. Communists and those who sympathized with them everywhere believed they must safeguard the Soviet Union, the champion of the international working class and, indeed (true believers affirmed), the guardian of the destinies of the whole human race. However they qualified it in practice, when Bolsheviks had said their aim was to overthrow the non-communist societies, they meant it, so far as the long run was concerned. After 1945 other communist states had come into existence whose rulers agreed, at least in words, and the result was a Europe, and a world, increasingly divided into two camps.

GERMANY DIVIDED

THE ORIGINAL COMMUNIST Europe of 1945 had been added to by other takeovers and by 1948 Hungary, Romania, Poland and Czechoslovakia had all ceased to have any non-communists in their governments, while communists dominated that of Bulgaria. Then, the opening of the Marshall Aid

programme was almost at once followed by what was to prove to be the first battle of the Cold War, over the fate of Berlin. It was decisive in that it apparently established a point at which, in Europe, the United States was prepared to fight. It does not seem that this outcome had been anticipated by the Russians, though they had provoked it by seeking to prevent the re-emergence of a reunited and economically powerful Germany, which would not be under their control. That conflicted with the western powers' interest – to reanimate the German economy, at the very least in their own occu-

West Berlin police greet Berliners returning to their sector of the city in 1953.

Time chart (1948–1974)						
	1948 Berlin crisis and air shuttle	1952 Nasser becomes president of Egypt		1959 Castro imposes a Communist régime in Cuba	1967 The Arab–Israeli Six Day War	
1940			1960			1980
	1950 Start of the Korean War	1955 Bandung Conference	1962 Missile crisis in Cuba	1964 Start of the Vietnam War	1974 The "Revolution of the Carnations" in Portugal	

An American aeroplane carrying food supplies arrives in West Berlin. Throughout the blockade, the British and Americans ran an air shuttle, with a plane taking off or landing every minute, to ferry supplies to the city.

pation zones and to do this before Germany's future political shape was settled, in the certainty that it was vital for the recovery of western Europe as a whole.

In 1948, without Soviet agreement, the western powers introduced a currency reform in their own sectors. It had a galvanic effect, releasing the process of economic recovery in western Germany. Following on Marshall Aid, available (thanks to Soviet decisions) only to the western-occupied zones, this reform, more than any other step, cut Germany in two. Since the recovery of the eastern half could not be integrated with that of western Europe, a revived western Germany might now emerge by itself. That the western powers should get on with the business of putting their zones on their feet was undoubtedly economic sense, but eastern Germany was thenceforth decisively on the

other side of the Iron Curtain. Currency reform divided Berlin, too, and thereby prejudiced communist chances of staging a popular putsch in the city, isolated though it was within the Soviet occupation zone.

THE BERLIN AIRLIFT

The Soviet response was to disrupt communication between the western occupied zones of Germany and Berlin. Whatever their original motives, the dispute escalated. Some western officials had already had it in mind before this crisis that a severance of western Berlin from the three western zones might be attempted; the word "blockade" had been used and Soviet actions were now interpreted in this sense. The Soviet authorities did not question the rights of the western allies to access to their own forces in their own sectors of Berlin, but they disrupted the traffic that ensured supply to the Berliners in those sectors. To supply them, the British and Americans organized an airlift to the city. The Russians wanted to demonstrate to the West Berliners that the western powers could not stay there if they did not want them to; they hoped thus to remove the obstacle that the presence of elected non-communist municipal authorities presented to Soviet control of Berlin. So, a trial of strength was underway. The western powers, in spite of the enormous cost of maintaining such a flow of food, fuel and medicine to keep West Berlin going, announced they were prepared to keep it up indefinitely. The implication was that they could be stopped only by force. American strategic bombers moved back to their wartime bases in England. Neither side wanted to fight, but all hope of cooperation over Germany on the basis of wartime agreement was dead.

THE FOUNDATION OF NATO

The blockade of West Berlin lasted over a year and defeating it was a remarkable logistical achievement. For much of the time, over 1,000 aircraft a day achieved an average daily delivery of 5,000 tons of coal alone. Yet its real significance was political. Allied supply was not interrupted nor were the West Berliners intimidated. The Soviet authorities made the best of defeat by deliberately splitting the city and refusing the mayor access to his office. Meanwhile the western powers had

The West German chancellor, Konrad Adenauer (1876–1967) (middle row, second from left), is among the members of the Council of Ministers attending this NATO Council meeting in 1955. It was during this meeting, when West Germany was formally admitted, that the North Atlantic Treaty Organization acquired its full significance as a defence against communism.

North Atlantic Treaty 1949

"The Parties agree that an armed attack on one or more of them in Europe or North America shall be considered an attack against them all and they consequently agree that, if such an armed attack occurs, each of them, in exercise of the right of individual or collective self-defence recognized by Article 51 of the Charter of the United Nations, will assist the Party or Parties so attacked by taking forthwith, individually in concert with the other Parties, such action as it deems necessary, including the use of armed force, to restore and maintain the security of the North Atlantic area. Any such armed attack and all measures taken as a result thereof shall immediately be reported to the Security Council. Such measures shall be terminated when the Security Council has taken the measures necessary to restore and maintain international peace and security."

An extract from Article 5 of the North Atlantic Treaty of 1949.

The Cold War

The Second World War had given rise to an alliance between countries of very different political tendencies. However, this alliance disappeared once the war was over. Although the United States and the Soviet Union were not to engage in direct conflict, their rivalry from 1945 onwards turned into a confrontation known as the Cold War, a term coined by a journalist reporting on an unfruitful meeting to control nuclear energy in 1946.

In 1947 disagreements between the superpowers came to the fore when the Soviet leaders rejected the Americans' Marshall Plan. Instead, the USSR created COMECON in 1949 and installed Soviet systems in the Eastern bloc.

During the long period of the Cold War, four main stages could be discerned. Each stage began with rising tensions, followed by a breakdown in relations, generally with a regional war, but eventually ending in more cordial relations. In the first stage (1945–53), both blocs took up irreconcilable positions and there was no dialogue at all between them. This stage culminated in the Korean War. Between 1953 and 1962, after Stalin's death, Khrushchev began talks, first with Eisenhower and then with Kennedy. The impact of the Cuban Missile Crisis in 1962 forced both sides to consider the dangers of a nuclear war. During the third stage (1962–73), overshadowed by the Vietnam War, the two military superpowers proposed limiting the acquisition of strategic weapons, which were ruining their economies. Between 1973 and 1989, attention was first focused on the world economic crisis, but the war in Afghanistan muddied the waters of their relations again. This phase differs from earlier ones in that East–West conflicts were stabilized, while North–South conflicts came to the fore. In 1989, the world view changed totally with the withdrawal of the Soviet troops from Afghanistan, Gorbachev's proposal for disarmament and the democratic changes in eastern Europe.

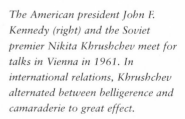

The American president John F. Kennedy (right) and the Soviet premier Nikita Khrushchev meet for talks in Vienna in 1961. In international relations, Khrushchev alternated between belligerence and camaraderie to great effect.

signed a treaty setting up a new alliance, the first Cold War creation to transcend Europe. The North Atlantic Treaty Organization (NATO) came into existence in April 1949, a few weeks before the blockade was ended by agreement. The United States and Canada were members, as well as most western European states (only Ireland, Sweden, Switzerland, Portugal and Spain did not join). It was explicitly defensive, providing for the mutual defence of any member attacked, and thus yet another break with the now almost-vanished isolationist traditions of American foreign policy. In May, a new German state, the Federal Republic, emerged from the three western zones of occupation and in the following October, a German Democratic Republic (the GDR) was set up in the east. Henceforth, there were to be two Germanys, it seemed, and the Cold War ran along an Iron Curtain dividing them, and not, as Churchill had suggested in 1946, further east, from Trieste to Stettin. But a particularly dangerous phase in Europe was over.

THE KOREAN WAR

The foundation of NATO suggested perhaps that as well as two Europes there might also be two worlds divided by Cold War soon seemed likely. In 1945 Korea had been divided along the 38th parallel, its industrial north being occupied by the Russians and the agricultural south by the Americans. The problem of reunification was eventually referred to the United Nations. After failing to obtain elections for the whole country that organization recognized a government set up in the south as the only lawful government of the Republic of Korea. By then, though, the Soviet zone had also produced a government claiming sovereignty over the whole country. Russian and American forces both withdrew, but North Korean forces invaded the south in June 1950 with Stalin's foreknowledge and approval. Within two days President Truman had sent American forces to fight them, acting in the name of the United Nations. The Security Council had voted to resist aggression, and as the Russians were at that moment boycotting it, they could not veto United Nations action. The Americans always provided the bulk of the UN forces in Korea,

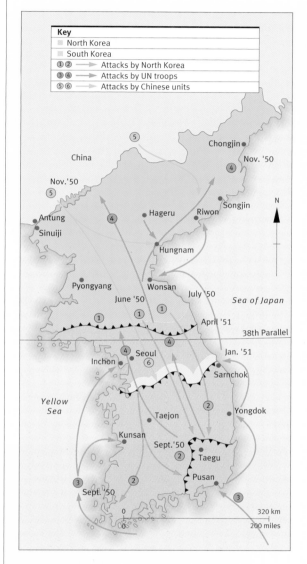

The Korean War

Key
- North Korea
- South Korea
- ①② Attacks by North Korea
- ③④ Attacks by UN troops
- ⑤⑥ Attacks by Chinese units

China · Chongjin · Nov. '50 · Nov. '50 · Antung · Sinuiji · Hageru · Riwon · Songjin · Hungnam · Pyongyang · Wonsan · June '50 · July '50 · Sea of Japan · April '51 · 38th Parallel · Seoul · Inchon · Jan. '51 · Sarnchok · Yellow Sea · Taejon · Yongdok · Kunsan · Sept.'50 · Taegu · Pusan · Sept. '50

320 km
200 miles

In 1950, the conflict in Korea became the first in which the risk of a nuclear war between the superpowers was apparent. Until then, diplomatic crises and local wars had created varying degrees of tension between East and West. The danger of another world war, however, had been remote, as the United States had a monopoly on atomic warheads. But when the Soviet Union successfully carried out its first atomic test in August 1949, the world realized that a nuclear holocaust was possible. Fears mounted when the two superpowers entered into conflict over Korea, even though they were not directly at war with each other, as the map shows.

The main strategic events of the Korean War are depicted.

but other nations soon fielded contingents. Within a few months the allied army was operating well north of the 38th parallel. It seemed likely that North Korea would be overthrown. When fighting drew near the Manchurian border, however, Chinese communist forces intervened and drove back the UN army. There was now a danger of a much bigger conflict. The question arose of direct action, possibly with nuclear weapons, by the United States against China. China was the second largest communist state in the world, and the largest in terms of population. Behind it stood the USSR; a man could (in theory, at least) walk from Erfurt to Shanghai without once leaving communist territory.

Prudently, Truman insisted that the United States must not become involved in a greater war on the Asian mainland. That much settled, further fighting showed that although the Chinese might be able to keep the North Koreans in the field, they could not overturn South Korea against American wishes. Armistice talks were started. The new American administration, which came into office in 1953, was Republican and unequivocally anti-communist, but knew its predecessor had sufficiently demonstrated its will and capacity to uphold an independent South Korea and felt that the real centre of the Cold War was in Europe rather than in Asia. Stalin's death in March 1953 made it possible for an armistice to be signed. Subsequent efforts to turn this into a formal peace have as yet failed; nearly fifty years

later, the potential for conflict remained high between the two Koreas. But in the Far East as well as in Europe the Americans had won the first battles of the Cold War, and in Korea they had been real battles; estimates suggest the war cost three million dead, most of whom were Korean civilians.

THE USSR AT STALIN'S DEATH

THE LEADERS WHO TOOK over in the Soviet Union after Stalin's death aimed at a reduction of tension with the West, because they felt their country was not ready for war. They also tried to improve relations with the neutral countries. The new American president, Eisenhower, remained distrustful of Russian intentions and in the middle of the 1950s, the Cold War was as intense as ever. Shortly after Stalin's death his successors revealed that they too had the improved nuclear weapon known as the hydrogen

A Soviet propaganda poster from 1950 shows Stalin advocating "the Leninist path to communism". The dam in the background is meant to illustrate the Soviets' ability to provide electricity for the whole of the USSR. In spite of an outward show of strength and prosperity, for most Soviet people poverty and suffering continued long after the end of the war.

КОММУНИЗМ-ЭТО ЕСТЬ СОВЕТСКАЯ ВЛАСТЬ ПЛЮС-ЭЛЕКТРИФИКАЦИЯ ВСЕЙ СТРАНЫ.
В.ЛЕНИН

ПО ЛЕНИНСКОМУ ПУТИ-
ИДЕМ К КОММУНИЗМУ!

bomb. This was Stalin's final memorial, guaranteeing (if it had been in doubt) the USSR's status in the post-war world. Stalin had carried to their logical conclusions the repressive policies of Lenin, but he had done much more than his predecessor. He had rebuilt most of the tsarist empire and had given Russia the strength to survive (just, and with the help of powerful allies) its gravest hour of trial. What is not clear is that this could only have been achieved or was worth achieving at such cost, unless (as may well be thought) to have escaped defeat and German domination was justification enough. The Soviet Union was a great power but, among the elements that made it up, it can hardly be doubted that one day Russia at least would have become one again without communism. Yet in 1945 its peoples had been rewarded for their sufferings with precious little but an assurance of international strength. Domestic life after the war was harsher than ever; consumption was for years still held down and both the propaganda to which Soviet citizens were subjected and the brutalities of the police system seem, if anything, to have been intensified.

THE WARSAW PACT

Another of Stalin's monuments was the division of Europe, clearer than ever at his death and confirmed in the next few years. The western half was by 1953 substantially rebuilt, thanks to American economic support, and was carrying a larger share of its own defence costs. The Federal Republic and the GDR moved further and further apart. On successive days in March 1954 the Russians announced that the eastern republic now possessed full sovereignty and the West German president signed the constitutional amendment permitting the rearmament of his country. In 1955 West Germany entered

NATO; the Soviet riposte was the Warsaw Pact, an alliance of its satellites. Berlin's future was still in doubt, but it was clear that the NATO powers would fight to resist changes in its status except by agreement. In the east, the GDR agreed to settle with old enemies: the line of the Oder–Neisse was to be the frontier with Poland. Hitler's dream of realizing the greater Germany of the nineteenth-century nationalists had ended in the obliteration of Bismarckian Germany. Historic Prussia was now ruled by revolutionary communists, while the new West Germany was federal in structure, non-militarist in sentiment and dominated by Catholic and Social Democratic politicians, whom Bismarck would have seen as "enemies of the Reich". So, without a peace treaty, the problem of containing the German power that had twice devastated Europe by war was settled at last. Also in 1955 came the final definition of land frontiers between the European blocs, when Austria re-emerged as an independent state and the occupying allied forces were withdrawn, as were the last American and British troops from Trieste, with a settlement of the Italo-Yugoslav border dispute there.

The peace treaty with Austria is signed in 1955. Aware of its vulnerable position between eastern and western Europe, Austria declared itself neutral.

Post-war Germany and central Europe

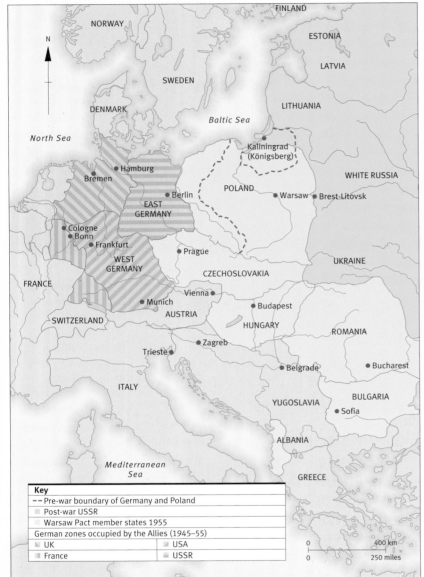

Key
-- Pre-war boundary of Germany and Poland
▨ Post-war USSR
▨ Warsaw Pact member states 1955
German zones occupied by the Allies (1945–55)
▨ UK   ▨ USA
▨ France   ▨ USSR

The Warsaw Pact was created as a reaction to the admission of a remilitarized West Germany into NATO. On 11 May 1955, the Warsaw conference was opened, with representatives from the USSR, Poland, Hungary, Czechoslovakia, East Germany, Romania, Bulgaria and Albania. On 14 May, they signed the "treaty for friendship, cooperation and mutual aid". In an annex to the treaty, the unified high command for their armed forces was created, and the Soviet general Koniev was appointed to the post of commander-in-chief.

In this map showing the situation in 1955, the three western zones constitute the Federal Republic (West Germany), while the Russian zone is the German Democratic Republic (East Germany), both set up in 1949. Berlin then remained under four-power occupation.

THE EMERGENCE OF TWO ECONOMIC SYSTEMS

After the establishment of communism in China, a division also appearing worldwide was that between what we may call capitalist and command (or would-be command) economies. Commercial relations between Soviet Russia and other countries had been encumbered by politics from the October Revolution onwards. In the huge disruption of world trade after 1931 the capitalist economies had plunged into recession and sought salvation in protection (or even autarky). After 1945, though, all earlier divisions of the world market were transcended; two methods of organizing the distribution of resources increasingly divided first the developed world and then other areas, notably East Asia. The essential determinant of the capitalist system was the market – though a market very different from that envisaged by the old liberal free trade ideology, and in many ways a very imperfect one, tolerating a substantial degree of intervention through international agencies and agreement; in the communist-controlled group of nations (and some others) political authority was intended to be the decisive economic factor. Trade between the two systems continued, but on a cramped basis.

Neither economic and political system remained unchanged. Contacts between them multiplied as the years passed. None the less, they long appeared to offer the world alternative models for economic growth. Their competition was inflamed by the politics of the Cold War and actually helped to spread its antagonisms. Yet, this could not be a static situation. Before long one system was much less completely dominated by the United States, and the other somewhat less completely dominated by the Soviet Union than was the case in 1950. Both shared (though in

far different degree) in the continuing economic growth of the 1950s and the 1960s, but were later to diverge as the market economies moved ahead more rapidly. The distinction between the two economic systems nevertheless remained a fundamental of world economic history from 1945 to the 1980s.

The entry of China to the world of what were called socialist economic systems was at first seen almost purely in Cold War terms, and as a shift in strategic balances. Yet by the time of Stalin's death there were many other signs that the prophecy made by the South African statesman Jan Smuts more than a quarter-century before that "the scene had shifted away from Europe to the Far East and the Pacific" had been realized. Although Germany continued to be the focus of Cold War strategy, Korea was dramatic evidence that the centre of gravity of world history was moving once again, this time from Europe to the Orient.

THE ASIAN REVOLUTION

THE COLLAPSE OF EUROPEAN POWER in Asia was bound to be followed by further changes as new Asian states came to be aware of their interests and power (or lack of it). Shape and unity given them by their former masters often did not long outlast the empires; the subcontinent of India turned its back on less than a century of political cohesion while Malaysia and Indo-China were already by 1950 beginning to undergo important and not always comfortable changes in their governmental arrangements. Internal strains troubled some new nations; Indonesia's large Chinese communities had disproportionate weight and economic power and anything that happened in the new China might disturb them. Whatever their political circumstances, moreover, all these countries had fast-growing populations and were economically backward. For many Asians, therefore, the formal end of European domination now seems less

Hindus take part in the Kumba Mela festival in India, which is alternately held in the holy cities of Hardwar, Allahabad, Ujjain and Nasik. Millions of pilgrims attend the festival every year, a sign of the continuing weight in Asia of ancient traditions, untouched by Western influence.

of a turning point that was once thought. The biggest changes came later.

Europe's control of their destinies had for the most part been fitful. Although Europeans had swayed the fate of millions of Asians, and had influenced their lives for centuries, their culture had touched the hearts and minds of few even among the dominant élites. In Asia, European civilization had to contend with deeper rooted and more powerful traditions than anywhere else in the world. Asian cultures had not been (because they could not be) swept aside like those of pre-Columbian America. As in the Middle Eastern world, both the direct efforts of Europeans and the indirect diffusion of European culture through self-imposed modernization faced formidable obstacles. The deepest layers of thought and behaviour often remained undisturbed even in some who believed themselves most emancipated from their past: nativities are still cast in educated Hindu families when children are born and marriages contracted,

and Chinese Marxists were to draw on an unassailable sense of moral superiority grounded in age-old Chinese attitudes to the non-Chinese world.

TWO ASIAS

For the purpose of understanding Asia's recent role in world history two zones of Asian civilization remain as distinct and significant as they have been for centuries. A western Asian sphere is bounded by the mountain ranges of northern India, the Burmese and Siamese highlands and the huge archipelago of which Indonesia is the major component. Its centre is the Indian Ocean and in its history the major cultural influences have been three: Hindu civilization spreading from India to the southeast, Islam (which also spread eastward across it), and the European impact, felt at first through commerce and missionary Christianity, and then for a much shorter era of political domination. The other sphere is eastern Asian, and it is dominated by China. In large measure this is a function of the simple geographical fact of that country's huge mass, but the numbers and, sometimes, the migration of its people and, more indirectly and variably, China's cultural influence on the East Asian periphery – above all, Japan, Korea and Indo-China – all form part of the explanation. In this zone, direct European political domination of Asia had never meant as much as it did further west, in either extent or duration.

INDIA

IT WAS EASY TO LOSE SIGHT of the important differences between eastern and western Asia, as of much else imposed by history, in the troubled years after 1945. In both zones

The fakir, or holy man, remains one of the symbols of traditional India.

there were countries that seemed to follow the same road of angry rejection of the West, expressed in Western nationalist and democratic jargon and appealing to world opinion on long-familiar lines. India absorbed within a few years both the princely states which had survived the Raj and the subcontinent's remaining French and Portuguese enclaves in the name of a truculent nationalism that owed little to native tradition. Soon, the Indian security forces were energetically suppressing any threat of separatism or regional autonomy within the new republic. Perhaps this should not have been surprising. Indian independence was, on the Indian side, the work of a Western-educated élite, which had imported the ideas of nationhood, equality and liberty from the West, even if it had at first only sought equality and partnership with the Raj itself. A threat to that élite's position after 1947 could often be most easily (and sincerely) understood as a threat to an Indian nationality that had in fact still to be created.

PROBLEMS FACING THE NEW GOVERNMENT

This was all the more true because the rulers of independent India had inherited many of the aspirations and institutions of the British Raj. Ministerial structures, constitutional conventions, division of powers between central and provincial authorities, the apparatus of public order and security were all taken over, stamped with republican insignia, and continued to operate much as before 1947. The dominant and explicit ideology of government was a moderate and bureaucratic socialism in the current British mode, and not far removed in spirit from the public-works-and-enlightened-despotism-by-delegation of the Raj in its last years. The realities that faced India's rulers included a deep

conservative reluctance among local notables who controlled votes to disturb traditional privilege at any level below that of the former princes. Yet awesome problems faced India – population growth, economic backwardness, poverty (the average annual per capita income of Indians in 1950 was $55), illiteracy, social, tribal and religious division, and great expectations of what independence ought to bring. It was clear that major change was needed.

Nehru (1889–1964) is shown here on the second anniversary of independence.

The new constitution of 1950 did nothing to change these facts, some of which would not begin to exercise their full weight until at least the second decade of the new India's existence. Even today, much of life in rural India still goes on virtually as it did in the past, when war, natural disaster, and the banditry of the powerful allowed it to do so. This implies gross poverty for some. In 1960, over a third of the rural poor was still living on less than a dollar a week (and at the same time, half the urban population earned less than enough to maintain the accepted minimum daily calorie intake required for health). Economic progress was swallowed by population growth. In the circumstances it is hardly surprising that the rulers of India should have incorporated in the constitution provisions for emergency powers as drastic as any ever enjoyed by a British viceroy, providing as they did for preventative detention and the suspension of individual rights, to say nothing of the suspension of state government and the submission of states to Union control under what was called "President's Rule".

A street in the Indian city of Agra throngs with cycles, motorcycles and pedestrians. Unlike that of more highly industrialized countries, India's agricultural revolution is still incomplete and has hardly helped to feed its rapidly expanding population. Because the birth-rate is high, the growth of the cities has caused only a minimal drop in the size of the rural population.

TENSION BETWEEN INDIA AND PAKISTAN

The weaknesses and uneasiness of a "new nation" made things worse when India quarrelled with its neighbour Pakistan over Kashmir, where a Hindu prince ruled a majority of Muslim subjects. Fighting began there as early as 1947, when the Muslims tried to bring about union with Pakistan; the Maharajah asked for Indian help and joined the Indian republic. To complicate things further, the Muslim spokesmen of Kashmir were themselves divided. India refused to hold the plebiscite recommended by the United Nations Security Council; two-thirds of Kashmir then remained in Indian hands as a running sore in Indo–Pakistani relations. Fighting stopped in 1949, only to break out again in 1965–6 and 1969–70. he issue had by then been further complicated by demarcation disputes and quarrels over the use of the Indus waters. In 1971 there was more fighting between the two states when East Pakistan, a Muslim but Bengali-speaking region, broke away to form a new state, Bangladesh, under Indian patronage (thus showing that Islam alone was not enough to constitute a viable state). It soon faced economic problems even worse than those of India or Pakistan.

For thirty years Kashmir has remained a source of tension and sometimes armed conflict, and it was the cause of heightened international alarm when, in 1998, a provocative test nuclear explosion by India at once provoked a similar test by Pakistan.

POLITICAL ALIGNMENT

In these troubled passages, India's leaders showed great ambitions (perhaps going at times so far as a wish to reunite the subcontinent) and sometimes blatant disregard of the

The problems of the young state of Bangladesh have been exacerbated by a series of natural disasters. The cyclones that regularly devastate the country also cause floods, such as this one in 1988.

interests of other peoples (such as the Nagas). The irritation aroused by Indian aspirations was moreover further complicated by the Cold War. India's leader, Nehru, had quickly insisted that India would not take sides. In the 1950s, this meant that India had warmer relations with the USSR and communist China than with the United States; indeed, Nehru appeared to relish opportunities of criticizing American action, which helped to convince some sympathizers of India's credentials as a progressive, peaceful, "non-aligned" democracy. It came as all the greater a shock, therefore, to them and to the Indian public, to learn in 1959 that Nehru's government had been quarrelling with the Chinese about the northern borders for the previous three years without saying so. At the end of 1962, large-scale fighting began. Nehru took the improbable step of asking the Americans for military aid and, even more improbably, of receiving it at the same time as he also took assistance (in the form of aeroplane engines)

from Russia. His prestige, at its height in the mid-1950s, was seriously diminished.

Logically, the young Pakistan had not courted the same friends as India. In 1947 the country was much weaker than its neighbour, with only a tiny trained civil service (Hindus had joined the old Indian Civil Service in much larger numbers than Muslims), divided geographically in two from the start, and almost at once had lost its ablest leader, Jinnah. Even under the Raj, Muslim leaders had always (perhaps realistically) shown less confidence in democratic forms than Congress; usually, Pakistan had been ruled by authoritarian soldiers who sought to ensure military survival against India, economic development, including land reform, and the safeguarding of Islamic ways.

It always helped to distance Pakistan from India that she was formally Muslim while her neighbour was constitutionally secular and non-confessional (at first sight a seemingly "Western" stance, but one not hard to reconcile with India's syncretic cultural tradition). This was to lead Pakistan towards increasing Islamic regulation of its internal affairs. Religious difference, though, was to affect Pakistan's foreign relations less than the Cold War.

THE THIRD WORLD

The Cold War brought further confusion to Asian politics when a new association of professedly neutralist or "non-aligned" nations emerged after a meeting of representatives of twenty-nine African and Asian states at Bandung in Indonesia in 1955. Most delegations other than China's were from lands that had been part of the colonial empires. From Europe they were soon to be joined by Yugoslavia, a country with its own histories of imperial and alien rule to rake over. Most of these nations were also poor and needy, more suspicious of the United States than of Russia, and more attracted to China than to either.

They came to be called the "Third World" nations, a term apparently coined by a French journalist in a conscious reminiscence of the legally underprivileged French "Third Estate" of 1789, which had provided much of the driving force of the French Revolution. The implication was that they were disregarded by the great powers and excluded from the economic privileges of the developed countries. Plausible though this might sound, the expression "Third World" actually masked important differences between the members of that group. The coherence of Third World politics was not to prove very enduring and since 1955 many more people have been killed in wars and civil wars within that world than in conflicts external to it.

THE COLD WAR IN ASIA

Nevertheless, ten years after the end of the Second World War, the Bandung meeting

The Bandung Conference

Held in Indonesia in 1955, the Bandung Conference was attended by representatives from 29 countries that had recently gained independence, with the aim of analysing their common political, economic and cultural problems. The following were affirmed at the end of the conference: the independence and equality of the Afro–Asian countries; a condemnation of colonialism; respect for human rights; a policy of non-intervention in the internal affairs of other countries; non-participation in collective agreements favouring the individual interests of a particular power; the right of every nation to defend itself; and the creation of the Non-Aligned Countries Movement.

    However, the policy of strict neutrality, advocated by Tito, was unlikely to be implemented. The radical countries – mostly African ones supported by Cuba – had aggressive policies giving priority to the anti-imperialist struggle. On the other hand, the moderate countries, led by India, emphasized the need to solve the East–West problems.

Egypt's President Nasser, with Nehru of India and Tito of Yugoslavia, was a key leader at the Bandung Conference.

In order to continue with the self-sufficient economic model that Tito (shown here addressing a rally in Skopje in 1953) had set up for Yugoslavia, the Yugoslav government had to seek aid from the West. Yugoslavia received large loans from the United States and the International Monetary Fund (IMF), which increased tension between Belgrade and the other countries in the communist bloc. Tito tried to develop a policy of neutrality and non-alignment in international affairs.

forced the great powers to recognize that the weak had power if they could mobilize it. They bore this in mind as they looked for allies in the Cold War and courted votes in the UN. By the late 1950s there were already clear signs that Russian and Chinese interests might diverge as each sought the leadership of the underdeveloped and uncommitted. At first this emerged obliquely in the guise of differing attitudes to the Yugoslavs; it was in the end to be a worldwide contest. One early result was the paradox that, as time passed, Pakistan drew closer to China (in spite of a treaty with the United States) and Russia closer to India. When the United States declined to supply arms during its 1965 war with India, Pakistan asked for Chinese help. It got much less than it hoped for, but this was early evidence of a new fluidity that was beginning to mark international affairs in the 1960s.

No more than the USSR or China could the United States ignore it. Indeed, the Cold War was to produce an ironic change in the Americans' role in Asia; from being enthusiastic patrons of anti-colonialism and demolishers of their allies' empires, they began sometimes to look rather like their successors, though in the East Asian rather than in the Indian Ocean sphere (where long and unrewarded efforts were made to placate an ungrateful India; before 1960 it received more economic aid from the United States than any other country).

INDEPENDENT INDONESIA

ONE VERY SPECIFIC EXAMPLE of the new difficulties facing great powers was provided by Indonesia. Its vast sprawl encompasses many peoples, often with widely diverging interests. Although Buddhism had been the first of the world religions to establish itself there, Indonesia has the largest Muslim population under one government in the world, while Buddhists are now a minority. Arab traders had brought Islam to Indonesia's peoples from the thirteenth century onwards, and more than four-fifths of the Indonesian population is reckoned now to be Muslim, although traditional animism perhaps matters as much in determining their behaviour. Indonesia also has a well-entrenched Chinese community, which had in the colonial period enjoyed a preponderant share of wealth and administrative jobs. The departure of the Dutch released communal tensions from the discipline an alien ruler had imposed just as the usual post-colonial problems – overpopulation, poverty, inflation – began to be felt.

SUKARNO IS DEPOSED

In the 1950s the central government of the new republic was increasingly resented; by 1957 it faced armed rebellion in Sumatra and elsewhere. The time-honoured device of distracting opposition with nationalist excitement (directed against a continual Dutch presence in west New Guinea) did not work any more; popular support for President Sukarno was not rebuilt. His government had already moved away from the liberal forms adopted at the birth of the new state and he leaned more and more on Soviet support. In 1960 parliament was dismissed, and in 1963 Sukarno was named president for life. Yet the United States, fearing he might turn to China for help, continued to stand by him.

American support enabled Sukarno to swallow up (to the irritation of the Dutch) a would-be independent state that had emerged from west New Guinea (West Irian). He then turned on the new federation of Malaysia, put together in 1957 from fragments of British imperial territories in Southeast Asia. With British help, Malaysia mastered Indonesian attacks on Borneo, Sarawak and the Malaysian mainland. Although he still enjoyed American patronage (at one moment, President Kennedy's brother appeared in

Communist prisoners at the notorious Salembra jail in Indonesia are given a lesson in politics as part of their "re-education".

London to support his cause), this setback seems to have been the turning point for Sukarno. Exactly what happened is still obscure, but when food shortages and inflation went out of control, a coup was attempted (it failed) behind which, said the leaders of the army, were the communists. It is at least possible that Indonesia was intended by Mao Tse-tung to play a major part in the export of revolution; the Communist Party, which Sukarno had tried to balance against other politicians, was at one time alleged to be the third largest in the world. Whether or not a communist takeover was intended, however, the economic crisis was exploited by those who feared one. The popular and traditional Indonesian shadow theatres were for months seasoning the old Hindu epics, that were their staple material, with plentiful political allusions and overtones of coming change. When the storm broke, in 1965, the army stood back ostentatiously while popular massacre removed the communists to whom Sukarno might have turned. Estimates of the number killed vary between a quarter of and a half a million, many of them Chinese or of Chinese extraction. Sukarno himself was duly set aside the following year. A solidly anti-communist régime then took power that broke off diplomatic relations with China (they were not to be renewed until 1990). Some of the losers of 1965 were kept in jail and a few were hanged as evidence of resolute prosecution of the struggle against communism and, no doubt, *pour encourager les autres*.

Paradoxically (and almost incomprehensibly, given Indonesia's problems), American support for Sukarno had reflected the belief that strong, prosperous national states were the best bulwarks against communism. The history of Far Eastern Asia in the last forty years can be read so as to offer support for that principle, but its successful expression

President Sukarno (1902–1970) of Indonesia is pictured.

in American policy was always far from unqualified. Difficulty lay in its practical application.

CHINESE POWER REASSERTED

PARADOXICALLY (AND for too long incomprehensibly, given Indonesia's problems), American support for Sukarno had reflected the belief that strong, prosperous national states were the best bulwarks against communism. The history of eastern and southeastern Asia in the last forty years can indeed be read so as to offer support for that principle, but it had always to be applied specifically in difficult and complex contexts. In any case, by 1960, the dominant strategical fact east of Singapore was the re-creation of Chinese power. South Korea and Japan had successfully resisted communism, but they too benefited from the Chinese Revolution; it gave them leverage against the West. Just as East Asians had always held off Europeans more successfully than the Indian Ocean countries, they showed after 1947 an ability to buttress their independence in both communist and non-communist forms, and not to succumb to direct Chinese manipulation. Some have linked this to the deep and many-faceted conservatism of societies that had for centuries drawn on Chinese example. In their disciplined, complex social networks, capacity for constructive social effort, disregard for the individual, respect for authority and hierarchy, and deep self-awareness as members of civilizations and cultures proudly distinct from the West, the East Asians drew on more than the triumph of the Chinese Revolution; indeed, that revolution is only comprehensible against a background dominated by something itself immensely varied in its expressions and far from adequately summed up by the cant phrase "Asian values".

THE CHINESE RECOVERY STARTS

With the Chinese Revolution's victory and installation in power in 1949, nonetheless, Peking was once more the capital of a formally reunited China. Some thought this showed that its leaders might again be more aware of pressure from the land frontiers in the north than of the threat from the sea that had faced it for more than a century. However this may be, the Soviet Union was the first state to recognize the new People's Republic (whose capital was soon officially termed Beijing), closely followed by the United Kingdom, India and Burma. Given Cold War preoccupations elsewhere and the circumstances of the nationalist collapse, the new China in fact faced no conceivable threat from the outside. Its rulers could concentrate on the long overdue and immensely difficult task of modernization; the nationalists, cooped up in Taiwan, could be disregarded

The former British Crown Colony of Singapore acquired a vigorous new autonomous government in 1959. In 1963 Singapore joined the Federation of Malaysia, but broke away as an independent republic in 1965. It is an active commercial enclave, boasting one of the best communications networks in Southeast Asia, and was one of the original so-called "Asian Tigers".

even if for the moment they were under American protection and irremovable. When a major threat appeared, as the United Nations forces approached the Yalu river frontier of Manchuria in 1950, the Chinese reaction was strong and immediate: they sent a large army to Korea. But the main preoccupation of China's new rulers was the internal state of the country. Poverty was universal. Disease and malnutrition were widespread. Material and physical construction and reconstruction were overdue, population pressure on land was as serious as ever, and the moral and ideological void presented by the collapse of the ancien régime over the preceding century had to be filled.

The peasants were the starting point. Here 1949 is not a very significant date. Since the 1920s land reform had been carried out largely by the peasants themselves in areas the communists dominated. By 1956 China's farms were collectivized in a social transfor-mation of the villages that was said to give control of the new units to their inhabitants, but actually handed them over to the Chinese Communist Party (CCP). The overthrow of local village leaders and landlords was often brutal; they must have made up a large num-ber of the 800,000 Chinese later reported by Mao to have been "liquidated" in the first five years of the People's Republic. Meanwhile, industrialization was also pressed forward, with Soviet help, the only source from which China could draw. The model chosen, too, was the Soviet one: a Five-Year Plan was announced and launched in 1953 and opened a brief period during which Stalinist ideas dominated Chinese economic management.

FOREIGN AFFAIRS

The new China was soon a major interna-tional influence. Yet its real independence was

An agricultural commune near Peking (Beijing) is shown. Many such collective farms were set up following Mao's land reforms of the 1950s.

long masked by the superficial unity of the communist bloc and its continued exclusion from UNO at the insistence of the United States. A Sino-Soviet treaty in 1950 was interpreted – especially in the United States – as further evidence that China was entering the Cold War. Certainly, the regime was communist and talked revolution and anticolonialism, and its choices were bound to be confined by the parameters of the Cold War. Yet in a longer perspective more traditional concerns now seem evident in Chinese communist policy from the start. At a very early point, there was visible a primary concern to re-establish Chinese power within the area it had always tended to fill up in past centuries.

The security of Manchuria is by itself enough to explain Chinese military intervention in Korea, but that peninsula had also long been an area of dispute between imperial China and Japan. A Chinese occupation of Tibet in 1951 was another incursion into an area that had for centuries been under Chinese suzerainty. But from the start the most vociferous demand made for regaining control of the Chinese periphery was for the eviction of the KMT (Kuomintang) government from Taiwan, seized in 1895 by the Japanese and only briefly restored in 1945 to control by the mainland. By 1955, the United States government was so deeply committed to the support of the KMT régime there that the president announced that the United States would protect not merely the island itself but also the smaller islands near the Chinese coast thought essential to its defence. About this issue and against a psychological background provided by a sense of inexplicable rebuff from a China long patronized by American philanthropy and missionary effort, the views of Americans on Chinese affairs tended to crystallize for over a decade so obsessively that the KMT tail seemed at times to wag the American dog. Conversely, during the 1950s, both India and the USSR supported Beijing over Taiwan, insisting that the matter was one of Chinese internal affairs; it cost them nothing to do so. Sensation was therefore all the greater when China was known to be in armed struggles with both countries.

CHINA AND INDIA

The quarrel with India grew out of the Chinese occupation of Tibet. When the Chinese further tightened their grasp on that country in 1959, Indian policy still seemed basically sympathetic to China. An attempt by Tibetan exiles to set up a government on Indian soil was stifled. But territorial disputes had already begun and had led to clashes. The Chinese announced that they did not recognize a border with India along lines drawn by a British-Tibetan negotiator in 1914 and never formally accepted by any Chinese government. Forty-odd years' usage was hardly significant in China's millennial historical memory. As a result, there was much heavier fighting in the autumn of 1962 when

A steelworker in a factory in Wuhan is pictured. The first Five-Year Plan plunged China into socialism, with the nationalization of both heavy and light industry.

This scene from the mountainous landscape of Tibet shows Mount Everest in the background and the Rongbuk monastery in the foreground. Chinese occupation of this thinly populated Himalayan country led to a brief war with India in 1962.

Nehru demanded a Chinese withdrawal from the disputed zone. The Indians did badly, though fighting ceased at the end of the year on the initiative of the Chinese.

CHINA AND THE SOVIET UNION

Almost at once, early in 1963, a startled world suddenly heard the Soviet Union bitterly denounced by the Chinese communists, who alleged it had helped India, and had, in a hostile gesture, cut off economic and military aid to China three years earlier. The second charge suggested complex origins to this quarrel, and by no means went to the root of the matter. There were Chinese communists (Mao among them) who remembered all too well what had happened when Chinese interests had been subordinated to the international interest of communism, as interpreted by Moscow, in the 1920s. Since that time there

had always been a tension in the leadership of the Chinese party between Soviet and native forces. Mao himself represented the latter. Unfortunately, such subtleties were difficult to disentangle because Chinese resentment of Soviet policy had to be presented to the rest of the world in Marxist jargon. Since the new Soviet leadership was engaged at the time in dismantling the Stalin myth, this almost accidentally led the Chinese to sound more Stalinist than Stalin in their public pronouncements, even when they were pursuing non-Stalinist policies.

In 1963, non-Chinese observers should also have recalled an even more remote past. Long before the foundation of the CCP, the Chinese Revolution had been a movement of national regeneration. One of its primary aims had been the recovery from the foreigners of China's control over its own destiny. Among these foreigners, the Russians were pre-eminent. Their record of encroachment

Collectivization in China

Before culminating in the commune – the maximum level of collectivization – Chinese agrarian development went through several stages. In 1955, the "semi-socialist production cooperatives" appeared, which brought together 30 or 40 families; in 1956, the "socialist cooperatives" formed groups of between 100 and 300 families, divided into brigades and teams; and finally came the communes.

During the Great Leap Forward 740,000 socialist cooperatives were grouped together into 26,000 communes with an average of 4,634 families in each. But from 1962, when this type of organization was deemed to be too large to manage and inefficient, the 26,000 communes were converted into 74,000, each of which encompassed only a third of the land of the old communes and employed just one-third of the workforce.

Within the commune, the smallest cell was the production team. Each team worked about 15 to 20 hectares of land and supplemented its production by food grown on private plots and animal husbandry.

A production brigade was made up of seven or eight teams, which were coordinated to carry out communal work. The commune itself was comprised of 12 or 13 brigades. Most communes had an important social services centre, which provided secondary education and hospital care. It also administered tax collection, public safety, the civil register and the commercialization of excess production.

In spite of the highly structured nature of their organization, Chinese communes were far from uniform, owing to differences in the environmental conditions in which they were located and the varying quality of their links to urban markets.

The first Chinese communes consisted of seven or eight families who shared tools and draught animals. The members of these "Mutual Aid Work Teams" later shared tractors, such as the one driven by these men in the Gao Kan commune in Senyang.

upon the Chinese sphere went back to Peter the Great and had continued through the tsarist to the Soviet era. A protectorate over Tannu Tuva had been established in 1914 by the tsars, but the area was annexed by the Soviet Union in 1944. In 1945 Soviet armies had entered Manchuria and north China and thus reconstituted the Tsarist Far East of 1900; they remained in Sinkiang until 1949, and in Port Arthur until 1955. In Mongolia they left behind a satellite Mongolian People's Republic set up in the 1920s. With something like 4,500 miles of shared frontier (if Mongolia is included), the potential for friction along its huge length was immense. The Soviet authorities complained of 5,000 Chinese border violations in 1960. An area about one-fifth of the size of Canada was formally in dispute, and by 1969 (a year in which there was much fighting and scores were killed) the Chinese were talking of a "fascist" dictatorship in Moscow and ostentatiously making preparation for war. The Sino-Soviet quarrel that came in the end to entangle the whole communist world was inflamed by Russian tactlessness, too. Soviet leaders seem to have been as careless as any Western imperialists of the feelings of Asian allies: one Soviet leader once revealingly remarked that when touring in China he and other Russians "used to laugh at their primitive forms of organization". The withdrawal of Soviet economic and technical help in 1960 had been a grave affront and one all the more wounding because of the moment at which it came, when China faced the first major domestic crisis of the new régime, in what were officially described as "natural disasters" caused by flooding.

Mao Tse-tung's personal experience must have counted for much in making this crisis. Although his main intellectual formation had been Marxist and although he found its categories helpful in explaining his country's predicament, he appears always to have diluted them with pragmatism. Mao was a ruthless power-seeker; his judgement of political possibilities appears to have faltered only in the years of success, when megalomania, vanity and eventually age took their toll. Even as a young man, he had advocated a Sinicized Marxism, rejecting Soviet dogma that had cost the CCP dear. The basis of Mao's world view seems to have been a vision of society and politics as an arena of contending forces in which human willpower and brute force could be deployed to bring about morally desirable and creative change – defined, of course, by an all-knowing leader.

After benefiting from the violent expropriations and the release of energy that marked the early 1950s, rural China had in fact been subjected in 1955 to a new upheaval. Hundreds of millions of country-dwellers were reorganized into "communes", whose aim was the collectivization of agriculture. Private property was swallowed in them, new goals were set centrally for production and new agricultural methods were imposed. Some of the new methods did positive damage (campaigns for the extermination of birds that fed on crops, for example, released population explosions of insect predators, which the birds had kept in check), others merely stimulated inefficiency. The cadres that ran the communes became more and more concerned with window-dressing to show that targets had been achieved than with food production. The outcome was disastrous; production fell catastrophically. When in 1958, a new surge of endeavour, the "Great Leap Forward", was proclaimed and an intensification of pressure on the communes

MAO TSE-TUNG'S CHINA

MAO'S RELATIONSHIP with his party had not always been untroubled, but his policy towards the peasantry provided a way ahead for it after disaster had overtaken urban communism. After a temporary setback in the early 1930s he was from about 1935 virtually supreme within the party. Rural influences predominated. A new way also seemed to be open for Mao to sway international events; the notion of a protracted revolutionary war, waged from the countryside and carried into the towns, looked promising in other parts of the world where orthodox Marxist belief that industrial development was needed to create a revolutionary proletariat did not look persuasive.

The split between the Soviet and the Chinese communist parties came during the 23rd Congress of the Soviet Communist Party in October 1961. In December 1962, Khrushchev, pictured here, publicly attacked China for allowing the imperialist enclaves of Macau and Hong Kong to exist on Chinese territory. Throughout 1963, the two parties sent mutual accusations to each other in the form of open letters.

followed, matters further worsened. By 1960, large areas were experiencing famine or near-famine conditions. The facts were suppressed; they were not known even to many of the ruling élite. Meanwhile, some estimates now say, as many as forty million Chinese may have died in a few years. Mao stubbornly refused to acknowledge the failure of the Great Leap Forward, with which he was closely and personally identified, and a hunt for scapegoats commenced within the party. In 1961, senior officials began, nonetheless, to gather irrefutable evidence of what had occurred. Mao's standing suffered as his rivals slowly put the economy back on the road to modernization without letting the true facts emerge.

GROWING CHINESE CONFIDENCE

In 1964, a striking symbol of one kind of success was the explosion of a Chinese nuclear weapon. Thus China acquired the expensive admission card to a very exclusive club. The ultimate basis of its international influence, nonetheless, was bound to be its huge population. Even after the setbacks of the famine, the population continued to rise. Five hundred and ninety million has been thought a reasonable estimate for 1950; twenty-five years later, it was 835 million. Although China's share of world population may have been higher at certain points in the past – perhaps it contained nearly 40 per cent of mankind on the eve of the Taiping rebellion – it was in the 1960s stronger than ever before. China's leaders talked as if they were unmoved even by the possibility of nuclear war; the Chinese would survive in greater numbers than the peoples of other countries. There were signs that the presence of such a demographic mass on the border of its most thinly populated regions alarmed the USSR.

THE CULTURAL REVOLUTION

Some of those in the outside world who felt positively unfriendly to the communist régime were heartened by such information, as they had been in the early 1960s about the true state of affairs (Chiang K'ai-shek is said to have wished to have launched an invasion from Taiwan but to have been restrained by the Americans), but the damage was for the most part successfully concealed by censorship and propaganda. Soon, too, Mao began again to seek to regain his ascendancy. He was obsessed with the wish to justify the Great Leap Forward and to punish those whom he saw as having thwarted it, and thus to have betrayed him. One weapon he deployed against them was the uneasiness of many communists over events in the USSR since Stalin's death. A loosening of the iron grip of dictatorship there, modest though it was, seemed to have opened the door to corruption and compromise in bureaucracy and party alike. The fear that something similar might happen if discipline were relaxed in China helped Mao to promote the "Cultural Revolution", which tore asunder country and party between 1966 and 1969. Millions were killed, imprisoned, deprived of their jobs or purged. The cult of Mao and his personal prestige were revitalized and reasserted; senior party members, bureaucrats and intellectuals were harried; universities were closed and physical labour was demanded of all citizens in order to change traditional attitudes. The young were the main instruments of persecution. The country was turned upside down by "Red Guards", who terrorized their seniors in every walk of life. Opportunists struggled to join them before themselves being destroyed by the young. At last even Mao himself began to show signs that he thought things had gone too far. New party cadres were installed and a congress confirmed his leadership, but he had again failed. The army in the end restored order, often at the cost, this time, of the students.

Yet the Red Guards' enthusiasm had been real, and the ostentatious moral preoccupations that surfaced in this still in some ways mysterious episode remain striking. Mao's motives in launching it were no doubt mixed. Besides seeking vengeance on those who had brought about the abandonment of the Great Leap Forward, he appears really to have felt a danger that the Revolution might congeal and lose the moral *élan* that had carried it so far. In seeking to protect it, old ideas had to go. Society, government and economy were enmeshed and integrated with one another in China as nowhere else. The traditional prestige of intellectuals and scholars still embodied the old order, just as the examination system had done as the century began. The "demotion" and demonization of intellectuals was urged as a necessary consequence of making a new China. Similarly, attacks on family authority were not merely attempts by a suspicious régime to encourage informers and disloyalty, but attempts to modernize the most conservative of all Chinese institutions. The emancipation of women and propaganda to discourage early marriage had dimensions going beyond "progressive" feminist ideas or population control; they were an assault on the past such as no other revolution had ever made, for in China the past meant a role for women far inferior to anything to be found in pre-revolutionary America, France or even Russia. The attacks on party leaders, which accused them of flirtation with Confucian ideas, were much more than jibes; they could not have been paralleled in the West, where for centuries there was no past so solidly entrenched to reject. In that light, the Cultural Revolution, too, could be regarded as an exercise in modernization politics.

THE NATURE OF THE CHINESE REVOLUTION

Rejection of the past is only half the story of the Chinese Revolution. More than two thousand years of a continuity stretching back to the Ch'in (Qin) and perhaps further also shaped it. One clue is the role of authority. For all its cost and cruelty, the revolution was a heroic endeavour, matched in scale only by such gigantic upheavals as the spread of

A flamboyant parade is held in Beijing in August 1968, during the Cultural Revolution.

Chinese people recite texts from the Little Red Book, in which Mao stressed the need to reduce urban–rural differences and the importance of "perpetual revolution".

alism, though not of Chinese individualism or collective radicalism.

The régime over which Mao presided benefited from the Chinese past as well as destroying it, because his role was easily comprehensible within its idea of authority. He was presented as a ruler-sage, as much a teacher as a politician in a country that has always respected teachers; Western commentators were amused by the status given to his thoughts by the omnipresence of the Little Red Book (but forgot the Bibliolatry of many European Protestants). Mao was spokesman of a moral doctrine which was presented as the core of society, just as Confucianism had been. There was also something traditional in Mao's artistic interests; he was admired by the people as a poet and his poems won the respect of qualified judges. In China, power has always been sanctioned by the notion that the ruler did good things for his people and sustained accepted values. Mao's actions could be read in such a way.

Islam, or Europe's assault on the world in early modern times. Yet it was different from those upheavals because it was at least in intention centrally controlled and directed. It is a paradox of the Chinese Revolution that it has rested on popular fervour, but is unimaginable without conscious direction from a state inheriting all the mysterious prestige of the traditional bearers of the Mandate of Heaven. Chinese tradition respects authority and gives it a moral endorsement that has long been hard to find in the West. No more than any other great state could China shake off its history, and as a result communist government sometimes had a paradoxically conservative appearance. No great nation had for so long driven home to its peoples the lessons that the individual matters less than the collective whole, that authority could rightfully command the services of millions at any cost to themselves in order to carry out great works for the good of the state, that authority is unquestionable so long as it is exercised for the common good. The notion of opposition is distasteful to the Chinese because it suggests social disruption; that implies the rejection of the kind of revolution involved in the adoption of Western individu-

WAR IN INDO-CHINA

The weight of the past was evident in Chinese foreign policies, too. Although it came to patronize revolution all over the world, China's main concern was with the Far East and, in particular, with Korea and Indo-China, once tributary countries. In the latter, too, Russian and Chinese policy had diverged. After the Korean War the Chinese began to supply arms to the communist guerrilla forces in Vietnam for what was less a struggle against colonialism – that had been decided already – than about what should follow it. In 1953 the French had given up both Cambodia and Laos. In 1954 they lost at a base called Dien Bien Phu a battle decisive both for French prestige and for the French electorate's will to fight. After

Population pressure and post-war recovery in South and East Asia

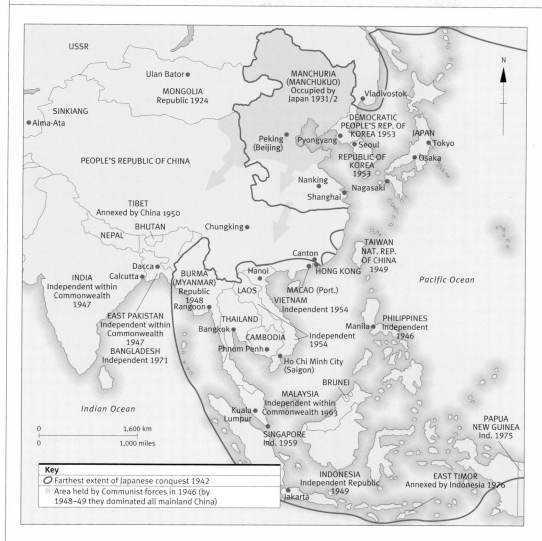

Although Chinese culture has been disseminated over the area shown on this map for centuries, that vast nation has had political influence over much of southern and eastern Asia. Only in the last couple of centuries was the region divided into areas of major European influence. Japan, which was particularly strong following the 19th-century Meiji Restoration, has also exerted a strong influence in the area.

Since the end of the Second World War, most southern and eastern Asian countries have gained independence from their old colonial rulers.

Key

○ Farthest extent of Japanese conquest 1942

▪ Area held by Communist forces in 1946 (by 1948–49 they dominated all mainland China)

Population pressure (persons per square km)

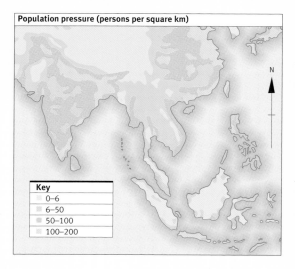

Key
- 0–6
- 6–50
- 50–100
- 100–200

Gross Domestic Product *per capita* in 1992

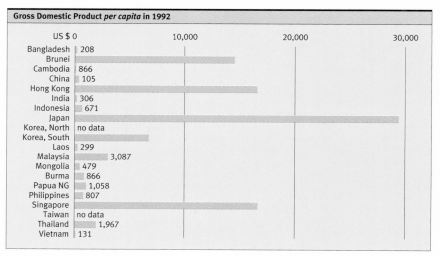

	US $ 0	10,000	20,000	30,000
Bangladesh	208			
Brunei				
Cambodia	866			
China	105			
Hong Kong				
India	306			
Indonesia	671			
Japan				
Korea, North	no data			
Korea, South				
Laos	299			
Malaysia	3,087			
Mongolia	479			
Burma	866			
Papua NG	1,058			
Philippines	807			
Singapore				
Taiwan	no data			
Thailand	1,967			
Vietnam	131			

A merican support for South Vietnam would eventually spill over to neighbouring Cambodia. There the government tried to match the ferocity of the communist guerrilla organization the Khmer Rouge. The heads of guerrillas are shown being carried from a battle zone.

this, it was impossible for the French to maintain themselves in the Red River delta. A conference at Geneva was attended by representatives from China, which thus formally re-entered the arena of international diplomacy. It was agreed to partition Vietnam between a South Vietnamese government and the communists who had come to dominate the north, pending elections that might reunite the country. The elections never took place. Instead, there soon opened in Indo-

China what was to become the fiercest phase since 1945 of an Asian war against the West begun in 1941.

The Western contenders were no longer the former colonial powers, but the Americans; the French had gone home and the British had problems enough elsewhere. On the other side was a mixture of Indo-Chinese communists, nationalists and reformers, supported by the Chinese and Russians who competed for influence in Indo-China. American anti-colonialism and the belief that the United States should support indigenous governments led it to back the South Vietnamese as it backed South Koreans and Filipinos. Unfortunately, neither in Laos nor South Vietnam, nor, in the end, in Cambodia, did there emerge régimes of unquestioned legitimacy in the eyes of those they ruled. American patronage merely identified governments with the Western enemy so disliked in East Asia. American support also tended to remove the incentive to carry out reforms that would have united people behind these régimes, above all in Vietnam, where *de facto* partition did not produce good or stable government in the south. While Buddhists and Roman Catholics quarrelled bitterly and the peasants were more and more alienated from the régime by the failure of land reform, an apparently corrupt ruling class seemed able to survive government after government. This benefited the communists. They sought reunification on their own terms and maintained from the north support for the communist underground movement in the south, the Vietcong.

By 1960 the Vietcong had won control of much of the south. This was the background to a momentous decision taken by the American president, John Kennedy, in 1962, to send not only financial and material help but also 4,000 American "advisers" to help the South Vietnam government put its military house in order. It was the first step towards what Truman had been determined to avoid, the involvement of the United States in a major war on the mainland of Asia, and in the end led to the loss of more than 50,000 American lives.

JAPAN IN 1945

ANOTHER OF WASHINGTON'S responses to Cold War in Asia had been to safeguard as long as possible the special position arising from the American occupation of Japan. This was virtually a monopoly, although there was token participation by British Commonwealth forces. It had been possible because of the Soviet delay in declaring war on Japan, for the speed of Japan's surrender had taken Stalin by surprise. The Americans firmly rejected later Soviet requests for a share in an occupation Soviet power had done nothing to bring about. The outcome was the the last great example of Western paternalism in Asia and a new demonstration of the Japanese people's gift for learning from others only what they wished to learn, while safeguarding their own society against unsettling change.

The events of 1945 forced Japan spiritually into a twentieth century it had already entered technologically. Defeat confronted its people with deep and troubling problems of national identity and purpose. The Westernization of the Meiji era had seeded a dream of "Asia for the Asians"; this was presented as a kind of Japanese Monroe doctrine, underpinned by the anti-Western sentiment so widespread in the Far East and cloaking the reality of Japanese imperialism. It had been blown away by defeat, and after 1945 the rolling back of colonialism left Japan with no obvious and credible Asian role. True, at that moment it seemed unlikely for a long time to have the power for one. Moreover, the war's demonstration of Japan's vulnerability had been a great shock; like the United Kingdom its security had rested at bottom upon control of the surface of the sea, and the loss of it had doomed the country.

American troops cross a coral reef to reach a beach during their campaign in the Pacific (1942–45). The sea battle in the Philippines was a disaster for the Japanese. Two Japanese naval chiefs of staff committed suicide when they saw that the Americans had taken the island of Saipan. As they advanced inland, American soldiers and marines were horrified to see women, old people and children throwing themselves off the cliffs, rather than face defeat.

The Showa emperor, Hirohito (1901–89), the 124th sovereign from the reigning family, became regent when he was 20 years old, and was crowned emperor in 1926. In 1936, the totalitarian and militaristic Taisei Yokusankai party won the elections, and tried to manoeuvre the emperor away from political matters. However, after the atomic bombs had been dropped, Hirohito was able to get the government to agree to unconditional surrender. The United States kept Hirohito on the throne as the only guarantee for the pacification and rapid reconstruction of the country, and in 1946, by the terms of the new constitution, he duly became a constitutional monarch.

Then there were the other results of defeat; the loss of territory to Russia on Sakhalin and the Kurile islands and the occupation by the Americans. Finally, there was vast material and human destruction to repair.

JAPANESE RECOVERY

On the asset side, the Japanese in 1945 still had the unshaken central institution of the monarchy, whose prestige was undimmed and, indeed, had made the surrender possible. Japanese saw in the emperor Hirohito not the ruler who had authorized the war, but the man whose decision had saved them from annihilation. The American commander in the Pacific, General MacArthur, wanted to uphold the monarchy as an instrument of a peaceful occupation and was careful not to compromise the emperor by parading his role in policy-making before 1941. He took care to have a new Japanese constitution (with an electorate doubled in size and now including women) adopted before republican enthusiasts in the United States could interfere; he found it effective to argue that Japan should be helped economically in order to get it more quickly off the back of the American taxpayer. Japanese social cohesiveness and discipline was a great help, even though for a time it seemed that the Americans might undermine this by the determination with which they pressed democratic institutions upon the country. Some problems must have been eased by a major land reform in which about a third of the cultivated area of Japan passed from landlords' to cultivators' ownership. By 1951 democratic education and careful demilitarization were deemed to have done enough to make possible a peace treaty between Japan and most of its former opponents, except the Russians and nationalist Chinese (with whom terms were to be settled within a few years). Japan regained its full sovereignty, including a right to arms for defensive purposes, but gave up virtually all its former overseas possessions. Thus the Japanese emerged from the post-war era to resume control of their own affairs. An agreement with the United States provided for the maintenance of American forces on its soil. Confined to its own islands, and facing a China stronger and much better consolidated than for a century, Japan's position was not necessarily a disadvantageous one. In less

than twenty years this much-reduced status was, as it turned out, to be transformed again.

The Cold War had changed the implications of the American occupation even before 1951. Japan was separated from the Russians and Chinese by, respectively, 10 and 500 miles of water. Korea, the old zone of imperial rivalry, was only 150 miles away. The spread of the Cold War to Asia guaranteed Japan even better treatment from the Americans, now anxious to see it working convincingly as an example of democracy and capitalism, and also gave it the protection of the United States' nuclear "umbrella". The Korean War made Japan important as a base and galvanized its economy. The index of industrial production quickly went back up to the level of the 1930s. The United States promoted Japanese interests abroad through diplomacy. Finally, Japan at first had no defence costs, since it was until 1951 forbidden to have any armed forces.

THE USA AND THE PACIFIC STATES

Japan's close connection with the United States, its proximity to the communist world, and its advanced and stable economy and society, all made it natural that it should eventually take its place in the security system built up by the United States in Asia and the Pacific. Its foundations were treaties with Australia, New Zealand and the Philippines (which had become independent in 1946). Others followed with Pakistan and Thailand; these were the Americans' only Asian allies other than Taiwan. Indonesia and (much more important) India remained aloof. These alliances reflected, in part, the new conditions of Pacific and Asian international relations after the British withdrawal from India. For a little longer there would still be British forces

In 1954 SEATO was set up to maintain stability in Asia and the Pacific. A meeting was held in Washington on 8 November 1954 to which representatives of the free nations were invited, together with Japanese prime minister Shigeru Yoshida (1878–1967), pictured here speaking at the meeting. Yoshida called upon the United States and other free nations to invest $4,000 million in Southeast Asia in order to reduce the risk of the region falling into communist hands.

east of Suez, but Australia and New Zealand had discovered during the Second World War that the United Kingdom could not defend them and that the United States could. The fall of Singapore in 1942 had been decisive. Although British forces had sustained the Malaysians against the Indonesians in the 1950s and 1960s, the colony of Hong Kong survived, it was clear, only because it suited the Chinese that it should. On the other hand, there was no question of sorting out the complexities of the new Pacific by simply lining up states in the teams of the Cold War. The peace treaty with Japan itself caused great difficulty because United States policy saw Japan as a potential anti-communist force while others – notably Australia and New Zealand – remembered 1941 and feared a revival of Japanese power.

ASIAN REJECTION OF WESTERN DOMINATION

American policy was not created only by ideology. Nonetheless, it was long misled by what was believed to be the disaster of the communist success in China and by Chinese patronage of revolutionaries as far away as Africa and South America. There had certainly been a transformation in China's international position and it would go further. Yet the crucial fact was China's re-emergence as a power in its own right. In the end this did not reinforce the dualist, Cold War system but made nonsense of it. Although at first only within the former Chinese sphere, it was bound to bring about a big change in relative power relationships; the first sign of this was seen in Korea, where the United Nations armies were stopped and it was felt necessary to consider bombing China. But the rise of China was also of crucial importance to the Soviet Union. After being one element of a bipolarized system, Moscow now became the corner of a potential triangle, as well as losing its unchallenged pre-eminence in the world revolutionary movement. And it was in relation to the Soviet Union, perhaps, that the wider significance of the Chinese Revolution most readily appeared. Overwhelmingly important though it was, the Chinese Revolution was only the outstanding instance of a rejection of Western domination that was Asia-wide. Paradoxically, of course, that rejection in all Asian countries was constantly expressed in forms, language and mythology borrowed from the West itself, whether they were those of industrial capitalism, democracy, nationalism or Marxism.

On 1 July 1997 the British colony of Hong Kong was handed back to China: two scenes from the farewell celebrations are shown here. At the handover ceremony at the Hong Kong Convention Centre (top), dignitaries from around the world were among the guests who watched the Chinese flag flying after the British Union Jack had been lowered. Later, a fireworks display lit up the harbour (bottom).

2 INHERITORS OF EMPIRE

THE SURVIVAL OF ISRAEL, the coming of the Cold War and a huge rise in the demand for oil revolutionized the politics of the Middle East after 1948. Israel focused Arab feeling more sharply than Great Britain had ever done. It made pan-Arabism look plausible. On the injustice of the seizure of what were regarded as Arab lands, the plight of the Palestine refugees and the obligations of the great powers and the United Nations to act on their behalf, the Arab masses could brood bitterly and Arab rulers were able to agree as on nothing else.

ISRAEL AND THE ARAB STATES

AFTER THE DEFEAT of 1948–9, in spite of the new spirit of pan-Arabism, the Arab states were not for some time disposed again to commit their own forces openly. A formal state of war persisted but a series of armistices established for Israel *de facto* borders with Jordan, Syria and Egypt that lasted until 1967. There were continuing border incidents in the early 1950s, and raids were carried out upon Israel from Egyptian

The Dome of the Rock in Jerusalem is an important Islamic shrine. In the period prior to the establishment of Israel, the struggle between the Jews and the Arabs was focused on the control of Jerusalem. Within the city, the Jewish and Arab quarters had long been mixed. In the war that followed the foundation of Israel, Jordanian forces occupied the old city and tried to blockade the Jews holding out in the new sector. The armistice of 1949 left Jerusalem divided, with an Israeli corridor to its sector of the city. From 1967, Israel occupied the former Jordanian sector. A unified Jerusalem is now the capital of Israel.

The post-Ottoman Near and Middle East

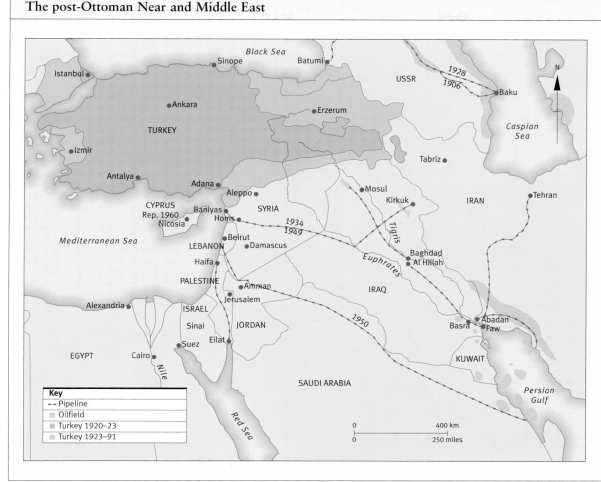

Key
- -- Pipeline
- ▪ Oilfield
- ▪ Turkey 1920–23
- ▪ Turkey 1923–91

In many of the Muslim countries in the Near East foreign colonial powers have weakened and disappeared since the end of the Second World War, while Arab oil wealth has grown rapidly. It has been a tumultuous period in the region. The establishment of the state of Israel in 1948 was followed by the Arab–Israeli wars. In 1956 the Suez crisis took place. Soviet troops invaded Afghanistan in 1979 and fought in the civil war there until 1989, while civil war also raged in Lebanon from 1975 until 1989. Following the Iran–Iraq war of 1980–1989, Iraq's invasion of Kuwait in 1990 sparked off the Gulf War.

and Syrian territory by bands of young guerrilla soldiers recruited from the refugee camps, but immigration, hard work and money from the United States steadily consolidated the new Israel. A siege psychology helped to stabilize Israel's politics; the prestige of the party that had brought about the very existence of the new state was scarcely troubled while the Jews transformed their new country. Within a few years they could show massive progress in bringing barren land under cultivation and establishing new industries. The gap between Israel's per capita income and that of the more populous among the Arab states steadily widened.

Here was another irritant for the Arabs. Foreign aid to their countries produced nothing like such dramatic change. Egypt, the most populous of them, faced particularly grave problems of population growth. While the oil-producing states were to benefit in the 1950s and 1960s from growing revenue and a higher GDP, this often led to further strains and divisions within them. Contrasts deepened both between different Arab states and within them between classes. Most of the oil-producing countries were ruled by small, wealthy, sometimes traditional and conservative, sometimes nationalist and Westernized, élites, usually uninterested in the poverty-stricken peasants and slum-dwellers of more populous neighbours. The contrast was exploited by a new Arab political movement, founded during the war, the Ba'ath party. It attempted to synthesize Marxism and pan-Arabism, but the Syrian and Iraqi wings of the movement (it was always strongest in those two countries) had fallen out with one another almost from the start.

NASSER'S EGYPT

Pan-arabism had too much to overcome, for all the impulse to united action stemming from anti-Israeli and anti-Western feeling. The Hashemite kingdoms, the Arabian sheikdoms, and the Europeanized and urbanized states of North Africa and the Levant all had widely divergent interests and very different historical traditions. Some of them, like Iraq or Jordan, were artificial creations whose shape had been dictated by the needs and wishes of European powers after 1918; some were social and political fossils. Even Arabic was in many places a common

Abdel Nasser (1918–1970) was one of the instigators of the Egyptian coup that overthrew King Farouk in 1952, and became president of the Revolutionary Council. Nasser was appointed head of government in 1954, a moment captured here, and president of Egypt in 1956. He played an important role in the Bandung Conference in 1955.

language only within the mosque (and not all Arabic-speakers were Muslims). Although Islam was a tie between many Arabs, for a long time it seemed of small account; in 1950 few Muslims talked of it as a militant, aggressive faith. It was only Israel that provided a common enemy and thus a common cause.

Hopes were first awoken among Arabs in many countries by a revolution in Egypt, from which there eventually emerged a young soldier, Gamal Abdel Nasser. For a time he seemed likely both to unite the Arab world against Israel and to open the way to social change. In 1954 he became the leader of the military junta that had overthrown the Egyptian monarchy two years previously. Egyptian nationalist feeling had for decades found its main focus and scapegoat in the British, still garrisoning the Canal Zone, and now blamed for their part in the establishment of Israel. The British government, for its part, did its best to cooperate with Arab rulers because of its fears of Soviet influence in an area still thought crucial to British communications and oil supplies. The Middle East (ironically given the motives that had taken the British there in the first place) had not lost its strategic fascination for the British after withdrawal from India.

EUROPEAN REACTIONS TO NASSER

The 1950s were a time of strong anti-Western currents elsewhere in the Arab world, too. In 1951 the king of Jordan had been assassinated; in order to survive, his successor had to make it clear that he had severed the old special tie with Great Britain. Further west, the French, who had been forced to recognize the complete independence of Morocco and Tunisia soon after the war, faced troubles that by 1954 had grown into an Algerian national rebellion, which was soon to become a full-scale war; no French government could easily abandon a country where there were over a million settlers of European stock. Moreover, oil had just been discovered in the Sahara. In the context of a stirring Arab world, Nasser's rhetoric of social reform and nationalism had wide appeal. His anti-Israeli feelings were not in doubt and he quickly had to his credit the success of an agreement with Great Britain for the evacuation of the Suez base. The Americans, too, increasingly aware of Soviet menace in the Middle East, looked on him for a while with favour as a spotless anti-colonialist and potential client.

He soon came to appeal to them far less. The guerrilla raids on Israel from Egyptian territory (the "Gaza Strip", where the most important Palestinian refugee camps lay) provoked irritation in Washington. In 1950, the British, French and Americans had already said they would provide only limited supplies of arms to Middle East states and only on such terms as would keep a balance between Israel and the Arabs. When Nasser carried off an arms deal with Czechoslovakia on the security of the cotton crop, and Egypt recognized communist China, second thoughts about him hardened. By way of showing displeasure, an American and British offer to finance a cherished project of internal development, a high dam on the Nile, was withdrawn. As a riposte, Nasser seized the assets of the private company that owned and ran the Suez Canal, saying its profits should finance the dam; this touched an old nerve of British sensibility. Instincts only half-disciplined by imperial withdrawal seemed for once to be coherent both with anti-communism and with friendship towards more traditional Arab states, whose rulers were beginning to look askance at Nasser as a revolutionary radical. The British prime minister, Anthony Eden, too, was obsessed with a

false analogy which led him to see Nasser as a new Hitler, to be checked before he embarked upon a career of successful aggression. As for the French, they were aggrieved by Nasser's support for the Algerian insurrection. Both nations formally protested over the canal's seizure and, in collusion with Israel, began to plan Nasser's overthrow.

The ancient statues at Abu Simbel in Egypt are relocated to make way for the Aswan High Dam. The dam, which was inaugurated in January 1971, impounds a vast reservoir called Lake Nasser and controls the annual Nile flood.

THE SUEZ CRISIS

IN OCTOBER 1956, the Israelis suddenly invaded Egypt to destroy, they announced, bases from which guerrillas had harassed their settlements. The British and French governments at once said freedom of movement through the canal was in danger. They called for a cease-fire; when Nasser rejected this they launched (on Guy Fawkes' Day) first an air attack and then a seaborne assault on Egypt. Collusion with Israel was denied, but the denial was preposterous. It was a lie, and, worse still, from the first incredible. Soon the Americans were thoroughly alarmed; they feared advantage for the USSR in this renewal of imperialism. They used financial pressure to force a British acceptance of a cease-fire negotiated by the United Nations. The Anglo-French adventure collapsed in humiliation.

The Suez affair looked (and was) a Western disaster, but in the long run its main importance was psychological. The British suffered most; it cost them much goodwill, particularly within the Commonwealth, and squandered confidence in the sincerity of their retreat from empire. It confirmed the Arabs'

hatred of Israel; the suspicion that it was indissolubly linked to the West made them yet more receptive to Soviet blandishment. Nasser's prestige soared still higher. Some were bitter, too, that Suez had at a crucial moment distracted the West from eastern Europe (where a revolution in Hungary against its Soviet satellite government had been crushed by the Russian army while the Western powers fell out). Nevertheless, the essentials of the region's affairs were left by the crisis much as before, animated by a new wave of pan-Arab enthusiasm though they might be. Suez did not change the balance of the Cold War, or of the Middle East.

THE REPERCUSSIONS OF THE SUEZ CRISIS

In 1958 an attempt was made by Ba'ath sympathizers to unite Syria and Egypt in a United Arab Republic that briefly bore fruit in 1961. The pro-Western government of the Lebanon was overthrown and the monarchy of Iraq swept aside by revolution that year, too. These facts heartened pan-Arabists, but differences between Arab countries soon reasserted themselves. The world watched curiously when American forces were summoned to the Lebanon and British forces to Jordan to help maintain their governments against pro-Nasser forces. Meanwhile, fighting went on sporadically on the Syrian-Israeli border, although the guerrillas were for a time held in check.

However, from Suez until 1967 the most important development in the Arab world was not there, but in Algeria. The intransigence of the *pieds noirs* (the French settlers) and the bitterness of many soldiers, who felt they were asked to do an impossible job there, nearly brought about a *coup d'état* in France itself. The government of General de

The Israeli offensive that began on the night of 29 October 1956, took the Egyptians completely by surprise. On 1 November, Israeli troops continued to advance through Sinai and one day later they occupied Gaza. Here, jubilant Israeli troops pose with a captured Egyptian lorry in Gaza on 2 November.

From 1954, the National Liberation Front fought for the political independence of Algeria. On 12 March 1962 a cease-fire was agreed: the republic of Algeria was recognized and guarantees for France's principal interests in the new state were made, along with agreements on future cooperation. Here, Prime Minister Muhammad Ben Bella gives a speech in the new Algerian National Assembly in 1962.

Gaulle nevertheless opened secret negotiations with the Algerian rebels and in July 1962, after a referendum, France formally granted independence to a new Algeria. Angrily, a million *pieds noirs* migrated to France, to embitter her politics. Ironically, within twenty years France was to benefit from over a million Algerian immigrant workers, whose remittances home were essential to the Algerian economy. As Libya had emerged from United Nations trusteeship to independence in 1951, the entire North African coast outside the tiny Spanish enclaves was now clear of European supremacy. Yet external influences still bedevilled the history of the Arab lands as they had done ever since the Ottoman conquests centuries before, but now did so indirectly, through aid and diplomacy, as the United States and Russia sought to buy friends.

The United States laboured under a disadvantage: no American president or Congress could abandon Israel. The importance of Jews among American voters was too great, although President Eisenhower had been brave enough to face them down over Suez, even in an election year. In spite of America's clean hands therefore, Egyptian and Syrian policy continued to sound anti-American and prove irritating. The USSR, on the other hand, had dropped its early support of Israel as soon as it ceased to be a useful weapon with which to embarrass the British. Soviet policy now took a steady pro-Arab line and assiduously fanned Arab resentment over survivals of British imperialism in the Arab world. Marginally, too, the Russians earned a cheap bonus of Arab approval in the later 1960s by harassing their own Jews.

THE OIL FACTOR

The context of the Middle East's problems was slowly changing. In the 1950s there were two important developments concerning oil.

One was a much greater rate of its discovery than hitherto, particularly on the southern side of the Persian Gulf, in the small sheikdoms then still under British influence, and in Saudi Arabia. The second was a huge acceleration of energy consumption in Western countries, especially in the United States. The prime beneficiaries of the oil boom were Saudi Arabia, Libya, Kuwait and, some way behind, Iran and Iraq, the established major producers. This had two important consequences. Countries dependent upon Middle Eastern oil – the United States, Great Britain, Germany and soon Japan – had to give greater weight to Arab views in their diplomacy. It also meant big changes in the relative wealth and standing of Arab states. None of the three leading oil producers was either heavily populated or traditionally very weighty in international affairs.

THE SIX DAY WAR

The importance of the oil factor was still not very evident in the last Middle East crisis of the 1960s, which began when a much more extreme government took power in Syria with Soviet support in 1966. The king of Jordan was threatened if he did not support the Palestinian guerrillas (organized since 1964 as the Palestine Liberation Organization, or PLO). Jordanian forces therefore began to prepare to join in an attack on Israel with Egypt and Syria. But in 1967, provoked by an attempt to blockade their Red Sea port, the Israelis struck first. In a brilliant campaign they destroyed the Egyptian air force and army in Sinai and hurled back the Jordanians, winning in six days' fighting new borders on the Suez Canal, the Golan Heights, and in Jordan. For defence, these were far superior

An oil refinery in Jeddah, Saudi Arabia, is pictured. The sectors that turned the 1950s and 1960s into growth years in the industrialized nations (the car industry, steel and iron works, petrochemicals, electronics and construction) were dependent on oil. This meant that underdeveloped countries that had access to large oil reserves, particularly those in the Middle East, were suddenly able to influence international politics in a new way.

The Israeli defence minister, Moshe Dayan (left), waits in a bunker in the Golan Heights during the Six Day War. The war was a tactical victory for the Israelis. They managed to surround the Egyptian Third Army, which suffered such heavy losses that President Nasser temporarily resigned.

to their former boundaries and the Israelis announced that they would keep them. This was not all. Defeat had ensured the eclipse of the glamorous Nasser, the first plausible leader of pan-Arabism. He was left visibly dependent on Russian power (a Soviet naval squadron arrived at Alexandria as the Israeli advance guards reached the Suez Canal), and on subsidies from the oil states. Both demanded more prudence from him, and that meant difficulties with the radical leaders of the Arab masses.

TENSIONS RISE OVER ISRAEL

The Six Day War of 1967 solved nothing. There were new waves of Palestinian refugees; by 1973 about 1,400,000 Palestinians were said to be dispersed in Arab countries, while a similar number remained in Israel and Israeli-occupied territory. When the Israelis began to plant settlements in their newly won conquests, Arab resentment grew even stronger. Even if time, oil, and birth-rates seemed to be on the Arab side, not much

else was clear. In the United Nations, a "Group of 77" supposedly non-aligned countries achieved the suspension of Israel (like South Africa) from certain international organizations and, perhaps more important, a unanimous resolution condemning the Israeli annexation of Jerusalem. Another called for Israel's withdrawal from Arab lands in exchange for recognition by its neighbours. Meanwhile, the PLO turned to terrorism outside the disputed lands to promote their cause. Like the Zionists of the 1890s, they had decided that the Western myth of nationality was the answer to their plight: a new state should be the expression of their nationhood, and like Jewish militants in the 1940s, they chose terrorism – assassination and indiscriminate murder – as their weapons. It was clear that in time there would be another war, and therefore a danger that, because of the identification of American and Russian interests with opposing sides, a world war might suddenly blow up out of a local conflict, as in 1914.

The danger became imminent when Egypt and Syria attacked Israel on the Jewish holy

day of Yom Kippur, in October 1973. The Israelis for the first time faced the prospect of military defeat by the greatly improved and Soviet-armed forces of their opponents. Yet once again they won, though only after the Russians were reported to have sent nuclear weapons to Egypt and the Americans had put their forces on the alert around the world. This grim background, like the possibility that the Israelis themselves might have nuclear weapons they would be prepared to use in extremity, was not fully discernible to the public at the time.

This, however, was not the only way in which the crisis transcended the region. The problems of the Ottoman succession left behind in 1919, of which Israel's emergence was only a part, had been successively further poisoned, first by the inter-war policies of Great Britain and France, and then by the Cold War. But it was now to become clear that there had been a much more fundamental change in the Middle East's world role. In 1945 the world's largest oil exporter had been Venezuela; twenty years later this was no longer so and most developed economies depended for much of their oil on the Middle East. In the 1950s and for most of the 1960s the British and Americans had been confident of cheap and assured supplies from the region. They had managed what once had looked a possible threat to their access to

Iranian oil in 1953 by overthrowing an unfriendly Iranian government, exercised informal controlling influence in Iraq until 1963 (when a Ba'ath regime seized power there) and had no difficulty in retaining Saudi Arabian goodwill. But the Yom Kippur War ended this era. Led by Saudi Arabia, the Arab states announced they would cut supplies of oil to Europe, Japan and the United States. Israel had to face the frightening possibility that it might not always be able to rely on the diplomatic support it had always found outside the region. It might not be able to go on counting on guilt about the Holocaust, sympathy and admiration for a progressive state in a backward region, and the weight of Jewish voters in the United States. It was not a good moment for the United States and its allies. In 1974, with 138 states members of the UN, there were for the first time majorities in the General Assembly against the Western powers (over both Israel and South Africa). Although for the moment the UN agreed to put a force into Sinai to separate the Israelis and the Egyptians, none of the region's fundamental problems was solved.

THE OIL CRISIS

The impact of "oil diplomacy" went far beyond the region, however. Overnight, economic problems that had been tolerable in the 1960s became acute. World oil prices shot up. Dependence on oil imports everywhere played havoc with balance-of-payments problems. The United States, floundering in what had become an Indo-Chinese morass, was badly shaken; Japan and Europe appeared to face full-scale recession. Perhaps, it seemed, a new 1930 was on its way; at any rate, the golden age of assured economic growth was over. Meanwhile, it was the poorest countries among the oil importers that suffered most from the oil crisis. Many of them were soon having to face rocketing price inflation and some a virtual obliteration of the earnings they needed in order to pay interest on their large debts to foreign creditors.

AFRICA

THE IMPACT OF HIGHER oil prices was notable in much of Africa. In the 1950s and early 1960s that continent had undergone a startlingly rapid process of decolonization. It had been exhilarating, but had left behind some fragile new nations, especially south of the Sahara. France, Belgium and Great Britain were the major imperial powers concerned with what was on the whole a perhaps surprisingly peaceful process. Italy had lost her last African territories in 1943, and only in Algeria and the Portuguese colonies was there much blood spilled in the process of liberation, the Portuguese finally giving up after domestic revolution in 1974; thus the Iberians who had led the European adventure of overseas dominion were almost the last to abandon it. There was plenty of bloodshed to come after the roll-up of empire, it is true, when African set about African, but troubles tended to arise for the French and British only when there were significant white settler communities to consider. Elsewhere, both French and British politicians proved anxious to retain influence, if they could, by showing benevolent interest in their former subjects.

THE LEGACY OF COLONIALISM

Africa owes its present form in the main to decisions of nineteenth-century Europeans (just as much of the Middle East owes its political framework to the Europeans in the twentieth century). New African "nations" were usually defined by the boundaries of former colonies and those boundaries have proved remarkably enduring. They often enclosed peoples of many languages, stocks and customs, over whom colonial administrations had provided little more than a formal unity. As Africa lacked the unifying influence of great indigenous civilizations, such as those of Asia, to offset the colonial fragmentation of the continent, imperial withdrawal was followed by its Balkanization. The doctrine of nationalism that appealed to the

Elated Algerians celebrate the declaration of their country's independence from France on 3 July 1962.

Westernized African élites (Senegal, a Muslim country, had a president who was a writer of poetry in French and was an expert on Goethe) confirmed a continent's fragmentation, often ignoring important realities, which colonialism had contained or manipulated. The sometimes strident nationalism of new rulers was often a response to the dangers of centrifugal forces. West Africans combed the historical record – such as it was – of ancient Mali and Ghana, and East Africans brooded over the past that might be hidden in relics such as the ruins of Zimbabwe in order to forge national mythologies like those of earlier nation-makers in Europe. Nationalism was as much the product of decolonization in black Africa as the cause.

ECONOMIC PROBLEMS

Its new internal divisions were not Africa's only or its worst problems. In spite of the continent's great economic potential, the economic and social foundations for a prosperous future were shaky. Once again, the imperial legacy mattered supremely. Colonial régimes in Africa left behind feebler cultural and economic infrastructures than in Asia. Rates of literacy were low and trained cadres of administrators and technical experts were small. Africa's important economic resources (especially in minerals) required skills, capital and marketing for their exploitation, which could only come in the near future from the world outside (and white South Africa long counted as "outside" to many black politicians). What was more, some African economies had recently undergone particular disruption and diversion because of European needs and in European interests. During the war of 1939–45, agriculture in some of the British colonies had shifted towards the growing of cash crops on a large scale for export. Whether this was or was not in the long-term interests of peasants who had

Maputo, seen here, is the capital and main port of Mozambique, Africa. Now a multi-party republic, Mozambique achieved independence from Portugal in 1975 after a 13-year war. The country's exports include rice, rubber, jute and precious stones.

previously raised crops and livestock only for their own consumption is debatable, but what is certain is that the consequences were rapid and profound. One was an inflow of cash in payment for produce the British and Americans needed. Some of this came through in higher wages, but the spread of a cash economy often had disturbing local effects. Unanticipated urban growth and regional development took place. Many African countries were thus tied to patterns of development that were soon to show their vulnerabilities and limitations in the post-war world. Even the benevolent intentions of a programme like the British Colonial Development and Welfare Fund, or many international aid programmes, unintentionally helped to shackle African producers to a world market. Such handicaps were the more grievous when they were compounded, as was often the case, by mistaken economic policy after independence. A drive for industrialization through import-substitution often led to disastrous agrarian consequences as the prices of cash crops were kept artificially low in relation to those of locally manufactured goods. Almost always, farmers were sacrificed to townspeople and low prices left them with no incentive to raise production. Given that populations had begun to rise in the 1930s and did so even more rapidly after 1960, discontent was inevitable as disappointment with the reality of "freedom" from the colonial powers set in.

DECOLONIZATION

In spite of the difficulties experienced along the way, the process of decolonization in black Africa was hardly interrupted. In 1945 the only truly independent countries in Africa other than Egypt had been Ethiopia (which had itself, from 1935 to 1943, been briefly

under colonial rule) and Liberia, though in reality and law the Union of South Africa was a self-governing dominion of the British Commonwealth and is therefore only formally excluded from that category (a slightly vaguer status also cloaked the virtual practical independence of the British colony of Southern Rhodesia). By 1961 (when South Africa became a fully independent republic and left the Commonwealth) twenty-four new African states had come into existence. There are now over fifty.

AFRICAN POLITICS

In 1957 Ghana had been the first ex-colonial new nation to emerge in sub-Saharan Africa. As Africans shook off colonialism, their problems quickly surfaced. Over the next

Official trade agencies were established in Kenya after the Second World War, ending the monopoly of European businesses over the rural economy. Cotton picking in Watamu is shown here.

Decolonization in Africa and Asia

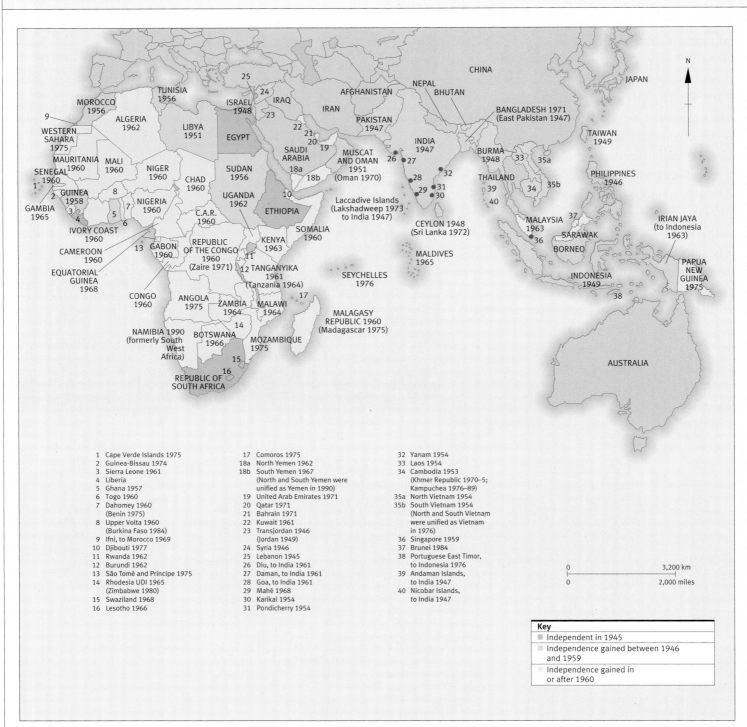

1	Cape Verde Islands 1975	
2	Guinea-Bissau 1974	
3	Sierra Leone 1961	
4	Liberia	
5	Ghana 1957	
6	Togo 1960	
7	Dahomey 1960 (Benin 1975)	
8	Upper Volta 1960 (Burkina Faso 1984)	
9	Ifni, to Morocco 1969	
10	Djibouti 1977	
11	Rwanda 1962	
12	Burundi 1962	
13	São Tomé and Príncipe 1975	
14	Rhodesia UDI 1965 (Zimbabwe 1980)	
15	Swaziland 1968	
16	Lesotho 1966	

17	Comoros 1975
18a	North Yemen 1962
18b	South Yemen 1967 (North and South Yemen were unified as Yemen in 1990)
19	United Arab Emirates 1971
20	Qatar 1971
21	Bahrain 1971
22	Kuwait 1961
23	Transjordan 1946 (Jordan 1949)
24	Syria 1946
25	Lebanon 1945
26	Diu, to India 1961
27	Daman, to India 1961
28	Goa, to India 1961
29	Mahé 1968
30	Karikal 1954
31	Pondicherry 1954

32	Yanam 1954
33	Laos 1954
34	Cambodia 1953 (Khmer Republic 1970–5; Kampuchea 1976–89)
35a	North Vietnam 1954
35b	South Vietnam 1954 (North and South Vietnam were unified as Vietnam in 1976)
36	Singapore 1959
37	Brunei 1984
38	Portuguese East Timor, to Indonesia 1976
39	Andaman Islands, to India 1947
40	Nicobar Islands, to India 1947

0	3,200 km
0	2,000 miles

Key
- ▪ Independent in 1945
- ▪ Independence gained between 1946 and 1959
- ▪ Independence gained in or after 1960

One of the crucial events in the modern world has been the access of various nations, mostly in the southern hemisphere, to political independence. As this map shows, decolonization effectively began in 1947 with the independence of India and Pakistan and ended around the mid-1970s. A number of countries have since changed their names or territorial boundaries, sometimes through unifications.

twenty-seven years twelve wars were to be fought in Africa and thirteen heads of state would be assassinated. There were two especially bad outbreaks of strife. In the former Belgian Congo an attempt by the mineral-rich region of Katanga to break away provoked a civil war in which rival Soviet and American influences quickly became entangled, while the United Nations strove to restore peace. Then, at the end of the 1960s, came an even more distressing episode, a civil war in Nigeria, hitherto one of the most stable and promising of the new African states. This, too, drew non-Africans to dabble in the bloodbath (one reason was that Nigeria had joined the ranks of the oil producers). In other countries, there were less bloody, but still fierce, struggles between factions, regions and tribes, which distracted the small

Westernized élites of politicians and encouraged them to abandon democratic and liberal principles much talked of in the heady days when a colonial system was in retreat.

In many of the new nations, the need, real or imaginary, to prevent disintegration, suppress open dissent and strengthen central authority, had led by the 1970s to one-party, authoritarian government or to the exercise of political authority by soldiers (it was not unlike the history of the new nations of South America after the Wars of Liberation). Often, opposition to the "national" party that had emerged in the run-up to independence in a particular country would be stigmatized as treason once independence was achieved. Nor did the surviving régimes of an older independent Africa escape. Impatience with an *ancien régime* seemingly incapable of

Kwame Nkrumah (1909–1972) was secretary of the 5th Pan-African Congress in 1945. He became the first prime minister of independent Ghana in 1957; in 1960 he declared Ghana a republic, and ruled as president until overthrown in 1966.

As leader of the dominant KANU Party, Jomo Kenyatta (c.1891–1978) negotiated the terms of Kenya's independence from Great Britain in 1963 and became the first president of the republic in 1964. Along with other anti-colonial African leaders, he took part in the organization of the 5th Pan-African Congress in 1945.

The emperor of Ethiopia, Haile Selassie (1891–1975), is pictured during his coronation in 1930. Haile Selassie was deposed in 1974 by the military revolution, which proclaimed a Marxist popular republic.

men" of the new nations can be seen as the inheritors of the mantle of pre-colonial African kingship, rather than in Western terms. Some were simply bandits, however.

AFRICAN ALLIANCES

Their own troubles did not diminish the frequent irritation with which many Africans reacted to the outside world. Some of the roots of this may not lie very deep. The mythological drama built on the old European slave trade, which Africans were encouraged to see as a supreme example of racial exploitation, had been a European and North American creation. A sense of political inferiority, too, lay near the surface in a continent of relatively powerless states (some with populations of less than a million). In political and military terms, a disunited Africa could not expect to have much weight in international affairs, although attempts were made to overcome the weakness that arose from division. One abortive example was that of 1958 to found a United States of Africa; it opened an era of alliances, partial unions, and essays in federation, which culminated in the emergence in 1963 of the Organization for African Unity (the OAU), largely thanks to the Ethiopian emperor, Haile Selassie. Politically, though, the OAU has had little success, although in 1975 it concluded a beneficial trade negotiation with Europe in defence of African producers.

providing peaceful political and social change led in 1974 to revolution in Ethiopia. The setting aside of the "Lion of Judah" was almost incidentally the end of the oldest Christian monarchy in the world (and of a line of kings supposed in one version of the story to run back to the son of Solomon and the Queen of Sheba). A year later, the soldiers who had taken power seemed just as discredited as their predecessors. From similar changes elsewhere in Africa there sometimes emerged tyrant-like political leaders, who reminded Europeans of earlier dictators, but this comparison may be misleading. Africanists have gently suggested that many of the "strong

The very disappointment of much of the early political history of independent Africa directed thoughtful politicians towards cooperation in economic development, above all in relation to Europe, whose former colonial powers remained Africa's most important source of capital, skill and counsel. But the economic record of black Africa has been dreadful. In 1960, food production was still roughly keeping pace with population growth, but by 1982 in all but seven of the thirty-nine sub-Saharan countries it was lower per head than it had been in 1970. Corruption, misconceived policies, and preoccupation with showy prestige investment projects squandered economic aid from the developed world. Even in 1965, the GNP of the entire continent had been less than that of Illinois and in more than half of African countries manufacturing output went down in the 1980s. On these feeble economies there had fallen first the blow of the oil crisis of the early 1970s and then the trade recession that

followed. The shattering effects for Africa were made even worse soon after by the onset of repeated drought. In 1960 Africa's GNP had been growing at the unexciting, but still positive, annual rate of about 1.6 per cent; the trend soon turned downward and in the first half of the 1980s was falling at a rate of 1.7 per cent a year. It hardly seems a surprise that in 1983 the UN Economic Commission for Africa already described the picture of the continent's economy emerging from the historical trends as "almost a nightmare".

Unsurprisingly, political cynicism flourished and many of the leaders of the

The African Union

The newly independent African countries have tried to maintain the ideals and principles of Pan-Africanism not as a formula for a narrow, absolutist political federation, but rather as a continental union that expresses the fundamental identity of the independent African peoples.

This attempt to move towards unity and mutual cooperation crystallized with the establishment of the Organization of African Unity (OAU) in May 1963, at the Conference of Heads of State and Government held in Addis Ababa (Ethiopia). Three factors led to

the establishment of the OAU: the continuation of the pan-African ideal of unity; the radicalization of the fight for complete independence for all the countries on the African continent; and the harmonization of the different existing tendencies in those countries that were already independent.

The constitutional charter set out the objectives and principles that were to govern independent Africa, as well as the rights and obligations of the members. Some of the most outstanding objectives were to collaborate in improving living standards for the people of Africa, to defend the sovereignty, territorial integrity and independence of member states, and to favour international cooperation based on the United Nations Charter and the Universal Declaration of the Rights of Man. Its principles include non-interference in the internal affairs of the member countries; peaceful solutions to disputes through negotiation, mediation, conciliation or arbitration; and non-alignment with the major blocs.

In 2002 the OAU became the African Union, with increased emphasis on socio-economic integration of the continent.

Emperor Haile Selassie of Ethiopia (right) greets President Julius Nyerere of Tanzania as he arrives in Addis Ababa to attend the 10th anniversary of the OAU.

The term *apartheid* was first used in 1948 by the South African senator Hendrik Verwoerd, when he asserted the need to maintain white supremacy in South Africa. One of the apartheid laws, the Reservation of Separate Amenities Act, decreed that all public services were to be destined for the use of either whites or non-whites; this affected buildings, beaches, parks, public benches, buses and even, as this picture shows, public conveniences.

independence era seemed to lose their way. Too many of them showed an almost complete lack of self-criticism and often a frustration expressed in the encouragement of new resentments (sometimes exacerbated by external attempts to entangle Africans in the Cold War). These could be disappointing, too. Marxist revolution had little success. Paradoxically, it was only in Ethiopia, most feudally backward of independent African states, and the former Portuguese colonies, the least developed former colonial territories, that formally Marxist régimes took root. Former French and British colonies were hardly affected.

SOUTH AFRICA AND RHODESIA

SCAPEGOATS, INEVITABLY, were sought on whom Africa's problems could be blamed. Increasingly, but perhaps explicably, given the completeness and rapidity of decolonization

in Africa and the geographical remoteness of much of it, they tended to be found near by and old ethnic differences emerged in civil war and massacre. But resentment also came to focus on the racial division of black and white in Africa itself. This was flagrant in the most powerful of African states, the Union of South Africa.

THE APARTHEID SYSTEM

The Afrikaans-speaking Boers, who by 1945 dominated South Africa, cherished grievances against the British which went back to the Great Trek and had been intensified by defeat in the Boer War. They had led to the progressive destruction of ties with the British Commonwealth after the First World War, a process made easier by the concentration of voters of Anglo-Saxon origin in the provinces of Cape Town and Natal; the Boers were entrenched in the Transvaal and the major industrial areas as well as the rural hinterland. South Africa, it is true, entered the war in 1939 on the British side and supplied important forces to fight in it, but even then intransigent "Afrikaners", as they increasingly called themselves, supported a movement favouring cooperation with the Nazis. Its leader became prime minister in 1948, after defeating South Africa's senior statesman, Jan Smuts, in a general election. As the Afrikaners had steadily engrossed power inside the Union, and had built up their economic position in the industrial and financial sectors, the prospect of imposing a policy towards black Africans that diverged from their deep prejudices was already inconceivable. The result was the construction of a system of separation of the races: apartheid. It systematically embodied and reinforced the reduction of black Africans to the inferior status they occupied in Boer ideology. Its aim was to guarantee the position of the whites in a land where industrialism and market economies had done much to break down the regulation and distribution of the growing black population by the old tribal divisions.

SOUTHERN RHODESIA SECEDES FROM THE COMMONWEALTH

Apartheid had some appeal – on even less excusable grounds than the primitive superstitions or supposed economic necessities of the Afrikaners – to white people elsewhere in Africa. The only country where a similar balance of black and white population to that of South Africa and a similar concentration of wealth existed was Southern Rhodesia, which, to the great embarrassment of the British government, seceded from the Commonwealth in 1965. The aim of the secessionists, it was feared, was to move towards a society more and more like South Africa's. The British government dithered and

missed its chance. There was nothing that the black African states could immediately do about Rhodesia, and not much that the United Nations could do either, though "sanctions" were invoked in the form of an embargo on trade with the former colony; many black African states ignored them and the British government winked at the steps taken by major oil companies to ensure their product reached the rebels. In one of the most shameful episodes in the history of a feeble ministry, Great Britain's stock sank in the eyes of Africans, who, understandably, did not see why a British government could not intervene militarily to suppress a colonial rebellion as flagrant as that of 1776. Many British reflected that it was precisely that remote precedent which made the outlook for intervention by a remote and militarily weak imperial sovereign discouraging.

Though South Africa (the richest and strongest state in Africa, and growing richer and stronger all the time) seemed secure, it was, together with Rhodesia and Portugal, the object of mounting black African anger as the 1970s began. The drawing of the racial battle lines was hardly offset by minor concessions to South Africa's black population

Pictured are two workers in a gold mine near Johannesburg in 1948. The gold industry, together with diamond mining, created most of South Africa's wealth. The country's economy grew at a tremendous rate from 1960 to 1970, with GDP increasing by 113 per cent, and the population by 34 per cent. This new wealth, however, was unevenly distributed among the population.

and its growing economic ties with some black states. There was a danger, too, that outside powers might soon be involved. In 1975, after the Portuguese withdrawal from Angola, a Marxist régime took power there. When civil war followed, foreign communist soldiers arrived from Cuba to support the government, while South African support was soon given to rebels against it.

ZIMBABWE

The South African government soon showed that it could take action. It sought to detach itself from the embarrassment of association with an unyielding independent Rhodesia (whose prospects had sharply worsened when Portuguese rule came to an end in Mozambique in 1974 and a guerrilla campaign was launched from that country against it). The American government contemplated the outcome if Rhodesia collapsed at the hands of black nationalists depending on communist support. It applied pressure to the South Africans, who, in turn, applied it to the Rhodesians. In September 1976 the Rhodesian prime minister sadly told his countrymen that they had to accept the principle of black majority rule. The last attempt to found an African country dominated by whites had failed. It was another landmark in the recession of European power. Yet the guerrilla war continued, worsening as black nationalists sought to achieve unconditional surrender. At last, in 1980, Rhodesia briefly returned to British rule before re-emerging into independence, this time as the new nation of Zimbabwe, with a black prime minister.

GROWING OPPOSITION TO APARTHEID

The emergence of Zimbabwe left South Africa alone as the sole white-dominated state and

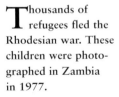
Thousands of refugees fled the Rhodesian war. These children were photographed in Zambia in 1977.

Black Africans travel on a train reserved for Europeans in protest against South Africa's apartheid laws in 1952.

the richest in the continent and the focus of black (which, in this context, meant non-white) resentment around the world. Although the OAU had been split by civil war in Angola, African leaders could usually find common ground against South Africa. In 1974 the General Assembly of the United Nations (UN) forbade South Africa to attend its sessions because of apartheid, and in 1977 the UN Commission of Human Rights deftly sidestepped demands for the investigation of the horrors perpetrated by blacks against blacks in Uganda, while castigating South Africa along with Israel and Chile for their alleged misdeeds. From Pretoria, the view northwards looked more and more menacing. The arrival of Cuban troops in Angola showed a new power of strategic action against South Africa by the USSR. Both that former Portuguese colony and Mozambique also provided bases for South African dissidents, who fanned unrest in the black townships and sustained urban terrorism in the 1980s.

CHANGE IN SOUTH AFRICA

International condemnation, the threat from the north and domestic unrest were no doubt among the reasons for changes in the position of the South African government. By the middle of that decade, the issue seemed to be no longer whether the more obnoxious features of apartheid should be dismantled, but whether black majority rule could be conceded by South African whites without armed conflict. A change was apparent when a new prime minister took office in 1978. To the dismay of many Afrikaners, P.W. Botha slowly began to unroll a policy of concession. Before long, though, his initiative slowed; continuing signs of hostility to South Africa in the UN, urban terrorism at home, an increasingly dangerous and militarily demanding situation on the northern frontiers in Namibia (allocated to South Africa years before as a UN trusteeship territory), and increased distrust of Botha among his Afrikaner

supporters (shown in elections), all led him back towards repression. His last gesture to relaxation was a new constitution in 1983, which provided representation for non-white South Africans in a way that outraged black political leaders by its inadequacy, and disgusted white conservatives by conceding the principle of non-white representation at all.

Meanwhile, the pressure of what were called "sanctions" against South Africa by other countries was growing. In 1985 even the United States imposed them to a limited extent; by then, international confidence in the South African economy was falling, and the effects were showing at home. Straws before the wind of change in domestic opinion could be discerned in the decision of the Dutch Reformed Church, to which many Afrikaners belonged, that apartheid was at least a "mistake" and could not (as had been claimed) be justified by scripture. There was also growing division among Afrikaner politi-

cians. It probably helped, too, that in spite of its deepening isolation, South African military action successfully mastered the border threats, though it was incapable of defeating the Angola government so long as Cuban forces remained there. In 1988 Namibia came to independence on terms South Africa found satisfactory and peace was made with Angola.

NELSON MANDELA IS FREED

This was the background against which P.W. Botha (president of the republic since 1984) reluctantly and grumpily stepped down in 1989 to be succeeded by F.W. de Klerk. He soon made it clear that the movement towards liberalization was to continue and would go much further than many thought possible, even if this did not mean the end of apartheid in all respects. Political protest and opposition were allowed much more

freedom. Meetings and marches were permitted; imprisoned black nationalist leaders were released. Meanwhile, an important change in the relations between the superpowers had produced agreements between the United States and the Soviet Union over ending the struggles in Angola and Mozambique and giving freedom to Namibia.

Suddenly, the way ahead opened up dramatically. In February 1990 F.W. de Klerk announced "a new South Africa". Nine days later, the symbolic figure of Nelson Mandela, leader of the African National Congress (ANC), emerged at last from jail. Before long he was engaged in discussion with the government about what might come next. For all the firmness of his language, there were hopeful signs of a new realism that the task of reassuring the white minority about a future under a black majority must be attempted. Just such signs, of course, prompted other black politicians to greater impatience.

By the end of 1990 de Klerk had gone a long way, taking his followers further than Mandela had taken his. He had even said he would rescind the land legislation that was the keystone of apartheid. In 1991, at last, the other apartheid laws were repealed. It was an interesting indicator of the pace with which events had moved in South Africa that the interest of the world was focused by then less on the sincerity (or insincerity) of white South African leaders, than on the realism (or lack of it) of their black counterparts and their ability (or inability) to control their followers. The hopes surrounding Mandela at the time of his release soon gave way to misgivings, even if once unthinkable steps towards a democratic South Africa had been taken.

The transition in South Africa was not a simple one. Although de Klerk had rescinded most of the apartheid legislation by the end of 1991, there were many among the white elites who resisted change. But neither the 1993 assassination of Chris Hani, a prominent left-wing ANC leader, nor strife in the black townships (often fuelled by rogue elements inside the state), could unmake the road to majority rule. Increasingly, the majority of South Africans of all races came to view Nelson Mandela – reverently referred to by his clan-name "Madiba" – as the guarantor of political stability and economic progress in a new multi-racial state. When he was elected president in 1994, Mandela spoke of a country reborn and a pride regained for all South Africans. But it was in the following year, when President Mandela put on the jersey of the all-white South African national rugby team – the Springboks – to celebrate their victory in the World Cup, that he became the symbol of national unity for whites as well as blacks. "Madiba magic worked for us," said the captain of the team. In 1999, as Mandela stepped down from the presidency, all of South Africa had reason to say the same.

LATIN AMERICA

BY 1900, SOME LATIN AMERICAN countries were beginning to settle down, not only to stability but to prosperity. Argentina was one of the richest countries in the world. To the original colonial implantations in the continent had been added the cultural influence of nineteenth-century Europe, especially of France, to which Latin American élites had been drawn in the post-colonial period. Their upper classes were highly Europeanized and the modernity of many of the continent's great cities reflected this, as they also reflected recent European immigration, which was beginning to swamp the old colonial élites. As for the aboriginal Americans, in one or two countries their suppression had been so complete as to produce near extinction.

LATIN AMERICA BEFORE 1914

Almost all Latin American states were primary producers of agricultural or mineral exports. Some were relatively highly urbanized, but their manufacturing sectors were inconsiderable, and for a long time they did not seem to be troubled by the social and political problems of nineteenth-century Europe. Capital had flowed into the continent, only briefly and occasionally checked by periodic financial disasters and disillusionments. The only social revolution in a Latin American state before 1914 (as opposed to countless changes in governmental personnel) began with the overthrow of the Mexican dictator Porfirio Díaz in 1911. It opened the way to nearly ten years of fighting and a million deaths, but the primary role was played by a middle class that felt excluded from the benefits of the régime, not by an industrial or rural proletariat, and that class was the main gainer, along with the politicians of the party, which emerged to monopolize power until the 1990s. Although most Latin American countries could display class conflict aplenty in their countrysides, they did not appear to suffer from the social bitterness of industrialized and urbanized Europe.

The problem of the division of land was enormous in early 20th-century Mexico; figures have been put as high as 470,000 landowners and 14 million landless peasants. The 1910 insurrection against President Porfirio Díaz had the support of the revolutionary peasant leaders, such as Emiliano Zapata and Pancho Villa, pictured here with his brigade. Villa presented a programme of agricultural revolution based on granting land to the peasants.

Getulio Vargas, president of Brazil 1930–1945 and 1951–1954, arrives in Rio de Janeiro to watch a parade in December 1934. As the leader of the Liberal Alliance, Vargas had spearheaded opposition to Brazil's oligarchical republic and set himself up as spokesman for the burgeoning industrial middle classes. His régime represented the first attempt at popular government in Latin America.

INSTABILITY BETWEEN THE WARS

Latin America's promising-looking societies survived the First World War prosperously. It brought important changes in their relations with Europe and North America. Before 1914, although it was the predominant political influence in the Caribbean, the United States did not exercise much economic weight to the south. In 1914 it supplied only 17 per cent of all foreign investment south of the Rio Grande – and Great Britain much more. The liquidation of British holdings in the Great War changed that; by 1919 the United States was the largest single foreign source of investment in South America, providing about 40 per cent of the continent's foreign capital. Then came the world economic crisis; 1929 was the doorway to a new and unpleasant era for the Latin American states, the true beginning of their twentieth century and the end of the nineteenth. Many defaulted on their payments to foreign investors. It became almost impossible to borrow further capital abroad. The collapse of prosperity led to growing nationalist assertiveness, sometimes against other Latin American states, sometimes against the North Americans and Europeans; foreign oil companies were expropriated in Mexico and Bolivia. The traditional Europeanized oligarchies were compromised by their failure to meet the problems posed by falling national incomes. From 1930 onwards there were more military coups, risings and abortive rebellions than at any time since the wars of independence.

INDUSTRIALIZATION

Nineteen thirty-nine again brought prosperity as commodity prices rose because of wartime demand (in 1950 the Korean War prolonged this trend). In spite of the notorious admiration of Argentina's rulers for Nazi Germany and evidence of German interests in some

Juan Domingo Perón, who was president of Argentina from 1946 to 1955 and 1973 to 1974, salutes the crowds in Buenos Aires in 1952, accompanied by his wife, Eva. Perón had been appointed minister of employment after the 1943 *coup d'état*. His 1946 election programme included agrarian reform and autarky.

other republics, most of them were either sympathetic to the Allies, who courted them, or subservient to the United States. Most of them formally joined the United Nations' side before the war ended, and one, Brazil, sent a small expeditionary force to Europe, a striking gesture. The most important effects of the war on Latin America, however, were economic. One, of great significance, was that the old dependence on the United States and Europe for manufactured goods now became apparent in shortages. An intensive drive to industrialize gathered speed in several countries. On the urban workforces that industrialization had built up was founded a new form of political power that entered the lists as a competitor with the military and the traditional élites in the post-war era. Authoritarian, semi-fascist,

but popular mass movements brought to power a new kind of strong man. Perón in Argentina was the most famous, but Colombia in 1953 and Venezuela in 1954 produced similar rulers. Communism had no such conspicuous success among the masses.

COLD WAR ANXIETIES

A significant change had also come about (though not as a result of war) in the way the United States used its preponderant power in the Caribbean. Twenty times in the first twenty years of the century American armed forces had intervened directly in neighbouring republics, twice going so far as to establish protectorates. Between 1920 and 1939 there were only two such interventions, in Honduras in 1924 and Nicaragua two years later. By 1936, there were no US forces anywhere in the territory of a Latin American state except by agreement (at the Guantanamo base, in Cuba). Indirect pressure also declined. In large measure this was a sensible recognition of changed circumstances. There was nothing to be got by direct intervention in the 1930s and President Roosevelt made a virtue of this by proclaiming a "Good Neighbour" policy (he used the phrase for the first time, significantly, in his first inaugural address) that stressed non-intervention by all American states in one another's affairs. (Roosevelt was also the first president of the United States ever to visit a Latin American country on official business.) With some encouragement from Washington, this opened a period of diplomatic and institutional cooperation across the continent (which was encouraged, too, by the worsening international situation and growing awareness of German interests at work there). It succeeded in bringing an end to the bloody "Chaco War" between Bolivia and Paraguay, which raged from 1932 to 1935, and it culminated in a declaration of Latin American neutrality in 1939 which proclaimed a 300-mile neutrality zone in its waters. When, in the following year, a United States cruiser was sent to Montevideo to stiffen the resistance of the Uruguayan government to a feared Nazi coup, it was more evident than ever that the Monroe doctrine and its "Roosevelt corol-

lary" had evolved almost silently into something more like a mutual security system.

After 1945, Latin America was again to reflect a changing international situation. While United States policy was dominated by European concerns in the early phase of the Cold War, after Korea it began slowly to look southwards again. Washington was not unduly alarmed by occasional manifestations

Post-war Latin America

Latin America has long been plagued by serious intermittent economic difficulties, agricultural problems, illiteracy and accelerated demographic growth, which have influenced politics, encouraging populism and demagoguery. For most Latin American nations, independence from colonial rule did not bring economic independence: their dependence on outsiders continues to grow and to influence domestic politics. The boxes on this map show the amount of economic aid (in millions of US dollars) received by Latin American countries between 1961 and 1964.

provided for communism by poverty and discontent should be removed. They provided more economic aid (Latin America had only a tiny fraction of what went to Europe and Asia in the 1950s but much more in the next decade) and applauded governments that said they sought social reform. Unfortunately, whenever the programmes of such governments moved towards the eradication of American control of capital by nationalization, Washington tended to veer away again, demanding compensation on such a scale as to make reform very difficult. On the whole, therefore, while it might deplore the excesses of an individual authoritarian régime, such as that of Cuba before 1958, the American government tended to find itself, as in Asia, supporting conservative interests in Latin America. This was not invariably so; some governments acted effectively, notably Bolivia, which carried out land reform in 1952. But it remained true that, as for most of the previous century, the worst-off Latin Americans had virtually no hearing from either populist or conservative rulers, in that both listened only to the towns – the worst-off, of course, were the peasants, for the most part American Indians by origin.

REVOLUTION IN CUBA

For all the nervousness in Washington there was little revolutionary activity in Latin America. This was in spite of the victorious revolution in Cuba, of which much was hoped and feared at the time. It was in a number of respects a very exceptional problem. Its island position in the Caribbean, within a relatively short distance of the United States, gave it special significance. The approaches to the Canal Zone had often been shown to have even more importance in American strategical thinking than Suez in the British. Secondly, Cuba had

Women from a village near Riobambas in the Ecuadorean Andes carry water from a pump funded by American aid back to their mountain homes in 1961.

of Latin American nationalism, for all its anti-Yanqui flavour, but became increasingly concerned lest the hemisphere provide a lodgement for Russian influence. With the Cold War came greater selectivity in United States support to Latin American governments. It also led, at times, to covert operations: for example, to the overthrow in 1954 of a government in Guatemala that had communist support.

At the same time United States policymakers were anxious that the footholds

been especially badly hit in the depression; it was virtually dependent on one crop, sugar, and that crop had only one outlet, the United States. This economic tie, moreover, was only one of several that gave Cuba a closer and more irksome "special relationship" with the United States than had any other Latin American state. There were historic connections that went back to before 1898 and the winning of independence from Spain. Until 1934 the Cuban constitution had included special provisions restricting Cuba's diplomatic freedom. The Americans still kept their naval base on the island (as they still do). There was heavy American investment in urban property and utilities, and Cuba's poverty and low prices made it attractive to Americans looking for gambling and girls. All in all, it should not have been surprising that Cuba produced, as it did, a strongly anti-American movement with much popular support.

FIDEL CASTRO

The United States was long blamed as the real power behind the conservative post-war Cuban régime, although after the dictator Batista came to power in 1952 this in fact ceased to be so; the State Department disapproved of him and cut off help to him in 1957. By then, a young nationalist lawyer, Fidel Castro, had already begun a guerrilla campaign against his government. In two years he was successful. In 1959, as prime minister of a new, revolutionary, Cuba, he described his régime as "humanistic" and, specifically, not communist.

Castro's original aims are still not known. Perhaps he was not clear himself what he thought. From the start he worked with a wide spectrum of people who wanted to overthrow him, from liberals to Marxists. This helped to reassure the United States,

which briefly patronized him as a Caribbean Sukarno; American public opinion idolized him as a romantic figure and beards became fashionable among American radicals. The relationship quickly soured once Castro turned to interference with American business interests, starting with agrarian reform and the nationalization of sugar concerns. He also denounced publicly those Americanized elements in Cuban society that had supported the old régime. Anti-Americanism was a logical means – perhaps the only one – open to Castro for uniting Cubans behind the revolution. Soon the United States broke off diplomatic relations with Cuba and began to impose other kinds of pressure as well. The American government became convinced that the island was likely to fall into the hands of the communists upon whom Castro increasingly relied. It did not help when the Soviet leader Khrushchev warned the United States of the danger of retaliation from Soviet rockets if it acted militarily against Cuba and declared the Monroe doctrine dead; the State Department quickly announced that reports of its demise were greatly exaggerated. Finally, the American government decided to promote Castro's overthrow by force.

Fidel Castro takes part in a press conference in Havana in January 1959. In April that year, during his trip to the United States, Castro announced, "We are not communists". A few weeks later, Cuban political parties were repressed, the elections were delayed and the régime appeared to show communist leanings. Some historians claim that it was pressure from the United States that brought about this apparent change of political direction.

THE BAY OF PIGS OPERATION

When the presidency changed hands in 1961 John Kennedy inherited a decision to overthrow Castro using Cuban exiles, who were already training with American support in Guatemala. Diplomatic relations with Cuba had been broken off. Kennedy had not initiated these activities, but he was neither cautious nor thoughtful enough to impede them. This was the more regrettable because there was much else that boded well in the new president's attitude to Latin America, where it had been obvious for some time that the United States needed to cultivate goodwill. As it was, the possibilities of a more positive approach were almost at once blown to pieces by the fiasco known as the "Bay of Pigs" operation, when an expedition of Cuban exiles came to a miserable end in April 1961. Castro now turned in earnest towards Russia, and at the end of the year declared himself a Marxist-Leninist.

A new and much more explicit phase of the Cold War then began in the western hemisphere, and began badly for the United States.

US president Kennedy and Soviet premier Khrushchev meet in Vienna, Austria, in June 1961 to discuss tensions over Berlin and differing views on Cuba.

The American initiative incurred disapproval everywhere because it was an attack on a popular, solidly based régime. Henceforth, Cuba was a magnet for Latin American revolutionaries. Castro's torturers replaced Batista's and his government pressed forward with policies which, together with American pressure, badly damaged the economy, but embodied egalitarianism and social reform (in the 1970s, Cuba claimed to have the lowest child mortality rates in Latin America).

THE CUBAN MISSILE CRISIS

Almost incidentally and as a by-product of the Cuban revolution there soon took place the most serious superpower confrontation of the Cold War and perhaps its turning-point. It is not yet known exactly why or when the Soviet government decided to install in Cuba missiles capable of reaching anywhere in the United States, and thus roughly to double the number of American bases or cities that were potential targets. Nor is it known whether the initiative came from Havana or Moscow. Although Castro had asked the USSR for arms, it seems likeliest that it was the second. But whatever the circumstances, American photographic reconnaissance confirmed in October 1962 that the Russians were building missile sites in Cuba. President Kennedy waited until this could be shown to be incontrovertible and then announced that the United States navy would stop any ship delivering further missiles to Cuba and that those already in Cuba would have to be withdrawn. One Lebanese ship was boarded and searched in the days that followed; Soviet ships were only observed. The American nuclear striking force was prepared for war. After a few days and some exchanges of personal letters between Kennedy and Khrushchev, the latter agreed that the missiles should be removed.

THE FAILURE OF THE ALLIANCE FOR PROGRESS

This crisis by far transcended the history of the hemisphere, and its repercussions outside it are best discussed elsewhere. So far as Latin American history is concerned, even though the United States promised not to invade Cuba, it went on trying to isolate it as much as possible from its neighbours. Unsurprisingly, the appeal of Cuba's revolution nevertheless seemed for a while to gain ground among the young of other Latin American countries. This did not make their governments more sympathetic towards Castro, especially when he began to talk of Cuba as a revolutionary centre for the rest of the continent. In the event, as an unsuccessful attempt in Bolivia showed, revolution was not likely to prove easy. Cuban circumstances had been very atypical. The hopes entertained of mounting peasant rebellion elsewhere proved illusory. Local communists in other countries deplored Castro's efforts. Potential recruits and materials for revolution turned out to be on the whole urban rather than rural, and middle class rather than peasants; it was in the major cities that guerrilla movements were within a few years making the headlines. Despite being spectacular and dangerous, it is not clear that they enjoyed wide popular support, even if the brutalities practised in dealing with them alienated support from authoritarian governments in some countries. Anti-Americanism meanwhile continued to run high. Kennedy's hopes for a new American initiative, based on social reform – an "Alliance for Progress" as he termed it – made no headway against the animosity aroused by American treatment of Cuba. His successor as president, Lyndon Johnson, did no better, perhaps because he was less interested in Latin America than in domestic reform. The initiative was never recaptured

after the initial flagging of the Alliance. Worse still, it was overtaken in 1965 by a fresh example of the old Adam of intervention, this time in the Dominican Republic, where, four years before, American help had assisted the overthrow and assassination of a corrupt and tyrannical dictator and his replacement by a reforming democratic government. When this was pushed aside by soldiers acting in defence of the privileged, who felt threatened by reform, the Americans cut off aid; it looked as if, after all, the Alliance for Progress might be used discriminately. But aid was soon restored – as it was to other right-wing regimes. A rebellion against the soldiers in 1965 resulted in the arrival of 20,000 American troops to put it down.

ANTI-AMERICANISM

By the end of the decade the Alliance had virtually been forgotten, in part because of the persistent fears of communism, which led American policy to put its weight behind conservatives everywhere in Latin America, in part because the United States had plenty of other pressing problems. One ironic result was

Pictures taken by the CIA in 1962 of missile launch pads in Cuba, such as these to the east of San Cristóbal, astounded and alarmed the US government. Close study of this image revealed between 16 and 32 missiles which could be made ready for action in less than a week.

do so no longer. Once the spur of an internal fear was gone there was little reason for governments not to try to capitalize on anti-American feeling.

LATIN AMERICA UNDER STRAIN

Yet the real problems of Latin America were not being met. The 1970s, and, still more, the 1980s revealed chronic economic troubles and by 1985 it was reasonable to speak of an apparently insoluble crisis. There were several sources for this. For all its rapid industrialization, the continent was threatened by intimidating population growth, which began to be obvious just as the difficulties of the Latin American economies were again beginning to show their intractability. The aid

The policy adopted by Havana after the Bay of Pigs affair became clear when, in a visit to Moscow, the guerrilla leader Che Guevara (1928–1967), who had become a minister in Castro's government, requested more aid from the Soviet Union. The aid sent by Moscow whipped up American public opinion against Cuba. It also enraged anti-Castro Cubans living in the United States, pictured here demonstrating near the Soviet embassy in New York in October 1962.

a new wave of attacks on United States property interests by governments that did not have to fear the loss of American support while the communist threat seemed to endure. Chile nationalized the largest American copper company; the Bolivians took over oil concerns; and the Peruvians American-owned plantations. In 1969 there was a historic meeting of Latin American governments at which no United States representative was present and *Yanqui* behaviour was explicitly and implicitly condemned. A tour undertaken by a representative of the president of the United States that year led to protest, riots, the blowing up of American property and requests to stay away from some countries. It was rather like the end of the previous decade, when a "goodwill" tour by Eisenhower's vice-president ended in him being mobbed and spat upon. All in all, it looked by 1970 as if Latin American nationalism was entering a new and vigorous period. If Cuba-inspired guerrillas had ever presented a danger, they appeared to

The denunciation of exploitation

"Look at the background: unreturned value, that is to say, that did not return to Chile in the great copper mines (…). Between 1930 and 1969, $3,700 million have crossed the borders of our country, which have gone to increase the strength of the companies that, on an international scale, control copper fields across the five continents. In 1969, $166 million did not return. I must stress that $3,700 million comprises 40 per cent of Chile's total wealth, of the effort accumulated over 400 years by the Chilean people. Forty per cent of that wealth has left the country from 1930 to 1969 and this fact cannot be forgotten. Chile also knows that altogether, in roughly the same period, as well as through copper, something like $9,600 million has vanished through iron, saltpetre, electricity and telephones, which represents the total value of Chile's wealth (…) ."

An extract from a speech given by the newly elected president of Chile, Salvador Allende, on 21 December, 1970.

programme of the Alliance for Progress patently failed to cope with them, and failure spawned quarrels over the use of American funds. Mismanagement produced huge foreign debts, which crippled attempts to sustain investment and achieve better trade balances. Social divisions remained menacing. Even the most advanced Latin American countries displayed vast discrepancies of wealth and education. Constitutional and democratic processes, where they existed, seemed increasingly impotent in the face of such problems. In the 1960s and 1970s, Peru, Bolivia, Brazil, Argentina and Paraguay all underwent prolonged authoritarian rule by soldiers and there were plenty of people willing to believe that only authoritarianism could bring about changes of which nominally democratic and civilian government had proved incapable.

In the 1970s, the world began to hear more of torture and violent repression from countries like Argentina, Brazil and Uruguay, once regarded as civilized and constitutional states. Chile had enjoyed a longer and more continuous history of constitutional government than most of its neighbours, which lasted until, in the 1970 election, a divided Right let in a minority socialist coalition. When the new government embarked upon measures that brought economic chaos and seemed to be slipping further leftwards, and even into a breakdown into lawlessness, the outcome was, in 1973, a military coup that had United States approval and undercover support. Yet many Chileans, frightened by what looked like a worsening situation, went along with it too, in the belief that the overthrown government had been under communist control. Chile's new and authoritarian military government soon showed it had no qualms in mounting a brutal and wide-ranging persecution of its opponents and critics, using the most savage methods to do so. In the end it rebuilt the economy and

even, in the late 1980s, began to look as if it might be able to restrain itself. But it drove ideological division deeper into Chilean society than the country had ever hitherto known, and that country became the outstanding symbol of dangers undoubtedly latent in other Latin American countries. Nor were all of these of the same kind. By the 1970s Colombia was already engaged in a civil war (still raging as the next century began) fed by struggles to control the country's huge production of cocaine, virtually partitioning the country.

ECONOMIC AND CULTURAL PROBLEMS

On a troubled and distracted continent there had fallen, to cap its troubles, the oil crisis of the early 1970s. It sent the foreign debt problems of its oil-importing countries (that is, most of them other than Mexico and Venezuela) out of control. In the next two decades, many economic remedies were to be

Salvador Allende (1908–1973) became president of Chile in 1970, and immediately faced a critical situation: the country had a huge budget deficit and an enormous external debt. A military coup, led by General Augusto Pinochet, overthrew Allende's socialist government in September 1973. Allende, pictured here just before his death, was killed during the fight for control of the presidential palace.

tried in one country or another, but all turned out to be unworkable or unenforceable. It seemed impossible to deal with runaway inflation, interest charges on external debt, the distortion in resource allocation arising from past bad government, and administrative and cultural shortcomings which nourished corruption. In 1979 the Argentinian government was overthrown by popular unrest, and in the next decade the Argentinians experienced an inflation of 20,000 per cent. Latin America still appeared to be, perhaps more than ever, an explosive, disturbed continent of nations growing less and less like one another, for all their shared roots, except in their distress. To the layers of differentiation laid down by Indian, slave, colonial and post-colonial experiences, all strongly reflected in differences of economic well-being, had now been added new divisions brought by the arrival in the 1950s and 1960s of the assumptions of developed, high-technology societies, whose benefits were available to the better-off, but not to the poor. Just as in Asia, though it has been less obvious, the strains of the impact of modern civilization on historically deep-rooted societies are now more visible than ever before, even if Latin America has been undergoing some of them since the sixteenth century. But in the 1980s they were expressed additionally through the terrorism displayed by radicals and authoritarians alike, and they continued to threaten civilized and constitutional standards achieved earlier.

In the 1990s, however, there took place what looked like a major restoration of constitutional and democratic government and economic recovery in the major states of Latin America. In all of them, military government was formally set aside. Eventually only Cuba was left as an overtly non-democratic regime. This helped to produce better hemisphere relations, and Argentina and Brazil both agreed to close their nuclear weapons programmes, while in 1991 they, together with Paraguay and Uruguay, agreed to set up a common market, Mercosur, which at once launched a major tariff-cutting exercise. In 1996, Chile adhered to it. This promising atmosphere was troubled only by a few attempted coups, while economic conditions held up. Unhappily those conditions began to falter continent-wide in the middle of the decade and by the end of it the IMF had to mount new operations to rescue both Argentina and Brazil from severe troubles. Ominously, although the former had tied its currency to the United States dollar (itself a source of some of its difficulties), Brazil was again beginning to show the effects of inflation, while Argentina's debt to foreigners had risen out of control. The international community braced itself to face a repudiation of unprecedented size, while, as 2001 came to an end, the population of Buenos Aires again took to the streets, and after some bloodshed and casting out three presidents in ten days, appeared to face a renewal of deflation and hard times.

The early 2000s showed clearly the winners and losers in the economic growth that was beginning to take hold in most Latin American countries. While the economies of many countries grew more rapidly than they had done since the 1950s, the domestic returns of these advances were very unevenly divided among the population. Brazil, for instance, is by most standards the most unequal society on earth. While the most advanced 10 per cent of its 170 million population has a living standard that equals the EU average, the poorest 50 per cent has seen little progress during the 1990s. The election in the early 2000s in many Latin American countries of left-wing governments reflects the preoccupation with growing inequality. But even the radical leaders – who span from the Venezuelan firebrand populist Hugo Chavez

In this view of Rio de Janeiro, the poverty of the well-established shanty town in the foreground contrasts sharply with the modern skyscrapers beyond, home to office suites and wealthy Brazilian families.

to the moderate socialist presidents Michelle Bachelet in Chile (elected 2006) and Luiz Inácio Lula in Brazil (elected 2003) – are unwilling to touch the market-oriented reforms of the previous decade, which are widely held to have produced the first economic progress these countries have experienced for more than a generation. It is therefore likely that the contradiction between economic growth and abject poverty will remain the key issue in Latin America's development for years to come.

3 *CRUMBLING CERTAINTIES*

IN THE 1970s, TWO giants still dominated the world, as they had done since 1945, and they still often talked as if the world was divided into their adherents or enemies. But changes had come about in the way they were regarded. Some believed the United States to have lost its once overwhelming military preponderance over the Soviet Union and perhaps any preponderance at all. The perception was wrong, but many, and even some Americans, shared it. Those easily frightened by signs of instability wondered what would happen if another confrontation arose. Others thought that a more even balance might make such a crisis unlikely. Other relevant changes, too, were difficult to weigh up. The two once more or less disciplined blocs, surrounded by small fry in danger of being swallowed by them, were showing signs of strain. New quarrels were beginning to cut across old ideological divisions. More interesting still, there were signs that new aspirants to the role of superpower might be emerging. Some people had even begun to talk about an era of détente.

SUPERPOWER DIFFICULTIES

ONCE AGAIN, THE ROOTS OF change go back some way and there are no sharp dividing lines between phases. The death of Stalin, for instance, could hardly have been without effect, although it brought no obvious immediate change in Russian policy, and even more difficulty in interpreting it. Subsequent changes of personnel led after nearly two years to the emergence of Nikita Khrushchev as the dominant figure in the Soviet government, and the retirement in 1956 of Molotov, Stalin's old henchman and veteran of Cold War diplomacy, from his post as foreign minister. There had then followed a sensational speech by Khrushchev at a secret session of the Twentieth Congress of the Soviet Communist Party. In it he denounced the misdeeds of the Stalin era and declared "coexistence" the goal of Russian foreign policy. The speech was soon given wide publicity, which shook the monolithic front communism had hitherto presented to the world, and for the first time alienated many communist sympathizers in Western countries who had been hitherto untroubled by Soviet realities – or, perhaps, the revelations allowed

Hungarian freedom fighters dismantle a statue of Stalin a few days after the Soviet invasion of 4 November 1956. Imre Nagy (1895–1958), the Hungarian premier who opposed the Russians, was deposed, later to be executed, and a new communist government was set up.

them to express an alienation they already felt at no cost to their consciences.

Together with announcements of Soviet reductions in armaments, Khrushchev's speech might have heralded a new mood in international affairs, had not the atmosphere in 1956 quickly been fouled. The Suez adventure called forth Soviet threats to Great Britain and France; Moscow was not going to risk Arab goodwill by failing to show support for Egypt. But the same year had also brought more anti-Soviet rioting in Poland and a revolution in Hungary. Soviet policy had always been morbidly sensitive to signs of deviation or dissatisfaction among its satellites. In

1948, Soviet advisers had been recalled from Yugoslavia, which was then expelled from the Cominform. Yugoslavia's treaties with the USSR and other communist states were denounced, and five years of vitriolic attacks on "Titoism" began. Not until 1957 did the two governments finally came to an understanding when the USSR climbed down and symbolically resumed its aid to Tito.

REVOLUTION IN HUNGARY

Yugoslavia's damaging and embarrassing survival as a socialist state outside the

Time chart (1950–1984)							
	1950–1952 Schuman Plan and the formation of the ECSC	1963 J.F. Kennedy assassinated	1973 Treaty signed between the United States and North Vietnam to end the war		1979 Iranian revolution Saddam Hussein becomes president of Iraq	1982 Falklands War	
1950						1980	
	1956 Soviet invasion of Hungary	1968 Martin Luther King assassinated Soviet invasion of Czechoslovakia		1976 Mao Tse-tung dies	Indira Gandhi assassinated	1984	

In August 1961 the Berlin Wall was erected along the demarcation line between the two sectors of the city, ending the exodus of thousands of East Germans. Here, another concrete slab is placed atop the wall in 1964.

Warsaw Pact, however, had made Moscow even more sensitive to tremors in the eastern camp. Like anti-Soviet riots in East Berlin in 1953, those in Poland in the summer of 1956 showed that patriotism, inflamed by economic discontent, could still challenge communism in places nearer its heartland. Similar forces help also to explain how disturbances in Budapest in October 1956 grew into a nationwide movement that led to the withdrawal of Soviet forces from the city, a new Hungarian government promising free elections and the end of one-party rule. When that government also announced its withdrawal from the Warsaw Pact, declared Hungary's neutrality, and asked the United Nations to take up the Hungarian question, the Soviet army returned. Thousands fled the country and the Hungarian revolution was crushed. The UN General Assembly twice condemned the intervention, but to no avail.

The episode hardened attitudes on both sides. The Soviet leadership could again reflect on how little they were liked by the peoples of eastern Europe and therefore became even more distrustful of Western talk of "liberating" them. Western European nations were again reminded of the real face of Soviet power and sought to consolidate their growing strength.

THE BERLIN WALL

In October 1957, *Sputnik I* had opened the age of superpower competition in space and gave a terrible shock to American confidence that Soviet technology lagged behind American. Soviet foreign policy in the Khrushchev era meanwhile continued to show recalcitrance, uncooperativeness, and sometimes remarkable confidence. Fearing the danger of a rearmed West Germany, the Soviet leaders were anxious to strengthen their satellite, the German Democratic Republic. The all too visible success and prosperity of West Berlin – surrounded by GDR territory – was embarrassing. The city's internal boundaries between west and east were easily crossed and well-being and freedom drew more and more East Germans – especially skilled workers – to the West. In 1958, the USSR denounced the arrangements under which Berlin had been run for the last ten years and said the Soviet sector of the city would be handed over to the GDR if better arrangements could not be found. Two years of drawn-out wrangling followed. As an atmosphere of crisis over Berlin deepened, the outflow of refugees through Berlin shot up. The numbers of East Germans crossing to the West were 140,000 in 1959 and 200,000 in 1960. When more than 100,000 did so in the first six months of 1961, in August that year the East German authorities suddenly put up a wall (soon reinforced by landmines and barbed wire) to cut off Berlin's Soviet sector from the western sectors. Tension increased in the short run, but in the long term the Berlin Wall may have calmed things down. Its gloomy presence (and the sporadic killing of East Germans who tried to cross it) was to be for a quarter-century a gift to Western Cold War propaganda. The GDR had succeeded in stopping emigration, though. Khrushchev quietly dropped more extreme demands when it was clear that the United States was not prepared to give way over the legal status of Berlin, even at the risk of war.

CONFRONTATION OVER CUBA

Substantially, this rhythm of mounting tension followed by détente was repeated the following year over Cuba, although the risk

was then far greater. The European allies of the United States were not so directly interested as they had been over a possible change in the German settlement, nor did the Russians seem to pay much attention to Cuba's interests. Moreover, in a virtually "pure" confrontation of the superpowers, the Soviet Union appeared to have been forced to give way. While avoiding action or language which might have been dangerously provocative, and while leaving a simple route of retreat open to his opponent by confining his demands to essentials, President Kennedy none the less made no conspicious concessions, and the withdrawal of American missiles from Turkey followed quietly after a little while. Immediately, Khrushchev had to be satisfied with an undertaking that the United States would not invade Cuba.

It is difficult to believe that this was not a major turning-point. The prospect of nuclear

In 1962 several conferences on disarmament were held in Geneva, attended by representatives from the United States and the USSR. The talks mainly centred on the importance of restricting the number of countries able to stock nuclear weapons and preventing costly arms escalation. However, even as the talks progressed, multiple-head missiles and ABMs (anti-ballistic missiles) were being developed.

war as the ultimate price of geographical extension of the Cold War had been faced by the Soviet Union and found unacceptable. The subsequent setting-up of direct telephone communication between the heads of the two states – the "hot line" – recognized that the danger of conflict through misunderstanding made necessary some more intimate connection than the ordinary channels of diplomacy. It was also clear that in spite of Soviet boasting to the contrary, American preponderance in armed strength was as great as ever. The new weapon, that mattered for purposes of direct conflict between the two superpowers was the inter-continental rocket missile; at the end of 1962 the Americans had a superiority in this weapon of more than six to one over the Russians, who set to work to reduce this disparity. The choice was made of rockets before butter and once again the Soviet consumer was to bear the burden. Meanwhile, the Cuban confrontation had probably helped to achieve the first agreement between Great Britain, the United States and the Soviet Union on the restriction of testing nuclear weapons in space, the atmosphere or under water. Disarmament would still be pursued without success for many years, but this was the first positive outcome of any negotiations about nuclear weapons.

KHRUSHCHEV FALLS

In 1964 Khrushchev was removed from office. As head of both government and party since 1958 it seems likely that his personal contribution to Soviet history had been to provide a great shaking-up. That had meant qualified "de-Stalinization", a huge failure over agriculture, and a change in the emphasis of the armed services (towards the strategic rocket services that became their élite arm). Khrushchev's own initiatives in foreign policy (besides the disastrous Cuban adventure) may have been the fundamental

Pictured during a reception in Moscow in 1962 are, from left to right: the Russian cosmonaut Yuri Gagarin, the Soviet premier Nikita Khrushchev, the Indonesian president Achmed Sukarno, and Leonid Brezhnev, who would replace Khrushchev two years later.

cause of the decision to remove him. Yet though he was set aside with the connivance of the army by colleagues whom he had offended and alarmed, he was not killed, sent to prison or even to run a power-station in Mongolia. Evidently the Soviet Union was civilizing its techniques of political change. The contrast with old times was striking.

Soviet society had indeed relaxed a little after Stalin's death. The speech at the Twentieth Congress could never be unsaid, even if much of it was aimed at diverting criticism from those who (like Khrushchev himself) had been participants in the crimes of which Stalin was accused. (Symbolically, Stalin's body had been removed from Lenin's tomb, the national shrine.) In the next few years there was what some called a "thaw". Marginally greater freedom of expression was allowed to writers and artists, while the régime appeared briefly to be a little more concerned about its appearance in the eyes of the world over such matters as its treatment of Jews. But this was personal and sporadic: liberalization depended on who had Khrushchev's ear. It seems clear only that after Stalin's death, particularly during the era of Khrushchev's ascendancy, the party had re-emerged as a much more independent factor in Russian life. The authoritarian nature of the Russian government, though, seemed unchanged – which is much what might have been expected.

DEFICIENCIES AND EFFICIENCIES IN THE SOVIET ECONOMY

Soviet authoritarianism may now make it seem odd that for a time it was the fashion to say that the United States and Soviet Russia were growing more and more alike, and that this meant that Soviet policy was becoming less menacing. This theory of "convergence"

Khrushchev attempted to transform Soviet agriculture. In 1954 he proposed to increase deliveries to the state by 40 per cent. This could only be achieved by farming virgin land in harsh conditions in Siberia and Kazakhstan. A large number of *kolkhozes* (collective farms), such as the one shown in this aerial view, were set up in these regions, thanks to the arrival in the "new lands" of hundreds of thousands of young people.

gave a distorted emphasis to one indisputable truth: the Soviet Union was a developed economy. In the 1960s some on the European Left still thought socialism a plausible road to modernization because of that. But often overlooked was the fact that the Soviet economy was also inefficient and distorted. Although Soviet industrial strength had long been evident in heavy manufacture, the private consumer in the Soviet Union remained poor by comparison with his American counterpart, and would have been even more visibly so, but for a costly system of subsidies. Russian agriculture, which had once fed the cities of central Europe and paid for the industrialization of the tsarist era, was a continuing failure; paradoxically, the Soviet Union often had to buy American grain. The official Soviet Communist Party programme of 1961 proposed that by 1970 the USSR would outstrip the United States in industrial output. That did not happen, although President Kennedy's proposal of the same

Built in Moscow in the 12th century, the Kremlin was originally a fortress, but its use as state headquarters has made it synonymous with Soviet and now with Russian government.

year to put a man on the moon was realized. Yet the USSR, in comparison with undeveloped countries, was undoubtedly rich. In spite of the obvious disparity between them as consumer societies, to the poor the USA and USSR sometimes looked much the same. Many Soviet citizens, too, were more aware of the contrast between their stricken and impoverished country in the 1940s and its condition in the 1960s, than of comparison with the United States. Nor was the contrast of the two systems always one-sided. Soviet investment in education, for example, may have achieved literacy rates as good as, and even at times better than, the American. Such comparisons, which fall easily over the line from quantitative to qualitative judgement, nevertheless do not alter the basic fact that the per capita GDP of the Soviet Union in the 1970s still lagged far behind that of the United States. If its citizens had at last been given old age pensions in 1956 (nearly half a century after the British people), they also had to put up with health services falling further and further behind those available in the West. There had been a long legacy of back-

wardness and disruption to eliminate; only in 1952 had real wages in Russia even got back to their 1928 level. The theory of "convergence" was always too optimistic and too simplistic.

SOVIET SPACE EXPLORATION

By 1970 the USSR had a scientific and industrial base that in scale and at its best could rival the achievements of the United States. Its most obvious expression, and a great source of patriotic pride to the Soviet citizen, was in space. By 1980 there was so much ironmongery in orbit that it was difficult to recapture the startling impression made twenty years before by the first Soviet satellites. Although American successes had speedily followed, Soviet space achievements remained of the first rank. Reports of space exploration fed the patriotic imagination and rewarded patience with other aspects of daily life in the USSR. It is not too much to say that for some Soviet citizens their space technology justified the revolution; the USSR was shown by it to be able to do almost anything another nation could, and much that only one other could, and perhaps one or two things which, for a while, no other could. Mother Russia was modernized at last.

SOCIAL STRAINS IN THE USSR

Whether Russia's modernization meant that she was in some sense becoming a satisfied nation, with leaders more confident and less suspicious of the outside world and less prone to disturb the international scene, is an entirely different matter. Soviet responses to Chinese resurgence did not seem to show that; there was talk of a pre-emptive nuclear attack on the Chinese border. Soviet society was beginning to show new signs of strain as well by 1970. Dissent and criticism, particularly of restraints upon intellectual freedom, had become obvious for the first time in the 1960s, as were symptoms of anti-social behaviour, such as hooliganism, corruption and alcoholism. But they probably held both as much and as little potential for significant change as in other large countries. Less obvious facts

may turn out to have been more important in the long run; in the 1970s native Russian speakers for the first time became a minority in the Soviet Union. Meanwhile, the régime was still one where the limits of freedom and the basic privileges of the individual were defined in practice by an apparatus backed up by administrative decisions and political prisons. The difference between life in the Soviet Union and the United States (or any western European nation) could still be reckoned by such yardsticks as its enormous expenditure on jamming foreign broadcasting.

The Soviet dissident scientist Andrei Sakharov (1921–1989) is pictured in 1989, three years after Gorbachev authorized him to return from "exile" in Gorky, where he had been since 1980. Many intellectuals, artists and writers who openly criticized the régime were put under house arrest or exiled from the USSR.

Under Brezhnev, the USSR was a conservative society and the state used censorship, repression and the highly efficient secret police force (the KGB, whose headquarters in Moscow is seen here) to prevent all but a few outbreaks of unrest. When minor disturbances erupted, they were rapidly quashed by the use of force.

AMERICAN SOCIETY

FOR OBVIOUS REASONS, changes in the United States were more easily observed than those in the Soviet Union, but this did not always make it easier to discern fundamentals. Of the sheer growth of American power there can be no doubt, nor of its importance to the world. In the middle of the 1950s, the United States contained about six per cent of the world's population but produced more than half the world's manufactured goods; by the year 2000 the economy of the state of California alone would be the fifth largest in the world. In 1968 the American population passed the 200 million mark (in 1900 it had been seventy-six million), only one in twenty of whom were not native-born (though within ten years there would be worries about a huge Spanish-speaking immigration from Mexico and the Caribbean). Numbers of births went up while the birth-rate dropped after 1960; the United States was unique among major

Built in the 1950s, Philadelphia's Penn Center – a complex of high-rise office buildings, hotels and shopping centres – symbolizes the rejuvenation of the city that took place during that decade. By the 1960s, the United States as a whole was enjoying the benefits of its post-war economic "miracle".

developed countries in this respect. More Americans than ever lived in cities or their suburbs, and the likelihood that they would die of some form of malignancy had trebled since 1900; this, paradoxically, was a sure sign of improvement in public health, because it showed a growing mastery of other diseases.

THE US ECONOMY

The United States' immensely successful industrial structure was dominated in 1970 by very large corporations, some of them already commanding resources and wealth greater than those of some nations. Concern was often expressed for the interests of the public and the consumer, given the weight in the economy of these giants. But no doubts existed about the economy's ability to create wealth and power. Though it was to be shown that it could not do everything that might be asked of it, American industrial strength was the great constant of the post-war world and underpinned the huge military potential upon which the conduct of American foreign policy inevitably rested.

Political mythologies still mattered in the 1950s. President Truman's second administration and those of President Eisenhower were marked by noisy debate and shadow-boxing about the danger of governmental interference with free enterprise, which lingers still. Yet this was largely beside the point. Ever since 1945 the federal government has held and indeed increased its importance as the first customer of the American economy. Government spending had been the primary economic stimulant and to increase it had been the goal of hundreds of interest groups; hopes of balanced budgets and cheap, business-like administration always ran aground upon this fact. What was more, the United States was a democracy; whatever the doctrinaire objections to it, and however much rhetoric might be devoted to attacking it, a welfare state slowly advanced because voters wanted it that way. These facts gradually made the old ideal of totally free enterprise, unchecked and uninvaded by the influence of government, unreal. They also helped to prolong the Democratic coalition. The Republican presidents who were elected in 1952 and 1968 on each occasion benefited from war-weariness; but neither could persuade Americans that they should elect Republican congresses. On the other hand, signs of strain were to be seen within the Democratic bloc even before 1960 – Eisenhower appealed to many Southern voters – and by 1970 something a little more like a national conservative party had appeared under the Republican banner because some Southerners had been offended by Democratic legislation on behalf of the black population. Twenty years later the Democratic-voting "Solid South" created by the Civil War had disappeared as a political constant.

The United States, which had access to enormous funds for basic and applied research, spearheaded the technological revolution of the 1960s and 1970s. Here, engineers and researchers demonstrate a drilling system that has huge implications for oceanographic research and the oil industry.

While pro-segregation white students shout abuse at her, Elizabeth Eckford makes her way between lines of US National Guardsmen in an attempt to gain entrance to the "white" high school in Little Rock, Arkansas, in 1967.

THE ELECTION OF PRESIDENT KENNEDY

Presidents could sometimes shift emphasis. The Eisenhower years leave an impression that little happened in the domestic history of the United States during them; it was not part of that president's vision of his office that he should provide a strong policy lead at home. Partly because of this, Kennedy's election by a narrow margin of the popular vote in 1960 – the arrival of a new man (and a young one, too) – produced a sense of striking change. It was misleading and too much was made at the time of the more superficial aspects of this. In retrospect, though, it can be agreed that both in foreign and domestic affairs, the eight years of renewed Democratic rule from 1961 brought great change to the United States, though not in the way in which Kennedy or his vice-president, Lyndon Johnson, hoped when they took office.

BLACK AMERICANS' PROBLEMS

ONE ISSUE ALREADY present in American politics in 1960 was what could still then be called the "Negro question". A century after emancipation, the black American was likely to be poorer, more often on relief, more often unemployed, less well housed and less healthy than the white American. Forty years later, this was still to be true. In the 1950s and 1960s, though, there was growing optimism about changing things. The position of black people in American society suddenly began to appear intolerable and became a great political question because of three facts. One was migration. This turned a local Southern question into a national problem. Between 1940 and 1960 the black population of Northern states almost trebled in a movement not reversed until the 1990s. New York became the state with the biggest black population of the Union. This not only brought black Americans into view in new places, but also in new ways. It revealed that the problem facing them was not only one of legal rights, but was more complex; it was one of economic and cultural deprivation, too. The second fact pushing the question forward on to the national stage lay outside the United States. Many of the new nations, which were becoming a majority at the UN, were nations of coloured peoples. It was an embarrassment – of which communist propaganda always made good use – for the United States to display at home so flagrant a contravention of the ideals she espoused abroad as was provided by the plight of many of her black citizens. Finally, the action of black Americans themselves under their own leaders, some inspired by Gandhian principles of passive resistance to oppression, won over many white Americans. In the end, the legal and political position of black Americans was

Martin Luther King

Martin Luther King (1929–1968) was born in Alabama, the son of a Baptist clergyman. While studying at the Theological School of Boston University, he founded the Student Non-Violent Coordinating Committee (SNCC) and, with the help of the Association for the Advancement of Coloured People (NAACP), he organized a series of boycotts against segregation in public toilets in Montgomery (Alabama) which brought him national recognition.

King led the non-violent civil rights movement with tremendous energy, culminating in 1963 in the great march on Washington, DC, where he gave his most famous speech in front of a crowd of almost 300,000 people of every race. "I have a dream," he declared, "that my four little children will one day live in a nation where they will not be judged by the colour of their skin but by the content of their character."

Nominated "Man of the Year" by *Time* magazine in 1963 and awarded the Nobel Peace Prize in 1964, King continued to organize acts of resistance in order to ensure that anti-segregationist laws were complied with. He did not agree with organizations that advocated violence as the only way to bring about change, nor did he accept Malcolm X's black nationalism. In 1968 King led a series of peaceful demonstrations in Memphis, and on 4 April he was assassinated in that city while he stood on a hotel balcony.

Martin Luther King delivers his "I have a dream" speech on the steps of the Lincoln Memorial in Washington, DC.

radically altered for the better. Yet bitterness and resentment were not eliminated in the process, but in some places actually increased.

THE CIVIL RIGHTS CAMPAIGN

The first and most successful phase of the campaign for equal status of black Americans was a struggle for "civil rights", of which the most important were the unhindered exercise of the franchise (always formally, though actually not, available in some Southern states) and for equality of treatment in other ways, such as access to public facilities and schooling. The success stemmed from decisions of the Supreme Court in 1954 and 1955. The process thus began not with legislation but with judicial interpretation. These important first decisions declared that the segregation of different races within the public school system was unconstitutional and that where it existed it should be brought to an end within a reasonable time. This challenged the social system in many Southern states, but by 1963 there were some black and white children attending public schools together in every state of the Union, even if others stayed in all-black or all-white schools.

Legislation was not really important until after 1961. After the inauguration of a

Children survey the aftermath of the race riots that shook Los Angeles in 1992. Three days of unrest followed the news that four local white policemen had been acquitted of the beating of a black motorist, Rodney King, although they had been caught on film.

successful campaign of "sit-ins" by black leaders (which itself achieved many important local victories), Kennedy initiated a programme going beyond the securing of voting rights to attack segregation and inequality of many kinds. It was to be continued by his successor. Poverty, poor housing, bad schools in run-down urban areas were symptoms of deep dislocations inside American society. And inequalities were made more irksome by the increasing affluence in which they were set. The Kennedy administration appealed to Americans to see their removal as one of the challenges of a "New Frontier".

SOCIAL AND ECONOMIC DIFFICULTIES

Even greater emphasis was given to legislation to remove poverty and its accom-

panying problems by Lyndon Johnson, who succeeded to the presidency when Kennedy was murdered in November 1963. Unhappily, the deepest roots of the black American problem appeared to lie beyond the reach of laws in what came to be called the "ghetto" areas of great American cities. Again, a long perspective is helpful. In 1965 (a hundred years after emancipation from slavery became law throughout the whole United States) a ferocious outbreak of rioting in a district of Los Angeles with a large black population was estimated to have involved at its height as many as 75,000 people. Other troubles followed in other cities, but not on the same scale. Twenty-five years later, all that had happened in Watts (where the Los Angeles outbreak took place) was that conditions had further deteriorated. The problem was (it was usually agreed) one of economic opportunity, but none the easier to solve for that. It not only remained unsolved but appeared to be running away from solution. The poisons it secreted burst forth in crime, a major collapse in health standards in some black communities, and in ungovernable and virtually unpoliceable inner-city areas. In the culture and politics of white America they seemed at times to have produced a near-neurotic obsession with colour and racial issues.

His own poor Southern background had made President Johnson a convinced and convincing exponent of the "Great Society" in which he discerned America's future, and perhaps this might have held promise for the handling of the black economic problem had he survived. Potentially one of America's great reforming presidents, Johnson nevertheless experienced tragic failure, for all his aspirations, experience and skill. His constructive and reforming work was soon forgotten (and, it must be said, set aside) when his presidency came to be overshad-

owed by an Asian war disastrous enough before it ended to be called by some "America's Sicilian Expedition".

THE VIETNAM WAR

AMERICAN POLICY in Southeast Asia under Eisenhower had come to rest on the dogma that a non-communist South Vietnam was essential to security, and that it had to be kept in the Western camp if others in the area – or as far away as India and Australia – were not to be subverted. So, the United States had become the backer of a conservative government in part of Indo-China. President Kennedy did not question this view and began to back up American military aid with "advisers". At his death there were 23,000 of them in South Vietnam, and, in fact, many of them were in action in the field. President Johnson followed the course already set,

In 1966, the Americans attempted to "pacify" rural areas controlled by the Vietcong through search-and-destroy missions in the lowlands. While refugees fled to the cities, the Americans also used chemicals to destroy the foliage that sheltered the rebels in the jungles. Here, American troops disembark from helicopters to launch an operation.

believing that pledges to other countries had to be shown to be sound currency. But government after government in Saigon turned out to be broken reeds. At the beginning of 1965 Johnson was advised that South Vietnam might collapse; he had the authority to act (given him, thanks to careful political management, by Congress after North Vietnamese attacks on American ships the previous year) and air attacks were launched against targets in North Vietnam. Soon afterwards, the first official American combat units were sent to the South. American participation quickly soared out of control. In 1968 there were over 500,000 American servicemen in Vietnam; by Christmas that year a heavier tonnage of bombs had been dropped on North Vietnam than had fallen on Germany and Japan together in the entire Second World War.

The outcome was politically disastrous. It was almost the least of Johnson's worries that the American balance of payments was wrecked by the war's huge cost, which also took money from badly needed reform projects at home. Worse was the bitter domestic outcry that arose as casualties mounted and attempts to negotiate seemed to get nowhere. The better-off young (among them a future president) sought to avoid conscription and Americans gloomily contemplated at home on their television screens the cost of a struggle viewable in their homes as no other war had ever been. Rancour grew, and with it the alarm of moderate America. It was small consolation that Russia's costs in supplying arms to North Vietnam were heavy, too.

DISILLUSION IN THE UNITED STATES

More was involved in domestic uproar over Vietnam than the agitation of young people rioting in protest and distrust of their government, or the idealism of conservatives outraged by ritual desecrations of the symbols of patriotism and refusals to carry out military service. Vietnam was bringing about a transformation in the way many Americans looked at the outside world. In Southeast Asia it was at last borne in on the thoughtful among them that even the United States could not obtain every result it wanted, far less obtain it at any reasonable cost. The late 1960s brought the end of the illusion that American power was limitless and irresistible. Americans had approached the post-war world with this illusion intact. Their country's strength had, after all, decided two world wars. Beyond them there stretched back a century and a half of virtually unchecked and unhindered continental expansion, of immunity from European intervention, of the growth of an impressive hegemony in the

A crowd of demonstrators gathers in front of the Pentagon brandishing posters with anti-Vietnam War slogans in 1967.

American hemisphere. There was nothing in American history that was wholly disastrous or irredeemable, hardly anything in which there was, ultimately, failure, and nothing over which most Americans felt any guilt. It had been easy and natural for that background to breed a careless assumption of limitless possibility. Prosperity helped to carry it over from domestic to foreign concerns. It was understandable that Americans should overlook the special conditions on which their success story had long been built.

THE END OF THE VIETNAM WAR

The reckoning had begun to be drawn up in the 1950s, when many Americans had to be content with a lesser victory in Korea than they had hoped for. There had then opened twenty years of frustrating dealings with nations often enjoying not a tenth of the power of the United States, but apparently able to thwart her. At last, in the Vietnam disaster, both the limits of power and its full costs were revealed. In March 1968 the strength of the rising opposition to the war was shown clearly in the primary elections. Johnson had already drawn the conclusion that the United States could not win, and had restricted bombing and asked the North Vietnamese to open negotiations again. Dramatically, he now also announced that he would not stand for re-election in 1968. Just as the casualties of the Korean War won Eisenhower election in 1952, so the casualties of Vietnam, on the battlefield and at home, helped (with the presence of a third candidate) to elect another Republican president in 1968 (only four years after Johnson won a huge Democratic majority) and to re-elect him in 1972. Vietnam was not the only factor, but it was one of the most important in dislocating the old Democratic coalition.

The new president, Richard Nixon, began to withdraw American ground forces from Vietnam soon after his inauguration. Peacemaking took three years. In 1970 secret negotiations began between North Vietnam and the United States, accompanied by further withdrawals, but also by renewed and intensified bombing of the North and its extension to Cambodia by the Americans. The diplomacy was tortuous and difficult. The United States could not admit it was abandoning its ally, though in fact it had to do so, nor would the North Vietnamese accept terms that did not leave them able to harass the Southern régime through their

The Vietnam War created hundreds of thousands of refugees, including these Eurasian and Afro-Asian orphans (pictured at an orphanage in An-Loi in 1972), left behind by the departing US forces.

Civilians are rounded up by US Marines inside the Citadel in Hué during the Vietcong's costly but politically successful "Tet Offensive" in early 1968. This surprise attack on South Vietnamese cities, launched to coincide with the Vietnamese New Year (Tet), was the turning-point of the Vietnam War. After months of optimistic reports from Saigon, the American people were dismayed to hear that the "defeated" Vietcong were occupying no less than 103 towns and had penetrated even the US embassy in Saigon. Although they were quickly repulsed, the effect on US policy-makers was decisive. They had learned that the communists would make any sacrifice to win. Victory cost North Vietnam and the Vietcong a total of nearly one million combatant deaths.

sympathizers in the South. Amid considerable public outcry in the United States, bombing was briefly resumed at the end of 1972, but for the last time. Soon afterwards, on 27 January 1973, a ceasefire was signed in Paris.

THE EFFECTS OF THE CEASEFIRE

The Vietnam War had cost the United States vast sums of money and 58,000 dead. It had gravely damaged American prestige, had eroded American diplomatic influence, had ravaged domestic politics and had frustrated reform. What had been achieved was a brief preservation of a shaky South Vietnam, saddled with internal problems which made its survival uncertain, while terrible destruction had been inflicted on the peoples of Indo-China, of whom three million died. Perhaps the abandonment of the illusion of American omnipotence might go some way to offset these costs.

It was a real success to have disentangled the United States from the morass and President Nixon justifiably reaped the benefit. The liquidation of the venture had followed other signs of his recognition of how much the world had already changed since the Cuban crisis. The most striking of these was a new policy of normal and direct American diplomatic contact with communist China. It came to a climax only in 1978, but two dramatic earlier events had preceded even the making of the Vietnam peace. In October 1971 the UN General Assembly had recognized the People's Republic as the only legitimate representative of China in the United Nations, and expelled the representative of Taiwan. This was not an outcome the United States had anticipated until the crucial vote was taken. The following February, there took place a visit by President Nixon to China that was the first visit ever made by

Henry Kissinger, the US diplomat and adviser on national security affairs, and Le Duc Tho, the North Vietnamese statesman, leave the International Conference Centre in Paris after their peace talks for Vietnam in October 1972. The following year, both men were awarded the Nobel Peace Prize.

an American president to mainland Asia, and one he described as an attempt to bridge "16,000 miles and twenty-two years of hostility".

When Nixon followed his Chinese trip by becoming also the first American president to visit Moscow (in May 1972), and this was followed by an interim agreement on arms limitation, the first of its kind, it seemed that another important change had come about. The stark polarized simplicities of the Cold War were blurring, however doubtful the future might be. The Vietnam settlement followed and this can hardly have been unrelated to it; Moscow and Peking both had to be squared if there were to be a ceasefire. China's attitude to the Vietnamese struggle was, we may guess, by no means simple; it was complicated by potential danger from the USSR, by the United States' use of its power elsewhere in Asia, notably in Taiwan and Japan, and by older memories of the strength of Vietnamese nationalism; its Indo-Chinese communist satellite could not be trusted.

Once seen by China as one of her tributary peoples, the Vietnamese looked back on a long history of struggle against Chinese as well as French imperialism. In the immediate aftermath of the American withdrawal, too, the nature of the struggle going on in Vietnam was more and more clearly revealed as a civil war over who should rule a reunited country.

RENEWED CONFLICT
IN VIETNAM

The North Vietnamese did not wait long to settle the matter. For a time the United States government had to pretend not to see this; there was too much relief at home over the liquidation of the Asian commitment for scruples to be expressed over the actual observation of the peace terms that had made withdrawal possible. When a political scandal forced Nixon's resignation in 1974, his successor faced a Congress suspicious of what it

saw as dangerous foreign adventures and determined to thwart them. There would be no attempt to uphold the peace terms of 1972 insofar as they guaranteed the South Vietnamese régime against overthrow.

Early in 1975 American aid to Saigon came to an end. A government, which had lost virtually all its other territory, was reduced to a backs-to-the-wall attempt to hold the capital city and lower Mekong with a demoralized and defeated army. At the same time, communist forces in Cambodia were destroying another régime once supported by the United States. Congress prevented the sending of further military and financial help. The pattern of China in 1947 was being repeated; the United States was cutting its losses at the expense of those who had relied on it (though 117,000 Vietnamese left with the Americans when the North Vietnamese army entered Saigon in April 1975).

Such an outcome was doubly ironic. In the first place it seemed to show that the

Pol Pot, pictured here with one of his Khmer Rouge soldiers, headed a notoriously bloodthirsty pro-Chinese régime in Cambodia from 1976 until 1979. In 1978 the Vietnamese invasion of Cambodia accelerated the deterioration of relations between Vietnam and China and led to the frontier war of February–March 1979. When the victorious Vietnamese overthrew his régime, Pol Pot became the leader of the communist resistance movement, which is active today.

hardliners on Asian policy had been right all along – that only the knowledge that the United States was in the last resort prepared to fight for them could guarantee the post-colonial régimes' resistance to communism. Secondly, the swing back to isolationism in the United States was accentuated, not muffled, by defeat and disaster; those who reflected on the American dead and missing and the huge cost now saw the whole Indo-China episode as a pointless and unjustifiable waste on behalf of peoples who would not fight to defend themselves. It was arguable, though, that better relations with China mattered much more than the loss of Vietnam.

CONFLICTING SIGNS IN THE US

As 1980 drew nearer many Americans were confused and worried; national morale was not good. Vietnam had left deep psychic wounds as well as helping to feed a counter-culture at home which they found frightening. In the 1960s, the first voices of note had raised the alarm over environmental dangers; the 1970s had brought the oil crisis and a new sense of exposure at a moment when, for the first time, America's Middle Eastern ally, Israel, no longer seemed invulnerable to her enemies. The disgrace and near-impeachment of President Nixon, after a scandalous abuse of executive power, had eaten away at confidence in the nation's institutions. Abroad, the behaviour of other allies (themselves worried and confused by American disarray) seemed less predictable than in the past. For the first time, too, Americans' confidence in the promise their nation had always been believed to hold out for mankind faltered in the face of what looked like blunt rejection by much of the Islamic world.

The situation was indeed not easy to read.

Yet the American democratic system showed no sign of breaking down, nor of not meeting many of the country's needs, even if it could not find answers to all its problems. The economy had, astonishingly, been able to continue for years to pay for a hugely expensive war, for a space exploration programme that put men on the moon, and for garrisons around the world. True, the black American's plight continued to worsen, and some of the country's greatest cities seemed stricken by urban

Richard M. Nixon (1913–1994) had been US president for six years when this photograph was taken in 1974 at the height of the Watergate scandal that cost him his political career. He is shown in the last minutes of his presidency, before his resignation in favour of Gerald Ford.

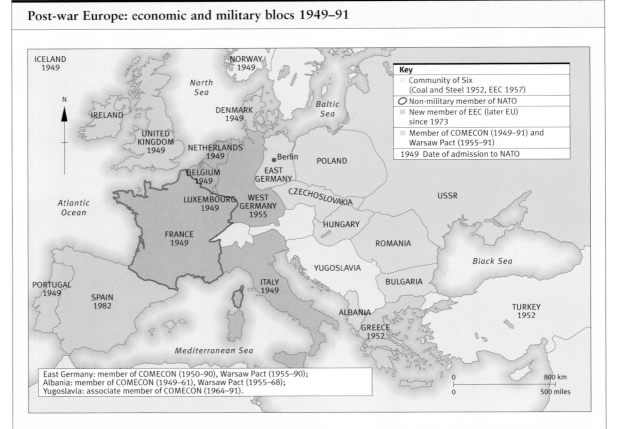

Post-war Europe: economic and military blocs 1949–91

Key
- Community of Six (Coal and Steel 1952, EEC 1957)
- Non-military member of NATO
- New member of EEC (later EU) since 1973
- Member of COMECON (1949–91) and Warsaw Pact (1955–91)
- 1949 Date of admission to NATO

East Germany: member of COMECON (1950–90), Warsaw Pact (1955–90);
Albania: member of COMECON (1949–61), Warsaw Pact (1955–68);
Yugoslavia: associate member of COMECON (1964–91).

Following the end of the Second World War, the division of Europe was evident on a political and military level, with NATO opposing the Warsaw Pact. It was also evident in the European countries' economic organization: western Europe, with the Marshall Plan and later the EEC, formed a stark contrast to the Eastern bloc countries, which were members of COMECON (the Council for Mutual Economic Assistance created by Stalin). Cuba, Mongolia and Vietnam were also members of COMECON, which was disbanded in 1991 when communism collapsed in Europe.

decay. Fewer Americans, though, seemed to find such facts as worrying as their country's supposed inferiority in missile strength to the Soviet Union (it was to be an issue in the presidential election of 1980). President Gerald Ford (who had taken office in 1974 on the resignation of his predecessor) had already had to face a Congress unwilling to countenance further aid to its allies in Indo-China. When Cambodia collapsed, and South Vietnam quickly followed, questions began to be asked at home and abroad about how far what looked like a worldwide retreat of American power might go. If the United States would no longer fight over Indo-China, would it, then, do so over Thailand? More alarmingly still, would it fight over Israel – or even Berlin? There were good reasons to think the Americans' mood of resignation and dismay would not last for ever, but while it lasted, their allies looked about them and felt uneasy.

TWO EUROPES

EUROPE WAS THE BIRTHPLACE of the Cold War and was for a long time its main theatre. Yet well before 1970 there had been signs that the terrible simplifications institutionalized in NATO and (even more rigidly) in the Warsaw Pact might not be all that was shaping history there. Although long insulated by Soviet power from external stimuli to change and by its command economies, there were signs of division in eastern Europe. The violence with which Albania, the tiniest of them, condemned the Soviet Union and applauded China when the two fell out in the 1960s had to be endured by the Russians; Albania had no frontier with other Warsaw Pact countries and so was not likely to have to take account of the Red Army. It was more striking when Romania, with Chinese support, successfully contested the direction of its economy by COMECON, asserting a national right to develop it in its own interest. It even took up a vaguely neutralist position on questions of foreign policy – though remaining inside the Warsaw Pact – and did so, oddly enough, under a ruler who imposed on his people one of the most rigidly dictatorial régimes in eastern Europe. But Romania had no land frontier with a NATO country, and one 500 miles long with Russia; her skittishness could be tolerated, therefore, because it could be quickly curbed if necessary. That there were clear limits to the dislocation of the old monolithic unity of Communism was clearly enough shown in 1968 when a communist government in Czechoslovakia set about liberalizing its internal structure and developing trade relations with West Germany. This was not to be tolerated. After a series of attempts to bring her to heel, Czechoslovakia was invaded in August 1968 by Warsaw Pact forces. To avoid a repetition of what had happened in Hungary in 1956, the Czech government did not resist and a brief attempt to provide an example of "socialism with a human face", as a Czech politician had put it, was obliterated.

POLYCENTRISM

Sino-Soviet tension combined with tremblings within the Eastern bloc (and perhaps the uneasiness of the United States over relations with Latin American countries) to lead to suggestions that the world as a whole was abandoning bipolarity for "polycentrism" as an Italian communist called it. The loosening of Cold War simplicities had indeed been surprising. Other complicating developments had meanwhile emerged in western Europe. By 1980 it was clear that one of the historic roles of its peoples was over since they by then ruled no more of the world's surface than their ancestors had done 500 years earlier. Huge transformations had taken place, and irreversible things had been done in those five centuries. Although Europe's imperial past was over, the discovery of a new role was well under way. Western Europe had begun to show some of the first, feeble signs that nationalism's grip on the human potential for large-scale organization might be loosening in the very place where nationalism had been born.

In the "Prague Spring" of 1968 mass demonstrations, such as the one pictured here, were held in Prague, demanding the liberalization of the régime. The arrival of Soviet tanks in August to quell the unrest, however, quashed the attempt at democratization.

General de Gaulle, pictured here greeting the German leader Konrad Adenauer in 1963, was, above all, a French patriot, determined to restore France to its former glory. His personal ambition for Europe was to free it from American patronage and to create an integrated organization based on respect for national sovereignty.

WESTERN EUROPEAN INTEGRATION

THE LEGACIES of common European experience have been traced by enthusiasts back to the Carolingian monarchs, but 1945 will do as a starting point. From that date, the continent's future for more than forty years was mainly determined by the outcome of the Second World War and Soviet policy. The likelihood of another great civil war in the west over the German question seemed remote since defeat and partition had disposed of the German problem and so quietened the fears of France. Soviet policy had then given the western countries many new reasons to cooperate more closely; the events in eastern Europe in the late 1940s struck them as a warning of what might happen if the Americans ever went home and the western European nations remained divided. The Marshall Plan and NATO turned out to have been the first two of many important steps towards the integration of a new Europe.

NEW EUROPEAN INSTITUTIONS

Western European integration had more than one source. The initiation of the Marshall Plan was followed by the setting-up of an Organization (at first of sixteen countries, but later expanded) of European Economic Cooperation in 1948, but the following year, a month after the signing of the treaty setting up NATO, the first political bodies representing ten different European states were also set up under a new Council of Europe. The economic forces making for integration were developing more rapidly, however. Customs Unions had already been created in 1948 between the "Benelux"' countries (Belgium, the Netherlands, and Luxembourg), and (in a different form) between France and Italy. Finally, the most important of the early steps towards greater integration emerged from a French proposal for a Coal and Steel Community. This came into existence formally in 1951 and embraced France, Italy, the Benelux countries and, most significantly, West Germany. It made possible the rejuvenation of the industrial heartland of western Europe and was the main step towards the integration of West Germany into a new international structure. Through economic arrangement, there came into existence the means of containing while reviving West Germany, whose strength, it was becoming clear, was needed in a western Europe menaced by Soviet land power. Under the influence of events in Korea, American official opinion (to the consternation of some Europeans) was in the early 1950s rapidly coming around to the view that Germany had to be rearmed.

THE ESTABLISHMENT OF THE EEC

Other facts, too, helped to ease the way to supranational organization in Europe. The political weakness symptomized by their domestic communist parties subsided in both France and Italy, mainly thanks to economic recovery. Communists had ceased to take part in their governments as early as 1947 and the danger that French and Italian democracy might suffer a fate like Czechoslovakia's had disappeared by 1950. Anti-communist opinion tended to coalesce about parties whose integrating forces were either Roman Catholic politicians or social democrats well aware of the fate of their comrades in eastern Europe. Broadly speaking, these changes meant that western European governments of a moderate right-wing complexion pursued similar aims of economic recovery, welfare service provision, and western European integration in practical matters during the 1950s.

Further institutions emerged. In 1952 a European Defence Community formalized West Germany's military position. This was to be replaced by German membership of NATO, but a major thrust towards greater unity, as before, was economic. The crucial step came in 1957: the European Economic Community (EEC) then came into being when France, Germany, Belgium, the Netherlands, Luxembourg and Italy joined in signing the Treaty of Rome. Besides looking forward to the creation of a "Common Market" embracing its members, within which barriers to the free movement of goods, services and labour were to be removed, and with a common tariff, the treaty also provided for a decision-making authority, a bureaucracy and a European

The expansion of the European Union (1957–2007)

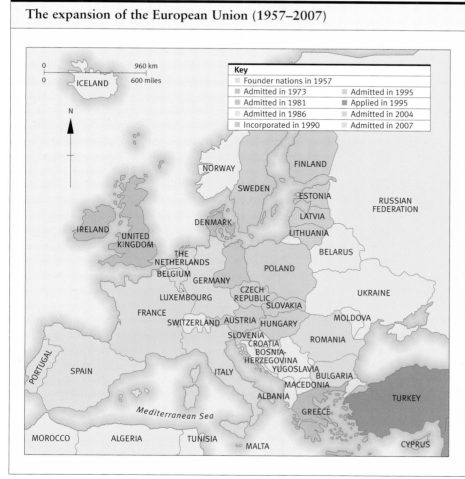

Key
- Founder nations in 1957
- Admitted in 1973
- Admitted in 1981
- Admitted in 1986
- Incorporated in 1990
- Admitted in 1995
- Applied in 1995
- Admitted in 2004
- Admitted in 2007

The European Economic Community was renamed the European Union (EU) in 1994. From an original six members in 1957, a series of enlargements had taken EU membership to 27 nations by the beginning of 2007. This map shows membership of the European Union and the date of each country's entry.

parliament with advisory powers. Some spoke of the reconstitution of Charlemagne's heritage. It spurred countries which had not joined the EEC to set up their own, looser and more limited, European Free Trade Association (EFTA) two and a half years later. By 1986, the six countries of the original EEC (by then it had become simply the EC – the word "Economic", significantly, had been dropped) were twelve; while EFTA had lost all but four of its members to it. Five years later still, and what was left of EFTA was envisaging merging with the EC.

Western Europe's slow but accelerating movement towards a modicum of political unity demonstrated the confidence of those who made the arrangements that armed conflict could never again be an acceptable alternative to cooperation and negotiation between their countries. Tragically, though recognizing that fact, Great Britain's government did not seize the chance to join in giving it institutional expression; later it was twice to be refused admission to the EEC. Meanwhile, the Community's interests were steadily cemented together by a Common Agricultural Policy, which was, to all intents and purposes,

a huge bribe to the farmers and peasants who were so important a part of the German and French electorates, and, later, to those of poorer countries as they became members.

FRANCE UNDER DE GAULLE

For a long time determined opposition to further integration, at the political as opposed to the economic level, came from France. It was expressed strongly by General de Gaulle, who returned to politics in 1958 to become president when the fourth French republic seemed likely to slide into civil war over Algeria. His first task was to negotiate these rapids and to carry through important constitutional reforms, which created the Fifth Republic. His next service to France was as great as any in his wartime career, the liquidation of her Algerian commitment in 1961. The legions came home, some disgruntled. The act freed both him and his country for a more vigorous international role, though a somewhat negative one. De Gaulle's view of European consolidation was limited to cooperation between independent nation-states; he saw the EEC as above all a way of protecting French economic interests. He was quite prepared to strain the new organization badly to get his way. Further, he in effect twice vetoed British applications to join it. Wartime experience had left de Gaulle with a deep distrust of the "Anglo-Saxons" and a belief, by no means ill-founded, that the British still hankered after integration with an Atlantic community embracing the United States, rather than with continental Europe. In 1964 he annoyed the Americans by exchanging diplomatic representatives with communist China. He insisted that France go ahead with its own nuclear weapons programme, declining to be dependent on American patronage. Finally, after causing it much trouble, he

View of the standard bearer in a French Foreign Legion parade in the 1940s outside the élite unit's headquarters at Sidi-Bel-Abbès, Algeria. Legionnaires first landed in Algeria in 1831 and were to form an emotional attachment to the country as their unit's homeland, which it remained until 1962. In April 1961 the 1st Regiment Etranger Parachutiste was disbanded when it rose against the government of Charles de Gaulle in protest against moves by France to negotiate with revolutionaries to bring an end to the war in Algeria.

withdrew from NATO. This could be seen as the coming of "polycentrism" to the Western bloc. When de Gaulle resigned after an unfavourable referendum in 1969, a major political force making for uncertainty and disarray in western Europe disappeared.

BRITISH UNCERTAINTIES

GREAT BRITAIN FINALLY JOINED the EEC in 1973, a registration, at last, of the facts of twentieth-century history by the most conservative of the historic nation-states. The decision complemented the withdrawal from empire and acknowledged that the British strategic frontier lay no longer on the Rhine, but on the Elbe. It was a significant turning point, though far from conclusive in an era of uncertainty. For a quarter-century British governments had tried and failed to combine economic growth, increased social service provision and a high level of employment. The second depended ultimately on the first, but when difficulty arose, the first had always been sacrificed to the other two. The United Kingdom was, after all, a democracy whose voters, greedy and gullible, had to be placated. The vulnerability of the traditional British economy's commitment to international trade was a handicap, too. Other handicaps lay in its old staple industries, starved of investment, and the deeply conservative attitudes of the people. Though the United Kingdom grew richer (in 1970 virtually no British manual worker had four weeks' paid holiday a year and ten years later a third of them did), it fell more and more behind other developed countries both in its wealth and its rate of creating it. If the British had managed a decline in international power and the achievement of a rapid decolonization without the violence and domestic bitterness visible elsewhere, it remained

unclear whether they could shake off the past in other ways and ensure themselves even a modest prosperity as a second-rank nation.

VIOLENCE AND UNREST IN THE UNITED KINGDOM

One obvious and symptomatic threat to order and civilization was posed in Northern Ireland. Protestant and Catholic hooligans alike seemed bent on destroying their homeland rather than cooperating with their rivals, and caused the deaths of thousands of British citizens – soldiers, policemen and civilians, Protestant and Catholic, Irish, Scottish and English alike – in the 1970s and 1980s. Fortunately they did not disrupt British party politics as Irishmen had done in the past. The British electorate remained preoccupied, rather, by material concerns. Inflation ran at unprecedented levels (the annualized rate 1970–80 was over 13 per cent) and gave new edge to industrial troubles in the 1970s, especially in the wake of the oil crisis. There was speculation about whether the country was "ungovernable" as a miners' strike brought down one government, while many leaders and interpreters of opinion seemed obsessed

Masked IRA activists carry the coffin of the hunger striker Martin Hurson in 1972. By that time, the IRA were killing police officers and British soldiers on leave and planting bombs in Belfast. In August 1971, the British government had decreed internment without trial for captured terrorists, but this only served to increase opposition to British rule.

with the themes of social division. Even the question whether the United Kingdom should remain in the EEC, which was submitted to the revolutionary device of a referendum in June 1975, was often put in these terms. It was therefore all the more surprising to many politicians when the outcome was unambiguously favourable to continued membership.

THE INFLATIONARY THREAT

More bad times (economically speaking) lay immediately ahead; inflation (in 1975 running at 26.9 per cent in the wake of the oil crisis) was at last identified by government as the overriding threat. Wage demands by trades unions were anticipating inflation still to come and it began to dawn on some that the era of unquestioned growth in consumption was over. There was a gleam of light; a few years earlier vast oil fields had been discovered under the seabed off the coasts of northern Europe. In 1976 the United Kingdom became an oil-exporting nation. That did not help much immediately; in the same year, a loan from the International Monetary Fund was required. When Mrs Thatcher, the country's (and Europe's) first female prime minister and the first woman to lead a major political party (the Conservatives), took office in 1979 she had, in a sense, little to lose; her opponents were discredited, as, many felt, were the ideas that had been long accepted uncritically as the determinants of British policy. A radical new departure for once really did seem to be a possibility. To the surprise of many and the amazement of some among both her supporters and her opponents, that is exactly what Mrs Thatcher was to provide after a shaky start to what was to prove the longest tenure of power of any British prime minister in the twentieth century.

Argentinian tank crews prepare to go into battle against their British counterparts on the Falkland Islands, which Argentina held for two months. The war cost 254 British and 712 Argentine lives.

THE FALKLANDS WAR

Not far into her premiership, Mrs Thatcher found herself in 1982 presiding unexpectedly over what may well prove to have been Great Britain's last colonial war. The reconquest of the Falkland Islands after their brief occupation by Argentine forces was in logistic terms alone a great feat of arms as well as a major psychological and diplomatic success. The prime minister's instincts to fight for the principles of international law and for the islanders' right to say by whom they should be governed, were well attuned to the popular mood. She also correctly judged the international possibilities. After an uncertain start (unsurprising, given its traditional sensitivity over Latin America), the United States provided important practical and clandestine help. Chile, by no means easy with her restive neighbour, was not disposed to object to British covert operations on the mainland of South America. More important, most of the EC countries supported the isolation of Argentina in the UN, and resolutions that condemned the Argentine action. It was especially notable that the British had from the start the support (not often offered to it so readily) of the French government, which knew a threat to vested rights when it saw one.

It now seems clear that Argentine action had been encouraged by the misleading impressions of likely British reactions gained from British diplomacy in previous years (for this reason, the British foreign secretary resigned at the outset of the crisis). Happily, one political consequence was the fatal wounding in its prestige and cohesiveness of the military régime that ruled Argentina and its replacement at the end of 1983 by a constitutional and elected government. In the United Kingdom, Mrs Thatcher's prestige rose with national morale; abroad, too, her

Margaret Thatcher was British prime minister from 1979 to 1990. Her neo-liberal economic policy was widely seen as an attack on the advanced British welfare state and particularly on the National Health Service, but the "Iron Lady" won ardent supporters as well as fierce opponents by breaking the power of the unions to obstruct the pace of change.

standing was enhanced, and this was important. For the rest of the decade it provided the country with an influence with other heads of state (notably the American president) which the raw facts of British strength could scarcely have sustained by themselves. Not everyone agreed that this influence was always advantageously deployed. Like those of General de Gaulle, Mrs Thatcher's personal convictions, preconceptions and prejudices were always very visible and she, like him, was no European, if that meant allowing emotional or even practical commitment to Europe to blunt personal visions of national interest.

THATCHERITE BRITAIN

In domestic affairs, Mrs Thatcher transformed the terms of British politics, and perhaps of cultural and social debate, dissolving a long *bien-pensant* consensus about national goals. This, together with the undoubted radicalism of many of her specific policies, awoke both enthusiasm and an unusual animosity. Yet she failed to achieve some of her most important aims. Ten years after she took up office, government was playing a greater, not a smaller, role in many areas of society, and the public money spent on health and social security had gone up a third in real terms since 1979 (without satisfying greatly increased demand).

Although Mrs Thatcher had led the Conservatives to three general election victories in a row (a significant achievement in British politics), many in her party came to believe she would be a vote-loser in the next contest, which could not be far away. Faced with the erosion of loyalty and support, she resigned in 1990, leaving to her successor rising unemployment and a bad financial situation. But it seemed likely that British policy might now become less obstructive in its approach to the Community and its affairs and less rhetorical about it.

The Spanish prime minister Felipe González (centre) signs the Treaty of Madrid in 1985. This formalized his country's entry into the European Community – Spain's membership would become valid on the first day of the following year.

THE GROWTH OF THE EC

THE 1970S HAD BEEN difficult years for all the members of the EEC. Growth fell away and individual economies reeled under the impact of the oil crisis. This contributed to institutional bickering and squabbling (particularly on economic and financial matters), which had reminded Europeans of the limits to what was so far achieved. It continued in the 1980s and, coupled with uneasiness about the success of the Far Eastern economic sphere, dominated by Japan, and a growing realization that other nations would wish to join the ten, led to further crystallization of ideas about the Community's future. Many Europeans saw more clearly that greater unity, a habit of cooperation and increasing prosperity were prerequisites of Europe's political independence, but some also felt an emerging sense that such independence would always remain hollow unless Europe, too, could turn itself into a superpower.

Comfort could be drawn by enthusiasts from further progress in integration. In 1979 the first direct elections to the European parliament were already being held. Greece in 1981, Spain and Portugal in 1986, were soon to join the Community. In 1987 the foundations of a common European currency and monetary system were drawn up (although the United Kingdom did not agree) and it was settled that 1992 should be the year which would see the inauguration of a genuine single market, across whose national borders goods, people, capital and services were to move freely. Members even endorsed in principle the idea of European political union, although the British and French had notable misgivings. This by no means made at once for greater psychological cohesion and comfort as the implications emerged, but it was an indisputable sign of development of some sort.

The West German chancellor Helmut Kohl (b.1930) and the French president François Mitterrand (1916–1996) are pictured at a European summit in Hanover in 1988. Kohl and Mitterrand had a close professional relationship, and often worked together to promote greater European integration.

4 NEW CHALLENGES TO THE COLD WAR WORLD ORDER

IN DECEMBER 1975 Gerald Ford became the second American president to visit China. The adjustment of his country's deep-seated distrust and hostility towards the People's Republic had begun with the slow recognition of the lessons of Vietnam. On the Chinese side, change was a part of an even greater development: China's resumption of an international and regional role appropriate to its historical stature and potential. This could only come to fruition after 1949 and by the mid-1970s it was complete. An approach towards establishing normal relations with the United States was now possible. Formal recognition of what had been achieved came in 1978. In a Sino-American agreement the United States made the crucial concession that its forces should be withdrawn from Taiwan and that official diplomatic relations with the island's KMT government should be ended.

CHINA AFTER MAO

MAO HAD DIED in September 1976. The threat of the ascendancy of a "gang of four" of his coadjutors (one was his widow), who had promoted the policies of the Cultural Revolution, was quickly averted by their arrest (and, eventually, trial and condemnation in 1981). Under new leadership dominated by Party veterans, it soon became clear that the excesses of the Cultural Revolution were to be corrected. In 1977 there rejoined the government as a vice-premier the twice previously disgraced Deng Xiaoping, firmly associated with the contrary trend (his son had been crippled by beatings from the Red Guards in the Cultural Revolution). The most important change, though, was that China's long-awaited economic recovery was at last attainable. Scope was now to be given to individual enterprise and the profit motive, and economic links with non-communist countries were to be encouraged. The aim was to resume the process of technological and industrial modernization. The major definition of the new course was undertaken in 1981 at the plenary session of the central committee of the Party, which met that year. It undertook, too, the delicate task of distinguishing the positive achievements of Mao, a "great proletarian

After Mao Tse-tung's death China entered a new phase. Before Deng Xiaoping took over the leadership of the Communist Party and the country, he had to overcome competition from the extreme Left. The Gang of Four, his principal rivals, were arrested and imprisoned; Mao's widow, Jiang Qing, is pictured here at her trial, at which she was sentenced to death (commuted to life imprisonment).

revolutionary", from what it now identified as his "gross mistakes" and his responsibility for the setbacks of the Great Leap Forward and the Cultural Revolution.

MODERNIZATION

For all the comings-and-goings in CCP leadership, and the mysterious debates and sloganizing, which continued to obscure political realities, and although Deng Xiaoping and his associates had to work through a collective leadership which included conservatives, the 1980s were to be shaped by a new current. Modernization had at last been given precedence over Marxist socialism, even if that could hardly be said aloud (when the secretary-general of the party pronounced in 1986 the incautious and amazing judgment that "Marx and Lenin cannot solve our problems", he was soon dismissed). Marxist language still pervaded the rhetoric of government. Some said China was resuming the "capitalist road". This, too, was obscuring, though natural. There persisted in the Party and government a clear grasp of the need for positive planning of the economy; but there was a new recognition of practical limits and a willingness to try to discriminate more carefully between what was and was not within the scope of effective regulation in the pursuit of the major goals of economic and national strength, the improvement of living standards, and a broad egalitarianism.

One remarkable change was that agricul-

ture was virtually privatized in the next few years in the sense that, although they did not own the freeholds of their land, peasants were encouraged to sell produce freely in the markets. New slogans – "to get rich is glorious" – were coined to encourage the development of village industrial and commercial enterprise, and a pragmatic road to development was signposted with "four modernizations". Special economic areas, enclaves for free trade with the capitalist world, were set up; the first at Canton, the historic centre of Chinese trade with the West. It was not a policy without costs – grain production fell at first, inflation began to show itself in the early 1980s and foreign debt rose. Some blamed the growing visibility of crime and corruption on the new line.

Deng Xiaoping (1904–1997) became a member of the Chinese Communist Party in 1925 and took part in the Long March. Deputy prime minister from 1952 and secretary of the Party's central committee, he resigned from political life in 1966 because of the personal criticism levelled against him during the Cultural Revolution. In 1973, he was appointed deputy president of the Party, and on Mao's death Deng effectively took over the leadership.

Time chart (1974–1990)					
	1974–1975 End of the dictatorships in Portugal and Spain	1980 Start of the Iran–Iraq war	1985 Gorbachev becomes general secretary of the Soviet Communist Party	1990 Iraq invades Kuwait Reunification of Germany	
1970				1990	
	1979 USSR invades Afghanistan	1981 Jaruzelski becomes prime minister of Poland	1989 Eastern Europe countries become democracies Tiananmen Square massacre (China)		

Pupils attend a school in China's Guizhou province. In 1949, China had illiteracy rates of up to 80 per cent, but the government's huge efforts to improve this situation have borne fruit: more than 90 per cent of the population now has access to primary and secondary education. By 2007, the combination of education reforms and adult literacy campaigns had reduced China's illiteracy rate to 10 per cent.

ECONOMIC DEVELOPMENT

There can be no doubt of the development policy's economic success. Mainland China began in the 1980s to show that perhaps an economic "miracle" like that of Taiwan was within her grasp. By 1986 she was the second largest producer of coal in the world, and the fourth largest of steel. GDP rose at more than 10 per cent a year between 1978 and 1986, while industrial output had doubled in value in that time. Per capita peasant income nearly tripled, and by 1988 the average peasant family was estimated to have about six months' income in the savings bank. Taking a longer perspective, the contrasts are even more striking, for all the damage done by the Great Leap Forward and the Cultural Revolution. The value of foreign trade multiplied roughly twenty-five times in per capita terms between 1950 and the middle of the 1980s. The social benefits which have accompanied such changes are also clear: increased food consumption and life expectancy, a virtual end to many of the fatal and crippling diseases of the old régime, and a huge inroad into mass illiteracy. China's continuing population growth was alarming and prompted stern measures of intervention, but it had not, as had India's, devoured the fruits of economic development.

INTERNATIONAL RELATIONS

The new Chinese line specifically linked modernization to strength. Thus it reflected the aspirations of China's reformers ever since the May 4th Movement, and of some even earlier. China's international weight had already been apparent in the 1950s; it now began to show itself in different ways. In 1984 came agreement with the British over terms for the reincorporation of Hong Kong on the expiration of the lease covering some of its territories in 1997. A later agreement with the Portuguese provided for the resumption of Macao, too. It was a blemish on the general recognition of China's due standing that among its neighbours Vietnam (with which China's relations at one time degenerated into open warfare, when the two countries were rivals for the control of Cambodia) remained hostile; but the Taiwanese were somewhat reassured by Chinese promises that the re-incorporation of the island into the territory of the republic in due course would not endanger its economic system. Similar assurances were given over Hong Kong. Like the establishment of special trading enclaves on the mainland where external commerce could flourish, such statements underlined the importance China's new rulers attached to commerce as a channel of modernization. China's sheer size gave such a policy direction importance over a wide area. By 1985 the whole of East and Southeast Asia constituted a single trading zone of unprecedented potential.

CHINA'S NEW CHALLENGE IN 1989

The new policy was not without costs, however. Growing urban markets encouraged farmers and gave them profits to plough back, but the city-dwellers began to feel the effects of rising prices. As the decade progressed, though, domestic difficulties increased. Foreign debt had shot up and inflation was running at an annual rate of about 30 per cent by the end of the decade. There was anger over evidence of corruption, and divisions in the leadership (some following upon the deaths and illness among the gerontocrats who dominated the Party) were widely known to exist. Those believing that a reassertion of political control was needed began to gain ground, and there were signs that they were manoeuvring to win over Deng Xiaoping. Yet Western observers and perhaps some Chinese had been led by the policy of economic liberalization to take unrealistic and over-optimistic views about the possibility of political relaxation. The exciting changes in eastern Europe stimulated further hopes of this. But the illusions suddenly crumbled.

As 1989 began, China's city-dwellers were feeling the pressures both of the acute inflation and of an austerity programme that had been imposed to deal with it. This was the background to a new wave of student demands. Encouraged by the presence of sympathizers with liberalization in the governing oligarchy, they demanded that the Party and government should open a dialogue with a newly formed and unofficial student union about corruption and reform. Posters and rallies began to champion calls for greater "democracy". The régime's leadership was alarmed, refusing to recognize the union, which, it was feared, might be the harbinger of a new Red Guards movement. As the seventieth anniversary of the May 4th Movement approached, activists invoked its memory so as to give a broad patriotic colour to their campaign. They were not able to arouse much support in the countryside although there were sympathetic demonstrations in many cities, but, encouraged by the

obviously benevolent attitude of the general secretary of the CCP, Zhao Ziyang, they began a mass hunger strike that won widespread popular sympathy and support in Beijing. It had started only shortly before the new Soviet leader Mikhail Gorbachev arrived in the capital; his state visit, instead of providing further reassuring evidence of China's international standing, only served to remind people of what was going on in the USSR as a result of policies of liberalization. This cut both ways, encouraging would-be reformers and frightening conservatives.

By this time the most senior members of the government, including Deng Xiaoping, seem to have become thoroughly alarmed. Widespread disorder might be in the offing; they believed China faced a major crisis. Some feared a new Cultural Revolution if things got out of control. On 20 May 1989 martial law was declared. There were signs for a moment that a divided government might not be able to impose its will, but the army's reliability was soon assured. The repression that followed two weeks later was ruthless. The student leaders had moved the focus of their efforts to an encampment in Beijing in Tiananmen Square, where, forty years before, Mao had proclaimed the foundation of the People's Republic, and they had been joined there by other dissidents. From

King Juan Carlos and Queen Sofia of Spain are shown on a visit to China. The Chinese government's attempts at liberalization in the 1980s were accompanied by several official visits from Western heads of state, with the aim of establishing trade relations. China needed foreign capital to accelerate its development; the rest of the world wanted access to the huge Chinese market of potential new consumers.

During the night of 30 May 1989 the student protesters encamped in Tiananmen Square erected this "Goddess of Democracy" plaster statue atop the Revolutionary History Museum. It faced a portrait of Mao over the gate to the old Forbidden City.

one of the gates of the old Forbidden City a huge portrait of Mao looked down on the symbol of the protesters: a plaster figure of a "Goddess of Democracy", deliberately evocative of New York's Statue of Liberty. On 2 June the first military units entered the suburbs of Beijing on their way to the square. There was resistance with extemporized weapons and barricades that they forced their way through. On 3 June the demonstrators

were overcome by rifle-fire, tear-gas, and a brutal crushing of the encampment under the treads of tanks that swept into the square. Killing went on for some days, mass arrests followed (perhaps as many as 10,000 in all). Much of what happened took place before the eyes of the world, thanks to the presence of foreign film-crews who had for days familiarized television audiences with the demonstrators' encampment.

Foreign disapproval was almost universal. Yet, as so often in China, it is hard to know what had really happened. Obviously China's rulers felt they faced a grave threat. It is probable, too, that they acted in a way deplored and opposed by many of their fellow Chinese. There was disorder, some of it serious, in over eighty cities, and the army encountered resistance in some working-class districts of Beijing. Yet the masses did not rise to support the protesters; they were more often hostile to them. Much was to be made in future years of Tiananmen as evidence of Chinese disregard of human rights, but it cannot, objectively, be confidently asserted that China would have been bound to benefit if the party had given way to the student movement. More Asian lives were shattered by banking fiascos in the 1990s than in China's troubles in 1989.

THE JAPANESE ECONOMY

WITHIN THE ASIAN TRADING ZONE, new centres of industrial and commercial activity were developing so fast in the 1980s as to justify by themselves the view that the old global balance of economic power had disappeared. South Korea, Taiwan, Hong Kong and Singapore had all shed the aura of undeveloped economies; Malaysia, Thailand and Indonesia, by 1990, looked as if they were moving up rapidly to join them. Their success was part of that of East Asia as a

The Asian Tigers

Four so-called "Asian Tigers" – Taiwan, South Korea, Hong Kong and Singapore – enjoyed high growth rates during the 1970s, which contrasted with the crisis that affected industry in developed countries. Today, these four territories are among the most highly industrialized in the world. After 1970, all enjoyed a steady annual growth rate of around 7 per cent, in spite of the fact that they were oil importers and possessed only very limited natural resources.

The most revealing change in their economies occurred in exports. From representing only 1.4 per cent of world trade in 1964, these reached 5.7 per cent in 1983 and 8.4 per cent in 1989. By that year, all four centres were among the world's top 15 exporters of manufactured goods, particularly in areas such as footwear, textiles and clothes, electronic components, plastics and toys. The remarkable economic growth of the Asian Tigers is explicable in part by cultural factors, but also by the availability of large, cheap workforces, which made it possible for their industries to expand rapidly in the 1970s.

Workers assemble televisions in the Tatung television factory in Taipei, Taiwan.

whole, and Japan had been indispensable to this outcome. The rapidity with which Japan, like China, recovered its former status as a power (and surpassed it) had obvious implications for its place both in the Asian and in the world balance. In 1959 Japanese exports again reached pre-war levels. By 1970 the Japanese had the second-highest GDP in the non-communist world. They had renewed their industrial base and had moved with great success into new areas of manufacture. Only in 1951 did a Japanese yard launch the country's first ship built for export; twenty years later, Japan had the largest shipbuilding industry in the world. At the same time it took a commanding position in consumer industries such as electronics and motor cars, of which Japan made more than any country except the United States. This caused resentment among American manufacturers – the supreme compliment. In 1979 it was agreed that Japanese cars should be made in England, the beginning of their entry to the European market. The debit side of this account was provided by a fast-growing population and by the ample evidence of the cost of economic growth in the destruction of the Japanese environment and the wear and tear of urban life.

THE CHANGES IN JAPANESE SOCIETY

Japan was long favoured by circumstances. The Vietnam War, like the Korean, was a help; so was American enforcement of a bias towards investment rather than consumption during the occupation years. Yet human beings must act to take advantage of favourable circumstances, and Japanese attitudes were crucial. Post-war Japan could deploy intense pride and an unrivalled willingness for collective effort among its people;

both sprang from the deep cohesiveness and capacity for subordinating the individual to collective purposes, which had always marked Japanese society. Strangely, such attitudes seemed to survive the coming of democracy. It may be too early to judge how deeply rooted democratic institutions are in Japanese society; after 1951 there soon appeared something like a consensus for one-party rule (though irritation with this quickly showed itself in the emergence of more extreme groupings, some anti-liberal). Mounting uneasiness was shown, too, over what was happening to traditional values and institutions. The costs of economic growth loomed up not only in huge conurbations and pollution, but also in social problems which strained even Japanese custom. Great firms still operated with success on the basis of group loyalties, buttressed by traditional attitudes and institutions.

Nonetheless, at a different level, even the Japanese family seemed to be under strain.

JAPAN'S NEW INTERNATIONAL STATUS

Economic progress also helped to change the context of Japanese foreign policy, which moved away in the 1960s from the simplicities of the preceding decade. Economic strength made the yen internationally important and drew Japan into Western monetary diplomacy. Prosperity involved it in many other parts of the world, too. In the Pacific basin, it was a major consumer of other countries' primary produce; in the Middle East it became a large buyer of oil. In Europe, Japan's investment was thought alarming by some (even though its aggregate share was not large), while imports of its manufactured goods threatened European producers. Even food supply raised international questions; in the 1960s 90 per cent of Japan's requirements for protein came from fishing and this led to alarm that the Japanese might be over-fishing important grounds.

As these and other matters changed the atmosphere and content of foreign relations, so did the behaviour of other powers, especially in the Pacific area. Japan increasingly assumed in the 1960s a position in relation to other Pacific countries not unlike that of Germany towards central and eastern Europe before 1914. It became the world's largest importer of resources, too. New Zealand and Australia found their economies increasingly and profitably tied in to the Japanese rather than to the old British market. Both of them supplied meat, and Australia minerals, notably coal and iron ore.

On the Asian mainland both the Russians and the South Koreans complained about the Japanese fishing. This added a new complication to an old story of economic involvement there. South Korea was Japan's second biggest market (the United States was the biggest) and the Japanese started to invest there again after 1951. This revived a traditional distrust; it was ominous to find that South Korean nationalism had so anti-Japanese a tone that in 1959 the president of South Korea could urge his countrymen to unite "as one man" against not their northern neighbour, but Japan. Within twenty years, too, Japanese car manufacturers were looking askance at the vigorous rival they had helped create. As in Taiwan, so in Korea industrial growth had been built on technology diffused by Japan. Furthermore, Japan's dependence on imported energy had meant a nasty economic shock when oil prices shot up in the 1970s. Yet none of this seemed for a long time to affect its progress. Japanese exports to the United States in 1971 were worth $6 billion; by 1984, that total had grown tenfold. By the end of the 1980s Japan was the world's second largest economic power in terms of GDP. As its industrialists turned to advanced information technology and biotechnology, and talked of running down car manufacturing, there appeared no reason to think that it had lost its power of disciplined self-adaptation.

FOREIGN POLICY

Greater strength had already meant greater responsibilities. The withdrawal of American direction was logically rounded off in 1972 when Okinawa (one of the first of its overseas possessions to be reacquired) was returned to Japan, a large American base there notwithstanding. There remained the question of the Kuriles, still in Russian hands, and of Taiwan, in the possession of the Chinese nationalists and claimed by the Chinese communists, but

Japanese attitudes on all these matters remained – no doubt prudently – reserved. There was also the possibility that the question of Sakhalin might be reopened. All such issues began to look much more susceptible to revisions or at least reconsideration in the wake of the great changes brought to the Asian scene by Chinese and Japanese revival. The Sino-Soviet quarrel gave Japan more freedom for manoeuvre, both towards the United States, its erstwhile patron, and towards China and Russia. That too close a tie with the Americans might bring embarrassment became clearer as the Vietnam War unrolled and political opposition to it grew in Japan. Its freedom was limited, in the sense that all three of the other great powers of the area were by 1970 equipped with nuclear weapons (and Japan, of all nations, had most reason to know their effect), but there was little doubt that Japan could produce them within a relatively brief time if it had to. Altogether, the Japanese stance had the potential to develop in various directions; in 1978 the Chinese vice-president visited Tokyo. Indisputably, Japan was once more a world power.

Industry in Japan employs one-third of the active population and is based on a structure in which huge ultramodern complexes co-exist with small family businesses. The motor industry, of which this Nissan factory forms a part, is one of the world's largest for utility vehicles and second only to the United States for saloon cars.

INDIA

IF THE TEST OF A NATION'S STATUS as a world power is the habitual exercise of decisive influence, whether economic, military or political, outside its own geographical area, then by the 1980s India was not a world power. This is perhaps one of the surprises of the second half of the twentieth century. India moved into independence with many advantages enjoyed neither by other former European dependencies, nor by Japan in the aftermath of defeat. It had taken over in 1947 an effective administration, well-trained and dependable armed forces, a well-educated élite, thriving universities (some seventy of them), had much international benevolence and goodwill to draw upon, a substantial infrastructure undamaged by the war and, soon, the advantages of Cold War polarization to exploit. The country also had to face poverty, malnutrition and major public health problems, but so did China. By 1980 the contrast between them was very visible; the streets of Chinese cities were by 1970 filled by serviceably (though drably) dressed and well-nourished people, while those of India still displayed horrifying examples of poverty and disease.

INTERNAL DIVISIONS

In considering India's poor development performance it is easy to be pessimistically selective. There were sectors where growth was substantial and impressive. But such achievements are overshadowed by the fact that economic growth was followed closely by population increase; most Indians remained little better off than those who had welcomed independence in 1947.

It has been argued that to have kept India together at all was a great achievement, given the country's fissiparous nature and potential divisions. Somehow, too, a democratic

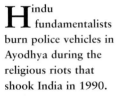

Hindu fundamentalists burn police vehicles in Ayodhya during the religious riots that shook India in 1990.

electoral order was maintained, even if with qualifications, and peaceful changes of government occurred as a result of votes cast. Even India's democratic record looked less encouraging after 1975 when the prime minister (and Nehru's daughter), Mrs Gandhi, proclaimed a state of emergency and the imposition of presidential rule akin to that of viceroys in the old days (one of the two Indian communist parties supported her). This was followed, it is true, by her loss of the elections in 1977 and her judicial exclusion briefly from office and parliament the following year, which could be thought a healthy symptom of Indian constitutionalism. But on the other side of the balance were the recurrent resorts to the use of presidential powers to suspend normal constitutional government in specific areas and a flow of reports of the brutality of police and security forces towards minorities. It was an ominous symptom of reaction to the dangers of division that in 1971 an orthodox and deeply conservative Hindu party made its appearance in Indian politics as the first plausible threat to the hegemony of Congress and held office for three years. That hegemony persisted, nonetheless.

DYNASTIC POLITICS

Forty years after independence, Congress was more visibly than ever not so much a political party in the European sense as an India-wide coalition of interest groups, notables and controllers of patronage, and this gave it, even under the leadership of Nehru, for all his socialist aspirations and rhetoric, an intrinsically conservative character. It was never the function of Congress, once the British were removed, to bring about change, but rather to accommodate it. This was in a manner symbolized by the dynastic nature of Indian

India has been torn in recent decades by political infighting between the Congress Party and the Janata Party, border conflicts with Pakistan and religious struggles. Prime Minister Indira Gandhi was assassinated in 1984. She is pictured here with her son Rajiv, who was himself assassinated during the election campaign of 1991.

government. Nehru had been succeeded as prime minister by his daughter, Mrs Gandhi (who had begun her divergence from his wishes by setting aside his request that no religious ceremony should accompany his funeral) and she was to be followed by her son, Rajiv Gandhi. When he was blown up by an assassin (he was not in office at the time), Congress leaders at once showed an almost automatic reflex in seeking to persuade his widow to take up the leadership of the party. In the 1980s, though, there were signs that dynasticism might not prove viable much longer. Sikh particularism brought itself vividly to the world's notice in 1984 with the assassination of Mrs Gandhi (once more prime minister), after the Indian army had carried out an attack on the foremost shrine of Sikh faith at Amritsar. In the next seven years, more than 10,000 Sikh militants, innocent bystanders, and members of the security forces were to be killed. Fighting with Pakistan over Kashmir, too, broke out again in the later part of the decade. In 1990 it was officially admitted that 890 people had died that year in Hindu–Muslim riots, the worst since 1947.

THE LEGACIES OF INDIA'S PAST

Once again, it is difficult not to return to the banal reflection that the weight of the past

For several months in 1984 armed Sikh extremists occupied the Golden Temple at Amritsar. The Indian army eventually laid siege to the building for three days, killing the extremists' leader, and leaving the 220-year old Sikh temple in ruins.

was very heavy in India, that no dynamic force emerged to throw it off and that modernity arrived slowly and patchily. As memories of pre-independence India faded, the reassertion of Indian tradition was always likely. Symbolically, when the moment for independence had come in 1947 it had been at midnight, because the British had not consulted the astrologers to provide an auspicious day and a moment between two days had therefore to be chosen for the birth of a new nation: it was an assertion of the power of Indian ways which were to lose little of their force in the next forty years. Partition had then redefined the community to be governed in much more dominantly Hindu terms. By 1980 the last Indian civil service officer recruited under the British had already retired. India lives still with a conscious disparity between its ingrafted Western political system and the traditional society on which that has been imposed. For all the great achievements of many of its leaders, devoted men and women, the entrenched past, with all that means in terms of privilege, injustice and inequity, still stands in India's way. Perhaps those who believed in its future in 1947 simply failed to recognize how difficult and painful fundamental change must be – and it is not for those who have found it hard to accomplish much less fundamental change in their own society to be supercilious about that.

THE ISLAMIC WORLD

INDIA'S NEIGHBOUR PAKISTAN turned more consciously to Islamic tradition and so soon found itself sharing in a movement of renewal which was visible across much of the Muslim world. Not for the first time, Western politicians had again to recall that Islam was strong in lands stretching from Morocco in the west to China in the east. Indonesia, the largest Southeast Asian country, Pakistan, Malaysia and Bangladesh between them contained nearly half the world's Muslims. Beyond those countries and the lands of the Arabic culture, both the Soviet Union and Nigeria, the most populous African country, also had large numbers of Muslim subjects (as long ago as 1906, the tsarist government of Russia had been alarmed by revolution in Iran because of its possibly disturbing effect on its own Muslim peoples). But new perceptions of the Islamic world took time to appear. Well into the 1970s the rest of the world tended to be obsessed by the Arab countries of the Middle East, and especially the oil-rich among them, when it thought of Islam much at all.

THE COLD WAR AND ISLAM

The world's limited perception of the Islamic states was also for a long time obscured and confused by the perspectives of the Cold War. The shape of that conflict sometimes blurred into older frameworks, too; to some observers a traditional Russian desire for influence in the area seemed to be a strand in Soviet policy now nearer satisfaction than at any time in the past. The Soviet Union had by 1970 a worldwide naval presence rivalling that of the United States and established even in the Indian Ocean. Following British withdrawal from Aden in 1967, that base had been used by the Russians with the concurrence of the South Yemen government. All this was taking place at a time when further south, too, there had been strategic setbacks for the Americans. The coming of the Cold War to the Horn of Africa and the former Portuguese colonies – especially the conflict in Angola – had added significance to events taking place further north.

THE MIDDLE EAST

Soviet policy, in a longer perspective, does not appear to have benefited much within the Muslim world from the notable disarray of American policy in the mid-1970s in the Middle East. Egypt had by then fallen out with Syria and had turned to the United States in the hope of making a face-saving peace with Israel. When in 1975 the General Assembly of the United Nations denounced Zionism as a form of racism and granted the PLO "observer" status in the Assembly, Egypt was inevitably more isolated from other Arab states. By this time, the PLO's activity across the northern border was not only harassing Israel, but also was driving Lebanon, once a bastion of Western values and now a PLO sanctuary, into ruin and disintegration. In 1978 Israel invaded southern Lebanon in the hope of ending the PLO raids. Although the

Muslim worshippers outside a mosque in Lahore, Pakistan, offer prayers during the first day of the Eid ul-Fitr religious festival in October 2006. People traditionally visit the homes of their relatives and friends during Eid ul-Fitr, which marks the end of the holy month of Ramadan.

The faithful reach out to touch the Iranian religious and revolutionary leader Ayatollah Khomeini (1900–1989), on his return to Tehran in February 1979 after 15 years in exile. Khomeini quickly set up an Islamic republic and imprisoned or executed those who opposed the new régime.

non-Islamic world applauded when the Israeli and Egyptian prime ministers met in Washington the following year to agree a peace providing for Israel's withdrawal from Sinai, the Egyptian three years later paid the price of assassination by those who felt he had betrayed the Palestinian cause.

The limited settlement between Israel and Egypt owed much to President Jimmy Carter, the Democratic candidate who had won the American presidential election of 1976. American morale was by then suffering from setbacks other than those in the Middle East. The Vietnam War had destroyed one president and his successor's presidency had been built on the management of American defeat and the 1973 settlement (and it was soon clear how little that settlement was worth). There was in the background, too, the fear many Americans shared of the rising strength of the USSR in ballistic missiles. All this affected American reactions to an almost wholly unforeseen event in 1979, the overthrow of the shah of Iran. This not only dealt a damaging blow to the United States, but also revealed a potentially huge new dimension to the troubles of the Middle East and the volatility of Islam.

THE IRANIAN REVOLUTION

Long the recipient of American favour as a reliable ally, in January 1979 the shah of Iran was driven from his throne and country by a coalition of outraged liberals and Islamic conservatives. An attempt to secure constitutional government soon collapsed as popular support rallied to the Islamic faction. Iran's traditional ways and social structure had been dislocated by a policy of modernization in which the shah had followed – with less caution – his father Reza Khan. Almost at once, there emerged a Shi'ite Islamic republic,

led by an elderly and fanatical cleric. The United States quickly recognized the new régime, but unavailingly. It was tarred with guilt by association, as the patron of the former shah and the outstanding embodiment of capitalism and Western materialism. It was small consolation that the Soviet Union was soon undergoing similar vilification by the Iranian religious leaders, as a second "Satan" threatening the purity of Islam. Some Americans were encouraged, though, when the particularly ferocious Ba'ath régime in Iraq, already viewed with favour for its ruthless execution and pursuit of Iraqi communists, fell out with the new Iran in a conflict inflamed (in spite of Ba'athist secularism) by the traditional animosity of Mesopotamian Sunni and Persian Shi'ite Muslims. It was in July 1979 that Saddam Hussein took over as president in Baghdad, and that looked encouraging to the CIA: it was thought that he was likely to offset the Iranian danger in the Gulf.

ANTI-WESTERN FEELING

The Iranian revolution implied more than just the American loss of a client state. Even though a coalition of grievances had made possible the overthrow of the shah, a speedy reversion to archaic tradition (strikingly, in the treatment of women) showed that more than a ruler had been repudiated. The new Iranian Islamic republic, although specifically Sh'ite, made universal claims; it was a theocracy where right rule stemmed from right belief, somewhat in the style of Calvin's Geneva. It was also an expression of a rage shared by many Muslims worldwide (especially in Arab lands) at the onset of secular Westernization and the failure of the promise of modernization. In the Middle East, as nowhere else, nationalism, socialism and capitalism had failed to solve the region's problems – or at least to satisfy the passions and appetites they had aroused. Muslim "fundamentalists", as they came to be called, thought that Mustafa Kemal Atatürk, Reza Khan and Gamal Abdel Nasser had all led their peoples down the wrong road. Islamic societies had successfully resisted the contagion of atheistic communism, but to many Muslims the contagion of Western culture to which so many of their leaders had looked for a century or more now seemed even more threatening. Paradoxically, the Western revolutionary notion of capitalist exploitation helped to feed this revulsion of feeling.

One of the most obvious effects of the Islamic revolution has been the change in women's clothing. These Iranian women, gathered in Masala Square in Tehran, have exchanged Western dresses for chadors.

ISLAMIC FUNDAMENTALISM

The roots of Islamic fundamentalism (to use that unsatisfactory blanket term) were varied and very deep. They could tap centuries of struggle against Christianity. They were refreshed from the 1960s onwards by the obviously growing difficulties of outsiders (including the USSR) in imposing their will on the Middle East and Persian Gulf, given their Cold War divisions. There was the mounting evidence for many Muslim Arabs that the Western principle of nationality advocated since the 1880s as an organizational remedy for the instability that followed Turkish decline had not worked; only too evidently, the wars of the Ottoman succession were not over. A favourable conjunction of embarrassments for the West was made more promising still by the recent revelation of the potency of the oil factor. But then there was also, since 1945, the growing awareness of pious Muslims that Western commerce, communications and the simple temptations offered to those rich with oil, were more dangerous to Islam than any earlier (let alone purely military) threat had been. This made for strain and uneasiness.

This was not all that fostered division. Sunni and Shi'ite hostility went back centuries. In the post-1945 period, the Ba'ath socialist movement, which inspired many Muslims and which was nominally entrenched in Iraq, had become anathema to the Muslim Brotherhood, which deplored the "godlessness" of both sides even in the Palestinian quarrel. Popular sovereignty was a goal fundamentalists rejected; they sought Islamic control of society in all its aspects, so that, before long, the world began to be used to hearing that Pakistan forbade mixed hockey, that Saudi Arabia punished crime by stoning to death and amputation of limbs, that Oman was building a university in which men and women students were to be segregated during lectures – and much, much more. By 1980, radical Islamists were powerful enough to secure their goals in some countries. Even students in a comparatively "Westernized" Egypt had already by 1978 been voting for them in their own elections, while some of the girls in medical school were refusing to dissect male corpses and demanded a segregated, dual system of instruction.

THE RADICALS' REJECTION OF STATE STRUCTURES

To put so-called "fundamentalist" attitudes in perspective (and at first sight it is not obvious to Western eyes why student "radicals" should happily espouse such obviously reactionary causes), they have to be understood in the context of a long absence within Islam of any state or institutional theory such as that of the West. Even in orthodox hands, and even if it delivered some desirable goods, the state as such is not self-evidently a legitimate authority in Islamic thought – and, on top of that, the very introduction of state structures in Arab lands since the nineteenth century had been in imitation, conscious or unconscious, of the West. Youthful radicalism, which had tried and found wanting the politics of left-wing socialism (or what was thought to be that, and was in any case another Western import) felt that no intrinsic value resided in states or nations; it looked elsewhere, and that, in part, explains the efforts shown first in Libya, and then in Iran, to arrive at new ways of legitimating authority. Whether the age-old Islamic bias against public institutions and towards tribalism and the brotherhood of Islam can be sustained remains to be seen. Even that brotherhood, after all, has to recognize that most Muslims in the world do not understand Arabic.

In 1969, young army officers led by Captain Muammar Gaddafi (b.1942) staged a military coup in Libya, overthrowing King Idris and establishing the Libyan Arabic Republic, an Islamic state with socialist and nationalist leanings. Gaddafi, who promoted himself to the rank of colonel, is accused of supporting terrorist revolutionary groups around the world, and oil-rich Libya has been involved in several clashes with the West.

While there is much potential for disorder, internecine conflict and even international danger in parts of the Islamic world, it is too tempting to simplify and misinterpret; the Islamic world is not culturally homogeneous. No more than the mythological "West" denounced in the 1980s by popular preachers in the mosques can Islam be identified convincingly as a coherent, discrete, neatly bordered civilization. Like the "West" it is an abstraction, occasionally a useful shorthand for expository purposes. Many Muslims, including some of a religious cast of mind, seek a footing in two worlds, committed in a measure to both Western and Islamic ideals. Each world represents a historical centre of dynamism, a source of energies, but this looks truer of Western civilization, however defined, than of any possible reading of Islam.

As for the disturbing violence of politics in many Arab states, it is often the outcome of a simple polarization between repressive authoritarianism on the one hand and the radical wave on the other. In the 1980s both Morocco and Algeria were to find their domestic order thus troubled. The situation was made the more dangerous and explosive by demography. The average age of most Islamic societies is said to be between fifteen and eighteen, and they are growing at very fast rates. There is just too much youthful energy and frustration about for the outlook to be promising for peace.

HOSTAGE-TAKING AND ITS IMPLICATIONS

This helps to explain why, soon after the Iran revolution, students in Tehran worked off some of their exasperation by storming the American embassy and seizing diplomats and others as hostages. A startled world suddenly found the Iranian government supporting the students, taking custody of the hostages and endorsing the students' demands for the return of the shah to face trial. President Carter could hardly have faced a more awkward situation, for at that moment American policy in the Islamic world was above all preoccupied with a Soviet intervention in Afghanistan. A severance of diplomatic relations with Iran and the imposition of economic sanctions were the first responses. Then came an attempted rescue operation, which failed dismally. The unhappy hostages were in the end to be recovered by negotiation (and, in effect, a ransom: the return of Iranian assets in the United States, which had been frozen at the time of the revolution), but the humiliation of the Americans was by no means the sole or even the major importance of the episode. Besides its wide policy repercussions, the retention of the hostages was a symbolic moment. It was a shock (registered in a unanimous vote of condemnation at the

UN) to the convention, evolved first in Europe and then developed over more than three centuries throughout the civilized world, that diplomatic envoys should be immune from interference. The Iranian government's action announced that it was not playing by the accepted rules. That was a blatant rejection of "civilized" assumptions, which forced some in the West to wonder for the first time what else Islamic revolution might imply.

FRUSTRATIONS

THE 1980s WERE TO bring startling changes, but few in the Middle East, where, as the decade began, they had seemed likely. Instead, a fundamental stagnation seemed to hang over the region. Tension had been high there in 1980, as it had been for years, and so were the hopes of most interested parties about resolving the problems presented by Israel's appearance as a successor state to the Ottoman empire in Palestine. Except perhaps among a minority of Israelis, these hopes were to be gravely disappointed. For a time, it had looked as if the Iranian revolution might transform the rules of the game played hitherto and some had indeed hoped so. Ten years later, though, it would still be very difficult to say what it had actually changed outside Iran, or what was the true significance of the uproar in the Islamic world that it had provoked. What had looked for a time like an Islamic resurgence could also be seen as merely one of the recurrent waves of puritanism which have from time to time across the centuries stimulated and regenerated the faithful. Clearly, too, tension owed much to circumstance; Israel's occupation of the third of Islam's holy places in Jerusalem had suddenly enhanced the sense of Islamic

A ticker-tape parade is held in New York City in 1981 in honour of the American hostages, following their eventual release by Iran after 444 days in captivity.

The Soviet army displays its nuclear missiles in Moscow's Red Square in a May Day parade, which was characteristically used as a show of strength.

solidarity. Yet the attack by Iraq on Iran in 1980 led to a bloody war lasting eight years and costing a million lives. Whatever else might have been behind it, it also mattered in that conflict that Iraq was Sunni, Iran Shi'ite. Once more, Islamic peoples were divided along ancient lines as well as by contemporary issues.

THE SUPERPOWERS

A CENTRAL REALITY OF international politics was about to reassert itself. For all the dramatic changes since the Cuban crisis, the American republic was still in 1980 one of only two states whose might gave them unquestioned status as (to use an official Soviet definition) "the greatest world powers, without whose participation not a single international problem can be solved". This participation in some instances would be implicit rather than explicit, but it was a fundamental datum of the way the world worked. History, moreover, has no favourites for long. Although some Americans had been frightened by Soviet strength after the Cuban missile crisis, there were plentiful signs by the early 1970s that the Soviet rulers were in difficulties. They had to face the truism that Marxism itself proclaimed, that consciousness evolves with material conditions. Two results, among others, of real but limited relaxation in Soviet society were an evident dissidence, trivial in scale but suggesting a growing demand for greater spiritual freedom, and a less explicit, but real, groundswell of opinion that further material gains should be forthcoming. The Soviet Union nevertheless continued to spend colossal sums on armaments (about a quarter of its GDP in the 1980s). Yet these could hardly suffice, it appeared. To carry even this burden, Western technology, management techniques and, possibly, capital, would be needed. What change might follow on that was debatable, but that there would be change was certain.

THE FUNDAMENTALS OF DÉTENTE

However, by 1980 there had grown even stronger the most compelling tie between the two superpowers. For all the huge effort by the Soviet Union to give itself greater nuclear striking power over the United States, superiority at such a level is a somewhat notional matter. The Americans, with their gift for the arresting slogan, concisely summed up the situation as MAD; that is to say, both countries had the capacity to produce "Mutually Assured Destruction", or, more precisely, a situation in which each of two potential combatants had enough striking power to ensure that even if a surprise attack deprived it of the cream of its weapons, what remained would be sufficient to ensure a reply so appalling as to turn an opponent's cities into smoking wildernesses and leave its armed forces capable of little but attempting to control the terrorized survivors.

This bizarre possibility was a great conservative force. Even if madmen (to put the matter simply) are occasionally to be found in seats of power, Dr Johnson's observation that the knowledge that you are to be hanged concentrates the mind wonderfully is applicable to collectivities threatened with disaster on this scale: the knowledge that a blunder may be followed by extinction is a great stimulus to prudence. Here may well lie the most fundamental explanation of a new degree of cooperation which had already been shown in the 1970s by the United States and the Soviet Union in spite of their specific quarrels. A 1972 treaty on defensive missile limitation had been one of its first fruits; it owed something to a new awareness on both sides that science could now monitor infringements of such agreements (not all military research made for an increase of tension). In the following year talks began on further arms limitations, while another set of discussions began to explore the possibility of a comprehensive security arrangement in Europe.

THE HELSINKI AGREEMENTS

In return for the implicit recognition of Europe's post-war frontiers (above all, that between East and West Germany), the Soviet negotiators had finally agreed in 1975 at Helsinki to increase economic intercourse between eastern and western Europe and to sign a guarantee of human rights and political freedom. The last was, of course, unenforceable. Yet it may well have had more importance than the symbolic gains of frontier recognition to which the Soviet negotiatiors had attached much significance. Western success over human rights was not only to prove a great encouragement to dissidents in communist Europe and Russia, but side-stepped old restraints on what had been

The Red Army pulls out of Afghanistan in 1989. The USSR lost 15,000 men in the war against the Islamic fundamentalist Mujahidin guerrillas, in which they remained embroiled for nine difficult years. Three years after the withdrawal of Soviet troops, Afghanistan's Marxist régime was toppled by Muslim forces.

Ronald Reagan campaigning for election as president in 1980. After successfully winning and then holding office (1981–1989) to much greater effect than expected by his critics, Reagan was able to ensure another Republican election success when his vice-president, George H.W. Bush, followed him in the presidency (1989–1993).

deemed interference in the internal affairs of communist states. Gradually, there began to arise public criticisms that were in the end to help to bring about change in eastern Europe. Meanwhile, the flow of trade and investment between the two Europes began almost at once to increase, though also very slowly. It was the nearest approach so far to a general peace treaty ending the Second World War, and it gave the Soviet Union what its leaders most desired, assurance of the security of the territorial settlement that was one of the major spoils of victory in 1945.

For all that, Americans were very worried about world affairs as 1980, the year of a presidential election, approached. Eighteen years before, the Cuban crisis had shown the world that the United States was top dog. It had then enjoyed superior military strength, the (usually dependable) support of allies, clients and satellites the world over, and the public will to sustain a world diplomatic and military effort while grappling with huge domestic problems. By 1980, many of its citizens felt the world had changed and were unhappy about it. When the new Republican president, Ronald Reagan, took office in 1981, his supporters looked back on a decade of what seemed increasing American powerlessness. He inherited an enormous budgetary deficit, disappointment over what looked like recent advances by Soviet power in Africa and Afghanistan, and dismay over what was believed to be the disappearance of an American superiority in nuclear weapons enjoyed in the 1960s.

NEW MIDDLE EAST ISSUES

In the next five years President Reagan was to restore the morale of his countrymen by remarkable (even if often cosmetic) feats of leadership. Symbolically, on the day of his inauguration, the Iranians released their American hostages, the close of a humiliating and frustrating episode (many Americans believed the timing of the release to have been stage-managed by the new administration's supporters). But this was by no means the end of the troubles the United States faced in the Middle East and the Gulf. Two fundamental difficulties did not go away – the threat posed to international order in that area while Cold War attitudes endured, and the question of Israel. The war between Iran and Iraq was evidence of the first danger, many people

thought. Soon, the instability of some Arab countries became more obvious. Ordered government virtually disappeared in the Lebanon, which became battleground terrain disputed by bands of gunmen patronized by the Syrians and Iranians. As this gave the revolutionary wing of the PLO an even more promising base for operation than in the past, Israel took to increasingly violent and expensive military operations on and beyond her northern borders. There followed in the 1980s a heightening of tension and ever more vicious Israeli–Palestinian conflict. More alarming still to Americans, Lebanon had descended further into an anarchy in which, following the arrival of United States marines, bombs exploded at the American embassy and its marines' barracks, killing over 300 people in all.

The United States was not alone in being troubled by these enduring ills. When the Soviet Union sent its soldiers to Afghanistan in 1979 (where they were to stay bogged down for most of the next decade), Iranian and Muslim anger elsewhere was bound to affect Muslims inside the Soviet Union. Some thought this a hopeful sign, believing the growing confusion of the Islamic world might induce caution on the part of the two superpowers, and perhaps lead to less unconditional support for their satellites and allies in the region. This mattered most, of course, to Israel. Meanwhile, the more alarming manifestations and rhetoric of the Iranian revolution made some think that a true conflict of civilizations was beginning. Iran's aggressive puritanism, though, also caused shivers among conservative Arabs and in the oil-rich kingdoms of the Gulf – above all, Saudi Arabia. There were indeed numerous signs of what looked like spreading sympathy for the radical reactionaries of the Iranian revolution in other Islamic countries. Fundamentalists murdered the president of

Egypt in 1981. The government of Pakistan continued to proclaim (and impose) its Islamic orthodoxy, and winked at assistance to the anti-communist rebels in Afghanistan (although uniquely among Islamic countries it had by the end of the decade accepted a woman as prime minister, and even, in 1989, rejoined the British Commonwealth).

NORTH AFRICA

More alarming evidence of radical Islamic feeling as the decade advanced became apparent in North Africa, less importantly in the bizarre sallies and pronouncements of the excited dictator of Libya (Colonel Gaddafi called upon other oil-producing states to stop supplying the United States while one-third of Libyan oil continued to find a market there, and in 1980 briefly "united" his country to Ba'athist Syria) than in Algeria. That country had made a promising start after winning its independence, but by 1980 its economy was flagging, the consensus which had sustained the independence movement was crumbling, and emigration to look for work in Europe seemed the only outlet available for the energies of many of its young men. In the 1990 Algerian elections, an Islamic fundamentalist party won a majority of votes for the first time in any Arab country. In the previous year a military coup in the Sudan had brought a military and militant Islamic régime to power there that at once suppressed the few remaining civic freedoms of the people of that unhappy land.

Nonetheless, for all the attractions of Islamic radicalization, there were plentiful signs by 1990 that moderate and conservative Arab politicians were antagonized enough for indigenous opposition to the fundamentalists sometimes to be effective. It remains hard to believe, even in the light of the World Trade Center attack, that sufficient leverage is available to the would-be revolutionaries, even

Members of the Islamic fundamentalist Taliban militia use force to ensure that the inhabitants of Kabul attend Friday prayers at the mosque in 1990. The Taliban have attempted to impose the rigid disciplines of sharia law (the sacred law of Islam) on the areas of Afghanistan under their control.

after setting aside both such political realities and deeper questions about the feasibility of successful Islamic revolution, when so many of its would-be supporters still sought, unknowingly, to realize goals of power and modernization systematically incompatible with Islamic teaching and custom. Libya could destabilize other African countries and arm Irish terrorists, but achieved little else. Because of preoccupations with changing circumstances elsewhere, the old Soviet-American rivalry was decreasingly available for exploitation. All that was left for the fundamentalists to look to were two potentially rich countries, Iraq and Iran, and for most of the 1980s they were fatally entangled in a costly struggle with one another.

SADDAM HUSSEIN

There was also growing evidence that the ruler of Iraq, patronized by the Americans and the major troublemaker of the Middle East, was only tactically and pragmatically a supporter of militant Islam. Saddam Hussein was a Muslim by upbringing, but led a formally secular Ba'athist régime actually based on patronage, family and the self-interest of soldiers. He sought power, and technological modernization as a way to it, and there is no evidence that the welfare of the Iraqi people ever concerned him. When he launched his war on Iran, the prolongation of the struggle and evidence of its costs were greeted with relief by other Arab states – notably the other oil-producers of the Gulf – because it appeared at the same time to pin down both a dangerous bandit and the Iranian revolutionaries whom they feared. It was, however, less pleasing to them that the war distracted attention from the Palestinian question and unquestionably made it easier for Israel to deal with the PLO.

Saddam Hussein (1937–2006) became president of Iraq in 1979. In 1980 he declared war on Iran, with the aim of liquidating the Iranian revolution: the conflict lasted until 1988. While final peace negotiations were still under way Hussein invaded Kuwait in August 1990. This provoked the brief Gulf War, involving a multinational UN force, in which Iraq was defeated. He was overthrown in 2003 and eventually executed in 2006 after being found guilty of crimes against civilians.

THE INVASION OF KUWAIT

During nearly a decade of alarms and excursions in the Gulf, some of which raised the spectre of further interference with Western oil supplies, incidents seemed at times to threaten a widening of armed conflict, notably between Iran and the United States. Meanwhile, events in the Levant embittered the stalemate there. Israel's continuing occupation of the Golan Heights, its vigorous operations in Lebanon against Palestinian guerrilla bands and their patrons, and its government's encouragement of further Jewish immigration (notably from the USSR) all helped to buttress it against the day when it might once again face united Arab armies. At the end of 1987, however, there came the first outbreaks of violence among Palestinians in the Israeli-occupied territories. They persisted and grew into an intermittent but what would prove enduring insurrection, the *intifada*. The PLO, despite winning further international sympathy by officially recognizing Israel's own right to exist, was nonetheless in a disadvantaged position in 1989, when the Iran–Iraq war finally ended. In the following year Ayatollah Khomeini died and there were signs that his successor might be less adventurous in support of the Palestinian and the fundamentalist Islamic causes.

During the Iran–Iraq war, the United States had favoured Iraq, in part because of American exaggeration of the fundamentalist threat. When, nevertheless, the Americans found themselves at last face-to-face at war in the Gulf with a declared enemy, it was with the Iraqis, not the Iranians. In 1990, after making a generous peace with Iran, Saddam Hussein took up an old border dispute with the sheikdom of Kuwait. He had also quarrelled with its ruler over oil quotas and prices. It is not easy to believe in the reality of these grievances; whatever they may have meant symbolically to Hussein himself, what seems to have moved him most was a simple determination to seize the immense oil wealth of

Kuwait. During the summer of 1990, his threats increased. Then, on 2 August, the armies of Iraq invaded Kuwait, and in a few hours subdued it.

There followed a remarkable mobilization of world opinion against Iraq in the UN. Hussein sought to play both the Islamic and the Arab cards by confusing the pursuit of his own predatory ambitions with Arab hatred for Israel. Demonstrations of support for him in the streets of Middle Eastern cities proved of very low value. Only the PLO and Jordan spoke up for him officially. No doubt to his shocked surprise, Saudi Arabia, Syria and Egypt actually became improbable partners in the alliance that rapidly formed against him. Almost equally surprising to him must have been the acquiescence of the USSR in what followed. Most startlingly of all, the United Nations Security Council produced (with overwhelming majorities) a series of resolutions condemning Iraq's actions and, finally, authorizing the use of force against her to ensure the liberation of Kuwait.

An American soldier passes dead Iraqi troops during the Gulf War. It had quickly become clear that the Iraqi army stood no chance of victory against the United Nations forces of around half a million drawn from several nations.

Iraqi anti-aircraft fire is used against American and allied bombers attacking Baghdad in January 1991. The Gulf War, called "the mother of all battles" by Iraq's president Saddam Hussein, had more than a human cost – it also caused severe environmental damage. The water in the region was polluted by millions of litres of spilt oil and the Iraqi leader ordered his troops to set fire to the oil wells.

THE GULF WAR

Huge forces were assembled in Saudi Arabia under American command. On 16 January 1991 they went into action. Within a month Iraq gave in and withdrew, after suffering considerable loss (allied losses were insignificant). Yet this humiliation did not obviously threaten Hussein's survival. Once again, the turning-point in the Middle East that so many had longed for had not arrived; it satisfied neither Arab revolutionaries nor Western would-be peace-makers. The greatest losers were the PLO, and Israel was the greatest gainer. Arab military success at Israel's expense was inconceivable for the near future. Yet at the end of yet another war of the Ottoman succession, the Israel problem was still there. Syria and Iran had already before the Kuwait crisis begun to show signs that, for their own reasons, they intended to make attempts to get a negotiated settlement, but whether one would emerge was another matter, even if, for the United States, it was clearly more of a priority than ever to get one.

Perhaps it was an advance that the alarming spectre of a radical and fundamentalist pan-Islamic movement had been somewhat dissipated. For practical purposes, Arab unity had again proved a mirage. For all the distress, unrest and discontent with which many Muslims faced the West, there was virtually no sign that their resentments could yet be coordinated in an effective response, and less than ever that they would do without the subtly corrosive means of modernization that the West offered. Almost incidentally, too, crisis in the Gulf appeared to reveal that the oil weapon had lost much of its power to damage the developed world, for, though one had been feared, there was no new oil crisis. Against this background, in 1991 American diplomacy at last persuaded Arabs and Israelis to take part in a conference on the Middle East.

THE END OF DÉTENTE

Great transformations had meanwhile taken place elsewhere and they also bore upon events in the Middle East. Yet they did so only because they shaped what the USA and USSR did there. In 1979–80, the American presidential election campaign had deliberately been used to exploit the public's fears of the Soviet Union. Unsurprisingly, this reawoke animosity at the official level; the conservative leaders of the Soviet Union showed renewed suspicion of the trend of United States policy. It seemed likely that promising steps towards disarmament might be swept aside – or even worse. In the event, the American administration came to show a new pragmatism in foreign affairs, while, on the Soviet side, internal change was to open the way to greater flexibility.

One landmark was the death, in November 1982, of Leonid Brezhnev, Khrushchev's successor and for eighteen years general secretary of the Party. His immediate replacement (the head of the KGB) soon died and a septuagenarian, whose own death followed even more quickly, succeeded him before there came to the office of general secretary in 1985 the youngest member of the Politburo, Mikhail Gorbachev – he was fifty-four. Virtually the whole of his political experience had been of the post-Stalin era. His impact upon his country's, and the world's, history was to be remarkable.

MIKHAIL GORBACHEV

The conjunction of forces that propelled Gorbachev to the succession remains unclear. The KGB, presumably, did not oppose his promotion, and his first acts and speeches were orthodox (although he had already, in the previous year, made an impression on the British prime minister as someone with whom business could be done). He soon articulated a new political tone. The word "communism" was heard less in his speeches and "socialism" was reinterpreted to exclude egalitarianism (though from time to time he reminded his colleagues that he *was* a communist). For want of a better term, his aim was seen by many foreigners as liberalization, which was an inadequate Western

Mikhail Gorbachev

In March 1985, Mikhail Gorbachev (b.1931) became secretary-general of the Soviet Communist Party. At the 27th Party Congress in February 1986, Gorbachev announced the revision of some of the state policies that were increasingly being questioned by the Soviet people. Gorbachev seemed to want to construct a constitutional democratic state based on upholding the law and respect for civil liberties. This implied the separation of the Party from the State and the removal of the effective centre of government from the Party to the State. This in turn meant the end of the one-party system. In foreign affairs, Gorbachev launched what has been called the "détente offensive", signing arms limitations treaties in an attempt to reduce the huge drain the Soviet military put on the economy.

Mikhail Gorbachev is pictured during the 1990 meeting of the Soviet Council, the year before his resignation.

attempt to sum up two Russian words he used a great deal: *glasnost* (openness) and *perestroika* (restructuring). The implications of the new course were to be profound and dramatic, and for the remainder of the decade Gorbachev grappled with them.

What actually happened in due course cannot have been in his mind when he started out. No doubt he saw that without radical change the Soviet economy could not provide the USSR with its former military might, sustain its commitments to its allies, improve (however slowly and modestly) living standards at home and assure continuing self-generated technological advance. Accordingly, Gorbachev seemed to seek to avoid the collapse of Communism by opening it to his own vision of Leninism, above all by making it a more pluralist system, and by involving the intelligentsia in the political nation. The possible implication of such a change of course seems to have been concealed even from himself. Essentially it was an admission that the seventy years' experiment in arriving at modernization through socialism had failed. Neither freedom nor material well-being had been forthcoming. And now the costs were becoming too heavy to bear.

A NEW SOVIET-AMERICAN RELATIONSHIP

Ronald Reagan was soon drawing dividends on Gorbachev's assumption of office. That Soviet policy was reflecting a new tone soon became clear in their meetings. Discussion of arms reduction was renewed. Agreements were reached on other issues (and this was made easier in due course by the decision of the Soviet leadership in 1989 to withdraw their forces from Afghanistan). In America's domestic politics, a huge and still growing

budgetary deficit and a flagging economy, which would under most presidents have produced political uproar, were for years virtually lost to sight in the euphoria produced by a seeming transformation of the international scene. The alarm and fear with which the "evil empire" (as Reagan had termed it) of the Soviet Union was regarded by many Americans began to evaporate a little.

Optimism and confidence grew as the USSR showed signs of growing division and difficulty in reforming its affairs, while Americans were promised wonders by their government in the shape of new defensive measures in space. Though thousands of scientists said the project was unrealistic, the Soviet government could not face the costs of competing with that. Americans were heartened, too, in 1986 when American bombers were launched from England on a punitive mission against Libya, whose unbalanced ruler had been supporting anti-American terrorists (significantly, the Soviet Union expressed less concern about this than did many western Europeans). President Reagan was less successful, though, in convincing many of his countrymen that more enthusiastic assertions of American interests in Central

Gorbachev and Reagan sign the Treaty of Washington in December 1988, ending the stockpiling of intermediate-range nuclear missiles. This represented the beginning of the end of the arms race and was also influential in moving several regional conflicts towards viable solutions.

Pictured is the National Textile Industry building in Sibernik in the former Yugoslavia. Before the outbreak of civil war, the country had a centrally planned economy, with around a quarter of the workforce employed in state-run manufacturing industries.

America were truly to their advantage. But he remained remarkably popular; only after he had left office did it begin to dawn that the decade had been one in which the gap between rich and poor in the USA had widened even further.

In 1987, the fruits of negotiation on arms control were gathered in an agreement over intermediate-range nuclear missiles. In spite of so many shocks and its erosion by the emergence of new foci of power, the nuclear balance had held long enough for the first stand-downs by the superpowers. They, at least, if not other countries seeking to acquire nuclear weapons, appeared to have recognized that nuclear war, if it came, held out the prospect of virtual extinction for mankind, and were beginning to do something about it. In 1991 there were to be further dramatic developments as the USA and USSR agreed to major reductions in existing weapons stocks.

EASTERN EUROPE

THE SUPERPOWER stand-down was a huge change in the international scene and cannot be disentangled from its many consequences for other nations. They have to be artificially separated to be expounded, but one could not have occurred without the other. At the end of 1980 there had been little reason to believe that the peoples of eastern Europe and the Soviet Union were about to see changes unmatched since the 1940s. What was already clear was that the European communist countries were finding it harder and harder to keep up even the modest growth rates they had attained. Comparison with the market economies of the non-communist world had become more and more unfavourable to them, although this did not appear to suggest any challenge to the verdicts of 1953, 1956 and 1968, or to Soviet power in eastern Europe. The carapace provided by the Warsaw Pact seemed still to be capable of containing the social and political change crystallized over thirty years (and more, if one counts the great unwilled changes of the Second World War and its aftermath).

At first sight, communist Europe had a striking uniformity. In each country the Party was supreme; careerists built their lives around it as, in earlier centuries, men on the make clustered about courts and patrons, or the Church. In each (and above all in the USSR itself) there was also an unspeakable and unexaminable past, which could not be mourned or deplored, whose weight hung over intellectual life and political discussion – so far as there was any – corrupting them. In the eastern European economies, investment in heavy industrial and capital goods had produced a surge of early growth (more vigorous in some than in others) and then an international system of trading arrangements with other communist countries, dominated by the USSR and rigidified by aspirations to central planning. It had also given rise to appalling environmental and public health problems, hidden as matters of state security. Increasingly and obviously, a growing thirst for consumer goods could not be met; commodities taken for granted in western Europe remained luxuries in the eastern European countries, cut off as they were from the advantages of international economic specialization. On the land, private ownership had been much reduced by the middle of the 1950s, usually to be replaced by a mixture of cooperatives and state farms, although within this broadly uniform picture different patterns had later emerged. In Poland, for instance, something like four-fifths of Polish farmland was eventually to return to private exploitation even under communist government. Output remained low, however; most eastern European countries could achieve agricultural yields only half to three-quarters those of the European Community. By the 1980s all of them, in varying degree, were economic invalids, with the possible exception only of the GDR. Even there, per capita GDP stood at only $9,300 a year in 1988, against $19,500 in the Federal Republic. Other problems, too, were arising. Investment in infrastructure was falling and so was their share of world trade. Debts in hard currency were piling up. In Poland alone, real wages fell by a fifth in the 1980s.

A NEW DIVERSITY

What had come to be called the "Brezhnev doctrine" (after a speech made in Warsaw in 1968) said that developments within Eastern bloc countries might require – as in Czechoslovakia that year – direct Soviet intervention to safeguard the interests of the USSR

When Alexander Dubcek (1921–1992) became first secretary of the Czechoslovakian Communist Party in January 1968, he began to implement liberalizing reforms, for which he received widespread public support. Observers in Moscow, however, quickly lost their patience with the "Prague Spring"; in August they sent 650,000 Warsaw Pact troops to bring the country back into line. Here, a young man stands on one of the invading tanks, brandishing the Czech flag in defiance.

Solidarity leader Lech Walesa addresses striking Polish workers at the Lenin Shipyard in Gdansk in 1980.

and its allies against any attempts to turn socialist economies back towards capitalism. Yet Brezhnev had also been interested in pursuing *détente* and his doctrine reflected realism about possible dangers to international stability presented by breakaway developments in communist Europe. Such dangers could be limited by drawing clearer lines. Since then, internal change in Western countries, steadily growing more prosperous, and with memories of the late 1940s and the seeming possibility of subversion far behind them, had removed some grounds for East–West tension. By 1980, after revolutionary changes in Spain and Portugal, not a dictatorship survived west of the Trieste–Stettin line and democracy was everywhere triumphant. For thirty years, the only risings by industrial workers against their political masters had been in East Germany, Hungary, Poland and Czechoslovakia – all communist countries.

After 1970, and even more after the Helsinki agreement of 1975, as awareness of contrasts with western Europe grew in the Eastern bloc, dissident groups emerged, survived and even strengthened their positions, in spite of severe repression. Gradually, too, a few officials or economic specialists, and even some Party members, began to show signs of scepticism about the effects of detailed centralized planning and there was increasing discussion of the advantages of utilizing market mechanisms. The key to fundamental change, nevertheless, lay elsewhere. There was no reason to believe that change was possible in any of the Warsaw Pact countries if the Brezhnev doctrine held, and had the Soviet army standing behind it.

THE POLISH CRISIS

The first clear sign that this might not always be so came in the early 1980s, in Poland. The Polish nation had retained, to a remarkable degree, a collective integrity by following its priests and not its rulers. The Roman Catholic Church had an enduring hold on the affections and minds of most Poles as the embodiment of the nation, and was often to speak for them – all the more convincingly once a Polish pope had been enthroned. The Church did so on behalf of workers who protested in the 1970s against economic policy, and condemned their ill-treatment. This, together with the worsening of economic conditions, was the background to 1980, a year of crisis for Poland. A series of strikes then came to a head in an epic struggle in the Gdansk shipyard. From them emerged a new and spontaneously organized federation of trades unions, "Solidarity". It added political demands to the economic goals of the strikers; among them, one for free and independent trades unions. Solidarity's leader was a remarkable, often-imprisoned, electrical union leader, Lech Walesa, a devout Catholic, closely in touch with the Polish hierarchy. The shipyard gates were decorated with a picture of the pope and open-air masses were held by the strikers.

The world was surprised to see, so soon, a shaken Polish government, troubled as strikes spread, making historic concessions. The crucial step was that Solidarity was recognized as an independent, self-governing trade union. Symbolically, regular broadcasting of the Catholic mass on Sundays was also conceded. But disorder did not cease, and with the winter, the atmosphere of crisis deepened. Threats were heard from Poland's neighbours of possible intervention; forty Soviet divisions were said to be ready in the GDR and on the Russian frontier. But the dog did not bark in the night; the Soviet army did not move and was not ordered by Brezhnev to do so, nor by his successors in the turbulent years that followed. It was the first sign of changes in Moscow that were the necessary premise of what was to follow in eastern Europe in the next ten years.

When John Paul II (1920–2005) – the first non-Italian pope since 1523 – visited Poland in June 1979 his tacit expression of the Church's opposition to communism boosted the strength of the Polish Solidarity movement. Here, the pontiff is pictured during a 1991 visit with Lech Walesa, the Solidarity leader who had become president of Poland at the end of the previous year.

FROM MARTIAL LAW TO DEMOCRACY

In 1981, tension continued to rise in Poland, the economic situation worsened, but Walesa strove to avert provocation. On five occasions the Russian commander of the Warsaw Pact forces came to Warsaw. On the last, the Solidarity radicals broke away from Walesa's control and called for a general strike if emergency powers were taken by the government. On 13 December, martial law was imposed. There followed fierce repression and possibly hundreds of deaths. But the Polish military's actions also made Russian invasion unnecessary. Solidarity went underground, to begin seven years of struggle, during which it became more and more evident that the military government could neither prevent further economic deterioration, nor enlist the support of the "real" Poland, the society alienated from communism, for the régime. A moral revolution was taking place. As one Western observer put it, Poles began to behave "*as if* they lived in a free country"; clandestine organizations and publications, strikes and demonstrations, and continuing ecclesiastical condemnation of the régime sustained what was at times an atmosphere of civil war.

Although after a few months the government cautiously abandoned formal martial law, it still continued to deploy a varied repertoire of overt and undercover repression. Meanwhile, the economy declined further, Western countries offered no help and little sympathy, and, after 1985, the change in Moscow began to produce its effects. Yet the climax came only in 1989, for Poland her greatest year since 1945, as it was for other countries, too, thanks to her example. It opened with the régime's acceptance that other political parties and organizations, including Solidarity, had to share in the political process. As a first step to true political pluralism, elections were held in June in which some seats were for the first time freely contested. Solidarity swept the board in them. Soon the new parliament denounced the German-Soviet agreement of August 1939, condemned the 1968 invasion of Czechoslovakia, and set up investigations into political murders committed since 1981.

CHANGES IN EASTERN EUROPE

In August 1989 Walesa announced that Solidarity would support a coalition government; the communist diehards were told by Gorbachev that this would be justifiable (and some Soviet military units had already left the country). In September a coalition dominated by Solidarity and led by the first non-communist prime minister since 1945 took office as the government of Poland. Western economic aid was soon promised. By Christmas 1989 the Polish People's Republic had passed from history and, once again, the historic republic of Poland had risen from its grave. Even more important, Poland, it soon turned out, led eastern Europe to freedom. The importance of

The Soviet economy had collapsed by the winter of 1990–91. Food shortages struck in the cities. Here, Muscovites queue for the few available products in a Russian supermarket in which most of the shelves are bare. Ration books were eventually introduced in some areas, but they had to be withdrawn owing to a lack of supplies.

events there had quickly been grasped in other communist countries, whose leaders were much alarmed. In varying degree, too, all eastern Europe was exposed to a new factor: a steadily increasing flow of information about non-communist countries, above all through Western television (which was especially easily received in the GDR). More freedom of movement, more access to foreign books and newspapers had imperceptibly advanced the process of criticism elsewhere as in Poland. In spite of some ludicrous attempts to go on controlling information (Romania still required that typewriters be registered with the authorities), a change in consciousness was underway.

ECONOMIC AND POLITICAL PROBLEMS

This change appeared to be underway in Moscow too. Gorbachev had come to power during the early stages of these developments. Five years later, it was clear that his assumption of office had released revolutionary institutional change in the Soviet Union too, first, as power was taken from the Party, and then as the opportunities so provided were seized by newly emerging opposition forces, above all in republics of the Union which began to claim greater or lesser degrees of autonomy. Before long, it began to look as if he might be undermining his own authority. Paradoxically, too, and alarmingly, the economic picture looked worse and worse. It became clear that a transition to a market economy, whether slow or rapid, was likely to impose far greater hardship on many – perhaps most – Soviet citizens than had been envisaged. By 1989 it was clear that the Soviet economy was out of control and running down. As ever in Russian history, modernization had been launched from the centre to flow out to the periphery through

authoritarian structures. But that was precisely what could not now be relied upon to happen, first because of the resistance of the *nomenklatura* and the administration of the command economy, and then, at the end of the decade, because of the visibly and rapidly crumbling power of the centre.

By 1990 much more information was available to the rest of the world about the true state of the Soviet Union and its people's attitudes than ever before. Not only were

As the economy of the Soviet Union collapsed, food shortages brought desperation to the cities, particularly in winter. Here, a pensioner picks over the contents of a rubbish dump on the outskirts of Moscow in search of food.

The Soviet Union and its successors

The USSR made its last territorial acquisitions during the Second World War, when it annexed territories along its western borders, including the three Baltic states. From 1945, the integrity of the 15 republics that made up the USSR was threatened only by minor border conflicts with China. Following the collapse of communism in 1991, the former Soviet republics declared their independence. All except the Baltic states are now members of the Commonwealth of Independent States.

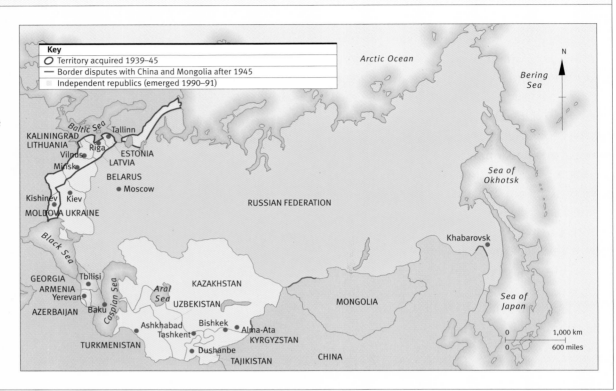

there now overt experiences of popular feeling, but *glasnost* had also brought to the Soviet Union its first surveys of public opinion through polls. Some rough-and-ready judgements could be made: the discrediting of the Party and *nomenklatura* was profound, even if it had not by 1990 gone so far as in some other Warsaw Pact countries; more surprisingly, the long unprotesting Orthodox Church appeared to have retained more respect and authority than other institutions of the Marxist-Leninist *ancien régime*.

But it was clear that economic failure hung everywhere like a cloud over any liberalizing of political processes. Soviet citizens as well as foreign observers began to talk by 1989 of the possibility of civil war. The thawing of the iron grip of the past had revealed the power of nationalist and regional sentiment when excited by economic collapse and opportunity. After seventy years of efforts to make Soviet Man, the USSR was revealed to be a collection of peoples as distinct as ever from one another. Some of its fifteen republics (above all Latvia, Estonia and Lithuania) were quick to show dissatisfaction with their lot. They were to lead the way to political change. Azerbaijan and Soviet Armenia posed problems that were complicated by the shadow of Islamic unrest that hung over the whole Union. To make matters worse, some believed there was a danger of a military coup; commanders who were as discontented by the Soviet failure in Afghanistan as some American soldiers had been by failure in Vietnam were talked about as potential Bonapartes.

THE CENTRE FAILS

The signs of disintegration multiplied, although Gorbachev succeeded in clinging to office and, indeed, in obtaining formal enhancements of his nominal powers. But this had the disadvantage of focusing responsibility for failure, too. A declaration of the Lithuanian parliament that the annexation of 1939 was invalid led, after complicated negotations, to Latvia and Estonia also claiming their independence, though in slightly different terms. Gorbachev did not seek to revoke the fact of secession, but won agreements that the Baltic republics should guarantee the continued existence of certain practical services to the USSR. This proved to be the beginning of the end for him. A period of increasingly rapid manoeuvring between reforming and conservative groups, allying himself first to one and then, to redress the balance, to the other led by the end of 1990, to compromises that looked increasingly unworkable. Connivance at repressive action by the soldiers and KGB in Vilnius and Riga early in the new year did not stem the tide. For by

then, nine Soviet republics had already either declared they were sovereign or had asserted a substantial degree of independence from the Union government. Some of them had made local languages official and some had transferred Soviet ministries and economic agencies to local control. The Russian republic – the most important – set out to run its own economy separately from that of the Union. The Ukrainian republic proposed to set up its own army. In March, elections led Gorbachev once more back to the path of reform and a search for a new Union treaty, which could preserve some central role for the state. The world looked on, bemused.

THE BERLIN WALL COMES DOWN

The Polish example had growing prestige in other countries as they realized that an increasingly divided, even paralysed, USSR

East Berliners clamber on the defunct Berlin Wall in November 1989. The collapse of the communist German Democratic Republic and German reunification were to follow the bringing down of the wall – events that had been unthinkable less than a decade earlier.

would not (perhaps could not) intervene to uphold its creatures in the communist party bureaucracies of the other Warsaw Pact countries. This shaped what happened in them after 1986. The Hungarians had moved almost as rapidly in economic liberalization as the Poles, even before overt political change, but their most important contribution to the dissolution of communist Europe came in August 1989. Germans from the GDR were then allowed to enter Hungary freely as tourists, although their purpose was known to be to present themselves as asylum-seekers to the embassy and consulates of the Federal Republic. When Hungary's frontiers were completely opened in September (and Czechoslovakia followed suit) a flow became a flood. In three days 12,000 East Germans crossed from these countries to the West. The Soviet authorities remarked that this was "unusual". For the GDR it was the begin-ning of the end. On the eve of a

carefully planned and much-vaunted celebration of forty years' "success" as a socialist country, and during a visit by Gorbachev (who, to the dismay of the German communists, appeared to urge the East Germans to seize their chance), riot police had to battle with anti-government demonstrators on the streets of East Berlin. The government and Party threw out their leader, but this was not enough. November opened with huge demonstrations in many cities against a régime whose corruption was becoming evident; on 9 November came the greatest symbolic act of all, the breaching of the Berlin Wall. The East German Politburo caved in and the demolition of the rest of the wall followed.

FREE ELECTIONS

More than anywhere else, events in the GDR showed that even in the most advanced

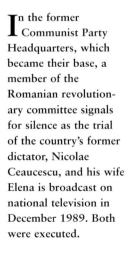

In the former Communist Party Headquarters, which became their base, a member of the Romanian revolutionary committee signals for silence as the trial of the country's former dictator, Nicolae Ceaucescu, and his wife Elena is broadcast on national television in December 1989. Both were executed.

communist countries there had been over the years a massive alienation of popular feeling from the régime. The year 1989 had brought it to a head. All over eastern Europe, it was suddenly clear that communist governments had no legitimacy in the eyes of their subjects, who either rose against them or turned their backs and let them fall down. The institutional expression of this alienation was everywhere a demand for free elections, with opposition parties freely campaigning. The Poles had followed their own partially free elections, in which some seats were still reserved to supporters of the existing régime, with the preparation of a new constitution; in 1990, Lech Walesa became president. A few months earlier, Hungary had elected a parliament from which emerged a non-communist government. Soviet soldiers began to withdraw from the country. Czechoslovakian elections in June 1990 produced a free government and it was soon agreed that the country was to be evacuated of Soviet forces by May 1991. In none of these elections did the former communist politicians get more than 16 per cent of the vote. Voting in Bulgaria was less decisive – there, the contest was won by Communist Party members turned reformers, calling themselves socialists.

GERMAN REUNIFICATION

In two countries, events turned out differently. Romania underwent a violent revolution (ending in the killing of its former communist dictator) after a rising in December 1989, which revealed uncertainties about the way ahead and internal divisions ominously foreshadowing further strife. By June 1990 a government some believed still to be heavily influenced by former communists had turned on some of its former supporters, now critics, and crushed student protest with the aid of

vigilante squads of miners at some cost in lives and in disapproval abroad. The GDR was the other country where events took a special turn. It was bound to be a special case, because the question of political change was inescapably bound up with the question of German reunification. The breaching of the wall revealed that not only was there no political will to support communism, there was no will to support the GDR either. A general election there in March 1990 gave a majority of seats (and 48 per cent of the vote) to a coalition dominated by the Christian Democrat party – the ruling party of the western German Federal Republic. Unity could no longer be in doubt; only the procedure and timetable remained to be settled.

In July the two Germanys joined in a monetary, economic and social union. In October they united politically, the former territories of the GDR becoming provinces of the Federal Republic. The change was momentous, but no serious alarm was openly expressed, even in Moscow, and Gorbachev's acquiescence was his second great service to the German nation. Yet alarm there must

In the East German town of Magdeburg, a mixed crowd turns out to listen to the chancellor of the FDR Helmut Kohl make a speech during his election campaign in early 1990.

Soldiers from a British battalion of the United Nations peace-keeping forces are seen on patrol in Bosnia during the civil war in the former Yugoslavia.

have been in the USSR. The new Germany would be the greatest European power to the west. Russian power was now in eclipse as it had not been since 1918. The reward for Gorbachev was a treaty with the new Germany promising economic help with Soviet modernization. It might also be said, by way of reassurance to those who remembered 1939–45, that the new German state was not just an older Reich revived. Germany was now shorn of the old eastern German lands (had, indeed, formally renounced them) and was not dominated by Prussia as both Bismarck's empire and the Weimar Republic had been. More reassuring still (and of importance to western Europeans who felt misgivings), the Federal Republic was a federal and constitutional state seemingly assured of economic success, with nearly forty years' experience of democratic politics to build on, and embedded in the structures of the EC and NATO. It was given the benefit of the doubt by western Europeans with long memories, at least for the time being.

YUGOSLAVIA

At the end of 1990, the condition of what had once seemed an almost monolithic East European bloc already defied generalization or brief description. As some former communist countries (Czechoslovakia, Poland, Hungary) applied to join the EC, or got ready to do so (Bulgaria), observers speculated about a potentially wider degree of European unity than ever before. More cautious judgments were made by those who noted the virulent emergence of new – or re-emergence of old – national and communal division. Over all of eastern Europe there gathered the storm clouds of economic failure and the turbulence they might bring. Liberation might have come, but it had come to peoples and societies of very different levels of sophistication and development, and with very different historical origins. Prediction was unwise and just how unwise became clear in 1991. In that year a jolt was given to optimism over the prospects of peaceful change when two of the constituent republics of Yugoslavia announced their decision to separate from the federal state.

The "Kingdom of Serbs, Croats and Slovenes", which had appeared as the successor to Serbia and Montenegro in 1918, had as long ago as 1929 changed its name to "Yugoslavia" in an attempt to obliterate old divisions, accompanied by the establishment of a royal dictatorship. But the new kingdom was always seen by too many of its subjects, Serbs and non-Serbs alike, as essentially a manifestation of an old historical dream of a "Greater Serbia". When its second king,

Alexander, had been assassinated in 1934 in France, it was by a Macedonian aided by Croats, acting with the support of the Hungarian and Italian governments. The bitterness of the country's own divisions had thus soon attracted outsiders to dabble in its affairs, and local politicians to seek outsiders' support; Croatians subsequently declared their own independence as a state when German troops arrived in 1941.

Besides its demographic and communal diversity (the Yugoslav census of 1931 distinguished Serbo-Croats, Slovenes, Germans, Magyars, Romanians, Vlachs, Albanians, Turks, "Other Slavs", Jews, Gypsies and Italians), Yugoslavia also displayed wide disparities of custom, wealth and economic development. In parts of it, the Middle Ages had barely faded away in 1950, while others were modern, urbanized and contained significant industry. Overall, what were mainly agricultural economies had been impoverished by fast-growing populations. Yet Yugoslav politics between the German wars had turned out to be in the main about a Croat–Serb antagonism and this was deepened by wartime atrocity and struggle in a three-sided civil war between Croatians, the mainly Serb communists (themselves led by the Croatian, Tito) and Serb royalists after 1941. This struggle began with a campaign of terror and ethnic cleansing launched against the two million Serbs of the new Croatia (which included Bosnia and Herzegovina). It ended in communist victory in 1945, and the effective containment of nationalities by Tito's dictatorship within a federal structure; this seemed to solve the old Bosnian and Macedonian problems and was likely to be able to ward off the territorial ambitions of outsiders. Forty-five years later and ten years after Tito's death, however, the old issues suddenly revealed themselves to be still vigorously alive.

FRAGMENTATION OF YUGOSLAVIA

In 1990 the Yugoslav federal government's attempts to deal with its economic troubles were accompanied by accelerating political fragmentation. Democratic self-determination finally undid the Tito achievement as Yugoslavs of different nationalities began to cast about to find ways of filling the political vacuum left by the collapse of communism. Parties formed representing Serb, Croat, Macedonian and Slovene interests as well as one in favour of the Yugoslav idea and the federation itself. Soon, all the republican governments, except that of Macedonia, rested on elected majorities, and new national minority parties had even begun to make themselves heard inside the individual republics. Croatian Serbs declared their own autonomy and there was bloodshed in the Serbian province of Kosovo, four-fifths of whose inhabitants were Albanian. The proclamation of an independent republic there had been a major symbolic affront to the Serbians – as well as of concern to the Greek and Bulgarian governments, whose predecessors had not ceased to cherish

Macedonian ambitions since the days of the Balkan wars. In August, sporadic fighting by air and ground forces had begun between Serbs and Croats. Precedents for intervention by outsiders did not ever seem promising – though different views were held by different EC countries – and prospects for it became even less attractive when the USSR in July uttered a warning about the dangers of spreading local conflict to the international level. By the end of the year Macedonia, Bosnia-Herzegovina and Slovenia had all, like Croatia, declared themselves independent.

THE SOVIET COUP OF 1991

The Soviet warning over Bosnia was the last diplomatic *démarche* of the régime. It was soon eclipsed by a much more momentous event. On 19 August a still mysterious attempt was made to set aside Mikhail Gorbachev by *coup d'état*. It failed, and three days later he was again in occupation of the presidency. Nonetheless, his position was not the same; continual changes of side in a search for compromise had ruined his political credibility. He had clung too long to the Party and the Union; Soviet politics had taken a further lurch forward – in the eyes of many, towards disintegration. The circumstances of the coup had given an opportunity, which he seized, to Boris Yeltsin, the leader of the Russian republic, the largest in the Union. The army, the only conceivable threat to his supporters, did not move against him. He now appeared both as the strong man of the Soviet scene, without whose concurrence nothing could be done, and as a possible standard-bearer for a Russian chauvinism that might threaten other republics.

While foreign observers waited to understand, the purging of those who had supported or acquiesced in the coup was developed into a

Demonstrators shake hands with a tank driver during the failed coup of August 1991 in Moscow. Gorbachev's opponents took advantage of his absence from the capital to stage their coup. They believed they would be welcomed by the masses, who would applaud a "return to normality", but they had badly misjudged the public mood and only a small minority supported the attempt.

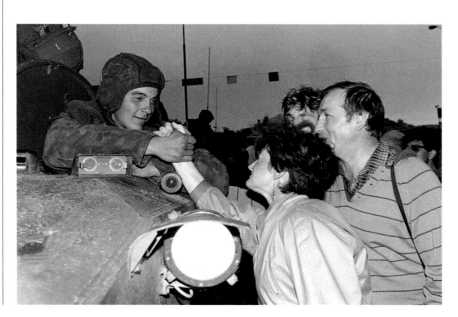

determined replacement of Union officialdom at all levels, the redefinition of roles for the KGB and a redistribution of control over it between the Union and the republics. The most striking change of all was the demolition of the Communist Party of the Soviet Union, which began almost at once. Almost bloodlessly, at least to begin with, the huge creation which had grown out of the Bolshevik coup of 1917 was coming to an end. There seemed at first good grounds for rejoicing over that, although it was not clear that nothing but good would follow.

THE SOVIET COLLAPSE

The fact that the end of communism might bring mixed blessings became clearer as the year came to an end. With the decision to abandon price controls in the Russian republic in the near future, it seemed likely that not only inflation unparalleled since the earliest days of the Soviet system, but also, perhaps, starvation, too, would soon face millions of Russians. In another republic, Georgia, fighting had already broken out between the supporters of the president elected after the first free elections there and the discontented opposition. Dwarfing all such facts, though, was the end of the giant superpower, which had emerged from the bloody experiments of the Bolshevik revolution. For nearly seventy years and almost to the end it was the hope of revolutionaries around the world, and the generator of military strength that had fought and won the greatest land campaigns in history. Now it dissolved suddenly and helplessly into a set of successor states. The last of the great European multinational empires disappeared when Russian, Ukrainian and Belorussian leaders met at Minsk on 8 December and announced the end of the Soviet Union and the establishment of a new

"Commonwealth" of Independent States (CIS). On 21 December 1991 a gathering of representatives from eleven of the former republics met briefly at Alma-Ata to confirm this. They agreed that the formal end of the Union would come on the last day of the year. Almost immediately, Gorbachev resigned.

It was the climax of one of the most startling and important changes of modern history. Of what lay ahead, no one could be sure – except that it would be a period of danger, difficulty and, for many former Soviet citizens, misery. In other countries, politicians were rarely tempted to express more than caution over the turn events had taken. There was too much uncertainty ahead. As for the USSR's former friends, they were silent. A few of them had deplored the turn of events earlier in the year so much that they had expressed approval or encouragement for the failed coup of August. Libya and the PLO did so because any return to anything like Cold War groupings was bound to arouse their hopes of renewed possibilities of international manoeuvre that had been constricted first by *détente* between the USA and USSR and then by the growing powerlessness of the latter.

Georgia, the birthplace of Stalin, became independent from the Soviet Union on 9 April 1991. In the 1990s attempts by ethnic groups in Abkhazia and South Ossetia to secede from Georgia resulted in bloody civil wars. Here, women from South Ossetia carry photographs of their husbands and sons who they claim were shot by Georgian soldiers.

5 OPENINGS AND CLOSURES

Well before the collapse of the USSR, it was clear that very little of the world would remain wholly unaffected by what was happening in Europe. Immediately, the end of the Cold War reawoke old questions of identity throughout that continent and beyond, as well as presenting new ones. Peoples began to see themselves and others afresh in the light of what soon turned out to be for some a chilly dawn; some nightmares had blown away, but only to reveal troubled landscapes. Fundamental questions about identity, ethnicity and religion could again be asked, and some of these questions were disturbing. Once again new determining circumstances were emerging in world history.

Almost incidentally, not only had one half of Europe's security arrangements disappeared with the Warsaw Pact, but the other half, NATO, had also been subtly changed. The collapse of the USSR, the major potential opponent, had deprived the alliance not only of its main role, but also of the pressure that had shaped it. Like a blancmange in a warm room, it began to sag a little. Even if, as some thought, a revived Russia were to emerge as a new threat at some future date, the disappearance of the ideological struggle would mean that potential opponents would have to think in new ways about it. There were soon excommunist countries seeking to join NATO. Poland, Hungary and the Czech Republic joined up in 1999, and Slovenia, Slovakia, Bulgaria, Romania and the Baltic countries followed five years later. In total contravention of the promises US president George H.W. Bush

August 1995 and Croatian Serb refugees move along a motorway near Banja Luka, after the Croatian millitary's Operation Storm in which almost the entire Serb population was forcibly displaced.

had given Mikhail Gorbachev in 1990, NATO had expanded not just up to the borders of the Soviet Union, but beyond them. The alliance had become an instrument for linking most of Europe (minus Russia) to the United States. But the purpose of its military power was by no means clear, even if in the mid-1990s the American government began to look to NATO as a machine for dealing with new European problems, notably in the former Yugoslavia; and for use outside the European area.

NATIONALITY AND ETHNICITY

AFTER THE COLD WAR, the fate of peoples in eastern and southeastern Europe seemed for the first time in the century entirely and evidently in their own hands. Like the old dynastic empires or the extemporizations of the German and Italian dictators in the Second World War, the communist scaffolding of the region had now collapsed. As much buried history re-emerged and more was remembered or invented, what appeared was often discouraging. Slovaks felt restive about their inclusion in Czechoslovakia, but Slovakia itself had a large percentage of Hungarians in its population, as did Romania. Hungarians could now agonize more openly over the treatment of Magyars both north and east of their borders. Above all, old issues escalated rapidly into new violence and crisis in the former Yugoslavia. In 1991, as all former republics of the Yugoslav federal state declared their independence, wars were being fought between local Serbs and the new governments of Croatia and Bosnia-Herzegovina. The Serb minorities were supported by the government in Belgrade, headed by the militant Serb nationalist Slobodan Milosevic, and by the remnants of the Yugoslav federal army.

A Muslim woman from the western Bosnian town of Prijedor cries over the body of a relative, at the cemetery in Prijedor in July 2006. The deceased was one of more than 300 civilian victims of the 1992–95 civil war who had been identified by DNA analysis after the bodies were exhumed from mass graves in the Prijedor area.

The civil war in Bosnia-Herzegovina led to the worst atrocities against civilians in Europe since the end of the Second World War, as the three main ethnic groups – Serbs, Croats, and Muslim Bosniaks – tried to control as much territory as possible, often driving out the other population groups as they advanced. At Srebrenica in 1995 Serb forces massacred several thousand Bosniak civilians, and Serbs besieged the Bosnian capital Sarajevo from 1992 to 1995. Both the EU and the United States were reluctant to intervene, and it was only military setbacks for the Serbs that made an agreement possible at Dayton, Ohio, in December 1995. From being a peaceful mosaic of different ethnic groups, Bosnia-Herzegovina had given rise to the term "ethnic cleansing" – the expulsion by force of people who were defined as enemies. Croatia made use of the decline in Serb military fortunes throughout the region to reclaim Krajina, driving out many of the majority Serb population there. Having gone from one disaster to

Swastikas deface Jewish graves in a recently renovated Dutch cemetery, while the perimeter wall bears the chilling graffiti message "Wir Sind Zuruck" (We Are Back). In recent years Europe has seen a rise in anti-Semitic attacks and vandalism.

another in his so-called "defence" of the Serbs, Milosevic was finally toppled in 2000 after his heavy-handed policy in the Albanian-dominated region of Kosovo had led to NATO intervention against his troops. Fearful of a repetition of the Bosnian atrocities, the Western allies had at last agreed to intervene.

EASTERN EUROPE AFTER THE COLD WAR

Thus, the early 1990s left millions of eastern Europeans facing grave problems and difficulties. Agreement was lacking on legitimating principles and ideas. Insofar as

the region had possessed "modernizing" élites, these, whether effective or not, were usually to be found in the old communist hierarchies. Unavoidably, professionals, managers and experts whose careers had been made within the communist structures continued to govern because there was no one to replace them. Another problem was the fickleness of populations now voting freely as the immediate euphoria of political revolution ebbed. There was nostalgia for the apparent security of the old days. As people cast about for a new basis for the legitimacy of the state, the only plausible candidate often seemed to be the nationalism that had so often bedevilled past politics, sometimes for centuries.

Old tribalisms had quickly resurfaced and imaginary histories were soon turning out to matter as much as what had actually happened in the past.

Some ancient confrontations had, tragically, been brought to an end by the Second World War. In the most horrifying and greatest instance, the Holocaust (as people had come to call the Nazis' attempt to extirpate the Jewish people) had ended the story of eastern Europe as the centre of world Jewry. In 1901 three-quarters of the world's Jews had lived there, mostly in the Russian empire. In those once Yiddish-speaking areas only a little more than 10 per cent of Jews now live. Nearly half of the world's Jews are now to be found in English-speaking countries, and another 30 per cent of them in Israel. In eastern Europe, communist parties anxious to exploit traditional popular anti-Semitism (not least in the Soviet Union) had encouraged emigration by harrying and judicial persecution. In a few countries this virtually eliminated what was left in 1945 of the Jewish population as a significant demographic element. Two hundred thousand Polish Jews surviving in 1945 had soon found themselves again victims of traditional pogrom and harassment and by 1990 those who had not emigrated numbered a mere 6,000. The heart of the old eastern European Jewry had gone.

NATIONALISM IN WESTERN EUROPE

In some western European countries, too, minorities showed a new recalcitrance. Basque separatists terrorized Spain. Walloons and Flemings nagged at one another in Belgium. Northern Ireland was probably the most striking instance. There, Unionist and Nationalist feeling continued throughout the

1990s to block the road to settlement. Anglo-Irish agreement in 1985 had acknowledged the Irish Republic's right to a role in discussion of the future of Ulster and set up new machinery to provide for it. One ceasefire ended tragically after a little less than eighteen months, but when a Labour government came to power at Westminster in 1997 it proved willing to take the important symbolic step of opening direct negotiations with Sinn Fein, the political movement that masked the terrorists of the IRA. Before the end of that year Sinn Fein representatives had been received by the British prime minister in London and in 1998, in cooperation with the Irish government, British initiatives succeeded, against the odds, in winning the acquiescence of the official leaders of Sinn Fein and of the Ulster Unionists in putting to an all-Ireland referendum proposals that went further than ever before in institutionalizing both safeguards for the Nationalist minority in the north and the historic tie of the north with the United Kingdom. This so-called Good Friday Agreement, of course, implied fundamental change in what the sovereignty of the Crown was to mean in the future (and incidentally went much further than the

Russians bearing extreme nationalist and anti-Semitic slogans stage a demonstration in Moscow in early 1990 to protest at the influence of Jews and foreigners and to demand a return to the norms and values of the pre-revolution era.

measures of devolution the British government was contemporaneously introducing in Scotland and Wales). Though the detail was potentially still very divisive, the principles of the new arrangements met with popular approval on both sides of the border. And while the British and Irish governments failed in putting together a Northern Ireland Executive representing all parties – and therefore had to return to direct rule from London – the province was spared the terrorist outrages that had dominated up to 1998.

AN EVER-CLOSER EUROPEAN UNION?

F ROM 1986 the passports issued to citizens of the member states of the EC had carried the words "European Community" as well as the name of the issuing state. In practice, however, the Community faced growing difficulties. Although the main central institutions – the Council of Ministers of Member States, the Commission and the Court of Justice – worked away, they did not do so without contention, while policy – notably over fisheries and transport – provoked well-publicized differences. Fluctuations in exchange rates were another source of awkwardness and institutional bickering, especially after the end of dollar convertibility and the Bretton Woods system in 1971 and the oil crisis. Yet in the 1980s there was solid evidence of encouraging economic success. The USA had resumed in the 1970s its pre-1914 status as a major recipient of foreign investment and two-thirds of what it attracted was European. Western Europe accounted for the largest share of world trade, too. Outsiders became keen to join an organization that offered attractive bribes to the poor. Greece did so in 1981, and Spain and Portugal in 1986.

THE MAASTRICHT TREATY

The latter turned out to be a decisive year, when it was agreed that a further step should be taken in 1992 to move beyond a mere customs union to a single, integrated, border-free internal market. After difficult negotiations the Maastricht Treaty of December 1991 put in place arrangements for the single European market and a timetable for full economic and monetary union to be achieved not later than 1999. Capital, goods, services and people were to move freely without let or hindrance across national borders at last. Once again, reservations and special arrangements had to be made for the cautious British. Margaret Thatcher's successor as prime minister, John Major, was something of an unknown quantity, but almost at once he found himself upholding his country's position in the

Despite having been at the heart of the European project since its inception, many French voters remain hostile to the surrender of national sovereignty, or the abandonment of it implied by binding supranational treaties, and against the globalization of the world economy – sentiments made clear by these placards in Provence. Maastricht was approved by a tiny majority, and in 2005 some 55% of French voters rejected the European Constitution.

Maastricht negotiations at the head of a party divided over it. The treaty that resulted opened the way to a single currency and an autonomous central bank to regulate it. Maastricht also gave citizenship of the new "European Union" (EU), which replaced the EC, to the nationals of all member states and laid down an obligation on its members to impose certain common standards in work practices and some social benefits. Finally, the treaty extended the area over which EU policy might be made by majority votes. All this looked like a significant accretion of centralized power, although in an effort to reassure the suspicious the treaty also set out agreement to the principle of "subsidiarity", a word rooted in Catholic social teaching; it indicated that there should be limits to the competence of the Commission at Brussels in interfering with the details of national administration. As for agreement over European defence and security policy, this was soon in hopeless disarray thanks to events in Bosnia.

Maastricht raised difficulties in several countries. The Danes rejected it in a referendum the following year. A similar test in France produced only a slim majority in its favour. The British government (notwithstanding special safeguards it had negotiated) was hard-pressed to win the parliamentary vote on the issue. In the governing Conservative Party a split that had appeared was to cripple the party when it next faced the electors. European voters still usually thought of protecting or damaging traditional sectional and national interests and these loomed larger as economic conditions worsened in the early 1990s. But Maastricht was in the end ratified by fifteen member states. Debate continued over allegations of encroachment on the independence of member states by the Commission at Brussels and the comparative fairness or unfairness of individual countries' use or abuse of the Union's rules.

A fishing boat from the Netherlands, laden with its catch, at sea in the English Channel. Overfishing remains a serious problem in European waters – in fact, worldwide – despite the fisheries policies dictated by the European Union; indeed, some critics argue the policies are greatly to blame.

THE EUROPEAN UNION

While the Maastricht process was created in part by the need felt by many member states – and especially France – for a deeper integration into Europe of the new and powerful united Germany, it soon took on a much wider significance. With communism gone in eastern Europe, the need for a truly *European Union* – as the Community called itself after Maastricht – stood out. It is a testimony to the strength of the institutions created over half a century of European integration that the EU managed both to introduce a common currency (the Euro, from 2002), alongside an EU Central Bank, and deeper cooperation on criminal justice, foreign policy, and military affairs, while moving rapidly towards membership for central and eastern Europe. In 1995 the Cold War neutrals Austria, Finland and Sweden joined, while the big step

The redevelopment of the eastern city of Dresden provides a fitting symbol of the reunified Germany. The Baroque Frauenkirche was left in ruins during the Cold War as a reminder by the authorities of the infamous bombing raid and firestorm that razed the city. In the early 1990s Dresdeners launched a successful international appeal to reconstruct the Frauenkirche and in summer 2004 the church itself was completed, although the surrounding Neumarkt area (pictured) is still undergoing sympathetic reconstruction.

eastwards came in 2004, with the accession of ten countries, among them Poland, the Czech Republic, Slovakia, Hungary, and – most astonishingly of all – the former Baltic Soviet republics Estonia, Latvia and Lithuania. In spite of continued disagreement about its constitution, budget, and plans for further expansion, the EU, with its 461 million population, had taken giant steps towards becoming the all-European union that its founders had envisaged.

NEW ECONOMIC REALITIES

Economic circumstances had changed, too. For all its importance, the Common Agricultural Policy (CAP) did not mean what it had meant in the 1960s; in some countries it was evolving from an electoral bribe to large numbers of smallholders to a system of subsidy for fewer, but much richer, agriculturalists. Within the new Union, too, national responses were not what they had been in the 1960s and even later. Germany now provided the driving force and much of the Union's financial support. Chancellor Helmut Kohl's greatest triumph, reunification, had confirmed Germany's natural position as Europe's major power. Yet this had been costly. Germany was driven into deficit on its trade account and dissatisfaction with the terms of reunification began to be heard. As time passed, more was also heard of the danger of inflation, an old nightmare for Germans, and of the load carried by the German taxpayer as former East Germans moved to the west and unemployment rose. Economic recession, indeed, cast long shadows in most member states of the EU in the

1990s, reminding their peoples of disparities and differences of economic strength between them. Everywhere, too, fiscal, budgetary and exchange problems came in the 1990s to undermine the confidence of governments.

There was thus plenty for politicians to take into account. Views were changing everywhere. For the French, for example, the deepest root of the European impulse had always lain in fear of Germany, which their statesmen had sought to tie firmly into, first, the Common Market and, then, the Community. As the German economy grew stronger, though, they had been forced to recognize that it would have the preponderant share in mapping Europe's future shape. De Gaulle's ideal of a Europe of nation-states gave way among Frenchmen to a more federal – that is, paradoxically, more centralizing – view of a Europe consciously built so as to give a maximum of informal and cultural weight in it to France – through, for example, appointments at Brussels. If there were to be a European super-state, France could at least try to dominate it. None the less, the French decision in 1995 to rejoin NATO was a clear break with the ways of de Gaulle.

A SINGLE CURRENCY

The German government after 1990 had soon sought to express its new influence by seeking to befriend its ex-communist neighbours. The rapidity with which German businessmen and investors got to work in those countries and the speed and eagerness of Germany's recognition of newly independent Croatia and Slovenia at the end of 1991 (it was the first country to do so) was far from reassuring to other EU members. How the EU was to expand was bound to be crucial for world history. A democratic and pluralist EU of almost 700 million, stretching from the Arctic Circle to Antalya and from Faro to Kerch, might be one conceivable outcome, but another is a break-up (not necessarily into its national components) of what Union there was. Eventually, the question will appear of whether to attempt to integrate Russia, which is, in spite of its size and its autocratic tradition, undeniably a European country with many of these resources – human and material – that the EU will need for the continued welfare of its citizens.

There has of course been some cultural convergence within the Common Market Community and EU over more than thirty years. Increasing standardizing of consumption, though, owed less to European policy than to shrewder marketing and growing international communication at a popular level (the outcome was often, as in the past, deplored as "Americanization"). And such slow convergence as had been consciously promoted in, for instance, agriculture had

The giant logo of the European Central Bank (ECB) standing in front of its building in Frankfurt. The euro became the official currency for 300 million citizens of the then twelve participating European Union countries (Austria, Belgium, Finland, France, Germany, Greece, Ireland, Italy, Luxemburg, the Netherlands, Portugal and Spain) on 1 January 2002.

been very costly and the CAP understandably irritated non-farming voters. The Union seemed feeble, too, in its handling of external affairs; it blatantly failed the severe tests posed by Yugoslavia's dissolution. Many uncertainties thus still hung over the future of Europe at the beginning of the twenty-first century. Among them was the project of a single European currency. Although the argument for it had always had a predominantly political flavour, it was asserted that great economic benefits would flow from its introduction and that lower prices and lower interest rates would be likely to follow. With equal assurance, it was pointed out that participating states would lose control over important aspects of their economic life. A common currency, in fact, implied further surrender of sovereignty. Politicians brooded over what voters might think when choices had to be made that would bring home to them the consequences of a monetary union. It was not hard to agree, though, that were monetary union to fail, and were enlargement not to take place, the EU could settle back into not much more than a simple customs union.

When Helmut Kohl was defeated in the German elections of November 1998 and Gerhard Schröder, the first socialist chancellor of united Germany took office, this had made no difference to the monetary union goal of the German government. The French government, too, stayed behind it. Denmark and Sweden firmly announced they would not wish to participate. In Britain, the new Labour government of Tony Blair, elected in a landslide vote in 1997, while cautiously positive to further integration, refused to join "until the time was right", and the right time was not to appear during their first ten years in office. But on 1 January 2002, most of the member countries introduced their first shared currency since the age of Charlemagne. In a telling avoidance of

offence to national susceptibilities, the possibilities of great historic names – crowns, florins, francs, marks, thalers and many more – were set aside and the new unit of currency was to be called a "Euro". By the mid-2000s, its notes and coins were the only legal tender among the 300 million citizens of the EU's participating member states, and was even adopted by states and territories *outside* the EU, such as Montenegro and Kosovo.

LIMITS TO EXPANSION?

The difficulties of enlarging the Union were by then much clearer. The longest standing candidate for admission was Turkey, of whom some asked whether it was a "European" country at all since most of its territory lay in Asia and most of its people were Muslim. Worse still, the modernizing Ataturk legacy was under challenge there after a sixty-year ascendancy. Islamists had always resented the régime's traditional secularism. Yet if the test of Europeanness was modernity in institutions (representative government and women's rights, for example) and a certain level of economic development, then Turkey clearly stood with the Europeans rather than with the rest of the Islamic Near East. Turkish treatment of political opposition and minorities (particularly the Kurds) nonetheless met with much disapproval abroad, and the record of the Turkish government as a guardian of human rights was questioned. Turkey thus posed yet again old and unanswerable questions about what Europe really was. Significantly, though, Turkey's old enemy Greece has become one of the key supporters of membership for Ankara, arguing both along economic and political lines, in spite of the unresolved issues over Cyprus (now a member of the EU in its own right).

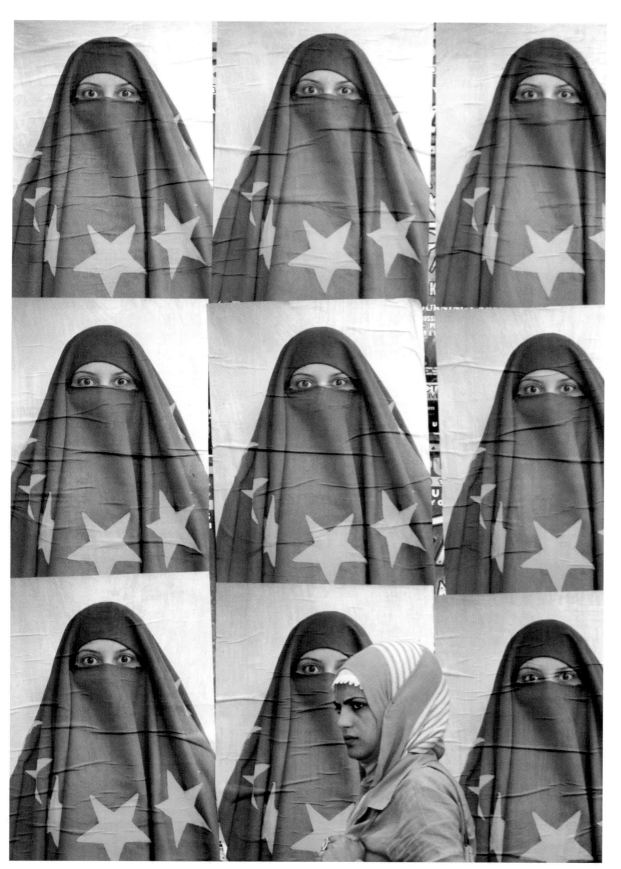

Istanbul, Turkey, where in recent years Islamists have gained ground aginst secular parties. One of the emotive symbols in the battle between Muslim radicalism and Kemalist secularism is the issue of women's headscarves, which have become identified with political Islam. This Turkish woman wearing a headscarf is walking past posters in which a woman is veiled by the European Union flag.

At the end of 2000, in negotiations at Nice, while the principle of further expansion was agreed upon, it was also agreed to change voting qualifications, but France succeeded in hanging on to the same "weighted" voting rights as Germany, now indisputably much the largest and wealthiest member state. Ratification of the Nice treaty had still to be obtained in national parliaments, of course, and the Irish government soon had to face the problem posed by losing a referendum on its proposal; this sent another shock through the system. Agreement at the end of 2001 that a special convention should take up the consideration of the working of EU institutions, and of possible changes in them, only slightly offset this. And when in 2005 referendums in both France and the Netherlands rejected the product of that convention, the somewhat extravagantly termed "European Constitution", the project of further deepening of the integration process seemed, again, to be in deep trouble. But while the popular rejection of the constitution treaty is yet another sign of the European Union still being an enterprise of and by the political élites, much of the content of the constitution will – perhaps for that reason – find its way into EU rules and regulations, even if an amended version of the proposed constitution were not to be brought back for referendums in the countries that have rejected it.

THE FUTURE OF THE EU

To an extent, then, the end of the Cold War seemed at last to have revealed that Europe was more than the geographical expression it had so long seemed to be. Equally, though, there seemed less point than ever in seeking some innate European essence or spirit, let alone a European civilization, the major source of a world civilization though it might

Members of the Jonge Democraten (Young Democrats), affiliated to the social liberal party Democrats 66, campaign in the streets of The Hague on the eve of the 1 June 2005 referendum on the European Constitution in the Netherlands. Despite the Dutch Prime Minister calling on voters to vote yes, the constitution was heavily rejected.

be. It was as ever a collection of national cultures resonating vigorously to their own internal dynamics, for, as the twenty-first century began, there was little sign of a European patriotism able, like the old national allegiances, to stir the emotions of the masses, for all that had been achieved since the Treaty of Rome. Participation by voting in elections for the European parliament had fallen everywhere except in those countries where voting was compulsory. Linguistic chauvinism threatened a new unworkability in the institutions of the Union – whose huge, disordered complexity already baffled those who sought political logic in them and undoubtedly contributed to a larger public sense of boredom with the idea of Europe. But much had been achieved. Above all, the Union was a community of

constitutional democracies and the first successful essay in European integration not based on the hegemony of a single nation. As the twentieth century ended, too, the EU was, even in rising economic gales, in the long run evidently an economic success. Including Switzerland (which, of course, the EU does not), western Europe already accounted for some 75 per cent of world trade (most of it between its own member countries) and 40 per cent of the world's GDP. Its own GDP was in that year larger than that of the United States and more than twice that of Japan. Europe was one of the three prime movers of the world economy that had emerged in the previous fifty years. If Europeans still seemed to worry a lot about where they were going, they were obviously a team many outsiders wished to join.

Crowds in Prague in the Czech Republic celebrate its accession to the European Unon on 1 May 2004, little over a decade since the creation of the state upon the peaceful split of Czechoslovakia into the independent Czech and Slovak republics.

The Oriental Pearl TV Tower, alongside (right) the Bank of China Tower, in the newly developed area of Shanghai known as Pudong. The entire district, opposite Shanghai's older Bund waterfront area, symbolizes the development of China since 1990. Pudong is home to the Lujiazui Finance and Trade Zone and is officially regarded as mainland China's financial and commercial hub.

CHINA: THE NEW SUPERPOWER?

THE YEAR 1989 had left much doubt about the future direction of China. Not only had the ruling Communist Party faced a significant challenge from below, which it could only overcome by the use of raw force; but the economy also seemed to be stumbling, with growth flattening out in many sectors. Deng Xiaoping, the man who had engineered the economic reforms ten years earlier and who, at the age of eighty-five, had returned to the centre of political decision-making as the 1989 crisis grew, now embarked on his last campaign. Visiting the southern provinces in 1992, Deng condemned those who saw political retrenchment as synonymous with economic retrenchment. The reforms had to be intensified, Deng said, and private enterprise should be given more room. By then, the 1989 stagnation was already a thing of the past, and from 1992 on China entered a phase of hyper-growth, with its GDP increasing by more than 10 per cent on average for the next fourteen years.

The explosion of economic growth in China may turn out to be the most important global event of the 1990s. Not only did it create a middle class of more than 200 million people with a purchasing power around the EU average, it also made China into the fourth largest national economy on earth. Most of this growth was in the private sector, but – after much restructuring – there was also some growth in the publicly owned or controlled sector by the early 2000s. China's economic model seemed to combine extreme capitalism with a very important role for the state and even the Communist Party. It blends rampant exploitation of the masses of young men and women who enter into the factories from the countryside with an emphasis on

political control of all companies, including those that are privately owned by Chinese or foreigners. Although gradually spreading north and west, the growth is still heavily concentrated in the south and east, along the coast and by the great rivers, repeating a pattern that has been visible since the earliest dynasties. While becoming a guarantor of regional economic stability, the regime has done little to make itself more accountable to its people through democratic reforms, and – as a result of the lack of transparency – corruption and the misuse of power among officials is rampant. The Communist Party of China seems to have found a development model that works, at least in good times, but it has little to fall back on in terms of legitimacy when times turn bad.

The end of the Cold War also transformed China's foreign relations. The 4,000-plus miles of shared frontier with the former USSR were now replaced for about half that distance by frontiers with the newly independent and much weaker states of Kazakhstan, Kyrgyzstan and Tajikistan. Meanwhile, in the later 1990s, concern over Taiwan, the problem that had long tied together Chinese internal policy and foreign

A lone Chinese man faces death as he tries in vain to block the path of a tank in Tiananmen Square on 5 June 1989. More than 100 student protesters died when the army destroyed their encampment, prompting the international community to impose sanctions on China.

relations, was clearly as alive as ever after nearly five decades in which the seemingly fundamental nature of the original clash between the nationalist regime there and the People's Republic had, in fact, been slightly blurred after the formal closure of American diplomatic relations with the Taiwanese nationalist regime and its subsequent exclusion from the United Nations. Yet in the 1990s, while Beijing still maintained its policy of reuniting Taiwan (like Hong Kong and Macao) to mainland China as a long-term goal, more began to be heard of alleged independence sentiment on the island. Beijing was evidently disturbed, alarm reaching its height during a visit by the president of the Taiwanese republic to the United States in 1995. The ambassador of the People's Republic in Washington was withdrawn and

an official newspaper proclaimed the issue of Taiwan as "explosive as a barrel of gunpowder". It was clear that if Taiwan formally declared itself independent of the mainland an invasion of the island would probably follow.

EAST ASIA AFTER THE COLD WAR

Taiwan, moreover, was only one source of uncertainty and nervousness in East Asia. An increasing instability and volatility was apparent in the region after the Cold War ended, even though these trends did not reach the same levels as in Europe. What the closing of that relatively well-defined and therefore clarifying struggle might mean was at first very hard to see. In Korea, for example, it

A Long March II F rocket carrying a Shenzhou VI spacecraft stands ready in October 2005 at the Jiuquan Satellite Launch Centre in Jiuquan, Gansu, prior to two Chinese astronauts lifting off for a five-day orbital mission to mark China's second manned foray into space.

changed very little, North Korea remaining obstinately locked in a confrontation with the United States and with the Republic of Korea in the south by its rulers' determination to maintain a command economy in virtual isolation. Economic mismanagement, the ending of Soviet aid in 1991 and, it appeared, some straightforward dynastic exploitation of power by the ruling dictator, brought North Koreans to the edge of starvation by early 1998. The North's problems remained unusually specific, detached somewhat from the regional trends, as South Korea could not be. That country was by the mid-1990s an established democratic regime with high growth figures and an impressive involvement in international trade.

A JAPANESE CRISIS?

While all of East and Southeast Asia, China excepted, went through a deep but, for most countries, temporary financial crisis in 1997 and 1998, Japan entered a recession after the Cold War that was to last for more than a decade. The economy often hailed in the 1980s as the world leader in productivity and product development was by the end of the century a shadow of its former self. Property speculation, and huge investment in non-productive activity or sectors generating very small returns, had encumbered its banks and financial institutions with unserviceable debts. The currency weakened sharply; speculation against it was immediate and crippling in a world of financial transactions more rapid than ever before. The prevailing business culture of Japan, firmly embedded as it was in official and financial networks that now proved unable to give decisive leadership, made solutions harder still to achieve as conditions worsened. The Japanese economy became a laggard in international terms, with

Downtown Tokyo in February 2007 and a woman looks at an electronic board of share prices displaying the news that the Nikkei-225 index of leading shares has lost 202.31 points (to 17,344.80) after retreating from a near 10-month closing high. After miraculous economic growth for several decades, Japan's economy suffered in the 1990s from the after-effects of speculative excesses in the stock and real estate markets in the 1980s. Despite government efforts to revive growth, not until 2005 did things really pick up again in Japan.

deflation and unemployment as results. The rapidly shifting governments seemed unable to stem the process, and some of them began pandering to nationalist sentiments to strengthen their authority. The recession in Japan meant that it could not be counted on to help pull the other economies out of their economic difficulties in the late 1990s, and even though the region as a whole was growing again in the early 2000s, some countries – such as Indonesia and the Philippines – did not regain their earlier growth rates. Millions of people from Hokkaido to Bali lost their savings and sometimes their livelihoods in the process.

CHANGES IN SOUTHEAST ASIA

The political shifts in Southeast Asia that followed the crisis were also significant. Authoritarian governments in some countries had exploited public resources in the interests of cronies of those in power and their families. In May 1998, after the Indonesian economy had shrunk by more than 8 per cent since the beginning of the year, and the currency had lost four-fifths of its dollar value, riots drove the president from power. Thirty-two assured years of a firmly controlled, corrupt, but formally "democratic" system came to an end. The successor governments made Indonesia a much more open society, but had little luck with rebuilding the economy. The result was increasing ethnic and religious strife in a country divided as Indonesia was between a large Islamic majority and significant Hindu, Christian and Chinese communities. The second most populous country in the region, Vietnam, moved in the opposite direction, further centralizing its politics while intensifying Chinese-style economic reform, in Vietnam called *doi moi* (Renovation). By the early 2000s Vietnam was the world's second fastest growing economy, but large parts of the country were still very poor and – as in China – the exploitation of the workforce in the name of capitalism with communist characteristics was intense. Altogether, what the extraordinary highs and lows of the East Asian economies had shown in the first decade of the twenty-first century was how integrated the global economy was becoming: economic shifts in Beijing or Jakarta would have an immediate effect on the world, and vice versa.

THE INDIAN SUBCONTINENT

INDIA, LIKE CHINA, DID not at once share the violent financial and economic cycles of many East Asian countries. In this respect, undeniably, past policies favoured it. Congress governments, though moving away somewhat from the socialism of the early years of independence, had long been strongly influenced by protectionist, managed, nationally self-sufficient, even autarkic ideas. The price had been low rates of growth and social conservatism, but with them came also a lower degree of vulnerability to international capital flows than other countries.

In 1996 the Hindu and nationalist Bharatiya Janata Party (BJP) inflicted a major defeat on Congress and became the largest single party in the lower house of parliament. It was not able to sustain its own government, though, and a coalition government emerged that did not survive another (very violent) general election in 1998. This, too, was inconclusive in that no clear parliamentary majority emerged, but the BJP and its allies formed the biggest single group in it. Another coalition government was the outcome, whose Janata supporters soon published an ominously nationalist agenda that announced that "India should be built by Indians". Some found this alarming in a country where

A motorist rides past a propaganda poster in Ho Chi Minh City, Vietnam. Like China, communist one-party rule has seen a command economy being reformed into a market economy at the direction of the state. From 1990 this reform – called Renovation – has delivered high economic growth after decades of stagnation. Vietnam is now one of the most promising emerging markets in Asia.

nationalism, though encouraged by Congress for a century or so, had usually been offset by prudent recognition of the real fissiparousness and latent violence of the subcontinent. Eventually, though, the new government surprised many by avoiding Hindu-nationalist excesses domestically and by stepping up the liberalization of the economy, leading to increased economic growth in some parts of the country. This growth continued under the new Congress-led government that – in another example of India's functioning democracy – surprisingly was voted into office in 2004. The new prime minister, Manmohan Singh – an economist of Sikh origin – stepped up the attempts at opening India's economy and making it more competitive internationally. By the mid-2000s, India seemed to be at the beginning of rapid economic expansion.

Though it seemed consistent with a determination to win domestic kudos by playing the nationalist card, it was nonetheless in the context of the running sore of the old quarrel with Pakistan that the world had to strive to understand the Janata government's decision to proceed with a series of nuclear test explosions in May and June 1998. They provoked the Pakistan government to follow suit with similar tests of its own; both governments were now members of the club of nations acknowledged to have deployable nuclear weapons. Yet larger contexts in which to set this fact (the Indian prime minister pointed out) were those of Indian fear of China, already a nuclear power and remembered by Indians as the victor of the Himalayan fighting of 1962, and a growing sympathy shown by the Pakistan government to Islamic fundamentalist agitation in other countries – notably, Afghanistan, where 1996 had seen the establishment of an intensely reactionary government in Kabul, under a Pakistan-supported faction named "Taliban". Some

gloomily pondered the notion that a Pakistani bomb might also be an Islamic bomb. In any case, there had been a huge setback to the curbing of nuclear proliferation so far achieved; there was universal alarm, ambassadors were withdrawn from Delhi and some countries followed the lead of the United States in cutting off or holding up aid to India. Such action, though, did nothing to deter Pakistan from following India's example. The world, evidently, had not rid itself of the danger of nuclear warfare by ending the Cold War. That danger, too, had now to be understood in a world that some thought much less stable than the 1960s had been and with India–Pakistan relations still bedevilled by the Kashmir issue.

Workers for the Bharatiya Janata Party (BJP), Indian People's Party, display a party flag from the windows of a police vehicle in Bhopal after they were arrested in May 2003 for allegedly forcing shop owners to close their shutter to support a protest against the lack of power supply in the state

A NEW RUSSIA

THE BIGGEST and most important of the CIS states, Russia, elected Boris Yeltsin president of the republic in June 1991 with 57 per cent of the votes cast in the country's first free election since 1917. In November the

Russian soldiers backed up against the wall of the US Embassy in Moscow in a firefight during the storming of the Russian White House in October 1993. When the parliament's vote to impeach the president was upheld, Yeltsin disbanded it and called in the army to take back the White House, whereafter parliament was reformed, renamed the Duma and moved to a new building.

Russian Communist Party was dissolved by presidential decree. In January 1992, after the dissolution of the Soviet Union, a programme of radical economic reform was launched, which in one bold stroke led to an almost complete liberation of the economy from previous controls. The economic result of this was, for almost all Russians, an unmitigated disaster. While a few insiders got very rich, most people lost their savings, their pensions, or their jobs. Energy consumption fell by a third, accompanied by rapidly rising unemployment, falls in national income and real wages, a drop in industrial output by half, huge corruption in government organs and widely ramifying crime. To many Russians, these abstractions were brought home in the savage detail of personal misery. Public health and life expectancy declined to less than sixty years for males in the early 2000s, a drop of five years in less than a decade.

In 1993 a new parliament containing many of his enemies had been elected to add to Yeltsin's difficulties. Others were posed by relations with non-Russian republics of the CIS (in which there lived twenty-seven million Russians) and by the clans of political interest which had emerged around bureaucratic and industrial foci in the new Russia, as well as by disappointed ex-reformers, of whom he had sacked a great many. It was not long before it began to be recognized that Russia's troubles were not solely attributable to the Soviet legacy, but owed much to the general state of Russia's historic culture and civilization.

In 1992 Russia had itself become a federation and in the following year a presidential and even autocratic constitution completed the country's constitutional framework. But Boris Yeltsin soon had to face the challenge of opposition from both left and right and, eventually, of insurrection. After he had suspended parliament's functions by decree "on gradual constitutional reform", over a hundred people were killed in the worst bloodshed in Moscow since 1917. Like his earlier dissolution of the Communist Party this was seen as presidential high-handedness. No doubt the president's personality made forceful action more congenial to him than patient diplomacy. Nevertheless, considering he had so little to offer Russians in the way of material comfort, as the economy was exploited by corrupt officialdom and entrepreneurs on the make, it was to the credit of his government, and to the Russians' love of their new-found political freedom, that he managed to fight off the neo-communist challenge and achieve re-election as president in 1996.

THE RUSSIAN BORDER AREAS

Two years before that a new problem had emerged, a national insurrection in land-locked Chechnya, an autonomous republic in the Russian federation with a predominantly Muslim population. Some Chechens deplored and would avenge, they said, the immorality of their conquest and suppression by

Catherine the Great in the eighteenth century and the genocidal policy carried out by Stalin in the 1940s. Their anger and resistance was stiffened by the brutality with which the Russians, alarmed by the dangerous example that might be set to other Muslims, reduced the Chechen capital to ruins and the countryside to starvation. Thousands were killed, but Russian casualties reawoke memories of Afghanistan and there were all-too-evident dangers of fighting spilling over into neighbouring republics. Ever since 1992, after all, a Russian garrison had been propping up the government of now-independent Tajikistan against the danger of its overthrow by Islamic radicals supported from Pakistan. Against this doubtful background, not much was left by 1996 of the hopes raised by *perestroika* and *glasnost*, and additional gloom was cast over the situation as it became clear that President Yeltsin's health was poor (and probably made worse by heavy drinking). By then events outside Russia, notably in former Yugoslavia, prompted gestures and very vocal reminders to Western powers that the country still aspired to play the great power role it felt was its due, as well as of the growing concern Russia felt over the implications of intervention there in the affairs of an independent sovereign state.

FROM CRISIS TO RE-CENTRALIZATION?

By 1998, however, the Russian government could hardly gather taxes and pay its employees. The year 1997 had been the first year since 1991 in which GDP had registered a real, if tiny, increase, but apparently the economy was still abandoned to the mercy of special interests as the state sold off more and more of its investments to private business, often on a corrupt and favoured basis. Huge

fortunes were rapidly made by some, but millions of Russians suffered unpaid wages, the disappearance of daily necessities from the markets, continuing price rises, and the irritations and hostilities that inevitably arose as high levels of consumption for some confronted poverty face-to-face in the streets. Then, in 1998, came a financial crash and a repudiation of foreign debt. Yeltsin had to replace a prime minister he had chosen for his commitment to market economics and to accept one imposed upon him by his opponents. Yet the next parliamentary elections returned a parliament less likely to quarrel with him and on New Year's Eve 1999 he felt able to announce his resignation.

His successor was already at that moment serving as his prime minister. Boris Yeltsin duly announced that the next president should be Vladimir Putin, and accordingly he took up office after the election of March 2000. A former member of the KGB, Putin by then had to his credit in the eyes of many Russians a success – temporary as it turned out – in pacifying Chechnya and the decline of the danger that its turbulence might spread beyond its original borders. It seems likely

Known to Chechen separatists as Dzhokhar and Russians as Grozny, the capital city of the Chechen republic was subjected to widespread artillery bombardment at the hands of the Russian army during a series of assaults in 1994–95 to seize the city from rebels during the First Chechen War. Sadly for the civilian residents of the city, the whole process was repeated in 1999–2000 with the Second Chechen War.

Russian president Vladimir Putin inspects the crew of a guided missile submarine, of the Arkhangelsk class, upon the vessel's return to the Northern Fleet at Severomorsk, north of Murmansk, in February 2004. The president had watched large-scale military exercises in the Barents Sea.

that outcry abroad over threats to human rights in Chechnya further helped to rally patriotic support behind Vladimir Putin, but he had also made a favourable impression in Western capitals. In spite of the misfortunes of a series of accidental disasters in his first months as president, which indicated the run-down state of Russia's infrastructure, there was a new sense that grave problems were at last going to be surmounted. In a more narrowly personal sense, that was no doubt true also for Yeltsin, who, with his family, was assured by his successor of immunity from prosecution for offences committed during his presidency.

Putin's presidency put a new vigour into Russian government after the lethargy of the last Yeltsin years. The new president, only forty-eight when he took office, projected an austere and reserved image that most Russians liked after his extroverted but often inefficient predecessor. Putin wanted to be known as a man of action. He immediately began recentralizing power in Russia and cracked down on the super-rich – the so-called oligarchs – when they would not do the bidding of the Kremlin. After his re-election in 2004 concerns were voiced about the pressure his government exercised on Russian media critical of the president's policies. While the events of 11 September 2001 had given Putin a welcome chance to portray his aggressive conduct of the war in Chechnya as a war against terrorists – and thereby avoid too vocal a Western reaction – he had little success in bringing the conflict to a close. His attempts at influencing Russia's former Soviet neighbour-states to take a more friendly attitude to the new Russia also mostly backfired. Putin's most important contribution is to have created some form of economic stability; by 2005, inflation had been stemmed and

Russian GDP was gradually increasing. Still, Vladimir Putin is likely to be seen as a transitional figure on the way to a new Russian society that re-takes its place among the world's great centres of power.

PAX AMERICANA QUALIFIED

TAKING A LONG backward look from the early twenty-first century, the United States, much more clearly than in 1945, was the world's greatest power. For all the heavy weather of the 1970s and 1980s, and a cavalier piling up of public debt through budgetary deficit, its gigantic economy continued to show over the long run a huge dynamism and seemingly endless power to recover from setbacks. Its slowing as the 1990s drew to a close did not check this. For all the political conservatism which so often struck foreigners, the United States remained one of the most adaptive and rapidly changing societies in the world.

Yet as the last decade of the twentieth century began, many old problems still remained. Prosperity had made it easier for those Americans who did not have to face those problems in person to tolerate them but it had also actually provided fuel for the aspirations, fears and resentments of black Americans. This reflected the social and economic progress they had made since the Johnson presidency, the last that had seen a determined effort to legislate black America out of its troubles. Although the first black state governor in the nation's history took up office in 1990, only a couple of years later the inhabitants of Watts, notorious for their riots a quarter-century before, again showed that they saw the Los Angeles police force as little more than members of an occupying army. Over the country as a whole, a young black male was seven times more likely than his white contemporary to be murdered, probably by a fellow black, and was more likely to go to prison than to a university. If nearly a quarter of American babies were then being born to unmarried mothers, then two-thirds of black babies were, an index of the breakdown of family life in the black American communities. Crime, major deteriorations in health in some areas, and virtually unpoliceable inner-city areas still left many responsible Americans believing that many American problems were racing away from solution.

THE CLINTON YEARS

In fact, some of the statistics were beginning to look better. If Bill Clinton (who took up the presidency in 1993) disappointed many of his supporters by the legislation he actually could deliver, the Republicans in Congress got much of the blame for that. Although, too, the burgeoning phenomenon of rapidly growing numbers of "Hispanic" Americans, swollen by legal and illegal influx from Mexico and the Caribbean countries, worried many people, President Clinton set aside recommendations to restrict immigration further. The population of Hispanic ancestry had

President Bill Clinton delivers his inaugural address after being sworn in on 20 January 1993 as the 42nd president of the United States by Supreme Court Chief Justice William Rehnquist in Washington, DC.

doubled in thirty years, and now stands at roughly one-eighth of the total. In California, the richest state, it provided a quarter of the population and a low-wage labour pool; even in Texas, Hispanics were beginning to use politics to make sure their interests were not overlooked. Meanwhile, in a modish figure of speech, Clinton could surf the economic wave. Disappointments in his domestic policy tended to be attributed by supporters to his opponents rather than to his own failures of leadership and excessive care for electoral considerations. Although the Democrats lost control of the legislature in 1994, his re-election in 1996 was triumphant, and success for his party in the mid-term elections was to follow.

Nevertheless, Clinton's second presidency was a disappointment. In his defence it can be said that he had at the outset inherited an office diminished in prestige and power since the Johnson days and the early Nixon years. The authority the presidency had accumulated under Woodrow Wilson, Franklin Roosevelt and during the early Cold War had swiftly and dramatically ebbed away after Nixon. But Clinton did nothing to stem the rot. Indeed, for many Americans he made it worse. His personal indiscretions laid him open to much-publicized and prolonged

investigation of financial and sexual allegations, which led in 1999 to an unprecedented event: the hearing of charges by the Senate against an elected president with the aim of bringing about his impeachment (coincidentally, in that year an attempted impeachment of Boris Yeltsin also failed). Yet Clinton's public opinion poll ratings stood higher as the hearings began than they had done a year earlier, and the impeachment attempt failed. Those who had voted for him were content, it seemed, with what he was believed to have tried to do, even if they were not oblivious to his defects of character.

FROM CAUTION TO INTERVENTIONISM

As the Clinton presidencies unrolled, the United States had also come to appear to squander the possibilities of world leadership which had come with the end of the Cold War. Whatever the average reporting of American newspapers and television bulletins, there had seemed then to be for a moment some hope that traditional parochialism and isolationism might be permanently in eclipse, and that the United States would work with other countries globally to improve conditions for all. Concerns which required continuous and strenuous efforts by the United States in every part of the globe could hardly be ignored. They were indeed to loom larger still in the next ten years, but this was soon obscured by the ambiguities of American policy. Clinton's aim was first and foremost to assist in the globalization of market economies and for other countries to learn from the success of the United States. While a multilateralist at heart, Clinton was much too careful a politician to risk going against an American public tired of the international campaigns of the Cold War.

Rwandan refugees being expelled from Zaire in the back of UN trucks, just a few of the estimated one million Rwandans who had fled there during the genocidal attacks in their country. Some 85,000 Hutus were reported to have fled into the hills of east Zaire to avoid repatriation.

Many issues that the United States could have taken a lead on, such as world poverty and global ecological issues, were therefore brushed under the carpet in return for his electorate viewing Clinton as "the feel-good president" – he made them feel good in return for doing very little except enriching themselves.

Soon, however, the peace-keeping activities of the United Nations were troubling American policy. While the fiftieth anniversary of the foundation of the UN in 1995 prompted Clinton to tell his countrymen that to turn their backs on the organization would be to ignore the lessons of history, his remarks were provoked by the action earlier that year of the lower house of the American Congress in proposing to cut the American contribution to the costs of UN peacekeeping – against a background, moreover, of American default on its subscriptions to the normal budget of the UN amounting to over 270 million dollars (nine-tenths of the total arrears from all nations which were owed to the organization). United States policy seemed to reach a turning point with the collapse of a UN intervention in Somalia in 1993 which had led to casualties among UN forces taking part, and to spectacular television footage of the maltreatment of the bodies of American servicemen by enraged and exultant Somalis. Soon, the refusal of American participation or support to UN intervention in the African states of Burundi and Rwanda showed what disastrous consequences could flow from American refusal to participate, or to permit forceful intervention with ground forces, in peace-keeping, let alone peace-making. In these two small countries, each ethnically bitterly divided for generations into a ruling minority and a subject majority, the outcome in 1995–1996 was genocidal massacre. Over 600,000 were killed and millions (out of a total population of only about thirteen mil-

lion for both countries together) were driven into exile as refugees. It seemed the UN could do nothing if Washington would not move.

After President Clinton had authorized limited airstrikes against Bosnian Serb forces to bring about the peace settlement that was finally signed at Dayton in 1995, there was much debate among scholars, journalists and politicians about what the world role of the United States should be. Much of this debate centered around the proper use of American power and the ends to which it should be applied, and even about potential wars of civilizations. Meanwhile, Clinton's diplomacy appeared caught between the wish to create a world more amenable to US ideological goals and a wish to avoid military casualties, first and foremost amongst Americans.

WEAPONS OF MASS DESTRUCTION

Among fresh international problems to be faced was the appearance of new potential sources of nuclear danger. North Korea's modest nuclear programme in 1993–1994 showed (and the Indian and Pakistani tests of

A newly arrived M1-A1 Abrams tank leaves just enough room for a cart as it moves from the port at Mogadishu to its new base in the east of the capital in November 1993. USS *Denebola* lay in port offloading M1-A1 tanks, Bradley fighting vehicles and an assortment of other heavy military equipment for several days.

1998 reaffirmed) that the United States was now one of a slowly growing group of nuclear-armed states (seven openly acknowledged and two others not), whatever its huge superiority in delivery systems and potential weight of attack. America had no reason any longer to believe (as had sometimes been possible in the past) that all of these states would make rational – by American standards – calculations about where their interests lay. But this was only one new consideration in policy making after the end of the Cold War.

THE MIDDLE EAST

In the Middle East, early in the 1990s American financial pressure over the spread of Jewish settlement on the West Bank looked for a time as if it might persuade the Israeli government, harassed by the intifada and its accompanying terrorism, that a merely military solution to the Palestine problem was not going to work. Then, after great efforts, helped by the benevolent offices of the Norwegian government, secret talks between Israeli and Palestinian representatives at Oslo

A Palestinian Hamas militant gestures in front of red graffiti in Arabic (which reads "Hamas") during fierce fighting in February 2007 in Gaza City between the warring Palestinian factions of Hamas and Fatah.

in 1993 at last led to an encouraging new departure. The two sides then declared that it was time "to put an end to decades of confrontation and conflict, recognize ... mutual legitimate and political rights, and strive to live in peaceful coexistence". It was agreed that an autonomous Palestinian Authority (firmly defined as "interim") should be set up to administer the West Bank and Gaza Strip, and that a definitive peace settlement should be concluded within five years. This appeared to promise greater stability for the Middle East as a whole; it gave the Palestinians their first significant diplomatic gains. But the continuing implanting of new Israeli settlements in areas occupied by Israeli forces soon poisoned the atmosphere again. Optimism began to wilt when there was no cessation of terrorist attacks or of reprisals for them. Palestinian bombs in the streets of Israeli cities indiscriminately killed and maimed scores of shoppers and passers-by, while a Jewish gunman who killed thirty Palestinians in their mosque at Hebron won posthumous applause from many of his countrymen for doing so. Even so, hope lingered on; Syria, Jordan and the Lebanon all resumed peace negotiations with Israel, and a beginning was in fact made in the withdrawal of Israeli forces from the designated autonomous Palestinian areas.

Then, in November 1995, came the assassination of the Israeli prime minister by a fanatical fellow countryman. The following year, a conservative prime minister, dependent on the parliamentary support of Jewish extremist parties, took office. His popular majority was tiny, but it was clear that, for the immediate future at least, it was unlikely that anything but an aggressive policy of further territorial settlement by Israel would be forthcoming and that the Oslo agreements were in question. Even the election of a new Labour government in 1999 did not lead to a return to the promise of the Oslo agreement.

The new negotiations, led by Bill Clinton in the waning days of his presidency, failed spectacularly in achieving any concrete settlement. Palestinian leader Yassir Arafat spent the remaining years of his life, to 2004, besieged by Israeli troops in his compound in Ramallah, after a new Palestinian uprising broke out in 2000. In 2006 the Islamist group Hamas – a party dedicated to the extermination of Israel – won control of the Palestinian parliament. Americans were evidently doing no better than other outsiders to the region in grappling with the consequences of the creation of the Zionist programme a century earlier, and the Balfour declaration of 1917.

THE USA AND THE MIDDLE EAST

Nor did United States policy in the Persian Gulf provide lasting solutions there. Sanctions authorized by the UN did no good in Iran or Iraq, and patient and assiduous effort by the latter had by the mid-1990s to all intents and purposes broken any chance of maintaining the broad-based coalition of 1991 against it. Saddam's government seemed untroubled by the sanctions; they bore heavily on his subjects, but could be tempered by the smuggling of commodities the regime desired. Iraq was still a large oil exporter and revenues from this source made possible some restoration of its military potential, while no effective inspection of the country's production of weapons of mass destruction, as ordered by the United Nations, was taking place. American policy was as far as ever from achieving its own revolutionary and evident goal of overthrowing the regime, even when (supported only by the British) it fell back again for four nights in December 1998 on open aerial warfare, to no avail. Nor did it help American prestige when suspicion arose that the timing of the bombing offensive might have some connection with a wish to distract attention from the impeachment proceedings about to begin in Washington.

The year 1998 had begun with President Clinton stressing in his State of the Union message that domestic conditions indicated that these were "good times" for Americans, but this was not proving true in foreign affairs. In August, American embassies were attacked by Muslim terrorists in both Kenya and Tanzania, with heavy loss of life. Within a couple of weeks there was an American reply in the form of missile attacks on alleged terrorist bases in Afghanistan and the Sudan (where the factory attacked was said to have been preparing weapons for germ warfare, a charge whose credibility rapidly faded). The embassy bombings were both linked by Bill Clinton to the mysterious figure of Osama bin Laden, a Saudi extremist, in a speech which also alleged that there was "compelling" evidence that further attacks against United States citizens were planned. When, in November, a Manhattan federal Grand Jury indicted Osama bin Laden and an associate on over 200 charges relating to the embassy attacks, as well as to other attacks on

In 1998 simultaneous car bomb explosions at the US embassies in the East African capital cities of Dar es Salaam, Tanzania, and Nairobi, Kenya, killed more than 250 people and wounded over 4,000. Here, a body is carried from the wreckage in Nairobi, where most of the deaths occurred.

Burqa-clad Afghan women look at carpets in Kabul in the immediate aftermath of the overthrow of the Taliban in 2001. During their five years in power the strict Islamists imposed draconian dress codes on women in public. Religious police patrols enforced these rules and any deviations could result in public punishment. In education, girls were deprived even of elementary schooling.

American service personnel and an abortive bombing in 1993 of the World Trade Center in New York, it caused no surprise when he failed to appear in court to answer them. It was believed bin Laden was hiding in Afghanistan under the protection of the Taliban régime, which had taken control of that country on the ruins of the Soviet war in the mid-1990s.

THE KOSOVO WAR

As 1999 began, Kosovo was at the centre of the troubles of former Yugoslavia. When spring passed into summer, a strategic commitment at last undertaken in March to a purely air campaign by NATO forces (but carried out mainly by Americans) against Serbia appeared to be achieving little except a stiffening of its people's will to resist and an increase in the flow of refugees from Kosovo.

The Russians were alarmed by NATO action, unsupported as it was by UN authorization, and felt it ignored their traditional interest in the area. The casualties inflicted on civilians – both Serbian and Kosovan – were soon causing misgivings in domestic opinion within the nineteen NATO nations, while the Serbian president, Slobodan Milosevic, had apparently had his confidence increased by Bill Clinton's assurance that there would be no NATO land invasion. What was going forward was indeed unusual: the armed coercion of a sovereign European state because of its behaviour to its own citizens.

Meanwhile, over three-quarters of a million Kosovan refugees crossed the frontier in search of safety in Macedonia and Albania, bringing stories of atrocities and intimidation by Serbs. It appeared that it was the deliberate intention of the Belgrade government to drive out at least parts of the non-Serb majority. Then came a disastrous mishap. Acting on out-of-date information – and therefore in avoidable error – American aircraft scored direct hits on the Chinese embassy in Belgrade, killing members of its staff. Beijing refused even to listen to the apology Clinton attempted to give. An orchestrated television campaign had already presented the Chinese people with an interpretation of the whole NATO intervention as a simple act of American aggression. Well-organized student mobs now attacked the American and British embassies in Beijing (though without going quite so far as the extremes experienced during the Cultural Revolution). Conveniently (the ten-year anniversary of Tiananmen Square was coming up), student steam was thus let off in anti-foreigner riots.

The depth of Chinese concern about America's world role can hardly be doubted, nor that China's involvement, like Russia's, in the Kosovo crisis was likely to make it harder for NATO to achieve its aims. The Chinese were strong believers in the veto system of the Security Council, seeing it as protection for the sovereignty of individual nations. They were also disinclined to view with sympathy would-be Kosovan separatists, sensitive as they had always been to any danger of fragmentation in their own huge country. In the deep background, too, must have lain thoughts of reassertion of their own historic world role, as well as the specific irritations of recent years. For a century after the Opium Wars, after all, China had never been without the humiliation of European and United States troops assuring "order" in several of her cities. Perhaps it had crossed the minds of some Chinese that it would be a sweet reversal of fortunes if Chinese soldiers should in the end form part of a peace-keeping force in Europe.

Thanks to the American president's wish to avoid at all costs the exposure of ground troops to danger, just as Bosnia had destroyed the credibility of the United Nations as a device for assuring international order, it now appeared that Kosovo might destroy that of NATO. Early in June, however, it appeared that the damage done by bombing, together with timely Russian efforts to mediate, and British pressure for a land invasion by NATO forces, were at last weakening the will of the Serbian government. That month, after mediation in which the Russian government took part, it was agreed that a NATO land force should enter Kosovo in a "peace-keeping" role. Serbian forces then withdrew from Kosovo and the province was occupied by NATO. It was not the end of the troubles of the former Yugoslav federation. In 2006 NATO soldiers were still there, and there was still uncertainty about the long-term future of Kosovo, even if the Serb minority was getting smaller as the Albanian majority used strong-arm methods to control the province. But by then there had been a notable change of mood and of government in Belgrade and the former Serbian president had been arrested and handed over to a new international court at the Hague, which had begun to try offenders against international law on war crimes and other charges.

FROM CLINTON TO GEORGE W. BUSH

As Clinton's presidency moved towards its close, he at different times asserted the need to reverse the decline in defence spending, indicated that the proposals for imposing limits on the emission of industrial gases damaging to the climate were unacceptable, and strove to reassure China by efforts to secure normal trading relations with her; China was to secure admission to the World Trade Organisation, in fact, in 2001. The Republican candidate in the presidential election of 2000, George W. Bush, emphasized in his successful campaign his anxiety to avoid the use of American troops on peace-keeping duties abroad and that he would authorize the building of a Nuclear Missile Defense system to protect the United States against "rogue" powers armed with such missiles. As

Former Yugoslav President Slobodan Milosevic appears at the war crimes tribunal at The Hague, Netherlands, in 2002. According to Chief Prosecutor Carla Del Ponte, Milosevic oversaw the murder of over 1,000 people and the displacement of more than one million in the former Yugoslavia. The trial was the first time that a head of state had appeared before a United Nations Tribunal.

Hijacked United Airlines Flight 175 from Boston crashes into the south tower of the World Trade Center and explodes at 9:03am on 11 September 2001 in New York City. The crash of two terrorist-hijacked airliners into the towers and their subsequent collapse killed nearly 3,000 people.

often observed, we shall always find what happens somewhat surprising, because things tend to change on the one hand more slowly and on the other more rapidly than we tend to think. That seemed to be as true as ever – when events on 11 September 2001 changed things anew.

9/11

On the morning of that beautiful autumn day, four airliners travelling on scheduled flights within the United States were hijacked in flight by persons of Islamic or Middle Eastern background and origin. Without attempting, as had frequently been the case in similar acts of air piracy, to ask for ransoms or to make public statements about their goals, the terrorists diverted the aircraft and, in a combination of suicide and murder, flew two of them into the huge towers of the World Trade Center in lower Manhattan, and another into the Pentagon building in Washington, the heart of American military planning and administration. The fourth crashed in open country, apparently forced down by the heroic efforts of some of its passengers to overcome the terrorists who had seized it. No one in any of the aircraft survived, the damage was immense in both the cities (above all New York) and 3,000 people perished, many of them not Americans.

It was immediately apparent that it would take time to discover the full truth about these tragedies, but the immediate reaction of the American government was to attribute responsibility in a general sense to extremist Islamic terrorists, and President Bush announced an implicitly worldwide war against the abstraction "terrorism". More particularly, Osama bin Laden was to be hunted down and brought to justice. In a sense, though, individual responsibility for 11

The cover of *Time* magazine on 1 October 2001 shows a photograph of Saudi Arabian-born terrorist leader Osama Bin Laden under the headline "Target: Bin Laden".

September was not the most important immediate consideration. Much more important was the excitement which erupted worldwide on the general relationship of Muslim radicalism – and perhaps of Islam itself – to such an atrocity. Because of this, the effects of what had happened were potentially even more important than the misery and terror they had brought to thousands and the physical and economic damage caused. A few such effects were immediately apparent in isolated anti-Muslim acts in several countries.

THE WORLD AFTER 9/11

It rapidly became a cliché that everything had been changed by the events of 11 September. This, of course, was an exaggeration. For all the eventual repercussions of what followed, many historical processes went on unaltered in many parts of the world. But the effect of the attacks was, undoubtedly, galvanic, and it made much evident that had only been implicit. Immediately and obviously, a huge shock had been given to the American consciousness. It was not to be measured only by the remarkable rallying of public opinion behind the president's categorization of what had happened as the beginning of a "war" – though one with no precisely identified enemy – nor, even, by the transformation of the political position of the new president, George Bush, which, at the beginning of the year, after a disputed election, had been questioned by many. It was clear now that his countrymen felt again something of the national rage and unity that had followed the attack on Pearl Harbor nearly sixty years before. The United States had endured terrorist attacks at home and abroad for twenty years. The tragedy of 11 September, though, was wholly unprecedented in scale and, unhappily, it suggested that other atrocities might be on the way. It was not surprising that Bush felt he could respond to a democracy's outrage in strong language and that the country overwhelmingly fell into line behind him.

It soon seemed likely that to the apprehension and bringing to trial of the shadowy figure of bin Laden would be added the aim of removing by force the threat of the "rogue states" whose assistance to terrorism was presumed to have been available and essential. The practical implications of this went far beyond the preparation of conventional military efforts, and began immediately with a vigorous and worldwide diplomatic offensive to obtain moral support and practical assistance. This was remarkably successful. Not all governments responded with equal enthusiasm, but almost all responded positively, including most Muslim countries and, more important still, Russia and China.

American soldiers patrolling in the Baghran valley, Afghanistan, during Operation Viper in February 2003. The mission was to search from village to village for weapons and signs of Taliban and al-Qaeda sympathizers.

The Security Council found no difficulty in expressing its unanimous sympathy; the NATO powers recognized their responsibilities to come to the assistance of an ally under attack.

Just as in the days of the Holy Alliance after the Napoleonic Wars Europe's conservative powers had been haunted by the nightmare of conspiracy and revolution, in the years following the hijackings there was an alarming hint of a similar exaggerated fear of Islamic terrorism. That what had happened had been carefully and cleverly planned, there could be no doubt. But little was actually known about what the organizing powers really were and what were their ramifications and extent. It did not, at first sight, seem plausible that merely the work of one man could explain these acts. But neither could it be plausibly argued that the world was entering upon a struggle of civilizations, although some said so.

That United States policy abroad – above all, in support of Israel – had given much encouragement to the growth of anti-American feeling in Arab countries could not be doubted, even if that was a new idea for many Americans. There was widespread resentment, too, of the offensive blatancy with which American communications had thrust manifestations of an insensitive capitalist culture on sometimes poverty-stricken countries. In some places what could be regarded as American armies of occupation, guests rarely welcomed in any country, could be depicted as the upholders of corrupt regimes. But none of this could plausibly add up to a crusade against Islamic peoples any more than could the immense variety of Islamic civilization be seen as a monolithic opponent of a monolithic West. What soon was achieved was the removal of the hostile Taliban regime in Afghanistan, by a combination of the efforts of its local and indigenous

Thousands of people march along the Embankment in London towards Hyde Park as they participate in an antiiwar protest in February 2003. The march is believed to have been the UK's biggest ever peace protest up to that time. Massive demonstrations took place at the same time throughout Europe, North America and Australia against the increasingly likely prospect of a US-led war on Iraq.

enemies and American bombing, technology and special forces. By the end of 2001 there was a new Afghan state formally in being, resourceless and dangerously divided into the fiefs of warlords and tribal enclaves though it seemed, and dependent on US and other NATO forces to fight its enemies. Elsewhere, the consequences of the ill-defined war on terrorism complicated events in Palestine. Arab states showed no willingness to cease to support the Palestinians when Israel attacked them invoking the crusade against international terrorism.

THE INVASION OF IRAQ

The most disastrous effect of the 11 September 2001 atrocities was the decision taken by President Bush and his main international ally, Britain's prime minister Tony Blair, to invade Iraq in 2003. The main cause of the invasion was the growing fear, especially in the United States, that Saddam Hussain's régime had, or would soon get hold of, chemical, bacteriological or nuclear weapons of mass destruction. Before September 2001 it would have been difficult to envisage a pre-emptive strike against a sovereign country based on (unfounded, as it turned out) suspicions of weapons' acquisitions, however unpalatable that country's régime was. But, for many Americans, the events of 9/11 changed that. They were now ready – at least for a time – to follow a president who wanted to make use of the sense of post-9/11 emergency to deal with other potential threats. Even if Bush and Blair realized that Saddam – for all his anti-Western bluff and bluster – had nothing to do with the attacks on New York and Washington, they thought his regime was an evil that had to be removed. In spite of stiff resistance from all the other members of the UN Security Council, and most of global public opinion, the United States and Britain started pushing for a UN resolution that would empower them to attack Iraq. When it became clear, in early March 2003, that no such resolution was forthcoming, the two countries, and some of their allies, decided to invade Iraq and remove Saddam's régime even without the support of the UN.

This second Gulf War lasted only twenty-one days in March and April 2003, but came to dominate international affairs at the beginning of the twenty-first century. It ended, predictably, with the removal (and ultimate trial, conviction and execution) of Saddam Hussain and the overthrow of his régime. But it also produced new fissures in world politics that proved difficult to plaster over, and lasting resistance in many areas of Iraq against what was seen as foreign occupation. In Europe, France, Germany and Russia opposed the invasion and spoke out against

it. China condemned it as a violation of international law. NATO encountered its biggest post-Cold War crisis, when it could not agree on supporting the invasion, and the United States was left with the new eastern European members as its staunchest supporters. But the biggest damage was done to the concept of a new post-Cold War world order in which consultations among the great powers and multilateral action should replace worldwide confrontation. The UN General Secretary, the Ghanaian Kofi Annan – a man the United States itself had worked hard to get elected – told the world that US and British action in Iraq was illegal. To him, and to many others, the real concern was not with Bush's determination to get rid of Saddam, but with what would happen elsewhere, when other countries were determined to get rid of their enemies and the biggest power on earth had set an example through unilateral action.

Bush and Blair would have escaped some of the criticism they came in for after the invasion of Iraq if the occupation of that country had been better planned. Instead, parts of the country fell into anarchy after the collapse of the régime, as basic services stopped and the economy faltered. Looting and lawlessness were widespread for months after Iraqis – much helped by a US tank – had toppled Saddam's statue in the centre of Baghdad. Even though relations between the main ethnic and religious groups in Iraq would have been difficult to handle for any post-Saddam authority, the lack of security and the economic chaos helped inflame the situation. The majority Shia Muslims – long oppressed by the former Baath regime's mainly Sunni leaders – flocked to their religious leaders for direction, many of whom wanted to establish an Islamic state similar to that in Iran. Meanwhile, a number of revolts started in the Sunni parts of the country, based both on Saddam loyalists, and, increasingly, on Sunni Islamists both from Iraq and other Arab countries. The new Iraqi authorities – a weak coalition government dominated by Shias – remained dependent on US military support, while the Kurdish northern part of the country set up its own institutions separate from those in Baghdad.

THE FUTURE OF AMERICAN HEGEMONY

By the end of the Cold War, the United States plainly exercised the first global hegemony in history. Its first attempts at exercising that hegemony had been stuttering, to say the least. The massacre of innocent lives on 11 September 2001 had set the United States on a direction that had led to the alienation of many of its friends and a war that it seemed unable to win fully or to withdraw from. As a result, soon after having won re-election in 2004, President Bush the younger was more unpopular than any other president in living memory, including President Nixon when he faced imminent impeachment. But in spite of the invasion of Iraq having undone both Bush's presidency and Tony Blair's prime-ministership, there were few others who could come up with better recipes for how to employ US power in the post-Cold War world. On the one hand, Americans themselves were divided between those who thought the lesson of Iraq was more isolationism or more multilateralism. On the other hand, more importantly, the rest of the world, while often complaining about the consequences of US unilateral action, had very little to put in its place when confronted with major crises. At the end of the post-Cold War era, the region in which civilization began had given birth to yet another twist in history's long tale. The dismal fate of intruders and invaders in Mesopotamia was nothing

new; the global predominance of one country clearly was. The United States had the power to remake international affairs. What she might do with it remained to be seen.

A statue of the dictator Saddam Hussein is pulled down in Baghdad city centre on 9 April 2003.

6 EPILOGUE: IN THE LIGHT OF HISTORY

The story told in this book has no clear end. However dramatic and disrupted, a history of the world cannot pull up short and come to a halt at a neat chronological boundary. To close with the year in which the author ceases to write is merely formal; it says nothing about the future of the historical processes then under way and thus severed in mid-life. As history is what one age thinks worth noting about another, recent events will acquire new meanings and present patterns will lose their clear outlines as people reflect again and again on what made the world in which they live. Even in a few months, present judgements about what is important will begin to look eccentric, so fast can events now move. Perspective is harder and harder to maintain.

This does not mean that the record is no more than a collection of facts or just a succession of events constantly reshuffled. Discernible trends and forces have operated over long periods and wide areas. In the longest run of all, three such interconnected trends stand out: the growing acceleration of change, a growing unity of human experience and the growth of human capacity to control the environment. In our day, for the first time, they have made visible a truly unified world history. Blatantly, the expression "one world" remains little more than a cant term, for all the idealism of those who first used it. There

Road crews work to repair a broken levee near Modesto, California, after a flood in 1997. Many people blame global warming for the unusualy extreme weather conditions that have struck many parts of the world in recent years. Although this is difficult to prove, we do know that the average temperature of the earth has increased by around 0.5°C since 1900 and is still rising. This is likely to result in a rise in sea levels that will cause flooding along some of the most densely populated coastlines in the world.

is just too much conflict and quarrelling about and no earlier century ever saw so much violence as the twentieth. Its politics were expensive and dangerous even when they did not break out in overt fighting, as the Cold War showed only too clearly. And now, just into a new century, new divisions are appearing still. The United Nations is still based, ironically (even if a little less firmly than fifty years ago), on the theory that the whole surface of the globe is divided into territories belonging to some 200 sovereign states. The bitter struggles of the former Yugoslavia may yet reopen and the simplicity upon which many would like to insist of an Islamic–Western clash of civilizations is cut across in a half-dozen ways by the tribal divisions of even so Islamic a country as Afghanistan.

SHARED EXPERIENCE

Much, much more could be said along the same lines. Yet that does not mean that humanity does not now share more than it has ever done in the past. A creeping unity has seized mankind. An originally Christian calendar (now often ideologically sanitized by the substitution of BCE and CE for BC and AD) is now the basis of governmental activity around most of the world. Modernization implies a growing commonality of goals. Clashes of culture are frequent, but were more evidently so in the past. What is now shared is at the humdrum level of the personal experience of millions; if society is a sharing of references, our world shares more than ever before, even if, paradoxically, people feel most acutely the distinctions between them in their daily experience. Yet when those who lived in neighbouring villages spoke significantly different dialects, when in the whole of their lives most of them would only exceptionally travel ten miles from their homes,

when even their clothes and tools might provide in their shape and workmanship evidence of big differences of technology, style and custom, that experience was in important ways much more differentiated than it is now. The great physical, racial and linguistic divisions of the past were much harder to overcome than are their equivalents today. This is because of improved communication, the spread of English as a global lingua franca among the educated, mass education, mass production of commonly required artefacts, and so on. A traveller can still see exotic or unfamiliar clothes in some countries, but more people over most of the globe now dress alike than ever before. Kilts, kaftans, kimonos are becoming tourist souvenirs, or the carefully preserved relics of a sentimentalized past, while traditional clothing is more and more the sign of poverty and backwardness. The efforts of a few self-consciously conservative and nationalist regimes to cling to the symbols of their past only bear this out. Iranian revolutionaries put women back into the chador because they felt the experience pouring in from the world outside to be corrosive of morality and tradition. Peter the Great ordered his courtiers into western

A tourist in the Philippines photographs people in traditional dress. In many regions of the world tourism has brought mixed blessings. Although it can often destroy traditional ways of life, it can also help to sustain village communities, along with some aspects of local cultural heritage.

Three women in Shanghai walk past a poster promoting the new James Bond movie *Casino Royale*, which made its debut in cinemas around China at the end of January 2007 – the first Bond film to earn approval from censors in China, which allows only 20 foreign films to be officially released each year. Bond, however, is already well known in China due to the widespread distribution of pirated copies of films.

European clothes, and Ataturk forbade Turks to wear the *fez*, to announce a reorientation towards a progressive, advancing culture and a symbolic step towards a new future.

GLOBAL FAMILIARITIES

However, the basis of shared experience now available is only secondarily a consequence of any conscious commitment. Perhaps that is one reason why it has been so neglected by historians, and has tended to lie below their horizon of interest. Yet in a relatively short time, millions of men and women of different cultures have been in some degree liberated from, for example, many effects of climatic differences by electricity, air-conditioning and medicine. Cities all over the world now take street lighting and traffic signals for granted, have policemen on point duty, transact business in similar ways in banks and supermarkets. Much the same goods can be bought in them as are available in most other countries (in season, the Japanese now sell Christmas cakes). Men who do not understand one another's languages service the same machines in different countries. Motor cars are everywhere a nuisance. Rural districts still escape some of these concomitants of modern life in some places, but big cities, which now contain a larger share of humanity than ever before, do not. Yet for millions of their inhabitants the experiences they share are also ones of squalor, economic precariousness and comparative deprivation. Whatever the differences in their Muslim, Hindu and Christian origins, and whether they shelter mosques, temples or churches, Cairo, Calcutta and Rio offer much the same misery (and, for a few, a similar opulence). Other misfortunes, too, are now more easily shared. The mingling of peoples made possible by modern transport means that diseases are shared as never before, thanks to the wiping out of old immunities. Aids has now

The impact of cinema

When Frenchmen Auguste and Louis Lumière projected their first film, *Workers Leaving the Lumière Factory*, in 1895, the event marked the birth of what was to become a new form of artistic expression, mass communication, education and popular entertainment. The cinema, now a massive industry, has been enormously influential throughout the 20th century and since.

Even in the early days of silent films, film-makers were already faced with the dual demands of artistic or testimonial quality on the one hand and commercial interests on the other. Directors such as Georges Méliès (1861–1938) in France, D.W. Griffith (1875–1948), Erich von Stroheim (1886–1957) and Charles Chaplin (1889–1977) in the US, F.W. Murnau (1888–1932) and Fritz Lang (1890–1976) in Germany and Sergei Eisenstein (1898–1948) in Russia laid down the artistic foundations for cinema. At the same time, Hollywood began to realize that the cinema was going to be big business and money became the objective of studios setting up as film factories. Cecil B. De Mille's 1927 biblical epic *The King of Kings* sold 800,000 seats.

This commercial–artistic polarity remained evident in the era of talking films – still mainly in black and white until 1945, although a Technicolor feature was made as early as 1935 by Walt Disney (1901–1966). Directors who continued to extend the frontiers of film art included the Frenchmen René Clair (1898–1981) and Jean Renoir (1894–1979), and the American Orson Welles (1915–1985). Others such as the German Ernst Lubitsch (1892–1947) and the Englishman Alfred Hitchcock (1899–1980) were able to impose a strongly personal style even while working within the big studios whose box-office driven productions pushed Hollywood's takings up to $1,700 million by 1946.

The political themes of early Soviet cinema, the Nazi propaganda films of Joseph Goebbels, and the more positive social messages of post-war Italian neo-realism already showed the power of film to influence human attitudes and behaviour. New Wave French directors of the 1960s displayed increasing ease in using the camera to "write" films that seemed to dissolve the boundaries between reality and imagination. Cinema's more recent marriage with television and video has vastly increased the ability of film-makers to project lifestyles, dreams or aspirations worldwide. For better or worse – and film continues to range between art and mindless entertainment – no other medium contributed so much to the advance of a global culture in the 20th century.

Charlie Chaplin is pictured on the set of his film The Great Dictator *(1940), in which he mocked Adolf Hitler.*

appeared in every continent (except, possibly, Antarctica), and we are told it is killing 6,000 people a day.

Even a few centuries ago a traveller from imperial Rome to imperial Loyang, the Han capital, would have found many more contrasts than a modern successor. Rich and poor would have worn clothes cut differently and made from different materials than those he knew, the food he was offered would be unusual, he would have seen animals of unfamiliar breeds in the streets, soldiers whose weapons and armour looked quite unlike what he had left behind. Even wheelbarrows

had a different shape. A modern American or European in Beijing or Shanghai need see little that is surprising even in a country that is still in many ways deeply conservative; if he chooses Chinese cuisine (he will not need to) it will seem distinctive, but a Chinese airliner looks like any other and Chinese girls wear fishnet tights. It is only a little while ago that junks were China's ocean-going ships, and looked wholly unlike contemporary European cogs or caravels.

Shared material realities advance the sharing of mental signposts and assumptions. Information and popular entertainment are now produced for global consumption. Popular groups of musicians tour the world like (though more easily and prosperously than) the troubadours who wandered about medieval Europe, presenting their songs and spectacles in different countries. Young people in particular cheerfully abandon their distinctive local ways in the indulgence of tastes binding them to other young people far away who have spare cash in their pockets – and there are now millions of them. The same movies, dubbed and subtitled, are shown worldwide on television to audiences that take away from them similar fantasies and dreams. At a different and more consciously intended level, the language of democracy and human rights is now enlisted more widely than ever to pay at least lip-service to Western notions of what public life should be. Whatever governments and the media actually intend, they feel they must say increasingly that they believe in a version of democracy, the rule of law, human rights, equality of the sexes and much else. Only now and then does there occur a nasty jolt, an exposure of hypocrisies in practice, the revelation of unacknowledged moral disagreement or of blunt rejection by cultures still resistant to contamination of their traditions and sensibilities.

THE STARK DIFFERENCES BETWEEN RICH AND POOR

True, millions of human beings still inhabit villages, struggling to get a living within highly conservative communities with traditional tools and methods, while all-too-visible inequalities between life in rich and poor countries dwarf any differences that existed in the past. The rich are now richer than ever, and there are more of them, while a thousand years ago all societies were by modern standards poor. Thus, in that way at least, they were closer to one another in their daily lives than they are today. The difficulty of winning one's daily bread and the fragility of human life before the mysterious, implacable forces which cut them down like grass, were things all men and women had in common whatever language they spoke or creed they followed. Now, a large minority of mankind lives in countries with an average per capita annual income of over $3,000, and millions of others in countries where the corresponding figure is less than one-tenth of this sum and there are colossal distinctions even among the poor. Such disparities are relatively recent creations of a brief historical era; we should no more assume they will endure for long than that they will easily or swiftly disappear.

The leading classes and élites, even in the poorest countries, have for at least a century looked to some version of modernization as a way out of their troubles. Their aspirations appear to confirm the pervasive influence of a civilization originally European. Some have said that modernization is only a matter of technology and that more fundamental matters of belief, institutions and attitudes remain stronger determinants of social behaviour, but this side-steps questions about the way material experience shapes culture. The evidence is growing that certain master ideas and institutions, too, as well as material artefacts and

The Declaration of Human Rights

"Article 10: Everyone is entitled in full equality to a fair and public hearing by an independent and impartial tribunal, in the determination of his rights and obligations and of any criminal charges against him.

"Article 11: (1) Everyone charged with a penal offence has the right to be presumed innocent until proved guilty according to law in a public trial at which he has had all the guarantees necessary for his defence. (2) No one shall be held guilty of any penal offence on account of any act or omission which did not constitute a penal offence, under national or international law, at the time when it was committed. Nor shall a heavier penalty be imposed than the one that was applicable at the time the penal offence was committed."

An extract from the *Universal Declaration of Human Rights*, published in 1948.

techniques, have already spread generally among mankind. Whatever the practical effect of such documents as the United Nations Declaration of Human Rights, the interest shown in drawing them up and signing them has symptomatically been intense, even when some signatories have little intention of respecting them. Such principles always turn out to be derived from the western European tradition, and whether we regard that tradition as greedy, oppressive, brutal and exploitative, or as objectively improving, beneficent and humane, is neither here nor there. Aztec and Inca civilizations could not stand up to the Spanish; Hindu and Chinese civilizations were only slightly more successful against later "Franks". Such statements can be true or untrue: but the facts are neither admirable nor repugnant. They register the fact that Europe reshaped an old, and made the modern, world.

This image of visitors to Luna Park, a Western-style fairground in Tehran, in 1994, demonstrates that certain global icons cross religious and cultural divides.

EUROPE AS A WORLD-SHAPER

Some "Western" ideas and institutions derived ultimately from Europe have often been deeply resented and resisted. Women are still not treated in the same way – whether for good or ill is here irrelevant – in Islamic and Christian societies, but neither are they treated in the same way in all Islamic societies which now exist, or within all of what we might call "Western" societies. Indians still take into account astrology in fixing the day of a wedding, while English people may find train timetables (if they are able get accurate information about them) or imperfect weather information, which they believe to be "scientific", more relevant. Differing traditions make even the use of shared technology and ideas different. Japanese capitalism has not worked in the same way as British, and any explanation must lie deep in the different histories of two peoples similar in other respects (as invasion-free islanders, for example). Yet no other tradition has shown the same vigour and attractiveness in alien settings as the European: it has had no competitors as a world-shaper.

Even its grossest manifestations – its material greed and rapacity – show this. Societies once rooted in changeless acceptance of things as they are have taken up the belief that limitless improvement in material well-being is a proper goal for them. The very idea that willed change is possible is itself deeply subversive, as is the notion that it may be a road to happiness. Large numbers of people now know that things have changed in their own lifetimes, and sense that there can and probably will be still further change for the better. A spreading attitude of unquestioning, not very reflective, acceptance that human problems are in principle manageable or at least remediable is a major psychological transformation; it was hardly foreseeable, let alone established, even among Europeans only a couple of centuries ago. Although for most of their lives millions of human beings still rarely contemplate the future except with deep unhappiness and misgiving – and that is when they can summon up the energy to consider it at all, for they are often still going hungry – in the normal course of events more millions than ever before do not go hungry, nor do they seem in any obvious danger of doing so. More people than ever now take it for granted that they will never know real need. A smaller, but still huge, number find it easy to believe that their lives will improve, and many more feel they ought to.

THE IDEA OF IMPROVEMENT

This change in outlook is of course most obvious in rich societies which now consume much more of the earth's resources than the rich could do even a few decades ago. In the Western world, for all its comparatively deprived minorities and underclasses, most people are now in this sense rich. Only about 200 years ago a typical Englishman would have been unlikely in the whole of his life to have been able to travel more than a few miles from the place where he was born except on his own two feet. Only 150 years ago he would not have had assured supplies of clean water. A hundred years ago, he still faced a good chance of being crippled or even killed by a casual accident, or by disease for which no remedy was known or existed, and for which no nursing care would be available to him, while many like him and his family ate meagre meals so lacking in balance and nourishment (to say nothing of being dull and unappetizing) that their like is now eaten only by the poorest in this country; and they could expect in their fifties and sixties (if they survived so long) the onset of a painful and penurious old age. Much the same could be said of other Europeans, and of North Americans, Australasians, Japanese and many others. Now millions of even the poorest worldwide can glimpse possibilities of changes in their lot for the better.

More important still are those who have come to believe that such change can be sought, promoted and actually brought about. Their politicians tell them so; it is now evident that peoples and governments implicitly believe it to be a matter of fact that many specific problems in their lives and the lives of their societies can be solved. Many go further and feel that, therefore, they will be. This cannot, of course, logically be taken for granted. We may well be at the end of cheap fossil fuel and plentiful water supplies. We may well also feel sceptical about rearranging the world to increase the sum of human happiness when we remember some of the twentieth century's attempts at social engineering, or the superstition and sectarianism, intransigent moralisms and tribal loyalties that still cost so much in misery and blood. Nevertheless, more people than ever now behave as if most of their problems are in principle soluble or remediable. This is a rev-

olution in human attitudes. No doubt its deepest origins lie far, far back in those prehistoric millennia of slowly growing capacity to manipulate nature, when pre-human beings learned to manage fire or to put an edge on a convenient piece of flint. The abstract idea that such manipulation might be possible took shape only much more recently, and at first as the insight of only a few in certain crucial eras and cultural zones. But the idea is now commonplace; it has triumphed worldwide. We now take it for granted that people everywhere should and will begin to ask themselves why things remain as they are when they evidently might be made better. It is one of the greatest of changes in all history.

An Egyptian vegetable vendor tidies her wares at the popular Imbaba market – just one of thousands of poor women to benefit from a partnership between a local credit organization and the Nobel Prize-winning Grameen Bank founded by Bangladeshi Muhammad Yunus. The small loans, which enable entrepreneurial activity, have a strong success record.

One of the dams for the Three Gorges hydroelectric power station is shown being built on the Yangtze river in China in the late 1990s. The power station will be the largest of its kind in the world when it is fully operational in 2009. Environmentalists fear that the scheme will seriously disturb the region's ecological balance and lead to the loss of a large area of wildlife habitats.

HUMAN MANIPULATION OF NATURE

The more invisible grounds for this change have been provided by mankind's increasing ability in the last few centuries to manage the material world. Science provided the tools for that. It now appears to offer more than ever. We stand at the edge of an era with the promise and threat of an ability to manipulate nature more fundamentally than ever (for instance, through genetic engineering). Perhaps there lies ahead a world in which people will be able to commission, as it were, private futures to order. It is now conceivable that they could plan the genetic shaping of unborn offspring, and buy themselves experience "off the shelf" as information technology becomes available to create virtual realities more perfect than actuality. It may be that people will be able to live more of their conscious lives, if they wish to do so, in worlds they have constructed, rather than in those provided by ordinary sense-experience.

Such speculations can be intimidating. They suggest, after all, great potential for disorder and destabilization. Rather than wondering about what may or may not happen, it is best to reflect firmly on the historical, on what has already changed human life in the past. Changes in material well-being have, for instance, transformed politics not only by changing expectations but also by changing the circumstances in which politicians have to take decisions, the ways in which institutions operate, the distribution of power in society. In only a few societies nowadays can or does religion operate as it once did. Science not only hugely enlarged the toolkit of knowledge humanity can use to grapple with nature, but has also transformed at the level of daily life the things millions take for granted. In this century it has accounted for much of a huge increase in human numbers, for fundamental changes in the relationships of nations, for the rise and decline of whole sectors of the world economy, the tying of the world together by nearly instantaneous communication, and many more of its most startling changes. And whatever the last century or so may or may not have done for political democracy, it has, thanks to science, brought a great extension of practical freedoms. Overwhelmingly Western in origin (in spite of early sallies by Asian civilizations), the expressions of scientific knowledge in better technology swiftly became global in their effect.

THE FUTURE OF SCIENCE

Only among the intellectual leadership of the richer societies has there been some qualification of the confidence evident and hardly challenged until 1960 or so, in human ability to manage the world through science and technology (rather than, say, through magic or religion), and so to satisfy human wants. Such qualification may prove to have much further to go. We now know more about the fragility of our natural environment and its susceptibility to change for the worse. There is a new awareness that not all the apparent benefits derived from the manipulation of nature are without their costs, that some may even have frightening implications, and, more fundamentally, that we do not yet possess the social and political skills and structures to ensure that humanity will put knowledge to good use. Discussion of public policy has only recently begun to give due weight to many of the concerns thus aroused, of which those most attended to can be summed up as "environmental" – pollution, soil erosion, dwindling water supplies, the extinction of species, forest depletion are among those most noticed.

Such awareness is evident in the attention given in recent years to the problem of "global warming", the rise in average temperatures on the world's surface, believed to be produced by changes in the atmosphere and stratosphere that affect the rate at which heat

is dispersed and lost from it. The facts themselves were until recently in dispute, but in 1990 a UN conference at Geneva conceded that global warming was in fact a growing danger, and that it was largely a matter of the accumulation of man-made gases in the atmosphere. This, it was agreed, had in a century already produced a measurable increase in average temperature; climate was in fact changing faster than at any time since the last Ice Age. At present, the authoritative consensus is that human agency has been a major contributor to this.

Argument continues about the likely rate of further increase and its possible consequences (in, for instance, rising sea levels) while work began on the preparation of a framework convention on man-made climatic change, which was ready by 1992. Its main aim was the stabilization of levels of emission so that in 2000 they should still be at 1990 levels. At Kyoto in 1997 this was turned into

Nunavut, Canada. A mother polar bear and her two-year-old cub on an iceberg in the open sea. Although the bears can swim over shorter distances, an increasing number are being taken out to sea as the ice breaks up due to global warming.

a regulatory agreement covering the emission of all major "greenhouse" gases (as they were called); it imposed levels of reduction for emissions and timetables that placed the main burdens on developed countries. The signing of the convention had been preceded by a warning from President Clinton earlier in the year that no such reductions would be acceptable to the United States, and President George W. Bush confirmed this in 2001. Meanwhile, signs of the bad effects of global warming multiply and the first attempts are already being made to seek legal remedies for damage caused by climate change.

A decade or so is hardly long enough to expect or find politically acceptable solutions to a problem of such magnitude. There seems to be no reason to assume that things will not get worse before they can get better, but, more important, also none that agreed solutions cannot be found. Humanity's confidence in science has, after all, been based on real success, not on illusion. Even if that confidence is now to be qualified, it is because science has made it possible to do so by giving us more knowledge to take into account. It is reasonable to say that while humanity may have been producing much irreversible change since it successfully displaced the larger mammals from their prehistoric habitats and if, consequently, some grave issues are now posed, the human toolkit has not been shown to be exhausted. Humanity faced the challenge of the Ice Ages with far poorer resources, both intellectual and technological, than it faces climatic change today. If our interference with nature has led to the appearance of new, drug-resistant bacteria by mutation through natural selection in the changed environments we have created, research to master them will continue. What is more, should further evidence and consideration oblige humanity to abandon the current hypothesis that global warming is

A technician works on a row of photovoltaic cells making up the largest solar energy plant in France, inaugurated in 2005 by the mayor of Chambery. PV or photovoltaics is a technology – such as found in pocket calculators – that converts energy from the sun into electricity. Large-scale incentive programmes, such as the ability to sell excess electricity back to the national grid, have accelerated the pace of solar installations in France, Spain, Germany, Japan and the United States.

Pathfinder reaches Mars

In 1877, Giovanni Schiaparelli, an Italian astronomer, observed some lines on the surface of Mars. Later Percival Lowell, an American, studied the planet for 15 years, declaring the lines to be "irrigation channels". At that point, science fiction took over: H.G. Wells' *The War of the Worlds* was published in 1898, and an enormous number of films have been made about aliens, frequently known as "Martians".

In 1976, the Viking I and Viking II space probes landed on Mars as part of a project costing $2,300 million. Twenty years passed before another space probe landed on the surface of the red planet. From July to September 1997, the NASA Mars Pathfinder probe explored Mars. The probe studied the soil and rocks on Mars, and provided a great deal of data suggesting that there was once a vast amount of water on the surface of the planet. In order to collect data, the Pathfinder probe had an exploratory vehicle called Sojourner. The size of a microwave oven, it moved at a little over 118ft (36m) per hour, propelled by solar power. As well as the on-board laboratory, Sojourner had a driving system oriented by laser rays, which enabled it to travel over the rough Martian terrain.

A section of the spacecraft Pathfinder, with its deflated airbags, is seen shortly after its landing on Mars.

mainly a man-made phenomenon – if, say, it were to become plausible to say that natural forces beyond human control or manipulation, such as those which produced the great Ice Ages of prehistory, were the determining forces at work – then science would apply itself to dealing with the consequences of that.

Even irreversible change does not in itself warrant any immediate abandonment of confidence in the power of the human race to pull itself out of difficulties in the long run. Although we may already have lost some choices for ever, the arena within which human choice can be exercised – history itself – is not going to disappear unless the human

Light decoration panels featuring British novel hero Harry Potter are displayed outside a Durga worship house in Calcutta, 2003. The four-day Durga Puja festival, in honour of the goddess Durga, is celebrated by Hindu worshippers around the world. The fame of schoolboy fiction hero Harry Potter cuts acoss religions and ethnicities and is evidence of the global appeal of certain stories and characters.

race is extinguished. That humanity's ambition should occur by natural disaster, independently of human action, is possible, but speculation about that is hardly useful (even actuarially) except over a limited range of cases (that the world should be hit by a monster asteroid, for example). The human being remains a reflective and tool-making animal and we are still a long way from exhausting the possibilities of that fact. As one scholar has strikingly put it, from the point of view of other organisms, humankind from the start resembles an epidemic disease in its successful competitive power. Whatever it has done to other species, though, the evidence of numbers and lifespan still seems to show that human manipulative power has so far brought more good than harm to most human beings who have lived. This remains the case, even if science and technology have created some new problems faster than they have yet produced solutions.

GLOBALIZATION

The power of humankind has almost imperceptibly encouraged the benign spread of assumptions and myths drawn from the historical experience of European liberalism into other cultures and of an optimistic approach to politics, even in the teeth of much recent and even contemporary evidence. That there may be huge prices in social adaptation to pay, for example, for effective response to global warming cannot be doubted, and it is fair to ask whether they can be paid without large-scale suffering and coercion. Nonetheless, confidence in our political culture remains high, to judge by the widespread adoption of much of it. Republics exist around the world these days, and almost everyone speaks the language of democracy and the rights of man. There are widespread efforts to bring to bear a rationalizing and utilitarian approach in government and administration and to replicate models of institutions that have been found successful in countries in the European tradition. When black men have clamoured vociferously against the white-dominated societies they lived in, they wished to realize for themselves the ideals of human rights and dignity evolved by Europeans. Few cultures, if any, have been able altogether to resist this vigorous tradition: China kow-towed to Marx and science long before it did so to the market. Some have resisted more successfully than others, but almost everywhere the individuality of other great political cultures has been in some measure sapped. When modernizers have sought to pick and choose within the dominant Western political model, they have not found it easy to do so. It is possible, at a certain cost, to get a selective modernity, but it usually comes in a package, some of whose other contents may be unwelcome.

For the sceptical, some of the best evidence of the ambiguous outcome for social well-being of the growth of uniformity in political culture has been provided by the continuing vigour of nationalism, whose success has been consummated virtually worldwide in the last hundred years. Our most comprehensive international (a word whose commonplace acceptance is significant) organization is called the United Nations and its predecessor was a League of Nations. The old colonial empires have dissolved into scores of new nations. Many existing national states have to justify their own existence to minorities that themselves claim to be nations, and therefore to have the right to break away and rule themselves. Where those minorities wish to break up the states that contain them – as do many Basques, Kurds, Quebecois, for example – they speak in the name of unachieved nationhood. The nation seems to have been supremely successful in satisfying thirsts other ideological intoxicants cannot reach; it has been the great creator of modern community, sweeping aside class and religion, giving a sense of meaning and belonging to those who feel adrift in a modernizing world in which older ties have decayed.

Once again, whatever view is taken of the relative waxing or waning of the state as an institution, or of the idea of nationalism, the world's politics are for the most part organized around concepts originally European, however qualified and obscured in practice, just as the world's intellectual life is increasingly organized around the science originating in Europe. Undeniably, cultural transfers can work unpredictably and thus have surprising consequences. Exported from the countries that first crystallized them, such notions as the individual's right to assert himself or herself have produced effects going far beyond what was envisaged by those who

first confidently encouraged the adoption of principles that they believed underlay their own success. The arrival of new machines, the building of railways and the opening of mines, the coming of banks and newspapers transformed social life in ways no one had willed or envisaged, as well as in ways they had. Television now continues the process which, once begun, was irreversible. Once European methods and goals were accepted (as they have been in greater or lesser degree, consciously or unconsciously, by élites almost everywhere), then an uncontrollable

Vietnamese Prime Minister Nguyen Tan Dung delivers a speech at Japan's upper house of parliament, or National Diet, in Tokyo, on 19 October 2006. Dung was in Japan on a five-day visit hoping to further boost trade ties with the major trade partner and aid provider to his communist country.

evolution had begun. Though continuing to shape it, humanity could no more than in the past determine the course of history for long. Even in the most tightly controlled essays in modernization, new and unexpected needs and demands erupt from time to time. Perhaps there now looms up the spectre that modernization's success may have communicated to mankind goals which are materially and psychologically unachievable, limitlessly expanding and unsatisfiable in principle as they are.

THE FUTURE OF HISTORY

Prophecy is not the historian's business, even if disguised as extrapolation. Guesses, though, are permissible if they throw light on the scale of present facts or serve as pedagogic aids. Perhaps fossil fuels will go the way that the larger prehistoric mammals went at the hands of human hunters – or perhaps they will not. The historian's subject matter remains the past. It is all he has to talk about. When it is the recent past, what he can try to do is to see consistency or inconsistency, continuity or discontinuity with what has gone before, and to face honestly the difficulties posed by the mass of facts that crowd in on us, in recent history in particular. The very confusion they present suggests a much more revolutionary period than any earlier one and all that has been said so far about the continuing acceleration of change confirms this. This does not, on the other hand, imply that these more violent and sweeping changes do not emerge

from the past in a way that is explicable and for the most part understandable.

Awareness of such problems is part of the reason why there now seem to be so many fewer plausible ways of seeing the world than in former times. For centuries, the Chinese could think untroubledly and unquestioningly in terms of a world order normally centred on a universal monarchy in Peking, sustained by divine mandate. Muslims did not, and still do not, find much place in their thinking for the abstract idea of the state; for them, the distinction of believer and non-believer is more significant. Many millions of Africans long found no difficulty in doing without any conception of science. Meanwhile, those who lived in "Western" countries could divide the world in their minds into "civilized" and "uncivilized", just as Englishmen could once distinguish "gentlemen" from "players" on the cricket field.

That such sharp disparities are now so much eroded marks the degree to which we are "one world" at last. The Chinese intellectual now speaks the language of liberalism or Marxism. Even in Jeddah and Tehran, thoughtful Muslims have to confront a tension between the pull of tradition and the need to have at least some intellectual acquaintance with the dangerous temptations of an alien modernism. India at times seems schizophrenically torn between the values of the secular democracy its leaders envisaged in 1947 and the pull of its past. But the past is with all of us, for good and ill. History, we must recognize, still clutters up our present and there is no sign that will come to an end.

Homeless Indian street dwellers in Calcutta stand beside a billboard advertising the latest mobile phone technology, April 2006. The Congress Party-led Indian government came to power in 2004 with the support of the country's poor farmers, having pledged to improve the lives of the huge numbers of Indians who live on less than a dollar a day. In countries such as India, developments enable technological leapfrogging to take place – for example, wireless networks will establish themselves in many places which have waited decades to no avail for cabled infrastructure.

INDEX

Page references to main text in roman type, to
box text in **bold** and to captions in *italics*

ACKNOWLEDGMENTS

PICTURE CREDITS

The publisher would like to thank the following people, museums, and photographic libraries for permission to reproduce their material. Every care has been taken to trace copyright holders. However, if we have omitted anyone we apologize and will, if informed, make corrections to any future edition.

KEY

b bottom; c centre; t top; l left; r right

AA: Art Archive, London
AGE: A.G.E. Fotostock
AISA: Archivo Iconografico SA
AKG: AKG-images, London
BAL: Bridgeman Art Library
BL: British Library, London
BLV: Bertelsmann Lexikon Verlag, Under Sublicence of Bertelsmann Picture Pool, Gütersloh
BM: British Museum, London
BN: Bibliothèque Nationale, Paris
BNM: Biblioteca Nacional, Madrid
BPK: Bildarchiv Preussischer Kulturbesitz, Berlin
CB: Corbis/Bettman
CP: Camera Press Ltd., London
DBP: Duncan Baird Publishers, London
FSP: Frank Spooner Pictures / Gamma
Getty: Getty Images
IWM: Imperial War Museum, London
JLC: Jean-Loup Charmet, Paris
KM: Kunsthistorisches Museum, Vienna
MP: Museo del Prado, Madrid
MEPL: Mary Evans Picture Library, London
MNCV: Musée National du Château de Versailles, Paris
NG: National Gallery, London
NMM: National Maritime Museum, London
NPG: National Portrait Gallery, London
NWPA: North Wind Picture Archives, Alfred, Maine
ON: Osterreichischen Nationalbibliothek, Vienna
RMN: Réunion des Musées Nationaux, Paris
SHMM: State Historical Museum, Moscow
UPI: United Press International
V&A: By courtesy of the board of trustees of the Victoria & Albert Museum, London
REX: Rex Features Ltd
SIPA: Sipa Press
SPL: Science Photo Library, London

6   Corbis / Neville Elder
10   Royal Geographic Society, London (Mr.264 H.9)
12   BAL / Lauros-Giraudon / Musée du Ranquet, Clermont-Ferrand
13   MP
14   BAL / Koninklijk Kabinet von Schilderijen Mauritshuis, The Hague
15   BAL / Giraudon / Louvre, Paris
18   Scala / Museo di Firenze com'era, Florence
19t   BAL / Národní Galerie, Prague
19b   BAL / BL (Add.24098, f.25v)
20   AA / Bibliothèque de L'Ecouen
21   NG
22   KM
23   AISA / Musée Carnavalet, Paris
24   MP
25   BPK / Jörg P. Anders / Staatliche Museen zu Berlin
26   Oronoz / BNM
27   Museo de América, Madrid
28   AKG London / Staatliche Kupferstich Kabinett, Dresden
29   AA / Frederiksborg Castle, Denmark
30   BAL / Science Museum, London
31   Scala / Pushkin Museum, Moscow
32   RMN / Gérard Blot / Louvre, Paris
33   BM
34   MP
35   RMN / Louvre, Paris
36   BAL / Guildhall Art Library, Corporation of London
37   MP
38   BPK / Staatliche Museen zu Berlin Preussischer Kulturbesitz / Gemäldegalerie, Berlin
39   Oronoz / Musée des Beaux Arts, Rouen
41   BAL / Wallace Collection, London
42   RMN / Louvre, Paris
43   Scala / Palazzo Vecchio, Florence
44   Giraudon / Bibliothèque de L'Arsenal, Paris
45   AA / Musée de Versailles
46   Lauros-Giraudon / Archives Nationales, Paris
47   NG
48   NG
49t   Scala / Galleria degli Uffizi, Florence
49b   RMN / Louvre, Paris
50   Scala / Galleria degli Uffizi, Florence
52   BAL / Giraudon / BN
53   BN
54t   BAL / National Gallery of Scotland, Edinburgh
54b   Oronoz / Musée de l'Histoire, Geneva
55   BAL / Bible Society, London
56   Scala / Galleria Nazionale d'Arte Antica, Rome

57t   NPG
57b   MP
58   Oronoz
60   RMN / Jean Schormans / Louvre, Paris
61t   Oronoz / Catedral de Toledo
61b   Oronoz / Coleccion Uria, Azcoitia, Guipuzcoa
62   BAL / Index / Museo Lazaro Galdiano, Madrid
64   BAL / Roy Miles Gallery, London
65   AKG, London
66   NPG
67   BM
68   BAL / The Trustees of the Weston Park Foundation
69   BAL / Giraudon / Château de Versailles
70   BAL / Philip Mould Historical Portraits Ltd, London
71   NG
72   RMN / Musée des Granges de Port Royal
73   AKG
74   BM
76   Oronoz / Embajada Francesa, Madrid
77   MP
78   AA / SHMM
79   Oronoz
81   AISA
82   Oronoz / Academia de Bellas Artes de San Fernando, Madrid
84   Musées Royaux des Beaux-Arts de Belgique, Brussels
85   ON (Cod. 1875, f.41v)
86   MP
87   RMN / Hervé Lewandowski / Louvre, Paris
88   BAL / KM
89   Oronoz / Biblioteca del Monasterio de El Escorial, Madrid
90   NG
91   BN
93   AA / BN
94   AISA / Musée de Versailles
95   Oronoz / Biblioteca del Monasterio de El Escorial, Madrid
96   MP
97   BAL / BL (Add.33733, f.9)
98   BAL / Giraudon / NG
99   BN (Turk. 524, f.218v)
100t   BAL / Stapleton Collection, London
100b   AISA / Historisches Museum der Stadt, Vienna
102   AISA / Musée de Versailles
103   AISA / Gallerie degli Uffizi, Florence
104   National Museum, Copenhagen / Niels Elswing
105   AISA
106   AISA / BN
107   V&A

109   TRIP / M. Jenkin
110t   BAL / Tretyakov Gallery, Moscow
110b   BN
111t   Novosti, London
112b   BAL / Stapleton Collection, London
113   BAL / Private Collection
114   AISA / Tretyakov Gallery, Moscow
115   AISA / Tretyakov Gallery, Moscow
116   John Massey Stewart / Tretyakov Gallery, Moscow
117t   AA / SHMM
117b   AISA
118   AISA / SHMM
119   Novosti, London
120   AISA
121   Lauros-Giraudon
122   OM
125   AKG
126   Oronoz / Musée des Beaux-Arts, Rouen
127   BN
128   BAL / NMM
129   BAL / Musei e Gallerie Pontificie, Vatican City
131   AKG
133   Oronoz / BNM
134   Werner Forman Archive, London / BM
135   AKG
136   BAL / Johnny Van Haeften Gallery, London
137   Rijksmuseum, Amsterdam
138   BAL / V&A
140   NPG
143   BNM (Ms 50, f.371)
144t   BNM (Ms 50, f.484)
144b   Museo de América, Madrid
146   Oronoz / BNM
147   Oronoz / Archivo General de las Indias, Seville
148   NPG
149   BN
150   DBP
152   AISA / BNM
153   North Wind Picture Archives
154   BM
155   BM
157   AA
160   Museo Municipal, Madrid
161   BAL / National Library of Australia, Canberra
162   Michael Holford / BM
163   Museum Boymans-Van Beuningen, Rotterdam
164   North Wind Picture Archives
165   BAL / City of Bristol Museum and Art Gallery
166   BAL / City of Bristol Museum and Art Gallery
167   NMM
168   Museum Boymans-Van Beuningen, Rotterdam / Willem van der Vorm Foundation

169t Oronoz / Biblioteca del Palacio Real, Madrid
169b BN
170t Oronoz / Biblioteca del Palacio Real, Madrid
170b RMN / Gérard Blot / Musée de Versailles
171 BM
173 North Wind Picture Archives
174 AISA / Union des Arts Décoratifs, Paris
177 BM
178 Maritiem Museum, Rotterdam
180 NMM
181 BAL / BM
183 Tasmanian Museum & Art Gallery, Hobart
184 Oronoz / Galleria dell'Accademia, Venice
186 Alinari-Giraudon
187t BAL / Rafael Valls Gallery, London
187b Museo del Prado, Madrid
188 BAL / Musée Condé, Chantilly
189 BAL / BM
190 Rijksmuseum, Amsterdam
191 AISA / Biblioteca Central de Cataluña, Barcelona
192 AISA / Biblioteca Central de Cataluña, Barcelona
193 BAL / Louvre, Paris
194 BAL / Christie's, London
195 Oronoz / Musei Vaticani, Vatican City
196 NPG
197t The Royal Society, London
197b Science & Society Picture Library / Science Museum, London
198 BN
199 AA / Tate Gallery, London
200t AISA
200b Muzeum Okregowew, Torunin
201 BAL / Biblioteca Marucelliana, Florence
202 NPG
203 BAL / Derby Museum & Art Gallery
204 AISA
205 AISA / Galleria degli Uffizi, Florence
206 BN
207 AKG / Erich Lessing / Musée des Beaux-Arts, Dijon
208 Musée Carnavalet, Paris / Habouzit
209 AKG / Erich Lessing / BN
211 AISA
212 AKG
213 Oronoz
214 AKG
215 Kunsthistorisches Museum, Vienna
216 Musée Carnavalet, Paris
217 BAL / Kunsthalle, Hamburg
219 Tate Gallery, London
220 Getty / Hulton
221 Index-BAL / NPG
222 BN
223 BN
225 BN
226 NG, London
227 BN
228t Scala / Museo del Passagio, Pallanza
228b Museo del Prado, Madrid
229 RMN / Musée des Beaux-Arts, Nantes
231t RMN / R. G. Ojeda / Louvre, Paris
231b MEPL

232t Oronoz
232b MEPL
233 BAL / Royal Holloway & Bedford New College, Surrey
234t Lauros-Giraudon / Musée National des Techniques, Paris
234b AISA
235 Walker Art Gallery, Liverpool / Board of Trustees of the National Museums and Galleries on Merseyside
236 BAL / Institute of Civil Engineers, London
237 JLC
238 Courtesy of Sheffield Art Galleries and Museums
239 Novosti, London
240 Peter Newark's Historical Pictures
241 BPK, Berlin
242 JLC
243 BM
244 BAL / Wallington Hall, Northumberland
245 BAL / Private Collection
246 MEPL
247 MEPL
249 JLC / Musée Carnavalet, Paris
250 NPG
251 NWPA
252 RMN / MNCV
253 © The Metropolitan Museum of Art, New York
254 BN
255 BN
256 AISA / Biblioteca Nacional, Madrid
257 Oronoz / Academia de Bellas Artes de San Fernando, Madrid
258 Peter Newark's Historical Pictures
259 BAL / Hall of Representatives, Washington D. C.
260 Peter Newark's Historical Pictures
261 Oronoz
262 NWPA
263 BAL / Private Collection
264 BAL / MNCV
265 RMN / MNCV
266 BN
267 JLC
268 RMN / MNCV
269 BN
270 BN
271t BN
271b Musée Carnavalet, Paris / Andreani
272 BAL / Musée Carnavalet, Paris
273 (l&r) BN
274 Musée Carnavalet, Paris / Berthier
275 AKG / Erich Lessing / MNCV
276 AKG
277 AA / Musée Carnavalet, Paris
278 BAL / New College, Oxford University, Oxford
279 Musée Carnavalet, Paris / Andreani
280t BAL / State Hermitage Museum, St Petersburg
280b RMN / Gérard Blot / MNCV
281 RMN / Louvre, Paris
282 Oronoz / Musée National des Châteaux de Malmaison et de Bois-Préau, Rueil-Malmaison
283 Deutsches Historisches Museum, Berlin
284 BAL / Biblioteca Nazionale, Turin

286 AKG / Steiermärkisches Landesmuseum, Austria
287 Museo del Prado, Madrid
288 AA / Fondation Thiers, Paris
289 Oronoz
291 Christie's Images, London
292 BAL / Lauros-Giraudon / Louvre, Paris
293 NPG
295 BAL / Lauros-Giraudon / Musée Carnavalet, Paris
296 RMN / Louvre, Paris
297 BAL / Wolverhampton Art Gallery
298 AA / Musée Carnavalet, Paris
299 RMN / MNCV
300t RMN / A. Danvers / Musée des Beaux-Arts, Bordeaux
300b RMN / Hervé Lewandowski / Louvre, Paris
301 Heeresgeschichtliches Museum, Vienna
302 Index / Raccolte Bertarelli, Milan
303t Oronoz
303b Historisches Museum, Frankfurt-am-Main
304 AKG / Museum Ostdeutsche Galerie, Regensburg
305 AA
306 Novosti, London
307 BN
308 BAL / Lauros-Giraudon / MNCV
309 Scala / Museo del Risorgimento, Milan
310 Scala / Museo del Risorgimento, Rome
311 Index / JLC / Musée Carnavalet, Paris
312 Bridgeman Art Library / Giraudon / Musée Carnavalet, Paris
313 JLC / Musée Carnavalet, Paris
314 BAL / Peter Willi Private Collection
315 Science & Society Picture Library / National Railway Museum, London
316t BN
316b Deutsches Historisches Museum, Berlin
318 AA / State Historical Museum, Moscow
319 Scala / State Tretyakov Gallery, Moscow
320 AISA / State Russian Museum, St Petersburg
322 AKG
323 AISA / State Tretyakov Gallery, Moscow
324t Index-BAL / State Tretyakov Gallery, Moscow
324b Giraudon / State Russian Museum, St Petersburg
325 AISA / State Tretyakov Gallery, Moscow
327 MEPL
328 Birmingham Museum & Art Gallery
329 AKG
330 AA
331 NWPA
332 BN
333t BAL / American Museum, Bath
333b BAL / Private Collection
335 Oronoz
336 BAL / Lauros-Giraudon
338 BN

340 DBP
341 NWPA
343t BN
343b AKG
344 MEPL
345 AISA
347 Peter Newark's Historical Pictures
348 Ardea London Ltd
349 AA
350 Museum of London
351 BAL / Houses of Parliament, Westminster, London
352 BAL / Victoria & Albert Museum, London
354 BAL / Bradford Art Galleries and Museums
355 Oronoz / BN
357 NWPA
358 BL / Oriental & India Office Collections. Mss Eurf.111/270 No.35
360 Getty / Hulton
362 AKG
363 AISA
364 AISA
365 AISA
366 AISA
367t AGE
367b AISA
368 AGE
369t AISA / Bibliothèque des Arts Décoratifs, Paris
369b AISA
370 Popperfoto
371 Zardoya / CP
372 Getty / Hulton
373 AISA
374 AISA
375 AISA
376 AISA / Museo Nacional de Historia, Mexico
377 AISA
378 AISA / Museo Municipal, Quito
379 AISA
380 AISA
381t AISA / Biblioteca de Ajuda, Lisbon
381b AISA
382 BAL / Private Collection
383 Punch Library, London
384 AISA
385 AISA
386 AISA
387 AISA
388 AISA
389 AGE
390 AGE
391 AGE
393 JLC
394 AISA
395 AISA
396 Zardoya / CP / Bassano
397t AISA / Bibliothèque des Arts Décoratifs, Paris
397b AISA
398 AGE
399 AISA
400 AISA / V&A
401 Getty / Hulton
402 AISA / BN
404 AISA / Musée Condé, Chantilly
405 AISA
409 AISA
410 AISA

411 AISA / Musée des Beaux-Arts, Orléans
412 AISA / Musée d'Orsay, Paris
413 AISA
414 AISA
415 Popperfoto
417 Getty / Hulton
418 AISA / BN
419 AGE
420 AGE
421 AGE
424 AA / Private Collection
425 AISA
426 AISA
427 AISA
428 AISA
429t AISA
429b Zardoya
430 Popperfoto
431 AISA / Museo d'Arte Orientale "Edoardo Chiossonè", Genova
432 AISA / Museo d'Arte Orientale "Edoardo Chiossonè", Genova
433 AGE
434 AISA
436 AISA
437 Kyodo News, Tokyo
439 AISA
440 AISA
441 AISA / Galerie de l'Imagerie, Paris
442 AISA
444 AISA / V&A
445 AISA
446 AISA
448 BL / Oriental & India Office Collections
450 AISA
452 AISA
453 AISA
454 Roger-Viollet
456 Roger-Viollet
457 Roger-Viollet / Branger
458 Zardoya / CP
460 AISA / Musée d'Orsay, Paris
462t Zardoya / CP
462b AISA
463 AISA
464 BAL / Giraudon / Bibliothèque de l'Assemblée Nationale, Paris
465 Roger-Viollet / Cap
466 AISA / BN
467 AISA
468 AISA
469 Popperfoto
470 AISA
471 AISA
472 AGE
473 Zardoya / CP
474 AISA
475 AISA
477 Popperfoto
478 AISA / Biblioteca Nacional, Madrid
480 AISA
481 AGE / Science Photo Library / JLC
482 AGE
485 Punch Library, London
486 AISA
487 AISA / Musée National du Château de Versailles, Paris
488 AA
489 Popperfoto
490 Getty / Hulton

491 AA / IWM
492 AA
493 AGE
494 JLC
495 AISA
496 Getty / Hulton
497 Zardoya / CP
499t AGE
499b AGE
500 Zardoya / CP / IWM
501 AA
502 AGE
503 Zardoya / CP / IWM
504 AGE
505 BAL / Novosti
506t Zardoya / CP
506b AISA
507 AISA
509 AA / Syndication International (Daily Mirror), London
510t Archive Photos / Image Bank
510b AISA
511 AA / IWM
512 AISA
513 Popperfoto
514 Getty / Hulton
515 AISA
516 AGE
518 Roger-Viollet / Harlingue
520 AISA / State Tretyakov Gallery, Moscow
521 Zardoya / CP
522 AGE
523 AISA
524 Roger-Viollet
525 Zardoya / CP
526t AGE
526b Popperfoto
527 AISA
528 Getty / Hulton
529 Archive Photos / Image Bank
530 AGE
531 AGE
532 CB
534 AISA
535 Roger-Viollet / Harlingue
536 CB
537 CB
538 CB / UPI
539 CB
541 CB
542 Getty / Hulton
543 CB
544 Popperfoto
545 Archives Ringart
547 CB / UPI
548 Getty / Hulton
549 CB / UPI
550 Zardoya / Magnum Photos / Koyo Kageyama
551 CB / UPI
553 AGE
554 CB / UPI
555 CB / UPI
556 CB / UPI
558 AISA
559t Zardoya / CP
559b AISA
560 AISA
561 AISA
562 CB / UPI
563 CB / UPI

564 Popperfoto
565 Zardoya
566 AGE
568 Roger-Viollet
569 Getty / Hulton
570 CB
571 AGE
573 Getty / Hulton
574 CB / UPI
575 CB
576 BAL / © VEGAP 1999
577 CB
578 CB
579 CB / UPI
580 CB / UPI
581 CB
582 CB
583 CB
584 CB / UPI
585 Zardoya / Magnum Photos / Robert Capa
586 CB
587 CB
588 CB / UPI
589 CB
590 Oronoz / Museo Reina Sofia, Madrid / © VEGAP 1999 / © Succession Picasso, Paris
592t CB / UPI
592b CB
593 AGE
594 CB / UPI
596 CB / UPI
597 CB / UPI
598 CB / UPI
599 CB / UPI
600 CB / UPI
601 Zardoya / Len Sirman Press
602 Zardoya / Magnum Photos / Koyo Kageyama
604 CB
605 CB
606 CB / UPI
607 CB / UPI
609 Getty / Hulton / Fred Ramage
610 CB / UPI
611 United Nations
612 Zardoya / CP
613 REX / United Nations
614 Getty / Hulton
615 AKG
616 David King Collection
617 Getty / Hulton
619 AGE
620 CB / UPI
621 Zardoya / CP
622 Zardoya / CP
623 David King Collection
624 Zardoya / CP
625 CB / UPI
626 Popperfoto
627 CB / UPI
628 AGE
629 CB
630 CB / UPI
631 Zardoya / CP
632 AGE
633 CB / UPI
634 Image Bank / Archive Photos
635 CB / UPI
636 Zardoya / Magnum Photos / Paul Fusco

638 CB / UPI
639 Magnum Photos / Robert Capa
640 SPL / NASA
641 AGE
642 Getty / AFP / Goh Chai Hin
643 Travel Ink / Peter Jousiffe
644 Panos Pictures / Alain le Garsmeur
645 Getty / Stone / Vincent Oliver
646 Axiom / Ian Cook
648 Zardoya / Magnum Photos / Hiroji Kubota
649 AISA
650 CB
652 Corbis / Eye Ubiquitous / James Davis
654t The World Bank, Washington D.C.
654b International Monetary Fund, Washington D.C.
655 AGE
656 Corbis / Reuters / Daniel Aguilar
657 AGE
658 CB
659 Getty / Taxi / Spencer Rowell
660 CB
661 Getty / Reportage / Kamoshida Koichi
662 AGE
663 Advertising Archives
665 SPL / Jerrican / Galia
666 CB
667 CB / UPI
668 SPL / James King-Holmes
669 SPL / Steve Gschmeissner
671 CB / UPI
673 BLV / NASA
674 AGE / NASA
677 NASA
678 Still Pictures / UNEP / Nutta Yooyean
679 Corbis / Reuters / Damir Sagolj
680 REX / SIPA
681 Panos Pictures / Paul Smith
682 AGE
683 Zardoya / Magnum Photos / Martin Parr
684 AGE
685 Panos Pictures / Alain le Garsmeur
686 CB
687 Network
689 CB / Reuters
690 BLV
691 CB
692 CB
693 Getty / Reportage / Paula Bronstein
694 Popperfoto
695 Network / Anthony Suau
696 Magnum Photos / Paul Lowe
697 Getty / Kael Alford
698 Photo European Parliament
699 Getty / Hulton
700 CB / Agence France Presse
701 Magnum Photos / Abbas
702 CB / A. Vonlintel
704 CB / UPI
705 CB / UPI
706 CB
707 CB / UPI
708 Magnum Photos / Cornell Capa
710 David King Collection, London
711 CB / UPI
713 REX / SIPA / Dieter Ludwig
714 AISA

715 CB / UPI
716 AISA
717 CB / AFP
718 CB / UPI
719 CB / UPI
720 Magnum Photos / Fred Mayer
721 CB / UPI
722 AISA
723 AISA
724 AISA
725 AGE
726 AISA
727 CB
729 David King Collection, London
730 AISA
732 CB / UPI
733 CB
734 CB
736 CB / UPI
737t Associated Press Ltd
737b REX / SIPA / Olivier Jobard
738 AISA
740 CB
741 CB / UPI
742 Bettmann / UPI
743 CB / UPI
744 AISA
745 CB / UPI
746 AISA
747 Magnum Photos / Marc Riboud
748 AISA
749 AISA
751t CB
751b CB / UPI
752 CB / UPI
753 CP
754 Magnum Photos / Ian Berry
755 CB / UPI
756 Magnum Photos / Peter Marlow
757 CB / UPI
758 REX / SIPA / Durand
759 REX
760 CB
761 CB / UPI
762 CB / UPI
764 Magnum Photos / Constantine Manos
765 CB
766 CB / UPI

767 CB / UPI
768 CB / UPI
769 CB / UPI
771 REX / SIPA
772 CB / UPI
773 CB
774 CB / UPI
775 CB / UPI
776 Magnum Photos / S. Raskin
777 AGE
778 AGE
779t CB
779b AGE / Mark Stephenson
780 AISA
781 CB / UPI
782 CB / UPI
783 Magnum Photos / Bob Adelman
784 Zardoya / Magnum Photos / Eli
      Reed
785 CB / UPI
786 CB / UPI
787 Magnum Photos / Ian Berry
788 Magnum Photos / Philip Jones Griffiths
789 CB / UPI
790 CB / UPI
791 CB / UPI
793 Magnum Photos / Josef Koudelka
794 CB
796 Getty / Hulton
797 CB
798 FSP / Gamma
799 CB
800 FSP
801 REX / SIPA / Alix
802 CB / UPI
803 Zardoya / Magnum Photos /
      New China Picture Company
804 AGE
805 Zardoya / CP
806 FSP / Chip Hires
807 Network Photographers /
      Christopher Pillitz
808 FSP
809 Zardoya / Magnum Photos /
      Richard Kalvar
810 Network Photographers /
      Roger Hutchings
811 CB / UPI

812 FSP
813 Getty / AFP / Asif Hassan
814 CB / UPI
816 CB / Reuters
817 AGE
819 REX / SIPA
820 REX / SIPA / Krpan
821 CB / Reuters
822 REX / SIPA
823 CB
824 Archive Photos / Reuters /
      Patrick de Noirmont
825 AGE / Network Photographers
826 CB / Reuters
827 CB / Reuters
828 REX / SIPA / Novosti
829 CB / Reuters
830 AISA
831 Magnum Photos / Josef Koudelka
832 Magnum Photos / Peter Marlow
833 Contifoto / Sygma / G. Dkeerle
834 FSP
835 Panos Pictures / Heidi Bradner
837 REX / SIPA / Jaques Witt
838 Magnum Photos / Leonard Freed
839 Network Photographers /
      Anthony Suau
840 REX / Sunday Times
842 CB / Reuters
843 CB
844 Corbis / Reuters / Ranko Cukovic
845 Getty / AFP / STR
846 Corbis / epa
847 Getty / Stephen Ferry
848 Corbis / Sygma / Terres Du Sud
849 Getty / AFP / Marcel Mochet
850 Corbis / Felix Zaska
851 Corbis / dpa / Boris Roessler
853 Getty / AFP / Cem Turkel
854 Getty / AFP / John D McHugh
855 Getty / Sean Gallup
856 Corbis / Tibor Bognar
857 Reuters / Archive Photos
858 Getty / ChinaFotoPress
859 Getty / AFP / Kazuhiro Nogi
860 Getty / AFP / Hoang Dinh Nam
861 Getty / AFP
862 Getty / Sean Ramsay

863 Corbis / Sygma / Patrick Chauvel
864 Getty / AFP / Alexei Panov
865 Getty / AFP
866 Getty / AFP / Alexander Joe
867 Getty / AFP / Hocine Zaourar
868 Getty / AFP / Mahmud Hams
869 Getty / AFP
870 Corbis / Reuters
871 Getty / Michel Porro
872 Getty / Spencer Platt
873 Getty / Time & Life Pictures
874 Getty
875 Getty / John Li
877 Getty / Mirrorpix / Daily Mirror
      Gulf coverage
878 Archive Photos / Reuters /
      David Ake
879 Sally & Richard Greenhill Photo
      Library
880 Getty / AFP / Mark Ralston
881 United Artists (courtesy Kobal
      Collection)
882 Archive Photos / Reuters /
      Kamal Kishores
884 Magnum Photos / Jean Gaumy
885 Getty / AFP / Khaled Desouki
886 Network / Saba / Robert Wallis
887 Getty / National Geographic /
      Paul Nicklen
888 Getty / AFP / Jean-Pierre Clatot
889 Archive Photos / Reuters / NASA
890 Getty / AFP /
      Deshakalyan Chowdhury
891 Getty / AFP /
      Toshifumi Kitamura/AFP
893 Getty / AFP /
      Deshakalyan Chowdhury

TEXT CREDITS

The publishers wish to thank the following for their kind permission to reproduce the translations and copyright material in this book. Every effort has been made to trace copyright owners, but if anyone has been omitted we apologize and will, if informed, make corrections in any future edition.

Page 43: an extract from *The Prince* by Niccolo Machiavelli, translated by George Bull (Penguin Classics 1961, revised edition 1975) copyright © George Bull 1961, 1975, 1981. Reproduced by permission of Penguin Books Ltd.

Page 204: an extract from *An Answer to the Question: "What is Enlightenment?"* from *Political Writings* by Immanuel Kant, translated by H.B. Nisbet. Copyright © Cambridge University Press, 1970, 1991. Reproduced by permission of Cambridge University Press.

Page 205: an extract from *Discourse on Method and the Meditations* by René Descartes, translated by F.E. Sutcliffe, 1968 (Penguin Classics 1968) copyright © F.E. Sutcliffe, 1968. Reproduced by permission of Penguin Books Ltd.

Page 211: an extract from *The Spirit of the Laws* by Montesquieu, translated and edited by Anne M. Cohler, Basia C. Miller and Harold S. Stone. Copyright © Cambridge University Press, 1989. Reproduced by permission of Cambridge University Press.

Page 321: an extract from *The Bronze Horseman* from *Narrative Poems* by Alexander Pushkin and Michael Lermontov, translated by Charles Johnston (The Bodley Head, 1984) copyright © The Literary Executor of the late Sir Charles Johnston. Reproduced by permission of The Literary Executor of the late Sir Charles Johnston.

Page 337: an extract from Volume One of *Democracy in America* by Alexis de Tocqueville. From the Henry Reece text, edited by Phillips Bradley, 1954. Copyright © Vintage Books, New York, 1945. Reproduced by permission of Vintage Books, a subsidiary of Random House, Inc.

Page 406: an extract from *The White Man's Burden* by Rudyard Kipling (Kyle Cathie, 1990). Reproduced by permission of A.P. Watt Ltd. on behalf of The National Trust for Places of Historic Interest or Natural Beauty.

Page 519: an extract from *"Left Wing" Communism: an infantile disorder* by Vladimir Ilyich Lenin (Bookmarks 1993). Reproduced by permission of Bookmarks.

Page 586: an extract from *Mein Kampf* by Adolf Hitler, translated by Ralph Manheim (Pimlico, 1992). Reproduced by permission of Random House UK Limited.

Page 656: an extract from *The Asian–African Conference, Bandung, Indonesia, April 1955* by George McTurnan Kahin (Cornell University Press, 1956). Reproduced by permission of the publisher, Cornell University Press.

Page 670: an extract from *The Cosmic Connection: An Extraterrestrial Perspective* by Carl Sagan, produced by Jerome Agel. (For further information: Jerome Agel, 2 Peter Cooper Road, New York, New York 10010, USA.)

Page 707: an extract from The North Atlantic Treaty. Reproduced by permission of the NATO Office of Information and Press from the *NATO Handbook* (1995 edition).